MADONNA

Also by Mary Gabriel

MADONNA

A Rebel Life

MARY GABRIEL

LITTLE, BROWN AND COMPANY

New York Boston London

Little, Brown and Company
Hachette Book Group
1290 Avenue of the Americas, New York, NY 10104
littlebrown.com

First Edition: October 2023

Little, Brown and Company is a division of Hachette Book Group, Inc.
The Little, Brown name and logo are trademarks of Hachette Book Group, Inc.

The publisher is not responsible for websites (or their content)
that are not owned by the publisher.

The Hachette Speakers Bureau provides a wide range of authors for speaking events. To
find out more, go to hachettespeakersbureau.com or email hachettespeakers@hbgusa.com.

Little, Brown and Company books may be purchased in bulk for business, educational, or
promotional use. For information, please contact your local bookseller or the Hachette
Book Group Special Markets Department at special.markets@hbgusa.com.

Copyright and permissions acknowledgments for this book appear on page 815.

ISBN 9780316456470
LCCN 2022943414

Printing 1, 2023

LSC-C

Printed in the United States of America

Why do we have to be sexy? Can't we just be powerful?[i]

—*Yesenia Ayala*

Contents

PART THREE: LOS ANGELES, 1985–1991

PART FOUR: MIAMI, 1992–1999

PART FIVE: LONDON, 2000–2009

PART SIX: LISBON, 2010–2020

Author's Note

Madonna: A Rebel Life is, ostensibly, a book about one person. But I found, during the five-plus years that I researched and wrote it, that it wasn't possible to re-create Madonna in a pop music vacuum. She is not just an entertainment icon, she is an artist who has changed cultural and social history globally. To tell her story, therefore, I had to tell *our* story as one century ended and another began, as she influenced the world and it influenced her.

That meant that the mound of material I had to work with grew exponentially, and the references attached to the text filled hundreds of pages. For this book, Little, Brown and I have decided to move that important but voluminous information online. The following URL will direct you to all the source material I used, from the individual references throughout the book, which can be found in the endnotes, to the bibliography, where full citations are available.

https://www.hachettebookgroup.com/titles/mary-gabriel/madonna/9780316456470/

Prologue

London, November 28, 2000

THE PEOPLE GATHERED inside the Brixton Academy seemed more than a little bored by the guest DJ, who had the difficult job of keeping the expectant crowd occupied, even if he hadn't succeeded in making it happy. He had barely finished his set when a familiar strain—just a few electronically generated sounds—produced a roar and then a sea of waving arms, cheers, and tears from nearly three thousand people standing shoulder to shoulder, some riding atop shoulders, at the start of what one critic called a "transcendent pop moment."[1] The song had only been available for a few weeks, but seemingly everyone in the audience knew it well enough to recognize the opening as Madonna's wonderfully quirky, wildly exuberant electropop track "Music" as well as the purely rhetorical question it asked: "Do you like to...boogie-woogie?"

For a few moments, a dreamy montage of photos and a voice-over narration calmed the mood inside the hall until a huge Union Jack was lifted high above the stage to reveal Madonna in a cropped leather jacket, rhinestone belt, and leather chaps, singing and dancing on a battered pickup truck amid a wolf pack of ripple-chested fellas—her raucous remake of that good-ol'-boy fantasy involving a flatbed full of hot chicks.

Her joy was infectious, the way it had been fifteen years earlier during her first US tour, when her record label tested the viability of this slightly strange dance-pop-R&B hybrid called Madonna. During that first outing, she seemed barely able to believe she was onstage and that the thousands of mostly young girls screaming her name were truly there to see *her*. Now, so many lifetimes later, she was back, showing that same delight as a crowd of slightly older, much gayer fans showered her with love. She returned it, throwing herself into the audience, where four dancers stood ready to catch her.

Madonna often said it was the process of creation she most valued: writing the song, conceiving and designing the tour, collaborating on the photo shoot or video, and, later, directing films.[2] But sometimes performances could be acts of creation, too, during which the audience became part of the work. That November night at the Brixton Academy was one of those occasions. The intensity of Madonna's twenty-nine-minute performance was matched by the commitment of the crowd.

Madonna hadn't performed in Britain in seven years. The limited space inside the Brixton Academy assured that she would have a relatively intimate gathering for her return. In the VIP section were Mick Jagger, George Michael, Ewan McGregor, director Alan Parker, designers Stella McCartney and Alexander McQueen, and Madonna's soon-to-be husband, director Guy Ritchie, among others. Filling the main audience were thousands of exuberant lesser mortals who had been invited or won tickets or paid exorbitant amounts at auction for seats in the hall. Outside, where Madonna's name was splashed across the building's facade, battalions of police manned barricades to keep at bay those dreamers who still believed they might be given entry. One report said Brixton, which for a half century had been the beating heart of London's Jamaican community, hadn't seen such a massive security operation since Nelson Mandela visited the neighborhood four years earlier.[3]

Knowing the venue would be too small to satisfy fans, Madonna had approached Microsoft's British network, MSN.co.uk, to see if it was interested in a novel idea: hosting a webcast of her concert. It was, and it soon launched what would be its first free live online performance. Madonna's Brixton show was streamed on huge outdoor screens in six cities, including New York and Paris, and on nine million home computers so that people in thirty-three countries could join the party, too.[4]

The webcast was not without glitches, in part because in those early days of broadband, many home systems weren't equipped to handle it, but a precedent had been set. Musical performance had a massive new global platform. MSN called it "the most ambitious web event in history." In 2018, *Guinness World Records* named it the largest internet pop concert of all time.[5]

By the time Madonna finished "Impressive Instant," her first song that night, she had truly defied pop gravity. Not just commercially: at that point she had sold more than 150 million albums worldwide and was the most successful female solo artist of all time.[6] And not just artistically: she had already transformed the traditional pop-rock concert format into a full-scale theatrical experience, raised music video from a sales tool to an art form, and put a woman — herself — in control of her own music, from creation to development to distribution. Her greatest achievement had been social.

In the early '80s, when Madonna became "Madonna," the pop and rock landscape was dominated by white men at record companies and radio stations and onstage, all targeting one important demographic: white men

and boys. The industry was designed to satisfy them. Rock celebrated heterosexual love, generally from a man's point of view. Women in the business were expected to be sexy but not sexual, with the aim of titillating an
audience raised on looking at women, not listening to them. Women
could play at being rockers if they liked, but they had to wiggle a bit for the
lads while doing so and maybe perform a private favor or two for the
record-company honchos.

If gays and lesbians wanted to make music, there were two rules: they
could not be out, and their lyrics had to be so obtuse as to render them
indistinguishable from heterosexual material. As for Black artists, a few
had broken through the racial divide to reach a white audience and thereby
garner crucial industry financial support, but mostly, Black artists were
represented by separate record labels, broadcast on separate radio stations,
and paid at vastly different rates. A white audience seeing a Black artist
onstage in the early '80s was still a novelty — though Michael Jackson,
Prince, and Tina Turner were testing those limits. To see Black and white
artists onstage together was rarer still.

That repressive system was the world Madonna entered at the start of
her career. Far from accepting it, she challenged it remorselessly and often
recklessly. Her youth had prepared her for the fight. It had introduced her
to racial harmony in music and racial animosity on the street; gay freedom
on the dance floor and homophobia away from it; the power of a woman's
sexuality and the sexism that tried to curtail that power; and, overall, the
cover that religions rooted in love provided the people who promulgated
such hatred. It was those lessons that would inform her life and art.

Packaged in the trappings of pop stardom, which made her ideas simultaneously more palatable *and* more dangerous, she set out to force open
every closet door and breach every racist and sexist barrier while offering
herself as actor, agitator, lightning rod. She also made herself an irritant,
sometimes even to her fans. She wanted to be loved, but not more than she
wanted to be heard. She had something she needed to say.

Young girls heard her message first. That vast army of adolescents who
were so easily ignored and from whom society expected so little heard her
admonition — girlfriend to girlfriend — to free themselves, be themselves,
dare to do *something,* the way she had done. Parents and the press were
amused at first but soon became alarmed by what they saw. Girls had
begun dressing like Madonna: leggings and lace, rags tied around
unbrushed hair. The adult concern focused on surface changes, how the
girls looked. Apparently of less interest to adults was what that mutinous
army, dismissed as wannabes, thought.

Feminist author Courtney E. Martin, who counted herself a member of
that cohort, said, "Madonna didn't teach me to be a heathen or a bitch or a

slut . . . She taught me to be brazen, unapologetic, and multi-dimensional . . .
It wasn't about the miniskirt; it was about the imagination."[7] Many girls
like Martin who listened to Madonna became powerful next-generation
activists — the riot grrrls and the girl power tribe, the postfeminists and
third wave feminists.

Within a few years, men and women, straight and gay, of all races
around the globe, had heard and understood Madonna and watched her
take body blows — repeatedly — for saying and doing what they didn't
quite dare to. She was particularly outspoken during the beginning of the
AIDS crisis, when the US government would not provide the funding
needed to find a cure for the disease, which at the start was killing men,
most of them gay, by the thousands. Madonna would lose some of the people she loved most to AIDS.

Hurt and furious, she used the megaphone of her celebrity and her personal wealth to try to remove the stigma and fear surrounding AIDS,
which affected not just those with the disease, but all gay men. Terror
became a partner to shame in those times. Being gay meant being not just
an outsider but also a pariah. Author Matt Cain recalled his frightened
twelve-year-old self in northwest England, grappling with his sexuality.

> It's difficult to overstate the emotional impact she had. When I was carrying
> around this "dirty secret" that I was gay and thought that everyone would
> hate me if it ever came out, I would go to my room, I would listen to
> Madonna, I would watch her videos, I would read her interviews, and I
> would feel like she was the only one who was on my side, sticking up for
> me. And then, things felt a little bit better because she was there for me.[8]

By the 1990s, even academics and intellectuals began to recognize that
this so-called pop singer, derided in much of the press as expert in little
more than the art of self-promotion, was an enduring and unique cultural
phenomenon and a multitalented artist. Universities offered courses on
Madonna. Scholarly papers and books examined her work and its impact.
Famous names began to court her personally and professionally.

In 1994, the lion of the macho school of new journalism, Norman
Mailer, interviewed Madonna after she had endured a particularly rough
patch following a disastrous appearance on *The Late Show with David Letterman*. Mailer reached two conclusions. The first, unpublished, described
Madonna with admiration as "a pint-size Wop with a heart built out of the
cast-iron balls of a hundred peasant ancestors."[9] His public declaration, in
Esquire, came soon after. There, Mailer called her "our greatest living
female artist."[10]

By the time she stood onstage at the Brixton Academy, Madonna wasn't a person as much as a concept. Just as the name Madonna once signified a gentle holy woman, it now denoted a celestial being from the entertainment sphere who spoke her truth, took shit for it, and kept standing. And yet there she was, looking every bit a normal person. More than normal. She was a mother.

After her first song, Madonna removed her jacket to continue her show in a T-shirt that bore the name of her newborn son—Rocco—on the front and the name of her four-year-old daughter, Lola, on the back. That simple gesture made a huge statement. Mothers weren't supposed to be rock or even pop stars, and if they were, they weren't supposed to flaunt it. Madonna did.

In that moment, she became the ultimate glamorous, glorious working mom: tough, muscled, defiant, aggressive, dancing like a dervish, and sexy as hell as she launched into the breakneck track "Runaway Lover," about a scoundrel of a man who had met his match in a woman. Her backup singers, Donna De Lory and Niki Haris, whose moves were usually so perfectly choreographed, danced during that song with abandon.[11]

Professionally, Madonna had much to celebrate. She had not had such a string of good fortune since the start of her career. During the previous five years, she had taken huge artistic risks with *Evita,* which required her to sing the film version of a beloved musical written by one of the masters of that form, Andrew Lloyd Webber—who, she knew, hadn't wanted her for the role. Madonna's performance earned her a Golden Globe.

She followed that challenging but commercial project with two albums that moved her in an entirely new and experimental direction. *Ray of Light,* created with reclusive British composer William Orbit, finally earned her the Grammy recognition that had inexplicably eluded her for the first fifteen years of her career. *Music,* which Madonna produced with Paris-based Afghan-Italian electrofunk composer Mirwais Ahmadzaï, mixed it up sonically and culturally in a way that reflected the direction her future work would take. Madonna emerged from those projects a more important artist.

In her personal life, she was as happy as she could dare to be. While filming *Evita,* she became pregnant by her partner, Carlos Leon. The birth of their daughter, Lourdes, nearly erased the pain that had shadowed Madonna's life after her own mother's death and all the death she had witnessed in the previous fifteen years as she watched her friends pass one by one in agony from AIDS. Lourdes—Lola—signified hope, a future. Light.[12]

Madonna herself was in every way reborn and able to give that loaded idea of family a try. She would do so with Guy Ritchie, the father of her second child, Rocco. His birth, in August of 2000, and Guy and Madonna's plans to marry, put Madonna in a settled and centered place she hadn't inhabited in thirty-seven years. She could be secure personally and bold creatively. Even the normally brutal tabloids gave her a (temporary) reprieve.

Sitting next to Mirwais on the stage in London, dressed in a cowboy hat and boots and singing "Don't Tell Me," Madonna seemed relaxed and happy. Her world was the one she wanted. It was a world of pushing boundaries, surrounded by people on all sides who could help her do that. Even the stage set had been a collaboration that helped tell her story.

That night, it was a quintessentially American tale of the Wild West, a look in the rearview mirror at an imaginary past as her life shifted from the United States to England. And to make sure it was told with humor *and* style, she had enlisted Italian designers Domenico Dolce and Stefano Gabbana to design a spaghetti western–themed set for the evening: golden bales of hay, golden cowboy hats, loads of rhinestones, and gold fairy dust.

Everyone got the joke. As Madonna danced in front of a filmed prairie with Donna, Niki, and four men in cowboy attire, the images were right out of pre-AIDS New York or San Francisco, when that look and those chaps were staples at gay clubs. "You like that?" Madonna asked the whooping and screaming Brixton crowd about the dancing before slowing her song to a halting repetition of its chorus: "Please don't, please don't tell me to stop." But stop she did. Madonna was out of breath. It had only been around three months since Rocco's birth. The Brixton set list gave Madonna a break with a slower song, "What It Feels Like for a Girl."

The word *girl* in the title didn't just refer to a female child. A girl in Madonna's song was anyone who felt powerless or voiceless, whether out of fear or because of tradition. Dropping to her knees, Madonna bowed her head to collect herself before beginning what one fan called "a fucking amazing song."[13] It was a feminist ode as bold and honest as "Express Yourself"—if more melancholy, because the ten-odd years between that earlier song and this one had not seen the big hand move very far toward dawn on the social enlightenment clock.

There was a sweet strength mixed with fatigue as Madonna sang. The crowd sang, too, with tears streaming down the faces of gay men who recognized their story in her lament. What no one in that audience could have known was how much worse the world would become in the very near future, and Madonna certainly couldn't have predicted that her picture-perfect life of November of 2000 would again deconstruct. That her attempts at happiness would once again be thwarted. That her work would once again be viciously criticized. That her personal decisions, which often provoked cruel reactions, would provoke the cruelest yet. And that she would have to start all over again—again.

"What It Feels Like for a Girl" and what it portended for the future were too somber a note to end on. So Madonna jumped back into the pickup truck and up onto its roof for a song she had been singing since 1983, which never grew tired: "Holiday." *The Guardian*'s Maddy Costa said that at that moment, "every person in the room [was] transformed into an over-excited teenager."[14]

To close the show, Madonna returned to the sounds the concert began with—"Music" and its distorted voice asking, "Do you like to...boogie-woogie?" The answer was not in doubt. Behind Madonna and her dancers, images of her various incarnations throughout her career sped by. It was daring to remind people of who she had been, because she risked being compared negatively to her younger self. But she must have known there *was* no real risk.

The forty-two-year-old woman onstage—surprisingly unadorned and slightly disheveled—looked every bit as beautiful, confident, and magnetic as those much younger selves. And that made the audience feel that they were okay, too. They weren't their twentysomething selves anymore, either. They were better.

PART ONE

Michigan

1958–1978

Chapter 1

Pontiac, 1958–1963

I don't think he had words for his pain.[1]

— *Madonna*

THE HOUSES WERE modest, the families inside young and frugal. In the summer, it felt like a neighborhood of children, whose adventures took place in small yards bordered by a chain-link fence, train tracks, and beyond that a sewer system that would, when they were old enough to climb the fence, become a new place to play.[2] When they were young, though, the yards were the extent of their world, and that was plenty. It was a world of motion and noise: cries and laughter, the sound of records and radios, the clatter and chatter from mothers cooking, cleaning, and hanging up clothes, and the shouted greetings of fathers, day and night, at the start and end of their shifts, mostly in GM factories. Only at twilight, after the children were in bed, did the streets grow quiet enough to hear the occasional TV laugh track through an open window and the continuous buzz of an electrical tower that loomed over the neighborhood, driving them all mad.[3]

Pontiac's Herrington Hills, like so many communities across the United States, was peopled with men and women busily rebuilding society after World War II. Theirs was the stuff of the American dream: faith, family, country. What made Pontiac unique was that its citizens were people of many ethnicities and races, all having been recruited in previous decades to come north to Michigan to work in the exploding auto industry. African Americans, Mexicans, Eastern Europeans, Italians, Irish — anyone and everyone from throughout the United States and abroad who wanted a union job and a settled future. In the late 1940s and early 1950s, GIs back from fighting joined the influx, and whole neighborhoods sprouted up to house them, just as schools were built to educate their children.[4] That was key to the dream. Having survived a hideous recent past, they wanted a better future for their children. They found it in Pontiac, where the school district became the best in the state.[5]

Silvio "Tony" Ciccone, twenty-four, and his new bride, Madonna Fortin, twenty-two, added to the Herrington Hills bustle when they moved into a small bungalow on Thors Street, in 1955. Their arrival came amid a second great wave of migration into the community, which filled it with people their age and at the same stage of life.[6] That meant that when Madonna began having children—five in five years, beginning with Anthony, in 1956, and Martin, in 1957—she was surrounded by mothers doing the same. The community of strangers became family, and that strengthened the young couple's bond as they embarked on what they fully expected would be a long and happy life together.

Tony Ciccone was the youngest of six boys born to Italian immigrants from the Adriatic region of Abruzzo who had settled in western Pennsylvania to work in the steel mills. His family was physically in the United States, but in every other way it had remained in Italy. The Ciccones lived among Italians, spoke Italian in the home and on the street, and filled their house with the dark and death-oriented Catholic imagery that made southern Italian churches so terrifying.[7] All the boys worked in the steel mills except Tony, who joined the air force and went to college. He exemplified the first-generation immigrant spirit. He was prepared to work hard, study hard, follow the rules—whatever it took to be American and raise American children who would enjoy opportunities vastly superior to his own.[8]

Madonna Louise Fortin would help him do that. She was a spirited, musical, and industrious young woman, one of eight children of French-Canadian stock. Her family lived in Bay City, Michigan, where her father had been successful in one of the region's biggest industries, lumber. They were considered upper class in that town of "sawmills and shipbuilders." The Fortins, too, were devoutly religious, but their version of Catholicism was less extreme than the Ciccones'.[9]

Tony and Madonna met in 1951 at the wedding of Madonna's brother, who was stationed with Tony at an air base in Texas. After a four-year courtship, carried on largely through letters while Tony earned an engineering degree, they married in Bay City in July of 1955 and settled in nearby Pontiac.

It wasn't the auto industry that drew them. Tony had a job in Chrysler's defense division. He was part of an elite class of scientists and engineers called upon to develop advanced systems to counter enemy technology.[10] It was a job that became more urgent after the Soviets launched the first man-made satellite, *Sputnik 1,* in 1957. The task facing Tony and his colleagues was to prevent war by making weapons so fearsome that no one would dare challenge them. In the process, they produced a technological and manufacturing revolution through the discovery of new materials and methods. It was a thrilling adventure for a young man determined to build himself a secure future.[11] Add to that a young family and a pretty wife, and Tony couldn't be blamed for thinking he had it all.

On August 16, 1958, during a visit to the Fortin family in Bay City, Madonna gave birth to the couple's first daughter, Madonna Louise. A tiny child with dark hair and green eyes, she would always be special in the Ciccone household because she was the first girl, because it was her nature to demand attention, and because of her name. It was an odd name, heavy with religious significance, and it was her mother's, bestowing authority on the child who had it.

Madonna—Nonni to her father—didn't occupy the coveted baby position for long.[12] Another daughter, Paula, was born in August of 1959, and a third son, Christopher, in 1960. The small Ciccone home on Thors Street burst at the seams with all those children.

Madonna's earliest memories as a toddler involve leaving the room she shared with her brothers and sister for the comfort of her parents' bed. "I think I must have done this a lot, gone in there, because they sort of sat up in bed and said, 'Oh, no, not again.'"[13] "Heaven" was how she described the kiss her mother planted on her forehead after she had climbed into bed to feel the night warmth of the sheets and the slightly cold silk of her mother's nightgown.[14]

The daytime household was infinitely rowdier. In the family's small living room, a record player spun Johnny Mathis, Harry Belafonte, Sam Cooke, and, most memorably, Chubby Checker's "The Twist." The whole family danced to that one.[15] But mostly the days involved children's play and children's fights and children's injuries. "I have a memory of my mother in the kitchen scrubbing the floor," Madonna said. "She did all the housecleaning, and she was always picking up after us. We were really messy, awful kids."[16]

Especially her older brothers. From an early age, they were troublemakers, setting fires, throwing rocks through windows. "I think my parents pissed a lot of people off because they had so many kids and they never screamed at us," Madonna recalled. "My brothers were very rambunctious...and my mother and father would never yell at them. They would just hug us and put their arms around us and talk to us quietly."[17] That may have been because the Fortin boys back in Bay City were wild, too. Or it may have been a matter of religion. Both parents' Christian beliefs informed every aspect of their lives.

Religion was fundamental to life in Pontiac, and because the population was so diverse, the congregations were, too. Catholic, Protestant, Baptist, Eastern Orthodox, Jewish, African Methodist Episcopal. A street might have a Catholic church on one corner and a synagogue on the other.[18] Life was lived as a cycle of religious observances. For the Ciccones, the church was *the* edifice outside the home. It was quite simply the ultimate lawmaker, and its tenets were not challenged. But inside the home, religion was embodied in the figure of Jesus Christ, whom Madonna senior treated as a living presence: someone to pray to, to feel protected by, to cherish.[19] Which is why what happened was so cruel.

Tony and Madonna had done everything right. They had lived good and generous lives, obeyed the dictates of church and state, and devoted themselves to their family. How, then, could it all unravel?

When Madonna senior was twenty-eight and pregnant with her sixth child, she discovered she had breast cancer.[20] As a younger woman, she had worked as an X-ray technician at a time when precautions weren't taken to protect medical staff from the effects of radiation.[21] The cause, though, didn't seem important. What mattered was the tragic result.

In stories about her mother, Madonna often recalled her religious fanaticism: "She would kneel on uncooked rice and pray during Lent. She would sleep on wire hangers. She was passionately religious. Swooning with it."[22] It is easy to imagine that the ferocity of Madonna senior's prayers and bargains with God only intensified after her cancer diagnosis. The prayers did not improve her physical health, but they gave her the strength to continue her pregnancy without cancer treatment and the inner reserve to hide her anguish from her children. "She was ill for a long time," Madonna recalled years later, "and she never allowed herself any sort of self-pity, you know. I don't think she ever allowed herself to wallow in the tragedy of her situation. So, in that respect, I think she gave me an incredible lesson."[23] But as a child, Madonna was mostly confused.

One of the most heart-wrenching stories Madonna has told of her mother's illness concerns a day when she wanted her mother to play with her. Madonna knew her mother was weak, but she didn't understand why.

> I remember she was really sick and sitting on the couch. I went up to her and I remember climbing on her back and saying, "Play with me, play with me," and she wouldn't. She couldn't, and she started crying and I got really angry with her, and I remember, like, pounding her back with my fist and saying, "Why are you doing this?" Then I realized she was crying...I remember feeling stronger than she was. I was so little, and I put my arms around her, and I could feel her body underneath me sobbing and I felt like she was the child. I stopped tormenting her after that.
>
> That was the turning point when I knew. I think that made me grow up fast. I knew I could be either sad and weak and not in control or I could just take control and say it's going to get better.[24]

Sometime after giving birth on July 1, 1962, to another daughter, Melanie, Madonna senior became so ill that she had to be hospitalized. And still, she maintained a facade of health when Tony brought the children to see her. "She was really funny, so it wasn't so awful to go and visit her there," Madonna said.[25] It became the place where the family came together, where they tried to re-create the warmth of home while talking to their mother in her iron bed and watching her grow gaunter with each visit. "My mother spent about a year in the hospital, and I saw my father going through changes also. He was devastated," Madonna said.[26] He knew what they didn't, that she would never come home.

Birthdays were big events for the Ciccones, but that year, they were different. Madonna turned five on August 16, 1963; Paula celebrated her fourth birthday less than a week later, and Christopher turned three on November 22, the day President Kennedy was assassinated. "One of the few memories I have of [my mother]," he said, is "a vague recollection of being pulled out of her arms in the hospital and not wanting to leave. And my father confirmed that, actually. She died right around my birthday."[27]

They learned about it in a phone call. On December 1, the family was in Bay City because the baby, Melanie, was staying with her grandmother. The kitchen phone rang: Tony answered, and when he hung up, he was crying. Their mother was dead, he said. Through his own tears, he told them not to cry. "I think he had to do that," Madonna said, "because I think he was falling apart."[28] Tony never spoke to the children about their mother's death. "He never said, 'How do you feel about it?' We never had a group hug," Madonna said. "We never had a cry. We never had... my father's very stoic and old school, and I think he was devastated too, and I don't think he had words for his pain."[29]

To Madonna, the news felt like "having your heart ripped out of your chest... the ultimate abandonment. It was a great mystery to me, where she went, and there was a part of me that was waiting for her to come back."[30] Tony, too, was desolate. At thirty-two, he was a single father with six children under the age of eight, one of whom was an infant.

The funeral for Madonna Louise Fortin Ciccone was held at Our Lady of the Visitation, the same Bay City church where she had been a young bride in white eight years earlier. Now she lay lifeless in an open casket with her lips sewn shut.[31] It was clear that she, or the lady who looked a little like her in the box, was gone. The light, it seemed, went with her.

> I know a place where no one ever goes
> There's peace and quiet, beauty and repose
> It's hidden in a valley, behind a mountain stream
> and lying there beside the stream I find that I can dream...

That song was Madonna's childhood favorite. She learned it from her mother. One day, she would sing it to her children, too.[32]

Chapter 2

Pontiac, 1964–1966

> Just the other day I found a photograph of me dressed in my
> mother's wedding gown when I was five years old. It was very
> strange.[1]
>
> — *Madonna*

For months after his wife's death, Tony moved the children around among
family members and neighbors. "My dad had to deal with so many things,"
Madonna said. "I went down the street and lived with this family for a
while. This poor woman had to put up with my rages and tantrums... The
woman had a daughter in a wheelchair with cerebral palsy who I thought
was luckier than me because she had a mom."[2]

Eventually, Tony hired a housekeeper to maintain order on Thors Street
so that he could keep the family together.[3] But he hadn't reckoned on the
fact that the children, who were unruly when their mother was alive, had
become even more so after her death. "We'd go through one housekeeper
after the other," Madonna said. "[We] hated them all."[4]

Madonna stepped into the breach of that revolving door of wardens to
become the pint-size woman of the house, or what she would call "the
main female."[5] It was a partnership; she and her father ruled the Ciccone
kingdom. Her older brother Martin said, "Madonna kind of assumed a
maternal role" for the younger children as they grew older, "feeding them,
making sure they were dressed, getting them ready for school."[6] She took
her job seriously to please Tony because she was terrified that she would
lose him, too.[7]

One of the attributes Tony instilled in his children—besides "honesty,
ethics, self-discipline, reliability, and honor"—was stoicism.[8] Madonna
tried to project that, but her body gave her away. "At that time, I had an
obsession with being ill, and I was constantly manifesting symptoms."
Sometimes she felt as though she had "ants crawling across [her] heart,"
which she assumed meant she had cancer.[9] She also developed a phobia
about leaving home and vomited if she had to spend the night elsewhere.[10]
Even at home, she couldn't sleep, and when she did, she had nightmares,

her feelings of loss exacerbated by guilt. "Children always think they did something wrong when their parents disappear," she explained.[11]

Gradually, however, as months turned into years, Madonna became stronger, bolstered by the discipline of the Catholic school she and her siblings marched off to every morning and the special attention she got from teachers who knew that she needed extra care.[12] And, at home, there was an almost military structure to their lives when their father was there: "He didn't like us to have any idle time," Madonna said. "If we didn't have schoolwork to do, he found work for us to do around the house. He thought we should always be productive."[13] Even in the minutes before the children fell asleep, he would sit in the hallway between the bedrooms telling the children stories to nourish their imaginations.[14] Madonna was Tony's best student. She absorbed all his lessons.

Among them was Tony's very deliberate effort to introduce his children to cultures outside their own so they would not be "prejudiced" or "unnerved by different people," Christopher said. Their house had a Black family on one side and a Hispanic family on the other. "We were also part of a...Catholic-Jewish organization," he said. "I celebrated Passover all my life, without realizing it was Passover. I thought it was Easter."[15]

Another anomaly in Tony's parenting was that he did not raise Madonna to be a girl. It most likely was not a conscious decision but the result of two factors: there was no female role model from whom Madonna might learn traditional femininity (what she called "manners and gentleness and... patience")[16] and his own intellectual drive. "My father never brought me up to get married and have kids," she said. "He actually brought me up to be very goal-oriented, to be a lawyer or doctor and study, study, study."[17]

The negative effect of not being schooled in the art of womanhood, however, was that Madonna could be accused of being too bold, too brusque, even vulgar. She behaved as she saw her older brothers behave. "I said what I wanted. I burped when I had to burp. When I liked a boy on the playground, I chased him. There was no one over me saying, 'Now, girls don't do that.' "[18] And so Madonna did, and in the process, she became "fearless."[19]

Madonna also learned that she possessed a power her brothers did not have. As early as age five, she recognized that if she *acted* feminine, she could get her way, a discovery she admittedly "milked...for everything I could."[20] For Madonna, it was more than a matter of getting things. Her charm earned Madonna *attention,* which was infinitely more valuable to a child struggling to be noticed in a household of similarly yearning children.[21]

That naive sexual awakening occurred around the time that she started to dance and sing. Her first mentors were on TV: Shirley Temple, whom she tried to copy, and the performers on *The Lawrence Welk Show,* a kitschy big-band variety show that simulated showbiz glamour with its floating bubbles, chandeliers, and ballroom dancing.[22] But her most important early lessons in music occurred in the neighborhood.

Pontiac, like its larger neighbor to the south, Detroit, was a town of cars and music, and neither was a matter of class or color. The immigrants who filled the auto-industry factories brought with them rich musical traditions, from the blues of the Mississippi Delta to the polkas of eastern Europe and everything in between. Some of it remained traditional, but some of the genres mixed, and new sounds were born. Children were introduced to music in church, even before they were introduced to pop or rock or soul or jazz or R&B or country.[23] And many of the same singers and musicians who played in the churches by morning played the clubs by night.[24] Music ran the pleasure scale from worship to wantonness in a single day without contradiction. It was all about the rapture.

Tony insisted that all the Ciccone children start with the basics and take piano lessons.[25] Of more interest to Madonna, though, was the music on the street. In 1963, the year her mother died, Berry Gordy Jr.'s Detroit music factory, Motown, became the undisputed center of the country's pop universe. Motown had ten singles on the Billboard top ten chart and eight more on the top twenty, representing an unprecedented tidal wave of music by Black artists. The Beatles arrived in the United States in 1964 to revolutionize the white sound, but even they didn't escape the Motown immersion. Their debut set included covers of early Motown songs, and they toured the UK that year with Motown artist Mary Wells.

The sheer number of stars arising out of Motown was so great that the Detroit talent pool seemed bottomless: Stevie Wonder, Martha and the Vandellas, Marvin Gaye, Smokey Robinson.[26] For children like Madonna, the Motown sound and story represented dreams realized. "Music was that area's only expression of self-assurance or escape," she recalled. "The music of the time was everything to almost everybody—listening and dancing to music, or aspiring to be this or that, was all people were interested in."[27] In Pontiac, she said, people had "yard dances [with] little 45 turntables and a stack of records and everyone just danced in the driveway and the backyard."[28]

Initially, Madonna had to fight to be admitted to the circle of friends in her neighborhood who were spinning those songs. "I had to be beaten up so many times by these little black girls before they would accept me, and finally one day, they whipped me with a rubber hose till I was like, lying on the ground crying. And then they just stopped doing it all of a sudden and let me be their friend, part of their group."[29] Once she was "in," Madonna and her friends formed imaginary girl groups, pretending they were on the road to stardom.[30]

During those early playful performances, Madonna assumed a persona. In the backyards of Pontiac, she didn't want to just dance and sing, as her friends did; she also needed to look like her friends to do justice to the music. "I was incredibly jealous of all my black girlfriends because they could have braids in their hair that stuck up everywhere," she explained. "So I would go through this incredible ordeal of putting wire in my hair and braiding it so that I could make my hair stick up."[31] From the start, the Madonna package involved song, dance, *and* style.

Through the mid-1960s, Madonna's and her siblings' lives involved a routine despite the chaos of their existence. There was school and church; tormenting housekeepers on the one hand and trying to please their father on the other; adventures involving various degrees of mischief (which Madonna the "rat fink" tattled on).[32] Also on the schedule were long summer visits with extended families: Tony's, in Aliquippa, Pennsylvania, and their maternal grandmother's, in Bay City. Both households had numerous uncles whom the children loved, but they considered the darkness of the Ciccone homestead frightening.[33]

Christopher said that, like other immigrant homes where hard-won possessions were valued, his Italian grandparents' house was filled with furniture covered in plastic.[34] By way of decoration, Grandmother Ciccone — Michelina — had decorated the home with rosaries, candles, and pictures of Christ. "If ever I go into her room, I find my grandmother on her knees praying to the Virgin Mary." Their grandfather Gaetano was a "heavyset, hunched-up old man who drinks too much." Christopher came to believe that his grandmother's ardent prayers were for the old man's death. After having six children by him, she slept in a separate room with seven locks on the door, which she kept bolted. When he finally died, Michelina believed he was haunting her, bolts be damned.[35]

By contrast, the Fortin family residence, in Bay City, was a true home away from home. Grandmother Elsie Mae Fortin was, according to Christopher, "a second mother to all of us." She wore feminine clothes, classic styles, and smelled of L'Air du Temps perfume. She was elegant, "a lady in every sense of the word."[36] Her husband, the children's grandfather, had died in 1959. But years later, the house was still redolent of his love for her. One birthday, knowing her favorite color was pink, he gave her "an all-pink kitchen: a pink stove, pink refrigerator, pink dishwasher." The atmosphere was warm, loving, and permissive, the way their mother had been. The children considered the Fortin home a haven.[37]

Packing his children off to visit their grandparents during the summer may have made Tony's life easier, but it was only a temporary reprieve as he juggled work and the needs of six growing children. He was also still a young man. In 1966, at thirty-five, he would have been expected to try to find a mother for his children, if not a companion for himself. In fact, there were several contenders. The Fortin family wanted him to marry a friend of Madonna senior, a Natalie Wood type the children thought looked like their mother.[38] Instead, he surprised them by announcing that he planned to marry one of the children's housekeepers, a twenty-three-year-old of northern European ancestry named Joan Gustafson.

The Fortin family was furious and forever after referred to Joan as "the Maid."[39] The children were equally disdainful. "She was really gung-ho, very strict, a real disciplinarian," Madonna said.[40] Christopher said the marriage occurred not long after *The Sound of Music* movie was released. He speculated that Joan may have expected the Ciccone clan to be as malleable as the von Trapp children. She was wrong. The children, he said, were "determined to make her life miserable."[41]

For Madonna, the entry of this woman into their lives reopened barely healed wounds and tore open new ones. "It was hard to accept her as an authority figure...My father wanted us to call her Mom, not her first name. I remember it being really hard for me to get the word 'mother' out of my mouth. It was really painful."[42] With Joan's arrival, Madonna also believed that she had lost her father.[43] "I felt in many ways that my step-mother stole him from me. I felt deserted," she said.[44] "I was just one angry, abandoned little girl."[45]

Madonna responded the way her mother did to her illness, the way her father did to his loss: with quiet resolve (and, unlike her parents, with bad behavior). Summoning all the courage she could muster, she professed a child's version of the adult survival strategy: "I don't need anybody. I can stand on my own and be my own person and not belong to anyone."[46]

Madonna met hurt with defiance, and she was helped in that regard by a song. In January of 1966, Nancy Sinatra's "These Boots Are Made for Walkin'" went to number 1 on the charts and shocked parts of America with its declaration of independence by a scandalous new breed of woman—a *Sex and the Single Girl* kind of woman—who had no time to waste on a double-dealing man. More shocking still, it was Frank's little girl, with her dyed blond hair, dancing in a black sequined minidress, black stockings, and high-heeled black boots.[47] As she did, she delighted in her power and made it clear that if any hearts were to be broken, hers wouldn't be one of them. Madonna said that Nancy Sinatra singing that song "made one hell of an impression on me. And when she said, 'Are you ready, boots? Start walkin',' it was like, 'Yeah, give me some of those go-go boots. I want to walk on a few people.'"[48]

Chapter 3

Pontiac, 1967–1969

Don't be afraid of me...I'm just a nice little girl.[1]

— *Patti Smith*

YOUNG MADONNA'S EMERGING awareness of pop songs came at a propitious moment, not just for her but also for American culture. It was a new era for women in music. Nancy Sinatra was just one of the many voices singing what women and girls generally didn't dare say. Like other aspects of pop and rock, that rebellious tradition was born in the blues with singers like Willie Mae "Big Mama" Thornton and Ida Cox, who delivered sassy, sexy declarations of independence from the no-account men in their lives. The lyrics were so hot in every way that they never quite made it into the white mainstream unless they were sanitized to the point of meaninglessness. Big Mama Thornton's growling indictment of a gigolo in her song "Hound Dog" became a nonsensical sensation when recorded by Elvis Presley.[2]

But in 1960, something began to happen in music. A new breed of female singer delivered an updated pop version of the saucy old blues sentiment. The Shirelles had a hit with the song "Will You Love Me Tomorrow." It was about a young woman deciding whether to have sex and it was revolutionary in every way.[3]

Cowritten by Carole King, "Tomorrow" was released the year the birth control pill was introduced, when women began considering sex without the risk of procreation. Sex for women, as it had always been for men, could be *recreation*. Of a sort. Culturally, a man's desire remained paramount, but the pill was a first big step on the path toward sexual freedom. It introduced the radical notion of choice into a woman's personal life.

The song was the first by a pop girl group to discuss sex so explicitly, and it shot to number 1 on the Billboard Hot 100 chart. That ranking was also a first: no girl group had had a chart-topping hit at that point—let alone a Black girl group.[4] "Tomorrow" and the Shirelles were a cultural and crossover sensation.[5] With their success, girl groups proliferated.

Most were Black or Latina working-class teenagers from New Jersey or New York City—young women like sisters Estelle and Veronica "Ronnie" Bennett and their cousin Nedra Talley, who as the Ronettes became the "first female superstars of rock." After their hit "Be My Baby" and a first album, they toured England in 1964 with the Rolling Stones as *their* opening act.[6]

The early girl group look was coiffed, clean, and demure. What that meant was that the lyrics they sang, which spoke to girls in a way no one had about their deepest desires and concerns, were shielded from undue scrutiny because the young women delivering them looked like "nice girls."[7] No one thought to listen to what those nice girls were saying.

Madonna began listening to girl groups a few years later, when Motown moved the sound to Detroit and made stars out of young women like Mary Wells, who had her first big hit in 1964 with "My Guy," and Martha Reeves, who with the Vandellas released "Dancing in the Street."[8] But the Motown sound and style for young women artists were epitomized by the Supremes.

Graduates of the label's "finishing school," then called the artist development department, they had learned to walk, sit, talk, and dress (in hats and gloves) — to be "ladies" in the whitest sense of the word.[9] The group had its first number 1 hit in 1964 with "Where Did Our Love Go" and ended the year with an appearance on the top TV variety program in the United States. On December 27, 1964, Diana Ross (age twenty), Mary Wilson (twenty), and Florence Ballard (twenty-one) sang "Come See About Me" on *The Ed Sullivan Show* and were catapulted to pop stardom.[10]

Around the time that the Motown sound flooded the streets, white girl groups like the Shangri-Las also emerged. They didn't train to be ladies. Because they were white, it was assumed they were bred for that role. The mischievous Shangri-Las, however, proved that race did not guarantee respectability. Their first number 1 hit was the 1964 bad-boy ode "Leader of the Pack," about a deadly motorcycle accident. It was considered so bleak and its sound so violent that it was banned in Britain and by some US radio stations.[11]

The Shangri-Las were not nice girls. They wore *pants and boots*. They also flirted with the audience and expressed their sexuality in a way that was forbidden to Black girl groups if they had any hope of crossover success.[12] The Shangri-Las' look and daring expression, combined with their lyrics, were powerful and thrilling in an entirely new way.

And then, if all those new sounds and images weren't head-spinning enough, a so-called British Invasion of women performers occurred in the United States in the mid-1960s. White, mostly blond, eyes outlined in kohl, wearing tight sweaters, miniskirts, and boots, they were women like

Lulu, Dusty Springfield, Sandie Shaw, and, coming on the scene in 1965, Marianne Faithfull. That wounded angel was just seventeen when she released the Mick Jagger–Keith Richards song "As Tears Go By." The British women offered alternative voices and "mod" looks.[13]

Madonna came of age at a time when a woman's self-expression wasn't exceptional; it was normal. Women and girls had voices people wanted to hear and ideas worth conveying about their dreams and desires, about love and that forbidden topic, sex; about fear and anger; even about death. And they sang words that girls understood in youthful voices they could mimic. Each memorized song amounted to a dose of empowerment shot directly into the psyches of millions of little girls.[14] The bold messages those young women delivered arrived at a time when Madonna needed them most.

The appearance of Joan on Thors Street in her new role as wife and step-mother upset the eccentric regimen of the Ciccone household. She immediately tried to organize the children, which only gave them more reason to rebel. "My stepmother was very young, and she just wasn't ready for a billion kids who were extremely unwilling to accept her as an authority figure," Madonna explained.[15] "It was a hard adjustment for all of us to make . . . We had some really rough times, I have to admit."[16]

The children gradually came to rely on one another, gathering in a bedroom for secret confabs. "You know how kids go to their parents when they have problems?" Madonna said. "Nobody really did that. They sort of went to me or my older brothers."[17] That may have been why Joan relied on her to help with the children. But Madonna regarded the work she had previously done willingly as drudgery now that Joan was asking her to do it. She also recognized that her brothers were given liberties that she wasn't.[18] "From that time on I felt like Cinderella with a wicked step-mother," Madonna said. "I couldn't wait to escape."[19]

In the meantime, Madonna developed defensive skills: she could be outspoken, belligerent, sarcastic, even cruel. She portrayed herself in the years after Joan's arrival as "the she-devil," struggling to gain the attention of her father, struggling to get what she needed amid so many grasping hands.[20] Madonna described the family household as "like living in a zoo."[21] Even her play became angry. "I played with my Barbie dolls all the time . . . And they were bitchy, man. Barbie was *mean* . . . Barbie would say to Ken, 'I'm not gonna stay home and do the dishes. *You* stay home! *I'm* going out tonight, I'm going bowling, okay, so *forget* it!' You know? She was going to be sexy, but she was going to be *tough*."[22]

The turmoil inside the Ciccone home was exacerbated that year, 1967, by turmoil on the street.

*   *   *

The high-water mark of the early civil rights movement was reached in 1963, when Martin Luther King Jr. previewed his "I Have a Dream" speech at Detroit's Cobo Arena and delivered the final version in Washington nine weeks later.[23] It moved the world, but words weren't strong enough to dislodge the racial hatred embedded in US society. Soon after King spoke, fifteen sticks of dynamite planted by white bigots exploded inside a Baptist church in Alabama and killed four Black girls. King's call for nonviolence all but perished along with them.[24]

Through 1964 and again in 1965, the year Malcolm X was murdered in New York, racial violence erupted in Miami, Cleveland, New York, Jersey City, Chicago, Philadelphia, and Los Angeles. In the summer of 1966, there was more violence, so much more that people in large cities began to dread the season. And then, 1967 exploded in what one historian called the "greatest urban riots of American history." There were more than 160 uprisings, eight of them major. The worst was in Detroit.[25]

It began before dawn on Sunday, July 23, when white police raided a party at an illegal club in a Black neighborhood.[26] Among the seventy-four people arrested were two Black soldiers recently returned from Vietnam.[27] After decades of discrimination, it was the last straw. Detroit and its surrounding communities, Pontiac among them, descended into five days of rage. Madonna, then nearly nine, remembered "all the white families were freaking out and moving out."[28]

At the time, the Detroit uprising was the worst in the United States since the New York City draft riots of 1863.[29] "The confusion, the misinformation, the prejudices, and the fear that was running high cannot be overstated," said local historian Mike McGuinness of the 1967 trauma. "The fear and racial tensions were driving many of the changes in where families chose to live. It sparked massive numbers of Caucasian families moving quickly out of Detroit and out of Pontiac."[30]

Madonna said later that she saw herself as the character Scout in *To Kill a Mockingbird*. "Basically, she was this little girl who was surrounded by all this insanity, from Boo Radley hiding behind the door to the sadness and violence all around. She was always asking her father questions. I wanted my father to be Gregory Peck."[31] Tony Ciccone was too busy. The family had begun welcoming more babies. Joan's first after marrying Tony died, but in 1968 she had a daughter, Jennifer.[32]

Unfortunately, 1968 was another inauspicious year. That spring, the violence of the previous summer began early, in April, after Martin Luther King Jr. was assassinated in Memphis. Again, cities erupted. Again people were killed and injured, neighborhoods ravaged. Robert Kennedy had joined the presidential race as an antiwar candidate, offering himself as a social healer, especially to Black communities. With his still-fresh grief after his brother's murder, his words felt, to a people in deep pain, almost spiritual. And then in June, he was killed, too. Another bloodied body on the television, more dreams dashed.

There seemed to be no end to the suffering, no hope at all. That summer, in Chicago, the Democratic National Convention, where Kennedy would have accepted his nomination, turned into a scene of shocking violence. Chicago police beat demonstrators as news cameras broadcast those images around the world. Democracy in America. Rebellion, assassinations, and war. Citizens hungry for order thought Richard Nixon could do the job. He was elected president.

Madonna was ten. That was the nation the children of her generation were introduced to when they became aware that they were part of a society, a country, and a political system. That was their imperfect heritage. The best that could be said of it was that the dark secrets that had been festering belowground for decades—in the case of modern racism, since the lies of Reconstruction a century before—were now exposed to the light of day.

Joan gave birth again in 1969, to a boy named Mario. The family had outgrown the Thors Street house, and there was no reason to wait around for more trouble.[33] In 1969, the Ciccones joined the white flight to safety and landed in a place called Rochester Hills.

Chapter 4

Rochester Hills, 1969–1972

Who do I think I am? Someone who I believe is more than what she is told she could be.[1]

—*Mona Eltahawy*

"THAT WAS THE first time I felt out of place," Madonna said. "Suddenly I lived in a white middle class suburb, and I suddenly became aware of the differences of people." The irony of Madonna's discovery—that it took a move from a racially and ethnically diverse enclave to a community of what she called white conformists for her to realize that people were "different"—was not lost on her as an adult.[2] As a child, however, she felt desolate and angry about the move, which is also ironic. For an American family in 1969, a move from Pontiac to Rochester Hills should have been an exciting step upward and outward.

Rochester, as the locals called it, was part of the 1960s building boom, in which landscapes near crowded and insecure cities were plowed under to make way for suburbs. It was like the post–World War II emergence of identical starter homes that blossomed overnight to house young families. The suburbs of the late '60s similarly sprang up where fields had recently yielded crops, but they differed from those earlier tract-house communities in that the homes were less uniform and more spacious. They were the communities those young families moved to when Dad graduated from the sales force to the executive suite. Families in places like Rochester weren't aspiring to a better life; they had already achieved it.

In 1969, Rochester had a charming historic town center, parts of which dated back to the nineteenth century. A smattering of houses had been built on the outskirts of town, but the new Ciccone family home was, at the time, on the outskirts of the outskirts, in an area still considered rural. It was a newly built two-story, five-bedroom, redbrick-and-aluminum-siding structure with a wagon wheel ornament on the front lawn—a popular totem of the pioneering American spirit. Compared to the family's former residence, on Thors Street, the house on Oklahoma Avenue was huge, as was its yard: more than an acre of land with a creek, rather than a train track and sewer system, at the back.[3]

All the things that should have made the home appealing were, to Madonna, depressing. "There weren't any more house parties, there wasn't music blaring from the house next door," she explained.[4] She had left a vibrant, densely populated neighborhood for a remote, culturally homogeneous backwater. "Her school was small. Rochester was white," explained Mike McGuinness. "The Italians would have been the darkest people in Rochester."[5]

The children were enrolled in St. Andrew Catholic Elementary School. For Madonna, a religious education and the rituals of Catholicism might have provided comfort because it was a culture she knew well. But in those mutable days, even that had changed. The mystery of the church, with its Latin mass and the priest as a figure apart, positioned midway between God and his flock, ended when the Second Vatican Council completed its work, in 1965. The idea was a good one—to make Catholicism more about the people than about "the Church." But the result of that modern approach was that the religious hierarchy became human and the church considerably less divine.

By the time Madonna arrived at St. Andrew, the contradictions between Christianity and modern Catholicism were too great to go unchallenged. A religion based on goodness was obsessed with sin; a religion that celebrated light as a metaphor for revelation was instead, in Madonna's words, "dark, painful and guilt-ridden." A prime source of such guilt was sex.[6] "When you are raised to believe that anything having to do with sex is forbidden and taboo," she said, "then of course that's all you want to know about."[7]

Madonna had hints from the time she was "tiny" that this thing called sex, which was shorthanded in adolescence to "boys," might be interesting. Her Italian grandmother, locked away behind her myriad bolts, had "begged" Madonna as a child "not to go with men, to love Jesus and be a good girl."[8] Tony Ciccone delivered the same message.[9]

It was Madonna's family members who were instructing her, but the authority behind them was the church. At the very moment when, biologically and emotionally, a child begins to experience a wonderful new sort of attraction for another person, church teachings would have those feelings shut down, the door to healthy development closed tightly against pleasure. And worst of all, neither the church nor the family offered any explanation.

Madonna bombarded her reticent father with new questions, many about gender-based rules that to her young mind were patently absurd. For example, in the dead of a bitter Michigan winter, girls and women were expected to wear skirts to church.

> I would say to my dad, "Will Jesus love me less if I wear pants? Am I going to hell?" I wanted to know why...girls had to act a certain way and boys

didn't...My whole adolescence was full of unanswered whys. Because they never got answered, I just kept lighting fires everywhere—metaphorically speaking.[10]

Without addressing points of theology at that stage, Madonna came to believe the church and her family were much harder on her than they were on her older brothers. If Catholicism was a religion of sinners, it seemed that women and girls were considered the most dangerous among them because the laws and customs designed to control them were the most severe.[11]

Madonna responded by rebelling. "I wanted to do everything everybody told me I couldn't do," she said. "I'd do *anything* to rebel against my father." She violated her father's dictates and Catholic school policy by rolling up the waistband of her skirt to make it shorter and switching her socks for nylons after she had left home.[12] "Probably about the same time as I began to rebel against the church and my family, my breasts started to grow," Madonna said. "So right around that time was when I really started to think about sex. About its presence, not about what I was going to do about it."[13]

It is interesting to put Madonna's childhood rebellion against the church in the context of her career. She never stopped rebelling against the church, but she also never lost her fascination with it, to the point where it is impossible to separate Madonna from Catholicism.[14]

Madonna often said that she would not be the person she was if her mother had lived; that loss was foundational to her life and future work. Another post under the House of Madonna is the church. The unresolvable conflict between its physical and spiritual beauty and the almost medieval rules with which it tried to govern nearly every aspect of believers' lives made Madonna who she was, and, given half a chance, it would have prevented her from becoming who she could be.

But Madonna was freed of the burden of a Catholic education by the state of Michigan. In 1970, the state passed a ballot initiative that banned state aid to private schools.[15] With eight children, the Ciccones simply could not afford to pay for religious schooling.[16] That meant that Madonna was headed to public junior high school.

In the Catholic imagination (if not in reality), junior highs were hormone factories where pimple-faced boys began to exert their socially sanctioned dominance. They were places where girls became objects, first of fascination and then of conquest; where cigarettes, booze, and drugs were staples of Friday night parties; and where, in general, juvenile delinquents were hatched and let loose on the land.

Madonna's older brothers, Anthony and Marty, were already the "wildest kids in the neighborhood," according to Christopher.[17] Without the stern oversight of priests and nuns, Tony and Joan would have been justified in fearing that the younger children would go the same way, so they instituted stricter rules at home. Madonna remembered being particularly beleaguered in that regard. "It was school, come home, housework, help with dinner, do your schoolwork, clean the house, take care of the little kids."[18]

If the children needed disciplining, Christopher said, Joan chased them with a wooden spoon. If they sassed or swore, Tony washed out their mouths with soap.[19] If Madonna talked too much or too loudly (her nickname at home was "the Mouth"),[20] she was reprimanded. "I remember always being told to shut up. Everywhere, at home, at school."[21] Tony also severely restricted Madonna's social life. "He never let me do anything. Not being able to go out when all my friends were going out, not being able to wear nylon stockings or lipstick or a bra or whatever was a tragedy to me," she said.[22] Tony expected his word to be the one that counted. "You'll do this because I say so." End of discussion.[23]

If moving to Rochester awakened Madonna to the idea of white exclusivity, her first year at West Junior High School opened her eyes to her family's social position. At Catholic school, she and her siblings wore uniforms, which created a sense of equality among students. At West, there were no uniforms; children of wealth were visibly cloaked in privilege. Meanwhile, Madonna and her sisters wore home-sewn dresses made from a single pattern. Madonna was aware that her family was, as she said, "living above our means." "My clothes were not as cool as everybody else's or as nice as everybody else's...I mean, I'd wear the same clothes every day...I just didn't fit in."[24]

Even if her classmates hadn't noticed Madonna's clothes, she appeared odd to them because she didn't fit the usual girl mold: she was flirtatious, but she wasn't submissive or deferential to boys. "They took my aggressiveness as a come-on," she said. "They didn't get it. And they didn't get *it,* if you know what I mean, so I guess they had to say things because they knew that was the only way they could hurt me."[25]

Without anyone to help her understand these dynamics, Madonna felt "overwhelmed...I'd handle it in a number of ways—either I'd get more arrogant...or I'd get upset and cry. You can get hurt by it, or you can give them the finger. But it still hurts."[26] Madonna called junior high the start of the angriest period of her life.[27] It was then that she perfected the defensive counterattack skills that she would use throughout her career as the schoolyard bullying continued into her adulthood. "It's about insecurity," she explained.[28]

*   *   *

It was a given in her household that Madonna would play a musical instrument. "My father was really big on that," she said. "There was always music in our house. Either practicing or records or the radio or someone singing in the bathtub...Noise."[29] Tony wanted Madonna to take piano lessons, but she hated them.[30] She persuaded her father to let her take dance lessons instead at a school that taught ballet, tap, and baton twirling. She called it a refuge for "hyperactive young girls."[31]

By the early 1970s, pop and rock music had become about performance as much as about sound. In the rock universe, there were "rock operas" (the Who's *Tommy*) and "rock musicals" (*Hair*). In the world of concerts, events went big: Woodstock, Altamont, Monterey Pop. And all those music festivals were filmed so that the unlucky millions who didn't see the shows in person could watch Jimi Hendrix, Janis Joplin, Jim Morrison, the Rolling Stones, Grace Slick and Jefferson Airplane, and Bob Dylan, among many others, become more than singers, rockers, guitar players, and folkie balladeers. They became cultural icons who courted controversy and made statements.

Many of the statements the artists made were political. It was no longer possible, amid the deeply unpopular Vietnam War, civil rights protests, and the murder of students by the National Guard at Kent State, to simply play a tune you could tap your foot to. *Serious* music had to say something. Devotees of that music listened to the new FM radio stations and their hipster DJs, who broke with rollicking AM radio DJ tradition by whispering into their studio microphones, as befitting the solemnity of the rock message.[32] The scene was *heavy,* as were its fans.

It was also, despite the presence of incredible talents such as Slick and Joplin, a manly man's world of phallic substitutes and the jackhammer rhythm of the male climax.[33] The gulf between rock and pop became an unbridgeable chasm. Rock was art, or so its practitioners and fans believed, and pop was—well, not art.

At the other end of the musical performance spectrum were new TV shows with kicky pop culture sensibilities, such as the irreverent comic variety show *Laugh-In* and *The Sonny and Cher Comedy Hour.*[34] On NBC, *The Monkees* portrayed the trials and tribulations of a boy band. ABC added a twist to that narrative. *The Partridge Family* was about a mom and her kids trying to make it as a rock band. Long before the days of video, therefore, pop-rock was a visual experience that ran the gamut from the sublime to the absurd.

Madonna's musical interests had expanded since Pontiac, but they remained firmly rooted in pop and soul.[35] By 1970, the girl group phenomenon had died.[36] In its place, Madonna began listening to boy bands that had emerged in the wake of the Beatles: the Box Tops, the Turtles, Strawberry Alarm Clock, Gary Puckett and the Union Gap.[37] But the music phenomenon that interested her most at that time was the Jackson 5.

Motown had signed the Indiana-based brothers in 1968, and the Jackson family proceeded to dominate the charts. The sound was infectious, exuberant, in the best pop tradition, but it also had weight, because unlike the white boy bands, the Jackson 5 sound updated the blues, R&B, and the northern soul Motown tradition. Madonna became fascinated by Michael Jackson—the way he sang, the way he moved onstage, his abandon, and the absolute joy of his performance. "I went through an 'I want to be like Michael Jackson phase,'" she said, recalling her feeling that "I can do everything he can do, only I'm a girl!"[38] His presence was also a nagging reminder that life was short, and she had better get moving. Jackson was already firmly in the spotlight, and he was Madonna's age.

Madonna began performing at West Junior High. "The talent show was my one night a year to show them who I really was," she said, "and what I could really be, and I just wanted to do totally outrageous stuff."[39] One year, dressed as a spy, she danced to the pseudo-noir song "Secret Agent Man," by Johnny Rivers.[40] But her biggest splash took place during her last year at West.

Madonna's brothers were FM disciples and listened in the basement to music by the Rolling Stones, Bob Dylan, Led Zeppelin, and the Who. That band's new song "Baba O'Riley" caught Madonna's attention, and she decided to use it in her eighth-grade performance.[41]

The night of the show, the West Junior High auditorium was filled with families waiting expectantly for their children to arrive onstage. The many Ciccones were seated in the second row. Christopher said Tony even brought his camera to memorialize Madonna's big night. First came the tap dancers, and a student playing the harmonica, and another who recited a poem.[42] And then the stage darkened, black lights and a strobe were lit, and the electronic marimba rhythms of "Baba O'Riley" filled the room. Madonna and her friend Carol Belanger, meanwhile, appeared out of the darkness, covered in green-and-pink hearts and flowers that they had created with fluorescent body paint. By the time a bass sounded, and Roger Daltrey launched into the Who's ode to dissolute youth, the hearts and flowers onstage were moving in an unmistakable exultation of adolescent sexuality.[43]

No one "can take their eyes off Madonna," Christopher said. "She's wearing shorts and a top that are also covered in paint, but as far as my father is concerned, she might as well be naked. According to his strict moral code, her appearance is utterly X-rated, and he puts down his camera in horror." [44] Nearly everyone was horrified, as Madonna and Carol danced to Daltrey's screams and continued to move while the music built to a berserk crescendo, crash-landed, and died.

The lights went up, but not to the warm applause that had greeted previous acts. Christopher described the audience as "dumbstruck." Madonna's performance was "the most scandalous one that anyone has ever seen in that conservative community."[45] In the car after the show, he said, everyone was silent, and once they arrived home, Tony took Madonna into the dining room. Known by the family as the "formal," that was where serious reprimands occurred. "When she finally emerges, her face is tearstained. Her performance is never mentioned again," Christopher said. But around Rochester, it was the talk of the town for about a month. Kids whispered to him, "Your sister Madonna is a slut."[46]

The audience at West had seen "Madonna," the future phenomenon, in embryo. They were the first to witness the artist who would make a career of combining pop culture with more complex art forms—in this case, the look of a show like *Laugh-In* with the music of the Who and the politically provocative message of the song. Music, dance, sex, politics, and an imaginative presentation. It's easy to see the seeds of Blond Ambition in her performance of "Baba" that night.

Madonna was grounded for two weeks, and then that summer, between eighth and ninth grades, her father shipped her off for a period to her grandmother's house in Bay City. Madonna "loved going there." Her grandmother's idea of child-rearing was liberal in the extreme. Madonna said she could go out with boys, drink beer, "have twelve desserts...and stay out past ten."[47] Nanoo, as they called her, let her sons, Madonna's uncles, smoke pot in the basement and practice their rock band in her garage.[48]

"I thought they were the coolest people in the world," Madonna said. "I remember that summer I was watching my uncles' rock 'n' roll band—wearing tight jeans for the first time in my life. I smoked a cigarette...I started plucking my eyebrows and I started feeling like, 'Yeah, this is it, I'm cool.'"[49] Madonna said her uncles were the first people to treat her like a grown-up. "When I got home, my stepmother went crazy and accused me of being a tart."[50] "I felt like I had really grown up—only to find out that I was a floozy." Madonna was crushed.[51]

She responded as she usually did when told not to do something: she did it anyway, and then some. "From that day I adopted the floozy look to the hilt," she said.[52] Padded bras, tight sweaters, heavy makeup, and eyebrow pencil to enhance a beauty mark.[53] And with that, Madonna started high school.

Chapter 5

Rochester Hills, 1972–1974

There's gonna be a woman musician in the next three or four years that's just gonna knock everybody's heads off... There's gonna be some girl who right now is maybe fourteen, and she's gonna blow everybody's mind. I just can't wait.[1]

— *Linda Ronstadt*

IN 1972, WHEN Madonna began high school, it seemed that anything was possible for a young woman. The victories chalked up by feminists were front-page news. After fifty years of lobbying by women's rights advocates, the House and Senate passed the Equal Rights Amendment, and by the end of the year, twenty-two states had ratified it. Title IX, which threatened to withhold federal funds if schools discriminated against women in education or sports, was codified into law. *Ms.* became the first mainstream feminist magazine. Its inaugural issue sold out in eight days.[2] Tennis star Billie Jean King graced the cover of *Sports Illustrated* for her athletic ability.[3] New York congresswoman Bella Abzug recognized 1972 for what it was—"a watershed year"—and asked, she presumed rhetorically, "Who'd be against equal rights for women?"[4]

It was a thrilling time. The reality the girls of Madonna's generation inherited was one in which women were strong and independent. When Helen Reddy's song "I Am Woman" was denied radio play after its May 1972 release, Reddy didn't cower and accept it. She used any occasion to sing what became a feminist national anthem until it reached number 1 on the Billboard chart in December and earned her a Grammy. Regarding her critics, she said, "For a lot of men, thinking about the women's movement makes them grab their groins. What can I say? I didn't say that we were going to cut their dicks off or anything, you know?"[5]

Feminism was the movement, but in popular parlance it became "women's lib." Its successes were the result of a combination of organizing, politicking, and hard work, enlivened by some headline-grabbing agitprop campaigns. The first such event occurred in 1968, and it was historic. Writer and activist Robin Morgan had the idea of performing a "zap action" to protest the Miss America pageant by parading sheep the way the pageant paraded women and releasing a "stink bomb," which was actually a hair product made by a pageant sponsor, inside Convention Hall in Atlantic City. But the action that captured the news was the so-called bra burning.

The story about the charred bras was written and filed by a reporter in advance of the pageant. In fact, no bras were burned. Nothing was burned. But women gathered outside the hall did ceremoniously deposit a variety of "torture devices," or artifacts of cultural misogyny—stenographer's pads, hair rollers, false eyelashes, wigs, high-heeled shoes, copies of *Playboy,* girdles, and bras—into a "Freedom Trash Can" as news cameras rolled, and police escorted the women away.[6]

The protest garnered more attention than the pageant and became a successful recruitment tool. Women around the country started forming feminist groups of their own. The women's movement thereafter operated on two levels, as *New York Times* columnist Gail Collins noted: the National Organization for Women scored legislative victories, and young activists took to the streets employing guerrilla tactics that ensured that women's demands remained in the headlines.[7]

Of course, the backlash against those "angry" women began almost immediately: conservative activist Phyllis Schlafly got to work in 1972 to defeat the ERA. And still, the dominant cultural message was that the role of a woman was to look good and support a man's ambitions. (The largest source of college scholarships for women were beauty contests, and the most popular "team sport" for girls was cheerleading.)[8] But for the first time since World War II's army of Rosie the Riveters, there was a counternarrative that said that women didn't have to shelve their dreams. And that was lucky for Madonna, because she didn't have a retiring bone in her body. The questions for her were how to manifest her strength in a conservative community that hadn't quite heard the same message and what form that show of strength might take.

Playwright Thulani Davis wrote in the *Village Voice* in 1980 that a blues singer is "the woman who left home, left early, at fourteen, fifteen, even eleven. She was not an outcast as much as a cast out, a been-gone, a faraway, a woman with a will to be outside of society, a fantasy. High or low, she could be something she could make up on her own."[9] That was Madonna at fourteen. Physically, she hadn't left home, but mentally, she was "been-gone." As soon as she entered high school, she decided to leave Michigan.[10] "I wanted to be somebody," she said.[11]

> I used to dance in front of my mirror to the Isley Brothers, to "Who's That Lady, Beautiful Lady, Sexy Lady"…I just assumed I was that sexy lady. Of course, I was desperate for that to be the truth.[12]

A survival tactic adopted while she struggled to give birth to herself was to live a double life: one intensely private, sad, angry, and insecure, the other a ballsy bravado performance for public consumption. What Madonna called her public-private "paradox"[13] helped her survive Rochester Adams High School.

Adams was one of the best public schools in the state, and its student body was even more affluent than West's. "They had nice houses and lots of bathrooms," Madonna said.

> I somehow gauged lots of bathrooms with being incredibly wealthy, instead of having to share one bathroom with eight children. And I could tell the difference between the sort of generic food that we had in our refrigerator—you know, buying food in bulk and there's no label on it?—and the serious labeling going on in other houses.[14]

To add to her humiliation, she had a job cleaning houses, which included those of her schoolmates. "It was gross. I had to clean the toilet bowls of boys I went to school with," she said.[15] "They were members of country clubs," she said. "I felt like a country bumpkin and I was resentful...because I felt like people were judging me all the time."[16]

Madonna wasn't part of the "Anglo-Saxon tribe" that dominated the school. "Being like everyone else was important, dressing like everyone else was important, having the same hairstyle, wearing the same makeup, dating the cool guy," she said. "I didn't understand it and I didn't like it and I didn't fit in."[17] And yet to others, she seemed to. A classmate at Adams said that when Madonna arrived in ninth grade, "she was the belle of the ball."[18]

Madonna the outsider was so convincingly inside that she moved immediately to the heart of the school's social scene by joining the cheerleading squad (which she scandalized by wearing flesh-colored tights so that when her skirt lifted during a flip, she looked naked).[19] She became part of the school's intellectual crowd through the French club. She worked as a lifeguard and a swim instructor. She sang in the school choir. She displayed her altruistic side by volunteering at a program for disadvantaged children.[20] And she assumed a heavy academic load, for which she received top marks. "The bitch never had to study, man, never, got straight As," her older brother Marty said. "I used to get up there and study all the time...I did it cause I was supposed to...She did it because she knew it would get her over to the next phase."[21]

On the face of it, Madonna was what her brother Christopher called "very popular...outgoing."[22] But schoolmate Wyn Cooper recognized the dichotomy in Madonna. "She kept to herself, but she was also a cheerleader, so she seemed to have almost two sides to her personality," he said. "I don't think anybody could quite figure her out. She was a little bit of an enigma."[23] Cooper was intrigued. "She took herself more seriously than most of us did at that age ... She read more than your average high school student."[24]

While Madonna was still a freshman, Cooper told her he was making a movie and asked her if she wanted to be in it. "She didn't have a problem with it," he said, adding that even at that age Madonna was willing to test her limits in front of a camera. In Cooper's film, that meant eating a raw egg.[25] His one-minute 8mm silent movie, *The Egg,* would be Madonna's first film. It involved two girls, three eggs, and a urinal.[26]

The film screamed surrealism—baby Dalí or baby Buñuel. Cooper said it was about nothing. Out of it, however, arose a friendship between the director (whose poem "Fun" would be the basis of Sheryl Crow's hit "All I Wanna Do") and his star.[27] It was also a new avenue of expression for Madonna. Film was, and would be, one of her greatest passions.

Madonna immersed herself in school life not only because she was hungry for knowledge but also because she wanted to escape a home where she found little cheer.[28] She described her older brothers as always in trouble and suffering the consequences. "I was really frightened by them but completely enamored of them as well," she said.[29] As for the younger children, there was one perpetually underfoot in need of attention.[30] Madonna's family obligations were so well known that a cheerleading coach who heard she wanted to go to a Friday night dance helped her out by calling Joan to say, not entirely truthfully, that cheerleaders were required to attend.[31]

From the outside, the Ciccones looked like the quintessential Middle American family. The house was filled with the accoutrements of warmth: "the spindle-backed chairs, the fake spinning wheel in the corner, the wooden icebox that held the records," Christopher said. "We went to church all the time. We went to Sunday school, we went to catechism, and during Lent we went to church every day."[32] But amid all that cozy rectitude there was a coldness. "I think our father ... spent most of his time preparing us for the rest of our lives," Christopher said. "The things I learned from him were honor, loyalty, and the value of the truth: all the things that surround the ideas of love and affection, but not love and affection themselves. Our father's concern was our survival. He taught us discipline."[33]

Christopher believed that any love his father had to spare went to Madonna, who occupied a special place in his heart because she was named after their mother.[34] But Madonna mostly remembered Tony's disapproval. "My father was always angry with me. He wanted me to have more humility, more modesty," she said. "He always felt I should be doing my homework or reading the Bible or meditating."[35] Instead, when her brothers weren't around, she went to their bedroom, in the basement, and listened to music. Bob Dylan's "Lay Lady Lay" made her cry. "I was going through adolescence, I had hormones raging through my body," she said.[36] But it was the singer-songwriter women who inspired her.

By the time Madonna was in high school, a new type of solo woman artist had entered the world of rock and pop, though it was difficult to categorize them as part of either genre. The best of them were poets with guitars and pianos whose lyrics reflected a woman's point of view. For the most part, their lyrics weren't overtly feminist, but their lives were. Women such as Joni Mitchell, Carole King, Judy Collins, Janis Ian, and Laura Nyro were examples of what an independent woman artist looked like and what she could do.[37]

Two other women with unique voices during that period were notable in a slightly different way. They added a dose of sexuality to their work. In the Mitchell-King-Collins songs, you had to search for the sex. In the work of Carly Simon (who wrote her own songs) and Linda Ronstadt (who mostly interpreted other people's work), sex was part of the package, and it was a new kind of woman-owned sex. It was sex as power. Sex as fun and funky. And in Simon's case, it was teasingly bitchy.

Madonna discovered all those artists, but the most important to her was Joni Mitchell.[38] "I worshipped her when I was in high school. *Blue* is amazing," Madonna said of Mitchell's most personal album at that point. "I would have to say of all the women I've heard, she had the most profound effect on me from a lyrical point of view." When *Court and Spark* was released, in 1974, Madonna said it was "my bible for a whole year. I knew every word of every song on that album."[39]

At the same time in high school, Madonna began to "gobble" books: F. Scott Fitzgerald, Ernest Hemingway, Flannery O'Connor, J. D. Salinger. Reading Salinger, she said, "gave me license to behave eccentrically in a way...and made me feel comfortable in being precocious."[40] She also consumed poetry, the more tragic and confessional the better.[41] Madonna and her younger sister Paula, with whom she made a pact not to do anything "conventional" with their lives, exchanged books of poetry in the room they shared with their little sisters—three to four beds in the room.[42]

Anne Sexton was their favorite. "First of all, she looked like my mother," Madonna said, "and second of all I thought her language and her ideas and her imagery were so bold and extraordinary and her voice was so unique." Though Sexton was "oppressed" and "incarcerated by the world," Madonna said, she had found freedom through writing.[43]

Madonna would say that Sexton was one of three women artists in whose work she heard the message: "Get out of here, there's a bigger life waiting for you, and there's a place where you're gonna feel more comfortable."[44] The other two were dancer Martha Graham and painter Frida Kahlo. Madonna would be introduced to them through a man named Christopher Flynn.

Chapter 6

Rochester Hills, 1974–1976

I said, "Oh my God, I've found it."[1]

— *Madonna*

AROUND THE TIME that Madonna met Christopher Flynn, the disparate pieces that would become Madonna the artist came together: sex, dance, and musical performance. In 1974, at the age of fifteen, Madonna had intercourse for the first time, began to study ballet in earnest, and saw David Bowie in concert. Of the three, the sex was probably the least transformative, but it was one of those things that ranked high on a teenager's to-do list. The other two, Flynn's classes and Bowie's music, were simply life-changing. Flynn would put Madonna on the path she needed to follow, and Bowie would be the lodestar toward which she traveled.

Flynn was in his midforties, around the same age as Madonna's father, when she turned up at his dance studio in downtown Rochester Hills. It was a strangely sedate place for him to be. Born John William White in New England, he had left home for military service and came back to go to school on the GI Bill. He enrolled at Harvard to study clinical psychology, but his heart belonged to dance. He had been exposed to it before joining the navy after seeing the Martha Graham company perform.[2]

To satisfy his stage desires while studying at Harvard, he acted and sang in theatrical productions. And then one day, an English professor asked him, "Why are you here, when it's dancing you really want to do?" That was the nudge John White needed, and he began to study ballet part-time in Boston. It was there that a member of the renowned American Ballet Theatre noticed him and suggested he come to New York. The decision to ditch academia for a dream was easy. Adopting the more artistic name Christopher Flynn, he said, "Forget Harvard. Off I went to become a dancer."[3]

Flynn didn't join the American Ballet Theatre. Instead he studied with Russian dancers who followed a strict ballet tradition in both style and culture.[4] But while Flynn absorbed those lessons and would be the ultimate disciplinarian with his own students, it wasn't Russian ballet he was after. Modern dance in the decade after World War II had exploded as an art form as well as a political and social statement. Flynn wanted to be part of that. Serendipitously, he met Robert Joffrey, whose company was so new that it had a mere five dancers and traveled the country in a station wagon. Flynn joined Joffrey's school first as a student, then as a teacher. Finally, he became Joffrey's assistant.[5]

By the 1960s, Flynn's emphasis in dance had shifted from performing to teaching, and he left New York for the Midwest. In Rochester he opened his own school and company, the Christopher Ballet, on the second floor of an old Masonic temple building on Main Street.[6] It was an unassuming location and could have been dismissed as a place where girls (few boys took ballet in those days) could learn grace on their way toward proper womanhood. But Flynn was not training debutantes; he was training professionals.

"I think Christopher was a radical ballet teacher in that he would use... any kind of imagery that might help a dancer think," said Peter Sparling, a dancer who would work alongside Flynn at the University of Michigan dance department.

> He was really going for a thinking dancer. He expected a lot of intellect and intelligence in the process of learning dance. And in that sense, he was working outside the typical boundaries. I think, too, that he was looking for expressivity. He was trying to encourage these young mostly women to break out of their shells and to find ways of expressing through their bodies without feeling confined or afraid. He saw dance and technique as a vehicle toward becoming a performer.[7]

Madonna discovered him through a girl in tenth grade who she thought was more intellectual than most students, more "offbeat." She was also a serious dancer. "So I attached myself to her," Madonna said, and learned about Christopher Ballet.[8]

Madonna had taken various dance classes, and she had performed in every talent show, play, or musical produced at Adams High, often to acclaim.[9] Her "breakout event" was a school talent show in which she sang and danced to "Turn Back, O Man," from the pop musical *Godspell*. Madonna received a standing ovation.[10] "I remember that when the audience stood for the curtain call, she was crying," recalled student Clara Bonell. "The sense of acceptance, I think now that this is what she most appreciated, most craved."[11]

Madonna *did* want attention and appreciation, but she wanted something else even more: the chance to become who she believed she could be. She also needed someone to help her find the way to do that. "Everyone used to say, 'You have such a nice voice,' and everything," Madonna said. "It still didn't make me feel like I could get out of the situation I was in in Michigan...I didn't know anyone in New York. I didn't have any famous relatives, and I had no money or anything. I just didn't have an inkling how I should go about doing anything."[12]

Enter Christopher Flynn. Madonna's friend invited her to observe a dance class. "It was beautiful," Madonna remembered.[13] And so was Flynn, not in a conventional way but because he was so unselfconsciously artistic. He was also mischievous, witty, and "worldly wise," according to Madonna.[14] His accent was less a result of geography than breeding. When he walked ramrod straight, stepping heel-to-toe into the studio, cigarette dangling from his fingers, he commanded attention. "He was seductive, not in a sexual way," said Peter Sparling. Rather, he was magnetic: "He had a way of pulling you into his story."[15]

Madonna told her father that she wanted to enroll. He said that if she wanted to take another dance class, she should get a job, because "I'm not paying for it."[16] She did and showed up at Flynn's studio one day ready to begin. Flynn recalled his first impression of her as "very young, barely out of adolescence, playing a little child, with short, kind of dishwater blond hair. You know, nothing special." She carried a doll "that was, oh, probably two feet long, a little girl doll, you know with a little dress and so forth, stuck under her arm. Looked like just the most innocent child in the world."[17]

Madonna was a teenager. She had weathered storms that had required her to accept adult responsibilities. She had the intellectual interests of a more mature young woman. She had experimented with sex.[18] Madonna was, in other words, no longer a child. And yet, interestingly, Flynn's recollection was that she appeared at his studio in character: in the guise of a vulnerable waif.

Her look broadcast to him that she was ready to start from scratch— that prior to arriving at his studio, she had accomplished nothing. Madonna "was a blank page, believe me...and she wanted desperately to be filled in," Flynn said. "She knew nothing at all about art, classical music, sculpture, fashion, civilization—nothing about life, really...But she had this burning desire to learn, that girl. She had a thirst for learning that was insatiable. It was something that would not be denied."[19]

Madonna's brother Christopher didn't know she was taking ballet, but he noticed that she had changed. "Madonna starts going out every Thursday night and coming home looking tired but happy," he said. "Soon after, she gives up cheerleading, loses weight, and starts wearing black sweats instead of her usual brown-and-gold plaid skirts and sweaters."[20] Her focus turned entirely to dance. She went through the motions of her life at school and at home, but her mind was on Flynn's studio. Madonna said,

> It was like a fantasy world that I'd stepped into.[21] I didn't know what I was doing, really. I was with these really professional ballet dancers...so I had to work twice as hard as anybody else and Christopher Flynn was impressed with me...I really loved him. He was my first taste of what I thought was an artistic person.[22]

He was also the first out gay man she had ever met. "I didn't understand the concept of gay at that time...All I knew was that my ballet teacher was different from everybody else. He was so alive. He had a certain theatricality about him."[23]

Flynn was a new breed in every way, but he did share some important characteristics with her father. Flynn was, according to Madonna, "very Catholic," extremely disciplined, and demanding of perfection. "He was brutal. He was ruthless, and he walked around with a stick and he hit you with it," Madonna said. "He would not tolerate laziness or complaining... But when you did something right, he did feed you compliments, once in a while."[24] That tough love was straight out of Tony Ciccone's playbook. Years later, Madonna said, "I'd say that after my father, the most powerful, important relationship of my life was with Christopher Flynn."[25] Indeed, Madonna the phenomenon had two fathers. Tony Ciccone gave Madonna discipline, a work ethic, and familial experiences good and bad from which to draw. Christopher Flynn gave her culture and a means of expression.

Flynn became a kind of wizard, revealing a vast and magical creative landscape and the rich tradition to be found in the arts and its history, from the paintings of Frida Kahlo at the Detroit Institute of Arts to the dances of Martha Graham that he loved so well. He did it because he recognized that Madonna wanted and needed that education. He did it because he recognized that that little girl was, as she believed herself to be, special.[26]

Madonna came away from Flynn's classes replenished and revived. Through dance, she said,

> I could go from being unmolded clay, and over time and with a lot of work and with people helping me, I could turn myself into something else. Before I started feeling devoted to dancing, I didn't really like myself very much... I spent a lot of time loathing myself...When I started having a dream, and working toward that goal, having a sense of discipline, I started to really like myself for the first time.[27]

Flynn also had a direct role in helping Madonna actually *see* herself differently. Once, when she was in his studio with a towel wrapped around her head, he took her face in his hands and said, "You know, you're really beautiful... You have an ancient-looking face. A face like an ancient Roman statue." Madonna was stunned because no one had ever said that. "I knew that I was interesting, and of course I was voluptuous for my age, but I'd never had a sense of myself being beautiful until he told me. The way he said it, it was an internal thing, much deeper than superficial beauty."[28] She added, "No one had woken up that part of me yet."[29]

Madonna and the *Egg* movie director, Wyn Cooper, liked to cruise the streets of Rochester in his 1973 Mercury Capri listening to music "while enjoying a little marijuana," as he described it. Their favorite album that year was David Bowie's *The Rise and Fall of Ziggy Stardust and the Spiders from Mars*.[30] It was rock opera from another planet. It was the poetry of despair. It was a celebration of androgyny and transvestism. It was a denial of class and a defense of artistic aristocracy. It was an homage to rock 'n' roll and a mockery of its practitioners' staggering self-regard. And it was great music rooted in the R&B and soul Wyn and Madonna knew so well. Bowie's next tour, to promote his album *Diamond Dogs,* would bring him to the Cobo Arena in Detroit in June of 1974, and Madonna wanted to be there. It would be her first concert.

The week before the show, after planning to see it for months, she finally approached her father to ask if she could go. "He said, 'Over my dead body.'" Madonna and a friend went anyway by sneaking out of the house and hitchhiking to Detroit.[31]

Bowie's tour was a postapocalyptic extravaganza. The set looked like a constructivist painting, a Gotham City of rakish skyscrapers, enlivened by many moving parts. A catwalk descended from the Cobo rafters as Bowie performed "Sweet Thing," and a cherry picker lifted him forty feet above the audience as he sang into a red telephone the haunting line "ground control to Major Tom" from his famous song "Space Oddity." Bowie himself called the performance "the first real rock'n'roll theatrical show that made any sense."[32]

In the audience, Madonna watched, rapt. "I remember just being frozen. Rigid. Like, staring up at this creature thinking, 'Oh my God, he's everything. He's male and female and beautiful and elegant and poetic and funny and ironic and... other-worldly'... And I recognized myself in him somehow and he gave me license to dream a different future for myself."[33] *She* could be that wisp of a man onstage who had invited thousands of strangers into his imagination. As for her father, Tony grounded Madonna after he discovered that she had disobeyed him, but she said it was worth it. Revelation such as she had experienced was well worth the cost.[34]

*   *   *

Madonna returned to school following her summer break no longer wanting to be part of the high school scene. "I belong in some *special* world," she recalled thinking.[35] "When I latched onto the dance thing, I was with older and more sophisticated people. I felt really superior."[36] She said she "hated the mentality of all the jocks...On the other hand, I hated the laziness and the sort of...spaced outness of everybody that was a pothead or an acid head." Neither did Madonna have time for boyfriends—or if she did date someone, it didn't last more than a couple of weeks. "I mean guys didn't understand me anyway," she said.[37]

Academically, however, she remained driven: she loved her French class, Russian history, and English classes. Those teachers had become mother figures to her.[38] And she continued her involvement with the school's theater projects, even founding the Adams High School Thespian Society. But all those activities were in service to one thing—what her brother Marty called the "next phase." She said, "I didn't have many friends; I might not have had *any* friends. But it all turned out good in the end, because when you aren't popular and you don't have a social life, it gives you more time to focus on your future."[39]

Fellow students remarked that Madonna looked different. She didn't bother with makeup. She wore her hair short and messy, dressed in strange clothes, and stopped shaving her armpits and legs. People asked one another, "What happened to *her*?"[40] But some of Madonna's teachers understood and applauded the change. "She was taking dancing lessons after school when a lot of kids were out having cokes and burgers and having a good time," said guidance counselor Nancy Ryan-Mitchell.[41] Said French teacher Carol Lintz,

> Something happened to her at this time, and it caused her to no longer think of dance as a social act, but rather as an artistic one. There she would be in the middle of the dance floor at one of those teen dances, by herself, dancing. People would ask me with whom she was dancing. I would answer, no one. Herself. She was dancing with herself. Just for the experience.[42]

In 1975 Madonna no longer traveled the roads of Rochester on a Schwinn bicycle.[43] She had passed her driving test, and her father gave her a red 1966 Mustang. (Christopher said that at that point the family driveway had so many cars it "looked like a parking lot.")[44] Madonna was free, independent, and confident—sometimes too confident. "I'd literally put my hand over her mouth to shut her up," said her friend Carol Belanger.[45]

One afternoon, when Madonna and Carol took her car to a nearby gravel pit to swim, bikers began dropping firecrackers on them. "Madonna yelled up and told them to knock it off," Carol said. "The next thing I knew, one of the biker girls came down and started hitting her in the mouth. We finally got away, but Madonna had a black eye and bruised cheek."[46] Christopher recalled later that day watching Madonna stroll into the house, beaten up, and acting as if nothing had happened. "I'd never seen anything like this," he said years later. "Her resilience was something that stuck with me. And it's never left me."[47]

Madonna's new assertiveness spilled over into her interactions with her stepmother. Madonna's name no longer featured on the chore list that Joan wrote up each morning. Christopher said Joan was afraid of her. Once, when Madonna came home late, he said, Joan slapped her. Madonna responded by doing the unthinkable: she slapped Joan back. Tony took her car keys away for a week and grounded her.[48] But the point was made. Madonna at sixteen was, like her older brothers, officially beyond Joan's control. What Joan didn't know, what none of the family knew, was that Madonna had become a member of a new family that encouraged and empowered her most audacious self.

As part of her education and because it was a great place to dance, Flynn took Madonna to a brand-new club in Detroit on Six Mile Road, below the city's racial no-go line.[49] Menjo's was the first Detroit disco to feature a DJ mixing records. A squat, nondescript industrial structure, it resided in the middle of a neighborhood of single-family homes, art deco apartment buildings, and stately Tudor residences, some of which had been left to ruin in the post-uprising flight from the city. The gay community adopted the area. "It's not like it's the Castro District in San Francisco," said Mike McGuinness, "but it's as close as you can get in Detroit during that time frame."[50] Menjo's, local historian Dave Decker said, "became the epicenter of gay life."[51]

Once inside the club, Madonna was overwhelmed by what she saw. To the ecstatic sounds of Vicki Sue Robinson's "Turn the Beat Around" and Hot Chocolate's "You Sexy Thing," "men were doing poppers and going crazy," she said. "They were all dressed really well and were more free about themselves than all the blockhead football players I met in high school."[52] Through the darkness, amid the pinpoint lights of the mirrored disco ball, she could see people of every color, age, and sexual orientation dancing together in what looked like one big undulating embrace. "I said, 'Oh my God, I've found it.'"[53]

Discos like Menjo's were sanctuaries, places away from rules and laws and reprobation. It was a world confined within four walls, but inside those walls there were no limits. At gay clubs in the 1970s, *everyone* was a star on the dance floor. Everyone had a particular look that telegraphed a desire or a story. Every night was a party. Every night was experienced as if it were the first and last. Participation required nothing more than a three-dollar entry fee and absolute abandon.

"I'd never been to a club," Madonna said. "I'd only been to high school dances, and no guys would ever ask me to dance, because they thought I was insane." She continued,

> I felt like such an outsider, a misfit, a weirdo. And suddenly when I went to the gay club, I didn't feel that way anymore. I just felt at home. I had a whole new sense of myself...Until that point, I kept seeing myself through macho heterosexual eyes...When Christopher introduced me to this life, I suddenly thought, "That's not the only way that I have to be."[54]

Madonna was unabashed in her fascination with Menjo's. "There would be boys off in the corner doing, well, *everything,*" Flynn said, "and she would just walk right up and stare."[55] She hadn't even really understood what made Flynn so different from other men in her life. She just knew she felt comfortable with him, enjoyed his lifestyle, and loved the way he treated her. And now she found a club full of men like him, and her joy in Christopher's company was multiplied.

> I started spending a lot of time with dancers, and almost every male dancer that I knew was gay. Then I went through another kind of feeling inadequate because I was constantly falling in love with gay men...I was so miserable that I wasn't a man.[56]

It was at that moment, at the age of sixteen, that Madonna began the love affair with gay dancers that would last throughout her career. And it was at that moment that they began loving her back. "She would clear the floor and we'd just start cutting loose," Flynn said.[57] "God, she was hot... She was total fun in that outrageous way. Boys practically knocked each other over to dance with her...She was wild, and her wildness excited them."[58]

The joy Madonna witnessed at Menjo's was the result of a revolution. After nearly a century of abuse, shame, and discrimination against gays, some protections were being codified into law. In 1973, the American Psychiatric Association dropped homosexuality from its list of mental disorders. In 1975, the federal government made it illegal to deny government employment to anyone based on sexual orientation. Also in 1975, California struck down its antisodomy law. (Although gay sex acts were still crimes in most states.)[59] And by 1976, there was a National Gay Task Force, a Lambda Legal Defense and Education Fund, and a Gay Rights National Lobby. It's likely that none of that would have happened if not for an uprising that took place during the early hours of June 28, 1969, in Greenwich Village.

A bouncer at a Mob-owned gay club on Christopher Street called the Stonewall Inn had looked through the peephole to see three policemen poised for a routine harassment raid. Normally, police would check identification, survey clothing for "unnatural attire," and exchange verbal abuse with the patrons. But a mayoral race was underway, and a new precinct commander wanted to make a show of being tough on homosexuals. Stonewall, with its drag queens, brown and Black teenage boys, and lack of a liquor license, made an easy target.[60]

That night in June, as the last of the many customers deemed to have broken the law were shuffled into a paddy wagon, police led a handcuffed lesbian toward a patrol car. Whatever the officers' intentions that night were, a ride in a patrol car rather than a paddy wagon could mean a trip to an alley and a sexual assault by the arresting officers. The woman in the squad car that June fought back by trying to escape. After three unsuccessful attempts, she shouted to the crowd outside the bar, "Why don't you guys do something?" The scene exploded.[61]

Some people searching for reasons behind the depth of the passion that night pointed to the full moon; some pointed to Judy Garland's death. But really, as in all rebellions, there wasn't *a* spark. The gay, lesbian, and trans people in the West Village were tired of being harassed and arrested for being who they were. A Stonewall patron said, "Being gay meant feeling hunted." That night they took a stand, and it became legend.[62] A voice shouted, "It's the revolution," as stones, beer cans, bottles, even bags of oranges from an Orange Julius store rained down on police.[63]

On Sunday night, after two days of mayhem, a tenuous truce was reached. The battle of Stonewall had been won. "It felt kind of good not to take that shit anymore," said Miss Major Griffin-Gracy, a trans woman who was arrested the first night of the uprising. "We aren't going anywhere; there are no closets to hide in. We burned the house down." Gay power. Gay rights. Gay love.[64] The first Gay Pride marches were held the following year. New York's began on Christopher Street. That time, the police were there to protect the revelers.[65]

There is nothing sweeter than freedom experienced by one long deprived of it, and that was the scene Madonna entered—one of sweet freedom. Mike McGuinness, who years later would be a Menjo's patron, said, "There is a certain magic to your first aha moment, 'This is my place.' To a certain extent in life, we're always trying to capture that in a bottle."[66] Madonna would make a career of reliving the thrill of her introduction to that scene, and she would do her best to bring her audiences along with her.

Aware that she had started studying ballet late, Madonna tried to make up for lost time by taking classes at a college in Detroit that allowed high school students to study dance and rehearse with older students. During her last year at Adams, she went to school in the morning and drove into Detroit in the afternoon.[67]

Madonna was so eager to leave high school that she finished her studies a semester early, in December of 1975, and danced full-time through the winter in Detroit and at Flynn's studio. But that was about to change, because Christopher Flynn had been hired to teach at the University of Michigan's new dance department.[68] Flynn and Madonna's guidance counselor, Nancy Ryan-Mitchell, wanted her to audition for the Michigan program, too.[69]

It was inevitable that Tony Ciccone would meet Flynn, because he was intervening in Madonna's life. Tony was also concerned because Madonna wanted her brother Christopher to study dance with Flynn. "I remember my father meeting him and knowing right away that he was gay and having an adverse reaction," she said. "I remember my father being a little bit weirded-out about that, like a 'don't bring him around [your brother]' type of thing."[70]

Christopher Ciccone was two years younger than Madonna and extremely artistic and sensitive. "At that point, I was playing the violin in high school. I was doing some scribbling as an artist. I didn't think of myself as an artist. It was—a creative need," he said.[71] He also didn't think of himself as a dancer, but Madonna encouraged him. Christopher called that introduction to Flynn's school "the greatest gift Madonna has ever given me."[72]

In fact, Madonna had sensed that her little brother was special. "He was so beautiful...I knew something was different, but it was not clear to me," Madonna said. It was when Madonna introduced her brother to Flynn that she understood. "I just saw something between them...But then I thought, 'Oh, I get it. Oh, OK. He likes men, too.' It was this incredible revelation, but I didn't say anything to my brother yet. I'm not even sure he knew...He was still a baby."[73]

Christopher Ciccone didn't know. "I was completely unaware of the world of homosexuality or being gay," he said. But he *was* interested in dance, though he was nervous about Tony's reaction. "My father wanted me to be an engineer, to be a doctor, to be a priest, anything but a dancer," Christopher said. Madonna promised to work it out with their father. In the meantime, Christopher went with Madonna to downtown Rochester each week to "observe" her class.[74] That bit of teenage skullduggery was the beginning of a bond between sister and brother that would produce a rich decades-long artistic collaboration.

After graduating from Adams High in 1976 with the school's thespian award and a spot on the honor roll, Madonna received a four-year dance scholarship from the University of Michigan.[75] She was the first of her siblings to go to college.[76] Madonna's father was "pretty damn proud," Marty said, but he wasn't sure if Madonna recognized it. They fought too much, and she felt such anger toward him. Father and daughter were ready for a break from each other, Marty said, and college gave them that distance. The family had high hopes for Madonna as she left for Ann Arbor. "We all knew she was going to really come into her own."[77] Madonna believed it most of all.

Chapter 7

Ann Arbor, 1976–1978

Behind every great man is a great woman, and behind every great woman is a gay man.[1]

—*Madonna*

ANN ARBOR WAS only an hour away from Rochester, but it might as well have been another planet. While Rochester prided itself on being a bastion of conservative America, Ann Arbor trumpeted its reputation as one of the most liberal cities in the United States. It was also home to one of the nation's most politically radical universities, the place where the national student protests of the 1960s were born.[2] Whereas Rochester was cloistered and protected from forces beyond its small borders, Ann Arbor was a way station for a notoriously subversive underground—from feminists to antiwar activists to civil rights heroes—as they traveled the country giving speeches, organizing, and generally raising hell. And though Rochester's cultural offerings were well regarded, they were mostly tried-and-true productions featuring local talent. By contrast, Ann Arbor and the University of Michigan were favorite and frequent stops for major international cultural figures from across the artistic spectrum. The city and school were, quite simply, an intellectual oasis in the northern snow.

Madonna arrived there in the fall of 1976 and settled into one of the women's dorms. "That was the deal her dad made: if she wanted to go to Michigan she had to live in an all-girls' dorm," said Madonna's friend Linda Alaniz, now a photographer, who arrived at Ann Arbor that same year to study dance.[3] Dancer Peter Kentes remembered walking by the dorms and seeing Madonna hanging out her window shouting greetings to guys on the street below, taunting, teasing, laughing at their surprised reaction, and flirting if they stopped to talk. It wasn't sex or a boyfriend she was after.[4] Hers was an expression of pure joy, of being "shot out of a cannon," as she would say.[5] Without father, stepmother, siblings, church, or classmates to limit her actions and desires, she could do what she wanted, dress as she wanted, *be* who she wanted. Kentes called her a "wild child."[6]

Madonna loved Ann Arbor and wanted to be part of everything: the

academics, the art, the performances, the poetry readings, the activist politics, the nightlife. She credited the University of Michigan with introducing her to a lifelong passion, foreign films.[7] "I fell in love with people like
Resnais, movies like *Hiroshima Mon Amour*...Pasolini's films. I watched all
the Visconti films, and Buñuel...and De Sica."[8] At that point, the university offered her the best of all possible worlds. It contained all the ingredients necessary to satisfy her insatiable appetite for knowledge and her
equally insatiable appetite for fun.

The university had had a dance program for many years, but only in
1974 did it establish a dance department. When Madonna arrived, two
years later, the department had fewer than one hundred students, and the
official dance building wasn't ready, so the students worked in an old gym-
nasium that was so decrepit it was overrun with mice. But in early 1977,
the new building opened, and it became a protective and creatively nurturing ecosystem within the larger university. "Students pretty much lived
here," Peter Sparling, the dance professor, said.[9]

The building looked like a small high school, with two levels and four
large dance studios. All the students—graduate and undergraduate
alike—crowded together in the halls, locker rooms, offices, and lounge.
The lounge was where Peter Kentes first saw Madonna. He was a twenty-
five-year-old graduate student who had been living in Los Angeles, trying
to make it as a dancer. She was an eighteen-year-old freshman who had
just left home. Despite their differences, they became friends because they
were both Christopher Flynn's favorites. Especially Madonna. Peter said
Flynn loved her and used her to demonstrate how he wanted a dance
performed.[10]

Each day Madonna had two ninety-minute dance classes—ballet and
modern—plus classes in dance composition, dance history, the study of
movement, and art history. In order for a dancer to earn a degree, one-
quarter of his or her course load had to be academic.[11] But the focus of
Madonna's life was Flynn's class. He created a blueprint that Madonna
would rely on and return to later in her own work.

Flynn was a tyrant about technique, about mastering the basics until
they became second nature. And yet, he said, his main goal was "to get
people to stop playing it safe."[12] Madonna, too, would be meticulous to the
point of obsession about practice, about working out every single detail of
a performance in advance. But that meticulousness, a kind of creative
insurance policy, was always in the service of risk. It *allowed* her to take
risks. In those early days at Michigan, however, her risks seemed more
prank than artistry.

Madonna, whom some students called Maddie, was a self-described
ham. "I did everything I could to get attention and be the opposite of

everyone else," she said. Amid dancers trained in a strict ballet tradition — pristine tights and leotard, hair in buns — she ripped her leotards, wore her short hair randomly chopped and intentionally messy, burped loudly during pliés, and, when it was hot, wondered why she couldn't just dance in a bra.[13]

"She was beautiful, and she had this kind of energy that was like, 'Look at me,'" Linda Alaniz said.

> One time, our Afro dance instructor...asked for dancers to perform in a church. During our rehearsal, the first thing Madonna does is walk up to the pulpit, pick up the microphone and...start singing at the top of her lungs, "Good golly Miss Molly, sure like to ball." We were all laughing, and the teacher went ballistic: "Get down from there right now, that's sacrilegious." She loved being the center of attention. There were so many sides of her that she wanted to get out there and even back then, she would recreate herself on a daily basis.[14]

Peter Kentes said that Madonna was unusual, if not unique. Once, her family visited her at school dressed for a Sunday outing, and Peter could see that she wasn't at all like them. But then he realized "she wasn't like us either." As a hobby, Peter cast horoscopes and offered to do Madonna's. What emerged was something he'd never seen in the hundred or so charts he'd read: the signs pointed unmistakably to fame and fortune. When he told Madonna, she replied blandly, "I know."[15]

Madonna wasted no time in finding her way around Ann Arbor. She had various jobs and, through them, became acquainted with town life. One of her most important discoveries was a gay disco. Located literally on the other side of the tracks, the Rubaiyat — or, in local speak, the Rube — was far enough from campus to feel like outlaw territory.

That year, 1977, disco was in its heterosexual heyday: *Saturday Night Fever* was a box-office hit, and discos had gone mainstream. But that didn't mean clubs were no longer transgressive. The Rube was, and Madonna went there often. "We'd dance, like, eight hours a day, eat, have a little nap, and go to the Rubaiyat until it closed," Linda said. "It was a safe place to go because you could just dance. You didn't have to worry about creepy guys picking you up, because it was a gay bar."[16]

Madonna never had money and was always scrounging for food, according to Kentes. She was very small and very thin, as per Flynn's directives.[17] But the overall impression Madonna gave was one of sinewy strength: she had muscled arms and legs and a powerful will that felt almost tangible. "She worked really hard, but she played really hard," Kentes said.[18]

*   *   *

The Michigan dance department was a seedbed for New York companies. Madonna's dream was to dance with Alvin Ailey, and that year her dream seemed less fanciful: she learned that Ailey offered a six-week summer program. With Christopher Flynn's support, she applied for a scholarship. One possible hitch—she needed to audition in New York. That problem was solved with the help of a local hairdresser and future dance student named Mark Dolengowski, whom Madonna had befriended while working at a pizzeria. Dolengowski agreed to take her on a whirlwind journey in his father's car across six hundred miles of winter roads in February in a single weekend so Madonna could return to school on Monday. "I remember it was a sixteen-hour trip," he said. "And I did all the driving."[19]

Madonna was accepted into the Ailey program.[20] "So all I needed to do was get some ditsy-esque job somewhere so I could pay my rent," she said. "When you live with dancers, you live like ten people in one dinky apartment and your rent's like twenty-five dollars a month."[21] She found a spot on the Upper East Side that suited her needs and prepared to live for the summer in the only city that mattered for an artist.[22] But the municipality that eighteen-year-old Madonna Ciccone discovered in June of 1977 was a dystopian nightmare.

New York in the mid- and late 1970s was the scene of so many horrendous crimes that the police department distributed public-service handouts warning tourists not to leave their hotels after dark. The brochures were part of a police union action designed to win concessions from the city, but the messages on them were true.[23] During the summer of 1977, the hell that was New York had never looked so frightening.

It was the summer of the Son of Sam murders, committed by an assailant who terrorized the city by preying on random couples, especially those that included young women with brown hair.[24] "Everyone was freaked out and I was worried about her," Dolengowski said.[25] It was also the summer when Puerto Rican nationalists exploded bombs in midtown.[26] And that was on top of the shootings, stabbings, tens of thousands of burglaries, and more than five thousand rapes recorded that year. Amid a crippling fiscal crisis and a police department overstretched by the Son of Sam case, one writer said, "Downtown was almost unpoliced."[27]

Then, at 9:36 p.m. on July 13, New York City went dark. A lightning strike triggered a series of outages that plunged the city into darkness. With the power out for twenty-five hours, the streets erupted in an orgy of arson and looting that resulted in the largest mass arrest in New York's history: nearly four thousand people were thrown in jail.[28]

If Madonna was frightened by the mayhem, her fear didn't diminish her ambition. She worked through the noise and the crime, driving herself to the point of exhaustion in the dance studio.[29] She left the city at the end of the program determined to return and become a leading dancer. "Once I got a taste of New York, I knew I had to be there," she said.[30] But before she did, she needed to hone her skills.[31] Arriving back in Ann Arbor, she also needed a place to live.

Whitley Setrakian was a New York City kid to the marrow. She had spent her childhood in a one-bedroom apartment on First Avenue in midtown. Her father, actor Ed Setrakian, moved out when Whit was a toddler, and she lived with her mother, an actor turned teacher. When Whit was eighteen, she left the city to go to college upstate at Brockport to study dance. Two years later, she and two male dancer friends transferred to the University of Michigan, a "real place" that produced real dancers.[32]

They found a two-bedroom tenth-floor apartment that would be affordable if they could find a fourth roommate. University Towers, as it was called, was a nineteen-story concrete box along a street of shops, restaurants, and bars not far from the dance building.[33] (The Towers' only claim to fame or art or anything other than academic desolation at that point was that Iggy Pop had lived there in 1970 to be closer to his heroin connection.)[34] Whit called the place a "sin against God" but moved in anyway and began searching for a fourth "victim" to share the space.[35]

"Someone said, 'Oh, there's a girl in the department who's looking for a roommate, too.' I remember the first time she came over, she was a little intimidating to me," Whit recalled. "She had a shirt on that was all cut up like she had taken scissors and cut it up on purpose. She sat on the couch opposite me and kind of just took over the room." Whit was struck by this younger newcomer's huge green eyes and her beauty. She found herself thinking it was terrifying and didn't know if she could live with it. Despite her reservations, Whit was overruled. Madonna moved in on September 9, 1977, at the start of her sophomore year.[36]

Madonna had a year on Whit in Ann Arbor, and she was able to show her the town's hidden secrets. Gradually, the two young women became close friends, if not a little like sisters. Madonna made Whit feel like they were "allies." They smoked pot together in a dance-building storage area they christened Zeet Lounge. They both had jobs at Miller's Ice Cream (on the stipulation that they wear bras). "In the basement of Miller's is where they kept all the food," Whitley said. "We would go down and get frozen fish and cans of soup . . . so that's what we lived on." When Whit got a job modeling for life-drawing classes, Madonna did, too, because it paid so well.[37]

And, of course, Madonna took Whit to the Rube. It was Whit's first gay club, and once there, Madonna insisted that Whit dance with her. As they did, everyone in the disco stopped to watch. "Just by dancing, Madonna's made herself the vortex of the room. There's nothing unusual about what she's doing," Whit said. "It's how, it's the intent, it's the charge... Madonna's a complicated person... and her dancing mirrors that."[38]

The roommates were also allies during quiet times. Whit had come to believe that Madonna was "perhaps the smartest person I know," in part because she was such a good listener. The two had conversations about everything: Whit's hometown, New York; the state of the world; school—in short, their lives, including the most intimate parts of them.

Whit, for example, introduced Madonna to masturbation, which Madonna tried to her delight and wonder.[39] "I'd had intercourse before I understood" masturbation, she said years later.[40] They referred to it jokingly as "the nightly ritual" and talked about it for hours.[41] They also talked about sex with women: Madonna said she had kissed a gorgeous woman with callused hands who played the conga drum for their class. And they talked about men because the two were, according to Whit, sexual "neophytes" despite their "big talk and freewheeling behavior." There was much to discuss on that confusing subject.[42]

The sexual liberation of the 1960s and early 1970s wasn't really a woman's sexual liberation. The terms of women's emancipation had always belonged to men. And because men were happy with the new, less restrictive sexual landscape, and because they controlled the social and cultural messaging, the fictional narrative that women were as free as men to have the sexual life they wanted was accepted as fact.

In truth, that tale was a pernicious lie that risked undermining all the other gains women had made, because if a woman didn't have the right to her own body, to say yes or no, then what did she have? Feminist Robin Morgan described the state of postliberation women best:

> The invention of the Pill made millions for drug companies, made guinea pigs of us, and made us all the more "available" as sexual objects; if a woman didn't want to go to bed with a man now, she must be hung up. It was inconceivable, naturally, that she might not like the man, or the Pill, or for that matter, sex. We know that "hip culture" and "radical lifestyle"—whatever those mean—have been hip and radical for the men, but filled with the same old chores, harassment, and bottling-up of inner rage for the women.[43]

Madonna's generation matured at a time when women were independent, strong, and able to imagine a future of their own choice. But no one told those young women and girls the bad news: their sexual desires were still secondary to a man's. Young women would be left to discover that when faced with the real-life dilemma of whether to have sex.

Whit said that she and Madonna spent "a fair amount of time" discussing that weird stomachache you get when you know some guy *expects* you to have sex.

> Even if you kind of want to, the fact that he expects it makes you immediately part of this universal sisterhood of reluctance. Women in the rice paddies. Women in the Amazon. Women in Siberia. Me and Maddie in the Dance Department. We are all one in those moments, liking, perhaps, the flirtation and the foreplay, not so sure about all the fluids and the soreness and the ineptitude of them and the danger of the babies.[44]

Whit's conclusion: "It's all very complicated." Madonna's was less sanguine. She declared the situation "fucked up."[45]

Whit went away over the Christmas break, and while she was gone, Madonna worked in the dance studio every day except Christmas, when she went home for a "tense and anxious" visit with her family. After her summer in New York, driven by a dream to return there, she rarely took a day off, even in snowstorms, when no one else was in the dance building. During term time, if she went out until 2:00 a.m., Madonna would still be up at eight and "in class before everyone else, warming up," Whit said.[46] She worked so hard that her spine was bruised from sit-ups, and she injured and reinjured her hip but danced through the pain.[47]

Before the holidays, Madonna had begun mentioning a guy named Stephen Bray, who tended bar at the Blue Frogge, around the corner from University Towers.[48] He was twenty-one, from Detroit, and planned to study at the renowned Berklee College of Music, in Boston. "He was real cute. Someone all soulful and funky looking, you couldn't help but notice," Madonna said.[49] Bray had noticed Madonna, too. The Blue Frogge, he said, "had the whole 1977 disco hustle *Saturday Night Fever* thing going on and she came in to dance with some friends."[50] His first impression on meeting her was that "I had encountered a force of nature."[51] "She stood out, quite. Her energy was really apparent. What direction she should put that energy *in* hadn't been settled, but it was definitely there."[52]

In Madonna's account of their initial encounter, she often said she offered to buy Bray a drink, a memory he disputed, saying, "It was the other way around."[53] Whoever bought that drink, in Steve Bray Madonna had met her first important musical collaborator. In a few years, he would join her in New York, and together they would create many of the early songs that for some people still define "Madonna."

Using Whit's identification to get into the club, Madonna hung around the bar while Steve worked, and she watched his band play around town. It wasn't a cover band; the Cost of Living played original material. Madonna told Whit with "NO SHIT" excitement that all the songs were worth recording.[54] Bray appreciated Madonna, too. He said she came to the band's gigs "dancing up a storm, and of course creating her own. In fact, I wonder if some people didn't come to our shows 'cause they knew she would be there dancing."[55]

The friendship turned into a romance at a time when interracial dating was still rare, even on an enlightened campus like Ann Arbor.[56] For Madonna and Steve, that was not an issue in the slightest. What was, was the familiar problem of birth control, which in those "liberated" times fell to the woman to work out. Madonna was broke. The rent and electric bills were due; her roommates were out of town, and she needed $35 to get a diaphragm from Planned Parenthood. She decided to ignore the bills and take what money she had to the clinic, walking three miles in a blizzard, "feet like frozen turds, tears streaming from [my] eyes, and 3 hours of anxious waiting." Once inserted, the device presented a new kind of worry. Madonna became a member of the sisterhood of reluctant women.[57]

"Now that I had my diaphragm we could fuck all the time—I haven't an excuse not to. Do I want to fuck all the time? Boy this subject really causes me a lot of anxieties," Madonna wrote to Whit. The sex, when she and Steve had it, was "much better than I thought it would be," she wrote. But she didn't want to "do it all the time like every other seemingly normal person wants to do." Madonna admitted that she liked Steve "more and more each day" and that seemed in her mind at odds with an active sexual relationship.[58] It was as if she feared that once the relationship became sexual, it would be *only* sexual, and that was so excruciatingly one-dimensional.

Bray, for his part, took a cautious attitude toward the affair. He thought perhaps Madonna considered him a novelty. "'He's interesting, he's a musician, that's different. I'm used to dancers and poetry students and that sort of thing, but this is different—I kinda like it,'" he imagined her thinking. "We were having a little bit of a friendship there and suddenly she was gone."[59]

When Whit returned to Ann Arbor, she and Madonna were selected to be in the annual end-of-year performance at the university's Power Center theater. It was a boost to Madonna's ego as well as a thrill because of the intense preparation: late nights working with lighting, sets, and sound, "practicing on the massive space, making sure we can function in the bright lights and not fall into the orchestra pit," Whit recalled.[60]

Collaboration of that sort, which would form such a crucial part of all Madonna's future work, was part of her training in Michigan. Dance professor Peter Sparling said,

> Madonna, I think, was raised in that tradition, where dancers also had to choreograph or work with choreographers, work with costume designers, work with set designers, work with musicians, lighting designers...That was definitely invested in her here.[61]

Despite all that activity, however exhilarating, Madonna felt anxious. She said Ann Arbor had come to feel too much like a "home away from home."[62] She wasn't independent enough to develop the mental and spiritual strength and maturity she needed to truly take charge of her life.[63] "Those were good days," she said. "But I knew my stay at Michigan was short term. To me, I was just fine-tuning my technique."[64]

Christopher Flynn also recognized that she was ready for a new challenge in a new place.[65] He told her to go. To drop out of school. To go to New York.[66] "He made me push myself," Madonna said. "He was constantly putting all that stuff about New York in my ear. I was hesitant and my father and everyone was against it, but he really said, 'Go for it.'"[67]

Tony Ciccone was *dead set* against it. "I recall some pretty bad scenes," said her older brother Marty. The idea that she would forgo a scholarship to go to New York—to do what?—was unthinkable to her father. He even said at one point, "You drop out of school, you'll no longer be my daughter." To which Madonna replied, "Fine, but when I'm famous, will I be your daughter again?" He said, "We'll cross that bridge when we come to it... *if* we come to it." "Oh, we'll come to it, all right," she said.[68] Tony's final word was, according to Madonna, "Well, you don't have my blessing and I'm not going to finance it so... you're on your own."[69]

As she weighed her next move, Madonna considered the naysayers at home and school versus the urgency of her art-fueled dreams, but there was really no contest. Girls are usually advised what *not to do* in order to protect themselves. Boys are told what they *can do* to get ahead. Madonna never accepted the girlie route. And in any case, if she wanted to be somebody, she needed to take a leap—and quickly—into the unknown. Kentes said, in general, Madonna didn't waste time.[70]

In the spring, Whit told Madonna she was considering a trip to Oregon for the summer to join the "long-hair element." That was when Madonna dropped her own bomb: she was leaving Michigan for New York. From her jobs, she had been saving money, which she kept hidden in a book of New York City Ballet photos. Whit recalled Madonna saying, "I've got almost enough for a ticket…and I think I can get someone to loan me the rest. So I'm gonna go and take all the classes I can take." When asked if she was coming back, Madonna said she wasn't sure, but she didn't think so.[71]

The two friends shared one last outing before they both left town, bicycling in June to a river swimming hole. Madonna rode ahead, coasting downhill with no hands along the Huron River toward their destination. Once there, joints were smoked, clothes were shed, and a day was spent blissfully in the water. And then, back in Ann Arbor, Madonna and Whit climbed a fire ladder onto the roof of a nearby building to take in the view.

As the sun set, they put their arms around each other and danced, crazy dances, end-of-school-year dances, until it was time to go. Before they did, though, Whit remembered a childhood ritual. When she and her mother were on the roof of their building, she would drop a penny down a pipe for good luck. She and Madonna both did it that day. And then it was over. Their school life together had ended. "If this is the last real day we spend together, well, that's okay—it's a good one," Whit thought.[72] In fact, it was their last day in Michigan, but not their last day together. They would meet again in New York.

Peter Kentes had a car, so Madonna called him to bum a ride to the airport. He and Christopher Flynn picked her up at the dance building, where she stood waiting with a bag, a small suitcase, and a large doll. "She was a little nervous, you could tell," Peter said. No one from her family was at the airport to see her off as she walked away toward her next adventure. But Christopher Flynn was. He believed she would "make it big," said Linda Alaniz, which in a way meant he would, too. Flynn lived vicariously through Madonna. In the car that day he turned to Peter and said with a mixture of hope, sadness, and admiration, "There goes our little Madonna."[73] And then she was gone.

PART TWO

NEW YORK

1978–1984

Chapter 8

New York, Paris, 1978–1979

Look what can happen in this country, they'd say. A girl lives in some out-of-the-way town for nineteen years…and ends up steering New York like her own private car.[1]
— *Sylvia Plath*, The Bell Jar

IMAGINE MADONNA AT nineteen standing curbside at LaGuardia Airport: petite, rail-thin, excited, bewildered, and more than a little afraid, dressed in a heavy coat despite the summer heat and carrying a big doll and a small suitcase. And imagine the jaded taxi driver flipping on the meter for the one-way trip to her destiny after hearing where she wanted him to take her: "to the middle of everything."[2] Without a doubt, he had seen other girls like her coming from nowhere on their way to someplace, girls who had taken a detour into the netherworld of New York. There was nothing to indicate that Madonna wouldn't be one of them. In fact there was every reason to believe that was the *only* place she could go. She was too young, too naive, too eager. She would be eaten alive. And so he took this little lost girl to Times Square, where she'd probably end up anyway. Forty-Second Street: the "porn capital of America," as the city's former mayor Abe Beame called it.[3]

Sin. Sex. Girls, Girls, Girls. Nudes. Private Booths. Sexual Aids. Red. At night, everything was red: the signs, the blinking lights, the silhouettes of naked women's bodies, the real women and the occasional male hustler standing in doorways in that infernal glow, all speaking the patois of seduction. And movies. Movies were big after *Deep Throat* made porn flicks mainstream and more profitable than many Hollywood productions. Movie marquees all promised X ratings—triple X if you were up for it.[4]

Even in the daylight, when Times Square was blanched and filthy, Madonna would have recognized the place for what it was—hell or something pretty close to it. She had just taken her first plane trip and her first taxi ride, and they had brought her there. "I can't believe how frightened I was when I look back at it," she said.[5]

The massive scale of New York took my breath away...I felt like a warrior plunging my way through the crowds to survive...I was poised for survival...But I was also scared shitless and freaked out by the smell of piss and vomit everywhere.[6]

There was only one thing to do, untethered and alone as she was. "I walked. I looked up and walked," she said.[7] With $35 left (about $140 in 2023) from the money she had saved for her trip, she wandered east along 42nd Street to Lexington Avenue, where she came upon an outdoor street market bustling during a sunny summer afternoon. "I'm sure I looked like a hick," she said.[8]

Soon she noticed that she had attracted a shadow. A man was following her. "I said hi to him and he said, 'Why are you walking around with a winter coat and a suitcase?' And I said, 'I just got off the plane.'" He asked her why she didn't bring her things home instead of lugging them around the market, and she told him she didn't have a home.[9]

"The angels were protecting me," Madonna told Howard Stern years later about what happened next.[10] The stranger, who she thought was in his late twenties, offered to let her sleep at his place while she got her bearings in New York. Madonna accepted. She stayed with the man, sometimes she said for five days, sometimes two weeks.[11] "I learned later that I couldn't be so open, but it was just my luck that I met a really nice guy. And he didn't touch me." As soon as she found dance students to share a place with, she moved in with them.[12]

Madonna was back at the Alvin Ailey American Dance Theater, which was formed in 1958 by Ailey as a small troupe of Black modern dancers. As it celebrated its twentieth anniversary, in 1978, the company had moved from the fringe to international renown.[13] Madonna didn't survive the first round of auditions, but eventually she won a work-study scholarship to join the troupe's third-tier company—or, as one writer called it, the equivalent of "the sub-junior-varsity team."[14] It was a start. "My calculation was that I knew I had to apply myself and work. And that devotion—and that ambition and that courage—was going to take me to the next step," she explained.[15]

The Ailey courses didn't begin until the fall, so Christopher Flynn advised her to go to the annual American Dance Festival, which had moved that year to Durham, North Carolina. Madonna auditioned and won a scholarship to attend.[16]

The ADF was a six-week intensive summer program in modern dance during which students interacted with the best dancers in the world by day and saw performances by the best companies at night.[17] It was a place to learn and make connections, which Madonna did. She took class that summer with Pearl Lang.[18]

It wasn't their first encounter. Madonna had met Lang in Michigan, where the older woman had been an artist in residence. Lang remembered Madonna from that time as "this very thin, dark little girl, pushing herself around, working very hard."[19] She did the same in Durham. At the end of the summer, Madonna asked Lang, "Do you think you're going to need any dancers in New York?"[20] Surprised by Madonna's directness, Lang said she was always looking for an understudy. Madonna expressed interest and Lang went home and forgot about her.[21]

Madonna, too, returned to New York, where she began what would be four years of rootlessness, seemingly moving every month or two from one rented space or squat to another. Most of them were rooms in other people's apartments. Some of them were mere portions of a room—a mattress on the floor. And all of them were wretched in a way that was peculiar to New York: stinking of the street, cigarettes, and past tenants; full of mold and soot; covered in grime and alive with cockroaches.

At the start of her New York sojourn, Madonna seemed to live mostly on the West Side, in places like West Harlem and Hell's Kitchen.[22] Home—or the place where she slept—wasn't important. Home was the dance studio. And in the early fall of 1978, that was at the Ailey School. "I thought I was in a production of *Fame*. Everyone was Hispanic or black, and *everyone* wanted to be a star," she said.[23]

Madonna's mood alternated between euphoria and depression. "The whole place was so intimidating," she said.

> I'd go to Lincoln Center, sit by the fountain and just cry. I'd write in my journal and pray to have even one friend. Even in the dance school, most of the kids on scholarship were inner-city kids who had a much different temperament than I did. I was kind of off to myself in a little corner. I had been used to being the big fish in the little pond [in Michigan] and all of a sudden, I was a nobody. I longed for that familiarity and being on top of everything.[24]

She had two forms of solace: dance and reading. Her social life, such as it was, revolved around classical music concerts in the park and performances at Lincoln Center. "I didn't know anything about pop culture in New York," she said of those earliest days.[25] Through it all, however, she still believed that "something was gonna happen. I wasn't really sure what shape it was going to take."[26] Her goal was to "conquer" the city.[27]

While at the Ailey School, Madonna said, she was told "that if I wanted

to master Ailey's technique, I should really study at the Graham School...
Needless to say, I arrived there within twenty-four hours of receiving this
information." She joined beginners' classes and was "entranced" by what
she found. It was the opposite of the Ailey atmosphere, where students
hungry for glory dreamed of the bright lights and applause. At the Martha
Graham School, Madonna found a conventlike environment. "The studios were spartan, minimalist," she said. "Everyone whispered, so the only
sounds you heard were the music and the instructors, and they spoke to
you only when you were fucking up." Though the technique was "physically brutal," she was excited by the challenge. "I was learning something
new every day. I was on my way."[28]

Madonna longed to meet Graham herself. There were rumors that the
eighty-four-year-old legend, who still choreographed dances, roamed the
building and that she sometimes sat in on classes. After positioning herself to
no avail in all the logical places where she might serendipitously meet Graham, Madonna ran into her one morning while sneaking out of class to use
the toilet. "I heaved open the heavy door to the hallway, stepped outside the
classroom, and there she was, right in front of me, staring into my face."[29]

Madonna had violated what she called the "cardinal rule...No one *ever*
left the tomblike classrooms until classes were over! [Graham] stopped dead
in her tracks to see who the violator was. I was paralyzed." Madonna had
rehearsed what she might say if she ever met Graham, how she might "win
her over." But upon encountering her in the flesh, the girl her family called
"the Mouth" was at a loss for words. "This was my first true encounter with
a goddess. A warrior. A survivor. Someone not to be fucked with. Before I
could clear my throat, she was gone...I was left shaking in my leotard."[30]

Like other young dancers, Madonna took class with as many different
types of teachers as she could. One of them was Marcus Schulkind, a
dancer and choreographer trained in the Graham technique whom she
met during her summer in Durham. Schulkind's studio at the time was on
Great Jones Street, in NoHo, then a drug-infested downtown wasteland
that was also home to some of the most cutting-edge and underground
work across the arts. Schulkind said of Madonna,

> She was really a brilliant dancer. I tell you this truly. She was musical, she
> had a great sense of line, she had really strong technique...[and] she reeked
> of potential. If you even saw her, you could see that...Once you started to
> have some contact with her...you just kind of went, "Wow."[31]

He considered Madonna already a "semiprofessional. So what's holding
her back is some of the attitude she had...the unbelievable snippiness and

comebacks that she would come up with in dealing with other people's power." Schulkind said studios in those days still operated as they had in the time of Balanchine. "The choreographer is God, and you should be happy to bow down to them, and there wasn't an atom of that in Madonna."[32]

Since her arrival in New York that July, Madonna had been hoping to make inroads into the dance world in a capacity other than that of student.[33] The competition, however, was ferocious, and Madonna was at a disadvantage—not just because of her attitude but also because her fellow students were mere teenagers. In August, she had turned twenty, which seemed ancient in the beginners classes at the Graham School and in the third-tier at Ailey. She had no time to waste. Her most important connection to date had been with Pearl Lang, so it was to Lang that Madonna went to see if she could join her company.

The *Village Voice* described Lang as "one of the few dancers it is safe to call great." She was the daughter of Jewish immigrants who had fled persecution after the Russian Revolution and settled in Chicago. In 1941, Lang began studying with Martha Graham in New York and in 1942 joined her company.[34]

Though Lang would continue to dance with Graham for decades, she formed her own company in 1952 and choreographed her own works. Most of her dances explored Jewish themes. Many of them derived from Yiddish literature, which she expressed with an emotional range that ran the gamut from abject despair to religious ecstasy. Lang described the essence of her work as the search for God.[35] The intellectuality, spirituality, and passion of Lang's dances, not to mention the rigor of the work, all appealed to young Madonna.

In November, Lang was teaching a class when Madonna suddenly appeared.[36] She welcomed her as a student but quickly recognized that she was "exceptional" and began to incorporate her into her own productions. It was Madonna's first paid dancing job in New York. Said Lang,

> She was very talented—very fragile, but fierce. Many people can do the acrobatics required, but she had a poetic quality about her...[She had] the power, the intensity, to go beyond mere physical performance into something more exciting.[37]

To supplement Madonna's dance income, Lang found her a job in the cloakroom at the Russian Tea Room, where she could earn a few dollars and get a meal.[38] "I'm pretty sure that was the one decent meal she was getting."[39] But Madonna soon lost that job in a test of wills over her cloth-ing. "I got fired for wearing fishnets," she explained.[40] Rather than be dis-appointed, Lang was amused. "I was fond of her for her arrogance, her hunger, and her spunk. Nothing fazed her. She was going to do some-thing, and nothing was going to get in her way."[41]

In the late fall, Madonna attended a party at the Upper West Side apart-ment Lang shared with her husband, actor Joseph Wiseman. The place was full of dancers and friends of dancers. One of them was a young man named Norris Burroughs. He watched Madonna dancing at Lang's place to the Village People's "Y.M.C.A." It was impossible to ignore her, even in a room full of exhibitionists. At one point she did a grand jeté (a midair leap with her legs spread), landed on all fours, and stretched her body like a cat. "It was one of the most subtly sexual things I'd ever seen," he said. She was also notable because of her outfit: a turquoise pullover and orange leopard-print tights.[42]

Later in the kitchen, as she and Burroughs introduced themselves, a fel-low who overheard her name said, "You mean like Lady Madonna?" to which Madonna said, "Get lost! I hate that shit! Every idiot says that!" Then she turned to Burroughs and said, "Do *you* have anything original to say?" He was shocked and excited by her boldness, even more so when she called him the next day. Madonna and Burroughs became an item.[43]

By the time Burroughs met Madonna, she was no longer a terrified ref-ugee washed up in New York. In a few short months, she had found a cir-cle of friends from dance studios around the city and had adapted to New York's pace and style. She had become a New Yorker. The town's intensity matched her own; the opportunities on offer were plentiful enough to sat-isfy her wildest dreams. And, after the initial shock of entry, the city even felt familiar. The writer Giuliana Muscio once described New York as "the largest 'Italian city' in the world."[44] And Madonna was in the deepest sense an Italian girl. New York felt like—*was*—home.

Whitley Setrakian had come back to the city that early fall for a family visit and discovered just how entrenched Madonna was. "I fucking belong here," Whit recalled Madonna saying. "Every day I'm here in this city I can't stop thinking of all the days I haven't been here. I feel like I'm run-ning a race and everyone's had a head start." When the subject of returning to Michigan came up, Madonna shot back, "No way, lady." Physically, too, she was a new Madonna. Her short, chopped hair was longer. She wore a large men's white T-shirt and Bermuda shorts, belt tight at the waist, battered Adidas, and sunglasses. "I've never seen her so happy and sure," Whit admitted.[45]

On the night of Whit and Madonna's reunion, Whit's father, Ed Setra-kian, invited them and one of their former Ann Arbor roommates to meet him at the actor's hangout Joe Allen, at the edge of Broadway. Ed was a stalwart of the New York acting scene. He'd been in movies and on Broadway and had written and directed plays. Three years earlier he had landed a role in the Robert Redford–Faye Dunaway thriller, *Three Days of the Condor.* He knew everyone and everything about the business.[46]

As they sat in a booth at the restaurant, where Madonna was making spitballs of her napkin and calling Mr. Setrakian Ed, though she'd just met him, Whit noticed him watching the door, as if waiting for someone. Then Whit saw who that someone was. Ed's old friend Al Pacino walked into Joe Allen and over to their table. "I thought it would be a neat idea to have Al come and join us," Ed said, recalling that night. "He likes to do things like that."[47]

Even Madonna was disarmed and temporarily stopped misbehaving. Sitting at their table was Al Pacino—post *Serpico, Dog Day Afternoon, The Godfather,* and *The Godfather Part II.* He wasn't just an actor. He was *the* actor. Whit said that when Madonna greeted Pacino, she softened her pronunciation of the letter *a* and dragged out the *l* in his name to say, knowingly, "Hello, *Ahlllll.*" She then unwrapped a stick of gum and ate it in slow, deliberate, bite-size portions. "I think the idea here," Whit said, "is to call attention to her mouth."[48]

Later, after the group had left Joe Allen and returned there, Madonna produced a pink plastic bubble-mix container out of her dance bag and began blowing bubbles. By that point, she had absorbed Ed Setrakian and Al Pacino into her circle of friends and excitedly invited them to a party at a club the following Tuesday. And with that, the evening was over. Ed offered to drive everyone home in his old Toyota convertible.[49]

Madonna was the first to be dropped off, at a building on Riverside Drive. She kissed Whit and their former roommate, hugged Ed, and poked her head in on Pacino's side to tell him she had enjoyed meeting him. An hour later Ed, laughing so hard he could barely speak, called Whit to convey what Al had told him: "That friend of your daughter's stuck her tongue in my ear! When we were driving home, she leaned over and stuck her tongue in my ear!" Having seen much worse behavior in his travels, Ed said of Madonna, "I thought she was delightful."[50]

The apartment where Madonna was deposited after Joe Allen was a five- or six-room shared space in a beautiful prewar building, but she told Norris Burroughs that she wanted to move out because her roommate was pressuring her for sex. Her next place, into which she moved in December of 1978, was another shared apartment, this time on West 125th Street near the subway, in Harlem. That lasted for around a month, until she moved into a New York University building. Again, that stay was short, and she went from living in a building with a Picasso sculpture in the courtyard to a tenement in Hell's Kitchen.[51] Madonna called the place "seedy. I kept getting mistaken for a hooker."[52]

Just as she lived anyplace she could, Madonna worked at any crummy job she could find. But one steady source of income was posing for artists. Burroughs said Madonna was a regular model at an open drawing class on Greene Street, in SoHo, and he attended some of the sessions. "It seemed to me that she was getting hit on a lot by horny artists, and she certainly was getting a lot of offers to pose privately."[53] Painter Anthony Panzera became one of Madonna's private clients. "This was her livelihood," he said. "She made a big ten dollars an hour."[54] It didn't seem to him that Madonna had a home, only a series of phone numbers where she might be reached. He called her a "vagabond."[55]

Not until Madonna had been in New York for a few months did her father call to say he wanted to come and see her.[56] It was clear from their conversations that he still didn't understand what she was doing. "First I was a dancer, and I would call him and say, 'Well, I'm dancing'...He's a sensible guy, and what's dancing to him?" she said. "He can't imagine that you can make a living from it or work at it or be proud of it or think of it as an accomplishment. He could never really be supportive about it."[57]

Madonna didn't think his understanding would improve if he saw how and where she lived. "The apartment was crawling with cockroaches. There were winos in the hallway. The entire place smelled like stale beer," she said. She didn't want him to come. He did anyway and took her to dinner at an Italian restaurant, with the goal of persuading her to move home and finish school. "What's going to happen if this fool's dream of yours doesn't work out?" he asked her. She said she was staying and to leave her alone. Reluctantly, he did.[58]

Madonna's work with Pearl Lang intensified in the early months of 1979, but she had begun to feel that she had learned all she could from Lang.[59] In fact, she had even started to question whether she wanted to be a dancer at all.[60]

> I had to dare myself every day to keep going...I wondered if it was all worth it, but then I would pull myself together and look at a postcard of Frida Kahlo taped to my wall, and the sight of her mustache consoled me.[61]

By the spring of 1979, she decided to try a fresh direction and began reading trade publications in search of jobs on the stage or in film.[62] In a city full of people pounding the pavement, traveling between dreams and dejection, she joined the "cattle call" at auditions for roles she had only a passing interest in but tried out for because you never know: an artist must leave space for possibility. And in any case, it was part of the learning process.

"Most of the people auditioning were much more professional than I was," Madonna said. "They brought sheet music, and they'd give it to the piano player, and I would just wing it and sing songs I knew from the radio, like an Aretha Franklin song."[63] No callbacks, no jobs. Madonna summed up the period with one word: "Discouraging."[64]

Meanwhile, tensions in Lang's studio increased as it became clear that Madonna's interest in dance had waned. She missed class to attend auditions; she bristled at Lang's direction. Lang retaliated against Madonna's disrespect by being more critical of her and forcing her to repeat steps again and again until in one instance Madonna slammed her head against the wall and shouted, "Is that better?"[65]

In late April, after not seeing him for several months, Madonna ran into Norris Burroughs on 34th Street, and he invited her to a May Day party in Tribeca. The party's cohost was a friend of his named Dan Gilroy. "Sounds groovy," Madonna said.[66]

Gilroy was an artist who worked with Burroughs at a T-shirt shop on St. Mark's Place, but his real love was music. He and his brother Ed rented an abandoned synagogue in Queens and performed as the Acme Band. They also had a two-man music-satire routine, the Bil and Gil Show.[67] Tall, lanky, and without pretense, Dan lived to create but wasn't necessarily looking for huge recognition. The doing was the important part. If someone liked it, all the better.

Madonna showed up at the party, and Burroughs introduced her to his friends. The "attraction between Dan and Madonna was instantaneous," Burroughs said. "Dan's laid-back sense of humor was an immediate turn on for Madonna." By mid-party, Burroughs spotted them off in a corner kissing.[68] Said Madonna, "I fell in love with him, and it turned out that he was a guitar player in a band. What happened is, I said, 'You have to teach me how to play an instrument.' "[69] In return, Madonna offered to pose for his paintings.[70] Soon, she made her virgin voyage to Flushing Meadows, Queens.

The synagogue—or the Gog, as the Gilroys called it—was a brick house at the end of a row of attached homes in a mostly Italian neighborhood of porches, chain-link fences, tiny yards with oversize lawn ornaments, and lovingly polished cars parked bumper-to-bumper curbside. "A rabbi had died, and his sister rented out the synagogue—not rooms, a whole synagogue," Madonna said. The brothers lived upstairs and created a studio in the basement.[71] The neighborhood was light-years from the sophistication and pace of Manhattan, but Madonna liked it. She said it reminded her of Pontiac.[72]

Dan, meanwhile, held up his end of the bargain with Madonna. He put a guitar in her hand, tuned it to an open chord, and taught her basic chord progressions. "That really clicked something off in my brain," she said.[73] In her search for a new direction, she found one in that guitar. As for Dan himself, Madonna said, "He was a very generous and patient teacher. He was the best thing that could ever have happened to me at that point in my life."[74]

That spring, two Belgian producers, Jan Vanloo and Jean-Claude Pellerin, caught a performance of Dan and Ed's *Voideville* show at Theater for the New City on Second Avenue. In the course of a conversation with the Gilroys, the Belgians mentioned that they were holding open auditions for backup dancers to tour with Patrick Hernandez, a French singer they represented.[75] Hernandez's song "Born to Be Alive" was written in 1976 but languished until 1978, when Vanloo and Pellerin discovered it. By 1979, it was a smash hit, and Vanloo and Pellerin were organizing concerts to promote it and expand Hernandez's repertoire.[76]

The timing was critical. In the late '70s, European producers were experiencing enormous success, especially in the States. In 1976, the Parisian producer Marc Cerrone had a major disco hit with "Love in C Minor." Italian Giorgio Moroder, who in 1975 cowrote Donna Summer's seventeen-minute orgasmic disco anthem, "Love to Love You Baby," returned in 1977 with the haunting "I Feel Love," again for Summer. But it was the "French Wonder Boys"—Henri Belolo and Jacques Morali— who arguably had the biggest immediate impact on pop culture. They created a song, a sound, and an iconic group: the Village People.[77]

Belolo said that he and Morali were walking down Christopher Street in 1977 when Morali "took a fancy to a Puerto Rican bartender dressed as a Native American." They followed him into a gay club, the Anvil. After a customer walked in wearing full cowboy regalia, Belolo recalled, "Morali turned to me and said, 'Oh God, are you thinking what I'm thinking?' " The Village People concept was born. Morali and Belolo then wrote "Y.M.C.A.," which, despite its explicit celebration of gay love, was so infectious that it became a global hit and was played at baseball games and US political rallies.[78]

In the spring of 1979, Vanloo and Pellerin were in New York, keeping an eye out for the next big thing. Having been told by Dan Gilroy about the Hernandez auditions, Madonna tried out for the show.[79] The producers needed thirty-five performers to fill various roles in the act; nearly ten times that number appeared at the tryout. Madonna stood out immediately.

"It's difficult to explain," Hernandez said, "but we knew right away that she had a particular aura."[80]

The producers separated her from the pack to speak with her alone. They wanted to see what other talents she possessed besides dance. "While she moved marvelously well, she said she didn't know how to sing at all, and to prove it to us she hummed 'Jingle Bells,'" Hernandez said. "But we were already seduced."[81] They invited Madonna to dinner at the Pierre, a hotel overlooking Central Park, and told her they wanted to take her to Paris and make a record with her on their label, Aquarius.[82]

"I could hardly believe it. I tried to be very calm when they told me what they wanted me to do, but underneath I was on cloud nine," Madonna said.[83] "I kept thinking, 'I can't believe it. Somebody noticed me.'"[84] Though presented with the offer of a lifetime, Madonna only conditionally agreed. Having become what she called "a very shrewd girl," she had them checked out. "I had a lawyer involved...I mean, I didn't go into the whole thing blindly." Madonna found that "everything they were doing was legitimate."[85]

Madonna's first taste of life as a pop artist was so outrageously luxurious as to be laughable. She went from traveling by way of the dangerous and dirty New York subway system and living in a stinking dive in Hell's Kitchen to flying on the Concorde to Paris, where she was installed in a ten-room apartment overlooking the Parc Monceau, near the Arc de Triomphe. The apartment in that staid, conservative district was home to Vanloo and his wife. It was also Hernandez's residence while the group prepared his tour.[86]

"They were very wealthy people and they really put me up. I mean I had a driver, and I had a maid and I had everything," Madonna said. As promised, she was given a vocal coach, but she only met with him a few times. "I hated him," Madonna said, "so I didn't want to get involved in that."[87] During the day she took dance lessons, and at night she, Hernandez, and the producers' wider circle inhabited the world of fashionable Paris: the restaurants, the nightclubs, the parties peopled with the international jet set.[88]

Madonna was miserable. Hernandez said the trouble between Madonna and her producers began as soon as she arrived.[89] She felt she had been placed in a gilded cage and given meaningless tasks to keep her busy, such as overdubbing vocals on prerecorded disco tracks and learning dance moves as part of the Hernandez act. But nothing she did was *original,* even though the point of the trip had been to shape her career.[90]

Despite her position of absolute powerlessness—she was a twenty-year-old nobody who had nothing—Madonna made her dissatisfaction clear.

She wanted creative intensity, work.[91] What Vanloo offered instead was what sulky little girls are always offered: *les petits bonbons*. "I was like a poor little rich girl," she said.[92]

> Every time I complained they just gave me more money. Well, I'm not a material person, I don't care about stuff like that. My idea of success...is feeling like I've accomplished something personally...I was very frustrated because I came from New York, like starving and kicking ass. I mean working my ass off to get somewhere and being involved with like this rush rush kind of lifestyle that New York is so famous for. And people in Paris, they take breaks all day, they drink wine all day...and I couldn't click into that lifestyle.[93]

Vanloo and Pellerin had no idea that Madonna would never accept being paraded around like an ingenue in a *Pygmalion*-style drama. She told an interviewer in 1984, "They were like taking me around to everyone saying, 'Look what we found in New York. Isn't she wonderful?...We're gonna make her a star.' "[94]

Hernandez put some of the blame for the disastrous Paris situation on Madonna "because she systematically refused all the songs that were proposed for her. She knew perfectly well what she wanted to do and wouldn't make any concessions. She was already a diva."[95]

If the producers chose to make Madonna's life a misery, she decided to return the favor. "I turned into a rebellious little kid," she said.[96] "They made me meet these awful French boys and I would throw tantrums."[97] She began hanging around with a Vietnamese boy who had a motorcycle and any Americans she could find, while refusing to abide the wealthy people the producers courted. "I remember the scandal she made at a restaurant one night when she demanded strawberries at any price," Hernandez said.[98] When the Hernandez ensemble finally "toured"—to one country, Tunisia—Madonna outraged the locals by "swimming in a one-piece body stocking."[99] "Once again I was forced into the role of enfant terrible," she said. "All I wanted to do was make trouble, because they stuck me in an environment that didn't allow me to be free."[100]

Lonely and perhaps looking for comfort or affirmation, Madonna called her father to say she was in France, but it was a conversation they might have had in Rochester, Ann Arbor, or New York. He didn't understand what her life had become, and so he couldn't help her.[101] But in an important way, the lessons he taught her as a child did. He had said that if she wasn't suffering, she wasn't trying hard enough. And he told her, "You have to work for something, and you can't have anything handed to you. If it's handed to you, it's not gonna last."[102] Madonna wasn't suffering in the right way in Paris, and she hadn't worked for what she was given. She knew she had to leave.

Madonna and Dan Gilroy had been exchanging letters. Hers expressed frustration, saying that she wanted "hard work and sweat," not to be treated like a pet.[103] His were funny and beseeched her to come back to Queens. "He was my saving grace," she said.[104] She knew New York was where she belonged.

At the end of the summer, Madonna became ill and said she wanted to return to the States for a vacation. The producers paid for a round-trip ticket on the Concorde, and she left her clothes in Paris, as if she planned to return.[105] She did not.

Vanloo and Pellerin were angry, but Hernandez said he thought Madonna was courageous to leave a career offered to her on a silver platter for a life of insecurity and want on the street. She believed she had a better chance of making it on her own. "She once told me, 'Success is yours today but it will be mine tomorrow,'" Hernandez recalled. "I mean, was she bluffing, or did she really believe what she was saying? Back then in Paris, Madonna was pretty insignificant, but she was resolute. Success was a certainty in her mind."[106]

Chapter 9

New York, 1979–1980

Often when you try to reinvent yourself, there are intermediary places in the reinvention... You think it's a place of arrival, but in fact it turns out to be a place of departure.[1]

— *Édouard Louis*

WHILE IN PARIS, Madonna was so consumed with anger and frustration that she may not have been able to recognize the valuable lessons she actually *had* received. The Hernandez producers hadn't made her a singer, but they had given her a priceless introduction to, if not a crash course in, the world of pop music, from record production to concert tour.

During the performance itself, Madonna had been required to move in an entirely new way. She was no longer a classical ballerina or even a modern dancer but part of a pop ensemble dancing to the breakneck pace of a three-minute song. For the "Born to Be Alive" number, Madonna was lead dancer. The choreography was simple and as frenetic as an aerobics workout. But it acquainted her with the relationship between dancing and singing and suggested the idea that dance at its most imaginative can be used to enhance and dramatize a song.

All those ingredients would be critical to Madonna's career, and she had discovered them in Paris. She had also made some crucial personal discoveries that would guide her. Even at that embryonic stage, she realized that only she could decide who she was as an artist—that she could not have a role imposed upon her. She had also come to believe that she *could* be a singer and possibly a musician.[2] She had written a little in Paris—not songs per se but poems and passages that could be turned into lyrics.[3] She had hoped for one kind of learning experience in France; she got another. From it, she would begin to build a career on her own terms.

Madonna returned to New York in August of 1979, not much better off materially than she had been when she left but with a mind broadened by new experiences and an imagination enlivened by new goals. She was nothing if not a pragmatist. Asking herself, Who do I want to be? How do I get there? she set about answering in a very deliberate fashion. She continued to dance, though she took fewer classes.[4] And while she once again lived in Manhattan, she caught the train to Queens as often as she could to satisfy two kinds of hunger: Dan was there, and it was where she could learn the skills she needed to become part of New York's music scene at a moment of colossal change and opportunity.

In the mid- to late 1970s, the popular music world was dominated by punk and disco. By the fall of 1979, both were officially declared dead. Though disco still thrived in Europe that year, it was killed off in the States in July during a Chicago White Sox doubleheader, when a local DJ, along with the son of the team's owner, offered fans discount tickets if they brought in a disco record to be destroyed. Between games, fifty-nine thousand records (and the field) were set ablaze in an act of cultural annihilation aimed at the music and the people who enjoyed it: gays, Blacks, and "elites." The straight white men who controlled the airwaves wanted to hear rock on the radio, not the Village People or Donna Summer or "white Negroes" like the Bee Gees.[5]

The "disco sucks" campaign was loud and pervasive, and, eventually, it won. In July, when the record auto-da-fé occurred in Chicago, six disco songs were in the Billboard top ten. By late September, there were none.[6] Straight white men post-disco could resume nodding their heads to music without the fear that they might be asked to move their feet. For the denizens of the urban underground, however, disco was alive and well. In fact, out of the commercial spotlight, it sizzled.[7]

Punk, by contrast, killed itself. It was a sad ending.

Long before it was called punk, the scene existed in New York as pure creative rebellion: art and attitude. Its musical parents were the sexually ambiguous Velvet Underground of the 1960s—Lou Reed, John Cale, Sterling Morrison, Maureen "Moe" Tucker on drums, and the chanteuse Nico. The band emerged as part of Andy Warhol's coterie and formed an integral part of his art theater. Next appeared the madman from Michigan, Iggy Pop, who for his first concert, in 1968, wore an ankle-length white nightshirt, white face paint, and an Afro wig made of twisted aluminum foil.[8]

In 1970, the New York Dolls appeared, a joyous, crazy, unalloyed contradiction. They were five straight white men who dressed in ruffles, taffeta, and high-heeled shoes.[9] After the Dolls, anyone could make music anywhere. Musical ability—even knowing how to play an instrument—wasn't as important as performance. In fact, the scene became performance art masquerading as rock music. "Physical presentation in performing is more important than what you're saying," said Patti Smith, the poet-mother of punk. "If your quality of intellect is high, and your love of audience is evident, and you have a strong physical presence, you can get away with anything."[10]

In March of 1975, the Patti Smith Group double-billed with Tom Verlaine's band, Television, at a place on the Bowery. The bar was owned by what Debbie Harry called a "big slow-talking hippie" named Hilly Kristal, who at the height of the beatnik and folk music craze in 1959, had run the Village Vanguard. Ten years later, he relocated his operation to a spot at 315 Bowery and called it Hilly's on the Bowery. Its clientele were the natives of that neighborhood: drunks and derelicts. In 1973, he wanted to get back into music and renamed his bar Country, Bluegrass, Blues, and Other Music for Uplifting Gourmandizers. It was shorthanded to CBGB & OMFUG, then CBGB, and then just CB's.[11]

It was a year after Hilly had renamed the place that the members of Television persuaded him to let them play on Sunday nights, even though their sound wasn't remotely what the club was looking for. Reasoning that "these kids have something to say and we should listen," Hilly gave them a stage. That was when true punk was born. The attitude was arty, ironic, individualistic.[12]

CBGB became the heart of the new music scene. Television and the Patti Smith Group played eight shows a week. By the end of their seven-week gig, the lines to get into the club stretched around the block. Blondie, with Debbie Harry doing a street-urchin Marilyn Monroe, performed at CBGB not long afterward, and in June the art-school band Talking Heads debuted with its pretend-preppie look, extreme eccentricity, and Tina Weymouth on bass. She occupied the gamine space between what one writer called "the crappily boyish Patti Smith and the ur-feminine Debbie Harry."[13]

Punk was freedom. It was street. It was anticapitalist. It was sexually fluid.[14] But mostly, it was about having fun — fun as an antidote to the dark reality of Richard Nixon, Watergate, Vietnam, environmental degradation, urban decay, crime, racism, drug addiction, sexism, homophobia. Surprisingly, despite all that ugly sociopolitical background noise, New York punk wasn't angry. It was only after punk was introduced to British audiences in 1976 by Patti Smith and by the Ramones that it became nihilistic.[15]

Writer and filmmaker Mary Harron, who helped launch *Punk* magazine, said the scene that was started as a joke in New York turned hardcore and humorless in Britain. Harron remembered seeing kids backstage "like nightmares...like little ghouls with bright red dyed hair and white faces. They were all wearing chains and Swastikas and things stuck in their head."[16] The father of that scene was Malcolm McLaren.

Co-owner of a London shop called Sex, McLaren had managed the Dolls before their demise and thus knew what was happening in New York.[17] Back in England, still inspired by that experience, he created a boy band out of some youths who hung out at his store. He called them the Sex Pistols. One writer said they began as "hangers of clothes" for the biker and S/M designs of McLaren's partner, Vivienne Westwood.[18]

The Sex Pistols were a brilliant invention. The image was so strong and so ghastly that they instantly embodied punk on both sides of the Atlantic.[19] And when, after just two years, the band split, the punk scene began to die, too. That left a void, because many of the artists who came of age playing at punk clubs were still playing and didn't want to stop.

Sire Records' Seymour Stein, who had a seer's knack for spotting talent and was an early and ardent supporter of punk (he had also signed the Ramones, Talking Heads, and the Pretenders), said the bands had to accept that this musical chapter was over. The do-it-yourself inventiveness would remain and evolve into New Wave. But the future, as he saw it, was pop.[20] Prophetic words. Within three years, Stein would sign Madonna.

Madonna had been immersed in music since she was a child—though not the kind of music being made in downtown Manhattan. To understand that complex and intimidating world, she needed mentors. Luckily, by 1979 there were a few strong and exciting women artists she could turn to.[21] New Wave bands, which integrated painting, film, and literature into their work and made irony central to their messaging, were largely devoid of the heavy sexist scene associated with rock and late punk. That meant that women didn't need to assume a goddess-whore role. They could make music.[22] After Patti Smith declared, "I wasn't born to be a spectator" and proved it, critics questioned a woman's ability onstage at their peril.[23]

Madonna had seen Chrissie Hynde, a Midwestern transplant, former art student, and music journalist, in Central Park performing with her band the Pretenders. With her shaggy black hair, black clothes, and leather pants, her look was strong and androgynous, her voice deep. She wasn't a "girl singer," she was a powerful artist. She had a jazz vocalist's understated, resolute stage presence and used her voice as an instrument, allowing it to alternately soar, stop, and whisper as she delivered her poetry above the racket of a 4/4 rock beat.[24] "She was amazing. The one woman I'd seen in performance where I thought, 'Yeah, she's got balls, she's awesome,'" Madonna recalled. "She didn't give me license to think that I could do it. But it gave me courage, inspiration, to see a woman with that kind of confidence in a man's world."[25]

Madonna also loved Rickie Lee Jones, Hynde's stylistic opposite, who had released her first album in 1979 to huge acclaim.[26] At a time when artists assumed the romantic trappings of dereliction, Jones didn't need to act poor; she *was* poor. She had lived on the streets of LA, and yet her music and lyrics were bright, even sweet in their world-weariness. In her fishnets, berets, top hats, and feathers, she was the un–rocker, an artist happy to exist outside genres as she played Carnegie Hall and made the cover of *Rolling Stone*—all without losing her dignity or denying her art.[27]

Madonna added Debbie Harry to the list of women artists she admired, because, like Hynde and Jones, she wrote her lyrics and was "in charge" of her life.[28] But of those three women, Harry had another quality that Madonna shared and thought she could develop. Dan Gilroy said, "Somebody [Madonna] talked to said, 'The camera loved Debbie Harry.' That made a huge impression on her...and I think she felt, 'Yeah, the camera loves me too.' Something clicked."[29]

Madonna's immediate job, however, was to clock the hours of hard labor that those women had already put in. "I decided, if I was going to be a singer, I had to earn it," she said. "I had to learn how to play an instrument."[30] While the Gilroy brothers worked their day jobs, Madonna practiced drumming—endlessly—by listening to Elvis Costello records.[31] After four hours of that, she'd switch to a guitar and then keyboards.[32] "I had a lot of pent-up energy inside of me from sitting around being a spoiled French brat."[33]

Working at the Gog with the Gilroys' equipment spared Madonna the humiliation that many women who wanted to play music faced. Record stores and instrument shops were boy caves. Joan Jett recalled getting her first guitar when she was thirteen and asking a guy in a guitar shop for lessons so she could "play rock 'n' roll...I was so into it and he looked at me like I was out of my mind, like I ate heads or something." When during her first lesson he led her through the chords of "On Top of Old Smokey," she quit and taught herself.[34] Madonna, by contrast, had a supportive environment during her "intensive musical training." She said, "It was one of the happiest times of my life. I really felt loved."[35]

Whitley Setrakian had been in Durham at the American Dance Festival and returned to New York in late summer to try out for a position in an annual choreographer's showcase held at Dance Theater Workshop. She had created a piece she wanted to present at the audition. After tracking Madonna down through numerous phone numbers, she asked her to join the performance. Madonna agreed, and they began rehearsing with a third dancer in a loft in SoHo that Whit shared with roommates. Madonna asked Whit if she could move in, too, saying she hated where she lived. The other roommates were eager but, that time, Whit said no.[36]

Madonna invited Whit to her place, possibly to soften her up by letting her see just how bad it was. It didn't work, but Whit *was* duly horrified by what she called Madonna's "tenement beast in the West 40s." The staircase and halls were so filthy that she feared touching them. The apartment

amounted to nothing more than a grimy couple of rooms and broken furniture.[37] Sitting in the part of the place that Madonna designated her own
by hanging beads, she told Whit the incongruent story of her high life in
Paris and her hand-to-mouth existence in New York. Then, after laughing about their "nightly ritual," she offered another non sequitur. Madonna
told Whitley that she had been raped.[38] It had happened downtown during
a perfectly normal day.

In SoHo, NoHo, and the East Village, the art and music scenes were
vibrant because artists could afford to live and work there unimpeded by
any sort of authority at all. The region was so derelict that police didn't
bother to venture below 10th Street.[39] The heroin trade in nearby Alphabet City was as open and well known as the diamond trade was in the Diamond District. People who chose to travel those streets were on their own,
and that suited the artists just fine. But more than occasionally, they were
the victims of crime. The art kids made easy targets. Madonna became one.

She has recounted the rape story a few times over the years—the first
time publicly in 1995—without going into detail because she said she
didn't want to be seen as soliciting pity. She said it happened during that
first year in New York on a hot summer's day. She was on her way to dance
class, wearing a large men's shirt and baggy shorts. Having found the door
to the class locked, she needed money for a pay phone to call up for entry.
Madonna asked a stranger for a coin. He gave it to her and offered to walk
with her to the phone booth. When no one picked up at the dance school,
he offered to let her call from his apartment, across the street. "I was like,
'Oh, that's really nice of you'...I trusted everybody," Madonna said.[40] But
the man didn't take her to his apartment. He put a knife to her back and
forced her to the roof of the building, where the assault occurred.[41]

There are as many reactions to rape as there are women who experience
that violence. Some women are "upset, some calm, some in a state of
shock—but every victim's life is disrupted in four ways: physically, emotionally, socially, sexually," according to one expert.[42] And most of them
work through their trauma alone. Madonna recalled,

I wouldn't have dared to call my father to tell him, because he would have
said, "What were you wearing?"...You don't want to tell people you were
raped. It's shame. You feel bad, you think, "Someone will think I did something wrong"...

But when life gives you a lemon, you have to make lemonade. I'd rather
not be a victim. I'd rather learn from all the things that have happened to
me...It's there like all the other experiences—the good, the bad and the
ugly. They make me who I am today.[43]

Madonna kept the rape private and dealt with it on her own—in her words, as a survivor. "That's *all* there is to it."[44]

No one at the Gog had money. Dan recalled crawling around looking for loose change to buy food.[45] For cash, Madonna had a steady modeling job with Anthony Panzera, and she began working part-time with Dan Gilroy and Norris Burroughs at the Gossamer Wing textile design company, painting silk fabric. "She was fun, you know," Dan said. "She'd be working at this design thing that I was doing, and she would break into a dance in the middle of the day. It was an incredible attention getter."[46] During lunch breaks, Madonna and Burroughs practiced guitar, and in the studio the Gossamer crew worked to the latest sounds: the Police, Blondie, Prince, Joe Jackson, and some of the '60s girl groups like the Shangri-Las and the Ronettes. Burroughs said that the Gossamer staff "talked about music constantly."[47]

It wasn't about new *songs*, it was about new sounds. Each group of artists was so idiosyncratic that it was as if music were being constantly reinvented. A partial list of 1979 hits shows just how many became classics: Blondie's "Heart of Glass," the Police's "Roxanne," the Knack's "My Sharona," the Clash's "London Calling," Talking Heads' "Take Me to the River," Dire Straits' "Sultans of Swing," and the Sugarhill Gang's "Rapper's Delight," to name just a few. It was a thrilling time to listen to music and a thrilling time to contemplate making it.

Dan and Ed's Acme Band rehearsed at night. "They'd get gigs in clubs like CBGB and Max's Kansas City and those downtown dives," Madonna said. "Well, their drummer quit on them one day and I said, 'I can play the drums'...They said, 'You cannot.' But see, I'd been like practicing so I played the drums [and] they let me be the drummer in their band. Then I started doing gigs with them."[48]

By the time Madonna had mastered the drums, she had also gained enough confidence with the guitar to try writing a song. One day, she surprised herself and did so.

> The words just came out of me. I was like, "Who's writing this?"...It was called "Tell the Truth." It was maybe four chords, but there were verses and a bridge and a chorus, and it was a religious experience.[49] I remember that moment so vividly, the hair standing up on the back of my arms...I felt like I'd been possessed by some magic.[50]

From that point, Madonna said, "I became really prolific...songs just came out of me...Pain and loneliness and love, everything that I feel. I mean my whole experience about leaving my family and coming to New

York was a very traumatic thing for me."[51] Like Anne Sexton's poetry, Madonna's lyrics covered personal terrain. "She is talking about loss, low self-esteem, things that had been inside her for who knows how long," Ed Gilroy said. "She had stability here, security here, a positive environment to reach back into those times and try and express herself...there was no holding back. It was completely out there."[52]

Music was Madonna's focus, but she hedged her bets by continuing to look at the trades for possible stage or film jobs. In late August of 1979, she saw an ad in *Back Stage* that called for a "dominant woman who knows how to act and dance" to play a "dominatrix type" in a low-budget film. Madonna read the ad and thought, "Oh great, I'm going to be a movie star."[53]

Movie cameras were everywhere in those days because New York had mounted a huge campaign to promote itself as a film-friendly location for Hollywood projects.[54] Aspiring filmmakers shooting Super 8 movies hoped to be the next Martin Scorsese after the success of *Mean Streets* and *Taxi Driver*. Others were just fooling around with B-movie genres—"pulp plots and ultra-violent thrills"—presented as the tongue-in-cheek step-children of slasher films like *Carrie* and *The Texas Chain Saw Massacre*.[55] The film Madonna read about in *Back Stage* seemed to be one of those. She was okay with that. Hadn't Sissy Spacek become a star after *Carrie*?

Madonna sent director Stephen Jon Lewicki photos taken by Dan back-stage at a *Voideville* show and a two-page handwritten letter describing herself. She ended the letter with the question "Is this all?" and a list of her vitals: height, weight, hair color, eye color, and phone number.[56]

Lewicki said he had received a pile of correspondence from women interested in the role. When he sifted through them, Madonna's photo fell out.[57]

> The picture of her, where she's putting lipstick on...really grabbed my attention...and then I read the letter...and it was the most personable com-munication that I got from anybody. She gave me her life story in two pages, handwritten, which is pretty amazing! It just seemed like it was a fated kind of thing.[58]

Madonna and Lewicki agreed to meet in Washington Square Park. Wearing a red miniskirt and her chin cocked tough, she announced upon seeing him, "Look, I'll do your movie, but there'll be no screwing." Lewicki said, "Who said anything about screwing?" She took out a mirror and began to apply lipstick with her little finger and repeated, "Just know, that you and I will not be screwing. Got it?" Lewicki realized that this was her audition. "I knew she was perfect for the role. She was *doing* the role."[59]

Madonna was hired, along with her dancer friend Angie Smit, who played bass guitar.[60]

A Certain Sacrifice was half Ken Russell's *The Lair of the White Worm,* half *Taxi Driver.* Madonna was cast as a dominatrix, but the script portrayed her as a victim—first of an attack by her "sex slaves" and then of a rape (not shown on-screen) by a psycho in a diner.

The hour-long production had moments of interest, but Madonna wasn't part of most of them. It wasn't her fault. *Sacrifice* was a young man's fantasy film. The part she played as written was a cliché: a helpless but willing accomplice who exposed her breasts at crucial moments. In the middle of shooting, Lewicki ran out of money. He left the project "to be continued," which meant he'd reassemble the cast when he had the cash.[61]

After practicing all night, Dan, Ed, Madonna, Angie Smit, and whatever other musicians were around often ended up at the Flushing Meadows International House of Pancakes. They'd say at the end of a studio session, "Want to do a breakfast club?" Dan recalled. "This sounded so catchy, so we decided on it for a band name."[62] With that, the Breakfast Club was born. Its look was New Wave. Angie filled the femme fatale slot, while Madonna was the hip but innocent street kid. Its sound referenced both punk and New Wave: it could be loud, fast, and aggressive or funky, witty, and engaging.

Madonna got to work to promote it. "She'd be up in the morning, a quick cup of coffee and then right to the phones, calling up everybody— *everybody,*" Dan said.[63] Her immediate goal was booking gigs, but she had also started thinking about record deals.[64] "I used to call different management companies, agencies, A&R people, club owners, you name it, and no one ever returned my calls," she said. "If someone did, ten to one it was some horny old man who was in charge of listening to tapes, and when he'd hear my voice, he'd want me to come in and bring the tapes, and then he'd put the make on me."[65]

The Breakfast Club's first gig was at the UK Club, in Manhattan, with Madonna on drums, Angie Smit on bass, and Ed and Dan Gilroy on vocals and lead guitar. No one but friends turned up, which might have been why the Gilroys agreed to let Madonna sing. She had been agitating to get behind the microphone, so they gave her one song.[66]

"I got up and I did that one song and the band got a standing ovation. It was like the best response," Madonna said. "It was called 'I Was Born to Be a Dancer.' So, once I got a taste of that—playing guitar, dancing around, singing, I said, 'No way. I'm not going back there again. I'm not playing those drums. I want to be [out] front.'"[67] "That microphone position," she said, "was looking more and more inviting."[68]

*   *   *

Though Madonna rehearsed at the Gog every day and stayed there most nights, she hadn't moved in. But after she became part of the band, she finally did. "It was a comfortable place for her," Dan said. "Here was this girl without work, bumming around, not knowing where to go. Here was a place with enough space to do her dancing. There was a washing machine and a dryer. Plus, it was in an Italian neighborhood. What more could she want?"[69] Madonna wanted *everything*. But she'd settle immediately for center stage.

She admitted that Dan had "created a monster...I was always thinking in my mind, 'I want to be a singer in this group, too.' And they didn't need another singer." In fact, they didn't *want* another singer.[70] Madonna's new goal added a layer of complexity to the band's relationships, with Dan torn between loyalty to his brother and satisfying his irrepressible girlfriend.[71] But for a while, he so successfully juggled their competing needs that they all enjoyed their time together.

Madonna occupied the Gog like a weather system, filling it with creative drive, love, lust, joy, tumult, tragedy, tantrums, and play.[72] "It was fun. It was a good year," Dan said.[73] "I love people who are passionate about their stuff. She was excited and intense about working and preparing for whatever—yoga, running, music, dance." Ed had written a song, called "Cold Wind," that he performed with Madonna as a duet. "She... worked so hard on my song," he said. "She gave me all her time and effort."[74]

Madonna was very much in learning mode, and the Gog was her academy. "Being part of a band teaches you about musicality," she said. "There's no better way to understand about arrangements. How to create a song, how to perform...To me, those early days were so essential to building me as an artist."[75]

On some songs at that time, Madonna's voice was small and searching. It seemed most naturally her own and had the most original sound. But she wasn't prepared to settle on it without first experimenting with a range of vocal styles. She tried out a different one on each of the songs she had written: Patti Smith on "Trouble," Rickie Lee Jones on "Oh Oh!," even the '60s girl group sound on "Baby Come Home." Her default voice, though, was Chrissie Hynde. Bassist Gary Burke, who played in the band, said Madonna "absolutely worshipped" her.[76]

In early January of 1980, friends from Michigan called Whitley Setrakian to say that they'd seen Madonna and the Gilroys playing at a club and that Madonna had invited them all out to the Gog to watch a rehearsal. Linda Alaniz was with Whit, so she agreed to go to Queens, too.[77]

As Madonna played the drums and the band "pounded away" in the Gog sanctuary, Whit endured the session more than enjoyed it. She was uncomfortable being there and was thoroughly unconvinced by the music. But years later, she admitted that her discomfort didn't stem from either boredom or disapproval. "There's no doubt about what I was feeling: pure, 100-proof, moonshine-quality jealousy. In the face of her power, her willingness to fail in the service of the larger goal, of her stark beauty and fuck-you drive," she said.[78]

Linda was also impressed by what she saw—"how fast Madonna was growing"—but she picked up a note of dissatisfaction in her friend that day in Queens.

> We were talking to her, and I asked her if she was happy. And she said, "What do you mean?" And I said, "Are you happy doing what you're doing?" Because I always remembered Madonna as never being happy. She always seemed like she was so impatient to move ahead.[79]

What Linda sensed was indeed impatience. Dan said the band might get one or two paying jobs a month and earn eighty dollars, which they shared.[80] "We made the circuit of all the shitty clubs," Madonna said. "We played on the audition nights and the nights where you don't get any money and you were the tenth band to play and you set up your shit at three in the morning and there were ten people in the audience, and they threw things at you. I went through all that."[81]

Eventually, the band got a break: a gig at CBGB. Dan and Ed's Acme Band had played there, but it was a first time for the Breakfast Club, and it would be one of Madonna's big early tests as a singer because some of the artists she and the band admired were sure to be in the audience.[82] There was also the possibility that a record producer might be there. The bar had become a recruiting ground for new talent.

The night the Breakfast Club was due to perform, Norris Burroughs said, Madonna seemed nervous. And as usual when she felt ill at ease, she acted out, that night by belching loudly midsong. Meanwhile, Angie Smit, who Burroughs said wasn't much of a bass player, "was making up for her mediocre musicianship by wearing lingerie onstage, which diverted attention from what Madonna felt was the group's main attraction, her." To add insult to injury, a blue-mohawked gent next to the stage made "catcalls and wolf whistles" at Angie during Madonna's song. Madonna left the stage after the show spitting mad, but not discouraged.[83] She just had more work to do to become the performer she wanted to be, and that meant changing her role in the Breakfast Club.

"The more songs I wrote, the more I wanted to be the front person of the band," Madonna said.[84] Bass player Gary Burke said that the Gilroys weren't interested in playing backup in Madonna's show.[85] Events worked in Madonna's favor, however. The musician she had replaced on drums, Mike Monahan, returned and relieved her of those duties.[86] She switched to keyboards, which put her closer to the spotlight.

With Madonna's ascent, Ed Gilroy began to feel that he had become an auxiliary to Madonna and Dan's enterprise.[87] Tensions also developed with the other band members. Angie quit, and Gary Burke and Mike Monahan had crushes on Madonna, which made it easy for her to enlist them on her side of any dispute.[88] Madonna had thus become the focus of the band's musical direction and its main source of turmoil. The Breakfast Club was coming undone.

That spring, the group had a show on West 24th Street, at Bo's Space. There was a noticeable difference between the response the Gilroys received for their sets and the applause the audience showered on Madonna after she sang her songs. "The crowd really went wild for those two numbers," Dan said.

> At the Bo's Space thing, I think that that was maybe the first time where she...felt like "Whoa, there's somethin' happening with me and my microphone that isn't happening when I'm behind a keyboard with someone else singing." And that night in bed...I felt a distance that I hadn't felt before. She was thinkin' about maybe she didn't wanna be in a band or she wanted to front the band.[89]

He was right: she did want a new role in the band. But the distance he felt was the result of something much deeper. That night at Bo's, Madonna experienced the adulation of a crowd, a mass outpouring of affection that, however temporary, was big enough and powerful enough to satisfy her hunger for love. One young man couldn't come close to matching it; it was love on that scale and intensity that she craved.

Soon afterward, Madonna, with support from Gary Burke and Mike Monahan, presented Dan and Ed with an idea that she thought would improve the band: she would be its lead singer. As far as the brothers were concerned, they wrote the bulk of the material, the band didn't require a lead singer, and they didn't want to be bit players in her show. The Gilroys said no.[90] She quit.

Madonna hated to say goodbye and avoided it whenever possible, but Dan had been such a critical part of her life at a difficult time that he deserved the dignity of hearing from her that she was leaving. She told him she planned to start her own band. "It was sad, sweet, and rather poignant," he said.

She did it rather well and I have always appreciated that. There had always been the sense that she was passing through.[91] I knew with that kind of drive and devotion to getting ahead, something had to happen.[92] So, you grab on to her as long as you can.[93]

Madonna, meanwhile, was back at what had become a familiar place for her: square one.[94] Gary Burke left the Breakfast Club and went with Madonna, as did drummer Mike Monahan, and the three briefly formed a band called Madonna and the Sky, until Mike quit to focus on his day job selling insurance. That meant she was without a home, without a job, *and* without a band. Christopher Flynn once said that Madonna had a way of turning a crisis to her advantage, "all it took was luck."[95] In 1980, at that very low and highly uncertain moment, luck appeared in the form of an old friend. Steve Bray reentered the picture.

Chapter 10

New York, 1980–1981

I had this thing that I would look into everybody's eyes because I was going to be somebody, and they were going to remember me.[1]

— *Madonna*

STEVE AND MADONNA'S relationship in Michigan had ended abruptly and without much explanation when she left Ann Arbor for New York, two years earlier.[2] But any hard feelings had disappeared by 1980, when he contacted her out of the blue. "I called Madonna up to say, 'Hey, I'm coming to New York.' And she had this band and she said, 'Well I need a drummer. I've got a set full of tunes and I actually have a gig.' I don't think she really *did* have a gig at the time," Steve said, but he told her he'd be in New York the next week.[3]

Since Madonna had last seen him, Steve had attended the Berklee College of Music, in Boston, where some of the world's greatest musicians — Quincy Jones, Keith Jarrett, Branford Marsalis, to name just a few — had trained.[4] His was exactly the fresh energy and perspective she needed, personally and musically. Madonna called Steve "a real musical wizard."[5] Dan Gilroy said, "Steve had chops, serious chops."[6] There was also the added comfort that he was from home.

Only two years older than Madonna, Steve had had the same childhood musical influences as she did. He was imbued with the Detroit sound and Detroit attitude. And though they would have experienced the city's social turmoil from different perspectives — he as a young Black child inside the city and she as a white one outside it — they had both lived through it. They had a shared history that involved rebellion, social justice, and the healing power of music. All that meant that when they began working together, they could skip the lengthy and often awkward trust-building preambles and get right down to creation.

Steve hadn't been in New York since he was seven. When he arrived in 1980, he said, "I was broke for the most part having arrived with nothing but lint in my pocket but in love with becoming a New Yorker."[7] He agreed to meet Madonna at the corner of 38th Street and Eighth Avenue. "There's this building converted to rehearsal studios," he said. It was the Music Building, where Madonna was semi-established, working with Gary Burke. "We met up and she played me the songs that they had," Steve said. "We just kind of jammed the first day. I was excited to find that she had written some solid songs."[8] Madonna had about fourteen of them at that point, and Steve said, "To me, that was really impressive, 'cause I've had a lot of training, but by then I still hadn't written one song. So, I thought, well this is great. If a person can come from dance school and decide to be a songwriter and *become* a songwriter merely by volition, then I think I can do that, too."[9]

Not long after their reunion, Madonna was forced to flee a squat in the Garment District when one of the electric space heaters she used to warm the place ignited a piece of carpet she slept on. "I woke up in the middle of the night surrounded by a ring of fire," she said. "Then my nightgown caught fire. So, I took it off, got dressed, grabbed a few things, like under-pants and stuff—all my important things like tapes and instruments were already over at the Music Building, three blocks away—and I went over to the Music Building and started sleeping there."[10] Steve didn't have a place to live, either, so he joined her.[11]

The place had opened the year before with sixty-nine rehearsal stu-dios.[12] "You weren't supposed to live there. It wasn't really set up—there was like a bathroom in the hallway with a toilet and a sink in it," Madonna said.[13] The sink was small, with one tap—cold water only. To use it, a per-son had to hold the faucet on with one hand and wash with the other.[14] "Trying to make that work and feel clean was a bit of a nightmare," she said. In fact, among the aspects of her poverty that Madonna hated most during that period was "having to go out to dinner with idiots so I could come home and use their bathrooms."[15] "I couldn't wait to live in a house and take a bath, like a bathtub is a glorious aspect of that time, and I pretty much wore the same thing every day. We had a little cracked mirror in the room. I sort of like could tell what I looked like a little bit."[16]

To sleep, she and Steve found pieces of foam rubber, which they placed on the floor between a set of drums as their headboard and amplifiers as their footboard. "There was no heat, and it was hot in the summertime, and bands were playing literally twenty-four hours a day, so if you wanted to go to sleep...it was tough luck for you because it was never quiet," Madonna said. "You'd hear them rehearsing the worst music in the world. The same stuff over and over and they never got better."[17] She believed that only a few of the musicians in the building would be successful.[18] She knew she would be one of them.[19]

Despite the squalor and the racket from their fellow occupants, Steve and Madonna loved the place. "Just being in that atmosphere was intoxicating," he said. "You could just taste the creativity."[20] Said Madonna, "We just played music all day. I remember getting up with Steve and... he'd be doing his drum exercises...and I'd be doing my yoga...and then I'd play guitar and I'd write a song...and he'd play something that he had written, and I'd make up the words for it."[21]

Part of the joy of that period was that they both had the freedom to experiment, to make the mistakes they needed to make, because no one cared what they were doing. "That's an important thing, because it allowed me to develop as an artist and to be pure, without any influences," Madonna said.[22] During that period, she lived music and lived *for* music. It was as simple as that.

Any rent she and Steve paid was minimal because it was split among all the musicians who used the rehearsal space. But even with their lodging expenses hovering between tiny and nonexistent, they were so broke that they only allowed themselves a dollar a day to live on. Steve described that period as "some very lean and desperate hours. We basically were eating yoghurt and [asking ourselves,] 'Should we put the peanuts in the yoghurt or have them as an appetizer?' "[23]

The local delis extended them credit, but Madonna admitted she also "stole a lot of food."[24] And "when we'd run out of money," she said, "I'd pass by the garbage can in the lobby of the Music Building, and if it smelled really good—like if there was a Burger King bag sitting on top that someone had just deposited—I'd open it up, and if I was lucky, there would be French fries that hadn't been eaten."[25]

To earn the little they had, Steve worked part-time at a record store, and Madonna had what he called benefactors. "I don't know what was involved...clearly it wasn't anything nefarious...because she would have had more money."[26] Madonna explained, "I used to borrow money from people—I'd let some poor sucker take me out to dinner and then I'd go, 'Can I borrow a hundred dollars?' I was always borrowing twenty-five, fifty, a hundred dollars from people."[27] Modeling was also a fallback. "I would shoot on down to the New School and throw off my clothes and pose for three hours and make some food money and then get back [to the Music Building] to rehearse."[28]

But as bad as things were, she didn't want to ask her father for help. "I had turned down a scholarship at the University of Michigan to come and do this, so I couldn't expect much sympathy."[29] Besides, Madonna was suffering, which according to Tony's rules, meant she was onto something. She explained:

Pain makes you grow...it makes you different from people who've had an easy life. It makes you more introspective...You have to go into a deep place inside of yourself to get through pain...You just become a different kind of a person. You can see it in their eyes. Can't you? I can always see it.[30]

As for Madonna and Steve's relationship, it had evolved from their romance in Michigan to something that would be more enduring but was, at the time, confusing to Steve. "Being Madonna's boyfriend is a difficult job," he said.

Some people are very up-front, and some people are, "You'll find out eventually that you're not my boyfriend, that I'm seeing twelve other people." That is more her approach...I just learned that it would probably be best not to really count on her in that area.[31]

Instead, they became a musical team that would nurture each other to greatness.

Once the band was assembled—Madonna, Steve, Gary Burke, and rotating guitarists—the issue of a name arose. Madonna wanted the group to be called Madonna. Steve threatened to quit. "It was too Catholic for one thing, and maybe just a little bit of ego coming out," he said. "It just seemed like, 'What about the rest of us?'"[32] Someone then suggested No Name spelled backward. Phonetically, it sounded a bit like Emmy. Madonna claimed that had been her nickname.[33] Emmy it was. Sometimes Emmy & the Emmys. Steve simply called them a "band of gypsies."[34]

Using the pay phone in the Music Building lobby, Madonna made calls every day trying to get performance dates.[35] They played anywhere they could and comforted themselves with the thought that they were at least on *a* track, if not the right track, because they got gigs. "If you define gigging as taking the subway to the show with your drums and getting paid about seven dollars or so, yeah, we were gigging," Steve later told Culture Club vocalist and filmmaker Helen Terry in her documentary *Naked Ambition*.[36] They played on Long Island, in New Jersey, and at what Madonna called "really crap clubs on the Upper West Side."[37] How bad was Emmy? "We kind of sucked. I mean we didn't suck *bad,* but we weren't that good," Steve said. "After a crashing, thunderous ending, there'd be"—he made a slow, vague sound—"three or four people's hands clapping."[38]

Madonna described their music as "deranged punk with minimal funk."[39] Unlike the Madonna of the Breakfast Club, Madonna at the start of Emmy was hard-core. Her new look was Manhattan, the Music

Building, the street. Madonna's style always reflected *where* she was as much as *who* she was. In later years, when she was criticized for her "re-inventions" (as if artistic evolution were a bad thing), the root of the criticism was often that she had "become" Hollywood or "become" British. The fact was, she had. Madonna's work, from her lyrics to her music to her physical presentation, was influenced by and reflective of wherever she lived and worked.

Music Building Madonna presented herself as stronger, more androgynous, than Breakfast Club Madonna. For a time onstage, she even went full-bore punk. "She belted. She screamed," Steve said.[40] "She'd dance on the tabletop and break up things. She didn't smash the guitar, she didn't do that, but she did pour champagne all over herself and her guitar on New Year's Eve."[41]

Despite all that thrashing around, Madonna's performance still looked like work, like she was trying to get the rock thing *right*. Madonna would say many years later of performing, "We're in the world of creating illusions and giving people the ability to dream and to be inspired or moved. So you don't want people to see the labor behind it."[42] In Emmy, she wasn't yet able to invoke that kind of magic.

She played guitar, an instrument she wasn't sure of, and that proved frustrating, because instead of abandoning herself to the performance, she was focused on "playing the right chords." The band decided to hire a lead guitar to free her up.[43] "If we'd found that right guitar player, I think that's when things would have taken off," Steve said. "But there are so many horrible guitar players in New York, and we seemed to get them all."[44]

There was only one artist management company in the Music Building when Madonna lived and worked there, and it occupied the entire second floor: Gotham Sound.[45] It was owned by one of the few women in the business, a twenty-nine-year-old named Camille Barbone. Her graduate school, as she described it, was ten years spent at PolyGram, Columbia Records, Epic Records, Buddah Records, and Arista, working all aspects of the business, from managing departments to scouting new talent. That was the job she enjoyed most, working with the artists. She thought the best way to do that would be to open her own studio.[46]

Camille was small, dark, tough, and wiry. The product of an Italian household—New York City cop father and housewife mother—she was driven to succeed in the boys' world of music, not in order to make a statement but because she belonged there. Having been around the business on both coasts, she knew the harassment and disrespect she would face as a "girl," but she had thick skin and was prepared to take it. She was a lot like

Madonna (they were even born on the same date, August 16) in that she viewed obstacles as temporary inconveniences.[47]

Gotham agent Adam Alter recalled being in the Music Building one day when Madonna skipped by and told him he looked like John Lennon. "I certainly immediately thought, 'What does she want from me?'" What she wanted was help with her career, and she told him so. Alter liked her energy but didn't think much of her band. He gave her a noncommittal maybe. But he was interested enough to mention Madonna to his partner, Camille.[48]

Madonna's first encounter with that partner was not unlike her first meeting with filmmaker Stephen Jon Lewicki. She came in character, as if auditioning. Madonna "knew I was a gay woman. She worked it," Camille said.[49] Their first conversation was full of sexual innuendo. Meeting Camille in the elevator, Madonna looked her in the eye and said, "'Did you do it yet?' For a minute I was taken aback," Camille said, "but I said, 'Do it yet? No, not yet.' And it became a running joke."[50]

Gary Burke had worked hard to get Emmy a gig at Max's Kansas City, and Madonna invited Camille to watch her perform.[51] But Camille didn't show up.

> She came storming into my office the next morning slamming things. I was completely and utterly intrigued. And I just said, "I'm sorry, I had a headache. I didn't make it to your gig." And she just lit into me. "It's my life, how could you do this to me? I set that gig up just for you." Just went off on me and I really enjoyed it and I really thought she was a star at that point in time.[52]

Camille promised she'd see Madonna's next performance and began writing the date in her calendar, but Madonna grabbed it and threw it at Barbone's chest, saying, "If it's important enough to you, you'll remember."[53] Camille did.

The Madonna she saw onstage at Max's was wearing men's boxer shorts, a man's pajama top, shoes, and socks. "I remember I think I took my shoes and socks off and threw them in the audience," Madonna said. "I was very crazy, but I had fun then, too."[54] Camille was shocked by what she saw. Not by the New Wavey getup or requisite bad behavior; it was Madonna herself. "She had been on stage for one and a half minutes with a lousy band, but there was something about her that was sensational," Camille said.[55] "She sparkled, in a very street way."[56]

Barbone had seen that before on stages in New York, but Madonna exhibited a unique quality that set her apart from other female punk and post–New Wave women working the circuit, especially those out of

Britain—the Slits, Poly Styrene, Siouxsie Sioux, the Raincoats—who confronted, if not assaulted, the audience with their sound and personas. "When Madonna was onstage, she gave the audience the feeling of being inside her and of knowing what she was feeling. It's a rare quality," Camille said.[57] "If it's possible to be fearless and vulnerable at the same time, she was...It was the thing that made her unstoppable. And very disarming."[58]

Camille came away from the show ready to make Madonna an offer. "I said, 'How would you like a manager?' And she just screamed, 'Yeaaah,' and jumped up in the air and kind of threw her arms around me."[59] Steve said Madonna and Camille spoke the same language: "It was, 'I'm going to make you a star' and the other person saying, 'I'm gonna be a star.'"[60] Madonna signed a contract with Gotham in March of 1981.[61] She was twenty-two.

Being represented by one of the few women managers at the start of her music career saved Madonna from a lot of the sexual harassment that was accepted and ignored because it was part of the industry and always had been. "Men looked at Madonna as someone they wanted to bed as opposed to sign," Camille said. "I brought her into the mainstream music business in a way that she didn't have to fuck for it."[62]

Camille had two immediate tasks: take charge of Madonna's career and get hold of Madonna's life. "She was a street savvy kid who'd pick up someone to go home with if she was hungry and needed a meal," Camille said. Sensing that Madonna was "wounded," she wanted to protect her.[63] Camille promised her $100 a week, rehearsal space, paying gigs, and she had Madonna's bicycle repaired.[64] Steve said that after so much suffering, Madonna saw Camille as a kind of savior.[65]

Camille also moved Madonna out of the Music Building and into what she said would be improved quarters. The ironically named Star Motel, across from Madison Square Garden, was the first. "I shared a bathroom with two fat Colombians and this old Irish drunk who'd just been released from an insane asylum," Madonna said. The Irishman wailed all night long. "It was quite scary." The place was so bad that Steve refused to visit her there. Madonna lived in the Star until she was robbed, after which Camille moved her to a place on West 70th. It was broken into, too, so Madonna moved to an apartment back up on Riverside Drive that belonged to a friend of Adam Alter.[66]

Despite the harrowing circumstances of her existence, Alter said, "Madonna was not much different from your average spoiled brat...She would stomp her heels and 'I want, I want, I want.' We wanted to give her those things...It was like watching a kid play."[67]

Around that time, Madonna called her twenty-year-old brother, Christopher. The years since he had set foot in Christopher Flynn's class hadn't been easy. He had bounced between universities—Western Michigan and Oakland University—studying dance and anthropology, playing violin, and reading intensely.[68] He was the proverbial searching loner. "At that time, I wasn't openly gay; I wasn't anything. I was just kind of an oddball," he said.[69]

He had begun dancing with a company in Detroit when Madonna summoned him. "She called and said, 'Come to New York. You're a dancer; you're not going to get work in Detroit. It's silly. Come to New York—I'll help you out.' It took me this long to decide," Christopher said, snapping his fingers. "I wasn't afraid. I figured Madonna needs me, thinks I belong there, so I'm going... That would be my first kick in the ass, as it were, from her."[70]

When he arrived at Riverside Drive, Madonna greeted him at the door, said he couldn't live there, and gave him a tab of Ecstasy, as if to soften the blow. Her room had a mattress on the floor, a sink in the corner, a naked lightbulb hanging from the ceiling, and a Sid Vicious poster on the wall. "I turned on the light, and the whole floor moved," he said. "That was new for me. I'd never seen a cockroach."[71]

Madonna found Christopher a place to stay with a dancer friend, Janice Galloway. From that point on, he didn't see his sister much. He left New York after two months to accept a job dancing with a troupe in Ottawa. But around a year later, he would be summoned back. And that time it would be for good.[72]

From the start it was clear that Gotham Sound wasn't interested in any member of Emmy except Madonna. Barbone said the band wasn't "record industry caliber."[73] Madonna did need backup musicians, though. "So, I took all my contacts and I just laid them at her feet," Camille said.[74]

Barbone and Alter would eventually allow Madonna one of her own picks, Steve Bray.[75] Madonna had finagled him into the band by breaking Camille's cardinal rule: no sex among the band members. Madonna slept with the previous drummer, Bob Riley, so that he would be fired and replaced by Steve. "I just couldn't believe she would be so crafty, so mean," Camille said. "Sex, to her, was really just a means to an end, it meant nothing more. I actually became a little afraid of her when she did that to Bob."[76]

In June of 1981, Madonna and the musicians Camille and Alter had assembled, plus Steve Bray, began recording a demo at Media Sound, which was housed in an old church on 57th Street.[77] Jon Gordon played lead guitar and acted as producer during recording sessions. Even at that stage, he said, Madonna wrote most of the melodies, lyrics, and chords herself and had a big hand in running the show. "We were all taking direction from her. She was open to suggestions, but she'd speak up very quickly if she didn't like the way things were going."[78]

Initially Camille and Alter were suspicious of Steve because he was an unknown and because of his history with Madonna.[79] But whatever hesitation they had disappeared quickly because by working with him Madonna was able to turn rough songs into demos that could be shopped around to record labels. "They had a personal connection, an emotional connection," Alter said. "We immediately had some interest in Madonna."[80]

The secret of selling Madonna was Madonna herself. Camille knew the demo alone would be just another tape that could be easily dismissed if the record executive who received it was hungover, depressed, or had had a fight with his wife or lover. But the demo and Madonna combined would make the music unforgettable. Camille began bringing Madonna to meetings. "Once you met her, you either loved her or hated her, but you knew she was fascinating," Camille said.[81]

At times, Madonna disrupted the gatherings with burps or inappropriate laughter, either to hide her insecurities or because the executives at the table annoyed her. Other times, she turned on the charm and had "men eating out of her hands," Camille said. "A simple word like 'Hi' delivered by Madonna, and men are reduced to stuttering and stammering. She had men lending her money and musicians rehearsing and giving their time without pay—and she wasn't sleeping with any of them."[82] But Camille feared that the music industry, so rife with sexual exploitation, would use Madonna's sexuality against her, that she wouldn't be strong enough to withstand the pressure to sell her sex rather than her talent.

Camille's concern was well placed, but she was wrong to think that Madonna would let anyone else, even Camille, use her sexuality to advance her career. At the time Gotham began promoting Madonna, Camille advised her to ditch her look and try something more Pat Benatar-ish, which Steve described as leotards and leg warmers.[83]

Benatar, who was five years older than Madonna, had struck gold in 1979 after working her way up the New York club scene. Five feet and one inch tall, with a shock of messy dark hair and a svelte body, she was a new kind of act that combined a rocky toughness with a poppy sexuality that the music industry loved. What Camille feared would happen to Madonna *did* happen to Benatar.

In those days of "jiggle TV" and *Charlie's Angels,* she was told to move her body in "sexual ways" and to be "hot." Benatar said that she went from making music "to having this sex-goddess...bullshit slammed in my face."[84] It sold. Within a year she had reached the top ten with the innuendo-filled "Hit Me with Your Best Shot" (not written by Benatar). She embodied a male fantasy of what a woman rocker should be, and she was who Barbone, despite her expressed concerns about sexploitation, saw as a template for Madonna.

At first, Madonna went along with it. Her sound became more generic. Some of the lyrics could be read as describing Madonna's life—if the listener happened to be acquainted with her story—but they were trapped in such conventional pop-rock arrangements that her edgy reality was utterly lost. The one interesting aspect of the future Madonna to emerge from the episode was her voice. Unlike the Emmy performances, during which Madonna performed vocally as Chrissie Hynde or Patti Smith, the Gotham tapes featured Madonna's natural voice. It was the small, girlish sound she had used in some of the songs she recorded at the Gog.

The look Madonna and Barbone concocted was a mixture of New Wave and hot rock chick. It came across as strangely schizophrenic and was probably an indication of a broader struggle for Madonna's artistic soul. The New Wave bit was boyish and involved big white shirts, shorts, and a Bowie-like cropped tuxedo jacket worn over an athletic jersey emblazoned with the letter *m*. The rock-chick look was bizarre: a cape made of dozens of foxtails, a leather cave-girl miniskirt, an off-the-shoulder cropped leather top, and a leather band worn across the forehead. Barbone thought it worked, that Madonna was ready.

On October 8, 1981, at Chase Park, on lower Broadway, Madonna made her first appearance in New York City as "Madonna." A week later, at a biker bar called Uncle Sam's Blues, on Long Island, she made a bigger splash.

Camille had asked Bill Lomuscio, whose band had a regular gig at Uncle Sam's, to listen to Madonna's tape. "It wasn't anything impressive," Lomuscio said, but he agreed to let her open for his band.[85] To generate buzz, Camille hired groupies.[86] She also asked *Interview* magazine photographer George DuBose to take pictures, with specific instructions not to photograph the band, just the "star."[87]

Madonna went through three changes of clothing for the performance, which was unusual for a dive bar's opening act. But the only one anyone would remember from that night, and the one that crowd of rowdies responded to, was Madonna as sexual animal. She appeared onstage covered in the famous foxtail cape and launched into song until, midway through the performance, she discarded the fur and finished her number—supine on the stage floor—in scraps of leather and fishnet stockings.[88] Said Lomuscio:

> Now, my band was the house band, and they were pretty popular. Out came
> Madonna and the band and three break dancers that Camille picked up in

Times Square and proceeded to blow my band off the stage...She was really phenomenal. She was a great talent. You could see it immediately, and after three songs, she was getting called back for encores and the band that I had was having a hard time getting on the stage.[89]

Lomuscio surrendered and began working with Gotham to promote Madonna. Camille booked her in clubs outside New York City to help spread the word about her. It worked; Madonna began to attract a fan base.[90] But at just that moment, Madonna had second thoughts. "I'd agreed with my manager to do rock, but my heart wasn't really in it," she said.[91]

The thing is that when I started out with my manager, I was...writing rock 'n' roll stuff and all the musicians that I worked with were really rock 'n' roll musicians and eventually, my songwriting started changing stylistically to more R&B, like black sounding stuff, and I started going back to what I had originally loved as a child in the first place, which is Motown and all the stuff that you listened to in Detroit.[92]

Madonna's changed attitude was attributable in part to Steve. He had a deal with musicians in the Music Building that if he played drums for them, he got keys to their studios.[93] "Madonna was working with Camille downstairs on rock 'n' roll," Steve said, "and I'm working on dance-oriented tracks upstairs." He asked Madonna to help him out with the vocals.[94] She did. "It took a while," Madonna said. "It took a lot of nights working from midnight to eight in the morning" until they began producing songs they liked.[95]

Another major influence on Madonna at that time was a young man she had begun dating who was part of the city's dance club scene. "He introduced me to a whole different lifestyle," Madonna said. "I didn't know about Studio 54 or Xenon's or—I didn't hang out in clubs. I just didn't know about that kind of life, and he started taking me to all these clubs and I started hanging out in DJ booths."[96]

In the process, Madonna discovered that A&R (artist and repertory) scouts for record labels didn't necessarily go to hear a band live: they went to clubs to hear what the DJs were playing, to see what moved the crowd. *That* was where they found new music.[97] So she undertook reconnaissance missions to watch that side of the industry in action. While there, she also found her way back onto the dance floor she loved. She said,

Just the feeling of the tribal, the community...That bass booming, people dancing, moving in unison. There's something really primal about it and inexplicable. I think it's in our nature to want to do that. To want to join together and move to a beat.[98] I thought, "Why can't I do that?" I wanted to make music that I would want to dance to.[99]

But that created tensions with Camille, who had invested time and money in promoting Madonna as a rocker. Years later, Camille said that assumption was natural because it was who Madonna was when they met. But Madonna saw it as a kind of blindness on Camille's part. "I don't think she understood my direction as an artist," Madonna explained.

> She wanted to push me toward a Pat Benatar mold, because she thought my image was more white rock. I would sing those funk songs and she would say it didn't fit my image. I thought, "Why couldn't I start a new genre?"[100]

Steve said a confrontation was inevitable because Camille was busily selling Madonna the rock star while Madonna was in the clubs shopping around her dance music.[101]

One might think that having been essentially homeless a few months earlier, Madonna would have made artistic concessions—at least for a while—to reestablish her health and physical well-being. But for Madonna, her creative health was all that mattered. As she had been when she left home, when she left the University of Michigan, when she left Pearl Lang, when she left Paris, when she left Dan Gilroy, she was prepared to leave Camille Barbone's protective bubble because it wasn't enough, artistically and spiritually.[102]

Camille believed she had done everything in her power to help her. "Madonna basically pushed me to my financial limit, my loyalty limits, my patience limits," she said.[103] "I knew she was using me. But what could I expect, really?"[104]

Camille turned to booze in search of solace, and her relationship with Madonna grew more troubled. They fought often and loudly and, in Madonna's case, dirty. She provoked Camille by calling her at all hours, wanting to go to a movie, taunting Camille by making out with a female friend in the back seat while Camille drove in the front. She even painted the words *sex* and *fuc* on Camille's poodles.[105] During one altercation, Camille was so angry that she punched the wall and broke her hand. "I'm a nasty drunk and most of the fights and insanity would ensue then," Barbone said. "I have to admit that she could no longer rely on me."[106]

On New Year's Eve in 1981, Madonna opened for former New York Dolls vocalist David Johansen at My Father's Place, on Long Island. The club was a storied spot for aspiring artists and had hosted everyone: Bruce

Springsteen, Linda Ronstadt, Blondie, even Bob Marley and Peter Tosh when they arrived in the States in the '70s from Jamaica. Johansen had launched a solo career after the Dolls and had done some recording at Gotham, hence Madonna's gig with him.[107] But by the end of their sets, they had become friendly, so Johansen trundled Madonna into a limo and took her to a bash billed as a "New Year's Eve Rock 'n' Roll Party" at a hotel near Times Square, where he was also due to perform.[108]

The party was being thrown by a new cable TV channel that had begun broadcasting that August. It was called MTV. Johansen and Madonna bypassed the throngs of people lined up around the block to get in and entered a canvas tunnel erected inside the hotel that led to the elevator. In the early hours of that new year, 1982, an icon of New York's musical past was about to introduce an icon of New York's musical future to the party.[109]

Chapter 11

New York, 1982

On a cultural level for me, rock music means "the music of the land of white people." Dance music is something that is democratic and ethnically mixed.[1]

— *François Kevorkian*

IN FEBRUARY, A lawyer summoned Camille Barbone and Bill Lomuscio to a meeting to discuss Madonna. And not just any lawyer. It was powerhouse entertainment attorney Jay Kramer, whose clients included music megastar Billy Joel and bestselling writer Stephen King. As she settled in to talk, Camille thought Kramer's invitation was a strategy session to, as he said, discuss "how you guys are working together and what the future is going to hold." She might have realized from Madonna's position in the room that the future was contentious. Madonna had folded her body into a sofa, out of the line of fire.[2]

Camille knew Madonna was being courted by others. "I didn't have enough juice to get her to the next level," she said. "I was falling apart from it. I knew she was going to go all the way to the top. And it blew my mind."[3] Under those circumstances, maybe it wasn't a surprise when Kramer told Camille at this meeting about Madonna's future that she wouldn't be part of it.[4]

She and Lomuscio argued that Gotham had a contract with Madonna. But Kramer, a three-thousand-pound legal gorilla, essentially told them, too bad.[5] "I spent everything that I had on Madonna's career. It bankrupted me," Camille said. The end of the relationship also destroyed her personally. "We were a team, a marriage that in better circumstances would have thrived." Camille was so devastated that she quit the music business and spent a year working in a nursing home. "I needed people to say, 'Thank you,'" she explained.[6]

Many years later, after a lawsuit Gotham brought against Madonna was settled, after Madonna offered and Camille declined an invitation to join her professional retinue, and after Camille had returned to the music business, she said of Madonna, "She wasn't intentionally malicious, but just incapable of seeing life from anyone else's point of view. She wanted what she wanted, and if you didn't give it, she turned her back on you."[7]

From Madonna's point of view, that was her prerogative. If a young man in her position fired his manager over creative and career differences, he wouldn't be accused of lacking empathy; he would be praised as decisive. Furthermore, Madonna had struggled so long on little more than grit and will that she wasn't about to surrender her dreams to someone else. It wasn't a matter of wants but of artistic needs.

After she left Camille, Madonna had nothing. "I lost the rehearsal space, I lost the band. She was paying my rent, so I was on my own again."[8] All Madonna had left were aspirations, talent, drive, and Steve Bray. "Steve was always like by my side, and we said, 'Forget this band stuff, this is ridiculous. We can write songs and play instruments between us. We'll make a tape on our own. And that's what we'll get record companies to listen to.'"[9]

They planned to circumvent the normal channels and go directly to the DJs and dance floors. In so doing, they tapped into the zeitgeist of the downtown art scene, where visual artists bypassed traditional galleries and took their work straight to the people—artists such as Keith Haring; Jean-Michel Basquiat; Jenny Holzer, who posted her first *Truisms* as free hand-bills; and graffiti bombers like the brilliant Fred Brathwaite—Fab 5 Freddy—who "showed" on walls and in the subway.

Maybe it was youthful impatience, but it felt like something bigger: a rejection of cultural elitism and the established caste system that might, but only *might,* lead to acceptance. It felt like young artists were taking control of their creative output by building their own artistic infrastructure to support it. Said Glenn O'Brien, writer, *Interview* editor, host of the berserk cable-access show *TV Party,* and future editor of Madonna's *Sex* book:

> It was one of those times when the establishment was so far removed from what was going on in the street and the kids. People would open new [music] venues because the old venues were closed. They started new record companies because the other record companies were out of touch...An alternative world opened up.[10]

Madonna's goal in that world was comparatively modest. "All I wanted was a song to get played on the radio," she said. "That's all I was praying for. One song."[11]

In the meantime, she landed back on Riverside Drive in an apartment owned by a friend's father,[12] while she and Steve continued to work in the Music Building, sneaking into studios to use the gear. "I would go to clubs and I would listen to what would make me dance," Madonna said. "And then I would go back, and I would work on my music. I mean, I was influenced by Debbie Harry, Talking Heads, the B-52's. So, to me the line was very blurred between what I was working on and what I was dancing to."[13] Eventually they had it. She and Steve produced a four-song demo: "Everybody," "Stay," "Don't You Know," and "Ain't No Big Deal."[14]

The arrangements were surprisingly lush, relying on DIY ingenuity to compensate for a lack of studio musicians. At one point in "Ain't No Big Deal," Madonna and Steve replicated the sound of a vocoder—a synthesizer used to distort vocals—by holding their noses while singing the chorus. The beat was compulsive, light, and danceable. Madonna's lyrics were layered into the track in a remarkably sophisticated bit of production.

Madonna and Steve threw everything they had into the demo—the sounds of Detroit, the discipline of Steve's musical studies, the music that made people move at the clubs, and their own lives and artistry, which were so perfectly in sync.[15] The tracks were alive: fresh, wild, exciting. There was no comparison between them and the plodding, predictable Gotham tapes. Not a moment of the Madonna-Bray demo felt tired. It was a joy to listen to because it had been a joy to create. It was the sound they had been looking for and a glimpse of what could be. "It was the first time I made a tape...that I was really happy with," Madonna said. "I wanted to take it out and let it be heard."[16]

While promoting their demo, Madonna came face-to-face with the ugly side of the business that Camille had tried to shield her from. "I was the starting-out artist begging for help and I would go to people who ran labels or influential DJs saying: 'Can you help me out? Can you listen to this song?...Can you sign me to your record label?' And a lot of people said: 'Yeah, if you'll do this,' and usually it was a sexual favor."[17] That sort of exchange was par for the course in the industry. "Everybody has heard of the 'casting couch,'" said a midlevel record executive. "But people probably don't have any idea that sexual harassment is five times worse in the music business."[18]

On one occasion, a record executive invited Madonna to his Upper East Side apartment. Once inside, past the warm introductions, he made the terms of their business agreement clear: a blow job for a record deal. Madonna excused herself and went into the bathroom.[19] A poor man had once shoved his prick into her mouth on the roof of a tenement, and it was called rape. A rich man wanted to do the same in his elegant apartment, and it was called business.

Madonna said she was "so broke and so sick of being broke, I thought, 'Wait, could I do it?'" The answer was no. "I couldn't. I couldn't bring myself to do it because I knew I couldn't look myself in the mirror if I did."[20] Horrified by the choice she was being forced to make, that legions of women were forced to make, she left.[21] "I just kept going on as I had," she said, "being a starving artist and waiting for my ship to come in."[22]

In 1982, there was a world downtown where Madonna was safe, a world apart populated by kids and artists who had rejected what society had become and the people who ran it. Ronald Reagan's election as president two years earlier had unleashed a powerful campaign against the "radical" advances of the '60s and '70s—the civil rights movement, feminism, and gay rights in particular—while envisioning an idealized 1950s-like future that was white, patriarchal, and religious.[23] Feminist critic Ellen Willis described Reagan's "Morning in America" as "an invitation to wake up screaming."[24]

And when John Lennon was shot dead outside his New York apartment a month after Reagan's election, those screams turned to anguish. "Some artists became intensely political, others intensely apolitical, and nearly all became, in one way or another, more hedonistic," said performance artist Ann Magnuson. "Our collective subconscious knew that our time was limited and so we played that time for all it was worth."[25]

The arena for the hedonism—in fact, for the life—in that aesthetic underground was the dance club. Historian and music critic Jeff Chang said that clubs became "a communal sacred space, a chance to escape the chafing oppression of the times."[26] Clubgoers may not have realized it, but they were continuing a tradition of the dance floor as political refuge and dance as political defiance that began in modern times forty years earlier.

The first "discotheques" arose as acts of rebellion in Germany in 1939, when sexually liberated young men and women defying Hitler's cultural nationalism became the *Swingjugend*—the Swing Kids. Their gatherings featured "disc jockeys" who played banned American jazz records at secret locations. As Nazism spread, so did the swing movement—in Vienna, Prague, Amsterdam, Brussels, and Paris, where *les Zazous* craved *le jazz hot*.[27]

That irrepressible spirit survived the war. When Whisky à Go Go opened in Paris, in 1947, it became the "blueprint for the modern disco." *Les Zazous* and the Swing Kids could now dance their hearts out legally, but Whisky and the clubs that proliferated in its wake retained an outlaw appeal, because that was their heritage.[28]

The best known of those early discos, in Europe and later in New York, became home to the international jet set, who weren't interested in defying political power so much as in defying the conservative social mores arising out of the war. Discos became palaces of promiscuity. They also became places where the wealthy and celebrated rubbed shoulders with a vast "other."[29]

As wild as those scenes were, however, it was in the New York gay dance clubs post-Stonewall where the flame of rebellion burned brightest. The gay clubs featured "the hottest, sexiest, most redeeming, and most deeply loving dance music there has been," according to Bill Brewster and Frank Broughton in their history of master spinners and mixers, *Last Night a DJ Saved My Life*. "And it was always funky beyond the call of duty."[30] Gay discos were largely underground and illegal because that was where nonheteros, in an intolerant world, could most freely conduct their lives and show their love.

One such disco arose in a SoHo loft where David Mancuso—the "founding father" of modern disco—entertained friends with his eclectic record collection. So many guests attended these gatherings that the space became a private club. On Second Avenue, mostly white gay men flocked to the "Vatican of disco," the Saint, where as many as five thousand danced, drugged, and had crazy sex on a balcony they called heaven.[31]

But true "Paradise" could be found in an old parking garage on SoHo's western edge. By 1978, when the Paradise Garage opened, New York had seen legendary disc jockeys test the limits of technology and sound as well as dancers' abilities and endurance. And many DJs were admired as artists. But Garage DJ Larry Levan was widely considered a genius and "almost universally revered as the greatest DJ of all time."[32]

He didn't simply play music: he created it in his booth above the dance floor, taking the thousands of mostly Black and brown men and boys below with him on a choreographed journey that lasted past dawn. He controlled their feet, their hearts, their minds.[33] Music producers, club and radio DJs, and musicians made the pilgrimage to King Street to discover new ways of making music and learn what was hot. If Larry Levan spun a record, record stores noticed. The next day, demand went through the roof. Record execs also noticed.[34]

Saturday night was *the* night at Paradise Garage. So on Friday night, many of the Garage street kids joined the dance party at a former roller rink in Chelsea called the Roxy. Beginning in June of 1982, every Friday night from 11:00 p.m. to 6:00 a.m. a young woman just arrived in New York from London named Ruza Blue, a.k.a. Kool Lady Blue, brought together two worlds in that unlikely spot—the hip-hop scene from up in the Bronx and the downtown punk and New Wave scene—for what she called Wheels of Steel nights.[35]

Artist Fab 5 Freddy, who was best known at the time for his fabulous painting of Campbell's soup cans along an entire New York City subway car, had straddled the uptown and downtown music and art scenes for a decade and advised Blue. "These two scenes had never been mixed on this level," he said later. "When you went to clubs, the downtown scene was pretty much predominantly white, and the uptown scene was black and Hispanic. And I couldn't imagine it was gonna work. I just anticipated kids from the Bronx beating the shit out of weird-looking punk rockers."[36]

Instead, he said, the break-dance kids — B-boys and B-girls (some so young they arrived with their mothers) — came into the Roxy and started moving. "The energy was right. And it seemed to me, from that point on, you had this great mix. You had punk rock kids with mohawks standing next to b-boys."[37] Added Freddy, "It was definitely the beginning of the urban cultural revolution."[38]

It worked because 1982 was a magical year for rap and hip-hop. Though rap had been rocking the South Bronx since 1974, and the first rap record was released in 1979, it wasn't until 1982 that rap *statements* were made by two of the all-powerful Bronx hip-hop masters: Grandmaster Flash and Afrika Bambaataa. Grandmaster Flash and the Furious Five recorded hip-hop's first political rap, "The Message," about the trajectory of a ghetto child's life. It was so powerful that one writer called it the decade's "Strange Fruit," in reference to Billie Holiday's 1939 song about lynching.[39] "The Message" became the sound of the street that summer, firing up boys and girls eager to be seen for what they were: strong, powerful young men and women.

And then, Afrika Bambaataa released "Planet Rock," and it lit the dance floor on fire. His goal had been to do with a record what Ruza Blue had done with the club. "I was trying to grab the black market and the punk rock market," he said. "I wanted to grab them two together." His method: producing "some funky mechanical crazy shit with no band, just electronic instruments."[40] The result was "the birth of electro-funk sound."[41]

DJ impresario François Kevorkian said Planet Rock "blew everything open. It was just this wild animal, a cyborg let loose. It was just the most astounding, bass-drum heavy, in your face mother fucking deadly record we'd ever heard." The record cost $800 to make and sold out its first run of fifty thousand in a week.[42] "Planet Rock" and "The Message" became Roxy anthems.[43]

The sound that emerged as the uptown and downtown scenes converged was a spectacular mix of rap, reggae, jazz fusion, R&B, punk nihilism, New Wave irony, Kraftwerk-inspired electronics, Giorgio Moroder–inspired disco, Elvis, country and western, and funk, with a whole lot of militancy and an equal amount of love mixed in. In the process, it heralded the "rebirth of dance" — dance as communication, dance as statement, dance in the Swing Kids tradition as a declaration of independence from the forces that would say, "DON'T."[44]

Madonna took up residence in the clubs. She especially loved the Roxy. She absorbed the culture — the music, of course, but also the new dance styles and the look. Though not immediately. It understandably took a while to process that revolutionary spectacle. A new boyfriend helped her gain entry. Leonard McGurr, known as Futura 2000, was a graffiti artist whom a friend said Madonna "zeroed in on...like a missile. Futura did not stand a chance. He was exactly her type—a light-skinned Black, creative, rebellious but not threatening. They had a really hot thing going for a while, and for a while he was devoted to her."[45]

Madonna proved to be a quick study, and in any case, the Roxy scene was not unlike her early days in Pontiac. The hometown kids had merely grown up, the sound had become more complex and radical, and the party had grown much, much bigger. And it *was* a party, one worthy of hip-hop's Caribbean roots. Madonna found her way and her legs on the Roxy dance floor, where that summer the dance of choice was the webo—Spanish slang for "ball shaker." "Part of the dance was, you dance with a girl, but you get really all up on her," Fab 5 Freddy said. "It was a very freaky, very hot dance. You would often see Madonna when she was dancing, she would have two or three guys all up on her doing the freak."[46]

After she had been around the club for a while, and after she had gathered a posse of girlfriends to dance with her, Madonna reclaimed that sexual aggression for herself. Freddy said,

> What I can remember, I would be at a club dancing with a girl and [Madonna] would come up and she'd be in back of me, trying to be freakin' and I'd be like, "Yo, baby what's up?" She was trying to turn the tables a little bit.[47] You could say she was a tramp but that was missing the point. She was never some dingy white chick who slept around with the guys. She was smarter than that...[She was] a strong woman with a sense of humor.[48]

Madonna said she and her friends were the "only white girls that could Webo at the Roxy." Kano, a graffiti artist who did posters for the club, paid tribute to Madonna and her crew by painting the phrase "Webo Girls" on the backs of their jackets, which Madonna translated as "girls with balls."[49] That was also when Madonna adopted her graffiti tag Boy Toy, which she thought Futura might have come up with. "I was a flirt, I toyed with boys," she explained.[50] The Roxy manager, Vito Bruno, said, "Madonna and her friends were the kind of kids you wanted in your venue...She was a standout."[51]

That was what Madonna did for recreation on Friday nights. On other nights, she was a regular at an edgy, arty club called Danceteria. Her goal there was pleasure and business. She hung around the club for a month until she summoned the courage to tell the DJ, Mark Kamins, that she had a tape. "I knew that once I gained his respect and got him to listen to my tape, he had a number of friends that were A&R people...I knew he was very well connected. I planned the whole thing."[52]

Kamins was a native New Yorker three years older than Madonna who had worked in clubs in Manchester, London, and Athens.[53] After being immersed in the punk, New Wave, and northern soul of England as well as in the heavily electronic Eurodisco of Greece, he returned to New York, where clubs featured those sounds plus R&B and the smooth glide path of his youth, jazz. Kamins worked a few clubs before landing at Danceteria, located in a Mafia-owned building on 37th Street.

"Danceteria was the center of the universe, the place where everybody believed in magic," said the club's cocreator Jim Fouratt, who had also cofounded the 1960s radical group the Yippies and the post-Stonewall Gay Liberation Front. "If you were on the cutting edge of music, art, video, or attitude, you were there."[54]

The club, which was illegal, closed after a police raid found the dance floor covered "an inch deep in pills and glassine envelopes."[55] In 1982, it was resurrected on 21st Street with its staff largely intact: LL Cool J (elevator operator), the Beastie Boys (maintenance), Karen Finley and Sade (bartenders).[56] It was a four-story house of worship for a congregation of art types who had gravitated to New York from all corners of the globe. Danceteria's famous elevator—itself a place to dance, drug, and love—lifted clientele through the club's four dimensions: first floor, live acts; second floor, DJs and dancers; third floor, video installations; fourth floor, lounge. Kamins said that Danceteria wasn't a club; it was a "nation. It was a new country, a new world.

> Danceteria was one of those moments in history where everybody was at the same place at the right time and everybody just fed off each other. All we had was the club. We lived from the club, we lived off the club. We could eat, we could drink, we could talk, we could party...Nobody was a genius, nobody had a plan for success. It was just pure creative evolution... It was just a melting pot, a Petri dish.[57]

The club was open from 8:00 p.m. to 8:00 a.m. Kamins worked his twelve-hour shift on the second floor, with three thousand records in his booth ready to keep the place moving.[58]

Madonna caught Kamins's attention.[59] Though she was "young and a little bit naïve," he said, "she always knew what she wanted to do. She had a tremendous desire to perform for people. When she'd start dancing, there'd be twenty people getting up and dancing with her."[60] Eventually, Madonna came up to the DJ booth and introduced herself.[61] "We became good friends," he said. "We started going out and she brought me the tape."[62]

There are varying accounts of how and when Mark Kamins played Madonna's demo tape. Whatever happened, the result was the same: the dance floor liked it.[63] He and Madonna also liked each other. Soon they moved into a small place on the Upper East Side together, though when she "moved in" with a man she was only half there.[64] She almost always had a residence elsewhere. Even with someone as potentially important to her career as Kamins, she wasn't about to play the role of acquiescent partner just to keep him on her side professionally. Her independence was too precious.

Kamins, meanwhile, began trying to interest record companies in her demo. He was an A&R man for Island Records (he had introduced U2 to the label) and so he brought Madonna and Steve Bray's song "Everybody" to Island's Chris Blackwell. But Blackwell turned it down. "He didn't like Madonna and he said, 'I'm not going to sign my A&R guy's girlfriend.' "[65] The demo was also rejected by Geffen Records. People mistrusted Mark's faith in Madonna because they thought he was in love with her.[66]

Mark's next approach was to Michael Rosenblatt, a young A&R man from Sire Records. Mark learned that he was looking for "upbeat dance club acts."[67] In 1982, the Go-Go's reached the top of the album charts with *Beauty and the Beat*. Their look was funky girl next door; the sound quirky, bubbly, fun. With its notes of darkness, Madonna's music was more complex, but she could, if necessary, fit into an emerging underground genre known as new pop.[68] Kamins invited Rosenblatt to Danceteria to meet Madonna.[69]

Rosenblatt was twenty-five and had been working for Sire for five years in various capacities, but his real job was cruising the clubs looking for talent. His first discovery was the B-52's at CBGB. His boss, Seymour Stein, signed them and awarded Rosenblatt more responsibility, which he described as being paid to smoke pot and listen to music.[70] His next big find was the British duo Soft Cell, whose song "Tainted Love" sold a couple of million copies. "When 'Tainted Love' was still a big hit, that's when I discovered Madonna," Rosenblatt said.[71] A friend of his had signed a new English pop duo that called themselves Wham! and the friend asked Rosenblatt to show them around New York.

So I was taking them to clubs on a Saturday night—I'm at the Danceteria second-floor bar with George Michael and Andrew Ridgeley, and I see this girl walk across the dance floor and up to the DJ booth to talk to Mark. I figured she had to be the girl with the demo. So, I walked up and introduced myself as an A&R guy, and we started talking.[72]

A couple of days later Kamins and Madonna went to Rosenblatt's office. He listened to the four-song demo she and Steve had produced. He listened again. "It wasn't amazing. But this girl sitting in my office was just radiating star power," Rosenblatt said.[73] "I *knew* that there was this star sitting there." Rosenblatt asked Madonna what she wanted to do. She replied, "I want to make records."[74]

"The wrong answer is, 'To express my art,'" Rosenblatt said. "You look for an artist who understands this is a business. There's nothing hippy about it. I'm going to spend millions. You have to be prepared to sell your parents to the Turks."[75] Apparently, Rosenblatt was convinced that Madonna was, because he said, "OK, let's go."[76]

They shook hands, and Rosenblatt wrote up a contract on a legal pad. Madonna would get a $5,000 advance for two twelve-inch singles plus royalties and publishing fees of $1,000 for each song she wrote. He then called Stein to tell him about the girl and the deal and get his approval.[77]

Seymour Stein had established Sire Records in 1966 and quickly moved to the center of the rock music universe. His parties were a who's who of talent, from Iggy Pop to John Lennon to Elton John.[78] But Stein's professional focus was on the outliers, the artists the major labels wouldn't touch and radio stations wouldn't play. In the mid-'70s, he scooped up bands in lower Manhattan—the Ramones, Talking Heads—and their counterparts in Britain. That was where he signed Chrissie Hynde, who was working in London as a music journalist, and her band, the Pretenders.[79]

By 1981, "Sire had become the hippest label in New York," following the trajectory of the downtown clubs by combining the remnants of punk and disco with New Wave and rap.[80] But being the best wasn't enough. In 1977, Sire had become part of Warner Bros., which wanted more hits without spending more money. Seymour worked the globe to find talent he believed in that wouldn't break the bank. "I was blowtorching the candle at both ends," he said. In 1982, at the age of forty, he began having chest pains and was told he needed open-heart surgery. It was then, he said, while stuck in a hospital bed wallowing in self-pity that he encountered his "Florence Nightingale."[81]

Rosenblatt had sent Madonna's demo cassette to Stein in the hospital, and Stein popped the tape into his Sony Walkman. "As penicillin dripped into my heart, I lay there and listened…I liked the hook, I liked Madonna's voice, I liked the feel, and I liked the name *Madonna*. I *liked* it all and played it again." He wanted Madonna and Mark Kamins to come to the hospital to see him.[82] Meanwhile, he prepared himself for the meeting by calling for a hairdresser and ordering up a shower. "All I was wearing was one of those embarrassing hospital gowns like some lobotomized weirdo in *One Flew Over the Cuckoo's Nest*."[83]

When Madonna appeared, she and Stein truly did make an odd couple. Stein said she was wearing "cheap punky gear, the kind of club kid who looked absurdly out of place in a cardiac ward." He immediately saw past her costume and recognized her drive.

> I could tell she wouldn't have cared if I was like Sarah Bernhardt lying in a coffin. All she cared about was that one of my arms moved, that I could sign a contract. What I saw there was even more important than the one song I heard. I saw a young woman who was so determined to be a star.[84]

He believed she could be, but he said he never imagined that he was "looking at a female Elvis."[85]

Stein was sold on Madonna, but he had to fight with the head of Warner, Mo Ostin, to sign her, because Ostin didn't want to spend even a few thousand dollars on a total unknown. Warner was, like the rest of the music industry, in a slump and reassessing its operation.[86] Stein assured Ostin that Madonna was worth the paltry investment, that she was going to be huge, but Ostin said no. Undeterred, Stein went around him and made a pitch to the head of Warner's international division, Nesuhi Ertegun. After some cajoling, Ertegun agreed to back the deal. That meant that Madonna's initial contract was with Sire and Warner Music International.[87]

In signing with Sire, Madonna didn't just get a record deal; she also gained artistic legitimacy. The label had a real avant-garde pedigree. It signed performing artists, not entertainers. And its parent company, Warner Bros. Records, was "perhaps the most admired record company in the world," having signed artists such as George Harrison, Miles Davis, Paul Simon, Elvis Costello, and Quincy Jones.[88] It was exactly where Madonna wanted to be, and she credited Stein for her good fortune.[89] "He was the only one who said I could go straight into the studio. Epic, Geffen, Atlantic, they all wanted more demos," she said.[90] She mused that that may have been because Seymour was a gay man who wasn't distracted by her sexuality or threatened by her strength.[91]

Madonna planned to record the single "Everybody" during the summer. Both Mark Kamins and Steve Bray felt they had the right to produce it. Mark argued that he should because he had gotten Madonna the Sire deal.[92] Steve countered that *he* had production rights because he had coproduced the demo and helped Madonna write the song. "I was really scared. I thought I had been given a golden egg," Madonna said. "It was really awful, but I just didn't trust" that Steve would do a good job.[93] "I went to Steve and said, 'How about producing it *with* Mark?'... He refused, so I said, 'You're out.'"[94]

Though she would suffer a case of buyer's remorse, Madonna calculated—perhaps at Sire's urging—that Kamins was more experienced and better known. And so to produce her first single, she picked him over the man who had inspired and supported her and who had shared her extreme poverty. Steve said that when "she got a single deal I was really very excited, 'cause I figured, 'OK, there's got to be more than six dollars in this for me.'" He was wrong.[95] Madonna had once abruptly left Steve in Michigan. Now *he* left *her,* saying, "Fuck you. Either I produce or nothing." He didn't speak to her again for two years.[96]

Much later, after Steve and Madonna had written many more songs together, he was philosophical about the rupture. "The relationship's too old to have something like that stand in its way," he explained.

> Exploited? Some people say that, but that's resentment of someone who's got that drive. It seems like you're leaving people behind or you're stepping on them, and the fact is that you're moving and they're not. She doesn't try to be polite. She doesn't care if she ruffles someone's feathers.[97]

He understood that later, but at the time that he was sidelined, Steve said, "it was very hard to accept."[98]

In October of 1982, Madonna's first single was released. "Everybody" appeared on both sides, the B side being a longer, club-friendly, bass-heavy dub version. While it is hard to imagine today, the sound was so unclassifiable at the time that Warner didn't know how to promote it—whether to a Black or white audience. Remarkably, it wasn't thought possible that it could be offered to both. To sidestep the issue, Madonna's face was left off the record sleeve, and no promotional pictures of her were made available, so that her race—her person—remained a mystery. Madonna, with her extraordinary physical presence, began her professional recording career as a disembodied voice.[99]

Leaving nothing to chance, Mark Kamins brought "Everybody" to Larry Levan at the Paradise Garage. He had never met Levan, but he knew his mythical status and the fact that if you wanted a hit on New York's hottest radio station, WBLS, it needed Larry's endorsement. Larry immediately played the nine-minute dub side and "loved it," Mark recalled. "I think that was the first record he ever played with a white girl singing." Larry, in turn, played "Everybody" for Frankie Crocker, the DJ at WBLS. Crocker put it on the radio.[100]

Within a month, the song was number 1 on the WBLS playlist and number 3 on the Billboard Dance Club Songs chart. Suddenly, "Everybody" was everywhere.

Camille Barbone heard it: "I was sitting in a nursing home visiting a friend's mom and the older people were doing calisthenics...to the radio and it was WBLS in New York City and it was Madonna, and I literally was transfixed. I couldn't believe what I was hearing. I walked right across the lobby of the nursing home, went as close as I could to the radio and just couldn't believe my ears."[101]

Fab 5 Freddy heard it: "I was walking down Avenue A and about twenty steps ahead of me were these three young Puerto Rican girls. They were really hot and sexy, and I was watching them walk down the street and they had a little boom box with them, and I remember I was watching them, and I was like—whatever this record is, these girls are really into it. They were singin' and walkin' and switchin' down the street. And as I get a little closer to them, I realized that this was Madonna's record."[102]

Madonna heard it: "At about seven at night I had the radio on in my bedroom, on [New York Latin music station] KTU, and I heard 'Everybody.' I said, 'Oh my God, that's me coming out of that box.' It was an amazing feeling."[103] Madonna started to cry. It had happened. She got her one song on the radio. She had done it.[104]

Chapter 12

New York, 1982

Boom, for real.[1]

—Jean-Michel Basquiat

MADONNA WAS FORCED to leave the apartment on Riverside Drive where she was living because Futura, unable to resist a clean wall, had graffiti-bombed her bedroom.[2] That unpleasant ending, however, was the occasion for a fresh beginning. With cash in hand from her record deal, and after years of transience and shared spaces, Madonna rented her own two-room place on 4th Street between Avenues A and B. She had a futon on the floor, a boom box in the window, a Roland synthesizer on a stand, a hissing radiator on the wall, and her own bathroom.[3] Palatial. Outside, life wasn't quite as copacetic.

The apartment was in Alphabet City, an area so derelict (there were nearly four hundred abandoned buildings and three hundred vacant lots) and dangerous that even hard-core New Yorkers wouldn't venture there unless they were on the prowl for smack.[4] Undaunted, Madonna assembled a crew of barely adolescent boys—lookouts for drug dealers—to act as Praetorian Guard and walk her down the street.[5] She was delighted by that arrangement and by her new home on the far fringes of civilization. "This is when I really started to enjoy myself, have a circle of friends," she said. "Things were looking up."[6]

Madonna's circle comprised the next generation of creative types who had arrived downtown around the same time as she did, in the late 1970s. The earlier generation in music—the Debbie Harrys, the Tina Weymouths, the Patti Smiths—had already been on the scene for several years (Patti Smith had even left it) by the time Madonna and her friends began going to clubs. And as much as those slightly older artists were revered, they represented a different artistic reality because their music was rooted in rock. The younger generation's inspiration came from the DJs and the dance floor. The new generation was also less white, more gender-fluid, and—for a time—less angst-ridden.

It was among that younger crowd in the early '80s that Madonna discovered her tribe. One of the first members was a future actor who would become a lifelong pal, Debi Mazar. "I was in Danceteria, working the elevator," Debi said. "She came into my elevator and a great song was spinning and she goes, 'Hey, you wanna dance?' and I was like, 'Yeah!' And I parked the elevator, and we had a great dance together."[7] "I was a good dancer because I was always hanging out with...black and Puerto Rican queens, who were fabulous," Debi said. "It was exciting because this was a white girl who could dance, like myself, and she was great."[8]

Debi, who was eighteen when she met Madonna, had been navigating New York City's streets since she was a child. At around age fifteen, fake ID in hand, she discovered the clubs. By sixteen, she graduated to coat check at the famous Mudd Club, which was for a time the ultimate spot for artists, DJs, and celebrities of both the underground and blue-chip varieties. As a joke, the Mudd Club owner, Steve Mass, gave the girl-child a promotion: Debi became attendant for the club's VIP door. "I really didn't know who the VIPs were. If David Bowie walked in, okay, I knew who that was, and of course Debbie Harry," she said. "But there were people walking in like David Byrne from Talking Heads—people that were famous in the downtown scene." Soon Debi was on a first-name basis with everyone who was anyone and a favorite pet of them all.[9]

Her aspiration as a teenager beyond club life was to do makeup: "I dragged my little makeup box from Brooklyn into the city," she said. She also began focusing on style—thrift-store and vintage styles because she couldn't afford new ones.[10] So when Madonna appeared in her elevator, young Debi put on her fashion-expert lens and sized her up as a "punk rock Midwestern girl" working the elevator, "hustling." "She was very raw, very sexual. She made direct eye-contact. She had her own style, and her style was really cool—she had that messy, dirty hair, but it looked beautiful. She had big eyebrows and tons of bracelets."[11]

By way of introduction, Madonna told her, "I'm going to be a star. I'm going to cut some records and you're going to do my make-up."[12] Debi had undoubtedly heard much stranger pronouncements and didn't balk at that one. "She became one of my first girlfriends," Debi said.[13] "Even though she wasn't from the streets of New York, she had this very sort of street energy, and we just had a great time running around together."[14]

Another friend who appeared in Madonna's life that year, someone who would be her companion onstage and off, was a New York University sociology graduate student from Long Island named Erika Belle.[15] "The first time I met Madonna was at a night club," Erika recalled. "I think probably the third sentence she said was, 'I'm going to be the most famous woman in the world.' And I just thought, 'Who *is* this chick?'" The two bonded over music, dancing, and fashion. "We were out every single night, of every single day."[16]

Erika said the serious club-dance action started around midnight and lasted until 4:00 a.m.

> We would just try to get on the floor and take up as much room as possible, and dance as hard as possible... There was lots of flirting, lots of fun. Sure, those were the days when girls were having sex on the dance floor, but Madonna never wanted to be known for that. She was always self-aware, in control.[17]

Many who knew Madonna said she approached sex and relationships as a man would.[18] Photographer Marcus Leatherdale was more specific. He said Madonna approached sex like a *gay* man. "She likes sex, no apologies... I think she's just a free liberated woman and was one of the first women I knew that actually would be fine with sport sex."[19]

In an interesting way, Madonna's approach to relationships reflected the masculine environment she was raised in. As a child she had chased boys on the playground, unaware that that sort of behavior was considered improper. As an adult she knew society frowned on sexually assertive women, but she didn't care.

Those who knew her understood, but those who didn't tut-tutted that she used sex to advance her career through a series of strategic seductions. When Seymour Stein heard those sorts of comments, he said he broke "out in a rash.

> Trust me, no big shot picked her up and sprinkled her in stardust... She is just a very passionate young lady, living it... It's funny how we don't cry foul when a twenty-four-year-old male rocker turns a trail of pretty women into a storyboard of high-voltage songs. Okay, now a girl was chasing her mojo through all these handsome, talented guys. Do you have any idea how much I would have loved to do that at her age?... The only guy she relied on in the early years and who never gets a mention was Martin Burgoyne.[20]

Martin Burgoyne truly is one of the unsung heroes in Madonna's story. His impact on her life was enormous. At the start of a career that would, within two years, lift her from the squalor of Alphabet City to the luxury of the Hollywood Hills, Martin provided the anchor, buffer, and friend-ship she needed to survive that potentially destabilizing ascent. His love for her was unequivocal, as was hers for him. Stein said that Madonna and Martin were "inseparable."[21]

It was serendipitous, then, that he lived next door to Madonna in her new apartment building. In that urban hell, he appeared to be a nineteen-year-old cherub dispatched directly from heaven. Madonna said that Martin

> was an ethereal creature who just had the ability to bring out the best in everybody. He was from another world because, while everybody was out there struggling and trying to make it and be somebody and, you know, get somewhere, Martin wasn't concerned with that. He lived day to day, and he was always having a good time.[22]

One friend said Martin "was really like a Madonna double...The sense of joy, the love of the music, the love of the art world...He might've been the better version of Madonna, now that I think about it."[23] For Martin, it was all about adventure. Fearlessness topped the list of the many qualities that he and Madonna shared.[24]

Born in England but raised near Orlando, Florida, Martin had moved to New York to study art at the Pratt Institute.[25] He immediately fell in with the downtown crowd. "You will never find a person that didn't like Martin," Marcus Leatherdale said. "He was cute, lovable, and very fluid sexually, so there was something for everyone. He was just everybody's teddy bear."[26] Martin's friend Jordan Levin said that he was much "lusted after, an incandescent boy even in the darkest after-hours clubs."[27]

Martin was around five feet nine, with a mass of blond curls crowning a boyish face. His personal style was eclectic: motorcycle boots, piercings, hats that weren't necessarily weather appropriate, and often leather lederhosen that made him look like a Bavarian youth. He also wrote pornographic poetry, which he composed in a notebook that he kept with him and recited aloud to friends. "That was his shtick, and yet he was this cute little angel. You would never think that he was a total filthy motormouth," Marcus said.[28]

Like Puck in Shakespeare's *A Midsummer Night's Dream,* Martin materialized in people's lives to raise the right kind of ruckus and buoy flagging spirits. Australian photographer Catherine Underhill was one beneficiary. She met Martin when she was twenty-three and suffering the loss of her lover, who had just died after a long illness. "Nobody at that time had dealt with anybody dying, so we were just really bad at it," she said. Amid that pain, Martin began showing up at the loft she shared with Danceteria doorman and famed showman Haoui Montaug.

> [Martin] used to completely drive me crazy...I was so depressed and so broken at that time, and he was like this woodpecker who was just like

"Hello, hello, hello. Get your shit together. Come on, let's have some fun." Eventually I gave in and maybe had a little fun... He just wanted to do things with joy.[29]

Madonna had already made her way to the clubs, but her presence at Martin's side gained her acceptance among the hard-core Danceteria crowd, which viewed her with suspicion as a career-minded provincial.[30] "The artistic freedom of New York intimidated me a little at first," she admitted. "It's very intense and very enclosed—like a world within the city—and I just had to spend a bit of time breaking into it."[31] Marcus Leatherdale called Martin "Madonna's ticket. She was with someone that everybody loved. She was a strong, forceful person, but not necessarily the most lovable person then, not compared to Martin."[32]

During that period, Madonna even began to dress like Martin. She had an androgynous little-boy look, with short-cropped hair, a boy's jacket and knee-length shorts, white shirts, dark socks, and flat shoes.[33] "He was very influential in the way that she dressed, or *inspirational* in the way that she dressed," said Madonna's brother Christopher.[34]

He was also crucial to the early days of the traveling road show known as "Madonna." Martin accompanied her to performances, to the studio, even to record company meetings. "At Sire, we used to joke that before Madonna even had a manager, she had a court of valets and minstrels following her everywhere," Seymour Stein said. Martin was foremost among them. Madonna "worked out all her early songs, outfits and moves, with Martin giving her honest feedback," said Stein.[35]

Among the people Madonna met through Martin, one of the most important was a twenty-six-year-old Moroccan-born jewelry designer raised in France named Maripol. She was the art director at the famed 59th Street fashion emporium Fiorucci, which was where the downtown club kids hung out when they woke up in the afternoon. Artist Kenny Scharf called it "the daytime nightclub."[36]

Its Milanese founder, Elio Fiorucci, believed that "less is more," meaning the less clothing the better. Fiorucci's women's line featured crop tops, corsets, and bras with exposed nipples. Another Fiorucci philosophy was "no boundaries," meaning that fashion belonged in the same creative sphere as all the arts. And finally, Fiorucci considered his fashions ironic and that his goal was to "rediscover, recycle, redefine"—in other words, reinvent. That philosophy extended to the store itself. Every three months it had a new theme and changed its look entirely. "Everybody thought it was the coolest place," Maripol said. "Because everything was connected, you know, art and music and clothes."[37]

Maripol began working at the store after she was spotted at a club by one of Fiorucci's staff, who asked her who made her earrings. Maripol said she did, and the staffer said, "I want three hundred pairs." With that, she launched her first line of jewelry.[38] By the time Madonna was introduced to her, six years later, Maripol *was* the Fiorucci attitude. Her designs repurposed items that had nothing to do with fashion. Her most famous were rubber bracelets that she originally made for Grace Jones in 1977.[39] In 1982, Maripol opened her own store, Maripolitan, and began selling her jewelry directly while still working as art director at Fiorucci. The rubber bracelets became so popular, Maripol said, that they were used as currency at Danceteria: bracelets for drinks.[40]

Maripol had met Madonna by chance one night at the Roxy. Fab 5 Freddy had wanted some "cute girls" to dance on the stage in their bras and asked Maripol to find them. "I turned around and saw Madonna," she recalled. "I asked her if she had a nice bra on, and she thought I was out of my mind!"[41] The next time they met was when Martin brought Madonna to Maripol's loft. "It became an instant friendship, definitely," Maripol said.[42] It also became a collaboration. Maripol had discovered the person who could best carry off her designs, and Madonna discovered the person who would help create her iconic early image. "Maripol's influence on Madonna's image can't be [overstated]," Christopher said. "She is responsible for creating her punk–plus–lace look."[43]

Catherine Underhill worked with Erika Belle and Martin at an unlicensed bar called Lucky Strike and gave Madonna a couple of her bartending shifts because she was broke.[44] During those nights, Madonna said, she and Martin stole enough money from the cash register to pay bills and finance a trip to England. "He was friends with Marc Almond [of Soft Cell], so we stayed at his flat in Earl's Court," Madonna said.[45]

The trip gave Madonna a crash course in post-punk Britain. Her memories of it were less about music than style. Everyone in New York fashion whom Madonna admired—at that point, this amounted to a few people, including Maripol and the Fiorucci crew—had come by way of London. The King's Road–Carnaby Street fashion heritage of that city had created a culture of clothing as spectacle. People didn't wear clothes to be appealing or comfortable or fashionable but to make an artistic statement. "I couldn't believe how seriously everybody took their looks and fashion and stuff," Madonna said. "It was all very exciting and, yes, influential to a certain extent."[46]

After the release of "Everybody," Madonna began receiving invitations to perform in discos and clubs—half-hour jobs that involved singing five of her songs live over taped music. The shows were known as track dates. She was shocked by the amount of money she could earn from just one of them. Tony Ciccone's work ethic, and his warning about the perils of getting something for nothing, nagged at her as she considered the money that would be rolling in. She needed to do something to earn it.

"I refused to just stand up there and sing," Madonna said, "so I auditioned some dancers and what I did was I choreographed dance performances to each of the songs instead of having a band."[47] Her first dance recruits were Erika Belle, Erika's friend Bags Rilez, and Martin. Martin was game for a while, but he was more interested in running the show than dancing in it. Madonna needed a replacement, so she called her little brother.

"Again, I get a phone call: 'Come to New York. I made this record. I want you to be a backup dancer.' And so I did...All she had to do is yank and I was there," Christopher said. "And of course when I got there, there wasn't a job." Madonna told him that between the time they talked and the time he arrived, she had hired someone else to replace Martin. "I was pissed off because I made $300 a week dancing in Ottawa, which was unheard of. It was a lot of money...So I left all that and I came to do this, and I thought, 'What the fuck? I just left a real job for you.'"[48]

It was the second time Madonna had summoned Christopher only to disappoint him. This time, though, she at least let him live with her. "We were in the Village, rats everywhere...drug dealers on the street, garbage cans with fires burning in them constantly, people breaking into your apartment," Christopher recalled. "Crackers and tuna fish is what we lived on. We had nothing!" Christopher had traded the ordered existence of a dance company in Canada for life in New York without a safety net.

While Christopher waited to see what fate had in store, Madonna began giving him survival lessons. "Don't look anybody in the eye, and most important, walk like you belong here. This is your street." Good advice, but it wasn't easy. "There is so much stimulus, and that's a nice word for it. There's shit everywhere," he said. "Especially in that part of the city at that time. It was utter chaos and a circus. The *Blade Runner* thing is what it looked like."[49]

Madonna wasn't afraid. "She was going to own this. She said out loud, 'This is going to be mine one of these days.' I was like, 'Yeah, whatever,'" he said, laughing at the recollection. "Who says that kind of stuff?" Gradually, Christopher stopped being frightened. He became so accustomed to his surroundings and the strange goings-on that he became part of the circus, too.[50]

In November of 1982 Madonna filmed her first video. It was for "Everybody" and was meant to be distributed "in-house" to skeptical Warner honchos in LA.[51] The idea was to replicate a night at a dance club. Madonna persuaded Larry Levan to let her use Paradise Garage. Ed Steinberg was hired to direct, and Madonna summoned her friends to fill the dance floor.[52]

Levan so loved "Everybody" and her performance that he booked Madonna for the regular Garage crowd. "They weren't known for having white artists onstage, but Madonna got to perform," said music producer Danny Tenaglia. "That was the great thing about the Paradise Garage: if they were going to put this white girl onstage, she was there for a reason. The crowd embraced her."[53]

During her show, a club assistant put on the wrong backup tape while Madonna was singing. She pretended nothing had happened and continued her performance. "I just felt she was already a kind of a sensation," said French DJ François Kevorkian. "You have to have nerves of steel to do that on your first live performance... You could see that no bullshit is going to get in her way."[54]

In late 1982, Madonna began dating Jean-Michel Basquiat, whom she met through Ed Steinberg. Writer Lucy Sante once said of Basquiat that he reminded her of what the French Romantic poet Arthur Rimbaud must have been like, living on "a parallel plane, so absorbed in his art and its demands."[55] Jean-Michel was boyish, two years younger than Madonna, but in some ways he already seemed like an old man because he carried the weight of the world on his shoulders—not that he wanted to, but no matter how much he tried to escape it, shit seemed to land on him.[56]

He had appeared on the downtown scene as a graffiti tag before he appeared as a person. SAMO©—meaning "same old shit"—appeared everywhere in New York City in the late 1970s. Though it wasn't Basquiat's intention, the tag acted as a kind of advertising campaign, building anticipation about the artist behind it. When he finally showed up at clubs and galleries, the people who met him weren't disappointed. Jean-Michel seemed incapable of banality. For the first group show he was invited to join, he arrived with a crumpled-up drawing in his pocket, which he stuck on the wall. In another show, he exhibited a rack of jumpsuits that he had painted in instead of the paintings themselves.[57]

Everything he did made a statement. Using visual elements as clues, he conducted a running cultural commentary about life in Reagan's America, about life as a Black man in that society, about the gallery world that Fab 5 Freddy described as "white walls, white wine, and white people."[58] Basquiat challenged that world by his very person as much as by his work. He understood it, but it didn't understand him.

"I remember going to a chichi party with Jean," Glenn O'Brien said, "and some rich guy coming over to us and saying to him, 'And what do you do?' Jean said earnestly [though not truthfully], 'I'm the manager of a McDonald's,' and the guy just turned and walked away." On another occasion, Glenn said, Jean-Michel was denied entry at the Mudd Club by a doorman who told him "no blacks were allowed in that night. They were trying to keep the drug dealers out."[59] But much worse than those slights directed at him as a Black man was the racism he experienced as a Black artist.

In 1981, Basquiat had his first solo show. It was at a gallery in Modena, Italy, and he made $30,000. Money meant nothing to him—he kept hundred-dollar bills stuffed in his pockets as if they were Kleenex—but it meant everything to gallery owners, and interest in Basquiat grew. In September of 1982 he was in Zurich for a show at Bruno Bischofberger's gallery. The experience was a little like Madonna's in Paris, where she was presented as a wild child from the streets of New York. In Basquiat's case, it was worse. He felt he was treated like a zoo creature. After picking him up at the airport, he said, Bischofberger gave him some canvases and invited people over to watch Basquiat paint. The dealer was no doubt genuinely excited to observe Basquiat's process. But the artist felt as though he was on exhibition as an exotic, and it got to him. Back in New York, Jean-Michel tearfully recounted the episode to Fun Gallery owner Patti Astor.[60]

It was at that time that Madonna met him. Basquiat would be the most complicated, troubled, and brilliant man she had known up to that point. She had also never been involved with someone who had suffered so much for his art. On his side, Jean-Michel's friend Armon Stewart said, Basquiat loved Madonna's independence and "that she seemed on her way to greatness without kissing ass."[61]

After his Zurich experience, Basquiat locked himself in at the Fun Gallery, preparing for a show there.[62] On the night of the opening, November 4, 1982, with hundreds of people gathered outside, Patti Astor said, Jean-Michel was suffering from "cocaine-induced paranoia."[63] He had what looked like a woven wastebasket on his head. (Glenn O'Brien thought "it looked pretty good.")[64] Inside the gallery, its walls covered in Basquiat's painted poems, a work called A Panel of Experts included the notation "Madonna©." He and the actual Madonna, meanwhile, had taken up position in a corner to argue.[65]

A lot can be forgiven of someone so gifted. Madonna knew who Basquiat was—the rarity of his kind of talent and the fragility of his soul. "I remember getting up in the middle of the night and he wouldn't be in bed lying next to me," she said. "He'd be standing, painting, at four in the morning, this close to the canvas, in a trance."[66] Sometimes she would watch him as his tools scratched the canvas, not wanting to speak for fear of intruding into that place where his mind had traveled.[67]

★   ★   ★

Madonna was scheduled to perform at Danceteria for Haoui Montaug's revue, the "No Entiendes" cabaret. The event was held once a month, and in the weeks between performances Haoui fielded requests from people who wanted to be in the show. "It was a very egalitarian lineup," said Catherine Underhill. "Madonna was always around. She was Martin's best friend, so obviously she was going to get a spot."[68]

Madonna's appearance there, on December 16, 1982, was billed as the "world premiere of Sire recording artist, Madonna," and though that wasn't true (she had performed at the Garage), it felt like it. She would be onstage before a crowd of ultimate hipsters who needed to be convinced that she was worth listening to.[69] "Everybody knew that Madonna was very ambitious—that was just what she was," Catherine said. "We knew that this could be the start of something big. This was a kind of a safe space for [Madonna and her dancers] to see if the way that they were going to present the song would work."[70]

Dressed as if for Halloween, wearing a tux and holding a bottle of champagne, Haoui was the perfect host as he goaded the semi-sullen crowd to "wake your fucking selves up. Pinch yourselves. Pinch the person next to you on the ass... *Everybody wake up.*" The curtains parted. Madonna and three backup dancers—Erika, Martin, and Bags Rilez—were seen sitting in the dark onstage. A voice in the crowd shouted, "Go on, girl!" And with that admonition, Madonna's performing career was launched.[71]

"When she came on... I have to say I was really surprised because it was *slick,* I mean for a show at Danceteria, it was like 'Wow, this girl like rehearsed,'" said Johnny Dynell, a DJ and nightclub promoter who was the insider's insider. "And Mark [says], 'Yeah, she's gonna be big, she's gonna be big.' And I was like thinking, '*God,* she really might be.'"[72]

Jean-Michel, meanwhile, was in Los Angeles staying at art dealer Larry Gagosian's Venice Beach house preparing for a March show at the dealer's West Hollywood gallery. Not long after he arrived, Basquiat told Gagosian, "My girlfriend's going to come stay with us." Gagosian recalled, "And I said, 'Well, who is she? What's her name?' 'Madonna.' I said, 'Madonna, what kind of name is that?' And I'll never forget: Basquiat says, 'She'll be the biggest pop star in the world.'"[73] Larry said okay, so Madonna flew to California for New Year's Eve.

It was her second trip to California. The first took place when she was fourteen. Her father and Joan had decided to pack all the children into a van for a cross-country trip. Each child was allowed a Rolling Rock beer box by way of a suitcase. That trip ended at the beach in Santa Monica with the van chock-full of volatile Ciccones stuck in the sand.[74] Madonna's

1982 trip, ten years later, held more promise. With Jean-Michel at work in the studio, she would be able to promote "Everybody" on the West Coast, and together they could play tourist.

Fred Hoffman, who was helping Jean-Michel create a series of large prints, said, "They were looking for fun and it was decided that they should go for lunch at the commissary on the lot of the Twentieth Century Fox studio." A reservation secured, the three of them drove to the movie lot, on the edge of Beverly Hills. The vast commissary was filled with people, many of them celebrities. Madonna and Jean-Michel surveyed the crowd, whispering to each other like children as they did so. "What they did share with me I have never forgotten," Hoffman said. "They assured me that someday they would be famous and that everyone in this commissary would know who these two aspiring young artists were."[75]

At first Jean-Michel worked furiously, documenting the exploitation of Black stars—from boxers to musicians to Hollywood actors. He felt duty bound to paint what he witnessed, because, he said, artists create "true historical documents."[76] It was a cruel reality, even in the California sun, which might have been why he took a break from painting to indulge in his second-favorite pastime, drugs.

One day Madonna found him at Gagosian's home (Larry was not there) with a group of women and a mound of coke. Madonna ordered the women out and booked herself into a hotel without him. Jean-Michel went into junkie mode, blaming his drug use and bad behavior on forces outside himself, but Madonna didn't buy it. She had no tolerance for what she perceived as a weakness, especially from an artist of such rare talent. She left him in Los Angeles and went back to New York.[77]

In trying to decipher the enigma called Madonna, one need only look to 1982 for clues. Her previous life experiences informed the content of her work, but the means of expressing those experiences—the artistry, the humor, the style—and the course of her future all started to come into focus that year. No longer stymied and struggling, searching as an outsider for a point of entry, she had become part of a radical art kingdom. Glenn O'Brien called it a "junior art world," a "rebel music scene."

> Suddenly the kids who lived by night in elegant poverty created an entire culture of their own. The motivations behind every artistic act were self-amusement and community...There was a viral outbreak of contagious fun and madcap genius.[78]

And then came what Susan Sontag called the "rebuke to life and to hope."[79] By the end of 1982, it even had a name.

Chapter 13

New York, London, Los Angeles, 1983

> I don't want to die. I can only assume you don't want to die. Can
> we fight together?[1]
>
> — *Larry Kramer*

THE ONLY THING that was certain was that gay men were dying of it.
Everything else about acquired immunodeficiency syndrome was a medical mystery. It began when confounding symptoms appeared in a few gay
patients in April of 1981 and received press attention as a curiosity in June
and July of that year. But media coverage of the disease disappeared once it
was identified as a niche illness, a "gay plague." And even when it began
appearing beyond that population, in intravenous drug users and their
children, there was scant coverage in the press. It was an illness that targeted two marginal groups: gays and addicts.[2]

The moralistic "wrath of God" murmurings started early, but it was
obvious to many in the scientific community that a tsunami was approaching that would engulf lives well beyond those demographic groups. By the
start of 1983, AIDS was believed to have a mortality rate of around 50 percent, and scientists didn't know with certainty what caused it, how to control it, or how far it had already spread.[3]

The effort to understand and contain the disease was complicated by
politics. Propelled by an emergent religious right that saw homosexuality
as an abomination, voters in 1980 had elected the first Republican-
controlled Senate since 1954. The White House and the Senate were not
willing to spend tax dollars on a disease they believed was rooted in sin.
They didn't even want to discuss it, because in order to talk about AIDS,
one needed to talk about gay sex, and that was not a conversation to be had
in Ronald Reagan's America.[4]

In the gay community, meanwhile, fear was pervasive. But just as powerful and widespread as fear was denial. The joy in living that accompanied post-Stonewall liberation was not easily relinquished, even on pain of
death.[5] Men who refused to believe that sex was killing them convinced
themselves that the AIDS scare was a plot hatched by conservatives to deny
gay men pleasure. Others, fearful *and* in denial, fled the epicenters of the

disease—New York, San Francisco, and Los Angeles—for what they thought would be safe harbor in other American cities and even in Europe.[6] Very few, however, found safety, and even fewer found acceptance.

Susan Sontag said that AIDS brought "to many a social death that precedes the physical one."[7] Indeed, one of the earliest and cruelest aspects of AIDS was the rejection of gay men by their families, by the broader society, by landlords and employers, even by hospital staff and mortuaries. Because so little was known about AIDS transmission, people with AIDS became pariahs. The human warmth that might have comforted them was largely absent, and that meant their fear of death was compounded by the likelihood of dying alone.

In March of 1983, one of the loudest voices and most effective organizers in the AIDS activist community, Larry Kramer, threw what AIDS historian Randy Shilts called "a hand grenade into the fox hole of denial" by writing an article in New York's main gay newspaper, the *New York Native*. Kramer said, "If this article doesn't scare the shit out of you, we're in real trouble." He laid out in numbers and unadorned language the seriousness of the crisis.[8]

Shilts said that after Kramer's article, AIDS activism became a political movement that employed many of the attention-getting zap-action tactics of the '60s and '70s, targeting politicians, the Catholic Church, and any person or group seen as an impediment to combating the disease. Coincidentally, state and federal governments at around that time began releasing paltry funding for AIDS research, and the Food and Drug Administration began the hunt for treatments. But it was too late for too many.[9]

Between the time the first AIDS cases were detected, in 1981, and the spring of 1983, tens of thousands of people had been newly infected. Young men in the prime of their lives prepared to die, some more publicly than others. East Village painter David Wojnarowicz wore a denim jacket inscribed with the message IF I DIE OF AIDS—FORGET BURIAL—JUST DROP MY BODY ON THE STEPS OF THE F.D.A.[10]

Bitter humor joined anger as an antidote to the melancholia of that era. So, too, did music and dancing. On the dance floor, men who were denied a human touch could still enjoy ecstatic communion, and they did so, packing clubs by the thousands.[11] Marvin Gaye's "Sexual Healing," the Weather Girls' "It's Raining Men," and Gloria Gaynor's disco stalwart "I Will Survive" took on new meaning.

With "Everybody" still going strong, Madonna began work on a second single. Sire brought in a heavyweight R&B producer who had a track record of hits with women vocalists to help create it: Reggie Lucas had coproduced songs with Roberta Flack ("The Closer I Get to You") and Stephanie Mills (the Grammy-winning "Never Knew Love Like This Before").[12]

The difference between a first-time producer like Mark Kamins and a seasoned pro like Reggie was head-spinning. Madonna had much to learn about record production, and Reggie was potentially the person to teach her while helping her grow as an artist. "I needed musical direction. I needed someone who had worked with black female vocalists. I needed someone to push me," she said. "Reggie was the obvious choice... I felt that his musical knowledge and my freshness would work."[13] Lucas said, "When Warner Brothers called me about working with Madonna, I was the big score.

> It seems ridiculous in retrospect, but I was an established professional and she was a nobody... Most of the people around Madonna at the corporate level did not get her and for the most part did not like her. You could see them recoil from her bohemianism.[14]

Unlike "Everybody," Madonna's second single contained two songs, "Burning Up," written by Madonna, on side A and "Physical Attraction," written by Lucas, on the B side. The sleeve for the single was designed by Martin Burgoyne as a series of graphic portraits of Madonna. It was inspired by Andy Warhol, the cover of the Rolling Stones' 1978 album, *Some Girls,* and vintage cartoons. Interestingly, in showing the many faces of Madonna, it seems to anticipate the changing looks that would characterize her career.

The record wasn't the breakout hit everyone had hoped for, so Madonna got to work to promote it. In New York she shadowed Warner dance-music promoter Bobby Shaw, who held weekly sessions with DJs to introduce them to new Warner releases and listen to the music the other labels were offering. They were informal Friday night gatherings: ten or fifteen guys smoking joints while enjoying music. It was unusual for an artist to attend, but Madonna wanted to learn the business—every aspect of it. "She was so aggressive. She wants to know things," Shaw said. "She would sit in my office and watch me *work*."[15]

Outside the city, Shaw scheduled performances for Madonna and her crew—Martin, Erika, sometimes Bags, and sometimes Christopher. Ferried either in Michael Rosenblatt's car or a limo hired by Martin, they could hit three clubs a night. "A couple songs, a coupla grand," Rosenblatt said.[16] Christopher said Martin's job was to collect the cash while he, Erika, and Madonna retired to practice their steps in a "shabby dressing room" that might be nothing more than the club owner's office.[17]

At Uncle Sam's Blues, on Long Island, the befuddled crowd simply stared at them. At a preppy bar in Sag Harbor, Madonna was so disgusted by the audience's indifference that she stopped the set, shouted "Fuck you," and walked off the stage. "Long Island didn't like us as much as Manhattan did," Christopher said. "And Manhattan didn't really like us that much either."[18] In search of more receptive audiences, they went farther afield but had little joy elsewhere. In Fort Lauderdale, they followed a dancing pantomime horse onstage. They performed at Casanovas in Hialeah, the Copa in Miami, and at another Copa in Key West, all to muted response.[19]

Hijinks helped. To enliven one dreary excursion, Erika, Martin, and Madonna dyed their hair a different color every day.[20] But even such antics didn't lift their spirits during their first professional trip abroad.

In late February of 1983, the group flew to England for two weeks of performances. In general, it was a low-budget trip with few expectations; Madonna was not a priority for the label. "I was staying in a real shit hole," Madonna said. "For the first couple of times I stayed in England I had to take a bath in the hallway, and I thought, 'OK, that's how it is here.'... It didn't dawn on me that people actually had bathrooms inside of their houses." Though she thought the city grim and surprisingly lifeless, she was, as always, game.[21]

Dressed in her "Webo Girl" jacket and Maripol rubber bracelets, Madonna charmed a series of gentlemen interviewers from music publications who had a hard time deciphering who or what she was: a white girl who sounded Black, who oozed sex but dressed like a boy? As to her music, one opined that "Everybody" "is the sound of young New York's graffiti sensibilities" and described her as a disciple of Afrika Bambaataa.[22]

She opened her "UK tour" in London at a Soho club called Le Beat Route, which was a hangout for the Georges—George Michael and Boy George—and was briefly known as "the hottest club on the planet."[23] That audience, too, was confused by what they saw. *Black Echoes* music magazine said that Madonna and her dancers "cocked their legs like a Samba train" and bumped their hips against one another's groins. "This explicit choreography caused the normally unflappable patrons to lower their glasses from their lips and gape."[24] At the Hacienda, in Manchester, Christopher said the crowd "threw stuff at us." By that point he had decided, "OK, this isn't going to last long."[25]

Back in New York, however, Seymour Stein, Bobby Shaw, Michael Rosenblatt, and just about everyone who worked with Madonna remained convinced of her talent and potential. Rosenblatt famously predicted that she would be "bigger than Olivia Newton-John." But, he said, "Nobody at Warner Brothers gave a shit at all. Madonna was just a little dance girl."[26]

Still, the company greenlit an album, and Sire once again called on Reggie Lucas to produce.

Jean-Michel Basquiat was in and out of New York in the first half of 1983, and so Madonna used his apartment as a place to work with Lucas on the album. Surrounded by Basquiat's art, they did so without interference from record executives. Madonna wrote six songs, and Reggie wrote two: "Borderline" and the aforementioned "Physical Attraction." When it came time to record them, most of the work was done at the Sigma Sound Studios in the Ed Sullivan Theater building, on Broadway.[27]

Carrying biographies of old film stars, which she read voraciously during that period, Madonna arrived at the studio prepared to absorb whatever she could from Reggie and collaborate as much as possible.[28] But as they worked together, Madonna came to suspect that Reggie wanted to mold this "new girl" into something she was not: the kind of singer he had worked with in the past.

Camille Barbone had wanted her to be Pat Benatar. Reggie Lucas wanted her to be Roberta Flack. Madonna also began to dislike Reggie's production decisions; she believed he cluttered up the album with too many instruments.[29] Around three-quarters of the way into the album, she said so. "I started going backward and stripping the songs down and making them more sparse," she said.[30] For her, simple was better.[31]

The album also needed another song. Madonna had expected "Ain't No Big Deal," from her demo with Steve, to be on the record, but he sold it to another artist, and that left Madonna's album lacking an eighth track. Seymour Stein told Michael Rosenblatt to take Madonna to LA to meet Warner executives and ask for the cash to record a new one.[32]

As late as that March 1983 meeting, Warner executives were still confused about where Madonna's music belonged. "Because she expressed an interest in black music," Reggie explained, "they said, 'Oh! Go sell it to the black people, then.' That's how she was visualized." Even at that moment, with the recognized crossover appeal of Michael Jackson and Prince, who traded dominant positions in the charts, the white men of Warner Bros. apparently couldn't comprehend the changed world they lived in.

Madonna was also up against an industry that understood the power of male artists but wasn't willing to make that same investment in women artists. She told a writer Simon Hills that year,

> Warner Brothers is a hierarchy of old men, and it's a chauvinistic environment to be working in because I'm treated like this sexy little girl...I have had to prove them wrong...That is something that happens when you're a girl. It wouldn't have happened to Prince or Michael Jackson.[33]

Madonna did what she needed to do. She convinced executives, from chairman Mo Ostin on down, that she was worth an additional few thousand dollars.

After her experience in LA, it became clear that Madonna needed a manager to represent her in future negotiations.[34] Seymour Stein had one in mind. He had known Freddy DeMann for years and gave him a call at his Los Angeles office asking if he wanted to meet Madonna. He said sure, thinking that "Madonna" was the name of a band. When Seymour told Freddy the "band" was a woman, he was less interested but agreed to see her anyway.[35]

In 1983, Freddy DeMann was one of the hottest managers—some said simply *the* hottest manager—in the business.[36] He had taken on Michael Jackson when the former child star was "ice cold" and guided him to superstardom. As Madonna and Michael Rosenblatt were ushered into Freddy's office, overlooking Sunset Boulevard, Jackson was racking up hit after hit from his album *Thriller,* which sold twenty million copies in the United States alone. Madonna had loved Jackson as a child. Now she sat in his manager's office hoping to take her place alongside him on DeMann's roster.[37]

Freddy was likewise impressed with Madonna. "When she marched into my office, I was absolutely knocked off my feet. I had never seen a more physical human being in my life."[38] During the course of the meeting, Freddy received a call he said he needed to take. It might have been a strategic interruption, because he popped a Michael Jackson video into the VHS player and told Rosenblatt and Madonna to watch it; it would be on MTV in two weeks. DeMann's move was both an introduction to Jackson's new video and a reminder of how fierce Freddy could be on his clients' behalf.[39] He had been part of the epic battle to get Jackson on MTV, which at that point didn't air videos by Black artists. Eventually MTV relented and played "Billie Jean," after which Jackson became a global phenomenon.[40]

Against that backdrop, Madonna settled in to watch Jackson's "Beat It," a choreographed gang battle shot on location in the streets of LA with real gang members. Music, dance, passion, and social significance—all the ingredients she craved. Rosenblatt looked at her afterward and said, "This guy's your fucking manager." She agreed.[41] But no commitments were made beyond plans to continue talking. Freddy had a partner, Ron Weisner, whom she needed to meet, too. Madonna was scheduled to perform at Studio 54 for Fiorucci's fifteenth anniversary party on May 19. DeMann and Weisner agreed to be there.

Madonna's Michigan friend Linda Alaniz had moved to New York to become a photographer and had kept in touch. "Every time she had a gig she would invite me," Linda said. "I went to the Cat Club, CBGB. And then she calls to say, 'You're not going to believe this, but I'm actually going to be performing at Studio 54!' "[42]

It had fallen to Maripol to organize the party. "I had a big budget, and I kept saying to my boss, 'I want this singer.' Everybody was like, 'No, no, who is that? Who is Madonna?' " Elio Fiorucci had his heart set on Jennifer Beals, from *Flashdance*. The film, about a woman from the Midwest who dreams of being a professional dancer, was the third-highest-grossing movie of 1983 and featured a soundtrack by Giorgio Moroder. Maripol refused. Why hire the actress who *played* an aspiring dancer when you can hire the real thing? "Finally, I won," she said.[43]

Maripol had a huge rubber cake with fifteen candles made: Madonna would emerge from the top of it.[44] The planning complete, the invitations were distributed. The party began at 11:00 p.m., with "Madonna and Dancers" appearing last.[45]

Studio 54 was in its second incarnation after its original owners, Steve Rubell and Ian Schrager, went to prison for tax evasion. But that night the club's original cast of characters was in attendance: Bianca Jagger, Michael Jackson, Liza Minnelli, Halston, even Henry Kissinger (who danced with seventeen-year-old Brooke Shields). Amid that crowd, Madonna focused on just one guest: Freddy DeMann. "I was so nervous because Michael Jackson's so incredible live and I thought, 'If [Freddy] thinks Prince is terrible—which he did—what can I do?' "[46]

All she really had to do was appear onstage. Catherine Underhill said that Madonna "was just gobsmackingly beautiful."[47] She had begun dyeing her hair blond and shedding the little boy look in favor of a street-urchin femininity that Erika Belle helped her create, with rags tied in her hair, shirts cropped to show her belly, miniskirts worn with bicycle shorts, and masses of Maripol's jewelry.[48]

Having been given passes by Madonna, Linda arrived at Studio 54 with her ex-boyfriend, Madonna's old Michigan friend the actor David Alan Grier. "We danced for a while, and then they rolled out this big white cake. And suddenly Madonna just pops out of the top and rolls down it, kind of tumbles out, and gets up and starts singing 'Everybody get up and dance and sing.' And the crowd went wild." Linda said she never remembered Madonna being truly happy, but that night, she was.[49] A Polaroid that Maripol took of Madonna, Erika, Bags, and a dancer named David shows Madonna as radiant.

The performance was a hit. Fiorucci even wanted to send Madonna to Paris to perform during Fashion Week. But most important, Freddy "liked the show."[50]

DeMann may have become more open to Madonna because in the months between their meeting in Los Angeles and the Fiorucci bash, he had lost Michael Jackson as a client.[51] Seymour Stein was afraid Madonna would sour on Freddy over the Jackson dismissal, but she was thrilled. "She said, 'Now he's free to devote all his time to me.'"[52] After the Fiorucci event, Madonna went to Weisner-DeMann Entertainment to talk business.

The two men had checked around the clubs to see if Madonna was popular. The answer came back: yes. And Warner executives told Weisner that they were prepared to "put their promotional weight behind her."[53] Despite those assurances and his own instincts, Weisner needed to be persuaded to take on Madonna because he simply didn't like her. "I don't mind hunger and aggressiveness, but it got to a point when it wasn't, well, cool," he said. To Weisner's mind, *he* was interviewing Madonna. Madonna thought the opposite was true. She was hiring Weisner-DeMann to manage her career.

It might have surprised Weisner that anyone, let alone a young woman with nothing but street cred to recommend her, would think herself in pole position in their negotiations. But Madonna had to let him and Freddy know from the start that *she* was in charge and that they would need to listen to and respect her. She said,

> Sometimes people think if you're a girl you're going to be a pushover and they can get away with more. They can kind of pull the wool over your eyes. You're not going to be as strong as a man in like getting what you want, demanding what you asked for. But, I just surprise them when they see that they're wrong.[54]

At the end of the two-hour session, Weisner was ready to commit. He said he knew Madonna would be a star, that she represented a new direction in music. She was what he called a "ground-floor artist, someone who was there first. And when you have the opportunity to work with someone who is doing something that no one else is doing—and that something is saleable—you dive in."[55]

In the moments after the handshake that sealed their deal, Freddy, who was Madonna's "point man" at Weisner-DeMann, got a taste of what life with Madonna would be like.

> That day she had three problems, three overwhelming problems that really bothered her. And I said, "Look, I'll take care of these now and I'll just make some calls," and she said, "You will?" and I made three calls and took

care of her problems. And she was impressed with that. The next day she called, and she had five problems, and then the next day she called, she had seven problems, and then the next day she called she had ten problems. I said, "How in the world can one person..."

"Well, I do."[56]

The first order of business was getting Madonna on MTV. Though just two years old, MTV had close to twenty-four million viewers. The record industry saw the phenomenon for what it was: a massive new sales platform. The broader cultural impact, though, went far beyond dollars and cents. MTV changed the way people experienced music. After centuries of *listening* to music, people wanted to *watch* it.

As simple as that sounds, it was revolutionary. It also meant that to be popular, artists whose medium was sound had to become actors as well. Some established musicians weren't able to make that transition, and others had no interest in trying. Some *new* artists, on the other hand, those who might not have made it in a world of records and radio alone, became wildly successful, the camera more than compensating for any deficits in musical talent. The video phenomenon also gave birth to a new generation of filmmakers who could be as experimental as they liked because the rules hadn't yet been written. Everyone involved was making it up as they went along. It was a great place to be.[57]

Madonna's first official video was for the song "Burning Up." To helm it, Warner Bros. turned to Steve Barron, director of Michael Jackson's barrier-busting fantasy video for "Billie Jean." Shooting would take place in LA.[58]

"Burning Up" would be an anomaly among Madonna videos because it is the only one told from a male point of view: it's about a girl, a boy, and a car. In the *song,* Madonna expresses her desires with urgency and intensity—it is an active pursuit. The video, however, became a showcase for female passivity.

In it she rolls and writhes on the road as if, in her longing for the man in the song, she is ready to sacrifice herself to oncoming traffic. She tugs at her white dress, ready to pull it off if that's what it takes to attract a cold fish of a fellow driving a blue convertible. Interspersed with those images, Barron inserted a few random surrealist touches.[59]

What is not seen in the video is the real drama of the shoot. At one point, Barron took Madonna off the road and had her lying in a rowboat in a lake. He shot from a crane he positioned thirty feet above. As he instructed the crane operator to move in for a closer shot, Barron saw to his horror that two of the crane's four wheels were off the ground and the eight-ton machine was teetering in Madonna's direction.[60] The crane operator slowly retracted the crane's arm. No one told Madonna. Instead, a trembling Barron called a dinner break to settle his nerves.[61]

"Burning Up" introduced Madonna to the MTV audience, but it was not *her* on offer. It was a standard-issue submissive female, a cliché, which meant that the audience, comprised overwhelmingly of young white males, loved it.[62] The video did not, however, produce record sales. It wasn't the music the boys were after; it was Madonna herself.

The previous fall, as part of the "Everybody" promotion, Bobby Shaw had taken Madonna to a New York club called the Funhouse to meet the DJ, John "Jellybean" Benitez. Jellybean was one of the city's most important club DJs, so much so that a cult of personality had developed around him.[63] Celebrities in the music industry—from producers to artists—loved him.[64] So did the street. Jellybean was as important to the Latin crowd that hung out at the Funhouse as Mark Kamins was to Danceteria hipsters.

Though Jellybean was Madonna's type, she wasn't immediately attracted to him.

> He had really long hair and was walking around in really short shorts. I thought he was a girl at first...Then I ran into him again at a show at the Ritz [hip-hop club]. Then I knew he wasn't a girl. He started dragging me around everywhere, introducing me to all these industry people. I liked the way he held my hand. That changed my mind. He wasn't such a wimp anymore.[65]

Jellybean and Madonna would become lovers, creative partners, and very good friends at a moment when their careers were taking off like rocket ships. "For both of us, a lot changed at that time and we found comfort in sharing that," he said.[66] "For about a year and a half, I loved her very much. She was everything to me, my woman, my favorite artist, the bitchiest, funniest smart-ass I had ever known."[67]

At that point in the music world, besides Steve Bray, Jellybean was the person who best understood Madonna. He was as hungry for success and as pragmatic about how to get it as she was.[68] He also contributed a critical new element to her work: he called it "Latin percussion."[69]

Jellybean, who was a year older than Madonna, was raised in the South Bronx by his mother, who had emigrated from Puerto Rico in the early 1950s. After dropping out of school, he took odd jobs before landing a dream gig deejaying at a salsa club in the Bronx. He played salsa to satisfy that crowd, but he also played R&B and disco. As his musical repertoire expanded, so did his world.[70]

Traveling the club circuit from the Bronx into Manhattan, he worked at the popular club Xenon before taking a job at the Funhouse in 1981, which had opened in 1979 as a gay club. It was struggling before Jellybean helped turn it around by reviving the Latin music scene. In the process, he became the "first Puerto Rican DJ megahero."[71]

The club, on West 26th Street, was open from ten on Saturday night to ten on Sunday morning. During those hours, neither the music nor the dancers stopped. "It was nothing but one long party," Jellybean said.[72] "It was an escape for a lot of those kids... That's all they had, that Saturday night. I remember seeing kids coming in, you know it was $12 to get in, they'd have eight singles and the rest in change."[73]

Black, Puerto Rican, and Italian youths arrived dressed to dance to the music coming from the DJ booth, situated absurdly in the open mouth of a twelve-foot-high clown face.[74] The look for both boys and girls was cutoff T-shirts, sweatpants, and bandannas tied around the forehead. The dance was freestyle; the music hip-hop, electro, salsa, New Wave, disco—anything to keep feet and hips moving and the crowd happy. Jellybean knew right away if it was. Dancers barked if they liked a song and booed if they didn't.[75]

Madonna's album was almost finished, but she needed three songs remixed and asked Jellybean to do it. He had been mixing records for artists since 1979, among them a seven-inch version of Bambaataa's "Planet Rock." She and the Sire team met Jellybean for dinner to discuss it.[76] That deal struck, Rosenblatt then offered him the same challenge he had given Reggie Lucas: find a song for the eighth track on Madonna's album.

Jellybean had one he'd been trying unsuccessfully to pitch to other singers. Called "Holiday," it was written by Curtis Hudson and Lisa Stevens of the club band Pure Energy.[77] Curtis said he wrote the lyrics in response to the state of the world in the early '80s: the wars, the economy, AIDS, drugs, crime.

> It was troubling to see so much turmoil and this confusion, and so it came to me like, if we just had one day that we could just stop everywhere, over the world, that would be like a really great thing. So, the lyrics came: "If we took a holiday..."[78]

Pure Energy wanted to do it themselves, but their record label wasn't interested. Eventually they turned to Jellybean to see if he could shop it around. He told them to come to the Funhouse to meet Madonna.

"When I first saw her, she had all these rags tied around her dress and all these accessories," Hudson recalled. "I was like, 'What is she *wearing?*'"[79] But "she told us she loved the song...And she pretty much asked us, could she do the song?" Pure Energy—Curtis, Lisa, and Curtis's brother Raymond—huddled. They figured, "maybe there's something between this song and this artist...[it] might be something magical."[80]

"Holiday" would be Madonna's last album track, and Jellybean would produce it. He had one week and a $5,000 budget. Though he had mixed records, he had never produced one. "I worked like twenty hours a day to finish it," he said.[81] "I created the whole thing in my head. I got together some musicians I knew, and I hummed the parts to them."[82]

Curtis and Raymond Hudson were among the musicians in the recording studio. The Hudson brothers knew the song. Curtis *wrote* the song. But Madonna stopped him during a practice session to ask if he had to play the guitar "full funk," the way he had written it. Curtis said his immediate reaction was annoyance, but then he had to admit he was impressed. "How many artists even pay attention to that?" he asked. (Ultimately Jellybean sided with Curtis, and the guitar part was recorded as written.) Madonna also wanted to put her mark on the vocals.

When it came time to record them, she asked to be left alone in the studio. Curtis had never heard anyone besides Lisa Stevens sing the words to his song, and he was anxious about Madonna's rendition. At first, he didn't like it because it wasn't as soulful as Lisa's had been. But he listened again, and then he got it. He thought, "Wow, OK, they sound good." She brought "a kind of innocence" to the lyrics, he said. It was the magic he had hoped for.[83] Jellybean, meanwhile, was interested in a different kind of magic. He had been testing Madonna's version of the song during off hours at the Funhouse, blasting it through the sound system to see whether it would rock the dance floor. He came away happy, too.[84]

As Madonna's first album came together, her professional team began to take shape. Jellybean advised her to become a client of his accountant, Bert Padell, whose firm had handled a range of celebrities from the Beatles to Robert De Niro. He also steered her in the direction of entertainment lawyer Paul Schindler, whose partner was Alan Grubman, the most fearsome entertainment lawyer in New York, according to Seymour Stein.[85] All those men would be helpful to Madonna, but through Warner Bros. she made her most important connection, a woman who would be at her side for decades: her publicist, Liz Rosenberg.

Madonna's male team comprised a panel of specialists who handled whatever crisis fell within their jurisdictions. Liz, by contrast (and because she was a woman), handled them all, and they would be legion. It would be Liz who—with a smile and good-natured sarcasm—batted off the continual attacks, managed the flood of requests, responded to the head-lined rumors, and engaged in some strategic spinning of her own. Beginning in 1983, no one got to Madonna professionally unless he or she went through Liz Rosenberg.

A native of Long Island, Liz had studied nursing, which was quite accidentally the perfect training for a publicist. Her love of music drew her to the business, where she worked as a secretary, a bicycle messenger, and finally as an assistant to the director of the Warner Bros. publicity department. In that job, she was allowed to be an agent as well. That was when she discovered Van Morrison.[86] Liz had many other clients—including Cher, Prince, Rod Stewart, and Van Halen—but it is safe to say that none required as much time and effort as the young woman from Michigan.[87]

Liz began each day with a call to Madonna, and Madonna began using Liz's office to conduct her own business. It was a home away from home occupied by a friend and—because Liz was ten years older than Madonna—a mother figure whom Madonna welcomed amid the forty-something men in suits buzzing around her.[88]

All those personalities were in place in time for the debut of *Madonna,* on July 27, 1983, a few weeks before Madonna's twenty-fifth birthday. With her photograph on the album cover, there was no longer any question as to who or what Madonna was: a young, tough, brooding white woman. Dressed in gear that reflected her two worlds—a mass of Maripol's rubber bracelets on one arm and Funhouse-ready studded bracelets and chains on the other—she came across as beautiful and mysterious. Madonna dedicated her album to her father and thanked, among others, "my darling Martin."[89]

The album included eight songs, three of which had been released earlier in the year: "Everybody," "Physical Attraction," and "Burning Up." To attract DJ interest, a promotion-only single was produced, with "Lucky Star" on the A side and "Holiday" on side B. Warner Bros. expected "Lucky Star" to be the album's hit. But the DJs loved "Holiday," and the song began climbing the charts.[90]

Though "Holiday" was a dance hit, *Madonna* languished in the pop album charts. It was a matter of competition, which Seymour Stein said was fierce because of a new wave of British artists. But it was also still a matter of race. Cyndi Lauper's "Girls Just Want to Have Fun" was released the day before "Holiday." It went to number 2 on the Billboard Hot 100 chart. Lauper was the star for the white radio audience.[91] Madonna was a star on Black radio. The KJLH–FM program director, Jim Maddox, whose LA station played R&B and soul, went so far as to say, "Black stations were the only ones that played her."[92]

Madonna saw herself as a catalyst for change. "I'm a white artist doing R&B music on pop stations. I think that's opening up a place for black and white audiences as well."[93] Music—sound—didn't exist within prescribed boundaries. Why should musical artists? Fans got it. The question was, Why didn't the industry get it? "I know this record is good," Madonna said, "and one of these days Warner Brothers and the rest of them are going to figure it out."[94]

Chapter 14

New York, Spokane, Manchester, Paris, Los Angeles, 1983–1984

Jeanne Wolf: What's your category? Where do you fit now?
Madonna: You want the title of the category?... New, that's what the category is. New.
Jeanne Wolf: What's new about it?
Madonna: Me.[1]

—Entertainment Tonight, *February 12, 1984*

MADONNA CELEBRATED HER album's release with a group of visual artists, some of whom were at the same exciting cusp in their careers. She had become one of Warhol's "art kids," young artists who used pop imagery, ideas, and techniques to make sometimes personal, sometimes political statements. The new art was at once deadly serious and wildly fun.[2]

One of those artists was Keith Haring, and he would become one of Madonna's closest friends. "We both sort of came from the same place," she said.

> I mean, I'm from Michigan and he's from Pennsylvania... And the first people that were interested in his art were the people that were interested in me and that is the black [and] Hispanic community... We were kind of odd birds... he was drawn to the same world that I was drawn to and inspired by it.[3]

Raised in what he described as conservative eastern Pennsylvania, Haring was, like Madonna, an outsider in his youth. While in art school in Pittsburgh, he heard a lecture by the artist Christo, who was best known for massive public projects that brought attention to spaces and places that were otherwise ignored. Keith came away from the talk inspired by the notion of taking art directly to the public.[4] That artistic awakening occurred around the same time as his sexual awakening. "Obviously, the only place to go is New York," he said.[5]

In a way it was easier to arrive alone in New York in 1978 as a young gay man than it had been to arrive as Madonna did that year—as a young straight-leaning woman. Skinny, bespectacled, and loose-limbed as a puppet, Haring moved to the West Village off Bleecker Street and found himself literally embraced by strangers. "The whole gay thing was everywhere," he told his biographer John Gruen. "I mean, it was almost too much. You couldn't go to the post office without cruising or being cruised, without being totally aware of sex."[6]

At the School of Visual Arts, he quickly fell in with a circle of friends. One was a surfer from California named Kenny Scharf. And even though Jean-Michel Basquiat wasn't a student there, SVA was where Keith and Jean-Michel met.[7] Haring had seen Basquiat's SAMO© tag. He said the words that preceded it "would stop you in your tracks and make you think...From the moment I saw Jean-Michel's drawings and the things he did on the streets, I knew he was a great artist."[8]

Keith, Kenny Scharf, Jean-Michel, and an SVA student named John Sex with a huge blond pompadour began employing a new technology—color Xerox—to make art. Keith became intrigued by the possibility of using it in the public square the way Barbara Kruger did with her "pasteups" and Jenny Holzer did with her *Truisms*. Both women used words and phrases, and in Kruger's case images, that were so ordinary they became disturbingly *extraordinary*.[9]

In 1980, Keith began experimenting with his own wordplay, plastering collages and fake *New York Post* headlines around the city: REAGAN SLAIN BY HERO COP or RONALD REAGAN ACCUSED OF TV STAR SEX DEATH; KILLED & ATE LOVER. He Xeroxed them by the hundreds and put them on lampposts around town.[10] From there, he began creating graffitied hieroglyphics: flying saucers, dogs, babies, penises. Like Christopher Flynn, who urged Madonna to drop out and go to New York, a teacher at the SVA told Haring he didn't need school anymore. He was already an artist.[11]

Haring's next academy became the street, where he joined the established graffiti scene with Fab 5 Freddy and Lee Quiñones, whom he called the "kings of the graffiti world." Freddy said the "posse" consisted of himself, Quiñones, Haring, Scharf, Basquiat, and Futura.[12]

Long before Martin Burgoyne introduced Madonna to Keith—she believes at the Funhouse—she had seen his work.[13] It was impossible not to. His "gallery" was the New York subway system. Keith could do thirty or forty drawings a day in white chalk on the blank black spaces where ads would eventually be pasted. Curator Jeffrey Deitch said Keith brought art to one of the "most hostile environments in New York, where even armed cops weren't safe...His drawings affected life there."[14]

Next, Haring had his "radiant baby" designs printed on buttons, which he distributed for free. In an age when logos turned people into walking billboards, New Yorkers "were walking around with little badges with the crawling baby with glowing rays around it," Keith said. "The buttons started to become a thing now, too; people with them would talk to each other."[15]

In the early '80s, Haring was everywhere. He created an anti–apartheid "Free South Africa" poster. At a nuclear disarmament demonstration in Central Park in 1982, he distributed to passersby twenty thousand anti-nuclear posters he had created. He also tackled sexual prejudices, especially involving gay sex. Because he did it in his "naive" style, he made what would otherwise be considered pornographic appear benign. He planted a message before the viewer had time to be offended. "I think that there's a lot of innocence in his work," Madonna said, "coupled with a sort of brutal awareness of the world."[16]

Only after Haring had made so many public statements did he show in a gallery. That was in 1982, the same year Madonna signed with Sire.[17] By then, he was living in SoHo, on Broome Street, and getting involved with the clubs frequented by artists in the East Village. "There was a very open sexual situation," Keith said, "because at that point, everyone was pretty much bisexual."[18] But it was Fab 5 Freddy who introduced him to two clubs that changed Keith's life and art. The first was the Roxy. After Freddy took him there, Keith began using hip-hop images in his work. Freddy then took Keith to Paradise Garage.[19] "I was never the same since entering that club for the first time," Keith recalled. Dancing there, he said, was "attaining another state of consciousness."[20]

Keith, like Madonna—like nearly all the artists and characters who peopled the downtown scene in the late 1970s and early 1980s—was a post-modernist. He and they rejected the modernist notions of purity in art, solemnity in art, elitism in art, and strict artistic genres, replacing them with street art, word art, graphic art, and "the self" as art. There was no distinction between high and low culture, commercial and fine art. Art could be anything, and anything could be used in the service of art.

Appropriation and replication weren't stealing and copying; they were tributes and tools. Irony and self-mockery were critical to the messaging. Though postmodern artists were utterly of the world, they existed simultaneously outside it, as observers and translators, bringing what they discovered to others through their work.[21] The person who exemplified that philosophy for young downtown artists was Andy Warhol.

In the summer of 1983, Keith Haring met Warhol, who was then fifty-five. Though *Forbes* magazine that year had featured Warhol in a story about millionaire artists, he didn't feel respected by the established art world. "It was very painful for him. And so, for Andy to then connect with this younger generation for whom Andy was *the* hero, he loved it," Jeffrey Deitch said.[22] Keith became part of Warhol's circle. "Madonna was around and we all kind of grew up together in this crazy swirl of activity," he said.[23] Deitch called them "the children of Warhol."[24]

But Madonna didn't meet Warhol through Haring. The introduction came through Marcus Leatherdale, during his thirtieth-birthday dinner at a chic place uptown called Club A.[25] "I sat her next to Andy and he was like 'Who's *shee*?'" Marcus recalled. "She was very quiet, and she was very polite. She actually left early. She seemed uncomfortable somewhat with the caliber of…with the people." It was an intimidating crowd: Andrée Putman, one of the biggest designers in Paris; models Tina Chow and Iman; Dianne Brill, whom Warhol called "the queen of the night"; and Robert Mapplethorpe (who Madonna later admitted "scared the shit out of me"),[26] among others. By comparison, Marcus said, Madonna was "kind of green and new in town."[27]

Though in a few years that would be exactly the type of gathering Madonna would embrace, at the time she was still finding her way and was more at ease with Keith, Martin, Kenny Scharf, Fab 5 Freddy, Debi Mazar, Erika, Maripol, Jellybean, and, of course, Christopher—in short, her tribe. Madonna marveled at the fate that brought them together. "I was attracted to creative people," she said.

> And somehow, we found each other in Manhattan. That's the crazy thing. We found each other and we connected to each other, and we moved around the city together. They supported my shows. I supported their shows. We were a unit. And I don't even know how it happened. It just did.[28]

In late 1983, though they were no longer romantically involved, Basquiat was part of Madonna's circle, too. He had returned from LA with a jacket from *Singin' in the Rain* that actor Gene Kelly had given him and a bigger basket of bad habits.[29] Basquiat had promised Madonna he'd give up heroin, but days after he made that pledge, she found him unconscious in his loft. She dragged him into the bathroom and turned on a cold shower. She told his friend Armon Stewart, "He just doesn't give a fuck about me, about himself, his work…anything…I can't be around this." From a safer distance, she would watch him create masterpieces as an artist and self-destruct as a man.[30]

★   ★   ★

That year, Madonna began spending much of her time away from New York. She was offered a role in a movie, *Vision Quest*. Producer Jon Peters inherited the project about a high school jock who falls for an older woman. Peters approached Madonna about basically playing herself—a club singer. If she agreed, shooting would begin in September in Spokane, Washington.[31]

The power of MTV had already affected the film industry. A movie hoping to appeal to the thirteen-to-thirty-five age bracket had to have an MTV look and a radio-ready and MTV-ready soundtrack. And that meant Madonna. She wrote two songs for the film: one was "Warning Signs," written with Steve Bray, with whom she had reconciled after their falling-out. It wasn't used in the film, but Madonna's other song, "Gambler," was.[32] She also sang "Crazy for You," written by John Bettis and Jon Lind.

The film's music producer, Phil Ramone, said part of his job was to keep Madonna from overpowering the film. He failed, but it wasn't his fault. When she sang "Crazy for You" during a nightclub scene, her performance was electrifying.

Jellybean Benitez had been in and out of Spokane, working with Ramone to produce the film's songs. Madonna used a break in filming to bring him home to Michigan to meet the family at Thanksgiving.[33] She hadn't been back for years and had spoken to her father only sporadically. But now that she had an album to show for herself, she could return feeling vindicated in her decision to leave.

As much as she had rejected the life she led in Rochester, it was Tony's approval she most craved. It was his lessons that had pulled her through some of her toughest times. And it was his work ethic that had helped her distinguish herself from the countless other hopefuls who approached their lives and dreams passively. He had taught all his children that if they wanted something, they couldn't wait for someone else to make it happen for them. Madonna had learned that lesson best.

But that didn't mean *he* understood *her*. "I came home with black pants, a black T-shirt, no jewelry at all, and my hair just sort of not combed—that's pretty conservative," she said. "And my father spent most of the time looking at me, going, 'You always dress like that? Is that a costume?'"[34]

There were two network television programs in 1984 that were considered mandatory stops on the road to pop stardom: *American Bandstand* in the United States and *Top of the Pops* in Britain. Madonna hit them both in January of 1984. *American Bandstand* had been broadcasting longer than Madonna had been alive—and with only one host, a perennially jolly fellow named Dick Clark. Handsome in a 1950s sort of way, with a radio broadcaster's voice, he was ageless. Even after more than twenty-seven years in the business, Clark still seemed to love introducing new talent to his massive late afternoon audience.[35]

Madonna arrived on Clark's show like an alien from the planet Funhouse. As she launched into "Holiday," dressed in a mix she called "pseudo–Puerto Rican punk rock freak out" and "motorcycle baby," the first part of her body to move was the forbidden zone around her hips.[36] The jolt she sent through the audience was palpable.

The young people who encircled her from a polite distance were straight out of a Christian college recruitment brochure: sweaters and dirndl skirts, creased slacks, sensible shoes. As she belly danced their way, a whoop went up from the crowd, and then that mass of inhibited hormones revolted. Tame by today's standards, the scene was as pagan as *Bandstand* got without intervention from network censors. Madonna's joy was infectious.

To the Middle American teenagers watching her, she epitomized cool, and she was generous enough to make them feel that they could be, too. That was her genius. Madonna approached an audience the way club DJs did theirs. She didn't perform *at* them; she transported them. By the end of her song—and even before she had blown them all kisses—the *Bandstand* studio audience was hers, the girls and boys at home in their living rooms were hers—hell, even Dick Clark was hers. So much so that when she famously told him that her dream was "to rule the world," he didn't bat an eye. It didn't sound so crazy.[37]

"Holiday," meanwhile, had gradually worked its way from the Black radio stations into the broader culture and its subconscious. Rock critic Dave Marsh said,

> For a few months in 1984, it seemed like you couldn't possibly escape this record. You could go hiking in Vancouver, chase kangaroos on the outback, go surfing in the Pacific or mingle with crowds of Bombay, and it seemed you'd still hear Madonna's shrill cry of "it would be so nice"!!![38]

In January of 1984, the song entered the Billboard top 20, a first for Madonna. It had also reached the Top 40 in the UK, which was Madonna's next stop.[39]

A producer from a scrappy new show called *The Tube,* on Britain's Channel 4 network, discovered her during a trip to the States in late 1983. "Once I got to New York and started talking to people, it became obvious that she was fucking hot," Malcolm Gerrie said, "so I went to this tiny club to see her." He called her performance "one of the horniest things I'd ever seen" and Madonna herself "very intimidating." Gerrie returned home intent on persuading the owner of the Hacienda, in Manchester, to do a special live edition of *The Tube* featuring Madonna. The answer was an enthusiastic yes.[40] But first came *Top of the Pops*.

That music showcase had been broadcast by BBC1 since 1964. Everyone who was anyone in the post–Beatles era had appeared on its stage. In fact, the same night as Madonna was scheduled to perform, Cyndi Lauper was on the show, lip-synching "Girls Just Want to Have Fun." Lauper jumped around the stage, ran up and down the set's staircase, and "played" the balcony railing with drumsticks. Her performance was just this side of crazy aunt.[41]

Madonna appeared with Christopher and Erika, all three in comfortable club waif wear, dancing to "Holiday" while she sang over a backing track. One writer called Madonna's performance "coolness personified." The crowd around the stage danced shoulder to shoulder, waving their arms in the air, twisting their bodies, seconds away from a full-on dance-floor explosion. And when the song ended, the shouts from the crowd were deafening.[42]

Madonna appeared at the Hacienda for *The Tube* the next night after taking the train up from London. Fans who had seen her on the BBC lined up outside in the damp, cold Manchester evening. She arrived for the show in a limo as long as a street, according to a fire-eater named Bob, who was there to keep the queue amused. Madonna's entourage included Christopher, Erika, Martin, three record company executives, and a chauffeur.[43]

Given the activity outside the club, one would have expected the scene inside to be raucous, but Manchester was a tough crowd with a deep rock tradition. While Madonna, Erika, and Christopher performed "Holiday" on a soundstage without a bit of ambience, the audience stood lifeless.[44]

Madonna quietly simmered, telling an interviewer after the show, "There's a lot more to me than can possibly be perceived in the beginning."[45] Johnny Black wrote in the British publication *Q* that when the manager and bassist for the band New Order came to the dressing room after the show offering "50 quid" for a private dance, she dropped the facade of politesse and "told them to fuck off."[46]

The stony club audience didn't reflect the broader reaction to Madonna's performance. *Tube* producer Malcolm Gerrie said that the next day, the show was "bombarded with calls. The switchboard just lit up with people wanting to know more about Madonna."[47] But Madonna wasn't there to hear it. With a "Let's get the fuck out of here," she and her crew left Manchester by train, bitching, Christopher said, "about England and the English."[48]

The trip Freddy DeMann had planned for them didn't end in England and didn't get any better for it. A boat-train trip in the freezing cold brought them to Paris. Martin's role was ostensibly that of road manager, but his real job was to keep spirits high. His efforts were wasted.[49]

Christopher said the group was supposed to perform at the Fiorucci Paris opening party, which was held in a club with an empty swimming pool called La Piscine. "We are made to stand on the bottom of the pool and perform with everyone else standing above us and watching," he said. "We are basically performing to a wall and it's ludicrous. In the midst of the second song, someone shoots tear gas into the room. We run to the nearest exit, tears streaming down our faces. It's pandemonium, everyone running everywhere." Having washed the gas from their eyes, they tried to salvage the evening by going to a dance club but were refused entry. Madonna and company left Europe, angry and deflated.[50]

By that point, Madonna was a minor celebrity in New York, but she was still able to ride her bicycle around town, eat in East Village restaurants with friends, and ride the subway. "I have a lot of young girl fans and they'll start squealing on the trains," she told an interviewer in May of 1984. "People come up and say, 'You look just like Madonna,' and I'll go, 'Thank you.' Or, they'll say, 'Are you Madonna?' and I'll say, 'Yes.' Then they'll go, 'No you're not!' and I'll say, 'OK, I'm not.' "[51] That was the fun part. Madonna could watch the world watching her. She was a fly on the wall of her own life. But that would begin to change after the release of her next video—the one for "Borderline."[52]

The director was an Arkansas native named Mary Lambert. Moving to LA after graduating from the Rhode Island School of Design in the late '70s, she found paid work directing special effects for commercials and unpaid work making what she called "weird films." In 1982, after seeing a video of Rickie Lee Jones's song "Chuck E.'s in Love" and thinking she could do that, she called her art school friends Tina Weymouth and Chris Frantz of Talking Heads and offered to make a video for their new band, the Tom Tom Club. She took the finished video to Jeff Ayeroff, head of creative affairs at Warner Bros.[53]

He liked Mary's work but wasn't interested in promoting the Tom Tom Club. He gave her another job, directing a video for a new artist named Madonna, and bought her a plane ticket to New York.[54]

After tracking Madonna down to an apartment on the Upper East Side, a place so barren that Mary didn't think anyone actually lived there, the two "hit it off. We bonded on the level of just being girls," Mary said. Lambert was tiny, with straight blond hair, cornflower-blue eyes, and a sweet southern accent. But she was tough, tough as Madonna.[55] "I came away thinking that [Madonna] was a piece of work, and that it was going to be fun," Mary said.

She had four or five different boyfriends at the time. One of them was a record producer, Jellybean Benitez, but he was really, really jealous of everybody. Of every*thing*...He was convinced that she was seeing other guys and that he wasn't going to be able to control her. And he was completely right, of course, on both counts.[56]

Madonna was headed to Los Angeles, so they decided to shoot the video there. "I knew the downtown L.A. area really well, because there were a lot of artist bars there," Mary said.[57] "There was no formula. We were *inventing* it as we went along."[58] What emerged was a video so powerful that the song became secondary to the images.

Madonna cast a hunky young Hispanic man to play her lover, and the story line gave her a second love interest, too—an older white convertible-driving fashion photographer. The video presented Madonna with a follow-your-heart or follow-the-money dilemma: love on a barrio rooftop or love in a photographer's studio; hanging with the sisters on the corner or accepting the loneliness that comes with being the prized possession of a rich man.

It was an allegory about the choice between freedom and security that young women make. Sadly—but inexplicably—they rarely get both. Mary distinguished between those two choices by shooting the neighborhood scenes (freedom) in color and the studio scenes (security) in black and white. The video was only tangentially related to the song's lyrics, but that didn't diminish its impact.

The "Borderline" video was the first in which Madonna played a girlfriend—not only a man's girlfriend but also a *girl's* girlfriend, which made the video relatable to a female audience in a way "Burning Up" did not. Also in contrast to that earlier video, Madonna's character didn't exist in the orbit of a man or men; she was the planet around which *they* turned. She came across as strong and vulnerable, beautiful and ordinary, sexy and chaste. She was something a woman rarely was on-screen: a complete person full of contradictions.

Mary Lambert brought the video to Freddy DeMann. "He was hysterical that I had combined black-and-white footage with color footage," Mary said. "He made me screen it for all the secretaries in his office and see how they reacted, because he felt I had crossed a line that shouldn't be crossed." The secretaries' opinions must have mattered, because the video was approved. Ayeroff said, "MTV jumped on it...and that was it. Away we go."[59] "Borderline" became Madonna's first Billboard top ten single.[60] The "Borderline" video also marked the moment when young women started to dress like Madonna.

⋆   ⋆   ⋆

By early 1984, it was known that she was white and New Wavey—another example of the new generation of women performers who pushed the limits of fashion decorum onstage. Cyndi Lauper existed at one end of the spectrum, with her bright red hair and bag-lady eccentricities. The Slits had been around for years, wearing underwear as outerwear, dreadlocks, and a grab bag of mismatched clothes. Lydia Lunch, of the same fashion ilk as the Slits, was darker—her clothes, her hair, her look. Exene Cervenka of the band X looked like a punk Louise Brooks. And then there was Annie Lennox. After the Eurythmics' 1983 hit "Sweet Dreams (Are Made of This)," she became a video sensation with her gender-bending technicolor androgyny.[61]

But as unique as those women's styles were, they were extreme, and they represented a step most girls and young women at that time were not prepared to take. Madonna's look, by contrast, was distinctive enough to make a statement and cause family dramas of the "You are not leaving the house looking like that" variety but not so radical that young women were frightened by it. Plus, she looked *good*. The rags in the hair, the mismatched earrings, the crosses, the crop tops, the miniskirts with bicycle shorts, the flat shoes and big athletic socks were *great*. And comfortable.

Just as the daughters of second wave feminism, who had been taught that they were equal to their brothers, started learning that that was not the case, they discovered Madonna. Her look gave them a rebellious way to express their simmering dissatisfaction and emerging defiance. Cyndi Lauper's "Girls Just Want to Have Fun" heralded a new feminism. The message wasn't the 1970s "I Am Woman" but a 1980s "I am free." But what did freedom look like? It looked like Madonna.[62]

Madonna had been writing songs throughout her travels and was eager to work on a new album. The experiences of the previous few months had made her more confident about her abilities in the studio and clearer about the direction she wanted to go with her music.[63] "The production won't be so slick," she told an interviewer in Britain. "I want a sound that's mine. There will be a more crossover approach to it this time."[64] She also knew whom she wanted to produce it. Madonna asked Warner executives if she could work with Nile Rodgers. It was an audacious ask. He had just finished working with David Bowie on his biggest-selling album ever, *Let's Dance*.[65]

Madonna wanted Rodgers not only because of Bowie, whom she revered, but also because Nile made dance records. Reggie Lucas produced songs people could listen to or sing along with. Nile Rodgers produced songs that made people move—all people: Black, brown, white, across the sexual spectrum.[66] "Nile has worked with so many kinds of musicians, and every record he's made is a great one as far as I'm concerned," she said. "I identified with him, too. He's a real street person, and we hung out at the same clubs. Even before I started to interview producers, I thought he was the one I wanted."[67]

Nile could make his guitar do anything. After he met bassist Bernard Edwards, in the late '70s, disco became his focus. He recognized the music's rebellious heritage and believed that after the dust of political protests had settled, and after the shaming of the first modern criminal president, Richard Nixon, it was time to dance.[68] Disco, he said, was more political and communal than the hippie mentality of the '60s, when "we talked about freedom and individuality, and it was all bullshit." With disco, he said, people "bonded through their bodies...Dance had become primal and ubiquitous, a powerful communication tool, every bit as motivational as an Angela Davis speech."[69]

His first big hit, "Dance, Dance, Dance," was released during the Son of Sam summer of 1977, when Madonna arrived in New York for her Alvin Ailey course. Rodgers and Edwards had just formed the band Chic and would go on to record a string of hits that sold tens of millions of records.[70] That Rodgers had reached this height was a testament to his survival skills. By his own admission, he was a "full-blown daily drug user [and] daily drinker." Cocaine and vodka. A bump and a swig.[71]

It wasn't his habits that ended Chic's disco run, though; it was white radio. Rodgers and Edwards then began focusing on furthering other artists' careers, working as producers with people like Diana Ross, Debbie Harry, and Bowie. A few years and several major albums later, Madonna came calling.[72] Rodgers knew of her through Jellybean but had never met her, so he went to the Roxy, where she was performing, to check her out. He expected to see a young Puerto Rican, but instead he was "startled" by what he saw.

> A toothsome white girl stepping. Stepping was what R&B bands like the Jackson 5 and most others used to do until the likes of Prince moved the scene to more rock-like performance...Now here was a white girl doing intricate choreography, all while crooning: "Holiday-ee, Celebra-eete.".... She was akin to a young, sexually aggressive, white Gladys Knight.[73]

He went backstage to meet her and found her "cute, but raw, and her toughness was impressive, even to a homegrown New Yorker like myself," he said. "She looked like she was living a hard life." Nile left intrigued, confused, and still unconvinced.[74]

Madonna, meanwhile, went to LA to talk with Warner Bros. about the album. Mo Ostin's son Michael, a Warner A&R man, had come across a song that he thought would be perfect for her. It was called "Like a Virgin." Billy Steinberg, who wrote the lyrics, said it was based on his own experience.[75] "I wasn't just trying to somehow get that racy word 'virgin' in a lyric," he said.

> I was saying…I've been battered romantically and emotionally…but I'm starting a new relationship and it just feels so good, it's healing all the wounds and making me feel like I've never done this before.[76]

Virgin wasn't a word one *heard* on the radio in 1984. Steinberg and Tom Kelly, who wrote the music, had been told that "no one will sing a song with that title."[77] But Michael Ostin suspected that Madonna would. As luck would have it, he had a meeting with her the next day. "When I played it for Madonna," Ostin said, "she went crazy."[78] She recalled,

> As soon as I heard "Like a Virgin," I knew that's what I wanted to call my album, just to tick everybody off. It was a loaded statement that I knew would be misinterpreted. People thought I was saying I just wanted to have sex, when it meant just the opposite. It celebrates the idea of feeling untouched and pure. I liked having the secret knowledge that what it said was good.[79]

That was when Warner executives called Rodgers to discuss the album. "After a few meetings where I was fully exposed to her now legendary blonde ambition…I knew I could take her to the next level," he said. "With this astonishingly charismatic girl who turned on every room of strangers we entered, I was sure that I could deliver the goods."[80]

Rodgers and Madonna got to work. She let him hear five songs she had written (of which four were composed with Steve Bray) and four that she wanted on the album that were written by other people.[81] After Nile listened to the demos, Madonna turned to him and said, "If you don't love all of these songs, we can't work together." Shocked by her ultimatum, he said, "Well, to be honest with you, I don't love *all* these songs, but I can promise you this: By the time we're finished with them I will."[82] That was assurance enough for Madonna.

They worked at the loft she shared with Jellybean on Broome Street and West Broadway in SoHo. Jellybean's life had shifted from mostly deejaying to mostly producing, which took him out of New York often.[83] Madonna's life had also become one of near constant travel to promote her work. Nile found their home devoid of furniture except for a mattress on the floor and a color television that Madonna said was the most extravagant thing she had ever purchased. Rodgers sent her a couch from his office and took a seat there.[84]

"Over the next few months, I grew as close to Madonna as I've ever been to a woman without being romantically involved," he said. "We spent every spare moment we could together until her record hit the streets."[85] Said Madonna, "He gave me the feeling we were really collaborating, and I felt free to say what I wanted."[86] Such was their collaboration that Madonna would be listed as a producer on the album.

Madonna's relationship with Nile would be a template for her work with future producers.[87] He called it "the perfect union...It was sexual, it was passionate, it was creative."[88] It was a little like a marriage. And like a marriage, it was not without conflict. Theirs began with the album's title. Nile wasn't sure about *Like a Virgin*. "I was like, 'Are you nuts?'" he recalled saying. "I didn't want to kill her career with it." Madonna argued that girls would relate to it because losing their virginity was all they talked about at a certain age.[89] As the song grew on him, he admitted that he couldn't get it out of his head. Finally, he told Madonna, "Let's do it."[90]

They also clashed about the album's song order. She wanted "Like a Virgin" to be the first single, but he thought "Material Girl" was better first out of the gate. After they recorded "Material Girl," Madonna, Nile, and all the musicians and backup singers gathered in the listening room to hear the final version. "It sounded great, you know, everybody loved it," said backup singer Frank Simms. "We were laughing, laughing, laughing. Madonna was laughing her stones off. And it was like, 'Oh God this is ridiculous. People are gonna love this.'" But even believing that it would be a hit, Madonna stuck to her guns. "It's funny: I'd worked with so many international superstars," Nile said, "but I'd never come across such an iron will before. Madonna won 'Like a Virgin' as the first single."[91]

While Nile's relationship with Madonna was good, she could be rude to the musicians who worked with them—mostly Chic alumni—because she expected everyone to have her obsessional work ethic. At one point, she was so abusive to a musician who had dared to take a bathroom break without her permission that Nile threatened to quit. Picking up his things and storming out, he got as far as the elevator, where Madonna ran him down and said by way of apology, "'Nile! Does that mean you don't love me anymore?'" Rodgers said, "How could I stay angry after that?" They started laughing and returned to the studio.[92]

In late May, after six weeks of work, *Like a Virgin* was ready, but Warner didn't want to release it because the single "Borderline" was, according to Nile, "taking off like a rocket" after the video's release. The record company wanted to build on that song's success and drive up sales of the first album, possibly by rereleasing "Lucky Star," which had been overshadowed the previous year by "Holiday." "Man, we sat on *Like a Virgin* for what felt like ages," Rodgers said, "and it drove Madonna crazy."[93] She hadn't been satisfied with the *Madonna* album in the first place, and it was ancient history for her artistically. She was no longer that woman. She was *Like a Virgin,* and she wanted people to hear *that* person on the radio.[94]

On the street outside the Paradise Garage, helmeted police stood several deep behind barricades for crowd control.[95] "There were kids outside selling tickets to it," Andy Warhol said, "although it was a free party."[96] The date was May 16, 1984; the event was Keith Haring's first annual Party of Life. It was a bold idea to celebrate life in the time of AIDS and even bolder to suggest that there would be future parties. "First" implied "second," yet dance floors around the city were emptying because the men who had filled them were dying. Haring decided to defy the disease and celebrate his twenty-sixth birthday by throwing a massive bash. "At that point, I had made a sufficient amount of money to have a sufficient amount of guilt about, and to want to share with my friends," he explained.[97]

Haring rented the Garage on a Wednesday night, when it was normally closed, and sent out invitations printed on handkerchiefs. "It didn't say Madonna was going to perform because that sort of happened last minute," he said. It did say that Larry Levan would DJ.[98] That, coupled with Keith as host, was enough to attract friends, street kids, celebrities who wanted to be friends, and Garage regulars to what was undoubtedly the hottest party in town.[99]

Keith secured Madonna's help by making a trade. He would give her a specially painted leather jacket in exchange for her music. She was happy to oblige. It gave her a chance to perform songs from her new album. "I immediately liked these two songs, 'Dress You Up' and 'Like a Virgin,'" he said. "We decided she'll sing those."[100] Keith's party would be the first time she would perform them for an audience. It was fitting that she did so at the Garage, where she had also debuted her first single, "Everybody."

For the show, Madonna wanted to sing from a brass bed covered with white lace and white roses. Keith's new assistant, Julia Gruen, was sent on a reconnaissance mission to find the bed, the lace, and the flowers.[101] Keith and the graffiti artist LA II, meanwhile, decorated the Garage with Keith's paintings and cotton banners, and spray-painted everything else in fluorescent colors. Keith also made T-shirts, which he gave away as party favors.[102] Paradise Garage had become a Keith Haring installation. Entering the club was like entering his mind.

On the night of the party, Keith welcomed the crowd resplendent in a fluorescent yellow velvet tuxedo designed by another Warhol art child, Stephen Sprouse. In fact, Sprouse's Day-Glo designs featuring Keith's hieroglyphics were everywhere that evening as three thousand people, some wearing Day-Glo necklaces, walked the Garage ramp to squeeze onto the two-thousand-capacity dance floor.[103]

Wearing a too-tight tuxedo below his imposing pompadour, John Sex took the stage first with the Bodacious TaTas — four gorgeous women who looked like Jayne Mansfield.[104] "Then the stage darkened and there was a big brass bed in the middle of the stage with Madonna," said Courtney Harmel, whom Keith hired to videotape the event. "She did 'Like a Virgin.'" Julia hadn't been able to find white roses, so white lilies were used instead, but the brass bed was, as requested, covered in virginal lace.[105]

For that song, Madonna wore a sheer loose dress of Maripol's with a tank top and blue pants visible underneath and layers of pearls around her neck. After "Like a Virgin," the stage darkened, and Madonna's sugary voice from the shadows wished Keith a Marilyn Monroe–style happy birthday. Then the lights rose again, and she reappeared, dazzling, in a second outfit: a Day-Glo pink suit designed by Stephen Sprouse that was covered in Keith's drawings. Like a New Wave Jackie Kennedy, Madonna launched into "Dress You Up," which she sang on and around the bed.[106]

In retrospect, it was an important performance on many levels, but at the time, the response was muted. "This was before 'Like a Virgin' and 'Dress You Up' had come out so people didn't know the songs. It was the first time they were hearing them," Keith said. "Six months later, when you heard those songs six times a day on the radio, it would have been a whole other thing."[107] Six months later, Madonna's performance of "Like a Virgin" would change pop culture history.

Chapter 15

New York, Venice, Los Angeles, 1984

If Sissy Spacek can be a country singer, why can't I be an actress?[1]

— Madonna

THAT SPRING, FREDDY DeMann organized a trip for Madonna to Paris, Munich, Bremen, and Morocco to promote her first album.[2] Warner's Jeff Ayeroff, meanwhile, was busily planning for the future. He contacted Mary Lambert about doing a video for "Like a Virgin." "We want to do something outrageous," he said. Rarely is a director given such freedom, so Mary said, "'Let's do it in Venice!' The idea of Madonna singing in a gondola was the most outrageous thing I could think of. And Madonna dug it, because she has the whole thing with the Catholic Church and her Italian heritage."[3] That city of saints and sinners, art and artifice, decadence and discovery would be the perfect backdrop for Madonna's song. Mary said,

> There's this famous yearly Carnival in Venice where everyone wears elaborate masks. I loved that idea, of things not being what they seem. Madonna's love interest in the video wore a lion mask, and that gave me the idea to get a real lion...Nobody else liked the lion. Madonna went along with it.[4]

Ayeroff eventually agreed, and a lion was shipped up from Rome.[5]

The video itself appears to be a fairy tale of the most traditional kind about a woman surrendering herself to a man. It begins with Madonna, a New York hipster, gazing out over the Hudson River. In an instant she is no longer in New York but in Venice, following a lion as it wanders around a Venetian palazzo. "We wanted me to be my modern day, very worldly-wise girl that I am," Madonna explained. "But then we wanted to go back in time and use like an ancient virgin. Me, back and forth."[6]

The contemporary Madonna, in East Village wear — including Boy Toy belt and beads — with her hair styled as a lion's mane and her green eyes made leonine with makeup, sings as she cruises Venice's canals writhing in a gondola. The "ancient" Madonna, all gauzy and pearled, exists inside the palazzo, wearing a wedding dress and representing the virgin of the song. Saving herself for her lover, she strips the furniture, though not herself, of its coverings.

Madonna's lover, meanwhile, exists as a mere suggestion. He wears a lion mask, in *Carnevale* tradition. Otherwise, he is a shadow passing through the room where Madonna sings in her wedding dress until he carries her off, *Beauty and the Beast*–style, presumably toward a romance-novel ravishment.

The video, like the song, is full of unanswered questions. Is he a beast or a gentleman? Is she an independent woman or a virginal bride? Or are they both? And isn't it all just for fun anyway? That was its intention, but the response the video provoked from some viewers was fury.

In the "Like a Virgin" video, Madonna presented her sexual-virginal, bad girl–good girl duality for the first time. That made her a target for the religious right, which had just powered Reagan to a second term. It also made her a target of feminists who were engaged in a raging debate about how much or even whether a woman's sexuality should be expressed publicly.[7] Madonna's work would eventually be pointedly political, but at that early stage she seemed to have merely stumbled into a controversy.

The Madonna who emerged visually out of 1984 had the help of two women who captured her on film. One was Mary Lambert, and the other was Susan Seidelman, who would direct Madonna in her breakout movie, *Desperately Seeking Susan.*

The script was written by Leora Barish, a sax player in the East Village who had moved to California to try her hand at writing. She brought it to her producer friend Sarah Pillsbury, who, with Midge Sanford, had a company, Sanford/Pillsbury Productions. "The only people who liked the script were women and gay men — that was it," Pillsbury said. "And there weren't any of them who could actually say yes or no to a movie getting made."[8] They needed a straight white man to back the project. Orion Pictures' Mike Medavoy did, offering a modest $4.5 million. Sanford and Pillsbury eagerly took it. They already had a director in mind.[9]

Ten years earlier, Susan Seidelman had enrolled in New York University film school. In those days for a woman, she said, the thought of being a film director "was like a fantasy, it wasn't an actual concrete goal."[10] She was inspired to try anyway and to focus on films with strong female leads. "To me it's a natural decision," she said. "I didn't want to work with territory that guys had already mined."[11]

She made her first film, *Smithereens,* about a punk groupie who used street skills to survive in lower Manhattan. In 1982, it was a surprise hit at Cannes. Seidelman was the only woman director at the festival that year in the running for the Palme d'Or, and hers was the only independent US film in competition.[12] After Cannes, she was in demand but for the wrong kinds of movies, which she described as "really dopey cheerleader or sorority scripts." When *Desperately Seeking Susan* landed on her desk, she liked the fact that the writer and producers were women. She also liked the story, because it dealt with the "idea of reinvention, the idea of somebody who comes from outside of New York, coming into New York to be who-ever she wanted to be."[13] Rosanna Arquette, then a major up-and-coming actor, had already signed on to the project. Seidelman agreed to direct.

In 1984, having so many women in front of and behind the camera on a feature film was unheard of (and would continue to be rare for decades). Seidelman saw it as a feminist cultural marker, however stealthy. "It's not coming across like a heavy, feminist, we-have-got-to-make-a-statement-about-women-struggling film. It's much more playful," she said. "The best way to get across a point anyway is with humor and irony."[14]

The film is about a "good-girl" suburban New Jersey housewife named Roberta (Rosanna Arquette) who fantasizes about a "bad-girl" free spirit East Villager named Susan, whose boyfriend is desperately trying to find her through personal ads. Several comic interludes and a bump on the head later, Roberta thinks she *is* Susan. And in a way she is, locked away in the suburbs, looking to get free. Seidelman said the story was about integrating those two aspects of the Roberta character so she could be whole.[15]

Seidelman lived near Madonna in SoHo and had been aware of her from Danceteria and the Paradise Garage. "I knew who she was. What she looked like," she said.[16] "She has an incredible face, almost like vintage movie stars like Garbo and Dietrich. A face you would like to look at blown up fifty feet high and thirty feet wide."[17] Seymour Stein told Seidelman that Madonna was interested in the Susan role. Seidelman agreed to audition her.[18]

Two hundred actors read for the part, and Orion was leaning toward Ellen Barkin to play Susan, but Seidelman wanted to see Madonna's screen test before a final decision was made.[19] If there was any serious hesitation about Madonna, her obvious suitability for the role outweighed it. "She got out of the cab, but she didn't have enough money to pay," Seidelman said. "So here she is meeting a bunch of movie people for a job, and the first thing she does is hit us up for cab fare. It was exactly what Susan would have done!"[20]

Seidelman continued,

Even when I was testing the other actresses—people like Melanie Griffith and Kelly McGillis—I just couldn't get Madonna out of my mind…She seemed more secure about who she was than anyone I'd seen…She was somebody who thought she was special and made *you* feel special…The key to the character of Susan was that she had to be so magnetic that people were irrevocably drawn to her. Madonna has that quality—it leaps out at you.[21]

At the same time, Madonna "was nervous and vulnerable and not at all arrogant—sweet, but intelligent and verbal, with a sense of humor…I just started seeing her as Susan."[22] Sarah Pillsbury did, too. "She just had that kind of sassy, bratty, sexy, Mae West-y thing."[23] Madonna was hired in July for nine and a half weeks of shooting, beginning in September. She would be paid $80,000. It was a nice chunk of cash, but it was still only one-fifth the amount earned by the designated star of the show, Rosanna Arquette.[24]

For Madonna, that didn't matter. The role wasn't about the money; it was about her future. She said at the time that she intended "to have a career as an actress as well as a singer, and I gotta start somewhere. This is a very good first project for me, and so it's important to me…and this is the right time."[25] Besides, she liked the script. It was a modern take on the classic films she loved, "caper comedies Claudette Colbert and Carole Lombard made in the Thirties. They give you a taste of real life, some poignance, and leave you feeling up at the end," she said. "None of that adolescent-fantasy bullshit."[26]

If the film felt authentic in its depiction of downtown, it was because Seidelman knew it well enough to cast real characters from the neighborhood. For crowd scenes on the street or in clubs, she posted handbills around the East Village. For supporting roles, she picked local personalities such as Keith's friend Richard Hell. Rockets Redglare, a former Sid Vicious bodyguard, played a cab driver. Performance artist Ann Magnuson turned up in the film, as did musician John Lurie and a new actor named John Turturro. "The idea of combining Hollywood actors and real people appealed to me," Seidelman said. "The film's about a clash of worlds and I thought the worlds should clash."[27]

Madonna's clothing was also less costume than actual street wear. Originally, she was given clothes for the film by a production designer, but she said neither she nor her character would typically wear those outfits. "They were from vintage shops, like Cyndi Lauper dresses," Madonna said. "I hated it! Stiletto heels and stuff." She created her own look. "Like one outfit will be my shirt, her skirt, my socks, their shoes," she said. "It's a combination."[28]

Madonna's performance in *Desperately Seeking Susan* is regarded as one of her very best. Critics looking for a reason to discredit her acting often say that as Susan, she did nothing more than play herself. Of course, that's nonsense. Even if she *were* the character she played, there are an infinite number of ways she could have done so badly. Seidelman suggested two factors behind Madonna's success in the film. One, because the director was a woman, she and the star had "a more down-to-earth relationship because there isn't the kind of sexual politics and games." She also argued that Madonna could and did act—and act well.

> She was saying scripted lines, she had blocking, she had to do all that stuff and make it seem natural, which is not easy. She could bring a lot of her persona to that role and it was a perfect blend of who she was then and the character she was playing. She had great ideas... One of my favorite little bits in the film is when she dries her arms under the hand dryer in the Port Authority bathroom. She just did that. She just turned the blower and dried her armpits. That was so Susan and so Madonna that it was just perfect.[29]

Though Seidelman said Madonna wasn't nervous, Madonna said otherwise. "I had a few scenes where I was really shittin' bricks," she said. "A few times I was so nervous I opened my mouth and nothing came out... I think I surprised everybody, though, by being one of the calmest people on the set... I think that had to do with the fact that I was in total wonderment: I was gonna soak everything up."[30] She also surprised Seidelman by her rigor. Shooting might last until midnight, with first call around 6:30 a.m. Madonna would get up at 4:00 a.m. to swim one hundred laps at the YMCA health club. She did that every day.[31]

It was part of her ongoing effort at self-improvement, because no matter how beautiful people said she was, she worried about her weight and was conscious of her height. "I come from a boring sort of middle-class lifestyle and I wasn't born with a perfect body," she said.[32] At five feet four, she felt "like a shrimp... Everything about me is average... It's the things inside that make me not average."[33] And so she worked to create a body that reflected that inner strength.

While filming, Seidelman said she needed a song for a club scene shot at Danceteria and asked if Madonna would bring in a tape. She and Steve Bray had just written "Into the Groove" and recorded it as a demo in his apartment with dogs barking and people yelling in the background. Madonna chose that one. She said,

> I wanted to test it out on all the extras... to see if it was a good song... So, I brought it in, and we played it, and we had to do take after take, and pretty

soon everyone was starting to like the song and they were saying, "What's this song, and where's it coming from?". . . I didn't go into this film thinking I'm going to get a hit song out of this, or an MTV video. No way![34]

As filming continued, Seidelman searched for another song for the club scene but couldn't find one better than "Into the Groove." Sarah Pillsbury finally called Freddy DeMann to get permission to use it. He had never heard of it.[35] Warner Bros. was reluctant as well. "They wanted us to use 'Material Girl' or 'Holiday,'" Madonna said. The film's producers insisted on the new song. "We ended up using the original 8-track demo Stephen and I had made."[36]

Erika Belle was there when Steve and Madonna worked on the song. At one point, he was having trouble with the bridge, and Madonna came up with "Live out your fantasy here with me." Erika said, "It just seemed to come out of her. I was awestruck."[37] That bridge was what the film was all about.

In the year between the making of Madonna's first album and her second, her life had changed massively, and her appearance reflected it. Prior to *Like a Virgin,* her biggest reveal was the odd bra strap and her belly button, which sent young men (and journalists) accustomed to *Playboy* or worse into paroxysms, as if they had never seen anything so forbidden. But at the beginning of her *Virgin* period, Madonna became more overtly sexual. "I guess the music I started to write had more of a seductive quality," she said, "and I unconsciously morphed into that. It also had to do with the fact that I was doing more photo shoots. I was being styled and dressed. Before that, I was doing everything myself."[38]

One of the people responsible for Madonna's changed appearance was thirty-year-old Steven Meisel, who photographed her for the *Like a Virgin* album cover and would continue to take pictures of her for decades.[39]

Meisel has been called the best "commercial photographer of our time."[40] The word *commercial,* however, seems misplaced. Yes, his photographs appeared primarily in magazines, but like the work of Warhol, Haring, and Madonna, they were no less works of art because they were widely accessible. Commerce merely provided an opportunity to create and a platform to show.

Meisel was from Madonna's Gog stomping grounds: Flushing Meadows, Queens. But he would have been an alien in the Dan and Ed Gilroy scene.[41] His best friend from Queens was Patti Smith's piano player, Richard Sohl, whose nickname was DNV—for *Death in Venice.* They had been making the gay and punk bar scene together since junior high school.[42]

"Yes, I went to every single club, every single hangout, every single after-hours drug place," Meisel said. "There wasn't one thing that I didn't do; there wasn't one place that I didn't go to."[43]

One former fashion editor said that Meisel and his group were "the coolest of the cool. Threateningly cool. They walked around like every mother's nightmare." Steven's look was black from head to toe, including around his eyes, which under his black sunglasses were outlined in kohl.[44] His bold look and attitude masked his extreme shyness. He rarely spoke; anything he had to say he could say through his pictures. Madonna's image became a powerful means of expression for them both.[45] "Before I worked with Steven," she said of that *Like a Virgin* cover shoot,

> I just showed up in the clothes I was wearing, stood in front of the lights, and got my picture taken. With Steven, a team of people descended on me, started to undress me. Someone grabbed my hair, another grabbed my face, another started helping me try on various bits of clothes, and they all seemed to be speaking a language I didn't understand, the language of Steve Meisel.[46]

In his work with Madonna, Meisel approached her as a Renaissance painter would a model. But unlike those Renaissance forefathers, Meisel treated Madonna as a collaborator. "He just really, really appreciates beauty, and he knows how to photograph a strong female. He's a diva himself," Madonna said.[47]

> He made me feel like I was part of something important. He treated each photo shoot like it was a small film and insisted that we create a character each time we worked, but then would make fun of the archetypes we created. He was the first person to introduce me to the idea of reinvention.[48]

Maripol was hired as Madonna's stylist for the *Like a Virgin* cover shoot, which took place at the St. Regis hotel, in New York. At the start, an art director involved in the project "had this idea, which was to have the Black Sabbath–type virgin. You know, like black lipstick, black this, black that," Maripol said. "And I kept saying to her, 'We should go for the real thing, come on!'" Madonna agreed.[49] On the album's front cover, she appears on a bed in her Maripol-designed wedding dress and Boy Toy belt, not inviting a lover to join her so much as daring him to.[50] In the back cover photo, the deed has been done. It is the morning after, and Madonna sits *déshabillé* on an unmade bed in her slip, not as an ecstatic ex-virgin but as a satisfied woman.

★   ★   ★

Earlier in the year, Madonna, Christopher, and Erika—accompanied by Martin Burgoyne—had been summoned by Jeff Ayeroff to the old Charlie Chaplin Studios in Los Angeles to shoot a video for "Lucky Star." It was basically a re-creation of their old track-date performances and just as bare-bones.[51] "I made 'Lucky Star' for $14,000 with a friend who was a pot grower from Bolinas, California," Ayeroff said, referring to Arthur Pierson, who was tapped to direct. The finished video went into the hopper in the event "Lucky Star" was rereleased as a single.[52]

By August of 1984, before *Desperately Seeking Susan* began filming, Warner was ready, and the label played its hand well. It aired the video on MTV to get phone lines to radio stations fired up with requests, so that when the single was rereleased, it was a hit. It worked. "Lucky Star" became Madonna's first song to breach the top five of the Billboard Hot 100, coming in at number 4.[53]

That phenomenon should have proved to video deniers just how powerful the new medium was, but skeptics remained. Madonna was invited to the fifth annual New Music Seminar, hosted by Haoui Montaug in New York, to advocate for video as a new way to reach audiences.[54] The other participants on the panel with Madonna were Lou Reed, Afrika Bambaataa, George Clinton, John Oates of Hall & Oates, Fred Schneider of the B-52's, and the Godfather of Soul, James Brown.[55]

Seated on the dais among those music veterans, wearing knee-length bicycle shorts and fingerless gloves, she argued, "Kids today worship the television, so I think it's a great way to reach them." She also said a performer was a performer whether or not a camera was pointed in their direction. But John Oates wasn't convinced. Adopting the purist rock line, he said with exasperation that it should be enough to be a musician without having to also be an actor.[56] He would share the stage with Madonna again the following month at the MTV Video Music Awards, when that camera he dismissed as superfluous made Madonna a star.

Chapter 16

New York, 1984

Gee, Madonna was just a waitress at the Lucky Strike a year
ago.[1]

—*Andy Warhol*

ONE WRITER COMPARED Madonna's performance at the MTV Video
Music Awards in September of 1984 to iconic music moments like Elvis
Presley causing jaws to drop in living rooms across America with his "pelvic thrusts" on *The Milton Berle Show* in 1956 and the Beatles' few minutes
on *The Ed Sullivan Show* in February of 1964, which created the template
for the ensuing twenty years of pop-rock music.[2] Another observer called
it "the award-show equivalent of Abraham Lincoln's Gettysburg
Address—the ideal against which all successors would be measured."[3] It
was, in other words, unforgettable.

The stage that night at Radio City Music Hall was filled with stars who
had been cajoled into helping launch the show. It was MTV's first awards
event, and if it was successful, MTV executives thought it could be the
fledgling music video industry's very own annual Oscar-Grammy ceremony. Bette Midler and Dan Aykroyd had agreed to host. To perform during the show, MTV lined up Rod Stewart (the dean of music videos simply
because he made so many of them), ZZ Top, Hall & Oates, Tina Turner,
Ray Parker Jr., Huey Lewis and the News, and the new gal, Madonna.[4]

Rather than one of the tracks from her first album, Madonna wanted to
sing the still unreleased single "Like a Virgin." Her first idea was to perform with a Bengal tiger (she had apparently soured on lions). When that
was a no go for obvious reasons, she suggested emerging from a wedding
cake, as she had at the Fiorucci party, when she tumbled out of a cake singing "Everybody."[5] The VMAs' producers agreed.

Before the show, Madonna and Christopher went to Maripol's, where
Madonna dressed in the wedding attire Maripol had designed for her album
cover. Strangely, Christopher said, they weren't alone. Cher sat in a corner
watching like a bridesmaid as Madonna readied for her big night.[6] Maripol
said that Madonna had "stage fright" because the hall would be packed with
artists and industry types. She believed "it was either break or make."[7]

★   ★   ★

From a distance, Madonna looked appropriately bridal atop the cake, singing a song that no one except the people who were at the Paradise Garage
earlier that year had ever heard. It was a song about a virgin, sung by a
woman wearing a bustier-and-tulle wedding dress and a belt that identified her as a Boy Toy. As she made her way down the cake, the unimagi-
nable became undeniable as she began to shed her bridal wear: first shoes,
then veil; after which she loosened her hair, boudoir-style. Madonna likes
to say that what happened next, when she famously rolled around the
stage, skirt up, panties and garters exposed for all the world to see, was her
attempt to retrieve a lost shoe.[8]

   That was the official story, which may be how she remembered it, or it
may have been a bit of damage control, because Madonna's handlers
believed she had gone too far. Such behavior, which would have been perfectly acceptable, even mild, at Danceteria or the Garage or Studio 54, was
considered beyond outrageous at the MTV Video Music Awards show.
The lost shoe story provided handy cover. But that's not what happened.

   Madonna went to the floor twice. The first time it was to retrieve the
two shoes she had kicked off to facilitate her descent down the cake. The
second time it was apparently for the hell of it—gyrating, crawling, rolling lustily on the floor, simulating masturbation while sullying that ultimate symbol of purity, a white wedding dress—with both shoes firmly on
her feet as she did so. That's when the audience was treated to a full view of
Madonna's derriere.

   Christopher watched from the Radio City green room, thinking of his
father and grandmother, who, like millions of other TV viewers, would
see the show at home and be stunned by what appeared to be the on-air
despoliation of a bride—by *herself*![9]

   In mocking the social covenant that traditionally codified a woman's
status as lesser, she declared liberation not in the language of feminist politics but in the language of sex. Madonna in her wedding attire claimed
that power as her own. Just the year before, *Time* magazine declared that
the sexual revolution was over.[10] Madonna showed that for women of her
generation, it hadn't even begun.

   In the full unpublished transcript of an interview Edwin Miller conducted with Madonna for *Seventeen* magazine not long after the VMA
show, she described what her actual thinking may have been going into
that night, and it was an interesting take on the notion that the promise of
marriage and the reality of marriage are two very different things. She said
she imagined herself on top of the cake "sitting on top of the world," but
she "ended on the ground, broken."[11]

   Whatever her plan had been, Madonna was pilloried in the press and by some of the other artists in the hall. Annie Lennox called her performance "very, *very* whorish...It was like she was fucking the music industry. It might have been parody on her part, but I thought it was very low."[12] Madonna said that when she found Freddy DeMann afterward, he was "white as a ghost. And he looked at me and said, 'Do you know what you just did?'...'Your career is over.'...I was just starting out and I was like, 'Oh, OK.'...I wasn't that apologetic. I was just like, 'Well, fuck it, I made a mistake.'"[13]

The VMAs controversy was Madonna's introduction to the vast cultural gulf between the downtown New York world she inhabited and the mainstream world she was about to enter. Madonna realized she had left her "little gay cocoon...From the dance world to the music world, my social strata was mostly gay men. That's who my audience was, that's who I hung out with, that's who inspired me...I left that world and went into the mainstream. Suddenly there was judgment."[14]

Cyndi Lauper, who was in the audience and was familiar with both worlds, recognized Madonna's segment for what it was. "I loved that — it was performance art," she said.[15] Lauper was right. Madonna was not merely a pop singer; she was also part of a rich tradition of creative women who used everything they had in their art, who simply *were* their art.[16] Madonna's performance about women, marriage, and sexuality arose out of that milieu. But most people didn't get it.

The VMAs would be the first of many episodes in Madonna's career in which she expressed herself using the methods common in the New York art world only to suffer the wrath of public opinion. The verdict time and again would be that she had gone too far, that her career was over. Time and again, the jury was wrong. Madonna's actions earned her detractors, to be sure, but they also earned her loyal fans and increased attention.

Maripol, who had stood behind a curtain onstage watching Madonna, said,

> I knew that day she had made it. Every journalist was rushing, running, going, "Oh my God, who is this girl with the white outfit rolling and crawling on the floor, with crosses in her ears, and her name is Madonna?"[17]
>
> When we left, the kids were waiting for Madonna in the street, cheering. As we went into the limo, I was watching her. She was looking at all the kids, and she was wondering why she was *here*. She wanted to be *there,* with them, in the street, yelling at herself. And I looked at her face, and it was pure innocence and pure joy.[18]

A young French fashion designer in the audience was excited by the performance, too. Jean Paul Gaultier said he was surrounded by "mostly businesspeople, who were horrified. There were just a few young fans—and me, who absolutely loved it. That is when I realized that she couldn't care less what others thought of her, and I also saw how powerful she was."[19]

Nile Rodgers also knew Madonna had arrived. He watched her performance while sitting with Mick Jagger and another friend in a recording-studio lounge, taking a break from making Jagger's first solo album. The friend dismissed Madonna as more style than substance. But Nile told him, "I wish I could bottle what she's got and give you a drink of that shit. Then I could produce your ass and we'd both have a lot more money."[20]

Madonna was at the VMAs because she was nominated for Best New Artist in a Video for "Borderline." She lost to Annie Lennox and the Eurythmics, but she stole the show.[21] Looking back from a distance of thirty years, MTV's Jocelyn Vena said, "That three minutes in 1984 was the point when Madonna became a superstar."[22] It was also when MTV's VMAs became "must-be TV." Bob Pittman, one of MTV's founders, said, "The first year, it was everything we could do to get talent to come to the event and fill the seats. By the *second* year, every act wanted to be on the bill."[23]

Like a Virgin was finally released on November 12, 1984, followed by the video for the title track the day after. The reviews were generally scathing. The *Los Angeles Times* said Madonna sounded like a "sheep in pain." In the UK, *NME* showed its disdain, saying she "isn't a musician and doesn't wish to be a singer...she's just earning her way as a saleswoman." What was she selling? "Undiluted *Cosmo* consumerism."[24] In *Rolling Stone,* Kurt Loder, who would in a later incarnation at MTV court Madonna assiduously, if not slavishly, dismissed her as an "*Interview* magazine wet dream of what's hip and happening in glittery Manhattan.

> Madonna's bare-bellied, fondle-my-bra image is strictly bimbo city, and of course it sells...[It] seems custom-designed to gag feminists of both sexes, as well as anyone with even a vestigial interest in rock, funk, soul, you name it. Take away the ravaged-tart trappings and there's nothing else to talk about.[25]

Interestingly, all those critics were men whose stinging remarks reflected the broad assumption that any music that appealed to an audience of girls and young women was inherently valueless. By contrast, Debby Bull, writing in *Rolling Stone* soon after Loder's piece, gave Madonna's album three and a half out of four stars, and called the song "Like a Virgin" "terrific."[26] Fans thought so, too.

"Like a Virgin" shot to number 1 in Australia, Canada, and the United

States (and stayed there for six weeks). The album, likewise, hit number 1 in the United States, and by February would go triple platinum — more than three million albums sold.[27]

Warner executives watched those figures mount to six million that year with excitement and regret. During their initial negotiations with Nile Rodgers, they had offered him a 3 percent royalty on the album, which he rejected. He wanted 2 percent "on the first two million copies and 6 percent retroactive after that." Stein said Warner executives were dumbfounded. Madonna's first album had only sold three hundred thousand copies, and Rodgers was betting his paycheck on millions. Warner agreed to the deal.[28]

Now, seeing that Rodgers had outsmarted them, Stein said Warner executives were so angry that they wanted Madonna to pay Nile's percentage, so she enlisted entertainment lawyer Alan Grubman to defend her. "He was a heavyweight Brooklyn Jew who delivered every legal slam in filthy language and personal insults," Seymour said. Grubman went to California to meet with the Warner chairman, Mo Ostin, who tried to "sweet talk" Grubman. "Bullshit!" Grubman shouted. "The artists did their jobs. *You* fucked up."[29]

"Any time Mo opened his mouth," Seymour said, "it was *bam!*"

When Mo could physically take it no more...Everyone knew the score. From here on in, Warner was going to accept pretty much whatever Madonna wanted. She was in charge now...all future Madonna negotiations would be conducted like a special convening of the U.N. Security Council.[30]

Said Seymour, "That stone-broke little blonde who'd come bouncing into all our offices a year before now had the world's biggest record corporation by the walnuts."[31]

From the distance of years, having watched Madonna's career, the music industry recognized the cultural importance of what one critic had called a "tolerable bit of fluff." Howard Johnson, writing in *Q,* said that with *Like a Virgin,* the "concepts of Madonna the Phenomena, Madonna the Superstar, and Madonna the cultural icon were born."[32]

Danny Weizmann, in *LA Weekly,* also writing with hindsight, pointed out that when *Like a Virgin* was released, the biggest-selling female artists (aside from Cyndi Lauper) were Black — Tina Turner, Sade, and Chaka Khan. Madonna's album was the

first pure entertainment record in several moons written and recorded by a white girl. It was also the first white girl's record to do the black drum-machine dance right. Every song on this album was a radio hit, and even the kids who made fun of her made fun of her a lot. She was on their minds.

It's hard to imagine how insane this record sounded...But back in 1984 the lusty positivity of songs like "Dress You Up" was so forward it was almost embarrassing. From that embarrassment a whole generation of girls and boys found a way to be.[33]

With the album's success, Madonna became part of a pop trinity. In 1984, for more than eight months, she, Prince, and Michael Jackson topped the Billboard charts with *Like a Virgin, Purple Rain,* and *Thriller* respectively. Those three artists, all born in 1958, all from that vast stretch of America between the coasts, would rescue the music business, rechart its future, and help rewrite the book on race and gender.

In November, Madonna made the cover of *Rolling Stone,* but the piece was a "hatchet job." In "Madonna Goes All the Way," Christopher Connelly dismissed her as a video entertainer who relied on sex rather than musical ability.[34] He also introduced the idea that Madonna used boyfriends to advance her career. He asked Dan Gilroy and Steve Bray to confirm his hunch. Both said it wasn't true. But once posed, the question became the answer, and it was used for decades by people looking to belittle Madonna's work and accomplishments.[35]

Neither Madonna nor her publicist, Liz Rosenberg, feared controversy. Said Liz, "She'd rather have that than apathy."[36] But for the record, and after numerous stories repeated Connelly's charge that she "used" men, Madonna told music writer Laura Fissinger, "If anybody wants to know, I never fucked anyone to get anywhere. Never."[37] Seymour Stein knew that to be a fact. Years later he wrote,

> I still believe to this day that she would have become a star without any of [the men around her]...she was more naturally powerful than any of us...If there is a trail of whimpering, wounded men along her path to the top, it is only because various guys tried to hold on to her, but as they'd all learn, she didn't *need* any of them.[38]

The VMAs performance, Madonna's second album, and the *Rolling Stone* cover all appeared during the nine-and-a-half-week *Desperately Seeking Susan* shoot. Suddenly, mobs of Madonna fans turned up, asking, "'Is this the Madonna movie?'" Seidelman said no one involved in the film was prepared for that onslaught, not Madonna and certainly not Rosanna Arquette, whose star turn was "being eclipsed by a novice."[39]

Madonna had learned a lot—about making records, about video, about film, about performing, about the business, and about the demands of celebrity. Before that year, she could say what she wanted, to whomever she pleased, without worrying that it would come back to haunt her. She was a civilian. But by the end of 1984, that was no longer the case.[40]

One person who helped her as she made her transition from club singer to international superstar and from New York to LA was photographer Herb Ritts. Madonna would come to regard him as a "big brother...a very lovable one," though when she met him, she dismissed him as a "real geek."[41]

They met when Herb was hired to shoot an ad for *Desperately Seeking Susan*. "She arrived early and marched into the studio with all her 'boy toy' belts and black lace, very definite," he recalled. "She said, 'I've seen all your work in *Lei* magazine. You're good.' Just like that. She knew who I was, though I'd only been shooting for a couple of years."[42]

Tatler fashion editor Michael Roberts remembered that day slightly differently. He said Herb was hired by *Tatler* to photograph Rosanna Arquette for a *Desperately Seeking Susan* article. During the shoot, Herb told Roberts, "Oh, there's this other girl in the next room. She's gonna be a star—she's the singer in this film." Roberts, who was also acting as the stylist, told Herb he didn't have time to style her because his focus was Arquette. Herb insisted. "She's really desperate for you to put something on her so she can have her picture taken too."[43]

All that Roberts had on hand were "a lot of colorful boxer shorts" for a menswear shoot. "So I went into Madonna's little dressing room and put the boxer shorts on her head, and she was so shocked and slightly affronted. But Herb got a picture...Somehow, they still looked good."[44] *They* didn't look good; she did. Through Herb's lens, Madonna looked fantastic even with the equivalent of a dunce cap on her head.

That was the start of her work with a man her brother Christopher called one of the most important collaborators of her career. The photographic face of Madonna, especially through the 1980s, was largely the result of Herb Ritts's camera, magazine cover after magazine cover, album after album. Ritts would later say that through the course of his career, Madonna was his most frequent subject.[45] He would also be one of her closest and most trusted friends.

Like Martin Burgoyne, Ritts was gentle, fun, generous, mischievous, always on, always up, and innocent.[46] Innocent, however, didn't mean cloistered. Herb's homes in California, whether a run-down beach house in Malibu or a house in Hillside, were magnets for a wide and wild circle of friends. His parties at the beach were open to anyone who wandered in ready to take acid, dance naked, and generally celebrate life on the beautiful side. His Hillside place was a hangout for LA's young gay scene.[47] His social life was, in other words, a sunnier version of Madonna's in New York.

But more important, Herb's artistic sensibilities were completely aligned with Madonna's. Both were artists who worked in the commercial (in Madonna's case pop) realm.[48] Both were pragmatists in business. Both used their art to celebrate beauty, love, and sexuality.[49]

The timing of Herb and Madonna's first meeting could not have been better. He would absorb her into his life as she entered the alien landscape of Hollywood, where nothing seemed real and everything and everyone was for sale. "He took me under his wing, he took me to all the best parties, he introduced me to all the right people, and even most of the wrong people," she said. It would be Herb Ritts who would photograph the next chapter of Madonna's life. Madonna called it being "Herbified."[50]

PART THREE

LOS ANGELES

1985–1991

Chapter 17

Los Angeles, 1985

Movie Mogul: She's fantastic. I knew she'd be a star.
George: She could be. She could be great. She could be a major star.
Movie Mogul: She is a star, George.
George: The biggest star in the universe, right now as we speak.[1]

—*"Material Girl" video*

ON NEW YEAR'S Day in 1985, Warner Bros. approved Madonna's idea for her "Material Girl" video. She wanted to re-create Marilyn Monroe's "Diamonds Are a Girl's Best Friend" performance in the 1953 film *Gentlemen Prefer Blondes.* It would be a tribute to Marilyn, a commentary on the materialism of the Reagan era, and the launch of Madonna's Hollywood period. She had shot videos and conducted business in LA, but that January her world would largely rebase there. What better and more playful way to announce her arrival than in the glamorous guise of the ultimate movie star icon?[2]

Mary Lambert, once again in the director's chair, wrote the script, in which twenty men in tuxedos try to woo Madonna with expensive gifts and money. Singing "Material Girl" and dancing among them, she refuses their blandishments while accepting their lavish trinkets. Meanwhile, a movie mogul played by Keith Carradine watches the film playback and is mesmerized by Madonna. Unlike the suitors in tuxes, he is smart enough to realize that it isn't things she wants but love. In the final scene he wins her heart with a bouquet of daisies and an old pickup truck. The video is a Hollywood comedy-musical of the old-school tradition, a pink-and-rhinestone tribute to midcentury glamour.

Madonna was terrific in it. Having finished *Desperately Seeking Susan,* she was comfortable with the camera and her role as comic actor. She was once again the good girl–bad girl—in this case the starlet looking for real love off the set while playing the manipulative materialist onstage.[3] "Madonna's always had a dual personality," Mary said. "A lot of her early videos... are largely about her straddling two different worlds."[4]

At various points in the video, Carradine's movie mogul lurks around the set in a leather jacket, discreetly eyeing his inamorata. In a case of life imitating art, one day during filming another leather-jacketed young man lurked in the shadows watching Ms. Ciccone. He was twenty-four and, after six films, considered by some to be the most talented actor of his generation. He was also one of the most difficult.[5] His name was Sean Penn, and he would be the love of Madonna's life.

Penn was born with righteous discontent and a fighter's spirit, in part because his family narrative was built on an injustice.

Sean's father, Leo, came from a family of Russian and Lithuanian Jewish immigrants who made their way by Greyhound bus from the East Coast to California to work in the orange groves. After the Depression, they scraped together the money to open a bakery in East LA. Leo Penn wanted to be an actor and had made inroads into the industry, but with the start of World War II, military duty beckoned. He enlisted and survived what a friend called "unbelievable shit" flying missions as a tail gunner over Germany.[6]

Leo returned to the States with a medal and a Paramount contract in hand and began living an actor's life, starting at the bottom and dreaming his way to the top. But just as he began shooting a career-making film, starring opposite Gregory Peck in *The Gunfighter,* he learned that he was blacklisted. Like so many others before the war, he had attended Communist Party meetings and performed at the Actors' Laboratory Theatre, which the FBI in its zeal considered a communist cell.[7]

By 1957, with the "Red" witch hunt over, Leo could work again, but his film acting career was finished. Instead, he wrote scripts, directed, and acted on TV and in theater. It was at the Circle in the Square, in New York, while playing the lead in *The Iceman Cometh,* that he met the love of *his* life. She was his costar, Eileen Ryan. Born Eileen Annucci, she was half Irish, half Italian, and 100 percent free-spirited and outspoken.[8] They married, returned to California, and had three sons: Michael, Sean, and Christopher.[9]

The Penns were an exceedingly close-knit family, forming a protective and loving ecosystem within a potentially hostile environment. Sean as an adult retained that stance, that defensive crouch, ready to do battle. Director Art Wolff said that Leo's blacklisting had a "real effect" on Sean. It was "part of why Sean has a jones about Hollywood...because of the way his father was treated, and then their pretending it never happened."[10]

With Leo Penn's earnings, the family moved to not-yet-tony Malibu in 1969, into a fixer-upper near the beach, where, Sean said, his life was "*Huckleberry Finn* with a surfboard."[11] High school revolved around surfing, tennis, politics, and law. Eileen said Sean read *Black's Law Dictionary* into the night and dreamed of being a lawyer. Instead, by the end of high school, he decided to be an actor. For two years, he studied Method acting with Peggy Feury at the Loft Studio. For money he worked on loading docks and in restaurants, parked cars, and washed dishes.[12]

When he was nineteen, Sean received his Screen Actors Guild card and left LA for New York to work in theater. Not long afterward, in November of 1980, Art Wolff picked him for a part in a play called *Heartland*. It was through that role that he was chosen for the film *Taps,* an intense drama opposite two other young actors, Timothy Hutton and Tom Cruise.[13]

Sean should have been happy. Instead, he said, he felt suicidal. He didn't think his style of acting belonged in movies, and he fought with the *Taps* director, Harold Becker. "There is an anger in Sean, and a pain in him, and clearly they come from the same well-springs that feed his talent," Becker said.[14] After *Taps,* Sean was offered a project with a director, a script, and a character that excited him. The film was *Fast Times at Ridgemont High;* the director was a twenty-eight-year-old NYU graduate named Amy Heckerling; the script was by *Rolling Stone* writer Cameron Crowe; and the character, Jeff Spicoli, was a stoner surfer.[15]

Sean became Spicoli. He discovered that if he could inhabit the character's look—the dress, the way he moved and spoke—he could become the character emotionally. He had to step into the character's body to discover the character's mind. He called it finding "the music of the character."

The film's release, in August of 1982, made Spicoli a star.[16] The image was so strong and the character so popular that Sean risked being typecast unless he broke that mold, which he did in his next picture, *Bad Boys*. He went from a laid-back surfer dude to a violent reform-school inmate. The director, Richard Rosenthal, said, "Sean was the only actor of his generation who can really become a different person for each acting job."[17]

Though only twenty-two, Sean believed he was ready for marriage. He was looking for his Eileen Annucci, a partner in art and life, an anchor to reality as he surrendered himself to his various roles, a person to help calm his rage. On the set of *Fast Times at Ridgemont High* he met Bruce Springsteen's sister Pamela, who had a small role in the film. In Chicago, on the set of *Bad Boys,* he proposed to her.[18]

Sean's career, meanwhile, bounced between the stage and the movies. And with each production, his reputation as a difficult actor who had no interest in playing the Hollywood game grew. He believed a *Rolling Stone* cover story invaded his privacy by reporting on his relationship with Pam Springsteen. The relationship ended soon afterward.[19] He refused to do a cover story with *People* because it wanted to feature him and his new girlfriend, Elizabeth McGovern.[20] They broke up, too. (She said she "needed a quieter life.")[21]

"Nursing that heartache," as he called it, Sean began an odyssey through

Europe alongside Harry Dean Stanton, Joe Pesci, and Robert De Niro.[22] It was on his return to Los Angeles from that trip that he met James Foley. The Brooklyn-born former film student had directed a romantic drama called *Reckless,* which the scriptwriter considered so bad that he cried after the first screening and later disowned it.[23]

Sean called Foley to say that he hadn't liked the film, either, but he saw something in the director's work that he *did* like. He asked Foley to look at a script he'd been attached to since 1983 called *At Close Range.* "It was in that period of *At Close Range* pre-production and Sean's sleeping on my couch that his next relationship happened," Foley said.[24]

When people working on the "Material Girl" video learned that Sean was coming over to watch them shoot, producer Sharon Oreck said, "The set was ablaze with rumors that this perfect couple would fall in love, get married, and have ten celebrity children."[25] Though Sean and Madonna had never met, he was already intrigued by her.

Sean's assistant, Meegan Ochs, who ferried him around town because his car wasn't working, had a cassette of Madonna's *Like a Virgin* album and played it as Sean mused aloud, " 'So who do *you* think I should marry?' Finally, I said, 'Well, I think you should marry Madonna.' He said, 'Who?' I said, 'The singer we're listening to . . .' So the joke became that we would get in the car and want to put some music on, and Sean would say, 'OK, play my wife.' "[26]

Meegan, meanwhile, was hired to work on Madonna's "Material Girl" shoot. She called Sean and said, "Guess what? I'm working on your wife's video."[27] Not long afterward, Sean and Foley were watching MTV, and the "Like a Virgin" video came on. Foley lived nearby so they decided to go to the shoot and "check out this chick."[28]

During rehearsals, the video's producer told Madonna through a walkie-talkie that "Sean Penn wants to come visit the set." She responded loudly enough for everyone on the soundstage to hear, "Only if he'll go out with me afterwards!" Meegan said, "So then, Sean and Jamie Foley showed up and basically spent the entire day playing with me, carrying me around piggyback—not a word to Madonna, nothing."[29]

But Madonna had spotted him.

> I was standing up at the top of these steps, waiting—they were doing some lighting—and I looked down and noticed this guy in a leather jacket and sunglasses kind of standing in the corner, looking at me. And I realized it was Sean Penn, and I immediately had this fantasy that we were going to meet and fall in love and get married.[30]

The shoot continued for hours, and still Sean was there.

> So I went outside to talk to him... There were people everywhere, so it was
> hard for us to have this conversation, but we were just kind of throwing
> questions at each other and being really provocative. I had given flowers to
> everybody in the cast and crew of the video, all the guys, and I had one left.
> So when Sean was leaving, I said, "Wait, I have something for you." And I
> ran upstairs and I got this rose for him.[31]

"Afterward," Sean said, "I was over at a friend's house, and he had a
book of quotations. He picked it up and turned to a random page and read
the following: 'She had the innocence of a child and the wit of a man.' I
looked at my friend, and he just said, 'Go get her.' "[32]

But Sean had to wait. Madonna left LA for Hawaii and her first solo
photo shoot with Herb Ritts.[33]

The "Material Girl" video was released in early February. Madonna
instantly became, and for some people would remain, a particularly shameless new Marilyn. Debbie Harry, who had also adopted a Marilyn look in
tribute to Monroe, called it "girl drag" and considered it an "act of transgression."[34] But few in the mainstream press got the joke or the cultural
commentary in Madonna's video. The headlines accompanying its
release implied that just when you thought Madonna couldn't get more
outrageous, the virgin-whore had revealed herself to be a brazen gold
digger.

Female fans largely understood the video as parody and the intention as
fun, but the press either did not or chose not to, because bad girls sold. The
boys occupying the media management chairs also missed the less-than-
subtle irony in "Material Girl." In their minds, Madonna had closed the
door on a dreary decade of feminism and opened an exciting new one in
which women could again be sex objects and dopey eye candy.

As a result, and much to her annoyance, Madonna was labeled the Material Girl.[35] The image appeared just as the world awakened to Madonna
and before she had a chance to properly introduce herself. And that self
was interested in neither money nor things. Madonna said around that time,

> I know my manager sometimes looks at me with dismay when he tells me
> I've sold six million records or sold out in seventeen minutes and I just say
> "OK." I'm glad that's not what interests me... I never had money until now,
> and I never felt the lack of it.[36] I always said I wanted to be famous. I never
> said I wanted to be rich.[37]

Rich might have been the easier path. That year, with the image of her dancing through a sea of tuxedos flickering across millions of television sets, fame came barreling down on her like an avalanche, and it was not at all what she had imagined.

Jellybean returned to New York, and Madonna stayed in Los Angeles. Their year-and-a-half-long relationship was ending.[38] "We were going to be married along the way," he said, "but there was no way, when you really think about it."[39] Without mentioning him by name, Madonna said in the inaugural issue of *Spin* that spring that her relationships always deteriorated because her boyfriends complained that she didn't spend enough time with them. "I disagree," she said. "I have a lot of shit to do right now...But I always say it's the quality of time and not the quantity."[40]

As word of the breakup spread, the press scoured the landscape for a new man in Madonna's life. As if on cue, Prince appeared on the horizon. After he released five albums as a relative cult figure to a loyal fan base heavily invested in funky-ass R&B, his sixth album, *Purple Rain,* heralded his breakout moment. His tour brought him to Los Angeles for six sold-out nights at the Forum.

On the night of his third concert, Prince sent a limo to collect Madonna. They had met the month before at the American Music Awards, where he won three top prizes for *Purple Rain*. Madonna presented one of them. The pairing was probably the work of the Warner Bros. publicity department. The two had helped the company's annual profits rise 51 percent the previous year. Madonna had started 1985 at number 1 with her *Like a Virgin* album, which had already sold more than three million copies. Prince's *Purple Rain,* at nine million copies, was the top-selling album of 1984.[41]

Their appearance together at the AMAs immediately sparked rumors of a possible romance. But from Madonna's perspective, any relationship she might have with Prince would be based on art, admiration, and business. The momentum was building for her own concert tour. Warner wanted to ride her album's popularity into midsize halls nationwide, and she had something to learn from Prince's tour as she planned her own.

From her earliest outings as "Madonna," she hadn't wanted to simply stand still and sing. She wanted to put on a show. Initially, that amounted to a few choreographed dance steps and some dramatic lighting. Now she needed razzle-dazzle.

Prince's Forum concert showed her what that looked like, from the fire-fly lighting to the showstopping video images to his dialogue with God, which he conducted in semidarkness from a bathtub. The stage itself was essential to the performance. Like Bowie's in Detroit, Prince's set was constructed for a theatrical production, with staircases and platforms.[42]

Near the end of the show, Madonna appeared onstage to join Prince and Bruce Springsteen for a concert finale of "Purple Rain."[43] But it was the party afterward that gave photographers what they came for—snaps of what one music tabloid called "the Queen and King of Rock." The article announced an imminent "royal wedding" and the birth of Prince and Madonna's child.[44]

The crazy kitsch coverage was great publicity for Warner Bros., but Prince may have taken it seriously. Five days after the Forum concert, Madonna and Prince had a post-Grammy dinner at a Japanese restaurant in the Hollywood Hills.[45]

Prince rented out the entire place for the duration of their three-hour meal, during which, with infinite delicacy and otherworldly reserve, he didn't eat and barely spoke.[46] "He was just sipping tea, very daintily," she said. "I was stuffing food down my face and I was like, 'Aren't you going to eat?'" He whispered, "No." "And I thought, 'Oh my God! I have this theory about people who don't eat. They annoy the fuck out of me.'"[47] To his mind it must have been a successful evening, because at a club afterward he asked Madonna to be his "girl." She didn't respond immediately. Writer J. Randy Taraborrelli said she was "waiting for the punchline" of what she assumed was a joke. When it was not forthcoming, she broke the silence by saying, "Hmmm...now *that's* food for thought, isn't it?"[48]

Madonna's actual romance had, remarkably, evaded the radar of the tabloid press. In early February, Sean Penn invited some people to Warren Beatty's place to watch a friend's movie and brought Madonna.[49] (She called the night "auspicious" because she met both Beatty and Sandra Bernhard—two people who would play a role in the end of her relationship with Sean—on that first date with him.)[50]

Not long after the Beatty party, Sean took Madonna to the Westwood cemetery to visit Marilyn Monroe's grave. A rose was there, which Madonna said had been left by Joe DiMaggio. "He really loved her," she added.[51] And Sean *really* loved Madonna. Foley said she became the center of Sean's life.[52] Penn's childhood friend Charlie Sheen agreed. "Sean's always been misunderstood. And probably most about how much he adores Madonna."[53] For her part, Madonna said, "I was crazy about him from the beginning...I felt he was my family already."[54]

Soon the tabloids picked up the scent. Madonna and Sean Penn were right out of the golden era of Hollywood, when high-wattage celebrities dated, married, and usually divorced—all in front of the camera. Marilyn Monroe and Joe DiMaggio. Elizabeth Taylor and Richard Burton. Singer

Eddie Fisher and seemingly every female star in Hollywood. Those stories made for huge sales at supermarket checkouts because they were real-life soap operas with highs and lows, heroes and villains. Sean was immediately cast as a villain.

One of the first Madonna-Sean stories to hit the tabs involved a hole Sean punched in a wall, supposedly during a fight over Prince.[55] The reconciliation story came soon afterward. In late March, *Rolling Stone* ran a note saying, "Madonna and new beau Sean Penn were declared an item when spied smooching in the corner of a party in Manhattan for comedienne Whoopi Goldberg."[56]

Sean began introducing Madonna to his world. She met his parents and brothers, his actor and writer friends, the eccentric characters he knew on the periphery of the entertainment world, even the musicians he'd come to know. "He brought Madonna to see us," said U2's Bono. "She was a cute cookie at that time. I don't think people realized she was as smart as she is. I'm not sure *I* did. But he spotted it from afar; and unless he's keeping that kind of company, he's gonna get bored."[57]

Sean satisfied her needs, too.

Martin Burgoyne, who had been on the set of the "Material Girl" video and watched the romance develop from the start, said Madonna's "other relationships weren't right because they weren't fifty-fifty. This one is. Neither one of them is in control; she can learn from him, and he can learn from her."[58]

Geography proved to be a problem as they embarked on projects in separate places. But more disruptive still was the emotional dislocation that would be a hallmark of their relationship as the work they pursued put them on entirely different trajectories. In 1985, Madonna was about to begin a joyous romp—her first concert tour—while Sean had committed to *At Close Range* with James Foley. Set in the backwoods of Tennessee, the black-as-pitch script was based on a true story and had Sean playing a confused redneck whose idea of conflict resolution was more violence.

At the start of their romance, Madonna and Sean thought they could surmount any obstacle, but the people closest to them weren't as sure. Madonna's brother Christopher said he understood her attraction to Sean. "He is a dead ringer for our father as a young man, is middle-class like Madonna but with a street-kid persona and presents himself as a bad boy and is a rebel—just like our brothers." Christopher called that a "recipe for disaster."[59] Meegan Ochs saw disaster, too, from Sean's perspective. "She was someone running at the limelight and he was running away from it. Oh my God, was that a conflict."[60]

★   ★   ★

Desperately Seeking Susan premiered on March 29, 1985, and Madonna the pop star became Madonna the movie star. There had been a moment when it wasn't at all clear that the film would succeed. Test screenings were inconclusive, and according to the *Boston Globe,* "the word was out among the exhibitors that *Desperately Seeking Susan* was a loser." Some local theaters skipped trade screenings and didn't plan to show the film at all.[61]

Then the movie's "Into the Groove" scene at Danceteria found its way to MTV. Sarah Pillsbury said, "It was so popular that DJs were playing 'Into the Groove' on the radio by recording it off of MTV."[62] The song went to number 1. That, coupled with great reviews from New York critics and word of mouth from viewers, saved *Susan.*[63] Opening initially on fewer than three hundred screens, in less than two weeks it was on seven hundred. It earned back its $4.5 million budget and then some in its first three days.[64]

For the film's US premiere, in Los Angeles, Madonna arrived in a white faux fur stole, cross earrings and necklace, a white bustier dress, and white elbow-length lace gloves. She was ecstatic. "I really felt like a little girl," she said. "All the cameras, the flashes, the crowd that applauded, it was just great."[65] After the premiere, outside the theater, she was still beaming— and carrying a jumbo-size bucket of popcorn as if she were a mere spectator and not the focus of the red-carpet attention.

The reviews, overall, were effusive. *Variety* recognized the film as a breakthrough:

> The whole picture reflects the fact that none of the producers, director, or writer is named Joe or Sam...Susan is totally free, as few movie female characters have ever been.[66]

Pauline Kael, in *The New Yorker,* said that Madonna "moves regally, an indolent, trampy goddess...She has dumbfounding aplomb."[67] The film even had a great reception at Cannes, where it showed out of competition on the festival's last night. Sarah Pillsbury recalled so much prescreening buzz that festivalgoers fought over tickets. "When we walked out [afterward] we were mobbed," she said.[68]

More important, audiences loved it. Madonna's Susan was one of the rare women on-screen whose destiny did not depend on a man and whose freedom did not come at a cost.[69] She was smart, tough, self-confident, gorgeous, and fun. She was for girls and young women what James Dean and Brando had been for boys and young men trapped in a social straitjacket in the 1950s.

But that was only one of many projects to hit the jackpot for Madonna that spring. She had six songs, five videos, and two films— *Vision Quest* had been released in February—in circulation.[70] Warner Bros. Records' euphoric head of marketing called it "almost unprecedented."[71] Madonna was everywhere. Magazines, TV, movies, posters, radio, record stores, shopping malls.[72] It was total-surround Madonna.

Freddy DeMann worried that she was overexposed. She was known by some in the industry as "McDonna...Over 1 million served." And while her albums had sold in the millions, she was compared unfavorably to Cyndi Lauper, whom one industry executive called an "artist," implying that Madonna was not. A *Billboard* magazine editor named Paul Grein famously predicted, "Cyndi Lauper will be around for a long time. Madonna will be out of the business in six months."[73]

In the glare of a thousand klieg lights, and as the object of love and loathing, Madonna brushed off the controversy, as she would do for decades, and began putting together a cast and crew for her first tour.

Chapter 18

Los Angeles, Seattle, Detroit, New York, 1985

Yes, Madonna, you have become an adjective. Of all the Madonna's of history, you are the Madonnaist.[1]
— *Barry Walters*

NOW THAT WARNER Bros. was banking on Madonna, the label wanted artists and crew with tour experience to support her. Madonna's New York dancers — Erika, Bags, and Christopher — would not join her onstage for her first major outing. Neither would the band members she had worked with in New York. Even Maripol was cut. Madonna would need a new designer-stylist. Forced to start nearly from scratch, she set up headquarters in LA, with Christopher as her assistant, and began assembling a cast of dancers, musicians, designers, choreographers, and support staff. It would be the first of twelve tours she would organize over the next thirty-five years.

For the Virgin tour, Madonna plucked talent from the shows of her compatriots Prince and Michael Jackson. Madonna hired Prince's Purple Rain tour set designer, Ian Knight. And from the Jacksons' massively successful Victory tour, which had ended the previous December, she wanted drummer Jonathan P. Moffett and keyboardist Patrick Leonard. Moffett would be her "go-to" drummer for the following decade. Leonard would be one of the most important collaborators of her career.[2]

That almost didn't happen. After his Jackson tour obligations were over, Pat wanted to get off the road and into the recording studio. But Freddy DeMann called Pat's manager to say that Madonna wanted him to be her tour's musical director. "My first response was, 'The girl in her underwear? No, no, no.' And they said, 'Would you talk to her?'"[3]

Madonna and Pat Leonard weren't an obvious fit. He came from a family of musicians — a jazz saxophonist father, classical musician sister — and had been playing piano, he joked, since he was in diapers. (His first "show" was at school at the age of five.) When he was sixteen, having been tossed out of school, music became his life. And that was where his story and

Madonna's converged. They both lived to create sound; to see where its magic could take them.[4]

They finally met during a party at his home in LA and ventured into his studio to listen to some of his music. She liked what she heard. "In fact, Madonna came up with a lyric on the spot," he said. It was for "Love Makes the World Go Round."[5] She called soon afterward and asked him to reconsider her offer to join the tour. Spelling out exactly what she wanted from him, "she said, 'I've never done this. No push back. Your show. You pick the players. You're in charge,'" Pat recalled. "So I kinda couldn't resist that." He said yes.[6]

Pat would be one of the few straight, white, married-with-children men in Madonna's life.[7] He would also be one of her staunchest defenders.

> When I started working with her, I used to get so burned, man, so pissed, when people would say, "How can you work with her?" I'd say, "What are you saying?"...She's a nice person. She's sweet. She's dedicated. She's fucking talented as hell...She's not this person everybody thinks she is.[8]
>
> I've heard the talk about how Madonna can't sing and I can tell you that's bull. She's a natural, intuitive singer with great intonation; and she puts across a vulnerable quality that you can't copy, and I know, because I've heard people try.[9]

With Moffett and Leonard signed to the tour, Madonna quickly rounded out the band.[10] Most were newcomers, but one, guitarist Paul Pesco, was a New York friend from as far back as the Patrick Hernandez auditions.[11] Their familiarity would be evident during the tour. Pesco performed the role of coconspirator in two of her steamiest stage routines.

Madonna left the musical coordination of that first tour largely to Pat Leonard. "She did not need to control everything," he said.

> She was a total pro. Like our relationship remained, it was always real open and real simple—you do what you do and I do what I do, and it's good. She knew how to allow space for things that she didn't understand.[12]

Madonna concentrated on the show's dancing, but she didn't want to choreograph it.[13] She offered that critical job to twenty-four-year-old Brad Jeffries. They had spotted each other at the American Music Awards, where he performed with Lionel Richie.[14] Two days later she called and invited him to dinner. Three minutes into the meal, she asked if he'd be interested in choreographing her tour. Without a second's hesitation he said yes.

They became friends, and when she decided to move out of her hotel and into an apartment, she chose the Chateau Beachwood, where Jeffries lived. "She was *incredibly* sexy and seductive," he said, "and had I not been gay, I am sure I would have been bitten, sucked dry, and wrapped in her steely cocoon when she was done with me."[15]

Madonna also selected two dancers who would double as backup singers: Lyndon B. Johnson, who had been on the TV show *Hill Street Blues,* and Mykal Perea, who had toured with Cher and Lionel Richie.[16] And with them, the performance cast for the show was complete. But their look onstage was critically important. To oversee that aspect of the production, Madonna turned to LA-based designer Marlene Stewart.[17]

Stewart specialized in creating characters. One fashion editor described her clothes as ranging from "fey to flamboyant," inspired by "Latin dancers, hippie vagabonds and medieval maidens."[18] Maripol saw Stewart's tour designs and thought they were too "Prince-ly...very *Purple Rain.*" In the end Madonna combined her own and Maripol's look with Stewart's: brocade jackets, cropped lace shirts, purple bra, miniskirts with bicycle shorts, black fringed rocker gear, and wedding white.[19]

With the team finally assembled, weeks of rehearsals began, focusing on dance in the morning and the band at night. Brad Jeffries and Madonna drove together. "Our routine was that I would walk over to her place, which was spartanly furnished with one Turkish rug, and collect her to start our day."[20]

One morning, Jeffries recalled, "We were standing in her kitchen eating cold leftover veggie pizza when her phone rang." Madonna picked it up and said, "'Hello,' listened for a minute or so, and then...said a very blasé, 'Really?' More listening. 'Cool,' and hung up." Jeffries asked who it was. "And she said in the most offhand way, 'That was my business manager in New York, and he just told me that I just made my first million dollars. Are you done with that pizza?'"[21] Jeffries attributed Madonna's casual response to her certainty that that would be only the first of "many more millions to come."[22] But that was only part of it. She truly didn't care about the money. She had more important things on her mind.

The announcement of Madonna's tour came in March. It would open in Seattle in April and end, twenty-seven cities and two months later, in New York. Despite her popularity, there was much anxiety in Warner executive suites. It wasn't clear whether she could endure the tour, dancing and singing twelve songs for seventy-five minutes over thirty-eight shows.[23] Warner also wasn't sure about ticket sales. Because Madonna was new and a woman, she was booked into smallish halls. Seats, however, sold out almost immediately, which caused a mad scramble to find larger venues.

Early press coverage described Madonna as the "bad girl of boys' dreams," but it soon became evident that she was the bad girl of girls' dreams.[24]

Two weeks after *Desperately Seeking Susan*'s premiere, Madonna's Virgin tour opened on April 10 at the twenty-eight-hundred-seat Paramount Theatre in Seattle. "As I stood near the theater's front entrance, I watched car after car pull up and drop off several young girls, all dressed like Madonna," recalled Ron Weisner. "I'd guesstimate that 75 percent of the audience was under the age of fifteen...When the show started, the kids went nuts."[25] Madonna said that first concert "took my breath away."

> It literally sucked the life out of me, sucked the air out of my lungs when I walked on stage. I sort of had an out-of-body experience. Not a bad feeling, not an out-of-control feeling, but an other-worldly feeling that nothing could prepare you for.[26]

For her opening act, Madonna had recruited the Beastie Boys, three rude youths from her Danceteria days who had made a name for themselves as white hip-hop artists. It was a controversial choice, because there was nothing remotely pop about them.[27] Adam "Ad-Rock" Horovitz said the job was "harder work than I ever really imagined." Madonna's fans weren't interested in rappers, and the band struggled to win them over.[28] On opening night, they were practically booed off the stage. "Freddy DeMann said, 'These guys suck. They need to go home.' And Madonna was like, 'These guys are staying.' She put her foot down," Horovitz said.[29]

When Madonna took the stage, the boos and the Beastie Boys were all but forgotten.

Since the days of Sinatra, Elvis, and the Beatles, images of young women and girls screaming over male stars were so common that they had become clichés. It seemed that women only became mobs when expressing their longing for men. But in Seattle, that mob was screaming for a *woman* because of what she represented. They saw her success as their own. They saw her strength as their future. They saw themselves doing whatever they wanted to do because she had paved the way.

A sixteen-year-old concertgoer told the *Los Angeles Times,* "She is living out our fantasies."[30] A seventeen-year-old at a Houston concert told *Time* magazine, "I like the way she handles herself, sort of take it or leave it. She's sexy but she doesn't need men, really. She's kind of there by herself." Another teenager at the same concert said, "She gives us ideas. It's really women's lib, not being afraid of what guys think."[31]

The concert began with the words "Don't be afraid, it's gonna be all right," while the concert video featured Madonna reciting her fairy-tale history:

I went to New York. I had a dream. I wanted to be a big star. I didn't know anybody. I wanted to dance. I wanted to sing. I wanted to do all those things. I wanted to make people happy...I worked really hard and my dream came true.[32]

Her reassuring words immediately put her audience at ease. In a roomful of wannabes, she revealed that she had been one of them, a member of that vast, powerless, voiceless, and overlooked multitude who subsisted on dreams.

During her show, Madonna laughed with the crowd, teased them, confided in them, embraced them in a way that was oddly intimate for such a large setting. After a manic three-song opener of "Dress You Up," "Holiday," and "Into the Groove," she became the naughty best friend, telling the crowd as she sat on a boom box that she wanted to introduce them to her special friend, her "box. Everybody has a box, right? You see, mine is different from other people's. Mine makes music, but you have to turn it on."[33]

The crowd roared. It was a dirty joke told by a girl to an audience of girls, whose sex education in school was about reproductive organs. Madonna acknowledged a vagina for what it was, a source of pleasure, and launched into "Everybody" with a few seconds of masturbatory grinding. *Masturbation? Whoa!!* Girls weren't even supposed to *know* about that. As the young audience screamed in delight, the adults stood horrified.[34] "We told her to 'go easy' on stage but of course she did the opposite," said Ron Weisner. "Afterwards the mothers all left the concert, and you could hear them talking in shock about what they'd just seen."[35]

Madonna lightened things up during her next number, "Angel." Hundreds of balloons bearing the message DREAMS COME TRUE dropped from the theater's rafters. The concert became a raucous birthday bash with balloons bouncing back and forth between audience members. As they played, Madonna disappeared for the first of three costume changes.

Christopher had joined Madonna on tour, though he no longer joined her onstage. "The thing that drives other people to perform in front of an audience was not in my DNA," he explained.[36] His official role was as Madonna's "dresser," which meant he was responsible for her costumes and ensuring that she changed them every four songs in less than a minute and a half.[37]

As stressful as that was, his unofficial job—"her brother with whom she can be Madonna of Thors Street and Oklahoma Avenue"—was much more taxing. *That* Madonna unleashed her pent-up anxiety in his direction, delivering a foul-mouthed tirade at top volume as fast as she could spit out the words.[38]

Arriving in the dressing room sweating, she would throw herself at him to be stripped, wiped down, and redressed from undergarments to gloves, while shouting: "What the fuck Christopher, you haven't pushed out the little finger! Fuck you, you piece of shit…Hurry the fuck up, or I'll fucking fire you right now." And then she was off, back onstage, "singing and dancing like there's no tomorrow" while he stood close to tears listening to the crowd cheer. Four songs later, she would be back in the dressing room to do it all again.[39]

Madonna's set list continued with "The Gambler" from *Vision Quest,* performed with uncharacteristic full-rock aggression, followed by "Borderline," "Lucky Star," "Crazy for You," "Over and Over," and "Burning Up." That number was truly shocking: the choreography had Madonna simulate a threesome with her male dancers until they apparently rejected her, at which point she focused her desire on Paul Pesco, playing guitar nearby. By the end of the song, she was kneeling before him, performing an unmistakable pantomime of a blow job.

The scene was full of symbolism, if you could get past the image of Madonna on her knees, because it was less his person that she was simulating oral sex with than his guitar—the almighty rock 'n' roll phallic stand-in.[40] It was Madonna as groupie, Madonna worshipping at the altar of rock, just as she had been Madonna the available "boy toy" or Madonna the grasping "material girl." It was parody aimed at the pervasive misogyny of rock music. Said Grace Slick that spring, "Madonna is conscious of what she's doing, and more than making fun of women, it makes fun of how stupid men are. She's saying, 'Let me twist that around.'"[41] And with that image implanted in their brains, Madonna abruptly said to her audience, "Thank you and good night."

But of course, that wasn't the end of the concert. Madonna had yet to be a bride. She returned for an encore with "Like a Virgin," and the crowd thundered back to life. That song was followed by "Material Girl," during which Madonna tossed fake hundred-dollar bills that bore the words LIVING IN A MATERIAL WORLD and ALTERED STATES OF MADONNA. It was all fun, all play, but Madonna was real. What she represented was real. That was her secret.

Each night, the concert ended with the tape of a man's voice—meant to be Madonna's father's—telling her to "get down off that stage this instant!" to which Madonna replied with a prerecorded "Daddy, do I hafta?" The girls in the crowd went mad. That was *their* father talking to *them* that very night. *Did it hafta end?* It did. Their parents were waiting for them in their station wagons, ready to drive them home to their structured lives. But everything had changed between the time they entered the theater and the time they exited, less than two hours later. The old structure no longer existed.[42]

Madonna planted a seed of rebellion in Seattle, as she would in all the cities she visited on her tour. She was the cool bad girl who had invited her audience to hang with her for a night, the smart older sister willing to help those girls sort out their lives at a delicate moment of transition.

Many of her fans were becoming young women. It was a confusing time, when even their bodies seemed to conspire against them by forcing them to endure a supposedly shameful and actually painful monthly period. At that fork in the road of female adolescence—at the juncture of girl and woman—one path led to submission and the other to self-fulfillment. And that second path was perilous because of the social forces arrayed against it.[43]

Madonna had walked that dangerous route ahead of them, clearing the land mines and taking the incoming fire. Being misunderstood, being demonized, being discounted as a vulgar, talentless fame hound—taking shit, as she liked to say—became part of what it meant to be Madonna. And it started in earnest that spring.

Press reports along her tour route called her a sexual menace. She was a "cocktease, a slut, a sleaze, a shameless wanton."[44] She was "a chief exponent of 'Bimbo Rock.' "[45] Speaking for many of his fellow critics about her tour, *Rolling Stone*'s Michael Goldberg wrote,

> Madonna was a sweaty pinup girl come to life. She wiggled her tummy and shook her ass…She rolled around on stage and got down on her knees in front of a guitarist. And when she raised her arms, her scanty see-through blouse also rose, revealing her purple brassiere…What Madonna is really about is sex, and there was plenty of that.[46]

Men in the music business, and no doubt men in general, saw a sexual presentation. They couldn't conceive that it wasn't sex Madonna offered her audience but power. Not the macho power that some women in rock imitated but a woman's power. Not a pretend penis but a full woman's body. The biggest cheers of the night would invariably come when she started dancing—because she *moved,* because she expressed herself physically without an ounce of restraint. Madonna showed the girls and young women in the audience that they could do that, too. *Own your body; do what you want with it; move it however you please.*

Madonna's stage performance was mild compared with depictions of sex on film and in rock videos. It was even mild when compared with those of some women who preceded her: Joan Jett and the Runaways performed in corsets, garters, bikini underwear, and heels in 1977. And it was chaste compared with Prince. Madonna might flash a bra and expose her midriff, but that was the full extent of her exhibitionism. Prince, by contrast, preferred black bikini underwear or G-strings and leg warmers to trousers.[47] Madonna said,

I try to have a thick skin, but every once in a while I read something that someone says about me and it's so slanderous and moralistic, and it has nothing to do with my music. There was this one review that said things about me that boys said to me in the seventh grade...."slut."...And "cheap coquette," a girl who made her way into lots of back seats in the drive-in theater...I remember guys saying that sort of stuff to me when I was really young. I thought suddenly that the whole experience was repeating itself all over again.[48]

The problem for Madonna's critics wasn't really her sexual presentation, it was who it was aimed at. As her tour progressed, it became clear that straight men weren't her audience at all. Like the poor groom left atop her *Virgin* cake at the VMAs, men in Madonna's oeuvre were kind of superfluous. "I do it because it turns *me* on," she told an interviewer.[49] And that was the message she telegraphed to her audience of women and girls.

What Madonna offered her young audience was a 1985 version of the "consciousness-raising" sessions at the start of second wave feminism, a decade before. Those women did a most radical thing—*they talked to one another.* By the mid-1980s, however, that dialogue had devolved into squabbles, and that left space for their detractors to label them "radical, bitter, man-hating, separatist" lesbians.[50]

Madonna introduced her audience to a new kind of feminism, a *lived* liberation. It was wild—sexy and sexual, outspoken and political, creative and loving. She also introduced her audience to a new kind of *femininity.*[51] Far from being soft and weak, Madonna showed that a feminine woman humped a boom box, rolled on the floor, and sweated profusely—the sweat of an athlete—while looking great in the process, not because she was so "pretty" but because she was so free.

Alarm bells that sounded in the press turned into foghorns in conservative communities. "Her ideas will only cause rebellion in our impressionable teenagers," wrote a concerned reader to *People* magazine.[52] The California group United Parents Under God said that Madonna "should be banned to save our children from ruin!"[53]

By September, Madonna had five songs on a "porn rock" list compiled by a group of Washington, DC, women who were bringing their case against sex and violence in music to Congress. "Dress You Up" ranked number 8 on its list of the fifteen filthiest songs in pop music. The offensive lyrics: "Gonna dress you up in my love / All over your body."[54]

Five days after the tour launched in Seattle, Madonna arrived in Portland, Oregon, to find the religious right picketing outside the Arlene Schnitzer Concert Hall. Placards called Madonna the daughter of Satan. Freddy told Christopher that she had received death threats, but neither man told Madonna. "From that moment on, I become hyperaware of what is going on around her," Christopher said, "extremely protective, even paranoid."[55]

As the tour traveled to California, Texas, Florida, Atlanta, Cleveland, Cincinnati, Chicago, St. Paul, and Toronto, the crowds inside and outside the auditoriums grew.[56] Warren Beatty would say that Madonna didn't want to live off camera. Christopher said he was wrong: Madonna didn't want to live off*stage*.[57] She agreed. "I love reaching out to people and I love the expressions in people's eyes and just the ecstasy and the thrill."[58]

Her tour was her first taste of adulation on a grand scale, and she would crave it again and again, no matter how grueling. Christopher said she was out of breath after the third song each night. During that first tour she realized that she needed to train for at least five months before considering another.[59] Thus began Madonna's lifelong workout regimen.[60] It wasn't so much aimed at ridding herself of the few pounds around her middle that the press loved to mention as increasing her stamina.

In late May, Madonna played to the most intimate crowd yet. She was at the Cobo Arena, in Detroit. Sean had brought his parents to her concert in Los Angeles, and now he was in Detroit to meet her family and help her through her emotional homecoming. In the audience were her grandmother, her father, Joan, Christopher Flynn, all her brothers and sisters, most of her aunts, uncles, and cousins, and teachers and school friends from Adams High.[61] "I was overwhelmed," Flynn said. "I still saw this little fourteen-year-old girl clutching her doll. Now she had everything she wanted."[62]

Opening the concert with "Dress You Up," Madonna seemed nervous. Her smile was tentative, her movements stiff. But by her second song, "Holiday," she was in the moment. Telling the crowd to get up on its feet, she shouted, "That goes for you, too, Grandma!"[63]

Madonna stopped that song midway to speak to the audience, recalling her childhood in Michigan, thanking her family and her teachers—the people she loved but had felt compelled to leave in order to follow her dream. "I gotta talk fast 'cause I might start cryin'," she said. She tried to collect herself, but she couldn't. Doubled over, her body shook with tears. "She's crying, and the band was getting choked up," Pat Leonard said.[64] When she finally finished "Holiday," Madonna's tears turned to joy. She spun alone on the stage, dancing and blowing kisses to the crowd.

The show was a slightly abbreviated version of the concerts she'd given up to that point, and her language and actions were tamed out of deference to her grandmother. The boom-box humping in "Everybody," for example, was shorter and less vigorous, and she didn't perform her most blatantly sexual number, "Burning Up." But the raw emotions she displayed that night easily compensated for any lack of outrageous behavior, especially when she sang "Crazy for You."

There were times in Madonna's career during live performances when she transcended the song and the moment. That song on that night was one of them. She was humble and solemn in her expression of what could only be seen as a declaration of love for Sean Penn. He represented her future as he sat among the people who comprised her past. Everything she desired for her happiness had come true — *more* than she could have hoped for — all her dreams except that one element: lasting love. She believed she had found it with him.

As she belted out the chorus, she held her hand over her face to hide more tears. And then, the woman whom detractors called a sexual predator assumed a position of utter vulnerability. She threw back her head, exposing and extending her neck. It was visceral. Animal. Poetic.

Madonna closed her show, as she always did, with "Material Girl." But in Detroit, rather than a recorded male voice ordering her to get off the stage, Tony Ciccone came out and pulled her off. Madonna had given him instructions in advance to "think back to those days when you were really mad at me," like the night of her "Baba O'Riley" performance in junior high.

> I said, "Think of that, and how you wanted to yank me off the stage." And he did, boy — he just about dismembered me. When I came offstage, I was so hysterical I just collapsed laughing. That was a total release. Because I felt like my father was finally seeing what I do for a living.[65]

The tour left Michigan and wound its way east before finally arriving in New York in June for five shows — three at the six-thousand-seat Radio City Music Hall, where the shows' collective eighteen thousand tickets sold out in a record thirty-four minutes — and two at Madison Square Garden, which would accommodate those fans unable to squeeze into the first three concerts. The Garden's nearly twenty thousand seats sold out on each night. It was unprecedented for a first tour by a female artist.[66]

But then, New York City was Madonna's home, and it largely understood her — not just the fans who lived there but also the city's media, which appreciated her artistic roots and was not appalled by the messaging. Wrote Barry Walters in the *Village Voice* of the people in the hinterlands who called Madonna a slut,

> I can't help but think that this attitude might be a wee bit misogynistic. Maybe Madonna in the privacy of her bedroom is a slut. Maybe she's a slut

in the privacy of other people's bedrooms. I, for one, do not care. For if Madonna's a slut, she's the most inspired, intelligent, foolish, euphoric, entertaining, liberating slut of the moment...

Underneath the artifice, Madonna is genuinely erotic, but all the conflicting iconographical baggage she carries around puts her sexuality in quotes. Both "sweet" and "sleazy," she makes the spectator aware that her "sweetness" and "sleazinesss" is what a society determined by masculine discourse requires from its feminine sex symbols.[67]

The audience at Madonna's opening night at Radio City was filled with her artistic family — Andy Warhol, Keith Haring, Kenny Scharf, Jean-Michel Basquiat, Futura, Fab 5 Freddy, Martin Burgoyne, Maripol, Debi Mazar, and Erika Belle. "The show was so great. Just so simple and sexy and Madonna was so pretty," Warhol wrote in his diary. "And afterwards we went downstairs where there was a private party."[68] Haring saw Madonna's concert every night, renting a limo and taking different people with him. "After each concert, we'd go out to eat," he said. "One night we went to Mr. Chow's and Madonna came with us. The media was driving her crazy, following her everywhere."[69]

Madonna was a huge story not only because of her tour but because she had become big business.[70] During her appearances, merchandise disappeared from vendors' tables as quickly as the tickets had from box offices. A Virgin tour concession operator said Madonna sold more T-shirts and memorabilia than Bruce Springsteen, the Rolling Stones, and Duran Duran. At her San Francisco show, $20 T-shirts sold "at the rate of one every six seconds."[71]

It was all part of a broader trend across the industry that exploded in the early 1980s. Merchandise had become an important part of the entertainment revenue stream.[72] Madonna helped take the trend to the next level, signing a merchandising deal to market Boy Toy clothes, which would be sold in malls and department stores from coast to coast.[73]

Girls loved the fashions. Madonnawear made them strong because — at least until the look was entirely co-opted — it broadcast rebellion in a way girls' fashions rarely did. The height, weight, and shape of the young woman who wore Boy Toy fashions also didn't matter. That was another aspect of Madonna's appeal and why so many girls dared to "be" her.[74]

To capitalize on the craze and Madonna's proximity, Macy's flagship store, in Herald Square, held a Madonna look-alike contest on June 6, with Andy Warhol and Maripol as judges. The event coincided with the tour's Radio City opener and the launch of Macy's Madonnaland department.[75] Around one hundred girls entered the competition.[76] Since Madonna's "Borderline" video, Maripol had seen her shop invaded by what she called "the Little

Madonnas."[77] But she found the Macy's event disturbing because it was a harbinger of the coming commercialization of Madonna's image.[78]

On the last night of Madonna's New York concerts, *ABC World News Tonight,* anchored by Peter Jennings, aired a segment on the tour and the artist's hold on young women.[79] Talking heads analyzed the Madonna madness, with the scale heavily weighted toward disapproval. It was left to pioneering feminist Betty Friedan to offer the sole adult support for Madonna. "She's courageous and gutsy . . . and I think her appeal is that she is feminine, she is herself, she is sexual, but she's *strong*."[80]

As for the new generation interviewed for the ABC piece, girls in all shapes and sizes, some wearing braces on their teeth, decked out in fingerless lace gloves, crosses, and "Susan" sunglasses, clearly adored Madonna. Reporter Betsy Aaron asked one young fan—no older than ten or eleven—"When you dress like this, how do you feel?" The beatific child responded with joy and remarkable self-assurance, "I feel *wonderful*."[81]

Girls all over the world felt the same way. Novelist Soniah Kamal was introduced to Madonna's music in, of all places, Jeddah, Saudi Arabia. A friend from the international school where she studied played "Lucky Star" for her and another girl. "Before we knew it we were jumping on the bed through 'Holiday' and 'Everybody,' yelling bits of the choruses we'd picked up," she recalled. The friend had a VHS tape of Madonna's Virgin tour performance in Detroit, and the three girls watched it in secret. Soniah said,

> I was mesmerized . . . Madonna was magic. Madonna was madness. The concert ended with a man—Madonna's real-life father—barreling on stage to drag her away as if she were a naughty girl. At that moment I felt akin to Madonna. *I was Madonna.* She understood my life, so I gave her my soul.[82]

When the concert ended, the three friends looked at each other. They rewound and played it again—three times—until Soniah's mother caught them.

In retrospect, Soniah said, Madonna represented "pure, unadulterated, raw sexual liberation" and hope. "Hope that sexy girls did not necessarily die bad deaths, hope that sexy girls lived to tell their tales, hope that sexy girls could rule the world. And do." Because Madonna did.[83]

Chapter 19

Nashville, Philadelphia, Malibu, 1985

I seem to be the girl they hate to love.[1]

— Madonna

IN LATE JUNE, with *Like a Virgin* selling eighty thousand copies a day and her tour wrapped, Madonna traveled to Tennessee, where Sean was filming *At Close Range*.[2] It would be the first time they would be alone together, without her screaming fans, without her entourage wandering in and out of her hotel suite, without her mind preoccupied by the thousands of things that could go wrong that night onstage. It was a rare moment of repose.

Not so for Sean. He was working, inhabiting his character, Brad Whitewood Jr., a confused and searching small-town hood with a hair-trigger temper. The cast and crew lived the movie, too. Actor R. D. Call said, "We were kind of isolated, secluded, off in the hills of [Franklin,] Tennessee, a world within a world within a world."[3]

Enter Madonna. "I remember just pandemonium at the Nashville airport upon her arrival," director James Foley said. "A horde of paparazzi following her. But she wouldn't come to the set, in order to keep the monsters at bay. She was very respectful of the process."[4] The photographers and journalists who followed her were not respectful as they staked out the Maxwell House hotel, where the film's cast and crew were staying. "There were weird things that were completely inappropriate," said Meegan Ochs, who was involved in the film shoot.

> Someone thinking that Madonna was pregnant and had had an abortion, sending her a huge bouquet of black balloons. As much as one can say Sean should have expected it, I don't think he was expecting how mean-spirited it was going to be. He was very taken aback by it and felt very protective of her...And that was the first time, I think, that he ever actually hit anybody.[5]

The incident in question occurred in Nashville soon after Sean and Madonna became engaged. The proposal was not an on-one-knee diamond-ring scenario. It was as innocent and childlike as they were. Madonna recalled the scene later that year during an interview with actor Harry Dean Stanton:

> Sean asked me to marry him but he didn't say it out loud, I read his mind… It was a Sunday morning and I was jumping up and down on the bed, performing one of my morning rituals, and all of a sudden he got this look in his eye and I felt like I just knew what he was thinking. I said, "Go ahead and say it, I know what you're thinking." No! What I said was "Whatever you're thinking, I'll say yes to." That was his chance. So he popped it… Then we went to the 7-Eleven and bought a whole bunch of jawbreakers and celebrated.[6]

But even the simplest outings during their stay in Nashville were fraught with peril because of the paparazzi. "I was involved enough with them on that occasion, and later in New York, to understand what it's like to have people who physically confront you with heavy pieces of metal, hitting your head sometimes," Foley said. "You're being assaulted."[7]

On Sunday, June 30, reporter Ian Markham-Smith and photographer Laurence Cottrell from Rupert Murdoch's *Sun* newspaper in Britain were hanging around the hotel parking lot looking to get a scoop on Madonna and Sean. As the couple walked by holding hands, Markham-Smith shouted questions, and Cottrell tried to take a picture. Sean, half protective fiancé, half his volatile film character, warned him not to, and when Cottrell persisted, Sean threw a rock at him, ripped his camera off his neck, and beat him with it. Markham-Smith tried to intervene and got a punch in the eye, which Cottrell captured on film.[8]

"Whatever it was that happened took about five seconds, but somebody takes a picture and suddenly it's all over the world and never goes away," said Sean's *At Close Range* costar, Christopher Walken. Sean was charged with assault and battery and freed to return to work.[9]

The film company became involved later that month when Cottrell sued Sean, Madonna, and Orion Pictures for $1 million, saying the assault was "instigated by and carried out with the approval of Madonna." Orion was named because the photographer reportedly claimed the attack was staged to get publicity for the movie.[10] That confrontation, just after Sean and Madonna's engagement, would set the tone for their marriage. It would be characterized by deep love and extreme distress, a good deal of it caused by the paparazzi.

Once upon a time, film studios managed access to actors. But in the 1950s, after the war, Italian photographers trying to scrape together a living found that if they hung around outside the famous Rome film studio Cinecittà or along the star-filled Via Veneto, they could take candid photographs of celebrities and sell them. They became known as paparazzi, after a character named Paparazzo in Federico Fellini's film *La dolce vita* who made a pest of himself by taking unauthorized photos of stars. The real-life mid-century paparazzi were in the best cases mere pests, but some were borderline criminal. They weren't at all averse to staging confrontations in order to provoke a celebrity punch and get a photo.[11]

By the 1980s, celebrities began referring to paparazzi as "stalkerazzi." In LA they drove "pap cars." In New York they worked on foot. In both cases, they looked for two kinds of pictures: the "circuit shot," which showed celebrities going about their daily lives, and the "exclusive," which could involve stealth on the part of the photographer (pointing a long lens at someone's home or backyard) and a high degree of intrusion.[12]

During the Reagan era, celebrity news became a major growth industry. Readers had a love-hate relationship with the wealthy and were eager to shell out a few coins to read about their latest romances, outrages, heartbreaks, and medical scares. The four major supermarket tabloids—*Star, Globe,* the *National Enquirer,* and the *National Examiner*—accounted for the biggest magazine circulation growth in the United States. Add to that glossy celebrity weeklies such as *People* and *Us* as well as the even glossier monthlies like *Vanity Fair*—under its new editor, Tina Brown—and the appetite for photos and celebrity gossip became bottomless.[13]

That was the environment during the early days of Madonna and Sean's romance. She was the hottest female entertainer on the planet; he was the hottest head in Hollywood. They would be pursued every moment, and none of their secrets was safe. They had decided not to tell anyone about their engagement except their most trusted friends and associates. Sean told Jamie Foley and Meegan Ochs. Madonna told Liz Rosenberg and Rosanna Arquette, who, Meegan said, "told someone, who told *everybody*. And that was the end of that."[14]

The terms of Sean's bail—$500—were set on July 2, which meant he was free to leave the state of Tennessee.[15] Madonna was due in Philadelphia where, on July 13, she would perform at the biggest event of her career in front of the largest concert audience ever assembled—more than a billion people. The show was called Live Aid, and it had been organized by Irish songwriter and former Boomtown Rats singer Bob Geldof to raise funds to help alleviate a famine in Ethiopia that would ultimately kill more than a million people.

Live Aid would be unprecedented, with twenty-one hours of music broadcast from JFK Stadium in Philadelphia and Wembley Stadium in

London, and featuring some of the best music talent in the Western world—Bob Dylan, Mick Jagger, Tina Turner, Elton John, Run-DMC, David Bowie, Sting, Black Sabbath, Sade, U2, the Who, Eric Clapton, Queen, Paul McCartney, Neil Young, the Pretenders, Patti LaBelle, and Madonna among them.[16]

Geldof also harnessed the power of the new satellite television technology to create a first-of-its-kind global spectacular—the show would be broadcast in 110 countries. In the United States alone, ratings showed that more than half of all TVs tuned in. As one writer said, not since an audience watched man's first steps on the moon was the world's attention so focused.[17]

The rehearsals for the show were extensive and exciting, with music legends coursing around the stage and drinking in hotel bars in the evenings. Madonna was reunited with members of her tour band, including Pat Leonard, Jonathan Moffett, and Paul Pesco, as well as people from the recording studio, among them Nile Rodgers, who would be part of Live Aid's house band.

Just a year before, in July of 1984, Madonna was shooting the "Like a Virgin" video in Venice. She hadn't begun working on *Desperately Seeking Susan.* She was still a relative unknown. Since then, she had traveled from obscurity to being part of music history.[18] Steve Bray said simply, "The person I knew in 1977 now owned the planet."[19] And then the person she had been in those early years resurfaced and threatened to destroy everything she had achieved.

On July 7, while Madonna was rehearsing Live Aid, *Penthouse* announced that it had nude photos of her and planned to publish fourteen pages of them. The year before, that magazine had shamed Vanessa Williams, the first Black woman to win the Miss America pageant, by publishing nude images of her. She was ultimately forced to relinquish her crown. Now the magazine that made a business of objectifying women was looking to take down Madonna by splashing photos from her difficult days in New York across its glossy pages.

On July 8, *Playboy* one-upped *Penthouse,* announcing it would publish seventeen pages of a nude young Madonna. Both were scheduled for the magazines' September issues, but the interest was so great and the competition so fierce that they couldn't wait. *Playboy* moved up its publication date to July 10, with *Penthouse* soon after printing five million copies, or 15 percent more than its usual run.[20] To keep the story alive, the magazines offered Madonna more than $1 million to strip anew for the camera.[21]

All the critics who had called Madonna a slut, who said she "plowed through boyfriends like party snacks," and all the parental and religious organizations that warned of her malign influence felt vindicated.[22] There is nothing more exciting to a sexist society than diminishing a woman of achievement. It not only embarrassed the woman but also warned those who emulated her: Don't try. You'll fail. The higher you go, the more humiliating the fall.

Without minimizing Madonna's actual rape, it's easy to imagine that the publication of the photos would have felt like a similar violation on a grander scale. The million-dollar offer echoed the Upper East Side record executive's contract-for-a-blow-job proposition. Madonna had survived the first and rejected the second and would do so once more that July with a very public rejoinder in the *New York Post*. Liz Rosenberg arranged it. She assured Madonna, who feared for her career when the story broke, "This is not a big deal. We're not gonna let it be a big deal."[23]

Madonna's classic response—MADONNA ON NUDE PIX: SO WHAT!—was splashed across the *Post*'s front page in type larger than the newspaper's nameplate. Its Metro edition read MADONNA: "I'M NOT ASHAMED." "That was the first time I was aware of saying 'Fuck you' with my attitude," Madonna said later. "You're trying to put me down because of this? I'm not going to let public opinion dictate my own feelings about myself. I'm not going to apologize for anything I've done."[24]

Music critic Greil Marcus said the scandal surrounding the photos was only the latest version of a type of harassment that had long been visited upon women in show business. "It happened to Louise Brooks, it happened to Marilyn Monroe. It's always been a scandal and people try and suppress the pictures, and say, 'Oh I was so poor.' ... Madonna said, 'What's the big deal?' "[25] In doing so, she directed the shame where it belonged, on the brutes behind it.

That was her public position. Privately, Madonna suffered because of the exposure and its impact on her family. Her grandmother in Michigan cried when she learned about the photos while watching a daytime TV talk show. And then there was the question of Sean's reaction so soon after their engagement.[26] "I can't say I wasn't devastated by the experience," Madonna told *Rolling Stone* the following year.

> Sean kept saying, "Look, this is all going to blow over," but nobody wants their skeletons to come out of the closet... The thing that annoyed me most wasn't so much that they were nude photographs but that I felt really out of control—for the first time in what I thought to be several years of careful planning... It took me by surprise.[27]

Pat Leonard said, "That whole week was full of rehearsals, flying around and being nuts, getting ready for the show—she only said one thing in reference to those photos. We were out to dinner at a restaurant in

Philadelphia, and I was making fun of her about something, and she said, 'Aw, Lenny, get off my back. I've had a rough week.' That's all she said."[28]

Three days after the *Playboy* photos were published, Princess Diana and Prince Charles kicked off Live Aid in London to the strains of "God Save the Queen." Two hours later, Joan Baez opened the tandem show in Philadelphia with a speech and a rendition of "Amazing Grace."[29] Christopher was backstage with Madonna, as was Sean, looking like his *At Close Range* character: plaid shirt, mirrored aviator sunglasses, a can of beer in hand. He was there to protect and reassure but also to savor the moment. He was surrounded, thanks to his future wife, by the musical geniuses he admired and some of his acting chums from LA.[30]

Madonna's performance was scheduled eight hours into the show, just after Kool & the Gang and before Tom Petty and the Heartbreakers. That meant she had plenty of time to be apprehensive. Everyone backstage, everyone she encountered that day, from stars to crew, had seen her naked. Probably most of the audience had, too, or at least she imagined so. "I really thought, I can't do this. I just can't, I can't go on," Madonna said.[31]

> It was the first time since the pictures came out that I was making a public appearance. Part of me felt about this big [she made a gesture to indicate an inch]. And another part of me was saying "I'll be damned if I'm gonna let them make me feel down. I'm gonna get out there and kick ass, get this dark cloud out from over my head."[32]
>
> So I decided to be a warrior and it worked and that was the first time that I really understood my power.[33]

The heat was intense, and Madonna was wearing layers of clothing—much more than she usually wore—topped off by a brocade jacket. After Bette Midler introduced her, Madonna bounded onto the stage and launched into a six-minute version of "Holiday." The sea of people before her was enormous. The outer fringes appeared as mere dots on the horizon. Lyndon B. Johnson and Mykal Perea joined her again as backup dancers and singers, and, as she had during her tour, Madonna stopped singing midway through "Holiday" to speak to the crowd. Her look was pure joy.

Backstage, Sean's was, too. "When she was on stage," Meegan Ochs said, "he had a big smile on his face." He saw her triumph and the love that washed her way from the crowd. That audience couldn't have cared less about the photos. All they wanted was her. It was the ultimate validation.[34]

Madonna kept the momentum going with "Into the Groove." By the end of that second song, she hadn't stopped moving for twelve minutes. Nile Rodgers said the heat was "scorching." She was sweating and winded.

But before she began her final song, she told the crowd that she would keep her jacket on in solidarity with them because they were hot, too. Someone in the audience shouted, "Take it off," and others joined the chant. Madonna responded with a broad smart-ass smile, "I ain't taking shit off today. You might hold it against me ten years from now." The crowd roared its approval.[35]

The TV censors, meanwhile, hadn't been quick enough to block her language, so the whole world heard her laugh off the skin-magazine scandal with vulgar defiance. As the censors scrambled, the Thompson Twins and Nile Rodgers joined her in singing "Love Makes the World Go Round," the song that she began writing on the first day she met Pat Leonard.[36]

But the media wasn't ready to give the subject a rest. The usual press scrum around Madonna looked to turn into a full-on assault as journalists struggled to confront her over the photos when she came offstage. She had given no interviews and allowed no photos, except for the ones taken by Keith Haring, who snapped her and Sean with his Polaroid.[37]

The official photo that would emerge from the event was one of solidarity, with Bob Dylan on one side of Madonna and Mick Jagger on the other, their arms draped big-brother-style across her shoulders. Tina Turner—herself no stranger to scandal—leaned in on the other side of Jagger's embrace. The concert raised $120 million for famine-hit East Africa.[38]

Madonna stored her *Playboy* and *Penthouse* experience in the mental compartment she drew from for inspiration. It was a protective and creative device: protective in that it allowed her to sequester painful memories and creative in that all experiences, good and bad, became material for her work. Christopher said that after the scandal, Madonna "had nothing to lose anymore, nothing more to hide . . . From now on she is free to be as outrageous as she wants."[39]

It might not have seemed possible during those early days in July when the story of the photos broke, but Madonna emerged from the episode stronger, as did women in general. The little girl from Pontiac had stood up to the giants of the porn industry and made the misogynists in the boardrooms look like schoolyard punks.

Having weathered his contretemps with the law and her skirmish with *Playboy* and *Penthouse,* Sean and Madonna rented a bungalow in Beachwood Canyon and began planning their wedding.[40] Their birthdays were August 16 and 17 (hers came first), so they wanted to hold the ceremony at midnight. Logistically that seemed too difficult, and they settled on Madonna's birthday for the occasion.

The setting would be a bluff overlooking the Pacific at the Malibu home of Elda and Dan Unger, friends of Sean's parents. It was selected for its proximity to the groom's home, where he and Madonna would stay the night before, and for its supposed privacy.[41] Sean and Madonna asked Wolfgang Puck to cater; Judge John Merrick, who had signed the warrant that led to Charles Manson's arrest, to officiate; DJ Terence Toy to entertain; and Herb Ritts to take photos.[42] Sean's brother Michael made the pink invitations, which featured an Edward Gorey–esque take on Grant Wood's painting *American Gothic,* with Madonna in a "Sean Toy" belt. It read in part:

> *The Celebration Will Commence at Six o'clock p.m.*
> *Please Be Prompt or You Will Miss Their Wedding Ceremony.*
> *The Need for Privacy and a Desire to Keep You Hanging*
> *Prevents the Los Angeles Location from Being Announced*
> *Until One Day Prior.*

The guest list included an eclectic mix of characters representing New York's downtown art world and what the *Los Angeles Times* called "a roster of Hollywood's hippest" actors, writers, and directors.[43] As anticipation in the press grew to a fever pitch, reporters frantically tapped people who might be on the list for details and scoops.[44] Andy Warhol said that Martin Burgoyne was being "wined and dined" by the tabs and *People,* and asked to reveal secrets about his best friend. He played the game well—divulging little while availing himself of the attention and free meals.[45]

The New Yorkers bearing pink envelopes who would travel together to LA included Keith Haring, Debi Mazar, Maripol, Diane Keaton, club owner Steve Rubell, Martin, and Warhol. Martin had invited Warhol to be his date because the older artist had recently become enamored of Los Angeles. He felt Hollywood offered a whole new level of kitsch inspiration and was thus overjoyed to be part of the wedding circus.[46] As gifts, he and Keith collaborated on paintings commemorating what Madonna called the "watershed moment" when she stood up to *Playboy* and *Penthouse* in the *New York Post.*[47]

The group planned its trip as if they were teenagers on a first outing away from their parents. Warhol said the choice of hotel wasn't based on comfort or proximity to the wedding venue but on which facility would be easiest to slip into with companions they might encounter in LA.[48] A sexually freewheeling New York contingent heading to closeted Hollywood was like an alcohol enthusiast entering a dry county: it was important to find a place to hide the bottles because you knew there would be some.

Andy noted those arrangements in his diary on July 29, four days after

Rock Hudson, matinee movie idol and star of the biggest show on television, *Dynasty,* gave his publicist permission to announce that he had AIDS. The story rocketed around the world. The press that hadn't wanted to mention AIDS suddenly could write about nothing else.[49]

Hudson's announcement brought much-needed attention to the illness, but it also triggered a wave of paranoia in Hollywood. The film and TV community panicked at the thought that other gay men in straight roles might have AIDS and infect their fellow actors during passionate scenes. Organizations such as the Screen Actors Guild and the Directors Guild of America began discussing whether people with AIDS should be required to reveal their condition.

Gay actors saw such talk as the start of what they feared would be a new blacklist, barring homosexuals from work the way the Red Scare blacklist banned so-called communist actors. The closet in Hollywood before AIDS was huge, filled with gays and lesbians worried that discovery would kill their careers. But the closet post–Hudson's announcement became the size of an arena. People were terrified of the backlash.[50]

That climate of fear and secrecy was what the New Yorkers anticipated when they made their plans for Los Angeles. Openness was better, but heartbreakingly, the tragedy of AIDS struck both the outed gay community and the closeted one. Three of the four men who traveled from New York to attend Madonna's wedding would die of AIDS within five years. Steve Rubell learned he was HIV-positive that year.

After a night at the Beverly Hills Hotel, the New York crew, wearing what looked more like costumes than wedding clothes (Keith was in a Vegas-style "sparkly suit," and Martin had had his hair done at the hotel salon that morning), traveled by limousine to Malibu. Martin's job at the wedding was to act as unofficial doorman, standing next to the blue-blazered gents checking IDs against the two-hundred-person guest list, because so many people who weren't on it were invited that they needed someone in the know to wave them through.[51]

Sean and Madonna had gone to extraordinary lengths to keep the wedding location secret. It had fallen to Meegan Ochs to call the guests one by one with the details.[52] Delivery trucks, caterers, and florists, too, were given limited information until the last minute. Far from insulating the event from prying eyes, however, the cloak-and-dagger approach ensured that it would be one of the most sought-after stories for reporters from around the globe.[53]

Security men armed with night-vision binoculars checked the perimeter for interlopers and found some. An Italian photographer in full camo and blackened face was ejected from the spot among the shrubs where he had been lurking since just after midnight. Sean also dispatched a hidden paparazzo. But the problem wasn't really the *hidden* reporters and paps: it was the ones who were all too visible.[54]

A battalion of eight choppers flew in circles above the Unger estate, making a pass over the grounds every three minutes. To put the scene in perspective, consider that the number of helicopters flying over the wedding and its two hundred guests was half the number that flew over the ninety thousand spectators at Live Aid in Philadelphia.[55] The Malibu sky was alive with metal and blades that were "dangerously close—too close to one another, and too close to us," said Joseph Vitarelli, Sean's school friend. "One of those things crashes and you wipe out half of Hollywood."[56] "It was like 'Apocalypse Now,'" Warhol wrote in his diary of the helicopters. "It was just the most exciting weekend of my life."[57]

The noise from the aircraft was such that people had to shout to be heard. "At first, I was outraged, and then I was laughing," Madonna said. "You couldn't have written it in a movie. No one would have believed it."[58] Sean fired off his .45 at the helicopters, despite Madonna's entreaty not to. He had also inscribed FUCK OFF in twelve-foot-tall letters on the beach below the Ungers' home so that photographers couldn't take pictures—their editors wouldn't allow such profanity. His message proved no deterrent, because photos are easily cropped.[59]

From the point of view of an East Village artist, Keith called the madness "really fun" and "a very normal family wedding."[60] Christopher Walken delivered the West Coast verdict: he said the wedding was like a Fellini film. "There were literally people jumping out of the bushes with cameras. Helicopters overhead like big dragonflies."[61] Thus began the wedding day of Madonna Louise Ciccone and Sean Justin Penn. It was Madonna's twenty-seventh birthday and the day before Sean's twenty-fifth.

The bride wore a strapless Marlene Stewart–designed dress with a ten-foot train and a pink sash—like a Girl Scout or a beauty queen—embroidered with roses and jewels. Under her veil, she wore a black bowler hat. "I don't know what that was supposed to mean," said a stumped Warhol.[62] For jewelry, she wore something very special: Maripol made her a single earring, a small star with gold chain and pearls. "I only made one piece, it was only for her, and I never made it for anyone else," Maripol said.[63] The groom wore a double-breasted Versace suit off the rack.

The wedding guests represented a sampling of Madonna's and Sean's worlds. Madonna's side included her extended family from Michigan, plus Christopher Flynn; her madcap downtown New York friends; the Warner Bros. team, including the chairman, Mo Ostin; music mogul David Geffen; her *Desperately Seeking Susan* colleagues Susan Seidelman and Rosanna

Arquette; and people in the entertainment world she had come to know, among them Cher (wearing a huge purple wig).[64]

Sean's invitees included his family plus a coterie of young Hollywood talent—Carrie Fisher, Charlie Sheen, Judd Nelson, Rob Lowe, Timothy Hutton, and the *Fast Times at Ridgemont High* screenwriter, Cameron Crowe. Also on hand were a few old-timers (or so they called themselves) such as Harry Dean Stanton and Robert Duvall.[65] Warhol was dizzy surveying the crowd, writing in his diary, "All these young actors seemed like they were in their father's suits, like Emilio Estevez and Tom Cruise. All these movie star boys with the strong legs who're 5'10" or so. I guess that's the new Hollywood look."[66]

Presided over by Judge Merrick, with James Foley as best man and Madonna's sister Paula as maid of honor, the ceremony lasted less than ten minutes amid the deafening clatter of helicopters. "The three of us knew pretty much what we were doing. But everybody else couldn't hear over the noise," Merrick said.[67] "Chariots of Fire" provided the soundtrack to the couple's first post-vows kiss. The bouquet was tossed, the garter retrieved. An electronic version of *Madama Butterfly*—composed by the father of the Sex Pistols, Malcolm McLaren—played as the guests downed Cristal champagne before their meal.[68]

Maripol sat at the head table with Madonna and Sean, but she said it was half empty because the bride and groom were wandering, as was Herb Ritts with his camera (he was the only person at the wedding allowed to have one). "I told Madonna that I didn't have anyone next to my chair, so she goes to Sean and whispers in his ear and Sean comes back with Tom Cruise!" Maripol recalled, laughing. "During the whole dinner, we were talking. He was really cute and smart and polite."[69]

Madonna had selected the music. "I wanted it to be really romantic," she said. It included classics from the repertoires of Bing Crosby, Ella Fitzgerald, Cole Porter, and Sarah Vaughan.[70] Madonna's music was represented by "Into the Groove." She felt sentimental about that song, telling an interviewer that it encapsulated her early life and career. "It also meant a lot to me that the guy I wrote it with and the guy that produced the record with me...Steve Bray, was somebody I'd been with since my childhood."[71]

Around ten, the party began to wind down.[72] Warhol said that Steve Rubell was "really out of it on I guess Quaaludes. And I think I saw Madonna kick him away from her."[73] Debi had splurged on a pair of Manolo Blahniks for the event only to see them destroyed. "I basically probably had my electricity turned off just to buy these shoes, and Rubell vomited on them," she said.[74] It was time to go.

Tom Cruise asked Maripol if he could hitch a ride to his car to avoid the paparazzi and threw himself into the back of the limo along with Martin Burgoyne, Keith Haring, Steve Rubell, and Warhol. Maripol sat on his lap. For Warhol, the wonderment of the day started all over again. "I just couldn't believe my eyes," he wrote.[75]

Madonna and Sean disappeared to honeymoon in Carmel, while the New York crew spent the remainder of their time in LA visiting celebrities—including Dolly Parton and Cher—and driving along impossibly clean, palm-tree-lined roads under bright blue skies.[76]

Back in dirty, gray New York, Warhol felt deflated. As he was walking down 66th Street, after his ride in from the airport, a woman shouted "Andy!" "When I didn't turn around," he said, "she screamed, 'Your mother's a whore.'"[77] He had officially left the fantasyland that was Hollywood.

Sean surprised Madonna with a 1957 Thunderbird convertible as a birthday-wedding gift, which she loved so much that a Thunderbird appeared in a video for her new album. The song and the album would be called *True Blue,* a phrase Sean used that had a very 1950s ring to it. In fact, at the start, the newlyweds seemed to exist in a 1950s or early-1960s world: she the actor and performer, he the sensitive film hunk, both of them traveling in intellectual and artistic circles. When they were together, they could live that dream. But just in case reality threatened to impinge, the house they bought in Malibu, set on fifty acres with an ocean view, was surrounded by a wall topped with spikes. (Sean said he had considered gun towers.)[78]

Madonna and Sean would both be in and out of New York for work, so it made sense to have an apartment there, too. Their timing made the task difficult because the *Playboy-Penthouse* ruckus was still fresh in people's minds. They tried to buy an apartment in the San Remo, on Central Park West, but were rejected by the co-op board (only Diane Keaton backed the application). Residents reportedly feared having tabloid targets in their midst.[79] Madonna and Sean then found a place at Harperley Hall, near Lincoln Center, where their application to buy was accepted.

Meanwhile, in October Sean returned to Tennessee to plead no contest to assault and battery charges, for which he received a ninety-day suspended sentence and a fine.[80] That same month, Madonna's past became an issue once again when Stephen Jon Lewicki released his film *A Certain Sacrifice.* Though it was PG even by 1985 standards, the media pounced on the film the way it had the *Playboy-Penthouse* photos because Madonna's breasts were visible for a nanosecond and she supposedly played a dominatrix.[81]

The episode was more annoyance than anything else. Madonna wanted to launch a serious film career after the success of *Desperately Seeking Susan,* and she didn't think the Lewicki film was very good.[82] She tried to block its release. When that failed, she did her best to ignore it. But the press reported what it wanted to report, even if the stories were invented out of whole cloth. Every rumored film project, every rumored quarrel with Sean, every rumored pregnancy (and when that imagined pregnancy didn't produce a bump, every rumored abortion) made headlines. Tabloid reporters even hounded Madonna's father, forcing him to repeatedly change his phone number.[83]

Amid all that nonsensical scrutiny, in November, Yoko Ono invited Madonna to a small dinner party for Bob Dylan at her New York apartment. Columbia Records had thrown a bash for him the previous night at the Whitney Museum of American Art, and Yoko gathered some of the attendees together in a more intimate setting—her kitchen. Dylan, David Bowie, Iggy Pop, Andy Warhol, Keith Haring, Martin Burgoyne, and Madonna, among a few others, stood around in a circle, eating store-bought chicken.[84]

It was poetic in a way that Madonna would end her year of equal parts adulation and abuse at Ono's place. Yoko was a groundbreaking artist who had suffered insults for decades. She was seen as an evil, manipulative woman, a feminist and foreigner to boot, and was held responsible for ending the fantasy of rock that was embodied in the Beatles. Worst of all, she refused to play wife to a rock genius. She had the nerve to want to be heard, too.

That year, she had released a seventh album, *Starpeace* (a comment on Reagan's Star Wars program), but it was widely panned outside New York. Ignoring the carping of the critics, she was busily planning a concert tour of Europe.[85]

This strong woman had continued to create despite life's tragic vicissitudes and had continued to take artistic risks even when she was the object of scorn. She was a survivor. She had integrity. She was steadfast. Sean might say she was true blue.

In December, Madonna and Sean took a page from the Lennon-Ono playbook. John and Yoko had been known to quietly visit hospitals and the needy, engaging in acts of charity to spread their love. Ahead of the Penns' first Christmas together, they visited Weill Cornell Medical Center to distribute gifts to children forced to spend their holiday in the hospital. Photographers were not allowed.[86]

Chapter 20

Hong Kong, Los Angeles, 1986

Nothing that I've said so far, nothing that I could possibly come up with, is as important as her. No movie, nothing is as important as her.[1]

— Sean Penn

THE TRADE PAPERS announced on November 7, 1985, that Madonna and Sean had signed to costar in the film *Shanghai Surprise.* Producer John Kohn, who had worked with Sean in the past, had sent Madonna a screenplay he cowrote based on the book *Faraday's Flowers,* by Tony Kenrick. It was a romantic comedy set in Shanghai as the Japanese prepared to invade on the eve of World War II. Madonna would play a missionary nurse, with Sean cast as a shady salesman of glow-in-the-dark neckties. With its gangsters, opium, colonial culture clashes, and burgeoning love between the saint and the scoundrel, the film had the makings of a 1930s-style romantic caper set in an exotic locale.[2]

Madonna and Sean had been looking for a dark comedy to do together, and so they met Kohn at an LA restaurant to discuss it. Not long after they were seated, Kohn's coproducer arrived: ex-Beatle George Harrison. "They nearly fell off their chairs with surprise," Kohn said. Sean and Madonna agreed to do the film.[3] "I thought it was a great script, and the idea of going to Shanghai was exciting to me, and the idea of working with my husband was exciting to me because he's a great actor," Madonna said.[4]

Her enthusiasm, however, was tempered by a case of pre-project jitters. Friends told her that costarring in a film with Sean was the surest way to end their young marriage. Madonna also feared that Sean wouldn't respect her as an actor.[5] Sean, too, had reservations, though for different reasons. *Shanghai Surprise* wasn't the kind of film he would normally make.[6] "Why did I do it? For love and money," he responded when asked by an interviewer about his participation in the film.

Well, put it like this, I was in a marriage with somebody who had a lot of money...And I certainly did not want to be anything less than a full participant in anything that we did. But that was the number-two thing. The number-one thing was: I had just got married, and she was asking me to do it.[7]

Madonna and Sean flew to Asia in early January. Four weeks of filming were set to begin on January 20 in Hong Kong and Macao, followed by four more weeks in London.[8] Sean wanted to see Shanghai to research the story's actual setting because the Chinese government wouldn't allow the film to be shot there. Accompanied by three government escorts, Sean, Madonna, and her brother Christopher visited it.[9]

"We were supposed to go to sleep but we couldn't sleep," Madonna said. "We ended up just walking around in the streets on this steel cold morning. It was still dark out, and the streets were filled with people doing tai chi. So dreamlike—you saw all these hands moving." No one knew who Madonna was, but her blond hair made an impact. "I'm like from outer space to them. A Martian. I loved that," she said.[10] In Hong Kong, she returned to earth.

Madonna was mobbed at the airport.[11] Sean called the situation "*insane.*" On the second day of filming, the press was so intrusive that Sean demanded the on-set publicist be fired for not being able to keep reporters at bay while they worked.[12] With one publicist gone, another appeared, but the paparazzi only grew more aggressive.[13]

On the set, Christopher said, the all-British crew took an "instant dislike to Madonna and Sean." They regarded them as "two troublesome brats."[14] With respect to the actual shooting, Madonna described a litany of woes. She said the area they filmed in was controlled by the Chinese mafia, which had to be paid off before the film crew was allowed to shoot.

Another time, we were in a village about an hour outside of the city with only one tiny road leading out. They blocked the road and demanded $50,000 to let us leave.[15] So it's two o'clock in the morning, it's cold, we're tired, we have to get up the next morning at six, and we couldn't get out of there because this guy was parked, and he wanted $50,000. That went on every day.[16]

In addition, because the story was set in summer but shot in winter, Madonna froze in lightweight dresses during outside scenes.[17] And then there were rats, power outages, and what she described as her growing suspicion that the director didn't know what he was doing. "We were on a ship without a captain," Madonna said, "and we were so miserable while we were working that I'm sure it shows."[18]

Madonna and Sean took turns being strong in the face of a terrible situation.[19] At other times the strain was so great that they took their frustrations out on each other. Christopher remembered waking up at three in the morning to screaming and crashing furniture from Madonna and Sean's suite next door. "Although I'm half-asleep, I can make out some of the words. 'I'm the actor, you're not. You should forget about acting.' ... And 'You don't know a fucking thing about handling the media, you paranoid control freak.'"[20]

After Christopher heard what sounded like a fist in a wall, he made to break down the door, but at that moment it opened, and Madonna flew into his room with Sean in pursuit. Christopher locked him out. "Sean is banging on the door yelling her name," Christopher said. "'Open the fucking door, Madonna, open the fucking door.'" Eventually it stopped. So did Madonna's sobbing. She and Christopher fell asleep in his room.[21]

In the morning, she was back on set looking professional and confident as if nothing had happened.[22] For his part, Sean admitted that he relied on booze to get him through the shoot. "I just said, 'I don't give a fuck.'"[23]

The filming next took them to Macao, a former Portuguese protectorate and gambling haven in southeastern China near Hong Kong. Looking for a little peace, they were assured that the Oriental hotel, where they would be staying, had been cleared of the press and intruders. Sean arrived at the hotel with a kickboxing coach, who doubled as his assistant and bodyguard, and was escorted to his room by two hotel security men. "As I approach the room, security drops back. There's a door to the left side of the corridor, and as we make a right into the room, somebody jumps out. We were not prepared for this," Sean said.[24]

Accounts vary as to what happened next. Sean said he and his kickboxing buddy "grabbed the guy, ran him through the room to the balcony and hung him over ... not with the intention of throwing him over." The hotel security men, meanwhile, recognized the interloper as a photographer. "We were pulled off him by security guys, and we went willingly; it wasn't violent. And we got arrested for attempted murder."[25]

Sean and his assistant were taken in by police for two hours of questioning, after which they were left to consider their fate on the stone floor of a Macao jail. "So we're looking at each other like, 'What do we do now?'" Sean recalled. "The cell door was ajar. We took off, got out ... And we were able to make a phone call to the production office."[26] After a series of calls among various players, including the Triad that ran Macao, an arrangement was made that allowed Sean to return to work pending an investigation. His friend was also allowed to remain free.[27]

With shooting in Asia finally wrapped, Madonna and Sean flew to

Berlin for the premiere of *At Close Range* at the Berlin International Film Festival. Sean stayed behind in Germany for a few days while Madonna, with a bodyguard and trainer, flew to London to continue filming *Shanghai Surprise*. The story of the Macao incident and the picture's troubled production having preceded her, the press awaiting her in Britain was rabid.[28]

Christopher had arrived in Britain ahead of Madonna and met her at Heathrow. All was calm coming out of the plane and through customs, but once the doors to the arrivals hall were thrown open, Christopher said, "all hell breaks loose. The hall is ablaze with exploding flashbulbs and the glare of TV cameras." As they pushed into the hall, Christopher estimated, there were around three hundred people bearing down on them. He, the bodyguard, and the trainer formed a protective wedge around Madonna and made their way slowly across the hall, pushing through the crowd for around fifteen minutes, toward a car awaiting them outside.[29]

Inside, it was impossible to see out the car's windows because bodies were pressed against the glass. They heard a thud on the roof. Then a paparazzo jumped on the car's hood. It was like a zombie attack in a horror movie. Madonna screamed, "Get me out of here!" But the driver couldn't move because the car was surrounded. Slowly, he inched the vehicle forward until its occupants felt a bump. A photographer had fallen off the car and onto the road. The paparazzi were thrilled. They had their exclusive. The headline wrote itself: MADONNA'S LIMO RUNS OVER PHOTOGRAPHER.[30]

Madonna's driver hit the gas, taking that moment when the press was distracted to make a break for it. Christopher turned around to watch as the paparazzi snapped away at the man on the ground. When he began to get up, one of their number motioned for him to lie back down; he hadn't gotten the picture. As much as Christopher disliked Sean for the Hong Kong fight with Madonna, he said his experience with the paparazzi that day made him feel a "flash of empathy for him. After all, I only had to endure the full force of the paparazzi for a few hours, but Sean is condemned to endure it for as long as he and Madonna are married."[31]

Producer George Harrison indirectly blamed Madonna and Sean for their problems with the media, grumbling that they didn't have a sense of humor about the press and didn't handle it the way the Beatles had.[32] It seemed that Harrison failed to recognize the changed relationship between the media and celebrities in the twenty years since he had been in the spotlight with the band. He also didn't understand the underlying misogyny of the Madonna coverage. He got a taste of it, though, during what he had hoped would be a peacemaking press conference.[33]

The hostility in the room was palpable. With Sean still in Germany, it was left to Harrison and Madonna to respond to seventy-five reporters shouting questions. Harrison, that supposed veteran of press encounters, grew immediately testy with the hostile inquisitors. "You're all so busy creating a fuss, then writing about it as if we've created it for the publicity," he said. One of the reporters asked him what he had expected of the press. To which he replied, "We expect nonanimals."[34]

For her part, Madonna handled the room with calm aplomb. Dressed as her *Shanghai Surprise* character, she was prim and gracious in the face of demands that she apologize for supposedly having mistreated the press. She refused but did so in such a way that by the end of the press conference, she had lowered the temperature considerably.

Despite her efforts, some reporters published pieces that were probably written in advance because they had already decided on the story: Madonna was a bitch. The *NME* reporter, however, said that Madonna was "as quick-witted, self-possessed and beautiful as I'd hoped she would be." Either way, bad girl or good girl, Madonna was unfazed by the commentariat. "I'm tough, ambitious, and I know exactly what I want. If that makes me a bitch, okay," she said.[35]

Returning to LA, Madonna headed back to friendly terrain—the studio—to work on her new album, *True Blue*. She wanted to create a girl group sound, like that of the Shirelles or the Ronettes. To help her, she recruited Steve Bray and Pat Leonard. "Madonna and I really adore that old school pop, and it was a huge part of why we clicked," said Steve.[36] Lyrics had become more important to her, too. Her new songs would be danceable because that was her signature style, but words were no longer used merely to support the rhythm. That was both because her emotional life had deepened and because of the changed atmosphere in the clubs.

By the mid-1980s, most gay men had finally accepted that AIDS was transmitted through unsafe sex and were willing to trade some of their prized freedom for a chance at life: monogamy rather than serial partners; gyms rather than bathhouses; vitamins rather than poppers.[37] Dance and music were still part of it, but the volume had been turned down, and the dance floor was less hedonistic. Madonna's album would reflect that. Just as she, the wild child, had epitomized the era of absolute freedom, Madonna the married lady represented a new reality: lust had, at least temporarily, taken a back seat to love.

And she was definitely in love. Madonna called Sean "my hero and my best friend."[38] She conceded in late 1985,

> I feel calmer now than I ever have before. What that means is that I can really concentrate on the important things. It's funny, now that I'm in love, all the songs I write I feel like I do it all for him. I do it for myself, but I do it

for him. I'm writing the lyrics or doing the music, or something that's creative, I think "Would he like it?"[39]

Hanging around, jiggling his car keys, "he" came to Pat Leonard's home studio in LA, where Madonna would record five songs. Sean "wanted to get her outta there as fast as he could. They were so into each other," said Bruce Gaitsch, who played guitar on the album.[40] In New York, Madonna recorded four more songs—including "Papa Don't Preach"—with Steve Bray in a studio he had set up in his apartment in Brooklyn.[41]

It could be argued that *True Blue* was actually the first "Madonna" album. It was certainly the first in which she wasn't a student working with a veteran producer and the first with her fingerprints on every aspect of the record, from writing to production to presentation. She would be coproducer with Pat and Steve, neither of whom had ever produced an album. "We argued a lot," Pat said. "But one day [in the late stages of the project] she held up the *True Blue* album cover and said: 'Whose picture is that?' The more feisty conversations stopped there!"[42]

Pat said that Madonna was in the studio for "every note," prodding them, questioning them. When he wanted to settle more comfortably into what he called the rules of pop, she demanded to know why they couldn't break the rules. "I found out after the first song or so that if you listen to what she says, it instantly becomes a 'Madonna' record—her instincts just turn into that, no matter what producer she's working with."[43]

Steve described the writing and recording as "a fantasy situation."

> We were working for this big label…and she had gotten to the point that she didn't really have to answer to them creatively, so we were left on our own to make this whole album…Doing whatever we wanted and letting them in the room when we finished was great.[44]

While Madonna was in the music studio, Sean became obsessed with a writer named Charles Bukowski. He had received Bukowski's poetry book *War All the Time* as a wedding present and in late 1985 set out to meet him. Sean wasn't disappointed. In the world of artifice that was industry LA, it was probably Bukowski's honesty that made him attractive. There was nothing he would not write or say. The word *unfiltered* didn't begin to describe him; foul-mouthed would be overly polite. His violence wasn't stylized; it was gut-wrenchingly ugly. Bukowski himself was a hard man, and it was written all over his craggy face.[45] It took a true romantic like Sean to see beauty in him.

By the time Sean met him, the sixty-five-year-old writer was married to his second wife, Linda, and living in San Pedro, California. He was out of the flophouses where he had lived and the dive bars that he often crawled home from, but his drinking habits hadn't changed, nor had his personality—neither of which mattered to Sean. If anything, it made Hank, as Bukowski was called, more intriguing. Sean loved the man.[46] Bukowski became one of Sean's major influences during his first year of marriage, but he also awakened the part of Sean that was most self-destructive.[47]

Sean had always been a drinker, but by that spring it consumed him.[48] His watering hole of choice was Helena's, a members-only supper club in the Silver Lake district of East LA run by a generous-spirited woman named Helena Kallianiotes.[49] The rules were few, and only one was rigorously enforced: no photographs. Helena herself manned the door, where on any given night she might welcome Jack Nicholson, Anjelica Huston, Susan Sarandon, Rob Lowe, Sarah Jessica Parker, Elton John, Rod Stewart, or Marlon Brando.[50]

Just after midnight on April 12, 1986, Sean and Madonna were there having a quiet supper. As always, there were several versions of what transpired that night. The most widely repeated had musician David Wolinski, whom Madonna had known in New York, stopping by their table to say hello and give Madonna a kiss on the cheek. Out of jealously, the story went, Sean jumped up, punched him to the ground, kicked him once he was down, and hit him with a chair. Restrained by other diners, Sean was forced to leave.[51]

Sean's version of the story put his actions in context. He said Wolinski had tried to make a pass at Madonna the previous year, and only Madonna's intervention kept Sean from hitting him at that time.[52] When they encountered Wolinski at Helena's, Sean still hadn't forgotten the punch not thrown. He said that as he and Madonna made to leave the club, Wolinski stood up to say hello. Sean accused Wolinski of trying to hit on Madonna the year before, and when Wolinski denied it, Sean snapped.

> I, stupidly, hit him...And *then* I made the mistake. He was bigger than I was, I didn't want him getting up, so I picked up a chair—not thinking, I just went from the misdemeanor handbook to a felony, assault with a deadly weapon...It was more of a threat than anything else, but I *did* make contact. And now I wish I had fucking slammed him, because I went to jail like I'd slammed him.[53]

Wolinski suffered face, leg, and back injuries. The LA city attorney filed charges against Sean. It was his third violent episode in less than a year.

The reasons were simple: a hair–trigger temper and an exaggerated threat response combined, in the Wolinski case, with a dangerous cocktail—booze and jealousy.[54]

Sean's history of jealousy was well known. As early as *Fast Times at Ridgemont High,* he had stood over Amy Heckerling's shoulder while she shot a scene in which his then girlfriend, Pam Springsteen, walked away from the camera. He wanted to ensure that the shot didn't linger unnecessarily on her behind.[55] While making *Racing with the Moon* with Elizabeth McGovern, he reportedly went berserk when he learned that she was alone in her trailer with a male reporter. Sean stormed over and rocked the trailer while they were inside.[56]

With Madonna, he was not only jealous but also what she called "protective." "He was like my father in a way," she said. "He patrolled what I wore. He'd say, 'You're not wearing that dress. You can see everything in that.' But at least he was paying attention to me. At least he had the balls."[57] At the beginning, she appreciated such behavior as a sign of Sean's love. But as it had with her father, it would become too much.

At Close Range premiered in Los Angeles on April 18, six days after the Wolinski incident. The film's party was at Helena's. Despite the skirmish, Sean remained in her good graces.[58] The film received positive reviews, especially for the acting, though some critics accused James Foley of prettying up the story's gritty reality. Any discussions of the film's supposed failings, however, were overshadowed by the success of Madonna's song for the picture.[59]

Madonna and Pat Leonard had written "Live to Tell" the previous year for a different movie. "I asked Madonna as a favor if she'd write lyrics for the song," Pat said. He had the music written, but while Madonna was still at work on the lyrics, the studio called to say it didn't want his song. "She said, 'Well, let me hear it, because Sean's got this new movie that he's working on.'" They recorded Madonna singing her lyrics over Pat's music, and she brought the song to Penn.[60]

Foley and Sean loved it and wanted it in their movie, but Madonna said, "'Who's gonna sing it?' And we all went, 'You're gonna sing it.'"[61] Pat added, "She didn't want to. She thought it had to be sung by a man because it's so low and unlike anything she'd attempted before." But finally, she agreed.[62] Foley also asked Pat to score his movie. "So I got fired, wrote that song, and got hired to do another movie, all in one day," Pat said.[63]

Madonna described "Live to Tell" as "about being very young and having to grow up quickly because you've seen certain things."[64] She credited Pat with encouraging her to "dig deep and explore areas of my emotional life that I possibly hadn't really gotten into yet...Pat had a dark side to him, and so that kind of brought out my dark side."[65]

The song that was used in the film was the demo she recorded with Pat.[66] Madonna told Warner Bros. that she wanted to release it as the first single from her next album, but the company feared that a soulful ballad would kill her momentum as an upbeat pop star. "They really said, 'It's over. It's over. You're doomed. You're putting out a seven-minute song that stops three times, that's just this weird dark thing,'" Pat said.[67] Madonna authorized the song's release anyway, along with an accompanying video.

That video caused fresh heartburn in Warner executive suites. It incorporated scenes from *At Close Range* and had Madonna singing on a bare stage with only a wooden chair by way of set. Madonna videos weren't supposed to look bleak. But she recognized that "Live to Tell" was a haunting song for a haunting time. It went to number 1 in the charts, and the video was put on heavy rotation on MTV. To those who doubted Madonna's talent, Pat said, "How many singers do you know who can do a rough vocal of a song they wrote two hours ago, and sell a million copies with it?"[68]

After her *Shanghai Surprise* duties, Madonna abandoned her 1930s coiffure by cutting off her hair and dyeing it platinum blond. She spoke of it as shedding last year's skin.[69] It was that look—sleek, clean, early Kim Novak—that Herb Ritts captured for the cover of *True Blue*. Madonna's first two album photographs looked New York: dark, rough, and moody. The Madonna of *True Blue* was bathed in California sun against an intense hand-tinted Pacific-blue background.

Much was made of Madonna's new image. There was a sense of betrayal in the way the media wrote about the change. Many writers had criticized or mocked her early look, yet they weren't prepared to let her move on. But change was essential to Madonna. As was true of her mentor, David Bowie, each new project required a new character that existed across a spectrum of media: music, videos, live performances, movies, even interviews. She might inhabit a character for a year—or three years—depending upon the needs of her work.[70] And each look generally involved a top-to-bottom renewal. Her radical change from the Boy Toy of her first two albums to the '60s girl group singer of *True Blue* was the first real example.[71]

In June, *True Blue* was released to critical acclaim.[72] It also had wild commercial success—better than *Like a Virgin*—going straight to number 1 in twenty-eight countries. One critic suggested the album was so popular because it was the first of Madonna's works "to invite listeners past the façade." The songs she wrote offered tantalizing clues about Madonna's life.[73] But it was a song she didn't write that garnered the most headlines.

"Papa Don't Preach" was written by Brian Elliot and brought to Madonna by Michael Ostin at Warner Bros., the same executive who found "Like a Virgin" for her.[74] The songs formed a pair. "Like a Virgin" is about the glory of love and sexual awakening. "Papa Don't Preach" is about the consequences. The song also fit comfortably with the other material on the album because it was an updated version of 1960s story songs. "We thought of it as a 'Harper Valley P.T.A.' kind of song and we just liked it," Steve Bray said. "I don't think she knew it was going to rock the Vatican."[75]

In the 1970s, during the heyday of women's liberation and in the wake of the Supreme Court's decision in *Roe v. Wade,* the subject of abortion was about a woman's right to choose whether to have a baby. In the '80s, that debate was overwhelmed by the religious right, which shifted the focus to the *fetus's* rights. The woman carrying the child became a troublesome bit player.[76] Madonna's song returned that woman to center stage — it was about what *she* wanted. The song "fit right in with my own personal Zeitgeist of standing up to male authorities," Madonna said, "whether it's the pope or the Catholic Church or my father and his conservative, patriarchal ways."[77]

That was not how the many sides of the abortion debate saw it. Because the young woman in the song keeps her baby, the right embraced "Papa Don't Preach" for its seemingly antiabortion stance, though it worried about the premarital-sex angle. Feminists denounced it as a "commercial for teen pregnancy."[78] Planned Parenthood's New York chapter went so far as to send a "critical memo" to radio and TV stations, advising them to "think carefully" before playing it. The chapter's executive director, Alfred Moran, told the *New York Times,* "Everybody I've talked to believes she has more impact on teenagers than any other entertainer since the Beatles. That's what makes this particular song so destructive."[79]

But of infinitely more importance were the discussions the song provoked. Writing in the *Boston Phoenix,* culture critic Joyce Millman said,

> "Papa Don't Preach" is Madonna's finest three minutes, not merely because it addresses teen pregnancy but because it suggests that a portion of the blame rests on parents' reluctance to discuss, not lecture about, sex... "Papa Don't Preach" opens a long overdue and desperately needed discussion... Female adolescence will never be the same.[80]

Madonna knew the song would be controversial. She called it a "message song that everyone is going to take the wrong way." She continued,

> When I first heard the song, I thought it was silly. But then I thought, wait a minute, this song is really about a girl who is making a decision in her life. She has a very close relationship with her father and wants to maintain that closeness. To me it's a celebration of life. It says, "I love you, father, and I love this man and this child that is growing inside me.". . . Who knows how it will end? But at least it starts off positive.[81]

The video for "Papa Don't Preach," which was Madonna and James Foley's second collaboration after "Live to Tell," premiered in Los Angeles in June. Filmed on Staten Island, it was shot in an environment that might have been any working-class neighborhood where family dramas played out against pop music soundtracks.[82]

In this case, Madonna—boyish in her blue jeans and black leather jacket, gamine with her short blond hair—plays a teenager in love with a handsome garage mechanic, portrayed by a young actor named Alex McArthur.[83] Danny Aiello, a veteran of the New York Italian-American school of cinema, plays Madonna's gruff but loving father.

Because it is a Madonna video, she is shown as two characters: the omniscient observer and the other Madonna—Staten Island Madonna—confronting the consequences of her young love. Observer Madonna is filmed alone on an empty stage, as in "Live to Tell," but in "Papa Don't Preach," she dances.

The five-minute mini movie is gripping. Her real-life friends Erika Belle and Debi Mazar appear in the opening scene, in which Madonna, hanging on the street wearing an ITALIANS DO IT BETTER T-shirt, first spots her soon-to-be boyfriend. Madonna had found the shirt and asked Foley if she could wear it. He called it a "masterstroke."[84] It wasn't just that the shirt made Madonna's character more authentic: the word *Italian* also instantly broadcast what she would be up against—a religious family and a strict father.

The video contains all the dramatic tension of the song—love, longing, excitement, confusion, isolation, fear—but never shame. And *that* was a breakthrough. In real teenage pregnancies, the girls are the "sinners" who literally carry their shame. Madonna's pregnant teenager has none.

Sean flew Martin Burgoyne and Erika to Los Angeles for the video's premiere. The *New York Times*'s Stephen Holden called Madonna's performance in the video "virtuoso . . . Like Michael Jackson's 'Billie Jean,' the song and its video have an iconographic resonance that could push

Madonna's career to an even higher plateau."[85] An MTV spokeswoman said that the video "received an unbelievable response."[86]

Madonna began to be compared with Bruce Springsteen for supposedly speaking to working-class women and girls the way he spoke to working-class men and boys. *Rolling Stone* anointed her the "pop poet of lower-middle-class America."[87]

Chapter 21

Los Angeles, New York, 1986

> I loved him, it seemed, forever, and nothing new could happen
> to that love. I'd forgotten about death.[1]
>
> —*Marguerite Duras*

MADONNA'S DANCE TEACHER Christopher Flynn had been in Los Angeles
for her wedding and left there contemplating a move west. He hadn't
been given tenure at the University of Michigan because he lacked an
advanced degree, and in any case, he had soured on the school. He hoped
to begin a new teaching career outside of academia, maybe start another
Christopher Ballet. Madonna encouraged him to come to Los Angeles to
do it.[2]

At fifty-five, he knew it wouldn't be an easy move, but he decided he
wasn't too old to try.[3] By August, he and his partner, Earl GeBott, had
found an apartment in Silver Lake, and Christopher took a job teaching on
a freelance basis. Madonna, meanwhile, introduced him to the city's theater scene, which was more gay-friendly than the film world.[4]

In a piece about Flynn's move, the *Ann Arbor News* said, "The pupil is
finally getting her chance to repay the teacher...It's like some sort of O.
Henry story still waiting for the ending to be written." Except that by the
time the article appeared, the ending had been written.[5] Flynn was diagnosed with AIDS before he left for LA. "He taught a couple of classes, but
he really wasn't into it," GeBott said. Instead the two men enlisted in the
AIDS fight, joining a group that provided people with AIDS the material
necessities of life.[6]

Madonna was still digesting the news of Flynn's illness when she learned
about Martin Burgoyne.

He had been ill but refused to acknowledge the cause. In July, he told
Keith Haring that he had been tested for AIDS and had been given the all-
clear. Haring knew that wasn't true. "When I looked at him, I saw death,"
he said.[7] Martin "kept telling everyone he had measles and we knew he
didn't have measles," said Catherine Underhill. To others, he said he had
the flu. No one knew for sure because he refused to leave his apartment.
"One or the other of us would go and bang on his door and try to get him

to open or take him food," Catherine said, "or get him to engage with what we knew was really happening."[8]

The tabloid reporters following Madonna wrote in early August that she was spotted on Columbus Avenue buying books for a "sick friend." Shortly afterward, Martin flew to Florida to be with his family. By the middle of the month he was back in New York and diagnosed with AIDS-related complex. It was a category that meant he was HIV-positive but didn't exhibit conditions then associated with AIDS. It was a limbo state that offered little comfort. Martin was twenty-three.[9]

He told Madonna about the diagnosis. It was the second time in a month that she heard such news from a man she loved. But with Martin it was different. Christopher Flynn had at least had a chance at life. Martin hadn't even begun. "It really ripped her up," said Freddy DeMann's assistant, Melinda Cooper.[10] Even from a distance, Martin had been a constant in her life. They spoke by phone. Sometimes he came to Los Angeles. Often, she was in New York. Her marriage meant that they were no longer joined at the hip, but her love for Martin had not diminished with Sean's entry into the equation, nor had Martin's for her.

After Martin stopped working with Madonna when her life shifted to LA, he supported himself by designing record covers for various artists in the United States and Britain. Catherine Underhill said,

> Martin had approached Madonna for money to set up a graphics business. She came back to him and said he needed to put together a business plan and to talk to her then. He was kind of offended that she just didn't want to give him the money straightaway. I actually thought it was really smart because it was gonna make him think through what he really wanted. But then he got sick.[11]

Madonna shifted into rescue mode. She rented an apartment for him on 12th Street; it had fewer stairs and was around the corner from St. Vincent's Hospital, which had become the primary health center in New York for people with AIDS. She also arranged to cover all his medical bills. "She absolutely provided for him. That enabled him not to be scared about money, to have the best medical care," Catherine said. Three friends—Catherine, Erika Belle, and Claudia Summers—acted as nurses. "He did not go gently into that good night," Catherine said. "It was not fair, and he never came to a point where it was okay."[12]

Madonna called Martin every day when she wasn't in New York and saw him several times a week when she was. She became an expert on experimental treatments for AIDS, including the drugs ribavirin and iso-prinosine, which weren't available in the States for AIDS patients but were sold in Mexico. She sent Sean there to get them. There was no time to waste.[13]

Martin's illness was tragic on many levels, but perhaps the saddest part was that that year, as Madonna settled into her relationship with Sean, Martin, too, had fallen in love. The man in his life was a twenty-two-year-old actor named Lawrence Monoson. "As far as I know," said Marcus Leatherdale, "he was the only person he actually had a relationship with, where he said, 'This is my boyfriend.'"[14]

Lawrence was in New York for rehearsals for a film called *Gaby: A True Story,* starring Liv Ullmann. "I do not remember exactly how I met Martin. We were just absolutely taken *immediately* with each other," Monoson said.

> I can honestly tell you he was like a magical child. Being with Martin was like having this open escort to New York. He was the most adored person I have ever hung out with. Ever...He had a beautiful spirit and a softness and a gentleness about him...Being with him, there was an anything-was-possible kind of feeling. It really was this whirlwind, crazy, novelistic romance.[15]

The backdrop to their romance, though, was death. Lawrence noticed it because it was so different from LA, where, he said, "AIDS wasn't part of the lexicon. It wasn't real. It existed as a newspaper article...In New York, it was visceral. People were disappearing from the street. It was, like, every week, 'Where is John?' 'Where is...' There was hysteria. It just happened so fast. It was devastating."[16]

Perhaps it was because of that disease and its hideous inevitability that Martin and Lawrence bonded so quickly and loved each other so intensely. But soon Lawrence had to return west. It was nearly time to go to Mexico City, where *Gaby* would be filmed.[17]

When they met, Martin still lived on 4th Street, and his apartment was filled with an eclectic array of memorabilia. "There was a cassette tape of the Partridge Family's greatest hits," Lawrence said. He asked Martin if he could have it, and Martin said, "Sure." Not long after that that, Martin became ill. He "disappeared into his apartment. I was calling him all the time...I went over to Martin's apartment and brought this soup because he had the flu. And he wouldn't let me in the door...I left the soup, and I went back to LA."[18]

While packing to go to Mexico City, Lawrence found the Partridge Family cassette and decided to take it with him. "I absolutely have no idea why I asked for it and then why I packed it for Mexico City." But one day during rehearsals, Lawrence played the Partridge song "I Think I Love

You." Director Luis Mandoki liked it and wanted to use it in the film. Lawrence was so pleased because it felt like Martin had become part of the project. He didn't realize it at the time, but that song in the movie and his memories would be all he would have of him. Lawrence never saw Martin again.[19]

Madonna's work kept her in New York for much of the late summer and fall. Sean's immersion in literature through his association with Bukowski had given him the idea to try writing himself. He wrote poetry and a screenplay, which he wanted David Rabe's help with. Sean had met Rabe in New York in 1983 and thought he was the "best playwright in America, period." Rabe was of the generation of artists who had served in Vietnam and, once back in the States, tried through their work to make sense of that horror.[20]

Rabe was too busy to look at Sean's script, but he had a play that he wanted Sean to read. It was called *Goose and Tomtom*. Rabe said it was set in an "apartment in the underworld...in reference both to a contemporary criminal underworld but, more importantly, to the mythical underworld, to Hades—which is where it *really* takes place, I think."[21]

The play was about a pair of tough-guy thieves who collaborate with a tough-girl sexpot named Lorraine to gather a treasure trove of jewels, which is then stolen by a rival gang. Sean loved the script and asked if he could show it to Madonna.[22] He wanted to play Tomtom opposite Madonna as Lorraine.[23]

Rabe wasn't convinced it would work, but he agreed, thinking, "This will be fun, it will definitely be interesting." Rabe had an arrangement with Lincoln Center's Mitzi E. Newhouse Theater that allowed him to produce a work in progress without any obligation to show it to the public. It was under the auspices of that deal that he got to work on his play.[24]

Soon, Barry Miller, who had primarily done TV, and Harvey Keitel joined the cast. When Rabe told Keitel he needed another woman in the play, Keitel suggested his partner, Lorraine Bracco. She hadn't acted, but Rabe liked her and gave her the part. "You can imagine what it was like for a little newcomer like me," Bracco said of her first rehearsal. But the actors coalesced easily, and Bracco's butterflies disappeared. "There was no tension," she said. "We weren't there for the money."[25]

Rehearsals lasted for three weeks and went so well that Rabe decided to show the production to an audience. Because Madonna had other professional obligations, the number of performances had to be limited to four— over Labor Day weekend. The audience would be by invitation only. The press pounced on that news as a sign that *Goose and Tomtom* wasn't any good. Given Rabe's agreement with the theater, he wasn't required to show it to anyone at all, much less an audience of hypercritical industry peers. But logic rarely impinged on the coverage of Sean and Madonna, and so the narrative became that the Penns were responsible for another failed project.

In fact, Lincoln Center treated the workshop as a real play, spending money it ordinarily wouldn't on such a short production. Rabe said that he suspected the creative types there, including Lincoln Center's director, Gregory Mosher, were essentially auditioning Sean and Madonna for future projects. Madonna made the grade. When Mosher later directed David Mamet's *Speed-the-Plow,* he chose her for the female lead. Rabe was also struck by Madonna's performance. After *Goose and Tomtom* had been staged many times in many places, he said, "Madonna was the best Lorraine I ever saw. Truth is, I think if that had been the production she was first seen in, then everybody would have said she was a wonderful actress, instead of the shit she's received."[26]

The egalitarian, noncommercial nature of the production was evident on the performance program. The actors were listed in alphabetical order, with the newcomer, Lorraine Bracco, first and Sean last. The audience, however, was dense with stars. On opening night, Madonna looked into the crowd and said to producer Barbara Ligeti, "Hey, big sister, what the hell did you just do to me?" Ligeti said, "I looked out from the wings and there...was Warren Beatty seated next to Cher seated next to Al Pacino."[27] Around one thousand people would see the performance, mostly celebrities and industry people but also friends. Tom Cruise, for example, for Sean; and for Madonna, Keith Haring, Andy Warhol, and Martin.

Madonna made a point of including Martin in everything and treating him as she always had. She would not let him become his illness.[28] On the play's opening night, Warhol said,

> Martin met me backstage and there was a big candy chocolate leg there from Krön [chocolatier] and everybody was eating it, and Martin was, too. And it's so sad, he has sores all over his face, but it is kind of great to see Madonna eating the leg, too, and not caring that she might catch something. Martin would bite and then Madonna would bite.[29]

When the group left that night for a cast party at Sardi's, Warhol and Martin rode in a limo with Sean and Madonna. "The big bodyguards were with them," Warhol said, "and they said to the photographers, 'If you take one picture, we'll kill you.'" For perhaps the first time ever, the threat worked. Or maybe the paparazzi were so horrified by Martin's ravaged face that they couldn't bring themselves to photograph it—it was simply too much reality for the grocery-store checkout line.[30]

Aside from that brief respite, the press coverage of the "Poison Penns" was fierce during that period.[31] In fact, if the press disliked Sean and Madonna individually, as a couple they were reviled. The New York *Daily News* called them "the most offensive people on the entire planet."[32] They were trailed by paparazzi looking to turn a "circuit shot" of them walking down the street into an "exclusive" by provoking Sean into a fight.

Lorraine Bracco said there was no possibility of going out during rehearsals. "You'd walk out and there was literally a wall of three hundred paparazzi screaming horrific things to Sean to try to get him agitated."[33] David Rabe recalled that a coproducer who walked home with them one night was "pale when he came in the next day, shocked by what he'd seen." According to him,

> the paparazzi are always acting like they just walk around asking, "May we take your picture?"...But these photographers were really insulting them verbally, calling her this and that, asking Sean, "Who do you think she was fucking last night?" I've never read *that* anywhere. There was a bounty, we were told...if they could get a shot of Sean coming at them, it was guaranteed extra.[34]

On August 29, the second night of the *Goose and Tomtom* run, *Shanghai Surprise* premiered in select theaters to savage reviews. A group of five paparazzi followed Madonna and Sean home from dinner into the courtyard of their apartment building. Sean told them to get out, that they were on private property.[35] A shouting match turned into fists flying and cameras snapping. Madonna exhorted Vinnie Zuffante, a photographer she knew, to tell his friends to stop. Zuffante said he couldn't because Sean was a "madman" and "this is news." At that moment, Sean turned to Zuffante and punched him in the eye. *Snap.*[36]

It was just another night for the paparazzi, and unfortunately just another night for the Penns. Since her tour ended, Madonna said, she hadn't had a

> moment's peace from the press...It's not even the taking of the pictures that bothers me, it's the element of surprise...Every time I go running in Central Park around the reservoir...I'm gliding along listening to music and all of a sudden they jump from behind a tree. They're always scaring me, so I have to deal with that constant fear...I feel like they might as well have taken a gun out and shot me, because it takes me at least an hour to come down from that shock.[37]

To the paparazzi, celebrities are fair game; they belong to their fans, and they are rich and deserve to be taken down a notch. Paparazzi seemingly have no regard for what the people they photograph are coping with personally. The night that Madonna and Sean were pursued into their courtyard, she was grappling with the knowledge that she was losing two of the most important people in her life.[38]

For most people in the early '80s, AIDS was an abstraction—an acronym that meant death. But for millions of others, those four letters represented a face, a heart, a body, a soul, or a loved one gone too soon. AIDS felt like theft committed in broad daylight, and when its victims cried out for help, none came—not for years, until an entire population of promise had been wiped out. The cruelty of that neglect was exacerbated by homophobes who felt emboldened by the disease to vent their hatred.

The same "pro-family" movement that waged a battle against women's rights mounted a campaign against gay rights, using AIDS as evidence of God's judgment. At the time, one in five US residents considered themselves "born again" Christians. The rock stars for that multitude were the media preachers. Thirteen thousand radio stations broadcast Christian programming. The Moral Majority's Reverend Jerry Falwell alone preached daily on more than three hundred TV stations and 280 radio stations in thirty-one states.[39] The message on all those platforms was antifeminist and antigay.

In fact, the tide had turned so wildly against gays that in some states, being touched by a gay person was a valid defense against a murder charge. In 1986, the Supreme Court upheld an antisodomy law in Georgia (twenty-five states had similar laws) stemming from a case in which police arrested two men in the privacy of their own bedroom.[40] And then the Vatican weighed in. Joseph Cardinal Ratzinger, the future pope, issued a letter to Catholic bishops on October 1, 1986, calling homosexuality "intrinsically disordered" and stating that those who engaged in the "intrinsic moral evil" of homosexual acts "shall not enter the Kingdom of God."[41]

Gay activists in New York, including many who were only too aware of the pedophile priests the church sheltered, were outraged by the cruelty, the hypocrisy, and lack of mercy. In response, they launched high-profile acts of civil disobedience.[42]

The time for quiet acquiescence in the face of official disregard and murderous disdain was over. By mid-September, even as deaths mounted into the thousands and the Centers for Disease Control and Prevention estimated that as many as one million Americans were infected with the virus, Ronald Reagan had only mentioned AIDS publicly once, and that was in response to a reporter's question about fellow actor Rock Hudson.

Activists in New York said Governor Mario Cuomo and Mayor Ed Koch were similarly doing fuck all to help. That year, AIDS activists adopted the logo SILENCE = DEATH.[43]

Meanwhile, the tabloids that pursued Madonna and Sean couldn't resist making Martin part of the story. On October 21, the *National Enquirer* ran a front-page piece with a picture of Sean and Madonna and the headline: MADONNA'S FORMER ROOMMATE HAS AIDS — SEAN IS TERRIFIED & FURIOUS. IT'S WHAT'S REALLY RIPPING THEIR MARRIAGE APART. Inside, among photos of Martin, Madonna, and Sean, the story claimed that Sean was worried that Madonna had AIDS, too.[44]

The impact of that vicious story was painfully clear to everyone who knew Martin.[45] A friend, Jordan Levin, visited him soon after the article was published and found him alternately frantic and weeping. Martin said, according to Levin, "'How can they say this about me?...Sean isn't angry at me. I saw them last week and he hugged me.'" Levin said, "I never experienced such raw pain in my life, and I didn't know how to deal with it."[46]

In early November, "Open Your Heart" was released and became the third number 1 single from *True Blue*. An upbeat, poppy song, it might have gone unnoticed as just another Madonna hit if not for the video accompanying it. The song is about an innocent seduction, but the video is set in a peep show. It features the *performance* of seduction, a woman putting herself on display so that strangers can imagine they possess her.

In the booths are a tabloid journalist, a grubby businessman, an "elegant" gentleman, and a hormonal young fellow as well as two gay sailors with their arms draped around each other and a lesbian averting her eyes from the only show in town—Madonna. It looks squalid and sad, like a crowded bar when the lights are switched on at last call.

The video's hope and happiness reside in a boy outside the peep show, fantasizing about the goings-on inside. Whereas the people who watch Madonna perform sit lifeless around her, the child dances, pretending that he *is* her.

The video was to have been directed by Sean, but French fashion photographer and filmmaker Jean-Baptiste Mondino, who would become one of Madonna's most important video collaborators, directed it instead. Shot over two days in a seedy part of LA, it sparked an entirely new kind of controversy because Madonna portrayed herself as a sex worker and because some of the clients watching her were gay and lesbian. "Open Your Heart" included the first overt references to homosexuality in her work.[47]

Madonna's video forced the viewer to recognize that desire manifests itself in many ways. In that context, the little boy outside the peep show might not be a heterosexual child lusting after the woman inside the theater at all. He could just as easily be a gay or transgender child trying, by mimicking Madonna's dance moves, to understand his own sexuality.

That possibility was not lost on gay, lesbian, and trans children, who existed in a world that told them they were abnormal and bad and that the stirrings of love they felt were wrong.[48] British writer Matt Cain, who was eleven when he saw "Open Your Heart," said, "Nobody would stand up and speak for us, and then Madonna was celebrating who we were and defending us and just shouting this message so loud and clear and so kind of joyfully."[49]

Many have speculated about what it means when, at the end of the video, Madonna and the child run off together. One critic bizarrely called it "lascivious."[50] Madonna said it was "about innocence versus decadence, really, and in the end, I chose innocence."[51] But in light of Madonna's fears about losing Martin, her flight with the child takes on another meaning and added poignancy. The video feels like Madonna's love letter to him.

When they began performing together in New York, she and Martin wore matching shorts, hats, jackets—little-boy clothes like the ones the child and Madonna wear in the video as they make their mad dash to freedom. Those were innocent times. They were children. They had dreams. One night when they both worked at Lucky Strike, pocketing money for tickets to England, Martin's friend Ward Capeci came in and showed them his new tattoo.

> Madonna wanted one too and ran and got a Sharpie. She asked me to draw a heart on her arm that "looked wet." Martin grabbed the Sharpie and wrote the words "pink-moist-love" inside the heart and then drew a poundcake on his own arm. He chose the name Poundcake for himself. He once told us that if he was ever to have a daughter, he would name her Cinnamon.[52]

And now he was dying. And though he would be gone, Madonna's "pink-moist-love" would be with him. Always. When she skips into the sunset hand in hand with that child in "Open Your Heart," she is skipping into a future filled with the sweetest memories.

Madonna was in LA when she learned that Martin didn't have long to live. She called Lawrence Monoson, who was in Mexico shooting *Gaby,* and said, "I think if you wanna see him you better fly to New York." As Monoson later recalled, "I, of course, asked the producers, 'Can I go to New York?' And they said, 'No absolutely not, we're in the middle of shooting a movie.'"

So this was a torturous, horrible moment because I was so unbelievably upset. I was a very young actor at the time, and here I'm, like, in love with this guy who's dying, and then there's this huge star who's mad at me, telling me I should go to New York. I was twenty-two, and I didn't know what to do, and I ended up not leaving, and that is something that has always been a pain to my heart.[53]

If Lawrence had gone and admitted the real reason for doing so, it could have been the end of his career—not necessarily because he left a movie shoot for personal reasons but because he would have outed himself. "I remember, there's a very famous manager, and she said, 'You wanna be a movie star? You stay in the closet,'" Lawrence said. "And that's what many people did and still do...It's a great source of pain and regret in my life. I would do things incredibly different now."[54]

Madonna and Sean, meanwhile, hopped on a plane and flew back to New York. "He was at home," Catherine Underhill said of Martin. "We knew he was dying. His parents were around. He was getting fluid on the lungs, and he couldn't talk anymore, but we realized...he was waiting for Madonna, and it was just really clear that he was not going to go until he saw her."[55]

They shifted Martin's body to keep him seated so he could breathe. They tried to make him comfortable while he waited. At 3:00 a.m., Madonna and Sean finally arrived. "She made sure that he knew she was there," Catherine said. "He couldn't really communicate, so she said what he needed to hear, touched him and held him." Sean and Madonna left, and Martin died immediately afterward.[56] "They had a very deep and profound love," Erika Belle said. "Once he heard her come into the room, he knew he could die."[57] The date was November 30, a day before the anniversary of Madonna's mother's death.

So many friends grieved Martin's passing, but they tried not to do it in sadness. "I remember we threw a really great party," Catherine said. "We didn't do sad memorials." Martin had helped bring Catherine back to life five years earlier, when her partner died. Since then, she had been Martin's other best friend. They had even planned to have children together if neither of them ended up with a permanent mate. When they made those happy plans, they couldn't imagine that death would come sooner.[58]

Madonna arranged a memorial for Martin on December 2. Hundreds of people were there, and many of the men among them already had what Martin called "the curse" or would be diagnosed with it shortly. Martin's friend and neighbor Karen Bahari sang "Over the Rainbow," at which point everyone who had been trying to be brave broke down in tears. Marcus Leatherdale, Steve Rubell, and Stephen Sprouse grabbed one another for a group hug. "We were all in tears, and they're both gone, too," Marcus said many years later. "I was the last man standing."[59]

Madonna wasn't there. She had returned to Los Angeles. She once said, "When you know someone's dying, you have to make your peace with it before they die." That was one of her earliest lessons in life, and that is what she tried to do with Martin.[60] But with Martin's death, there *could* be no peace. After Christopher Flynn's diagnosis and Martin's loss, amid the mounting numbers of men dead from AIDS and the powerful backlash against gays, Madonna became a fierce and unwavering gay rights activist.[61]

Director Joel Schumacher recalled her commitment. He had written a script about a woman whose gay brother had AIDS.

> About thirty of the most famous actresses in Hollywood—who love to be connected to the correct liberal causes—turned me down flat. And many of those actresses were first championed by gay audiences. I was shocked by their attitude. But Madonna read the script and called me herself to fight for the role. She was not frightened to be associated with the subject matter at all. Unfortunately she wasn't old enough for the sister... but I'll always be touched by her passion.[62]

Remembering those times many years later, Madonna told music writer Charlotte Gunn, "I came to the LGBTQ community and put my arms around them. While everyone else was running away from them, I was running towards them."[63]

Chapter 22

New York, Los Angeles, Osaka, Tokyo, Miami, 1986–1987

When times are bad, people want to dance their troubles away.[1]

—Robert "Kool" Bell

THE WIDE RELEASE of *Shanghai Surprise* was a disaster. The prerelease publicity had been so bad, with recriminations flying between the parties, that its failure was assured. The *Rolling Stone* headline read: MADONNA FIRST FLOP: SHANGHAI SURPRISE A BONA FIDE BUST. The *Boston Globe* said: "Boy, did they stink up the screen in this one."[2]

There is a good chance that if the early buzz about the picture and its stars hadn't been so dreadful, the film might have done okay. It must be said that Sean was uncharacteristically terrible. He hadn't trusted the director. He hadn't wanted his marriage to be the stuff of on-screen romance. And he admitted he was drunk through most of the filming.[3]

Madonna, by contrast, was completely believable as a comedic actor. Because of her, the film was watchable and at times even charming. The poor reception amounted to a case of self-sabotage on the part of the production team (George Harrison included), the studio (which failed to screen it for critics), and Sean and Madonna (who broadcast their dissatisfaction). More's the pity, because as Madonna's second film, it made her debut in *Desperately Seeking Susan* seem like a fluke and would set the tone for coverage of her future film projects.[4]

Madonna had been inundated with scripts but wasn't interested in most of them. She refused to do anything that required nudity or involved violence. Amid so much sadness in her life, she said, "Everything I do has to be some kind of celebration of life...I just love those films where the woman gets away with murder, but her weapon is laughter. And you end up falling in love with her."[5] "I was really excited about doing a real physical, screwball comedy so when Jamie brought this up, it was like my reward." Jamie was director James Foley, and the film in question would be called *Who's That Girl*.[6]

Madonna agreed to play a ditsy blonde who is wrongly convicted of murdering her boyfriend. Upon her release from prison, a Rolls-Royce–driving young lawyer, played by Griffin Dunne, is asked by his soon-to-be father-in-law (the real murderer) to escort her to the bus station to get her out of town. The running gag involves Madonna, Dunne, and a 160-pound cougar named Murray. In the end, true love triumphs, and the real scoundrels are apprehended.[7]

Foley and Madonna both liked the concept, but it required work, which required time, and that was something they didn't have. Warner Bros. had greenlit the project late, meaning that preproduction elements weren't properly finalized when filming began in October. Foley said the night before the shoot he realized there were also problems with the script. It was "lousy," but it was too late to do anything about it.[8] And the misery continued on the set. Filming was plagued by bad weather, and during street shoots in Manhattan, hordes of paparazzi and tourists jostled each other for a view, shouting "Madonna! Madonna!"[9]

Police were employed to manage the crowd and provide security, which included four sharpshooters with sniper rifles in case the four cougars who played Murray made a run at the crowd. "Cougars by instinct will go for the weakest of your species when they're hungry," said producer Bernie Williams, "and they're always hungry, because we skip their dinner the night before." Madonna was required to climb into the back of the Rolls with the ravenous cat.[10] "It's always twice as hard, whatever I'm doing, if the cougar's around," she explained, "but it also looks great on camera, so it's worth it."[11]

Foley said that Madonna's attitude put the rest of the cast and crew at ease.[12] An *American Film* reporter on set said Madonna treated everyone as a "quasi-sibling."[13] But reporters who were *not* on set described Madonna as fighting with her costars, filing for divorce from Sean, and having an affair with a male model. Oh, and her career was over.[14]

One of the most joyous songs on *True Blue* is called "Where's the Party." Madonna said it was her "ultimate statement about what it's like to be in the middle of this press stuff with everybody on my back and my world about to cave in. Whenever I feel like that—and it does get to me some-times—I say, 'Wait a minute, I'm supposed to be having a good time here, so where's the party?' It doesn't have to be this way. I can still enjoy my life."[15]

She needed a party; the world needed a party; the gay community espe-cially needed joyous respite amid so much agony and fear. Madonna decided to go on tour.

Madonna's Virgin tour, two years earlier, had visited relatively small theaters, auditoriums, and halls. In 1987, the venues needed to be much,

much bigger. But the tour's promoter worried that Madonna was still too new (and too female) to fill the arenas where the boys—Michael Jackson, Prince, Bruce Springsteen, U2—entertained tens of thousands of fans. Pat Leonard, who would again be musical director, worried about larger spaces, too. How could he fill a sports venue with dance-club music?[16]

Madonna was excited by the challenge, which she described as "being able to make a show interesting in a stadium, where you're not *supposed* to be interesting, where it's like just this big mega show, real impersonal. I wanted to make it really personal, even though people would be sitting really far away from me."[17] That sort of connection with the audience was why Madonna went onstage, and it was why her fans loved her. She said,

> When you're an actor, you do your work and you go home, and people deal with what's up on the screen. When you're a singer, obviously it's you. That's what music is all about. It's a lot more accessible. You're saying, "This is me," so people know you intimately. They see you onstage, being vulnerable, sweating, singing, crying, dancing, whatever it is. Or just standing still. But it's a statement: "This is me. And here I am for all you people."[18]

Madonna's second tour would be a grand production, visually cacophonous, and continually in motion. It would feature seven costume changes, two huge video screens, three dancers, three backup singers, and a band.[19]

Like her film, the tour would be called Who's That Girl, because she said the public seemed preoccupied with trying to discover which of her various personas was *her*. "And I'm not like any of them. I'm all of them. I'm none of them."[20]

One ingredient in Madonna's recipe for keeping a concert interesting for herself was to rework her songs—the way they were played and sung—and to offer novel interpretations of them through her performance. There was a risk of alienating audiences by doing so, because conventional wisdom in concert planning said that fans wanted to hear songs performed the way they sounded on an album. Madonna took a chance by forcing her audiences to hear and see her work in a new light.[21]

Music would be the foundation of the show, but dance would make it a performance. For choreography, Madonna turned to a thirty-two-year-old named Shabba-Doo—Adolfo Quiñones—who had "danced his way out" of the infamous Cabrini-Green housing project, on Chicago's North Side, and into stage productions and films. Madonna had seen his star turn in the 1984 picture Breakin', about B-boys. She liked his ideas. She liked his moves. "And I was dubbed the choreographer," he said.[22]

Joining Shabba-Doo onstage with Madonna were two dancers. Angel Ferreira, an LA native who had trained in ballet, discovered hip-hop while working as an extra in the movie *Beat Street,* and appeared in the film *A Chorus Line.*[23] The third dancer was thirteen-year-old Chris Finch. Madonna wanted a character in her show like the child in the "Open Your Heart" video. Finch became more than a tour dancer; he became a little brother. Madonna called him "the ideal man. He does everything I ask him to do and never complains."[24]

During the Virgin tour, Madonna had been the only woman onstage. But because the Who's That Girl tour featured material from her *True Blue* album, she decided to employ female backup singers to help re-create the '60s girl group sound. Debra Parsons would only join Madonna on that tour, but the other two women—Niki Haris and Donna De Lory—would form an inspiring onstage sisterhood with her for nearly two decades.[25]

Donna, twenty-two, was born into the music business. Her father was an LA-based producer and manager. Her mother had been a singer and dancer, but like Madonna's mother, she died of breast cancer when Donna was a child. Donna came to Madonna's attention through Pat Leonard when she sang the original demo for "Open Your Heart."[26] Pat liked her voice and tipped her off about the audition for the tour—not that it was a secret. When Donna arrived at the SIR rehearsal studios, she said, "I saw every singer that I knew in L.A. there!"[27]

Donna didn't know what to expect from Madonna. She recalled,

> From the beginning the industry rumors were discounting her success, as if she couldn't have just earned it. So going in, when I met her, it was like, "Oh, my gosh, that's not the case. She is extremely savvy and talented. She is the source of the whole vision."[28]

The women at the audition were asked to sing in groups of three with Madonna. "The girls that I was with were not blending too well, and I thought that it was over for me," Donna said. Pat then asked her to sing the bridge to "La Isla Bonita" with Madonna. "She had her back turned when we were singing," Donna said of Madonna. "Then she stopped and said, 'Why aren't you singing?' Pat spoke up for me and said that I *was* singing and that our voices blended perfectly together." Donna got the job.[29]

Twenty-four-year-old Niki Haris was born in Michigan. Her father, too, was in the business, as a jazz pianist. She had wanted to be a history teacher and only turned to music to support herself, but it quickly became a career. Niki had worked with, among others, Whitney Houston and the Righteous Brothers. It was while she was in Las Vegas with that group that

Freddy DeMann called with an urgent request: "Can you learn seventeen songs and seventeen dance moves in five days?" A backup singer who had been hired for the tour didn't work out, and Madonna needed a replacement.[30]

Niki said there were two hundred women at the audition. She didn't think she had a chance, and wanting to get back to Las Vegas quickly, she asked Madonna to move her to the front of the queue. She did. "Then basically she said, 'Everybody can go home, I found what I need.' "[31] Niki was in the back of the limo with Madonna when she called the Righteous Brothers' Bill Medley to ask if she should come back to Las Vegas for one more gig or find someone to replace her. He asked how much Madonna was paying. After Niki told him, Medley said, "Stay and go make that money."[32]

Christopher, meanwhile, would be Madonna's assistant while she was preparing the tour, and on the road he would reprise his role as her dresser. Debi Mazar would do her makeup, just as they had imagined during their Danceteria days. And Madonna's youngest brother, seventeen-year-old Mario, was given a minor job, mainly so he could experience the show. With that, the cast and crew were assembled, and weeks of rehearsals began.

During rehearsals, Madonna worked seventy hours a week.[33] "Every single movement she did on stage was evaluated and staged and really meticulously laid out," said Jeffrey Hornaday, the tour's stage director.[34] Her day also included a new workout regimen with trainer Rob Parr, who helped her build a body that could withstand the rigors of a tour. She lifted weights, swam, bicycled twenty-five miles a few times a week, and ran hundreds of stairs at Pepperdine University.[35]

Madonna was burning the candle at both ends. While involved in tour preparations, she also fielded inquiries about films. There were magazine cover requests, queries about commercials in Asia, and social causes seeking her support. *And* she was a married lady juggling the demands of her career with the needs of her husband.

Madonna was a poster child for the do-it-all, have-it-all woman who in the mid-'80s was under attack by pop psychologists and the political and religious right. Bestselling books advised women that they risked infertility if they had careers. One book claimed that if something wasn't done to stop ambitious women, the United States faced demographic Armageddon.[36]

The message was hardly subtle. Powerful voices wanted to put women back into a preliberation box. Madonna, through her example, said, Crush the box. You can do it all. You can get an education; you can have a career;

you can have a home life.[37] Of course, it was easier for her than it was for most women, as she readily admitted, because she had the money to hire help if she wanted to. But during her marriage to Sean, she tried to stay grounded. In an interview with Vicki Woods for *Vogue,* a magazine in which women were shown in airbrushed perfection, she said,

> You know those cut-off jeans I wear? Sean would bring someone back to the house, and I'd be wearing those with my hair all erghh and washing clothes—I mean, I would be looking like a hag. And he'd bring in a friend and drag me over and say, "Look at her and she's one of the richest women in America!"[38]

In fact, Madonna and Sean's life together was, in some ways, surprisingly normal. They visited Sean's parents once a week. His brothers were around. Her brothers were around. She had given Sean an Akita puppy that grew almost immediately into a terrifying dog that Sean named Hank, after Bukowski. Bukowski himself was often at the house, drunk and sick, according to Christopher. "The moment he arrives, my sister escapes into the bedroom, disgusted," he said. "She loathes few things more than an undisciplined drunk."[39]

And whether she was at home or on the road, Madonna read: James Joyce, Henry James, Thomas Mann, Honoré de Balzac, Guy de Maupassant, Françoise Sagan, Marguerite Duras, V. S. Naipaul, and Alice Walker, to name just a few. Before she moved into the Malibu home she shared with Sean, she dreamed of a room lined with books the way other young brides might dream of the perfect kitchen.[40]

She also consumed movies. Christopher said that when Sean was away, he and Madonna watched them together. When Sean was home, Christopher left the pair to sit in front of the TV alone.[41] At those moments, they were not Sean Penn, bad-boy actor, and Madonna, superstar. They were just a young couple wrapped around each other on the sofa. Those were the moments to treasure.

Sean's acting kept him in LA working on a film directed by Dennis Hopper called *Colors* about city cops and drug gangs.[42] "There was so much shit going on," Sean said, "but nobody was talking about it because it was all happening on the other side of the Harbor Freeway."[43] That's the road that divided ravaged South Central from the wealthy white Westside and the Santa Monica Mountains, an area containing "one of the largest concentrations of affluence on the planet."[44]

South Central had once been a center of cultural wealth and community rivaling the glory days of Harlem. It had since become a war zone, with a daily body count of gang members and civilians. Police only exacerbated the situation. The antagonism between the men wearing gang colors and the men wearing law-enforcement uniforms was visceral and deadly.[45]

The South Central story was one that white Angelenos, behind their security walls and ARMED RESPONSE! signs, did not want to read, let alone watch on a movie screen.[46] The movie industry in general did not recognize "Black films" as a viable genre. Aside from 1970s pictures like Melvin Van Peebles's *Sweet Sweetback's Baadasssss Song* and Gordon Parks's *Shaft,* films about modern Black urban life did not exist. It would be several years before Spike Lee's *Do the Right Thing* and John Singleton's *Boyz n the Hood* made it to theaters.

That was the culture Sean and Hopper encountered when they began their film. They wanted to make a movie in a war zone where they weren't welcome about a subject people would prefer to ignore. Amazingly, Orion Pictures approved it. What no doubt sold the story was that South Central was merely the backdrop. The film was about two white cops working the gang squad: Sean as the hothead rookie and Robert Duvall as the wise elder.

As always, Sean rehearsed his role intensely, cruising with an LAPD gang squad member named Dennis Fanning. Sean was told to ride along with him if he wanted to see some action. "Dennis was jacked," Sean said. "He was the guy." Together on patrol, Fanning and Sean became what Fanning called a "shit magnet...Shootings, stolen cars, all kinds of shit. We rode around off and on for three months. So the more we rode around, the more shit we got into, the more Sean became the character."[47]

Madonna was no longer married to the backwoods redneck of *At Close Range:* she was now married to a trigger-happy cowboy from the LAPD. Early on, she knew what Sean's "internship" with Fanning would mean. She pulled Fanning aside and said, "Sean is very impressionable, so I want you to *please* be very careful with what you're teaching my husband." But it was too late. Fanning said,

> Sean actually thought he was a fucking cop...He was walking like one, he was talking like one, he was hanging out with us...he'd get drunk and fucken party, man. He'd shoot off guns, go chase bad guys, pull up on a corner and just sit there, see how many different crimes he could spot: see who was dealing dope, who was stealing cars, who was doing what—just for the fun of it.[48]

It was nearly a year since the incident at Helena's when Sean attacked David Wolinski, but the case hadn't reached court. In late February of

1987, it did. Sean pleaded no contest to one count of misdemeanor battery. He was fined $1,700 and given a year's probation.[49] And then in April, on the set of *Colors,* Sean noticed a man on a skateboard taking pictures and confronted him. The two exchanged "motherfuckers" and spit. Sean hit him and hit him again.[50] On May 1, Sean surrendered to face parole violation charges and was ordered back in court for a hearing in June.[51]

While awaiting arraignment, Sean went on the Sunday of Memorial Day weekend to Bukowski's house, where booze featured big in the evening's entertainment. On the way back to Malibu at two in the morning, he was driving fifty in a thirty-five-mile-per-hour zone and ran a red light within sight of a police car.[52]

"I take off. Within a few minutes, it's like daylight—because of helicopters overhead," he said. "I pull over, get arrested for drunk driving." Sean was locked up until the morning and released on his own recognizance. The police at that time didn't know about his parole violation. Sean knew that as soon as they found out, he was headed to jail. The pretend cop had become an actual criminal.[53]

His latest episode occurred as Madonna finalized plans to head out on tour. The dissonance between her personal life and her professional life had never been greater. Her husband was bound for a jail cell, and she was destined to woo the world.[54]

Who's That Girl opened in Japan for five sold-out shows. Not since the Beatles in 1966 had any Western rock or pop star caused such pandemonium there. Thousands of fans, with one thousand police in place to restrain them, turned up at the airport to greet her. Outside the stadium in Osaka, where she would perform two concerts, thousands more who weren't able to get tickets stood in a crush of bodies hoping to be allowed in anyway. In Tokyo, her next stop, a mini typhoon caused the opening of her three-night gig at Korakuen Stadium to be canceled. Mikal Gilmore, who covered the tour for *Rolling Stone,* said the normally well-behaved Japanese fans nearly rioted.[55]

The next day, the weather cooperated, and the concert was on.[56] The audience's first glimpse of Madonna came through a white screen. That silhouette was enough to elicit a roar that ebbed and swelled over the following hour and thirty minutes. During that time, Madonna was onstage for all but the few minutes it took to change costumes. She did not stop, even as sweat poured down her face and back. She worked the stadium the way she had worked the clubs, determined to hold that vast audience in her thrall.

Writing in *Rolling Stone,* Gilmore said, "Although it may come as a major surprise to many of her critics, there has probably never been a more imaginative or forceful showcase for feminine sensibility in pop than Madonna's current concert tour." He said Madonna was the first woman to ever star in a show of that scope, which he called a "fusion of Broadway-style choreography and post-disco song and dance that tops the standards set by previous live concert firebrands like Prince and Michael Jackson."[57]

Madonna started the show with "Open Your Heart," which announced her intention: by the end of the evening she would make the audience love her. Wearing a black bustier with gold disks and tassels at the nipples, she danced alongside her thirteen-year-old partner, Chris Finch. One more song in that costume—"Lucky Star"—before she changed into a flouncy blue Debbie Reynolds dress out of a late-'50s movie and launched into a series of songs from *True Blue*.[58]

Niki Haris, Donna De Lory, and Debra Parsons, having taken up positions behind her in similar attire, sang backup while performing the hand gestures made famous by early girl groups. When Shabba-Doo appeared as a greaser trying to win Madonna's affections during the song "True Blue," the imagery was a perfect tribute to that earlier musical era. It was also a poignant reminder of the behind-the-scenes drama of her life.[59]

Madonna had written the song for Sean after their marriage during a time of pure happiness, and now she performed it in a time of dread as he prepared to go to court for sentencing. Onstage, she didn't sing the bridge as much as shout it to him, wherever he was.

The romance of that number became rebellion in the next. Madonna slipped on a leather jacket over her powder-blue dress—she was both tough and feminine—to sing "Papa Don't Preach." At the opening chords of the song, the largely female audience screamed in delight. "Papa Don't Preach" spoke to Japanese girls trapped in a patriarchal system that barely acknowledged them.[60]

The song as recorded was plaintive. The song as performed made demands. Madonna stomped her feet repeatedly in a brilliant bit of choreography (and percussion). "I really lose myself," Madonna said of her dancing during that song. "I'm throwing a tantrum. I'm stepping on every man who ever told me to do something I didn't want to do."[61]

Images projected on the screen behind her featured a rogues' gallery of oppressors: the church, the pope, Ronald Reagan, Richard Nixon, and the patriarchy's scientific masterwork—the atomic bomb. Interspersed with those images were various casualties of those men and their system: Malcolm X, Martin Luther King Jr., Robert Kennedy, hungry children, student protesters, the planet. "Papa Don't Preach" ended with the screen frozen on the words SAFE SEX. She took it upon herself to spread that gospel to the world.[62]

It was incumbent upon Madonna to perform some songs from her earlier albums, but she couldn't play them straight. Dipping into a phone booth, she changed into a dress and hat that made her look like a punk Minnie Pearl. She was covered in dime-store junk: dice, plastic baby dolls, a fake lobster. Her pink hat was topped with grapes, a flower, a small chair, and a feather. To complete the look, she wore lavish cat-eye glasses.[63]

In that attire she began a set with "Dress You Up" and continued with a slapstick rendition of "Material Girl." Shabba-Doo and Angel Ferreira joined her onstage, also wearing comical getups. Projected behind them as they sang about the virtues of "cold hard cash" were symbols of materialism: dollar signs, the abbreviation IRS, and the words BANK OF AMERICA and HOLLYWOOD. For her next song, "Like a Virgin," she upended marital tradition by ravishing the groom, Chris Finch. Madonna would tell critic Gene Siskel that that three-song medley was her favorite part of the show.[64]

Then she transitioned from a marriage theme to a visual commentary on the paparazzi. In her life, one had followed the other. Against a projection of the *New York Post* headline MADONNA: "I'M NOT ASHAMED," from the nude-picture episode, she danced in silhouette with two male dancers posing as paparazzi. Each photograph the dancers took sounded like a gunshot. That bit of theater was her lead-in for one of the poppiest songs of the night, "Where's the Party." It would be followed by the most sober, "Live to Tell."[65]

For that song, Madonna stood alone in the spotlight with a massive image of her face as Marilyn Monroe on the screen behind her. She was dwarfed by the weight of that image, which had haunted her from the moment she dyed her hair blond and declared herself a Material Girl. While performing "Live to Tell," she demonstrated why the comparison was a false one. Marilyn was desirable in life because she was vulnerable; she was made mythical in death because she was tragic. Madonna could be the former but never the latter.[66]

Dramatizing "Live to Tell" onstage, using only her voice and very few movements, Madonna trod that Monroesque path uncertainly until a point when she, too, appeared dead. She stopped, slumped to the floor for what felt like an excruciatingly long period—actually less than a minute—before being reborn strong and defiant. Gilmore said that during her Tokyo performance, when she "rises from the floor and stands with her head erect, a decidedly feminine yowl—in fact, the loudest roar of the evening—greets the motion. It is an acclamation that will be repeated on several other nights in the weeks ahead."[67]

Madonna's rebirth was complete in the next number, "Into the Groove." It was a rousing send-off for the show, as she and her gang deserted the stage. But as she had with the Virgin tour, she came back not with a token encore but with an additional set. Dressed in red, she and Angel Ferreira danced a flamenco to "La Isla Bonita."[68]

The theme song from the film *Who's That Girl* followed. Madonna stood alone onstage chanting again and again, "Who's that girl? Who's that girl?" until it was impossible not to ponder the meaning. Then she walked offstage, leaving the question unanswered. Writer Vince Aletti called that part of her performance brilliant.[69]

She returned for "Holiday." *That* song was her closer. As dark as Madonna could go, and as dark as her life could become, she would never end on a down note. She would leave the audience happy.[70]

After her show, with tens of thousands of cheering voices still ringing in her ears and still charged by that energy, Madonna, the world's most controversial female entertainer, showered, ate sorbet, and settled down with a book.[71] That was who she was, too.

Madonna left Japan on June 23, the day Sean appeared in LA's Municipal Court. Wearing a suit and aviator sunglasses, he stood before the same court commissioner, Juleann Cathey, who had generously given him probation on the Wolinski charge. In June she wasn't as lenient. She ruled that Sean had violated his probation on two counts: reckless driving and punching the skateboarder on the *Colors* set. Pleading no contest, he told Cathey he would obey the law "from now on." But that assurance wasn't enough to keep him out of jail.

She sentenced Sean to sixty days. He was also fined, ordered to undergo six months of counseling for violence and alcoholism, and had his probation extended for two years. He was told to surrender to authorities on July 7 "with his toothbrush and overnight case." In the meantime, he would be allowed to travel to Berlin to act in a Cold War–era film directed by his father called *Judgment in Berlin* and to see his wife in Miami.[72]

On June 27, Madonna opened the North American portion of her tour at the Miami Orange Bowl before a sellout crowd of more than sixty-four thousand people. Before she arrived, Sean had taken a penthouse at the Turnberry Isle Country Club and filled it with white lilies and white orchids.[73] He had seen the tour rehearsals, and Madonna consulted with him on the show, but Miami would be the first time he would see her perform it before an audience.[74] Though there were critics who panned it, some of the most important were effusive about Who's That Girl. Wrote music veteran J. D. Considine:

> I've seen the Springsteen Stadium tour, I've seen Dylan and the Grateful Dead, and I was at Live Aid. Out of all those shows, Madonna's is the only

one I'd want to see again . . . You need a larger-than-life show if you want to come off in a stadium, and Madonna does.[75]

Madonna had finally risen above the pop condescension. There would always be writers who criticized her in the same terms they used in 1983, as if her work had never evolved and as if she had never matured. But the balance of the coverage of her music had tilted toward respect, and Sean had been there to see it happen.

Under the terms of his sentence, Sean was to begin serving his jail time on July 7, but his two-week furlough was extended because principal shooting on his father's film wouldn't begin until July 15.[76] The commissioner granted the extension on that basis alone. Sean was to go to Germany, work with his father, and come back to California to serve his time. But that's not exactly what happened. Before going to Germany, he made a detour to New York for Madonna's Madison Square Garden concert. It was a benefit for AIDS research and a tribute to Martin Burgoyne.[77]

Chapter 23

New York, Leeds, Paris, Turin, Los Angeles, 1987

Someday this plague will be over and we will survive as a people to tell the tales. Don't forget to tell how much we honored life. Don't forget to tell how hard many of us fought for it.[1]

— *Connie Norman*

NEW YORK HAD changed drastically in the few short months since Martin Burgoyne's death. Andy Warhol had also died. People noticed he was sick when he missed Sunday mass, and then he was gone, dying in February during a routine medical procedure involving his gallbladder. It was a most banal ending for a man who had fundamentally changed how art was created and how it was perceived. "It is hard to imagine what N.Y. will be like without Andy," Keith Haring wrote in his journal. "How will anybody know where to go or what is 'cool'?"[2]

The city's club scene had changed, too. Danceteria was closed. The Funhouse was closed. Paradise Garage would close later that year. Heroin had gotten the better of Larry Levan, whose dance floor was decimated by AIDS. At the Vatican of gay clubs, the Saint, membership renewal letters came back so often bearing the words *addressee unknown* and *addressee deceased* that women were invited to join. But the ladies couldn't save it. It, too, would soon close.[3] Pre-AIDS Manhattan was dead. The boarded-up clubs existed as heartbreaking reminders of what had been.

When Madonna's tour rolled into New York City in July, she used her only appearance there—a concert at Madison Square Garden on July 13—to raise money to fight the disease. In doing so, she became the "first major American pop star to stage such a large-scale fundraiser" for AIDS. Pop acts were generally afraid of being associated with something so "dirty," and rock bands were afraid of tarnishing their phallic image by being associated with a sexually transmitted disease.[4] Madonna wasn't afraid. She thought it was her duty.

Others did, too. Burt Lancaster, Angela Lansbury, Joan Rivers, and

Elizabeth Taylor, among others, raised money for AIDS research and promoted safe sex.[5] But they did not have the impact Madonna had when speaking to a young audience. Said Matt Cain, "Elizabeth Taylor, she was older than my grandma. Madonna was speaking as a woman who we knew was out there having sex...so she was on our level...With Madonna, it seemed so kind of raw and emotional, and she was so passionate about it. It really made an impact."[6]

If, in 1987, Madonna adopted an outspoken stance on AIDS, it was because there was simply no time to lose. The disease had to be confronted in the boldest, starkest language. That was the message of AIDS activists in new groups like ACT UP—the AIDS Coalition to Unleash Power. It had formed that spring and immediately launched a high-profile campaign of civil disobedience because, as historian Lillian Faderman said, many of its members had AIDS and had nothing more to fear—certainly not arrest and definitely not disgrace.[7]

Part of Madonna's contribution to the fight was to use unequivocal AIDS messaging in her show. During "Papa Don't Preach," the final image that flashed behind her as she sang read SAFE SEX.[8] It had been an utterly alien message in Japan, but even in the States, where the phrase was more generally known, it was still considered controversial, because it could be seen as condoning teenage sex, extramarital sex, sex for purposes other than procreation, and that giant bugbear, homosexuality.

In addition, it was unnerving because the message wasn't just "safe gay sex"; it was "safe sex" period, which implied that heterosexuals were at risk. The AIDS message to heteros had been, broadly, "Don't worry." For example, *Cosmopolitan* magazine, that self-declared authority on women's sexuality, informed its readers that "most heterosexuals are not at risk" of contracting AIDS because HIV could not be transmitted in the "missionary position."[9]

Amid so much fear, confusion, and misinformation, someone had to deliver the unadorned facts. Contrary to *Cosmo's* message, Madonna said, "Worry," and she made the point repeatedly during her show.[10] And just in case fans didn't get the message, she distributed a brochure to concertgoers. In comic-book style and in very clear terms, it described how AIDS was spread and how it could be prevented. Madonna also included a personal handwritten note:

> Right now there is no cure for AIDS but there is a way to stop it from spreading. Don't let fear keep you from knowing the facts.
>
> Read this booklet—then give it to your best friend. It just might save his or her life...It just might save your own. Love, Madonna.[11]

Madonna graduation photo from Adams High School, Rochester, Michigan, December 1975 *Photographer unknown. Universal History Archive Universal Images Group. Getty Images*

Madonna cheerleading at Adams High School in Rochester, Michigan, circa 1972 *Michael Ochs Archives. Getty Images*

Christopher Flynn,
Ann Arbor, Michigan,
1978 *Photo by Linda
Alaniz. Copyright Linda
Alaniz*

Madonna at the dance
building, University of
Michigan at Ann Arbor,
1977 *Photo by Peter Kentes.
Copyright Peter Kentes*

Madonna posing at the University of Michigan at Ann Arbor, 1978 *Photo by Linda Alaniz. Copyright Linda Alaniz*

Madonna, New York City, 1979 *Photo by Michael McDonnell. Hulton Archive Getty Images*

Madonna, New York City, 1983 *Photo by Amy Arbus. Copyright Amy Arbus*

Left to right: Jean-Michel Basquiat, Andy Warhol, and Fred Brathwaite (Fab 5 Freddy), New York City, January 1984 *Photo by Patrick McMullan. Getty Images*

Jean-Michel Basquiat, *A Panel of Experts,* 1982. Acrylic and oil pastel on paper mounted on canvas, *The Montreal Museum of Fine Arts, copyright the estate of Jean-Michel Basquiat, ADAGP Paris/IVARO Dublin 2022*

Keith Haring drawing in the New York City subway, 1983 *Photo by Tseng Kwong Chi. Photo copyright Muna Tseng Dance Projects, Inc. Art copyright Keith Haring Foundation*

Martin Burgoyne and Madonna, New York City, 1983 *Photo by Marcus Leatherdale. Copyright Marcus Leatherdale*

Madonna with (left to right) David (surname unknown), Erika Belle, and Bags Rilez at Studio 54 for Fiorucci's fifteenth-anniversary party, May 1983 *Photo by Maripol. Copyright Maripol*

Debi Mazar, New York City, May 1992 *Photo by Ron Galella. Ron Galella Collection. Getty Images*

Madonna and Jellybean Benitez, Like a Virgin event, 1984 *Photo by Andy Warhol. Andy Warhol Museum © 2023 The Andy Warhol Foundation for the Visual Arts, Inc. / Licensed by Artists Rights Society (ARS), New York*

Madonna premieres "Like a Virgin" at the first Party of Life at Paradise Garage, New York City, 1984 *Photo by Tseng Kwong Chi. Copyright Muna Tseng Dance Projects, Inc.*

Martin Burgoyne and Maripol at the Private Eyes nightclub, New York City, September 1985 *Photo by Patrick McMullan. Getty Images*

The US government wouldn't produce a brochure on AIDS and safe sex for another year.[12] "Gay lives were not seen as valuable," said British AIDS activist Matthew Hodson, who would be diagnosed with HIV the following year. "That was why what Madonna did was so important, because she was kind of saying, gay lives matter. At that point to say gay lives matter was a radical statement."[13]

She made it personal at Madison Square Garden when she dedicated "Live to Tell" to Martin. As she sang it, the hall fell silent.[14] So many people in the Garden that night knew someone with the disease, and so many men in the venue had it or feared they did. In his journal that spring, Keith Haring described his own fear: "My friends are dropping like flies and I know in my heart it is only DIVINE INTERVENTION that has kept me alive this long."[15]

Madonna's song spoke eloquently of that dark reality and the grieving people who would survive to tell of it. But it also spoke of hope, because that spring there was some. The Food and Drug Administration had approved a drug—AZT—that didn't kill the virus but supposedly extended the life expectancy of people with AIDS. It was hugely expensive and therefore out of reach for most of the people afflicted with the disease, but it was a first hint of light, a first possibility of...possibility.[16]

Amid all that raw emotion, as Madonna sang in memory of her dear lost friend, many of the nearly seventeen thousand people who heard her responded with tears of grief and thanks. That was why the criticism of her concert in the *New York Times* was so stinging. Jon Pareles said that the show "wasn't exactly moving" but was enjoyable as "shallow, kitschy pop entertainment."[17] Said Madonna with resignation afterward, "There are still people who, no matter what I do, will always think of me as a little disco tart."[18]

Meanwhile, the concert raised $400,000 for the American Foundation for AIDS Research—amfAR. Liz Rosenberg said that the group had helped Martin, and Madonna had "made a vow that she would do a benefit as soon as she went on tour."[19]

Sean left New York for Germany, where he met up with his mother and father on July 21 to appear in his father's film.[20] At the end of the month, he returned to California. His next stop would be jail.[21]

His first cell was in a private facility at the Mono County Jail, in Bridgeport, which the tabloids described as a "spa." He couldn't bear being cast as a pampered coward, so he called his lawyer and asked to be transferred to LA County Jail.[22] The preferential treatment stories continued even after Sean was moved. "The press is saying I got *sushi* dinners. Bullshit. In L.A.

County Jail, they stick a finger up your ass and tell you, 'OK, you don't have a gun.' There isn't a sheet in the place that doesn't have shit stains on it."[23]

Sean was placed in protective custody, where he was alone in a cell for all but thirty minutes a day: he was allowed a ten-minute phone call and one twenty-minute visit. He could not leave his cell without a "belly chain" and ankle irons. "I'll tell you there's nothing like being in jail and hearing the screams of somebody who's going to be in there for the rest of his life," he said. "At night, you're trying to sleep and you hear these fucking primal screams."[24]

The inmate nearest to Sean had generated even bigger headlines than he did. Richard Ramirez, the so-called Night Stalker serial killer and serial rapist, had murdered at least thirteen people. Sean said, "Ramirez and I had one thing in common: we're both insomniacs. I'd look across at him and he'd look across at me." Sean and Ramirez also took showers at the same time because they were high-profile inmates, and both had received threats. Ramirez asked Sean for his autograph, and they agreed to exchange them. Ramirez wrote to Sean: "Stay tough and hit 'em hard again. Richard Ramirez, 666." He drew a pentagram and the devil. Sean wrote to Ramirez,

> *Dear Richard: It's impossible to be incarcerated and not feel a certain kinship with your fellow inmates. Well, Richard, I've done the impossible. I feel absolutely no kinship with you.*[25]

Sean thought he'd be like a monk in a cell with plenty of time to read, which he did: the essays of Montaigne, a novel by William Burroughs, Raymond Carver short stories, and the collected works of James Thurber. He finished what he could emotionally handle (Montaigne and Thurber) in two days.[26] That left him with plenty of time and nothing to do but write. While in jail, he began a one-act play called *The Kindness of Women*. The plot involved a troubled marriage, extramarital pit stops, and liquor.[27]

As Sean completed his first week in jail, Madonna's film with James Foley, *Who's That Girl,* opened on August 6. Ten thousand people turned up in Times Square to see her before the show's premiere, at the National theater. She looked like a movie star, yet she also looked like a girl dressing up as a star. That was her charm. She was still within reach.

Unfortunately, that media event would be the highlight of the film's opening. *New York Times* critic Vincent Canby said the movie was so bad "you might even suspect that there's a Cyndi Lauper 'mole' among

Madonna's advisers, someone bent on wrecking a career before it's decently gotten started." By contrast, her videos, especially "Open Your Heart," which Canby called "a tiny, comic, sexy classic," showed Madonna's potential. "In Madonna, Hollywood has a potent, pocket-sized sex bomb. So far, though, all it does is tick."[28]

James Foley blamed himself and the script for the film's poor reception. He said, "She gave me her trust and I squandered it."[29]

Madonna was able to put the film behind her because her tour left the States soon afterward to play in sold-out stadiums in Europe. Her first stop was Leeds, in the hard-core northern England region that had shown scant interest in her during her earliest UK appearances. Now Madonna performed before seventy-three thousand screaming fans. When the concert moved to London's Wembley Stadium, the anticipation for the show was so great that fans nearly rioted. She performed there for three nights before more than two hundred thousand people.[30]

Madonna's appearance in France only occurred after some high-profile intervention. She wanted to perform at the Parc de Sceaux, an elaborate Versailles-like garden surrounding a seventeenth-century château that was often used for cultural events. Local officials were hesitant; they thought the concert would be too large and too loud and that Madonna would be too racy.

Claude Chirac, the twenty-four-year-old daughter of France's prime minister, Jacques Chirac, persuaded her father to help Madonna secure the site. "I took daddy aside and made him listen to my records and watch my videos," she said. The prime minister and the mayor of Sceaux having been persuaded, Madonna performed before 130,000 people, the largest audience that had ever gathered in France for a pop concert.[31]

Chirac, that stalwart conservative, also threw a party for Madonna at his private residence in the Hôtel de Ville, in Paris. The French press snapped away as Chirac hugged her and as she presented him with a check for 500,000 francs, or around $85,000, for AIDS charities.[32] It wasn't a token gesture but an acknowledgment of the work French researchers had done on AIDS. The Institut Pasteur had led the way in AIDS research by discovering the virus that caused the disease.[33]

Madonna wrapped up her tour with two shows in Italy. The first was in Turin, where she was greeted as daughter, sister, and lover. Before the concert, twelve people were injured in a stampede as a mostly male crowd struggled against police barricades to see her. "It was lots of straight men, and it was all about the sexuality," Pat Leonard said. Police had to erect roadblocks around her hotel to keep them at bay.[34]

Madonna's joy in Italy was evident. No doubt she was happy that the grueling tour was almost over, but there was also a sense that she was home. The frenzy of the crowd and the boisterous display of exaggerated machismo were all so familiar. She had even met some of her distant relatives from Abruzzo. Two days later, on September 6, the tour ended in Florence amid more mob scenes—so many that a small hospital was set up to treat injuries.[35]

Madonna returned to the States triumphant. One and a half million people in three countries had seen her show, earning her more money per concert than any act in history.[36] As the first woman to headline a stadium tour, she demolished an entertainment barrier for women.[37] Within a month, *Forbes* magazine ranked her number 7 on its list of the world's highest-earning entertainers. Among women, she was number 1. At a time when the value of art, more than ever, was based on money, she was a masterpiece. At a time when the entertainment industry was focused on blockbusters, she was one.[38]

Sean was released from jail on September 17, after serving forty-seven days of his sixty-day sentence. Awaiting him was a gift from *Penthouse:* a special two-year anniversary issue of its infamous nude spread on Madonna. The 1987 version (also the cover story) featured more old pictures and an updated text designed to aggravate Sean as much as possible.[39]

It described him as a "petulant and pugnacious young method actor, two years her junior and a minor player in the bread-winning scenario [who] distinguished himself by consummately playing an asshole on screen, and even more consummately off screen." Madonna didn't get a pass, either. After first commending her for embodying fantasies of "boys the world over," it hinted that those days were numbered.

> Already there are rumors...that her hair has begun to fall out alarmingly, due to heavy bleachings of recent years. Others speak of the ugly sagging holes, three in each earlobe, that have started to gape from the weight of too much gaudy jewelry worn for too long, and they speak, too, of little wrinkles at the corners of the eyes.

The magazine said that Madonna stood at the verge of irrelevance for a woman who (according to *Penthouse*) had built her career on her looks: the following year, she would turn thirty.[40]

Two friends collected Sean from jail with a pizza, which he ate en route to Malibu to see Madonna. Years later, when asked whether she was happy to see him, he said, "Not particularly...Listen, it's not a comment on her. Just a comment on the state of the marriage at the time. Going to jail is not good for any marriage."[41]

Together again, Sean and Madonna fought—a lot. Sean's friend David Baerwald, who lived in the Malibu house while Madonna was on tour, had a ringside seat. He said that although their fights were terrible, they were fascinating because they were conducted in code. "You would be in the car with them, and one would be going, 'Well, number three!' and the other would say, 'Yeah, but you number-foured my number two!'"[42]

The code was designed to thwart eavesdroppers. "A lot of times the press would make up the most awful things that we had never done," Madonna said. "Then sometimes we *would* have a fight and we'd read about it, and it would be almost spooky, like they'd predicted it or they'd bugged our phones...It can be very scary if you let it get to you."[43]

Divorce rumors had been circulating almost since the pair were married. Once the wedding tent was packed away, happiness was never again the story line attached to Madonna and Sean.[44] They were "cast" in the tabloid version of their lives as rich, arrogant brats who wanted to bask in celebrity glory without paying celebrity dues.[45] The scrutiny became unbearable. Madonna coped by working harder. Sean coped by drinking more.

After Sean returned home from jail, the press became a convenient scapegoat when he and Madonna publicly discussed the problems in their marriage. But it was clear that there were deeper issues undermining the relationship. In the three years since they had met, Madonna had gone from being an up-and-coming pop star to being the wealthiest female entertainer in the world. It would have been nearly impossible to ride that wave and stay balanced.

During that time, their expectations for their relationship had also diverged. She wanted it to be a marriage of equals. He no doubt believed in the concept, but he had a strong streak of traditionalism that required him to be the "man."

Sean's mother once said, "Sean creates pain in others so he can fix it. If it isn't there and it doesn't need to be fixed, he can't be the hero."[46] With Madonna, he had tried to be the hero by protecting her from the paparazzi. But before Sean's appearance in her life, she hadn't needed protecting. She understood the press and how to deal with it. Sean, in his assumed chivalry, had created a problem and may have believed he could fix it. He failed, and that failure was intolerable. He said the situation made him feel "diminished."[47]

In late November, the denouement the tabs had been awaiting began. Liz Smith's New York *Daily News* column quoted Madonna as saying, "We're just not communicating anymore." The last straw, according to the piece, was Sean's mysterious four-day disappearance before Thanksgiving. Not long afterward, Liz Rosenberg issued a statement saying the marriage was over.[48] Sean's publicist, Lois Smith, said the same: "The two of them have called off the marriage . . . It is really too bad because these two people love each other."[49]

Madonna's lawyers filed papers in Santa Monica on December 4, citing irreconcilable differences. She stayed in New York, surrounded by family. Her sister Melanie had a place in Brooklyn, and Christopher stayed at Madonna's apartment with her. (The tabs staking out the building reported that he was a new boyfriend.) Sean, who had been in New York, returned to LA and reportedly went directly to Helena's, where he got drunk, snarled at the crowd inside, and peed on the building's facade.[50]

Mission accomplished, the press worked overtime to report the story: DIARY OF A MAD MARRIAGE: JEALOUSY, BOOZE AND BRAWLING SINK HOLLYWOOD'S MOST OUTRAGEOUS COUPLE, read the cover of *People*'s December 14, 1987, issue.[51] And then, four days after those headlines, an Associated Press bulletin announced that Madonna had withdrawn her divorce petition. She and Sean would stay together.[52] The frenzied scramble to cover *that* plot twist amounted to the tabloid equivalent of a treasure hunt. *What had happened to make her change her mind?*

The answer—or answers—were obvious. They were still in love. Madonna and Sean might be rebels, but both took marriage very seriously. Neither was a quitter. And divorce hurt.[53] They had also had a scare. Biographer J. Randy Taraborrelli said that after Madonna filed for divorce, she discovered she had a lump in her breast. She was twenty-nine, the age her mother was when she had been struggling with breast cancer. Madonna called Sean, who went with her to the doctor, where they learned that the lump was benign. But Sean said, "Nothing sobers a man like knowing your wife might have cancer. I finally got the message that I had to get serious about my life, about Madonna's life, about our marriage."[54]

After a trauma, celebrities through their representatives often ask the press for privacy while they reassemble the shattered pieces of their lives. Sometimes, the press acquiesces, however briefly. No such luxury was afforded Madonna and Sean. If anything, the pursuit worsened. With blood in the water, the tabloid sharks circled.[55]

Madonna chose to ignore it as much as possible.[56] She even tried to accommodate them. One friend recalled waiting to cross the street with her in New York while surrounded by paparazzi. Madonna finally said, " 'Okay, guys, I think you got enough—whaddaya say?' and one turned to another and said, 'She asked nice—we should go.' And the other one said, 'Fuck her!' and just kept on taking pictures."[57]

Another new wrinkle in her life was the exuberant fans—loonies—who increased in number after her tour and after the extensive coverage of her personal life.[58] In January of 1988, a man crashed his pickup through the gate of her Malibu home and roamed around the grounds. Sean made a citizen's arrest. Not long afterward, Madonna's brother Mario and Sean discovered two teenagers and a twenty-year-old man prowling the property. Sean, who had just returned from the grocery store, hit the elder intruder on the head with a bottle of salad dressing and once again made a citizen's arrest.[59]

Madonna recognized the increased danger but tried to live as if it didn't exist. "I've become much more tolerant of people and human error," she told journalist Kristine McKenna. "Being constantly scrutinized and criticized as I am, you simply have to become tolerant—and a bit passive, I suppose. Either that or you spend all your time telling people to fuck off. It's easy to get into that habit."[60]

In January, amid the gate-crashers and the paparazzi, Madonna took a commercial flight to New York by herself. "It was the first time I'd done anything like that in a long time," she said.

> I don't travel with a huge entourage but I usually have my secretary or some kind of security person with me—and it was very hard for me to force myself to travel alone. I was so frightened...I have friends who are celebrities who live very sheltered lives and won't go anywhere without their bodyguards, but living that way would drive me insane.[61]

It was a matter of art as much as it was security and sanity. She saw how remote her contemporaries Michael Jackson and Prince had become because they isolated themselves from the world. "I think you really have to fight the temptation to go into hiding and surround yourself with people who protect you and *keep life out from you*," Madonna said. "I didn't struggle my way out of Michigan so I could crawl into a hole."[62]

Madonna had flown to New York because she was involved in a movie called *Bloodhounds of Broadway*. It was an ensemble picture based on stories published in the late 1930s by newspaperman Damon Runyon. Though it was a small film compared to some of the projects she'd been offered, Madonna accepted because everything about it felt right.[63]

The director, Howard Brookner, was from home—Madonna's artistic home—and it had been a long time since she had been in that free and loving environment. A former habitué of Paradise Garage, Howard had been part of Warhol's circle and counted among his friends some of the very best in New York's gay writer underground. The dean of that school was William Burroughs, from whom Howard picked up a heroin habit and about whom he had made his first documentary, which Madonna loved.[64]

Howard began working on his new film in 1987. It would combine four Runyon stories set in clubs and restaurants around Broadway on New Year's Eve in 1928, the last New Year's bash of the Jazz Age before the world descended into the Great Depression.[65]

When Howard chose those stories and that era for his film, he was on the verge of his own cataclysm. In the spring, he was diagnosed as HIV-positive. He told no one but his longtime partner, Brad Gooch, and because he was asymptomatic, he was able to "pass" as healthy, just as he was able to pass as straight when dealing with entertainment industry types. In the summer he went to Los Angeles to meet with, among others, Columbia Pictures chairman David Puttnam. Howard returned with a piddling $4 million to make his first feature film, but it was enough. It was literally a lifeline.[66]

At the time Howard pitched it, studio executives didn't know whom he had in mind to play the showgirl Hortense Hathaway. Karen Allen had been cast, but she took another job instead. Howard learned that Madonna was interested and called her. She told him she was in.[67] Meanwhile, Matt Dillon, Jennifer Grey, Randy Quaid, Steve Buscemi, and William Burroughs also joined the cast. Shooting was set to begin in the West Village and New Jersey by early October. It would continue into the new year.[68]

The project was fun for everyone involved because there weren't designated stars and there wasn't a lot of money on the line. The New Jersey shoot occurred in Union City, in a Knights of Columbus hall. "So while we're shooting, there were all these Knights of Columbus guys playing cards in our green room," the associate producer and screenwriter, Colman deKay, told writer Matthew Rettenmund.[69] Dressing rooms were separated by shower curtains.[70] Madonna, he said, was "totally game."[71]

The film was on, but Howard's condition was worsening. He had begun taking AZT, but he felt the drug interfered with his thinking. In his estimation, the film was more important than his health, so he stopped taking it. "It was a very clear choice, a very Howard Brookner choice," Brad Gooch said, "reckless but incredibly dedicated."[72] By early January, Howard had trouble seeing, walking, and raising his arm.[73]

Madonna noticed that he wasn't eating, and when he began asking her about Martin's death, she knew. "But I wasn't going to press him. He had a right to keep it private," she said. "Later, when he phoned and said, 'I have to tell you something,' he couldn't get it out. I said, 'I already know.' I think it was kind of a relief that I knew and that my feelings about him weren't going to change."[74] From then on, Madonna offered him her love and support. "Howard had a connection of the heart with Madonna that broke through the barriers of celebrity," Brad said.[75]

Chapter 24

New York, 1988

It was really a matter between me and God. I would have to live the life he had made me to live. I told him quite a long, long time ago there would be two of us at the Mercy Seat. He would not be asking all the questions.[1]

—*James Baldwin*

THE *BLOODHOUNDS* SHOOT wrapped in February of 1988, just in time for Madonna to start work on a project that couldn't have been more different, not only in terms of style but also in terms of the personalities and the stakes. She began rehearsing David Mamet's play *Speed-the-Plow.* Critic David Ansen said that Madonna had three formidable obstacles to overcome: she was a "pop star invading the sacred realm of the theater, a relative novice among acting professionals, and a woman invading the macho world of Mamet." She understood the challenge. "I knew I was up against a lot," she said. "I'm from a world they have no respect for. It was a really good experience for me to prove myself in that context."[2]

The first film Mamet wrote and directed, *House of Games,* had been released in the fall of 1987. Madonna was so impressed that she sent him a fan letter.[3] During lunch with director Mike Nichols, she mentioned the film, and Nichols told her that Mamet had a new play with a great woman's part in it and that she should contact the director. She asked who that was. He told her, Gregory Mosher.[4]

Madonna knew him from Lincoln Center, where she and Sean performed in *Goose and Tomtom.* She called Mosher and asked if she could read for the Mamet part.[5] "I was blindly driven to do it," she said. "Things just come up in my life and I feel like I'm supposed to do them...I believe there are no accidents, that everything happens for a reason."[6]

The drivers throughout Madonna's life were her desire to learn and to work. Fear played a role, but she called that a catalyst. And she craved respect and love. In *Speed-the-Plow,* she would work, learn, and test herself on a massive stage under the scrutiny of a terrifying literary giant. And if she was good enough, there might be love from the audience and respect for her as an artist. Madonna wanted the role badly and pursued it "like a motherfucker," she said.[7]

By the mid-'80s, New York theater, like Hollywood films, was about blockbusters. Andrew Lloyd Webber had transformed the stage with "megamusicals"—*Jesus Christ Superstar, Evita, Cats,* and *The Phantom of the Opera.* After those experiences, Broadway audiences wouldn't settle for less than full-on razzmatazz.

Drama was largely relegated to off-Broadway and seen by much smaller audiences. And that meant that the art of playwriting was diminished, because even great writers had limited opportunities to see their work performed. By 1988, David Mamet—along with August Wilson and David Rabe—was one of the few celebrated American playwrights actively working.[8]

Mamet was a small man, solid as granite. With his crew cut and economy of expression, he was an intimidating blend of machismo and intellectuality. He has been described as both a "coiled snake" and silly, as well as unpredictable and contradictory.[9]

All those traits made their way into his work, which, starting with his breakthrough play, *American Buffalo,* in 1975, was written in a most idiosyncratic style. An actor in a Mamet play had little room for interpretation. The playwright wanted his dialogue delivered *as written* in the rhythm Mamet intended. It was he, the author, speaking. The actors were not meant to interpret.[10]

Speed-the-Plow would be Mamet's first major stage work after his 1984 Pulitzer Prize–winning *Glengarry Glen Ross.* On either side of that play, he had written screenplays for some of Hollywood's biggest films, from *The Postman Always Rings Twice* to *The Untouchables.* He hadn't enjoyed it.[11] *Speed-the-Plow,* a critique of Hollywood, was written in the '60s, but what he had learned since then, while working in film, hadn't changed his opinion. Using his unforgiving language to describe a trivial episode involving three characters, Mamet would expose the artifice and deceit at the heart of Hollywood.[12]

If Madonna had merely wanted to make her mark in theater, it would have made sense for her to take a role in a big song-and-dance show that was certain to be a hit and a boost to her career. But Madonna didn't do what "made sense." She did what she needed to do to grow as an artist. In this case, she took on one of the most daunting projects in the theater, working with one of its most difficult writers under the brightest possible spotlight. In the theater world, a new Mamet play was an event because it happened so rarely. Madonna said, "I knew I was jumping into the fire," but she loved Mamet's work and she wanted the part. "It's as simple as that."[13]

The character Madonna sought was Karen, a seemingly prim, upright, and clueless temporary office worker who is seduced by a Hollywood producer as part of a bet he makes with a friend. But Karen is not an idiot. She is as Machiavellian as the men, and her character is the axis around which the work rotates. In Mamet's play, she represents Art—an anathema to the movie-business suits. And she represents Woman, as in the seductress whose very presence complicates, if not destroys, men's lives and work.[14]

Mamet regular Joe Mantegna and stage veteran Ron Silver were cast as the male leads. Thirty women auditioned for the part of Karen. The director, Gregory Mosher, had been impressed by Madonna's performance in *Goose and Tomtom* two years earlier, but he wasn't sure about her as Karen.[15] "It's obviously a part that has nothing to do with brassiness and selling yourself," he said. "But the character does need the strength that it takes to be pure, and Madonna's strength just astonishes you when she walks in the room."[16]

The Madonna who appeared for the audition was a brunette. After her tour, she dropped her *True Blue* blond gamine persona. She said she felt more serious, more mature, and more Italian as a brunette.[17]

Mosher and Mamet made her read for the role several times in various locations.[18] The men may have been surprised by what they saw. Mamet said he was "blown away" by her audition.[19] Said Mosher, "She was mesmerizing…It was like nothing I've ever seen from her in the movies. We didn't hire a rock star, we hired an actress. She really earned this."[20] Madonna got the part.

Her costars befriended her—inviting her home to dinner, giving her advice—but they didn't coddle her. "They were there for me, but they never went out of their way unless I asked for it…They didn't give me any training wheels."[21] Both Silver and Mantegna were conscious of the enormousness of Madonna's fame—it occupied the stage like a fourth character, one Mantegna called Godzilla—and how difficult that made her work.[22] "She's very talented, but because she's such a huge star she doesn't have the luxury of starting at the beginning and building a foundation as an actress," Mantegna said. "All her mistakes are so public."[23]

Rehearsals lasted six weeks, during which Mamet didn't offer the actors much in the way of insight into the characters.[24] Madonna thought that was particularly true of Karen.[25] She came to realize during rehearsals that the way she perceived Karen and the way Mamet and Mosher perceived her were very different. "I saw her as an angel, an innocent," Madonna said. "They wanted her to be a cunt."[26]

David kept changing my lines to make me more and more a bitch…So in the middle of this process I was devastated that my idea of the character wasn't what she was at all. That was a really upsetting experience. It was like getting trampled on every night.[27]

Despite all that, Madonna decided she would "make it work if it kills me."[28]

The play had been planned for a three-hundred-seat theater at Lincoln Center, but as word spread that Madonna was in it, the show sold out. The producers decided to move it to Broadway and the one-thousand-plus-seat Royale Theatre. By opening night, more than $1 million worth of advance tickets had been sold for Madonna Ciccone's Broadway debut.[29]

Meanwhile, downtown at the Orpheum Theater, in the East Village, actor and comedian Sandra Bernhard was in a one-person show called *Without You I'm Nothing*. It was a performance about fame, music, sexuality, obsession, and honesty during which she stripped, swore, shouted, alternately abused and adored her audience, and alternately abused and adored herself. It was a lot like Madonna's work in that she became various characters, trafficked in irony, and pushed the audience's every button on the way to outrage.[30]

Sandra had invited Madonna to see her show, and she came on Easter Sunday, April 3. "I first met her in L.A. through mutual friends, nothing too exotic," Sandra said, "but we didn't click until she came to see my show in New York."[31]

> She was so sweet, so excited, and then I went to see her show, and we just started hanging out...It seemed like the right thing at the right time. It was really an important time for her because she wasn't single yet but things with Sean were disintegrating, and I don't think she really had any friends in that world who could understand her success and not be threatened by it and not feel competitive.[32]

Bernhard was loudmouthed, irreverent, smart, *and* warm and generous. She was also *of* Hollywood but not "Hollywood." She had worked as a manicurist in Beverly Hills while doing the comedy-club circuit in LA before being cast at the age of twenty-eight as a deranged fan in Martin Scorsese's 1982 film, *The King of Comedy*. It was a breakout role that should have led to something bigger, but it didn't.[33]

It seemed the industry didn't know what to do with a tough, sarcastic, sexually ambiguous comic who didn't give a shit what the fellas in the executive offices thought of her. When good film roles failed to come her way, she returned to stand-up comedy, doing shows of her own devising.[34]

Madonna embraced the easy friendship Sandra offered. "I had a lot of evenings free and so we just started hanging out," Madonna said. "She was just what I needed. We became really good friends."[35] Sandra called Madonna "a defining friendship in my life . . . And I think we were a really good example of two women being friends."[36]

Female friendships in Hollywood were rarely acknowledged. In the '40s and '50s, many love affairs between women were whitewashed and folded neatly in the closet on the "bosom buddy" shelf. Incredibly, thirty years later, two women in the business could not have a friendship without being suspected of being lovers.

Madonna and Sandra did their best *not* to dispel the rumors, because the nature of their relationship was nobody's business. In a 1991 interview, Madonna said, "I think in the very beginning there was a flirtation, but I realized I could have a really good friend in Sandra, and I wanted to maintain the friendship."[37]

Just as Madonna prepared to open on Broadway surrounded by men in a play that made her feel like a victim, she took refuge in the friendship of women. She began hanging around New York with Bernhard and her *Bloodhounds of Broadway* castmate Jennifer Grey. After the tabs had exhausted the Bernhard–Madonna rumors, they seized on Grey as Madonna's new paramour. "It became a question of whatever female I had a close relationship with who is an outspoken girl—which Jennifer is—then I must be sleeping with her," Madonna explained.[38]

Speed-the-Plow was previewed for the press in April and opened to the public on May 3. Madonna sent all the crew—from the dressers to the stage doorman—flowers to wish them luck.[39] The event may have marked the first time that David Mamet was not the only marquee star of his show. Around town, the play was generally known as the "Madonna play," and it was her name, alongside his, that was murmured in anticipation as people waited outside the theater, on 45th Street.[40]

During the play's run, the Royale was *the* place to go in New York for stargazing. The theater was packed with celebrities.[41] But many others who bought tickets for the show were Madonna fans, young people "who for the most part had never set foot in a theater before."[42] It was a storming of the Bastille that no doubt changed lives the way a first trip to an art museum does for children who have never seen a painting. That cultural phenomenon went largely unnoticed, however, in the rush to cover celebrities at the show and in the critical frenzy to find fault with Madonna.

Entertainment Tonight gleefully ended its segment on *Speed-the-Plow*'s opening night by saying that critics offered "generally scathing reviews of Madonna's performance." The *Daily News* headline read NO, SHE CAN'T

ACT. WCBS-TV called her "ineptitude" "scandalously thorough."[43] Other critics tut-tutted that Madonna seemed wooden, that she didn't emote. In other words, that she acted the way David Mamet intended.[44]

Notably, however, the *New York Times*'s chief theater critic—the "butcher of Broadway," Frank Rich—loved the play. He wrote that *Speed-the-Plow* was "by turns hilarious and chilling...wire taut from start to finish." He said that Madonna "serves Mr. Mamet's play much as she did the Susan Seidelman film *Desperately Seeking Susan,* with intelligent, scrupulously disciplined comic acting."[45]

Madonna wasn't overly bothered by the critics, which like the paparazzi seemed to be a necessary evil. "I expected it because I get it with everything I do," she told the *New York Times.* "There are people who are violently opposed to the fact that I exist on this earth."[46] In speaking with author Harry Crews during the play's run, she said, "To be accepted as an actress, I'm just going to have to work very hard, do everything I have to do...That's the way it works. That's the way it has always worked."[47]

Jackie Onassis was one of the notable celebrities in the audience, an appearance that raised more than a few eyebrows because of rumors that year that Madonna was involved with her son, John F. Kennedy Jr. The prospect reawakened all sorts of Marilyn–Madonna fantasies in the tabloid world.[48]

JFK Jr. had been at the periphery of Madonna's life since her Virgin tour, when he was part of the backstage crush at Madison Square Garden, and again during her Who's That Girl performance there. But the connection had grown because of Herb Ritts, who had become involved with the Kennedys after taking photographs for the Special Olympics at the request of Senator Ted Kennedy, in 1987.[49]

Herb made friends with the younger generation of Kennedys, and because the people in Herb's circle usually found their way into Madonna's, she was recruited to help with the Special Olympics, too. In the fall of 1987, she recorded "Santa Baby" for the Special Olympics' first *A Very Special Christmas* album.[50]

Sometime at the end of that year, when she was separated from Sean, Madonna bumped into JFK Jr. and later began a relationship with him. Published accounts say that each talked about the other with friends: Madonna was bemused by the possibilities of the romance, and Kennedy was confused by how strongly he felt about her. He told one friend that he was "a little obsessed with her." To another he admitted that he was in love. But the affair seemed to have been brief and discreet, as evidenced by the lack of tabloid coverage during a period when the press was ravenous for news about the state of Madonna's marriage.[51]

★   ★   ★

Sean's film *Colors* had premiered on April 15. Critical reviews registered from mixed to positive, but the response from the audience was tremendous. In LA, lines outside theaters stretched around the block. The film made $45 million. That was only a third of what some of the top-grossing pictures made that year, but for such a risky project, it was a blockbuster. *Colors* was Sean's only hit movie during his marriage to Madonna. All the better, then, that it made a statement. Secure in the knowledge that it had, he left the States for Thailand to costar in a movie written by David Rabe and directed by Brian De Palma called *Casualties of War.*[52]

The film was based on the true story of five US soldiers on a reconnaissance mission in Vietnam who kidnapped a Vietnamese girl, raped her, stabbed her multiple times, then shot her dead. The psychopathic patrol leader, Sergeant Tony Meserve, considered the kidnapping a "morale booster" for the squad—or what he called "a little portable R&R." One of the squad members refused to participate in the attack and ultimately testified against the four others, who were court-martialed.[53]

Sean wanted to play the conflicted fifth serviceman, but that role went to Michael J. Fox. Sean was cast as "the pariah" Meserve. Years later, Sean found the role so disturbing that he couldn't watch himself in it because he had so convincingly inhabited the character, with all his murderous rage and pathological misogyny.[54]

The shoot was a long one that involved two weeks of on-site training with two military advisers. After that came months in the jungle, living out the horror of the story day after day. The inhumanity and brutality of the film were gut-wrenching. The next year, during a small test screening for industry types, six people walked out midfilm, and those who remained greeted the ending with silence.[55]

For the actors involved, the project was profoundly disturbing. "We were in hell," said Fox. "You're physically exhausted, and because of the material, you're emotionally in a bit of a state." Fox said that little things kept him tethered to reality, like seeing De Palma get out of his Volvo every day. It was difficult to cling to sanity while shooting what critic Hal Hinson would call "one of the most punishing, morally complex movies about men at war ever made."[56]

Sean returned to the States in late June. David Baerwald said he didn't know Sean was back until he got up one morning at the Malibu house and found him in the kitchen. Except it wasn't Sean. He was still Meserve. "He'd be going round the house, raging," Baerwald said.[57] Having been that damaged character for so long, he couldn't shed him. Like a returning vet, Sean was an alien in what had been his world.

★ ★ ★

As June turned into July, Madonna felt oppressed by her role in *Speed-the-Plow*.

> I was depressed the whole time I was doing it because Ron [Silver] and Joe [Mantegna] had the good parts. They were victorious in the end, and I felt like a loser at the end of every night.[58]
>
> It was just grueling...night after night, that character failed in the context of the play...to continue to fail each night and to walk off the stage crying...It just got to me after a while. I was becoming as miserable as the character I played.[59]

Madonna also felt the tedium of being stuck in one place doing the play over and over again for months.[60] She said she "would look out my window in the theater and see tons of people outside waiting for me every night. And I would find myself enviously watching some anonymous woman just carrying a shopping bag, walking down the street, just slowly window shopping and taking her time, with nobody bothering her."[61]

That Madonna survived the ordeal at all was attributable in part to Sandra Bernhard and Jennifer Grey. They brought her back to herself by just being girlfriends. They could be silly and reckless, which is what Sandra and Madonna were when they appeared on *Late Night with David Letterman,* on July 1.[62]

Bernhard was the guest, but Madonna showed up dressed in an identical outfit: cutoff jeans, white T-shirt, white socks, and black shoes.[63] "Sandy started playing up that we were girlfriends, and I thought, *Great, OK, let me go for it,*" Madonna said.

> Because, you know, I love to fuck with people. Just as people have preconceived notions about gay men, they certainly do about gay women. So if I could be some sort of detonator to that bomb, then I was willing to do that.[64]

The joke became "news" as the press ran with the story that Madonna and Sandra had all but confirmed that they were lovers. It was a delicious new scandal, which didn't trouble Madonna in the least.

> The fact is, she's a great friend of mine. Whether I'm gay or not is irrelevant... If it makes people feel better to think that I slept with her, then they can think it. And if it makes them feel safer to think that I didn't, then that's fine too.[65]

The performance was typical of a Bernhard appearance on *Letterman.* Having been on his show many times before, she had developed a schtick that was as sexually provocative as possible.[66] The Madonna–Bernhard episode was more of the same except for the hints at lesbianism. The references were minor—a couple of throwaway lines in an eleven-minute-plus segment—but it became the story and a new way to report on Madonna and Sean's struggling marriage. The tabs eagerly implied that she was leaving the young tough for a woman.[67]

By that summer, Howard Brookner was in the AIDS wing at St. Vincent's Hospital. He had finished the rough cut of *Bloodhounds of Broadway* just in time. The disease had affected his brain, and he was half blind and confined to a wheelchair.[68] Madonna appeared at St. Vincent's one afternoon to see him and "created a stir" in what was essentially a death house filled with terrified young men hooked up to all manner of tubes and humming monitors.[69]

Climbing onto Howard's bed and giving him a kiss on the mouth, Madonna then visited other patients, moving from bed to bed, getting into bed with some of them, offering a touch, a joke—whatever the person needed and could handle.[70] "It was like Judy Garland visiting another sort of Oz," Brad Gooch said.[71]

She had taped a public service message that would air in August. It tried to dispel myths about AIDS and offered safe-sex tips that boiled down to one essential: wear a condom.[72] That summer, Keith Haring went even further. "I didn't want to have sex anymore," he said.[73]

The month before Madonna's message aired, Haring was having trouble breathing. He developed Kaposi's sarcoma spots on his leg and arm. A New York doctor told him what he already suspected: he had AIDS.[74] "I went over to the East River and sat and cried and cried and cried," he said. "But then, it's like, you have to go on... You've got to figure out how you're going to deal with it."[75]

Keith could afford AZT, but he knew its limitations and that it might kill him before AIDS did because it was so toxic. Meanwhile, his lesions spread; one appeared in the middle of his forehead.[76]

Keith gave his pain voice through his art, which became much more political and angrier.[77] He wasn't hurt and raging over his own situation alone. He mourned the loss of the world he had emerged from in New York, the world he and Madonna had shared, the world where people lived art and talked art and made art.

By the mid-'80s, the art establishment, which had never fully understood that scene, had dismissed the organic movements arising from the street in favor of art that reflected the "greed is good" and "I create nothing; I own" ethos made famous that year in Oliver Stone's hit movie *Wall Street*. In the art world, that was manifest in what Keith called the faux intellectuality of conceptual art cooked up by dealers.

Keith didn't fit that mold. Neither did the people he knew and respected, especially Jean-Michel Basquiat, who had fallen out of favor and was accused of gimmickry. Having no idea who Basquiat was, what he had endured, or his historical significance, *Time* magazine's supposedly venerable critic Robert Hughes dismissed him as "the Eddie Murphy of the art world." Keith said it was "completely racist, ridiculous."[78] But it struck Basquiat to the core.

After Warhol's death, Basquiat spiraled out of control and turned to his old friend heroin. Glenn O'Brien said, "He had a habit big enough to get into the Rolling Stones."[79] Keith saw him earlier in the summer of '88. Basquiat told him that he had kicked heroin "definitely." Keith, in turn, told him he had AIDS but that he was feeling great.[80] The two friends were lying. That moment was the last the two artists shared. Jean-Michel died of a drug overdose in his studio on August 12. He was twenty-seven.[81]

Basquiat had countered the greed of the art world with humor and the bitter tongue of racism with genius.[82] And therein lay the rub. He was nobody's boy, and the establishment hated him for it.

Chapter 25

Los Angeles, 1988–1989

Music is healing. Some secrets r so dark they have 2 b turned in2 song 1st b4 one can even begin 2 unpack them.[1]

— *Prince*

MADONNA'S COMMITMENT TO *Speed-the-Plow* ended on August 28, 1988, and she returned to Los Angeles. After such an emotionally draining period, and after months of being Karen, she needed a place to collect herself so that she could begin creating her own art rather than interpreting someone else's. Malibu was not that place. In her absence, her home had become a free-range testosterone preserve. Sean hadn't shed his *Casualties of War* persona and had surrounded himself with friends nearly as pumped up as he was. He said that things between him and Madonna began falling apart.[2] Madonna had to face that very sad fact every day.

She turned thirty that summer, four days after Basquiat's death. The following month, she began work on a new album that would reflect her more mature and more conflicted woman's reality. "My first couple of albums, I would say, came from the little girl in me, who is interested only in having people like me, in being entertaining and charming and frivolous and sweet," she said. "This new one is the adult side of me, which is concerned with being brutally honest." She would call the album *Like a Prayer*.[3]

Returning from her tour the previous fall, Madonna recalled being so "burned out...I said to myself, 'Hey, I don't ever want to hear any of my songs ever again and I don't know whether I'll ever write another one.'" But Pat Leonard invited her to see a new studio he had built. "Within an hour, we'd written this great song," she said.[4] And then, while on Broadway, she wrote another. "Because of the state of mind I was in," she said,

> I dealt with a lot of sadness in my life that I hadn't dealt with in a long time, things like my mother's death and certain relationships. I started to explore all of that every night when I would do the play. Especially for the last scene, when I had to walk onstage being really upset and frightened. I would sit in

my dressing room with all the lights off, waiting for that scene, and I would force myself to think of something really painful. I did it every night, and I purged myself that way. It was like a goal I set...Forcing my fears.[5]

As Madonna dug deep into herself to revisit her past, she had help from her father. That year, Tony had given his eldest children copies of letters their mother wrote to him when he was in the air force, before they married. Christopher said he only read one of them because his mother's religious beliefs were so devout that it was "difficult for me to grasp." The letter, he said, was "loving and sweet...All about how God is keeping her love for my father alive, God this and God that." He and Madonna never discussed the letters, and Madonna did not mention them in interviews from that period.[6] But they very likely had an impact on her during that anguished time.

Madonna's mother loomed as large in her life as any living person, and she had never stopped yearning for her. When she began her new album, which she would dedicate to her mother, those letters may have acted as a balm as the love she struggled to keep alive in her own marriage survived on life support. It also can't be a coincidence that *Like a Prayer* was Madonna's first real musical foray into the Catholic imagery her mother embraced or that it connected belief and passion with family.[7]

On *True Blue,* Madonna had traveled back to the good times of her childhood—the girl groups, the joy of music, and the security of love. On *Like a Prayer,* she would journey to the dark side of that era, when her world fell apart, as it seemed on the verge of doing again. She would write all the lyrics on her new album herself. For the music, she turned again to her two most trusted collaborators, Pat Leonard and Steve Bray.[8]

Madonna worked on the album for five months, mostly in Burbank, at Pat's Johnny Yuma studios. "We called it her divorce album," he said.[9] On some days, Madonna "wore sunglasses all day in the studio. She was going through very hard times."[10]

Of the eleven songs on the album, two would be written with Steve, eight with Pat, and one with Prince. Pat said for most of the album, he would get to the studio by 8:00 a.m., and Madonna would come in around eleven, at which point she'd hear the music he'd been working on. "I would just put [on] the track, the chord changes, some kind of drumbeat, bass line—something simple—and say, 'Here's the idea, here's what I have for the day,'" he recalled.

She would listen, then we would talk a little bit. Oftentimes I'd say, "Here's the verse and here's the chorus," and she'd say, "No, it's the other way around, switch 'em." So I'd switch 'em...She'd start writing lyrics and oftentimes there was an implied melody. She would start from that or if there was nothing but a chord change, she'd make up a melody.[11]

Madonna said, "I don't think he's ever written a melody that I just *took* and said, 'OK, that's finished, I'll just slap some words on it.' It always needs to be worked."[12]

The source material for her lyrics came from art and from life. In just that past year, she had had inspiration and experience enough for a lifetime: her troubled marriage, Broadway, Howard Brookner's illness, her new friends and the deaths of old ones, her disorienting fame and the intense reaction to it, and her personal evolution from girl to woman. Madonna said in early 1988, "There's a side of me I'm finding less and less inhibited about expressing, and that's a side that has to do with a real pain and sadness that I feel."[13]

If the words didn't come, she stopped. "Ultimately you can't force it. But there is a certain amount of discipline required. When I have to write an album, I sit down and say, 'This is it.' . . . I give myself a block of time. But every once in a while, it's really tough."[14]

It wasn't tough for *Like a Prayer*. The lyrics poured out of her. Pat said she wrote the verses, chorus, and bridge for each song in about an hour. "And then she'd sing it. We'd do some harmonies . . . and usually by three or four in the afternoon, she was gone."[15] When they wrote the single "Like a Prayer," he said, "it felt like being on fire."[16]

> I think there was a point when we realized that it was the title track, and the lead track, and it was going to [be] a powerhouse. It became obvious that there was something unique about it . . . There is something different when you write something and you just have a sense that you can't break this, you can't really ruin this. It exists already.[17]

Madonna described that song as the voice of a young girl who was passionately in love with God.[18] To impart that, she said, she wanted to do something "really gospel oriented and a cappella with virtually no instrumentation, just my voice and an organ . . . Then we came up with the bridge together, and we had the idea to have a choir."[19]

The introduction of a choir, with its multitude of voices, raised the message of the song to the level of an accepted truth, what Saint Augustine called an expression of not just one but many hearts.[20]

For "Like a Prayer," Madonna used Andraé Crouch and his Los Angeles Church of God Choir. They had performed on Michael Jackson's "Man in the Mirror," which was released earlier that year. In fact, by the time Crouch worked with Madonna, he had become a "pop/rock gospel" phenomenon. He was criticized by some gospel purists, but he didn't balk at working with either Jackson or Madonna. "I play what God gives me to play," he said.[21]

Madonna, he said, told him she wanted something "very churchy, so I tried to blow up what she did and make it as powerful as I could." That became the theme of the single: blow it up. Bassist Guy Pratt called the recording process for the song "an out of body experience...As I was playing, Madonna was going: 'Guy, more! More!'" He called the result "the maddest bass performance on a pop record ever" and the best he's ever done.[22]

Pratt called Madonna "formidable...There were all these top L.A. session guys being very quiet and deferential." Madonna had earned that respect. While recording "Oh Father" with six musicians, he said,

> I think we did one run through, and I don't think we were recording. And Madonna stood in the control room, and she sang it, and she'd never sung it before. And at the end of it, she then gave the whole band notes, which were all absolutely correct. Not like "Make it more purple," they were really understandable like "Guy just hold the duck eggs...." She'd sung the song for the first time, nailed it, and clocked everything everyone was doing.[23]

Madonna had begun writing "Oh Father" while on Broadway "in a very, very dark state of mind." She called that song her most "autobiographical work, with a little bit of drama thrown in. It's boring to be *completely* autobiographical."[24] The subject wasn't just her father, she said. It was "me dealing with all authority figures in my life."[25]

That song was the only one that Pat and Madonna did for *Like a Prayer* that was not written during their two-week marathon.[26] "He came to New York," she said, "and...we got together in this really dingy, awful little studio in the garment district...and that's what came out of me."[27]

Pat felt that "Oh Father" was the most "real" song they ever wrote together.[28] They had planned to go back in and fix the vocals. "But then we'd listen to them and say, 'Why? They're fine,'" Madonna recalled. "So I decided not to go back and clean them up. There are weird sounds that your throat makes when you sing: p's are popped, and s's are hissed, things like that...and I didn't fix them...Because I think these sounds are emotions, too."[29]

One of the most curious songs on the album was the one Madonna recorded with Prince. At some point, she had been in Minnesota working with him on what they hoped would be a musical. When that didn't materialize, they continued to throw around ideas. It felt like something might happen.[30] Then, during *Speed-the-Plow,* Prince came to see her.

He had made a tape of bits of songs they'd worked on together. "Love

Song" was one of them. Madonna thought it was "great" and wanted it on her new album. "It seemed to relate to all the other songs because it's about a ... hate-love relationship."[31]

Prince agreed, and they began sending tapes back and forth, experimenting with the music and Madonna's words.[32] "It was fun because in this song it is only my musical influence and his. I didn't have Pat or Steve's help. I played the keyboards myself and because I don't know that much, it kind of came out strange and interesting."[33]

Prince also appeared via his guitar on other tracks on the album: "Like a Prayer," "Act of Contrition," and "Keep It Together."[34] Steve Bray said that in the last song Madonna was dealing with the impact of her success on her family.[35] Other songs on the album also arose out of family issues. "Oh Father" was one, "Promise to Try" another.[36]

"I played the piano and she sang," Pat said of that song. "She was right at my shoulder, next to the piano, with no headphones."[37] Madonna said the song wasn't about "one thing. It's my father talking to me, it's me talking to me."[38] It was also about Madonna's mother, "a yearning to have her in my life but also about trying to accept the fact that she's not ... I do talk to her often. I mean, I always have. I don't know if she can hear me or not, but I tell her things that a girl can only say to her mother. Private things."[39]

In light of what Madonna called her roller-coaster marriage, the fourth "family" song on the album, "Till Death Do Us Part," could only be seen as a window into her life with Sean. She described the song as being about "a destructive relationship that is powerful and painful. In this song, however, it's a cycle that you can't get out of until you die ... Now that's where the truth stops because I would never want to continue a terrible relationship forever and ever and ever until I die."[40]

The song was, as Madonna said, "brutally frank" in its depiction of domestic violence. Other singer-songwriters at the time were tackling equally difficult subjects. In 1987, Suzanne Vega had a hit single with "Luka," about child abuse, and MC Lyte released "I Cram to Understand U (Sam)," about crack addiction (which she wrote when she was twelve). In 1988, Tracy Chapman had a hit with her bleakly beautiful "Fast Car," about inescapable domestic misery. In the case of "Till Death Do Us Part," the broader story — the social commentary — was largely overlooked by critics in favor of the tantalizing clues it seemed to provide about Madonna's life.

If the critics missed the song's powerful statement on abusive relationships, however, women on the receiving end of such blows didn't. Madonna's was a clear-eyed and unsentimental description of the life they led and the fears they faced. And it wasn't judgmental. She merely stated the facts, and in them was an implied choice: leave or stay. It was up to the woman. If the song felt shockingly real and intimate, it was because Madonna was in the process of making that decision herself.

Madonna didn't offer advice in "Till Death Do Us Part." She saved that for what would be her first true feminist track: "Express Yourself." "The message of the song is that people should always say what it is they want," she explained. "Sometimes you feel that if you ask for too much or ask for the wrong thing from someone you care about that that person won't like you. And so you censor yourself."[41]

"Express Yourself" made the personal political by grabbing power for women and daring anyone to try to take it away.[42] "We didn't invent feminism," said Steve Bray, who wrote the song with her, "but this was a call to action...To have co-written a song about telling one's truth and demanding to be treated as an equal and as a partner—I couldn't be more proud."[43]

Madonna had turned to her most trusted musical collaborators to create her album, and she turned to Herb Ritts to shoot the cover. It would be his third. In 1986, he photographed her for *True Blue,* and in 1987, he shot the cover for her first remix album, a collection of songs called *You Can Dance.* Both albums featured Madonna's face. For *Like a Prayer,* he ignored it in favor of her famous midriff.

The front cover photo, with its suggestive image of blue-jeaned hips, was a tribute to and appropriation of images used by the Rolling Stones on their *Sticky Fingers* cover and on Bruce Springsteen's more recent *Born in the U.S.A.* On the back, Ritts paid tribute to the feminine beauty those boys couldn't touch. He shot Madonna praying in the dark silk slip that would become famous in her "Like a Prayer" video.

Among the surprises for those who purchased the album was the scent of patchouli oil that arose from the packaging, like incense in a church, and an insert titled "The Facts About AIDS." After a brief introduction denouncing antigay bigotry and violence against people with AIDS, it laid out in blunt language the risky behavior that spread the disease.

> You can get AIDS by having vaginal or anal sex with an infected partner.
> You can get AIDS by sharing drug needles with an infected person.
> You can get AIDS by being born to an infected mother.[44]

The reference to anal sex in 1988 was staggering. To mainstream America, it was beyond the pale. To young people navigating the dangerous waters of their sexual awakening, it was a lifeline. Savas Abadsidis, the future editor of the magazines *HIV Plus* and *The Advocate,* was fifteen when Madonna released her album and its "The Facts About AIDS" insert. He said he read it "cover to cover...Madonna would ultimately teach me more about sex than I ever learned at school."[45]

Like a Prayer introduced an entirely new sound for Madonna. Steve Bray said it was the first time that lyrics and musical experimentation were more important for her than the beat.[46] It was where "Live to Tell" had taken her, and that was largely away from the dance floor. But the album was risky commercially, because dance music dominated the radio. Thanks largely to Madonna, Michael Jackson, and Prince, a new pop format called "urban crossover sound" was born. It broke down the market-driven racial barriers—or "apartheid radio"—that kept white kids from listening to Black music and Black kids from listening to white music.[47]

And thanks in part to Madonna, a new generation of young women pop singers was climbing the charts—Paula Abdul, Debbie Gibson, Shanice Wilson, Alisha, and Tiffany among them—while Janet Jackson was *burning up* the charts. And then there was Whitney Houston. Her debut album, released in 1985, when she was twenty-one, stayed at number 1 for fourteen weeks. For a time, she owned the radio.[48] The music business awoke to the notion that men weren't the only people who bought records—that there was a vast female audience out there that record executives could no longer afford to ignore.

Madonna faced a new kind of pressure. Pat Leonard said he felt like he was in the "hot seat" while making *Like a Prayer.* "I had managers checking in, and the record company checking in, asking to hear stuff." If the record company worried about the risk of releasing an album as innovative and out of sync with the market as *Like a Prayer,* Madonna didn't. "I didn't try to candy coat anything or make it more palatable for mass consumption, I guess. I wrote what I felt," she said.[49] She had never taken the road most traveled. After *Like a Prayer,* she occupied a musical lane of her own.

In the fall of 1988, Madonna met with Warren Beatty to discuss his next movie, *Dick Tracy.* He needed a hit. A film released the previous year that he starred in with Dustin Hoffman was a bomb, and the chatter in the industry—fairly or not—was that *Ishtar* was Warren's $51 million disaster.[50] *Dick Tracy* could be the film to resuscitate his career. Casting Madonna as his leading lady would give him credibility with a young audience, for whom he was, at fifty-one, older than their fathers and just about as interesting.[51]

It was galling to him because, since his breakthrough film, *Splendor in the Grass,* released in 1961, he had been the prince of Hollywood, an

American Casanova. (His biographer Peter Biskind estimated that by the late '80s Beatty had had sex with nearly thirteen thousand women, not counting "quickies" and "drive-by blow jobs.") He epitomized the '60s one-sided sexual revolution, seducing everyone in his path and everyone in his professional circle.[52] But that wasn't working the way it once had. He needed to resurrect his winning formula.

From the start of his career, with *Splendor* and his costar, Natalie Wood, Beatty established a pattern that worked marvelously for him. He and the leading lady would fall in love. The press would leap on the story, which was usually messy, sometimes involving a jilted husband, public quarrels, and nearly always a conquest for Beatty as the woman succumbed to his charms. The film would benefit from the coverage. And when the picture ran its course in the theaters, Beatty's relationship would end, too.[53]

So why on earth would Madonna want anything to do with him? Because, as an artist, he was fearless and brilliant—not as an actor so much as a visionary who pushed film into new aesthetic and political dimensions.

If Beatty's career as a Valentino began in 1961 with *Splendor in the Grass,* his position as a film industry force began in 1967 with director Arthur Penn's *Bonnie and Clyde.* It is hard to describe how revolutionary that picture was at the time. The Depression-era outlaws of the title were depicted as populists, taking from the rich what had been taken from the people. Released during the Vietnam War and civil rights protests, *Bonnie and Clyde* was not only seen as glamorizing rebellion but also as justifying violence. Beatty himself said that the film's message was "You better give the have nots some money, or they'll shoot you."[54]

Bonnie and Clyde became a major hit, though most critics—seemingly terrified to endorse it—gave it a tepid response. Not Pauline Kael. She praised it in *The New Yorker* as the best American film since 1962's *The Manchurian Candidate.* Roger Ebert called it "a milestone in the history of American movies, a work of truth and brilliance."[55] After *Bonnie and Clyde,* an American "new wave" of films that catered to a younger, hipper audience swept Hollywood.[56]

Beatty hadn't just been an actor in the film; he was also a driving force as its producer. He emerged from the project a multimillionaire and one of the industry's most powerful men.[57] Several heralded films later, Beatty made *Reds,* about the radical American journalist John Reed, who had covered the Russian Revolution and became a communist activist and sympathizer. *Reds* was Beatty's baby. He starred in it, produced it, and directed it. Critics were split on whether it worked. But in February of

1982, it was nominated for twelve Academy Awards. Beatty won Best Director.[58] That was his last film until the misbegotten *Ishtar*, in 1987.

He knew everyone in the film business—old Hollywood and new. He knew the business as a winner and as a loser. If Madonna wanted to make it in the movies, she had in Warren Beatty the perfect teacher. While he divulged nothing about himself (one of his closest friends said that in forty-five years he never opened up), he loved to talk about movies.[59]

In 1987, Beatty had turned fifty. His father had just died, and others in his circle were extolling the virtues of marriage—or at least parenthood and a steady(ish) woman. There was also the specter of AIDS, which gave the boyos in Hollywood pause. Against that personal backdrop, he turned his professional attention to *Dick Tracy*.[60]

As the film's story line developed, it became about a good guy fighting a corrupt system and a middle-aged man struggling between the tug of a wife and child and the temptation of a seductress. It was, in other words, a comic-book version of Warren Beatty's state of mind.[61]

Beatty circumvented the problem of hiring a director and leading man by doing both jobs himself. For the female leads, he initially turned to the edgy *Blade Runner* actor Sean Young to play the wholesome Tess True-heart. For the steamy Breathless Mahoney, he ran through a list of blond temptresses before considering Madonna.[62]

Madonna wanted the role. She saw Breathless Mahoney not as a scheming dark force in Tracy's righteous world but as "a girl. She's scared. She's a seductress in a lot of pain."[63] "I've probably been preparing for this role all my life."[64] "Everybody said I'd be perfect for the role."[65]

One wonders if Sean Penn was among the "everybody" who thought it was a good idea. He had been part of the Hollywood boys' club. He knew what it meant if Madonna took the role, because *everyone* in Hollywood knew what it meant. It was a parlor game for onlookers: How long would it take before Madonna joined Warren's list of conquests? Sean reportedly once told her, "Do anything you want, just never make a film with Warren Beatty."[66]

Freddy DeMann also didn't think she should do it. But when Beatty offered, Madonna took the part. With Al Pacino, Dustin Hoffman, James Caan, Mandy Patinkin, and Paul Sorvino signed on, Disney gave its blessing to the film. Shooting would begin in February of 1989.[67]

Having only been in town for three years, Madonna had graduated into the upper ranks of establishment Hollywood. She was in big-budget movie-star territory, on a first-name basis with the biggest actors, producers, and directors in the business. In the world of entertainment more broadly, Madonna was without parallel, even if all one cared about was money. For the second year, she made it into the top ten on the annual

Forbes roster of highest-paid entertainers. She was also once again the top-earning woman on the list.[68]

Sean was set to open on November 16 at the Westwood Playhouse, in Los Angeles, in David Rabe's *Hurlyburly*. The play's producer, Barbara Ligeti, called it a "scathing indictment of Hollywood."[69] The story is told through the perspective of two casting agents who inhabit a world where everything is negotiable and everyone is for sale. Women in the play are regarded by the men as little more than broads and bitches. Cocaine features large in the men's lives, as do lying, cheating, and violence. As despicable as the men are, though, they are mere bit players in the most corrupt game of all—the movie business itself. In Rabe's play, the industry is the villain and the men just as much victims as the dames.[70]

An anti-Hollywood play was not without risk, especially because it was performed in the belly of the beast—reportedly at Sean's request, so he could be near Madonna. But Ligeti and Rabe wagered that the industry loved nothing more than a story about itself, and it appeared that they bet correctly. Tickets sold, even though Los Angeles was not a theater town.[71]

Sean was proud of his acting in that play. He believed it was the moment when his craft and his ability to express himself came together.[72] That could be why he was so angry with Madonna.

She had been attentive throughout the play's rehearsals. But on opening night, some accounts said she arrived late with Sandra Bernhard. Afterward, at a party in Century City, at the 20/20 nightclub, Sean was visibly upset and reportedly called Madonna an obscenity, saying, "How could you do this to me?" Partygoers heard the commotion coming from a private room, with Madonna screaming back.[73]

The fight was unique in that it was so public, but it was just one more drama during those last months of 1988 as their marriage frayed. "They would be stormy and then calm and happy," said Rabe. During the *Hurlyburly* period, he remembered, there had been a party at their home. "Madonna played her first tapes of *Like a Prayer,* and we listened, and it was very exciting…There was a lot that seemed to me like they were very happy and very much in love. And then, well…"[74]

Throughout the holiday season, Madonna appeared at the theater to watch Sean's play and take him home afterward.[75] And as she worked on her album, Sean was there to listen and encourage her to be as bold and frank as she needed to be. Madonna said Sean even loved her song about domestic violence, "Till Death Do Us Part."[76] But after she accepted the *Dick Tracy* role, he suspected that she was drawn to the glitz and glamour of the industry, willing to trade her artistic integrity for entrée into that world.[77]

She wasn't. Mainstream Hollywood was a step she had to take to become the artist she thought she could be. And maybe, after being disrespected for her film work for so long, she thought the cachet of Beatty and Disney would insulate her from the critics. But more important was the simple fact that she loved the movies, especially those feel-good pictures made during Hollywood's golden era.

Sean, however, only saw betrayal. At one point, he moved back into his parents' home. Drunk, he would reportedly call Madonna and leave angry messages. Early Madonna biographer Mark Bego quoted a person with access to the recordings who said, "He left one message for her toward the end—'You can continue to suck the big dick of Hollywood if you want to, but you can count me out!' "[78]

It was an extremely difficult time for them both. Sean had befriended the reclusive Hal Ashby, director of some of Hollywood's most memorable films of the 1970s, among them *Harold and Maude* and *Being There*.[79] The fifty-nine-year-old director and the twenty-eight-year-old actor played pool at Sean and Madonna's when she was out of town.[80]

For a young man, there was much to learn from Ashby about film. But more important, there was much to learn about life. For a short time, it looked as though Sean might be able to work with Ashby on a film. But Ashby died on December 27, 1988. He had been suffering from pancreatic cancer for three months. Sean, who had been with him for much of that time, was devastated.[81]

Shortly afterward, something happened in Malibu. According to Sean's biographer, Richard T. Kelly, the morning after Ashby's death, Sean and Madonna had an argument at breakfast. He asked her to leave. Madonna said she would come back later for her things, but Sean threatened to cut off her hair if she tried to.[82] Sean said that Madonna "took it quite seriously" and went to the police. "A SWAT team surrounded my house and came in every door...She felt the responsible thing to do would be to inform them...that there were firearms in the house." Sean said that when police arrived, he was eating cereal. He was not arrested.[83]

The story as reported later described a violent episode the previous night, which seemed to have been based on a British tabloid report published in January of 1989 that others picked up and repeated. Even gossip columnist Liz Smith repeated the story while admitting she had "no evidence that this happened." Others justified their reporting by saying, "When there are so many articles and so much press, there has to be something."[84]

In 1989, Madonna denied the reports, but because she didn't elaborate, her denials weren't taken seriously. And when her complaint to the sheriff's department was withdrawn, it was whispered that she merely wanted to keep Sean out of jail. Since then, Madonna and Sean have both denied the stories. In 2015, Sean successfully sued a director for repeating them. With police records expunged in 1992 as part of a routine procedure, it is impossible to verify details of that night or, because of Sean's lawsuit, even relay what was reported at the time.[85] But whatever occurred, it was the end of Madonna and Sean's marriage.

Liz Rosenberg found Christopher in New York and asked him to fly to LA to help his sister. "I call Madonna at once and ask how she is," Christopher said. "She says she is OK, but her voice is small and I know she isn't." She said she needed to find a place to live, that she had taken refuge at Freddy DeMann's house in Beverly Hills. Telling her he'd be there in the morning, Christopher packed his bags for California. For the next decade, he would be at his sister's side almost continuously.[86] He once said, "I was born my mother's son, but I will die my sister's brother."[87]

Madonna collected Christopher at the Bel Age Hotel in her Mercedes 560SL convertible, which she would own for ten years without ever lowering the top. She looked weak and tired, but she didn't want to talk about "it," meaning Sean. She was focused on houses. She needed one quickly, and she left the search and the decorating to Christopher. Madonna told *Vogue*'s André Leon Talley that her little brother "has the most impeccable taste of anyone I know." Said Christopher, "She has her own vision. I offer her different ways of looking at things. Other people do, too, but it's different with us. We fight a lot, and either she wins or I win, but we don't let up. Neither of us is afraid to be direct."[88]

Christopher looked at twenty-five houses before finding one on Oriole Way, high in the Hollywood Hills. "The home has the feeling of a great New York penthouse, except the view is better and there's a pool," Christopher said.[89] A British writer unaccustomed to such environs described the house's view as "heart-stopping" and the neighborhood as one where "the second most common profession is gardener, the first being pangalactic celebrity."[90]

Oriole Way didn't need work, so Christopher busied himself filling it with stuff—from the most elaborate antiques to the most basic kitchen utensils. He had never shopped on such a scale before, but it was easy. As soon as he announced that he was buying on behalf of Madonna, "it opened every door." Madonna had only one request. "She demanded good sheets," he said.[91] They both agreed the kitchen was critically important. "In an Italian home, socializing always centered around the kitchen." And when he raided the shops along Melrose Avenue for antiques, he chose Italian furniture, which he and his sister preferred. "It's grand without being gaudy like French furniture," he explained.[92]

More critical than sheets, eighteenth-century chairs, and colanders, however, was the art. The most striking piece was a massive gold-framed early nineteenth-century Jérôme-Martin Langlois mythological scene of nude figures once commissioned for Versailles. Christopher hung it on the ceiling in the main sitting room.[93] And Madonna had her own art collection, which she had begun building with her first Sire paycheck.[94] "Her collection felt very personal and very particular," said curator and photography critic Vince Aletti. "No matter how much advice she paid for, the results on the wall were never predictable. She had an exquisite small Dalí that is one of the most beautiful I've ever seen."[95]

Indeed, by 1989 her home featured museum-quality pieces that had been given to her — Keith Haring and Andy Warhol works among them — and that she had purchased without regard to their future monetary value, simply because they spoke to her. These included paintings by Fernand Léger, Frida Kahlo, Diego Rivera, Tamara de Lempicka, and Picasso as well as photos by Tina Modotti, Edward Weston, Irving Penn, Man Ray, Weegee, and Herb Ritts. Throughout her life, art would be her one material indulgence. She said collecting it was "like a disease."[96]

Frida Kahlo's *My Birth,* painted when the artist was living in Detroit in 1932, was a centerpiece of Madonna's collection. In the painting the adult Kahlo emerges from her mother's vagina. "This sense of being born whole, of being born grown-up is something absolutely crucial, I think, to what Madonna's about," said music writer Greil Marcus. "And obviously if you can create yourself, you can continue to re-create yourself."[97]

Christopher had the house ready in two weeks, allowing Madonna to move in before her divorce was finalized.[98] The terms were simple. Madonna wanted her legal name changed from Penn to Ciccone. She kept all her money and the New York apartment. Sean kept his money and the house in Malibu.[99] The residences "were the only things that we both put up cash for; everything else was separate and stayed separate," Sean said.[100] Before their marriage he had refused to sign a prenup, which he called a "death warrant on a marriage. Nor am I, under the worst circumstances, going to take a penny of somebody else's change."[101]

While the lawyers filled in the details, the real work of rebuilding a life began. Madonna said that the divorce left her feeling like a "total failure — as any good Catholic girl would." It would take a few years before that sense of failure became mere gnawing sadness and for the terrifying recognition that she had lost the love of her life to morph into numb regret. For the first year, Madonna said, "every time you turn the radio on or see a color or experience a smell, it reminds you . . . and you just crumble." She said it was "like a death."[102]

Both she and Sean conducted public postmortems on their relationship, and both accepted responsibility for its demise. Sean described his marriage to Madonna as a

> period of insufficient peace... You have to understand: When Madonna and I got together... she hadn't even gone on tour yet... My understanding of the direction that Madonna was choosing was a misunderstanding. And the degree to which she would be choosing, and chosen for, such an intense spotlight was... a surprise. A big surprise...
>
> I started to get the idea very shortly after we were together, but by then, there's that heart thing that gets involved. You don't walk away so easily just because something is a little difficult.

Sean said that at the start it wasn't even clear whether Madonna's career would last. But if anything, the spotlight on her grew brighter. "I don't think anyone else is carrying around that sort of Beatles—or Elvis Presley–size persona."[103] To cope with her celebrity, Sean drank. "I was pretty young when all this was going on," he said several years later. "I think I numbed myself pretty well."[104] Asked if the marriage ever stood a chance, Sean said, "No wa-ay. Under the circumstances of what happened with her? No way."[105]

> I just wanted to make my films and hide... I was an angry young man. I had a lot of demons and don't really know who would have lived with me at that time. I was just as badly behaved as her... Who was it that said, "Men are vain, particularly young men." That was me.[106]

The marriage didn't end, he said, "without both of us, to the best of our abilities, giving it a scout's try to make it work out."[107]

For her part, and in hindsight years later, Madonna said she hadn't been ready to be married. "I was completely obsessed with my career and not ready to be generous in any shape or form."[108] "Sean really wanted a wife, someone to be more nurturing than I was prepared to be. I was fighting that conventional idea of how a woman behaves."[109]

She also blamed herself for being naive about the press, because she hadn't anticipated how pathological their pursuit would become. "When I started out with Sean I broadcast our relationship."[110]

> I wanted the whole world to know that this is the man I loved more than anything. But there's a price to pay for that... Once you reveal it to the world—and you're in the public eye—you give it up, and it's not your own

anymore. I began to realize how important it is to hold on to privacy and keeping things to yourself as much as possible . . . So if you ask, Did I complicate things by being very public about [my feelings]? Yes, I did.[111]

Madonna took title to her new home on January 18 and encountered her wedding scene all over again; helicopters buzzed overhead taking pictures of the place.[112] She let them. She had a life to attend to. "It was an incredibly traumatic time for her," Sandra Bernhard said, but "she has this uncanny ability to bounce back . . . She's incredibly strong."[113]

Explained Greil Marcus,

After about three or four or five years of her career, she was probably the most famous woman in the world. She didn't have a nervous breakdown, or if she did, nobody knows about it. She didn't become a junkie. She did get married. But who went crazy? Her husband. *She* didn't go crazy. She seems to have been born for fame, for pressure that usually breaks people.[114]

Chapter 26

Los Angeles, 1989

If art like this is a crime, let God forgive me.[1]

—Lee Quiñones

THE DIVORCE WAS finalized on January 25, 1989, the same day Pepsi announced an unprecedented agreement with Madonna. She would release her new single, "Like a Prayer," during a Pepsi commercial in exchange for $5 million and Pepsi's sponsorship of her next tour. The ad marked the first time a record would premiere in a commercial and the first time a TV, commercial would be given a global launch. Pepsi said it would be seen in forty countries—or "just about every TV set on the planet Earth"—with an estimated viewership of 250 million people. Freddy DeMann called the marketing campaign around the record and the commercial the "pop-world equivalent" of a new Star Wars film.[2]

By 1989, commercials and advertisements featuring celebrities and their work had become cultural events. Andy Warhol and Keith Haring illustrated ads for Absolut Vodka. Spike Lee created an ad starring Michael Jordan for Nike. Miles Davis and Lou Reed appeared separately in Honda scooter commercials. But no industry relied more on famous boosters than the one peddling soft drinks. In a country where, per capita, people drank more soda pop than they did water, celebrities were needed to build brand loyalty, especially in the teenage market, which grew in value by billions of dollars each year. Pepsi and Coca-Cola were engaged in a hot and high-profile "cola war" that pitted their beverages and their ad budgets against each other. And that necessitated attracting more and bigger stars.[3]

Since 1984, Pepsi had featured entertainers in its ads—Michael Jackson, Tina Turner, David Bowie, Lionel Richie, and the Miami Sound Machine. It had even considered Madonna in 1985, but the *Playboy* and *Penthouse* scandal erupted, and she was deemed too controversial.[4] By late 1988, controversy (apparently) be damned, Pepsi considered her a must-have. Rival Coca-Cola had signed George Michael for a Diet Coke commercial directed by Stephen Frears. Pepsi's retort was the Madonna deal.[5]

Releasing her new song during a commercial was risky on many levels, not least because it bypassed the crucial radio market. "At first I thought, is it really Madonna doing this?" said Warner's Tom Ruffino. "But I've never met an artist who was so in tune with her own career; she plots it out very carefully. I realized that this would be an enormous way to achieve immediate recognition for the record from millions of people."[6]

Madonna defended the decision, saying, "As far as I'm concerned, making a video is also a commercial...[and] record companies just don't have the money to finance that kind of publicity."[7] Besides, she said, she liked the idea of fusing art and commerce, which made the former more "accessible" and elevated the latter.[8]

The Pepsi spot would be directed by Joe Pytka. He was perhaps best known in the late '80s for an unforgettable public service ad he did—the campaign was called This Is Your Brain on Drugs—that involved an egg, a frying pan, and a terrifying sizzle. The Madonna job came his way after he shot Michael Jackson's video for "The Way You Make Me Feel" and a Jackson commercial for Pepsi. But Madonna wasn't sure she wanted to work with Pytka, at least not until he brought choreographer Vincent Paterson onto the project.

Pytka said that Madonna told him she would not sing or dance in the Pepsi ad.

> The contract didn't call for that, but I wanted Vince to work with the other performers in the piece just to give it some energy. And she walked onto the set while he was rehearsing the other dancers. And she came over to me and asked me to introduce her to Vincent and the next thing I know, she's in there dancing.[9]

That introduction was, for Madonna's career, the most important part of the commercial. Paterson would go on to choreograph some of her iconic performances, from her Blond Ambition tour to parts of the film *Evita*.[10]

Madonna and Vincent Paterson, like Madonna and Pat Leonard and Madonna and Steve Bray, were compatible in part because of their backgrounds. Paterson, too, was raised in a conservative household steeped in Catholicism, which he credited with introducing him to the notion of theatricality. Though white, he grew up in Philadelphia in a mixed-race neighborhood where he learned to dance on the street. And, like Madonna, he became a little parent after his father left Vincent's mother and eight children.[11]

They were also sympathetic artistically. Paterson's first love was theater. As a result, his dancers performed as characters who expressed themselves through movement. And finally, Paterson drew inspiration from the same well as Madonna—old films, fashion, photography—and he thrived on collaboration.[12] "She is the first person I've ever synthesized so completely with as an artist," he said.[13]

The story told in the Pepsi commercial is a clever mix of past and present: a woman haunted by her past and a child dreaming of her future. The segment begins with black-and-white home-movie-style footage of Madonna as a child (played by eight-year-old Heidi Marshall) over which Madonna's voice sings the opening phrases of "Like a Prayer."[14]

On-screen, the past then becomes present, with the young Madonna gobsmacked, watching mature Madonna on TV, cool as hell dancing in the street, in a diner, and inside a club. Mature Madonna also dances with children in a Catholic school and in a crowded church, where a congregation and choir raise her song to the heavens. Pytka ends the spot with the adult Madonna holding a Pepsi can and the young Madonna holding a vintage Pepsi bottle as the older says to the younger, "Go ahead, make a wish."[15] It is Madonna telling her younger self to be brave.

Though Madonna was the star, Paterson embedded her in the crowds she danced with so thoroughly that the commercial feels like a generous celebration of everyone participating. He said he took his cue from Madonna in that regard.

> I've worked with a lot of people in this business. She has the best grip on success that I ever [encountered]. I first noticed it, actually, when we were doing this Pepsi commercial. We shot a scene in a Catholic school in a hallway. It was Madonna amidst, maybe, twenty schoolgirls that were from seven to thirteen years old. And, instead of going out to the trailer to hang, there was a little break, and she said, "Hey can you open up one of these classrooms?" They opened up a classroom and she took all the girls in there for a half hour and they all just sat and talked.[16]

The commercial was beautiful and inspiring. Pepsi executives were so excited that they prepurchased $10 million worth of airtime.[17] But there was a problem they were not aware of. Madonna had shot a separate video for "Like a Prayer" that would appear on MTV. It, too, was beautiful and inspiring, but it was also more controversial than anything Madonna had ever done. If the Pepsi ad marked a commercial milestone, the video for the song marked a cultural one.

The previous December, Madonna met Mary Lambert for dinner and asked her to direct the video for "Like a Prayer." Since 1986, when they had last worked together—on "La Isla Bonita," from *True Blue*—Mary had largely stepped away from video to concentrate on films. She spent much of 1988 in Maine directing an adaptation of Stephen King's *Pet*

Sematary. Horror wasn't her first choice; doing a movie with a female pro-
tagonist was, but in the late '80s, that kind of film was a hard sell. It seemed
the only place a woman could tell a woman's story was in video, through a
woman's song.[18]

Mary agreed to rekindle her creative partnership with Madonna. "By
that time we were really solid friends and we really trusted each other,"
Lambert said. After dinner, "we got in whatever...Mercedes she was
driving at the time and just drove around Hollywood. We drove up to
Mulholland and we listened to ['Like a Prayer']...pumped up on her car
stereo."[19]

The video they made for "La Isla Bonita" three years earlier involved
three sets, five hundred extras, and a four-day shoot in downtown LA.[20] In
it, a virtuous Madonna is shown in her room longing to be part of the
vibrant street life. It was like the story lines they had done so well before.
"Like a Prayer" would be different.

It would also involve a choice, although this time the choice would be
about right and wrong. It was also about religious and sexual ecstasy and
the idea that there was no need to choose between them, because a person
could relinquish herself to both. And it was about patriarchy and the choice
a woman must make to either submit to or to defy it. "That was all part of
the dialogue," Mary said. "We wanted to take certain things that are a
given or a convention and say, why couldn't it be this?...I knew there was
going to be some controversy, but I wasn't prepared for how much."[21]

The song "Like a Prayer" could have been filmed in many ways, but
Madonna wanted to give it the look and feel of LA's literary and cinematic
noir tradition and use religious imagery to tackle racism and bigotry.[22]
Racial tensions at the time were headline news.

That April in South Central, the LAPD's already aggressive antidrug
program graduated to a military-style scorched-earth campaign that did
not discriminate between crack dealers and civilians in making arrests,
gunning down "suspects," or reducing homes to ruins.[23] In New York,
meanwhile, there were so many cases of police brutality against Blacks that
Harlem minister Reverend Lawrence Lucas called the city the "most
polarized" and "racist" in America.[24]

Race hatred was so potent across the country that it was even injected
into the 1988 US presidential campaign. The infamous Willie Horton ad,
featuring a Black rapist who escaped a Massachusetts prison, helped
George H. W. Bush defeat his Democratic challenger, Massachusetts governor Michael Dukakis, whom he portrayed as weak on crime.

Other artists besides Madonna had also begun to tackle race in their
work. In the summer of '88 Spike Lee was in Bedford-Stuyvesant shooting his first political film, *Do the Right Thing,* about a neighborhood that

finally exploded under the burden of racism. Madonna's "Like a Prayer" and Lee's *Do the Right Thing* would both pose troubling questions. They also focused on an individual's responsibility to confront racism wherever he or she finds it.

To help tell the story, each used music: Madonna chose her own, while Lee picked Public Enemy's "Fight the Power." At the time, Public Enemy was called the "world's most dangerous band."[25] "I think those guys in Public Enemy are heroes," Madonna said. "They're not afraid to say things." She thought Spike Lee was a hero, too.[26] That was what was in the air as Madonna worked on "Like a Prayer."

Her video told a simple tale of a moral awakening through a spiritual one. Madonna plays a woman who sees a gang of white men assault a white woman. Hiding and afraid to get involved, she watches as a Black man comes to the woman's assistance. For his troubles, he is arrested by police and charged with the crime. Having taken shelter in a church, Madonna prays to a statue of a Black saint who looks like the Good Samaritan she just saw being arrested. She thinks she sees the saint crying.

"She lies down on a pew and falls into a dream in which she begins to tumble in space with no one to break her fall," Madonna said. She is caught by a strong woman who sends her back to the clouds and tells her to do what she knows is right. Madonna's character is still dreaming when her religious and erotic feelings merge and the statue of the saint becomes a man. At that moment, Madonna slices her hands with a knife. "That's the guilt in Catholicism that if you do something that feels good, you will be punished," she explained.[27]

The song of a choir washes over Madonna as religious ecstasy merges with sexual ecstasy. Madonna awakens knowing she has the strength to do what is right—to speak about what she saw and free the innocent man. The entire cast takes a bow, Madonna said, because the story isn't just one character's, it is everyone's.[28] Everyone has a role in ensuring that good and love triumph over evil and hatred.[29] That was Madonna's scandalous message.

It was the video's imagery that proved so shocking, including Madonna dancing in a slip in front of burning crosses. "I grew up in Arkansas, at a time when there was a lot of racial tension and violence, [which] was really offensive to me," Mary said. "One of the reasons I used a burning cross in 'Like a Prayer' was to force people to deal with the image I grew up with."[30] And then there was the image of Madonna humbling herself by kissing the feet of the statue and the saint returning her kiss when he comes to life in her dream. Though they rarely said so, critics' hostility was inflamed by the fact that the saint was Black. Said Mary Lambert several years after the video's release:

Interracial unions are still controversial in this country, especially within the broad demographic of MTV and national television. In "Like a Prayer," it's not just Madonna having an affair with a black man. The religious imagery makes it much deeper than that.[31]

Greil Marcus called the video "blasphemy on about ten levels at once, which as a story is as upsetting a piece of public work [as] you're going to see anywhere...You have interracial sex, you have sex between a human being—a woman played by Madonna in the video—and a saint, a black saint, who may not be a saint at all; he may be Jesus. That's just for starters."[32]

Madonna's embrace of Black culture and her sounding off on racial issues weren't just controversial for whites. Important Black figures such as the feminist bell hooks criticized Madonna for what she called the appropriation and commodification of Black culture. She said that Madonna's use of Black people in the video was exploitative, that the woman who caught Madonna as she fell through the air was a "modern mammy," and that the choir was like the "singing black slaves in the great plantation movies." But hooks conceded that she was speaking from the perspective of an older generation and that young Black women were "diehard" Madonna fans.[33]

To those younger women, Madonna was an inspiration. Author Joshunda Sanders said that in the video for "Like a Prayer," Madonna had

> power and clout to spare, and she chose to subvert the idea that blackness was something white women should stay as far away from as possible...She was down without trying to be. She was a sister in white-girl skin...She kept my attention because of her interactions with people of color in her videos and concerts...Madonna was the first non-black artist of my generation to really place herself in the center of blackness and black art without mocking it or trying to supplant it. She even moved a little like a sister...
>
> As a white artist who was unafraid to express her affinity for black culture in a time before it was cool, Madonna set the stage for a new generation of women—celebrities and regular folks alike—to express themselves outside of racial classifications.[34]

Religion was the other point of controversy in the video, and yet Madonna's interest in it was real and profound. "My Catholic upbringing is probably the foundation of everything I do right now," she said at the time.[35] She was a staunch critic of the church, but her criticism was from inside the family, spoken as a Catholic. Madonna said she prayed "constantly...I pray when I'm in trouble or when I'm happy."[36]

The church was also where Madonna believed she experienced her first feelings of sexuality and eroticism. And it was the place where she was first exposed to art.[37] All those personal elements came together in her video. She even looked like herself. The brunette who appeared on-screen was the woman Madonna Ciccone, not the star Madonna.

If the video emerged full of depth and meaning, its production, from the moment the actors were cast, was comic, chaotic, and at times terrifying. Sharon Oreck's O Pictures produced the six-minute piece, which was the biggest and most expensive her company had ever made. Worried Warner executives called her twenty times a day, she said, to check on its progress.[38]

The scene at O Pictures, meanwhile, was bedlam. Oreck recalled arriving at work one day to find the place full of tall, well-built young Black men dressed as Christian martyrs auditioning for the role of the saint. It was up to Mary Lambert to explain the part to them. In her book *Video Slut,* Oreck described that scene:

> "OK, so you're a plaster statue of a saint…and Madonna, who's confused and morally conflicted, comes in and she prays for your help," Mary explained.
>
> "I see," the actor she was speaking to replied.
>
> "Then she kisses your feet."
>
> "I see."
>
> "OK, and then you change from a plaster of Paris statue to a real live man!" injected a casting assistant named Luke. "And then you escort her up to the altar!"
>
> "That's cool," the actor replies.
>
> "And then you pat her head and then you get on top of her…and then… you have sex!" Mary said.
>
> "Whoa! OK. Wait a minute…so I'm a plaster saint in a church and I come to life so I can, er,…fuck Madonna?"
>
> "Yes," Mary replied. "Exactly!"

The actor looked around the room to see if anyone was laughing. No one was. "OK," he said, then assumed the pose of a statute. Mary called, "Action!"[39] (The actor Leon Robinson was eventually selected to play the arrested man and the saint.)

Costumes for the video were much less complicated than usual. Madonna needed just two: a coat and a slip. Marlene Stewart gave Madonna one of her own coats and found at the Western Costume Company a chocolate-brown slip that had been designed in the '50s to be worn by Natalie Wood. The slip still had Wood's name attached.[40]

The church interior and assault scene were shot on soundstages at Raleigh Studios, in Los Angeles, but Madonna's flight across the dunes at the start of the video and the cross-burning sequence were shot at night at Fort MacArthur, part of Los Angeles Air Force Base.[41] The cross burning took delicate negotiations to ensure that the base knew what the video crew was up to and that the video crew knew whether anything explosive had been buried in the vicinity of the twenty six-foot-tall crosses they planned to ignite.[42]

There was also the question of social sensitivities. Fort MacArthur was around twelve miles from South Central, and the sight and smell of burning crosses would surely cause alarm if not anger. Ahead of filming, the crew mimeographed announcements and stapled them to telephone poles in the neighborhood explaining the nature of the shoot.[43]

The police arrived anyway. At four in the morning, during the cross-burning scene, a line of police vehicles with lights flashing appeared on the set. Sharon Oreck met with them to explain what was happening, who was involved, and to assure the officers that everything was under control. It wasn't. Fuel was leaking from one of the crosses, and everyone in the cast and crew was freezing. In addition, the fog was coming in, and Madonna had stepped on a cactus while dancing barefoot in front of the crosses. She kept dancing until the song ended and Mary Lambert called "Cut!" Then, slumping to the ground to check her foot, Madonna yelled *"Keeeeriiistt!"* Oreck said the foot looked "like shredded wheat."[44]

The next shot in those predawn hours took them to another location — a University of Southern California swimming pool into which Madonna was to jump from a forty-foot-high diving board as part of the " 'plunging into grace' dream sequence." An Olympic diving coach hired to talk Madonna through the jump gave not very convincing reassurances that she "will not die." Madonna hugged her tearful team before beginning her ascent up a three-story ladder to the board. Her first thought when she reached it was "Oh God, it's really far." Her second was "What the hell?"[45]

Still wearing her brown slip, she stood at the edge of the diving board, fists clenched, listening to Mary Lambert shout instructions through a bullhorn. "Remember: you are blissful, ecstatic, and serene!" Mary then called out "Roll camera...and action." Madonna stood frozen to the board. Mary shouted, "We're rolling. *Jump!*" Madonna didn't move. Mary screamed into the bullhorn, "Madonna! The fucking camera is running! Jump and we'll let you go home!" That did it. Madonna was at the board's edge, and then she was gone.[46]

The film crew heard a splash and waited an eternity before they spotted her climbing out of the pool, her brown slip bunched around her waist as she crawled, hyperventilating, into a fetal position. Oreck began to ask

Mary if she needed another take, but Madonna stopped her. From her spot on the tile floor, she said, "There will not be a fucking second take!"[47]

Two days later, Oreck and Mary looked at what they had shot at USC. Nothing. The camera had run out of film. They didn't get Madonna's jump. Oreck said that a second camera caught it, but the angle showed Madonna falling through the air, terrified, exhausted, and shouting obscenities. Mary went silent for a minute, then said quietly, "We don't really need it." The video for "Like a Prayer" would not include a pool sequence.[48]

The video took four nineteen-hour days to shoot and a week to edit. "After that we sat and lived with it for a while, to be sure about our editing choices," Mary said.[49]

Pepsi, meanwhile, had built anticipation for its Madonna ad. During the Grammys, on February 22, it released a commercial for the commercial, saying "No matter where you are in the world on March 2, get to a TV and see Pepsi present Madonna." Madonna's single and Mary Lambert's video would be released the day after the ad's premiere.[50]

The first hint of trouble came from MTV. When the video arrived at the channel's offices, the senior vice president for music and talent, Abbey Konowitch, said, "I don't know what we're going to do with this." The problem was the cross burning.[51] Pepsi executives heard whispers of a possible hiccup and summoned Freddy DeMann, who did what he was unofficially paid to do during moments of crisis: obfuscate. "They said, 'Send us the video!' I didn't want to send them the video," Freddy recalled. "And I didn't. The commercial ran, then MTV premiered 'Like a Prayer' the next day. And of course Pepsi...pulled the commercial," initially from just MTV.[52]

The company feared that consumers would confuse the video with the commercial and associate the Pepsi brand with that controversial imagery, which is exactly what happened, thanks to religious provocateurs.[53]

Madonna's video was denounced by the Reverend Donald Wildmon, whose Mississippi organization, the American Family Association, had led a highly publicized boycott of Martin Scorsese's movie *The Last Temptation of Christ* the previous year. In a bizarre misinterpretation of the "Like a Prayer" video, Wildmon said it was "repugnant" to Christians because "Madonna, who represents Christ, is shown in a scene suggesting that she has sex with the priest, obviously to free him from sexual repression."[54]

Meanwhile, a well-known Texas antiabortion campaigner, Catholic bishop René Gracida, seconded Wildmon's objection, and in Rome, the pope accused Madonna of being "anti-Christian." He had the most immediate impact; Warner Bros. pulled the video off Italian TV after a Catholic group threatened legal action. "I knew that we were pushing some big buttons," Mary Lambert said, "but I sort of underestimated the influence and bigotry of fundamentalist religion and racism in this country and the world."[55]

Madonna and Mary had given leaders of the religious and political right the gift they needed to rally the faithful at a time when a majority of Americans—65 percent—said they had a negative view of the TV evangelists who had spent the previous decade preaching the Gospels in exchange for billions of dollars in donations. A series of scandals involving tax fraud, hush-money payments, defrauding the faithful, and soliciting prostitutes had rocked the world of religious showmen and women. The broader religious right movement, fighting for its life, sought to regroup around more serious and pious sorts.[56]

The year Madonna made her "Like a Prayer" video, the powerful Christian Coalition welcomed a new leader: a squeaky-clean-looking twenty-eight-year-old named Ralph Reed. In defense of the family and the Bible, he pledged to use what he called "guerilla warfare" against pornography, obscenity, and assaults on religion. Attacking art that was found guilty of any of the above proved both easy and lucrative.[57] First under fire in the new culture war were recipients of federal art funding. Robert Mapplethorpe was one of them.

Mapplethorpe had died of AIDS in early 1989, and an exhibition of his work, funded in part by the National Endowment for the Arts, was traveling to six cities. The prospect energized the religious and political right. They pointed in horror to the part of the show that included homoerotic photographs of nude Black men and sadomasochistic imagery. Their outrage became front-page news after Republican senator Jesse Helms dutifully displayed the "dirty" pictures on the Senate floor. The Christian Coalition took out full-page ads in the *Washington Post,* the *New York Times,* and *USA Today* asking Congress "not to underwrite porn, obscenity, or attacks on religion."[58]

Even though Madonna's video was not federally funded, it kept the controversy over art, sex, race, and religion alive. The forces of "good" could not stop her video from airing. It was a matter of free speech. But they could go after her commercial by threatening Pepsi: that was a matter of business. Reverend Wildmon led a boycott charge against the company, while Bishop Gracida upped the ante by threatening to boycott Pepsi *and* its holdings: Taco Bell, Pizza Hut, and KFC.[59] Pepsi had been drawn into a religious war. It capitulated. On April 4, a month after the commercial's launch, the company announced that it would pull it off the air in the United States and drop its sponsorship of Madonna's tour.[60]

The religious right (or "new right," as they wanted to be called) emerged emboldened, having successfully taken on one of the richest companies in America over one of the biggest stars in the world.[61]

But Madonna also came out of the fracas a winner. Other promoters would step into the breach and fund her tour, and her "Like a Prayer" single hit number 1 in thirty countries, including Italy (despite the pope).[62] And when her album was released, it earned plaudits that her work had never before received.[63] The self-declared dean of rock critics, Robert Christgau, called the album "thrilling."[64] J. D. Considine, writing in *Rolling Stone,* said,

> What you hear...is as close to art as pop music gets...*Like a Prayer* is proof not only that Madonna should be taken seriously as an artist but that hers is one of the most compelling voices of the Eighties.[65]

By the early spring of 1989, *Bloodhounds of Broadway,* the film Howard Brookner believed was more important than his health, was taken away from him. Columbia Pictures sold the film to Vestron Pictures, which informed Howard, who was then bedridden with AIDS, that he would not have the final cut. That news was the last straw. "Howard decided to die," Brad Gooch said. "It was a very clear decision. Suddenly the movie wasn't the movie he wanted to stay alive to see."[66]

Brad considered it a very bad sign when Howard stopped taking phone calls, including Madonna's. She had helped Howard with his hospital bills.[67] But then one day that spring he and Howard had a fight, which delighted Brad because it was a sign that Howard was still capable of passion, which meant he was still capable of life.

Madonna had sent Howard an advance copy of *Like a Prayer.* "Howard kept telling Tony [his nurse] to turn up the volume, turn up the volume," Brad said, "until the entire apartment was filled with overwhelming sound." Brad was writing on deadline and asked Howard to turn it off. Howard refused, saying, "I loooooovvve her. I looooove this album. It's just like her." Even as Brad threatened to leave, Howard wouldn't turn down the volume. "Get ouooooo-out!" Howard yelled joyously. He had made his choice. It was Madonna.[68]

Howard died on April 27 and was buried three days later, on his thirty-fifth birthday. The *New York Times* noted his passing in an obituary that bravely stated, at a time when many families of gay men fearing shame chose not to reveal it, that he had died of AIDS.[69] Howard left taped to his refrigerator a sweet goodbye filled with melancholy but not a drop of regret:

> There's so much beauty in the world. I suppose that's what got me into trouble in the first place.[70]

Chapter 27

Los Angeles, New York, 1989

I think there's no such thing as too much freedom—only too little nerve.[1]

—*Ellen Willis*

TOUGH, EVEN FORMIDABLE, was how Madonna emerged from the first months of 1989. The hypocrisy of the commentary about her "Like a Prayer" video was so thick it was nearly suffocating. The attacks on it—and on any socially challenging art at that time—weren't about art at all. They were assaults on freedom, on the "other," and on any beliefs that did not fit a narrowly defined fundamentalist idea of virtue. More incredible than those attacks, though, was that such intolerance had prevailed. But that was only because it was *allowed* to.

The choice of the second single to be released from Madonna's new album was no doubt made long before the ruckus over "Like a Prayer" occurred, but the choice would prove to be inspired. "Express Yourself" was Madonna's admonition to women to speak their minds and claim their power. The song's video broadened that into a general statement on rebellion. Filmed in April of 1989 in Los Angeles, it was directed by a twenty-six-year-old named David Fincher.

Since Michael Jackson's "Beat It" first aired on MTV, in the spring of 1983, music video had become a refuge for aspiring filmmakers, but only rarely did the videos rise to the level of art. The directors who could claim that distinction were well known, and perhaps the best known among them was Fincher. By the time he began working with Madonna, he had directed dozens of videos and was considered a genius of the medium.

Fincher's professional introduction to filmmaking was as an apprentice at George Lucas's Industrial Light & Magic visual effects company, where he learned on model sets how to move a camera. He graduated to production assistant on the 1983 film *Return of the Jedi*.[2] It was at the age of twenty-two that he made a name for himself with a thirty-second spot for the American Cancer Society that is referred to in industry lore as the "smoking fetus" commercial. Like Joe Pytka's This Is Your Brain on

Drugs ad, Fincher's commercial was so effective that he gained instant credibility as a director.

It was around that time that MTV was born, and Fincher, like so many other young camera freaks, knew he could make a video.

> From third grade, I was making movies in 16mm, and every year, in film class—and everybody took film—they'd give you a song, a 45 and they'd say, "Make a film to this song."...So when MTV came along, people went, "We want you to make a film to this song," and I thought, "I actually know how to do that. That may actually be the only thing I do know how to do."[3]

David soon joined five other young people to form a company called Propaganda Films, which would specialize in videos and commercials. Propaganda changed the music-video landscape because it was the first video "brand" and because it was the home of the most cutting-edge artists. All its directors were part of the MTV generation. They understood the medium's brief history and its vast potential—not to sell songs but to spark thought.[4]

Fincher, along with Mary Lambert, James Foley, and Jean-Baptiste Mondino, would be critical to early Madonna videos. But Fincher occupied a special place. Madonna at one point called him her most important collaborator. As she transitioned to her more mature work, he would be to Madonna what Josef von Sternberg was to Marlene Dietrich, a director who understood her darkness and her innocence and used both elements in his film; a director who merged her work with his own so perfectly that together they created art neither could have made alone.[5]

Madonna said that when she and Fincher met to discuss the "Express Yourself" video, they threw around ideas and imagery: everything "we could possibly conceive of."[6] It was immediately clear that they spoke the same language. Like Madonna's, Fincher's sensibilities came from photographs, paintings, classic movies—the grander, more mysterious, and more nuanced the better. He didn't flinch, therefore, when Madonna said she wanted the visuals in her video to be based on two works of art.[7]

The first was a 1921 black-and-white photograph by the social reformer Lewis Hine called *Power House Mechanic*. It depicted a man grappling with a machine, pitting his work-hardened body against the intransigence of steel.[8] The second was a silent film from that same era—Fritz Lang's *Metropolis,* released in 1927. "I definitely wanted to have that influence, that look," Madonna explained. "All the men, the workers, sort of diligently, methodically working away."[9]

Lang's film described in images a world of extreme wealth and the grinding inhumanity toward labor that made that wealth possible. It was the world of industrial capitalism. His characters were also the stuff of archetypes, among them a mad scientist and a woman who played two characters, one representing the saintliness of Womanhood and the other its wantonness. Below them was the Worker—the sleeping giant—who represented restrained brawn, but not *tamed* brawn. His potential for rebellion was palpable, and it seemed only a matter of time before it was unleashed.

Metropolis was anticapitalist and antiauthoritarian, attitudes that resonated in 1989. It was a time of worldwide rebellion as the Berlin Wall fell, the vast Soviet empire crumbled, and protesting students were mowed down in Beijing's Tiananmen Square. In the United States, 1989 marked the birth of the one percenters, the aristocracy of wealth that emerged out of 1980s deregulation and runaway capitalism, while workers' wages stagnated. Madonna and Fincher's video referenced Lang and those modern realities and added a feminist angle. The revolution that would overthrow evil empires would also liberate Woman, not as an act of benevolence but because she demanded it.[10]

Fincher once said his approach to filming came from a "voyeuristic place." He liked to position the camera as far from the action as possible so the viewer didn't sense the presence of a director. He wanted audiences to feel that they were peeking around a corner into the shadows. Clarity wasn't his goal, because he was not out to reassure. "Some people go to the movies to be reminded that everything's okay," he said. "I don't make those kinds of movies. That, to me, is a lie. Everything's not okay." That sense of unease in troubling times was at the core of his video with Madonna.[11]

As coproducer on the video, Madonna oversaw the details, from set building to costumes. "I had meetings with make-up and hair and the cinematographer, and you know, everybody . . . just every aspect," she said. Fincher was just as detail-oriented; his work ethic and need for control were just as extreme.[12] While shooting, he was firm and quiet. There were no theatrics.[13] But Madonna recalled one dispute with him during the project.

It was his idea for her to crawl like a cat, lick from a bowl of milk, and pour the milk over herself. Madonna thought the idea was too adolescent. "But I'm glad that I gave into him," she said.[14] The sequence helped describe the feminist theme of the video, which she shorthanded as "pussy rules the world."[15]

Madonna spared no expense. With its $5 million budget, the five-minute video was at the time the most expensive ever made.[16] Fincher brought in cinematographer Mark Plummer, who had worked with him and Mondino. To choreograph, Madonna called her Pepsi mate Vincent Paterson.[17] And she auditioned dozens of male actors and models to appear as laborers in her industrial netherworld.

That scene could have been a Herb Ritts photo shoot, and in fact, Herb was there on the set with her. The men in the video are wet, sculpted, subterranean slaves to the same machine and desires that she serves as she roams around aboveground in her pristine gown and lifeless luxury. Styled as a platinum-blond 1930s film goddess, Madonna looks in those parts of the video like a figure in a Tamara de Lempicka painting.[18]

The men are, on the surface, as quintessentially male as the woman is quintessentially female, and they all exist within an established and seemingly immutable social structure. But in Fincher's and Madonna's hands, that world becomes a jumble of what-ifs and why-nots. She wears a man's suit and stands boldly at the pinnacle of power; the laborers display a homoerotic sensuality; the industrialist is left vulnerable and alone.[19]

Among the scenes Paterson choreographed was a segment that required Madonna to be topless, though for the purposes of the video she would be covered with a bedsheet. Paterson said she was "very uptight" about it on the first day of filming, but by the second day she was relaxed.[20]

> That's the beauty of her and that's the reason I love working with her. She's not afraid to make statements. She's not afraid to make comments on political situations, or sexual role playing, or cross dressing, or fantasy. And in fact, the further you go, the further she wants to go with you.[21]

One of the video's most memorable moments was an example of just such audacity: Madonna grabbed her crotch during a mocking send-up of an industrialist. She had made a similar gesture during her Who's That Girl tour, but it was quick and easily missed. In "Express Yourself," it was a showstopper.

Madonna had been kidding Vincent about Michael Jackson's crotch grabbing, and at one point during rehearsals, while standing at the top of the steps, she yelled down to Paterson, "Hey, Vincent. What should I do with my left hand?" He called back, "Why don't you grab your balls? You've got bigger balls than anyone else here." She did.[22]

In that instant, the message was as clear as it was unequivocal. With the grin of a victor, Madonna claimed ownership—for herself, for women, for the disenfranchised and abused—of the power that had been mystically awarded to the male organ to justify eons of cultural, social, political, and religious domination. Madonna's gesture put the almighty penis in its place. It was just a dick.

⋆   ⋆   ⋆

Warren Beatty had been prowling the set of the "Express Yourself" video, as Sean once did on the "Material Girl" set.[23] Her big-budget cinematic confection with Beatty, *Dick Tracy,* had begun filming in February and coincided with her run-in with the religious right over "Like a Prayer." It is likely that Disney executives worried about what Madonna was up to with Fincher and whether her clerical critics would appear in Burbank to protest her inclusion in a film from family-friendly Disney.

During the best of times, Madonna would have been a risk, and not just because she was so controversial. There was the lingering question of whether she could act. Barry Diller, the chairman and CEO of Fox, had no doubt on that score.

> Madonna is a movie star without a movie. You want to know why she's such a movie star? Because she's incapable of doing anything that's not interesting. If she's in a photograph, it's interesting. If she sings a song, it's interesting. Her videos—all interesting.[24]

Diller predicted that within ten years, or by the year 2000, she would "find the right movie to prove it."[25] But Madonna didn't have that kind of time. She wanted to prove it yesterday. She candidly told an interviewer that spring, "I really want to be recognized as an actress. I've learned that if you surround yourself with great writers, great actors, a great director, and a great costumer, it's pretty hard to go wrong."[26]

That is what she thought she had in *Dick Tracy.* Madonna built protections for herself into the *Tracy* project. Though she took the job at union scale—$1,400 a week—she persuaded Disney to give her a percentage of the gross as well as a percentage of video and merchandise sales. She would also make money on the soundtrack and compilation albums. All that would add up to millions.[27] Madonna made sure Madonna was taken care of. And with that, she embarked upon her new role: Hollywood movie star and Warren Beatty's lover.

On June 1, 1989, *Rolling Stone* announced in its Random Notes section, "Madonna's name can now be added to Warren Beatty's list."[28] The revelation was surprisingly late, because the affair had begun many months earlier, not long after her divorce. Sean dismissed the relationship as the ultimate "cliché."[29] For the media, that was its attraction.

The entertainment press reported on the affair with fanzine delight, the way gossip queen Louella Parsons would have done in the '30s. "As his *Tracy* capers prove... Warren Beatty still has the power to get the girl," wrote *People.* Calling Madonna "the far-famed pop princess," the magazine reported that the two made "very public displays of necking on the set, trotting off together to L.A. restaurants, cuddling at Hollywood gatherings."[30] Madonna and Beatty had given each other "cute" nicknames that also made their way into the press: he was Old Man; she was Buzzbomb.[31]

But even in its playful reporting, *People* and other publications, as well as those witnessing the relationship firsthand, saw it as an affair of opportunity. Each had something to gain professionally from the liaison.[32] Madonna said she spent a couple of hours a day picking Beatty's brain. "He doesn't talk a lot but when he does it comes out in paragraphs," she said.[33] "He has infinite knowledge about what makes a good movie, a good director."[34] The press story line on what Beatty got out of the relationship involved a once powerful man seeking to revive his career.

"A romance with the biggest female star in the universe — more than twenty years his junior — is clearly a canny career move for him," said Christopher, who liked Beatty but could see the situation clearly.[35] "It could not be more obvious: he was looking for relevance, and she was looking for stature."[36]

And yet careers aside, there were genuine feelings between them. After her stormy ride with Sean, Beatty offered Madonna safe harbor. "He's very protective," she said.

> He's not easily shocked, either — which is great — by the things that have happened to me. He's just been through so much that in a way it's comforting.[37] Obviously somebody who hasn't experienced it would be more threatened by my fame than he is. You can't understand being hugely famous until it happens and then it's too late to decide if you want it or not. Warren's been a sex symbol for so long he's just not surprised by anything.[38]

As a child, Madonna had had a poster of Beatty in her bedroom, and she knew about his relationships with some of the world's most celebrated women. That part of his history intrigued her. "They're all very accomplished, talented, remarkable women," she said.[39] She admitted, however, that his past was, at times, intimidating. "I mean, how can I ever be as fabulous as Brigitte Bardot when she was twenty-five . . . Or any of those people," she said. "Then there is the other side of me that says I'm better than all of them."[40]

Madonna and Beatty came from two different worlds. It was as if she had stepped back in time, into the 1960s that Helen Gurley Brown described in her book *Sex and the Single Girl*. Once, Madonna came home to find that Warren had delivered a roomful of goodies for her: lingerie, perfume, makeup, dresses, shoes, and bras. He barely knew her, yet he knew her size from head to toe. A card read simply FROM WARREN.[41]

What Madonna didn't know was that that largesse was part of his MO. Leslie Caron, who left her husband for Beatty, said Warren liked to take charge of a woman's life. "He wanted total control of her, her clothes, her make-up, her work," she said.[42] Maybe Madonna intuited his intentions, because her first response was annoyance. "I'm not some little starlet that you can buy things for and control," she told him. "I'm a very wealthy person. I can buy my own underwear." Her second response was to see the gesture as generous, if over-the-top and dated in a vintage *Playboy* magazine sort of way.[43]

The filming of *Dick Tracy* took place in a warehouse in downtown Los Angeles and on the Universal Studios backlot. Beatty's idea visually for the picture was both surprising and stunning; his movie actually looked like a cartoon— or a Red Grooms painting. The color palette was basic, as if the set designer had used only seven Crayola crayons. Even the normally critical shades of black and white were used sparingly. The result was supreme simplicity. Each camera frame felt like a comic strip, and every one was magnificent.

If the set was simple, however, the characters and costumes were positively baroque. The villains Pruneface, the Rodent, Little Face, and the Brow were marvels of makeup-department ingenuity. Flattop's face comprised fourteen prosthetic devices and could take up to four hours to construct. In fact, nearly all the major male characters except Beatty were transformed to varying degrees into grotesque cartoon creations.

Beatty chose not to make his face into a square-jawed replica of Dick Tracy's. Lest anyone think the decision was a matter of vanity, he explained that masking his face would have made his emotions unreadable. (Interesting, because the most consistent emotion he registered in the film was befuddlement.) Beatty kept his own mug and reportedly only allowed himself to be shot between 10:00 a.m. and 2:00 p.m., the hours he believed he looked best. His character's concession to the comic-book genre was a bright yellow coat and matching yellow fedora.[44]

Madonna's Breathless Mahoney wouldn't be disfigured by prosthetics, either. (Though the other character she played, the Blank, was.) She would be the archetypal bombshell, occupying the sexual landscape between Mae West and Marilyn Monroe. And for that, she had to go blond. "I begged Warren...because it took me so long to grow my hair out and I really wanted to have dark hair," she said. "And then I had to change it so I had a bit of an identity crisis."[45]

As the film's story line developed, the fact that Tracy was a detective sometimes felt tangential to the plot. Beatty seemed saddled with that occupation out of loyalty to the cartoon. His Dick Tracy wasn't chasing criminals, necessarily; he was chasing a traditionally female dilemma—should he or shouldn't he? Should he go for the sex or hold out for marriage? Beatty called his movie a "love triangle" involving Dick Tracy, Breathless Mahoney, and Tess Truehart. "My film is about a guy torn between love and duty," he said. "My Dick Tracy is human. In this story he's all goofed up by temptation."[46]

Two days into the filming, one-third of Beatty's on-screen love triangle—Sean Young, who played Tess—left the picture. Some said Warren fired Young because her role required her to appear nurturing toward the child in the story, the Kid, and she seemed to hate children.[47] She alleged that she was punished for spurning Beatty's advances, a charge he denied. Beatty and the studio scrambled to replace her, which they did with acclaimed actor Glenne Headly. The cast change meant that the first two days of filming had to be reshot.[48]

Madonna's method of working on her own projects was economical. She would use the first best recording or the first best shot. Beatty's method of working was characterized by what she described as maddening indecision. "He does lots of takes," she said, "and once he's got what's in the script, he says, 'Okay, let's fuck it up. Do anything you want.' He likes to push you, to exhaust everything in your head that you want to do."[49]

Mandy Patinkin, who played a nightclub piano player named 88 Keys, said that in one scene he, Al Pacino's character, and Madonna's were in a verbal and physical tussle over a song.

> There was no reason to think we hadn't gotten it. Everyone was tired, and I couldn't tell why we were doing it over again. Finally, Al started improvising. He really laced into Madonna, and all of a sudden she just broke down. It was unlike all the other takes. Warren said, "Cut" and gave them hugs. That wouldn't have happened unless he gave it time to happen.[50]

Madonna recalled being "pissed. Al kept slapping me in the stomach, being really rude. He made me cry, and Warren never really stopped him."[51] It was one example of Beatty, the director, seemingly ignoring the well-being of his leading lady–lover. There were others. Madonna told writer Peter Biskind, who was on set for the shoot, that Beatty

> wanted to pour me into my dresses. He insisted I get fatter. I gained ten pounds. We were at Western Costume, and he'd say, "Tighter, tighter, cut it down lower." I felt like a mannequin, a slab of beef. He would walk around me like a vulture, making me feel like the ugliest thing in the world, I was treated that way on the set—the lust factor.[52]

Madonna may not have been prepared for that kind of disregard—if not disrespect. All the films she had been in (except *Shanghai Surprise*) were convivial and collaborative. Working in that hierarchical, patriarchal *Dick Tracy* environment opened her eyes to Hollywood's essential misogyny.

Dick Tracy wasn't a musical, but music would be a major part of the film and its success. Three albums emerged from the movie: *Music from the Motion Picture Dick Tracy; Dick Tracy Original Score,* composed by Danny Elfman; and *I'm Breathless,* by Madonna.

Normally, Madonna considered writing and performing songs for movies the least difficult part of a film. Not so with *Dick Tracy.* Beatty wanted Breathless Mahoney to sing original songs and turned to Tony Award–winning composer and lyricist Stephen Sondheim to create them. Sondheim wrote five songs for the film, three of which Madonna would sing.[53]

"Dumbfounded" was how she described her reaction when she sat beside Sondheim as he played her the songs. "And then, forget about making them my own, just to learn to sing them—the rhythmic changes and the melodic changes—it was really tough." Madonna used a vocal coach and an accompanist to slow down the songs so she could understand them. "I could hardly hear the notes, you know what I mean? So it was really a challenge."[54]

The songs weren't the only difficulty Madonna had with Sondheim. She was unused to his method. He didn't want her help writing lyrics or finding a melody. All he wanted from Madonna was her voice. She had been in a similar situation with Mamet: Madonna wasn't meant to interpret but to conform. As much as that was against her nature, she tried because she had something to learn from Sondheim.

He had been the lyricist for some of modern musical theater's most legendary productions, beginning with *West Side Story,* in 1957.[55] Madonna said she'd never paid much attention to Sondheim's work, much less appreciated it. That disregard turned into "respect and admiration" after she began to learn his songs. She called them "*unbelievably* complex...There's not one thing that repeated itself."[56]

Madonna's album *I'm Breathless* included three of the Sondheim songs that appeared in the movie—"Sooner or Later," "More," and "What Can You Lose"—as well as music "inspired by" the film. She turned to Pat Leonard for help with the bulk of those. Beatty wanted them to create songs that sounded like they were written before 1939. To illustrate what he meant, he gave them the names of old artists and records he liked. He even went to Pat's studio and played the piano so they could hear the sound he was after.[57]

Madonna and Pat wrote five original songs and coproduced eight tracks.[58]

Among them were a couple of subversive numbers she managed to sneak in. "Hanky Panky" was one. Humorously extolling the virtues of spanking, it came out of Madonna's line in the film: "You don't know if you want to hit me or kiss me, I get a lot of that."[59]

Shooting on *Dick Tracy* wrapped on June 28. Madonna was free to play. She and Sandra Bernhard, along with a few other gal pals, formed an eyebrow-raising posse. Female entertainers going out on the town in LA were supposed to do so on the arms of men. The boys could travel in packs—the Rat Pack, the Brat Pack—but not the women. On the cusp of movie stardom, Madonna seemed to revel in violating that social order.

With Sandra and her mates, whom either they or the press dubbed the Snatch Batch, Madonna could be as vulgar and outrageous as she pleased. She could be a *real person,* without regard for the industry that monitored actors' lives for fear that certain types of behavior, usually of the gay or lesbian variety, might jeopardize a studio's investment. "I think that's why she likes Sandra so much," a friend who had been part of the group told *Vanity Fair.* "She can be totally obnoxious with her and not worry about being a star... To put it bluntly, though, sometimes when they're together they can be a nightmare."[60]

Beatty remained in the picture romantically, but not very comfortably. He and Madonna fought often and in public. That wasn't unusual for Beatty. Some of his longest affairs were the most tempestuous. But Madonna's friends sensed that she wasn't in love with him. Christopher went so far as to say that love didn't "come into the equation."[61] Bernhard said Madonna complained that Beatty was a "pain in the ass... She didn't really take him down, but I thought she was pretty dismissive. It was just more the way she is in general, which is the real tough chick, she's gonna be the toughest guy in the room."[62]

If Beatty wanted to be seen with her, he had to go where she went. Among her favorite places was a club in South Central called Catch One. It was the oldest disco for gay Black men in Los Angeles and, at the time, the largest dance palace for gay Black men in the world. One writer said that Catch One was classed among "the nation's churches for worshippers of ambitious dance music and sexual liberty."[63]

Beatty was ill at ease. He refused to dance, so Madonna did so with Bernhard or Christopher or whoever was in the room. A cinematographer who saw them at Catch One said, "I'd never seen Warren like that, sitting there, this gray man in the corner. He just could not keep up with Madonna."[64] And it wasn't only at dance clubs. Producer Julia Phillips recalled seeing Madonna at Freddy DeMann's fiftieth birthday party that year, and she, too, was shocked. Phillips said she spotted Madonna standing with a "short, bespectacled man with good hair...It takes me a moment to recognize Warren. Warren is usually tall and dominates the room, but in this situation he is a dim bulb in the aura of her supernova."[65]

Beatty's biographer Peter Biskind said that Warren "was accustomed to being worshipped by women, to being completely in control." But he "was on dangerous ground with Madonna."[66] While still involved with her, Beatty opened his dog-eared black book and rekindled a relationship with a young woman who adored him.[67]

Beatty's bruised ego may not have felt overly important to Madonna that summer. Herb Ritts learned that he was HIV-positive in July. His longtime friend Richard Gere said it was the only time he saw Herb "off balance...That was the first time I think I ever saw him feeling that he didn't have the resources to deal with something."[68]

By the time Herb was diagnosed, tens of thousands of people had died of AIDS, but even more were still alive, battling the disease with the very few treatment options available. AZT was one, but it had potentially deadly side effects. Some people pinned their hopes on herbal remedies and experimental drugs, but even if they worked in the short term, the long-term prognosis for the disease did not change. At that time, being diagnosed as HIV-positive felt like a death sentence.

Serendipitously, that month Madonna proposed a project that might help take Herb's mind off his health, however briefly. Warner wanted another single released from *Like a Prayer,* and she had chosen "Cherish." It was an ode to unabashed love written the previous year during the heady days of her reconciliation with Sean.[69] Warner wanted a video for the song, so she asked Herb to direct it. It would be his first, and under the circumstances, it took some persuasion before he would agree to do it.

It wasn't that Herb didn't know how. He had been on the set of nearly every one of Madonna's important video shoots since *True Blue.* He knew the drill, but he had never held the camera. "She kept asking me, and I said I really didn't know the first thing about moving imagery," Herb recalled. There was also the question of whether he was able, physically and mentally at that terrible moment, to embark on such a project.[70]

Herb left town to photograph model Stephanie Seymour in Hawaii. He had been fascinated by mermaids since seeing the film *Splash,* and he put Seymour in a long, iridescent tail designed by stylist Sharon Simonaire.[71] While on site, he also practiced shooting moving images with a Super 8 camera. Two weeks later, back in LA, he told Madonna he would direct her video. Then he asked Simonaire to make him more tails.[72]

He wanted them for men who would swim in the ocean with the power and grace of real fish, not merely lounge on the sand, as Seymour did. The costumes were complicated, Simonaire said, because they had to be "aerodynamic." But Herb "wasn't thinking that way. He just saw these images of men frolicking in tails."[73]

On July 22, Herb assembled his cast and crew at one of his favorite beach spots, Paradise Cove in Malibu. The place lent itself to a color shoot—the sea, the sun, the sand. It was a natural. But Herb decided to shoot in black and white, which he did so effectively and with such rich depth that the video *looks* as if it is in color. Especially the warm tones, which seem to glow gold against Madonna's skin. Unadorned, clean, fresh, nurturing, and *beautiful,* Madonna in Herb's video is an earth mother—or sea mother—albeit a saucy one.

The video's feeling is light, free, simple. A day at the beach. But in view of Herb's condition, when Madonna sings "Cherish the thought of always having you, here by my side," it becomes heartbreaking. What had been a pop ditty and a bit of visual play become a loving message to a friend who fears for his life and an admonition for him to hold on. She could not lose him, too. "You can't get away, I won't let you."[74]

Throughout the video, Madonna remains at the water's edge, while offshore, three mermen swim in the sea with a merchild. The men represent male beauty—as perfect as any Renaissance sculpture or any Tom of Finland image—as well as the sheer wonder and power of nature. In the age of AIDS, they are healthy. In a time of cruel discrimination, they are free. The only connection between them and Madonna is the child.

Midway through the video, the merchild, shivering in the water, is transported into Madonna's arms. She holds him, plays with him on the beach, and poses for Herb's camera unselfconsciously, the way a young mother would in a home movie.

The seeming effortlessness of the video masked the difficulty of the shoot. The three mermen spent hours—much of it in the water—encased in forty pounds of rubber from the waist down. Two of them suffered hypothermia because Herb refused to stop filming. "He'd just make us all keep going," said Simonaire. "It was sheer determination."[75] No matter; Herb could do whatever he wanted. "Madonna appeared to love him," said Sharon Oreck, the video's producer. "And at that time, Madonna didn't appear to love anybody."[76]

At a moment when he feared for his own ending, the shoot gave Herb new life. He was so excited by the medium of film that he would go on to direct thirteen videos and more than fifty commercials.[77] For culture more broadly, the impact of the video was to introduce gay imagery to an MTV audience weaned on women in bikinis. "The woman who introduced Herb Ritts to video is definitely someone doing gay men a favor," said writer Michael Musto.[78]

Keith Haring had been in Los Angeles in early July. The trip was a birthday gift for his friend Gil Vazquez, who had never been to California, and so Keith "did Hollywood." Renting a red Jaguar convertible, they visited celebrity friends. "We hang out a lot with Pee-wee Herman. We have dinner with Madonna, Sandra Bernhard, and Warren Beatty at Sandra's house," Keith said. They spent the Fourth of July holiday at Dennis Hopper's watching Spike Lee's new movie, *Do the Right Thing.* Later, they stopped at Beatty's, where only Warren and Madonna remained after a barbecue.[79]

Keith seemed carefree and unburdened, and he was. He had given an interview to *Rolling Stone* in which he told the world what only his friends at that point knew. A decade before, Keith had repudiated the shame associated with being gay, and now he rejected the shame associated with having AIDS. The first had made him whole, and the second would make him free.

The *Rolling Stone* piece was aptly called "Keith Haring: Just Say Know." In the interview, he described the pain of losing friends to AIDS, his terror upon discovering that he was HIV-positive, and his renewed terror when he began developing symptoms.[80] He also injected a new idea into his discussion; he spoke of AIDS in terms of life. "Nothing is trivial. It adds another kind of intensity to the work that I do now; it's one of the good things to come from being sick."[81]

Keith said he knew in speaking out that he was potentially jeopardizing his work, some of which involved children and religious spaces. But he said it was necessary to do so because of those other children, the gay children whose fear and confusion about their sexual awakening were heightened because of AIDS. "Now there *has* to be openness about all these issues," Keith said, before adding his hope that out of the AIDS crisis and with more honest conversation gays would finally be seen for what they were: normal.[82]

The article was astonishing, coming at a time when politicians, religious leaders, the courts, and large segments of the public showed contempt for gays and exhibited little concern for AIDS. Keith's interview was a powerful rejoinder. What made it more remarkable still was that he articulated his message without malice; from start to finish, his interview was an expression of love. In the wake of it, Madonna called Keith an "incredibly great, courageous, brave human being."[83]

That kind of honesty would simply not occur in the movie business. "Nobody wants to offend anybody," Madonna said of Hollywood.

"Everyone is afraid in this town. This is a town full of very self-centered, selfish people who make their entire living out of putting their best face forward."[84]

In December, Madonna had a chance to speak her mind—to take a stand—and use Disney as a vehicle to do so. Beatty wanted another original song for *Dick Tracy*. After spending a summer back among her fold— amid the changing attitude in the gay community and away from the institutionalized homophobia of Hollywood—Madonna created her first indisputable musical celebration of gay culture.[85]

Madonna said her best songs were the ones she wrote in a couple of hours. "Vogue" was one of them. She wrote it on a plane on the way to New York. Beatty had wanted a song Breathless Mahoney might have written. "She was obsessed with speakeasies and movie stars and things like that," Madonna said of her character. "The idea for the lyrics came through that request. Coincidentally, I was going to Sound Factory and checking out these dancers who were all doing this new style of dancing called vogue-ing."[86] "I thought it was a really cool dance, very presentational, elegant, all about vanity."[87]

The Sound Factory opened that March on West 27th Street. It wasn't Paradise Garage, but it made a valiant effort to resurrect that club's spirit. One of the Garage's co-owners was behind it, and Junior Vasquez, who had studied at Larry Levan's knee, anchored the DJ booth.[88] "There's nothing better than going to the Factory on a Saturday night," Madonna said. "I like to sit on a speaker and watch humanity just pulsating, and everybody is one. It's so cool. That's what moves me. That's the kind of music I want to make."[89]

The voguing phenomenon was born in nineteenth-century Florida as the cakewalk, a dance in which enslaved people mimicked with exaggeration and humor the manners of their plantation overlords. It became associated with gay culture in the 1920s and '30s during the Harlem Renaissance, when blues singers were openly lesbian, and gay authors wrote of their forbidden love in barely coded language. But the fullest and most public expression of that rich subculture occurred at early drag balls.[90]

Then, beginning in the 1960s, when Blacks in general were taking to the streets and demanding their rights, those balls became less about masquerade and more about real life. The people who attended were so removed from wealthy white society that to show up "in costume" might simply mean dressing up as a Wall Street banker, a preppy college student, or a high-society dame. For the mostly poor young people who attended the balls, that garb was tantamount to fantasy wear. Unintentionally, the balls had become political theater.[91]

By the 1980s, another type of performance that fed voguing came onto the streets via the corrections facility on New York City's Rikers Island. Voguer Benny Ninja said that because men weren't allowed to have "dirty" magazines in those facilities, they used fashion magazines for titillation. "One of the queens sitting in jail trying to pick up guys said, 'You keep looking at her, and I can *be* her,'" Ninja said. "And he started posing like the women...Once [posing] left prison, or Rikers Island, it hit the streets of Harlem. The younger generation saw it...and then a whole world opened up."[92]

These drag balls were dominated by Black and Latinx gay men and trans folk who separated themselves into "houses" structured as families, with "parents" and "children." Houses formed creative as well as protective havens for young LGBTQ people abandoned by their biological families. Said Jennie Livingston, director of the 1990 film about the scene, *Paris Is Burning,* "The ball people I film could have turned out spiteful or angry, but instead they opted for a wildly creative life. The balls are a response to homophobia and racism, but one full of optimism and spirit."[93]

In the 1980s, the houses began competing in staged events, pitting their styles against one another using elaborate gestures they had seen in ancient and popular culture: fashion magazines, television, even Egyptian art. With each new influence, the performance became more elaborate, until in the late '80s it incorporated high-fashion poses and stylized B-boy moves.[94]

Junior Vasquez was associated with the Harlem ball-culture scene, and through him, the houses of vogue dancers came downtown. People who ventured into the Sound Factory's back bar early on a Sunday morning could see men, elegantly arrayed, transform themselves into members of the haut monde while striking the exaggerated poses they had seen in fashion magazines.[95]

And then, in May of 1989, SoHo shop owner Susanne Bartsch introduced voguers to a larger audience when she invited members of the various houses to perform at the first annual Love Ball, held at New York City's Roseland Ballroom. The fundraiser for AIDS research attracted people from across the arts and the fashion industries. For many of those in the packed ballroom, it would be the first time they had seen voguers twist their bodies into pretzels and form picture frames out of limbs.[96]

After the Love Ball, voguing became a "thing." Malcolm McClaren released a single in July called "Deep in Vogue." Keith Haring was so inspired by the Love Ball that he did a voguing series in the fall of 1989 and created a poster for the Chicago Voguers' Ball.[97] But it would be Madonna who would introduce that underground scene to the world.

DJ Shep Pettibone was recruited to help her write "Vogue." He and Madonna had been friends since her early days in New York. Shep had honed his technique at the time when the Bronx was vibrating to the mag-ical sounds of Grandmaster Flash, Kool Herc, and Afrika Bambaataa.[98] Like those masters, he remixed and re-created to such an extent that he invariably made an entirely new work of art. One critic called him the "new form's Charlie Parker." Shep's work had taken him to radio stations and clubs that played R&B and so-called urban music. Most recently, he had deejayed at the Sound Factory and had worked on Madonna's remix album, *You Can Dance*.[99] He was, therefore, uniquely qualified to help her with her song.

Madonna and Shep worked in a basement on West 56th Street, where someone had created a "home recording studio," in part by making a closet into a vocal booth. When Madonna arrived, she handed him her lyrics, and they made a few changes to his music to make them fit her words. But Shep felt the song still lagged in the middle. He suggested a rap. "You know, bringing in movie stars and stuff?" he recalled. They came up with a list of names: Madonna rapped them and left Shep to finish the song in New York.[100]

Around a week later, he sent "Vogue" to Warner. It became the twelfth track on *I'm Breathless* and the album's first single.[101] Shep thought it was good, but he didn't think it would be a huge hit—at least not until New York's most respected DJ, Frankie Crocker at WBLS, played it and declared on air afterward, "Well, you've never heard anything like *that* before here on WBLS." Shep called that "a pretty defining moment."[102] But Crocker's endorsement wouldn't occur until April of 1990. In the meantime, Madonna had work to do.

Chapter 28

Los Angeles, 1990

Question: If you were a gay man, would you be a top or a bottom?
Madonna: I am a gay man.[1]

MADONNA'S FIRST DECADE in the spotlight was a triumph. In December of 1989, she won MTV's Artist of the Decade award. *People* magazine named her one of the twenty individuals who defined the decade. The *Los Angeles Times* named her one of the top twenty artists of the 1980s.[2] In fact, if there was a list of important cultural figures during those ten years, she was on it. Gene Sculatti, who had been writing about music since the '60s, said that Madonna's songs "defined" the eighties sound. "It was black-rooted...[and] forced radio to devise a whole new format to accommodate her."[3] And that format sold.

Madonna overtook the Beatles for most consecutive top five singles, with sixteen in a row, prompting Mark Rowland to write in *Musician* magazine,

> As the decade draws to a close the votes are tabulated and the winner is... Madonna. She, not Bruce Springsteen, is the biggest. She, not Michael Jackson, is the baddest. She, not Prince, is the nastiest. She, not Pepsi Cola, is the shrewdest. She, not The Who, has earned our respect...You can't argue with her triumph. It is complete. Even when her films blow dead air or her marriage breaks up or her records bomb—that's never happened—she's the winner.[4]

From that position of power, and with few if any limits on what she could say or do, Madonna began putting together a four-month world tour.

She had been working on the tour since September of 1989. It began with sketches on yellow legal pads that she shared with Christopher in her Oriole Way kitchen. "We sat down and started talking about the show," he recalled. "About what to do, some creative stuff. Here's a song. What order should the songs be? What do you think?"[5]

He decided after her last tour that he no longer wanted to be her dresser. He needed more. In New York, he painted, showed in a gallery, and generally lived an entirely creative life. "She couldn't help but think of me as an artist," he said. Art was what he wanted to contribute to her show. "You know I can do this," he told her. "And she was like, 'Well, you've managed to give me an environment to live in' as her designer. It was all very clinical. [She said,] 'OK, you can be art director.'" In the bargain, she also wanted him to continue as her dresser and oversee costumes. The deal agreed, Christopher moved in with Madonna so they could work fourteen-hour days.[6]

When Pepsi was still involved in the project, the show's name had been the Like a Prayer World Tour.[7] Afterward, Madonna and Christopher decided to call it Blond Ambition. "There were a couple of reviews in the press accusing her of being somebody who had blind ambition," he said. Next they agreed that the show wouldn't be a pop or rock concert. It would be theater. "I'd seen enough theater in my life and enough dance performances, and I knew what the ground rules were," he said. "In a way, what we were doing was a bit of an opera. It was a roller-coaster ride of sorts emotionally. That's how I looked at it."[8]

Neither Ciccone was capable of thinking small when it came to art, so they created not one stage set but five different *worlds,* "all based on hydraulics," Madonna told Glenn O'Brien. "One is going down and another is coming up." Christopher said the men in suits who oversaw budgets balked at the scope of the plan, but Madonna got her way entirely.[9]

One world that Madonna and Christopher imagined was recognizable as the *Metropolis* tribute from her "Express Yourself" video. "It's very hard and metallic," Madonna said. "That's the heavy-duty dance music." The next set was a religious environment with columns that rose from the floor, a cathedral window that dropped from the rafters, votive candles, and an illuminated cross. The next world belonged to *Dick Tracy* and was vaguely art deco. "And then after that we do what I call the camp section," she said. "Then it gets really serious again and we go into our *Clockwork Orange–Cabaret* set."[10]

Chris Lamb, a Jackson tour alum who was hired as the Blond Ambition production manager, said the move from the "jeans and the steam" of the first section to the "grand staircases and culture" of the others required coordination and engineering on a scale few shows achieved "before or since."[11]

Madonna's first choice as tour choreographer was a New York acquaintance, the "punk ballerina" Karole Armitage. In 1989, Armitage had choreographed the film version of Sandra Bernhard's stage show, *Without You I'm Nothing.*[12] For musical director, Madonna chose Jai Winding because Pat

Leonard couldn't go on the road.[13] Winding had worked closely with Pat and Madonna on *Like a Prayer* and on the Who's That Girl tour, so there was a continuity in his taking the position.[14]

Niki Haris and Donna De Lory returned as Madonna's backup singers, and she wanted eight dancers. She didn't care if they were classically trained or had learned their moves on the street.[15] "It was very important to us that it wasn't about being a perfect dancer," Christopher said. "They each had to bring their own personality to the performance."[16] Madonna put out a dance call.

Madonna World Tour 1990
Karole Armitage, Choreographer
Open Audition for
FIERCE Male Dancers
Who know the meaning of
TROOP STYLE, BEAT BOY and VOGUE
Wimps and Wanna-be's need not apply![17]

Madonna began her search in New York.

Luis Camacho, a nineteen-year-old from the Lower East Side, had heard that Madonna was looking for voguers, so he sent her a tape.[18] At the Sound Factory not long afterward, Madonna met him and his best friend from the Fiorello H. LaGuardia High School of Music and Art and Performing Arts, José Gutiérez. Madonna watched José and Luis dance at the club, and then invited them to the dance call in Manhattan to see what else they could do. She described their audition:

> Luis came, and Luis will try anything. He was not so great at everything, but he was willing to try it, and I loved him for that. Jose wouldn't do a god-damned thing. Jose sat in the back with his hands on his hips...He was just like, "The fuck I will." So of course I loved him for that. I thought, "Now this guy has balls."[19]

Said Luis, "We carried our flamboyance as a warning. Yes, we have earrings on. Yes, we have eyeliner on. But don't mistake any of this for weakness."[20]

Their hubris got Madonna's attention, but it was their ability that got them the job. "She didn't realize they were trained dancers when they freestyled for her at the club," said dancer Kevin Stea. "So when they actually picked up choreography at the audition, and had technique, it blew her away because she thought they were just street dancers. They were locked in at that point for sure."[21] José was eighteen when he auditioned and would turn nineteen on tour. "Imagine that, right?" he said. "Dancers work for all of their lives, and it takes years to try and achieve enough credibility to be even considered for a job like that."[22]

Madonna also hired Salim "Slam" Gauwloos out of the dance call in New York because of the way he danced but also because of the way he looked. He could be the seductive laborer played by Cameron Alborzian in the "Express Yourself" video and a stand-in for Warren Beatty during the tour's *Dick Tracy* segment.[23]

Salim, who had studied ballet in Belgium, was from a strict home in Antwerp: Muslim Moroccan father, Belgian mother, rigid schooling. In that environment he had had to conceal who he was: a gay youth who wanted to dedicate his life to art. In 1987, at the age of seventeen, he won a dance scholarship to New York.[24] Three years later his life changed again. "I'm working with an iconic artist like Madonna."[25]

Madonna invited Salim, José, Luis, and a fourth dancer who only lasted a week to Los Angeles, where she was assembling the rest of her troupe.[26]

Normally an LA dance call would attract the usual suspects—the 150 or so male dancers in the city who were considered "professional." And that group was "*very,* very white," said Kevin Stea, who, as half-Chinese, was an outlier. "The look was often blond and buff, and there was a limited pool of people."[27] But for Madonna's tour, seemingly everyone who had ever taken a dance step appeared at the tryout. Hundreds of men of every size and skin tone lined up on the sidewalk outside Landmark Studios.

Madonna and her team reviewed groups of forty dancers at a time. The dancers had only a few minutes to make an impression. She would select at most one, maybe two people from each group for a callback, and sometimes she selected none at all.[28]

Twenty-year-old Kevin Stea was a student at the University of Southern California studying business and film. He called himself "book smart, not street smart." He had just returned to the United States from school in Singapore and turned to dance for fun after a heavy academic career.[29]

"I remember seeing [Madonna's] ad, and I had just had the roughest summer of my life. I had no money to eat. I had no money to get around." Home was an abandoned Victorian house with no floors in the dining room, no hot water, and people breaking down the door to rob him. Arriving at Landmark Studios in search of a paycheck and the possibility of travel, Kevin was shocked by what he found. "I'd never seen so many people at an audition. It was madness."[30]

Niki Haris taught his group simple choreography. "Some basic club moves—Robo Cop, Running Man, Roger Rabbit," he recalled. "Of course, I was standing right next to Niki, and as I did it, she pointed me out and said, 'Look, guys, this is how it's done.' I guess that's how I got noticed." That first day, Madonna narrowed down the number of potential dancers to around 160. "We had another day or two of auditions at another location," Kevin said. Dancers were eliminated until thirty remained for the final cut.[31]

Kevin was naturally competitive, and by that point he *wanted* the job. Madonna had already pulled three dancers forward. Those remaining were told that they could freestyle for that part of the audition. "That's when I was like, 'Those guys probably already have a job. If I'm going to go out, I'm going to go out with a bang.'"[32] He decided to do everything he knew, perform every style, every trick he could think of, one on top of the other. "And she wasn't even watching," he said. "So I was like, 'Okay, I gave this my all.'...As I walked out, Niki and Chris were by the door, and they pointed me out and said, 'Oh, that was really great. You did a really fantastic job. It was really good.'"[33]

He left deflated, thinking that he didn't get the job. Then he got a call from Christopher, saying, "Hey, I want you to be assistant choreographer. Are you up for that?" Kevin wasn't sure what the job entailed, but he assumed it meant he wouldn't be touring—that he would be working in LA with Karole Armitage, whose choreography he didn't understand. "I wasn't instantly elated," but he told his agent, who was, so Kevin accepted the offer.[34]

The three dancers Madonna was preoccupied with during Kevin's audition had, indeed, been hired for the tour. They were Carlton Wilborn, Oliver Crumes, and Gabriel Trupin.

At nearly twenty-six, Carlton was the old man of the group and "didn't really care about the gig," he said, because he had been offered a spot on the road with Whitney Houston. But Whitney delayed her tour, so he answered Madonna's call wearing a biker jacket, a caftan, and more than a little attitude. "I went to the audition for Madonna with a lot of confidence because a major icon had already said yes to me," he told Heath Daniels in an interview for *Queerty* years later.[35] "I was a little bit different to the other guys because I had had a full career already...I had come from a professional company, Hubbard Street Dance Chicago, I had already been touring, I'd already been in newspapers."[36]

But even with his level of experience, Madonna shocked and disarmed him. "I remember getting home, and I had a message on my answering machine...It was like, 'Hi, I'm trying to reach Carlton. This is Madonna.' I was like, '*What the fuck?* She called my house!'" She invited him to Club Louie, a gay dance joint. Some of the other dancers would be there, too.[37]

It was a chance to get a sense of whether she would enjoy them during their many months together and whether the dancers would enjoy one another. Carlton realized then that this job would be different.[38]

"She's an underground artist that has been given a lot of money to fund her projects," he said. "So the way she goes at things is like this fearless, raw, edgy street kid, doing her art." He said even with "tons of money" she didn't abandon her "balls out way of doing things."[39]

> With regards to what we were saying on a social level, and the fact that it would be a somewhat evergreen experience—I had not thought about that at all...I didn't know when I said yes to going on tour that she would be positioning us to take a stand for the gay community...I didn't know it was going to be about the LGBT community, and empowerment. It's been a blessing that I did not foresee.[40]

Oliver Crumes was the only unequivocally straight dancer hired for the show and a self-declared homophobe at that. A seventeen-year-old Compton kid, he had danced in a music video and taught hip-hop. "I heard about the audition through some students," he said.[41] Oliver didn't have much experience in dance or life, but he had style: piercings, peroxide-blond hair over cocoa-colored skin. And he had mastered survival skills, playing it tough and cool. But inside, he was a baby. When he learned he got the job, "I went home, and I said, 'Mom, I made it.' And I dropped down on my knees and started crying. And that was it."[42]

Twenty-year-old Gabriel Trupin was the "unofficial favorite child" of the tour, said Kevin. "There was something about him that was always peaceful, like this peaceful bright presence." What no one knew was that he was HIV-positive. "He was open about being gay with his friends and with most family, but he was not flamboyant by nature," said his mother, Sue Trupin. "And he was ashamed about having become infected. I think he took refuge in dance as a way to be most fully himself and, like any artist, to express his deepest feelings."[43]

He wasn't the only tour dancer with that secret. Carlton and Salim were also HIV-positive, and they were afraid to reveal themselves, too.[44] Said Carlton, "I was diagnosed in 1985 on tour with Hubbard Street Dance Chicago in Hawaii. I moved to L.A. in 1989, largely because of my diagnosis...because I thought, if I'm going to die in a year, I need to make my life as amazing as I can right now. That's really where I was."[45]

Hiding his status during the Blond Ambition tour was a constant source of pressure. He'd look in the mirror and say to himself, "You know that you're a liar." He added, "Nobody in that crew, in that team, nobody knew my secret." While on tour in Japan, he would have a close call.

Experiencing a cramp, he was sent to a doctor, who saw that something wasn't right. The doctor said he would have to tell Madonna. "And I was like, 'There's no *fucking way* you will tell them anything.' I was *pet-ri-fied* after that... The internal storm was just trying to fake your way to be accepted. Faking that you're strong, faking that you're confident, faking that you think you look good... Faking, almost all of it."[46]

Salim said he was diagnosed when he was eighteen, six months after he arrived in New York, in 1987. He was feeling ill and didn't have medical insurance, so he went back to Belgium for treatment. The doctor fixed what ailed him, and then he got a call to return to the hospital.

> So, me and my mom went... and that's where he told me, "I'm sorry, sir, I'm sad to tell you that you're HIV[-positive]."... When you have somebody telling you, "You know, listen, you're only going to live five to ten years..." Everybody was dropping like flies. I totally blanked it out. I didn't want to talk to anybody about it... It was such a dark time in my life.[47]
>
> Escaping on the tour was the perfect way not to deal with it. Madonna was so vocal about HIV and AIDS. Every time she mentioned it, I crumbled. When people talked about who died, I wondered, "Am I next?" But when I was dancing, I didn't think about it.[48]

If the Blond Ambition tour had a raw and profound intensity—which it did—it was partly because, like Keith Haring and Herb Ritts and thousands of other people with AIDS, Carlton, Salim, and Gabriel were making the most of the time they had left.

Madonna helped them. She created a small family. Call it the House of Madonna. "I look at the dancers and say, 'They're me.' I transfer me as a little girl onto them. I view them through all of my feelings of being deserted and not being emotionally supported or loved. And I say, 'Now I'm going to be their mother in the way I didn't have one.'"[49] Kevin said he considered the Blond Ambition cast and crew his "first dance family." His mother was in another state raising his brother, "so having Madonna around really did sort of fill that space for me... I knew I could rely on her."[50]

But the dancers helped Madonna, too. "It was Peter Pan and her lost boys," Liz Rosenberg told *Vulture*'s Matthew Jacobs. "Although she talked of being maternal, she was also one of them."[51]

The dancers' first performance together was on Madonna's "Vogue" video, which was filmed on February 10 and 11. Madonna asked David Fincher to direct it as penance for some advice he gave her concerning an earlier song.

Fincher told *The Guardian* that he had talked Madonna into releasing

"Oh Father" as a single in the fall of 1989 so that they could make a video for it.[52] Like the song, the video is dark. Whereas "Papa Don't Preach" is about a young woman's difficult but loving relationship with her dad, "Oh Father" hints at abuse and neglect after the death of the child's mother and as the child tries to become the mother. Flash-forward to the video's adult Madonna, who is portrayed as being in an abusive relationship with a hard-drinking young man. The images seem painfully autobiographical. Fincher even allowed Madonna to direct part of it—a sequence in the snow with her younger self.[53]

"Oh Father" was exquisite. Fincher and Madonna were both happy with it.[54] But Fincher said no one saw it because the song didn't reach the top ten. It was Madonna's first single since "Holiday" not to enter the upper reaches of the Billboard chart.

> So she came back to me and said, "You screwed me up. You wanted to make this video for the song, and no one liked the song, and I went to bat for you and now I have to make a video by Tuesday." And I said, "What's the song called?" And she said, "Vogue." And I said, "Okay, we'll get a bunch of stuff together and we'll make a video on Tuesday."[55]

Fincher came in "very, very prepared," said Kevin Stea. "He ran a very tight set. His sets were so simple in person and then you see them on camera, how they came to life...just brilliant." Fincher credited the director of photography, Pascal Lebègue, for much of its success. He said Lebègue, who had worked with Madonna and Mondino on "Open Your Heart," "literally showed up off the plane with his light meter...and he walked in and said, 'This, this, this, this' and we shot the video for like sixteen hours and we were done."[56]

The video is composed of two parts: still poses and dancing. Madonna and Fincher had selected the poses that she and the dancers would assume in advance, poring through books that they then brought to the set filled with sticky notes.[57] They shared the images around, and then Salim said Fincher took individual shots of the dancers. "It was all close ups," he said.[58] Luis called the experience "amazing...I was just a kid from 'el barrio' and this was my first foray into the Hollywood scene."[59]

Karole Armitage, with Kevin Stea assisting, was to choreograph the video, but there was creative tension during rehearsals between her and José and Luis, and between her and Madonna. At one point, José refused to dance. "He grabbed a cigarette and stood in the doorway and said, 'Karole, tell us when you're done.' The next day she was gone," Kevin said.[60]

In a bind, Madonna called on Vincent Paterson. He was in Cuba working on the Sydney Pollack film *Havana* with Robert Redford and begged off, but Madonna insisted. Paterson finally agreed and flew in for a rescue mission.[61]

Paterson wanted José and Luis to imagine the simplest vogue steps, something the entire world could do. They did face-framing gestures. Paterson opened the video with those. "José and Luis kept giving steps," said Kevin, who acted as Paterson's assistant, "and Vincent kept staging it and saying, 'That's good. This is great.' And they expanded it from there. Vincent had a clear view of what needed to be created to make a video."[62]

At the start of the rehearsals, only José and Luis were voguers. By the time the cameras rolled, they all were. Oliver Crumes was allowed to add a bit of his specialty, hip-hop, in a solo dance with Madonna.[63] His moves inject a present-day street style into the performance without sacrificing the dazzling homage to the past that is at the heart of the video.

In their cravats, waistcoats, silk scarves, and evening attire, the male dancers are midcentury elegance personified, posing on an old soundstage with vintage cameras and various props. Donna De Lory flits around with a feather duster and maid's outfit when she and Niki Haris aren't singing backup. Madonna, meanwhile, transmogrifies from Marilyn to Veronica Lake to a living Tamara de Lempicka painting to Lana Turner to Marlene Dietrich.

Fincher was in his element in the video because of his own love affair with '30s and '40s Hollywood RKO black-and-white movies. It was an inspiration he would nurture for decades—the artifice and the artistry that seduced the public while beneath them the machinations of the movie business destroyed lives. That was what the ballroom culture was about, too. It was the glamorous skin that covered poverty, ostracism, despair, and death. But as long as one looked good and the music played, that dark reality—like the dark reality of Hollywood, like the dark reality of AIDS—magically disappeared.

By the time the video was shot, Madonna had fired the fourth dancer she brought from New York and decided to hire Kevin Stea to go on tour as dance captain and assistant choreographer. He had become close to the other dancers, particularly the New York gang, because they were so different from anyone he had ever known. "LA was much more DL—down low—on everything, being gay, expressing yourself flamboyantly," he said, "partly because the LA dance community was really commercial."[64]

In Singapore, when he was in school, "you didn't even *talk* about being gay. It was obviously portrayed as wrong and illegal to be gay. And at USC, it was all frat boys and frat culture," Kevin said. By contrast, José,

Luis, and Salim were *out,* "using their sexuality and flamboyancy as a shield and armor and sword. [That] was completely foreign and alien to me."[65] Kevin spent as much time with them as he could. The group had, in other words, begun to coalesce. "I think she noticed that. So on the 'Vogue' video she actually, in between takes, when she had curlers in her hair, pulled me aside and asked me if I wanted to go on tour with her."[66]

> The truth is I didn't really know how big of a job I'd landed... I almost turned her down! I had other commitments... She was like, "So you wanna go on tour with me?" and I said, "Maybe. I'll have to get back to you." She was shocked! She said, "What! What have you got?" and I said, "Well I'm doing something with a choreographer I really like named Marguerite," and she was like, "Fuck Marguerite!"[67]

Kevin was persuaded.

On February 16, just days after Madonna completed the video for "Vogue," Keith Haring died of AIDS. He had been diagnosed with lymphoma and was no longer able to talk. "He was sort of scratchy and screeching, with no sound coming out," his assistant, Julia Gruen, said. "It was heartbreaking."[68] Madonna called Keith from California. Hers was the last phone call he was able to take. "He said what hurt him the most was how people did not want to touch door knobs after he touched them. The discrimination then was next level."[69]

Madonna had felt close to Keith not only because of their early shared experiences but also because, as they became famous, they both faced the same criticism: people said they had sold out. "I watched Keith come up from the street base, which is where I came up from," Madonna said, "and he managed to take something from... an underground counterculture and raise it to a pop culture for mass consumption. And I did that too."[70] It wasn't a matter of selling out. As artists, they simply wanted to share their work with the biggest audience possible and inspire as many people as they could.[71]

Madonna said that Keith had been a comforting kindred spirit. "I really can't compare myself to many people... and I don't feel that many people can relate to where I've come from and to where I've landed. So when I think of Keith and his life and what he's achieved... well, I feel that I'm not alone."[72] After the deaths of Martin, Basquiat, and Warhol, Keith was one of the last artists from Madonna's early New York circle remaining. And then, at the age of thirty-one, he was gone, too. She would use her tour to remember him.

★   ★   ★

Rehearsals continued in California. Contrary to Madonna's reputation as a bitch, Carlton said many years later that she was great to work with.

> Someone the other day [said], "I bet it was crazy, when she was being really intense in the rehearsals, making people feel bad." But that's not what she does, at all. She has [one] personality that she knows makes her money—a bit brash and snappy and in your face—and then she has who she is: just a chill, regular person. It was also a special time because she was single, didn't have any children, and hadn't really come against any extreme pushback, so she was very free.[73]

If there *were* any problems, however, cast and crew could take them to Christopher. He was known as the "pope" within Madonna's world. Next to her, he was the power, and because of his proximity to his sister he was treated as the tour's consigliere, advising people, settling disputes, passing messages to Madonna from timorous staff.[74] "He felt like part of the team, part of the band, part of us, though his official title was art director," Kevin said. "He was very supportive."[75]

Christopher was effective in his role because he understood his sister. "When we were working together," he said, "our differences in opinion or creatively were easily worked out. I mean that. A lot of that was because I knew how to handle the situation and I knew from experience the last person who spoke to her at night would win in the morning. I made it a rule to be the last person to speak to her at night."[76]

One such situation involved a major staff change. Madonna's decision to take Karole Armitage off the "Vogue" video meant that she was off the tour as well.[77] Madonna turned once again to Vincent Paterson. Having choreographed Michael Jackson's Bad tour, he had experience working on the scale of the production that Madonna and Christopher imagined. But she didn't want a Bad tour remake. She wanted something entirely new.[78]

Her instructions to him were " 'I want you to break every rule you can think of. Then, when those are done, make up some more and break those too.'" Paterson said, "So that is how I went into the tour, with complete artistic freedom to do whatever the fuck I wanted."[79] What *Madonna* wanted was to make provocative statements about sexuality and religion, according to Paterson, and "fundamentally change the shape of concerts."[80]

Paterson had three weeks to create or complete eighteen dance numbers before the troupe began three weeks of stage rehearsals. The dances ranged from voguing to hip-hop to classical ballet. Some of the dances involved movement Madonna had never performed in public, Paterson said—"some modern partnering work, lifts."[81] "When we worked on the 'religious' section of the show that included 'Like a Prayer,' I wanted the guys to raise her above their heads in a lift," he said. Madonna told him, " 'I don't want to be lifted like some girl.' " To which he replied, " 'No, Madonna, it's not like a girl…It's like a QUEEN.' And she said, 'OK boys, lift me!' "[82]

Dance rehearsals lasted from noon until 8:00 p.m. with no breaks. Madonna came up with the vignettes, what she hoped to say in each number, and then Paterson and a dancer or two would work on it and present it to her. Carlton said Madonna's instruction to the dancers was always the same: "Give me more of you. Give me more of you." She wanted personalities onstage, not moving mannequins. "We all had stories to tell," Oliver said.[83]

After eight hours of dancing, Madonna headed to music rehearsals with Jai Winding and the band. That schedule continued for three weeks, until the operation moved to a soundstage at the Disney lot, where the show and the people in it came together. Paterson said,

> We usually had some kind of rehearsal where I'd put the dancers on the stage and Madonna would work things out with all the mechanics of the set changes and then try to run through one or two songs, and each day, build a few more and then run that section, and then onto the next, and begin the pieces again. Finally, a week and a half later, we got to the point where we could run the show.[84]

Most days, he said, they would go through the entire hour-and-forty-five-minute show twice.[85] "I had no idea how exhausting the show was until we both decided she [would] watch the show once while I ran through it," Paterson said. "And I tell you, man, by the fourth song, I did not want to come back. I was so dead. And then she said you get that second gust of wind…and it carries you."[86]

Madonna sang and danced through nearly the entire show, which was made easier by using a hands-free headset microphone. The technology had been around for decades, mainly for use by airplane pilots, but in 1979 Kate Bush brought it to the stage by rigging up a cradle for her microphone out of coat hangers.[87] The idea didn't catch on until Madonna used a more sophisticated version of Bush's apparatus in the Blond Ambition tour. After that, the "Madonna mike" was ubiquitous.

Between her previous tour, in 1987, and Blond Ambition, Madonna had matured as a singer, thanks in part to her work on the Sondheim numbers for *Dick Tracy*. Even she recognized the change in her voice and her abilities. She told Paterson that she wanted to sing some of her old songs on tour because she could finally do them justice. "Where before I sang them," she said, "now I can really *perform* them and can really *sing* them because my voice is so much stronger."[88]

The first full uninterrupted performance of Blond Ambition was a "friends and family" show for industry people and select invitees. In the Disney studio that day, sixty people watched from small chairs in an otherwise vast and empty space. On the road, the cast would perform for tens of thousands of fans, but for that first show, size didn't matter. It was the response that counted. "They were flabbergasted," Kevin said, "*blooowwwn away*."[89]

Most pop and rock concerts, as they had developed by 1990, burst with pulsing lights, strategic gusts of fog, and blasts of color. The effects were assembled as diversions to make performers more visually stimulating. It was a case of smoke and mirrors. Then a group of street artists from Quebec revolutionized the nature of live performance. Cirque du Soleil's first US tour opened in LA in 1987. It made a huge impression because it freed performers from the gravitational limitations of the stage to create a new kind of performance that was visually stunning without relying on techno-hijinks.

Madonna's show used all that—the precedents in pop and the innovations of other art forms like theater, opera, modern dance, ballet, burlesque, film, painting, sculpture, and the circus—to create a cohesive theatrical production with changing characters and sets and a narrative that was alternately gripping, dramatic, provocative, funny, and thrilling. Perhaps most innovative and surprising of all was that, despite the lockstep precision and masterly staging, the show felt like a bunch of friends having fun, which meant the audience would, too.

"It's hard to quantify or really express the difference between touring shows before and after this show," said Kevin Stea. "It wasn't like the audience was just left being wowed. They were left being touched, which is really a testament to Madonna's willingness to be vulnerable."[90]

The people gathered in the studio that day saw the future of pop culture. "It inspired a generation that is now in charge and creating," Kevin explained decades later.[91] The *New York Times* said that, with Blond Ambition, Madonna became the "principal architect of the contemporary pop spectacle."[92]

The fact that dance rehearsals began at noon did not mean that Madonna, Christopher, and Vincent Paterson had the luxury of a good lie-in. All of them had work to do before rehearsals, especially Madonna, who also had businesses to run—Boy Toy for music, Siren for film, Slutco for videos.

She employed hundreds of people. Those at the top, closest to Madonna, were mostly women whom she considered her close friends.

"People comment on it. They say, 'Do you realize all of your friends are on salary to you?' And I say, 'Oh, my, I really hadn't thought of that, but maybe you could flip it around and think, 'Well, maybe I only work with people I really like.'"[93] Her formula, which was built on trust, apparently worked. *Forbes* featured a photograph of her on its cover that October, next to the headline AMERICA'S SMARTEST BUSINESS WOMAN?[94]

Madonna also used the morning "free time" to exercise. "She's major," said Paterson. "She gets up in the morning and does the Lifecycle machine, runs eight miles, does the reverse climber, and then goes and does the show...I mean she's buffed."[95] Madonna described intense physical exertion as a form of escape, like meditation, from which she emerged feeling "more in control."[96]

With the release of the single "Vogue" in March of 1990, Madonna became the woman with the most number 1 hits in music history.[97] The "Vogue" video helped put her there. Decades later, it would be recognized as representing a "seismic shift for queer culture in the broadest sense."[98] But at the time, Madonna was criticized by some as a cultural imperialist who robbed the less powerful of their art in order to enrich herself.[99]

The criticism of Madonna's appropriation of other art forms would resurface throughout her career, but the fact that it endured did not give it legitimacy. *All* artists appropriate. It is called inspiration.[100] Artists must look beyond themselves for ideas or their art will stagnate. There is simply no other way to do it. In Madonna's case, her work always reflected what she read, watched, listened to, and looked at. It also was reflective of the places where she lived and society's attitudes toward social issues at any given moment.

The claim that Madonna did not properly credit the men who vogued was also off the mark. Those men were *in* her video. It was their video, too. They helped choreograph it. She took José and Luis out of the clubs and gave them and their art a global platform. It was not theft; it was a tribute.

As always, there were more people who appreciated Madonna's work than disparaged it. "Vogue" was a huge hit and the video a sensation. The *Paris Is Burning* director, Jennie Livingston, said,

> I remember being in a drugstore and there was a white woman with two children, and one of the kids said, "Look Mommy, Johnny's voguing!" I was shocked, and that was really all because of Madonna...What impressed me was how many people from the ball world loved it and embraced it.[101]

Writer and producer Louis Virtel said, "Madonna accomplished something astounding with 'Vogue'—she ushered an audacious, unapologetically queer art form into mainstream America."[102]

Madonna's *I'm Breathless* album was released on May 22 and went to number 2 on the charts, helped largely by "Vogue." Warren Beatty was so pleased with the album that not long after its release he threw a party at his home to toast it and her. At one point, he played a song that Madonna and Pat Leonard had written called "Something to Remember." He asked everyone in his home to stop talking and listen. Even the waiters holding trays stood still and silent as those at the gathering looked at Madonna, understated and elegant in a backless black gown, her hair in a twist.[103]

When the song ended, Beatty walked to Madonna, whispered to her, and applauded. His guests did, too. That who's who of Hollywood actors and industry executives added words of congratulations as they gathered around her. "She stood there and just accepted it all graciously," Jack Nicholson said. "This beautiful, unpredictable, amazing young woman with tears in her eyes, and I thought—Jesus! What a star."[104]

But in a way, that night and her "Vogue" video signaled the end of Madonna's Hollywood romance. That year she would say she no longer needed what Hollywood had to offer.

Chapter 29

Los Angeles, Paris, Tokyo, 1990

When you meet your idol, you can be disappointed...When I met her, I was not disappointed.[1]

—*Jean Paul Gaultier*

OVER THE COURSE of Madonna's career, she encountered certain people whose artistic and social sensibilities so closely matched her own that they seemed fated to work with her. One of them was born in a working-class suburb south of Paris, the only child of a bookkeeper and a school cafeteria cashier. The magic in his life came via his grandmother, a nurse who ran a beauty salon out of her house, dabbled in mysticism and alternative healing, and had a wardrobe filled with corsets in various shades of pale pink. Decades later, the boy would turn those corsets into iconic fashion statements on his way to becoming the most important French couturier of his generation. His name was Jean Paul Gaultier.[2]

He and Madonna had known of each other long before they began working together. Madonna had worn his fashions as early as the premiere of *Desperately Seeking Susan,* in 1985. For his part, he had listened to her music and watched her career from the start: he had seen her singing "Holiday" on TV and watched from the audience as she rolled around onstage during her "Like a Virgin" performance at the VMAs. And, in 1987, they met briefly when Madonna visited his boutique after her Who's That Girl Paris concert.[3] There was, in other words, a mutual appreciation because they both experimented wildly, rebelled regularly, and, perhaps most important, brought a ribald sense of humor to their work.[4] But it wasn't until late 1989 that their intense decades-long collaboration began.

In October of that year, on the eve of Gaultier's summer runway show in Paris, Herb Ritts called him to ask if he wanted to design the clothes for Madonna's next tour. Gaultier thought it was a joke. "I keep on working as if nothing had happened," he said. But throughout his show, as he put the finishing touches on his designs before the models wearing them hit the runway, he had a nagging feeling. "What if it wasn't a joke?" He called Herb, who assured him it wasn't and gave Gaultier Madonna's phone number in Los Angeles. Jean Paul called, and Madonna answered.[5]

She told Gaultier she wanted to work with him because she liked that he played with gender by blurring the line between masculinity and femininity. "I thought he was very provocative, that he was making a political statement with his fashions in a way no one else was," she said. Around a week later, Madonna sent him costume ideas. Several weeks after that, on November 23, Gaultier was in New York meeting her and Christopher in the penthouse of the Carlyle hotel. "I ring the doorbell, heart pounding, one hundred and fifty sketches under my arm," he recalled. Madonna opened the door herself. Behind her, the film *Cabaret* was playing on a large screen, and on a table lay a biography of Louise Brooks that she was reading. Both were clues to her thinking, and both would inspire a portion of her show.[6]

Gaultier and Madonna's connection was instantaneous. "It was like two kids playing together!" she said.[7] "It was a real collaboration," he added, "one of friendship and complicity. She was frightened of nothing, and our vision was in complete harmony and symbiosis—a love affair was born."[8]

Gaultier had a few days in New York, so Madonna invited him to Thanksgiving dinner at her sister's place in the city. They also met to talk budgets (without advisers). And they celebrated their new artistic union with a night at the Sound Factory. In fact, Jean Paul was on hand when Madonna first saw José and Luis. That magical moment—when the face of hip Paris fashion met the voguers of New York—was typical of Madonna's world. The remarkable was almost a given.[9]

By November 27, Gaultier was back in Paris "working flat out" on the designs that Madonna had selected. Christopher said everything had to be made in triplicate and double-sewn and strengthened so the clothes wouldn't fall apart during the show. That meant Gaultier's atelier had to produce 358 costumes for Madonna and the Blond Ambition cast—in four months.[10]

As a boy, while fitting his teddy bear, Nana, with a tiny cone-shaped bra he had created ("I imagined he was a Marilyn Monroe"), Gaultier pictured himself designing costumes and sets for the Folies Bergère cabaret. Fashion, music, and performance were, for him, linked from the start. Clothing was not a sheath to cover a rigid body but a living, vibrant thing capable of telling stories and delivering messages.[11]

When he was seventeen, he sent some drawings of his designs to Pierre Cardin. The next year, Cardin offered him a job as an assistant.[12] The atelier was perfect. Cardin, who had dressed the Beatles, told Jean Paul that fashion had to reflect the age in which it was produced. He also told him that "anything was possible." One can only imagine the thrill the younger man felt hearing that formula in such a revered place. Unfortunately, it only lasted for eight months. When Cardin cut staff, Gaultier was laid off.[13]

His next professional stop was the very traditional House of Patou, in Paris. But Jean Paul felt stifled there.[14] As soon as he could break free, he went to London to get a firsthand look at punk. He was attracted to its "allusions to sex, torn fishnet stockings, black, kilts, bondage straps, mixing of genders and materials." He said, "It spoke to me, suiting me much better than some of the ossified couture conventions."[15] Rebellion, however, whether in fashion or politics, rarely pays a living wage, so Gaultier returned to work for Pierre Cardin.[16]

Around that time, he met the man who would become his business partner and the love of his life, Francis Menuge. Francis encouraged Gaultier to go out on his own and promised to join him: he made jewelry and ran the business, and Jean Paul designed clothes. "It was like the baby we had together," Gaultier said. Their first ready-to-wear collection was presented on the runway in 1976, when Gaultier was twenty-four.[17]

From the start, Gaultier broke every rule of French fashion, not just in his designs—which included jewel-studded bustiers, ballet skirts, fishnet stockings, and sneakers—but also in his materials. His clothing was made from place mats, canvas, upholstery fabric, toile, and leather. That first show was almost ignored by the fashion press in France, but the people who saw it were stunned. *Vogue*'s Lucinda Chambers said, "It wasn't about clothes, it was about being in someone else's head." Even the presentation was revolutionary. His models were characters—people from the clubs and the streets, like Madonna's dancers.[18]

It took two years for Gaultier's designs to garner serious attention and another seven years before he opened his first boutique, in 1985. By then he had made major statements on several hot-button topics.

About gender: men wore skirts and women wore trousers and masculine suit jackets.

About race: at a time when runways were still occupied by white women, he hired women of color.

About ethnicity and culture: Gaultier's designs combined African, Asian, Caribbean, traditional French, the designs of Inuit people and Hasidic Jews, the eccentricity of King's Road in London.

About body image: his models came in all shapes, sizes, and ages.

In words that might have been spoken by Madonna, Gaultier said, "I don't think I was ever concerned with shocking people. Was I conscious of the fact that it could be shocking? Yes. But I just wanted to show what I found fair or normal or beautiful. If anything, I was the one who was shocked, by certain kinds of intolerance."[19]

Two things happened in 1989 that changed Gaultier's life. First, Francis Menuge had been diagnosed with AIDS, and that year the disease began to destroy him. Menuge was Gaultier's life. Jean Paul would say, "1+1=1; Francis et Jean Paul = Jean Paul Gaultier." He wondered how he could continue without him.[20] The second life-changing event was his collaboration with Madonna. Gaultier called her "my feminine ideal."[21]

A "Gaultier woman," according to the editor of *Vogue Paris,* Carine Roitfeld, wore makeup and was feminine but she was also "a bit of a tom boy...She's not afraid of anything, she feels good about herself, about her relationship with men, her sensuality and sexuality."[22] She was feminine *and* masculine.[23] Gaultier said, "Madonna concretized that spirit of modern women, strong, and at the same time fragile, but more macho than macho, sometimes."[24]

It would be natural to think that Gaultier's Madonna association helped him survive his worries about Menuge, but Gaultier denied it. Work did, however, help, because in creating he kept one aspect of his partnership with Menuge alive. He had come to the conclusion that, in the age of AIDS, "nothing could be worse than to cancel out desire...It should be talked about and shown." He would do that in his Blond Ambition creations.[25]

Gaultier's collection was built around the corset. The iconic design he created for Madonna turned those articles of satin restraint into symbols of strength. Not since 1905, when French designer Herminie Cadolle created a metal bra for Mata Hari, had such power been given to a woman's undergarment.[26] "Instead of signifying oppression, it seemed to become a sign of women's liberation, of women assuming power, sexual power included, over their own bodies," said fashion historian Valerie Steele. "As a male designer, he could not have done that entirely by himself; the collaboration with Madonna was crucial."[27]

But it wasn't just undergarments that Gaultier reworked for a new kind of woman. He also re-created the power suit, which had been the fashion statement arising out of second wave feminism. With their linebacker shoulder pads (to show that women were tough) over blouses with bows (to show that they weren't unapproachably so), those suits were costumes worn by women the way a boy might wear his father's too-big suit. The look was aspirational, about growing into power.

In the late '80s, some women decided they didn't need to aspire to *be* men or look like them to be powerful. At the 1988 Olympics in Seoul, gold medalists Jackie Joyner-Kersee and Florence Griffith Joyner were examples of gorgeous, strong athletes who were also feminine. Gaultier said, "I think that real fashion always comes from things that are happening in society."[28] That is the direction he took.

One day, a young woman who worked with him arrived at his atelier in an open Chanel jacket with only a lacy bra underneath.[29] Inspiration. Gaultier designed a suit that acknowledged the faux masculinity of the '70s and early '80s and countered it with real femininity by allowing undergarments—corsets and garters—to be visible. People looking at his design no longer saw the suit; they looked beyond it to the corset. They looked past the "man" to discover the power and beauty of woman.

The work on Madonna's costumes, meanwhile, had progressed enough by December 29 to allow her to travel to Paris for a fitting. Gaultier called the day she arrived D-Day. Popping "Vogue" into the cassette player in his studio, Madonna started dancing to see whether she could move freely enough in his clothes to perform in them. She could.[30]

Among the costumes she tried on that day were a pin-striped suit over a salmon-colored corset with conical bra cups; a marabou-trimmed minidress (something Santa's helper might wear); a black sports bra and bicycle shorts with garters; a full-length dress with a bustier top and a diamond on the tip of each breast; a circus-performer sequined corset; and her famous golden corset, which she would wear for "Like a Virgin."[31]

Throughout the following three months, the fittings for Madonna, Niki, Donna, and the dancers continued, with suitcases full of clothing flying between Los Angeles and Paris and Jean Paul or one of his staff close behind. Niki and Donna had as many changes of clothing as Madonna did, in nearly matching styles. The seven male dancers had several costume changes as well, among them priests' robes, yellow topcoats and black underwear with satin codpiece inserts, and bowler hats.[32] The conical bras that José and Luis would wear during "Like a Virgin" had been designed by Gaultier for his North African collection in 1984. "It was entirely her idea" to put them on men, he said.[33]

On February 28, with less than a month before the finished costumes were due in LA, Gaultier discovered that a hand-embroidered bodysuit no longer fit Madonna because she had lost the weight she gained for *Dick Tracy*—ten pounds. All her costumes had to be remade. The already difficult schedule became much more so because Gaultier was also preparing his women's collection for the runway. Collection deadline: March 19. Tour deadline: March 20.[34] Gaultier said the pressure on his eight-person team was so great that they consumed 350 aspirin a day along with more than seven hundred tubes of water-soluble vitamin C, four hundred cartons of cigarettes, and untold gallons of coffee during their months of work.[35]

Miraculously, the costumes—all 330 pounds of them—were completed on time and delivered to Los Angeles with a note that belied the excruciating labor behind them. It read, "Love and kisses, Jean Paul."[36] It also belied the cultural importance of the moment. Gaultier and Madonna were about to set a new standard for pop and rock performers' appearance onstage. Said Valerie Steele, "No one since then can dress her-or-himself without at least implicitly referring back to the Gaultier-Madonna collaboration."[37]

Madonna's work with Gaultier also brought Paris high fashion into the mainstream, just as she had introduced New York street culture to the world. The previously remote runways of Paris, Milan, and New York became hip to a new generation.[38] And that would make Madonna an object of idolatry in the fashion industry. Designer Karl Lagerfeld said,

> Who can seriously claim to have been influential in the realm of female beauty? Certainly no fashion designer in the last few years. All have contributed their ideas, but compared to Madonna, that hardly counts.[39]

Often when observers who wanted to be generous but feared being mistaken for a fan deigned to compliment Madonna, they said she had a genius for finding the right collaborators. It was backhanded praise implying that she—like other clever women—simply knew how to find good help. The fact was, Madonna did have a gift for discovering talent. What elevated this above canny shopping was that the people she hired worked *with* her, not merely *for* her, and the association usually made them both better artists. That happened on the Blond Ambition tour with her decision to hire an unknown filmmaker to shoot the event.

Madonna had wanted to document it because, she said, "I was really proud of what I'd done on the stage, and I thought, I wish I could capture this on film."[40] Originally, it was to be an HBO documentary focused on the tour's performances. Madonna asked David Fincher to direct it, but he dropped out at the last minute because he was hired to direct his first feature film, *Alien*[3], with a whopping $50 million budget. She then pivoted to a novice she had never met: twenty-five-year-old Alek Keshishian.[41]

Born in Beirut and raised in New England, Keshishian had directed a "pop opera" version of *Wuthering Heights* for his senior thesis at Harvard, parts of which featured Madonna's music. After graduation he made the logical move to music videos and dreamed of working with the woman herself. Knowing that was unlikely to happen, he said to himself, "Go on with your life, Alek." But then, he said, "out of the blue, one afternoon at the end of March...the phone rings."[42]

He picked it up and heard a voice say, " 'Hi Alek, it's Madonna.' As if that was normal," he recalled. She had seen a tape of his *Wuthering Heights* and liked it so much that she told her agents at CAA, "I want to see everything this kid does." She gradually built a collection of his music videos — a small collection, because he hadn't shot many — and concluded that he filmed "dance better than anybody." When she finally saw Alek himself in clubs, her interest grew. "I liked the people he was with; I liked the way he looked. I liked the way he danced, I knew he was educated," she said, "and I felt I had something in common with him."[43]

Four days after his fairy godmother call, Alek was seated next to Madonna in first class on a plane headed to Japan as she proceeded to insult him, test him — in short, abuse him. He felt like he was on a school bus next to the class bully and wondered how to respond. Then he thought, "Fuck it, I didn't have the job four days ago. And so I began bantering back and I think that kind of connected us."[44] "I could keep up a banter with Madonna better than anybody in her company. It was like an old Howard Hawks movie. Very fast."[45]

Arriving in Japan, Alek experienced what he called the "most insane five days of my life." By the third day he was having panic attacks. "I wondered what the fuck I was doing."[46] Madonna had invited him to make a movie but fought with him over what he could film. "I filmed her yelling at me not to film her," he said. "I figured it was better for me to be fired from this movie than to be a flunky being told when to turn the camera on and off."[47]

The only person around who seemed willing to help him was Christopher. Alek asked him how to deal with his sister, and Christopher advised him to check her mood as he would the weather. "If she says 'Hi, how are you?' that's a better sign than if she just says 'Hi.' If she doesn't look at you or doesn't even say hi, you know it isn't a good day. You must never get in her face. You must make her feel as if all your ideas, in actuality, came from her."[48] And then Christopher said, "Just get on with it." And that's what Alek did.[49]

He started by trying to find the story, the focus of his film, and getting to know the group that would essentially be his cast. "[The dancers] were like, 'What the hell is going on?' " Alek said. "And I would interview them in the mornings in bed...Because they were impossible otherwise to grab...but that gave a certain vulnerability to them, actually, and I think they opened up much more quickly."[50]

Alek said those interviews were the catalyst for the film's direction. "I was like, wait a second. These are all amazing kids...In some ways they're broken, they're misfits in the world and Madonna is playing their mother."[51] He showed Madonna what he'd shot — thirty hours of footage in Japan — and she agreed. "I couldn't give a shit about the live show," she recalled thinking. "This is life! This is what I want to document."[52] She told Alek, "Let's concentrate on that."[53]

He would shoot the behind-the-scenes footage in 16mm black and white and the concert footage in 35mm color. The film crew amounted to two people with cameras, two sound people, two gaffers for the backstage footage, and twenty-two cameras to shoot the concert scenes. "Everyone around Madonna was telling her, 'Don't be crazy. Look at what happened with *Rattle and Hum*,'" Alek said. That U2 documentary hurt rather than helped the band's reputation because it was criticized as a film about bloated egos. "She decided to go with my opinion, rather than the others," he recalled, even when that meant that New Line Cinema bowed out of the project because the film would be shot partly in black and white.[54] Madonna decided to bankroll the $4 million film herself.

The intrusions of the cameras took some getting used to. At the start, while still in Japan, Madonna slammed the door on Alek's crew more than once. If she told him to stop filming, he would tell the cameramen to shoot anyway.[55] Soon, she said, she considered the camera "a kind of third eye" in the room. And by the last leg of the tour — Europe — Alek said, "To a certain extent I had carte blanche . . . It's really brave of her."[56]

The camera people and technicians who worked with Alek wore black to be as unobtrusive as possible, and they didn't talk to Madonna, nor did she talk to them.[57] Among her only rules was that she would not do anything twice. "Today, with reality TV," Alek said decades later in an interview with *Queerty* writer Jeremy Kinser, "you do a run-through, then they film it again and again for coverage, so they're improving . . . Madonna, if she walked through a door and I didn't get it, I knew not to ask her to do it again." Because that was another rule: she wouldn't "act" for his camera.[58] Niki Haris said that wasn't the case for others in the cast and crew. "Put a camera in front of people, people start wanting their best side, trying for the right angle, being nearest to Madonna so you're sure you'll be in the shot. A lot of that shit was going on."[59]

The film did not create scenarios, but in a few cases it went right up to the edge of invention in order to provide context for a remark or a scene. In the case of Madonna's friend Moira McFarland, who showed up at a concert, Alek arranged that encounter after Madonna mentioned Moira in a comment about her childhood. In another case, Alek learned that dancer Oliver Crumes was estranged from his father, so Alek set up and filmed their meeting "because that was an important emotional beat for him."

And when Madonna spoke to her own father on the phone, Tony Ciccone had agreed in advance to the call.[60]

But among the hundreds of hours of footage Alek and his crew shot, those interventions were few. Fiction simply wasn't necessary with such rich, picaresque reality. Alek saw the movie as Felliniesque—a mix of outrageous and intriguing characters in bizarre locations who made even the most mundane occurrences appear fascinating.[61] Madonna saw the film as Warholian. As early as the '60s, Warhol had been obsessed with tape recordings that captured a subject's activities around the clock. He then graduated to films that might show a person for hours on end doing absolutely nothing.[62]

The true antecedents of the Blond Ambition tour film, however, were the first reality television show, PBS's *An American Family,* which filmed the dissolution of the Loud family in California during a seven-month period in 1971, and D. A. Pennebaker's *Don't Look Back* documentary. In that film, about Bob Dylan's 1965 British tour, one of the most private men in music allowed himself to be filmed as petulant, arrogant, and downright mean while poets, musicians, journalists, and women paid homage to his brilliance. It was a courageous film, which Dylan's fans and the critics loved because of its unvarnished honesty.[63]

Madonna's tour film would be similarly daring, just as revealing, and therefore potentially dangerous. "I had a lot of resistance," Alek said. "Her advisors were telling her, 'What the hell are you doing listening to this kid?' "[64] Liz Rosenberg said she was "totally against it because I don't think the world needs to see what goes on backstage...I'm old fashioned in feeling protective and wanting everyone to see the best of Madonna." Freddy DeMann feared Madonna was overexposed. "But Madonna didn't agree, and when she doesn't agree, she has a doll and she squeezes it in all the right places and I feel pain," he said.[65]

Not everyone wanted to be on camera, and some people made themselves scarce. Dancer Carlton Wilborn was hesitant, he said, "because I was so riddled with secrets back then. No one knew the quandary I had" about being HIV-positive.[66] Vincent Paterson also avoided Alek's crew, as did production manager Chris Lamb. He didn't want to be seen being berated by Madonna. "Ya know, when she has something to say, she doesn't mince words," he said. "Sometimes you get it between the eyes."[67]

But those who made themselves available became stars. Niki and Donna came across as Madonna's friends, expressing themselves onstage and off boldly, unapologetically, joyously. They didn't take shit, and they didn't hover in the background. It was obvious that Madonna didn't require it, because her star wouldn't be diminished by sharing the spotlight with two strong women.

The seven male dancers made an even bigger impact by being trailblaz-ers in two ways. At a time when dancers were largely animated manne-quins selling products or, in the case of women, props selling sex in music videos, Madonna's dancers were unique and powerful personalities and recognized as such.[68] Audiences screamed when Madonna appeared. But after several concerts had taken place, and after fans had read media cover-age about the dancers, they screamed for them, too. And that was partly because of the other way in which the dancers were trailblazers: there wasn't a white Anglo-Saxon among them, and only one of them was heterosexual.

The tour and film were very much statements about homosexuality, yet they were no statement at all—or, as Alek said, "We made a really gay movie without the subject matter being gayness."[69] "The sort of daring progressive message in this movie was that you can be gay and human," said Kevin Stea.

> Up to this point, being gay was to be the other and be subversive and per-verse. And all of a sudden, there's this huge message that you can be gay and happy and successful and be full of life and be young. You didn't have to be hiding in the back alley or some sleazy bar, hiding out and married and pretending.[70]

Of Alek's contribution, he said, "Being gay himself and sharing the humanity of our community is what gave this movie long-lasting legs and power and iconic status."[71]

The film that would become *Truth or Dare* in some parts of the world and *In Bed with Madonna* in others showed Madonna and her team at work, at play, at rest; joyful, melancholic, loving, spiteful, threatened, adored; growing together and growing apart; and, most important of all, changing contemporary culture. That crew of young men and women would inspire generations of performers, choreographers, musicians, filmmakers, and people. People who struggled with their sexuality, people who felt power-less because of their race, people who longed to see themselves represented as accepted and valued members of society saw in the Blond Ambition tour and in the film that documented it the story of their dreams fulfilled.

Chapter 30

Tokyo, Houston, East Rutherford, London, Nice, 1990

Gender roles are my palette, not my chains.[1]

— *Nadya Tolokonnikova*

ON APRIL 13, 1990, the Blond Ambition tour opened before thirty-five thousand people at the new Zozo Marine Stadium, outside Tokyo. "When I heard her singing to an audience for the first time, it was like: 'Oh shit, she's fucking performing now,'" Carlton Wilborn recalled. The show was *on*. But just as it had with the Who's That Girl tour, the rain came down in buckets—this time during all three Tokyo concerts. By the third night, with strong winds and the temperature hovering around forty-five degrees Fahrenheit, advisers told Madonna to cancel. She refused. "When I saw the kids in front getting soaked, the decision was made."[2]

Jean Paul Gaultier, on hand to see his costumes in action, was left disappointed on that score. The only concession Madonna made to the weather gods was to do the show in civvies: tour jackets, combat boots or tennis shoes, and heavy tights. Otherwise, Gaultier's precious designs would have been damaged on the very first night. By the third, they would have been unusable. The water was so deep and the surface so slick that Madonna could hydroplane across the stage. "I'll bet you didn't know you were going to get an ice-skating show, did you?" she asked the crowd. Her joke masked her worry. "I just wanted everyone to get through the show and not get hurt," she explained.[3]

They did, Donna said, because Madonna had prepared for every eventuality. She recalled thinking at times during rehearsals, "Oh, my God, do we have to run through this three times in one day?" The reason became clear that night in Tokyo. "She knew all the things that could possibly go wrong, and that's why we had to be on automatic when we were out there. You had to be so in the moment and be able to make quick decisions. How can you fix the choreography because that person's slipping around?" Madonna's safety was also a concern. "Niki and I were like, 'We got you.'"[4]

The dancers, by contrast, had close to zero concern about the weather. Madonna said they "were so excited to be performing for an audience, the world could have been blowing up and they wouldn't have cared." The audience didn't seem to mind, either. Huddled under umbrellas and covered in ponchos, they clapped and screamed throughout the show. Vincent Paterson said that had never happened in Japan, even when Michael Jackson performed.[5]

From the concert's opening moments, as lights pulsed like beating hearts and gears the size of small cars turned to awaken the industrial setting for "Express Yourself," the scene was electric.[6] That song announced the concert's message: freedom. "Freedom as an artist, freedom as a human being, freedom with regards to fuckin' speak the truth," said Luis.[7]

In the song "Express Yourself," some lines could be interpreted as describing womanly submission. But in performance, gender expectations were flipped entirely. It was the women who offered men a "big strong hand" as Madonna, Niki, and Donna lifted the male dancers to their feet. It was the women who were the sexual aggressors — on top in simulated sex acts. And it was the women, not the brawny bare-chested lads, who represented power.[8] "There were a couple moves we did in that opening routine where we would go all the way back and bend," said Donna. "I remember having so much energy and adrenaline and feeling so strong."[9]

"Open Your Heart" followed, with Madonna singing in the Gaultier corset she had worn under her "Express Yourself" suit and Oliver Crumes dancing alone on a platform above her. It was remarkable that Oliver, young and inexperienced as he was, had the strength and confidence to carry off a skillful solo routine on what was then the biggest stage in the world. If "Express Yourself" was an admonition to women to take charge of their lives and say what they wanted to say, "Open Your Heart" beseeched men to free themselves of the prison of conventional masculinity.[10]

The theme of the next number? Girl power. In cropped warm-up jackets and hoods, Madonna, Niki, and Donna played street fighters as they sang "Causing a Commotion." Madonna asked the audience, "What do you do when people fuck with you?" Her answer: "You put 'em in their place." It was another tough-chick lesson in empowerment before she launched into the final number of the opening set, "Where's the Party."[11]

That song, written by Madonna during the height of her paparazzi problems, was a reminder to herself to have fun, keep things in perspective, and train her eye on the bigger goal — her life's journey. And with that, her stage narrative returned to the place where her journey began: her childhood — specifically, her sexual awakening, which the church and her father considered sinful. The second act of Blond Ambition would be the point at which the show became truly theatrical and unlike any previous pop spectacle. Kevin Stea called it "the heart of the tour" because it was the essence of Madonna.[12]

It opened with "Like a Virgin" and one of Madonna's most infamous performances. To the sound of North African music, she arose from beneath the stage in a golden corset, on a bed of red velvet, with José and Luis wearing Gaultier's cone bras standing beside her like eunuchs. "The first time we saw the costumes, we loved them!" said Luis. "The fact that they were so over the top and would cause [controversy] is what appealed to me the most." The two dancers had choreographed their part of the segment, basing it on their voguing.[13]

As a young woman during her Virgin tour, in 1985, Madonna had simulated masturbation. As a more mature woman in her Blond Ambition tour, she didn't hint at it; she embraced it. After Luis and José lowered her onto the bed, she began a masturbation sequence that lasted a full minute and grew more frenzied thanks to lighting director Peter Morse's decision to use strobe lights to dramatize her climax.[14]

Madonna later explained that in the masturbation scene she was ridding herself of the guilt the Catholic Church had made her feel about sex. Calling out God onstage directly afterward, Madonna sought understanding, if not forgiveness. She got neither. Dancers dressed as priests forced her to repent for her sin. Wearing a hooded black robe and a heavy cross, she writhed on her knees in another kind of ecstasy, the religious ecstasy of a penitent. And with that she began "Like a Prayer."[15]

Donna and Niki, dressed as nuns, and the male dancer-priests joined her in a tight formation, like worshippers crowded together in church. As Madonna sang, Carlton was her dance partner, at one point lifting her into the air in a nearly full arm extension.[16] He was so nervous about the routine that he never participated in late-night dinners and early morning clubbing with the other dancers if they had a concert the next day. "I was trying to stay steady and focused," he said. "I was the dude holding the multimillion-dollar brand over his head. I was partnering Madonna and carrying her around and I took it very seriously."[17]

The chorus of the song was sung by the entire troupe. It was the most moving portion of the concert up to that point, the one in which the group worked united, without the hierarchy of Madonna's celebrity. They were so in sync that all of them—Madonna, the singers, and the dancers— appeared as one body, one voice, one spirit.[18]

The group then left Madonna alone onstage to sing "Live to Tell" in front of a stained-glass cathedral window that had been lowered into place. "Oh Father" followed, with Carlton acting as a priest who first punished Madonna, then rejected her. Having tried and failed to please the church, she removed her cross and dropped it on the floor before entreating her secular father to accept her. The song she sang was "Papa Don't Preach."

Seven dancers joined her onstage for that performance, which mixed modern and classical ballet. When Madonna left them, they continued a dance that was as beautifully choreographed and performed as that of any professional troupe. One would not expect to see a display of such artistry and seriousness on a pop stage, and no doubt many in Madonna's audience never had.[19]

It is tempting to regard the third section of the show as a descent from the sublime to the ridiculous, but Madonna, Christopher, and Vincent Paterson made the *Dick Tracy* portion of the concert not only entertaining but also hilariously wicked—and not just because of Madonna's rendition of "Hanky Panky."

From the start of the set, the theme was old Hollywood, with searchlights fanning the hall as they would before a movie premiere. Madonna, in the spotlight, arose onto the stage, lying on a piano and singing "Sooner or Later." Wearing a long sheer black dress over a spangled corset, she enthusiastically assumed the role of a '40s torch singer. For "Hanky Panky," she shed the dress and became a sassy burlesque star.[20]

Salim appeared onstage at that point as Dick Tracy. Like Warren Beatty, he played Tracy as befuddled. But when he began dancing, he emitted more sexuality in two minutes than the professional lothario Beatty did in the entire movie. The routine was built around slapstick gags and one-sided comic banter, because Salim's character didn't speak. He also didn't sing. When he and Madonna performed "Now I'm Following You," he lip-synched Beatty's part of the duet.[21]

It was when Madonna and Salim disappeared for a costume change that the action in the spotlight became truly cheeky. Six dancers dressed in yellow topcoats took the stage for a bare-legged Rockettes-style kickline that raised the possibility that there was nothing under their coats. Sure enough, when they opened them, all they were wearing were black briefs with codpieces. Pairing up in couples, they danced together with their yellow coats flapping and their underwear-clad bodies in each other's arms, while a voice-over repeated the word *dick* and Madonna's voice said, "My bottom hurts just thinkin' about it."[22]

The scene was classic Madonna. Take what might have passed as acceptable, even sweet entertainment—a PG plug for the film *Dick Tracy*—and turn it into a subversive cultural event. In 1990, it was nearly unheard of for men to be seen onstage dancing arm in arm and unthinkable that mostly gay men in their underwear would do so. The scene was jaw-dropping and unforgettable—though, interestingly, few critics noted it because the straight press was fixated on Madonna's antics back on the bed.

That West Village *Dick Tracy* revue finished, Madonna returned to the stage for "Material Girl" (she, Niki, and Donna appeared under hair dryers in curlers and monogrammed bathrobes), followed by "Cherish" (which featured three mermen—José, Kevin, and Luis—and Madonna briefly playing the harp).[23] Such whimsy prepared the audience for her next message of the evening.

Performed *West Side Story*–style, the number pitted tough girls—Madonna, Niki, and Donna—on one side of a courtship ritual opposite tough guys, played by Gabriel, Salim, and Carlton. Madonna and the gals sized up the men, but Madonna hesitated, saying, "You know, you never really get to know a guy until you ask him to wear a rubber."[24] That act moved directly to "Into the Groove." In the context of safe-sex messaging, the line "Boy you've got to prove your love for me" was no longer just about dancing.[25]

"Into the Groove" was followed by "Vogue" and "Holiday" before the troupe launched a truly spectacular finale.[26] Madonna appeared alone onstage in a boned corset and bowler hat—part Liza Minnelli in *Cabaret,* part Malcolm McDowell in *A Clockwork Orange*—singing the beginning verses of Sly and the Family Stone's 1971 hit, "Family Affair." Gradually, the dancers rose through the floor carrying wooden café chairs to a welcome from Madonna, who, in a Cockney accent, declared the dancers, Niki, and Donna her family. And with that, they began "Keep It Together," a song about Madonna's flight from Michigan and her realization that she needed and loved the people she had left behind.

Visually, the performance was cacophonous. The dancers' costumes, comprising leather straps instead of shirts, and the chairs they used as props made the dance a moving puzzle of heavily linear parts that repeatedly locked together and then unlocked. The routine involved complex choreography that required precision timing and acrobatic ability. The potential for one missed step and an ensuing disaster hung over the routine. And yet the performers pulled it off.

"We spent so much time rehearsing the chair routine for 'Keep It Together,'" Donna said. "It felt like the whole sentiment of the song—with us being together and being at the end of the show." Kevin called that number his favorite. "The choreography was phenomenal, and it really felt like we *were* a family onstage . . . In that number we knew we had survived the show, so there was cathartic joy."[27]

As the song ended, everyone descended through the floor except Madonna, who sang the line "Keep, keep it together; keep people together forever and ever" solo for a full five minutes. By the end, the sound of those words echoed like a Gregorian chant.[28]

★   ★   ★

Just as the cast felt cathartic joy at the end of the show, so did the audience as it streamed out of concert venues, heads filled with images and sounds and, more important, ideas. Critics would focus on the controversial heterosexual sex in the concert because it allowed them to avoid the much more complex and culturally radical aspects of the show.

Onstage for just under two hours, women and men—gay, straight, and bi; African American, Dominican, Puerto Rican, North African, Asian, and white; many from humble backgrounds; most of them young—demolished stereotypes, defied sexism and bigotry, and claimed power and dignity for themselves as artists. During those precious minutes, they made audiences not only *see* society's invisible outsiders but also respect and esteem them. Historian Cindy Patton said that the Blond Ambition tour "unleashed" Madonna as the "queen of gender disorder and racial deconstruction."[29]

What Madonna did in the show for *women* was to throw a hand grenade into the patriarchy's centuries-old deceit concerning the extent and nature of a woman artist's power. Women onstage had long been feared as shameless temptresses. (In the seventeenth century, the pope banned musical education for women because it was so morally dangerous *for men*.)[30] Blond Ambition Madonna gave men a new reason to tremble. She was fierce. She did not ask permission to make a spectacle of herself. And she did not apologize for her brazenness. She owned it with fuck-you relish.[31]

After nine shows in three Japanese cities, Madonna's tour returned to the States to open in Houston on May 4. It was a daring choice, because Texas was home to some of her most vocal religious critics.[32] But it was also home to some of Madonna's most fervent fans. Kevin Stea described the opening as "insanity...they screamed for ten minutes straight, and we could not hear the music to start the show!"[33]

When the performance finally began, that excitement multiplied and became transcendent. "The power I felt onstage as a team, as a group, as a unit transmitting the energy back to this audience, giving us and charging us with everything they have—it's the reason why I'm still dancing today," said Kevin more than thirty years later. "I've been chasing that dragon ever since...It was really an epiphany."[34]

As the tour traveled through North America, the passion of the crowds grew, not just for Madonna but also for the show's entire cast. Signs appeared outside and inside venues saying WE LOVE MADONNA, WE LOVE LUIS, WE LOVE CARLTON, WE LOVE JOSE. "It was something I wanted my whole life," said Luis.[35]

The attention paid to the dancers displayed the hunger among Madonna's fans for a narrative about gay men that did not involve death. And yet Madonna often reminded people that while celebrating life, they should not ignore darker realities.

On the last tour date in the States, in East Rutherford, New Jersey, just outside New York City, Madonna dedicated the concert to Keith Haring and donated the $300,000 raised that evening to amfAR. As she described Keith's death and praised him for being out and being open about having AIDS, Salim and Carlton stood behind her, listening to her words: "In memory of Keith, let's tell each other the truth...Let's face it together." It was easy for her to say, but they couldn't. Salim said he felt himself dying inside.[36]

The European leg of the tour opened in Sweden and wended its way to Paris in early July, where Jean Paul Gaultier awaited it. To coincide with the tour's arrival, he mounted an exhibition of Christopher's paintings at his shop on the rue du Faubourg Saint-Honoré. Frédérique Lorca, who worked as Gaultier's communications director, said,

> We had planned to let [Madonna] in through the back...But the media found us out. I'd never witnessed such a crazy scene. Photographers and journalists were lying on the ground, perching in plants. They swept through everything in their paths: shops, bookstore stands, garbage cans, grandmothers doing their shopping who had no idea what was going on.[37]

The French couldn't get enough of Madonna.[38] The official reception on her next tour stop, in Italy, was much cooler. Long before the tour arrived there, prominent Catholics mounted a campaign to stop the show. One Catholic group, Associazione Famiglia Domani, urged Rome's cardinal to ban it. Unions threatened to strike if Madonna performed. Even Pope John Paul II weighed in, calling Blond Ambition "one of the most satanic shows in the history of humanity."[39]

Madonna invited the clergy to attend her concert and judge for themselves. The fusion of religious and erotic imagery in Italian art is as old as the Renaissance. Madonna's show was merely the twentieth-century version. "The moral is," she said, "be strong, believe in freedom and in God, love yourself, understand your sexuality, have a sense of humor, masturbate, don't judge people by their religion, color or sexual habits, love life and your family."[40] Her explanation caused a fresh scandal.

Madonna was forced to cancel her second show in Rome because of the potential strike and poor ticket sales. After receiving death threats, she was also moved to a villa outside the city for her protection. At Ciampino

Airport, as she prepared to leave Rome for Turin, she held a news conference. Declaring herself a proud Italian American, she said her "blood boils when I am misunderstood or unfairly judged for my beliefs...

> My show is not a conventional rock show but a theatrical presentation of my music, and, like theater, it asks questions, provokes thought, and takes you on an emotional journey, portraying good and bad, light and dark, joy and sorrow, redemption and salvation. I do not endorse a way of life but describe one, and the audience is left to make its own decision and judgment.[41]

Madonna also reminded her Catholic critics that he who is without sin should cast the first stone. Her reminder came not long after the church condemned the lifesaving use of condoms and needle exchanges to protect people from AIDS and amid accusations of child sex abuse that had been leveled against priests.[42]

When Madonna's tour rolled into Britain for three sold-out concerts at Wembley Stadium, she waded into the middle of another social debate. The UK was in the midst of what one writer called a "moral panic" over homosexuality. Two years earlier, the Thatcher government codified a law—Section 28—that "prohibited the promotion of homosexuality." It was aimed at keeping anything to do with homosexuality out of school curricula, but its effect was chilling across the culture.[43]

"People forget how homophobic society was at that time," said Matthew Hodson, one of the most influential gay activists in Britain.

> The government thought being gay was a choice and that people could therefore be persuaded to become gay by seeing positive images of homosexuality. That's what Section 28 was about, trying to erase us from view. The thinking behind Section 28 was, "We can't allow anyone to say anything nice about gays because then people will think it's OK to be gay and it's not OK to be gay."[44]

Madonna's concert was seen as not only promoting homosexuality but also normalizing it. One of her tour sponsors in the UK, the Abbey National Building Society bank, was criticized by the country's right wing for funding the concert's satellite broadcast.[45]

By that time, Madonna was so disgusted by the various attempts at censorship she had encountered that she defied British broadcasting rules by saying *fuck* fourteen times—in one minute—during a live BBC Radio 1 broadcast of her show. The station's mistake was to warn her in advance not to curse. A BBC spokesman said with characteristic understatement, "Our warning had quite the opposite effect."[46]

★　　★　　★

Near the end of Madonna's Los Angeles tour dates, back in May, Warren Beatty had given her a $30,000 diamond-and-sapphire ring as part of a "semi-proposal." She put it on the middle finger of her left hand. There was an obvious lack of commitment on both sides of the costly gesture.[47] Madonna discussed it with Christopher in an offhand, should-I-or-shouldn't-I-marry-him way that lacked the passion or even interest one would expect concerning such a decision.[48] The timing was also curious. Not only were she and Beatty moving in opposite directions, they weren't getting along all that well.

Kevin Stea recalled being at Beatty's in March with Madonna and his fellow tour dancers to celebrate Warren's birthday. "He did not want us there...Madonna delighted in it because it seemed she loved fucking with Warren. Like, 'Love me, love my friends. Get into it. Stop being such an old curmudgeon.'"[49] Beatty then infuriated Madonna by missing her tour opening in Houston after she had sent a plane to collect him. When he turned up at her LA show a week later, Beatty's biographer Peter Biskind said, she was "abusive." Finding him backstage, she shouted, "Don't hide back there, Warren. Get over here. You stink, you pussy man."[50]

A cynic might think that Beatty's gift of the ring during that tour stop had less to do with romance than finance. *Dick Tracy* was about to open in theaters. A big rock on Madonna's hand would get the press pumping out stories and possibly secure Madonna's cooperation during that important period. The pressure on Disney was enormous because the film's competition in the blockbuster sweepstakes that summer was fierce: *Another 48 Hrs., Die Hard 2, RoboCop 2, Days of Thunder, Total Recall.*[51]

Dick Tracy's prerelease publicity campaign hit every possible demographic, including kiddies, through a movie promotion deal with McDonald's. In the magazine world, Madonna and Beatty appeared together or separately on the covers of *Vanity Fair, Cosmopolitan, Harper's, Entertainment Weekly* and *Us* (several times), *Rolling Stone,* and *Premiere.* There was also a (disastrous) Barbara Walters TV interview with Beatty during which he refused to speak, a segment on ABC's *20/20,* a syndicated TV show about the film's creation, and MTV promotions. In addition to all that, Disney mounted a major advertising campaign.[52]

Dick Tracy delivered—sort of. It made more than $50 million in its first week, breaking Disney's own one-week earnings record. But that was only half of what *Batman* had brought in the year before, and it was below analysts' expectations. Ticket sales mounted, eventually totaling more than $100 million domestically and around $60 million internationally. But the experience left the Disney chairman, Jeffrey Katzenberg, wondering whether such costly films were worth it.[53]

Nearly every review of the film lauded its art direction. Vincent Canby, in the *New York Times,* and Sheila Benson, in the *Los Angeles Times,* gave the film and everyone in it rave reviews.[54] But Peter Travers, in *Rolling Stone,* wrote that compared to *Batman,* the film felt "emotionally impoverished" except for Madonna, who, he said, was the only character to radiate any real human emotion. He also noted that Beatty "never allows Madonna to complete a song without cutting away to car chases or gunshots."[55]

Madonna had issues with the finished product, too. "This is going to sound really horrible, but I have to admit I've never really seen the movie," Madonna said. "I saw a lot of bits and pieces, and I did see an early cut, and I saw about half of it at a premiere in Washington, D.C., but then I had to leave." She told a *Los Angeles Times* interviewer, "You could say I have a lot of unresolved feelings about it. I remember being very upset that all of my big music scenes were cut up the way they were. I learned a lot about filmmaking from Warren, but obviously it didn't make me a big box-office star, did it?"[56]

The Blond Ambition tour's final concert, on August 5, in Nice, was broadcast live on HBO.[57] The show followed the performance script, but Madonna went off-piste as often as possible in the language department, at one point riffing on freedom of speech by saying, "Fuck, fuck, fuck, fuck, fuck" and paying tribute to Roseanne Barr, who had recently grabbed her crotch after singing "The Star Spangled Banner" at a baseball game—a gesture that became a national story and nearly ended Barr's career.[58]

But Madonna's bad-girl behavior seemed almost token. That final night had a sweetness that the others didn't. When it came time to wrap things up, she brought out all the people who had worked the tour—onstage and off—and thanked each one individually before they stepped off the stage. Christopher, who was at the end of the line, picked Madonna up and twirled her around as she said, "Without my brother, I'm *nothing!*" And then, turning to the group that had already left the stage, she shouted, "Without *them* I'm nothing!"[59]

It was a rare and generous acknowledgment by a star that a show wasn't "I" but "we." Then, when everyone was gone, Madonna remained onstage alone, singing a cappella the final words of this magnificent tour: "Keep, keep it together; keep people together forever and ever."[60] Vincent Paterson said that song, "Keep It Together," was what Madonna was "all about as a person."

> She's about family, about having those people around her...It's everybody working together and supporting each other, believing in each other and

caring for each other...That seems to me to be the way she works and the closest to what she is as a real person.[61]

HBO's *Madonna: Blond Ambition World Tour Live* special, directed by David Mallet, would become the most-watched nonsports event in the channel's eighteen-year history, with nearly a quarter of all subscribers, or more than four million households, tuning in.[62]

For the people on the tour, especially the dancers, the reentry into real life was beyond sobering. "I wanted it to continue forever. Who wanted to get off that ride? Not me," said Luis.[63] "Getting off the plane, I didn't get into a Mercedes limo. I got into my father's Ford Reliance."[64]

Kevin Stea had even less.

When he landed in LA, he realized with an "Oh, shit!" that he had spent all his tour money. "All of it," he said years later, when he could laugh about it. "For me, having *any* money was an excess of money. For me to have thousands and thousands coming in...It wasn't hard to spend if you like clothes as much as I do." With only $800 in his pocket and a duffel bag full of exquisite duds, he moved into his car—a Hyundai Excel—for two or three days while he looked for a place.[65]

But the greatest loss for them all was emotional. Salim remembered being so torn up that he cried. Oliver, whom his fellow dancers had chided over his homophobia, was changed by the tour. He may have begun as a gay basher, but he ended up loving his dance mates. "Each one of us would have taken a bullet for each one of us," he said. "That's how close we were."[66]

For her part, Madonna was relieved the tour was over because it had been so exhausting, but she was deeply sorry to say goodbye to her tour family. She said her maternal instincts were awakened by her interactions with her dancers, especially when they left her. At that point she realized she wanted children, because even if they moved on one day to start their own lives, they would still be hers.[67]

The air was heavy with endings that August. Gaultier's love, Francis Menuge, died. And while Gaultier's star had risen immeasurably because of the tour—he had become the fashion world's equivalent of a rock star—he had second thoughts about his career. "When he died, I thought I'd done what I wanted—even beyond what I'd imagined was possible," Gaultier said. "And so I did think, after all, 'Why carry on? Maybe it's best if I stop now.'" But realizing "it's the only thing I know how to do," he chose to continue.[68]

Madonna, obviously, would, too. She was no longer simply a star or even a superstar. She finished the tour an icon. "She's kind of like the

epitome of everything that's considered important now in popular culture," journalist Kristine McKenna said that year. "I think societies need
goddesses and god figures and she's very much one."[69] Communications
professor and lesbian activist Lisa Henderson said that for many in the
LGBTQ community, especially the young generations, Madonna had
become "the emblem of sexual resistance, an embodiment of the same
in-your-face sexuality evoked [beginning that year] by Queer Nation's
slogan, 'We're here, we're queer, get used to it.'"[70]

She also emerged from the tour as more than a singer or even a singer-
songwriter. She was not a Celine Dion, Paula Abdul, Whitney Houston,
or the new gal on the block, Mariah Carey. Said Vincent Paterson, "She's
not a recording star, which the rest of them are.

> She's an artist, and that's what sets her apart...she pushes the limits on her-
> self and pushes the buttons on everybody else...I don't think she has con-
> cerns about pleasing people. I think the most important thing is to be true
> to herself and what she believes in.[71]

Chapter 31

Los Angeles, Paris, New York, 1990–1991

This movie will definitely be one of the all-time classics, like
The Wizard of Oz.[1]

— *Madonna*

BACK IN LOS Angeles, Alek Keshishian spent six weeks looking at the 250
hours of tour footage he had shot for *Truth or Dare,* which he reduced to a
three-hour rough cut to show Madonna. She wanted to keep all three
hours. Saying, "It's not *Gone with the Wind,* honey," Alek told her that was
impossible.[2] He managed to cut it back to under two hours, but Harvey
Weinstein, whose company, Miramax, would distribute it, said he wanted
to lose fifteen more minutes. On Madonna's behalf, Alek said no.[3] In the
battle between the two entertainment titans, Weinstein versus Madonna,
Alek bet on Madonna.

Barry Alexander Brown, *Truth or Dare*'s editor, recalled Weinstein floating some ideas during a test screening of the film. Madonna turned to him
and said, "Listen, I put up the money for this movie. I don't care what your
point of view is. I never want to hear it. Who the hell are you to tell me
what kind of film I should be doing?" Brown said Weinstein "crumpled."
Said Liz Rosenberg, "I think [Weinstein] was a little afraid of her...He
understood he was not in a position to give her shit."[4]

By contrast, Alek and Madonna's relationship was familial. He said he
would "pick her up in my Volkswagen with the bad brakes, and we'd go
out to dinner." Theirs was an exciting exchange generally, because they
knew they were creating something grand. "You have to understand: back
then there wasn't Instagram; there wasn't Facebook," Alek said years later.
"So in a way she was a double pioneer.

> She was a pioneer in terms of what she believed, that nobody was really say-
> ing or putting out there. [And] she was...foreshadowing what was gonna
> happen with social media...Now celebrities curate themselves, and they
> present you behind-the-scenes stuff, which is obviously what they want you
> to see. In this, I think Madonna was braver. She said, "Show it."[5]

Madonna described her philosophy as: "If I'm going to make a documentary and tell the director that I want to reveal truths, then I'm not going to say, 'But this is where I draw the line.'"[6] "There were plenty of scenes I felt edgy or uneasy about, but they're still in the film...Maybe all the moments aren't necessarily flattering, but they're the highs and the lows of the movie."[7]

Madonna was under pressure from the people in her professional orbit to cut "almost anything that you squirmed in your seat about."[8] She did not. She also kept the scenes that made *her* uncomfortable. She said if she asked herself, "Is that how I am? How I talk? How I act?" then she knew the scene was good.[9] The problem was that her embrace of warts-and-all reality involved other people who might not have wanted to be so open.

The episodes that caused Madonna's advisers to squirm included one in which she insulted Hollywood heavyweight Kevin Costner, who came backstage and called her show "neat." She responded on camera by making a gagging motion. "To go to my show, which I think is very disturbing and moving, and then come backstage and say it was 'neat,' I felt that was a slap in the face to me," Madonna explained later. "So basically, I was slapping him back."[10] (A decade later, she publicly apologized to Costner during an LA concert he attended with his daughters. "That meant more to me than you could ever know," Costner said.)[11]

A scene with a childhood friend who asked Madonna to be the godmother of her baby also made for awkward viewing because Madonna was clearly caught off guard.[12] Another disturbing encounter involved Madonna's hairdresser, Sharon Gault, who, Madonna learned, believed she had been drugged and possibly raped when the tour was in New York. Madonna's response, which seemed to amount to giggles, either indicated that she hadn't clearly understood what happened or that she *had* understood and responded with shocking indifference.

There was also a difficult sequence involving Madonna's older brother Marty, who was filmed showing up so late to visit Madonna in her hotel that she refused to see him. She suspected he had made a detour into a bar.[13] As difficult as the scene was, it showed that Madonna was like any other person coping with a family member's substance abuse. "He is an alcoholic," she said. "He's very tortured, and I speak to him, but it's hard for me because I find myself being very judgmental...In Alcoholics Anonymous it's called a codependent...We have a strained relationship. I know he loves me, and I love him, but it's difficult."[14]

A visit Madonna and the film crew paid to her mother's grave hurt and infuriated Christopher, who saw it as a desecration of their mother's memory.[15] Madonna defended the visit, saying she hadn't been to the grave for decades. "That's what this film was about. I was on a mission to film my life. So it gave me the opportunity to deal with an issue that I'd been avoiding or running away from all my life because it was so painful."[16]

But the part of the film that was perhaps most controversial and consequential involved the game truth or dare. "It all started out at a dinner with the film crew," Donna De Lory said.

> We were drinking Sangria and hanging out. Everyone got really into it. The truth ones were really fun because after spending so much time together you got to know [people] better…Everyone was kissing everyone. It was crazy.[17]

Nothing was off-limits, even when the game was being filmed. Answering a truth challenge, Madonna declared to the world that Sean was the love of her life. On a dare from Donna, she performed fellatio on a bottle of mineral water. And so when Salim and Gabriel kissed on a dare, it wasn't a big deal. "It's a hot kiss," said Salim. "Like if you see that, even as a straight guy, you wanna kiss a guy after you see that kiss."[18]

But for Gabriel, while the kiss itself wasn't a problem, filming it was, and he asked that it be cut from the movie. "In his early twenties, he wasn't there yet; he wasn't ready," his mother, Sue Trupin, said. "It wasn't a statement that he wanted to make. It was her statement."[19]

The kiss he shared with Salim remained in the film. For millions of people, it would be the first time they had seen men kissing passionately, and for the gay men and boys among them, it was a thing of beauty. "I must have received two thousand messages from people around the world telling me how their lives changed by seeing a gay kiss on the big screen," Salim said. Decades passed, and he still received those messages.[20]

Gay activist Matthew Hodson, who saw the film three times in the theater, said, "Outside of porn, it would have been the first time I'd seen handsome gay men kiss unproblematically…[*Truth or Dare*] is incredibly affirmative about being gay…I wanted to hang with them, these gorgeous people."[21]

As for Madonna's decision to include the scene and showcase gay life, Hodson said,

> There is a long history of famous women who have been gay allies. With them it was like they had lots of friends who were gay…and they were going to stand by their friends and that's obviously right and important. What Madonna did was much more radical and more brutal. Because she said it's not enough that I have gay friends and that I support them. I need to change the world…
>
> My perception is that her agenda was: people will not defeat HIV while homophobia persists, and one of the ways we can tackle homophobia is to

bring homosexuality into every household in the country. I think that's what she set out to do. I think she was an era-defining gay ally.[22]

Matt Cain was sixteen when he saw the film. He said he left the theater feeling like he'd been "shot in the arm with some kind of class A drug. I was walking taller. I felt stronger. I felt like I was wearing the body armor she had on."[23]

Madonna gave Alek control of the film's final cut.[24] In August, when it came time to screen it for her, Warren Beatty, Freddy DeMann, Warner executives, and a small group of friends, there was a sense of déjà vu. Madonna had once again ventured into potentially career-ending territory. She loved it, but the reaction in the room became more critical by the minute. Beatty was described as "silently furious."[25] He was the only person in the film who hadn't signed away his editing rights in a consent agreement. Madonna said,

> There were phone conversations I thought were really moving and touching and revealing, but Warren didn't know we were recording. It wasn't fair, plus it's a federal offense... Ultimately, I don't think he respected what I was doing or took it seriously. He just thought I was fucking around, making a home movie.[26]

The next day, Madonna received a letter from Beatty's lawyer threatening legal action if some of the scenes weren't cut. They were, but the letter marked the end of their relationship.[27]

The Madonna-Beatty romance had been on life support for some time. Christopher said that as soon as filming began on *Truth or Dare,* at the start of the tour, the relationship began to cool. Problems that already existed— jealousy, for one—were exacerbated. Christopher said that he once found Beatty in the middle of the night rummaging through the wastebasket in Madonna's home office in search of what Christopher assumed was evidence of infidelity.[28]

Beatty's biographer said Madonna was likewise convinced that Warren's philandering hadn't abated. He denied the affairs "to her face" and then insisted that *she* be faithful to *him.* Madonna told him to "go to hell."[29] Said Madonna, "While Sean was competing with me in the career department, I think Warren felt that my image as a sex symbol was the competitive thing... We mutually didn't trust each other. That was the bottom line."[30]

Beatty also didn't understand *Truth or Dare,* which was evident from the scenes he appeared in. At one point, Alek and his crew filmed Madonna in her New York kitchen having her throat examined by a doctor. Beatty sits in the corner providing a running commentary on how inappropriate that is. During his mumbling monologue, he utters what is perhaps his second-most-famous line (the first being "What's new, pussycat," which he used to seduce women). Beatty says of Madonna, "She doesn't want to live off camera."[31]

Unmoved by his criticism, Madonna later said that if Beatty found living in front of a camera so terrible, it's "perhaps because he has a lot of secrets. Me, I don't give a fuck."[32] "He comes from a different school of thought, that if you reveal too much of yourself, no one is going to find you interesting anymore. I think that's bullshit."[33] Asked by Patrick Goldstein of the *Los Angeles Times,* "Do you think [Beatty] underestimated you?" Madonna replied, "Yes. But he's always underestimated me."[34]

Call it Madonna's revenge, but she didn't cut the scene with Beatty in which she called him "pussy man." It wasn't a reference to his sexual adventures. She said he was "a wimp."[35] On the other hand, she did see Beatty's role in the film as valuable. He was the "objective counterpoint," the straight man asking the question the audience might be asking: "Why are you doing this?" She explained one of the reasons:

> What I really wish would happen from *Truth or Dare* is that movies would be made about gay lifestyles that wouldn't be these art-house movies like *Longtime Companion* [the first feature film about AIDS] that nobody saw … What I hope is—maybe I'm being too idealistic—that my movie changes things in Hollywood in that direction.[36]

After the Blond Ambition tour, Madonna's embrace of gay culture became even more open and radical. The first indication of that occurred on September 6, when she made her second-most-famous appearance at the MTV Video Music Awards. Accompanied by her full Blond Ambition cast, all of them dressed in eighteenth-century attire, she launched into a wildly new interpretation of "Vogue."

Nothing approaching that production had ever been attempted at the awards show. The elaborate period costumes, the ensemble theatrical presentation, and the joyous expression of art and power by women, gay men, and people of all races and ethnicities challenged the very foundation upon which the white male MTV empire was built. "We just came out and rocked," Carlton said.[37]

Since Madonna's "Like a Virgin" appearance, in 1984, outrage of some sort was expected at the VMAs. What she and her dancers offered was artistry and attitude—this is who we are: deal with it. The costumes were extraordinary, as was the choreography. For that, Madonna had again turned to Vincent Paterson, who created the concept of Madonna as Marie Antoinette surrounded by courtiers.[38]

The troupe was still tight. They knew each other so well that they worked as a unit—one big blur of creamy satin, tight breeches, heaving bosoms, and snapping fans—as they posed and played with Madonna as *la reine* at the center. The fact that it was a reunion added to both the dancers' and the viewers' excitement. It was appropriate that it was a performance of "Vogue," because that was where their journey together had begun less than a year earlier.

Of course the routine was racy, with Madonna's breasts getting much of the attention as her dancers nuzzled them. The overall effect, though, was fun and fabulous.[39] It wasn't just her gay fans who loved it. At McGuire Air Force Base, in New Jersey, troops preparing to ship to the Middle East for the first Iraq War gathered around a TV in a lounge littered with soda cans, hooting and hollering while watching the show. "Madonna's the '90s. She's what we're looking for," said one soldier. "She's awesome, the way she dresses—or doesn't dress."[40]

Going into the VMAs, Madonna had the distinction of having the most nominations. But as the *Los Angeles Times* reported in a killjoy article that called her VMAs "Vogue" performance "shameless," Madonna was "shut out." She lost Video of the Year and Best Female Video to Sinéad O'Connor, Best Dance Video to MC Hammer, Best Choreography to Janet Jackson, and Best Art Direction to the B-52's. "Vogue" came away with wins for the boys: Best Editing, Best Cinematography, and Best Direction for David Fincher.[41]

The next night, Madonna and company repeated their performance at a benefit for AIDS Project Los Angeles, held at the Wiltern theater, and received a seven-minute standing ovation.[42] Madonna was one of four people honored for her contribution to AIDS-related causes. The others were artist David Hockney, Congressman Henry Waxman, and actor Ian McKellen.

In her acceptance speech, she said she was honored to receive the award but felt she didn't deserve it because it "is easy to lend your name to a celebrity fund-raiser if you're famous, and it's very easy to donate money to AIDS research if you're rich." She said the people who deserved recognition were those who, in the face of "truly frightening" homophobia, had the courage to say they were gay and the "warriors" brave enough to say they had AIDS. She dedicated her award to the people she had loved and lost to the disease, "to the thousands I have heard about and to the millions I will never know."[43]

One of the people she was speaking to and about was Christopher

Flynn. Nearly blind and ravaged by the disease, he died around a month later. They had had a sweet moment together the year before at an AIDS Project Los Angeles danceathon that he helped organize. Flynn kicked off the proceedings by saying, "As your oldest living disco partner, I claim the first dance."[44] Madonna didn't attend his funeral. Christopher said she feared it would become a circus. Instead, she issued a statement saying, "Christopher Flynn was my mentor, is my higher power, and will remain an eternal inspiration."[45]

Martin Burgoyne, Keith Haring, and Christopher Flynn, the gay men who had nurtured Madonna's early career, were gone. In every way, that year felt like the end of one era and the beginning of a new one. Appropriately, she issued a farewell of sorts to that decade with her first greatest-hits album, *The Immaculate Collection*. Featuring sixteen of her most famous songs, it recapped her career from the beginning and, with the album's lead single, foretold her immediate future.

"Justify My Love," written by Ingrid Chavez with contributions by Madonna and Lenny Kravitz, was Madonna's first vocal foray into a mature woman's sexuality. It is a woman speaking to her lover so intimately that the listener is made to feel like an eavesdropper. The new Madonna, post–Blond Ambition, was headed deeper into controversial territory. As a mischievous calling card, she dedicated *The Immaculate Collection* to the pope. He would be hearing from her again.[46]

Madonna flew to Paris in November to shoot the video for "Justify My Love." "When Madonna called me about filming," the director, Jean-Baptiste Mondino, recalled,

> I said, "Why don't you come over here? It would be nice to do something simple." We locked ourselves in the [Hotel] Royal Monceau for two days and one night without any idea of what we were going to do. The only idea I had was for her to come in with a suitcase...
>
> We rented the whole floor and [gave] everyone their own room; there was no set. That's why the video shocked people. You could see it was not a fake. We didn't think we were going to do something wild. None of what you see was planned. But when I started to edit, I said, "This is never going to be shown."[47]

The floor of the hotel set aside for filming soon filled with friends and friends of friends. Jean Paul Gaultier designed the clothes, from Madonna's trench coat to the bondage wear worn by some of the characters in the video. Mondino drew from his acquaintances in the city's fashion demimonde for the cast, among them legendary muse and model Wallis Franken, boyish androgyne and Gaultier model Amanda Cazalet, and Brazilian actress-model Luciana Silva. From the States came Debi Mazar, fresh from acting in Martin Scorsese's *Goodfellas,* Blond Ambition dancers José and Luis, and Madonna's new consort, Tony Ward.

She had begun dating Tony in August, around the time her relationship with Beatty officially ended. At twenty-seven, Ward was the un-Beatty.[48] He had worked as Herb's model and muse for years, helping him to find his "edgier imagery." Herb's camera assistant, Mark McKenna, called him a "lonely, distraught, poet, James-Dean-type character."[49]

Madonna had known him since the "Cherish" video shoot—Tony was one of the mermen—but not until her thirty-second birthday, that August, did they connect. Within a month he had moved into her house, and not long afterward, they were headed to Paris.[50] Ward "had no problem posing nude or posing nude with girls or posing nude with guys," McKenna said. "His sexuality didn't hold him back from anything."[51]

"Justify My Love" unfolds as a travelogue of desires. Madonna arrives for her erotic journey weary, carrying a suitcase as she wanders down a hotel corridor, where her character meets a man played by Tony. Along the hallway, in open-door rooms, exists a fun house of sexual practices, all merely hinted at: the viewer is allowed to glance into the chambers but not stay for a visit.

Madonna's encounter with Tony in their own room is steamy, but no more so than any film involving consenting adults, except that Madonna's bra and panties are of better quality and Ward wears considerably more crosses than the average bloke about to score. The "deviance" in the video that would cause such a panic in the States occurs as fantasy: Madonna kissing Amanda Cazalet in front of Tony; Wallis Franken, as a slim butch woman topless but for suspenders, playfully reminding Tony who's boss; and assorted flashes of gay men, lesbians, androgynous and trans folks not doing much of anything but existing.

That was apparently outrage enough for the censorious-minded, because what else was there to criticize? Nudity? Not much. Sex? Not really. But in the often blurred black-and-white images there was titillating possibility aplenty. And then there was Madonna's voice. Her whispered lyrics were arguably the dirtiest thing in the video as she instructed Tony to "justify my love"—to prove that *he* was worthy of *her* attentions. The video was erotic in the best French tradition, and unlike porn, it was life-affirming. It ended with the woman—Madonna—happy. In it, sexuality was not either-or: it was "and."[52] "I think everybody has a bisexual nature," she said. "That's my theory. I could be wrong."[53]

⋆   ⋆   ⋆

Anticipation built before anyone had seen the video, thanks to gossip columnists. MTV stood eager, ready to receive—and it punted. Once programming executives viewed it, the channel announced that the video was not appropriate to air.

Misogyny was to MTV what American football was to ESPN: it was central to the channel's success. MTV's censors had from the start condoned images of disposable and interchangeable young women who existed only for the use and abuse of men. Madonna saw those videos as "cruel to women. It's an image that I've grown up with that I think is unfair." She said that, by contrast, Tony Ward in her "Justify My Love" video "knew what was happening to him...fully understood it and was into it...

> The sexuality in my videos is all consented to. No one's taking advantage of each other...I suppose people would say, "You emasculate men in what you do." Well, straight men need to be emasculated. I'm sorry. They all need to be slapped around. Women have been kept down for too long. Every straight guy should have a man's tongue in his mouth at least once.[54]

Incredibly, the video did not debut on MTV but on an ultraserious news program, ABC's *Nightline*. It was a show on which government and military officials appeared, on which the weightiest issues of the world were discussed, on which anchor Ted Koppel's baritone sounded—no matter the subject—*grave*.

On December 3, 1990, when Madonna appeared at 1:00 a.m., after *Monday Night Football* and with a US attack on Iraq imminent, it wasn't Koppel in the anchor chair but his colleague Forrest Sawyer. Despite the hour, the looming war, and a substitute inquisitor, the interview would become the second-highest-rated show in *Nightline*'s then ten-year history.

The program presented "Justify My Love" in its entirety with a warning beforehand from Sawyer that it contained "graphic portrayals of sexuality and nudity." And then Madonna herself defended the work. Clothed in rectitude—a stiff, high-collared dark jacket—she was part priest, part headmistress. It was a side of Madonna rarely on display.

She fully admitted that she had thought she could "bend the rules a little bit" after MTV, on so many occasions, allowed her to air what it had originally rejected.

> Half of me thought that I was going to be able to get away with it and that I was going to be able to convince them. And the other half thought, No,

with the wave of censorship...and the conservatism that is sort of sweeping over the nation...there was going to be a problem.[55]

One of the things that confounded Sawyer, he said, was Madonna's apparent cavalier regard for her star status. Instead of becoming more cautious, she had become more reckless. She had a huge career to lose, and she didn't seem to care.

She explained that she wasn't a star searching for brighter and bigger spotlights but an artist pushing boundaries.

> I think that's what art is all about, experimenting...It is my artistic expression, and for me a video is the filmic expression of the song...And you've got to listen to the words of the song. It's about a woman who is talking to her lover, and she's saying, "Tell me your dreams—am I in them? Tell me your fears—are you scared? Tell me your story—I'm not afraid of who you are." And so, you know, we're dealing with sexual fantasies and being truthful and honest with our partner.[56]

The very idea that a woman *had* sexual fantasies was discounted by some at the time. In the sexual arena, even fantasy belonged to men, according to a bestselling book that said that men had sexual fantasies and women had "relationship fantasies."[57] In her video, Madonna was not only convincingly engaged in her own sexual fantasies, she encouraged the man in her life to broaden his own.

Madonna then used her *Nightline* platform to describe what she called the hypocrisy of censorship in what passed as acceptable mainstream entertainment: images of "violence and humiliation and degradation," none of which appeared in her work. She said she believed in warning labels and agreed that not all material was appropriate for children. But she said sexuality shouldn't be the only area to be censored and sequestered. "I think MTV should have their violence hour, and I think they should have their degradation-to-women hour," she said with disdainful irony.[58]

Madonna's *Nightline* appearance, and her video, triggered an avalanche of commentary. Among the many things she said during her interview that resonated with the gay community was her use of the word *heterosexual.* She employed that word the way straight people talked about "homosexuals" and in doing so made heterosexuality just another color on the sexual spectrum.[59]

As for the video, Don Baird, writing in the *San Francisco Bay Times,* said that when he watched it,

I held my head in my hands in utter disbelief...Never has a pop star forced so many of the most basic and necessary elements of gayness right into the face of this increasingly uptight nation with power and finesse. Her message is a clear Get Over It, and she's the most popular woman in the world who's talking up our good everything.[60]

Said lesbian activist Lisa Henderson, "Madonna is one of us. Even her rampant heterosexuality cannot change that."[61] "She shimmies into our... imagination...and makes us face things we didn't think it was possible to learn from pop music."[62] The fact that Madonna's video was embraced by both gay men *and* lesbians was in itself notable. In *OutWeek,* Michael Musto wrote that Madonna was the first superstar to appeal equally to both.[63]

Some women praised Madonna for raising the important question of why degrading and abusive images are considered "entertainment." Said Harvard professor Lynne Layton in the *Boston Globe* in defense of Madonna at the time, "This is indeed a hypocritical culture, and the hypocrisy has everything to do with unequal gender relations and with an open distaste for any version of femininity that threatens not to know its place."[64]

But as intensely as "Justify My Love" was praised, it was criticized with equal passion by the mainstream press, by the church, and by moral stewards on the right *and* left.

From the right, a reader of *People* magazine wrote:

So, Madonna "draws the line at violence and degradation of women"? Well, millions of people draw the line at promiscuity, group sex, bisexuality and homosexuality—all of which were portrayed in her latest video.[65]

And from the left, in that same magazine, another reader said:

Madonna has set the feminist movement back at least one hundred years. Right back to the days when the only businesses women ran were brothels.[66]

Some gays and lesbians faulted her for not being explicit enough. And others faulted her because she was too central to the action, too blond, too perfect.[67]

There were also dismissive comments from all sides about Madonna wading into "political" issues. The subtext of those criticisms was that she was just a "girl" and, worse, a showgirl who didn't look like a "serious woman." And yet she was political to the marrow and had a track record to prove it through her charitable work, her creative work, the protests she had participated in, and the people she inspired.[68] Said Madonna around that time,

> It excites me to be a political person. I'm incensed by the prejudices in the world...if I can do something with my celebrity to make people see things that ordinarily they may not pay attention to, then I feel responsible to do it. But I want to have fun while I'm doing it.[69]

In November of 1990, *Rolling Stone* declared Madonna "a one-woman bonfire of the vanities." It called her an "AIDS activist," a "crusader for freedom," a "rebel gender bender," a "postfeminist," and a "mascaraed amazon."

> Madonna is more than her baby-breathless voice, trademark navel, stallion's nostrils. Nonetheless, her look is a crucial medium of her message. And what is that message, echoed endlessly in the sighs of her global fan club? Express yourself.[70]

Madonna had stirred political, social, and cultural passions. She had become an object of idolatry and hatred. Research papers were written about her; Madonna courses were taught at Harvard, UCLA, Rutgers, Princeton, and the University of Texas; analyses were published that searched for the source of the Madonna phenomenon in Freud, Marx, Catholicism, and feminism.[71] But really, the answer could be found in Michigan.

In December, Madonna went home for Christmas. There, to her sisters, she wasn't "Madonna." They called her Louise.[72] She recalled that Christmas as one of the happiest moments of that most eventful year.

> Nobody brings up the fact that I'm a star. Not one word. At first I thought, "Well, how come I'm not getting any special treatment?" But even though I had to sleep on the floor in a sleeping bag...the trip was really such a joyous thing for my father.[73]
>   It still hasn't dawned on him who I am...He lives in his own world and generally the things that happen to me pass right by him. I think that's good because it means he can have an OK life and not be bothered.[74]

Back in New York, the holiday season continued with a New Year's Eve party that was neither as convivial nor as reassuring as Christmas at home.

A palm reader told Madonna to expect more broken hearts, a life without children, and a possible career change because what she was working on didn't suit her. Madonna was "devastated." She did what she never did: she got drunk, vomited, passed out, and missed her own party.[75]

What she was working on was a Woody Allen film called *Shadows and Fog*. She had a tiny part in what was a small film featuring the kind of disproportionately high-profile cast that Allen's films attracted in those days. For Madonna, it was another learning experience. Allen managed to direct his film without being a "tyrant."[76] From his partner, Mia Farrow, who was surrounded by children, she received a lesson in family. Madonna concluded, "The fulfillment you get from another human being—a child, in particular—will always dwarf people recognizing you on the street."[77]

Madonna, however, wasn't ready for children. First, she did not want to have a child without a father she could depend on.[78] Second, she wasn't yet willing to give up her career, even temporarily. She still had something to prove, mostly to herself. "My drive in life is from this horrible fear of being mediocre," she said. "My struggle has never ended, and it probably never will."[79]

That year, Madonna would become "somebody" at some of the biggest events on the entertainment-industry calendar.

Chapter 32

Los Angeles, Cannes, New York, Evansville, 1991

You only live once, but if you do it right, once is enough.[1]
— *Mae West*

MICHAEL JACKSON HAD called Madonna about doing a song together for his next album, *Dangerous*. "So we got together, and he played me a bit of music," she said.

> It was a very unfinished track, and he said he wanted to call the song "In the Closet," and I said, "Really? You want to call this song 'In the Closet'?" He said, "Yeah." And I said, "Do you know what that implies?" and he said, "Yeah," and he sort of giggled a little bit, and I said, "Well, you know I like to deal with those kinds of ironic, innuendo kind of things, so if you wanna go that way..." So he said yes.[2]

Madonna wrote some lyrics and gave them to Jackson. "He didn't like them. And I think that...all he wanted was a provocative title, and ultimately he didn't want the content of the song to sort of live up to the title."[3] Madonna lost interest. "I'm not going to get together and do some stupid ballad or love duet—no one's going to buy it."[4]

In the meantime, she was preparing for her first Oscar performance. In March, she was to sing Stephen Sondheim's "Sooner or Later" from *Dick Tracy,* which was nominated for Best Original Song. When Jackson asked her whom she was taking to the ceremony, she said no one. "He said, 'Well, I'll be your date.'"[5] And with that simple offer, a pop culture moment was born.

At thirty-two, Jackson had been eclipsed somewhat by his little sister, Janet, and her record-breaking $50 million deal with Virgin Records. Not to be outdone, just days before the Oscars, he broke her record by signing a deal with Sony Music worth potentially hundreds of millions of dollars. An appearance with Madonna would show the world that he was back, bigger than ever. For Madonna's part, arriving with Jackson would be the best possible way to snatch the red carpet out from under every other celebrity and prove that she didn't need the box office to make her a Hollywood star.[6]

And that was why the Academy of Motion Pictures Arts and Sciences didn't allow Madonna and Michael to walk on the red carpet. The pairing would have made *the* picture of the night, and neither star was even up for an award. Instead, they were told by academy officials to arrive at the Shrine Auditorium's back door. With its whiff of "servant's entrance," that directive to a Black man and a formerly blue-collar woman could have been interpreted as a slight. In fact, it was the ultimate acknowledgment of their status: they were simply too big for the annual Oscar walk of fame. The paparazzi found them being hustled by security into the building, Madonna's white-gloved hand in Michael's black-gloved hand.[7]

As a couple, they were dazzling. One commentator said, "It was like looking at the sun."[8] Part of what made them so irresistible was that they were clearly enjoying the spectacle they created. She said their relationship in general was about "making fun of the crazy world that we were working and living in."[9]

That night, Madonna embodied midcentury Hollywood. Her blond hair long and wavy like Veronica Lake's, she wore a strapless body-hugging "pearl-encrusted" white Bob Mackie gown and white stole along with $20 million worth of Harry Winston diamonds. Jackson wore an off-white jacket with faux-pearl beaded lapels, a diamond brooch instead of a tie, and a black armband studded with black Swarovski crystals. Below the waist he went full-tilt cowboy: black leather pants and gold-tipped cowboy boots.[10] Befitting their status, the pair was seated in the spot reserved for Hollywood royalty: front row, aisle.[11]

That was the easy part. Madonna also had a job to do. Under the brightest lights, in front of an audience of entertainment luminaries, she took the stage alone to sing "Sooner or Later." Nervous didn't begin to describe how she felt. "I had four minutes to be perfect and three billion people were watching me on television," Madonna said. "That's a fairly daunting situation." She also felt the audience "was probably not particularly interested or respectful of me and what I do. And many things could have gone wrong. I had to climb up out of the floor. I had a dress that was so heavily beaded that to walk straight in it was a feat. And my head was like, 'Oh God, if I can just hold this together.'"[12]

People saw Marilyn in her performance, but Madonna had studied Rita Hayworth's movements, especially those in her "Put the Blame on Mame" number in *Gilda,* during which she peeled off a glove in a mock striptease.[13] Rising up through the stage with her back to the audience, Madonna, too, peeled off a glove and wiggled and vamped her way to the microphone before turning her back on the audience again to begin her song.

Her nerves were apparent in the trembling hand she held aloft after she'd turned to face the crowd, but she regained her composure during her routine as she alternately slinked and strutted around the stage. About four and a half minutes into the number, some vigorous movement dislodged a costly earring, which hung in her hair. Undaunted, she continued. When the song ended to enthusiastic applause, she freed the earring from her hair and threw it into the crowd. Confident and sassy, she glamour-walked off the stage. She had done it.[14]

"Sooner or Later" earned an Oscar, but it was one of the few bright spots for *Dick Tracy.* (It also won Best Art Direction–Set Direction and Best Makeup.) Ironically, the night belonged to Madonna's *Truth or Dare* foil, Kevin Costner, whose film *Dances with Wolves* won seven awards, including Best Picture and Best Director. The night also belonged to Whoopi Goldberg. She became the first Black woman since 1939 to win an acting Oscar when she picked up a statuette for her supporting role in *Ghost.*[15]

Madonna had been at the Oscars for someone else's film. But on May 13, she appeared at Cannes to promote her own. *Truth or Dare* was released the week before in the States, and she chose to premiere it in Europe at the most storied film festival in the world, albeit out of competition. Among the films by American directors under consideration for that year's Palme d'Or were the Coen brothers' *Barton Fink,* Spike Lee's *Jungle Fever,* and David Mamet's *Homicide.* Screening outside the main competition was John Singleton's breakthrough South Central drama, *Boyz n the Hood,* and Sean Penn's directorial debut, *The Indian Runner.*

Between the American contributions by people Madonna loved, respected, or had worked with and the European entries by directors whom Madonna admired, such as Lars von Trier and Krzysztof Kieślowski, she was more at home at Cannes than she had been at the Shrine Auditorium. But then Madonna always appeared more at ease as an artist in Europe.

Her work was accepted there without the bitter commentary (aside from the lobs thrown by the Vatican) that she often received in the more puritanical United States. Her sense of irony was more broadly appreciated. And she, as a woman, was better understood. Not that Europe was less chauvinistic; it was simply that a woman expressing her sexuality was nothing new there. France, for example, had never been burdened by a "Victorian era" of sexual denial and repression.[16] That was why Madonna's appearance at the festival was so remarkable—with the help of Jean Paul Gaultier, she managed to shock even that sexually sophisticated audience.

Crowds anticipating her arrival had waited all day along the Promenade de la Croisette, outside the Palais des Festivals. *In Bed with Madonna,* as the film was called at Cannes, was to be screened at midnight. On either side of the red carpet, security men stood shoulder to shoulder. One French journalist said the festival had never seen a security operation of that scale. Behind that line were hundreds of photographers, and behind them row upon row of fans.[17]

Before the crowd had even seen her, fans knew she had arrived. The song "Crazy for You" blasted over the PA system outside the palais. Then the woman herself appeared on the red carpet with Alek Keshishian, Jean Paul Gaultier, Liz Rosenberg, and a phalanx of bodyguards. The frenzy around her was intense, but she, on Alek's arm, seemed calm, smiling broadly as she took it all in and proceeded toward the palais stairs, where scores of men in black tuxedos awaited her. For a time, she was swallowed up among them. But one photo-savvy gentleman instructed those crowding Madonna to back away so the fans and the paparazzi could get a clear view of her. And that's when it happened.[18]

Wearing a long, loose Gaultier-designed rose-colored kimono, her blond Oscar hair replaced by dark curls, which *New York Times* critic Vincent Canby said looked like rolls of 35mm film, she turned to the crowd and opened her kimono. Underneath was nothing but a white bullet bra and girdle—the underarmor of the 1950s starlets who had famously walked those very steps.[19]

Cannes was home to topless beaches and streets where women routinely wore as little as legally possible, but when Madonna dropped her kimono from her shoulders, a gasp arose from the crowd as if it had never seen anything more shocking. She stood under the flashing lights of hundreds of cameras in her Gaultier underwear, giving them what they wanted, more than they wanted, and giving the world an unforgettable photograph that encapsulated the spirit of the paparazzi side of the festival. Glamour, sex, and mischief, mostly of the female variety.

As the image sank in, the gasp of the crowd turned into a roar of delighted disbelief. A BBC journalist said that not since a young Brigitte Bardot appeared in Cannes had one woman caused such a commotion.[20] That was in 1953, when the then eighteen-year-old Bardot opened her coat to reveal a tiny dress and then showed up on the beach in a tinier bikini.

Madonna's display caused the crowd, which Canby described as "dangerously large," to push into the paparazzi, who in turn pushed past the security line. The crush was so intense that Madonna barely made it into the theater. "I was smacked against a glass wall with a bunch of other people who were around Madonna," Liz Rosenberg said. "It was very scary." The *Los Angeles Times* reported that police sealed the venue and those ticket holders who were not already inside were locked out.[21] Said Spike Lee, "If the police weren't there, there'd have been a riot."[22]

Madonna remained in the South of France at the festival for five days, and everywhere she went, mayhem followed. Paparazzi in cars, on scooters, in helicopters, and on foot caused traffic jams.[23] It was impossible to ignore them—not just for Madonna but also for the other celebrities in town, whom the press found less interesting. One of those was Sean Penn. After he split with Madonna, the paparazzi who had dogged him dropped him just as quickly. In their absence he rebuilt his life.[24]

By the time Sean arrived in Cannes, he had directed his first film, a dark movie called *The Indian Runner,* about family ties frayed beyond repair by misfortune and violence. And he had become a father. The month before the festival, actor Robin Wright gave birth to their daughter, Dylan Frances.

It was inevitable that Madonna and Sean would meet in Cannes, which they did at a party for Spike Lee's *Jungle Fever.* Sean was seated in a VIP area when Madonna appeared. Producer Don Phillips described an awkward scene during which Madonna seemed to try to jump into Sean's lap. "Sean kind of jumped away. But everything in that place stopped."[25]

Sean described the encounter as friendly, saying that if others were tense about it, he was not. He had moved on in his life. He told an interviewer that year that he appreciated and liked Madonna; they just couldn't live together.[26] Madonna had moved on, too, but with more sadness. She told *Vanity Fair* that April that she watched Sean's movies "because sometimes that's the only way I can see him."[27]

Truth or Dare was wildly successful. For eleven years, it claimed the title of the highest-earning documentary of all time, despite having an R rating (ostensibly because of foul language). Thirty years later, it was still the fifth-highest-grossing documentary of all time.[28] *Rolling Stone*'s Peter Travers called it "the most revealing and outrageously funny piece of pop demythologizing" since Bob Dylan's 1965 concert film, *Don't Look Back.*[29] *Village Voice* critic Robert Christgau declared himself a Madonna "convert" after seeing it.[30] Culture critic Elayne Rapping wrote,

> Her sense of humor, irreverent and lusty, is a celebration of female freedom from sexual constraint of all kinds. Her sexual bravado . . . cannot possibly be misunderstood as the behavior of a sexual object.[31]

But many other critics saw in Madonna's film the tale of an ego run amok, an exhibitionist out of control, a "shallow, superglitzed Amway saleswoman," or what Jack Mathews in the *Los Angeles Times* that spring called "the media's first slut savant." The conservative *National Review,* which said Madonna surrounded herself with "blacks and homosexuals," lumped her in with "Marilyn Monroe and other sexpots" as "self-absorbed little bores who talked in cliches about 'art' and 'truth,' when they weren't talking about themselves."[32]

The film, in other words, did its job. It got people talking and thinking about Madonna. More important, it got people talking about what she had to say. The *New York Times*'s Stephen Holden said, "The movie reveals more clearly than any of her previous controversies the ways that Madonna uses her celebrity to make political statements."[33]

Truth or Dare's commercial success shocked some of the dancers depicted in it. Kevin Stea and Oliver Crumes believed Madonna owed them money because their contracts stipulated that they would be paid an agreed-upon fee if a feature film arose from the tour. Gabriel Trupin was distraught because his request to remove his kiss with Salim was ignored, and he was essentially outed against his will.[34]

The three dancers would ultimately file suit and reach a settlement with Madonna. Gabriel did so without much time left to live. He died of AIDS in 1995 after his twenty-sixth birthday. "If he had lived longer, I know he would have come to peace with *Truth or Dare*. He would have been quite amused and even proud of the juicy kiss," his mother, Sue Trupin, said. "Initially, yes, he did feel 'betrayed and unpaid' (hence the lawsuit), but by the end he was way beyond bitterness or regret."[35] It was a sad coda to their work together, because the dancers and Madonna loved one another and because it supported the narrative advanced by her critics that Madonna used people for her own purposes.[36]

Even before the lawsuit, a *Washington Post* reporter asked Madonna to respond to charges that she "exploited" gay men. Madonna responded, "In a revolution, some people have to get hurt. To get people to change, you have to turn the table over. Some dishes get broken. That's the only analogy that I can think of. It's the means to an end."[37] In her fight against homophobia, her brother Christopher would be one of those broken dishes.

British actor Rupert Everett once said of Christopher, "For anyone who came into contact with Madonna, to know her at all you had to know him. The one was incomprehensible without the other. He was her dark side and she was his."[38] Madonna told a French journalist that spring, "My brother is my best friend and my confidant... He's everything to me... I trust his judgment and I respect what he says."[39] But when it came to outing him during an interview with what was the most important gay magazine in America, *The Advocate,* she failed to ask that most trusted sibling what he thought about the idea.

Don Shewey, who conducted the interview, had written the first review of a Madonna album in *Rolling Stone* back in 1983. At that time he wasn't a fan. But through the years, there were markers in her career that made him think she had moved beyond the "cheerful pop disco" of that first album and into territory deserving of respect. "Live to Tell" was one of them; "Vogue" was another. In the meantime, Shewey's longtime partner, Stephen Holden, had written about Madonna and become friendly with Liz Rosenberg. When the LA-based *Advocate* asked Liz if Madonna would sit for an interview, she said yes immediately and that she wanted Don to do it.[40]

Though *The Advocate* was a national publication, Shewey said its circulation was small. However, his agent sold his "Madonna: The X-Rated Interview" to the Los Angeles Times Syndicate, which in turn sent it to nineteen countries, where it was translated into eleven languages. The interest didn't merely stem from the fact that it was a Madonna interview; that spring she had given dozens of them. It stemmed from the fact that Shewey's conversation with her was remarkably candid as she talked about herself, about the entertainment industry, about gay culture, and about her affinity for gay culture in terms rarely if ever used by a celebrity.[41]

"She was great and totally forthcoming," Shewey said. Nothing was off the record, and he was not required to run the interview past her for pre-publication approval of quotations, though she did contact him about two subjects they had discussed. One was Michael Jackson and her mention of his song "In the Closet," which she wasn't sure he wanted disclosed. The other was the fear she had expressed that Christopher might get AIDS. "They asked me to take that out," Shewey said. He agreed.[42]

What they did not ask him to remove was Madonna's disclosure that her little brother was gay. When asked how her family felt about Christopher's sexuality, Madonna said her father was "probably not really comfortable with it" but that her brothers and sisters accepted it.[43] Reading those words, Christopher was "incensed." Years later he wrote,

> Without asking me, without giving me a say in the decision, she has taken it upon herself to out me. I know that she hasn't for a moment considered whether my homosexuality is public knowledge, the reality that our grandmother doesn't know about it, and neither does our extended family... Besides, it has always been my choice whether, when, or where to come out, not Madonna's.[44]

He said that when he confronted her, she didn't understand why he was upset. In the early '90s there was pressure for people to come out because secrecy perpetuated a sense of shame, and shame bolstered the homophobic argument that there was something "wrong" with being gay or lesbian. The discussions had become so impassioned that prominent homosexuals were the targets of outing threats by activists.[45] Madonna supported that opinion, telling Shewey, "Maybe all these queens who are running this town should come right out, and maybe they'd all see that it wasn't such a horrible thing."[46]

To Madonna's mind, Christopher had no reason to hide who he was. And in a utopian world, it wouldn't be a problem. But in the real world, it was. Around a week after the *Advocate* article appeared, a reporter from the *National Enquirer* called Christopher to tell him that the newspaper planned to run a story saying that he had AIDS. He knew he didn't, but he had himself tested. When the results came in negative, the story disappeared, though the insinuations lingered. Madonna became a target, too.[47] As they had during Martin Burgoyne's illness, the tabs chased the tale that *she* had AIDS. Annoyed and disgusted, Madonna said, "If this is what I have to deal with for my involvement in fighting this epidemic, then so be it."[48] "You better be strong if you're gonna be in this fight—that's all I can say."[49]

Madonna teamed up with Steven Meisel on a photo shoot for *Vanity Fair*'s April issue that was inspired by the famous Bert Stern images of Marilyn Monroe. They were dreamily sexy in an early-1960s sort of way. For *Rolling Stone,* they joined forces for something bolder: a pictorial published in June called "Flesh and Fantasy." Using Brassaï's "secret Paris" photos from the '20s and '30s as inspiration, the pair re-created the sexual underground of that city—the cabarets, the drug dens, the brothels, and gay nightclubs.[50] The spread included the most explicit published photos of Madonna since her *Playboy-Penthouse* exposure. Madonna had sat for those early photos as a matter of survival. The *Rolling Stone* shoot, on the other hand, was fun, so much so that Madonna began considering collaborating on a book of erotic photos with Meisel.

Eight months earlier, the powerful Simon and Schuster editor Judith Regan had approached her about writing a book of erotic fantasies. Simon and Schuster had just published a national bestseller called *Women on Top* by Nancy Friday, an author who specialized in books about women's sexual fantasies. Without a doubt, Madonna's would be a global bestseller. The discussions reached the point where Regan thought they had a deal. They did not. Madonna was merely in a listening and thinking mode.[51]

Madonna said she had been approached by several publishers with the idea of writing a book of erotic imaginings. "It had nothing to do with photographs and illustrations or anything," she said. "And so I was throwing that idea around because I was actually flattered, and I said it seemed like something challenging to do, to actually write a bunch of short stories, erotica, sort of in the vein of Anaïs Nin, but today and in my language."[52]

Coincidentally, around that time, Madonna had begun trying to persuade Steven Meisel to do a photo book of his own. "And he said, 'Why
don't you do one with me?'" So she decided to marry the erotic fantasy
idea to Meisel's images.[53]

Her fantasy book, however, was just one of many items on an ambitious
to-do list that she described that spring in response to a journalist's question about her plans.

> I want to act in more movies. I want to direct movies. I want to produce
> movies...I want to develop a lot of my favorite books into screenplays. I
> want to make movies about people who inspire me. I want to get more
> involved in theater and performance art. I want to write a book of erotic
> short stories. I want to, um, tons of things. I want to be an entrepreneur and
> find struggling artists and help them with their careers. I'd like to have a
> baby—that takes some time, you know. I mean, there's tons of things
> to do.[54]

It was quite a list, and Madonna would accomplish most of it, beginning
with acting in another movie. She felt she could be a stronger actor after
Truth or Dare because it had made her more comfortable in front of a
camera.[55]

In May, the tabloids reported seeing twenty-seven-year-old Oakland A's
outfielder Jose Canseco leaving Madonna's apartment early one morning.
The *New York Post* published photos and ran a story implying that the married baseball star was Madonna's latest conquest. What Madonna wanted
from him was baseball tips.[56] She had agreed to act in Penny Marshall's
film *A League of Their Own.* Like *Desperately Seeking Susan,* it would be a
rollicking opportunity to showcase strong women.

The film was based on the true story of female baseball players recruited
during World War II to fill the fields left vacant when male players went to
war. As many as 545 women played in the All-American Girls Professional
Baseball League, which existed for eleven years, from 1943 to 1954. Though
required to be coiffed, made up, and in skirts on the field, the women nonetheless proved themselves to be formidable athletes. Their directive from
league organizers was: "Look like women. Play like men."[57]

Marshall had been wanting to do a sports movie when she discovered
the incredible story of the women's league. But, she said, it was hard to
persuade a studio to back it. "An all-girls period baseball? Naw," she
recalled of the reaction she received. By 1991, she had a directing deal with
Columbia Pictures, and it finally agreed to let her have her movie.

Marshall's route to the director's chair in the days when that was an almost exclusively male occupation was nearly as implausible as a woman pitcher's trip to the mound. She had been the costar of the popular mid-'70s sitcom *Laverne & Shirley* and had directed several episodes of it. But movies were something she merely stumbled into. When the director of the 1986 Whoopi Goldberg comedy, *Jumpin' Jack Flash,* left, Marshall was asked to step in.[58]

She soon proved to the studio and herself that her ascent wasn't a fluke. In 1988, her film *Big,* starring Tom Hanks, grossed more than $150 million. Marshall became the first woman director to cross the $100 million threshold.

Hollywood accepted Marshall, despite her sex, because she was so good, and that was the theme of her baseball movie. It was about women who succeeded in a man's world at a man's game. To that end, she insisted that actors demonstrate proficiency on the field and be approved by a coaching staff. Only then could they read for the part.[59]

When the actor chosen to play Mae "All the Way Mae" Mordabito dropped out of the film, Marshall contacted Madonna to discuss the role of the showgirl turned baseball player. "I needed a dancer," Marshall recalled. "So I went to see her." They didn't have much time, because Madonna was on her way to Cannes. "So she stopped in New York, and we went to St. John's [University], where the coaches tried her out and they said, 'Trainable,' and I said, 'You're in.'"[60]

One of Marshall's other hires was twenty-nine-year-old Rosie O'Donnell. Born on Long Island, she was the eldest daughter in a family of five who lost her mother (whose name she bore) to cancer just days before Rosie's eleventh birthday. Like Tony Ciccone, Rosie's father didn't speak of his late wife, and like Madonna, Rosie became the family's little mother. The parallels in her early life and Madonna's were remarkable, down to Rosie's statement, "My whole life revolves around my mother's death. It changed who I was as a person."[61]

Eschewing college for comedy, at twenty Rosie began working the club circuit and moved quickly to television. In 1986, she had a role on an NBC sitcom, and two years later, she had her own stand-up comedy show on VH1.[62] When Penny Marshall began casting her baseball movie, Rosie wanted in. It would be her first film.

Rosie demonstrated her powerful arm during tryouts at the University of Southern California.[63] "I didn't know who [Rosie] was, but she was a great player," Marshall said. "She was multitalented."[64] Marshall added a story line to the script that teamed relatable Rosie with the larger-than-life Madonna, thinking they would balance each other out. "I said, 'You two have to become best friends.'"[65]

Rosie said she and Madonna "were sisters from the moment we met."[66]

Mo and Ro.[67] Before they met, however, Rosie was so terrified that she was nauseated. She had watched *Truth or Dare* and saw that Madonna had a sense of humor, so she announced by way of introducing herself, "I have a vibrator," to which Madonna responded, "Panasonic?" She also told Madonna that her mother had died when she was young, "and I totally understand what motivates you."[68] Said Madonna,

> Rosie and I speak the language of hurt people…My friendship with Rosie has nothing to do with image. I cannot explain the mystery of what happens when you become best friends with someone. I can only say that we are tortured by the same things, we laugh at the same things, and I love her madly.[69]

Marshall cast Oscar winner Geena Davis as the female lead. It would be her first movie since her work in the feminist groundbreaker *Thelma & Louise,* which premiered that May. After that film, Davis's criterion when taking a role was "What are the women in the audience going to say when they see this movie?" Speaking with journalists about *A League of Their Own,* she described it as another "feminist film," prompting one reporter to ask, "Can we *write* that?" Davis recalled, "It was so insane how shame-filled [that word] was then."[70]

Unlike *Thelma & Louise,* with its blatant rejection of the status quo, *A League of Their Own* was stealth feminism. That made it almost more powerful, because nothing in it would alienate the timid audiences that desperately needed to hear and see a life-affirming tale of women's empowerment. For the women watching Marshall's movie, life in the early '90s was very much like that of their sisters in the early 1950s—only with even less security.

In 1991, most working white women were still employed in low-wage clerical or retail jobs, and women of color were mostly confined to even lower-paying positions. Meanwhile, women with careers were being actively encouraged to ditch them and return home as a "new traditionalist," which *Good Housekeeping* magazine (with more than a little self-interest) called "the biggest social movement since the sixties."[71]

The difference between that fantasy of 1950s traditionalism and 1990s reality was that the men involved no longer shared the responsibility for a family's well-being. In the "good old days," the gold-standard marital contract involved a stay-at-home mom who managed the house and family and a working dad who paid the bills. But that changed in an unexpected way as a result of agitation by women's groups in the '70s to make divorce easier to obtain.

The idea had been to give women a pathway out of bad and abusive marriages. It did, but it also freed men from family obligations, even their traditional obligation of financial support, because judgments about alimony and child-support payments weren't enforced in those days. That meant that women were left with neither the time nor the money to raise a family. And yet they were told they "had it all."[72]

"Postfeminists," who subscribed to the neoliberal belief "If I'm okay, you're okay, and if you're not, it's not my problem," said that women should stop playing the victim and stop their "harping" about oppression and inequality because there was none.[73] This when just over 16 percent of all households in America were headed by a single woman, yet those households comprised nearly half of all American families living at or below the poverty line.[74]

A film such as *A League of Their Own*—if women had the time and means to see it—could be both antidote and inspiration. It showed average women making choices, taking chances, and succeeding. And, best of all, the story was true.

The film is about the formation of the all-girl league, but the narrative focuses on the competition between two sisters, played by Geena Davis and Lori Petty, and the drunken coach, played by Tom Hanks, who is assigned the task of making the Rockford Peaches into a professional ball club. In the film, he is not the team's savior but rather an impediment to their success. It is the women who help and challenge each other.

Each of the players has a backstory. Madonna's Mae is a New York dance-hall performer. Rosie O'Donnell plays her soon-to-be best friend, Doris Murphy. There is a former beauty queen, an Italian homemaker, and any number of other atypical baseball stars who at first share little beyond a need to do *something* and a desire to win.

The training for the roles was intense: three months, six days a week, four hours a day with a University of Southern California baseball coach.[75] (*Sports Illustrated* would later "compliment" the cast by saying "nobody in *A League of Their Own* throws like a girl.")[76] Once shooting began, the physical demands of the job were great. The women did their own stunts, from Davis's splits while making a crucial catch to Madonna's headfirst slide into home plate.[77] And then there was the temperature in Evansville, Indiana, where the film was shot. With some exaggeration, Rosie estimated it to be "106 degrees, 120 in the field."[78]

With the stands at times filled with five thousand sweltering extras, Rosie took it upon herself to entertain them, doing thirty-minute stand-up routines, some of which involved poking fun at Madonna. Once, when Madonna was bitching about the heat, Rosie turned a hose on her. At other times, Rosie sang her own rendition of "Like a Prayer."[79] She was embraced by the community. Madonna was not. Locals said she wasn't friendly, though in that conservative environment they were undoubtedly predisposed to dislike her. A local pastor had published a letter in the *Evansville Courier* asking Madonna, as what he called the world's most famous sinner, to visit his church.[80]

Stranded together in ruby-red Indiana, where billboards along country roads featured religious scripture and outsiders were treated with polite but deep suspicion, the cast members entertained one another. "There was one gay bar that, uh, became a hangout," Hanks said. "Madonna found it."[81] Rosie said Madonna celebrated her thirty-third birthday at the bar.

> There was a guy doing Madonna, doing "Vogue." And she went up there with a roll of twenties and started handing him money. [The performer] started taking the money and thinking, "Who's this little dark-haired woman giving me money?" And then it clicked that it was Madonna. [The dancer] started to cry.[82]

It was in Indiana that Rosie told Madonna her secret. Rosie was dating a "lovely" man named Michael, but she knew she wasn't interested in men.

> So here I was VG, very gay, dating a man and I went to Madonna for advice...I was questioning and unsure. My gay life was blossoming, but I didn't quite know what to do when she told me, "Rosie, just follow your heart"...I was so inspired that this one tiny, incredibly muscular, Italian girl with the eyebrows could be such a powerful advocate for women, for the LGBTQ community, and most of all, for herself.[83]

To entertain that self away from her film family, Madonna had the company of a new boyfriend: twenty-two-year-old white rapper Robert Van Winkle, a.k.a. Vanilla Ice. The year before, his song "Ice Ice Baby" became the first rap single to top the pop chart.[84] Though their relationship wasn't long-lived, like her brief affair with Tony Ward it would be immortalized in art. Vanilla Ice would be among those featured in the erotic fantasy book that Madonna had begun planning in earnest during breaks in filming. She did so as a new character, a woman she called Dita.

Dita Parlo was an early twentieth-century German actress and anarchist who had starred in Jean Renoir's 1937 film, *La Grande Illusion,* and in Jean Vigo's 1934 film, *L'Atalante.* She would be Madonna's next and by far most controversial persona, one she would inhabit off and on for the next several years as her life took her far from the conservatism of Indiana, the closeted dread of Hollywood, and the art-as-commodity atmosphere in New York. Madonna—Dita—was headed to Miami.[85]

PART FOUR

MIAMI

1992–1999

Chapter 33

Washington, Olympia, New York, Miami, 1992

You paint a naked woman because you enjoyed looking at her,
you put a mirror in her hand and you called the painting *Vanity*,
thus morally condemning the woman whose nakedness you had
depicted for your own pleasure.[1]

—*John Berger*

IT IS IMPORTANT to understand the broad social context in which Madonna
embarked on her next artistic adventure in order to understand its outsize
impact. Though arguably her most personal work—not in its revelations
so much as in the fact that she did it entirely for herself—Madonna's *Sex*
book would become a cultural inflection point. She dropped it, so to
speak, at a time of massive change—when the facade of civility that characterized American democratic society had begun to crack and crumple,
when relations between men and women were strained at times to the violent breaking point, and when the right launched a multifront battle "for
the soul of America" in "defense of the family" during the run-up to the
1992 presidential election.[2]

Madonna's *Sex* book would land like a bomb in the middle of that social
upheaval, delighting and enlightening people who were inclined toward
liberation and mortally offending and frightening untold others. The latter
group far outnumbered the former, and it wasn't just the religious right or
conservatives who were offended. Women, men, gays, lesbians, Blacks,
and whites expressed alarm and confusion. *What is she doing? Why is she
doing it? Does she mean what she is saying?* Or worse, *Does she* know *what she is
saying?* For the first time, Madonna would emerge damaged after being at
the center of a controversy. She had finally gone too far, pushed too hard,
challenged too much. Though normally preternaturally attuned to the
times, she apparently failed to recognize the delicacy of the moment.

Maybe it was the approaching millennium, which loomed for some as a
terrifying milestone. Or maybe people were unnerved by new technology
as computers foretold a future of cognition faster than the human brain
and information more plentiful than society's ability to absorb it. Or

maybe it was that people, amid another recession and subsequent job losses, had finally awakened to the realization that the trickle-down theory, in which rising markets floated all boats, was a fiction, and they'd had enough.

The vast majority of people accepted what came their way, as they always had. But in the early '90s, rumblings of discontent arose from a vocal minority and manifested themselves in new and organized ways.

The decade saw the mobilization of angry white men who believed that their power was threatened by women and minorities. After the Reagan administration repealed the 1949 fairness doctrine, which had required political balance in broadcasting, that anger was stoked by a new kind of evangelist, the radio talk show host, who flooded the airwaves with a gospel of misogyny, racism, and homophobia. Rush Limbaugh was the grand wizard of that set. Twenty million people listened to his diatribes against "feminazis," racial and ethnic minorities, and gays.[3]

Aligned with those vitriolic radio personalities were religious conservatives, who, in 1991, migrated to satellite television. Three years before Fox News, Paul Weyrich, the "Robespierre of the right" who coined the term "moral majority," launched National Empowerment Television. NET, as it was known, broadcast alarming tales of liberals destroying the Christian way of life to millions of subscribers twenty-four hours a day.[4]

Some men, inspired by such talk or simply in thrall to their own demons, expressed their anger randomly and violently, while others formed militias to prepare for a "white man's" war.[5] But women were angry, too. In late 1991, one high-profile example after another showed just how far women had *not* come, despite postfeminist claims and society's reassurances to the contrary.[6]

In October of that year, a Yale-educated attorney named Anita Hill sat before the Senate Judiciary Committee to describe in excruciating detail four years of alleged sexual harassment by her former boss Clarence Thomas.[7] Even more sobering than her words was the image of a lone and dignified Black woman testifying before a panel of white men who accused her of lying, of being a "scorned woman" inspired by the movie *The Exorcist*. Hill took a lie detector test and passed. Thomas refused to take one. Her words were ignored. He was confirmed to the Supreme Court.[8]

Just as Hill's testimony ended, a sex scandal involving the US military exploded. Eighty-three women were assaulted during the annual Tailhook convention of navy aviators in Las Vegas, among them twenty-six female officers who were mauled and stripped as they were forced through a gauntlet of two hundred navy men and Marines in a hotel corridor.[9]

The navy had long tolerated the gauntlet, and that year's would have likely been ignored, too, if Lieutenant Paula Coughlin had not complained to her superiors and if a San Diego reporter hadn't learned of her ordeal. He also obtained a copy of a letter discussing it among navy brass. The story, and the attempted cover-up, became national news.[10]

And then in December, there was a fresh reason for outrage. The nephew of Senate Judiciary Committee member Edward Kennedy stood trial for rape. It was a sensational story that broke the previous spring, when William Kennedy Smith was accused of raping a twenty-nine-year-old single mother he had met at a bar and invited back to the Kennedy compound in Palm Beach, Florida. The accuser, like Anita Hill, was portrayed as loose, possibly crazy—in short, a slut trying to bring down a good man.

Many people bought that argument. A much-heralded article in the *New York Times* written by a twenty-three-year-old woman and published in the lead-up to the trial argued that the concept of date rape was a "neo-puritan" feminist "preoccupation," a "fiction," a "cliché" that "infantilizes women."[11] People who were eager to maintain male privilege over a woman's body and people eager to maintain the illusion that women had the same rights as men embraced her argument, the jury among them.[12] Smith was acquitted.

That shameful trifecta was just the start of a decade of scandal. Women were under assault, no matter their class, age, race, level of education, occupation, or marital status. The government didn't protect them. The courts didn't protect them. The police and social services didn't protect them. Families could not protect them. It became clear in the '90s that women had to protect themselves. As a result, three things happened.

First, a new political class arose, as a historic number of women won seats in Congress and as the new Clinton administration filled its ranks with women, including Janet Reno, the first female attorney general, and Ruth Bader Ginsburg, the second woman to serve on the Supreme Court.[13]

Second, a younger generation of women outspokenly defended their rights. In 1991, two books appeared that became bestsellers: Naomi Wolf's *The Beauty Myth* and Susan Faludi's *Backlash*. Together they undermined the Panglossian postfeminist argument that women lived in the best of all possible worlds. And then, in early 1992, two activists, Rebecca Walker and Shannon Liss, heralded a new feminist movement, the third wave.[14]

Unlike postfeminism or even second wave feminism, the third wave was an inclusive feminism that championed all sexual identities, classes, and races around the globe.[15] Third wavers also emphasized that a woman's body and a woman's sexuality are central to a woman's humanity.[16]

With that influx of energy, feminism was revived after lying dormant for much of the 1980s. In April of 1992, the National Organization for Women organized a pro-choice march on Washington because reproductive rights were under renewed assault. Hundreds of thousands of women responded to NOW's call. It was, at the time, the largest protest ever held in the capital.[17]

Not long after, a new brand of *cultural* feminism also appeared, and it would be the third feminist development. The first National Riot Grrrl Convention was held in DC, and while it only attracted two hundred people, it represented a revolutionary step in the way women created and performed music, expressed themselves, and interacted with one another.[18]

The riot grrrls, like the third wavers, arose in 1991 out of anger. The catalyst was a date-rape list of predator males posted in a bathroom at Evergreen State College, in Olympia, Washington.[19] The movement grew from a few girls talking to one another to a larger group communicating by mail to girls strapping on guitars and expressing themselves through music.[20] Their look and their lyrics were in-your-face—sexual, tough, ironically girly. And they used their bodies as billboards. Bikini Kill's Kathleen Hanna scrawled SLUT across her stomach to own the word used against women.[21]

After the DC convention, in July of 1992, grrrl power went global.[22] The message: "The revolution starts inside you...You don't have to take shit from anyone—be who you want, say what you want...Every girl is a Riot Grrrl."[23]

The third wavers and the riot grrrls were born after the mid-'60s. They had grown up in the world that Madonna created. Many of them had been in her audiences, seen her videos, bought her records, and absorbed her lessons.[24] Even if they objected to her or were suspicious of her because she was commercially successful, they had heard her, watched her, and grown up knowing that being a girl, being in a band, and being a pop star didn't preclude one from being political, even radically so. Young women and grrrls had voices and used them.

They became part of the vociferous chatter in the early '90s occurring across the political, social, religious, and gender divides. Though the concerns expressed were many, the underlying theme that bound the people expressing them (except for gay male activists) was women and sex—specifically, who controlled them and it.

Enter Madonna and her book. She would raise the temperature—as she always did—by challenging women on all sides of the feminist debate, by testing gays and lesbians who might question her motives, and by demonstrating to men of the left and right that a woman's sexuality is hers to express as she sees fit, not as they expect or demand. And she would use herself to illustrate what that kind of woman looks like. It is safe to say that in doing so she made the situation a whole lot messier and her own life a lot more difficult.

In the fall of 1991, Madonna was back in New York for "meeting after meeting" with Steven Meisel to discuss their book: its look, locations for shoots, people they wanted to work with. Mostly, though, Meisel needed to know what Madonna considered erotic.[25] It was not a simple question to answer. If they intended to mine the depths of what excited her, they needed to explore her subconscious. Because unlike sex, eroticism is more about feelings than about actions, and as such, it requires discovery. That effort would make her book art. It would be a story of Madonna's journey, one she hoped would help others embark on their own.

By the time Meisel agreed to the project, he had a reputation as one of the world's most provocative photographers. That summer the New York City Police Department had dispatched officers into the subway system to destroy safe-sex posters he shot that showed men in erotic poses.[26] He was also one of the world's most respected photographers, among the few regularly referred to as a genius.[27] And he had become known as one of the world's most difficult. A Condé Nast editor called him "self-destructive." A *Vogue* editor put it more gently: "He was ahead of his time, and that scared people."[28]

He did not frighten the beloved and legendary editor Franca Sozzani at the Italian magazine *Lei,* however. She adored Meisel *and* his work. When she moved to *Vogue Italia,* in 1988, to become editor in chief, she assigned him every cover—for the next twenty years.[29]

Meisel's sensibilities were the opposite of those of the light-infused Herb Ritts, who also worked for Sozzani. A former art director at *Vogue Italia* said of Meisel, "There's a sense of death in his pictures, the drive to recreate something that time forgot."[30] That darkness spoke to Madonna during the early '90s, after her sunny California period ended in divorce and amid the tragedy of AIDS. He was able to capture her innate sadness, even when she was smiling.

A quality Meisel did share with Herb, however—perhaps a quality all great photographers share—is that he made the people he photographed feel safe, comfortable, and part of a collaboration. The level of trust that Madonna required to make any art—a song, a video, a movie—was present in Meisel's whitewashed Park Avenue studio.[31]

He was the perfect partner for Madonna as she explored her fantasy life. For his part, he was ready for a project like *Sex.* In late 1990, he said,

I'm not having as much fun as I would like to or that I used to. I'm sort of in a transitional period in my life because I don't go out and do drugs and fuck all night long anymore, yet I'm not quite ready for dinner parties.[32]

To art-direct the book, Madonna and Meisel turned to Franca Sozzani's former art director at *Vogue Italia,* Fabien Baron.[33] In 1990, he had opened a New York design studio, where he created iconic ad campaigns, including an infamous heroin-chic spread for the perfume CK One. He would also help relaunch *Interview* magazine and, in 1992, redesign *Harper's Bazaar.*[34] When Meisel asked him if he wanted in on the Madonna book, he said yes. He loved Meisel's work, and he, too, trafficked in provocation.[35]

To edit the book, Madonna chose her old friend from the Warhol-Basquiat days, Glenn O'Brien. He had helped define the '70s and '80s New York downtown scene.[36] As editor of *Interview* during three crucial periods, he set the tone: "cool, streetwise, mischievous."[37] In the early '90s, his hip credentials remained impeccable. He was also a workaholic, though perhaps "the world's most louche," according to novelist Jonathan Lethem.[38]

In the spring of 1990, O'Brien had reconnected with Madonna on a cover story for *Interview.* The ease and depth of the piece reflected his deft questioning and her pleasure in their encounter. The next year, she asked him to be the editor of her book. They spent around a week together, then communicated by fax, which he described as sending Madonna "assignments" to "clarify her feelings."[39]

Hiring these three men meant that for Madonna's first book project, she would work with one of the best and most avant-garde photographers in the world, one of the edgiest art directors in the business, and a writer who had helped create and define art and culture in New York. *Interview* editor at large Christopher Bollen said, "Glenn had a trait known to geniuses: the confidence to assume that whatever he spent his time working on was the best and baddest thing going down."[40] Madonna's book at that moment was it.

Warner Bros. rarely established ground rules for Madonna's projects, but during those days of the religious right's steaming-hot culture war, companies did their best not to wander onto the battlefield, and so Warner, perhaps considering her the more accommodating adversary, took a chance and issued directives. Madonna could not show sex with children or animals or the desecration of religious objects. "None of those things happen to be my sexual fantasies so that wasn't a problem for me," she said. "I didn't have to censor anything."[41]

Madonna then sent out a casting call for people to "act" in her photo drama. The requirements for the job were that they had to be willing to be naked and kiss her. "Most of the people in the book were friends of mine or Steven's," Madonna said.[42] He called on, among others, Isabella Rossellini, whom he had shot for a cover of *Vogue Italia,* and Naomi Campbell, because she wasn't afraid of the content of his work.

Madonna summoned "Justify My Love" alumni Tony Ward and Wallis Franken, and forty-seven-year-old German actor Udo Kier, who had worked with avant-garde directors she admired. "I was in New York and my agent said, 'There's something secret going on,'" Kier recalled. "'Steven Meisel, the photographer, wants to see you, he is doing a book—it has something to do with Madonna.'

> Then I went there...There was a woman sitting there with no make-up. Madonna. I didn't recognize her right away. She said, "I liked you in *My Own Private Idaho.*" And then we started talking a little bit. I understood very quickly what she wanted—she wanted me to play her decadent husband...I came back to Los Angeles and her manager called and said: "Are you ready for hardcore sex?"[43]

Others gathered in New York for the shoot in late 1991 included gay porn star Joey Stefano and twenty-year-old NYU graduate psychology student Tatiana von Fürstenberg, daughter of fashion designer Diane von Fürstenberg. Once the cast and crew were assembled, Madonna, Meisel, and their friends began to play, taking photos first in New York at the Vault fetish club, the Gaiety gay burlesque theater, the Chelsea hotel, and Meisel's studio.[44]

Sex would be another example of Madonna's gathering ideas from society's outliers—in this case, "erotic minorities"—and taking them mainstream.[45] For the book, she invited readers to examine more closely areas she had already covered—gay sex, hetero sex, group sex, masturbation—and open their minds to new areas, especially lesbianism and the mysteries of sadomasochism, both of which were deeply misunderstood.

The image of the lesbian as masculine, unattractive, and humorless was as common as the image of the gay man as a pansy and just as destructive. That lesbian cliché had been used to frighten heterosexual women away from second wave feminism. The campaign was so effective that it speeded the second wave's demise.[46]

By the early '90s, the social climate had changed—especially on the coasts. Young feminists considered themselves "pro-sex," and that meant "claiming feelings they had been historically told they did not or should not have."[47] In that climate, the "lipstick lesbian" was born, and a thriving club scene along with her. "We've moved from an era defined by Artemis—who was sort of the Birkenstock goddess, if you will...and into the era of Aphrodite," said Kay Turner, a folklorist and, at the time, a fellow at the Wilson Center. "The discourse now is about being touched, and it's catalyzed by the presence of Madonna in our culture. Although she's not technically a lesbian, she's the figure lesbians gravitate toward."[48]

The women in clubs like the Girl Bar, in Hollywood, or the Clit Club, in New York, embraced sexual and social exploration. For every fashion-model type in dress and heels on the dance floor, there was also an androgyne in motorcycle gear. For every woman seeking candlelit romance, there was a woman in leather seeking a bondage encounter. The point was that the looks and desires of lesbians were as multitudinous as those of their hetero sisters. But that complexity wasn't recognized outside a small circle of enlightened women.

"For mainstream society, there have traditionally been only two images: man-hating bulldykes and titillating porn, made by and for straight men," Urvashi Vaid, executive director of the National Gay and Lesbian Task Force, said that year.

> The curious thing about both of those images is that here we are, women who love other women, and to the rest of the world, all they see is the lack of a man. They have to insert the man, as someone that we supposedly really need, or even as someone we supposedly hate, because it's indifference to men that drives them mad...In a society obsessed with men's relationships, lesbians are like people speaking a foreign tongue.[49]

Madonna offered herself as translator, using her body and her imagination to introduce readers to the many facets of lesbianism and lesbian love. S/M was one of them, and its practitioners—female and male—were even more misunderstood.[50] People outside that world saw it as a sick power dynamic between those who cruelly administered pain and those who weakly submitted to it. Among practitioners, it was about consent, trust, and exploring boundaries.[51]

In the post-Stonewall era, S/M in the gay community involved sexual exploration as well as self-discovery. "S/M play is about healing the wounds that keep us from fully living; its intensity cauterizes our hurt and mends our shame," wrote Mark Thompson in his 1991 book, *Leatherfolk*.[52] In the late '80s, people who practiced that kind of S/M called it "sex magic." Thompson said they saw it as a "shamanic journey into the 'other world'...It is in that secret inner place where the healing occurs."[53]

While the broad heterosexual society reacted to S/M with confusion, if not revulsion, a "leather lifestyle" had emerged in the clubs, and for some it was political.[54] S/M lesbians especially saw themselves as central to the fight against sexual repression. Wrote Wickie Stamps in *OutWeek* in 1991, "It is the S/M lesbians—female, queer and on the sexual fringes—who constantly remind us that what we are engaged in is a 'sexual' revolution."[55]

The photographs shot in late 1991 by Meisel and Madonna in New York explored those arenas: Madonna being dominated and made love to by butch women; Madonna S/M role-playing in a fetish club; Madonna having ambiguous sex with women who looked like boys and more ambiguous sex with boys who looked like women; Madonna as a schoolgirl being raped by two men in a gym.

Of all the images in the book, that would be the one that she was forced to explain most often, which she did by saying it was a rape *fantasy,* one that women, for many complicated reasons, undeniably have. The difference between Madonna's fantasy and actual rape is that she was laughing. "I'm playing the coquette, the virgin or whatever, and they are the bad boys. They take me but only because I give them the opportunity to," she said.[56] Besides, Madonna explained, nothing in the book was off-limits.

> I don't think a painter goes, "How far am I going to go with this?" I think you have a feeling, an idea, an expression of something and you see where it takes you. I don't think about boundaries, I only think about my original inspiration and where I want to go. My boundary is that I'm honest, that it feels real. If it ceases to be what I believe in, then I know that I've overstepped the boundary.[57]

In the preface, Madonna delivers two messages. "Everything you are about to see and read is a fantasy, a dream, pretend...Nothing in this book is true. I made it all up." She also delivers a safe-sex message, saying that because the book is fantasy, it takes place "in a perfect world, a place without AIDS." In the real world, she says, wear condoms.[58]

Those are the last words written by "Madonna." The rest of the book is written by the various characters she inhabits in her photos. The text appears as poems, random thoughts, and page-long "insights" that one might be tempted to call Madonna's philosophy of sex, except that she wrote them in jest.[59] There is also a series of letters from Dita to "Johnny" about a mutual lover named Ingrid.[60]

On December 31, 1991, Madonna threw a bacchanalian New Year's Eve bash at her New York apartment during which she was topless except for two leather straps, befitting the erotic explorations in her book.[61] Sandra

Bernhard was there with her twenty-seven-year-old girlfriend, a lithe and boyish Cuban American from Miami named Ingrid Casares. She and Sandra had begun dating that June. "But the moment Ingrid meets Madonna, as far as Ingrid is concerned, Sandra is history," Christopher said.[62]

Ingrid was from one of the most prominent Cuban families in Miami. Her Havana-born father, Raul Casares, had cofounded a window company in the late 1970s.[63] The timing could not have been better. By the early '80s, Miami was the transit point for one-third of all illegal drugs sold in the United States. It was also the nation's money-laundering capital, with billions of dollars in narco money pouring into Miami banks. A prime destination for all that dirty cash was property, and a city of skyscrapers—monuments to the coke trade—arose in South Florida.[64] Like many of the other legitimate businesses in Miami, Raul Casares's company expanded as the city did. In 1990, he founded his own firm, which became one of the nation's largest window companies.[65]

Ingrid was the second of three daughters. As a teenager, she began using cocaine and would continue to, as she said, party hard for around fifteen years, into the mid-'90s. Supported by her extremely wealthy father, she studied English and public relations at the University of Maryland and wandered through various jobs before moving to Los Angeles, where she worked as a booker at the Wilhelmina modeling agency. In Miami, she had been a "minor celebrity," according to Tom Austin, who covered the city's nightlife for the alternative newspaper *Miami New Times*. "She was just a girl around town."[66] In LA, through Sandra Bernhard, she joined the city's lesbian chic set.[67]

Writer Jonathan Van Meter described Ingrid as occupying "an odd and singular place in America's celebrity culture: Best Friend to Very Famous Sexually Ambiguous Women." She described herself as an "excitement junkie. The adrenaline. I need it 24/7." She was also, according to an ex, k.d. lang, a self-declared "star fucker." "To me that's more respectful than someone who denies it," lang said. And Ingrid was loyal, discreet, and "trustworthy on a very deep level to people who have lost trust, people in the public eye," lang explained.[68]

Madonna said that when she met Ingrid, "I thought she was the sweetest girl. Sandra was on the verge of breaking up with her, and I felt sorry for Ingrid. She likes to work out the way I do, so I started to ring her up and we'd go for a run or whatever...The way it came out in the press made it sound like I was trying to steal [Sandra's] girlfriend." It must have seemed that way to Bernhard, too, because Ingrid's arrival in Madonna's life signaled Sandra's exit.[69] In an interview in 1994 with Sheryl Garratt for *The Face,* Madonna said, "I've never had a sexual relationship with Ingrid, that's the irony. But she is a very good friend, and I've grown to love her.

So it's a tragedy what happened with me and Sandra, but I got a good friend out of it. You win some, you lose some."[70]

At that point, Christopher was Madonna's most constant companion. Ingrid would be the other. In fact, she and Madonna would become inseparable.

While Madonna was scouting additional locations for *Sex* in January of 1992, her search brought her to Ingrid's home turf, Miami. Madonna fell in love with a house on Brickell Avenue. "I knew I just had to have it," she said.[71] The price was just under $5 million and, once again, Christopher was asked to renovate. His job involved restoring the 1930s Spanish-style home to its original look. Madonna, meanwhile, had her white Mercedes convertible with red leather interior shipped from LA. And, to get around on the water, she bought a small speedboat that she called *Lola, Lola* and docked it at her house.[72]

Madonna's LA place was her work residence. Miami was for playtime, Christopher said. "Everyone was just having a good time, recharging. It was before it became super, super touristy, and you could walk around anywhere, and no one would really bother you." Compared to their move from New York to Los Angeles in the early '80s, Christopher said, "the transition from LA to Miami was so much easier."[73] With Latin music in the streets, cabaretlike clubs crowded with people of every race, origin, and sexual predilection, and fashion worn as artistic expression rather than as a sign of wealth, the city felt like home.

Miami, especially Miami Beach, but most particularly South Beach, was a place apart. If the rest of the nation was in a lather about sex and scandal, Miami Beach happily bathed in it. "Sex," said writer Steven Gaines, "is the city's favorite pastime. In South Beach, two is never enough." It was a place without judgment. No permissions were needed, because everything was allowed.[74]

When word spread that a tropical Shangri-la existed three hours by plane from Manhattan, gay men fleeing the darkness of AIDS cashed in their insurance policies, gathered up their savings, and pumped themselves full of steroids to live life to the fullest while they still could. Beginning in the '80s, Miami Beach became the main destination for gay men with AIDS, and a culture grew up around them.[75]

Artists found their way south, too. Sensing that the New York that had nurtured them had turned into a relative creative wasteland, they fled to the deco district in South Beach. Artists of all kinds interacted with one another and the colorful locals for daily doses of inspiration. "It's an end-of-the-world place," said author and artist Brian Antoni, who bought a house in South Beach. "If you can rent a space for three dollars a square foot, you can make your dreams come true."[76]

That world—created by elderly Jewish residents, artists, gays, straights, and trans people—was warm and generous, partly because life felt so fleeting. The neighborhood that was sometimes called "God's waiting room," because of the high number of aged and ill residents, gave birth to a new culture, a South Beach culture. They all shopped at the same thrift stores and developed an eccentric style that would eventually be appropriated by fashion designers.[77]

That part of the South Beach story began in the mid-80s with a Bruce Weber photograph of nude models taken for a Calvin Klein Obsession fragrance ad. Weber used the roof of the Breakwater hotel on Ocean Drive as a backdrop, positioning the models like sculptures in winter light so bright it was almost North African. "That picture captured the imagination of the industry here in the States," said Louis Canales, a renowned New York stylist. Photographers searching for that same clarity descended upon the island. Photo labs, stylists, assistants, and models soon followed.[78]

"What was amazing was that within one square mile, you had twenty-five hundred models living, working, and going out and partying through the entire winter season," said Canales. "The energy was palpable."[79]

Recalled Brian Antoni,

Everything was cooking…It became like Studio 54, the whole island. Everything became a party. Now everyone wants money, [but] back then everyone was just so excited about turning the beach into something special. Everyone felt part of it. You knew everyone, and everyone supported everyone. There was a pride in it.[80]

Art deco hotels were refurbished to house the flood of newcomers, and restaurants appeared to feed them. But most crucially, the club scene exploded. Some of them, like the gay cabaret and dance club Warsaw Ballroom, were so risqué that they would have been unthinkable elsewhere.

Louis Canales was the creative genius behind what was less a club than a bacchanalian circus. He had built platforms in the Warsaw so "all these very creative people could express themselves." Among them were the '70s porn star Kitten Natividad, who could, according to Canales, fold towels with her breasts. Another was Lady Hennessey Brown: she pretended to pull twenty feet of scarves from her vagina. Dancing girls and muscled men—some wearing costumes—snaked around the dance floor, distributing condoms and drink tickets.[81]

"I've been to every club in the world," said Brian Antoni. "The Warsaw is the best club I think I've ever been to in my life.

I remember one night leaving and being really tired and leaning against the wall on the outside. It was like the whole wall was pulsing and sort of sweating. I felt like I was leaning against a living organism, like a living heart...If you could capture all the dreams, all the sadness, all the happiness, people dancing the last dance, it was all encapsulated in that place...Why is the party good? You never know, but whatever the recipe was, it was there.[82]

The year that Madonna discovered Miami Beach, forty-five-year-old fashion designer Gianni Versace discovered it, too. "Last time I visited here was five years ago," he told Tom Austin in January of 1992. "Everything has changed so much. At this moment, Miami to me is heaven. I want to stay forever."[83]

While other multimillionaires protected themselves in communities of their confreres, Versace chose to live in the midst of the South Beach tumult and the street culture, which was his inspiration. He found a derelict 1930s mansion at 11th Street and Ocean Drive. It was the only private residence on that stretch of cafés, restaurants, and bars.[84]

The Casa Casuarina cost $8 million, but the home he envisioned— filled with marble and mosaics—would require $30 million in renovations and a year to complete. In the meantime, the transvestites ejected from the residence by its new owner held a "fuck Versace" party. It was also a farewell party of sorts, because it signaled the end of one era in Miami Beach and the start of a star-studded new one.[85]

"Before Madonna and Versace, it was just local; it wasn't serious," said Antoni. "It was just people. It may have been serious, but we weren't taken seriously by the world." With their arrival, everything changed. "Madonna was the straight priestess, and Versace was the gay priest. They arrived at the same time, so it was the coming together of the king and queen. What more could we ask for? They were the holy two."[86]

The air in Miami reminded Versace of home. He was born in Reggio Calabria—another end-of-the-world place—at the toe of Italy's boot. He learned his love of fashion from his mother, who was Reggio's best dressmaker. In his twenties, Versace took the family tradition north to Milan to try to break into the fashion business. It was an audacious move, because as a southern Italian he would have been considered unsophisticated, and as a Calabrian, he would have been suspected of having Mafia ties. Neither was true. He was cultured and elegant, and thirty years of investigations never produced a link between Versace and the Mafia. But those prejudices made his job much more difficult in an extremely competitive culture.[87]

Versace was part of a new generation of Italian fashion designers challenging the dominance of Paris. The Italian look was simpler, leaner, more sensual than the French, and in the '70s it was epitomized by Giorgio Armani's designs. Versace mastered that style, working with various designers in Milan, and then he went a step further. Like Gaultier, who was on a nearly parallel creative path in Paris, Versace drew inspiration from pop culture. His look was hip, young, reflective of the social changes and the political turmoil in Italy at that time. By 1975, *Vogue Paris* called his designs Italy's cutting edge.[88]

Within three years, Versace was ready to break out on his own and called his siblings to Milan to join him. His twenty-three-year-old sister, Donatella, gave up language studies at the University of Florence to help him with his runway shows and accessories. His older brother, Santo, brought his accounting skills to the Versace family enterprise as financial adviser.[89]

Versace's first runway show, in 1979, was criticized as "gimmicky," but his clothes appeared in magazines and attracted attention. In 1982, Versace stores began opening in Sydney, Paris, LA, and New York.[90] By 1986, the company was selling $220 million of clothes and products a year. In 1987, it began operating out of a Rizzoli family mansion that the company purchased in Milan. The young man from Calabria had become Milanese fashion royalty. But that ascent had come at a cost.[91]

When Versace appeared in Miami in late 1991 to open his latest boutique, he had been pushing himself for more than fifteen years and was exhausted. Miami Beach revived him—the warmth, the beautiful people, the music, the freedom. If Milan meant business; Paris, style; New York, status—then Miami Beach meant sex. For Versace, South Beach would be both release valve and inspiration, as it was for Madonna.

Those two, Versace and Madonna, would supercharge the South Beach scene. The Versaces and the Ciccones—Donatella and Gianni and Madonna and Christopher—would have a working relationship, and then they would become like family.

Chapter 34

Miami, Portland, New York, 1992

I'd rather walk through a fire than walk away from one.[1]

—*Madonna*

WHATEVER MADONNA AND Steven Meisel had originally envisioned for their *Sex* book changed under the new influences in Miami. The bondage-and-S/M direction was reinforced. "It was a big thing in South Beach, because when you're sick like that [with AIDS], you look for fetishes," Brian Antoni explained. "Pain makes you forget. Pain makes you feel."[2] And the mood of the book was transformed entirely. In Miami, the photographs became sun-drenched and unselfconscious. It was sex as play, sex as adventure, sex as a lark. It was South Beach sex. "The whole thing was like performance art," Madonna said.[3]

> We were out of New York, away from the usual environment... For the first time [Steven Meisel and I] were both kind of free of the constraints of lighting and all. We basically just ran around in cars. When we would find a place we liked, a pizza parlor or a burlesque club, we'd just run out.[4]
>
> I felt like a little girl. It was a rush... The idea of taking off your clothes and running through the streets naked is very liberating... I think everybody should run through the streets [naked] at least once... If you can do that, chances are you can have a lot of fun in other areas of your life.[5]
>
> I just had the best time, and I know Steven did, too. Free from everything. We could do what we wanted. Nobody was watching... Nobody knew that I was me.[6]

In Florida, Madonna the ferocious child abandoned Dita in favor of more frivolous personas: a '60s-era Angie Dickinson blonde hitchhiking in nothing but pumps and purse. A socialite stopping in for a slice of pizza, which she ate after dropping her fur to the floor to reveal her nude body. "Customers really didn't seem to mind I was naked," Madonna said, "but the woman who owned the pizza parlor turned on an alarm to summon the police, so we kind of got out of there pretty fast."[7]

On the beach, she became a naked Brigitte Bardot; curbside, she was topless in gold lamé shorts getting it on with her tattooed boyfriend, Vanilla Ice; or that same woman, sans shorts, in a garden threesome with Big Daddy Kane and Naomi Campbell. She also became a character in a beachside ménage à trois with Isabella Rossellini and Ingrid Casares.

The images themselves were familiar because they were the stuff of fashion photography. Decades earlier, photographers Guy Bourdin and Deborah Turbeville created similarly explicit shoots for advertising. But it was Helmut Newton, the father of "porn chic," who perhaps came closest to the Madonna Florida photographs. In a mid-'70s series for the magazine *Oui,* he shot, among other images, a seminude woman on US Route 1 in Florida and a nude woman at a drive-in joint in Palm Beach with a hamburger in her vagina.[8]

The photographs in *Sex* were also familiar because, by 1992, nudity, bondage, and sexual violence were favorite advertising industry gimmicks used to sell everything from fragrances to skin creams to blue jeans to cigarettes. Anyone anywhere of any age could see them by opening just about any magazine. Meisel's own shots for *Vogue Italia* included many of the ideas in Madonna's book.[9]

And yet despite the ubiquity of those kinds of images, Madonna's managed to shock. The fact that a woman of her stature would depict *herself* in erotic scenarios was unheard of. Music writer John Aizlewood said, "Nobody in Madonna's position has done anything so brave and as bonkers."[10] But that wasn't the book's most unsettling aspect. It was the changed point of view that made the photos so destabilizing. Madonna's *Sex* may have been the first major book of female sexual imagery ever published that was not created to titillate a heterosexual man.

Women in porn—and, arguably, advertising—were made to do everything except express their own desires. They were dolls or puppets, controlled by men to portray male fantasies, which were then sold as *the* fantasy. Woman was the focus, but she had no real part except to do as she was told. Feminist Catharine MacKinnon described that story line as "Man fucks woman; subject verb object." Madonna and Meisel's images made the woman the subject. It was her fantasy and her gaze for her arousal.[11]

Cultural historian Susan Bordo said,

> Madonna modeled the possibility of a female heterosexuality that was independent of patriarchal control, a sexuality that defied rather than rejected the male gaze, teasing it with her *own* gaze, deliberately trashy and vulgar, challenging anyone to call her a whore, and ultimately not giving a damn what judgments might be made of her.[12]

After they had taken the last photograph, Steven Meisel declared, "We've covered it. We've gone as far as we can in public...I don't think anyone else needs to do another photo essay on erotica—this is it. *Basta!*"[13] He had taken twenty thousand shots. Madonna spent a month examining them.[14]

Fabien Baron's job was to use those images to produce a book that maintained interest in one subject for 128 pages. "Same subject, same person, and each page she's nude!" he said. Like Madonna's concerts, the book was organized roughly around "acts"—bondage, pansexuality, sexual awakening and masturbation, and the Florida outdoor fantasies, with some gay men's erotica thrown in the middle of her sunny frolicking.

Madonna also challenged Baron to make the book something other than a book. She wanted it to be a physical metaphor for the contents, as well as a joke. The final idea was to produce it with a hard metal cover and soft cardboard pages.[15] It would be tactile, sensual, like a person, like Madonna: get past the tough exterior and find the "pink-moist-love," as Martin Burgoyne had called it. Even the book's heat-sealed Mylar bag would have significance. Baron said the book could be unwrapped like "a sex toy." Some said the wrapper was like a condom package. Nicholas Callaway, whose Callaway Editions produced *Sex,* said, "We wanted there to be an act of entering, of breaking and entering."[16]

Design decisions made, Callaway took over. His task: make 750,000 copies of the book in five colors and five languages with a comic-book insert. The metal covers were created from 750,000 pounds of aluminum—one pound for each book—and each cover was stamped and numbered. Callaway said that for the kind of book Madonna wanted, he would normally produce 250 limited-edition copies. She wanted hundreds of thousands in fifteen days.[17]

When Madonna was still in the Midwest working on *A League of Their Own,* Shep Pettibone visited and gave her a tape with a few tracks he had made. She liked them, so he wrote a few more. After their collaboration on "Vogue," he had worked with Madonna on her hugely successful greatest-hits album, *The Immaculate Collection,* but they hadn't done an album of original material together.[18] That changed when her film duties ended in October. She returned to New York to put words to Shep's music for her fifth studio album, *Erotica.*[19]

Madonna wanted to get as far away from LA and God's country, Indiana, as possible. Dita was looking for an edgy, raw sound—more "Justify My Love" than "Something to Remember." Musically, she wanted to go to Harlem, and not even to a dance club in Harlem but to an alley there.

She was so determined that at one point when Shep gave her what he thought was a great batch of songs, she said, "I hate them . . . If I had wanted the album to sound like that, I'd have worked with Patrick Leonard in LA." She told him to start over.[20]

The album would be Madonna's first entirely New York recording since *Like a Virgin*. Though she had been working on some of the lyrics for a year, most of the writing was done at Shep's Manhattan penthouse, where he had a home studio. She would arrive at two in the afternoon and stay until eight or nine.[21] "Madonna composed a lot of the lyrics lying on the floor on her stomach with her legs up, writing in her notebook," he said.[22]

At the start, Shep had to operate around Madonna's schedule. "I'd work with her for a week and then she'd go off to work with Steve Meisel on her book for two weeks," he said. The first songs they wrote were "Deeper and Deeper," "Erotica," "Rain," and "Thief of Hearts." Those songs, though, would change significantly over the following nine months, influenced by developments in Madonna's book, new sounds and experiences in Florida, and the artists she brought into the album project.[23]

Some were from what seemed like her distant past, and some were members of a new generation who could help her get the street sound she was after. "I'm not at all interested in working with people who are a part of the establishment, or who come set in their ways," she said that year. "I'm a pioneer. I want to dig up new ground, and I don't want to be safe — as an artist, that is the only thing that is going to make me happy."[24]

One of the people from her past who joined her on *Erotica* was bass player Doug Wimbish, whom Madonna had known since her early days at the clubs. He had played bass on Grandmaster Flash's "The Message" and was a member of the house band at Sugar Hill Records, the label that launched rap in 1979. By the time he was in the studio with Madonna on *Erotica,* he had worked around the world with major artists.[25]

Like Madonna, though, his roots were New York, and he and she related on that level. Wimbish said Madonna was essentially an "underground" artist and that was evident on her new album. "It was a very interesting community of cats that worked on this Madonna record."[26]

Andre "Dre" Betts was among the most interesting and most important to her album. "She knew Dre had something special," Wimbish said.[27] Betts, he added, was "just straight ghetto at times . . . He's really raw and honest."[28]

Betts came to Madonna's attention through Lenny Kravitz when they joined her in the studio on "Justify My Love." In 1992, she called him again to say she'd be in New York and asked whether he wanted to work. "I'm like, 'Yeah of course.'" She told him to find a "low-key" studio. He described the place he discovered on West 21st Street as "a hole in the wall for real"—with its own resident rats.[29] She arrived in a "fur coat all the way down to her ankles," and they got to work. It was during that session that Madonna and Betts wrote the song "Where Life Begins."

Having already acquainted fans with masturbation, she used her new song to introduce them to cunnilingus. At that time, among heterosexuals, if oral sex was mentioned at all, it was understood to be an act performed by a woman on a man. Madonna decided it was time for a little sex education.

In "Where Life Begins," she offers an alternately sweet and wickedly funny introduction to the practice. Betts recalled watching her write the song. "She's blushing and she's got this smile on her and she goes, 'Gosh!' and I'm looking at her like, 'What the hell are you writing?' "[30]

Betts wasn't shocked. He described his own music as having

a hypnotic/sexual sort of feel...My roots go way deep into hip-hop, but street hip-hop rather than the poppy side. That was the problem I was having with my music at the beginning—a lot of people didn't get it—but Madonna seemed really open to it.[31]

He would cowrite four tracks with Madonna, while Shep Pettibone and his assistant Tony Shimkin collaborated with her on the other ten.

Normally Madonna worked quickly, and if the first take was good, she went with it. Shep said the lead single, "Erotica," was an exception. It turned into "four different songs throughout the process."[32] The one that ultimately made it onto the album didn't appear until the mixing process at the end. "When we realized it was going to be the first single and started working on the remix, it took on a different, darker vibe," Shimkin said. "That's when the character emerged, this Dita, when she ad-libbed the speaking parts. Then the character became something that took over."[33]

"Erotica" introduces the album the way a master of ceremonies at a club in Weimar Germany would have prepared an audience for an evening of depravity. Madonna as Dita addresses the listeners, laying the ground rules and instructing them to shed their prejudices and inhibitions. She speaks the lyrics close to the microphone, she said, "so it sounds like I'm talking in your ear...And I use cheap microphones so it sounds dirty and raw."[34]

"Deeper and Deeper" places Madonna in the clubs of the late '70s, before AIDS decimated the dance floor. It is an updated version of the kind of Giorgio Moroder–Donna Summer disco number that got everyone moving their bodies together in the first place. It is nostalgic in that way. Joyous, too, in part because of a Latin section that breaks into the disco beat and in part because of the lyrics. When Madonna sings "But my love is alive / and I'm never gonna hide it again," gay dance floors explode, resolutions harden, closet doors dissolve.[35]

The overall tone of the album, however, represents a new kind of blue. It is *the* blues through a filter of pop and the electronic club music out of Chicago known as house. Music journalist Paul Mathur said of the album, "This sort of arresting sadness is Madonna's forte... There's no 'Live to Tell' here, but... 'Words,' 'Rain' and 'Waiting' just about compensate."[36]

"Rain" is the album's love song. Deceptively pure and simple, it describes the awakening of love and the patient longing for its return. Throughout the song, Madonna alternates voices: channeling the beautifully tragic Karen Carpenter while singing the verses, and in the chorus, she is early Madonna, her voice thin and yearning.[37] Both those voices feel ordinary in an AM radio kind of way, yet the song is sublime.

"Words" and "Rain" were written by Madonna and Shep Pettibone. From the start of "Waiting," it is clear that Madonna has switched partners and is working with Andre Betts. Unlike those other songs, "Waiting" features the voice of a mature, cynical woman. Betts's arrangement traverses the worlds of jazz, ska, R&B, and the blues. Madonna's vocals travel right along with it. It was a thrilling departure for her and an indication of where she would go musically well into the next decade.

By the time the crew working on the album had reached the midway point, Tony Shimkin said everyone was burned out. He and Shep took a break—Shep traveled to Jamaica, and Tony went to the Caymans. They returned with their heads filled with reggae. That was when they wrote "Why's It So Hard," which marries Madonna's most direct political and social message on the album to a Trench Town beat.[38] The lyrics themselves cover territory from Madonna's earlier song about family, "Keep It Together," but the family in question in the new song is bigger—humankind—and the message one of tolerance.

Madonna told British talk show host Jonathan Ross that year,

> When I write music...in my mind there's a little movie playing, and I always envision scenarios and characters, and of course it's not always something I've experienced but I always say it in the first person, so it seems like it's a personal thing...I always try to write songs so they can be read on lots of different levels. So you could appreciate them superficially, and if you go deeper, you see something else.[39]
>
> Behind everything I do, there's a tongue-in-cheek comment on myself or a more serious message on the social level.[40]

That was what Madonna did on "Bad Girl." On one level, the song could be about Madonna's failed relationships, or it could reflect the cautionary tale that society tells in books, film, and television about the "bad" single woman who drowns her sorrows in alcohol, broken and alone. People wanting to hear an apology from Madonna for her own supposed misbehavior could find a hint of contrition in the song. Except that the woman isn't sorry: she is merely tired and confused.[41]

The decision to cover Peggy Lee's 1958 song "Fever" came after another song they had written didn't work. Following an overnight stint in the studio, Shep developed a new bass line, and Madonna came in and started working on the lyrics by singing the words to "Fever." "At first we thought: This is cool, and it was. It sounded so good that we decided to take it one step further and actually cover the tune," Shep said.[42]

That song was finished just before Madonna's thirty-fourth birthday, which she celebrated by throwing herself a party on a boat circling Manhattan. "Picture about fifty people dancing on a boat with disco blasting out of the portholes and you get the idea," Shep said. He spent his time on the water thinking about *Erotica* and how people would respond to it. "It was definitely a different album for her."[43]

The recording and mixing process, carried out at the Soundworks studio, took three and a half months, from early June into September of 1992.[44] Madonna would have already raised record-company concerns with her lyrics, but as usual she went one step further by adding a last-minute track that would earn the album a parental advisory label.

During the final week at Soundworks, Andre Betts finished mixing "Waiting" and wanted Madonna to hear it. The guys in the studio had watched her interact with Betts over many weeks and were sure the two were involved. "They would ask me, 'Did you do it? Did you have sex with her?' I'm like, 'Helllllll no.' And they're like, 'You're lying, you're lying.'" So while waiting for Madonna, Betts grabbed a microphone and free-styled a rap he called "Did You Do It?" It is a fantasy about having sex with Madonna in a limousine and enjoying similar escapades with other women.[45]

When Madonna came back to the studio, she was accompanied by "four guys in suits" from Warner. She wanted to hear "Waiting," but Betts's song was set up to play. He hit the button. "I'm thinking, 'Man I don't know how this is going to go down, but it doesn't matter, I'm already paid and this is the last week'... When I hit play, man, she leaned over behind me and she literally had tears in her eyes and goes, 'You are fucking crazy.'" She called him later and said she wanted the song on her album.[46]

On September 12, Shep left Soundworks with a master copy of *Erotica*.[47] The album was light-years beyond *Like a Prayer* and a major step forward

on the path of musical experimentation. It was also Madonna's latest feminist statement. She called it a "female-in-charge kind of record... [a] real
female-in-the-world today, like a woman of the '90s who is intelligent,
has her own career, and has shit happening."[48]

Madonna herself had become a "female in charge." That year, she had her
first-ever business card printed, because she had officially entered that
world.[49] After a year of negotiations led by Freddy DeMann, she signed a
deal with Time Warner to create a multimedia company: music, music
publishing, films, TV programs, books, merchandise. Calling it Maverick,
she described her company as "an artistic think tank" modeled on the
Bauhaus in Germany and Andy Warhol's Factory in New York.[50]

> There's a group of writers, photographers, directors and editors that I've
> met along the way in my career who I want to take with me everywhere I
> go. I want to incorporate them into my little factory of ideas. I also come in
> contact with a lot of young talent that I feel entrepreneurial about.[51]

With a reported advance of $60 million (Freddy DeMann said the con-
tract was worth "dramatically" more), the deal was reportedly the biggest
signed by a performer up to that point, even topping Michael Jackson's
record-breaking agreement with Sony the previous year. Madonna also
renegotiated her own contract with Time Warner. She would receive a $5
million advance on each of her next seven albums (up from $3 million) in
addition to 20 percent royalties. (Michael Jackson earned 22 percent.)[52]
Entertainment companies had become like sports franchises, in which
executives are willing to spend a fortune to secure the services of the best
players. Having sold more than $1 billion worth of records and videos dur-
ing the first decade of her career, Madonna was one of those players. The
fact that the deals on offer were so rich reflected the amount of money
newly available after a series of mergers that created entertainment conglomerates. Warner Bros. had merged with Time, Inc., in 1989 to become
one of the world's largest communications companies.[53]
Maverick's films, TV programs, and books would be a sixty-forty joint
venture between Madonna and Time Warner, but the record label was hers
alone.[54] DeMann would be Maverick's president, with Veronica "Ronnie"
Dashev as chief operating officer and Madonna overseeing every critical
decision. "Nothing goes by me without me knowing about it," she said.[55]

> I'm not one of these dumb artists who is just given a label to shut her up...
> I'm not going to be invisible or simply phone in my partnership. There's no
> honor or satisfaction in palming the work off to someone else.[56]

I want a real record label with real artists. I don't want to be Prince and have everybody be a clone of me. That's not having a label, that's having a harem!...I want artists who are going to have a life of their own and who have a point of view.[57]

Joining Maverick Records was a twenty-year-old born in Jerusalem named Guy Oseary. He had been in school with Freddy DeMann's daughter at Beverly Hills High. At seventeen, he began learning the record business by hanging around Freddy. When Maverick formed, he came in as an A&R man. "I'm like the most fortunate kid in the world," he said at the time.[58]

Oseary would be critical to Maverick's success. He would help Madonna find and sign some of the label's biggest names, including the British electronic punk and rave band the Prodigy; singer-songwriter Meshell Ndegeocello, who would inspire the neo-soul movement; and a young Canadian named Alanis Morissette, who couldn't find a company willing to record her album *Jagged Little Pill.*[59] Maverick did. Released in 1995, the album would go on to sell more than thirty million copies and win four Grammys.[60]

With the Maverick deal struck, and the *Sex* book slated as its first publication, Madonna began work in Portland, Oregon, on a new movie, *Body of Evidence.* She was drawn to it because of its director, Uli Edel, whom she admired for his films *Christiane F.* and *Last Exit to Brooklyn,* and Willem Dafoe, who was attached to costar. Madonna felt the film was the best she'd been offered because she would play the lead in a drama. When asked if she thought the script was misogynistic, she said, "I think you'd be hardpressed to find a script that wasn't...so that to me is a reflection of society." What annoyed Madonna more was that one of the characters was ashamed that he was gay.[61]

The movie is about an attractive thirtysomething gallerist who, having been made sole beneficiary in her elderly lover's will, plies him with cocaine that his heart cannot tolerate and sex that his body cannot endure. He dies, and she is charged with murder. Willem Dafoe plays her eager and smitten lawyer, and Madonna's *Speed-the-Plow* costar Joe Mantegna plays the prosecutor.

The film was merely the latest in a series of movies in the neo-noir mold—*Body Heat, Fatal Attraction,* and *Basic Instinct* among them—that revolve around scheming beautiful professional women (in other words, *unnatural* women) who seduce weak-willed but basically upright, usually married, men and destroy their lives. Somebody always ends up dead, usually the woman.[62]

What would distinguish *Body of Evidence* from those earlier films is that audiences saw *Madonna,* not her character, as the villain. That was especially true in the sex scenes, which even decades later were considered explicit.[63]

Madonna agreed to do them because she thought they were integral to the story.[64] But that didn't make them easy to shoot. She said there were "fifty guys hanging around with walkie talkies and headphones, and people you don't know." During two scenes, Madonna asked Edel to create a "comfort zone" by playing music. He chose Led Zeppelin.[65]

> I don't think anyone will tell you that love scenes aren't difficult to do, because it's hard to pretend to make love to someone you don't know that well.[66] Willem and I were absolutely faking it; there was no penetration or anything like that. But if you're sitting on someone's face, you are sitting on someone's face. You can't really fake it.[67] After two weeks of being naked simulating sex...I just want to go home for a week and not take my clothes off.[68]

Most of the filming occurred in Portland, but in late April it shifted to Olympia, Washington, and the state capitol. Washington's secretary of state tried unsuccessfully to stop the shoot because *Body of Evidence* was "filled with sex and violence."[69] His objections were overruled, and filming proceeded until it was stopped again by much more significant events: Evergreen State College students protesting the Rodney King verdict.[70]

The whole country stopped when that verdict was announced. The year before, King had been beaten by three white police officers after he refused to stop his car and pull over. He'd been watching a basketball game with friends and feared he'd be sent to prison if police discovered he had been drinking. The police officers kicked King, who did not resist arrest, and struck him fifty-six times with their batons. The story might have ended there, except that the assault was videotaped and broadcast nationally.

Four police were charged—the three officers involved in the beating and their commanding officer, who was on the scene. On April 29, 1992, after their trial had been moved from racially diverse LA to reliably white Simi Valley, a jury acquitted the men on all counts. It could not decide on an assault charge for one of the four, and that resulted in a hung jury. When the news hit the street, South Central exploded, and the insurrection spread to Long Beach, Pasadena, and Hollywood. Within a week, ten thousand people had been arrested, and sixty-four were dead.

Madonna was in Los Angeles when the violence began. "I was scared, riveted to my television," she said. "In a way I applauded it. I'm not for violence or anything." But Madonna believed that racism and police brutality in LA had reached the point where an uprising was "the only avenue to take to wake people up...to shake up all the rich white people and say, 'Look, this shit is happening next door to you. You can't pretend it doesn't exist.' "[71]

It wasn't possible to arrest enough people to calm racial tensions in America. A much easier path was to co-opt the messenger. That June, rapper Ice-T was pressured by Time Warner to withdraw the song "Cop Killer" from his latest album. He predicted that "they"—the entertainment industry, the government, the police—would try to shut down rap entirely. There was evidence that that was the case. In *Can't Stop Won't Stop,* his history of rap and hip-hop, Jeff Chang said that after the King rebellion, record labels dropped rappers with political messages as quickly as they had signed them. And then they hit upon a lucrative alternative, one that made rap a favorite genre for white audiences, too.[72]

Labels began promoting rappers and rap producers who extolled the virtues of wealth over rights. Gang colors were replaced by Tommy Hilfiger logos. But to maintain rap's outlaw appeal, its lyrics needed someone to vilify. And that someone was Woman. Though misogyny had long been part of rap, as it had long been part of rock, by the end of 1992, babes and bling became *the* rap message, and much of it was violent.[73] To the men in executive suites, the decision was easy. Women in music, like women in movies, were expendable, which was what happened with Madonna's film.

In the last week of shooting, Madonna said Edel changed *Body of Evidence*'s ending. As originally written, Madonna's character was acquitted and then revealed to be guilty. Edel apparently decided that letting a woman get away with murder would not sit well with audiences, and so he killed her off. A violent fight in which she is tossed around like a rag doll, shot several times, then sent crashing through a window into the water below did the trick. The bitch was dead. "I fought it every step of the way," Madonna said of the change. "But I had no control. Woman who has sex must die: that is the theme of that movie."[74]

The baseball movie Madonna filmed the previous year had a happier ending. *A League of Their Own* opened in June to mixed reviews but a huge box office. By the end of the summer it would earn more than $100 million. Working with Shep, Madonna had written a song for the film: "This Used to Be My Playground."[75] The sweet, melancholy ballad reached number 1 in the States and was in the top ten in twenty other countries.[76]

While Madonna was in Portland in May, she learned that forty-four photos from her *Sex* book had been stolen. Though the book had been produced under strict security, pictures were being offered to the tabloids for a starting price of $100,000. Madonna's lawyers contacted eighteen publications threatening massive lawsuits if they dared publish the images. The FBI then set up a sting in a Los Angeles hotel room. A man was arrested, but he wasn't the person who stole the pictures. That person, allegedly a woman who worked in a New York photo lab, remained at large.[77]

News of the theft and the possibility that more photos might surface only added to the frenzy ahead of the release of Madonna's new album, book, and movie. "She's the only person I know whose publicity gets publicity," said Warner Books publisher Nanscy Neiman.[78] In all that chatter, one word was used to describe all three projects: *sex*. And two questions: How much and what kind?

Madonna revealed one answer on September 24: sex for her was mischievous *and* purposeful. Jean Paul Gaultier was in Los Angeles at the Shrine Auditorium hosting a benefit for amfAR chaired by Madonna and Herb Ritts. It was his first Los Angeles show, and more than six thousand people paid $500 each to be there. As befitting a Gaultier extravaganza, the models came in all shapes, sizes, colors, and ages, from the diminutive TV psychologist Dr. Ruth (in a black rubber nurse's uniform) to Raquel Welch to prostitutes, bikers, and Madonna.[79]

The show's set, with its gaslights and benches, recalled a street in Paris. Models wearing 140 different Gaultier designs paraded the faux avenue for an hour and a half. Madonna came last. "I was supposed to wear a top and jacket like Jean Paul's," she said, "but at the last minute, I decided it was better to go out topless!" Dressed in a dark jacket, long slim skirt, beret, and her gold Dita tooth, a grinning Madonna strolled alongside Gaultier to the end of the runway. Stopping before the crowd at their feet, she dropped her jacket to reveal naked breasts accentuated by suspenders. The image, meanwhile, appeared on two massive screens positioned to accommodate people too far from the runway to see.[80]

The *Los Angeles Times* reported that the Warner Bros. chairman, Bob Daly, was in the audience and "did not look amused." But seemingly everyone else was. "The audience was astounded," said model Tanel Bedrossiantz. "As for those of us who were watching backstage...well, our jaws just collectively dropped."[81] Madonna's performance received a standing ovation, and the image of her outrage ricocheted around the world. She had done her job: AIDS was in the headlines, as was her good friend Gaultier.

Madonna's shocking gesture was part play, part celebration. After nearly a decade of official disregard of AIDS, attitudes were finally changing. The year before, in November of 1991, one of the most beloved players on the

NBA circuit, Magic Johnson, announced he was HIV-positive. It was another Rock Hudson turning point in the way the disease was perceived. In Johnson's case, it meant that HIV/AIDS was no longer a "gay" thing. It wasn't even a "dirty" thing, because Johnson was a seemingly wholesome, all-American athlete and role model who had contracted the disease doing what athletes (with social approval) did: he had sex with several women.[82]

New York–based amfAR had been organizing a December 1991 fundraiser in Los Angeles, where Madonna would be awarded the first amfAR Award of Courage. In the wake of Johnson's announcement, money poured in, as did celebrities who were newly willing to be associated with the cause.[83] In fact, it became positively fashionable, as little red ribbons began appearing on the lapels of tuxedos at awards ceremonies that year.[84] Politicians took notice, and they, too, began to embrace AIDS research and gay rights as a cause.

A decade after the disease was first identified, New York's new mayor, David Dinkins, took the step Ed Koch never dared to and named a citywide coordinator for AIDS-related matters. Democratic presidential candidate Bill Clinton vowed to appoint a cabinet-level AIDS czar and launch a massive scientific effort to find a treatment, if not a cure. Clinton spoke at a fundraiser in Hollywood organized by six hundred gays and lesbians—unprecedented for a presidential candidate at the time—and said, "I have a vision of the future, and you're part of it."[85]

With so much political cover, the entertainment industry finally began to crack open closet doors. Former Fox chairman Barry Diller and the MCA president, Sidney Sheinberg, formed Hollywood Supports, a group dedicated to ending discrimination against gays and people with AIDS in the entertainment industry. Soon, studios offered same-sex domestic partner benefits.[86] But the biggest statement came from entertainment mogul David Geffen. On November 18, 1992, at the annual Commitment to Life benefit for AIDS Project Los Angeles, he said, "As a gay man..." Whatever he said after that wasn't nearly as important as those four words.[87]

Some questioned his timing. He had just sold Geffen Records for $750 million. "He was finally in the 'fuck you' position," said journalist Richard Natale. "He had the wherewithal for his social conscience to take over."[88] Whatever his motives, Geffen's announcement, at least among nonactors, gave other people the courage to come out. From studio design departments to script rooms to executive suites, the secrets everyone knew but didn't share were suddenly spoken of openly. Except among actors.

At that point, gays began to appear in Hollywood films as something other than murderers and maniacs, but they were played by heterosexual men. Tom Hanks, for example, would win an Oscar for playing a gay man dying of AIDS in the 1993 film *Philadelphia*. And so it went. If gay actors wanted work, they had to keep their sexuality hidden. It would not be safe for them to declare themselves for another twenty years.[89]

Four days after Madonna's runway exhibition in LA, amid a culture that had begun to recognize nonheterosexual "lifestyles," she released the single "Erotica." Three days after that, her "Erotica" video landed. She was about to test just how far society was willing to go to broaden its sexual horizons.

Essentially a live-action version of her book, the video was shot by Fabien Baron using a Super 8 camera while Steven Meisel took still pictures of Madonna and friends in New York and Florida. In the video, Dita—gold-toothed, masked, hair slicked back, riding crop in hand—sang "Erotica" as black-and-white images flickered past like those in an inexpertly made home movie or early porn film. No single frame remained on-screen long enough for the viewer to truly absorb it, but there was enough there to cause alarm.[90] If "Justify My Love" was what happened in bright hotel rooms, "Erotica" revealed the dark goings-on in the cellar. MTV showed the video, but only after midnight and only three times.[91] Madonna didn't fight the decision.

> MTV plays to a huge audience and a lot of them are children and a lot of themes I'm exploring in my videos aren't meant for children, so I understand that they say they can't show it and I accept it. But that's where I am right now in my life.[92]

That, however, was the last concession Madonna would make, as evidenced by the book party she threw on October 15, a week before *Sex* was published. Held on the fourth floor of the Industria Superstudio in New York City's West Village, it featured a naked woman functioning as a sushi platter, S/M enactments, gay sex, lesbian sex, group sex, and eight hundred guests overwhelmed by the magnitude of the spectacle.[93]

Andre Betts recalled walking up to the party and seeing wrestler Hulk Hogan trying to get in. "I'm thinking this will be a regular party, whatever," Betts said. "The first thing I saw was a naked person suspended in the air on chains, and I say to myself, 'Oh shit.'" Next, he saw a tub of popcorn with a naked woman in it and, beyond her, a row of doors. His friend looked into the first one and saw a woman masturbating. Behind a second door, a couple was having sex. Betts's friend moved to a third door and found a similar scene, but with two men. "And he freaked the freak out. He's like, 'Oh shit! I've never seen that before.' And there was two doors left and he goes, 'Hell no, I don't know what I might see in those doors.'"[94]

Rumors circulated that Madonna would arrive nude. Instead, she appeared as a gold-toothed Bavarian shepherdess with a little lamb. Betts said Madonna didn't "do anything crazy that night. She was like, 'I've had enough, I want to chill.' "[95]

The *Erotica* album was released on October 20 and *Sex* the next day. The book overshadowed the album. It would have been impossible for it not to. *Sex*'s launch was unprecedented: 750,000 copies went on sale simultaneously in Japan, Britain, France, Germany, and the United States. The price was $50 a copy.[96] Efforts began immediately to block its sale.

Sex was banned in Ireland and parts of Australia. Police in India seized it as it arrived at airports. French police confiscated twenty-five thousand copies to determine if it was pornographic (it was eventually released for sale). Likewise, in Britain (home of the topless Page 3 girl in daily tabloid newspapers), the Crown Prosecution Service investigated whether *Sex* violated the UK's obscenity laws, while a British parliamentarian called for the "vile, obscene, pornographic book" to be banned outright.[97] Fat chance of that. The rush to buy it was breathtaking.

In the hours before the book's release, at the stroke of midnight, hundreds of fans stood in the rain outside Books Etc. on Charing Cross Road in London awaiting a silver van with a *Sex* logo to arrive. The *Daily Mirror* reported that by midday, "po-faced businessmen could be seen sneaking out of WH Smith's [bookshop], fumbling with large plastic bags." One of the stores reported selling eighteen hundred copies in a single hour. By the second day, all one hundred thousand copies available in Britain were gone.[98]

Major bookstores in Paris, too, sold out their allotment of *Sex* in a few hours. In Canada, it became the fastest-selling book in history. In the United States, *Sex* sold five hundred thousand copies in one week and topped the *New York Times* nonfiction bestseller list, despite Madonna's statement on the first page that the stories weren't true. Harvard Business School was so impressed by Madonna's publishing feat that it invited her to lecture on the subject. She declined.[99]

Liz Rosenberg rightly feared that *Sex* promised a whole new level of controversy. "There's a lot to hate in that book," she told *Vanity Fair*'s Maureen Orth. She also worried about the reaction. "Psychos might see there's a message in it for them." Freddy DeMann was worried, too. "Warner Books is shitting in their pants," he said.[100]

Criticism of Madonna's book ranged from the expected outrage in the press to scorn from the too-cool-to-be-shocked crowd, and that stung. Madonna didn't mind being hated, but she hated even feigned indifference. *Rolling Stone* called *Sex* an "anticlimax," complaining that it was physically difficult to use (it was hard to turn the pages), the photos were campy, and the text was "so dumb...that it makes the dialogue from an X-rated Ginger Lynn movie sound like vintage Anaïs Nin."[101] Martin Amis, seemingly annoyed that Madonna refused his interview request, said, "There is the feeling that *Sex* is no more than the desperate confection of an ageing scandal addict."[102]

Some critics on the left took issue with it politically, saying the shots that included Naomi Campbell were racist because Madonna was so white. Others claimed she did not feature enough gays and lesbians or that the S/M scenes weren't authentic enough or that she was too central—to her own fantasies! Penn State professor John Champagne felt the book was homophobic because it only showed one penis, and it was soft.[103]

Men who purchased the book looking for titillation came away feeling confused, annoyed, betrayed, and in some cases terrified. The book depicted sex that they recognized but, strangely, weren't invited to be part of. During a televised interview, the late journalist Richard Carleton of *60 Minutes Australia* told Madonna he was frightened by her book because he had never seen anything like it.

> Madonna: You have so. Oh, please.
> Carleton: No.
> Madonna: You've never read *Playboy* magazine, or *Penthouse,* or anything like that?
> Carleton: Yes, but it was different with you.
> Madonna: Why?
> Carleton: Well, there was the picture of you astride the mirror masturbating. I thought that was horrible.
> Madonna: Why?
> Carleton: It just strikes me as horrible.
> Madonna: I think people's reactions to specific situations in the book is much more a reflection of that person than me...I mean, you were scared of that picture, what does that mean? Are you frightened of a woman that can turn herself on? Are you frightened of a woman who is not afraid to look at her genitals in the mirror?
> Carleton: A little bit, yes, that's right.[104]

The type of woman Carleton feared possesses the vagina dentata of myth and legend—a vagina with teeth. Such a woman in control of her sex was believed to have the power to eat men alive.[105]

After her book was published, Madonna joined Hillary Clinton as one of the two most vilified women in the United States. One spoke of political freedom, the other of sexual freedom, and both expressed themselves without apology and with no sign that they planned to stop, despite withering and often frightening criticism. The *National Review* called Hillary "that smiling barracuda"—a vagina dentata by another name.[106]

Like her songs, videos, and safe-sex messages, Madonna's book didn't include didactic lessons in sexual politics. Instead, she teased and cajoled people into pondering what they might not otherwise consider. "It's *supposed* to be funny," Madonna told music writer Barbara Ellen.

> I do think you need to bring humor to it...But no one got the subtlety, no one got the humor...It was never meant to be this incredibly hot, arousing, erotic piece of porn. In fact, I was poking fun at everybody's prejudices about other people's sexualities and their own sexuality.[107]

Even as she publicly defended her book, though, Madonna was stunned by the reaction. "People who don't think the controversies and the press affect her are wrong," Christopher said. "There is definitely a cost."[108] A few years later, during a *60 Minutes* interview, Madonna told Charlie Rose that after the *Sex* controversy,

> I lost confidence in humanity. I thought that people were being unbelievably cruel to me for no reason. And I lost confidence in...being able to feel there was a certain level of behavior that I could depend on in other people. A certain decency. When I lost confidence in that, I began to lose confidence in myself.[109]

What Madonna described in her book was so much a part of her world in New York and Miami that she didn't think it needed an introduction.[110] It did, which she offered in interview after interview after the fact. "My thing is not for everybody to have more sex," she said. "My thing is to feel comfortable with who you are, whether you are gay or you are straight or whatever."[111]

> I didn't start out trying to change people's views. I just started out expressing my ideas about sexuality, and now it sort of turned into a kind of mission or something, a sort of crusade, because everyone's saying what I'm doing is wrong and bad, and I'm saying no, there's nothing wrong with what I say or what I do.[112] Everyone's afraid, and I'm telling them not to be afraid.[113]

For all the people who criticized her book, however, there were legions of others who appreciated her courage. Blond Ambition tour dancer Carlton Wilborn said,

At the core of what she represents is the secret longing of every human being: we all have quiet thoughts, we all have hungry thoughts, but most of us have been conditioned to think it's inappropriate to let this be known. So when you have an example of somebody who is living their life against all the constructs that are blasted through the world and the media, it's intoxicating.[114]

Chapter 35

New York, Los Angeles, 1992–1993

Wishing a woman off the face of the earth is just another way of admitting she rules it.[1]

—*Mim Udovitch*

MOST CERTAINLY, MADONNA was not the first woman to use her art to describe sex from her point of view and to suffer for it. In 1926, that glorious norm buster Mae West wrote a play called *Sex* under the pen name Jane Mast (interestingly, she didn't hide behind a man's name in choosing a pseudonym). The play was about a prostitute in Montreal and the hypocritical society that tolerated the commerce surrounding a woman's body but not the woman herself.[2]

Newspapers refused to carry ads for the play because of the title, and critics denounced it because of its content. But pesky free-speech protections meant that the Broadway theater where it was performed was packed for a year until police finally found a reason to raid it and arrest West and the entire cast for indecency. Noting that West refused to shutter the play after the raid, the judge accused her of showing contempt for his courtroom. She replied, "On the contrary, Your Honor, I was doing my best to conceal it."[3]

Once released, West continued to incite. Her 1927 play, *The Drag*, was considered the first about homosexuality that showed gay men in a positive light. Her play *Pleasure Man*, performed in 1928, included female impersonators. It was raided—twice. When West and her cast were sent to the hoosegow again, many of the men were still dressed as women.[4]

West's films and plays so alarmed church and political leaders that a new decency code for movies was established to contain her and the artists who might emulate her. That repression worked. In 1933, Mae West topped the box office. In 1934, Shirley Temple did. A powerful woman's sexuality was replaced by a sexualized child's.[5]

Few women besides Mae West had enough power in the entertainment business to bring their own vision to the screen or stage, and that would remain true until the late 1970s. Painters and photographers did, however, mostly because what they created didn't require massive financial support *and* because they could be easily ignored. The early and mid-twentieth century produced provocative works by Georgia O'Keeffe, Frida Kahlo, and Helen Frankenthaler, among many others. And then, in the 1960s, some artists began to get more explicit. Twenty-four-year-old painter Betty Tompkins was one of them.

By 1969, Tompkins was thoroughly bored by what she saw in New York galleries. "It seemed totally formulaic, repetitive," she said. "All these guys weren't pushing any ideas, and what idea they had was so easy to look at. You saw it. There was nothing else to see; there was nothing to think about." Her work involved appropriation—choosing something that existed in the "real world," transforming it, and sending it back to be seen in a new light.[6] One day, in search of inspiration, she looked through her husband's porn collection and realized that if she eliminated the heads, hands, and feet and concentrated on the "money shots," the genitals, they became "aesthetically gorgeous" shapes.[7]

Galleries weren't interested. "They'd say, 'Come back in ten years when you've found your voice.' And I'd say, 'I'm screaming here. This is my voice!' But it was the times." When she sent her work to a group show in Paris, the paintings were confiscated at the airport. The same occurred in Tokyo. Feminists in the art world also rejected her work because, though abstracted, the paintings were considered too sexual and were derived from porn. It was thirty years from the time when a dealer ran out of Tompkins's bedroom studio in horror to the time when another dealer said he wanted her work. That would finally happen in 2002.[8]

In 1979, the artist Judy Chicago exhibited her grand and glorious installation *The Dinner Party*. The aim of the work, which took five years to produce and involved contributions from four hundred people, should have been heralded as *the* artistic statement arising from second wave feminism. On plates set around a huge triangular table, it pays tribute to thirty-nine women of historical significance—Sappho, Christine de Pisan, Sojourner Truth, Emily Dickinson, and Georgia O'Keeffe among them. On floor tiles and surrounding wall hangings, 999 other women are acknowledged.[9]

Chicago's decision to depict the thirty-nine principals in designs that looked like female genitalia was so controversial that it nearly cost the artist her life and resulted in the work being hidden from view after its initial tour was finished. In 1990, after dismissing it as "pornography," Congress refused to authorize funding to give *The Dinner Party* a permanent home at the University of the District of Columbia. The work was mothballed—except for one 1996 show at UCLA—until the Brooklyn Museum gave it a home in 2002. It was put on permanent exhibition there five years later.[10]

In the late '80s, artist Marilyn Minter was looking for a subject that was not traditionally a "woman's" subject and simultaneously trying to "repurpose" her own troubled history.[11] Though unaware at the time of Tompkins's art, she had come to the same conclusion: women didn't paint porn, and they most certainly didn't paint hard-core porn from a woman's point of view. "Nobody has politically correct fantasies. And nobody talks about it," Minter said. She wondered whether it would change the meaning of sexual imagery if she painted it herself.[12]

Minter created her lush images and was immediately ostracized. The reaction to the first exhibition of her new work, in 1992, as Madonna was finishing her *Sex* book, was outrage. "My show was closed a week early," she said. "I got dropped out of shows. I got excoriating reviews."[13] She also received anonymous phone calls and threatening letters because she was seen as "colluding with the porn industry."[14] "I'm doing clinic defense outside of Planned Parenthood, and at the same time I'm called a traitor to feminism," she said.[15]

By contrast, Cindy Sherman exhibited her Sex Pictures series at the same time to critical acclaim. The work was powerful, but it showed sex as "dismal" and made a statement about male privilege. Minter's work did not. She unapologetically and without irony celebrated sex and was pilloried for it.[16] Years later, Minter said,

> I thought it was a healthy thing... I wasn't thinking about pushing the envelope: I was just making my vision... It's the most threatening thing in the world, women owning their sexuality. It's like the world will come to an end... There was a long period I couldn't get anyone to come to my studio... Then there was a point when everyone who came to my studio offered me a show.[17]

But that took twenty years.[18]

Madonna, in other words, was not alone in the direction she had taken. But the reaction to her *was* unique. Despite the abuse those other women suffered, they did so as artists. Madonna was not given that dignity. She was denounced as a silly exhibitionist and sex fiend.[19]

Once, when asked by editor Richard Goldstein why he wrote *Giovanni's Room,* a novel about homosexuality published in 1956, James Baldwin said that he had wanted to "clarify something for myself" and that if he hadn't written it, "I would probably have had to stop writing altogether."[20] In the discussions of Madonna's book, rarely if ever did anyone consider whether there was something in it that she, as an artist, needed to clarify for herself.

By that point, Madonna had inhabited all the stereotypes that patriarchal society concocted for women—dutiful daughter, gamine, blond
bombshell, adoring wife, bitch—in her pursuit of a new woman, a person
who exercised her power freely, joyously, even wantonly, if that's what she
wanted. Her quest was what French philosopher Hélène Cixous described
as the search for a "feminine imaginary...an ego no longer given over
to an image defined by the masculine."[21] *Sex* was her breakthrough. In
128 pages, she returned the power of a woman's sexuality to its rightful
owner.

Like all major artistic statements, the book appeared before the broader
society was ready for it. British gay rights activist Matthew Hodson
recalled seeing *Sex* when it was published and thinking, "'Oh love, put it
away'...I was like, 'You are just selling your body, and is that a useful
thing to do for your sisters?'

> I look back on that now, and I think, here's a woman who's just absolutely
> owning her body and owning her sexuality and saying, "I'm not going to do
> what you want me to do, what you expect me to do, what you think is
> polite for me to do, what you think someone with my level of power and
> fame should do. I'm going to do what I feel is right"...I now see what she
> was doing, and now I think it's incredible.[22]

But that would take thirty years.

Amid the deluge of coverage of Madonna's book, *Erotica* proved to be the
poor, nearly forgotten stepchild. When it *was* mentioned, it was swept up
in the condemnation of *Sex* as part of a dirty package. But some people
could see past the controversy of the moment and recognize the album for
what it was. Writing in *Rolling Stone,* Mim Udovitch called *Erotica* Madonna's "finest full-length recorded work to date—as an act of faith in, among
other things, the power of art to bring about social change, its passion, sincerity, and scope are virtually unmatched."[23] In *Melody Maker,* Paul
Mathur wrote,

> *Erotica* is one of the best records you'll hear all year. She's finally pulled it
> together...It should be her proudest moment. It should be, but the rest of
> the territory she's fenced for herself just keeps on popping up, clouding the
> delights.[24]

Upon its release, the album charted at number 2, but *Erotica*'s overall
sales would not rise to Madonna levels. It would eventually sell six million
copies, considerably less than *Like a Prayer*'s nineteen million.[25] "She just

freaked everybody out," Doug Wimbish told writer Lucy O'Brien many years later.

> She was bringin' it from her point of view as a woman, bringing it to the forefront for *real*. That set the template now for your Christina Aguileras, Britneys, Beyoncés.[26] You wouldn't have some of the lanes that are out there now without her putting that record out. Fact.[27]

During that extremely difficult period, Madonna's friends circled around her. Ingrid Casares, especially, was indispensable. She never questioned Madonna's actions, never disagreed with her, and, according to Christopher, always said exactly want Madonna wanted to hear. Ingrid gave Madonna unconditional love when she most needed it, and their bond of friendship was cemented.[28]

Her family supported her, too. Madonna went home for Christmas at the end of that traumatic year, having graduated from a sleeping bag to an air mattress. Her father did not criticize her over her work, but he did ask her, "Why did you feel the need to do that?" Madonna didn't answer because to do so would have meant admitting that her actions were partly a rebellion against him.[29] Maybe he knew that anyway and hoped she had gotten it out of her system. His Christmas gift to her was a statue of the Virgin Mary and Christ child.[30]

The gay and lesbian community also largely stood by her. While some revived the criticism of Madonna as a sexual tourist and cultural appropriator, more saw the bravery of publishing a book celebrating the joy of queerness and otherness.[31] "She was being slut-shamed before the word was even invented, and we really understood that," said writer Matt Cain. "So we loved her even more."[32]

Virginia Woolf once described nineteenth-century composer and women's rights activist Dame Ethel Smyth as "one of the icebreakers, the gun runners, the window smashers. The armored tanks who climbed the rough ground, drew the enemies [sic] fire."[33] That was Madonna's role — smashing through boundaries so others could follow. She told a Japanese interviewer that December,

> Anger fuels a lot of what I do. I'm angry about the sexism in this world. I'm angry about racism. I'm angry about homophobia. I'm angry about the injustices of life, and so I write about them, and I challenge people's ideas about them.[34]

Asked by the interviewer what she wanted, Madonna said, "Creative freedom to do what I want." Asked what she lacked, Madonna said, "Peace of mind."[35]

*　　*　　*

Peace did not come.

Body of Evidence premiered on January 7, 1993. The film had been rated an adults-only NC-17, but after the controversy surrounding *Sex,* the film's distributors and producers had its erotic scenes edited to secure an R rating.[36] Eliminating bits of exposed flesh, however, failed to insulate *Body of Evidence* from the *Sex* scandal. The film received scathing reviews.

Rolling Stone's Peter Travers said it was terrible. "There is no sign of [Madonna's] stage charisma. Her character is a...nonentity...Willem Dafoe gives his first boo-rating performance...All the actors should fire their agents."[37] As bad as that review was, it was surprisingly fair. Travers's was one of the few that meted out the blame for the film's failings among several parties. Others hung it squarely on Madonna. She called those reviewers "relentlessly cruel."[38]

The criticism of the movie and her part in it was so intense that it was as if all the hatred for her that had been building during the previous decade finally exploded as pure naked rage. Audiences cheered when Madonna's character died at the end of the picture.[39] Critics stumbled over one another to describe how badly she acted, how insipid her dialogue, and how wooden her sex scenes.[40]

Steve Allen, who as the first host of *The Tonight Show* had helped create the late-night television talk show genre, offered one of the most pointed, culturally revealing, and frankly terrifying criticisms of Madonna in the wake of *Sex, Erotica,* and *Body of Evidence.* Writing in the *Journal of Popular Culture* in the summer of 1993, he called her the Marquis de Sade's "ableist and most influential present defender.

> There is a clue to this in the sort of wardrobe and costume she affects. There is nothing in it of the sweet, feminine, even Victoria's-Secret sort, in which the purpose is to glorify and enhance the natural factor of womanly beauty. What we see in Madonna, by way of contrast, is much use of black and of leather, of the sort associated with sadomasochism. Then there are the absurd conical, metallic-looking brassieres, a dehumanizing element when contrasted with the natural beauty of the well-formed breasts with which some women are gifted by nature.

Referencing what he called a "prescient short story" by James Thurber, Allen said it was "instructive because it is based on the sobering realization that the world would really be better off had some people never lived, whatever the degree of their momentary popularity." So as not to be accused of threatening Madonna, Allen made sure to add that Thurber did not advocate murdering the people he found disagreeable.[41] Others did. Hate mail and death threats addressed to her came in by the bagful.[42]

That was because sex in the late twentieth century was not an act but rather the very foundation of an economic, political, and social system, according to French philosopher Michel Foucault. Therefore, any "transgression of that sex — hetero-matrimonial — is a transgression against the order of things broadly." In speaking of it, he said, a person places themself "outside the reach of power, he upsets established law; he somehow anticipates the coming freedom."[43]

Madonna knew that she would be punished and that anything she did creatively would suffer because she transgressed that status quo with her book. She did not wallow in public displays of self-pity, which she described as "I've been punished! Boo-hoo. Get out the violins."[44] But she did say, wearily, "It would be nice if everybody could listen to my music and watch the movies and read the books, or whatever, without anyone telling them how they should think or feel, or accept it or not accept it, and then judge for themselves."[45]

That was Madonna's brave public face. Privately, she described herself as at "rock bottom...It was a really rough time. I mean I had to really work hard to rise above it and not take it personally."[46] Christopher said, "It was definitely a low point, probably the lowest point in her career."[47]

Appropriately and with gallows humor, Madonna started the new year at work on a video for "Bad Girl." Her old friend and creative soulmate David Fincher agreed to direct what would be the video for the third single from her *Erotica* album.

The previous November at the Roxbury club in LA, Madonna had gathered a group of friends — Debi Mazar, Ingrid Casares, Sofia Coppola, Udo Kier, Seymour Stein, Guy Oseary, and transgender actor and Warhol alum Holly Woodlawn, among others — to film a video for "Deeper and Deeper."[48] She wanted to combine the sensibilities of the 1920s Jazz Age with the 1970s disco world.[49] Both were times of abandon, and both amounted to last dances before the fall. In her notes for the video, she called it a "trippy hallucinogenic trip down memory lane" and an "anything goes pre-AIDS free for all."[50]

In the video, directed by Bobby Woods, Madonna's character appears strangely out of place as she enters the club world of disco balls and bell-bottom trousers. She is an amalgam of an F. Scott Fitzgerald flapper, Warhol star Edie Sedgwick, and Swedish actress Ingrid Thulin. Her character exists — as Madonna did in life — at the center of the action but also apart from it.

A second story line, set in an apartment, involves Madonna with her girlfriends, eating bananas while watching a man in his tighty-whities strike muscle poses on a bed. She also uses that setting to premiere a huge blond afro wig of the type Marlene Dietrich wore in *Blonde Venus*. It would feature in Madonna's next tour.

Like *Truth or Dare,* the video is shot in both black and white and color: the "real" scenes appear in black and white, and the club scenes, which represent "performance," appear in color. The video is also layered with deeper meanings and references, including nods to Goethe's *Faust,* Visconti's *The Damned,* various Warhol films, and Madonna's own video for "Vogue." Because of the infectious soundtrack and bizarre goings-on, the video is as fun to watch as it no doubt was to make. But Madonna's overall attitude in it is sad and slightly beleaguered. She would remain in that state in the video for "Bad Girl."

Fincher's *Alien*[3], which he chose to make rather than film Madonna's Blond Ambition tour, had been a critical disaster. Said one writer, after *Alien*[3], the wunderkind director's "name was mud." Since then, he had only directed a Michael Jackson video and a Nike commercial and wasn't sure he ever wanted to make another movie.[51] Madonna, of course, was in the midst of her own critical backlash. From that very low professional point, with little to lose, the two decided to work together.

The video for "Bad Girl" would be loosely based on *Looking for Mr. Goodbar,* which was one of those mid-'70s movies in which a "liberated" woman ends up dead after picking up the wrong guy. In the video, Madonna plays a strung-out magazine editor named Louise Oriole who, as the song reveals, drinks early, smokes too much, and seeks solace with strangers.[52]

In a nod to "Express Yourself," Madonna and Fincher's first collaboration, a hungry cat appears. In the new video, though, instead of pouring its milk over herself, Madonna licks cat food from her finger and washes it down with white wine. In an homage to Wim Wenders's 1987 film, *Wings of Desire,* Christopher Walken plays an angel who hovers over Louise protectively and with concern — even shedding tears — as he observes her dissolute ways.[53]

The character's need to self-destruct, however, proves stronger than her angel's power to preserve her. A serial killer is on the loose, and Louise has the bad luck to pick him as her sex partner for the evening. The video opens with Louise's corpse on the bed and ends with it being wheeled out of her apartment building on a gurney. Relieved of the burden of her life, she takes her place next to Walken as an angel, merrily swinging her legs as her life on earth ends and her life in the clouds begins.[54]

★   ★   ★

Madonna promoted her "Bad Girl" single on *Saturday Night Live* on January 16. The host was her *Goose and Tomtom* costar Harvey Keitel. At that time, the film division of Madonna's company was looking for cutting-edge material, and Keitel and director Abel Ferrara were shopping around just such a movie. That year, the pair had made a sulfurous film called *Bad Lieutenant.* Corrupt is too polite a word to describe the character Keitel played. His performance, as usual, was frighteningly good, and the film, despite being so violent and ugly that it was nearly unwatchable at times, became a critical favorite. Madonna loved it, too.

Dangerous Game, the movie Keitel and Ferrara hoped to make next, would be a film within a film — the story of a movie production and a parallel story about the disintegration of the lives of the people involved in it. The script landed at Maverick, and Madonna was interested. She saw it as similar to *Day for Night,* François Truffaut's much-heralded 1973 "movie within a movie."[55] She wanted not only to produce it but also to play the main female character, a woman named Sarah who is caught between two warring male egos — the director, played by Keitel, and an actor, played by James Russo.

The project seemed to be a good one. It had a provocative director, a massively talented costar in Keitel, and a challenging subject. In Madonna's interpretation of the script, her character destroyed the Keitel-and-Russo bond, which represented the exclusive male club of filmmaking. She emerged triumphant as a "new star." She called the role a "great feminist statement...I thought I could take that and do a great performance."[56] She must have been so seduced by the script that she failed to consider the director. If she had examined Abel Ferrara's history, she would have seen warning lights flashing crimson. Ferrara's own wife called him a "misogynist" and said that he "hates" women.[57]

Ferrara was part of the second wave of Italian American filmmakers, men like Quentin Tarantino.[58] Their work was tough, violent. They were also, like their mentor, Martin Scorsese, men's men. The bonds between Scorsese and his actors and crew were the stuff of film legend. They represented that oldest of Italian gangs, the *ragazzi* — the boys from the neighborhood — whose allegiance is first and foremost to one another.

Keitel, though not Italian, had that kind of relationship with Ferrara. So did Ferrara with the rest of his crew, from scriptwriter Nicholas St. John to cinematographer Ken Kelsch. There was also a strong current of ex-military running through the crew.[59] Added to all that testosterone were Ferrara's demons at the time.

He described himself as "spinning out of control...living that kind of go-for-broke life." He had been drinking and using drugs for so long that he didn't think he could direct a movie sober. Things got worse when filming moved to LA. He hated that town. "In L.A. film is commerce, man," he said. "It's a factory town."[60] Ferrara wasn't about to bow to Hollywood convention.[61]

In the film, Sarah (Madonna) is starring in a movie about a woman who, in finding God, rejects the life of sex, drugs, and booze she shares with her husband, Frank (James Russo). The husband has no desire to change. With increasing violence, he declares that he needs that life the way his wife needs her religion. The secondary plot — about the making of the movie — belongs to its director, played by Keitel. It is the story of more sex, drugs, and booze, the dissolution of *his* marriage, and his efforts to cajole his actors into enacting his vision.

Madonna had researched her part by visiting battered women's shelters, and Ferrara gave Madonna and James Russo copies of the script, which they duly memorized. "I knew, everyone knew, except for these two guys [Madonna and Russo], that none of that dialogue would ever make it to the movie," said Kelsch.[62] Ferrara's idea of directing was to give his actors "space so they could rage...just turn the fucking camera on and let them succeed." That had been his method with Keitel in *Bad Lieutenant*,[63] and that was the path he took in the new picture.

The movie, which started out as a film within a film, became a film within a film within a film. The third layer was about Madonna. "I forced her to confront many of the issues in her life," Ferrara said.[64] Much of that part of the movie was reportedly included without her knowledge. Ferrara used a video camera to shoot rehearsals without indicating that the footage would make its way into the finished film. He believed that what he got from Madonna in those moments was "great...She's totally cool. She didn't know the camera was on. She's alive. This chick is really alive."[65] Alive, yes, but as a plaything for the men in the film, who take turns abusing her emotionally and physically.

Ferrara deliberately chose James Russo to play opposite Madonna in a part that required him to scream at her, strike her, and ultimately shoot her at point-blank range. Ferrara knew the authenticity he sought would be bolstered by Russo's casting because he was a close friend of Sean Penn.[66]

Russo was part of the pack of young men gathered around Sean in Malibu after his dramatic breakup with Madonna. He would have been privy to the details of the couple's unraveling. The aggression he showed Madonna's character after Ferrara threw out the script and the cast improvised was queasily intimate. At one point Russo's character comes at Madonna with a pair of scissors as if to cut off her hair, just as Sean had threatened to do.

Ferrara's direction, Keitel's on-screen direction, and Russo's performance combine toward seemingly one goal: to pulverize Madonna. In the film, Keitel calls her a bad actress who is in the movie because they need her money. Russo hit her. "He cracked Madonna a really good one," Kelsch recalled of one scene.[67] Ferrara, too, got a swing in off camera after Madonna fought with him about his directing, about actors being drunk on the set, and about the general misogynistic atmosphere. "I fucking hit her on the set, even though I promised myself that I wouldn't ever touch her," he said. "She made it sound like I almost killed her. I pushed her."[68]

He told writer Andrew Morton that he also violated her by using "the ugliest, smelliest film crew member to simulate having sex with her for a scene." It was a scene that never even made it into the movie. And when, during one rehearsal, she was completely broken down, Madonna confided on film to Keitel the story of her own rape on a rooftop in 1979. (That segment *did* make it into the picture.) It was the only full description of that terrible day that she has publicly given, and it came amid another type of assault—on her as an artist.[69]

It was too much. Her book, the reactions, the movies she had been in. Madonna had lost control of who she was and what she wanted to say. "I think she realized it was time to sort of step back and rethink what was happening, and the people she was involved with, and what everyone was telling her to do," Christopher said. Madonna took a "recess" to decide how to "resuscitate her career." Christopher would help her.[70]

Madonna trusted him completely at that point. She trusted his artistic sensibilities, his judgment concerning her work, and the fact that he cared deeply for her welfare. She told Australian journalist Molly Meldrum that she would never act in a film that she directed because she wouldn't be able to see herself clearly. "That's where my brother comes in," she said. "I need somebody to be a stand-up guy to tell me what works...We rarely disagree, but when we do disagree, if you think I'm tough, meet my brother. But we work it out."[71] Christopher had long been Madonna's private adviser. That year, 1993, he would become her public adviser on a grand global stage.

Chapter 36

Los Angeles, London, Rio de Janeiro, Atlanta, 1993

What people fail to realize is how much guts it takes to do what we do, what any artist does...How much guts it takes to put yourself on the line and say, here's my work, here's my heart and soul.[1]

—*Madonna*

WHEN SHE WRAPPED her Blond Ambition tour, Madonna had vowed never to tour again. "I was spent. I was exhausted. I was sick of traveling. I wanted stability."[2] But stability did not come. Quite the opposite. So three years later, she decided once again to take her chances on the road. The stage was an environment she could control; it was where she communicated the message that *she* wanted to send.

Christopher would be the show's director as well as art director. "That was when she allowed me to be fully in charge," he said. "It wasn't easy to get there. Her manager, Freddy, did not want it. She was unsure about it; we haggled over pay," he said. "I'm like, 'After twenty years we're still arguing over money?'" Once the disputes were settled, they got to work.[3]

The title they chose, the Girlie Show, came from an Edward Hopper painting of a naked woman onstage in a burlesque house. Madonna's other inspiration was more contemporary. She said she went to a strip club in Miami and saw a pole dancer who was so talented and had "such a great vibe about her" that she decided to use a similar performance to open her show.[4]

Unlike the Blond Ambition tour, the Girlie Show would not have a pointed social message, aside from the fact that its three main women—Madonna, Niki Haris, and Donna De Lory—exuded girl power and were surrounded by a multiracial, sexually diverse cast, which was for some still a *radical* statement.[5] The Girlie Show would be art and entertainment, pure and simple. Christopher called it the "pinnacle of our collaborative work together. It was opera; it was theater; it was cabaret. Louise Brooks, that was the inspiration…I was living with Madonna at that time…I was actually redoing the Castillo del Lago."[6]

Though her life was no longer centered on Los Angeles, Madonna had bought a new house there. The nine-story late-1920s mansion, set on four acres of land with fountains and a pool overlooking the Hollywood Reservoir, was once owned by gangster Bugsy Siegel and used as a gambling den in the 1930s. With several terraces, a massive sitting room, nine bedrooms, a library, a wine cellar, rose gardens, palm trees, a pool, and a 160-foot tower, it was the grandest home Madonna had ever owned.[7]

Castillo del Lago's architectural style was Spanish colonial, but Christopher undertook $3 million in renovations—almost equal to the home's $5 million price tag—and transformed it into an Italian palazzo, beginning with a paint job. Inspired by a church they had seen in Portofino, he had the place painted in horizontal white-and-terra-cotta stripes. Far from hiding in the landscape, the house, located directly under the famous Hollywood sign, rested like a Ligurian jewel in the heart of the hills.[8]

In July of 1993, at Sony Pictures Studios, in Culver City, Madonna and Christopher began three months of work on her fourth tour. It would be shorter than Blond Ambition—thirty-nine performances—with only five shows in the United States, three of them in New York. But the tour would take Madonna and crew farther afield, to countries she had never performed in, among them Turkey, Israel, Australia, Argentina, and Brazil. She wanted to entertain cultures with "different expectations, different ways of expressing pleasure and bewilderment." She also said she wasn't interested in "preaching to the converted, so basically, I'm going to the places where I have the most enemies. That's why I'm starting in London."[9] The tour would open there on September 25 and end in Tokyo in December.

Since their earliest days in New York, Madonna and Christopher had spent hours together watching movies. Among their favorites were old comedies and musicals. That was where they started searching for choreography, costume, and stage-set ideas as well as themes for the tour.[10]

Gene Kelly featured in some of the films they watched, so Christopher suggested, "Why don't we just go right to the source?" Madonna's first response was incredulity. But Christopher persisted. "Why not? Just try to find him." So Madonna tracked down the eighty-one-year-old Hollywood legend, and he returned her call in around twenty minutes. "I was so nervous talking to him," she said, that she could barely say his name. "Ge…Ge…Ge…Gene?"[11] He agreed to come to the studio to see what they had up to that point. Madonna described it:

He started talking to me about how he'd worked with Marlene Dietrich once, and she'd asked him to stage a show for her, and he said [to her], "You know, you really must do a number dressed as a man in a tux and top hat. You really must; you're the only person that can do that." And so I had the idea, but I wasn't sure, and he kind of gave me the courage to do it.[12]

In her show, Madonna would become Dietrich in a comedic send-up of "Like a Virgin" that was completely off-the-wall and brilliant.

Madonna's search for dancers to help her create her spectacle was unconventional. In early July, she posted flyers in lesbian bars in Manhattan that said she wanted "three very special girls, androgynous, pretty boyish girls...that can dance: well!"[13] And then she called Blond Ambition dancer Carlton Wilborn. "She said, 'Hey, I'm planning to go back out. I'm going to be doing auditions in LA. Do you happen to know any dancers who you think I should see?'" he recalled.[14]

Carlton had been acting in the years since the Blond Ambition tour, but he was still in touch with the dance community. He thought about it, offered a few suggestions, and then they hung up. "She called me back in ten minutes and said, 'Oh, my God, I didn't even think to ask you. Are you interested in going back out?'" He was. She also asked him to run the LA auditions. He agreed and choreographed the dances that would be part of the tryout.[15]

The number of dancers auditioning for the Girlie Show was even greater than the number who had tried out for Blond Ambition. By 1993, people knew what going on tour with Madonna meant. Carlton said the group was broader as well because Madonna recruited men *and* women and because she sought different qualities.[16] For the Girlie Show, she wanted dancers who would be able to play characters, not just be their larger-than-life selves, the way her Blond Ambition dancers so famously were.[17]

She still wanted people with personalities, though. The Girlie Show dancers had to be "open-minded" and "willing to take chances." They also had to have a sense of humor: she asked them to tell her a funny story. "If they were really embarrassed and couldn't do it, I didn't pick them," Madonna said. They also had to agree to shave their heads—though she didn't plan to have them do it for the tour. "I just wanted to see how far they were willing to go for me."[18]

Eight dancers, including Carlton, were chosen in New York and Los Angeles—four men and four women. Despite their differences, there was a homogeneity about the group. With their close-cropped hair, they looked like a military unit, which is how they operated: precisely, flawlessly, submerging their individuality to the group's goal.

Christopher called a young Brazilian named Alex Magno and asked him to try out for the job of choreographer. Madonna had seen his work in footage of an LA dance company. The challenge for his Girlie Show audition was to create a dance for "La Isla Bonita" and teach it to the dancers the following day, with Madonna watching. That gave Magno one night to prepare a performance that could change his life.[19]

He created the steps and taught them to the entire Girlie Show troupe. When the number ended, Madonna took him aside and put her hands on his shoulders. She said she liked his work, but she wanted to be clear about how *she* worked. If she ever asked him why they were doing certain steps, he needed to have a reason. He recalled her saying,

> "I am a performer that relies on a character, this is more a theatrical piece than just dance steps so every dance step must have a reason. So if I say I don't like the step I don't want you to take offence ... If you can do that then you're cool."[20]

He said he could absolutely do that. "So I got the job," said Magno.[21]

He wouldn't be alone. In addition to Madonna, Christopher, Niki Haris, and Carlton Wilborn, who all made contributions to the choreography, Jeffrey Hornaday, the man who choreographed the Who's That Girl tour, was back as stage director. The show would require many hands with many talents, because what Madonna was creating was something entirely new.[22]

Madonna had no interest in singing her songs as they appeared on her album. She told Jai Winding, who was back in the musical director's seat, that she wanted the band to create new songs out of old ones to support the story being told onstage. They did, beginning with "Erotica." "I just thought it was amazing," Madonna said. "And then I shape it and edit it ... that's basically how every song went."[23] By the time the tour began, some of her songs were unrecognizable and were thus reborn.

To create the show's fifteen hundred costumes, Madonna and Christopher selected a relatively new Italian duo. The Sicilian Domenico Dolce and Milanese Stefano Gabbana, who were partners in business and in love, began collaborating as Dolce & Gabbana in 1985. They produced their first ready-to-wear collection three years later and opened a showroom in New York in 1990. They were on the fashion radar, but not on the level of a Gaultier or Versace.[24]

Madonna's association with them came through Steven Meisel, who had photographed their collection. Her interest went public when she caused a sensation by attending their spring-collection show in Milan in October of 1992.[25] It wasn't until August of 1993 that she settled on them to design the costumes for her tour. Their aesthetic, which was heavily indebted to mid-twentieth-century movies, matched the tour's needs. The fact that their designs were less provocative than Gaultier's also attracted Madonna. She wanted the costumes to enhance the show, not become the show.[26]

In fact, Madonna's Girlie Show look was not in the least bit outrageous or even "sexy" in the traditional sense for women entertainers. The new Madonna was androgynous: thin, wiry, with blond hair cut short like a boy's. She downplayed the significance of the look, saying her hair was less a style choice than a necessity because she had damaged it by switching the color between pink and blond in Miami.[27] Whatever the reason, Dolce & Gabbana worked well with her latest incarnation and within the structure of the show.

Their designs ran the gamut from decadence to elegance: sequined hot pants and bras, tuxedos and top hats, jerseys and jeans, long skirts with bustles, and military coats with epaulets. Unlike the Gaultier costumes, which were works of art, the Dolce & Gabbana costumes were wearable fashion. The concert, meanwhile, gave them the professional break they had been waiting for. After the Girlie Show, Dolce & Gabbana became famous.[28]

The tour opened on September 25, 1993, at Wembley Stadium, in London. "I'll never forget that night," Christopher said.

> I was standing right at the end of the stage...and there were eighty thousand people in the audience. The music began, and there was this rush of energy coming toward the stage, and it hit me like somebody hit me with a bat...It sort of knocked me off my feet, and then she rose on that little platform, and it was even more intense.
>
> I think at that point I realized what a drug it was for the person onstage, for her. For me, but they weren't doing it for me...I always did my best to temper what I was feeling because I knew it wasn't for me...But it was unbelievable.[29]

Christopher left the stage and went to the light booth, where he wrote a note: "You're fucking amazing." He folded it up, handed it to a crew member, and told him to run to Madonna and give it to her. "I knew she knew that what we were doing was remarkable and would never happen again and had never been seen before. I could not have been more proud."[30]

The show opened with circus music and colored spotlights playing across the surface of the stage's heavy curtain. Above the stage the illuminated tour title, THE GIRLIE SHOW, lit up the darkness like a marquee. The extravaganza on offer was theater, commedia dell'arte, cabaret, burlesque—an Italian *spettacolo.* It was a world the audience was invited to enter by a Pierrot figure onstage and by dancer Carrie Ann Inaba, wearing only a G-string as she slowly descended a twenty-foot pole in an aerial ballet.[31]

To whispers of "Erotica," the Pierrot figure wandered off, and Inaba disappeared backstage. It was then that Madonna arose from the floor wearing black sequined hot pants, a black fringed vest, knee-high stack-heeled boots, and elbow-length black gloves. She was also carrying a riding crop. The audience saw her from behind in a halo of light and fog, but that was enough. It erupted in cheers that continued after she turned to face them as Dita singing "Erotica," her eyes covered by a domino mask.

That introduction was the last of Dita. Having shed her vest and mask, Madonna made a dramatic march downstage, a drum beating out each step until she stood in a black bra and sequined hot pants to give her first smile of the evening—warm, generous, beautiful. With that she launched into "Fever" and a threesome with dancers Carlton Wilborn and Michael Gregory, for which they were punished by descending into the "flames of hell."

It was during the third number that Madonna's intention to breathe new life into old material became clear. She reappeared in an elaborate head-dress with Niki, Donna, and all the dancers to perform her classic song "Vogue." Except in the Girlie Show, "Vogue" became South Asian and had nothing to do with fashion poses or even voguing in the Harlem sense of the term. By exchanging New York culture for Indian (or Thai or Balinese; it could have been any one of them), the dance showed that the concept of voguing—the expression of stylized beauty—manifests itself in many cultures in many ways and always has.

Unlike Blond Ambition, the Girlie Show contained few overt references to religion—just subtle reminders that religion forms part of who Madonna is. One of those references occurred during "Rain," which Madonna sang with Niki and Donna. Bathed in blue light, the three appeared in long black choir robes. And, like a choir performance, the moment was about harmony: three women's voices, perfectly layering over and around one another, weaving through several songs: "Rain," "Here Comes the Sun," and "Just My Imagination." It was gospel; it was the Beatles; it was '60s soul; it was a prayer, which ended what was referred to somewhat inexplicably as the dominatrix part of the concert. (The only S/M reference in the segment was Madonna's riding crop, which she did not use.)

During the interlude between "Rain" and Madonna's reappearance, all eight dancers performed with umbrellas in a number choreographed by Gene Kelly.[32] That performance ended with Madonna's voice shouting, "I'm going to take you to a place you've never been before." With that, the stage turned into a disco, and Madonna, astride a giant mirrored disco ball, descended from the rafters in a Marlene Dietrich blond afro wig and blue hot pants.

Niki and Donna joined her for "Express Yourself," followed by "Deeper and Deeper." Early in that song, a man ran onstage from the audience and tore off his shirt and pants. It wasn't immediately clear that he was a dancer until, given a colored boa, he was joined by his dance mates—all draped in similar accessories. The stage became a living Gay Pride rainbow flag as Madonna, Niki, and Donna sang.

After a reggae-heavy version of "Why's It So Hard," Madonna paid tribute to people with AIDS and those she had lost to the disease. She said later that she wondered whether fans in non–English-speaking countries would understand, but she decided to do it anyway "out of respect for my friends and out of respect for people who have AIDS or have died of AIDS . . . I just have to do it."[33]

During the Blond Ambition tour, Madonna's AIDS statements haunted her HIV-infected male dancers. During the Girlie Show, it was Niki who was moved. Her sister, Tammy, was dying, and there was nothing she could do to help her.[34] She was not alone. When Madonna sang "In This Life," her melancholy tribute to Martin Burgoyne and Christopher Flynn, many in the audience who had lost people to AIDS or were in the process of losing them cried. It was the concert's "Live to Tell" moment, and it was followed by more drama.[35]

While Madonna disappeared for a costume change, her voice recited the lyrics to her controversial remix of "Justify My Love." Written in 1990, it was called "The Beast Within" and described the triumph of love over evil.[36] Onstage, the song became a dramatic dance featuring Carlton Wilborn and Christopher Childers. Carlton was cast as the beast who, resorting to seduction and aggression, tries to ruin Childers's goodness. Carlton explained that the beast is "that dark entity that exists in the world . . . The work of the Beast, the work of the devil is to kill, steal, and destroy. That's its job." He said the performance's message was a warning: "Be acutely aware."[37]

Madonna returned to the stage to strains of Marlene Dietrich's 1930s song "Falling in Love Again." In top hat and tux, sitting on a trunk amid chandeliers, she sang in a heavy German accent a melody that the crowd knew by heart but may not have recognized. It was "Like a Wurgin," as Marlene Dietrich might have sung it in her comedies.

The slapstick continued with "Bye Bye Baby" and "I'm Going Bananas," featuring Madonna, Niki, and Donna, and "La Isla Bonita," which involved the entire troupe dancing on a catwalk. And then, to the sound of toy-soldier martial music, the dancers returned in long military coats against a backdrop of an American flag. Madonna, the drill sergeant, flanked by Niki and Donna, called "Attention," and the dancers fell in line to perform "Holiday" as streamers descended from the rooftop. The party was over, but Madonna refused to leave. After a mad scramble worthy of Buster Keaton or the Three Stooges, Niki finally carried Madonna away.

The audience did not budge as it applauded and awaited an encore. Fans knew that in Madonna's concerts, those final segments often involved her biggest artistic productions, and that night was no exception. She appeared in a white ruffled blouse, a beige vest, and a long bustled black skirt to sing "Justify My Love." She and her similarly attired company then reenacted the Royal Ascot scene from the 1964 film *My Fair Lady*—until they began to vogue, twist, and do the monkey. Not until Baz Luhrmann's 2001 musical, *Moulin Rouge!,* would a pop spectacle be as mischievously culture-bending. "That was just visually stunning," Donna recalled. "I mean, who does that?"[38]

But that wasn't the end of the show, either. Madonna returned in cutoffs and a white sleeveless undershirt to sing Sly and the Family Stone's "Everybody Is a Star" followed by her first single, "Everybody." That was her cue to introduce the band, Niki and Donna, and the dancers. And *that* was the end of the show—sort of.

Pierrot, who had wandered onstage throughout the night, reappeared to say goodbye. Dancing, blowing kisses, demanding applause, he finally revealed himself to be Madonna. Beaming in her clown costume, she sang just one line, "Everybody is a star," then waved to the crowd, winked, and disappeared behind the curtain.[39]

Those expecting the Girlie Show to be a stage version of *Sex* would go home disappointed. The Madonna on display was a comic performer. It was a role she relished.

At the end of that first show, with the noise of the crowd still roaring in their heads, the two kids from Pontiac looked at each other and said, "This is fucking amazing; this is fucking awesome." Madonna and Christopher were backstage surrounded by actors and British celebrities. "It was impossible to deny how good it was," he said.[40] Niki Haris recalled the concert as "joy, joy, joy. We all loved each other. It was just about great music."[41]

Some critics in Britain, however, were brutal in their assessment. A writer in *Melody Maker* asked rhetorically if Madonna had taken "another step down that path signposted 'No Way Out: Career Over.'"[42] Keith Cameron, in *NME,* said,

The most startling aspect to this whole affair is that Madonna considered it worthwhile in the first place...this is the soulless, humourless and

damn-near pointless sound of a woman now spreading herself too thin...
One hesitates to say that at thirty-five she's too old for all this.[43]

In her 1991 book, *Feminine Endings,* feminist music critic and scholar
Susan McClary wrote, "What most reactions to Madonna share...is an
automatic dismissal of her music as irrelevant. The scorn with which her
ostensible artistic focus has been trivialized is often breathtaking."[44] That
observation was still apt two years later, as it would be twenty years later.
But some critics in 1993 saw the Girlie Show for what it was. *The Guardian's* Caroline Sullivan called it "simply a brilliant entertainment."[45]

As the Girlie Show traveled to cities where Madonna had never performed, passions ran high and divided generations. Young people lapped
up the liberation she preached. Older people resented what she represented: invading US culture.

By 1993, there were fifty billion television sets in houses around the
world, on which audiences watched *Cheers, LA Law, Roseanne,* and Vanna
White on *Wheel of Fortune.* US films dominated global box offices. US
bestsellers in translation filled bookshelves. And US brands from Nike to
Levi's to McDonald's were ubiquitous. Madonna was one of the biggest
"brands" of all.[46] To some critics, she wasn't a person but a multinational
corporation that sold social chaos. As her tour moved to new countries,
figures in authority prepared for the worst.

In San Juan, Puerto Rico, Catholic churches urged followers to tie black
ribbons to trees to "ward off the effects of Madonna's" performance, and
on the night of the show, churches remained open so the religious could
pray away the demon woman.[47] Before her concert in Tel Aviv, she
required a military escort while visiting the Church of the Nativity in
Bethlehem because some Christians expressed outrage over her use of religious symbols.[48] A judge in Argentina denied efforts to ban her shows, but
he did impose age restrictions.[49]

In all the cities where officialdom feared Madonna's malign effect, fans
awaited her eagerly. Attendance records were set and broken—360,000
tickets sold in Australia, 100,000 in Canada, 120,000 in Argentina, nearly
140,000 in Mexico. In Rio de Janeiro, some of the 120,000 ticket holders
had to be let into the Maracanã Stadium early because they were so packed
together that firemen feared for their safety in the crush.[50] It was Madonna-
mania of the kind seen in her first concerts in the States.

While Madonna was on tour in November, *Dangerous Game* premiered in
New York. The movie received good reviews after its European debut, at
the Venice International Film Festival. In fact, among critics who saw the

film there, Madonna's performance was generally lauded for its authenticity. The *Los Angeles Times* called it a possible "breakthrough film."[51] Madonna herself thought she was "good in it" but that the movie itself was "shit."[52] It was a *Body of Evidence* experience all over again, except worse.

Even though Madonna's company, Maverick, produced the film, Ferrara had the final cut and murdered Madonna's character, which she said hadn't been in the script. She said he also edited out her verbal and physical responses to the violence she suffered so that she appeared in the finished film as a silent, simpering cinematic cliché of an abused woman. "When I saw the cut film, I was weeping," she said.

> It was like somebody punched me in the stomach. He turned it into *The Bad Director*. He's so far up Harvey Keitel's ass, it had become a different movie. If I'd have known that was the movie I was making, I would never have done it, and I was very honest with him about that. He really fucked me over. So *c'est la vie*...I keep coming to the same conclusion: that I have to be a director. I feel like I'm constantly being double-crossed.[53]

The film was distributed in limited release before it quickly disappeared entirely. Ferrara blamed Madonna for killing it.[54]

Dangerous Game capped a year of crushing lows and glorious highs. Even for observers, Madonna's change in altitude was dizzying. A favorite parlor game in the entertainment press was predicting not whether she would crack but when.[55]

Madonna loathed the idea of appearing tragic, much less *being* tragic. Rather than brood, she said her "skin grew at least six inches thicker," and she became philosophical.[56] She said she did not feel any shame about her life or harbor any regrets about her choices. "Any mistakes I've made are war wounds I wear proudly because they've shaped me more than anything else."[57] She said she remembered a time when she didn't have so many enemies.[58] But that was also a time when she didn't have as many fans.

That year, 1993, folklorist Kay Turner published a book called *I Dream of Madonna*. It was a collection of dreams that women between the ages of thirteen and sixty-one in the United States, Canada, Britain, and France had had about Madonna. In their nightly imaginings, they saw her as sad and happy, a savior and someone needing rescue, a mother and a child, a saint and a sinner. They saw her in all her guises and manifestations. She had helped them, and they, in their fantasies, helped her. She was the stuff of their dreams because she was the "worst nightmare" of the granddaddy of theoretically sanctioned misogyny, Sigmund Freud. She represented a way out of his mess.[59]

★   ★   ★

Near the end of her tour, in December of 1993, Madonna began working on another album. *Erotica* had been overshadowed by controversy, and she was distracted by several other projects while recording it. That would not be the case with her new work. She was quieter, more introspective, partly because of the battering she had taken the previous two years. She said that during that period, she forced herself to take a long, hard look in the mirror to determine what was most important to her as a woman and as an artist.[60]

Despite the accolades from millions of fans during her tour, the voices that resonated most loudly and were most distracting belonged to her critics. "It was hard to be so profoundly misunderstood and not be destroyed and go back to work," she said. "So I would say my state of mind, what I wrote about was a reaction, a reflection, or a response to that."[61]

The album, which would be called *Bedtime Stories,* was a musical version of that nighttime storytelling ritual. It is Madonna comforting herself as she tries to quell the anxiety of the day. Like the Girlie Show tour, it would not make pointed political statements. She said the key to the album lay in the track "Secret," which would be its first single. She described it as being "about self-love and a spiritual awakening. I saw the same line over and over again, 'Happiness lies in your own hand.' And that's something that I really—I really came to realize in the past few years."[62]

Musically, Madonna sought to continue the direction she began to take in *Erotica,* especially the sound she created with Andre Betts. Normally she worked with one or two producers. For *Bedtime Stories,* she found herself drawn to several. The R&B, hip-hop, and urban contemporary music scene—new jack swing—had thrown up a fresh generation of talent and was particularly rich at that moment. She was also intrigued by the experimental composers behind the house sounds that filled British and French ravers' heads as well as trip-hop, an electronic–hip-hop fusion, which kept their feet moving. Hungry for inspiration and collaboration, Madonna wanted to taste it all, so she came up with what she called a wish list of people to work with: Kenneth "Babyface" Edmonds, Dallas Austin, Dave "Jam" Hall, and Nellee Hooper.[63]

Babyface and Dallas Austin were part of the new R&B sound out of Georgia that had been dominating the pop and R&B charts. "The Atlanta scene, it was like the black version of Seattle," said Jonathan Van Meter, who at the time was editor of the R&B and hip-hop magazine *Vibe.* "A zesty, sort of yeasty bubble coming out of one place."[64]

In the late '80s and early '90s, grunge, which originated in the Pacific Northwest, offered an alternative to the corporate rock of arena bands by producing a new kind of music that combined DIY garage-band and punk traditions with heavy metal. It was the music of alienated white youth.

The Atlanta scene, by contrast, was Black, joyous and infectious. People such as Dallas Austin, Babyface, the girl group TLC, and Grammy award–winning Toni Braxton were ruling the radio with a new sound that was as fresh as Motown had been in the '60s and at times as soulful as early Aretha. "The songs Babyface was writing then were so good," Van Meter said. "All of a sudden it felt like prettiness was allowed to come back into music again. It was really inventive, and it wasn't caught in the crosshairs of the New York hip-hop gangster wars. It didn't feel angry."[65]

Madonna was interested in the Atlanta sound because she liked that it brought her back to her Detroit musical roots and challenged her with a new way to interpret her beloved R&B. It also allowed her to dabble in hip-hop, which was in many ways where the postmodern mentality of high and low culture—including sampling, appropriation, and conversion—had traveled. That movement had started in the street, and it returned there through music.[66]

Some attributed the young musicians' decision to work with Madonna to the allure of a healthy paycheck and a brighter spotlight. That might have been the reason they got into the project, but by the time they were working with her artist to artist, it was a situation of intense creativity and mutual respect.[67] "At the time, I felt that most black artists, even if they didn't admit it, they really did look up to and admire and take ideas from Madonna," explained Van Meter, who came to know the Atlanta artists as they passed through *Vibe*.

> I feel like people appreciated her absolute admiration and interest and participation in [the Atlanta sound]. I know there's that age-old thing of, like, the white artist who does Black music and gets all the credit. There is a history of that in this country. But I didn't feel that about her. I felt like Dallas Austin and all those Atlanta guys all wanted to work with her. I felt like they were all psyched.[68]

Madonna's lodestar for *Bedtime Stories* would be honesty: about herself, about relationships, about the world. She did not, she said, put herself in a "strait-jacket creatively."[69] The only subject that was off limits was sexuality. "Sex is such a taboo subject and it's such a distraction that I'd rather not even offer it up," she said.[70] "I didn't want to give the critics any sort of ammunition...Let's just say that part of my personality's in hibernation... at least for the sake of my record."[71]

The work on *Bedtime Stories* was the most complicated Madonna had undertaken, not just because it involved so many producers but also because those producers were spread out geographically—in New York, Los Angeles, Atlanta, and London.[72] It also presented a challenge for

Madonna because each of the people she worked with inhabited his own creative orbit and had his own distinct style. "It was really hard for me to glue the sound together and make one kind of theme happen through the music, sonically and lyrically," she said.[73]

Madonna went to the first person on her wish list, Babyface, for what he called "lush ballads." Working in a small studio he had built in his house in Beverly Hills, they wrote three songs—two of which appeared on the album: "Forbidden Love" and "Take a Bow."[74]

"Forbidden Love" was, as the title suggested, about desire denied, either by a person or by social or religious strictures. But in an interesting twist, the song didn't bemoan the rebuff. It included the whispered line "Rejection is the greatest aphrodisiac." One had the sense that the love in the song wasn't so much lost as deferred and therefore made more delicious. It was a song that would have resonated with her gay fans in the way "Deeper and Deeper" did, but more quietly.

"Take a Bow," which would become one of the biggest hits of Madonna's career, continued the rejection theme, but its ending was more definitive, if not tragic. It was also more mature. Madonna said in an interview about the album,

> I tend to collect thoughts, and as I go through life...a lot of times it takes me a long time before I can come to terms with, maybe, a relationship I had years ago, and I finally find a way to talk about it or write about it.[75]

Babyface said he had jotted down ideas for the music and presented Madonna with a "beat and the chords."[76] By the time they got into the studio in New York, his notations had grown to include Japanese influences and, at Madonna's suggestion, a full orchestral string section. The result would be romantic, gorgeous, and tender.

It was Babyface who introduced Madonna to another person she wanted to work with, twenty-three-year-old Dallas Austin. Austin was edgier than Babyface, but the four songs he worked on with Madonna—"Survival," "Secret," "Don't Stop," and "Sanctuary," which sampled Herbie Hancock—belied the younger artist's reputation as "street."[77] All four were sweet and smooth, echoing the early-'80s sound of artists like Womack & Womack.

Madonna covered personal disappointments in her ballads with Babyface. The songs written with Dallas Austin, by contrast, were about *recovery* from disappointment. "Survival," which would be the first track, was one of two responses on the album to people who might ask Madonna post-*Sex,* "How you doing?" The answer was "Getting by." The voice on the track was small and young. Singing backup, Donna De Lory and Niki Haris provided depth.

"Secret" was the soul of the album, according to Madonna. Musically, it combined a Latin guitar, an orchestral string section, and Dallas Austin's drums. Lyrically, it offered a new take on love: not only is self-love okay, it is also necessary in order to love another person.

Madonna's decision to include British composer Nellee Hooper on an album dominated by American R&B was less of an aberration than it appeared. He was a member of the Bristol-based band Massive Attack, which pioneered trip-hop, and he produced the British hip-hop band Soul II Soul, which could have fit easily into the Atlanta scene. Also, he had a history of working with powerful women, including Sinéad O'Connor, on "Nothing Compares 2 U," and Björk, on her first album, *Debut.* In fact, it was because of that album that Madonna became interested in him.[78]

Though Hooper would work on several *Bedtime Stories* songs at the remixing stage, his signature song was "Bedtime Story." Madonna was a Björk fan and wanted her to write something for the album. When Hooper conveyed the message, Björk hesitated. She was *not* a Madonna fan. "I couldn't really picture me doing a song that would suit her," she said. "But on second thought, I decided to do this, to write the things that I had always wanted to hear her say that she's never said."[79] The trippy, almost hallucinogenic song was unlike anything Madonna had ever done. It, along with "Sanctuary," pointed to the direction she would take on her next album, years later.

It was Freddy DeMann who recommended Dave "Jam" Hall. Hall's roots were in the gospel scene in Nashville, but he was raised in New Jersey and was part of the early hip-hop and new jack swing pioneers in the Bronx. He had worked with Mariah Carey on her huge 1993 hit "Dreamlover" and with the exciting newcomer Mary J. Blige on her 1992 debut album, *What's the 411?*[80]

Madonna recorded four songs with Hall. The first was the romantic orchestral track "Love Tried to Welcome Me." Of all the songs on the album, it sounded like one of her famous first-take recordings. Its raw vocals set against the lush strings, soft percussion, and wandering acoustic guitar made it the most sexual song on the album.

"Inside of Me" featured Madonna's little-girl voice. In the wake of *Erotica,* the breathy intro and heavy breathing throughout could be interpreted as sexual, but Madonna said the song was about her mother.[81] Madonna's third song with Hall, "I'd Rather Be Your Lover," was the album's funkiest. Though not necessarily danceable, it was down and dirty in the best

R&B tradition, and it was impossible not to move to it. It also included a guest rap—a first for Madonna—from Meshell Ndegeocello.

Ndegeocello had signed with Maverick in 1993 after more than two years of being turned down by other record companies. "People at those other labels said my music was too eclectic," said Ndegeocello, a bisexual Black woman. "They said they didn't know how to market me. They said some of the songs were sexy, but I wasn't glamorous or sexy enough to put them across." Madonna had met Meshell through Andre Betts and loved her sound and respected the artist.[82]

Though Madonna said she wanted to steer clear of sex on *Bedtime Stories,* the fourth song she recorded with Dave Hall was a delicious commentary on the subject that would become a signature of her career. She called it "Human Nature."

> It's my definitive statement in regards to the incredible pay-back I've received for having the nerve to talk about the things that I did in the past few years with my *Sex* book and my record. It's getting it off my chest. It is defensive, absolutely. But it's also sarcastic, tongue-in-cheek. And I'm not sorry. I do not apologize for any of it.[83]

"Human Nature" was Madonna at her cheekiest, wittiest, ballsiest, and righteously angriest—in other words, the Madonna her fans loved best. It was Madonna as social satirist. It was Madonna as Mae West. It was the Madonna you don't fuck around with.

When Madonna began work on *Bedtime Stories,* she recorded the first version of "I'd Rather Be Your Lover" with Tupac Shakur. That collaboration didn't make it onto the album, but the two began dating.[84] Tupac was an anomaly in the rap community. He didn't accept the music business's post–Rodney King focus on rap that extolled the virtues of money over social change.[85] He was raised in Baltimore by his Black Panther mother, Afeni Shakur, to be what he called the "Black Prince of the revolution."[86]

After the release of his highly political first album, *2pacalypse Now,* he moved to LA, and his lyrics focused on gang life. He became a kind of Charles Dickens chronicling a society eating itself alive.[87] "He rapped our pain," said rapper Big Syke. But Tupac couldn't remain a mere observer for long. In South Central, you had to take a stand, pick a side, get a gun.[88]

In 1993 he earned street cred by being arrested in Atlanta for shooting two off-duty policemen who, he said, were "harassing a black motorist." Tupac got off when an investigation revealed that the police were drunk, had instigated the fight, and, according to a prosecution witness, had used a gun stolen from an evidence locker to threaten Tupac. The incident cemented Tupac's reputation in the rap and gang community, but it also put him on the radar of police nationally. One of his lawyers said, "People in law enforcement not only disliked Tupac but despised him."[89]

It was around the time of his run-in with Atlanta police that Madonna met him. Twenty-two-year-old Tupac was in New York filming a movie in which he played a gangster. He used a Haitian music promoter named Jacques Agnant as inspiration for the part. Madonna knew Agnant—he popped up in music studios where she worked on her new album and at clubs she frequented—and through him met Shakur. She and he played opposite parts in Tupac's undoing: Agnant had a part in the episode that brought Tupac down, and Madonna would try to cushion the fall.[90]

The episode began in mid-November, when Agnant introduced Tupac to a nineteen-year-old woman. Tupac and the woman had sex, and then four days later she came to Tupac's hotel, where, she alleged, Tupac, Agnant, and a third man raped her. They were arrested, and Tupac and the other man (but not Agnant) were also charged with weapons violations. Tupac denied his role in the rape and believed that Agnant was an informant who set him up.[91]

While he awaited trial—a period of one year—Madonna's relationship with him deepened. It wasn't exclusive, and for her it may have been an attempt to rescue a man she saw as full of potential but who tempted fate so often that it was bound to catch up with him. He was a little like Basquiat: he was as gifted as he was ill-suited for the role he was cast in, and it was almost impossible to imagine that he would survive it.

Chapter 37

New York, Miami, Los Angeles, Ronda, 1994

My comfort is that all the great artists since the beginning of time have always been completely misunderstood and never fully appreciated until they were dead. They didn't understand van Gogh and they crucified Christ... So there you go, that's my solace.[1]

— *Madonna*

IN MID-MARCH OF 1994, Madonna's first song since *Erotica* was released. It was a gentle ballad called "I'll Remember," written with Pat Leonard for Alek Keshishian's college romance movie *With Honors.* For many people, the song represented Madonna's having rediscovered her way, and they rewarded her by sending it to number 2 on the charts. Two weeks later, she appeared on *The Late Show with David Letterman,* and all bets were off. The cascade of abuse that had rained down on her after her *Sex* book became a cyclone. To many, she wasn't just a slut; she was a crazy slut.

Madonna hadn't been on Letterman's show since she turned up with Sandra Bernhard six years earlier and teased viewers with suggestions of lesbianism. Letterman had invited her back many times. "I kept saying, 'I don't have anything to promote; what's the point?'" she recalled. "And he said, 'Just come on the show and we'll have a good time, just be silly and have fun.' And I said, 'Oh, what the hell.' Just the kind of mood I was in."[2]

Madonna had spent the hours before the *Letterman* taping with Tupac. "He got me all riled up about life in general so when I went on the show, I was feeling very gangster," she said. She had also smoked a joint, which lessened her self-control.[3] In the green room before the show, meanwhile, Letterman's writers discussed what she should say. Madonna recalled their suggestions:

Rag on this, make fun of his hair... They gave me a list of insults, basically. So in my mind, he knew that that's what the game plan was, that we were going to fuck with each other on TV. I told some of the writers I was going to swear, and they went "Oh, great, do it, we'll bleep it and it'll be hysterical."[4]

Letterman's monologues often poked fun at Madonna's sex life. The comments were cheap shots, locker-room stuff, except that they were made with some regularity on national television. Madonna decided to call Letterman's bluff. If he wanted to talk sex, he had to do it her way and to her face.[5]

Appearing in a sheer black blouse, long black skirt, and combat boots, Madonna handed Letterman a pair of her panties and told him that they were worn. He quickly put them in his desk.[6] "I don't think he knew what he was getting into," she said. "He's kind of like a yuppie version of Beavis and Butt-Head, you know, '*Oooooooh, gross.*'"[7] Though usually obsequious with guests, Letterman quickly turned bully.

First, he pressed her to kiss a man in the audience, which she refused to do. When he persisted, she called him a "sick fuck." That was less than two minutes into her appearance. Then *she* began to bully *him.* "Can't get through a show without talkin' about me or thinkin' about me," she said. "You're always fucking with me on the show." She repeated that line twice more.[8]

The camera panned the audience to show reactions and lingered on a middle-aged couple from Appleton, Wisconsin, who squirmed as they listened to her. Letterman reprimanded Madonna, saying, "This is American television...people don't want that in their homes at eleven thirty at night." The audience was with him, cheering and applauding at Madonna's expense. "Wait a minute," she said. "People don't want to hear the word *fuck*?" Letterman mock-confided to viewers that there was "something wrong with her." The studio audience sounded an ominous low boo.[9]

Letterman had mostly played along until Madonna threw away the Top Ten List that she was supposed to read and said, "Why can't we just talk to each other? Why do we have to have all this contrived bullshit? Fuck the tape, fuck the list, everything—"

Letterman interrupted, saying, "It seems like we know almost everything there is to know about you."

To which Madonna replied, "Really? You don't know a goddamned thing."[10]

His comment unleashed the suppressed rage that had been growing inside her after years of what she saw as mistreatment by critics and the media. "That was a time in my life when I was extremely angry...about everything," she said of her *Letterman* appearance. "I felt like a victim. So I lashed out at people."[11]

Letterman made himself an easy target. The conversation devolved into an exchange initiated by Madonna about peeing in the shower. The camera panned again to the couple from Wisconsin, who had become the conscience of America. They were not amused. Madonna's *Letterman* appearance had become a righteous "man versus female monster" event. It was a small-screen *Fatal Attraction.* Whenever Letterman defended his manhood or the nation's morality against Madonna's assault, the audience applauded wildly. When Madonna spoke, the unstated response was *Kill the bitch.* The hostility felt frighteningly real.[12]

By that point, Madonna said later, she had detached herself from the person she was onstage. "I have no control over that person."[13] She refused to leave to make way for the next guest or allow Letterman to cut to a commercial. He, in response, became more aggressive, making cracks about her supposed predilection for NBA players. When she said she was interested in someone named Dave, Letterman asked "David Dinkins?" The random mention of the Black mayor of New York City could be interpreted as a "wink, wink, nudge, nudge" reference to the fact that Madonna dated Black men.[14]

Bandleader Paul Shaffer, perhaps sensing disaster, signaled to his musicians to play a cutaway number. An audience member shouted, "Get off!" Madonna snapped back that she wasn't going anywhere. Shaffer's band then began to play Hitchcock music. Finally the network broke in with a commercial, and when the show returned, Madonna was gone.[15]

During her appearance, she said "fuck" thirteen times—though each one was bleeped. Shaffer said later, "We were all amazed by it, shocked by it, really. And it was kind of shocking to hear the words she said on national television." Letterman expressed outrage, too. But it was all show. The segment was taped, and if the outrage had been real and the need to preserve American morality paramount, it wouldn't have aired. Instead, CBS ran it and reaped a ratings bonanza, capturing a quarter of all viewers in that competitive late-night time slot.[16] It was a little like the *Sex* book. Though denounced as abhorrent, it flew off the shelves.

Madonna said she immediately regretted her performance. "I couldn't believe how freaked out people were...You can show a person getting blown up, and you can't say 'fuck'? It's such hypocrisy." Still, the reaction got to her. "I can't tell you how intimidating it all is, and how, if you're not an incredibly resilient human being, it can crush you, no question about it."[17] "Since the David Letterman show, the news is that I've lost my mind."[18]

Norman Mailer watched the show and thought Madonna comported herself well but that Letterman—and the press afterward—acted like a schoolyard thug. "Madonna, once again, was being called sick, sordid, depraved, unbalanced, out of control, offensive, outrageous, and stupid. So wrote all the boozers, cokeheads, and solid suburbanites who do the TV columns." When the coverage migrated to news pages, it remained moralistic. Mailer told *Esquire* he wanted to do a story on Madonna. He would write to her rescue.[19]

Miami was Madonna's escape hatch and refuge. She once told an interviewer, "I don't know how to relax...I'm a certifiable workaholic...I'm a perfectionist—I'm anal retentive...I have insomnia and I'm a control freak."[20] In Miami she (mostly) wasn't that person. She said that as soon as she arrived there, "it's like taking a Valium."[21]

She had a daily ritual of covering herself in honey and jumping into Biscayne Bay, where she floated until the honey melted away, at which point she made a wish. She had also found a mother figure whom she described as an "older Cuban woman...I feel sort of unconditional love from her. I cry on her shoulder about men, about working too hard, about wanting to have children. I've never had that in my life." And she went to church.[22]

Though Madonna disagreed with almost every policy emanating from the Vatican, she had found a Catholic church down the street from her house, St. Jude Melkite, and went there, she said, with her "surrogate mother...She loves the priest, the priest comes over to my house all the time, Father Gabriel, and they're really sweet...It's very comforting, it really is. Because you get the understanding of how it used to be. A sense of community."[23]

In Miami, Madonna could live a normal enough life. She could go shopping, or even to the movies, without a bodyguard. Once, while she was in a theater, three girls in front of her turned around to ask if anyone ever told her she looked like Madonna. Madonna said, yes, she heard that a lot. She thanked them, and they all returned to watching the show.[24]

And she could have a social life. "If you wanted something private," Christopher said, "you went to your [own] house or you went to Versace's house. Otherwise, people generally hung out at the clubs on Washington...We had drag queens in tow, and we had people who weren't fancy traveling with us and hanging out. We were nondiscriminatory."[25]

The clubs in Miami were like Madonna's favorites in New York. They were even populated by many of the same people. "I feel like I take a lot of shit, and so does the gay and dance community. I feel comfortable there," she said. "I'm not going to feel comfortable in a country club in Connecticut. I'm a freak to those people. I want to go where other people can go and feel like we're different, but we're not freaks. We're just different."[26]

Madonna's friendships in Miami had also solidified, including the one with Donatella Versace. Madonna "hung out with the top photographers at the time, which were the same ones I was working with," Donatella said. "We moved in the same circles and saw each other at parties. For a while it was just 'Ciao, Ciao.' Then one day she called me and said, 'We need to talk.'" It was the period after *Sex,* and as part of her recovery and rehabilitation, Madonna asked Donatella to help her create a new image. She wanted to ditch Dita. Donatella gave her a Jean Harlow look as well as emotional support during that troubled period.[27] In return, Madonna agreed to become the face of Versace.

She would be shot that summer by Steven Meisel for Versace's 1995 spring-summer collection and by Peruvian photographer Mario Testino for the fall-winter collection. Testino called that photo shoot a turning point in his career, in part because the ads ran in *Vanity Fair* with the headline VERSACE PRESENTS MADONNA PHOTOGRAPHED BY TESTINO. "For the first time," he said, "I was part of the group of photographers that are known by their surname: Avedon, Newton, Penn."[28]

Madonna's appearance was also a breakthrough for Versace, after which celebrities lined up to be part of the house's ad campaigns. By way of thanks, Donatella had a cake made for Madonna's birthday that was so large it had to be cantilevered into the pool at Casa Casuarina. As it floated, men in Versace swim briefs cut slices and waded through the water to distribute them to guests.[29]

It was only natural, then, that after the ugly scene on *Letterman,* Madonna would flee south to her protective social bubble and her beautiful home. And it made sense that, angry about being used and abused for playing Letterman's game, she would be attracted to the baddest ass in the NBA. It was soon after *Letterman* that she met Dennis Rodman in Miami.

Jonathan Van Meter had followed Madonna's work since he saw a poster for her first album at his local record store in 1983 and bought the first issue of *Spin,* which featured a photo of Madonna by Herb Ritts. "It was a constant stream from there. I fed my addiction constantly like a weirdo," he said. By the time he was editor of *Vibe,* a decade later, he was still a fan, so much so that he wanted Madonna on the cover. Liz Rosenberg told him that Madonna didn't want to sit for another interview, but if he could find something interesting for her to do or someone interesting for *her* to interview, she'd agree to the cover.[30]

Like her friend Spike Lee, Madonna was an avid NBA fan. There were even rumors in the press that she wanted to buy a team. And of course there were rumors that she counted several NBA players among her boyfriends. During a Knicks–San Antonio Spurs game in 1994, a *USA Today* reporter asked her what she thought of the Spurs' flamboyant player Dennis Rodman. Madonna replied, "He's like the Madonna of basketball."

Jonathan Van Meter read that quotation and knew whom he wanted Madonna to interview. He called Liz Rosenberg and told her his idea. Madonna agreed to do it.[31]

The first week in April, Van Meter and photographer Melodie McDaniel, whom Madonna chose to shoot the cover, flew to Miami and appeared at Madonna's home on Brickell Avenue, also known as Millionaires' Row. Recalling his impressions, Van Meter said,

> It was the first time I'd ever been to a house where there was an enormous circular driveway with perfectly manicured grass growing up between the cobblestones. It was the first time I'd ever seen true master-of-the-universe kind of decadent living. I was really amazed by it. It had a huge wooden door, and the house was filled with gardenias floating in water bowls, and there were gardenias planted all around the house, so there was this incredibly intoxicating smell. I remember floating into her house.[32]

Madonna was in the kitchen with her entourage—including assistant Caresse Henry, Ingrid Casares, and Liz Rosenberg—as she held forth on Letterman. "She hopped up on the counter in the kitchen—she was so tiny—and she put her feet in the kitchen sink, and that's where she sat perched while she talked to the people in the room about the David Letterman reaction," Van Meter said. "She was incredibly defensive. She was just so annoyed."[33] In fact, she wouldn't let it go for weeks. In the meantime, however, she had a rendezvous with Dennis Rodman for *Vibe,* which was to begin with a photo shoot.

Melodie McDaniel had scouted places in Overtown, Miami's Harlem. The look she was going for was gritty, and she settled on an old garage and the exterior wall of a deli for the backdrop. Madonna, Rodman, Melodie, Van Meter, and a few other people then descended upon Overtown for the shoot. Security was light and was no match for the crowd. Interestingly, the excitement was less for Madonna than it was for Rodman.[34]

"At one point Dennis Rodman started to change his clothes right in front of everybody in broad daylight in public, completely naked," Jonathan said. After the faux outrage Madonna was subjected to on Letterman, Rodman's fuck-you-I'll-do-what-I-want-to attitude appealed to her. There was a "sexual energy and tension between the two of them that was just very obvious," Jonathan said. He recalled thinking, "Whoa, what's happening here?" The photos taken, Rodman came by Madonna's house a few days later for his interview. Jonathan gave her his tape recorder and a list of questions, then Madonna and Rodman went outside onto the lawn for a couple of hours.[35] That was the start of a brief but steamy relationship between them.

Van Meter, meanwhile, returned to *Vibe* with a transcript of the conversation filled with notations from Madonna along with potential cover photos of the two of them. He wrote the introduction and the headline: GAME RECOGNIZES GAME. "It was all ready to go; it was almost on the printer. We were thrilled," he said. Then, abruptly, the magazine's publisher, producer Quincy Jones, decided he didn't want to run it. "The idea of a big black man and a little white woman on the cover didn't sit well with Quincy Jones," Jonathan said.[36]

Vibe had been created as a "black *Rolling Stone,*" a place where Black musicians and Black cultural figures could get the kind of coverage—including covers—that they didn't get in white publications. The magazine was only around ten issues old, and though all but one of the covers had featured a Black artist, the previous issue had showcased the Beastie Boys. Jones didn't want a second cover in a row to present a white person. Jones also received complaints from Spike Lee and Eddie Murphy. Both were being profiled in what would have been the Madonna-Rodman issue, and both felt *they* should be the cover. "There were seven different crosscurrents happening," Jonathan said, "and finally Quincy said, 'Nope, I'm putting my foot down.' We had a huge fight, and I quit my job over it." Madonna's interview with Rodman was not published.[37]

At home in New York, while Jonathan was "licking his wounds," his boyfriend answered the phone and told him, "It's Madonna." She wanted to know what happened. She was angry, but not at him. In fact, she sent him white flowers and a note that said, "What we risk reveals what we value." She appreciated that he had fallen on his sword on her behalf.[38]

Meanwhile, Norman Mailer received the okay from *Esquire* to proceed with his article about Madonna and the cooperation of the woman herself. The two met in New York. Like the Rodman encounter, it began with a photo shoot—in photographer Wayne Maser's loft in SoHo. Seventy-one-year-old Mailer wasn't keen on being photographed with a woman half his age. He was aware of what he called the "shrinkage that visits a senior citizen."[39]

His discomfort grew when he was positioned next to her in front of a white canvas for the shoot. She stood in a green evening gown, and Mailer watched Maser pull down her strap and unceremoniously expose her breast. A self-described "secret gentleman," Mailer was disturbed by the lack of respect shown the lady and by standing alongside her in that state. He said, "Now we had portly Norman Mailer standing next to diminutive Madonna, in a green gown, one breast showing, a small nose ring in her left nostril."[40]

The encounter continued later that week at Madonna's apartment. The two icons represented different generations and perspectives, yet they had an elucidating meeting of the minds.[41] They traded ideas about work, sex, family, religion, politics, fame, porn, women's rights, and human rights. Mailer asked whether Madonna thought she spoke for all women. She said no.

> I've been accused for years and years, especially at the beginning of my career, of setting the women's movement back because I was being sexual in a traditional way, with my corsets and push-up bras and garter belts...and feminists were beating the fuck out of me: "What are you doing? You're sending out all the wrong messages to young girls. They should be using their heads, not their tits and their asses." My whole thing is you use all you have, all you have, your sexuality, your femininity, your—any testosterone you have inside of you, your intellect—use whatever you have and use bits and pieces wherever it's good.[42]

Mailer interrupted her. "Very well said," he commented, "but in the name of what?"

Madonna: In the name of what?

Mailer: Well, you're a revolutionary. What will this revolution be in the name of?

Madonna: In the name of human beings relating to human beings. And treating each other with compassion.

Mailer: And for that, you feel that the stereotyped male notions of how to treat women have to be broken down.

Madonna: Yes.

Mailer: Destroyed.

Madonna: Yes.

Mailer: What about female attitudes about men?

Madonna: That, too.

Mailer: But the female movement offers almost no compromise with men.

Madonna: Well, that's a problem, but you've got to start somewhere.[43]

Mailer said he embarked on the interview with Madonna to discover who she was. His conclusion may have surprised even himself. He identified her as the cultural offspring of Marilyn Monroe and Andy Warhol, and yet more than, or deeper than, either one.

> She gives us something Marilyn never could, something less attractive but equally valuable; she dramatizes for us how dangerous is any human's truth

once we dare to explore it; she reminds us that the joys of life bed down on broken glass.

As for Warhol, Mailer said that with her work she filled the "void" that he "enshrined in the ice of his technique," transcending artistic mediums and raising them to new heights. Especially video. Mailer called that perhaps "the only new popular art form in American life." And he called Madonna the master of the form.[44]

He ended their session by saying, "I want to leave you with an idea. I've come to the conclusion that you are a great artist." Madonna gasped. "It's on the record now," he said. "That's going to be the theme of this piece, that what we have among us is our greatest living female artist."[45]

It was not something that Madonna, especially during that controversial period, was accustomed to hearing. In fact, it was not something that she had *ever* heard. What do you say when someone confirms your own suspicion? She answered the only way she could. She simply said, "Thank you."[46]

In 1994, Madonna finally sold her Oriole Way home and moved into Castillo del Lago after Christopher's renovations were completed. Los Angeles was a place where Madonna went to work. "It's a city of making deals," she said. "Everyone's on the make here."[47] The city didn't inspire her, she said, so when she was there, she spent a lot of time at home.[48] That lack of distraction made it easier for her to concentrate on the task at hand, her album *Bedtime Stories*.

Madonna worked with Nellee Hooper and his fellow Brit programmer-producer Marius de Vries of Massive Attack in Encino at Chapel Studios. On his first day at the studio, de Vries recalled, he arrived to find a young woman in the corner who looked like an employee. He said hi and continued to set up his equipment. It was Madonna. Far from being offended, de Vries said she "enjoyed it."[49] Marius would be one of Madonna's studio partners off and on for the next twenty years as she moved toward more experimental music.

Hooper and de Vries were the last producers Madonna worked with on the album, and only then, she said, did she get "a grip of what the sound of the whole record was, so I had to go back and redo a lot."[50] It only took around two and a half weeks. De Vries said Madonna knew the sound she wanted.[51]

In August, she was able to slip away from LA and headed to Miami, where Christopher had organized a party at her house. It was the place where they celebrated holidays (with Christopher as chef), of which her birthday was one. In fact, birthdays among their crowd in Florida were occasions for major celebrations, each designed to outdo the last. One constant for nearly all of them was a Cuban singer named Albita. She was so beloved that Gianni Versace would have her sing to him over the phone when he was traveling.[52]

"I arranged for Albita to come and play at the party," Christopher said. "I also arranged for a bunch of drag queens to come." Madonna, meanwhile, had invited her Miami friends and her wider orbit, which included a group of NBA players. "It was a funny, weird mix of people that probably should never have happened," Christopher said.[53]

All went well during the performances, and everyone seemed happy, so Christopher ducked into the house for a respite. When he returned, all the drag queens were in the pool.

> Apparently, the basketball players had had enough of them and pushed them into the water. They were floating around, wigs floating around. I was really angry. There was nothing funny about it, and [the players] were kind of laughing...I said, "Madonna, get these stupid fuckers out of the house... Why would you invite them knowing who was coming and how they would respond?" That was the end of the party. I had to get into the water to fish all these men out and had to deal with—I don't know if you know what it takes for a drag queen to get dressed and then get made up and the hair and the corsets and all the other crap.[54]

Madonna's worlds had collided, to the detriment of the queens. Apologies for those disrespected or hurt by it were made and accepted. In fact, reconciliation was in the air that late summer.

Madonna had been invited to present the Video of the Year award on September 8 at the MTV Video Music Awards, where she typically stole the show with a shocking statement or performance. She asked herself whom she should appear with.

> I thought if I come out with anyone there has to be a symbolism...And I thought, wouldn't it be great to come out with David Letterman, because everyone thinks we're in this huge world war. And so I called him up and... I said, "Dave, are you ready to bury the hatchet?" He goes, "There is no hatchet."[55]

The award Madonna was to present was the last of the evening. She and Letterman came out arm in arm, he in his usual suit and tie, she as her

Bedtime Stories Jean-Harlow-via-Versace persona. "He was so nervous," Madonna said. "He was so sweet the way he was gripping my arm as we walked out on the stage."[56] When they reached the podium, Madonna said to the audience, "And you thought we wouldn't last." Holding Madonna by the hand and having performed his duties for the evening, Letterman leaned toward her and stage-whispered, "I'll be in the car; watch your language." He kissed her and left.[57] "I have to say I adore him," Madonna said later.[58]

Aerosmith, meanwhile, was the surprise winner of the Video of the Year award. The lead singer, Steven Tyler, possibly hoping to reclaim the outrage mantle from Madonna or perhaps "shame" her, said, "Madonna, baby! I saw your book, *Erotica* [sic]." Holding up two fingers in a clearly rehearsed routine, he turned to guitarist Joe Perry and asked, "Now, Joe, why do you suppose Madonna uses these two fingers to masturbate with?"

"I don't know. Why, Steven?" Perry asked.

"Because they're mine," Tyler answered.

Madonna, who had stepped aside, pushed through the band members and said, "Wait a second. If I used your fingers, then it's *not* masturbation."

"What would it be?" Tyler asked, confused.

"Sexual abuse," she responded.

Tyler shrank back from the microphone, speechless and chastened. Madonna had had another VMAs moment.[59]

The next day, she got to work on her own video, which would be the first for her new album. "Secret" was shot over three days in Harlem by Melodie McDaniel, who had photographed Madonna and Rodman for *Vibe* and who was one of the few women of color directing videos at that time. It was McDaniel's short film about a voodoo baptism that made Madonna choose her for "Secret." McDaniel said it was its "rawness" that attracted her.[60]

Madonna chose Harlem as the video's backdrop because people who didn't know the area thought of it as a "ghetto where everybody is sad, and people are full of despair and there's no hope." She said when she walked in Harlem she saw beautiful people and happy children. "I thought since this song is about uncovering a secret, I liked combining that."[61]

McDaniel settled on the Lenox Lounge as the scene of Madonna's musical performance in the video. She also looked for colorful local characters—old men, children, women, trans people—to fill out the small cast, which included actor Michael K. Williams in one of his first roles. Marc Jacobs designed the costumes, and Brigitte Echols, a young woman with punk DNA, was hired as stylist.[62]

For the duration of the video shoot, one corner of Harlem was transformed into "Madonna world." Her crew installed a mobile home and trailers. Security roamed the set, as did her entourage, which was aug-mented by famous friends. Donatella Versace even popped by for a visit.[63] The shoot, however, did not start well. McDaniel hadn't been clear about how she wanted Madonna to look. When Madonna emerged from her trailer, glamorous and clean, she was the opposite of what the director envisaged. McDaniel summoned the courage to explain her concerns to Madonna, who shot back, "Why the fuck didn't you tell me? Wasting all this time!" Madonna retreated to her trailer and came out looking like she'd just crawled out of bed after a night in the club. Perfect. "I've seen her be hard on people," McDaniel said, "but it wasn't being mean. There's no room for dilly-dallying around."[64]

Echols, meanwhile, watched Madonna with fascination and concluded that, even more than the director, the key relationship for her while film-ing was with the cinematographer, who in that case was Pascal Lebègue. Lebègue had also been director of photography on the videos for "Open Your Heart," "Vogue," and "Justify My Love." Echols said Madonna had a deep understanding of lighting, the best angles for a shot, and how to interact with Lebègue's camera.[65]

Madonna's character in the video is a singer in a small nightclub per-forming with a small ensemble for a small audience. It is a simple, intimate scene. The video references previous Madonna videos: a pool hall is a reminder of "Borderline"; Madonna climbing a staircase recalls "Papa Don't Preach"; "Like a Prayer" is invoked in a scene in which Madonna, in a white slip, undergoes a voodoo baptism and is lifted up by the hands of a religious figure. What is new to the "Secret" video is domesticity. It ends with Madonna finding happiness with a man who may or may not be her husband and a child who may or may not be hers.

The video was one of the rare moments in the pop culture of the time in which a white person was in the minority and one of the *very* rare instances in which a white woman is shown living in a Black community without fear. It was especially poignant because one of the most famous Black men in America, O. J. Simpson, was about to stand trial in the stabbing death of his white ex-wife, Nicole Brown Simpson. Among the many debates that case ignited was one about interracial relationships.[66]

Just a few years before, in 1991, a National Opinion Research Center poll found that one in five whites thought interracial marriage should be illegal. Author Earl Ofari Hutchinson, who wrote a book on the subject, said the Simpson case reinforced "ancient white fears of black men as hypersexual and dangerous."[67] In Madonna's video, skin color is meaning-less. The characters find love where they find it.

The "Secret" video aired on MTV on October 4 and helped propel the single, the first from *Bedtime Stories,* to the top five globally. In Britain,

Madonna made history: "Secret" was her thirty-fifth consecutive top ten single. No other artist had had so many straight hits. The song made another kind of history, too. Madonna became the first artist to offer a single from a new album as a download. In doing so, she included a prescient message by way of introduction:

> Hello, all you cyberheads! Welcome to the '90s version of intimacy. You can hear me, you can see me, but you can't touch me.[68]

"Secret" was a hit, but the album *Bedtime Stories,* also released in October, wasn't. In true Goldilocks fashion, some critics who had denounced her *Erotica* excesses now said her album was too tame, that she had not taken enough chances.[69] Others praised it. Stephen Holden, in the *New York Times,* went so far as to call it "easily Madonna's best album."[70] Barbara O'Dair, in *Rolling Stone,* said, "The record verily shimmers...*Bedtime Stories* says 'Fuck off, I'm not done yet.'"[71] The album hit number 3 in the States but sold only slightly more than *Erotica.* Madonna still hadn't won back her audience.

In November, Tupac Shakur finally stood trial on sexual assault and weapons charges. While the jury deliberated, on November 30, he went to a studio in Times Square to contribute a rap on another artist's record. Three men followed him into the building and shot him five times—once in the head. They hadn't killed him.[72] Determined to show up for the jury and fight again for his life, he appeared in court the next morning in bandages and a wheelchair. He was acquitted on three sodomy counts and the weapons charges but convicted on two counts of sexual abuse. He said he wasn't guilty but that he was to blame for failing to prevent the young woman's assault by others.[73]

Rather than pay the $3 million bail and risk the streets, where whoever had tried to kill him might do so again, Tupac surrendered himself to the court and was transferred to Rikers Island to await sentencing.[74] He used his time in jail to get a grip on his life. Part of that was making amends to people he had wronged, Madonna among them. He told Kevin Powell, who interviewed him at Rikers for *Vibe,*

> I was letting people dictate who should be my friends. I felt like I was this big Black Panther type...I couldn't be friends with Madonna. And so I dissed her, even though she showed me nothing but love. I felt bad, because when I went to jail, I called her and she was the only person that was willing to help me. Of that stature.[75]

On the day he met with Powell, Tupac also wrote a letter to Madonna asking that she visit and explaining why he had broken up with her. Addressing his words to "M," he wrote that for her to be seen in the company of a Black man would only make her seem more exciting, but if he appeared with a white woman, he risked disappointing "half of the people who made me what I thought I was." Shakur said he hadn't meant to hurt her and wanted to explain that while he still had the chance. "Please be careful Madonna. Everyone is not as honorable as they seem. There are those whose hearts bleed with envy and evil. They would not hesitate to do you harm."[76]

In February of 1995, Tupac would be sentenced to the maximum-security prison in Dannemora, New York, where he would remain until the fall. A year later, he would be murdered in a drive-by shooting in Las Vegas. He was twenty-five. No one has ever been arrested in his killing.[77]

Even before Tupac's arrest, shooting, and sentencing, Madonna had begun thinking about changing her life.[78] "I did my sexual rebellion thing. I took it as far as I could go...I've been naked in every state and country," she said. "There's nothing more!...I worked it out of my system."[79] She began searching "for meaning and a real sense of purpose."[80] In November of 1994, she said she wanted to have a child. "I look forward to making the sacrifices."[81]

Finding a man to have a child with, however, was fraught with peril. Whenever people came into Madonna's circle, in whatever capacity, she had to assess their intentions.

> I immediately go, "OK, what are their motives? What could they gain from this?" I have a whole filing system, and I watch for it. But I'm fooled sometimes, believe me—I think people have the best interests and they don't... It doesn't keep me from having friends or allowing people to get close to me, but it does add a whole other layer of anxiety to the normal ones when you're getting to know someone.[82]

There had been men in her life she had considered having a child with: she had discussed it with her bodyguard Jimmy Albright, whom she began dating after the publication of *Sex*.[83] The tabloids even suggested that she wanted to have a child with Sean. They were spotted holding hands on the set of *Body of Evidence* when his relationship with Robin Wright was "undergoing problems."[84]

And then one September day while jogging in Central Park, Madonna met a thirty-year-old Cuban American named Carlos Leon. "She was running, I was on my bike," he said. "I had seen her a few times before speaking to her." He stopped to say hello, they talked, and that was the end of it until Madonna called him. He was dumbfounded. "Can you believe this?" he asked his friends.[85]

A bicycle-racing fanatic and personal trainer, Carlos was one of two sons born into a rock-solid Catholic family. Raised on Manhattan's West Side, he was taught religious values at home and in parochial schools, and he had a Cuban work ethic. Like Madonna, he didn't drink or do drugs. Unlike Madonna, however, he had not fled his family. Even when he no longer lived with them, he visited his parents daily.[86]

He told them he was dating Madonna, and they thought he was joking. "When they showed up, we thought it was a look-alike or something," his father, Armando, said. But Madonna soon became part of the family, eating dinner with the Leons, listening to Cuban music, talking late into the night. In November, she spent Thanksgiving with Carlos and his extended family at the Miami Beach home of his great-aunt. The Miami Cuban connection may have cemented the relationship for Madonna. She told an interviewer that fall, "I was Spanish in another life. I am Cuban-Spanish. I love Cuba."[87]

Not long after Madonna met Carlos, she mused aloud during an interview, "I'll probably never find someone who has everything, who's like a combination of every incredible novel I've ever read, and every great movie I ever saw...but I want to get pretty damn close. Then I figure my friends can fill in the rest." She also realized that she would be a difficult partner for any man.

> It's like, "Be there when I want you, but get the fuck out of my face when I need my space," and there aren't a lot of people who can deal with that...I have a crazy schedule, I'm always all over the place, so I need someone who's more stable, but then I get pissed off and angry because they're not out being ambitious like I am...You want somebody to be there for you, but as soon as they say they will, you think they're a wimp...A really nice, kind person saying, "I'm going to love you for the rest of your life" and I'm like, "What's *wrong* with you?"[88]

Carlos was apparently the right combination of attentive and aloof, content and driven. And he ticked the macho box as well as Sean did but without as much drama. He also had a "strong sense of self," which Madonna said was necessary to weather the comments and attacks that would inevitably arise because of his association with her.[89] Madonna told Christopher that she was in love with Carlos. Having watched her life spin out of control, her friends greeted Leon's arrival in it with relief. Liz Rosenberg called him a "stabilizing influence."[90] The timing could not have been better. Madonna was about to embark on the biggest film project of her life.

As early as 1987, Madonna had met with directors and producers to discuss a possible film version of Andrew Lloyd Webber and Tim Rice's stage musical *Evita,* based on the life of the late Argentinean first lady Eva Perón.[91] In 1994, British director Alan Parker's name became attached to the project. He had directed more than a dozen terrific films, among them *Midnight Express, The Commitments,* and *Mississippi Burning,* and had the skill to film Eva Perón's story. Madonna felt it was her destiny to portray her. "I just knew that no one could understand what she went through better than I," she said.

> I related to her commitment, discipline and ambition [and] that bravery required for a girl of fifteen to come from the pueblos and go to Buenos Aires to find her way in entertainment and later in politics. Her suffering as a child was a catalyst to make a better life. I understood that. Because of her enormous impact, her detractors tried to tear her down and desecrate her image. People were frightened of the power she had and undermined her accomplishments by calling her a whore. I can certainly relate to that.[92]

Madonna went to Spain in November to shoot a video for "Take a Bow," which would essentially be an audition tape for *Evita.* The director she chose to work with was a relative newcomer, Michael Haussman.[93]

In Paris for Fashion Week, Madonna met him at the Ritz to discuss the project. She still hadn't settled on an idea, so she told him, "OK, here's the song: It's about a girl in love with a public figure. Write something, but just don't make it dark." During small talk over dinner, she asked him what he'd been doing, and he told her he'd been filming corridas—Spanish bullfighting. "And I just saw this sparkle in her eye and suddenly I just kind of went with it," he said, adding that he was "pretty sure the whole thing was written that night."[94]

The subject was exactly where Madonna's mind and heart were at that time. She was in love with Hispanic culture because of Miami and her new boyfriend, Carlos Leon.[95] The video would also show Alan Parker how she might perform in a period piece set in a Latin country. She left it to Haussman to put it together. He knew whom he wanted to play the matador: the famous toreador Emilio Muñoz. Haussman was told, however, that Muñoz would never do something so commercial. And indeed, he held out. Haussman waited for four days at a Seville hotel before Muñoz even agreed to talk to him.[96]

Meanwhile, People for the Ethical Treatment of Animals got wind of the fact that Madonna's video would include a bullfight.[97] It became so controversial that Haussman had police in his London office to check for letter bombs, and one of the video's producers received a death threat.[98]

In the face of that kind of opposition, and with MTV censors in mind, Haussman conceded that he could not stage a bullfight in which the bull was killed. Haussman described the problem to Muñoz. The toreador's reply was "Let me think about this." And with that, he disappeared for two days while Madonna made her way to Spain. "The drama was just fantastic!" Haussman said. Finally, Muñoz resurfaced and announced to the Spanish press, "I'm going to fight this bull, and I'm not going to pick [stab]...him. It's going to be the first time it's ever done and I'm going to do it." That announcement was Muñoz's answer to Haussman's request. He agreed to do the video.[99]

"Take a Bow" was shot over five days in Ronda, Spain, a fifteenth-century town in the province of Málaga. The bullfight took place in the city of Antequera, in Andalusia. Unlike the video for "Bad Girl," which abandoned the music-video format altogether and became a short movie, the "Take a Bow" video intersperses dramatic scenes with shots of Madonna singing. It thus remained firmly in the music-video camp, albeit on an elevated level.

The costumes, which intentionally evoke Eva Perón, were designed by John Galliano, Donatella Versace, and famed French-Egyptian shoe designer Christian Louboutin. The details in the costumes and in *every* aspect of the shoot had to be exquisite—Madonna made sure of that. "When you want something done right and you care about something, so often you're perceived as being a bitch," she said. "But...it's your ass on the line. You're being judged for it, so you've gotta make it the best it can be."[100]

The bullfight required five cameras working from various angles because it simply could not be directed: the bull did as it pleased.[101] Haussman filmed ten hours of footage, which had to be edited down to five minutes. "Take a Bow" was a good video, possibly a great video, but it was not a work of art. The video Madonna would shoot after it was.

At the time the "Take a Bow" video was released, Madonna was already working on a video for her single "Bedtime Story." She had chosen Mark Romanek, who was part of the Fincher world at Propaganda Films, to direct it. Romanek didn't want to make music videos: he wanted to make art that included music. His videos were basically poems come to life with color, movement, and sound, aided by technology that toyed with reality.[102]

He had directed more than a dozen videos by late 1992, when Madonna had first approached him to direct the video for her *Erotica* song "Bad Girl." She was staying at the Sherry-Netherland in New York because work was being done on her apartment. Romanek said she didn't have anything personal in the hotel except a small painting. It was no doubt Frida Kahlo's *My Birth,* because she often carried it with her when she traveled.[103]

He found the painting dark and disturbing and, because he didn't know Madonna, felt confused and surprised by her taste in art. "I might even have said to her, 'Wow, it would be great if you and I could do a video that looked like that someday.' And she said, 'Yeah.'" He declined the "Bad Girl" project, and she shot the video instead with David Fincher. But Romanek said he filed away the idea of re-creating the painting.[104]

Several months later, Madonna approached Romanek again, about directing a video for another song from *Erotica,* "Rain."[105] He agreed to do the video if he could make it "futuristic."[106] Madonna allowed Romanek's imagination to run wild. The idea he eventually came up with was simple: Madonna filming a music video.

Romanek's influences in creating the video's look were Japanese fashion designers like Yohji Yamamoto and Rei Kawakubo. For the filming, he borrowed an idea from a commercial Jean-Baptiste Mondino did with Catherine Deneuve for Yves Saint Laurent. "The way they colored the film and overexposed her face—it just was, at that time, just jaw-dropping how beautiful it was."[107]

Romanek had the look, the technique. All he needed was a setting.

Very late in the process I decided to make it appear as if it's all occurring in Japan because I thought it was interesting for Madonna to be the only Occidental in the video, which would make her more of an outsider... And then it came time to decide who would play the part of the director.[108]

At first, they considered Jean-Luc Godard. "When you're working with someone like Madonna, that's a possibility. In any other instance you'd say, 'Yeah, that's not going to happen.'" Godard, however, wasn't available. Next Madonna faxed Federico Fellini. He was ill, but he faxed Madonna a handwritten personal note in reply.[109] It began to look as though finding a director to play a director would be difficult, so they decided to look for a Japanese icon to play the part. They chose composer Ryuichi Sakamoto. "He's as big in Japan as Madonna is in America and Europe," Romanek said. Sakamoto flew in from Tokyo.[110]

At the Santa Monica Airport, Romanek created a studio and allowed the guts of the film shoot—the wires, the cameras, the lighting—to be seen. The Japanese cast, meanwhile, was allowed to roam in front of the camera and around Madonna as she sang and waited between shots. "It was very Zen, very stripped away," he said. "She was this accessible, vulnerable creature surrounded by the high-tech and the global."[111]

There is very little action in the video. What makes it so intoxicating is Romanek's use of the clean, cold colors inspired by the Mondino commercial to enliven an otherwise stark set and Madonna's blanched, almost bleached face. She is reduced to her essence: short black hair, intense blue contact lenses, pink lips, gapped teeth.

"Rain" would be the most experimental video Madonna had done up to that point. So when it came time to find a director for the video to accompany her most experimental song to date, she turned again to Romanek. "Bedtime Story" was, if nothing else, enigmatic and would need a director who had the vision to retain its mystery. This time, Romanek said yes immediately. He heard in that song the same dark, surreal qualities he had seen in the painting at the Sherry-Netherland hotel.

> I knew that Madonna had a vast knowledge of art and art history, and I went crazy, frankly, doing reference research on surrealism...I searched out very specifically a lot of the female surrealist painters at the time because there was quite a strong group...I thought it was important that the video had a very feminine attitude toward these artistic images.[112]

Among the painters who influenced the production were Leonora Carrington, Remedios Varo, the male artist René Magritte, and Frida Kahlo, because she had inspired the collaboration in the first place. Romanek also drew inspiration from British artist Lucian Freud and Russian filmmaker Andrei Tarkovsky.[113]

Romanek created a huge reference book and began showing the images to special-effects houses to see whether what he wanted to do was even feasible. He was told that it might be if new software was written to make his vision a reality. "A lot of it was on the edge of what was really possible to do," Romanek explained.[114]

Working with cinematographer Harris Savides, who had also shot "Rain" and "Take a Bow," Romanek and Madonna created a living surrealist painting with a touch of sci-fi at the beginning and end, as a Promethean creature named Ciccone, M., is birthed fully grown. That laboratory coldness warms when the video becomes a "painting" of Madonna as a sunflower, interspersed with images of a child, a sumo wrestler, and whirling dervishes. In a bit of technological wizardry, Madonna's face appears disembodied in twin mirrors, and at one point her eyes become singing mouths and her mouth becomes an eye. One of the most beautiful images in the video depicts a pregnant Madonna giving birth to a flock of doves; another occurs later, when she flies down a hallway, to the amazement of a child.

The "Bedtime Story" video, which took six days to shoot but months to plan and edit, is disturbing, marvelous, and unforgettable. It was acknowledged as more than a video when it became part of the permanent collection at the Museum of Modern Art in New York and the Museum of the Moving Image in London.[115]

Madonna had set out that year to return to pure creativity, without the drama and distraction of controversy. Controversy found her anyway, but it didn't paralyze her. On the contrary, she was on the move, traveling a path of experimentation that would occupy her for decades—after, that is, a short detour. First she had a musical and a baby to make.

Chapter 38

London, New York, Los Angeles, San Remo, Miami, 1995

The goals of feminism can never be achieved through evolution, but only through revolution. Power, however it has evolved, whatever its origins, will not be given up without a struggle.[1]

— *Shulamith Firestone*

DIRECTOR ALAN PARKER was at home in England for Christmas in December of 1994, having been in Hollywood meeting with potential cast and crew for his next film, *Evita*. Michelle Pfeiffer was attached to star, and Parker very much wanted her to have the part. But by the time they met, she had had a second child and couldn't embark on the months of travel that would be required for the film. That meant that as Parker tucked into his holiday meals, he was without an actor to play the character who was the heart and soul of his movie.[2]

It was then that he received "out of the blue" a letter from Madonna and a copy of her video for "Take a Bow." Parker had worked with her before on a possible remake of Marlene Dietrich's *The Blue Angel,* but that film, like so many Hollywood projects, didn't materialize. And though her name was associated with previous *Evita* film projects, he hadn't asked whether she was interested. Her letter told him in four handwritten pages that she was. He called it "extraordinarily passionate and sincere. As far as she was concerned, no one could play Evita as well as she could, and she said that she would sing, dance, and act her heart out, and put *everything* else on hold to devote all her time to it should I decide to go with her."[3]

By 1994, *Evita* was synonymous with blockbuster musical theater, but its beginnings were as humble as Eva Perón's. Lyricist Tim Rice had heard about Perón on his car radio in 1973. He and his fellow English collaborator, composer Andrew Lloyd Webber, had just had a huge success with their musical *Jesus Christ Superstar* and were casting around for a new project. Rice listened again to the radio broadcast and thought Eva—"Evita"—might be it.[4]

Maria Eva Duarte de Perón was a daughter of Argentina's provinces whose inauspicious life began with rejection. She was born the illegitimate child of a domestic, Juana Ibarguren, and a bourgeois businessman, Juan Duarte. When the businessman died, Eva and her mother were cast out, and the child was denied the right to his name. Eva took it anyway when she left her mother's home at fifteen to try her luck in Buenos Aires. Using all that she possessed—brains, charm, and determination—she lived with various men and built a moderately successful acting career. Then, at the age of twenty-four, she met one of Argentina's most powerful figures, the forty-eight-year-old widower Colonel Juan Perón. Eva became his mistress.[5]

At that young age, she was thrust into the middle of the country's political upheaval. During the first year she lived with Perón, he was arrested by the country's ruling junta, freed by a rebellion, and elected president. Marrying Perón, young Eva became a surprisingly formidable first lady. On the one hand, she was a glamorous globe-trotting ambassador for Argentina; on the other, she was a savior for the country's poor. She opened schools, hospitals, and homes for the old, the destitute, and the vulnerable. Having been poor herself, she knew what people needed most and provided it: shoes, cooking pots, sewing machines.

Some of her biggest battles were on behalf of women, and they were fought on two fronts: the personal and the political. Through her, Argentinean women gained access to contraceptives and the right to divorce. They also won the right to vote. Eva managed to accomplish all that in a staunchly Catholic country with entrenched patriarchal traditions. She proved such a skilled politician that at the age of thirty-two, in 1951, labor groups wanted her to become Argentina's vice president. She could not accept the position. Evita had developed cancer and died the following year, at the age of thirty-three. In death she was as polarizing as she had been in life. Her supporters' love turned to veneration, while her enemies set out to destroy her legacy.[6]

In 1976, Rice and Lloyd Webber undertook their first *Evita* project, a concept album. When its single "Don't Cry for Me Argentina" was released in Britain, it went to number 1 on the charts. Alan Parker heard it at that time and immediately recognized the story's movie potential. But Rice and Lloyd Webber wanted to do a stage production first. So *Evita* opened in the West End in 1978, where it remained for eight years and more than three thousand performances. In 1979, it opened on Broadway and stayed there for more than fifteen hundred shows, earning seven Tony Awards.

During those years, while audiences flocked to the theater to see it, film directors struggled to bring Eva's story to the big screen. But each time they came close to getting a green light, the project collapsed.[7] In fact, the cinematic history of *Evita* was so tortured that it almost seemed cursed. And with each iteration, Eva Perón became more of a caricature than a real person—a dreaded "ambitious woman." Madonna said that Eva became just one more woman whose life was told from a male perspective, and it was a distorted tale indeed.

> They were completely frightened by the kind of power that she had. And it's always easy, it's the most obvious and predictable way out, to call a woman a whore and imply that she has no morals and no integrity and no talent... It's the oldest trick in the book, and Sir Andrew Lloyd Webber and Sir Tim Rice fell for it, and... Well, it was extremely popular, that story.[8]

In reality, Eva should have been a feminist icon. Whatever her flaws, and no matter her intentions or her husband's fascist political leanings, she fundamentally changed the lives of women in Argentina and, by her example, throughout Latin America, if not the world. That was part of what interested Madonna in the project.[9] But of even greater interest to her was restoring Eva's personhood. She wanted to strip away the myth and tell the story of the woman who had accomplished so much. "I certainly don't see her as a saint. But what I tried to do is flesh her out and show her humanity and her sadness and pain."[10]

Despite having been fascinated by the role for a decade, Madonna did not jump into the project. Before writing to Parker, she engaged in some serious soul-searching. "It was really hard for me to decide to do it," she said. "I had to give a lot of things up."[11] There was also hesitation about Madonna on the part of executives at Disney, which would distribute the film, and Cinergi Pictures, which would finance it.[12] Meanwhile, the creative types on the project had mixed views about her participation. Tim Rice said he supported Madonna.

> I wanted someone accustomed to putting over a story and emotion in song. Madonna acts so beautifully through music. Better actresses like Meryl Streep weren't right because they're not singers. They can hold a tune, but they're not brilliant interpreters of songs.[13]

But he said Andrew Lloyd Webber, who had a casting veto, argued against her. "He felt that she had been rude to him, so it was a clash of two giant egos," Rice said. "He was also worried because he didn't think she could sing the part." Alan Parker was also hesitant, despite Madonna's impassioned letter.[14] After several meetings that Madonna described as "nerve-racking," all sides went away to think about it. Parker had a script to write, and Madonna immersed herself in books and newsreels about Eva Perón and Argentina while promoting her *Bedtime Stories* album.[15]

On January 30, 1995, Madonna appeared with Babyface at the American Music Awards to sing "Take a Bow." None of her songs from *Bedtime Stories* was nominated for an award, but the performance presented an opportunity to reintroduce the song she had released in December.

A string orchestra supported her and Babyface as they stood yards apart from each other on raised platforms. Wearing a red Manchu-style cheongsam, Madonna gave one of her most understated and yet moving performances. After the AMAs, "Take a Bow" went to number 1 on the Billboard Hot 100 chart, where it stayed for seven weeks, longer even than her previous record-setter "Like a Virgin."[16] With its success, Madonna displaced Carole King as the woman songwriter with the most number 1 hits, a position King had held for thirty years, or most of Madonna's lifetime. The video for "Take a Bow," meanwhile, would earn Madonna the MTV award that had eluded her since 1987—Best Female Video.

Madonna and Babyface took their show on the road in February, traveling to San Remo for the Italian city's annual music festival. Onstage, festival organizers had positioned Babyface behind Madonna. She called him closer and made him a partner in her performance. Babyface's manager, Ramon Hertz, told music writer Lucy O'Brien that the kind of respect Madonna showed her fellow artist was rare in the business.[17]

Madonna's next stop was the BRIT Awards to perform "Bedtime Story." The single languished on the US charts, becoming her worst-performing song since 1983, but British audiences immersed in rave culture were more receptive to its ethereal sounds. Of all her new songs, "Bedtime Story" was the most difficult to perform. She did it in Britain by using a remix, created by Junior Vasquez of Sound Factory fame, that turned it into a dance-club number.[18]

Madonna performed between two wind machines and lights that transformed her waist-length blond hair extensions into flames and her diaphanous Versace gown into a parachute. Behind her were two seemingly identical male dancers. The crowd danced, too, and when the song ended, the applause was deafening. "Bedtime Story" soared to number 4 on the British charts and remained there for thirteen weeks.[19]

Mark Romanek's video for "Bedtime Story," meanwhile, was released directly to select cinemas on March 10. It appeared on MTV eight days later to coincide with a midnight pajama party Madonna held at the New York City nightclub Webster Hall, during which she danced in a nightgown with fans and read the children's book *Miss Spider's Tea Party* to her fifteen-hundred-strong jammie-clad audience. Writer Michael Musto called the evening a "kooky and engaging...New York moment," more fun than the *Sex* book launch party, held three years earlier.[20]

Those forty minutes at Webster Hall and Madonna's appearances in Europe would be her "tour." The night of her pajama party, she told Freddy DeMann that she would not go on the road to promote *Bedtime Stories,* even though she stood to make tens of millions of dollars by doing so. She had to focus on *Evita.* She had finally been offered the part, and she accepted.[21]

Speculation began immediately in the press. Could she carry a $60 million movie?[22] The lady herself approached the subject objectively.

> I've been in four very successful films — *Desperately Seeking Susan, Dick Tracy, A League of Their Own,* and *Truth or Dare.* I've also been in four or five stinkers — some of which weren't *my* films at all, though they were promoted as such. Obviously, I haven't hit my stride in movies, but let me say this: I'm not particularly interested in becoming a great big movie star. I *am* interested in becoming a good actress. If one comes with the other, that's fine.[23]

One would think that Madonna would refrain from doing anything to jeopardize her role by making tremulous *Evita* producers even more nervous. But where creativity was concerned, she never allowed self-restraint to interfere with a project, and in the duality that was Madonna, naughty almost always followed nice. In April, she was at work in Los Angeles on a Spike Lee film called *Girl 6* in which she plays a stripper who runs a phone sex operation. And in May, she made a video for "Human Nature" that would feature a return trip to the land of S/M. The video amounted to a final "Get over it. I am who I am" from Madonna before she became Señora Perón.

Madonna shot the video with trusted collaborators Jean-Baptiste Mondino and cinematographer Harris Savides. The choreographer, however, was a twenty-three-year-old newcomer named Jamie King. Madonna had spotted him at the AMA show, where he choreographed and performed a twelve-minute Prince tribute that included seamless onstage costume changes, flying musicians, and King himself as Prince's doppelgänger.[24]

King's energy was undeniable, and his production was more Broadway show than awards-ceremony routine. It felt *big.* After the AMAs, Madonna called him to say she had a job for him if he was interested — working on her next video. A month later, he was with her looking at comic book–like bondage illustrations by Eric Stanton, an artist who had had one show in his lifetime — in 1984, at Danceteria. Madonna wanted his work to visually inspire the video. Other than that, King said, "She was like, 'Just go for it Jamie, just go crazy' and I did."[25]

Jamie King's rise was, without an ounce of hyperbole, meteoric. Born in 1972 in Verona, Wisconsin, King was a mixed-race gay child in a conservative, mostly white town that had been known at various points in history as a leper colony, the site of a poor farm, and the home of the county's mental hospital.[26] "School was hard in the sense that people didn't always understand my ethnicity and the mix," he said. "My cards were dealt for me; I was already an outcast. I have always felt different, but I have also always felt that anything is possible."[27]

MTV saved him. When he was ten, he began watching videos and saw in them a highway out of Verona. In his bedroom, surrounded by pictures of the "class" of '58 — Michael Jackson, Prince, and Madonna — he fantasized, and in his basement, he watched and copied video dance routines. "Then, I would change all the choreography. I would take what I had learned and make it my own." At sixteen, he enrolled in a dance school and eventually won a scholarship to the Edge Dance Studio in LA.[28]

At twenty, he accepted a life-changing job dancing with Michael Jackson on his Dangerous tour. "The shows I direct and the spectacles that I create, they are influenced by Michael 100 percent," he said. "I learned from him that you give all of yourself; you leave it on the stage. That is how the audience falls in love with you."[29]

After two years with Jackson, King got a call from Prince, who wanted him to rework his dance shows. They started small, with King choreographing weekly performances at Prince's LA club, Glam Slam West. That was where King learned how music was made and how choreography created the bridge between sound and movement. And *that* lit King's creative fire. He knew what he wanted to do with his life.[30]

Prince's first big job for King outside the club was to choreograph the tribute at the AMAs, which was where Madonna spotted him and why she called. Incredibly, the last of the three megastars on the posters King had on his bedroom wall wanted to work with him. He had earned it. Said Madonna, "No one knows more about music and movement than Jamie King."[31]

He would remain with Madonna for the next twenty years as creative director on seven tours and creative soulmate on important nontour performances. He would also work with other top pop talent and, in the process, became *the* leading creative force in the music-tour business.[32] His first project with Madonna would be the video for "Human Nature."

Though Madonna was back in *Sex* territory, her look had changed entirely. In *Sex,* despite her leather gear, she was soft and feminine. In "Human Nature," she was fierce, her hair in cornrows, her body in skin-tight patent leather. Jean-Baptiste Mondino's assistant, Dustin Robertson, recalled watching her emerge from her trailer in a leather body suit and stiletto boots, and confidently navigate the equipment-cluttered stage. "*Silence* hushed over the entire set," he said. "She was *stunning.*"[33]

Eric Stanton's influence on the video was mainly confined to the look of the costumes (leather and latex), the introduction of bondage elements (chains, body-suspension gear, bondage hood, ropes, and whip), and the presence of white cubes. At various points in the video, Madonna and her dancers appear inside the cubes, as if inhabiting comic-book frames. The set is beyond stark—completely white—with only a chair, the cubes, and a mirror to break up the space. That simplicity means that the action focuses entirely on Madonna and her dancers' bodies, which are so angular and expressive that they seem at times to form words and at other times to create kaleidoscopes. Just as the "Bedtime Story" video is a moving paint-ing, the "Human Nature" video is a moving illustration.

The video operates on two levels, one in which Madonna sings the song and another in which she delivers a sotto voce monologue. Like the song, the video is very funny, with Madonna mugging for the camera as she describes society's shrill, hypocritical, and judgmental reaction to her. The boxes that Madonna and her dancers squeeze into do not fit them, yet soci-ety has put them there anyway.

The "Human Nature" video shows Madonna at her most powerful. She has risen above sexuality. She now possesses and exhibits pure strength. It is the Madonna of Blond Ambition made razor-sharp by anger. Whereas that younger self tested the limits, the older self bursts through them, has the scars to prove it, and has survived with her humor intact. And in the process, she has not backed down, apologized, or tried to make herself acceptable. "Her refusal to bow her head and accept a tragic fate as the price for her sexuality...has made her, at least to some, a very scary lady," wrote Mim Udovitch in *Rolling Stone.*[34] For others, she had become an obsession.

In early 1995, Christopher noticed a small Persian rug missing from Castillo del Lago and said a door had been forced open. Madonna attrib-uted the theft to ghosts because the house was believed by locals to be haunted.[35] Then in April, a thirty-seven-year-old man named Robert Hoskins scaled the wall of the house and wandered around the property before being chased off by Madonna's security guard Basil Stephens. The next day the man returned, loitering outside and ringing the call box.

When Madonna's assistant Caresse Henry answered, she said he threatened to kill her, Madonna, and anyone else in the place.[36]

Basil Stephens arrived at the gate and confronted him after Hoskins left a note to Madonna scribbled on a religious tract that said "I love you. You will be my wife for keeps." Stephens told Hoskins to take his note and leave. "He said, 'Give her the note or I'll kill you,'" Stephens later testified in court. "I walked toward him, and he said, 'Tell Madonna I'll either marry her or kill her...I'll slit her throat from ear to ear.'"[37]

Stephens called the police, got his gun, and chased Hoskins, who escaped, but not before Madonna encountered him after she bicycled up to the gate. Though she had never seen him before, she noticed him because "he had a really crazy look in his eyes and he was staring at me in a very strange way."[38] Said Stephens, "I've had many people come up [to the estate]...but none was as credible a threat as this."[39]

After the publication of her *Sex* book, Madonna joked about attracting predators. "There are so many psychos out there bothering me anyway, what's five more?"[40] But in the years since, the invasions had become more frequent and more dangerous, and not just for Madonna. Riot grrrl Mia Zapata of the punk band the Gits was raped and murdered in 1993.[41] The month before Hoskins's appearance, twenty-three-year-old Tejano music star Selena was shot dead in Texas by the head of her fan club. The news of her murder generated hours of media discussion about the very real dangers celebrities face.[42]

After the Hoskins gate incident, and though she had only lived there a short time, Madonna put her LA house on the market because she believed it "attracts negative energy."[43] In the meantime, she hired more security.[44] Two months later, Hoskins reappeared. Again he scaled the eight-foot wall and jumped into the compound's grounds. When Basil Stephens confronted him, Hoskins lunged. Stephens shot twice, hitting Hoskins in the arm and abdomen.[45]

Before he was wheeled away on a gurney to Cedars-Sinai Medical Center, Hoskins told police on the scene that he was Madonna's husband and "had a right to be there." In his possession was a wooden heart that said "Love to my wife Madnna [sic]."[46] He was charged with five felonies: stalking, three counts of making terrorist threats, and assault. After being released from the hospital, he was ordered held pending trial.[47]

Madonna, meanwhile, invited her dancer friend Carlton Wilborn to live at Castillo del Lago. Niki Haris had told her that he was between jobs and needed a place to stay. "She gave me the run of the place," Carlton said, "and an account at the local grocery store down the street." Though his invitation was "open-ended," it lasted just three months. He moved when he booked his first regular role on a network TV series.[48] With

Carlton's departure, the fabulous mansion under the Hollywood sign was left vacant. Madonna's life in the States kept her in New York and Miami. *Evita* would bring her to London.

The *Evita* cast came together quickly. Alan Parker had long wanted Spanish actor Antonio Banderas to play a narrator "everyman" named Che.[49] With the casting of Welsh actor Jonathan Pryce as Juan Perón, Parker had his principals by the time he finished the first version of his script, in May. It called for 146 changes to the stage version of *Evita*'s score and lyrics.[50]

Parker also wanted a new song. He felt the complicated sung dialogue in the scene between Eva and Juan when she discovers she has cancer wouldn't work dramatically on-screen. "So we decided to simplify that and put in a new song, which also gave us a shot at getting the Oscar, because you can only win an Oscar with a new song," Tim Rice said. The result was "You Must Love Me," which became, after "Don't Cry for Me Argentina," the signature song of the movie.[51]

Madonna, meanwhile, began three months of training at the Manhattan apartment of vocal coach Joan Lader. One aspect of *Evita* would be easy for her. As a veteran of music videos, she knew how to lip-synch, which she would be required to do in *Evita* because the entire soundtrack was prerecorded. The difficulty came in learning to extend her vocal range. She needed to take her voice to places it had never been, for long periods of time and with complete control, because *Evita* was "operatic." Madonna was so shocked by the higher register she was able to achieve as a result of training that she didn't recognize her own voice. She asked Lader, "Where did that come from?"

"God," Lader replied.

Madonna excitedly called her friends and sang to them.[52]

Madonna arrived in London in September to begin rehearsals for *Evita*. "I'm starting to get nervous," she told a *Cosmopolitan* writer before she left.[53] Later she admitted, "I had no idea what I was in for when I was asked to be in this movie."[54] The film contains no spoken dialogue—every word in it is sung—so it was not merely a matter of learning a few difficult songs. She had to learn a few difficult songs as well as a long, difficult musical script. The challenge became clear on October 2, when the cast began recording the score. Parker called that nightmarish day "Black Monday."[55]

Musical supervisor David Caddick had decided to start with "Don't Cry for Me Argentina," which required Madonna to sing with an eighty-four-piece orchestra. Andrew Lloyd Webber was on hand to observe, and he was, Parker said, "apoplectic about everything."[56] Madonna, meanwhile, was overwhelmed. "I was in the recording studio with strange producers and writers, a huge orchestra and huge shoes to fill," she said.[57] "I was so nervous because I knew that Andrew had reservations about me, and here I'm singing the hardest song in the piece."[58] Parker saw that she was close to tears and realized that "three worlds were colliding...music and theater, pop, and film."[59]

That night, he and Lloyd Webber met for dinner to discuss the situation. They decided they needed to bring Madonna into the conversation, too. At her hotel, the three concluded that per Lloyd Webber's request, the conductor would be changed, and per Madonna's, she would record her vocals at another studio, more like those she was accustomed to working in. They all agreed that she would sing in the afternoons every other day to save her voice. "Over a period of four months, working seven days a week, we put in over four hundred recording hours preparing the forty-nine musical sections that were required for playback on set," Parker said.[60] By the end of that process, he concluded that Madonna sang the role "far better" than the original stage Evitas, Patti LuPone and Elaine Paige.[61]

While her work went better than she had expected, Madonna's personal life suffered for it.[62] Carlos Leon had come to London to see her, but they fought, and he left. When she arrived back in New York, she confided to Christopher that she didn't think Carlos respected her. She told her brother that she had never given anyone as much love as she gave Carlos but that he was like a spoiled child.[63] She also felt that he was extremely jealous.

> I mean, when I'm looking through a magazine, I'm careful not to comment on attractive pictures of guys. I understand this. Men who are with me have to endure my image...So I'm always reassuring my men. I say, "You're the one. I'm here with *you*." Of course, he looks at other women all the time. So I'm often left to wonder, *Why am I censoring myself for him?*[64]

She was so angry after their London fight that she changed her apartment locks and returned Carlos's belongings.[65] With that, during a break from *Evita* duties, she escaped to Miami. Ingrid Casares was the promoter for a new South Beach club called Liquid, and it was finally opening.

The club's owner was a New Yorker named Chris Paciello, who had arrived in Florida the year before, over Labor Day weekend. "By weekend's end, the unemployed twenty-three-year-old had made a deal to buy a nightclub," wrote South Beach historian Steven Gaines. In any other town, a cash transaction for a bar with previous Mafia ties might have raised eyebrows. In Miami Beach, it didn't. Organized crime had been part of the island culture since its inception as a resort.[66]

Within two months, Paciello reopened the bar as a small club called

Risk. It continued to be a "mob hangout," said Tom Austin, who covered the scene in his Swelter column for the *Miami New Times*.[67] For the opening, a contingent of "junior mobsters" came down from New York.[68] Compared with the narco multimillionaires across the causeway, though, the Brooklyn brigade seemed quaint, as if a Scorsese movie had come to town. Chris Paciello was the magnetic young star. What no one knew was that he was on the run from a murder charge.[69]

Paciello, whose real name is Christian Ludwigsen, was part of a gang of teenagers associated with the Bonanno crime family in Bensonhurst, Brooklyn, but he also "freelanced" for various families, according to Frank Owen, an expert on the Mob and Miami Beach. After a series of small jobs, kid stuff, the Bensonhurst gang hit a bank in 1992 and stole $300,000. Then in 1993, they robbed a home thought to contain a safe with a bundle of cash in it. The robbery went wrong, and the woman of the house, Judith Shemtov, was killed. Prosecutors said Paciello planned the robbery and drove the getaway car.[70]

The murder of a civilian in her home brought the police down on the crew, and it was reportedly then that Paciello turned up in Florida with enough cash to open Risk and enough style to begin attracting South Beach clubgoers, Ingrid Casares among them. She and Paciello met at Risk and hit it off. He said they had a lot in common: they both liked "money and women."[71]

In April of 1995, after only a few months in operation, Risk burned in a fire that investigators suspected was caused by arson, though that was never proved. Paciello received $250,000 in insurance money, which he used to open Liquid. "The big question back then in South Beach was 'How do I make Madonna a partner in my club?'" Steven Gaines wrote. "Everybody wanted Madonna to invest, not for the money, but because of her fame... That's what Chris Paciello did. He is smart because he made Ingrid Casares his partner, and that's how he got Madonna."[72]

Madonna had no financial stake in Liquid, but the possibility that she would be there, that it was "her club" because of Ingrid, was enough to keep the nondescript (by South Beach standards) nightspot filled when it finally opened. Said author and artist Brian Antoni, Madonna "was a walking VIP room."[73]

Paciello worked for eight months to renovate and staff Liquid. In the meantime, Ingrid introduced him to all the right people.[74] Rumors had him romantically linked to Madonna, though Christopher wasn't sure his sister was ever involved with him in that way.[75] "He was a handsome guy. I flirted with him; everyone flirted with him," Christopher said.

At the time, nobody knew his history. I certainly didn't. Madonna didn't. Ingrid didn't seem to, and nobody seemed to care. Miami at that time was a sort of bought-and-paid-for city, so you could basically live there untouched by anything in your past.[76]

Liquid's opening was billed as Christopher Ciccone's thirty-fifth birthday party. Ingrid and Paciello sent out ten thousand invitations and alerted the national media.[77] If a bomb had been dropped on South Beach that night, much of the entertainment and fashion worlds of the United States, Great Britain, and Italy would have been wiped out. The concentration of A-list celebrities gathered above a Payless shoe store on 14th Street and Washington Avenue rivaled that of an Oscar party.[78]

Calvin Klein, Shakira, Michael Caine, Barry Diller, British film director John Schlesinger, and supermodels Naomi Campbell and Kate Moss were all there. Tom Austin called it "a watershed gathering," the first time that international celebrities coalesced in one place on the Beach. That was also the start of the stratification of South Beach club society, when money and fame, but mostly fame, became the ticket for entry.[79]

Ingrid had poached Junior Vasquez from the Sound Factory in New York to act as DJ, and Chris Paciello had hired the best bartenders, the best waitstaff, and the best doormen—New York club veteran Gilbert Stafford and South Beach veteran Louis Canales. If any notables appeared at the rope line, the two men knew them.[80] For the mere mortals waiting at the door, the scene was apocalyptic. "It was the hardest door I have ever dealt with in my life," said Brian Antoni.

> It was like that last helicopter out of Saigon. We linked arms because we couldn't get through the crowd. This guy was getting us in. They lined up security guards, and some girl grabbed me, like she was desperate [to get in]. She grabbed me, and her nails came off in my hands. That's how bad it got.[81]

Steven Gaines said, "For one white hot moment, Liquid became the international cynosure of celebrity, as close as Miami Beach would ever get to having its own Studio 54."[82]

As they did at Studio 54, drugs fueled much of the nightlife. Christopher said the drug scene in Miami Beach generally was "way bigger" than in New York or LA. "It was cocaine, coke. It was coming directly from Colombia or whatever, super high quality." Christopher's use was recreational. "If I went out and came home at four o'clock in the morning, [Madonna] was like, 'Where were you?'" She had little patience for people who used drugs, her brother and Ingrid included.[83]

Before Liquid opened, Madonna and Chris Paciello intervened to get Ingrid into drug rehab. "Madonna was not going to tolerate my being self-destructive," Ingrid said, "and [she] didn't speak to me until I was ready to get help." Paciello told Ingrid that if she got clean and stayed clean, she could become the club's official face, the front person who attracted celebrities and the club's talent. It worked. Ingrid's new drug became work and the club.[84]

Madonna's Miami home was the place where she had fun. The place where she felt *safe* was at her sister Melanie Henry's, in Los Angeles. She told Forrest Sawyer during a return visit to ABC's *Nightline* that December,

> When I'm desperate, I run to her house because she has to me the warmth of a family and a real nurturing environment around her and she's not connected to the business and so I can go to her house and lie on the couch and watch stupid movies with her son—you know, dinosaur movies—and really, in a way, feel safe and away from everything.[85]

Asked by Sawyer if Sean was still her one true love, she said yes. Did anyone come close? "No." *Could* anyone come close to him? Madonna said, "Why not?" The problem was not meeting men: "It's a problem meeting one of them who's not an asshole." The main issue for Madonna was that she wanted to have a child. She said that, according to her biological clock, it was "*time*...But now I have to do this movie. Then after this movie, I'm going to put an ad in the *New York Times, Village Voice*...and who knows who's going to apply for this fatherhood gig."[86] In fact, Madonna had reconciled with Carlos. The ad would be unnecessary.

Chapter 39

Los Angeles, Buenos Aires, Budapest, London, 1996–1997

If you want something bad enough the whole earth conspires to help you get it.[1]

— *Madonna*

MADONNA BEGAN ONE of the most pivotal years of her life in a witness box. The man arrested for threatening her life, Robert Hoskins, was on trial in Los Angeles, and both the prosecution and the defense insisted that she appear in court to testify. She had no desire to be in the same room with Hoskins, and she missed her first court date, claiming fatigue and illness after being in London for *Evita*. Furious over what she believed was a celebrity's invocation of privilege, deputy district attorney Rhonda Saunders wanted Madonna arrested and held on $500,000 bond (three times more than what was required of the defendant). The judge in the case instead gave Madonna until January 2 to appear in court. If she failed to do so, he said, she would be arrested and held on $5 million bond.[2]

Hoskins watched intently as Madonna strode to the witness box in compliance with the court order. The defense argued that he was harmless, that he should be tried for what *had* happened, not what might have happened, and that if he was guilty of anything it was mere trespassing. Madonna did not think of him as a trespasser. "I feel sick to my stomach. I feel incredibly distressed that the man who threatened my life is sitting across from me and has somehow made his fantasies come true," she told the court. "I'm sitting in front of him and that's what he wants." She kept her eyes closed or averted so as not to meet his gaze as she answered lawyers' questions for an hour about her life and her movements — in short, about whether she had somehow provoked the fellow.[3]

Basil Stephens and Caresse Henry also testified. Hoskins did not take the stand. On January 9, a jury convicted him on all counts. One of the four women on the jury said that as far as they were concerned, "there was no doubt" about his guilt, but the men on the jury needed "a little convincing [about] what would or wouldn't scare" a stalking victim.

Madonna's testimony was compelling enough to eventually convince them. "We all walked away feeling she was frightened," said the jury foreman, John J. Utech.[4]

Madonna left Los Angeles for New York immediately after the verdict and reportedly spent the entire next day and into the early morning with Sean at the Carlyle hotel. They had appeared together at the VH1 Fashion and Music Awards in December. He surprised Madonna by presenting her with the Most Fashionable Artist of 1995 award. Their smiles were warm and genuine. They fell into each other's arms with what looked like relief and stayed there. Sean had just finished work on one of his most emotionally difficult films, *Dead Man Walking,* and he was separated from Robin Wright and living apart from her and their two children.[5]

After their Carlyle meeting, the press speculated that Madonna wanted to have Sean's child and had tried to persuade him to be the father. Perhaps, but throughout their lives at moments of crisis, they would come together. Sean was extremely protective of her, and she may have wanted that kind of reassurance at that moment of extreme distress — what she had just endured with Hoskins and what she was about to endure. Three days later, Madonna left for Buenos Aires.[6]

The passions Madonna and the film aroused in Argentina were evident before she even arrived at her hotel. Walls along her route from the airport to the city bore graffiti that said VIVA EVITA! FUERA MADONNA! (Madonna Out!) A vocal contingent of Peronists was appalled at the idea of her playing their sainted Evita. One of Eva Perón's elderly aides even threatened to kill her.[7]

Once Madonna arrived at her hotel, though, her fans were even more vocal than her detractors. Hundreds of them camped outside during the day, making egress nearly impossible. She eventually employed seven security guards to protect her and block the "MDs" — mad dashers — who broke out of the crowd to try to touch her or tear at her clothing. During the night the "children," as she called them, stood outside her windows calling to her to come to her second-floor balcony. Finally appearing, she told the group, "If you really like me, let me get some sleep." They didn't get the message.[8]

The press had also gathered. Madonna suspected that hotel staff had been bribed for information and that locals were paid to stage events — pretending to be hit by Madonna's car, in one case — in order to create a story. Alan Parker said that paparazzi in helicopters "formed an adjunct army." Their goal was to catch Madonna and Antonio Banderas in an affair. When that didn't happen, the headlines out of Buenos Aires were that the Argentinean people did not want the film or Madonna in it. Back in the States, Freddy DeMann heard reports that Madonna had received death threats. He ordered her back home. On the contrary, she told him: by the sixth day, things were improving. She could even sleep with the help of earplugs and a move to a higher floor of the hotel.[9]

Madonna felt enormous pressure and believed the entire production rested on her performance. Before filming began, in February, she arranged for an Argentinean journalist to schedule interviews for her with people who knew Eva Perón. She had read as much as she could but wanted to hear stories both from people who loved Evita and from those who despised her.[10] Her days were thus filled with meetings with Peronists, artists, and historians in the hope that they would help her understand her character and that one of them might help open the door to the most important meeting of all—with the president of Argentina, Carlos Menem.[11]

If the film crew had any chance of using the country's equivalent of the White House—the Casa Rosada—to shoot Evita's famous balcony scene while Madonna sang "Don't Cry for Me Argentina," they needed his approval. So far, despite interventions by Parker, the film's producers, and the British embassy, that permission had not been secured.[12] Through an elderly Peronist, Madonna pressed for an interview with Menem to see if she could persuade him.

On February 4, she learned that he would meet her discreetly on an island in the Paraná Delta. He could not be seen consorting with the enemy after being quoted in the press saying that he couldn't imagine Madonna as Evita and he didn't think the Argentinean people would accept her in that role.[13]

Menem loved celebrities. A notorious playboy, he felt at home in the world of big names and air-kisses. Maureen Orth, who interviewed him, described him as looking like an "aging lounge lizard from a night club in the provinces...But women adore all five feet four virile inches of him." And he, in turn, adored them.[14] The sixty-five-year-old bachelor, therefore, prepared to greet the world's biggest female pop star.[15] Instead, he met Eva Perón.

Madonna prepared for their encounter by dressing as the late Argentinean first lady. She exuded late-1940s style in a knee-length silk dress and black-and-white leather strap shoes, her hair in a chignon topped by a black horsehair hat with gray lace. Menem was disarmed by what he saw. He told Madonna she was the very image of Evita.[16]

Their meeting, attended by a few of Menem's staff, began in the early evening in the garden of an estate lent to Menem, with Madonna doing the talking—about her passion for Eva Perón—and Menem doing the looking. She said he couldn't take his eyes off her. Or maybe he didn't see

Madonna at all; he saw Evita sitting beside him. The bugs drove them inside, and it was then that she played for him "You Must Love Me," the new song from the movie. While Menem listened, Madonna said, she saw a tear spill from his eye.[17]

Their conversation veered away from the film into the areas of religion, desire, death, even magic, which was when Madonna finally asked him if he would change his mind and allow the film to be shot from the famous balcony. There was silence, then Menem turned to Madonna and said, "Anything is possible." She left at eleven that evening, still uncertain whether her mission had succeeded.[18]

Later that month, not long after filming began, Madonna was summoned to a second meeting with Menem. Alan Parker, Antonio Banderas, and Jonathan Pryce accompanied her. "After much small talk and diplomatic dancing," Parker recounted, "Madonna suddenly said to the president, 'Let's cut to the chase here. Do we have the balcony or don't we?' Menem smiled and nodded. 'You can have the balcony.'"[19] The scene shot there would be *the* pivotal moment of the film.[20]

On March 10, Madonna did it. She stood on the balcony of the Casa Rosada in the spot where Evita had stood many times addressing her people. But instead of speaking to them, Madonna lip-synched "Don't Cry for Me Argentina" as the film's soundtrack blasted out over the crowd. Alan Parker said that when she appeared on the balcony and began the song, "the crowd went crazy, as did all the crew."[21]

The four thousand extras below had time-traveled to 1951 to experience what the generation who had known Eva Perón felt: love and loss in equal measure. The tears in the extras' eyes were real. Madonna said she was so happy she couldn't speak and felt as though Evita was inside her.[22]

After a second night's shoot on the balcony, Parker said,

> It was impossible not to be moved...Suddenly it wasn't just the illusion and replication of film. It was strangely real. We shot throughout the night, and as the sun came up in the morning, we all quietly hugged one another. I think we all felt that we had, in five weeks, done all that we had set out to do and more.[23]

Five days later, with the Buenos Aires filming wrapped, Madonna went to New York and Miami to collect herself before flying to Budapest, where the shoot would continue. By the time she left for Hungary, Madonna knew. She wrote in her diary on March 19, "The only thing that matters [is] growing inside me."[24] Madonna was pregnant.

A doctor in New York had performed an ultrasound and showed her what she described as a "tap-dancing" creature "spinning around in my womb...I heard its heartbeat and fell instantly in love." The only people she told were Carlos; her assistant Caresse; and her trainer, because her routine might need to be changed. She also told Parker. "Are you sitting down, Alan?" she asked him in a call to Budapest. "I'm pregnant."

"How much?" he asked in reply. "When is it due?"

They both hoped against hope that she could finish the film without her pregnancy becoming an issue. Parker calculated the film schedule against her October due date. The last shot was scheduled in late spring. They might just make it.[25]

Madonna arrived in Budapest in late March, exchanging the brutal heat of Argentina for the brutal cold of Hungary. Because Budapest was an architectural stand-in for midcentury Argentina, she had to dress as if she were in South America, which meant wearing thin summer clothing during hours-long exterior shoots. There were also problems with locations. Parker wanted Eva's funeral to be filmed inside a basilica, but the local bishop would not countenance the slut Madonna inside his house of God. "The bishop can kiss my ass," Madonna wrote in her diary. "I'm not groveling for one more person in the name of this movie. There is no more skin left on my knees."[26]

Madonna carried her mother's memory with her as a talisman. She once said that, to her, her mother had become an almost mythical, Christlike figure. Her own pregnancy, however, made her mother more real in her life, and this made filming Evita's death scenes, in early April, so much more painful. Madonna had to experience as an actor the suffering of a person with cancer. "I kept thinking what my mother must have felt when my father told her she was dying. And how she stayed so cheerful and never gave into her sadness even at the end."[27]

By early April, Madonna was three months pregnant, and her costumes were becoming tight. Parker had to let some of the crew in on her secret because the production schedule was changed to accommodate her. The responsibility Madonna already felt concerning the picture had only grown. They had all worked so hard, and now she feared she would destroy what they had accomplished.[28]

Carlos, meanwhile, had joined her in Budapest as physical and emotional support. Madonna also called her father to tell him the news. By then, the world's press knew, too. Judgment was rendered on all sides, with the scale tilted heavily toward cynicism: Madonna's pregnancy was a career move; she did it for "shock value"; Carlos was a mere sperm donor. Jokes were made and questions raised about Madonna's fitness as a mother.[29]

At the heart of that cruelty, from the right and the left, was not just

Madonna's reputation as a "wanton woman" but also the fact that she had chosen to be a single mother, with Carlos in the role of partner and father, though not husband. "I believe that most people would be more comfortable if I got married and the marriage failed. I believe that divorce is more socially acceptable than single motherhood," she said.[30]

As she often did, Madonna had marched onto a political battlefield. This time, the fight was about marriage. In 1993, Hawaii's highest court ruled that denying same-sex marriage was "probably" discriminatory. That decision inspired hope among gays and lesbians and struck terror into the hearts of the religious right and social conservatives. In 1996, Congress passed, and President Bill Clinton signed, the Defense of Marriage Act, which codified marriage as a union between a man and a woman.[31]

In the wake of that, anyone who challenged "family values" was considered dangerous, especially if that person was a role model and gay ally like Madonna. It wasn't merely that she would be a single mother. Millions of women raised children on their own. But family-values types comforted themselves with the notion that those women would choose marriage if the opportunity arose. Madonna's choice wasn't open to interpretation. She clearly stated that she wasn't interested in a husband at that moment. Wrote feminist Joanna Russ the following year,

> Like the masterless man of medieval Europe, who owed fealty to no lord and thus posed a danger to the feudal hierarchy, the man-less woman — that is, the woman committed to no man — is a danger to patriarchal hierarchy and is named and treated as an enemy.[32]

And so Madonna was.

Filming moved to Shepperton Studios, outside London, in May, and while the accommodations and work environment were more congenial than they had been in Hungary, the scenes were extremely physical. The dance numbers featuring a young Eva had been saved until the end. Madonna's greatest fear was that all that activity might harm the baby.[33] She reassured herself by thinking, "If it's happening this way, then nothing will get in the way of it — this baby's coming no matter how many hours I stand on my feet."[34]

Madonna said she could not fully concentrate on her child until she rid herself of Eva. But the baby had a way of demanding attention. While shooting a scene during which Eva delivers a speech to a group of labor leaders, Madonna felt the baby's first kick. She had to fight the urge to laugh. On May 20, she learned that the little kicker was a girl.[35]

Sean Penn and Madonna at the Live Aid concert, Philadelphia, 1985 *Acetate by Andy Warhol based on photo by Keith Haring. The Andy Warhol Museum. © 2023 The Andy Warhol Foundation for the Visual Arts, Inc. / Licensed by Artists Rights Society (ARS), New York*

Andy Warhol and Keith Haring, *Untitled, 1985 Synthetic polymer, Day-Glo, and acrylic on canvas. Image courtesy Keith Haring Foundation. © 2023 The Andy Warhol Foundation for the Visual Arts, Inc. / Licensed by Artists Rights Society (ARS), New York*

The Breakfast Club, left to right: Ed Gilroy, Stephen Bray, Dan Gilroy, and Gary Burke, 1987 *Photo by Jim Shea. Copyright Jim Shea*

Christopher Ciccone, 1990 *Photo by Morris Sipa. Shutterstock*

Herb Ritts, Madonna's close friend and photo and video collaborator, Los Angeles, May 1990 *Photo by Ron Galella. Ron Galella Collection, Getty Images*

Jean Paul Gaultier holding a Madonna doll dressed in an "Express Yourself" costume, Paris, October 1990 *Photo by Ian Cook. Getty Images*

Steven Meisel, one of Madonna's most important photo collaborators, New York City, April 1993 *Photo by Steve Eichner. Getty Images*

Truth or Dare cast: bottom row, Jose Gutierrez; middle row, left to right, Luis Camacho, Oliver Crumes, Carlton Wilborn, Madonna; top row, left to right, Kevin Stea, Donna De Lory, Gabriel Trupin, Salim Gauwloos, January 1991 *Photo by Michael Ochs. Getty Images*

Madonna performing "Like a Virgin" during her Blond Ambition tour, Wembley Stadium, London, July 1990 *Photo by Duncan Raban Popperfoto. Getty Images*

Alek Keshishian and Madonna arrive at Christopher Ciccone's exhibition at the Wessel O'Connor gallery, New York City, November 1991 *Photo by Ron Galella. Ron Galella Collection. Getty Images*

Dino De Laurentiis, Madonna, and Alek Keshishian at the Cannes film festival, May 1991 *Photo by Jean-Claude Deutsch. Jacques Lange Paris Match. Getty Images*

Madonna and Rosie O'Donnell in *A League of Their Own*, 1992 *Moviestore/ Shutterstock*

Donna De Lory, Madonna, and Niki Haris performing in the Girlie Show, New York City, October 1993 *Photo by Steve Eichner. WireImage. Getty Images*

Madonna in the
video for "Erotica,"
1993 *Photo by Araldo
Di Crollalanza.
Shutterstock*

Ingrid Casares, New
York City, 1999 *DMI The
LIFE Picture Collection.
Shutterstock*

Carlos Leon, Madonna, and Spike Lee at a Chicago Bulls game at Madison Square Garden, New York City, March 1995 *Photo by Keith Torrie. New York Daily News Archive. Getty Images*

Madonna and Christopher Ciccone at the seventieth annual Academy Awards, Los Angeles, 1997 *Photo by Kevin Mazur. WireImage. GettyImages*

Nine days later, at four in the morning, the film shoot ended. Eighty-four days. Three countries. More than six hundred film crew and forty thousand extras. Madonna could retire her brown contact lenses, false teeth, and forty-two different hairstyles. There would be more work to do—on the soundtrack album, for example—but she no longer needed to *be* Eva Perón.[36] She called the timing "incredibly poetic…I waited so long for this movie, and it finally happened. I wanted so badly to have a child, and I got pregnant while making the movie. Suddenly God gave me two gifts that were very important to me."[37]

Madonna's pregnancy was easy, she said, and she continued a workout routine to keep her body fit.[38] She also practiced yoga. It was a bridge between her body and her mind as she prepared for motherhood with a more intense exploration of spirituality than she had undertaken up to that point. Religious beliefs had long been part of her self-education. She had studied the Gnostics and early Christians, Buddhism, and Hinduism. She told an Italian journalist, "Although I am Catholic in my bones, I am looking for something else in my blood."[39]

Madonna's childhood was filled with unanswered questions because she had no one to ask. Vowing to be the mother she never had, she would need answers to her own daughter's questions. When she was six and a half months pregnant, she sat next to film producer Susan Becker at a dinner party in LA and explained her dilemma. Becker mentioned that she was taking a class from a rabbi. "She said it was so inspiring and that I should come along," Madonna recalled. "I asked her what it was about. She said, 'Life.' I asked her what it was called. She said 'Kabbalah.'"[40]

The word *Kabbalah* is Hebrew for "received tradition" and refers to a five-thousand-year-old mystical belief system encapsulated in a twenty-three-volume thirteenth-century book written in Aramaic called the *Zohar,* or *Book of Splendor.*[41] It is not a religion so much as a philosophy of living based broadly on simple principles: every cause has an effect; everyone has a purpose and must work to find it; and people should love their neighbors as they do themselves. A person who lives by those principles will grow closer to God.

Traditionally, the teachings were reserved for Orthodox Jewish men over the age of forty who had prepared for years to receive such wisdom. But by the time Madonna was introduced to it, there was an outpost for the study of Kabbalah in Los Angeles run by a rabbi named Philip Berg and his wife, Karen. The LA center brought Kabbalah to people of all faiths, ages, and genders.[42]

Madonna went to a class and was attracted to the ideas and to being in a classroom, where she could sit quietly and anonymously in the back and learn.[43] The teacher that day was an Israeli rabbi named Eitan Yardeni. "I knew at this moment my life would never be the same," she said.[44]

She began attending classes, vigorously taking notes as she heard answers to the questions that she had often posed. "Life no longer seemed like a series of random events. I started to see patterns in my life. I woke up. I began to be conscious of my words and my actions and to really see the results of them."[45] She was also inspired by the stress Kabbalah placed on service. "What are you doing to help? What are you doing to make the world a better place?" she explained.[46] Before Kabbalah, Madonna said, she inhabited a

> me me me universe, not thinking before I spoke, not thinking before I acted...just not thinking. I thought I was a bad-ass-motherfucker—rebel-outside-of-it-all type of a person...I just didn't care about anyone but myself, really. I wasn't a total pig or anything, I think I was a decent human being, but I just didn't think of the big picture, that's all. My life was very small picture.[47]

She believed Kabbalah was exactly what she needed to help prepare for her new role as mother.

Outside Good Samaritan Hospital in Los Angeles, media trucks created a pop-up campsite as journalists staked out the doors, attempted to infiltrate the hospital, and tried bribing staff. Inside, in an eighth-floor suite, Madonna was giving birth. Five people were cleared to be with her: Carlos, Madonna's sister Melanie, Christopher, Liz Rosenberg, and Madonna's assistant Caresse.[48]

Her labor began at three thirty in the morning on October 14, 1996. Carlos and Melanie remained at her side throughout. Though Madonna had wanted a natural childbirth, by three thirty in the afternoon, doctors recommended a cesarean section, and Madonna agreed. The baby was born at one minute after four. Lourdes Maria Ciccone Leon. Madonna said that when her own mother was ill, she "always wanted to go to Lourdes...She never made it. So for sentimental reasons, I named my daughter that."[49]

Madonna called her daughter "the greatest miracle of my life." Carlos was simply beside himself, roaming the halls of the hospital in a T-shirt that said I GOT MY FIRST HUG AT GOOD SAMARITAN HOSPITAL.[50] The news shot around the world. Agence France-Presse journalists were on strike, but they filed one story anyway: the news of Lourdes's birth.[51]

Madonna and Carlos brought Lourdes—whom they called Lola—home to a small Spanish-style house that Madonna had purchased in Los Feliz, a family-friendly neighborhood.[52]

Madonna existed there in a very un-Madonna place: tranquility. She had completed the biggest, most difficult professional project of her life and produced her most beautiful creation—her daughter. Both involved living outside herself. In the case of *Evita,* she became another person. In the case of motherhood, Lourdes displaced Madonna as the most important person in her life. "I think how amazing to have someone in my life who's a part of me in a way that no one else can be, no matter how much you love them. There's also the feeling of responsibility that's different from any other love," Madonna said.[53] Madonna had loved many people, but Lourdes was the first one she lived for.[54]

Speculation in the entertainment press meanwhile was that Madonna might retire, at least for a while, to inhabit her new persona, "Material mom."[55] But because she was an "artist mom," that wasn't possible. After the year she'd been through, she had something to say.[56]

On December 19, Madonna learned that she was nominated for a Golden Globe Award for *Evita.* She was up against acting legends Glenn Close, Debbie Reynolds, and Barbra Streisand as well as relative newcomer Frances McDormand in the Best Actress in a Motion Picture—Musical or Comedy category. *Evita* had also been nominated for Best Motion Picture—Musical or Comedy; Best Director—Motion Picture (Alan Parker); Best Actor in a Motion Picture—Musical or Comedy (Antonio Banderas); and "You Must Love Me" for Best Original Song—Motion Picture (Andrew Lloyd Webber and Tim Rice). It was the recognition Madonna and her film colleagues had hoped for, and it set up *Evita* for the Oscars, because the Golden Globes were often a harbinger of that even more coveted prize. In the wake of the nomination, Madonna's settled tranquility vanished. She called herself a "ball of nerves."[57]

The movie had been rolled out strategically, beginning with the soundtrack, in November. The album would eventually chart in the top ten in fifteen countries, hitting number 2 in the United States and number 1 in Great Britain. In early December, Bloomingdale's stores around the United States opened "Evita boutiques," selling everything from snoods to stoles. Estée Lauder promoted Face of Evita makeup: flame-red lipstick and nail polish. Finally, on December 14, the film itself premiered in Los Angeles, at the Shrine Auditorium.[58]

Dressed as Eva Perón in a red velvet Givenchy dress, jacket, and foot-high veiled hat, Madonna arrived at the premiere with Carlos and Liz Rosenberg. More friends and family were inside the hall among an invited crowd of two thousand people. Outside, thousands of fans stood crushed together on risers along the red carpet and shoulder to shoulder in the street. Celebrity guests told reporters that they had never seen a premiere like it. The press attention and the fans' excitement made the event feel more like an awards ceremony than a movie debut.[59]

The enthusiasm hadn't diminished after the screening.[60] At the after-party, the talk was all about Oscar. The consensus was that at the very least Madonna would be nominated.[61] Asked by Matt Lauer on NBC's *Today* if she would be "terribly disappointed" if she wasn't, Madonna said, frankly, "Yeah."[62]

The film opened in select theaters on Christmas Day. *Evita* was not spared the passionate love-her-or-hate-her response to everything Madonna did. Critics of note praised it, but the commentary didn't end with reviews. Articles analyzed the film in the context of musicals, Eva Perón's life and legacy, and Madonna's voice, acting ability, and appearance. The amount of press was extraordinary.[63]

And then, on January 19, at the Golden Globes, *Evita* won Best Motion Picture—Musical or Comedy; "You Must Love Me" won Best Original Song—Motion Picture; and Madonna won Best Actress in a Motion Picture—Musical or Comedy.[64] Emotional and clutching her award, Madonna said, "I have been so incredibly blessed this past year and I have so much to be thankful for."[65]

Standing at the podium as an award winner was a rare occurrence for Madonna. Despite having been responsible for iconic videos that helped make the medium an art form, she had never won a Video of the Year Award. Despite having written more number 1 songs than any woman in history, having more consecutive hit singles than the Beatles, and having sold (at that time) more than one hundred million records worldwide, she had not won a Grammy for her music. Recognition was something she received from fans, not from the entertainment industry. But then, the Golden Globes were not bestowed by the industry; they were awarded by the Hollywood Foreign Press Association. Indeed, when it came time for the industry to render a verdict on *Evita* and Madonna, it and she were largely shunned.

On February 11, Oscar nominations were announced. *Evita* was nominated for Best Original Song, Best Sound, Best Art Direction, Best Film Editing, and Best Cinematography. It did not garner a single nomination in the major categories. Call it the Madonna curse: even when she was good—*really* good—she wasn't good enough. Call it the curse of the powerful woman: in 1992, Barbra Streisand's film *The Prince of Tides* had been considered worthy of seven Oscar nominations, but she was not nominated for Best Director. Sometimes the slights from the overwhelmingly white boys' club that constituted the Academy of Motion Picture Arts and Sciences just felt petty.

Madonna was in a good enough place personally and felt secure enough in what she had accomplished professionally to rise above that disrespect. She told Academy Award show organizers that she would like to sing "You Must Love Me" during the event. On March 24, she did. As she took the stage to sing live with a full orchestra (which had made her so nervous in London), before an auditorium filled with stars (which had so unnerved her when she performed "Sooner or Later"), she appeared self-assured, poised, serious. It was a new Madonna. She seemed greater than the night as she sang "You Must Love Me" to the academy that had rejected her.[66]

Tim Rice and Andrew Lloyd Webber won the Oscar for Best Song. It would be *Evita*'s only Academy Award. And with that and a few foreign premiere events, Madonna put the film behind her. The project had been "fulfilling on every level," she said, but she was ready to return to the "instant gratification" of writing and recording her own music.[67]

Madonna returned to the studio with her priorities realigned. "I just started to look at life differently," she said. "Probably what I started to focus on more than anything was living in the moment."[68] Gone was her anger, the rehashing of past wrongs and disappointments, and her tendency, if not her need, to provoke. She was happy.[69] She had been while working on other albums, too—*True Blue,* for example—but that happiness had depended upon a man. Madonna was finally happy with herself. The love she wanted to sing about was bigger than romance. It was as big as the world and as small as her daughter. She needed to find people to help her express that.

At first, she returned to her *Bedtime Stories* partner Babyface because there was an essence in that earlier album that Madonna wanted to build on. But she wasn't able to take her music far enough with him, and in the end she didn't use the songs they wrote.[70] She then returned to her old collaborator Pat Leonard. They met in Florida to create four songs—"Sky Fits Heaven," "Nothing Really Matters," "Skin," and "Frozen."

"Frozen" would be the first single from the still untitled album. It was drawn from Madonna's own experience, but the visual images it evoked, she said, were inspired by the film *The English Patient*—specifically, the scene in which the character played by Ralph Fiennes struggles across the desert to find help for his dying lover. "Oh, to be loved in that way," Madonna said. "Oh, to love someone that way."[71]

Those were Madonna's Pat Leonard songs. For others, she looked for new collaborators. Rick Nowels was one.[72] He had worked on Celine Dion's Grammy-nominated album *Falling into You.* At Barneys New York, while tie shopping for the awards ceremony, he saw Madonna. "I got up the nerve to walk over and introduce myself," he recalled. "It was very intimidating...I told her what a great songwriter she was, and she was very gracious and appreciative."[73] Two weeks later they were in Los Angeles working together.[74]

Madonna drove herself to Nowels's Hollywood Hills studio every afternoon. Being able to drive, she often said, was one of the only reasons she liked living in LA.[75] It was in the cocoon of her car that Madonna heard her music as a listener would, stuck in traffic. It was there that she could hear what it needed.

Nowels and Madonna wrote nine songs in ten days, three of which would appear on her album.

"To Have and Not to Hold," a song about misbegotten love, had a strong bossa nova beat and was all about the rhythm, while "The Power of Goodbye" was about the words. "It was deep, poetic, and intelligent," Nowels said. "When she's on and at her best, she's on a par with Joni Mitchell or Paul Simon."[76] "Little Star," a song about Lola, was written at the end of a frustrating day. "I was panicking a bit," Nowels told writer Lucy O'Brien. He began playing three chords and Madonna began singing. An hour later, they had a song. The next day, on the way to the studio, Nowels played it in his car. "I started crying," he said, "it was so beautiful."[77]

With Nowels's contributions, Madonna had seven songs for her album, but she needed more, and she needed someone to help shape the recording as a whole. She asked British producers Goldie and Tricky, as well as the band the Prodigy. "They all basically turned [up] their elitist noses at me and said, 'Oh, we can't work with you. You're a big pop star.'" Then a forty-year-old Brit named William Orbit came to Madonna's attention.[78]

Born William Wainwright, Orbit was raised in East and North London, where he struggled as a child to decode Jimi Hendrix by playing his records at half speed. As a young adult in the '70s, he lived in squats on a diet of Mars bars and a daily tab of acid while trying to build a music career. By the '80s, that career followed two paths: he became a remixer of other artists' work, including Madonna's, and he created his own music, recording three groundbreaking albums of ambient soul fusion under the name Strange Cargo.[79]

In the process, Orbit became a legend in the British rave underground. The electronic music for that fluid landscape was born in gay dance clubs in Chicago in the early '80s and blossomed later in Europe, where each country produced its own flavor. It was the sound of the space age—or the new internet age—rooted in funk, soul, and disco. It was also the soundtrack for a subculture of spontaneous gatherings so large and so countercultural that the British and French governments passed laws making them illegal.[80]

Orbit had been talking to Guy Oseary about his music. Oseary told him Madonna was looking for material and suggested he send her some tapes. "I didn't take it very seriously, so I didn't send anything," Orbit said. "Then he rang again."[81] Orbit put thirteen tracks of what he called "half-formed ideas" on a digital audiotape and sent it to her. Five days later he was sitting in his garden when Madonna called. At the end of their conversation, she invited him to New York.[82]

Tall, lanky, with a gap-toothed grin, Orbit arrived at her apartment in early June during a rainstorm, dripping wet and carrying a plastic bag of music samples. "I'd been closeted away in my studio for a long time," he said. "I was excited just to be out—let alone with Madonna, and in New York all of a sudden."[83] Madonna told writer Johnny Black that Orbit looked "like a drowned rat. He looked really fragile. He was very humble and unassuming and endearing, like a little boy. As soon as I met him, I liked him."[84]

She listened to some of the tracks he brought and was blown away.[85] He listened to some early versions of the songs she wanted on her album. "I thought, 'Golly, this is strong. This is potentially going to be a really interesting project,' " Orbit recalled.[86] They booked studio time at the Hit Factory, where they focused on the vocals. "That was pretty exciting," Orbit said, "because that was the first time I heard her sing her parts."[87] By the end of those sessions, Madonna was convinced that Orbit was the person to help guide her album. "I like to work with people who take chances," she said. "Usually they're undiscovered because once people are successful, they don't like taking risks."[88]

Madonna called Orbit "a complete madman genius."[89] "William has no pretenses and doesn't care whether people think he's cool or not."[90] "When I got into the studio with him, I felt like I'd been shot out of a cannon. I had so many ideas."[91] For his part, Orbit said, "I walked into Madonna World and emerged, blinking, five months later."[92] The album they would create together would be called *Ray of Light*.

Beginning in mid-June, Madonna and Orbit worked together at Larrabee Studios, in North Hollywood, constructing, destroying, and reconstructing the tracks she had made with Nowels and Leonard and creating new ones of their own.[93] "It really was a sort of throw-the-rules-out-the-window type of record making for me," Madonna said.[94] "I was in freefall for the first time."[95] But achieving that state wasn't easy.

Orbit had never worked with state-of-the-art equipment. He said the experience "wasn't so much a learning curve as a learning cliff."[96] Madonna described it as a culture shock.

> We had lots of problems. Things went haywire and everyone got frustrated because we were working with samples and synth sounds and Pro Tools and not with live musicians, and shit would keep breaking down and nobody would know how to fix it.[97]

Orbit had also never worked with someone like Madonna. "The first day, I was in paralysis," he told music journalist Johnny Black, "because I was used to going off and being left to get on with it, but she said, 'I'm not the kind of girl that leaves the guy to get on with it. Get used to it.' It took me a while to get used to someone looking over my shoulder."[98] Once he did, he said, the experience became

> very pure; it was all about making that record and nothing else... The moment I saw her jumping into the tracks in such an artistic way, I instantly thought how great it was going to be. She's an amazing person, producer and it was a true collaboration. It's important to get this across; I don't like it when people assume that I was the clever one doing the whole job.[99]
>
> She didn't put her name there out of vanity, she was fucking in there with me and it wouldn't have happened without the two of us.[100]

Madonna's musical goal for the album, she said, was to raise electronica to a new level "by actually investing it with emotion."[101] And that meant leaving it raw. The tendency for people working with computers, Orbit said, was to "perfect everything, because they can." Madonna's mantra was " 'Don't gild the lily,' in other words, keep it rough, and don't perfect too much... you can lose the character of it, and she always had an eye out for that."[102]

The studio itself was small and cramped and filled with as much equipment as the bridge of a spaceship—if that spaceship were in a club basement. Orbit and Madonna were the cocaptains of a talented crew, among them engineer Pat McCarthy, whom Madonna credited with keeping everyone calm, and Marius de Vries, whom she had invited back from *Bedtime Stories*.[103] Orbit was the "band." "Every guitar you hear is me," he said. "On a lot of tracks I did everything."[104]

Pat Leonard helped produce, too. Part of his job involved bringing a classical sensibility to the album, particularly with string and woodwind sections—twenty violins, six violas, six cellos, four double basses, two flutes, and an oboe—which were conducted by cellist Suzie Katayama on "Frozen" and "The Power of Goodbye."[105] And they had daily contributions from Lourdes, who, Orbit said, made "a beeline for the knobs and buttons. We'd look away and the whole sound had changed."[106]

Guy Oseary appeared occasionally, too, to save them from "some goofy ideas," Madonna said, and push them further on songs they thought were done.[107] But only once did someone from Warner Bros. Records turn up while they were working. Orbit said, "I do remember Madonna telling him, 'This is art. This is how we are doing it. We'll let you come and have a good listen...when it's done.'"[108]

Though the album was inspired by birth—Madonna's rebirth after her trying '90s, her experience with *Evita,* and Lourdes's arrival—the theme of many tracks was death and how to move past it. "The Power of Goodbye" was one of them. "Mer Girl" was another.[109] Madonna began writing the lyrics during a trip to Michigan for her grandmother's birthday. While she was out for a run, it started to rain as she passed a cemetery. "There was the blackest sky you've ever seen. I went against the instinct to run away, and just stayed there as the rain got to the leaves, and everything became heavy and muddy."[110]

When she returned home, she had the place to herself and wrote six lines for what became "Mer Girl." Once back in LA, she heard the music Orbit had written for it and got to work finishing the song. Lying on her bed listening to his music on a boom box, she said, she wrote and rewrote the lyrics. "Then I went into the studio and did it."[111]

The vocal booth at Larrabee wasn't a booth at all. It was a cozy sitting room with a chair, a Persian rug, a side table with fresh flowers, and a microphone.[112] Madonna entered that area and recorded her song in one semiwhispered take. "She stepped out...and everybody was rooted to the spot," Orbit told music writer Danny Eccleston. "It was just one of those moments. Really spooky."[113] "Mer Girl" was the most haunting song that Madonna had ever recorded. Orbit said that though there was "outside pressure to change it," she refused.[114]

Madonna explained that in writing a song, she first asks, "Is it my truth, does it come from the heart?" Second, will it touch people emotionally?[115] "I'm trying to affect people in a quieter way," she said of her album. "I set out to be honest about where I am now."[116] "Shanti/Ashtangi" was an example of that. The song included the prayer Madonna said before yoga every day, which she had learned by studying Sanskrit.[117]

"Drowned World/Substitute for Love," another Madonna–Orbit collaboration, concerns Madonna's relationship with fame "and coming to terms with the idea that there was a time in my life when I thought fame was going to give me everything I needed." She had since realized that "while it's really great and I've had a lot of great experiences…it does not take the place of true love."[118] The version of that song that ultimately appeared on the album was a demo. Like "Mer Girl," it was left just as it was.[119]

Susannah Melvoin, who was a Prince associate in the '80s, shared a writing credit on "Candy Perfume Girl." Before *Ray of Light,* Orbit had given her some tracks and asked her to write lyrics. "Candy Perfume Girl" was one, written while she was mourning the death of her brother from a heroin overdose.[120]

The single "Ray of Light," which Madonna called "a song about celebration" and "looking at the world for the first time with a feeling of real hope," also bears other artists' fingerprints.[121] The lyrics are based on a song written in the '70s by Clive Maldoon and Dave Curtiss, which Maldoon's niece Christine Leach sang for Orbit over music he had written. It would appear on Madonna's album with credits for Maldoon, Curtiss, and Leach.[122]

One of the criticisms that followed Madonna throughout her career was that she chose other people's material, made minor changes, and called it her own. Pat Leonard told writer Barry Walters that was nonsense.

> Her sensibility about melodic line—from the beginning of the verse to the end of the verse and how the verse and the chorus influence each other—is very deep. That's not common. Say, "Live to Tell," for example, our first big single. The melodies I wrote are still there and she sings them for the most part, but it's where she departs from them that turned it into a song. Many times she's singing notes that no one would've thought of but her. Some of it can be perceived as naiveté because she's picking a note you wouldn't choose. But who needs the "correct" note? You need the right note that tells the story, and she's great at that. She certainly made me look better. All I have to do is look at all the other people I wrote with over the years and how that went.[123]

Orbit agreed. He called Madonna "the consummate songwriter."[124]

When the album was finished, Orbit said, Madonna invited Warner executives to a listening party.

> As we were waiting outside in a little sitting room, picking on strawberries and biting our nails, I realized, "Shit, Madonna has no idea about how

they're going to respond! She's nervous!" I did not expect her to feel that way because she never shows it. As it turned out everybody loved it.[125]

That, he said, was "another thing about Madonna. I've never met anybody who has more ability to make things happen . . . just by the sheer force of her will."[126]

Chapter 40

Washington, Los Angeles, Miami, Milan, London, 1997–1998

I'd like to live forever. If there's anything I'm afraid of, it's missing what will happen tomorrow.[1]

— *Gianni Versace*

JOURNALISTS LIKE TO affix handy labels to decades. It's a way of keeping the present tidy for historians trying to understand the past. In 1995, a *Chicago Tribune* reporter named Steve Johnson did just that. In an article called "Making Sense of the Nineties," he noted that Tom Wolfe had called the '70s the "Me Decade" and that the '80s had become known as the "Yuppie or Greed Decade." Johnson himself called the '90s the "Tabloid Decade."[2] At a moment when society might have been better occupied focusing on a future dominated by technology that few understood and the portentous year 2000 bearing down like a meteorite, the public and the press were consumed by scandal. Instead of pondering the universe, they were digging elbow-deep through the mud.

That was because such "news" was everywhere. By 1997, the type of stories and sordid details that only tabloids would have covered five years earlier were splashed across the front pages of newspapers. Much of it emanated from Washington. In 1994, Republicans took control of Congress for the first time in forty years and launched thirty-seven investigations of the Clinton White House. There were accounting scandals, the suicide of a White House lawyer, and alleged cover-ups of alleged fraud allegedly involving Hillary Clinton. And finally, the impeachment of Bill Clinton for allegedly lying about his affair with a White House intern.[3]

Not since John F. Kennedy had there been so much talk of presidential sexcapades, which went largely unreported while Kennedy was alive. In Clinton's case, the scandals, which involved several women, were everywhere: TV, newspapers, the internet.[4] Hillary blamed the stories on a "vast right-wing conspiracy," which did indeed fuel and fund the firestorm. But the real problem was Bill Clinton himself. He was a tabloid dream.

In that environment, the coverage of celebrities became more aggressive. They were stalked, ambushed, and assaulted by paparazzi and "videographers" feeding a bottomless public appetite for dirt. In 1995, Brad Pitt and then twenty-three-year-old Gwyneth Paltrow, who met that year on the set of David Fincher's film *Se7en,* were caught sunbathing nude in St. Barts by a paparazzo with a telephoto lens. Madonna contacted Paltrow to offer support, and the two became friends. "She's experiencing the upsides and the downsides of being famous for the first time," Madonna said. "That's a lot for someone to take...So I'm happy to help her." (It was the second such big-sisterly gesture. When Paltrow was twelve, Madonna wrote her at the behest of Sean's father and told her to stop smoking.)[5]

In 1996, George Clooney, who at the time was among the biggest names in the entertainment industry, launched an offensive after pictures of him and his girlfriend appeared on the tabloid TV show *Hard Copy.* He said he would boycott that program as well as *Entertainment Tonight* and by inference any other organization that violated his privacy. Madonna joined the effort after a fee of $350,000 was offered to the paparazzo who could snap shots of Lola. "Because of Madonna's baby and now George, actors are joining the ranks," a Clooney publicist said. "It's truly a history-making move."[6]

Some news organizations backed off, at least temporarily, especially concerning coverage of children. But the need to sell papers and keep eyeballs on screens meant they had to find a new target. That favorite fallback—the gay and lesbian community—became one. Gay life had changed dramatically since 1995. The Food and Drug Administration that year approved a new class of drugs called protease inhibitors, which, when taken in combination with other drugs, made HIV/AIDS a livable illness for people who could afford the medications. At the same time, gay men and lesbians became a political bloc working to end legal restrictions that kept them from living as full citizens.[7]

Like all cultural advances, these were met with resistance. The Clinton administration had promised to help, but then, faced with bitter opposition from the right, backed down. The White House response to discrimination in the military was a policy called "Don't ask, don't tell," which essentially meant that gays could remain in the military if they stayed in the closet. Clinton called it "an honorable compromise." Meanwhile, antigay rhetoric and antigay violence were on the rise. FBI statistics showed that in 1996–97, though crime overall declined by 2 percent, hate crimes against homosexuals were up 10 percent.[8] In the public square, outing celebrities became a favorite tabloid pastime.

Is-she-or-isn't-she stories about Rosie O'Donnell filled tabloids in the late '90s.[9] Questions about whether Jodie Foster was a lesbian appeared then, too. Both women were single mothers who horrified the family-values crowd.[10] And then Ellen DeGeneres, whose eponymous series was one of the most popular on prime-time television, became *the* lesbian story. In 1996, tabloids began reporting that her character would come out on the show, which meant that Ellen the actor would, too.[11] "I had never had that much media attention," DeGeneres recalled. "It was really scary for me."[12]

Amid that controversy, Madonna called Ellen "out of the blue. We had never met. I just all of a sudden get a call saying, 'It's Madonna, and I just wanna say that I'm behind ya, I'm with ya, I support you.'" They talked about why it was so difficult to come out and that in a business built on an entertainer's ability to make audiences love them, they risked being rejected for who they were. Madonna told Ellen, "Things come to you when you let go and you don't care and [don't] need the validation any-more." DeGeneres said that advice gave her courage.[13]

On April 14, 1997, *Time* magazine's cover featured DeGeneres and the headline YEP, I'M GAY. And six days later, Ellen said so again on her show as her character came out before forty-two million viewers. Advertisers withdrew support, hate mail poured in, and ABC attached a parental advisory warning on the thoroughly wholesome sitcom. Still, the deed was done. Ellen had made her statement and in doing so changed the enter-tainment industry. Actors didn't, however, rush to follow her out of the closet. Her bravery cost her her show. The following year, the Emmy-winning series would be canceled.[14]

There was one place in the States besides New York and San Francisco where gays, lesbians, and trans people could live and love with impunity. And that was South Florida. Incredibly, despite the concentration of star power in and around Miami Beach, the paparazzi had not overwhelmed it, nor had the morality police tried to shut it down.[15]

Gianni Versace was the king of that scene, and his Casa Casuarina, on Ocean Drive, was the place where international celebrities mixed with Miami's most colorful locals. It was in every way a court in the European tradition—a gay court, consumed with fashion, art, love, sensuality, and sexuality. Parties around Versace's mosaicked and gold-inlaid pool were bacchanalian. And when the party wasn't at Versace's, it was at a club. For Gianni, that meant mostly the Warsaw Ballroom.[16] Donatella was part of the Liquid scene, along with Ingrid Casares, Naomi Campbell, Kate Moss, Gwyneth Paltrow, Madonna, and Christopher. One friend said that Dona-tella was "living a rock star's life. She was full on." She used bodyguards in Miami Beach, but Gianni never did. It was his kingdom. People loved him.[17]

In 1994, Versace was diagnosed with inner ear cancer, but by 1996 it was in remission. "I realized that it was possible that at not even fifty years old I could just…go," he told *The New Yorker* writer Andrea Lee in 1997. "I said to myself, 'Well, every day that I live from now on—it's my party.'"[18] In 1997, sales from his company hit $1 billion, and his brother wanted to take the company public. He had come a long way from Calabria. At times it seemed too far. Miami Beach helped him rediscover who he was. Having been in Paris on July 6 to present his latest collection at a show at the Ritz, Versace flew to Miami for two weeks of relaxation.[19]

On July 15, at eight fifteen in the morning, Versace walked, as he did most days, to the News Cafe at the corner to buy coffee and magazines. He told his lover Antonio D'Amico he'd be back in a few minutes. At eight forty he was at his front gate when a man in a baseball cap walked across the road, climbed the steps, and put the barrel of a gun to the back of Versace's head. He pulled the trigger. Twice. Versace lay dead on his steps in a black T-shirt and shorts. The gunman fled on foot up the street.[20]

The man in the hat was a Californian named Andrew Cunanan. He had been on a killing spree since April, murdering four men (three of whom he knew and one of whom, a stranger to him, he killed while stealing the man's truck) in three states before arriving in Miami, where he had holed up in a cheap hotel under an assumed name. The night before he killed Versace, he had been at Liquid.[21]

Cunanan was a professional con artist who lived off wealthy older gay men. He told friends in California that he had met Versace, but it was never clear that he had. The line between fantasy and reality in Cunanan's life did not exist. People who knew Versace doubted there was any connection before their fatal encounter.[22]

Madonna was in the studio in Los Angeles working on the track "Swim" when Donatella called her from Rome, "distraught," to tell her about Gianni. William Orbit said Madonna got off the phone, finished her vocal, which "is probably why it has such an emotional impact," and left the studio.[23] As Donatella flew from Italy to Miami, Madonna headed there to meet her. She would be at Gianni's house, which was by then a crime scene, when Donatella arrived.[24]

The last time Madonna saw Versace had been just before Easter, when she went to Casa Casuarina with friends and Lola. "He had kicked cancer, he was proud of his latest collection, and life was good," she said. Madonna tried to persuade him to start doing yoga. He didn't commit, but he seemed interested. And then he was dead.[25]

Donatella landed in Miami at three thirty in the morning, identified Gianni's body, then arrived at Casa Casuarina around dawn. "Madonna was waiting for me inside," she said.

I will never forget that she was trying to comfort me during these hours. There were FBI agents everywhere in the house. They interrogated each of us and opened all the drawers, a nightmare. My brother had just been murdered, and we were being treated like suspects. But that's probably what FBI agents have to do.[26]

Madonna invited Donatella to stay at her place, but Donatella said no, she would remain at Gianni's surrounded by police, the international press, and fans. Meanwhile, her brother's killer was still at large.[27] Wanted posters were plastered all over South Beach as police hunted for Cunanan. Eight days after Versace's murder, he was found dead in a houseboat up the beach. He had ended his killing spree by shooting himself.

The two bullets that took Versace's life didn't just kill a man: they also killed what Miami Beach had been. "As soon as celebrities realized they just couldn't walk around South Beach, it was over. I think for a while they thought of South Beach as a Garden of Eden," Brian Antoni said.[28] In the wake of Versace's death, Madonna said, she felt "a great sense of vulnerability. I became incredibly paranoid." But then, she said, she realized "there aren't enough bodyguards in the world to protect me…If someone wants to kill me, they're gonna kill me. And if it's my time, it's my time. My best protection is good karma, and that's all there is to it."[29]

The family cremated Versace's remains in Miami and buried them at his home at Lake Como, but Donatella wanted his funeral to be held in Milan at the world's third-largest Catholic church, the Duomo di Milano. The haute Milanese scoffed at the notion that this poor southern Italian tailor would be buried there, wrote Deborah Ball in *House of Versace*. The church feared a "gay pride spectacle," but in the end it agreed.[30]

The funeral was Gianni Versace's last big show. On July 22, black Mercedes began arriving at the cathedral to disgorge pop culture royalty.[31] Versace had wanted to be a Medici prince.[32] He was, in fact, a modern-day Caravaggio—rough, sexual, even vulgar compared with his more polished Italian designer rivals. But he, better than they, reflected the time. He captured the street as Caravaggio had during the Renaissance. It was his inspiration, and he made it art.

The tabloids, meanwhile, feasted on the story of Versace's death, a tale of homosexuality, violence, decadence, and wealth. Bill Clinton's dalliances, by comparison, seemed boring. But the press had not finished with Versace when an even bigger story exploded. Madonna was at Gloria Estefan's birthday party in Miami on August 31 when she heard that Princess Diana, her lover Dodi Al-Fayed, and a driver employed by the Ritz named Henri

Paul were killed in a car accident in a Paris tunnel while being chased by the paparazzi.[33] Diana, a mother of two boys, was thirty-six.

Diana Spencer had been hounded by the press for fifteen years. The British tabloids were relentless in their pursuit of her because she had made the mistake of living as a human rather than as a royal. It may not have been her intention, but her life—going to the gym, playing with her children, having boyfriends when her marriage to Prince Charles ended—challenged not only the monarchy but also the tabloid press. Traditionally, it was their job to unmask as ordinary those who were considered extraordinary. Like Madonna, Diana exposed *herself,* and the tabloids never forgave her. Madonna said that she and Diana had planned to meet so Madonna could give her tips on surviving that vicious coverage. They didn't have a chance.[34]

On September 4, an unusually somber Madonna used the MTV Video Music Awards to commemorate Diana. She did not berate the paparazzi or the tabloid editors; rather, she told the audience to examine its own role in the tragedy. The public's hunger for gossip and scandal kept the paparazzi and the tabloids in business. "Until we change our negative behavior," she said, "tragedies like this will continue to occur."[35]

Four days later, Madonna and Christopher attended the Versace memorial service at the Metropolitan Museum of Art in New York. Madonna read a poem she wrote for Gianni, and Elton John and Whitney Houston sang. But most poignant of all was Donatella, who gave her first public remarks since her brother's death. Remembering "the adventures that came with being his little sister," she said, "Each time Gianni would ask me to do what back then seemed like these impossible things, I'd tell him I couldn't do it. He'd tell me I could, and I did." Christopher recalled thinking as he listened that that was how he felt about Madonna.[36]

Donatella invited a small group of people from the memorial back to the house Gianni had purchased off Fifth Avenue: Madonna, Christopher, Lisa Marie Presley, Luciano Pavarotti, and Courtney Love among them. Madonna left early, and Christopher said that he, Love, and Donatella retreated to Donatella's sitting room to do lines of coke. "Meanwhile, Donatella keeps saying, 'Chreestopher, Chreestopher, play "Candle in the Wind" for me,'" Christopher recalled. That was the song Elton John famously sang at Diana's funeral.[37]

During Fashion Week in Milan several weeks later, it was Madonna's "Candy Perfume Girl" that Donatella wanted to hear. The song—written by Susannah Melvoin as she mourned her brother's death—hadn't been released, but Donatella featured it blasting over speakers as Naomi Campbell and Kate Moss appeared on the runway for the first Versace show without Gianni. After the show, Donatella sobbed uncontrollably about her loss and the recent past. To the crowd, though, that song and that show heralded the future.[38]

Madonna was back in Miami to spend the Thanksgiving holiday with Rosie O'Donnell and their families and to host Liquid's second anniversary party.[39] She decided to give *Ray of Light* a test run. "It was midnight," Ingrid said.

> There was a big cake and fire-eaters, drag queens, people on stilts—you name it. The crowd was totally mixed: straight, gay, Latin, Cuban, black, white. Then all of a sudden, you heard the very beginning of "Ray of Light." Once people realized that it was her, they went really crazy. Even the mayor of Miami started dancing. At six o'clock in the morning, I was still pushing people out.[40]

The sound introduced a new Madonna, and so did her look. Her hair was long, wavy, and unkempt—a henna-tinted Alanis Morissette or Fiona Apple. Unlike those women, however, Madonna appeared less earthy than ethereal. She said she was "obsessed with India" at that moment.[41] The inspiration could have been her study of Hinduism and yoga, which she pursued with her usual obsessiveness, or Arundhati Roy's book *The God of Small Things,* which was a huge hit that year. Roy's influence as a brilliant young activist Indian artist had filtered throughout pop culture, even into fashion.[42]

But whether the impulse to shed layers of artifice was external, internal, or both, in her latest incarnation Madonna was simply luminous. "Ever since my daughter was born," she said, "I feel the fleetingness of time. And I don't want to waste it on getting the perfect lip color."[43]

It was that version of Madonna who met Mario Testino in Miami after Thanksgiving to shoot the cover for *Ray of Light.* It would be their second cover together after her 1995 collection of ballads, *Something to Remember.*[44]

There was a naturalness to Testino's images: like a photojournalist's, they captured a fleeting moment. And indeed, his last big photo shoot before Madonna had been with Princess Diana. Appearing in the July 1997 *Vanity Fair* a month before her death, the pictures showed her as Diana Spencer, stripped of the trappings of royalty. Seen through Testino's lens, Diana was at her most human and her loveliest. He would do the same for Madonna on *Ray of Light.*[45]

Madonna's image in the Testino photographs was as infused with gold as Herb Ritts's shots for *True Blue* had been cool white. The story was light, which made her decision to go dark for the first video from her new album so curious. Or maybe not, after the events of that past summer.

Madonna became a woman in mourning, a Goth wraith in a desert so cracked and parched the only thing it could give birth to was bones. She soon found a director to help her realize that vision.

She had seen an obscure video for the Aphex Twin song "Come to Daddy." Directed by Chris Cunningham, it is mesmerizing in its nihilism. It is *A Clockwork Orange* crossed with *Children of the Corn* and Edvard Munch's painting *The Scream,* which comes to ghoulish life out of an abandoned TV set lying in the debris field of a British housing estate. The video is visually cacophonous, postapocalyptic, and terrifying. And it perfectly reflects the music — it *becomes* the music — in a way that videos rarely do.

Madonna wanted Cunningham to direct the video for "Frozen," which would be the first single released from her album. At twenty-seven, he knew Madonna as a singer his little sister listened to and was surprised when she wanted to meet with him in London. "She was really nice, though, and I got lucky again because the track was quite cinematic and I knew I could do something with it," he said.[46]

They started with clothing. Jean Paul Gaultier had designed a Gothic line inspired by Marilyn Manson and Frida Kahlo that Madonna wanted to use for the project.[47] She saw Martha Graham's aesthetic in them; her dance in the video, like Graham's onstage, would exist within the movement of the fabric.[48]

As for the location, Madonna imagined her character as a "mystical creature in the desert…the embodiment of female angst."[49] To bring that image to life, Cunningham planned big. He would use helicopters to film a desert full of bodies — all of them Madonna — that split up into ravens and dogs. But bad weather forced him to scale back his aspirations.[50] In fact, the Mojave, where the team gathered in January, was unforgiving. It was freezing and pouring rain, and Madonna was barefoot throughout the shoot.[51]

During her work on the "Frozen" video, Madonna spent her first night away from her daughter, which added to her anxiety. "And then I thought, 'I'm going to give my daughter a lot by being a creative person and being happy with what I've accomplished.' A lot of our parents are bitter that they gave things up so they could raise us."[52]

The irony was that the video could have been shot anywhere, because the intrigue resides in its special effects: Madonna, black-haired, with mehndi designs painted on her hands and wrists, hovers above the ground like a figure in a surrealist painting; her cloaklike dress spawns ravens, and a bounding dog, and replicas of herself.

The video aired on MTV on February 16. Six days later, Warner Bros. released *Ray of Light* in Japan. And on March 3, it was released in the United

States and Europe. After singing Andrew Lloyd Webber songs in *Evita,* Madonna had returned with a cutting-edge album that no one expected. Once again, she took a relatively underground phenomenon—electronica, or ambient music—and made it mainstream. In the process, she reflected the millennium zeitgeist and its emphasis on spirituality to counter the technology that was overtaking people's lives.

In the wake of *Ray of Light,* Madonna was praised for her daring. The new album marked a watershed moment: it was her *Sgt. Pepper's Lonely Hearts Club Band,* when the Beatles went psychedelic; or *Bringing It All Back Home,* when Bob Dylan exchanged his acoustic guitar for an electric one; or her *Private Dancer,* when Tina Turner showed the world who she was when freed from the malevolent shadow of Ike. Like those works, *Ray of Light* didn't just represent a new direction for the artist who created it; it represented new musical pathways more broadly.

Kurt Loder, on MTV, said the album "constitutes a new sonic vocabulary in popular music."[53] Stuart Maconie, writing in *Q,* said, "Madonna has always had the courage to fail...Compared with the output of her peers... she deserves immense credit...She remains the only pop aristocrat who's keeping her ears open."[54] *Rolling Stone's* Rob Sheffield initially wrote that the album was "sluggish" at times.[55] Then, admitting that it needed to be listened to and digested properly, he published a reassessment. "Even those of us who'd devoted our lives to worshipping Madonna weren't prepared for an album this great," he said.[56] Writing about *Ray of Light* in *Q* years later, Dan Gennoe said, "In one deft move her legacy was secured."[57]

Critics embraced Madonna's album with fervor, ostensibly because it was a breakthrough. But she had had those before, to less critical acclaim (e.g., *Erotica*). What made *Ray of Light* easy to champion was that it was the least political album she had ever made, even compared to her debut, which showcased a young woman's sexual power. There were no statements in *Ray of Light* concerning women's rights, race, sex, or homosexuality. Even her religious references were benign.

In her new persona as a golden-maned goddess, Madonna was not unlike the female folk singers of the late '60s and early '70s. It was an archetype, however transformed, that men everywhere, from corporate offices to newsrooms, could cheer, because she was a woman they had seen before. And that woman appeared to like them.

Madonna had been braced for critics to hate *Ray of Light.* When they surprised her with their enthusiasm, she took their compliments in stride. "If you buy into the good stuff [critics say] you end up getting hurt by the bad stuff," she said. "I'm grateful, thank you very much, but I'm more interested in what my fans say."[58]

The fans loved it, too. *Ray of Light* debuted at number 1 on album charts in the UK, Germany, Italy, Belgium, Israel, and Finland—seventeen countries in all. In the United States, it was deprived of the top spot by the soundtrack for the film *Titanic*. But Madonna still managed to set a US record for the most albums sold by a female artist in a single week—more than 370,000. It was her most successful album since *Like a Prayer,* a decade earlier. The singles, however, didn't do as well because they received very little radio play.[59]

By 1997, radio was dominated by two companies—Clear Channel and Infinity Broadcasting—both of which made centralized decisions about programming that dictated what listeners in hundreds of markets heard. One Clear Channel executive said the playlist focused on hits, some of which were broadcast as often as sixteen times a day. Gone, for the most part, were DJs like Frankie Crocker in New York, who took it upon himself to introduce listeners to new music that might just change their world. Radio had become corporatized, homogenized. It wasn't even clear if the people making the decisions *liked* music.[60]

Madonna's professional demands increased after the release of her album. But with Lola in her life, she responded to them differently. She told Robert Hilburn in the *Los Angeles Times* that year, "When my publicist says you have to do this and this, I go, 'No. I don't.'... Where I'm going to be and how much time I am with [Lola] is always going to come into the picture before I make any decision."[61]

But even after paring things back, Madonna told journalist Ingrid Sischy that she was overwhelmed.

> I'm like a chicken with my head cut off. I'm making my record, planning videos, doing photo shoots. I'm doing interviews. I'm trying to take care of my daughter. I'm reading scripts for movies, and Guy's [Oseary] calling me up, going, "You've got to listen to this and make a decision by tomorrow morning." And I'm like "O.K." I have no free time.[62]

To make it all work, Madonna became more obsessed with her schedule. "Sometimes, as a friend," Alek Keshishian said, "I want to shake her and go, 'Stop making the lists, and who cares that between two and three o'clock you've got to make the following twelve phone calls?'" But he admitted that it was that "structure" that kept Madonna sane. "It's her way of making sure she doesn't go into a place that's dark and negative."[63]

She also revamped Maverick. Freddy DeMann had been the person with the experience and connections she needed in the '80s. But by 1997, the entertainment world had changed, and so had the players in it. Freddy's generation had left the front lines to occupy emeritus positions in plush offices. He had not done that, but Madonna decided it was time that he did. His departure came in several choreographed steps.

Freddy was made chief executive of Maverick Records, and Guy Oseary was elevated to minority owner.[64] Next, after fifteen years as her manager, Freddy was replaced in that job by Madonna's assistant Caresse Henry. By the following year, he would be out entirely. Madonna bought him out of Maverick for $25 million and parted ways with her industry father.[65]

From that point on, Maverick became Madonna and Oseary. He was a vital connection to the latest in music, film, and video. The label that began six years earlier with a $10 million advance from Warner had generated more than $750 million in sales. That might not have happened without Oseary's instinct for talent.[66]

When Madonna formed Maverick, she described it as a creative think tank, and that was still the case. She influenced the artists her label signed as much as they influenced her. It was through a band Maverick signed that year, the Prodigy, for example, that she met a director she would work with for the next twenty years.

Thirty-two-year-old Jonas Åkerlund had directed the Prodigy's controversial video for its equally controversial song "Smack My Bitch Up." The video begins with an Åkerlund trope, which is to play with the camera angle and therefore the viewer's perspective. He often shot scenes from below or above, but in this case, he shot outward—meaning he presents the action as if the viewer is the main character. And "we" are a despicable person indeed.

The video follows a drunken, drugged-out sod through an evening of booze, dope, unwanted groping, fighting, puking, and generally boorish behavior that culminates in luring a prostitute home. Given the preceding minutes, and the music-video tradition of abusing women, the likelihood of an *American Psycho* scenario seems assured. Åkerlund's brilliant twist is to reveal the antagonist to be a woman and to end the video without violence.

Åkerlund's decision to show men how they looked during a night of debauchery by inserting a woman into a male role was considered *outrageous*. Some women, no doubt reacting to the title even more than to the video's content, denounced it as misogynist. Some European countries banned it outright because of its depiction of drug use. MTV aired it only during late-night slots and then, amid the general uproar, pulled it entirely. Åkerlund said,

> I remember I came here [LA], and Jay Leno, who had one of those *Tonight* shows or whatever they're called, he was making "Smack My Bitch Up"

jokes in his opening monologue for, like, five nights in a row. I couldn't believe that a music video could have that impact.[67]

Madonna thought the video was "brilliant."[68] She called Åkerlund and offered him a job directing the video for her single "Ray of Light." Six months and five treatments later, they landed on the right one. The video would depict a single day as the world barreled toward the new millennium.[69]

The finished video is beyond frenetic as it depicts the nightmare pace of survival in the modern world: the congested subways, clogged highways, packed streets, frantic stock-exchange floors, and crowded classrooms. Nothing is savored because no one has the time. Superimposed on that scene is Madonna—her famous navel back in the spotlight (even in "middle age" and after a baby). She exists in the video outside and above that mad quotidian reality but is still lashed by its speed. Finding no peace in the universe, she lets loose a blood-curdling scream on the dance floor.

Åkerlund once called his style "in your face." He described himself as a "vampire," saying he found "peace of mind...in a dark environment."[70] And he advised potential clients that if they wanted something normal, "I'm not their guy."[71] But his work evinced an overwhelming sense of wonder. And that wonder was at the heart of "Ray of Light."[72] "Looking back," he said, the video "was a life-changing moment for me."[73]

Madonna's artistic life had tipped toward Europe. She was excited by the visual work she did with Chris Cunningham and Åkerlund and the musical work she did with William Orbit and Marius de Vries. She was also listening to new sounds coming out of Britain and France. Where it wasn't "happening," she told MTV's Kurt Loder, was in the United States, because "there's a different premium placed on being creative in Europe. The premium here is based on selling—there's a competition to *sell* in America. There's a competition in Europe, especially in England, to be creative. So I think that gives people a lot more freedom."[74]

Her personal life drew her across the Atlantic, too. Madonna had grown fond of London while working on *Evita*.[75] And during her months in the studio with Orbit, she'd come to love his self-deprecating humor and intelligent banter about everything from astronomy to literature, as well as his utter lack of macho posturing. Asked around that time to describe her ideal man, she said he would be like Oscar Wilde: "The fop, the long hair, the suits, too witty for his own good, incredibly smart, scathingly funny—all that."[76]

By the fall of 1997, Madonna and Carlos's romantic relationship was over, though they were devoted to each other because of Lola. "It's important that she sees us as really good friends who respect each other,"

Madonna said.[77] When asked about whether he and Madonna had a "contractual agreement," Carlos snapped, "We love each other. We trust each other. More people should try it."[78] Carlos saw Lola three or four times a week in New York and spoke with her on the phone every night if Madonna was in Los Angeles or Miami. Except for the fact that they didn't share a residence, they were in every way a normal family with loving grandparents, cousins, uncles, and aunts on both sides.[79]

Settled in that regard, Madonna was ready to begin dating, and Alek Keshishian had someone in mind: a thirty-two-year-old former art student from England. Andy Bird was not unlike the fop of Madonna's imaginings, and he was on his way to Los Angeles to try to sell a comedy script he had written. Before he left, he traveled to Paris to meet Keshishian. "While I was there, he was on the phone and suddenly said, 'Andrew, say hello to Madonna'...I took the phone and said 'Hello' and there was a little giggly voice at the other end." Bird wasn't sure it *was* Madonna, but whoever it was seemed nice. He took her number and said he'd call.[80]

By the time he reached LA, they had spoken often. "Our conversations were a first thing in the morning, last thing at night kind of deal," he said. "There was certainly a degree of intimacy at that point. By the end, we were actually saying 'I miss you' when we hadn't spoken for a few hours."[81]

Bird's first actual meeting with Madonna occurred at a *Rolling Stone* cover shoot in October of 1997, during which Madonna, Tina Turner, and Courtney Love posed as three generations of women in rock. "I had to wait outside because I couldn't smoke in the studio," he said. "I was wearing a fake-fur coat a mate had given me." Leaving the studio with him for a dinner party—their first date—Madonna reversed her car into a wall. He was nervous and relieved that she was, too.[82] Their jitters didn't last. "For both of us there was a real sense of familiarity," he said. "You know, when you feel you've met someone before."[83]

Madonna's relationship with Bird grew more serious, and in November of 1997 they went to London, where Madonna house-hunted, met Bird's parents, and scouted schools for Lola.[84] In the meantime, she rented a house in South Kensington and had a blissful few days until the paparazzi discovered her.[85] "I thought after the Princess Diana thing...that I was going to be left alone," she said. Instead, "it was a nightmare...I would love to live in London, but I don't think I could handle the whole press thing. It's pretty intense. It's more intense even than New York, where the attention kinda comes and goes. In London, it's every day."[86]

Bird had no idea how to handle the onslaught. He was followed by paparazzi. His parents' home made the cover of a tabloid after he and

Madonna visited. Newspapers posted phone numbers that people who knew Bird could call with information about him. A radio program had a special line dedicated to public comments on "Madonna's latest choice of boyfriend," he said. As hard as it might be to believe, he said, he went into the relationship thinking that he and Madonna were like any other couple.[87]

Bird changed. He said he became paranoid and withdrawn. "I was frightened to answer my phone," he explained. "We still really cared about each other, but I was becoming much more aware of how difficult life would be with her."[88] Madonna's video for "Drowned World/Substitute for Love," directed by Walter Stern in London, illustrated how difficult her life already was.[89]

It depicts Madonna hounded by the paparazzi, fans, even hipsters in clubs. The scenes shot on the street showing her in a limousine flanked by paparazzi on motorcycles caused consternation in Britain, where she was accused of cashing in on Diana's memory. But she wasn't describing someone else's past. It was her own besieged present.

On June 21, five days before Madonna began filming her video with Stern, Sting and his film producer wife, Trudie Styler, asked her and Andy Bird down to their country home for a luncheon. Bird was seated downtable, "sulking," while next to Madonna was a young film director named Guy Ritchie.[90] He was not an Oscar Wilde type. Quite the contrary: he looked the part of a London tough, right down to the scar across his lower cheek. "I couldn't even tell you specifically what my thoughts were," she said.

> It was just... You know when people say "He turned my head"? My head didn't just turn—my head spun around on my body!...In my business, I get to meet all kinds of incredible people, fascinating people, glamorous people and sexy people and highly intellectual people...They're interesting, but not very many people stop you in your tracks...I had a whole premonition about my life in fast-forward. That's only happened to me once before.[91]

That had been on the set of the "Material Girl" video, when she imagined marrying Sean Penn. What sealed it for Madonna concerning Ritchie was that he made her laugh "immediately. He's very funny."[92] And confident, "very, very confident," she said. "Cocky, but in a self-aware way."[93]

Ritchie, ten years younger than Madonna, had just finished his first feature film, which he wrote and directed and for which he would earn the sobriquet "the British Tarantino." *Lock, Stock and Two Smoking Barrels* is a comedy about a gang of East End lowlifes who stumble from one botched caper to another, leaving a pile of bodies in their wake. The film was the antidote to the rom-coms and period pieces coming out of Britain at that time. It also gave the public relations gurus under Tony Blair, who had rebranded Great Britain "Cool Britannia," something to crow about. With its driving rock soundtrack and hip young cast, Ritchie's movie was cool, and it changed British film culture. Said the director, "I just wanted to make something a bit more contemporary than fucking Shakespeare."[94]

The young man himself took creative license with his past, perhaps to sell his picture. Ritchie told a reporter in 1999, "I've lived in the East End for thirty years...I've been in a load of mess-ups...I've been poor all my life."[95] In reality, his father, Captain John Vivian Ritchie, was an advertising executive, and his mother, Amber Parkinson, was a former fashion model. When Ritchie was five, his parents divorced, and both married aristocrats. Guy was raised in the home of his mother's husband, Sir Michael Leighton, on an estate near Shrewsbury. What education he had was at a boarding school.[96]

It was through his father's connections in London that he got a job at a Soho film company, working first as a gofer and then making music videos.[97] What he really wanted to do was make a movie. "I'd read that Steven Spielberg made his first movie by the time he was twenty-six," Ritchie said. "So I wanted to shoot a narrative by the time I was twenty-six. And somehow I did it, I made a short film called *Hard Case*."[98] The twenty-minute movie, released in 1995, was a teaser for his first major film, three years later.

Trudie Styler, who knew Ritchie's adman father, had seen *The Hard Case* and was impressed enough to help finance Guy's first feature. "Once she was in," Ritchie said, "all the other investors suddenly decided to join up."[99] It was also because of Styler that Guy was at the luncheon with Madonna. "I was very pally with Trudie at this point because we'd just made the film," he said.

> On my way to the train station, I called and said, "So who else is coming for lunch?" She said, "Just a couple of people." And I said, "Well, who?" And she said, "Madonna." I gotta tell you, it did knock my socks off a bit.[100]

Just as Madonna did, he said they hit it off immediately. And just as Madonna did, he said it was based on humor. "She's dry. She's funny," he said.[101] But that was the end of it for the moment. Madonna and Guy were both involved with other people and went their separate ways.

⋆   ⋆   ⋆

In September, the MTV Video Music Awards finally rewarded Madonna with the top prize, Video of the Year, for "Ray of Light." In fact, she—and Maverick—dominated the night. Her video was nominated for eight awards and won, in addition to Video of the Year, Best Female Video, Best Direction (for Jonas Åkerlund), Best Choreography, and Best Editing. Her video with Chris Cunningham, "Frozen," won Best Special Effects. Never had so many awards rained down on Madonna. She was in a position to be beneficent.[102]

Her acceptance speeches were gracious. Her performance of "Shanti/Ashtangi" displayed her regard for Hinduism, though she managed to enrage a group of Hindus anyway. They issued a statement accusing her of polluting the world's oldest religion. "By wearing the sacred marking while wearing clothing through which her nipples were clearly visible and while gyrating in a sexually suggestive manner with her guitar player," they said, "Madonna offended Hindus and Vaishnavas throughout the world."[103]

Though she was a kinder, gentler version of herself, Madonna still called out hypocrisy where she saw it. In response to the criticism, she replied, "If they're so pure, why are they watching MTV?"[104]

Chapter 41

Los Angeles, Miami, 1999

> Madonna's on this journey and if you're smart you'll get on
> board for the ride. But it doesn't matter if you do or you don't,
> because she's going to get there anyway.[1]
>
> — *William Orbit*

MADONNA ARRIVED AT the Grammys in February of 1999 having been
nominated for six awards. In her sixteen-year career, the National Academy of Recording Arts and Sciences had not rewarded her for her music.
That night, as she took the stage to perform, it seemed like it might. For
the occasion, Madonna was surrounded by people she loved. Rosie
O'Donnell hosted the show. Christopher was backstage helping organize
his sister's performance. William Orbit was at her side onstage, as were
Niki Haris and Donna De Lory. It was the three women's first public
appearance together since the Girlie Show, six years earlier. Her new
"friend" Guy Ritchie was there, too.[2]

Ritchie's film *Lock, Stock and Two Smoking Barrels* had been released to
general acclaim, including praise from the British Academy of Film and
Television Arts, which nominated it for the BAFTA Award for Outstanding British Film.[3] Paparazzi on both sides of the pond had reason to cheer
Madonna and Ritchie's evening in the Grammy spotlight. He was the
hottest filmmaker in Britain at that moment, and she was at the pinnacle of
her career.

Madonna performed "Nothing Really Matters." In the few short
months since she appeared at the MTV Video Music Awards in Indian
attire, she had adopted a new look from a new book. She had read Arthur
Golden's *Memoirs of a Geisha* and become obsessed with Japan's geisha culture. "The whole idea of geisha is a great metaphor for being an entertainer, because on the one hand, you're privileged, but on the other hand
you're a prisoner," Madonna said.[4] When she appeared at the Grammys,
she did so as a modern geisha in an oxblood-red Gaultier-designed cropped
kimono with a PVC sash and red twelve-inch platform shoes.

Her performance finished, the awards began to roll in. *Ray of Light* won
four: Best Pop Vocal Album, Best Dance/Electronic Recording for the

title single, Best Short Form Music Video, and Best Recording Package. Madonna, still dressed as a geisha, took the stage with William Orbit to accept the top pop prize. She expressed what seemed like genuine shock and delight, as did Orbit, who shyly admitted he'd had a "hankering" for a golden gramophone.[5]

And with those accolades, amid the rise of a new generation of pop stars, Madonna left that world. Arguably, she had done so in 1989 with *Like a Prayer,* but she had never before protested her assignment to that category. In 1999, she did. She hated being called a pop star. She was, she said, a performance artist.[6]

Madonna had considered many movie roles since *Evita,* but the first she committed to was with her friend Rupert Everett. *The Next Best Thing* is about a straight single woman who becomes pregnant after a drunken evening of sex with her gay best friend. The film challenged the notion of what constituted a family by showing a man and a woman who are not married raising a child and by showing a gay man as an exemplary parent. The film was thus a political statement masquerading as romantic comedy and called to mind the social messages delivered in Madonna's most danceable songs.[7]

Madonna and Rupert Everett had known each other since 1985, when he met Sean Penn while stopped in a car next to him at a traffic light on Sunset Boulevard. Through lowered windows, the two actors exchanged greetings and phone numbers. Three days later, Sean called to say that his girlfriend wanted to meet Everett, and they agreed to have dinner. Rupert had thought he was beyond being starstruck, but that night proved him wrong.

> At seventeen I had sat with David Bowie downstairs at the Embassy Club. At eighteen I had dined at La Coupole in Paris with Andy Warhol and Bianca Jagger... Yet everything was a pale imitation of the impact Madonna had... there was an energy field around her, like a wave, that swept everyone up as it crashed into the room.[8]

He didn't find her conventionally beautiful, he said. But she had a

> tenderness and warmth that made your skin bump... She was raucous, but poised, elegant but common... She was mesmerizing. She oozed sex and demanded a sexual response from everyone. It didn't matter if you were gay... By the end of the meal, I had fallen in love.[9]

Everett left town for several years to work in Europe but returned to LA in 1989 with a dog named Mo and set about looking for a movie. It was then that he reconnected with a newly divorced Madonna. And it was then that Everett became one of the very, very few actors to come out as gay.[10]

It was a dangerous, even reckless decision that for a few years derailed his career. But he said it helped that he was English, because all Americans "think everyone English is gay...One more English fag, give him a chance."[11] In 1994, Robert Altman did, casting Everett in his hit comedy about the fashion industry, *Ready to Wear*—or, as it was called outside the United States, *Prêt-à-Porter.* Everett's career was back on track. In 1997, he became a modern-day matinee idol by costarring with Julia Roberts in the film *My Best Friend's Wedding.*

It was a huge success, grossing nearly $300 million. He was Rock Hudson for a new generation. He was out, but his primary on-screen relationship was still with a woman. The film became a template for directors who wanted to acknowledge homosexuality without *really* acknowledging it. It was, however, a step forward because it represented a new front in the gay revolution. Gay men had become part of a positive pop culture narrative. In 1998, the TV series *Will & Grace* premiered, featuring prime time's first gay male character in a lead role (played by a straight actor)—though again, as the best friend of a heterosexual woman in a white, wealthy urban fantasy world.[12]

The reality of living as a gay, lesbian, or trans person was much grimmer. That year, Kimberly Peirce's film *Boys Don't Cry,* about the 1993 rape and murder of a twenty-one-year-old trans man in Nebraska named Brandon Teena, was released. It painted a heartbreaking picture of the peril young people outside the hetero norm faced if they dared to commit that simple and most beautiful act of falling in love.

And then, lest Americans comfort themselves with the fiction that in five years society had moved beyond such cruelty, another twenty-one-year-old, Matthew Shepard, died in the fall of 1998 after being beaten, tied to a fence, and left in a Wyoming field in near-freezing temperatures. The hideous brutality of that case, and the soaring number of attacks on gays, lesbians, and trans people, triggered calls for Congress to extend existing hate crime legislation to include them. The measure was defeated. Congress essentially told the community to fend for itself, as it had during the first decade of the AIDS crisis.[13]

In September of 1998, Madonna spoke at the fourteenth annual AIDS Walk Los Angeles. She warned the crowd of twenty-eight thousand against complacency, saying that while the new AIDS drugs were welcome, they in no way solved the health crisis that had killed nearly five hundred thousand people in the United States alone, the overwhelming majority of them gay men. Tens of thousands more people were living with AIDS, and the $30,000-a-year cost of the new drug treatments was beyond many of them. And that meant the disease was still a threat. She called for education for the young people who were once again practicing unsafe sex; she called on Congress to fund needle exchanges to cut the risk of AIDS to IV drug users; and she called in general for people to care.[14]

Amid that renewed focus on AIDS and the continued and dangerous discrimination against gays, Madonna signed on to do the movie with Everett. He had been in another $300 million picture, *Shakespeare in Love,* for which her friend Gwyneth Paltrow would win an Oscar. With Everett's string of successes, Madonna's star turn in *Evita,* and renowned British director John Schlesinger (of *Midnight Cowboy* and *Marathon Man* fame) at the helm, *The Next Best Thing* went into production with high hopes that it would be another winner. Four months of shooting began in Los Angeles in April of 1999. Everett said it was clear on the first day that "we were aboard a sinking ship."[15]

Sex was an issue. The producer refused to include a gay sex scene, and Madonna refused to do a hetero one. Even to kiss her love interest in the film, Benjamin Bratt, she required a drink to get into character, and then two. According to Everett, she began to "improvise" after said libation until Schlesinger shouted, "Will someone pour a bucket of water over that slit!" Everett said Madonna and Schlesinger "were at war...He pushed her too hard and didn't realize when she was being good." Then Everett accidentally knocked him over, causing the seventy-three-year-old director to chip his coccyx. After a while, Schlesinger became so disinterested in the movie that he slept during shooting.[16]

The film that emerged delivered a message that needed airing, but it was otherwise a waste of talent. There were moments of intense drama and moments of honesty. But there was little humor and not nearly enough warmth, given the subject.

The Next Best Thing was not, however, a complete loss. Everett persuaded Madonna to do a cover of Don McLean's classic song "American Pie" for the movie's soundtrack. She resisted, then relented, and was happy she did. "In a way, as we move into the twenty-first century, we are saying goodbye to a lot of things, the way they used to be," she said. "It turns out to me to be kind of an apologetic song."[17]

The millennium that had been looming finally arrived. It was greeted with trepidation: governments and industries around the world prepared for what they feared would be a cataclysmic technological failure as the dates on computer systems switched from 1999 to 2000. Doomsayers predicted planes falling from the sky, riots in the street, and food shortages. In short, the apocalypse.[18]

In South Beach, the end of the century had already arrived. It began with Versace's murder and ended with Chris Paciello's arrest in December of 1999 on federal murder, robbery, and racketeering charges.[19] "He was the golden boy, the South Beach club lion," recalled Brian Antoni. "Our gay god was killed. Then we realized [Paciello] was involved in a murder. It's gone. Paradise is over. It's the end."[20]

Paciello had been the subject of a two-year investigation by the FBI, the DEA, the IRS, the US attorney in Brooklyn, the Florida state attorney, and the Miami Beach police.[21] The New York charges involved, among other things, the robbery that ended in Judith Shemtov's murder. Local and federal authorities in Miami were interested in the fire at his first club, Risk, and allegations that he laundered mob money through Liquid.[22]

After his arrest, Paciello proclaimed his innocence, saying he was just a kid from a bad neighborhood. The community seemed to agree. On December 15, seventy people from the Miami Beach celebrity circuit arrived in limos to support him at his bail hearing. It was like an episode from the new hit TV show *The Sopranos*.[23] Friends promised millions of dollars to back his bail, but gradually, under the weight of the evidence against him, offers shrank, and some evaporated entirely. Bail was a moot point anyway, because Paciello was headed to pretrial detention in New York.[24]

Within a year, he would plead guilty to bank robbery and his role in the Shemtov murder. He was reportedly given a reduced sentence of seven years for providing evidence against New York mobsters. To pay his legal bills, he sold parts of the empire he and Ingrid had created, which included a club called Bar Room and a West Palm Beach Liquid. The original Liquid, in South Beach, remained open, but its VIP room was less illustrious. The toughest door in the world was now accessible to anyone.[25]

In the meantime, the crowd that had made Liquid famous prepared for one last party at the end of its wild decade. Donatella and her brother Santo had put Gianni's mansion on the market that summer, but before it was sold, she decided to throw a New Year's Eve bash there. Rupert Everett called it "the last party of the old century."[26]

Donatella invited seventy-five people from the world of fashion and entertainment for dinner in the courtyard. Tarps were hung from trees to shield guests from prying paparazzi and tourists on Ocean Drive, where the noise was deafening. News trucks stood ready to report the carnage when computers crashed as 1999 became 2000. The South Beach version of a town crier couldn't wait. Rollerblading up and down Ocean Drive, a man had written on his chest in yellow body paint his forecast for the future: WE'RE ALL FUCKED.[27]

Madonna, Guy Ritchie, Guy Oseary, and Gwyneth Paltrow, who were all staying at Madonna's, arrived by boat at South Beach and hopped into a car with a police escort to avoid traffic en route to Donatella's. Once there, they were directed to the back door—the same door Madonna had entered the morning of Gianni's murder.[28] His death haunted the festivities, as did the recognition that the life they had all shared in South Beach was over.[29]

Rupert Everett, who had become part of the Madonna-Versace gang after renting an apartment on Ocean Drive, found Donatella alone in the garden when he arrived. She admitted she was depressed. So, apparently, was Guy Ritchie, who seemed uncomfortable in that scene, with drag queens and shirtless men dancing on platforms.[30]

Ingrid, who had just lost Chris Paciello to prison, wasn't depressed as much as frantic that she was losing Madonna, too. Madonna had begun to distance herself after the Paciello revelations. "It wasn't about being disloyal or anything," Christopher said. "It was about self-preservation, because God knows what other shoe would drop...Thank God Madonna was never financially involved with [the club]."[31] Everett said that Guy Ritchie was another source of anxiety for Ingrid. That night, Rupert said, she "held on doggedly to the fraying lasso around Madonna's neck."[32]

There was also evident tension between Christopher and Guy. That visit was the first time the pair had met. "I thought he was Sean Penn lite," Christopher said.[33] "He was a fairly decent guy at the time. I thought he was a little bit of an idiot, but whatever. He was an English tough guy. He reminded me of Sean, that fake I'm-a-tough-guy shit, and I can see that a mile away."[34] Everett said, "Guy and Chris were from different planets, and in a way the one's success relied on the other not being there."[35]

Donatella's feast turned into dancing, and sometime well after midnight the party moved to Bar Room. Before they arrived, some in their group had taken Ecstasy.[36] By four, the party was raucous, with Madonna and Gwyneth dancing on a table, Christopher and Gwyneth dancing on the floor, and Madonna and a nineteen-year-old stranger dancing close and slow. It was too much for Ritchie. He strode across the dance floor, kicked the teenager in the leg, and made to hit him. Christopher intervened. "Guy got kind of weirdly frisky," Christopher said. "I guess he was trying to bond with me." Ritchie had come up behind Christopher and began lifting him up and down.

> I was, "Dude, what the fuck? Put me down: we're not dancing, but if you want to dance, we can dance." And I pushed him against the wall and started grinding on him, which totally freaked him out...I think he was trying to exercise his dominance over me because he knew how close Madonna and I were at that time.[37]

Madonna alone—and maybe Gwyneth Paltrow—seemed to thoroughly enjoy the evening. Madonna called it the best New Year's Eve ever.[38]

On January 1, as tourists gathered to take pictures of the spot where Gianni Versace was murdered, Donatella locked the Casa Casuarina and never returned.[39] Madonna would sell her Miami home two months later. Rupert Everett said, "La belle époque was officially over."[40] One century had ended, and another had begun. Madonna would start hers in another country.

PART FIVE

LONDON

2000–2009

Chapter 42

London, Los Angeles, New York, Dornoch, 2000

Do fortysomething baby-mamas still have the divine right to get down? (The answer is yes.)[1]

— *Dimitri Ehrlich*

MADONNA BEGAN HER life in England by embracing American iconography in a way she never had in the States. On February 11, a video she shot in a studio in London with a German director named Philipp Stölzl aired on MTV. After her recent forays into Hinduism and the world of Japanese geishas, she reappeared in blue jeans, tank top, and tiara as hootenanny Madonna, hometown beauty queen Madonna. Without a trace of irony, as she literally wraps herself in the US flag, she is "American Pie" Madonna.

Rupert Everett had had to persuade her to cover the Don McLean classic for their movie, which she did by roping in William Orbit on production and Everett on backup vocals.[2] It was a crazy idea, coming in the midst of Madonna's most experimental album and as she moved away professionally from American sounds and American collaborators. The song might have languished in the land of radio nostalgia after its release had it not been for the video's premiere. That video, featuring photos and footage of forgotten Americans in all their socio-economic, racial, and gender diversity, combined with that song, told the story of where the United States was at the start of the new century: weary but hopeful.

"American Pie" became an unlikely hit, reaching the top of the dance chart in the States and number 1 on pop singles charts in eight countries, including England and Germany. When asked what he thought of Madonna's having recorded his song, McLean said, "I have received many gifts from God, but this is the first time I have received a gift from a goddess."[3]

The song would be one of Madonna's inspirations as she made her transition from the States to England and embarked on her next album. Called *Music,* it would be an even more radical departure from pop than *Ray of Light,* and it would be her first album created outside the United States with exclusively European producers. That is what made Madonna's next persona so interesting, even sweet. *Music* Madonna would be a cowgirl.

By September of 1999, Madonna and William Orbit were at work on her eighth studio album. Theirs was a demonstrated winning combination. After their bounty of Grammys for *Ray of Light,* they picked up another for "Beautiful Stranger," a single they wrote for the Mike Myers spy spoof *Austin Powers: The Spy Who Shagged Me.*[4]

But nine songs into their work on the new album, Madonna feared it sounded too much like the old one. She told an Australian interviewer, "I'm as interested in being entertained as I am in entertaining people . . . I think that's the secret to everyone's longevity — to stay hungry, to stay curious, and to be excited by your work."[5] Madonna wasn't. She decided to start over with another artist. His name was Mirwais Ahmadzaï.[6]

Mirwais had been looking for a US record label and was impressed by what Maverick did for the Prodigy, so he asked a friend to give Guy Oseary a copy of his 2000 hit single, "Disco Science."[7] The friend did, and Oseary passed it to Madonna.

> And I just said, "Oh my God, this is what I want. This is the sound." . . . I said, "Please find out . . . if he wants to work with me and collaborate, just try out one song together." And we did. And then I wanted more. And then we did two. And then I wanted more. And then we did three. And then that was it.[8]

Madonna's and Mirwais's sensibilities — artistically and politically — were the same, as were their goals: to use music to change culture.

Born in 1961 in Switzerland to an Italian mother and Afghan father, Mirwais moved to Paris with his family when he was six. Musically, he traveled a path similar to William Orbit's, through Jimi Hendrix, the Rolling Stones, Kraftwerk, and punk. By the time Mirwais was twenty, he was in a band called Taxi Girl, which writer Martin James, in his history of French music, called "one of the most influential bands to have come from the synth and electro pop era." By 1987, it was over. Heroin killed it. Mirwais called the band "very tragic."[9]

After a brief detour into acoustic folk music, Mirwais returned to electronica and, in early 2000, just before he met Madonna, charted with "Disco Science," which he said was rooted in the French disco tradition and influenced by Giorgio Moroder.[10] Within three weeks of hearing his single, Madonna was working with him.[11]

But there was a problem. They couldn't understand each other, because she didn't speak French, and he seemed not to speak English. "I wanted to rip my hair out," Madonna said. With Mirwais's manager acting as translator, they struggled to make it work. Madonna was *determined* to make it work, because she believed Mirwais was "a genius."[12]

Beyond their communication problems, Madonna described their artistic challenge as marrying her songs, which she called "conservative" in structure, to her producer's extremely "unconventional" methods.[13] They began with the very first song they created, "Impressive Instant." "It was the most complete of the demo tracks I sent her," Mirwais said.

> She said that she had an idea for lyrics. When we got to London, I asked her to sing it for me...She improved my track! I was amazed.[14] Normally, it takes about six months to a year for people I'm working with to understand my ideas. With Madonna, the first time she heard it, she loved it. She had a chemical reaction to it.[15]

Some of his radical ideas included dehumanizing Madonna's voice, either through Auto-Tune software or a vocoder. At the time, neither was used in mainstream music to distort vocals. Madonna upped the ante during the song's bridge with nonsensical wordplay. "I thought, 'Oh, fuck it, let's just have fun.'" *Billboard* would call "Impressive Instant" her "weirdest sonic excursion ever."[16]

On other songs on the album, Madonna said, all the effects were eliminated. "There's no reverb, there's no delay...it's just really dry and up front and in your face, and that was something I hadn't done since my first record."[17]

Music writer Caroline Sullivan said that for a pop singer, having vocals left untouched was "tantamount to stripping naked."[18] Madonna said that only Mirwais could have persuaded her to do it, because she trusted him completely. "I listen to his stuff and I think, 'This is the future of sound.'"[19]

The trust Madonna felt for Mirwais was one element of her success generally. Having arisen out of the New York art scene, where collaboration was paramount, she knew that an artist, even a great artist, needs input from other people. There would always be exceptions, but the milieu in which her talents developed had emphasized art as a community endeavor. "I never think I can do whatever I want to do," Madonna said. "I think, 'This is my dream. Let me gather around the people I think are gonna most support my dream, and let's see what happens.'"[20]

That is what she did with *Music*. She went back to William Orbit and told him about Mirwais, that she wanted him to be the lead producer on her album because she wanted to go in another musical direction. Orbit wasn't offended that he had been pushed aside in favor of another sound and another man. "God no," he said. "As long as she uses good people." In his estimation, Mirwais was one.[21]

Working mostly at SARM Studios, in London, Madonna and Mirwais decided to begin the album with three songs that she said "make you feel like you're taking off on a rocket."[22] "Music," "Impressive Instant," and "Runaway Lover" informed the listener that they had left the ashram of *Ray of Light* and were firmly back on the dance floor.[23]

The lyrics for the single "Music" came to Madonna at a Sting concert after watching the audience come alive when he started performing songs from his old days with the Police. "The energy in the room changed. It ignited the room," she said. The audience of strangers sang together, celebrated a shared history together. "It really moved me. And I thought, 'That's what music does to people.' It really does bring people together, and it erases so much. And so that's how I came to the hook of that song."[24]

For the next three tracks, which Madonna called "I-love-you-but-fuck-you" songs, the album drops tempo. These are the soaring Orbit collaboration "Amazing," the apologetic "Nobody's Perfect," and "I Deserve It."[25] That track showcases Madonna's voice at its most naked and Mirwais's production at its most minimalist. It is stripped down instrumentally to a strumming guitar and vocally to a quiet, vulnerable Madonna untouched by technology. She sounds like a woman in her bedroom singing to herself.[26]

The next group of songs expresses personal rebellion and/or revelation: "Don't Tell Me," "Paradise (Not for Me)," "Gone," and "What It Feels Like for a Girl." A listener coming across that last title would assume it's about sex. In fact, it is about a girl's struggle (or a powerless individual's struggle) to be recognized as a person—what it feels like to *be* a girl. It would constitute one of Madonna's most powerful feminist statements.

The song arose from two sources: external and internal. The external source was a backing tape Madonna's cowriter Guy Sigsworth sent her. On it was dialogue from the film *The Cement Garden,* in which actor Charlotte Gainsbourg's character explains the difference between the way boys and girls are perceived. She says girls secretly aspire to *be* boys—to have their power, even look like them—but for boys to want to look or act like a girl is considered degrading. Those words made Madonna think of the masquerade of a girl's life, during which she pretends to be one thing—limited, frail, acquiescent—while housing a spirit that soars, a mind that hungers, and a body that can be fierce if it is allowed to be.[27]

Aspects of that masquerade were present in Madonna's own life that year. In February, she discovered she was pregnant, which led to discussions between her and Guy Ritchie about how to proceed, together or apart, and if together, whether to raise a family in England or the States. Madonna's life still moved between both. "Of course, being the girl, I made the first compromise. It's that extra thing that women have...there's an extra accommodating chromosome that we have. I picked up my life and my daughter [and moved to England]...It was a huge sacrifice for me."[28] And yet it had been expected.

Madonna said her generation had been told to "grab life by the balls, be super-independent, get a great education, follow our dreams, kick ass, all that stuff."[29] But men and the greater society hadn't heard the same message. To be desirable, women, no matter how accomplished, were still expected to be lesser. "The song is really a realization about the politics of the sexes. It's a complaint. It's also about traditional feminine behavior, this kind of thing," she said, curling her hair around her finger and batting her eyes. To get along, women had to play along.[30] Madonna called that realization a "bitter pill." And that, too, inspired her song.[31]

After Sigsworth sent Madonna his "sketch" for the backing track, he went to the studio to hear the lyrics she had written. "As soon as she started singing it...I knew that what we were doing was artistically great," he said.[32] Madonna said with more humility, "I just knew that I had something true."[33]

Madonna's early song "Express Yourself" was a feminist anthem written by her younger kick-ass self. "What It Feels Like for a Girl" was written by her slightly older self after she realized the depth of misogyny's roots and the height of the obstacles women face to surmount it. She hadn't given up—far from it. She had just become a bit more cynical than the young woman who joyfully grabbed her crotch and called it power. The *way* Madonna sang her song reflected that change. "Express Yourself" is emphatic. "What It Feels Like for a Girl" is sung with a girl's voice, one that barely dares to speak. Said Sigsworth,

> Most singers want themselves as loud as possible till it's almost painful in the mix. Madonna's not like that. She likes to hear herself *in* the music, not on top of it....She's very aware of the musical context.[34]

To test whether she had reached that listener, Madonna played the music in her car for what she called her "Pussy Posse": her nanny, her personal assistant, and her girlfriends. Sigsworth said,[35]

> In practice it comes down to, if she likes it, and maybe a small group of friends, then that's it. She never even asks the record company whether they like it. What are they going to say? She knows better than they do.[36]

★   ★   ★

Madonna had purchased a house in London but sold it almost immediately over security concerns. Her next move was to a rental in Notting Hill, which would become command center for Madonna, Inc. When she traveled, her entourage traveled with her. She said at that point she hadn't been alone in twenty years. The house, which looked like a small hotel, was big enough to accommodate her clan.[37]

The paparazzi kept close tabs, praising Madonna for walking the streets without bodyguards, donating clothes to a local charity shop, washing Ritchie's car outside his house, and generally living as a normal single mother. "She's amazingly ordinary," a neighbor said with admiration. The *Daily Mirror* declared that June: "In the UK all we want is for our stars to be ordinary...We just want to hand her her own British passport and be done with it."[38] The period represented Madonna's honeymoon with the British press and public. She even earned a pet name, Madge, which could be an acknowledgment of her everywoman ways or, as Ritchie tried to convince her, a diminutive of "Her Majesty."[39]

While Madonna was busy with her album, Ritchie was occupied with a new film, *Snatch,* starring Brad Pitt.[40] Sony Pictures Entertainment had given Ritchie and his producer partner Matthew Vaughn $10 million to make the picture. It wasn't a fortune, but it was ten times the budget for *Lock, Stock and Two Smoking Barrels.* Ritchie felt considerable pressure because he believed people were "sharpening their knives," hoping his second film would be a failure.[41] That was pressure Madonna understood. "Guy works almost as hard as Madonna does," Rupert Everett said, sounding very much like Martin Burgoyne had when describing Sean. "That's a good thing for her...He has got a serious career going, so he's dealing with all his own stuff."[42]

Madonna herself acknowledged that her respect for Ritchie's talent was part of the attraction. Seeing Ritchie work made her "feel very proud," she said.[43]

> I think the recipe for a good relationship/marriage is that two people really enjoy their life and love what they're doing...If you're both busy and working, then you're going to spend some time apart and when you come back you are filled with new experiences to share.[44]

Ritchie's film career was going swimmingly, but Madonna's had faltered — again. *The Next Best Thing* premiered in Los Angeles on March 3 with only slightly less fanfare than *Evita.* In 2000, fans and paparazzi wanted a glimpse of Madonna and her new beau. The premiere, however, would be the film's high point.[45]

The reviews were terrible. Critics were seemingly delighted to announce that Madonna's star turn in *Evita* had been a fluke. In their telling, *The Next Best Thing* proved that she *was* a terrible actor. Everett said he had "never read such bad reviews in my life." Many actors, he added, had won *awards* for much worse performances.[46]

The film also damaged director John Schlesinger, who said Madonna's "outrageous" demands—among them that she didn't "want her bare arse to be seen"—had contributed to his post-filming heart attack.[47] And it damaged Everett. "It blew my new career out of the water," he said.[48] Even the gay best friend roles dried up.[49]

Everett left Los Angeles for the sprawling Kibera slum, in Nairobi, to do a film for Oxfam. The trip put his professional plight into perspective. He came back, he said, haunted by what he had seen. "I lived in denial for a year. Then one day at the beginning of 2001, I woke up and wrote a letter to all the richest people I know. Without that much effort, I raised a considerable amount of money." Madonna, Elton John, and George Michael were the most generous, he said. Everett, the gay best friend, took on a new role as an advocate and activist for international aid and AIDS.[50]

Madonna seemed to take the bad film reviews in stride. They were, at that point, to be expected, and she had much bigger things to think about that year: her baby, her daughter, her boyfriend, and her album. She had decided to release "Music" as the first single. Jonas Åkerlund was called back into service to direct the video. In it, Madonna wanted to lampoon the bling-and-babes videos produced for entertainers like Snoop Dogg, so they filled a limo full of gals and set out for a night of clubbing. The fact that Madonna was four months pregnant while doing so made the joke sweeter still.[51]

The original cast included the kind of leggy models who might appear in a man's video as vacuous space fillers. To play the limo driver, Madonna had wanted her friend Chris Rock, but Åkerlund told her to look at Sacha Baron Cohen. He wasn't yet known in the States but had a hit show in England as a character named Ali G. Madonna loved him, and he was hired to be her driver for the evening, complete with Tommy Hilfiger hat, red Tupac tracksuit, and a limo with a license plate that read MUFF DADDY.[52]

As the shoot began in Los Angeles, it didn't work for Madonna. "All the pretty, model-type girls were too stiff, and none of them had any personality," Madonna explained. "So I said, 'OK, I'm gonna call my girls.'"

"She called me at the last minute. 'Come on, do me a solid,'" Niki Haris recalled. "She's pregnant, and I'm like, 'Okay, no problem. I'm there for you, babe.'" Debi Mazar was, too.[53]

In the video, the three friends, bedecked in furs and jewels—with

Madonna in her *Music* cowboy hat—make their club tour, with commercial breaks in the form of Åkerlund-created cartoons of Madonna as a street-fighting superhero. At a strip club, she assumes that persona as she liberates the dancers from their poles and they join her, Niki, and Debi in the car.[54] The laughter from the back of the limo was real. Sacha Baron Cohen's ad-libbing in character "had us rolling the entire time we were shooting," Madonna said.[55]

Before "Music" and its video were released in August, the song was leaked and made available on Napster. The file-sharing program, created by an eighteen-year-old college student named Shawn Fanning, allowed fans to download music for free. By July, nearly twenty million users were on the service. Soon there would be sixty million. One Warner Music Group executive called Napster "the end of the world." For him and his ilk, it potentially was. If it continued to grow, it would destroy the business model that had supported record empires for more than a century, empires that by 2000 were dominated by just five global music groups. It was truly a case of David and Goliath.[56]

Almost immediately, artists whose material was leaked and companies whose products were shared by Napster filed suit against Fanning and his financial backers. Meanwhile, entertainment firms, Maverick among them, struggled to position themselves in Fanning's brave new world.

Guy Oseary invited a Napster executive to meet with him and Madonna to discuss a possible million-dollar investment.[57] Madonna considered the likes of Napster "inevitable" and potentially "a great way for people to hear your music who wouldn't have the chance to hear it on the radio."[58] The Maverick-Napster talks, however, ultimately broke down because of the many lawsuits against Napster and pressure from the recording industry.[59]

In the end, the leak didn't hurt sales. In what Mirwais called a "small victory for underground music," "Music" became Madonna's first number 1 US hit single since 1994's "Take a Bow."[60]

Madonna put her Los Feliz home on the market in June and bought a new one—Diane Keaton's place on Beverly Hills's Roxbury Drive. It was Madonna's first move into the heart of storied old Hollywood. Roxbury was where the mid-twentieth-century stars had lived—Jimmy Stewart, Jack Benny, Lucille Ball, Rosemary Clooney, Hedy Lamarr. Madonna once again turned to Christopher to design it. But her relationship with her brother was strained over money (he said she owed him some from his work on her Miami house) and his lifestyle.[61]

Christopher's fate had been intertwined with hers since he joined her in New York, fifteen years earlier. He had been at her side as adviser, protector, friend, family member, tour director, and interior designer, and in the process he had been so busy that he hadn't developed a career apart from her. "People didn't really know what I did for her," he said. "She never really talked about me, ever, except when she outed me in the *Advocate* magazine."[62]

In the mid-'90s, after the Girlie Show tour, Christopher began to branch out by making music videos, taking design jobs, and creating his own freewheeling social circle. He said Madonna thought he had a drug problem. Communicating by fax because she didn't like confrontations, they worked through their difficulties, but their relationship had changed. The foundation of trust had developed fissures.[63]

By 2000, Christopher had sold his New York apartment and moved to Los Angeles, and though he had a job designing a restaurant, he was broke. When he and Madonna agreed to terms on the Roxbury project, he accepted. It should have been easy. He had designed eight residences for her at that point. But at Roxbury he wasn't just working with Madonna. Ritchie had a say in the house, too, and that complicated the job and Christopher's life.

Christopher said that every decision had to be run past him. For every set of chairs, wall color, or fabric, Madonna insisted that her brother present several possibilities for Ritchie's approval. Most difficult were those parts of the house that Ritchie considered his own. Speaking to Christopher about a closet, Ritchie told him, "Nothing mincey, mate. Nothing twee." It was a word he used "over and over, and I got the message."[64] "When I started interacting with Guy on a personal level, and I'm putting that in quotes, I realized how much he hated me." Pausing, he added, "I think it was more about her than me being gay."[65]

Christopher was eight years older than Ritchie, genuinely streetwise, acerbic, and, however estranged, intensely loyal to Madonna. He believed that Ritchie wanted to control her—having deluded himself that he *could* control her—and that Christopher stood in his way.

> I do really think he thought in his head, "I'm gonna take this [Madonna] and train it, retrain it to be mine."...For a good period of time, she gave into it. She felt like she needed to [relinquish] a certain amount of her power to make him happy...I understood, so I never spoke ill of Guy to her. I would never do that.[66]

And so the two men had contretemps that Madonna did not witness and about which, at least from Christopher's side, she was not told.[67] An early example occurred at the house. Christopher was standing in the driveway when Ritchie pulled in with his car.

> There was plenty of room for him to drive past me, and as he drove...he turned the wheels toward me...And I didn't move, and he stops right in front of me and rolls the window down and says, "What the fuck is wrong with you? I could have run you over." I'm like, "What the hell's wrong with you?...Do you think because I'm a fag I'm going to run screaming out of the way for you?" That was how I felt at that point. He was constantly challenging me.[68]

Interestingly, Ritchie didn't seem to have a problem with Carlos Leon, who was very much part of Madonna's life. "It's shocking how civilized they are to each other," Madonna said. And that was important to her. Madonna loved Carlos. She considered him one of her closest friends and someone she could rely on. At one point that year, she needed to be in New York, so Carlos flew to London to take care of Lourdes, whose schedule at the age of three was no longer as flexible as it had been because she was enrolled in a French school.[69]

By August, a heavily pregnant Madonna said she felt like a "walking furnace."[70] With her album due to be released and Guy's movie about to premiere, being nine months pregnant was even more of a burden than it might have been. But as with Lourdes's birth and *Evita,* the good came with the good, and Madonna did not want to quibble about such favorable fortune. "A baby is always going to interrupt *something,*" she said.[71] Referencing her album and her baby, she added, "We'll see what pops out first."[72]

Rocco won. At seven months, doctors discovered that Madonna had a condition called placenta previa, which could cause maternal hemorrhaging and a blockage of the baby's blood supply. Labor was extremely dangerous, so Madonna scheduled a cesarean section for two weeks before her due date, in September. In the meantime, she was told to stop all yoga and exercise. "I hung around the house and did nothing but talk on the phone and read, which was like a death sentence to me," Madonna said.[73]

Just into her eighth month, on August 10, she began bleeding and was rushed to Cedars-Sinai Medical Center. Guy, who was at a screening of *Snatch,* met her at the hospital.[74] Rocco was delivered the next day by cesarean.[75]

In deciding on a name, Madonna and Ritchie wanted to give the baby an Italian first name because he would have an English surname. "We went through the list of my Italian relatives," Madonna said, "and he was thinking about Rocco," which was the name of one of Madonna's uncles. The choice was made when they watched Visconti's 1960 film, *Rocco and His Brothers*. "It was a great name, and it sounds good with Ritchie," Madonna said.[76] Rocco John Ritchie: the child's middle name was in honor of Guy's father.

Rocco remained in the hospital for five days. "I sat in a little room next to intensive care, reading books and running in there every three hours," Madonna said.[77] The day they brought him home from the hospital, which was Madonna's birthday, she found a crumpled paper bag next to her breast pump and went to throw it away before noticing that there was a small box and a card inside. "It was a really sweet letter that [Guy] wrote to me, about everything we've been through and my birthday, and the baby and how happy he was." She opened the box to find a diamond ring. "I never liked big rocks on my finger," she told a journalist that fall. "Well I do now!"[78]

Around a month later, on September 19, Warner and *Us* magazine invited six hundred people to the gay dance club Catch One, in South Central, for the launch of Madonna's album *Music*. The venue was her choice.[79] The crowd streaming in was eclectic. On the sidewalk, Divine stopped for the cameras, as did Hugh Hefner (amid a fluffle of Playboy Bunnies) and rainbow-dreadlocked funkster George Clinton. He said he planned to take off his clothes once inside.[80]

Madonna and Guy Ritchie appeared, too, wearing T-shirts promoting each other's projects: his a red *Music* tank top, hers a black one bearing the title *Snatch*. But what grabbed more attention was Madonna's jewelry. She wore a diamond necklace that spelled BABY and a ring that suggested wife. "I wouldn't say it's an engagement ring," she said. "We talk about marriage, but we can't decide whether it's something that's necessary."[81]

The party was a success, as was the album. Featuring Madonna as a cowgirl in photos shot by Jean-Baptiste Mondino, it went to number 1 in the States, selling more than four hundred thousand copies the first week.[82]

In Europe, the album included a bonus track, "American Pie." In Asia, it included "Cyber-Raga," a Madonna-penned prayer written with British-based underground musician Talvin Singh. And on the Mexican edition of the album, there was a Spanish-language version of "What It Feels Like for a Girl." *Billboard* magazine would call *Music* a "globalist, Warholian pop art take on Americana."[83] Andrew Harrison, writing in *Mixmag* that spring, said,

The strangest thing about this woman is also the most obvious. It's the one we still can't accept, even though she's been in this game for sixteen years, sold millions of records and still holds herself to standards long abandoned by her contemporaries in the pop stratosphere. It's this: she's in it for the music.[84]

And indeed she was. With her album, she hoped to awaken the industry from what she called the "doldrums." Charts were dominated by teen pop and commercial hip-hop and rap. "It's scary," she said. Aside from a few artists, "no one's doing anything interesting or daring...If this record happens, it might mean that people are ready for something different."[85]

She didn't hope to win over the Britney Spears generation. "I'm not a teenager anymore and I won't pretend to be one to sell records," Madonna said. But it was a big world, and she was confident that there were people in it like her who were interested in music as art and statement, if she could reach them.[86]

Music would be her third studio album without a tour. It was time. "I need to take a trip around the world, sing a few songs," she said. To test the waters, she scheduled two small performances in November: one at the Roseland Ballroom, in New York, and the other at the Brixton Academy, in London.[87]

Madonna enlisted "Human Nature" choreographer Jamie King to help. He had gone from strength to strength since their 1995 video together, most notably with his work on Ricky Martin's 1999 star-making first world tour.[88] But before Madonna thought big or even medium, she thought very, very small—the size of a TV screen. She took her new music to *The Late Show with David Letterman*.

On November 3, Madonna appeared there as a guest for the first time since her disastrous 1994 fuck-fest. During that show, she was dressed in gangsta chic. In 2000, she came out in rodeo wear and let not a single f-word and only a couple of s-words (for which she apologized) pass her lips. Even when Letterman playfully tried to provoke her, she didn't bite. She was too nervous. That night, she was expected to play guitar and sing with only her twenty-four-year-old guitar teacher, Monte Pittman, onstage to support her.

It was a first for them both. Not long before, Pittman had left Texas for Los Angeles, looking to break into the music business. In the meantime, he got a job at a music store selling guitars and sweeping floors. He thought he'd be happier giving guitar lessons, so he had a card made up, quit the store, and waited for students. The third person to call him was Guy Ritchie. "I didn't know who he was. It turns out he and Madonna were dating," Pittman said. Ritchie was laid up with knee surgery, so Madonna bought him a guitar to amuse himself with while convalescing. "He started taking lessons," Pittman said, "and he got pretty good at it." In August of 2000, just after Rocco's birth, Guy bought Madonna a guitar, and Pittman became her teacher, too.[89]

A month after the lessons began, she called Monte to ask if he wanted to join her on Letterman's show. "I thought she was pulling my leg at first," he said, "but she was serious."[90] With Pittman beside her, before an audience of millions, she carefully—like the student she was—strummed her way through "Don't Tell Me." Brow furrowed, she concentrated so intently on the guitar that her singing sounded disconnected from the music. "I can't believe I had the balls to do that," Madonna said a few years later. "I was so bad...A lot of times, you just have to face your fear."[91]

The song Madonna performed that night arose out of a demo recorded by her singer-songwriter brother-in-law, Joe Henry. Henry was part of Madonna's life even before he married her sister Melanie: he and Madonna were friends in high school. Christopher called him one of her most important collaborators, though he, too, remained largely behind the scenes, even after she began recording his songs.

Henry's interests had taken him to the land of indie-country music, while hers traveled through pop. On "Don't Tell Me," their worlds converged in a song Madonna loved because of its defiance.[92] It would be *Music*'s second single and the subject of one of Madonna's cleverest, most playful, and most exhilarating videos.

Camp in the gayest sense of the term, North American in the most iconic, it was joyously subversive on every level. Reuniting the "Human Nature" team of Jean-Baptiste Mondino, choreographer Jamie King, and Madonna, the video was, in King's words, a "beautiful collaboration."[93] Mirwais called it "Electronic Cowboy."[94]

It begins straightforwardly: Madonna in a straw cowboy hat, plaid shirt, blue jeans, rhinestone belt, and silver-toed cowboy boots walking down a road in the vastness of the desert Southwest with a nearby cowboy astride a bucking bronco. Except she isn't on a road, and he isn't in the desert. The camera rolls back to show Madonna on a moving walkway on a stage, the great outdoors a movie-within-a-movie behind her. The cowboy on his bronco? A billboard. Commentary on the artifice of western films and mythology established, Mondino, Madonna, and King begin to have fun.[95]

Gradually, four wranglers appear on the billboard, dancing in sand and scrub until Madonna joins them in a line dance—she onstage, they in the billboard. Reality and fantasy meld, and they join her for a dance straight out of the West Village. The video ends with Madonna back on the imaginary road and the billboard cowboy still trying to control his steed.[96]

Vogue writer Liana Satenstein recalled seeing the "Don't Tell Me" video when she was eleven. "It was mind blowing...country music never hit close to home. It was all Garth Brooks singing about driving a truck with a fat engine and cracking a warm beer by the lake. But Madonna took the genre and spun it on its head." She credited Madonna with launching the "giddy-up pop" of the later 2000s.[97] The bridge Madonna built between country music and pop made it easier for Taylor Swift in the coming decade to cross over.

The artist who appeared in the video and on *Letterman* was warming up for her return to the stage. On November 5, the Roseland Ballroom was packed with a standing-room-only crowd of three thousand people. Many of them had won admission through radio-station contests, but the hall was also filled with celebrities whose invitations were sent by Madonna and her team: Gwyneth Paltrow, Rupert Everett, Rosie O'Donnell, Donatella Versace, Ben Stiller, Adam Sandler, and of course Madonna's two Guys—Oseary and Ritchie—among them.[98]

Lourdes and Rocco were backstage as Madonna prepared for her show. "'This isn't how I usually do it!'" she thought. "There I was, getting ready to go out and be Superwoman, while what I really was feeling like was a mom!...You know, it's kind of strange, jiggling children on your knee when you're wearing a rhinestone outfit." [99] Adding to the strangeness was her fear. Madonna always felt nervous before a performance, but that night was different. It had been a long time since she had been onstage, and every aspect of her life had changed. But, she said, "if I'm afraid of something, I have to do it." And so she did.[100]

The fans gathered inside Roseland were *ready* and had been for seven years. Jamie King choreographed the microconcert by elaborating on the Madonna-as-cowgirl theme of the "Don't Tell Me" video. Dolce & Gabbana created the set—a truck covered in a US flag, bales of golden hay, illuminated horseshoes, silver cacti.[101] Madonna emerged from a pickup truck with four bare-chested men. Mirwais, Donna De Lory, and Niki Haris soon joined her onstage.

Niki had had a dark couple of years. Her grandfather had died in 1996 and her sister in 1998. "It was a time when I thought my mother would never smile again," she said. And Niki had broken her leg and was confined to a wheelchair for almost a year. By the time she was onstage at Roseland, she said, "I was joyful that I could move...and it felt good to just sing."[102]

The audience went crazy. The production seemed small, and Madonna's voice sounded tentative, but it didn't matter. What mattered was that she was back, and she was dancing, and so was the crowd. During her five songs and twenty-five minutes, no one stood still.

For the concert, Madonna wore a tank top with BRITNEY SPEARS written in rhinestones across her chest, and at the after-party she wore a T-shirt bearing Britney's image. Before her return to the stage, questions arose about where Madonna fit in the new Britney-centered universe. Entertainment writers invented a bizarre competition between the eighteen-year-old, who in two brief years had become the top-selling female pop singer in the United States, and forty-two-year-old Madonna, who had carved out the lane Spears occupied.

But Spears wasn't Madonna's competition: for better or worse, she was her offspring—like the Spice Girls, whom Madonna famously defended, saying, "I love the Spice Girls...I was a Spice Girl when I started out. Give them a chance and see how they develop."[103] Unlike Spears, the Spices had safety in numbers. Madonna worried about Britney as she watched the paparazzi descend upon her and saw the story line shift from delight to disrespect on its way to despoliation.[104] Madonna told reporters who asked her about Spears, "Can I just say that I find it really irritating that everyone beats up on Britney Spears? I want to do nothing but support her and praise her and wish her all the best."[105]

Madonna's next stop was London's Brixton Academy, on November 28. The event there would be larger, with thirty-five hundred people in the audience and nine million viewers watching online around the world. The production was geared toward that bigger platform. The stage was larger, the sets both cleaner and more glamorous (more than $1 million worth of Dolce & Gabbana glamour), the performance tighter. A twelve-piece string section would accompany Madonna and Mirwais on "Don't Tell Me."[106] "Brixton was really about joy, because she was in joy," Niki said of Madonna. "She was in love with Guy. It was good. Things were good."[107]

Madonna exchanged her Britney T-shirt for one that bore the names of her biological offspring: Rocco on the front and Lola on the back. In her movement, her energy, and her gloriously disheveled appearance, she blew a meteor-size hole through the clichés about motherhood robbing a woman of her energy and appeal. She looked fantastic, and she knew it. "I don't want to sound immodest," she said, "but I don't think that having a child has made me unsexy. There's nothing sexier than a mother. Susan Sarandon, Michelle Pfeiffer—I mean those women are *sexy*. If you're sexy, you're sexy, whether you have no children or five."[108]

Maddy Costa, who was in the audience for *The Guardian,* wrote that Madonna didn't look like "any forty-two-year-old mother of two any normal person knows." Nor did she act like one. "She is the saucy

Madonna we know and love, swivelling her hips, lasciviously whispering 'kiss me' while muscly blokes in fashion-error trousers lick her. It's seven years since Madonna has played in this country...you immediately remember why she is talked about and why she is so loved."[109]

Fans streaming out of the concert agreed. British TV personality Tara Palmer-Tomkinson called the show "the best gig I've ever been to. She said she felt as if she'd won a Willy Wonka golden ticket." A radio-station competition winner described it as "incredible. Sensational. Fantastic...I can't even recover."[110] Guy Ritchie's Conservative Party activist step-mother, Shireen, left the event imagining Madonna as a role model for future female Tory leaders.[111]

Madonna and her gypsy caravan of managers, publicists, assistants, nannies, children, and boyfriend didn't linger in London. *Snatch* opened in Los Angeles on December 6, its red carpet filled with British tough-guy actors and Hollywood hipsters.

The film received the mixed reviews expected of a new director whose first outing had been met with surprise and praise on both sides of the Atlantic. Many said Guy hadn't moved on from that movie. But those reviews felt like grumbling for grumbling's sake. *Snatch* was, if anything, more inventive than *Lock, Stock and Two Smoking Barrels*. It had a singular subject and style that transcended Ritchie's earlier influences: Quentin Tarantino's movies and Hong Kong Triad films. And in the all-important box office category, it did very well. The $10 million movie would eventually earn more than $80 million. For the moment, Guy Ritchie had Hollywood's attention, and it had nothing to do with Madonna.[112]

Madonna had had a fairy-tale year, during which she experienced intense creativity, a new romance, the birth of her second child, and a shocking lack of controversy. Everyone seemed to love her, even the rabid British tabloids. She comported herself well at a party at Prince Charles's home at Highgrove House. She said often and with genuine enthusiasm that she liked British pubs. She used English idioms and expressed them in an English accent (at that point, she was given high marks for trying).[113] And when the British press got wind of her plan to marry Ritchie on an estate in Scotland, the UK press *adored* her. It was a real-life version of the then popular "rebellious woman coming to her senses and marrying" movies. It was a made-for-the-press event, even if much of the reporting was based on rumors.

Speculation about a Ritchie-Ciccone union had intensified after Rocco's birth, when the press spotted the ring on Madonna's left hand. It became frenzied in the face of repeated denials by the couple. On

December 7, that speculation ended. In the tiny village of Dornoch, in the Scottish Highlands, banns were posted: "Entry number 2000/34 Guy Stuart Ritchie/Madonna Louise Ciccone. Proposed date of marriage 22/12/2000." December 22. The news from humble Dornoch made headlines around the world.[114]

After considering other locations, they decided on Scotland because of Guy's grandfather's military service in the Seaforth Highlanders regiment. The events would begin with Rocco's christening, on December 21, at the Church of Scotland's Dornoch Cathedral, followed the next day by his parents' marriage, at Skibo Castle. The spot was a favorite for celebrity weddings not only because of its beauty but also because the facility's seventy-five hundred acres provided a buffer between guests and prying eyes and its fifty-one rooms could accommodate friends and family.[115] Madonna said she and Ritchie "wanted to create an environment that is cut off from the world."[116]

The guests were asked to remain at Skibo for five days, during which the women would enjoy themed luncheons and engage in lady-of-the-manor activities at the estate's spa while Ritchie and his mates would play country gentlemen, indulging in grouse and pheasant shooting on the grounds. Nights were given over to black-tie dining and drinking in cavernous rooms warmed by roaring fires. The event was in every way the kind of upper-class British wedding in the country beloved by film audiences, complete with several eccentrics from Madonna's world to add spice to the gathering.[117]

Madonna, meanwhile, had enlisted her talented friends to help with the proceedings. Sting would sing at Rocco's christening. Jean-Baptiste Mondino would act as the week's official photographer. And twenty-nine-year-old Stella McCartney, Madonna's maid of honor, would create the wedding dress. At that time, McCartney had a fashion-design career but was still best known as Paul's daughter. Her success was suspect because of her rock royalty name, and cynics suggested that she wasn't a serious designer.[118] That narrative was far from the truth. In fact, what attracted Madonna to Stella was that she had done the work, struggled to make something of her own, and succeeded.

McCartney and Madonna met in 1995, just after McCartney graduated from Central Saint Martins College of Art and Design, in London.[119] McCartney described their meeting:

I was running a bath and was totally unprepared. I thought, "Oh my God, she's here"—panicked and ran downstairs to let her in. There were paparazzi everywhere taking her picture, which really flustered me. When I ran back upstairs the bath had over run and had started to flood my flat. It was a nightmare![120]

Unfazed by the plumbing disaster, Madonna came away thinking that McCartney was "a genius."[121] In 1997, she was named head designer at the Paris label Chloé and became one of the first designers with a major house to eschew animal-derived materials. She wasn't interested in putting women in hair shirts to make a statement about the environment, animal cruelty, and sustainability. She wanted to make gorgeous clothes *and* be responsible in the process.[122]

On December 20, sixty-some christening and wedding guests began arriving in Scotland, either at Inverness Airport or at a Royal Air Force base slightly farther away. Paparazzi assembled in the rain and fog to snap away as celebrities from the film, fashion, and financial worlds, along with family members, disembarked from private airplanes to be whisked off in black Range Rovers to the castle.

The list included some people who had been at Madonna's first wedding, among them her father; her stepmother, Joan; her sisters, Paula and Melanie; her brother Christopher; her brother-in-law, Joe Henry; Liz Rosenberg; and Debi Mazar. Among the friends who hadn't been around in 1985 were Gwyneth Paltrow, Ingrid Casares, Jean Paul Gaultier, Rupert Everett, Donatella Versace, and Alek Keshishian.[123] Ritchie's guests included his mother; his father; his stepmother; his stepbrother, Oliver Williams; Trudie Styler and Sting; actors Jason Statham and Jason Flemyng; and his two best men, London club owner Piers Adams and film producer Matthew Vaughn.

At Madonna's request, the officiant at the wedding ceremony and Rocco's christening would be the Reverend Susan Brown. The first woman in the UK to take charge of a cathedral, she was so "forward-thinking" that the press made her an honorary Spice Girl: Holy Spice. She was also known to travel around the village on Rollerblades. Prior to the ceremonies, Brown received hate mail and vile telephone messages from what one newspaper called "religious extremists." "There are still a lot of people against women in the church," she explained.[124]

On the day of Rocco's baptism, the fleet of Range Rovers that had collected guests at the airport drove forty of them to the church. Outside the Skibo Castle grounds, a pack of journalists and fans, who had stood day and night in the damp and bitter December cold, jumped into action and followed the convoy to Dornoch Cathedral, where they were once again forced to huddle outside for a passing glance or wave of a gloved hand.

Inside the church, which Christopher said was positively hot with candles, godparents Trudie Styler and Guy Oseary stood in attendance as Reverend Brown christened the baby, who was resplendent in a white silk gown with gold embroidery designed by Donatella. Sting sang "Ave Maria."[125]

Despite extraordinary efforts by the local police and the presence of seventy guards from a private security firm, two intruders managed to make their way into the cathedral. One man was arrested during the ceremony after he was found inside the church, where he had been hiding for twenty-four hours. A second was arrested outside, after the service, carrying a bag of waste. He had been hiding in the cathedral for *three days* to film the baptism.[126]

The interlopers' images didn't survive to tell the tale, but photos of Madonna and Guy emerging from the church with Rocco made newspapers around the world. An estimated five hundred journalists and photographers had waited for just that picture, along with around one thousand fans and villagers. For a moment, Madonna seemed to step back into her *Evita* character as she waved regally and happily to the cameras and the crowd.

The next day, December 22, at around six thirty in the evening, guests were told to take their seats at the foot of the grand staircase in Skibo Castle's Great Hall. A bagpiper performed as the guests gathered, but once the wedding ceremony began, French pianist Katia Labèque began to play. Four-year-old Lourdes was the first person to appear. Wearing a dress designed for her by Stella McCartney, she tossed red rose petals.[127]

Guy Ritchie entered, wearing a teal blazer, his family's tartan kilt (Rocco had a matching kilt over his diaper), his grandfather's military pouch at his waist, and antique diamond cuff links that Madonna had given him. Ritchie's best men followed, and Stella McCartney appeared next, wearing silk pants and top. Having taken their places near a stained-glass bay window on the staircase, they and Reverend Brown awaited Madonna.[128]

She appeared in a strapless ivory satin gown with an eighteenth-century corset bodice and an antique lace veil covering her face. Resting on her veil was a tiara studded with 767 diamonds that had been loaned to her by Asprey & Garrard. On her wrists, she wore three-inch-wide pearl-and-diamond cuff bracelets from Adler of London, and around her neck was a thirty-seven-carat diamond cross made for her by the house of Harry Winston in New York. Understandably, the guests gasped when they saw her.[129]

Despite her rebellious Rollerblading reputation, Reverend Brown conducted the service with solemnity as she led the couple through prayers, a statement of marriage, and their vows. She concluded the ceremony by beseeching Madonna and Guy to "cherish, honor, delight in family and always keep and hold to one another."[130]

"Who would have thunk it?" Madonna asked writer Hamish Bowles in retrospect about her marriage. "The last thing I thought I would do is marry some laddish, shooting, pubgoing nature lover and the last thing he thought he was going to do was marry some cheeky girl from the Midwest who doesn't take no for an answer!"[131] By the time they said "I do," Madonna believed those differences didn't matter. She called Guy her "soul mate."[132]

After the ceremony, the wedding party enjoyed champagne before moving into the dining room, where a Scottish band played traditional music. The lads toasted Ritchie during the meal with a slide show and a salty telegram from actor Vinnie Jones, who could not make it.[133]

Throughout the week, Christopher said, toasts had featured homophobic humor, which grated on him. What if Black guests seated at the table had been regaled with racist jokes? And if that was not okay, why were gay jokes okay? Christopher was shocked and saddened that the so-called humor was treated with such equanimity by his gay-rights–champion sister, who seemed prepared to accept that display of bigotry as part of her new life with her husband. Christopher looked at Madonna and thought, "Who is this person?"[134]

During one dinner, he couldn't take it. "I am really thick-skinned. I don't care if people call me a faggot. I don't give a fuck," he said. "But they were so relentless. I was like, 'You know what?' I got up and left the table and walked out of the dining room into the hallway to deal with the heat and the feeling." Trudie Styler came, too, and told him she understood his anger. "On the other hand, Rupert Everett, a fellow traveler, was laughing," Christopher recalled. "I was like, 'Do you hear what they're saying?' Jesus Christ."[135]

Christopher got his revenge at the wedding dinner when Madonna asked him to make a toast. "You really don't want me to do that," he told her. She insisted. The brother of the bride then stood and said, "I'd like to toast this happy moment that comes only *twice* in a person's lifetime ... And if anybody wants to fuck Guy, he'll be in my room later." The only people who didn't laugh were the bride and groom.[136] "The wedding was a sign of things to come," Christopher said. "At that point I realized that this was not going to be a good thing for me."[137]

Wine and dessert consumed, the group descended to a disco that had been created in the castle basement. Madonna's favorite Miami DJ and frequent remixer, Tracy Young, did the honors with the music. Young was one of the few women at the top level of the DJ circuit and one of the only women remixers who worked with major talent.[138]

★   ★   ★

The five days in Scotland cost Madonna around $1.5 million.[139] Money hardly mattered. Christopher's toast aside, she described the week as "truly a magical religious experience...it was like summer camp, no one wanted to leave, no one wanted to leave each other."[140]

Madonna emerged as a new persona. She became someone called Mrs. Ritchie and insisted quite rigorously on being called that. She and the mister spent their honeymoon at Sting and Trudie Styler's country estate, in Wiltshire, and remained there through Christmas. Christopher came up from London to help celebrate, as did Elton John and David Furnish. Christopher had known them for years, but with Guy there, he felt like "the odd man out." He began to feel that he had reached the end of something—incredibly, perhaps, the end of his relationship with his sister.[141]

Bookmakers, meanwhile, were placing bets on the longevity of Madonna and Guy's marriage. At that point the odds were one in three that they would make it five years.[142]

Chapter 43

Los Angeles, Barcelona, London, New York, 2000–2001

He who transgresses not only breaks a rule. He goes somewhere that others are not; and he knows something that others don't know.[1]

— *Susan Sontag*

THE PREVIOUS MONTH, between Madonna's Roseland performance and her Brixton show, the United States had fallen into an unprecedented political crisis. The presidential election of November 7, 2000, which pitted Republican George W. Bush against Democrat Al Gore, did not produce a clear winner. The election came down to a few hundred votes in Florida, where Bush's brother was governor.

At that point in modern US history the political tensions surrounding an election—not the campaigning but the election itself—had never been so high. As Madonna prepared to take the stage in cowboy gear in Brixton, embracing her American roots, the American democratic experiment was in peril. What no one could have foreseen was that that election was the start of decades of profound social and political crisis. Madonna's playful excursion into the US heartland had just begun, but it already felt like a nostalgia tour.

In the end, the fate of the election fell to nine people: the justices of the US Supreme Court, who were asked to decide whether to end a Florida vote recount. On December 12, the majority of justices—all appointed by Republicans—agreed that it should stop. Bush won. The religious right was thrilled. After working for twenty years to elect an advocate for their values, they finally had.[2] Gore accepted the court's decision, but his angry supporters did not.

On January 20, 2001, Bush used his inaugural address to try to unite the country. Protests by thousands along his inaugural parade route, however, showed that would not be easy. At one stage, anti-Bush demonstrators were so loud that they drowned out the marching bands. Not since 1969, when anti–Vietnam War protests marred Richard Nixon's inauguration, had citizens witnessing a transfer of power in the United

States seen such a display. Black clouds obscured the dawn of the new century.[3]

That was the climate of social and political upheaval that Madonna and her family returned to in January of 2001, when they arrived in Los Angeles after the wedding and holiday festivities in Britain. Her work over the next two years would reflect that chaos. It would be her most blatantly political and angriest to date and among her most controversial. The backlash she would encounter would be the fiercest since her sexual statements of the early '90s.

The politics and anger were her own, but the expression of them was Ritchie's. His influence pervaded her work the way Sean Penn's had when *True Blue* Madonna channeled early Hollywood. That was an easy fit, because that was who Madonna was, too. Ritchie's East End shoot-'em-up, bust-'em-up persona was more of a stretch. She nonetheless assumed it gamely, adopting the angry British working-class chav look and attitude. It reflected the unsettled times, and it was interesting to her because it was entirely new and therefore worthy of exploration. But most of all, it was a way to please Ritchie. She was crazy in love. Musing aloud to an Australian journalist in January of 2001, she said she missed him if they were separated for even a few hours.[4]

Snatch had opened nationally in the United States to respectable reviews and ticket sales, and scripts poured in for Guy's consideration. In the meantime, he found a project to work on with "the Missus."[5] He wanted to direct the video for "What It Feels Like for a Girl." Madonna said it was the song on the album he responded to the most.[6]

Rather than the album version of the song, however, Ritchie used a remix that stripped out the lyrics except for Charlotte Gainsbourg's narration and a couple of lines from the chorus.[7] Madonna's description of a girl's frustration in navigating the limitations imposed upon her was gone. Instead, he offered a man's take on a woman's anger.

The result was not without interest. Rarely at that time did films or videos feature a woman's rage independent of male rejection or outside a futuristic or horror-genre setting. In Ritchie's video, Madonna, convincingly and with relish, plays a woman hell-bent on mayhem for the fun of it. Adopting "boy zone" trappings—tattoos, fast cars, a gun—she robs, menaces, mows down, and immolates archetypal oppressors: moneymen, hoodlums, jocks, cops.[8]

But without the lyrics, there is no context for Madonna's rage and therefore no meaning. She becomes a feisty conduit for a man's violent fantasy. And for that she must die. As she herself said, bad girls always do in the movies. In the video, she drives herself and an elderly woman she rescues from a convalescent home head-on into a lamppost.

The video also contains flourishes that are alternately silly and offensive. On the silly side, Madonna's hotel room number, 666, alerts viewers to the demon woman within. On the offensive side of the ledger is Ritchie's decision to hang an OL' KUNTZ GUEST HOME sign on the building where Madonna picks up a frail old granny for her drive to the death. That sign in that context with that elderly woman is jaw-dropping.

MTV banned the video when it was released, citing violence, gunplay (though the gun is clearly a water pistol), and the suggestion of suicide. Despite previous controversies having helped record sales, "What It Feels Like for a Girl" sank like a stone.

A Madonna-camp insider told a British newspaper that the Ritchies had so much fun making the video that they decided to work together again.[9] BMW was hiring A-list directors to make eight short film advertisements featuring its cars.[10] In each, Clive Owen plays a driver who ferries characters around LA, a hostage to their whims and hair-raising circumstances. David Fincher's production company organized the project and picked the directors, Ritchie among them. Madonna signed on as a passenger. For her troubles, she was reportedly paid more than $1 million, ten times what Ritchie was said to have received to direct the ad.[11]

Payback was sweet—not that that was Ritchie's intention, but the commercial just so happened to be about a superstar bitch taken down several notches by Owen. His job, according to BMW, was to "scare the snobbery out of her."[12] During seven of the video's nine minutes, Madonna is flung around the back of the car while Owen speeds through downtown LA as if his BMW were the Batmobile. When he finally delivers Madonna to her venue and into the arms of the waiting paparazzi, he turns the car so violently that she flies out the passenger door onto the red carpet. Seeing her on her back on the ground, the paparazzi get a shot they never expected. The traumatized superstar has peed herself.[13] In Ritchie project number 1, Madonna dies; in number 2, she is humiliated. After seeing the BMW commercial, Liz Rosenberg told writer Matthew Rettenmund that she recalled thinking, "This man hates her."[14]

The previous summer, while Madonna was heavily pregnant and stuck at home, she thought, "There's absolutely nothing remotely cool or cutting edge about me right now." She told *Rolling Stone's* Jancee Dunn, "It's a funny place to find yourself in when you think of yourself as having some kind of revolutionary spirit." Her concerts in New York and Brixton helped restore some sense of self. But she needed more.[15]

It had been so long since Madonna was on the road that she had a huge mental file of images and ideas to choose from.[16] Two, however, were uppermost in her mind: the 2000 Ang Lee film, *Crouching Tiger, Hidden*

Dragon, and punk rock. Madonna wanted to fly like the characters in Lee's film and burrow deep underground to resurrect the early British punk scene. "Guy turned me on to all these old documentaries of the Sex Pistols," Madonna said.

> It's just such a cool look and I love the attitude. It's so much fun and so refreshing when you think about what's going on in the music business right now...And I love the idea of getting out there and just thrashing away on an electric guitar.[17]

The concert tour she envisioned would include four acts—punk, *Crouching Tiger,* cowgirl, and Latin. Her two encores would feature a pimped-out *Foxy Brown* version of "Holiday" and a full-cast performance of "Music."

From conception to execution, the concert would take three and a half months to create. Part of that time would be spent building a new team. She had changed. The times and technology had changed. She decided she needed a different group to help her make that transition.[18]

Madonna had thrown around preliminary ideas with Christopher, as she had since her Virgin tour. But when she began working on what would become her Drowned World tour, she decided that he would not be part of it.[19] Yes, Christopher had felt a personal distance growing between them with the entry of Guy Ritchie into her life. But the first indication that the distance was also creative came when Madonna asked her friend David Collins to redesign her New York apartment. It was the first of her homes that Christopher had worked on and the one he felt most attached to. "I walked in there and saw what [Collins] had done," he said. "That was another moment, like a knife to my heart. It really hurt me...It was just another sign that she had lost her respect for me."[20]

Next came the news that he wouldn't have a role in her tour. "I understood that she wanted to go with somebody else," he said.

> We'd been working together forever and why not bring somebody new in? But it was the fact that she never even said anything, that I had to find out from a friend.[21]
>
> When I asked her about it, she was very defensive. She went into this thing, "I made you, you have your life because of me." It was just kind of "I don't owe you anything." I didn't feel like I deserved to be cut off like everybody else. I had watched her cut out people who were super important in her world, just cut them out without any sort of looking back, and I figured that couldn't happen to me. And then it did. I am just like everybody else, nothing special.[22]

Christopher wasn't like everyone else. He was still Madonna's brother and someone she cared for and worried about. But she had decided to entrust her tour to twenty-nine-year-old Jamie King. Choosing King as choreographer and creative partner was easy not only because of the quality of his work but also because of the *way* he worked, which perfectly suited Madonna as she juggled the demands of career and family. "He's always thinking of the artist first in ways that I don't think anyone else was," said King's friend and colleague Kevin Stea.

> So when the artist walks out onstage, or even just for rehearsal, everything is magically perfect and working perfectly and in place where it should be and everybody's ready...so what the artist experiences is comfort, ease, and this sense that you're taken care of. That's attractive to every artist.[23]

And that was exactly what Madonna needed if she was to embark on a world tour. "I guess she was tired of the — not conflict with me, but my second-guessing her about creative decisions," Christopher said. "I guarantee you [King] never said no to her. And that's what she was looking for at that point. She just wanted someone to say yes and leave her alone."[24]

There would also be a new man in the role of music director, a Paris-born twenty-three-year-old raised in Reading, England, named Stuart Price.[25] Under the stage name Jacques Lu Cont, Price was an underground electronic musician who also dabbled in dance and rock music. He had what Madonna loved: a DJ vibe. While in Germany in February, staying in what he called "one of the worst hotels I think I'd ever been in," Madonna rang to offer Price a job playing keyboards on her tour.[26]

It would be a departure from his musical roots. His pianist parents taught him classical music. Pop and rock came via the Pet Shop Boys and Erasure. He didn't begin paying attention to Madonna until around her "Justify My Love" period, when it became clear to him that she was "using these good producers and coming up with unique music."[27]

The leap from vaguely listening to Madonna to intensely working with her was made through some remixing he had done with Mirwais. "When Madonna was looking for a live keyboard player, he recommended me," Price said.[28] From there, he graduated to tour musical director. "There was a certain direction she was looking for, and she put me in control of making music the right side of cool," he told music writer Lucy O'Brien.

> For me, it was an opportunity — there's no other major artist on that level who'd take the risk of having someone like me, not well known, control the music. I didn't have a burning desire to be an MD, but with her it was different. Her style of working was so different.[29]

For example, he said, on the song "Holiday," he suggested she insert a bit of a bootlegged song by the French house artists Stardust right into the middle of it. "Madonna said, 'Yeah, fuck it, let's do it.' You don't see Whitney or Tina Turner doing that," Price said.[30]

Price would be one of Madonna's closest and most crucial musical collaborators during the next five years, both in the recording studio and onstage, as would her guitar teacher, Monte Pittman—the latter not for five years but for two decades.[31] During the Drowned World tour, Pittman would be her most important onstage counterpart, playing off her and with her the way her dancers and backup singers had in previous concerts.

With that trio of twentysomething young men—King, Price, and Pittman—in place, Madonna called Niki and Donna back out on the road. Both had been working on their own music in the intervening years. Donna had her own band, so she knew from a different perspective how hard it was to put a tour together, to be the boss, to count on people. She said,

> I was even more humbled, and I respected her more, and then I respected her being a mom and seeing her go through all that...She's like all of us humans, women. We have fear...But she has so much courage. And the determination. She has a mission, and when you were aligned with her you felt that mission and purpose.[32]

Niki wasn't as eager to go out again. Her surgeries on her leg had left her with one slightly longer than the other. "I knew it was coming to an end for me," she said.

> I always say the Drowned World tour was my Muhammad Ali tour, because you see those films of Muhammad Ali and you say, "He should not be fighting anymore." And that's what I felt like at that moment when I was forty years old, trying to dance next to eighteen-, nineteen-year-olds with an injury. I could still sing, but physically it was just kicking my ass.[33]

Still, Madonna at that point was family, and despite her misgivings, Niki said yes.[34]

How the people onstage *looked* was nearly as important as how they sounded, and for that Madonna turned to stylist Arianne Phillips. Drowned World would be her first of many tours with Madonna as well as countless other projects, from videos to live performances. They had met in 1997 during the *Rolling Stone* Women of Rock cover shoot. Phillips was there as Courtney Love's stylist, and Madonna invited her to work on her "Frozen" video.[35]

By 2000, she had styled some of Madonna's most important videos, including those for "Ray of Light," "Don't Tell Me," and "Music." Then, in 2001, she answered the phone and heard, "Hi, Ari, we're going on tour."[36] It would be a massive undertaking before, during, and after. "I work with a big crew — just the prep side alone can reach twenty-five people." Phillips also styled the dancers, the backup singers, and the band. For Drowned World, that meant 265 costumes.[37]

Jean Paul Gaultier was enlisted to create designs for three segments of the show. For the opening act, he returned to his punk roots: kilts and bondage straps. For the Latin act, he designed a fabulous backless dress that was a cross between costumes he had made for Luc Besson's film *The Fifth Element* and for Peter Greenaway's *The Cook, the Thief, His Wife & Her Lover*. Gaultier then switched to his geisha designs for the *Crouching Tiger* portion of the show. The latter required him to create a kimono with twenty-six-foot sleeves.[38]

Dean and Dan Caten, Milan-based Canadian brothers behind the brand Dsquared2, were asked to re-create the look they had designed for Madonna's "Don't Tell Me" video for the country portion of the concert. That became a design-engineering feat. "She calculates how high she can lift her leg according to the weight of the pant," Dean Caten said.[39]

But clothing was only part of the cast's costuming. Hair told another part of the story, and in the punk part of the show, Madonna wanted the people who hadn't already shaved their heads to get mohawks. Niki said no. "Black folks weren't really into mohawks," Haris said. "The only mohawks I saw were on, like, Aryan youth. I fought her tooth and nail."[40]

It wasn't the first time Madonna had asked Niki to become something she wasn't. Niki said that during their early years together, Madonna wanted her to complement her physically onstage, so she told her to lose weight, especially around the hips, and pressured her to exercise "to make my body be something it wasn't, that it wasn't supposed to be. I'm a curvy, beautiful, brown-black woman. When I think about what that young girl inside of me went through in those years, it felt cruel." The mohawk episode "triggered" that pain.[41]

"It got really hairy for a while," Niki said. "She felt like I was fighting her, and how could I do this to her, and she thought I was her friend. I was like, 'Okay, Madonna, if this is going to give you some joy, I'll do it.'"[42] But when Madonna wanted Donna to shave her head entirely and lose her luxuriant hair, Niki stepped in to save her. "Donna's in the dressing room crying her eyes out, and I threw some Bantu knots in her hair. She looked like an African girl. Madonna said, 'Oh, I love this.' We got away with that."[43]

* * *

Rehearsals began at Sony Pictures Studios in LA in late March. Under Jamie King's direction, Madonna's show was more of a multimedia extravaganza than a theatrical one. King liked to use videos as an adjunct to the activity onstage. Lighting was also more dynamic than it had been in Madonna's previous shows.[44] All those elements required an infinitely more complicated preparation.[45]

In April, rehearsals moved to the LA Forum, where the dancers, musicians, and technology finally came together. At that point, Madonna announced the tour: Europe and the States, six countries in all, with extended residencies at each venue.[46] "In Europe we wanted to stay in the same city for a week at a time so the kids wouldn't have to change planes so much," Caresse Henry said. "Madonna builds *everything* around her family."[47]

Unlike the intimate Girlie Show, Drowned World looked big and was big. Two jumbo jets were hired to move one hundred tons of equipment, fifteen hundred storage trunks, and the 4,900-square-foot stage. Nearly two hundred people, some of them on-site but most of whom traveled, were involved in the show.[48] On previous tours, Madonna traveled with the cast and crew. For Drowned World, she flew separately in a private plane with her family and stayed in a separate hotel.[49]

Drowned World was scheduled to open on June 5, 2000, in Cologne, Germany, but it was canceled at the last minute because of technical problems. Instead, it opened at Barcelona's Palau Sant Jordi stadium four days later to shouts of "Torero, torero" from the eighteen-thousand-strong audience. The last time Madonna had performed in Spain was for a video in which she struggled to win a bullfighter's heart. In 2001, she *was* the bullfighter.[50]

Such was the excitement over Madonna's first tour in eight years that it sold out almost immediately at every stop along its route. But fans hoping to be reunited with the Madonna of the '80s and '90s—the unbridled joy, the sex, the love—were disappointed. Drowned World Madonna went dark. (The tour's name and the song title from her *Ray of Light* album were derived from a 1962 J. G. Ballard science fiction novel about a planet ravaged by global warming.) Drowned World Madonna also went straight. (Though androgynous, her dancers didn't make a gay statement; they were too otherworldly.) And, as a woman, Madonna was angry. She was past cajoling the world into recognizing a woman's power. In Drowned World, she was prepared to kill for it.

Glimmers of the old Madonna surfaced briefly during the concert. But in her new show, she was a guitar-playing rocker, removed from the crowd, removed from her sister backup singers, removed from her dancers. For the first time in her career, she appeared at times lonely onstage, even sad. By the tour's end in September, its themes of violence, despair, and chaos would seem prescient. But at the start it just felt confusing.

Christopher saw the "friends and family" preview performance in Los Angeles before it went on the road and said, "I had to go outside. I couldn't watch it. It was like, 'What the hell? This is so dark and weird.' "[51] Niki feared they would be booed off the stage. "Noises and music are two different things," she said, "and there's a lot of [noise] going on." Madonna told Niki to trust her.[52] That was the message to her fans, too: trust that she was taking them someplace—to yet another place—where she thought they needed to travel.

The concert opened onto a futuristic *Mad Max Beyond Thunderdome*–type stage, with toughs played by Stuart Price, Niki, Donna, Monte Pittman, and a few of the tour's dancers spitting and snarling in full punk regalia. Finally Madonna appeared in the mist, standing like a warrior in a kilt, torn sheer shirt, and dog collar, singing "Drowned World/Substitute for Love." She did not move. She did not dance. There was no embellishment in her song. She sang it direct and raw. She was strong, defiant, and at the same time vulnerable, even small. The performance was unlike any other Madonna concert opener. Also absent was a smile. This was a Madonna who had seen the future, and it was not pretty.[53]

When the next song, "Impressive Instant," began, she was surrounded by dancers in gas masks and headlamps who carried her off her platform and down to the stage. A lengthy skirmish between Madonna and the dancers ended in a standoff, but not before she was given an honorary penis by a dancer who put a pipe between her legs and let its fog spew out onto the crowd.[54]

At that point the show became a rock concert and an homage to the guitar—what Donna Gaines in *Rolling Stone* once called "the wank itself."[55] The audience heard her before they saw her playing a black electric Les Paul. In playing it, she was claiming it, that ultimate symbol of macho rock.

Madonna transformed "Candy Perfume Girl" into something the Doors might have performed. It was hallucinogenic, but rather than appear onstage as a trippy hippie, tour dancer Tamara Levinson performed as a depraved dystopian contortionist with a mohawk. Madonna finished the song with her guitar and a scream: "Fuck off, motherfuckers."[56]

The concert lightened up with a playful rendition of "Beautiful

Stranger," which Madonna sang with Niki and Donna. It was one of only three moments in the concert when they re-created their electrifying sisterhood. In the Girlie Show, Donna explained, Christopher "really loved us three together." In Drowned World, Jamie King was more interested in acrobatic dancers and screens. "All that three-girl stuff," Niki said, "he was like, 'Uh-uh, that's not going to happen.'" For most of the concert, while singing backup, Donna and Niki were relegated out of sight, away from Madonna, above or behind the band.[57]

The punk segment of the show ended with a frantic rendition of "Ray of Light," after which a recording of "Paradise (Not for Me)" filled the arena while on-screen, samurai swordsmen silhouetted against a Japanese flag moved slowly and Madonna transformed herself into a geisha as she and they prepared for battle in the next portion of the concert.[58]

Madonna appeared onstage in a black kimono, its famous fifty-two-foot wingspan held aloft by two men who moved them like banners as lighting director Peter Morse illuminated them with Japanese kanji characters. "That was one of those magic moments," he said. It had been an enormous technical challenge.[59]

Singing "Frozen," Madonna stood still as the fabric waved and the light danced until her sleeves were yanked off her shoulders and carried away like battle flags. Once freed, she and her dancers began a hybrid performance of martial arts moves and gestures from the jiuta-mai geisha dance.[60] The concepts of dominance and submission were about to be challenged.

Madonna's geisha sang her vocodered apology, "Nobody's Perfect," to a sword-wielding samurai who seemed uninterested in her contrition. Three-quarters of the way through the song, he chopped off her ponytail with his sword and held it aloft as if it were a scalp. After fleeing offstage, Madonna reappeared in a red kimono, singing her song of escape, "Mer Girl."[61]

"Mer Girl" segued into "Sky Fits Heaven," and with it, Madonna took flight. Held in place by cables, she flew more than twenty feet off the ground and became a martial arts fighter in a spectacular aerial dance, as she and two flying women took on three samurai. Madonna and the women having won that battle, she returned to earth and "Mer Girl."[62]

Images on-screen, meanwhile, were difficult to watch. They showed Madonna's geisha persona being beaten. Her eyes blackened, her nose bloodied, she offered a half smile. Yes, she had taken a licking, but it hadn't killed her. As she ended "Mer Girl" onstage, she ripped off her black wig, shook out her blond hair, picked up a shotgun, and killed a samurai. Descending through the floor, she brandished her gun over her head with one hand, like Charlton Heston at a National Rifle Association convention.[63]

The Japanese-style anime that ended Madonna's geisha segment opened with Charlotte Gainsbourg's voice-over from "What It Feels Like for a Girl" as the audience watched, on-screen, scenes of more violence against women, this time including rape.

To the entertainment industry, that kind of violence is okay, because it isn't "real," even though actual women actors are subjected to the aggression. The end of Madonna's anime made just that point. The director of the cartoon is heard ordering the shoot stopped so that he can adjust a camera. The cartoon man ravaging the cartoon woman takes that opportunity to apologize for what his job requires him to do. She replies with a chirpy, "Oh, no, it's all right." That is what girls do—excuse the inexcusable—because that's Hollywood, because that's life.[64]

Madonna returned to the stage for her cowgirl segment, which was without violence. Having slayed the dragon and made her feminist point, she climbed onto a bale of hay and enjoyed herself with "I Deserve It," "Don't Tell Me," "Secret," and "Gone." She played guitar, rode a mechanical bull, and led a line dance. She followed that North American Wild West tribute with one to South America.[65]

Madonna had included a Latin element in her concerts since her first tours because she loved the sound. By 2001, it was also good business. The music industry was experiencing a Latin explosion that had begun in the mid-'90s with Selena and grew after her murder with the emergence of performers like Ricky Martin, Gloria Estefan, Shakira, and the 1997 album and 1999 film celebrating Cuban music, *Buena Vista Social Club*. In 2000, Madonna's record label launched a Latin division, Maverick Musica.[66]

Madonna's Latin segment opened with her singing "What It Feels Like for a Girl" in Spanish, followed by "La Isla Bonita." For that song, she played Spanish guitar and was joined onstage by her musicians and dancers in an ecstatic performance. Her previous concerts always felt like a group of friends performing for the enjoyment of other friends—the audience. That wasn't the case with Drowned World until "La Isla Bonita."[67]

Madonna's encores traditionally included some of her most memorable moments, and that tour was no exception. Niki and Donna had asked Madonna to close the show with "Holiday." Madonna agreed to make it one of two closing songs.[68]

Dressed identically (except for Madonna's Versace fur coat), singing in perfect harmony and moving in lockstep as they always had, the three displayed a purity of sound and a generosity of spirit unlike anything else on offer that night. The crowd went crazy, not merely because the piece was nostalgic but also because it was still so damn good.[69]

That was not the last word. Madonna reserved "Music" for her final encore. It concluded with a calisthenic workout requiring Madonna, Niki, Donna, and the dancers to do killingly fast-paced deep knee bends.[70] When the performance was choreographed, Madonna knew about Niki's injury—she had even had special shoes made for her so that her legs were of equal length—yet Madonna had included her in that grueling routine. Niki said she went into "a kind of trance and just let God lift me up through the whole thing."[71]

At the end of past concerts, Madonna remained onstage offering prolonged goodbyes to the audience. During Drowned World, she didn't. She left that final moment to a recording of Sacha Baron Cohen as Ali G. Appearing on-screen as Madonna departed, he said, "What iz u still doing here? Go on, piss off. She ain't coming back." The show was over.[72]

The tour moved from Barcelona through Europe, and by mid-June, it was in Berlin. Madonna had been on the road for less than a month, but she was exhausted and experiencing throat trouble. Stella McCartney, Ingrid Casares, and Gwyneth Paltrow swooped in to join her in Germany for a little support and R&R. Surprisingly, they chose to spend Madonna's day off in a poignant way. On June 24, they traveled to nearby Oranienburg to tour the Sachsenhausen Nazi concentration camp. "She did not say anything, she prayed," reported *Bild Zeitung* in a front-page story on Madonna's visit.[73]

Her spirits were revived in Paris, where she was met by her French creative posse—Mirwais, Jean Paul Gaultier, and Jean-Baptiste Mondino—whom she greeted from the stage. And then on to London, where the mood turned sour again and Madonna's nerves frayed. During one performance, a drunk stormed the stage and came within inches of her before he was wrestled to the floor by her tour manager and a bodyguard.[74] British music and entertainment writers were generally positive about the concert, but the British tabloids ridiculed the show and obsessed over the domestic drama offstage.[75]

Press reports had started to describe Madonna and Guy's quarrels. On the eve of her return to the States and a difficult twelve-city, twenty-eight-performance schedule, they fought during dinner at a West End restaurant. A columnist wasn't wrong when he speculated that "the most famous woman in the world" could never be happy "playing the little woman for very long." And Ritchie "will certainly never be happy being Mr. Madonna...no macho man is going to put up with [it]."[76]

Ritchie attended almost every show on the tour. It was his most prolonged exposure to Madonna as "Madonna," and it occurred on the road, where the magnitude of her celebrity was overwhelming to anyone witnessing it for the first time. The experience was a first for her, too. Never had she toured with a husband and children. Having them near gave her strength, but they also increased and complicated her workload. "There isn't a second in my day that isn't taken up looking after my family or thinking about my show," she told *People*.[77] When corners had to be cut, her family's needs overrode her tour's.

Jamie King recalled, "We'd be in the middle of rehearsal...and, say, in the middle of doing 'Holiday,' Lourdes would come in and Madonna would stop everything and ask what kind of day she had at school."[78] Choreographer Alex Magno said Madonna's priorities had changed since her last tour. During the Girlie Show, she managed every detail and knew everyone involved, "even the guy that was cleaning the floor." Now, he said, her work was her husband and family.[79]

The tour arrived in New York in July for six nights at Madison Square Garden. Those concerts felt like home. During one of them, Lourdes had a playdate in a toy-filled room adjacent to her mother's dressing room at the Garden. Carlos minded her and her playmates while Madonna performed. In the audience were row upon row of Madonna's friends. That show of support provided a boost, but it wasn't enough. Suffering from exhaustion and laryngitis, she canceled a concert in New Jersey.

Regrouping, she continued on to Boston, and then to Florida in August, where Guy surprised her onstage with a birthday cake. Rumors circulated that, now that she was forty-three, the Drowned World tour would be her last.[80] If it were, Madonna would go out on top. More than seven hundred thousand people would see the tour. Based on its gross proceeds of nearly $77 million, it was the most successful tour by a solo artist that year. She had proved that, despite having reached an age at which the music world put women out to pasture, she was not *a* force but *the* force.[81]

Arriving in LA in September, she planned to wrap up her tour with four performances. But on the eleventh of the month, four passenger planes commandeered by men with boxcutters flew into formerly impregnable symbols of US power. Not since the Japanese bombing of Pearl Harbor, in 1941, had the United States been attacked to such deadly effect on its home turf. It was a moment that would change everything nearly everywhere. It was the millennial catastrophe some had been anticipating.

Madonna was scheduled to perform that day, but she postponed it. Concerts around the country and the world were shuttered. Everything closed down as people tried to make sense of what had happened and braced for the possibility of what was to come.[82] The dust had not settled when the stunned world awakened to the needs of the attacks' victims. Rescue teams and charities mobilized to rush help to the sites of carnage. Entertainers organized benefit concerts. Madonna returned to the stage in LA on September 13 and donated the proceeds of her last tour dates, around $1 million, to the victims and their families.[83]

Some of her tour's cast were reluctant to perform. The atmosphere of fear after the attacks was pervasive, especially at large venues that might be targets. "We were scared," Donna said.

> But her manager said, "Madonna's going on, and she understands if you don't want to go, but she would really appreciate you standing in solidarity with her." Meanwhile, dogs were sniffing the arena for bombs. It was really scary. But when we got in front of the audience, and everyone was holding up pictures of New York and the towers, it was just—you were just crying through the whole thing. It was the right thing, of course, to be together.[84]

Madonna toned down some of the violence in her show post-9/11 — she didn't murder her onstage foes; she hugged them. She also went off script.[85] Joe Henry said that in the middle of her show, "she dismissed the dancers and acrobats, the full band and backing singers, and came to the front of the stage with just her guitar player, Monte . . . I remember it as the most visceral and human moment of the whole show." They sang "Don't Tell Me" before the rest of the cast rejoined them to continue the performance.[86]

On September 14, Madonna dedicated five minutes to talking about the attacks. "Everyone here in this arena is angry and sad. Everyone wants to know why and wants to know what they can do," she said. She told her audience to look in the mirror and consider their own behavior, whether they terrorized people in their lives, whether they were bigoted. "It's not just [Osama] bin Laden," she said.[87]

She then called for a moment of silence to pray for the victims, the people trying to help them, and "everyone who thinks it is right to kill in the name of God." *Los Angeles Times* reporter Greg Braxton said the Staples Center went completely still. "The moment ended as the audience erupted into cheers. Picking up a guitar, Madonna said: 'If you want to change the world, change yourself.'"[88]

On September 15, the last night of her tour, she had more to say. As news of the attacks turned to news of possible US retaliation, she stopped the concert and urged the White House to show restraint, telling the crowd, "Violence begets violence . . . What happened was horrible, but I'd like to think of it as a wake-up call. There's terrorism every day all over the world." Fans began shouting "USA, USA." Madonna said,

> OK, USA—but start looking at the world, change yourself… We're not doing this show because we want to forget, but because we want people to remember how precious life is.[89]

Chapter 44

Malta, Los Angeles, London, 2001–2002

I think life is tragic and, as an artist today, you can't avoid the tragedy. It's not necessarily political, it's just a problem of despair.[1]

— *Mirwais Ahmadzaï*

ON SEPTEMBER 20, nine days after three thousand people were killed and more than six thousand injured in the 9/11 terrorist attacks, US president George W. Bush stood before a joint session of Congress and declared an open-ended, borderless "war on terror." Seventeen days later, the United States invaded Afghanistan to hunt down Osama bin Laden and the Al Qaeda leadership behind the attacks and to punish the Taliban government for having harbored them.

Just as they had after Pearl Harbor, young people marched into military recruiting offices and volunteered to fight. Just as they had after Pearl Harbor, the vast majority of Americans rallied around the flag. And that flag was everywhere: porches, yards, apartment windows; in shops and on poles on Main Streets; fluttering off pickup trucks on the highway; pinned to lapels. Any politician who did not wear a flag pin was not just unpatriotic, they were un-American.[2]

For a time, the anger and social tensions that had characterized the '90s and greeted George W. Bush's election disappeared in the face of those much larger circumstances. Americans gave the government a "stack of blank checks," as author Naomi Klein put it, allowing it to rescind rights, wage war, and spend tax dollars to establish a surveillance state. Dissent, sometimes even discussion, equaled disloyalty.[3] The question of political allegiance was no longer "Are you a Democrat or a Republican?" After 9/11, it became "Are you with us or against us?"[4]

It didn't take long for people with a social agenda to twist the facts of the crisis for use against their enemies. Christian crusader Jerry Falwell said of 9/11, "The abortionists, and the feminists, and the gays and lesbians and the ACLU made this happen." To his mind, they had weakened the American backbone, and their sins had brought down the wrath of God. And that was just the start of the vitriolic scapegoating.[5]

*   *   *

Maybe the Mediterranean sounded like a good escape. Two weeks after her tour, despite a pulled abdominal muscle and fatigue so severe that she was near physical collapse, Madonna was headed to Malta and Sardinia to shoot a movie with Guy. They had decided to remake Lina Wertmüller's 1974 Italian classic, *Swept Away*. Filming would begin on October 1, 2001.

The idea came from their friend, actor Steven Weber. After watching their BMW commercial, Weber said Madonna and Guy should do a movie together and suggested *Swept Away*.[6] The film was about gender roles, class prejudices, and what transpires when two strangers are freed from their moorings together on a deserted island.

It wasn't a stretch that Weber thought of that film when watching Ritchie's BMW ad. Wertmüller's movie is also about bringing an uppity bitch to her knees. Guy wasn't a fan of "artsy-fartsy movies" and had never heard of *Swept Away,* but Madonna had seen it at school and wanted to watch it again with Ritchie. He "loved the film after he got past the first twenty minutes," she said. "As soon as they got to the island, 'cause he loves Greece and Italy and fishing...he tuned in." They decided to do it, with a few major tweaks.[7]

The original film is sexually explicit. That is the language the two stowaways speak to each other because they have little else in common. Under Ritchie's direction, the emphasis shifts from the physical to the emotional, according to Madonna. He didn't particularly like sex scenes in films, and she wasn't thrilled about rolling around naked with another man in front of her new husband.[8]

Ritchie also did away with the original film's political subplot. In Wertmüller's movie, the female lead is a right-wing bigot, which raises the tension in her relationship with a lower-caste crewman. Madonna's character in Ritchie's script is mostly annoyed about a lack of material things and reduced to what Steven Daly in *Vanity Fair* called "comfort-deprived whining."[9] The effect of Ritchie's decision was not unlike what happened in his video for "What It Feels Like for a Girl" when he omitted the lyrics: he denied both the movie and the video the opportunity to make a political or social statement.

The five weeks of filming allowed Madonna, Ritchie, and the children to be together in one place for an extended period. She called that a "plus, a real plus." As for the film, she told one interviewer that it was "a labor of love between me and my husband."[10] To another, however, she called it a huge test, "and I so deserve a medal" for surviving it.[11]

The work itself was difficult. Shooting occurred outside, much of it on the water, during the Maltese winter. Madonna recalled being seasick.[12] The sex scenes, such as they were, were uncomfortable for everyone, including Adriano Giannini, who played the crewman his father, Giancarlo Giannini, had portrayed in the original. "We saved the physical stuff to the very end of the shooting," Madonna said. "And I think everyone expected, like, bombs to go off. The whole crew was waiting for Guy's head to explode off his body."[13]

Most challenging for her, though, was being directed by Ritchie, whom she didn't feel she could question the way she might someone else. "He has the final say," Madonna said. "I did have to accept that, full stop."[14] Madonna said she learned "thousands" of life lessons making the movie on set and off. She learned not to talk shop during "husband-and-wife time." She learned not to bring their personal problems onto the film set. "So I learned about restriction and patience," she said, "and not just getting my way and having it out when I wanted to do it, which is the kind of person I am."[15]

Fifteen years earlier, Madonna had made a movie with her first husband. At the time, she said she strove to show him that she was a good actor. In 2001, she felt the same way about her second husband and their movie.[16] Though he had less film experience than Madonna did, Ritchie didn't seem to feel he had anything to prove to his wife. "I'm confident. And that's all you can be," he said.[17]

Ritchie and Madonna left Malta believing they had made something good, or at least telling each other that they had.[18]

For many reasons, September 11 among them, there was no question of returning to the States. By November, Madonna agreed with Ritchie that home would be England. "Basically, Guy threatened to leave me and I said, OK," she recalled half jokingly of the decision. They relocated what he called their "big old team"—eight or nine people, including two nannies and Madonna's assistants—to London.[19]

Madonna found a Georgian terrace home near the Marble Arch, at the edge of Hyde Park. It had five reception rooms, a library, eight bedrooms, fifteen-foot-high ceilings, and a large drawing room. It was also secure because the points of entry were limited: the house was attached on either side to other residences, and the busy street outside afforded little space for loitering.[20] Ritchie foresaw a "pretty normal life" there.[21]

During their first year of marriage, he and Madonna had both made concessions, but she was expected to and seemed prepared to make more of them. She told a reporter that she dressed more modestly than she did before because Ritchie didn't want her to wear revealing clothes. She didn't stay in New York as much because she said Guy was "totally freaked out" by the city. And though a longtime vegetarian, she learned to shoot birds so she could share the activity with her husband at a storied estate they bought in the British countryside.[22]

The Wiltshire home was Ritchie's fantasy because he considered his childhood spent on his stepfather's estate the best time of his life. Madonna admitted that it took her a while to appreciate it, but eventually she did.[23] Like other married women, Madonna as Mrs. Ritchie had chipped away at who she was to become the woman her husband wanted her to be. It was an act of love. She had done as much before, but it didn't work and never lasted. The real Madonna was still in there, and she needed to let off steam.

Madonna used an appearance at the televised Turner Prize presentations at the Tate Britain on December 9 to do just that. Each year Britain's highest recognition for a visual artist is presented to an artist of significance by a person of significance. Madonna was asked to present that year's award. From the start, the ceremony's organizers annoyed her. They wanted to read her speech beforehand, and when she said no, they tried to wheedle the contents out of her. "So then I just got insulted," she said.[24]

Next, she was asked how she wanted to be introduced. "And I said, 'Mrs. Ritchie.' And they said, 'Oh, no, we can't do that because everyone knows you as Madonna.' Come on, can't we play a little bit? It was ridiculous."[25] Clearly, organizers had not done their homework, because they beseeched her not to swear during the presentation. Madonna said she considered that an "invitation" to do so.[26]

On the night of the award presentation, as Madonna walked toward the podium, she was visibly annoyed, mustering at best a strained smile. She took the opportunity to plug her new greatest-hits album, *GHV2,* which included music from her previous four albums, and to laud Stella McCartney, who had designed the clothes she wore that night. And then she delivered a cogent statement on the meaninglessness of awards.[27]

"It's a little bit strange handing out a prize for the 'best artist' because there's no such thing as the 'best' anything; there are only opinions." She said awards never made an artist better, and while the prize money—in this case, £20,000—was handy, it would not change the artist's life for long. And then she said,

> What I do know is that art is always at its best when there is no money, because art has nothing to do with money and everything to do with love. And like love it can be inspiring, inexplicable, provocative, and sometimes infuriating. Nevertheless, we cannot live without it, so that is why I'm here. Not because I think that one artist is better than another but because I want to support any artist who not only has something to say but the balls to say it. In a time when political correctness is valued over honesty, I would also like to say, "Right on, motherfuckers. Everyone, everyone is a winner."[28]

Madonna announced the award recipient that night, installation artist Martin Creed, and reminded the audience that the woman presenting the prize was "Mrs. Ritchie, thank you very much."[29]

Britain's Channel 4 broadcast the ceremony live, and its censors weren't quick enough to override her language.[30]

Far from settling in to married life, in 2002 Madonna went into creative overdrive. She began by joining the most iconic of all British film productions. She had agreed to write and perform the theme song for the next James Bond movie, *Die Another Day,* and make a cameo appearance in the film as a rapier-wielding character named Verity. Madonna said she played the "one woman who's not interested in [Bond] in the movie. I liked that."[31]

In the Bond movies, more than in almost any other nonmusical film franchise, songs are a crucial part of the production and the film's success. Released before the movie, they set the tone and whet the appetite for audiences who wonder what 007 — in 2002, actor Pierce Brosnan — would be up to next. Shirley Bassey had sung the theme for *Goldfinger* in 1964, and from that point on, music, like cars, martinis, and women, became integral to the Bond mystique.[32]

Die Another Day would be the twenty-second Bond film, but not since 1985 and Duran Duran's "A View to a Kill" had there been a chart-topping Bond song. Producers thought Madonna could deliver another. Teaming up with Mirwais, she began working on it in February. She said it was about destroying one's ego. It would make references to Sigmund Freud, and unstated references to Kabbalah.[33] French composer Michel Colombier, meanwhile, joined them to direct a strings section that provided a bridge between the Madonna–Mirwais electrodance creation and the traditional Bond orchestral sound.[34]

The song would also appear on Madonna's new album, which she had been writing since just after the September 11 attacks. The US Congress was poised to spread its war on terror to Iraq, and the British prime minister, Tony Blair, had vowed to support Washington. "I was very agitated by what was going on in the world around me," Madonna said.[35] "Mirwais is also very political, seriously cerebral and intellectual. All we did was sit around, talking politics all the time."[36]

On her new album, *American Life,* Madonna did not directly confront the war. She wrote about what she knew best—fame and celebrity. As it happened, those were the fantasy worlds that many people living in fear had retreated into. With reality itself so grim, reality TV provided a mindless respite. Shows like *Survivor* and *Big Brother* made stars out of people willing to eat worms and act bratty.[37]

Her album also asked listeners to think about their priorities at a time of enormous social change. After 9/11, some on the right called for a "vast relearning," which meant amending or eliminating civil rights protections to bolster the new security state, and circling the wagons domestically by reemphasizing a man's role as protector and woman's as wife and mother. Wall Street, meanwhile, responded to the trauma by accelerating the scavenger capitalism born in the 1980s.[38]

Changes of that scale occurred with shockingly little commentary from citizens because the multitude's attention was elsewhere. Celebrity—the dream of achieving it and the obsession with the lives of people who had— consumed them.[39] Madonna said she wanted to "shout from the rooftops that we...have to wake up to reality."[40]

> I'm saying celebrity is bullshit, and who knows better than me?...In America, more than any other place in the world, you have the freedom to be anything you want to be. Which is all well and good, but it only works if you have a value system and we do not seem to have one anymore. It's whatever it takes to get to the top.[41]

Four songs on her new album—"American Life," "Hollywood," "I'm So Stupid," and "Nobody Knows Me"—dealt with the subject of celebrity. They would be the record's most controversial, especially "American Life," partly because Madonna rapped a verse to express the relative meaninglessness of the things fame had brought her.[42]

The rap was Mirwais's idea to cover an instrumental portion at the end of the song. "He just told me to do stream-of-consciousness, whatever I was thinking...It was just total improv and obviously it was sloppy at first, but I got out all my thoughts and then I wrote everything down...and then I perfected the timing of it."[43]

"Hollywood," which began with humble guitar picking, was an act of self-sabotage, a giant middle finger to the movie and music industries, especially the latter. As a middle-aged woman, Madonna already had trouble muscling her way onto the conglomerate-owned radio stations, which favored manufactured sugar-pop stars. In her song, she told her fans to "flip the station, change the channel." Revolt.[44]

Confessional songs have been part of popular music for as long as love songs have. They are where artists go when love turns sour. Madonna's "I'm So Stupid" was a new kind of confessional song. In it, she described her stupidity as she chased an empty fame dream. Her voice was all hard *r*'s, while Mirwais's music relied on a primitive drum machine. It was an alley song, a dare-me song, an "I'm outta here" song.

"Nobody Knows Me" described the aura of mystery that continued to surround her, despite years in the spotlight. Challenging the very media that she should have courted—magazines and television—she characterized the stories they sold as a "social disease." In the staccato delivery that was a hallmark of Mirwais's work, Madonna swore off them and said she slept much better for it.

Madonna saw those celebrity songs as "clearing away what isn't important. And once you clear away the cobwebs you can see the things that do matter."[45] That process made way for a song called "Mother and Father," which recognized the anger she still carried because of her mother's death and her father's abandonment. Madonna tried to convince herself in its lyrics that she should move past the hurt so she could find love.

That love was the subject of three songs: "Love Profusion," "Nothing Fails," and "Intervention." All three were acoustic guitar–heavy, traditional, and intimate. Any of them, especially "Nothing Fails," might have been a lead single on the album if Madonna had been interested in making a hit rather than a statement.

Those songs, like the fame songs, were wake-up calls. Real love, according to Madonna, was something one worked at.[46] "X-Static Process" described the struggle involved in making love work and not losing oneself through compromise in the process. Written with Drowned World tour music director Stuart Price, the song was a sequel to "What It Feels Like for a Girl." The voice was the same, as was the confusion, but "X-Static Process" is sung by a grown woman, and the dilemma is resolved. She finds herself and discovers her self-worth.

It is the album's most beautiful song, as pure in its delivery as it is powerful in its shockingly honest message. For those who watched uneasily as Madonna tried to become a person called Mrs. Ritchie, it was a revelation: she wasn't entirely comfortable in that role herself. "X-Static Process" became one of her most important songs of that period.

The last track on the album, "Easy Ride," which Madonna wrote with Monte Pittman, came "full circle" back to fame, her career, and the fact that her achievements weren't the stuff of magic but the result of labor, courage, and commitment.[47] Her reward, according to the song, was simple pleasures. For her that meant art, children, home. Madonna began her album denouncing the entertainment-industry machine and ended up offering an alternative to its candy-coated fantasy: simple living.

"The whole reason I got into the music business wasn't because I thought I had a spectacular voice. It's because I had something to say," Madonna said. "Never did I write a song and say, 'This is too risky,' or 'This is too pop.' It's just, 'Is this what I wanna say? Do I love this sound? Is this where I am right now?' "[48] With the songs on *American Life,* she could answer yes to those questions. She saw it as her first mature political album.[49]

Madonna's musical work was interrupted by her return to the stage. She had read Australian playwright David Williamson's play *Up for Grabs,* about the 1990s art-market gold rush. At its core, the play puts forth the idea that art is valued for its cost rather than its mystery because many of the people involved in its creation and sale are only interested in pursuing the evil twins fame and money. The concept was close to Madonna's heart. It was the subject of her Tate speech and one she was grappling with on her album.

David Williamson was Australia's leading playwright, but he was best known outside his country as a screenwriter for the films *Gallipoli* and *The Year of Living Dangerously.* He was not a Madonna fan, but he understood what it meant when his London agent called him to say that she wanted to play the lead in a West End production of his work. "I wanted to have at least one sell-out West End show in my career," he said. Madonna was his ticket. He traveled to London to meet with her because before she agreed to do the play, she wanted him to make major changes to the script.[50]

The plot as written involves an art dealer who tries to make a name for herself by selling a painting for a bundle. To do that, she puts up her own assets as a guarantee and embarks on a high-stakes game pitting five people—two couples and a corporate art adviser—against one another to drive up the price. In the process, she degrades herself by literally putting her body on the line in her scheme of deception and seduction. In the original version of the play, her gamble pays off. She dupes the corporate bidder into paying an inflated price and thereby secures her place in the galaxy of art dealers.

Among the changes Madonna sought was the main character's name. She wanted to be called Loren rather than Simone. She wanted the action shifted to New York from Sydney, and she wanted the painting in question to be by Jackson Pollock rather than Australian artist Brett Whiteley. She also wanted the price tag to be $20 million, not $2 million. "Two million for a painting is peanuts in New York," she told Williamson. And she didn't like the ending.[51]

In the play, the Loren/Simone character sleeps with a woman, straps on a dildo during sex with a man, lies, and cheats—all in pursuit of a sale—and gets away with it. Madonna asked Williamson, "What kind of audience are gonna love someone who does that?" He said Australian audiences did. "They like amoral cheats?" Madonna asked him, adding, "In our country, you do something bad, you pay. Retribution then redemption."[52]

At first glance, that comment, coming from Madonna, appeared to indicate that she bought into the favored narrative that bad girls (or boys) deserve punishment. But it could also be interpreted as Madonna following *her* favorite narrative: the journey from darkness to light. Either way, she didn't want her character to be rewarded for her misdeeds. Madonna told Williamson that she wanted her to go broke, lose her home and husband, and then "remake her life." Such was her power and his hunger that he agreed to the changes.[53]

Madonna's people announced her participation in the play in February.[54] The entire ten-week run at the eight-hundred-seat Wyndham's Theatre sold out in ten days. The ripple effect was felt from the West End to Broadway. Theaters had been hard hit by post–September 11 security fears. Audiences were reluctant to congregate in public settings, where they might make an attractive target for another attack. Robust ticket sales and the participation of a star of Madonna's caliber gave the industry a boost it desperately needed.

Rehearsals began in April. Laurence Boswell, a veteran of West End shows that featured marquee celebrities, was chosen to direct. He told Dominic Cavendish of Britain's *Daily Telegraph* that nothing prepared him for what he encountered with Madonna.

> It was utterly, utterly stressful. As soon as it started, my life disappeared. She has people in London. She has people in New York. She has people in Los Angeles...From the minute I signed up, twenty-four hours a day, seven days a week, I was answering questions...So, in the simplest terms, you're lifted into Madonna-land, which is...incredibly intense.[55]

If Madonna made Boswell's life difficult, it was because she was nervous. She had not been on a theatrical stage since 1988, when she performed in David Mamet's play *Speed-the-Plow.* Once again, she chose to challenge herself under the brightest, harshest spotlight, and in the case of London, to open herself up to the ridicule of critics who had theater running in their veins. If critics did not believe Madonna belonged in movies, they most certainly did not believe she belonged on a London stage. Knowing that, she put herself to the test anyway.

In *Up for Grabs,* she was one of seven cast members, the other six being theater veterans. As an opening-night gift, she had placards made for her fellow actors' dressing-room doors. Sian Thomas was "Fiona Fucking Shaw." Michael Lerner was "Laurence Fucking Olivier." "It was kind of a joke," Madonna said,

> because Sian Thomas is a real grande dame of the theater...and so we would tease her about that a lot and then Michael Lerner was always

spouting and interrupting in rehearsals...And I used to say to him, "Who are you, Laurence Fucking Olivier?" And it's a joke, all done in fun, and so we just got into calling each other names...everyone got to be an alter ego.[56]

Madonna's alter ego was "Judi Fucking Dench." She was identified in the play's promotional material as yet another character, "Madonna Ritchie."[57]

Preview performances were scheduled to begin on May 9 but were postponed for several days because of technical difficulties. Matinees were also canceled so that Madonna could work on her album.[58] That meant that by the time the play opened to the public, on May 14, the anticipation was explosive. Hundreds of fans stood outside Wyndham's, on Charing Cross Road, for eight hours in the rain trying to buy scalped tickets.[59]

Audience members lucky enough to have a seat on opening night greeted Madonna's entrance onto the stage with wild applause. David Williamson said Madonna "was momentarily thrown. After a minute or two, everyone calmed down and she had her first line."[60] There was hardly a minute in the ninety-minute play when she was not onstage. And though nearly everyone agreed—from fans to critics—that she appeared nervous and that her voice didn't carry, she was rewarded at the end of the night with a standing ovation.[61]

Without doubt, that was less a reflection on the play than on what a *Guardian* reviewer called "some hollow concept of celebrity."[62] Fans who had only seen Madonna from a great distance at Wembley Stadium were thrilled to see her in an intimate setting. An army of friends who turned up for opening night—Donatella Versace, Sting, Trudie Styler, Elton John, and Stella McCartney among them—threw their support behind her.[63] Guy Ritchie was there, too, but rather than reassure her, he made Madonna more nervous because she said she wanted to impress him.[64]

David Williamson called opening night "bizarre. Every celebrity you could think of was there. I overheard Sting being interviewed at the end and he declared the play very witty. I'll take that from Sting."[65] Critics were, however, unconvinced. Said one, "Madonna made her West End stage debut last night and it was, frankly, a belly flop. She tries hard but she's as flat as a flounder."[66] A *Guardian* critic wrote, "Madonna is not positively bad: just technically awkward."[67]

The *Sunday Telegraph* critic was one of the few who went gently on Madonna: "The most striking aspect of her performance is the amiability, even sweetness, that she projects. If she is putting it on, she is a brilliant actress indeed. If not, she is no more than competent. But under the circumstances that is good enough."[68]

Fans didn't care about the critics. If anything, as the play continued and criticism mounted, they became more rabid. By its last weekend, in July, the crowds standing outside the theater were so great that police erected barricades and patrolled the area from the sky in helicopters. In those days of heightened security, Madonna's presence created an additional threat. "They were at their wits' end!" Laurence Boswell said. "It was like a riot."[69]

The play's run ended on July 13. In words that echoed her reaction to *Speed-the-Plow* thirteen years earlier, Madonna said of her work in London, "I ended up with a headache every night from crying...Sometimes I'd show up for work in a happy mood, and I'd just think, I don't want to be sad; I don't want to go where my character has to go tonight—but I can't fake it. The part was exhausting."[70] There was talk of moving the play to Broadway, but Madonna said no. She needed a break. She needed creative and spiritual restoration.[71] The Ritchie family packed up and headed back to Los Angeles.

In that city utterly lacking in spirituality, Madonna found sustenance in Kabbalah. She had been studying it since 1996, and by 2002 it had become an integral part of her life, her family's life, and her work. She once said of her pre-Kabbalah self, "What was I thinking before I was thinking?...I don't miss being an idiot."[72]

The Madonna who wrote *American Life,* who had political and social statements to make, did so through the lens of Kabbalah. It taught, she said, that "the only thing that matters in life is your relations with people...The philosophy is, if you really stripped [it] down,...love your neighbor as yourself." She said it also taught that "nothing is what it seems, and the more tinsel there is on something, the less real it is."[73]

Madonna tried to structure her life around Kabbalah's teachings. If a change in her attitude wasn't always evident, the outward trappings of her belief were on display. She wore a red string on her wrist to ward off evil. She drank pricey Kabbalah water. "It's from Canada and certain kinds of prayers by highly enlightened persons affect the molecular structure of the water," she told writer Steven Daly.[74] She associated with Kabbalists and worked to persuade her friends to attend classes, too.[75]

Though she still considered herself a student, the Kabbalah Centre leadership in LA seemed to some observers to use her as a trophy, placing her and Guy at the center of its social activities. "After service on Friday, there would be a dinner and of course at the head rabbi's table would be Madonna and Guy sitting next to him," Christopher said. "All these other people would be in the room who had been doing it for years, but they had never been able to sit with the rabbi. So what they were teaching was completely at odds with what they were doing."[76]

Another troublesome aspect of Madonna's Kabbalah studies involved ego. Control of one's ego is a central tenet. Supporting a community or working for the broader good can only be achieved if people suppress their personal desires. In the context of marriage, however, that raises worrying issues. The suppression of a woman's ego was traditionally part of the marriage contract and had long been sanctioned by the world's major religions. During those delicate first years of marriage, when Madonna wanted, as she often said she did, to please Ritchie, Kabbalah validated self-denial as a way to do so.

After the constraints of the play and the conservatism of the London theater scene, and amid a home life steeped in a marital tradition that she accepted willingly but could not help but chafe against, Madonna swung wildly back toward the razor's edge with two projects that August. Both were meant to fulfill seemingly conventional obligations: a fashion magazine photo shoot and a video for "Die Another Day." Both could have been accomplished quickly and easily in exchange for generous pay and critical approval. In each case, Madonna chose to take the most difficult path, regardless of money and criticism.

The first project was for *W* magazine. That spin-off of the fashion industry mainstay *Women's Wear Daily* was where photographers who made statements, not pictures, showed their work and where designers who wanted their clothing to be associated with the ultrahip in fashion, film, and art hoped to see it. That Madonna had never appeared in the magazine before was something of a mystery.

As early as 1989, *Vogue*'s legendary editor Anna Wintour chose her to be the first celebrity to grace that magazine's cover. Since then, she had appeared on the covers of magazines around the world. By 2002, Madonna *was* fashion. Everything she wore became a trend; every designer she worked with became a star; every fashion show she attended became a media event.[77]

Thirty-seven-year-old photographer Steven Klein, even more than Steven Meisel, was an un-fashion fashion photographer. A Klein image was about his vision first, the subject second, and if clothes were involved, they were only there to illustrate and enhance priorities 1 and 2.[78] "It's my world and the world beneath the surface," he said. Shades of gray were his natural palette; subterranean his preferred location; despair, violence, and filth his favored motifs. Sexuality in Klein's world tended toward S/M and what curator Neville Wakefield called "sexual surrealism."[79]

Inspired by Picasso and Francis Bacon, Klein had studied painting at the Rhode Island School of Design. He had no interest in becoming a photographer, but photography had been part of his life since childhood.[80] In

1985, after leaving RISD, he concluded that he wasn't a good painter, and, in need of cash, he picked up a camera to shoot an ad campaign for Christian Dior in Paris. A year later, he moved to New York and set up a studio.[81]

Klein was magnetic, what one writer called "unnervingly seductive." Of his subjects, he said, "I like them and I fear them—I *do* fear them... but at the same time I desire them"—though not sexually. Klein said, "I keep myself out of that equation."[82]

He wasn't every fashion magazine's photographer, but for those unafraid of provocation—*W* among them—he was *the* young master. He had done shoots with Brad Pitt, David Beckham, and Justin Timberlake that showed those pinups in their least flattering light—and made them more interesting figures in the process. He had an idea that he wanted to shoot Madonna, too.[83]

Over the course of several months in 2002, he and Madonna exchanged emails. Klein's attitude toward his work matched hers on almost every level. If he was the un-fashion photographer, he was also the anticelebrity photographer. *New York*'s Simon Dumenco wrote that Klein was "selling a darker version of celebrity at a particularly idiotic, giddy juncture in pop culture."[84] It was the same dark side of fame that Madonna would cover in *American Life.*

Meanwhile, Klein told *W* magazine about the possibility of a shoot with Madonna, which she expressly did not want to be about fashion. "If I don't feel that I'm creating something that means something," she said, "I don't want to do it." With that in mind, Klein and Madonna began to talk about a performance piece documented in photos.[85]

For one day in August, over a period of ten hours, using fifteen cameras and sets worthy of a film shoot, Klein took pictures of Madonna. In them, she wore clothes by some of the world's greatest designers: Yves Saint Laurent's Rive Gauche, Dolce & Gabbana, Prada, Christian Lacroix. But that wasn't what arrested the viewer's attention. It was Madonna as a contortionist atop a table; Madonna sitting on a filthy mattress like a woman in an asylum; Madonna in a heavy ceremonial dress and beaded face veil, paralyzed into immobility by the weight of her garment; a wedding dress aflame while Madonna, in a beaded mask, stretches like a panther and watches it burn.[86]

According to writer Vince Aletti, the shoot that would appear over forty-four pages in *W* finally elevated Klein into the pantheon of "auteur" fashion photographers.[87] After that shoot, he would also join Madonna's court. He became one of her closest friends and her photographer of choice on magazine shoots, album covers, concert tours, and a short film. Klein would be to Madonna in the 2000s what Herb Ritts had been to her in the

'80s and Steven Meisel and Mario Testino were to her in the '90s. Klein said he "connected" with Madonna because she was willing to go where his pictures took him, and that was very, very far.[88]

Not long after her work with Klein, Madonna and a team of artists from the Swedish video-directing collective Traktor began her second big commercial project: shooting the video for her James Bond single. One of the Traktor team, Ole Sanders, had been in Prague working on a Prodigy video when he received a letter and an unfinished song from Madonna. "We initially thought it was a joke, as the letter was long and handwritten," Sanders said. "But the song sounded suspiciously like her." Sanders had a drink to settle his nerves and arranged to go to London to see parts of the Bond film and meet with Madonna.[89]

That encounter ended with all sides interested. Through emails, Sanders and colleagues Mats Lindberg and Pontus Löwenhielm offered ideas to which Madonna responded with "concise, unequivocal and occasionally entertaining" comments.[90] After all that back and forth, the video's messages became simple and crystal clear. One, according to Madonna, was "Don't fuck with me." The other was "Pain is an illusion and death is just a doorway."[91]

The three Traktor directors, with Madonna's regular cinematographer, Harris Savides, shot the video in Hollywood over the course of six days. It incorporates references to the Bond film (North Korean villains, Madonna's character Verity, and iconic Bond props) as well as to the meaning of Madonna's song. The video's sets represent two battlegrounds: an interrogation room where Madonna fights an external enemy and a space inside Madonna's head where she fences with herself.[92]

Madonna was banged around a good deal during the shoot. She is thrust against a wall; her torso is slammed onto a table; her head is dunked into icy water; her body is dragged roughly by two men. And in the next instant, she performs a dance of pure mad sexual defiance. Covered in sweat and dirt, bruised and battered, trapped in a seemingly hopeless situation, she leaps onto a table, hangs from a chain, and rolls on a floor of broken glass.

In the video (and in reality), Madonna performs in a room full of men, but she seems the toughest of them all. During the shoot, when the director called "Cut" at the end of the interrogation segment, there was silence followed by a gasp at her strength and audacity—then applause.[93]

In the fencing segment, "enlightened Madonna" vanquishes "ego Madonna" by killing her. In the interrogation segment, Madonna also wins, but to do so, she has to die. At the start of the story, her tormentors laugh at her while they beat her. After she has overcome her fear, she laughs at them.[94] The video depicts Madonna as having been electrocuted, but instead of her body, her tormenters find burned into the electric chair the Hebrew letters she had tattooed on her arm: lamed, aleph, vav.

Michael Berg, one of Madonna's Kabbalah advisers in Los Angeles, explained that the letters form one of the seventy-two names of God and are associated with curtailing the power of the ego. The tefillin straps that she wraps around her arm as she prepares to die on-screen, he said, represent an end to selfishness and a desire to share. The use of both the Hebrew lettering and the tefillin caused a minor uproar because, for observant Jews, the name of God should never be used in a vehicle as worldly as a music video and a Gentile woman wearing the tefillin crossed the line into sacrilege.[95]

Madonna had offended Catholics, the Christian community as a whole, Hindus, and now Jews. Parts of that community, who were already indignant over the "fast-food" version of Kabbalah being offered by the Berg family at the Kabbalah mother ship in Los Angeles, were exasperated anew by her display. But other religious scholars weren't so sure that her performance was entirely bad for Judaism.[96]

"It vibrates with piety and blasphemy, a great combination," said Rodger Kamenetz, a retired professor of religion and an expert on modern Judaism. "There's a sense of violation and a sense of homage, and that's complex." Others hoped she might inspire lapsed Jews. "If the biggest rabbis in the United States said you should keep kosher, nobody will pay attention," said Rabbi Ephraim Buchwald, director of the National Jewish Outreach Program in Manhattan. "But Madonna..." There was no need for him to finish his sentence.[97]

Swept Away was released in the United States on October 11 to horrendous reviews. The *Washington Post* said of the film, "It's as awful as you've heard and as bad as you've imagined." *Rolling Stone* declared, "It's the movie that's a shipwreck."[98] The film remained in cinemas for three weeks and disappeared with only $600,000 of its $10 million cost recouped from US ticket sales.[99] It was scheduled to be released in the UK, but Columbia TriStar scrapped the plan. Critics there had already pronounced the film a disaster.[100]

The flood of negative press hadn't receded by the time Madonna's Bond song, "Die Another Day," was released as a single, on October 22. It was as if music critics felt obligated to dislike it as much as film critics had trashed *Swept Away*. Madonna had been hired to update the Bond brand for the new century, which was precisely the excuse critics used to pillory her. They thought she and Mirwais strayed too far from the hallowed Bond tradition.[101]

But as always, the fans told the story of a Madonna song's worth. In the States, "Die Another Day" hit number 1 on the Billboard Hot Singles chart and number 8 on the Billboard Hot 100. That was Madonna's thirty-fifth song in the top ten of that chart, which pushed her past the Beatles and one song behind Elvis. She also displaced fellow Detroiter Aretha Franklin to become the female artist with the most Top 40 hits ever. Finally, "Die Another Day" did what the film's producers hoped it would. It became the highest-charting Bond song since 1985.[102]

In November, the film premiered at Royal Albert Hall, in London, and for once Madonna wasn't the main attraction: Queen Elizabeth was there. Madonna was visibly giddy when she was introduced to her, even after Her Majesty admitted she didn't know who Madonna was.[103] Madonna could hardly be offended; everyone else knew exactly who she was. That fall, *Vanity Fair* called Madonna "the biggest imported star [London] has seen since Wallis Simpson." And *she* was an American for whom a British king had abdicated the throne.[104]

Die Another Day would make more than $400 million at the box office. It was the most financially successful film Madonna had ever been in. And with that, her feature film acting career was over, but not her love of cinema. Within a few years she would begin directing movies, including one about that other American — Mrs. Simpson.

In the years after Herb Ritts's AIDS diagnosis, he worked like a demon, trying to outrun the clock. He shot fashion photography; he shot portraits of his famous friends; he shot in Africa, where he found a subject grand enough to satisfy him. But through it all, his health had deteriorated. He didn't complain, but his friends could see it happening. He was thinner inside his Prada suits, and his face almost always had a Band-Aid on it to cover a Kaposi's sarcoma lesion.[105]

In December of 2002, Ritts was hired by *Vanity Fair* to photograph Ben Affleck riding a motorcycle on a parched lake bed at El Mirage, California. The bike that Affleck rode around in circles kicked up thick dust that settled like a cloud as fog rolled in. Everyone felt it in their lungs, and some of the crew got sick from it. Herb did, too. Within days he was at UCLA Medical Center with pneumonia, checked in under the name Mike Scooter. Two days later, he was on a ventilator.

So many people converged on the hospital that staff tried to limit Ritts's visitors. Madonna wasn't allowed in until his partner, Erik Hyman, rescued her from waiting-room hell and snuck her into Herb's room.[106] Despite Maria Shriver's rosaries, k.d. lang's Buddhist beads, and Madonna's Kabbalah bracelets, which they all clung to at a bedside vigil, by Christmas Day Herb was in a coma. The next day, he was dead.[107]

Three hundred people gathered at LA's Paramount Theatre to remember him. Madonna delivered a eulogy, recalling the twenty years she had known and loved Herb, the work they had done together, and, more important, the fun they had. Her voice cracked as she described him and as she tried to convince herself and the crowd that he wasn't gone. "Just because we can't see Herb doesn't mean that he's not here. And just because he's gone from our sight doesn't mean that he has ceased to exist."[108] He had merely walked through the door of death before they did.

Museum curator Malcolm Rogers said, "Herb immortalized a world that was immensely creative. A world without barriers of class, race, or sexuality...He celebrated this world—and celebrated, I think, is the right word, for his work is essentially joyful." Herb and his work existed in what he called the golden hour, which was the light he liked to shoot in. That was the light he gave to his friends, and that was why they loved him. In a dark world, his memory was something to cling to.[109]

Chapter 45

Los Angeles, London, New York, 2003

I'd like to change the world, not conquer the world.[1]

— *Madonna*

Someone once said of pioneering feminist Margaret Fuller that she had as many skins as an onion. That had long been true of Madonna, yet it still perplexed people. Who was she? If anything, in 2003 it became more difficult to say. At various points in her life, she simultaneously inhabited two diametrically opposed personas. In high school, friends were bewildered by her extrovert-introvert dichotomy. While endeavoring to conquer hetero Hollywood, an effort that culminated in *Dick Tracy,* she challenged that closeted culture with her grandest artistic tributes to homosexuality: "Vogue," the Blond Ambition tour, and *Truth or Dare.* During the period of her most outrageous sexual adventures, she made the PG film *A League of Their Own.*

In 2003, she would project an even more complex combination. She was, on the one hand, an adoring mother and wife, a figurehead for a religious group based on ancient Jewish mystical texts, and the tweed-clad lady of an English country manor. On the other hand, she adopted Che Guevara's iconic beret-clad image for her latest musical persona as she challenged the US government on war and US society on its obsession with celebrity.

The two Madonnas confused her audience. That year, the twentieth anniversary of her professional debut, would be one of her least understood and most criticized. What troubled critics was what had always troubled them about Madonna. She wasn't either-or; she dared to be everything.

Throughout the entertainment world after September 11, benefit concerts brought in millions of dollars for its victims, and artists wrote patriotic songs and verse that memorialized, even romanticized, that tragic day. White House officials encouraged Hollywood executives to promote "patriotism and loyalty" on the big screen.[2] Few questioned aloud *why* the attack had occurred. Bruce Springsteen did with his album *The Rising,* but he could be forgiven because he had made a very public show of support for the victims' families and because he was historically red, white, and true. Besides, he was almost a folkie at that point, a performer in a genre that sanctioned such soul-searching.[3] In the US entertainment world generally, however, stars were expected to leave their politics at the stage door. A poll taken in 2002 found that most Americans disapproved of actors injecting it into their work.[4]

Traditionally, for pop culture figures it was more acceptable to be a scoundrel than to have a political opinion. Frank Sinatra had Mafia ties, which was okay for a young man from New Jersey. But it was not okay for him to be known as the civil rights advocate he was. His activism was considered more potentially damaging to his career than associating with criminals. That unspoken rule was even more ironclad for women. Folk singers like Joan Baez could perform at as many protests as would have her, but a female pop artist was expected to exist in a fantasyland called neutrality.

Madonna had always been an anomaly in that regard. She said what she wanted about whatever she pleased, however injudiciously, and dared the suits to try to stop her. But she hadn't done that in almost a decade, not since her *Sex* period. After 9/11, with the Bush administration hankering for an expanded war, into Iraq, she could remain mum no longer.[5]

Madonna decided to make an antiwar statement. The inspiration was filmmaker Michael Moore. She had seen her friend and fellow Michigander at a performance in London in November during which he criticized the "comfortable class," who even in the face of atrocities—whether school massacres or a reckless rush to war—did nothing. "Nobody wants to get their hands dirty...Nobody wants to get hurt. We've all given up," he exclaimed.[6] Madonna said afterward, "I felt like, 'Okay, I'm ready to go! I'm starting a revolution by myself!' I felt so inspired."[7] She enlisted Jonas Åkerlund to help her.

In February 2003, in Los Angeles, they began shooting a video for "American Life." By then, war in Iraq was a foregone conclusion. The secretary of state, Colin Powell, had just delivered a speech to the United Nations justifying a US invasion based on the belief—what he called the "evidence"—that Saddam Hussein's government possessed weapons of mass destruction.[8] Madonna said,

> I felt the threat of war looming over us, and...I wanted to make a video that was going to wake people up and say, "Hey, stop being distracted by all of your entertainments, TV, fashion shows, you know, superficial life. There's a real war going on here, or about to go on here, and we have to do whatever we can to stop it."[9]

And it wasn't just Iraq, she said. "At any given moment there's at least thirty wars going on [in] this world and I'm against all of them."[10] She and Åkerlund created a visual commentary on war and the culture of selfish ignorance that allowed it to happen. It was released on March 31, 2003. The timing could not have been worse.

After threatening to invade Iraq for nearly a year, on March 20, the Bush administration did so. It did not have the support of the international community. Even many Americans failed to see the necessity of war. But in those "you're with us or against us" times, voicing such concerns was dangerous.[11] For an entertainer, it was potentially career-ending.

In late 2002, Sean Penn took a very public stance against the war, buying a full-page ad in the *Washington Post* in which he accused President Bush of taking a "simplistic and inflammatory view of good and evil" and begging him to save the country from a "legacy of shame and horror." Other reliably left-wing actors had taken similar positions, but Sean crossed the line when he went to Iraq to see what was happening.[12] He returned even more outspokenly opposed to the invasion. As a result, he said, he was dropped from the lead in a film because he would not promise to stop his antiwar campaign.[13]

Then, in early March, a three-woman Grammy Award–winning Dallas group, the Dixie Chicks, made an antiwar statement during a concert in London. Singer Natalie Maines said, "We do not want this war, this violence, and we're ashamed that the President of the United States is from Texas." That free speech cost them corporate sponsors and triggered a radio boycott of their music and a sales boycott of their records. Fox commentator Bill O'Reilly called them "callow, foolish women who deserved to be slapped around."[14] Afterward, entertainers feared that they would be "Dixie Chicked" if they said too much. Antiwar entertainers became like gay actors in Hollywood. Only their friends knew for sure where they stood.[15]

Madonna's antiwar statement was bigger and more inflammatory than Sean's or Maines's.[16] The Drudge Report website said she had created one of "the most shocking anti-war, anti-Bush statements yet to come from the show business industry."[17]

In her video, models dressed in "commando chic" (which was, in fact, all the rage on the catwalk that season) parade before an approving, well-heeled audience while images of war appear on huge video screens behind them. Meanwhile, in a public bathroom nearby, Madonna and a group of agitated women prepare for battle. After carving the words PROTECT ME into a toilet stall, Madonna and her comrades move out on their mission.[18]

Back at the fashion show, children wander onto the runway only to be shooed away by soldier models, much to the amusement of the crowd. At that point, Madonna and her femme fighters roar onto the runway in a modified Mini Cooper and spray the audience with a water cannon. The audience is delighted. Soon gravely injured US soldiers crawl along the runway, and still the crowd is amused. Nothing penetrates their shield of privilege.[19]

The injuries on the runway become more horrific: a young woman runs along it with her clothing aflame; the bodies of men dressed as US soldiers are tossed about in the air. Meanwhile, on a video behind them, maimed children roam bombed streets, and grieving mothers cradle dead babies. The callow fashionistas are on their feet. *Bravo! Bravo!* At that point, Madonna tosses a hand grenade to a man in the front row who looks like President Bush. This finally gets the crowd's attention, and everyone gasps in anticipation of an explosion. None comes. The grenade is a lighter, which "Bush" uses to fire up his cigar.[20]

The video was made while the invasion was still being debated. By the time Madonna released it, the war had begun.[21] She withdrew the video after one day, saying, "Due to the volatile state of the world and out of sensitivity and respect to the armed forces, who I support and pray for, I do not want to risk offending anyone who might misinterpret the meaning of this video."[22]

Madonna's decision also coincided with the dramatic end of one of the most fraught early episodes of the war. A nineteen-year-old West Virginia soldier named Jessica Lynch was captured by Iraqi forces during an ambush in late March. On the day Madonna pulled her video, US Special Forces rescued Lynch in a raid that received wall-to-wall media coverage. By then, Lynch had become everyone's daughter. Releasing an antiwar video at that moment would have been seen as unforgivable.

The Madonna of 1989, 1993, or even 1996 would likely have stood by the video. But Madonna the wife and mother could not. Her destiny was no longer her own. She told an interviewer that spring that she didn't want to "compromise" her family.[23] She told another, "I did it because I didn't want people throwing rocks at my children on the way to school. I did it for them, not for me."[24] Madonna's decision nonetheless shocked her fans and the music world.

Five years later, journalist Sal Cinquemani wrote, "The backlash Madonna likely would have suffered...would have made the whipping she endured following *Sex* seem like harmless roleplay."[25] But he wished she had not pulled the video, which he said turned her song "into a startling comment on the obscenity of war and materialism—one that would have undoubtedly been looked back on as brave."[26]

On April 16 she released a second version of the video, also directed by

Åkerlund, in which she sang in front of the flags of many nations.[27] The album *American Life* was released soon afterward. The cover featured Madonna as an amalgam of Patty Hearst and Che Guevara—with a beret on her head and the added touch of a razor-blade kiss over her eyebrow. It topped the charts in fourteen countries but didn't sustain that early interest and became the lowest selling of all Madonna's studio albums.[28]

Critics attacked its music. Madonna and Mirwais had sought to keep it raw, even to the point of discordance. "Too much electronic music has been used for fashion and is overly popularized," Mirwais said.[29] But most critics didn't make the connection between the lyrics' message about the danger of celebrity culture and the album's intentionally blemished sound.

Madonna's lessons on the hollowness of fame were also generally dismissed. Comments by the *Washington Post*'s David Segal were typical of the criticism: "The stardom-as-mortal-burden idea is among the more insipid cliches out there, and it's especially absurd coming from Madonna."[30]

Even the sincerity of her antiwar stance was met with skepticism. Jessica Winter, in the *Village Voice,* wrote a withering critique, saying she did not believe Madonna was protesting the war but rather profiting from it as "an ugly American, loud and ignorant and hopelessly cocooned by good fortune."[31]

Madonna promoted her album in dozens of interviews and television appearances in the United States and Europe as well as at record stores— HMV on Oxford Street in London, where five hundred people crammed into the shop to hear her, and Tower Records on 4th Street in New York, before a smaller crowd. She also promoted the album at a Paris restaurant for her celebrity friends and regular folks who won a radio-station competition.[32]

She was trying to cut through the morass of controversy and misinterpretation, but it was exhausting. She told a Swedish interviewer that spring, "I've pretty much grown to expect people to not understand what it is I'm trying to say, so if they do it's a pleasant surprise."[33]

Two extremely different projects helped Madonna survive that spring. On April 24, the week her album was released, she appeared on the gay-friendly TV sitcom *Will & Grace.* She had agreed to do the show in January, and taping began in mid-March. If the timing for her "American Life" video was terrible, the timing for her appearance on *Will & Grace* was exceptional, albeit accidental.

That very month the *New York Times* ran its first same-sex wedding announcement when playwright Tony Kushner married magazine editor Mark Harris. Their marriage wasn't legal; it was a political statement made as the Supreme Court considered an issue that would fundamentally affect gay life — whether sodomy was a crime. If it ruled that it was not, then gay men were not criminals and could live their lives freely and openly.[34]

Gay rights, like women's rights and civil rights, progressed in fits and starts. The battle for equality, much less security, was far from won. At that critical moment, Madonna supported the community by appearing on a prime-time television show that portrayed a gay man in a positive light.

Several days later, she returned to the safety of her downtown roots at Jeffrey Deitch's SoHo gallery, Deitch Projects, where she was the subject of a provocative photography, video, and sound installation.[35] Deitch had already worked with Steven Klein on a photo exhibition. "He said, 'I have another idea,'" Deitch recalled. Klein told him he wanted to do a show based on his *W* magazine photo shoot with Madonna the previous summer. Deitch challenged him, saying, "'We've got to think bigger. If you're doing this project with Madonna, it's not just hanging your photos.' He agreed, and he ran with it."[36]

It became an installation called *X-STaTIC PRo=CeSS,* a reference to Madonna's song on *American Life* and the fact that she often found the process of creating, during which a work is imbued with possibility and still belongs to the artist, more rewarding than the finished result. The entire gallery was redesigned by the architectural firm LOT-EK into a series of bijou theaters in order to house five works from the Klein-Madonna photo shoot. Klein had enlarged the images and made them more than mere photographs. They became moving pictures using computer-generated imagery.[37]

Deitch said,

> What was especially interesting for me was how engaged Madonna was, not like the normal artist I work with who comes in and hangs out. She personally got involved in every aspect of the show: the layout, the visuals, the sound, the graphics, the text. And I've never experienced this from any artist in the several hundred exhibitions I've put on: she edited the press release word by word, line by line, changing punctuation, commas. She was that focused.[38]

The title *X-STaTIC PRo=CeSS* was also her decision. "That's completely, 100 percent Madonna," Deitch said.

> Even the choice of the gallery attendant had to be approved, so it was all a unified artistic statement. And that's what she does with her concerts, her books. I'm not sure there's anyone else who goes to that extent to unify every aspect... It was a total work of art.[39]

The centerpiece of the show was a CGI version of a photograph Klein took of Madonna wearing a beaded mask and kneeling in an industrial space, with a coyote straining on a leash nearby as a wedding dress burns like an eternal flame. The image was housed in a specially fabricated "shed" that made it appear to be actual activity taking place in another room or another dimension. Madonna's voice could be heard reciting passages from the book of Revelation.

Madonna considered Klein an artist, but Klein said he would "never consider what I do art." That was because he didn't see a hierarchy in his activities—fashion photography versus art photography. He simply created.[40] It was a position Jeffrey Deitch understood. "I saw that there was a whole new group of younger people primarily who did not differentiate between aesthetic stimulation in art, music, fashion, writing. It was all equivalent." And that felt familiar.[41]

Deitch, like Madonna, came out of the downtown scene of the late '70s and early '80s, that glorious "convergence period" when art crossed every border and artists came together to create revolutions. He wanted to restore that sense of wonder. "I was thrilled with the reaction," Deitch said of the show. "It brought in this whole new audience who loved it."[42]

New York Times art critic Roberta Smith, however, called the images "derivative... tacky and overwrought. They are not art; at best they are stills from some unusually egregious music videos."[43] Separately, Deitch himself was criticized by the art establishment. "They said that I'm selling out, I'm not serious," Deitch recalled. "But no, I always saw Madonna as somebody who extended what an artist can be today. Because there is a visual, conceptual attitude about everything she's done, and the visuals of Madonna are so strong." He added, "She's a performance artist who had a genius to take it mainstream."[44]

Madonna would turn forty-five in 2003, and the chatter about her having passed her use-by date was as pervasive as it was cruel.

In March, Lynette Holloway, in the *New York Times,* declared at the start of a feature article on Madonna that she "may be looking at the final stages of a long career." Apparently ignoring the fact that the year before, Madonna had surpassed the Beatles' milestone of having the most top ten hit singles of any recording artist in history, Holloway offered, "It has been so long since Madonna has had a hit that radio stations are wondering if listeners want to hear her new material." She quoted a radio trade publication executive who said it wasn't clear whether Madonna was still relevant or whether she appealed to that crucial consumer cohort, the "kids." But, he added magnanimously, she "deserves the benefit of the doubt." It was the equivalent of "Hey, give the old broad a shot."[45]

Asked by NBC's Matt Lauer to respond to that article, Madonna said:

I don't see the point of writing those kinds of articles. At the end of the day, what is the relevance of Aretha Franklin? What was the relevance of Frank Sinatra? What is the relevance of all artists? Do we have to fit into an age group and appeal to a specific audience to have relevance? That's absurd. It's disrespectful and absurd.[46]

Madonna was not in any way at the "final stages" of her career. By May, she had begun talking about another tour. It was too early to give up on *American Life*.[47]

On June 23, she premiered a video for the album's second single, "Hollywood." The song topped US dance charts after its release, in late May, and did well in Europe, but it failed to chart in the Billboard Hot 100. It was Madonna's first single in twenty years not to. She hoped the video would breathe new life into the song.

Shot in early June in Los Angeles with her "Open Your Heart" and "Justify My Love" team of Jean-Baptiste Mondino and Pascal Lebègue, the video illustrates Madonna's vision of Hollywood, which she called a "city of dreams, a city of destruction, of superficiality, whatever. It's a place to go and get distracted from what's really important in life . . . You can lose everything. You can lose yourself."[48]

Mondino found "artifice" to be such a broad category that they decided to focus on showing "the beauty, the scariness, the sexiness, and the loneliness" as well as the humor of the city.[49] They did so in part with an homage to the late French photographer Guy Bourdin, who also inspired some of Madonna's *Sex* book shots.

The video opens in a tacky motel room, a place where Hollywood dreamers frequently find themselves and from which some never depart. Looking like a 1930s corseted ingenue, Madonna straddles a TV set. Between her legs, the screen features a "show" of Madonna hitchhiking, trying to catch a ride to glory. The video then switches to flash card–like scenes of Madonna as various "old Hollywood" icons: working the phone like a wanton Rita Moreno, dancing in a pink satin outfit in a pink mirrored dressing room like Rita Hayworth, lounging like Jean Harlow or Mae West in a posh hotel. Madonna herself appears getting Botox injections and playing with a large blue yoga ball like a doll on Benzedrine.[50]

The Technicolor tour of Hollywood's desperate spaces is a little like Mondino's tour through a Paris hotel in "Justify My Love," except that it is Madonna in some form in all the "Hollywood" sets. In the earlier video, she seeks pleasure. In the later one, she seeks fame. In "Justify My Love," she finds satisfaction. In "Hollywood," she finds clarity. The Madonna

astride the television finally has the good sense to pull the plug. The calm
that descends on the room and on the viewer shows Hollywood and its
trappings to be what they are—a gaudy illusion.[51]

Having finished the video, Madonna had two more showcases lined up
for her song. On July 30, "Hollywood" was featured in a Gap ad she did
with hip-hop star Missy Elliott. It was an odd marriage—not Madonna
and Elliott but Madonna and Gap. A brand associated with blue jeans and
T-shirts being promoted by a star associated with haute couture? A
shopping-mall brand sold by a woman who had just released her most controversial album in ten years?

Unlike the tremulous Pepsi of 1989, Gap was a company that thought
provocative ads for its highly unprovocative clothing were a good thing. It
had used counterculture figures before to great success, from footage of
Beat writer Jack Kerouac to ads featuring LSD king Timothy Leary. In
2003, Gap, the world's largest clothing retailer, needed a boost from
Madonna, the world's biggest star.[52] It had followed the market and focused
on "trendy, teen-oriented clothing," but that market was saturated, and
Gap had suffered two years of falling sales. What it sought was someone to
make the brand look cool again.[53]

Madonna could do that. She was a walking klieg light—just signing her
brought Gap priceless columns of news coverage. And she would resonate
with the traditional Gap customers, people in their midtwenties to early for-
ties, who needed clothes for themselves *and* their children. BabyGap and
GapKids would benefit from the appearance of one of the world's best-
known celebrity moms. The September issue of *Harper's Bazaar,* which hit
the newsstands in early August, featured Madonna resplendent in Gap, diamonds, and a hint of black fishnet. The message: Gap moms are exciting.[54]

Madonna stood to gain from the ad, too. She reportedly received $10
million for her services and was given a showcase for her music, which
would be a mash-up of "Hollywood," "Into the Groove," and a bespoke
rap by Missy Elliott.[55] The Gap campaign included eight weeks of TV and
print ads beginning in late July, plus a second campaign in early
September.

The TV commercial opens with Madonna in tank top, jeans, heels, and
what a Gap executive called "twenty million dollars' worth of ice," walking
through a film-studio lot, singing "Hollywood."[56] A sneakered Missy Elliott
appears in more Gap gear—bomber jacket, T-shirt, jeans—rapping. The
two women bounce off each other musically and physically as they make
their way toward a soundstage and a dance-off between them and their
crews.

The imagery was all about generations—how the two women move
differently, sing differently, yet come together. For the purposes of the ad,

what binds them is Gap clothing, but the bigger message is that they are both strong women: one white and middle-aged, one Black and young, expressing themselves in an atmosphere of mutual respect. Missy Elliott said,

> I always dreamed of working with Madonna 'cause I always felt like if I had any kind of connection with any artist it would be Madonna. What she do in her field, she's edgy, she's not scared to take risks, and that's pretty much me on the hip-hop rap side.[57]

On August 28, one month after the Gap ad premiered, Madonna and Missy Elliott appeared together at the annual MTV Video Music Awards. Madonna sang "Hollywood." The next day, she and it were in newspapers around the world.

Madonna had tried to ignore the commentary about her age and about the fresh pop talent eclipsing her in record sales, but ignoring it hadn't worked. She used the VMAs to take control of the narrative, to give that younger generation her blessing, so she could move on. She was scheduled to perform the opening number with thirty-two-year-old Elliott and two pop princesses—twenty-one-year-old Britney Spears and twenty-two-year-old Christina Aguilera.

The sugar pop that launched Spears and Aguilera in the '90s was dead. Four years before, Spears had sold twenty-five million records. Her most recent album before the VMAs, released in 2001, sold less than half that. Aguilera was in the danger zone, too. Her transition from cute to "trashy" had nearly killed her career. It was a perilous moment for both women.[58] Emerson College professor Kristin Lieb, who specializes in music marketing, said that the industry considered female pop stars "short-term person brands" who are every bit as disposable as that sounds.[59]

The VMAs number would be built around a wedding theme. Spears and Aguilera would appear as brides in white singing "Like a Virgin," as Madonna had done in 1984, when they were still in diapers. Madonna would appear as the groom, dressed in black, singing the cautionary tale "Hollywood" to the young women who risked being gobbled up and destroyed by the fame game.

The segment was short on production values but full of referential moments. A figure stood atop a cake as Madonna had once done, her face covered by a veil. When the veil was lifted in 2003, it was Spears. Aguilera came from around the side of the cake and gave the song a more fulsome sound before the two of them descended to the floor and rolled around, re-creating Madonna's infamous display. Mendelssohn's wedding march interrupted their folly, signaling Madonna's appearance atop the cake.[60]

The concept incorporated Madonna's hopeful past with "Like a Virgin" and her cynical present with "Hollywood," and it signified her position in the entertainment hierarchy: she had become "the man." But all those good, potentially poignant ideas were lost in a kiss, or a pair of kisses. Madonna had ingested a bit of bad advice and spoiled her message.

It was choreographer Jamie King's suggestion. "I wanted her to do a kiss on the MTV awards—kiss Britney, kiss Christina—and she was like, 'What?' I said, 'It's a marriage, and at the end of the marriage you kiss.'"[61] Madonna was game, and so were the younger women. It was to be a quick kiss bestowed on both young women by the "groom," who was, coincidentally, their musical mother. During the actual performance, however, Britney opened her mouth.[62]

Madonna said she was caught off guard, but "I'm a showgirl...We learn to roll with the punches...If someone comes at you with their lips slightly parted, you have to kiss them." Asked by Oprah Winfrey if she was making a sexual statement, Madonna said, "I made those statements ten years ago."[63]

Both kisses combined might have been missed in a blink. But photographers captured the moment, and MTV, knowing from rehearsals that *a* kiss, but not *that* kiss, was coming, stood ready with its cameras to pan the crowd for a reaction. It settled on Spears's ex-boyfriend Justin Timberlake, whose expression was enigmatic but was described by the press afterward as a disapproving frown. Guy Ritchie most definitely *didn't* approve, according to Madonna, but the camera missed his response.[64]

Immediately after the kiss, the third Madonna musical offspring, Missy Elliott, appeared onstage to join the trio. At that point, the stage came to life, and the image became one of women as power, women in charge of their own destinies, even if Spears and Aguilera looked a little lost in the mix. The segment ended with the four joining hands and singing the line in "Hollywood" that lambasted radio stations.[65]

Unfortunately, no one remembered that part of the performance. The Britney-Madonna kiss became the story. The *Entertainment Tonight* presenter breathlessly reporting after the show even ignored the night's winners and led with "Can you believe Britney's open-lip lock with Madonna? The room was blown away!" It was not the first time two celebrity women kissed on camera. But the VMAs kiss felt bigger than Jennifer Aniston and Winona Ryder smooching on *Friends* for ratings. It felt like a cultural turning point.[66]

It was a most unfortunate episode. The problem wasn't the act—for some young women, it was no doubt as exciting to see that kiss as it had been for some young men to see Gabriel and Salim in *Truth or Dare*. The problem was the environment. The kiss furthered the soft-core-porn "lesbian" fantasy of blonde on blonde, which didn't exclude men; it was done *for* men. Madonna, who had never advocated a woman's sex "for" anyone but herself, who had put her career on the line to defend that freedom, seemed to have given its inverse her seal of approval that night.[67]

In their 2008 book, *The Porning of America,* Carmine Sarracino and Kevin M. Scott wrote that Madonna "has been arguably the most influential figure in the last three decades urging women to take control of their own sexual and professional lives." But, they wrote, she has "also been part of the general sexualization of American culture, and of young women in particular."[68] By 2003, in pop culture, an "empowered" young woman meant one thing: she was "hot." You can deliver a message, but you can't control how it will be received or used. That kiss that night turned into one of those confusing moments.

In the whipsaw world that was Madonna's life, her next stop was back in London for the launch of her first children's book, and even *that* was controversial, with critics questioning whether she could be entrusted with a child's imagination.

Madonna hit upon the idea of writing children's books because the ones she read her children were without "moral messages." She was also tired of the passivity taught to girls through books.[69] The feminist lessons she embodied had been easily co-opted. Maybe if she reached a younger audience, they had a better chance of taking root.

Madonna told her stories using Kabbalah as her guide.[70] The first, *The English Roses,* illustrated by Jeffrey Fulvimari, was about five eleven-year-old girls based loosely on Lourdes and her British friends at school. The lessons they learned were about jealousy and envy. Proceeds from the book's publication went to Spirituality for Kids, a Kabbalah Centre program that tried to provide children with the spiritual tools they need in life.[71]

More than a million copies of *The English Roses* were printed in thirty languages for publication in one hundred countries. In the United States alone, it was sold in fifty thousand locations. Not surprisingly, it immediately topped children's book charts nearly everywhere. In the UK, where a bespectacled Madonna in a floral-pattern dress presided over the private book launch–tea party, it was second only to J. K. Rowling's fifth Harry Potter book, which was released at the same time. Within a month, *The English Roses* eclipsed it, topping UK hardcover fiction bestseller lists.[72]

The book's promotion took Madonna into the land of women's TV and domestic magazines. During those interviews, she invited readers into her home. She said she and Guy based their lives around the children. "We get up with them in the morning. I get my daughter ready for school. I spend time with my son before he goes off to his daycare. Either Guy or I am always with them at dinner, and we spend evenings together."[73]

She said Guy called her "wife" or "wiff," or "the Missus" or even "mum." She said she distanced herself from some old clubbing friends because "I'm on a spiritual passage and they're not."[74] She also said she wanted another child. "But because of my exercising and this, that, and the other, I've kind of screwed up my cycle a bit and I'm going to the doctor's to make sure I'm OK to have a baby."[75]

On *The Oprah Winfrey Show,* another side of maternal Madonna was revealed. At the start of that year, she had befriended a seventeen-year-old Canadian named Kerri Yascheshyn, who was dying of liver cancer. They met through the Make-A-Wish Foundation, but after their initial encounter, Madonna kept up the friendship, calling Kerri every day. The child died on February 9, and soon afterward her friend wrote to Oprah describing Kerri and Madonna's relationship. "Madonna was Kerri's angel," she said. "She is the reason Kerri woke up every morning."[76]

But neither those moving disclosures nor Madonna's professions of domesticity and spirituality convinced some commentators that she should call herself a children's book author. One of the most powerful TV news personalities in the United States at the time, Diane Sawyer, pinioned Madonna with her eyes during an interview and asked, "What moral right do you have, after writing *Sex,* to do a children's book?" Taken aback, Madonna answered,

> I don't understand that question. I have a right to write any book I want about anything. The books I am writing now are a reflection of who I am and what I value in the world, and when I published *Sex,* that was a subject that I was interested in exploring.[77]

Undaunted, Madonna released the second book in her series, *Mr. Peabody's Apples.* Its November launch was even wider, and its stay at the top of the *New York Times* bestseller list was longer. Critics dismissed it as weak.

Chapter 46

Los Angeles, New York, Dublin, London, 2004

I don't want people to dress like me anymore...I want them to think like me.[1]

— *Madonna*

BY THE END of 2003, four singles from *American Life* had been released, including "Nothing Fails" and "Love Profusion." The reception was mixed for all of them, but not on the dance floor. *American Life* became the first album ever to have seven top ten songs on the Billboard Hot Dance Music chart. Madonna's core fans were out there. She would go on tour to find them, and unlike Drowned World, this show would give them what they wanted.

She had reportedly thought of calling her tour the Whore of Babylon, but given the war in Iraq, where Babylon is located, and the absolute certainty that the word *whore* would ignite a controversy, Madonna went with the name Re-Invention. It was a word she loathed because it had been used to belittle her artistic evolution, yet she chose it because it suited what she had in mind. She decided to cover some of her old songs by reinventing them. The idea was a win–win. Her fans had long wanted to hear her sing their favorites, and she kept things interesting for herself by remixing them.[2]

It had only been two years since Drowned World, but Madonna was ready for the therapy a tour provided. Re-Invention would be longer, and include more performances, than either of her two previous tours.[3]

There was also another reason to get out there. The download future had arrived. Warner Bros. Records was the first of the major labels to sign on to Steve Jobs's iTunes scheme, which would charge listeners just ninety-nine cents per song. The cost to the artist was enormous. For each download, Apple took twenty-two cents, which left a mere seventy-seven cents to be split among the record label, music publisher, and the artist.[4] Tours were becoming the best way to reach the most ears and earn the most money.

Amid those industry changes, Madonna had begun negotiating her exit from Maverick Records in the summer of 2003. Meeting with Time

Warner chairman Richard Parsons, she said she wanted $60 million to sell her 30 percent stake in the company. Parsons balked, saying the record label was only worth half that. The wrangling continued with suits and countersuits until June of 2004, when Warner bought Madonna's share of Maverick for $17 million. Guy Oseary became the CEO.[5]

The Maverick buyout freed Madonna from a burden that had once been a joy. "It's really hard to have children and a relationship and two careers, really, and run my record company and try to have a social life," she said.[6]

After Maverick, Madonna created a smaller operation comprising manager Caresse Henry, assistant Angela Becker, and publicist Liz Rosenberg.[7] Madonna called them the Semtex girls, which she defined as "a girl who is dynamic, a girl who explodes, a girl who doesn't know the meaning of nine to five, a girl who is unstoppable and doesn't take no for an answer...I rely on them as much as they rely on me. I can't do what I do without their help...We're a team." She added, "Guys can be Semtex girls, too."[8]

When Madonna began planning her next tour, she did so by sitting down with Caresse and Jamie King. Madonna wanted to "revisit" her old songs, incorporate elements of Kabbalah, and express her disapproval of war. In short, she said she wanted to "enlighten and entertain the audience...One of my goals was that every person in the audience should leave knowing that each of them could make a difference in this world." She also wanted to express her appreciation to her fans for sticking by her for twenty years. "I think this show is my personal thank you to them."[9]

A call for "strong and versatile" dancers went out in February. "Choreography will be unpredictable...anything goes!" the ad said.[10] Auditions were held in New York that month and in Los Angeles in March. "You get unbelievable dancers, the best," Madonna said. "But I also do get a lot of cuckoo people who like to dress up like me. People who think they look like me. People who've just been released from a lunatic asylum."[11]

What she sought were individuals who were actors and performance artists as well as dancers. "We always give them combinations to do, but then I always let them freestyle or show me what *they* do," Madonna said. "I'm always drawn to the people who have something *very* special that I've never seen before, even if it doesn't fit in with what I'm doing. I end up building the show around it. So it's great."[12] Out of thousands of people trying out for the tour, twelve dancers and one skateboarder were chosen.[13]

She was helped in her selection by Jamie King, who would again be tour director and the show's main choreographer, as well as by a young woman named Stefanie Roos. Roos had worked with Madonna on some of her most important videos, beginning with "Human Nature," and served as Madonna's doppelgänger when she wanted to watch a performance from the point of view of the audience. With each project, Roos's responsibilities grew. On the Re-Invention tour, she was assistant director and assistant choreographer.[14]

In addition to King and Roos, Madonna summoned back Stuart Price as musical director, Monte Pittman on guitar, and Arianne Phillips to style the show, with costumes by Jean Paul Gaultier, Christian Lacroix, Stella McCartney, and Karl Lagerfeld at Chanel.[15] Donna De Lory got the call to reunite with Madonna as backup singer.

Donna had had a daughter, Sofia, the year before. Another artist might not have been inclined to take a single mother with a one-year-old, a nanny, and the inbuilt uncertainty of that situation on a world tour. But Madonna was at that stage in life, too. Donna said when she first told Madonna about her pregnancy, Madonna supported her 100 percent.

> She said, "It's a miracle, a blessing. This is where you're supposed to be.". . .
> In the early days, I used to go to her room to get pimple cream, and now I'm asking advice about being a mom. So there's a beautiful story there of that evolution and her as a big sister.[16]

Donna joined the tour. "I loved the work, but it was very stressful, obviously . . . I would literally run off the stage, go out to the motorcade, and go home and put my kid to bed . . . I'd give her a bath in my full makeup and sweaty costume and put her to bed." Madonna, she said, wrote her notes saying, " 'I know how challenging this is.' She would always show that compassion."[17]

Niki had had a daughter, too, a baby she named Jordan Ann. Those three mothers on the road would have given a whole new meaning to woman power, but Niki didn't join the Re-Invention tour. Professionally, a change had occurred during the Drowned World tour, when Niki's and Donna's roles were diminished under Jamie King's direction. That change was exacerbated by a growing rift between Niki and Madonna.[18]

Niki said with fame, and under Kabbalah and Guy Ritchie's influences, Madonna had become distant personally.

> As the SUPERSTAR atmosphere enveloped the environment, the line between the haves and the have-nots increased. The superstar illusion was out of hand for *me*. She was inaccessible. It went from being a superclose friend watching movies in bed together to me having no access to my sister

friend. Now I know I simply missed my friend, and I understand what we now call being *canceled*. I didn't understand then.[19]

Madonna and Guy had bought a new home on Sunset Boulevard with seven bedrooms, twelve bathrooms, a home movie theater, a pool house, a tennis court, and a gym, all situated on a one-acre-plus lot in Beverly Hills.[20] There, Madonna's social life increasingly reflected her spiritual life, and it was as suffused with Kabbalah as her mother's and grandmother's homes had been suffused with Catholicism.[21] By 2004, Madonna had been studying Kabbalah for seven years, but, she said, only recently had it come to "inform" her life.

> It took me a long time before I could go from the girl sitting in the back of the class wowed by all the information, keeping notes, to thinking, there is a point to this life, now I know why there's chaos and suffering and pain in the world, and I can actually do something about it.[22]

Madonna had taken the Hebrew name Esther after the "courtesan who became queen" and saved the ancient Jewish people from annihilation. It wasn't a name she used but one she adopted for the same reason a Catholic chooses a confirmation name — to identify her "metaphysical" self.[23]

Her studies at the Kabbalah Centres in Los Angeles and London were as intense and consuming as her physical workouts were in the '80s, when she learned she could transform her body through hard work.[24] Madonna's goal in her spiritual studies was to, among other things, be "more liberated from my ego, less concerned what people think of me." She would make that easier by choosing to surround herself, personally and professionally, with like-minded individuals.

Madonna reportedly distanced herself from some people who did not study Kabbalah and tried to persuade others to study it.[25] "When she was living on Roxbury, that was when she was getting into it," Christopher said. "When she was on Sunset, that was when she was trying to get everybody else into it."[26]

Christopher said she "blackmailed" him into taking classes. "I use that term in an artistic sense. Maybe another word is better." He was about to finish decorating the house on Sunset, and worrying that his drug use had become more than recreational, Madonna refused to pay him unless he went to the Kabbalah Centre. They settled their money dispute, and he went with her to classes.[27]

"She thought it would be helpful, and in many ways it was. I did get a number of things that were useful to me, but as an institution I just can't be part of it." He said the environment the Bergs cultivated seemed antithetical to Kabbalah's teachings. "It was all celebrities," Christopher said. The studies amounted to "breaking down your ego in a room full of egotists."[28]

Christopher had suspected that part of Jamie King's appeal for Madonna was that he was so agreeable. In 2003, he noted that his sister began wanting only "yes" people near her. "She was just kind of tired of people disagreeing with her, like me. 'Why is there a life-sized photo of you in the kitchen?' I was too close."[29] Some old friends also didn't fit in with her new life, Niki among them.

That year, Debi Mazar and Madonna threw Niki a baby shower, but Madonna called and told her she was "really out of it" and had been so busy that she couldn't make it. Then phone calls went unanswered, emails, too. "The abruptness of how it ended—I thought, 'Wow, I thought we were sisters. I thought we were beyond just employment,'" Niki recalled.[30]

Echoing Christopher, Niki said she recognized that the new people around Madonna were intent on pleasing her rather than challenging her. "I watched, as they say, the court change," Niki said.

> I watched all the disciples that stood around her change. All the virtue signaling. I remember when everyone had red strings around their arm. It's like, "None of y'all are studying Kabbalah...I got it, it makes you feel closer to Caesar."...
>
> The deepest part of me has nothing at all but gratitude. I'm a Black woman from a seriously oppressed culture in America, in Michigan, where I didn't even know to dream to be on stages like that...But I think she and I both knew it: if we didn't separate, there was going to be a big blowout. It's just better. Let's just call the whole thing off.[31]

Donna said,

> The last time the three of us performed together was Drowned World. It was 9/11. I knew that it was harder for Niki. She had her own issues with her ankle, physical things...I think it was just natural. Niki comes from this whole jazz background. We're both artists in our own right. She was doing jazz festivals with her dad as well as her dance singles, and I think she just thought that would be more sustainable for her.
>
> And the way things had evolved with Madonna, they were more like buddies, like best girlfriends. [Madonna and I] stayed professional. We'd hang out, but it was always professional. But Niki had more of a buddy relationship with her, and that had changed.[32]

For Donna, not having Niki on the tour "was really hard. I missed her so much. I missed what we had onstage first and foremost. Niki missed it, too, realizing that we all weren't going to do this again. But I was happy for her that she was more at ease in her life."[33]

Siedah Garrett was picked to replace Niki. She was an LA-born singer-songwriter who had cowritten Michael Jackson's hit "Man in the Mirror" and had recorded and toured with him.[34]

The last piece to be finalized before rehearsals began in earnest was to find a director willing to document the tour. Twelve years after Alek Keshishian's *Truth or Dare,* Madonna wanted to create a similar "visual journal" that depicted her as a wife, mother, and more mature artist.[35] Madonna had asked Keshishian to do it, but he declined. Now that she had a family, he wouldn't be as free to shoot as he had been.[36] Madonna asked Michael Moore. He wanted to, but he was making *Fahrenheit 9/11.* He asked her to delay the tour, but that was impossible.[37] Madonna then asked Jonas Åkerlund, and he said yes.

With that, Madonna and her crew were ready to work, and that was her favorite part of the process. "When you're putting together a show," she said, "it's like life during wartime. Everyone has to pay attention. No one can fuck up." She said she wished she could live with "this kind of mindset all the time. I love it. I love the energy of it. And I love the idea that we're creating something together, that there's a unity."[38]

The concert would, as usual, be broken into "acts," starting with a Versailles segment that would, appropriately, begin with "Vogue." Madonna had not worn costumes from that era since performing that song at the VMAs after the Blond Ambition tour. The show then segued into a military segment, which was a reenactment of her withdrawn "American Life" video. By 2004, opposition to the Iraq War was widespread, and statements like Madonna's could be made without fear of retribution. The military, or martial, section was followed by a circus-themed act and what she called her Scottish tribal segment, the latter featuring Madonna and cast in kilts.

The connection between the various acts was the notion of one world — that the peoples of the world were all capable of sharing love but impeded from doing so internally, by emotional wounds or self-constructed barriers, and externally, by forces that stoked fear. Madonna's message was: Think big by going small. Help the world by helping yourself. Help yourself by loving the people around you.[39]

Madonna's most globally themed and spiritually based show to date would occur at a time of great religious polarization, when factions from Asia to the Middle East to North America had retreated to their corners, preparing for a fight. In the United States, a fundamentalist Christian message had taken hold in the aftermath of 9/11 that spread widely as evangelicals greatly expanded their pop-culture presence.

By 2003, contemporary Christian music was the industry's fastest-growing segment. *Seventeen* magazine added a faith section, and the publisher Harlequin launched a new Christian romance series.[40] The bestselling Left Behind end-of-days fiction series, written by Reverend Tim LaHaye, the cofounder of the powerful Christian-right group Council for National Policy, and evangelical Christian writer Jerry B. Jenkins, sold sixty-two million copies and spawned a children's series and two films.[41] Mel Gibson's 2004 movie, *The Passion of the Christ,* earned more than $600 million at the box office globally.[42]

What those latter books and films had in common was an adversarial narrative based on Christianity and three apparent means to protect it: vengeance, violence, and oppression. Madonna's tour would offer a spiritual counternarrative about tolerance, peaceful coexistence, and love. All three were as difficult to find in the world at-large as they were at times in her own life.

The Re-Invention tour opened at the Forum in Inglewood, California, on May 24, 2004, and was scheduled to end four months later in Lisbon. The million or so fans who bought tickets encountered the Madonna they knew and loved. Though her concert was at times difficult politically, she exuded the warmth and inclusivity that had been absent from Drowned World. She engaged with her cast onstage and with her vast audiences in the halls. She opened her heart, and they returned the gesture.

The concert began ominously with five minutes of Steven Klein's *X-STaTIC PRo=CeSS* photos of Madonna on billboard-size video screens and her voice reading from the book of Revelation. Just as the weight of those images and words began to feel oppressive, she offered an alternative. The strains of "Vogue" could be heard. That freedom anthem had offered relief during the darkest days of AIDS, and now it offered relief amid the religious crusades mounted against anyone identified as "other" in the United States and beyond.[43]

Madonna rose through the stage, seated on a platform, wearing an eighteenth century–style corset and thigh-high boots. One of the most stunning visuals in Madonna's career was created during that opening. While on her platform, she moved into an Ashtanga yoga headstand, her booted legs silhouetted against the bright white of the video screen.[44]

From the start it was clear that Re-Invention would not include the elaborate staging of Madonna's early tours. In fact, there were even fewer sets than there had been in the sparse Drowned World tour. What made the concert unique was the stage itself.

At the center was a forty-two-foot-wide, ten-foot-high turntable. The front of the stage was crisscrossed by moving walkways. And, fifty-eight feet above, was a grid that allowed dancers to drop from the sky, Madonna and company to perform twenty feet above the audience on a suspended cat-walk, and the show to move in what seemed like four dimensions.[45] That added dimension came from King's reliance on screens. He had five video screens, the largest weighing seven tons, custom-made for the tour.[46]

The screens could become rooms in front of which Madonna and her dancers performed, artworks that morphed before the audience's eyes, religious symbols, battle scenes, words, or giant disco balls. It was visually stunning, though the theatricality of the performance was diminished—except when Madonna and her dancers performed "American Life."[47]

That segment was the concert's most complex. It showed clips from Madonna's censored video on-screen behind the performance as the danc-ers battled onstage and reenacted the fashion show of the video, this time decked out in religious garb because that was the new battlefield.[48]

Singing "American Life" at Madison Square Garden in the aftermath of 9/11 was as moving and heartbreaking as singing "Live to Tell" in that same arena during the worst of the AIDS crisis. The audience in New York, where the carnage began, held small US flags aloft. It wasn't so much an act of patriotism as an act of remembrance.[49]

The world had come to believe that Washington went to war knowing that Iraq did not possess weapons of mass destruction, and the citizens of some of the countries that supported the US invasion suffered gravely as a result. Just that March, ten bombs were planted on commuter trains in Madrid, killing 191 people. The attack was directed by Al Qaeda in Iraq in retribution for Spain's support for the war. And then, the following month, the pain on all sides of the war turned to fury.

From the start of the so-called war on terror, there had been criticism over the arrests and torture of suspects at CIA black sites around the world. That extrajudicial detention became de facto US policy when the prison at Guantánamo Bay, Cuba, began holding suspects in 2002. But even that prelude did not prepare the world for images broadcast by CBS News in April of 2004 from a prison west of Baghdad.

They showed US service members physically, psychologically, and sex-ually abusing Iraqi detainees. The photographs were terrifying in their inhumanity. The actions of those men and women in uniform fueled anti-American sentiment globally. Whatever moral high ground the United States had occupied after September 11, whatever those flags held aloft in New York once represented, was lost in the cells at Abu Ghraib.

Performing in a military uniform, Madonna slowed her song consider-ably from her album track so that every word mattered. When she sang "this type of modern life is not for me," she no longer meant just money, fame, and the obsession with celebrity; she also meant war and the degradation that came with it.[50]

During one of her six New York shows, Michael Moore was in the audience. Madonna stopped the performance to recognize him. At the time, he was being lambasted for his film *Fahrenheit 9/11,* in which he questioned the official September 11 story, the justification for the invasion of Iraq, and the business community's support of the war. The film had just won the Palme d'Or at Cannes, which only increased the attacks on Moore because he was seen as being embraced by European critics of US foreign policy. From the stage, Madonna thanked her friend for "sticking his neck out, for going against the establishment, for giving us all hope." She added, "The world needs more people like you."[51]

Interviewed after the show, Moore said he was "stunned" by what she said. "It was like everything kind of went into slow motion in my head... I think a lot of people tonight were very moved by what she said, the songs that she sang, the video up on the screen." He cited an image of Israeli and Palestinian boys walking arm in arm that was projected behind her as Madonna covered John Lennon's song "Imagine." "Man, everybody had tears in their eyes around me because everybody wants to live in that world," Moore said. "Everybody is sick and tired of the way it is." Not everyone. Some booed Madonna's remarks about war. One man said, "I thought I was coming to a music show. I didn't think I was coming to a political Democratic convention."[52]

Guy and the children followed the tour along its route. After the concerts, while Madonna changed out of her costume, he played host to special guests who gathered backstage. In Chicago, it was Madonna's father and stepmother, Joan. During that concert, when Madonna sang "Mother and Father," from *American Life,* she did so flanked by screens showing the Catholic imagery she grew up with. She sang the song to Tony Ciccone, who told Madonna after the show that it was "probably the most positive concert you've ever put on."[53]

During *Truth or Dare,* Tony had, at times, felt like a prop. In film footage Åkerlund shot during the Re-Invention tour, he was a person. That was because Madonna finally understood him. She told an interviewer that year that after she had her own children, his plight as a single parent "fell on my head like a brick—all the sacrifices my father had made for my very big family. I felt really bad for all the hard times I gave him."[54] He in turn said he understood *her* most controversial periods as being part of her growth. Theirs was a new, calmer relationship. But she still wasn't his favorite singer. Madonna said he preferred Celine Dion, who looked like her cousin Loretta.[55]

Because Madonna's tribe was now British—or Scottish by marriage—an Edinburgh-based bagpiper named Lorne Cousin was recruited for the show. Cousin had a day job as a lawyer but took a few months off with his firm's permission to tour the world with Madonna. His most important part of the concert came during "Into the Groove," when he not only played bagpipes while Madonna sang but also did a solo dance with her.[56] Missy Elliott also had a cameo in that song, appearing on video doing her Gap rap.

In Ireland, the tribal part of the show was a huge hit. It was Madonna's first time performing in that country, and nearly seventy thousand people bought tickets to stand in a field outside Slane Castle to hear her.[57] When the cast and crew arrived to rehearse, the stage was wet and the weather cold. Madonna tried coaxing the turbulent clouds overhead to cooperate, first singing the 5th Dimension's song "Aquarius/Let the Sunshine In" and then praying to God to delay the rain until eleven thirty that night. Neither the song nor the prayer worked, though there was a full moon visible between the thunderclouds.[58]

Madonna was terrified for herself and for the dancers, but there was no possibility that the show would be canceled. "I felt so much love and joy in the audience," she said. "I couldn't believe the people...just stood there for six hours in the rain" before the show.[59] Fellow Detroiter Iggy Pop was her opening act. Seemingly oblivious to any form of pain or discomfort, he performed his segment shirtless. And then it was Madonna's turn.

When she sang "Nothing Fails," she stood outside the stage canopy and was pelted with rain. The dancers weren't bothered by the elements, either. They were awestruck by the size of the crowd and the dazzling setting with a castle as a backdrop. "The rush of danger involved, and the eighty thousand fans, made it worthwhile and possibly the most incredible show we had done," said dancer Mihran Kirakosian.[60]

The concert ended with two songs: "Music," for which the entire cast was dressed in kilts, and "Holiday." Twenty years before, Curtis Hudson said, he wrote that song in response to a world gone mad. As of 2004, it had not become saner. As she performed it in front of flags of every nation, with confetti shooting out over the crowd, Madonna returned to her message of unity. One world, one people. Hope.

Concert reviews along the way were generally positive.[61] David Segal, the *Washington Post* writer who had been so critical of *American Life,* said,

> Madonna has created a new performance hybrid, one that lifts and blends elements of Broadway, Cirque du Soleil, Rock the Vote rallies, art installations, extreme sporting events, church sermons, disco dances and

gun-spinning military drills...Here's the weird part: it's not a mess. It's actually kind of amazing...It's hard to leave this epic extravaganza feeling anything less than awe.[62]

Based on Billboard statistics, Re-Invention was the highest-grossing tour of 2004, earning $125 million and selling out all but one of its fifty-six dates.[63] Young women performers, who feared their careers would reach an expiration date when they were in their thirties, were inspired. Beyoncé, Jennifer Lopez, Lil' Kim, and Kylie Minogue, among many others, had taken early career cues from Madonna. With Re-Invention, they had a template for their later years.[64] The Sugababes' Heidi Range said, "She's the ultimate role model for a woman in the music industry." Pink said simply, "She was my god."[65]

Madonna's young wannabes, who were now adults, were inspired, too. As Re-Invention arrived in London, Barbara Ellen wrote in *The Observer* that for twenty years Madonna

> has been an inspirational global totem for the women who have grown up with her. It would appear to be the case that Madonna has become more and more important to these fans as the years have gone by...For many it is a strange mixture of comforting and exciting just to feel that Madonna's still around, doing her thing, putting out great records, loving her children, digging her man, practising her dance routines...Unlike most men, who have spent over twenty years debating whether Madonna was too slutty (or not slutty enough) for their tastes, it was always more about friendship than sex for us...
>
> Add to that the music, the style, the humor and the sanity (see Prince and Michael Jackson for what could have happened) and not for the first time Madonna, circa 2004, starts looking positively indispensable.[66]

Gay fans, too, embraced the return of their Madonna. After feeling alienated by the darkness of Drowned World and its hard-rock heterosexuality, they could see Re-Invention Madonna as one of them. She was singing the songs they loved, and their lives paralleled hers once again.

In June of 2003, the US Supreme Court ruled that sodomy was not a crime, which opened the door to the possibility of gay marriage. On Valentine's Day in 2004, the San Francisco mayor, Gavin Newsom, officiated at a wedding ceremony for two women. That ceremony, and Newsom's order earlier that month that San Francisco's marriage license application eliminate references to gender, changed history. In February alone, more than four thousand same-sex couples were married in San Francisco. It wasn't the end of the fight, but it was a major victory.[67] Madonna's life trajectory took her on the path many of her gay fans hoped to travel. They, like her, wanted stability in a legal lifelong relationship, something that had once seemed out of reach.

It had taken Madonna many years to feel at home and accepted in England.[68] By 2004, she was. In November, she was inducted into the UK Music Hall of Fame. The Rock & Roll Hall of Fame, in the States, didn't consider admitting artists before the twenty-fifth anniversary of their first record. That meant Madonna had four years to go. The Brits had no such requirement. She was honored as the only woman inducted at the hall's inauguration, along with the Beatles, Bob Marley, Elvis, U2, Cliff Richard, the Rolling Stones, Queen, Michael Jackson, and Robbie Williams.

British visual artist Tracey Emin presented Madonna with the award, while Gwyneth Paltrow, in a Blond Ambition gold corset, and Stella McCartney, wearing a "Material Girl" pink gown, contributed a filmed tribute for the ceremony.[69] The three women would reunite with Madonna in December to help celebrate her fourth wedding anniversary at the Ritchies' country house, Ashcombe.

During her tour, Madonna confessed to Jonas Åkerlund's camera, "I got married for all the wrong reasons. And when my husband didn't turn out to be everything I imagined he'd be, I just wanted to end everything."[70] That line was seized upon by reporters looking for evidence that Madonna's second marriage was on the brink of collapse. Inconveniently for that narrative, her quotation continued and said the opposite.

> It's not easy having a good marriage. But I don't want easy. Easy doesn't make you grow. Easy doesn't make you think. I thank God every day that I'm married to a man that makes me think. That's my definition of true love.[71]

Madonna was committed to making her marriage work, and the country estate in Wiltshire was part of that. There, Guy could play at being a landed gentleman, and Madonna could play at being a country lady with a bohemian bent. Ashcombe was that kind of place. Its previous owner, photographer Cecil Beaton, called it "essentially an artist's abode" where he entertained H. G. Wells, Salvador Dalí, and Diana Vreeland, among many other notables. "We played; we laughed a lot; we fell in love," Beaton wrote of his sanctuary.[72]

Madonna and Guy had fallen in love with the eighteenth-century estate, set on more than one thousand acres of rolling hills not far from

Stonehenge. The original house was long gone, but part of a stable and the laundry building remained. The Ritchies restored them and, having made the laundry into a residence, called Ashcombe home. "I go for lots of long walks, ride my bike," Madonna said.

> It's a very physical place, a place for adventure. You can choose to go there to work in a very undistracted way and a very contemplative way, or you can go there and get lost in the environment. I always feel really melancholic when I'm driving away. You feel protected... It's a kind of buffer against the world.[73]

So thoroughly and convincingly would Madonna inhabit the role of country gentlewoman that the following August, the pride of Pontiac, Michigan, would come in second in the Town & Country festival's "face of rural England" competition.[74] She would also be ranked number 10 that year on *Country Life* magazine's annual Power 100 of the Countryside list.

For their anniversary party at Ashcombe, Madonna invited her friends to put on a show. She found a play called *The Town Wench, or Chastity Rewarded,* which a British film producer had created for one of Beaton's parties in 1937. A scene from that play, which Madonna called "really funny and so bawdy," would be her and Guy's contribution to the evening.[75] "Gwyneth and Stella and Chris composed a song together, which was brilliant," Madonna said, "a spoof on 'American Life,' only they called it 'American Wife.' Gwyneth did a fantastic rap and Stella sang background vocals and, well, Chris played the piano."[76]

The Chris at the piano was the Coldplay lead vocalist, Chris Martin. Paltrow had become an American transplant to Britain after marrying him the previous year and having her first child. Since then, the creative triumvirate of Madonna, Paltrow, and McCartney had grown closer. They were formidable women walking the tightrope of motherhood (McCartney was pregnant), marriage, and career and helping one another remain aloft and balanced.

Madonna was especially in need of support. After fifteen years of working together, she had fired her close friend and manager, Caresse Henry. Kabbalah was reported at the time to be the reason. Some people said Henry thought Madonna was too involved with it; others said Madonna believed that Henry had violated Kabbalah's teachings of faithfulness by having an affair with Madonna's security guard while both had other partners.[77] Whatever the reason, it was a sad parting.

Madonna told an interviewer that fall, "I need to calm myself. I don't have a manager anymore, so now I'm my own everything." That, coupled with domestic duties, left her exhausted. "That's really my problem now," she continued. "I no longer have time to be creative."[78] And that was where her friends came in and why their folly was so nourishing.

The story coming out of that weekend was an old one: a tired wife and a happy marriage. By the same time the next year, that would no longer be the case.

Chapter 47

London, Tokyo, 2005

Fuck everything, let's dance.[1]

—Madonna

ONCE SETTLED AGAIN in Britain, Guy was back on creative terra firma, shooting a new gangster movie called *Revolver* with his pal Jason Statham.[2] Madonna could have used a break, but Warner wanted another album, which she was contractually obligated to provide. She told them, "I don't have any more ideas, I'm tapped out." Her pleas were ignored, so she went to Stuart Price's apartment to play around without a particular direction in mind. The single that would become "Hung Up" was the startling result. She said it "resonated so monstrously" that she decided to make a dance album.[3]

> I didn't want to over-think things too much...I made a lot of political statements in my show and in my film...so I moved to another area and that's "God, I really feel like dancing right now.".... It's not just a reaction to what I was doing work-wise, but also a reaction to what was going on in the world. I just wanted some relief.[4]

She told Price, "Let's just keep writing in this direction and see what happens."[5]

When Stuart listened to a song, he heard where other music might be slotted in to add another dimension to the track. On "Hung Up," he wanted to use a portion of the ABBA classic "Gimme! Gimme! Gimme! (A Man After Midnight)."[6] But it wasn't at all certain that ABBA's Björn Ulvaeus and Benny Andersson would allow him and Madonna to sample the song. "I had to send an emissary to Stockholm with a letter and the record, begging them, imploring them, and telling them how much I worship their music," Madonna said. They took time to think about it but eventually said yes.[7]

That song set the tone for the album. *Confessions on a Dance Floor* would be Madonna's disco album. It would be informed by the past—Giorgio Moroder, Marc Cerrone, Chic, the Bee Gees, and, yes, ABBA—but re-created to suit the times. There would be no ballads. There were no breaks between songs. The goal was to keep bodies moving.[8]

Dancing was another casualty of the post–September 11 world. The British government banned even legal raves because they supposedly presented a terrorist target.[9] And yet the world needed to dance in 2005 the way it needed to dance during previous periods of social turmoil, going back to the days of disco's founding, during World War II. "I wanted to lift myself and others up with this record," Madonna said.[10]

Price lived in West London's Maida Vale neighborhood in a two-room flat with a low attic studio reached by a ladder. It was there that he and Madonna wrote her album. Surrounded by piles of records and old equipment, she recorded her vocals seated in a broken chair.[11] "I couldn't have made this record anywhere else but up here," she said.[12] "It was so liberating...I want to be in a small place with no furniture. I want to keep it...the way it was when I started, sitting on the floor and scribbling in my notebook."[13]

The music emanating from that attic would soon be heard around the world, but for the moment it was their secret. "The guy next door says, 'Was that Madonna going into your house yesterday?'" Price recalled. "I said, 'No it's just my friend.' 'Nice car,' he said, and I said, 'She really does well for herself.' They haven't quite cottoned on."[14]

Though he was nearly twenty years her junior and from a different planet culturally and socially, Price enjoyed a friendship with Madonna that was warm, comfortable, and genuine. At that point, they had worked together for five years on two tours, numerous special performances, remixes, and one song for *American Life:* "X-Static Process." Madonna considered Price a "brother." She recalled arriving at his place after he'd been up all night working.

> Stuart would answer the door in his stocking feet...I'd bring him a cup of coffee and say, "Stuart your house is a mess, there's no food in the cupboard." Then I'd call someone from my house to bring food over for him. And then we'd work all day.[15] Usually, I work with people in the studio and we have a slightly more formal relationship. That's not how it is with Stuart and me.[16]

Price said that during the five or six weeks they spent in his apartment, they were

> like two kids...They always say that an album sounds like the time that you had making it. I know that with [*Confessions*] it was a super-productive time, but it was also really fun and natural. And I think that comes across in the way it sounds.[17]

Making a record, he said, is "95 percent mistakes... You're just waiting for the 5 percent of magic to happen. And the more comfortable you can make someone feel, the greater the chance that that's gonna happen." That's what he did with Madonna. He made a safe space so they could get down to the magic.[18] "She has this thing where she can turn the microphone on, open her mouth and one of those melodies comes out and you go 'Blimey! That's how you've done it!' "[19]

Their relationship left room for disagreement because it was fostered in an atmosphere of trust. Madonna said songwriting was "very intimate... especially when you write lyrics and sing them in front of someone for the first time... To me, singing is almost like crying, and you have to really know someone before you can start crying in front of them."[20]

What they did in the studio together was laughably simple, direct, and real compared with the layers of production and market analysis that went into creating most big albums at the time. In the early 2000s, a song-testing service called HitPredictor (purchased by radio giant Clear Channel) could forecast a song's success by test-marketing chopped-up two-minute remixes. Another service, Hit Song Science, used a computer program to overlay an entire CD onto previous "hit clusters" to determine whether the "songs conform to the mathematical pattern of past hits."[21]

Music factories, meanwhile, found, cultivated, and trained the talent that sang the songs. In South Korea, "cultural technology" was developed that even dictated the color of eye shadow a pop star should wear in order to be most appealing to a particular regional audience.[22] That was the world that existed outside Stuart Price's sanctuary.

"Hung Up" would be the album's lead single. It declares with manic intensity that Madonna and Price are taking the listener hostage to their sound, not just while they're listening to the album but also afterward, when its choruses and emphatic beats continue to occupy the brain the way dancers stumbling onto the street still hear and feel a club's throbbing bass.

The lyrics of "Hung Up" are nearly lost to the strength of the music, but they, like those of most of the songs on the album, tell the story of a relationship in trouble. In "Hung Up," it is the frustration of waiting for a call that never comes and a declaration that it is too late for the absent lover to make amends. There is no moping involved. Madonna's boots are made for walkin', because—"ticktock"—there is no time to waste.

An alarm clock introduces the next song, "Get Together." The impatient lover of "Hung Up" has met someone new. Is it love at first sight? Is that even real? Maybe not. But it feels as good as the silky song sounds. It seemed almost impossible after "Hung Up" that the next song on the album could be as good. But it is. "Get Together" describes romance de-romanticized and yet still worth seeking on a dance floor.[23]

"Sorry" begins with expressions of apology in five languages, but it is not the singer who is sorry. As in "Hung Up," there is a ne'er-do-well in the picture trying to apologize his way out of a misdeed. The singer won't have it. The takedowns in "Sorry" are classic. Vocal backup on the song is provided by Neil Tennant of the Pet Shop Boys.

An anomaly on the album is the Madonna–Stuart Price song "I Love New York." It is a silly song, but it reminds her fans that no matter how far she has wandered into the British countryside, she still considers New York home. "It is more a state of mind than a place," she explained.[24] "New York is my favorite city because that's where I learned to breathe."[25] "When I walk down the street anywhere people say, 'Oh, there's Madonna,' but in New York the cops are like, 'Hey, you're back.' "[26]

Madonna and Stuart Price were joined on the song "Jump" by Madonna's brother-in-law, Joe Henry, who brought Madonna the idea.[27] Like Henry's previous song "Don't Tell Me," "Jump" is about freedom. In a few simple verses, it describes Madonna's career, her rush toward new challenges, her fearlessness before the abyss, and her need to move on after she has learned what she can from a person or place, because again, the clock is ticking.

The song "How High" appears after "Jump" for the fun of it, according to Madonna. It returns to the fame question. "I'm not a reluctant pop star," she told Simon Garfield of *The Guardian* that year. "I'm very grateful and happy for everything that I have and for things when they go well." But, she said,

> When I'm standing at the golden gates, I'm sure God doesn't give a shit how many records I've sold or how many number one hits I've had. All he gives a shit about is how I behaved, how I treated people. So understanding that, and still doing my best making records, is the conclusion I've come to.[28]

Confessions would not be a Madonna album without controversy. Rabbis criticized her for the song "Isaac," which they said was a song about sixteenth-century Kabbalist Yitzchak Luria.[29] She called it absurd that these men who had never heard the record accused her of blasphemy. "It's interesting how their minds work, those naughty rabbis," she said.[30]

In fact, the song is named for her friend Yitzhak Sinwani, a Yemeni Jewish singer who taught at the Kabbalah Centres in LA and London. Madonna had heard him sing and was so moved that she cried. She and Price invited him to the studio to record without knowing what they would do with the results or what *he* would do. Singing in the Hebrew dialect Yemenite, Sinwani performed "Im Nin'alu," a popular Yemeni song whose lyrics say that if doors on earth are closed, the gates of heaven remain open. Madonna said his performance was "flawless." She told Stuart they could take bits of it and create their own song around it.[31]

Madonna wrote "Push" in part for Guy Ritchie. It isn't a romantic song but an appreciation of the tension he brought to her life, which made her question who she was and what she was doing. Interestingly, she pays tribute to Sting's old band the Police in the song, because it was through him that she met Ritchie.[32] Overall, in concept and execution, "Push" is a strange song right to the very end, when Madonna and Price turn a straightforward melody into a Celtic weave with calls and answers and echoes. That portion of the song sounds like Madonna's internal rationalization that the tension Ritchie represents is a good thing.

Madonna ends her album with "Like It or Not." It is a perfect ending to a nearly perfect album. Madonna delivers her message as a saucy Peggy Lee would have: she is who she is, and she has no intention of fundamentally changing. Its pairing with "Push" made for interesting tea-leaf reading about the future of her relationship with Ritchie.

While Madonna worked with Price on her album, she edited her Re-Invention tour film, *I'm Going to Tell You a Secret,* with Jonas Åkerlund. She recalled Michael Moore telling her before filming began, " 'Just remember one thing: you write the script in the editing room. Don't freak out, and just shoot as much as you can' and we did." That meant the task before them was daunting. Working in Stockholm, they had around 350 hours of footage to sort through and cut down to two hours. "Just trying to figure out what I wanted to say with the film and whose stories I wanted to follow and letting things go was tough," Madonna recalled. "The hardest thing to do is edit."[33]

Madonna felt more involved in the creation of that film than she had in any other visual work in her career. "From every aspect — pre-production and filming to film stock and cameras used to editing and post-production — I loved it."[34] Her goal was to make an entertaining film that was also political, provocative, and spiritual, because, she said, "It's subversive to be spiritual!"[35] And she wanted it to be revealing about her life as an artist and as a working wife and mother, because that was subversive, too.

In the 2000s, women who had chosen the career paths opened to them by second wavers faced difficult now-or-never decisions as they reached their thirties. Their options boiled down to (1) career but no children, (2) children but no career, or (3) career *and* children with the prospect of doing justice to neither.[36]

Working-class women had balanced those tasks for centuries, but the media that targeted women with disposable incomes and the political ideologues who wanted to influence them created standards for a figure called Mother that were impossible to meet. She must be nurturing, patient, wise, a whiz in the kitchen, CEO and crisis manager of the home, attractive for her husband, available to him sexually, a hostess to their friends, and great at her job.[37] Examples of celebrity supermoms filled the pages of entertainment magazines: Angelina Jolie, Demi Moore, Julia Roberts, Michelle Pfeiffer. They all looked beautiful. They all expressed fulfillment. They all made it look easy. Madonna was there to say that it wasn't.

In an interview for *Ladies' Home Journal* published in the summer of 2005, she said that days were long, schedules were complicated, she didn't sleep much, and she had given up on a social life. "When you have a husband, two kids, and a lot of jobs, you just don't go out that much." For fun, she said, she danced with her children "like lunatics" before they went to sleep.[38] Sounding very un-Madonna, she said part of making her marriage work was learning to "bite my tongue . . . That's the whole give and take about marriage . . . You suddenly have to think of somebody else before you make decisions, before you speak."[39]

She listed her priorities as "making my marriage and my children and my spiritual life work" as well as what she called "the big picture." By that she meant finding answers to the questions that bedevil humankind: Why is there war, famine, illness? Why do people blithely live their lives from entertainment to entertainment, immersed in materialism?[40]

Early in her career, she said, she tried to help people by encouraging them to be self-confident and follow their dreams, but she muddied her message with her overt sexuality.

> One minute I was saying believe in yourself, and the next I was saying just be sexually provocative for the sake of being sexually provocative. Now that's confusing . . . So I didn't exactly help people by being an exhibitionist. I think I hurt myself, too, because I ended up devaluing my original message, that anybody could do anything—it's about what's on the inside.[41]

By 2005, she had grown. She said she didn't consider herself "holier than thou" or a "righteous soul," but having experienced the best and the worst, she was in a position to "help people, share what I know. I think about everything I do, how is this going to affect people? . . . Am I part of the problem, or the solution?"[42] That was why, when Bob Geldof called, she couldn't say no.[43]

★   ★   ★

The year had begun with desperate appeals for aid. The deadliest tsunami in recorded history hit Asia on December 26, 2004, killing 230,000 people within the first hours of its impact and devastating Indian Ocean communities in Sri Lanka, Thailand, Indonesia, the Maldives, and India. The destruction was a humbling reminder to residents of planet Earth that they only existed through the grace of a force much larger than themselves—nature.

At the same time, Africa was suffering a more protracted and persistent tsunami of AIDS, poverty, and debt. Though the postcolonial generation of leaders who were most closely linked to corruption were largely gone, the new, more technocratic African heads of state could not make strides toward anything approaching self-sufficiency, much less prosperity, because of crippling debts racked up by previous governments and an epidemic out of control.

The leaders of the industrialized nations, the Group of Eight, were scheduled to hold an annual summit in Scotland in July of 2005. In 2004, partly in anticipation of that event, U2's Bono and screenwriter Richard Curtis began working on a campaign called Make Poverty History. But they feared that nothing short of a cataclysm would get the G8's attention. And then came the tsunami in Asia. George Clooney organized a celebrity telethon to raise funds for tsunami victims, which Madonna participated in. *The Guardian* wrote that once the focus on Asia subsided, Bono and Curtis's Make Poverty History campaign took off.[44]

The G8 meeting coincided with the twentieth anniversary of the original Live Aid concert, and Bono and Curtis wanted its organizer, Bob Geldof, to help produce a second megaconcert. After much prodding, Geldof agreed. It would be called Live 8, in a pointed reference to the G8 leaders' scheduled gathering. Geldof and Bono worked the phones and lined up talent. It was Geldof's job to recruit Madonna, who was "identified as essential."[45] Madonna recalled his approach:

> When Bob Geldof started writing me letters, I thought, "Oh no, I just finished recording, and I just finished my film, and I promised my children I'd go to the countryside." They'd just finished school and they were really mad at me. Bob was like [screeches] "Africa's more important than your children!"...I said, "OK, let me think about it" and the next thing I read in the newspaper that I was doing it and I hadn't even answered him yet...I didn't regret that I did it, it turned out to be an amazing thing.[46]

Organizers wanted the G8 leaders to agree to provide an additional $50 billion in aid (half to Africa and half to the rest of the world's developing countries), cancel the debts of poor nations, and restructure the conditions imposed on aid recipients. In an open letter to the G8 leaders, Geldof said, "Do not disappoint us. Do not create a generation of cynics."[47] To maximize the pressure, the concert was scheduled to be held four days before the G8 meeting.

Live 8 began on July 2 in Tokyo and Johannesburg and moved with the sun to Europe—Moscow, Paris, Berlin, Rome, London, Cornwall, and Edinburgh—before closing later in the day in Barrie, Ontario, and Philadelphia. Millions of people saw it in person, and billions—the largest-ever global audience—watched it on TV.[48] Stuart Price said that during rehearsals in London's Hyde Park the previous day, "Everything was going wrong. Everyone was shitting themselves, but when that stage finally revolved around, it was one of the most magical moments I've ever had."[49]

Madonna was scheduled to appear onstage with twenty-four-year-old Ethiopian student Birhan Woldu. It was the image of Woldu as a starving infant during Ethiopia's famine in 1985 that inspired the first Live Aid. She had grown into a radiant young woman. When Geldof asked her whom she wanted to appear with at Live 8, she said Madonna because she was the only celebrity on the roster she recognized.[50]

With the London Community Gospel Choir, Donna De Lory, and new backup singer Lisa Fischer, Madonna sang "Like a Prayer" while holding Woldu's hand. The young woman appeared overwhelmed by the crowd before her and was quietly led offstage. Madonna continued without her through that song and into "Ray of Light." She closed her segment of the show with "Music" as two hundred thousand people, including the paparazzi, clapped their hands along with her.[51]

Live 8 was criticized by some as the Global North's monument to feel-good liberalism.[52] And while some of that criticism was well placed, the concert did achieve a couple of its goals. It brought the issue of poverty to the attention of the world, and it greatly increased pressure on G8 leaders. They responded by erasing the debt that eighteen of the world's poorest nations owed to international lenders and committing to increase development aid by $50 billion within five years. It wasn't as much as some people wanted, but campaigners cheered the results as a start.[53] The experience had another outcome as well. It made some of the entertainers involved into committed activists, Madonna among them.

After the concert, Madonna left with her family for the country. Five days later, on July 7, terrorist attacks in central London shut down that city the way New York had come to a standstill after 9/11. The London attacks, too, happened during the morning rush hour, but the targets weren't symbols of power: they were part of the mass-transit system—the London Underground and a city bus filled with "ordinary people" going about their day. Fifty-six people were killed, including the four bombers, and nearly eight hundred were injured. Not since World War II had there been as deadly a single strike on the city.[54]

All the July 7 bombers were British citizens, three of them second-generation Pakistanis and the fourth of Jamaican heritage. All four were Muslim. In the search for motives, religion was often mentioned, but beyond that there was befuddlement, even in the official House of Commons report on the attack, which was issued the next year after a lengthy investigation.[55] Rarely in the official search for a motive was anger mentioned as the driver of the terrible deeds—anger over decayed communities, a lack of opportunity, the discrimination the attackers felt as second-class British citizens, and the suspicion they aroused simply because they were brown and Muslim.

On July 21, it happened again. Another team of four bombers attacked the London Underground and a bus, though their bombs failed to detonate. What became clear was that the reservoir of rage and disaffection was much deeper than the authorities—not just in Britain, but around the world—understood. Globally, in 2005, there were nearly forty terrorist attacks that killed hundreds of people. The perpetrators were almost all young men. The dead were almost all civilians. Some communities came to fear the young people whom they had previously ignored. Madonna did the opposite. She would give youths from disenfranchised communities who expressed themselves through art rather than violence a role in her new work.

Madonna had begun taking horse-riding lessons that year at a stable in Richmond Park, in southwest London. She so enjoyed it that she rented all the necessary gear and asked to take two of the stables' horses to Ashcombe. From that point on, riding became part of her life. It was one of her favorite physical exercises and the activity at Ashcombe that made her feel most alive and most like herself. It also connected her to her mother. She once said that her most treasured possession was a picture of her mother laughing while riding a horse. She had stolen the photo from her father and brought it to New York when she left Michigan.[56]

As a surprise for her forty-seventh birthday, Guy had asked friends to bring four horses to their estate for a group ride. Madonna had shot the cover for her *Confessions on a Dance Floor* album with Steven Klein and finished the mixing with Stuart Price. She was ready to relax.[57] "Everything was perfect, the sun was shining...the sky was blue," she said. One of the horses in the pack was a polo horse, a Thoroughbred. "My friend said to me, 'Oh God, you've gotta try this horse. He rides like a deer.' And I said, 'Really?'...She's like, 'Yeah, yeah, get on him, get on him.' And I said, 'I don't really know how to ride a polo horse.' 'No, no, no he's so tame, he's so lovely.' "[58]

Madonna hopped on. "I was literally on it for a minute and got thrown off."[59] "He went crazy, and I went down. I was thinking, 'I'm graceful, I'm a dancer, I'm going to land, I'm going to roll and it's going to be fine.' "[60] But the surface below was like concrete. Madonna lay on it "motionless." Fearing that she was unconscious, friends rushed to reach her and pull the horse away. "I don't think her riding friends even knew what had happened until they saw Madonna on the ground," a source identified as an "insider" told the *Daily Mirror*.[61]

Madonna said that she tried to stand up, but her "whole skeleton just collapsed on me. I just fainted."[62] Rarely did Madonna's body disobey the dictates of her mind. In the case of her fall, it did. She was hurt badly.

Rushed to Salisbury District Hospital, she appeared in the emergency room in her riding gear, shaking, in obvious pain but lucid. Guy arrived around ten minutes later.[63] Madonna said she broke her collarbone, her scapula in two places, four ribs, and a left knuckle. "I cried a lot...mostly from pain because when you can't set bones it's very painful." Madonna said Guy was in the room, but she screamed at him—and for morphine—so much that he finally left.[64]

That evening, she was released from the hospital and flown by helicopter back to London with her hand in a cast, her arm in a sling, a bag full of painkillers, and instructions not to dance or exercise for three months. "If the horse had landed on top of Madonna or trodden on her, it could have been an awful lot worse," a source told a British newspaper at the time. "Although she's in excruciating pain, she did get off quite lightly." As for Guy, he was "absolutely mortified...It was a lovely treat which went sadly all wrong."[65]

"I guess the universe wanted me to slow down for a minute," Madonna reckoned.[66] "It was the most painful thing that ever happened to me in my life, but it was a great learning experience."[67] The immediate lessons? She wasn't bionic, and she could not take certain pain medications because they turned her into a monster.[68]

At first, far from listening to the universe or her doctors, she had no intention of slowing down. Her downtime lasted a few hours. The day after the accident, she flew to Paris for another birthday party.[69] But her injuries were real, and as much as she would have liked to ignore them, she couldn't. Madonna stopped what she was doing and let her body heal.

During her recovery, she said, she made bargains with God:

"I'll never be pointlessly depressed again...I'll never be ungrateful..." I found a new gratitude for the fact that I can do what I do and I have the strength I have. The accident fueled my energy and my desire to dance and to connect with people, and to be in a positive frame of mind—and to take people with me![70]

She could not do that without a strong body. Rebuilding it became her focus.[71] "I had to do a lot of Pilates to rehab my shoulder joint and get the use of my arm back," she said. "My Pilates instructor was a dancer, so my workout became much more ballet oriented." Once upon a time, Madonna said, "physicality, feeling strong, feeling empowered was my ticket out of middle-class Midwest culture. So I equate movement and strength with freedom." That was her goal again.[72]

There were reports that Madonna felt Ritchie hadn't been sympathetic enough during her ordeal. "Guy just wasn't there for her," a Madonna associate told *People*. "His cold manner was devastating to her. It was the beginning of her understanding that he was not a partner in every sense of the word." For his part, Ritchie was surprised by her "neediness," said a friend of the couple. "She's used to being able to do the impossible. But she didn't have superhuman powers to heal herself, and neither did Guy, and they both suffered for it."[73]

Serious illness and injury nearly always exact a toll on a relationship, if for no other reason than that they alter lives and plans in unexpected ways. There was, in any case, no evidence of a strain in their relationship in mid-September. Madonna threw a birthday party for Ritchie at a Moroccan restaurant in Mayfair during which reporters noted that the couple had a "steamy make-out session."[74] But not long afterward, the mood darkened when *Revolver,* Guy's comeback movie after the disastrous *Swept Away,* was released in Britain, on September 22.

Leicester Square was jammed with fans waiting in rows along the red carpet for Guy and Madonna to arrive. Two things happened when they did. Though the film was Guy's, the press attention was for Madonna. It was her name photographers shouted. And when the couple didn't stop for fan photos or autographs, boos began. Some of the fans had waited since that morning, and they were bitterly disappointed at being "snubbed."[75]

The film's reviews amounted to more boos. The *New York Times* offered the most positive spin: "Mr. Ritchie deserves credit for chutzpah."[76] But other critics were less generous. "*Revolver* is a humorless, leaden, car crash of a movie...with a disturbing sense of its own self-importance."[77] The *Guardian* reviewer wrote: "After *Revolver, Swept Away* now looks like *Citizen Kane.*"[78]

"Deep down he blames her for his career nosedive," Madonna biographer Lucy O'Brien quoted a friend as saying.[79]

The promotional phase of Madonna's new album release was derailed by her accident, the first casualty being her video for the lead single, "Hung Up." At one point, she and director Johan Renck, her collaborator on the video for "Nothing Really Matters," wondered whether they would need to scrap the very physical concept they had envisaged.[80] But she wouldn't let that happen. "When I shot the video, none of the bones had gone together," she said. "Pharmaceuticals and my will got me through the shoot."[81]

The video encapsulated Madonna's intent for her album: to provide "some kind of relief from all the insanity in the world."[82] Choreographed by Jamie King and Stefanie Roos, it pays homage to *Saturday Night Fever*, with Madonna playing both John Travolta in his famous strut along 86th Street in Brooklyn and his dance partner, Karen Lynn Gorney, as she prepares for a disco competition. But those references were the end of the nostalgia. Shot in Los Angeles and London, the video reflects the times by going into neighborhoods most associated with violence to find artists doing their best to escape it.[83]

Renck and Madonna incorporated a dance that was popular in the Paris banlieues and employed one of its ablest practitioners, Sébastien Foucan, to perform it. Parkour began as a French military training exercise in which a person—a traceur—uses only their wits and body to surmount obstacles, climb walls, and leap from high places. In the mostly immigrant ghettos of suburban Paris, traceurs defied the barrackslike walls that surrounded them and the oppression they endured by, in some cases, literally taking flight. In the English-speaking world, parkour became known as freerunning.[84]

The companion to those movements in Madonna's video was born half a world away in South Central. Krumping began there in 1992, the year of the Rodney King riots. It was a way to work out aggression without violence and involved dancers in mock confrontation. If parkour was about breaking free, krumping was about standing one's ground. Madonna asked famed krumper Marquisa Gardner—Miss Prissy—to appear in her video.[85]

Both parkour and krumping had been featured in films: Parkour in two movies Luc Besson was involved with, *Yamakasi* (2001) and *District B13* (2004), and krumping in David LaChapelle's *Rize* (2005). Though critically acclaimed, they did not reach a mass audience. "Hung Up" showcased for the world those underground cultures and the largely unrecognized paths young people took to avoid conflict, blow off steam, express themselves, and have fun—all things Madonna wanted to do, too.

*　　*　　*

Warner Music Group, meanwhile, watched and waited. In the spring of that year, Madonna had called the company's then CEO, Edgar Bronfman Jr., and said, "I want to come in and play my record." It was not the way Bronfman liked to do things. Hearing an album for the first time with the artist in the room was potentially disastrous. But after listening to *Confessions on a Dance Floor,* he was ecstatic. "She gave us a great record," he said, one that the company would use to market music in a new way.[86]

Bundling, or making music available on nontraditional platforms, had been tested since the iTunes store opened, in 2003. But by 2005 it had still not generated significant revenue. Warner hoped Madonna's album would point the way.[87] Recognizing the changed industry and increased competition, she didn't balk at the prospect. "You must join forces with other brands and corporations," Madonna said. "You're an idiot if you don't."[88]

In the download world, singles were paramount, the way they had been in the '50s and '60s, during the heyday of 45s. Madonna had a dynamite single, "Hung Up," that Warner bet would work on several platforms. They set the plan in motion. She would team with MTV for "branding opportunities." She would allow her song to be featured in episodes of *CSI: Miami* and *CSI: NY* and in a commercial for Motorola's cell phones. The phones were the first to offer iTunes, and "Hung Up" was the first Madonna song available on Apple's digital store. She would also license the single's use as a ringtone to cell-phone carriers in the United States and Europe.[89]

The bundling formula was so successful that within a year Warner Music Group, using the *Confessions* template, cornered the market on premium bundles. The humble ringtone became a major revenue driver, with worldwide sales in 2005 reaching $2.5 billion. The future for the music industry looked a lot less dire.[90] And with that grand entrance into a brave new world, Madonna launched weeks of travel, talk, and performance as anticipation built for the release of her "Hung Up" video, on October 27.

Until that moment, the song was praised as a celebration of disco past. The video showed that the tradition of dance as expression, as release, as survival, and as political statement was alive, well, and unforgettable.[91] It opens with Madonna warming up in a studio, freerunners on a rooftop doing the same, and people waiting at an LA bus stop krumping after the arrival of a boom box playing Madonna's song inspires them to dance. The scene is repeated across the globe—in the London Underground, in what is meant to be a noodle shop in Shanghai, and in a video arcade in Tokyo. The power belongs to whoever has the best moves. Eventually, all those characters converge on a dark, wet London street, where Madonna as Travolta appears and the real party begins.

The video was a lasting showcase for "Hung Up," but the biggest one-off event for the song and Madonna's rehabilitated body was the televised MTV Europe Music Awards, held in Lisbon on November 3. Only three months after her accident, she was scheduled to headline the show. She was so nervous that she rehearsed her performance thirty times. *Rolling Stone's* Neil Strauss wrote, "She not only stole the show but, nearing fifty...still managed to be the best-looking woman on the stage that night."[92]

Wearing a purple leather jacket, purple boots, a purple leotard, fishnet stockings, and tinted shades, Madonna emerged with her dancers from a giant disco ball. "I didn't know if I was going to be able to dance again," she told *Harper's Bazaar*. "So, to come out of that, I felt so much inspiration and so much joy just to have my body back and to feel strong again."[93]

She was all legs and attitude as she let her dancers—some of whom had been in her video—control the floor while she sang. She also indulged in a group grope that involved the most sensuous moves she had performed onstage since the Girlie Show. Her old pal Sacha Baron Cohen, by then an international star and the night's cohost, commented dryly on her performance, saying it was "very brave to open the show with a transvestite."[94]

Madonna felt great, but how were tabloid readers to know? The dominant story on those pages was about the state of her marriage. She and Ritchie were described as fighting constantly. Reports said they barely spoke, that he was "fed up" with her "diva behavior."[95] Ritchie didn't like her new album, which in fact she confirmed to *The Guardian,* saying, "He thought it was 'shit.' "[96] (He was notably left off the acknowledgments.) Reports also surfaced that she and Stuart Price were more than creative collaborators.[97]

That rumor hurt, because it indicated that people hadn't listened to what she was saying or understood who she had become. According to author J. Randy Taraborrelli, while Madonna was signing an autograph at *The Ellen DeGeneres Show,* she told a fan,

> It's as if everything I have ever said about being fair and decent and honourable—all of my spiritual beliefs—means nothing. How could anyone believe that I'm the kind of person who would do this to my husband and my family? *That,* to me, is what's really shocking.[98]

The tabloid industry of the 1980s that had hounded Madonna during her first marriage seemed quaint when compared with the tabloid industry of the 2000s. The internet had become a giant grocery-store aisle filled with celebrity gossip, and the digitization of photographs meant that anyone, anywhere, could take a picture and have it posted online in a matter of minutes.

Uncensored websites had become the new tabloids—Perez Hilton launched his in 2005. *TMZ* appeared that same year as an interactive blog featuring celebrity gossip. That was also the year YouTube appeared. Embarrassing or compromising moments caught by photographers that had previously disappeared after a few months became short YouTube movies that never went away.[99] Print tabloids became more aggressive in their "reporting" to compete with the internet. That year, Rupert Murdoch's *News of the World* was accused of tapping Prince William's phone messaging service. It was the first of many such scandals.

Madonna's appearance on British broadcast legend Michael Parkinson's show helped calm the tabloid waters a bit as far as she and Ritchie were concerned. Speaking frankly, she acknowledged that marriage wasn't easy, that she had learned to say "I'm sorry" even if she didn't mean it, and that Ritchie was "nonchalant"—as in unimpressed—about her career.[100] But she said, "When you're hugely famous, you need some kind of reminder that this is not real, something else is."[101]

November 9, the day after she recorded her Parkinson interview, *Confessions on a Dance Floor* was released. *Rolling Stone* called it "pure groove."[102] Joan Morgan, in the *Village Voice,* wrote, "Call the chirren y'all. Madge is taking it to church." She called *Confessions* "easily dance record of the year."[103] There were dissenters, of course, and US radio–programming conglomerates didn't give *Confessions* airtime because the music was not "mainstream." Madonna's fans took notice and signed a petition called "End the Madonna on U.S. Radio Boycott."[104]

Music journalist Caroline Sullivan noted that in a few years the US market would "rediscover dance music (and retitle it EDM, electronic dance music), but that would be too late for *Confessions* singles."[105] Happily, the fate of the album didn't rest with US broadcasters. Charting in forty countries, *Confessions* earned recognition in *Guinness World Records* for the Most Charts Topped Around the World—Same Album.[106] Madonna celebrated by popping a bottle of bubbly and crying tears of joy.[107]

Part of that good fortune came down to hard work. She embarked on a mini promotional tour at venues more befitting a newcomer than the biggest star on the planet. She appeared in Mannheim on the high-ranking but utterly bizarre TV show *Wetten, dass...?* (Want to bet that...?) and the French reality TV talent show *Star Academy.*[108] After a couple of small club dates in London, she traveled to Japan, performing at the intimate Tokyo venue Studio Coast and appearing three nights later on the TV variety series *SMAP×SMAP* during its Bistro segment, in which five chefs—some of them dressed as Madonna—were interviewed about food.[109]

Returning to London in time for the UK premiere of her Re-Invention tour film, *I'm Going to Tell You a Secret,* Madonna received a standing ovation before and after the show.[110] And though critics took issue with the Kabbalah elements in the movie, and most agreed that *Truth or Dare* was superior, they generally seemed to enjoy the ride. *The Guardian*'s Rupert Smith began his piece with two sentences: "I love Madonna. I can't help it—it's probably genetic."[111]

Madonna had not had so much positive press since *Ray of Light*. Even the snide remarks about her age disappeared for a few news cycles. Maybe watching her battle back from serious injuries had silenced her critics. Maybe her record was just that good. Madonna thought so. Guy Ritchie knew her well enough to know what that meant. "He said to me the other day, 'Am I going to lose you again for another six months?'"[112] Her answer was yes. She wanted to tour, even though her children were still roadweary from the last one and even though she knew how difficult it would be for Ritchie. She told *Rolling Stone* that fall,

> It's hard for a guy to be traipsing around the world with a girl. No one wants to be anybody's trailer bitch...You have to be a pretty evolved man to go on the road with me and not for a moment have this glimpse of yourself as someone who's lost their identity.[113]

And yet she was prepared to do it again.

Chapter 48

Los Angeles, London, Lilongwe, Rome, Moscow, Tokyo, 2006

While other female icons fade, fold, or fossilize into camp, for better or worse, Madonna seems determined to do something unsettling and new: spin to the center of the dance floor till the end.[1]

— *Emily Nussbaum*

FIGURATIVELY SPEAKING, MADONNA stood alone when she opened the Grammy Awards ceremony in February of 2006. An animated version of her shared the stage with the CGI band Gorillaz before she joined her dancers and band for "Hung Up." But she, as a phenomenon, was alone, as in unrivaled, because of her achievements, her culture-altering work, and her lifetime of norm busting, which made the path easier for the artists who followed her.

That younger generation was in the Staples Center that night watching a woman who was old enough to be their mother perform with vitality, urgency, and joy. What they did not see was the cost. Just as she had learned to dance past her riding injuries, she learned to conceal the anguish in her personal life. Confiding in fashion designer Isaac Mizrahi, she said,

It is a struggle to balance my career with my children...I'm always going, "Oh God, I'm a crap mother." I want to get home and put my kids to bed. And then sometimes, if I'm spending a lot of time with my children, I think, "Oh God, I just want to be an artist." And you know it's hard...I guess I always feel like there is so much more to do, so much to learn, so much to know.[2]

Centuries of women artists before her had experienced just such a moment of sad awakening when they realized the difficulty of giving themselves over to a creative life while trying to raise a family and that in the end they would be forced to choose. Madonna refused to make the choice. That was her new challenge—to prove that it could be done, that a woman could be a wife, mother, and artist and do all three *well*. As she performed that night in LA, that was her latest battle, which she fought alone.

Guy had remained behind in London. Madonna explained his absence in a special Grammy-themed episode of *The Ellen DeGeneres Show,* saying, "He works and I work, and we can't always coordinate our working schedules together." Asked if the rumors that she and Guy had split were true, she answered indirectly, saying, "He's still calling me every five minutes."[3]

While Madonna batted away questions about her marriage in LA, Ritchie's friends seemed happy to talk about what they described as a husband left by the wayside of his wife's ambitions. "It's as if work is the only thing that interests her," one said. "Guy's spending a lot of time at home alone."[4] Actor Vinnie Jones said Madonna's fame "shook" Ritchie. "He didn't know what he was getting into."[5] To "de-stress," a friend said, Guy "turns up at the martial arts centre at the end of the very hardest class—just for the fights."[6]

An aide to Madonna didn't waste time worrying about Guy. "It is fair to say their relationship has been under huge strain because of Madonna's excessive workload recently. She has thrown herself 100 percent into promoting her album and has little time left to spend with Guy. He'll get over it."[7] The fact was, he didn't seem to.

Madonna returned to London after the Grammys—and after undergoing a hernia operation—in time to attend the BRIT Awards, where she was nominated in two categories: International Album and International Female Solo Artist.[8] "Sorry," the second single from her album, had been released the previous week and became Madonna's twelfth number 1 single in the UK. The awards ceremony would be a celebration of her dominance of the British charts. Ritchie didn't want to attend. The *Daily Mirror* quoted a source as saying,

> She wants the whole world to see they are together. But Guy clearly has other ideas. Like all relationships, theirs is going through a bit of a bad patch but he doesn't see why he's to pretend everything is OK just to keep her happy...It's a game he's just not willing to play.[9]

Days before the February 14 BRITs, Madonna declined a table at the ceremony for herself and her guests because it wasn't clear whether Ritchie would be there.[10] He finally relented, but organizers were reportedly told that he and Madonna would only attend briefly. "She made it clear they would take their seats, she would present the Best Album prize, collect her [International Female prize], then leave," a BRIT Awards source told the

Daily Mirror. They remained at the ceremony for thirty minutes, during which Ritchie was described as "miserable."[11]

In January, Madonna had reassembled the dancers and choreographers from her "Hung Up" video to shoot the video for "Sorry." Directed by Jamie King, Madonna leads her female dancers, "Music"-style, out on the town and ends up at a roller-skating rink like the old Roxy in New York. Her dancers are every bit as eclectic as that famous club's clientele had been. A mix of genders, ages, ethnicities, and religions, they also appear to be as much fun. Madonna had a relationship with them that she hadn't had with a dance crew since Blond Ambition. It was only natural, then, that when she began planning her tour, some of them would be part of it.

Her tour preparations took the family to Los Angeles and out from under the scrutiny of the British tabloids. Ritchie's father told a newspaper that they had vowed to recommit to their marriage for the sake of Rocco and Lourdes. After they spent a few weeks in Los Angeles, the change of scenery appeared to have worked. "They seem to have left the bumps they were having over here behind them," said John Ritchie. "They're able to go home at night and be together."[12]

During rehearsals, Madonna's life was as stable as it could be. For a period of several months, she was (sort of) tied to one region, working long but (sort of) steady hours. And she was happy.[13] "I like the creation of everything, like being able to wear my rehearsal clothes and be sweaty and not having to worry about how I look and just get into what it is I'm trying to say and do."[14]

Madonna had decided that she wanted each concert to be as immersive an experience as a night at a disco. She didn't want her audience to feel they were watching a show but that they were *part* of a show, "inside a disco ball," she said. "We want to devise a sound system that's surround-sound, because the standard system in a sports arena is crap for people watching, and it's crap for people on stage."[15]

Finding the crew to help her realize that dream was easier than usual. She reassembled the core group from her Re-Invention tour onstage and off. By that point, they were all tight and knew that the only thing Madonna expected was perfection—and that meant work. Rehearsals were held from nine to nine Monday through Saturday.

Five of the fourteen dancers and freerunners who would tour with Madonna in 2006 had been part of her Re-Invention cast: Jason Young, Daniel "Cloud" Campos, Mihran Kirakosian, Reshma Gajjar, and Tamara Levinson, who was on her third tour with Madonna, having joined her first on Drowned World. They would form the backbone of the performance. The nine new dancers would represent her shift in emphasis from war and religious tensions to dance as a form of personal, social, and political expression.

The Confessions tour would be joyous. It wasn't a denial of the world's troubles: it merely provided a respite from them and showed — through movement and the life stories of some of the dancers — how people survived. Comparing the Re-Invention and Confessions tours, Reshma Gajjar said, "Re-Invention felt like a deep breath in, and Confessions felt like an exhale."[16]

Among the newcomers was Compton native Charmaine Jordan (later known as Charm La'Donna). When she was recruited to join the tour, the seventeen-year-old was a senior in high school known for her legendary street dance moves. "I had never left the United States before," she said. "Then suddenly, it was eight months with Madonna."[17]

Twenty-three-year-old Algerian-born Sofia Boutella grew up in Paris and studied ballet before switching gears and joining a break-dancing crew. The Confessions tour would be her next school.[18] "When I started dancing with Madonna, I was a complete tomboy, first of all," Boutella said.

> I did ballet, and then I did hip-hop because I wanted to break all the rules... Then I started dancing with her, and she gave me a pair of heels for the first time... She taught me so much... She cares so much about what she does, the way she does it... Every number that I've ever done with her, she always asks me, "Are you okay dancing with this? How do you feel?" She would, like, go on her knees and fix your shoe.[19]

Sébastien Foucan, the Paris-born freerunner of Guadeloupean descent who had appeared in Madonna's "Hung Up" video, also joined the tour. By 2006, he was the grand master of the form. That year he would film his breakthrough role, challenging Daniel Craig in a parkour chase in the opening segment of the James Bond film *Casino Royale.*[20]

For her Confessions tour, Madonna's dancers would each be encouraged to be creative individuals, the way her Blond Ambition crew had been. She would make sure that audiences knew their names, their stories, and their dance moves. "Madonna has a great idea of what each and every one of the dancers bring to the performance," said Mihran Kirakosian. That was because she trusted them, one artist to another.[21]

Donna De Lory agreed to go back out on tour with her now three-year-old daughter. "It got more challenging," she said. "I was older. I needed more. My kid needed more." Madonna accommodated her needs. "I asked for a car so I could have my nanny and my kid with me. I think the band was a little resentful," Donna said, "but I got what I needed to do that gig... That's where that understanding was [one mother to another]. It wasn't spoken."[22]

Singing backup with Donna would be actor and recording artist Nicki Richards. When Stuart Price called to ask Richards if she'd be interested in touring with Madonna, she answered, "Um, yeah!!!"[23] Having passed the audition, Richards joined the tour and joined a family. She thought of young dancer Charmaine Jordan as a little sister. She thought of Donna as "a tiny little angel here on earth." She thought of Madonna as the high bar she aspired to. "My discipline muscle got kicked up a few notches!...I don't know if I've ever worked so hard in my life. I felt respected, encouraged and challenged."[24]

For the first time since Blond Ambition, Jean Paul Gaultier would be the sole designer for Madonna's show. By 2006, he was no longer the enfant terrible of the Paris fashion scene: he was the ranking couturier, having inherited Yves Saint Laurent's coveted spot closing Paris Fashion Week.[25] He had also become head designer at Hermès—and, coincidentally, that season he was showing women wearing riding helmets, carrying riding crops, and draped in leather and lace.[26] That would do nicely for the opening of Madonna's show, which had an equestrian theme.

Despite her accident, horses were still very much part of Madonna's life. She had begun taking lessons with the British Olympic equestrian William Fox-Pitt on her Welsh cob horse, Tom.[27] And earlier that year, she did a photo shoot for *W* with fellow horse lover Steven Klein using six stallions. In the shoot, Madonna, Catherine the Great–style, paid homage to the beasts.[28] Jamie King decided to make her accident and recovery part of the concert by using Klein's photographs, X-ray images of injuries like Madonna's, Gaultier's designs, and his own choreography.[29]

Madonna seemed completely focused on rehearsals. But in truth, her attention was split. The previous fall, she received a call that changed her life. A businesswoman from Malawi named Victoria Keelan had heard about Madonna's program Spirituality for Kids, which had expanded beyond mere consciousness-raising to providing aid to children in need around the world. Madonna said Keelan told her, "If you're in the business of helping children, we have over a million orphans here in Malawi and the problem is insane."[30]

Keelan sounded exhausted as she described the situation: there weren't enough orphanages to house the children; they were "sleeping under bridges, hiding in abandoned buildings, being abducted, kidnapped, raped."[31] Keelan said, "It's an emergency. And they need your help."[32]

A few months earlier, during an interview after Live 8, Madonna was asked if she'd ever been to Africa. She answered in two ways. She said she hadn't, not "because it's difficult. I would do it if the time is right and I could really go there and effect real change." Her follow-up response was telling. "I do know, to a certain extent, what's going on there from Bill Clinton and Christiane Amanpour, who are both friends of mine. But obviously nothing is like actually being there and witnessing it."[33]

What was amazing about her answer was its guilelessness concerning the celebrity bubble she inhabited and the fact that she didn't try to hide her ignorance. You don't learn if you pretend to know. She did the same with Keelan. Madonna admitted she knew nothing about Malawi, saying, "I don't even know where that is." Keelan told her to get a map and hung up on her.[34] Madonna found one and began studying the country.[35]

The tiny southeast African country, squeezed between Tanzania, Mozambique, and Zambia, could be missed entirely amid such giants. But within its borders existed a diversity of terrain—mountains, highlands, woodlands, plateaus, and swamps—and species representative of an entire continent. During the 1960s liberation movements against colonial rule in Africa, it declared independence from Britain. Having been called Nyasa-land, it renamed itself Malawi.[36]

The country was primarily Christian, with Catholicism the dominant strain. Its ten main ethnic groups each spoke their own language, but most Malawians spoke the official languages, Chichewa and English.[37] Their lives were largely rural and agricultural: more than 80 percent of the land was worked by subsistence farmers. Fishing was another major occupation. Madonna learned that Lake Malawi, the ninth largest in the world, contained eight hundred species of fish.[38]

Though the land and the lake were rich, the people of Malawi were poor. On several international financial indicators, it ranked near the bottom, even compared to its African neighbors. It also had among the highest infant mortality and maternal mortality rates in the world. All that—the poverty and the death—was attributable to AIDS.[39]

The new epicenter for the plague was sub-Saharan Africa. The World Health Organization reported in 2005 that 64 percent of the world's HIV-infected people lived there, and that 59 percent of those infected were women.[40] The effect of those tragic circumstances was borne by children. Twelve million of them under the age of seventeen had lost one or both parents to AIDS, and millions more were born with the virus. The WHO reported that 90 percent of the world's HIV-infected children lived in sub-Saharan Africa, and only one in ten received even the most basic medical attention.[41]

As small as it was, Malawi in 2005 had the distinction of being the ninth most AIDS-affected country in the world. One out of every twelve people was HIV-positive, and nearly one million people had died of AIDS. Most of the infected and the dead were women.[42] As a result, Malawi had become a country of children: 43 percent of its population was under the age of fourteen. It was also a country of orphans: estimates of the number of children without parents ranged from five hundred thousand to one million.[43]

The tragedy of Malawi would have been overwhelming if not for its people. They had relatively nothing materially. They were dying of a disease imported from foreign lands, and in 2003, after being shunned by foreign donors because of political turmoil, the country was plunged into famine. And yet its people were *kind*. Marcus Westberg wrote of Malawi,

> As a photojournalist and travel writer, I am wary of cliches and generalizations. But few countries have been awarded a more appropriate slogan than Malawi, which is known as the "Warm Heart of Africa.". . . If you were to ask me where in the world I would feel the most comfortable walking up to a stranger—any stranger—to start a conversation, my answer. . . would unhesitatingly be Malawi.[44]

After receiving Victoria Keelan's phone call and immersing herself in the country's story, Madonna created a foundation called Raising Malawi, to which she donated millions of dollars. Its focus would be to support Malawi's orphans and vulnerable children. In April, she went to Malawi with Keelan to see the situation for herself.[45]

She found there a level of poverty and need that she had never experienced.[46] She visited people living with AIDS, who were receiving all the wrong medications. She saw orphans in the streets without any support whatsoever. She saw children in orphanages lying on the ground in their own urine because there were too few staff to attend to them. She held year-old AIDS babies who weighed just three pounds. "You think, 'How can I save them all, how can I make their lives better, what is their future?' "[47] She was reminded of New York in the early '80s. AIDS-related death was everywhere; what was lacking was understanding and action. "It was like history repeating itself," she said.[48]

Amid all that grief, Madonna was confounded, even shocked, to find the "warm heart of Africa" that Westberg described. "You get really confused when you go there," she said.

> There's so much love and so much joy and such a sense of community—and yet people are dropping like flies. And we are over here [in the West] with access to every kind of medication, and an infrastructure, and people are educated, and everyone's miserable. So you're like, "Well, wait a minute. Who do we need to save?". . . It's a question of consciousness and

where your head is at. And for most people around the world, our heads are up our asses.[49]

No doubt Madonna was viewed by the people she met as another celebrity *mzungu*—a white person who would come and go, maybe donate some money but not her time and certainly not her heart. But Malawi was made for Madonna. As a child who had lost a parent, she was unable to turn her back on its orphans. As a young woman who had lost people she loved to AIDS, she could not ignore the plague's youngest victims. As a mother, she could not abandon a country of innocent children in need of so much.[50]

When she returned to the States, she spoke with Harvard public health expert Dr. Jim Yong Kim, who worked extensively with AIDS in Africa. She also met with Dr. Paul Farmer, a liberation theology activist who had worked to bring health care to the world's poorest countries. She talked to Bill Clinton about getting medicine to Malawi. She met with economist Jeffrey Sachs, who that year with the United Nations would launch his Millennium Villages Project to improve living conditions in targeted sub-Saharan African villages. Madonna agreed to sponsor one in Malawi. She also invited a group of eight teachers from Malawi to Los Angeles and paid for training that prepared them to help children in the classroom and out.[51]

When word got out about Madonna's interest in Malawi, the press greeted it with cynicism. She mocked the coverage, saying, " 'Oh God, she's so horrible, she's thinking about her fellow man! Damn her!!'...I don't understand that," she told Matthew Todd at *Attitude*. "You know some people think I fell off my horse as a publicity stunt. If you're a celebrity, everything you do is suddenly perceived as a way to get attention...If you're in a position...where you can help people, then why don't you?"[52]

Madonna's concert tour would reflect what she experienced in two ways. "In Africa, everybody dances and everybody plays music," she said. "When people are busy making music and dancing, they're kind of too busy to hate and fight."[53] And AIDS would once again become part of her message. She would use "Live to Tell" as she described the menace that had not disappeared, that was in fact killing millions of people and infecting millions more largely without global attention or even recognition.

Madonna's seventh tour would visit three continents for sixty shows and be seen by more than one million people. It was her largest and longest ever. Rehearsals in Los Angeles were held in a place lovingly referred to by the tour's crew as the "bunker." It was so secure that entry badges were color-coded and changed daily.[54]

Madonna appeared every day around one, after spending mornings with her children and on the phone taking care of business. Once she arrived, her manager, Angela Becker, greeted her with a list of questions that needed answers and problems that needed solving. No matter how big the tour had become, Madonna was involved in every creative decision.[55]

Consuming cans of Red Bull while she worked, she practiced harder than anyone in the room, at once taking chances that might be expected from a daring newcomer and showing the complete control of a veteran. "There are three choreographers, but she never looks at them," Gaultier said. "She's actually better than they are. Almost all of the show comes from her."[56]

Except the music. Madonna so trusted Stuart Price that she essentially gave him free rein musically on the tour. She wanted to eliminate the space between the performance and the audience to create a "club." Price's idea for the music was similar. He would have a live band onstage, but he would manipulate its sound the way he would if he were manning a disco booth. "It was imposing the DJ club dynamic onto live music," he said. The music would be as unpredictable as it is during a night on the dance floor.[57]

All the tour dancers arrived with expertise in some area, but during the rehearsals they were challenged to learn something new. Victor Lopez, among others, discovered freerunning, which he would introduce to LA and perform for the rest of his life.[58] And *all* the cast — dancers, singers, and band — had to learn to navigate the tour's gargantuan stage.

With a footprint twice the size of the Re-Invention stage, it existed on several levels, including a main stage, a sixty-foot catwalk into the audience, and satellite stages hovering just over the crowd. Above the stage, out of sight, the workings to control the show's many parts were so complex that a journalist writing about its design said with only slight exaggeration that "an air traffic controller is needed" to direct it.[59]

If all went as planned, the concert would last two hours and consist of four sets: equestrian, Bedouin, rock, and disco. There would be no encores.[60]

Like the Re-Invention tour, Confessions opened with Steven Klein's photographs of Madonna, this time from their horse shoot earlier that year. Displayed as a triptych, the images captured the animals' muscled restraint.[61] Onstage, meanwhile, dancers reenacted the human-horse relationship of domination and submission as a 1.5-ton disco ball covered in $2 million worth of Swarovski crystals descended to "hatch" Madonna in full equestrian garb. While singing "Future Lovers," which included a sample of Donna Summer's "I Feel Love," she tamed, through gentle S/M play, "horses" in the form of male dancers.[62]

Then, left alone on the stage—the band, Donna, and Nicki Richards stood some distance behind her—Madonna began "Get Together." It would be her real welcome to the audience, sung as she prowled the catwalk deep into the crowd. "Do you think we can change the future? Do you think I can make you feel better?" That was the essence of the show. She would challenge her fans to open their minds and leave them feeling hopeful.[63]

Most of the concert featured new material, but Madonna reworked "Like a Virgin" yet again for the Confessions tour. X-rays of broken bones, horses' hooves, and riding accidents appeared on screens behind her as she sang and rode a horse's saddle on a pole positioned on a satellite stage. Her performance, high above her audience, gave new meaning to the song her audiences knew so well. In the early '80s, she was a virgin transformed by love. In the 2000s, she was a woman strengthened by adversity.[64]

The segment would have been memorable enough, but Stuart Price picked up the tempo, and Madonna went at it with the saddle and pole. It wasn't as explicit as Madonna on her bed of red in the infamous Blond Ambition masturbation sequence, but it was thrilling in its own way because it was so dangerous and so beautiful. Madonna on the saddle, lying back with her leg extended into the air, looked like a piece of moving sculpture.[65]

The Girlie Show had been Madonna's Weimar-era cabaret. In a way, Confessions was another—not visually as much as emotionally. The concert made viewers feel as though they were part of an underground society, protected from a world deficient in understanding, love, and humor. Sitting on a platform in front of Stuart Price, Madonna channeled Joel Grey's "Mesdames et messieurs" introduction from *Cabaret* when she said, "Ladies and gentlemen, welcome to our show. The night is young, and the show has just begun."[66]

At that point, she sang "Jump." Sébastien Foucan, Victor Lopez, Daniel "Cloud" Campos, and Levi Meeuwenberg began the parkour/freerunner moves that represented escape. The photos on the screens behind them showed what they were escaping from: barrackslike ghettos in the banlieues, desolate LA streets, New York tenements, mercantile Tokyo, graffiti, modern life. The message of the number was "Go." Madonna did, disappearing through the floor while her four dancers tossed their bodies through the air as if the laws of gravity had no bearing on their reality.[67]

With that, the equestrian segment ended and the Bedouin section began. It would be about empowerment, and its first set was the show's most controversial. It opened with three dancers telling their stories of survival.[68]

Campos described being a boy who was hit so hard by his father that his body flew across the room. "We all fall to the floor at some point. It's how you pick yourself up. That's the real challenge," his voice said, while he enacted his words in freerunning movements onstage.[69]

Sofia Boutella came next, flinging her body around the stage while on-screen behind her, blood drops appeared on flesh. She said,

> There was a time I suffered so much I wanted to get it out of me. I would cut my arms. Not to kill myself. I don't want to die. I know I am lucky to be on this earth. I did it so the physical pain would calm the pain that was eating me inside . . . I am blessed by God to tell myself I suffer that much to become who I am today.[70]

And finally, Leroy Barnes Jr.: "I was never out to kill anybody, especially when I made that decision to gangbang. I just wanted to fit in. But one day, I was forced to do something that opened my eyes." Barnes described the pressure he felt to avenge a "homie's" murder. "We pulled up to the corner. Then he placed a chunky-ass gun in my lap. He said, 'You know what to do with it. It's time to get a poppy for the hood.' But I wasn't out to kill anybody."[71]

Madonna had chosen dancers with histories for her tour, people who not only danced the dances of the street—whatever street they were from in whatever country—but also had stories that society ignored and that belied the joy and beauty of their art. Those three dancers "lived to tell." And then Madonna appeared onstage to sing that song.

Organ music played, and a giant mirrored cross arose from the stage with Madonna "crucified" on it, wearing a sheer chiffon blouse, velvet pants, and a crown of thorns with two red "blood" beads. She sang while an LED display overhead, like a doomsday clock, counted the number of African children orphaned by AIDS until it reached twelve million.[72] She ended the song facedown on the floor as two web addresses appeared on the screens: one for Raising Malawi and one for the Clinton Foundation.[73]

With her next songs, Madonna remained in the world of seemingly intractable problems. During the performance of "Forbidden Love," pairs of bare-chested male dancers, one tattooed with a Star of David and the other tattooed with the Islamic star and crescent, engaged in "armed" conflict before they embraced.[74] The singer Yitzhak Sinwani then blew a ritual shofar to introduce the next song, "Isaac," which he sang in a duet with Madonna.

While they sang, Sofia danced in a cage, wearing a long blue cape to represent traditional Islamic women's garb, as a falcon spread its wings on the screen behind her. The cage door opened, and Boutella was freed.[75] For the next song, it was Madonna's turn behind bars. Standing her ground and batting away the excuses that men give for their misbehavior, she sang "Sorry." A posse of women entered the cage to fight alongside her, prowling the enclosure like panthers. Four male dancers met them for a dance-off. The result: Chicks 1, Fellas 0.[76]

The tour's dancers took the stage during the interlude between the Bedouin and rock sections of the show. Freerunning had dominated the first half of the concert, and now it was the krumping contingent's turn. Performing to a remix of "Sorry," Charmaine Jordan and Barnes bent and jerked their bodies in rhythmic aggression as images of political, religious, and military leaders appeared on the screens behind them. Interspersed among those faces were pictures of dying children, child laborers, child soldiers, melting ice caps, raging fires, urban decay, and war.[77]

The Confessions tour wouldn't have been complete without the closing song, "Hung Up," which inspired the album and brought Madonna back to her disco roots. She began the song, then disappeared, leaving the band playing, disco lights swirling around the arena, and the dancers freerunning down the catwalk, off the secondary stages, and into the audience. Madonna, meanwhile, changed into her "Hung Up" costume—purple leotard, cropped jacket, and tinted shades.[78]

With the entire cast back on the main stage, the dance became a tableau vivant of intertwined bodies, a living abstract painting in oranges, purples, blues, and reds.

The Confessions tour was Madonna's most thematically complex since Blond Ambition and the Girlie Show as well as the most technically complex ever. There were so many moving parts and so many people engaged in death-defying acts that everything had to be split-second perfect. People disappeared into the floor, rampaged up scaffolding, or sped down the catwalk on roller skates, jumping over one another, mock fighting. There were very few moments in the two-hour performance when calm descended.[79]

After twelve weeks of rehearsals, it was ready.[80] The twenty-seven performers and 106-member crew packed up the show and hit the road.[81]

The tour began on May 21 at the Forum in Inglewood, California. Unlike Re-Invention, the Confessions tour didn't linger in every city; it stayed in most of them for only two nights. Madonna performed four or five nights a week.[82]

At Madison Square Garden, she told a cameraman that Guy couldn't "wait for this tour to be over...I can't blame him. It's tough on him and the kids. I keep saying I'll never do it again, but after every tour ends I'm somehow ready to go back and do another."[83] By July, she was willing to accede to Ritchie's wishes. She announced that she would cut her tour short by eliminating her last dates, scheduled for September in Australia. The strain on her family was too great.

The tour arrived in England for eight nights, in time for Madonna's forty-eighth birthday, on August 16.[84] After the concert in London, she and Guy went to a party at the Loungelover club, in Shoreditch, where she shocked her friends with a tearful tribute to her husband. "I care for Guy deeply and he is the love of my life. He has changed my life for the better since I met him. I can only thank him for all his support." One party guest said, "It was incredible to hear her open up and let people know such personal feelings...Guy was beaming and it's clear they're very much in love."[85]

Actor Mark Strong, who appeared in Ritchie's film *Revolver,* said of Guy, "The fact that he's stayed sane and is such a lovely bloke is a miracle. I read this bullshit written about him and her and it bears no relationship to reality. He is thoughtful, kind and funny, yet the way he's portrayed is unbelievable."[86]

Before the tour's arrival in continental Europe, critics were mostly laudatory. That changed after a show in Rome on August 6. The city's Catholic, Jewish, and Muslim leaders united in public condemnation of Madonna over her "Live to Tell" crucifixion segment. A Vatican spokesman called it profane.[87] In Düsseldorf on August 20, prosecutors threatened to arrest her for blasphemy, and a Lutheran bishop called for a boycott of her show.[88] In Moscow in September, her concert was condemned by the Federation of Jewish Communities of Russia and the Russian Orthodox Church. The former called for a boycott, the latter a ban.[89]

It was Madonna's first performance in Russia, and the cast could feel the hunger for her message of freedom there. In European cities where Madonna had appeared many times, fans were loud, both in the audience and on the street. Nicki Richards said that in Moscow, fans didn't know if it was okay to approach the cast. "I'd walk out of the hotel, and they'd just watch silently, until I said, 'Hi'...Then the enthusiasm came pouring out...I hugged and cried with more people in Moscow than anywhere else."[90] During the concert, which was surrounded outside the venue by ten thousand soldiers and riot police, Madonna added "Give Peace a Chance" to the set list. "She meant it from the heart; we all meant it," Nicki said.[91]

The tour ended in Tokyo on September 21. They had been on the road since May, but Madonna asked some of the dancers to give just a little more. Jonas Åkerlund had scheduled the video shoot for "Jump" in Japan and wanted to showcase freerunning. The dancers were exhausted from the flight, from the tour, from putting every bit of themselves out there as they traversed the globe. On top of it, the shoot was outdoors, and it was raining.[92]

The show's four freerunners dug deep and did it, jumping from rooftops and stairwells, swinging high from lampposts and telephone poles, dancing through gritty daytime streets and surreal neon nightscapes. The awe-inspiring images were a fitting coda to the tour—testimonials to the power of the individual to surmount all obstacles and the power of art to uncover beauty in the most unlikely places.

It was finally time for the cast to say goodbye. Confessions would be Donna De Lory's last outing with Madonna. She wanted to have another baby and pursue her own music. And, sadly, she no longer felt needed. During the tour, Donna said, "I was on the riser behind the keyboard player. I could have been drinking champagne back there and nobody would know. I missed that so much, being out there and being part of the show." It was time to move on. "Six tours—I felt really good about it."[93]

Confessions was a massive success. It grossed nearly $200 million, at that point the most ever for a tour by a woman artist and second only to the Rolling Stones tour that year.[94] Professionally, no one could touch Madonna. Personally, it was another matter.

Chapter 49

Lilongwe, London, 2006–2007

If you aren't willing to fight for what you believe in, then don't
even enter the ring.[1]

— Madonna

In October, Madonna took her second trip to Malawi, traveling with a
retinue that included Guy Ritchie and pediatrician Sonia Sachs, who is
married to Jeffrey Sachs, founder of the Millennium Villages Project. A
camera crew accompanied them as they visited orphanages around the
country. Madonna wanted to make a documentary to help raise awareness
of Malawi's plight. Her Raising Malawi foundation had made an initial
commitment to provide funds to feed, house, and educate as many as four
thousand children.[2] It was her second charitable enterprise after Spirituality for Kids, and it, too, was linked to the Kabbalah Centre. For people
looking for an excuse to condemn Madonna's philanthropy, that association provided one.

By 2006, the Kabbalah Centre was under scrutiny for the apparent dis-
connect between its beliefs and its practices. Critics saw it as a cash cow not
unlike those of the television evangelists who preach piety and godliness
while living lavishly off the funds given by donors. Madonna alone was
said to have donated around $5 million to the center. But her name was
more valuable to it than her money. Her very real and very public dedication to Kabbalah made the teachings attractive to other A-list celebrities
trying to make sense of their lives.[3]

The teachings undoubtedly inspired and improved the lives of many,
Madonna included. What attracted criticism was that the emphasis of the
Kabbalah Centre, as run by Philip and Karen Berg and their two sons,
Yehuda and Michael, appeared to have shifted over time from a focus on
giving to a focus on getting. As money rolled in, some asked whom it ben-
efited. Critics looking at the Bergs' three Beverly Hills homes and their
Centre-subsidized existence believed they found a partial answer.[4]

Michael Berg had accompanied Madonna and Guy on their Malawi
visit in his role as cofounder of the Raising Malawi foundation. His

presence received more press attention than Sonia Sachs's and was used to undermine the legitimacy of the trip, especially in the British press.

Journalists had been investigating the London Kabbalah Centre and reporting on items sold in its shop: "blessed, restoring" face cream (£78); 1.5-liter bottles of Kabbalah water, with "centuries of wisdom in every drop" (£4); and the book of wisdom, the Zohar (£289). A rabbi at the Central Synagogue in London, Barry Marcus, said, "There's not a single Rabbinic authority on this planet who endorses what they're doing; the condemnation of them is universal." He also noted that the Zohar could be picked up at any religious bookshop (£35).[5]

The bad press didn't discourage Madonna; it made her angry. She noted the hypocrisy in the way the Kabbalah Centre was covered compared to the coverage of the documented and in some cases prosecutable Christian evangelical excesses and the financial and sexual abuse scandals involving the Catholic Church.[6] Her argument, however cogent, didn't persuade the press to change its coverage.

The Kabbalah link to Madonna's Malawi visit was *the* story, overshadowing the need she had hoped to expose and the work she had undertaken. That is, until the press picked up another story: an adoption. She had tried to keep it quiet, but on October 4, a Malawi government spokeswoman announced that Madonna intended to adopt a baby boy.[7] "I didn't realize the adoption was causing any controversy," Madonna said, "until I came back and there were a million film crews in the airport and press camped outside my door."[8]

Madonna had long wanted another child, and adoption had always been a possibility. Having finally decided to go that route, she applied to an international adoption agency and waited.[9] In the meantime, through Raising Malawi, she had come to understand the depth of Malawian orphans' needs and felt that she had come to know some of them through footage sent to her by Nathan Rissman, the director of her documentary.[10]

He was an unlikely choice to direct a film in Africa: Rissman had worked as her gardener. "He's a brilliant, lovely guy...He did everything, and he did it with humility. And everybody just grew to love him," Madonna said. He had made movies of Lourdes and Rocco that he sent to Madonna to cheer her up if she was away. "So one day I said, 'I need somebody to document [Malawi]' and then I looked at him and I said, 'And I think that person is you!'"[11]

Rissman went to Africa ten times over the course of two years, sleeping on floors of huts "and waking up with chickens on his head," Madonna said. "People opened their hearts to him."[12] That compassion came through in his footage for the film that would be called *I Am Because We*

Are, based on the African philosophy of ubuntu—"A human is a human through other humans."[13]

Madonna watched Rissman's videos over and over until she started to feel "connected" to the children in them.[14] David Banda was one such child. Madonna said she first saw him being carried by an eight-year-old girl. "I became transfixed by him." She had been that young girl caring for an infant after the death of her mother, and she had been that young boy, seemingly alone in the world. Madonna asked who he was.[15]

She finally met David at the Home of Hope orphanage, where five hundred orphans were cared for by the Reverend Thomson John Chipeta, whom Madonna called a "saint" who "cannot turn anyone away." Madonna said the orphanage didn't have enough food or medicine, and when she asked about laundry facilities, she was told that the children only had one outfit each, "so they didn't do laundry."[16]

David was one of the youngest of Chipeta's orphans. At thirteen months old, he had already survived malaria and tuberculosis. When Madonna met him, he had pneumonia. He, like the other children, had no diaper and was "basically going to the bathroom on himself," Madonna said. The next day she came back with a truckload of Pampers and the wish to adopt David.[17] "The look of pure joy on her face was beyond words, not unlike when her children were born," a witness to their meeting told *People* magazine.[18]

David was born into a family that had lost two of its three children to malaria. His mother, Marita, had died, too, six days after giving birth to him. His desperate father, Yohane Banda, placed his five-week-old son in an orphanage, hoping he would survive. "I was alone with no money," Banda said. "I didn't want him to die like the others."[19]

Though Banda said he visited his son twice a week, sometimes with the child's grandmother, Madonna said she was told that during his first year of life, David hadn't been visited by any members of his family. "If somebody had said to me, 'Oh his dad comes every week, or his granny visits on a regular basis and he's well looked after,' I would have not given [adopting him] another thought," she said. "The thing that was so disturbing to me was that from the time that he was filmed...to the time that I actually met him, his health had declined enormously." "He could hardly breathe."[20]

Madonna received permission to take David to a clinic, where doctors put him on a bronchial dilator and injected him with antibiotics. Her next job was to determine whether the adoption would be allowed.[21] Malawi's minister of children told her it might be, but she needed David's father's written approval.[22]

Madonna and Guy met Yohane Banda, a thirty-two-year-old farmer, at the High Court in Malawi's capital, Lilongwe. In the low brick building, which had no electricity, Madonna, speaking through an interpreter, promised to give David a good life and to bring him back to Malawi to see his family.[23] She said,

> He looked into my eyes and said to me that he was very grateful that I was going to give his son a life and that if he had kept his son with him in the village, he would have buried him...I didn't really need...any more confirmation that I was doing the right thing and I had his blessing.[24]

People quoted David's grandmother as saying, "God has heard our prayer. May he bless this kind-hearted woman abundantly."[25]

US citizens began adopting children internationally in large numbers after World War II. These were ordinary citizens moved to compassion by the devastation of that conflict, and the children adopted were usually European—white—like their adoptive parents. During the next US war, in Korea, it took an act of Congress for an evangelical couple from Oregon to be able to adopt eight Korean orphans and bring them to the States, thereby opening the door to transnational, cross-cultural adoptions.[26] By the mid-2000s, more than forty-five thousand children from developing nations were adopted, most of them by US citizens.[27] But not every developing country allowed international adoption or had the legal structure in place to accommodate it. Malawi was one of them.

Ordinarily, a person wanting to adopt a child there had to become "Malawian" by living in the country for eighteen months prior to adoption. That wasn't feasible for Madonna, so she and Guy were given interim permission on October 12 to assume temporary custody of David. They could take him out of Malawi in a foster-care capacity while the eighteen-month adoption process continued. In the meantime, a social worker was to check on David periodically at Madonna and Guy's London home before the final adoption was granted. The main thing for Madonna was that David was safe and that she could begin caring for him.[28]

The contrast between her private exultation and the shrill and venomous public response was unprecedented in Madonna's life, even after she had been on the receiving end of twenty years of personal and professional attacks.

Human rights activists in Malawi protested, saying that she and Guy had circumvented a law designed to protect children from human traffickers. They wanted the court to order them back to Malawi. Within days, sixty-seven rights groups from Africa and abroad had filed court documents to block the adoption.[29]

Some groups pressured Yohane Banda to rescind his approval, telling him from their position of supposed superior understanding that he didn't know what he had done. He begged to differ. "As David's father, I have no problem, so what is their concern?" he asked. "What I want is a good life, a good education for my child."[30] Of the people newly concerned with David's welfare, he wondered, "Where were they before all this happened? . . . My son's been taken by a kind-hearted woman, but they want to bring him back to the orphanage."[31]

Banda's wishes were ignored, and the high-minded outrage continued, as did the pressure on Banda as activists and international media descended upon him, telling him he would never again see his child and that Madonna was not the good woman she seemed to be. The people against the adoption soon got what they wanted: Banda relented and said he hadn't understood the documents he signed.[32]

Malawi's minister of children disagreed. "We explained every detail and Madonna explained her intentions. He was asked several times in court if he understood what was going on and he said he did."[33] Madonna did not blame Yohane Banda; she blamed the international press, who "brought nothing but chaos to his life. I did think his [initial] reaction is the true reaction, and that is 'thank you for giving my son a life.' "[34]

Madonna herself was also under attack in stories that revealed less about the adoption than the underlying racism in US and British society. The press was unabashedly obsessed with David's skin color. ABC News would run a story called "Black Babies: Hollywood's Hottest Accessory?"[35] In London, a TV presenter in a segment on Madonna said, "What do you give the woman who has everything? A little black baby, it seems."[36]

Adoption rights activists, meanwhile, charged that Madonna and Guy had been given VIP treatment while other families had to wait much longer for a child.[37] Some accused her of perpetuating imperialism as a rich white woman swooping into Africa to save a poor Black child.[38] Images of the Middle Passage and slave markets were invoked. Lost in the frenzied discussion were the facts: a little boy was being offered a home by a family who loved him.

When David arrived by private plane in London accompanied by Lourdes's nanny, Shavawn Gordon, and her husband, Nathan Rissman, they were surrounded by paparazzi swarming like vultures with no regard for the child's safety or welfare, which was supposedly at the heart of their concern. The fact that Madonna hadn't herself traveled to London with the child triggered yet more righteous ire.[39] Madonna said of the adoption blowback, "It crushed me. I have to say it was one of life's great disappointments."[40]

The uproar might not have been so loud if news of Madonna's desire to adopt hadn't come when it did. That fall an ad campaign appeared, initiated by the model Iman, to help the AIDS charity Keep a Child Alive. In it, a number of entertainers, most of them white, adopted tribal markings and declared themselves African. In theory, the ad was meant to show that, au fond, everyone has African DNA. In practice, it came across as privileged entertainers telling dying Africans, "I feel your pain."[41]

Africa had become so "hot" for celebrity branding that otherwise apolitical entertainers like Jessica Simpson and Paris Hilton had either gone there or were considering a trip.[42] In the PR world, supporting an African cause had become as essential to one's career as launching a celebrity perfume had been earlier in the decade. Madonna's adoption of David was, cynically, seen as part of that, even though her "brand" needed no artificial bolstering.

When Madonna wasn't criticized for adopting David as a career move, she was accused of doing so to copy the "yummy mummy" Angelina Jolie, who had adopted her first son, Maddox, from Cambodia in 2002 while working as a goodwill ambassador for the United Nations High Commissioner for Refugees.[43] Her decision was transformative: Jolie went from wild child to earth mother. In 2005, she adopted a second child, Zahara, this time from Ethiopia. She also had a child with Brad Pitt, delivered in Namibia in the spring of 2006. World leaders praised her. *Esquire* called her "the best woman in the world."[44] By contrast, in the adoptive mommy story, Madonna was cast as villain.[45]

Gala magazine turned the Angelina–Madonna saga into a catfight, publishing an interview with Jolie in which she appeared to criticize Madonna. Jolie said the article was edited to omit her support for Madonna. "I have been horrified by the attacks she's been subjected to," Jolie said in a statement. "All that should count is the happiness of her little David."[46]

Madonna issued a statement, too, saying, "I expect to be given a hard time about many of the things I do. I know they are provocative, and I prepare myself, but I did not expect the media, the government, or any human rights organizations to take a stand against me trying to save a child's life."[47] Guy responded to one critic, saying, "How dare anyone question her motives? . . . It's so preposterous that anyone would be critical of Madonna for wanting to share her love and wealth."[48]

By the end of October, Madonna had scheduled several high-profile interviews to "set the record straight."[49] During her first TV interviews about the adoption saga — with Kirsty Wark on BBC2 and Oprah Winfrey in the States — she was obviously in pain and struggled to compose herself. With great understatement she called the period a "real low point in my life."[50]

Some good did come of the controversy. The adoption coverage put Malawi on the map. Suddenly the small country and its oversize AIDS crisis was recognized even by people who limited their reading to entertainment magazines and the tabs. Madonna had wanted to shine a spotlight on Malawi, and she succeeded. She also began a dialogue about family, both the kind that shares a home and the one we're all part of—the one that shares a planet. Wrote Caitlin Moran in the London *Times* in early November of that year,

> In a single act of altruism, she has managed to ignite a debate that encompasses immigration, Africa, working mothers, modern parenting, international adoption law, race, money and fame.[51]

Former Labour Party parliamentarian Oona King, who herself had adopted a child from abroad and who as a government official had visited African orphanages and knew the conditions there, similarly defended Madonna. "We would not even be thinking about the countless African orphans but for Madonna's intervention."[52]

Madonna was fierce in defending her own actions, but she was fiercer still in defending the people she loved. After being initially knocked over by the gale of criticism coming her way, by December she was back on her feet. She and her adoption saga were favorite topics of television comedians, but she dared to show up at the British Comedy Awards anyway to present a prize to Sacha Baron Cohen for *Borat*. After introducing her, the evening's host, Jonathan Ross, said, "Congratulations on your lovely little black baby, David. [Audience laughs]...When I went to Africa all I came home with was a wallet." Madonna snapped, "Well, you might go home with a black eye."[53]

Over Christmas and New Year's, Madonna and Guy gathered up their children and escaped London and the world's media, taking a rare family holiday to an island in the Indian Ocean. They had to go that far to have the peace and quiet they needed to enjoy one another as a family. David was very much part of it. Madonna said the family called him "King David."[54]

During some press encounters, Madonna mentioned a little girl named Mercy, who was just a few months younger than David. She had met Mercy and David at around the same time and wanted to bring her home, too. Though Mercy's fourteen-year-old mother had died and her eighteen-year-old father had disappeared, her grandmother wouldn't allow it.[55] Madonna had just been through the fight of her life for David, but she refused to abandon Mercy, no matter how long it took. When she met those children, she said, "I held each of them in my arms [and] I whispered in their ears that I would look after them." She was determined to keep her promise.[56]

Madonna's Indian Ocean holiday was "lovely," but her mind was on New York. The artist in her wanted to live there, and she wanted Lourdes to be closer to Carlos.[57] The vacation also hadn't helped her marriage. "It's as if he thinks it's his duty to put her in her place every now and again," an insider was quoted as saying of Ritchie. "She just gets tired of it. She wishes he was nicer to her."[58] For his part, Ritchie wanted a regular life, what he called a "husband and wife thing."[59] That wasn't going to happen. Madonna settled in London when they returned, but not as a homemaker and certainly not as the lesser half in her marriage. She had decided to direct a movie and make a new album.

The movie decision hurt. That was Guy's career—one that, after early triumphs with *Lock, Stock and Two Smoking Barrels* and *Snatch,* had struggled. Following the disastrous *Swept Away* and the poorly received *Revolver,* he wanted to make another film, he said, "in the same genre as *Snatch.*" Madonna's entry into his world at that moment risked undermining his film because, good or bad, the attention would undoubtedly be on hers.

Madonna's work with Nathan Rissman on the Malawi documentary *I Am Because We Are* reawakened her interest in directing. She was the film's writer and the creative force behind the project. As its producer, she secured interviews with former president Bill Clinton, Archbishop Desmond Tutu, Jeffrey Sachs, and Dr. Paul Farmer. Rissman directed on-site, but Madonna decided what appeared on-screen. The finished film, like her concerts, videos, and records, would be the result of a collaboration, but it was essentially hers.[60]

Madonna had worked alongside directors for more than two decades, most recently with Jonas Åkerlund on the 2005 tour film *I'm Going to Tell You a Secret* and had had her first experience as a director in 1990 with David Fincher on the "Oh Father" video. In 2007, she was ready to do it again. To say that out loud, however, took courage. In Hollywood, only 9 percent of feature film directors were women. "I was afraid to just say, 'I want to be a director,'" she recalled. "But then one day I said, 'OK, stop dreaming and do it.'"[61]

She began with a commercial. That spring, she directed a television spot for a fashion line she developed for the Swedish retailer H&M. Around ninety seconds long, with thirteen characters (Madonna among them), it was as quick and clean as her "Human Nature" video and nearly as funny.[62]

Madonna felt ready to tackle something bigger. It would be a feature film called *Filth and Wisdom*. She considered it her "film school."[63] She came into it with ideas, mostly based on Kabbalah's notion that good and bad do not exist, that all is good because "bad" helps one learn and therefore grow. She kept that concept but adapted her script after meeting a mustachioed Ukrainian punk gypsy named Eugene Hütz.[64]

Born Yevgen Oleksandrovych Nikolaev-Symonov, he emigrated from Ukraine to Vermont with dreams of being a musician. He eventually landed in New York, where he formed the underground band Gogol Bordello. "I heard that she…had been an admirer of the band for some time," he said. "Then one day my phone rang, and I picked up and she was there!" Within two weeks they were working together.[65]

Madonna and Hütz approached the film the way they might if they were in a music studio, bouncing around ideas. "She comes with her creative energies flowing and is also very spontaneous. She's probably one of the most powerfully spontaneous people I have ever met," he said. "So we quickly put the script for the movie together and went to work."[66]

Hütz played a struggling musician who moonlights as a cross-dressing dominatrix. He shares a flat with two women, one a ballerina (Holly Weston) who moonlights as a pole dancer and the other a pharmacist (Vicky McClure) who, while administering medicines to relatively well-off customers, is obsessed with the needy in Africa. A fourth figure, a blind poet neighbor named Professor Flynn, played by Richard E. Grant, is based on Madonna's mentor Christopher Flynn, who lost his sight to AIDS.[67]

All those characters have high goals: art, saving humanity, or both. But more immediately, they are engaged in a desperate fight for survival and a search for human warmth. "If you break it down, it's about the struggle of being an artist," Madonna said. "I feel like the three main characters in the film are basically me."[68] The eighty-minute movie was shot in London during two weeks in mid-May. Hütz needed to get back on tour with his band, and Madonna had a record to make.

Rather than the musical avant-garde of Europe, Madonna's next album, her last with Warner Bros., would involve the cream of the US mainstream. In February, Tim Mosley—Timbaland—announced that he was collaborating with Madonna on a record. One of the biggest producers in the business, he had worked with Missy Elliott, burnished his reputation to a lustrous gold with Justin Timberlake, and expanded his repertoire by producing Coldplay's Chris Martin (Mr. Gwyneth Paltrow) and Björk. Along the way, he created a slick new production-heavy sound that mixed hip-hop and R and B.

By sheer coincidence, Timbaland was looking to work with Madonna at the same time as she decided she wanted to work with him.[69] She had begun her new album with Pharrell Williams but wanted additional songs that had more of a groove to their sound. Timbaland was the natural choice. Guy Oseary then suggested that Justin Timberlake join the team. And that, too, made sense. It was the sound that the two Tims had created on Timberlake's 2006 *Future Sex/Love Sounds* album that Madonna was after. With *Ray of Light,* she had wanted to make electronica warm. Timberlake and Timbaland had made it sexy.

Timberlake said, "I thought she could essentially do the whole record with Pharrell...and I asked Tim, 'How do we fit in?'"[70] They decided to do what had worked for Timberlake's album by "co-producing together" and "just throwing, you know, Madonna in the mix."[71] *Throw Madonna into the mix of her own album?* She wasn't a guest artist; she was *the* artist. Without realizing it, Timberlake had foretold the album's biggest problem.

Pat Leonard once said that Madonna had a way of making every song she worked on a "Madonna song." That wasn't the case on what would become *Hard Candy.* Her eleventh studio album was not a "Madonna album." Its credits told that story: they were like the ingredients on processed-food labels — mind-numbing in their complexity and far removed from their sources. Madonna was all but lost in the overproduction of a sound so mainstream that it was nearly elevator music.

In the past, if Madonna's collaborators were well known, it was only to people in the underground music world. But the team she chose to work with on her new album were *only* unknown in the underground. Pharrell Williams and his musical partner Chad Hugo — the Neptunes — were responsible in 2003 for nearly half the songs on US radio.[72] What was she thinking? In one interview, she said she was fulfilling an obligation "to deliver [an] album every two years" to Warner.[73] In another, she admitted that she didn't know.

> I didn't have any idea what kind of music I wanted to make. I just knew I wanted to collaborate with Pharrell and Justin. I needed to be inspired and thought, Well, who's making records I like? So I went, "I like that guy and I like that guy." It's not like we hit it off right away...I had ups and downs before everybody got comfortable.[74]

The album's development was the opposite of her experience with Stuart Price on *Confessions.* The intimacy of that project was replaced by cold studios and teams of egos who made music *for* artists but not necessarily *with* them. "It's more like writing a TV show than writing a song," said

John Seabrook in his book *The Song Machine.* "The producer is the undisputed king of the song-writing process." *King* being the operative word. Fewer than 5 percent of music producers were women.[75]

"With this album, I had a lot of strong-minded men in the studio," Madonna said. "They had ideas as to how they thought I should sound, how I should sing. There were a few times along the way that I had to remind them that nobody tells me how to sing."[76] At one point, she was so angry with Williams that she cried. "I was in a sensitive mood," she explained.

> I was singing in the studio and I didn't understand the rhythm that he wanted me to sing in, and he was kind of giving me a hard time and I was sort of taken aback by the way he was talking to me, so…I said, "You know what? We need to talk.".…So, we went upstairs and I'm like "You can't talk to me that way!" and then I just burst into tears, and he was like, "Oh my god, Madonna has a heart!" and I was like "What?!" and I started crying even more, and then we had it out. Now I love him…but I think we had to go through that.[77]

Williams said that after that episode he and Madonna became "seriously tight. She's probably the best person I've ever collaborated with."[78]

The Madonna-Williams song "Candy Shop" opened the album, and it would set the tone for its other confections. Its sex-as-sugar story had been covered in James Mtume's 1983 R&B classic, "Juicy Fruit." But "Candy Shop" wasn't "Juicy Fruit." The composition wasn't clever enough to support the humor or sexy enough to support the innuendo. Unfortunately, most of *Hard Candy* remained at that too-easy, too-sweet level. But there were exceptions.

The second track, which would be the album's first single, was one: "4 Minutes." Madonna and Timberlake wrote the lyrics after Timbaland played them the beat. "He gave us a bit of the music and we started writing the lyrics, we came up with the melody and he started writing more music," she said. "That's really how all the songs were written, piecemeal."[79] As for the subject, she explained that it was a warning that humans were running out of time to save the planet.[80] She wrote the next track, "Give It 2 Me," "so I could have a great time doing it in a stadium."[81]

"Heartbeat" was a Madonna song in subject and sound. The discordant opening, during which her voice dared to wander off key and stagger as it did in "Bad Girl," announced that there would be nothing formulaic about it. "Heartbeat" was one of the rare songs on the album in which Madonna was given the space she needed to be herself.

"Miles Away" was potentially another one. The lyrics were strong enough to override the heavy and yet surprisingly empty beats. With another musical treatment, it could have been one of her best and most moving songs, but the coldness of the sound nearly killed it. Maybe that coldness was brilliantly intentional. Madonna said the song was "inspired by Guy" but written for anyone dealing with the emptiness of long-distance relationships. "You have to work hard to make it work."[82]

"She's Not Me" and "Incredible" remained in "Miles Away" territory in that Madonna's fans searched them for clues about her personal life. The songs told the story of a woman alternating between anger and heartbreak as she tried to make sense of a tattered relationship. But the music didn't hint at angst of any kind. The young men Madonna worked with set her lyrics to music that might have been written for an assembly-line pop singer, and, inexplicably, Madonna acquiesced.

"Beat Goes On," which features vocals by Kanye West, comes along at a critical moment to break up the monotony of the first half of the album. His participation was serendipitous. Madonna was working in a studio in Los Angeles, and West was recording down the hall. Guy Oseary suggested that Madonna invite him to join her on a song, and she did.[83] The result was what might be called a fine mess. Madonna said it was written with a sense of urgency. "Kanye only had four hours. I had to finish it before he had to catch an airplane," she explained. "But you know what? Right now, I'm operating in the mode of 'live every day like it's your last day.' So there's a sense of urgency in everything I do."[84]

By the end of the album, Madonna's fans were left to fantasize about what might have been had she worked with other collaborators. But the biggest element missing from *Hard Candy* was Madonna. Maybe she was trying to figure out who she was musically after a decade of testing the boundaries with William Orbit, Mirwais Ahmadzaï, and Stuart Price. Maybe, preoccupied by her marriage, her children, her films, and Malawi, she was otherwise engaged. Whatever the reason, for the first time in her career, Madonna seemed AWOL from her own record.

Madonna and Guy had been visited every six weeks by social workers assessing two-year-old David's development. They were asked "all kinds of invasive questions," fingerprinted several times, and forced to undergo psychological evaluations. "Everybody who goes through adoptions has to do this, so I'm not alone," Madonna said. "But you know, I'd do it again. Because David is amazing."[85]

In April, she took a break from her projects to return to Malawi with David and Lourdes. The previous time she was there, she was criticized for bringing a film crew. That spring, Madonna was criticized for arranging a private trip "shrouded in secrecy." Part of it involved reuniting David and his father, which she wanted to do outside the glare of the media. Another reason for her visit was her effort to adopt the little girl she had met the previous year, Mercy James.[86]

In the year since she first traveled to Malawi, Madonna recognized that things had already changed and that progress, though slow, had begun.[87] Over the course of several weeks, she visited the organizations she wanted to help and met the people who needed it while ten-year-old Lourdes volunteered in orphanages with HIV-infected children. "She so came into her own," Madonna told *Interview* editor Ingrid Sischy, "and was so responsible and stayed for eight hours every day and worked tirelessly. I thought, 'Why am I babying her so much? She's capable of so much more.' ... After you go to Africa, you drop all that silliness."[88]

One of Madonna's most ambitious projects involved helping girls Lourdes's age. She had purchased land and hired an architect to design a school.[89] Oprah Winfrey had opened the doors that year to a school she built in South Africa that would provide a free education and boarding to African girls. A *Newsweek* article about it sniffed, "$40 million for a school of impoverished girls in Africa does seem a bit, well, extravagant."[90] Was the problem the fact that the school was in Africa? Or that it was for girls? Ninety percent of the graduates of Oprah's so-called vanity project would go on to attend international universities, Oxford and Stanford among them.[91]

Madonna worked to finish her album in September, but in the middle of the month, she and Guy went to Tel Aviv for the Jewish New Year, Rosh Hashanah. It wasn't their first such trip. They had traveled there in 2004 as part of a Kabbalah Centre event and to visit Jewish holy sites.[92] During that visit, they were together except during religious observances, when men and women were separated. During their latest trip, the press noted that while Madonna participated in religious services and Kabbalah events, Guy spent his time on the beach.[93]

Rumors of divorce followed Madonna that year. Few, however, thought the divorce would be from her record company. She had been with Warner for twenty-five years, ever since Seymour Stein signed her from his hospital bed, in 1982. She had earned the company billions of dollars, and it had given her the freedom to develop as she needed, no matter how risky her projects were. The relationship hadn't soured, but the times had changed.

When it came to relationships, whether creative or personal, as soon as Madonna recognized that she needed to change direction, she ended them. That was what she did with Warner. The record business she once knew no longer existed. The internet had killed it. Radio conglomerates had killed it. Her experience with *Confessions* was the last straw. Warner hadn't been able to use its muscle to get her singles from that album on the radio, despite her record-breaking concert tour and the songs' chart-topping performance in Europe. Madonna had to adapt.[94]

Having concluded that "there's one thing you can't download and that's a live performance," in October she announced that she had signed with the concert promoter Live Nation and was leaving Warner. The news reverberated through the music world and the entertainment business. Coming as it did on the same day that Radiohead announced it would release its *In Rainbows* album as a digital download and allow users to decide what they wanted to pay, Madonna's announcement felt like a call to a revolution that was already underway.[95]

There had been signs. Napster was the first, followed by iTunes. The concentration of radio play to a few set lists controlled by megaprogrammers was another. MTV, meanwhile, had largely abandoned music videos in favor of reality TV. Record stores became obsolete because of downloads and Amazon. By 2006, most of the big chains were bankrupt. But until Madonna's deal with Live Nation, record companies retained one asset that kept them alive: the talent. Where could an artist go? Madonna pointed the way.[96]

She signed an industry first: a ten-year, 360-degree deal that covered recording, touring, merchandise, music-related TV and film projects, licensing, and sponsorships. In return, she received a $17.5 million signing bonus and a contract worth $120 million in cash and stock. Madonna would be the "founding artist" in Live Nation's new Artist Nation division.[97]

Some entertainment business insiders mumbled that Live Nation might not see a return on its investment. But others recognized the value of having a trendsetting artist like Madonna endorse Live Nation's business model. And there was the income Live Nation would make off the Madonna brand, even when she wasn't touring. Her H&M fashion line, developed just that year, had already earned $20 million from its trench coats, casual wear, and daytime dresses. Future such deals would benefit Live Nation. The company wasn't investing in a performer but a "cross-capitalized entertainment platform."[98]

Madonna made a long bet, too, but it wasn't entirely a leap into the unknown. The chairman of Live Nation's music division, who was also the president of its global touring division, was an old friend. Arthur Fogel had produced Madonna's previous three tours: Drowned World, Re-Invention, and Confessions. She called him a "touring genius."[99]

Within five years, Live Nation would dominate the multibillion-dollar tour industry, not only organizing tours but also owning venues and

Guy Ritchie and Madonna at the launch party for *Music,* Los Angeles, September 2000 *Photo by Ron Galella. Ron Galella Collection. Getty Images*

Madonna at Brixton Academy, London, November 2000
Photographer Unknown. Shutterstock

Madonna performing during the Drowned World tour, Los Angeles, September 9, 2001 *Photo by Jeffrey Mayer. WireImage. Getty Images*

Madonna performing during the opening night of the Re-Invention tour, the Forum, Inglewood, California, May 2004 *Photo by Kevin Mazur. Getty Images*

The Madonna and Steven Klein collaboration *X-STaTIC PRo=CeSS,* New York City, March 2003 *Photo by Stephen Lovekin. Deitch Gallery FilmMagic. Getty Images*

Steven Klein, Madonna's longtime friend and one of her most important collaborators, Tokyo, September 2006 *Photo by Jun Sato. WireImage. Getty Images*

Mirwais and Madonna at a performance of "American Life," Tower Records, New York City, April 2003 *Photo by Kevin Mazur. WireImage. Getty Images*

William Orbit, Madonna's collaborator on *Ray of Light* and *MDNA*, among other musical projects, March 2010 *Photo by Laurie Mayer. Copyright Laurie Mayer. Image provided by William Orbit*

Jonas Åkerlund, Madonna, and Stuart Price at the premiere of *I'm Going to Tell You a Secret*, New York City, October 2005 *Photo by Kevin Mazur. Getty Images*

The Confessions tour arrives in Moscow, September 2006 *Photo by Maxim Marmur. AFP, Getty Images*

Madonna directing her film *W.E.,* Central Park, New York City, September 2010 *Photo by Ray Tamarra. Getty Images*

Madonna performing on the opening night of the MDNA tour, Philadelphia, August 2012 *Photo by Kevin Mazur. WireImage. Getty Images*

Maluma and Madonna, 2019 Billboard Music Awards, Las Vegas, May 2019 *Photo by Kevin Winter. Getty Images*

Lourdes Leon and Mercy James during a visit to the Mkoko Primary School, Malawi, April 2013 *Photo by Amos Gumulira. AFP, Getty Images*

Mercy James at the opening of the Mercy James Institute for Pediatric Surgery and Intensive Care, Blantyre, Malawi, July 2017 *Photo by Amos Gumulira. AFP, Getty Images*

Rocco Ritchie, London, September 2017 *Photo by Ray Crowder. Getty Images*

David Banda and Madonna at the WBA Lightweight Championship fight, Brooklyn, May 2022 *Photo by Cassy Athena. Getty Images*

merging with critical stakeholders like Ticketmaster.[100] Madonna had helped put Live Nation in that position, but her association with it—while financially beneficial—would greatly complicate her life. Her tours would be longer, her branding obligations greater. The test would come the next summer, when she embarked on her first tour for Live Nation just as she was about to become a single mother.

Chapter 50

Des Moines, New York, Berlin, Cannes, London, Cardiff, Buenos Aires, 2008

> People always talk about how stardom changes you, but they
> never talk about how it can change the people close to you.[1]
>
> — *Madonna*

THE UNTHINKABLE HAPPENED in January of 2008 in Iowa. A Black man
won the Iowa presidential caucus, defeating his main rival, a woman. The
man was Barack Obama. The woman was Hillary Clinton. And the race
had the potential to make history. For liberals, and for people who did not
agree with the direction in which the United States had traveled since
9/11, the fact that a Black man and a woman were serious contenders for
the White House was beyond exhilarating.

In that season of hope, it was impossible to remain on the sidelines of history. The stakes were too high. Madonna campaigned for Hillary. Though
she liked and admired Obama, she felt solidarity with a woman, particularly
one with a survivor's spirit.[2] As writer Dina Honour said, both women had
walked "through the flames rather than succumbing to them."[3]

Even the most frivolous events felt purposeful that year. The big story of
New York Fashion Week wasn't the usual material excess and design outrage but Gucci's decision to eschew a grand-opening party for its new
Fifth Avenue flagship store and join forces with Madonna to host a benefit
for Raising Malawi and the UN children's fund, UNICEF. Gucci said in a
statement that it "wanted to give something back." The world's most
famous fashion journalist, Suzy Menkes, wrote in the *New York Times* that
the gathering "might just mark a new phase in the glossy and glamorous
luxury world."[4]

In the past, Madonna had supported other people's initiatives: AIDS
Project Los Angeles, ACT UP, amfAR, Live Aid, Live 8, and Live Earth (a
series of benefit concerts intended to help combat climate change), as well
as countless celebrity charity events, voting drives, and political campaigns. The UN benefit was the first she had organized herself, and it was
for the cause closest to her heart — Malawi and its children.

The February 6 event was held in a forty-two-thousand-square-foot transparent tent erected on the north lawn of UN headquarters, in Manhattan. Madonna arranged for entertainment from Alicia Keys, Rihanna, Timbaland, and the African Children's Choir. Chris Rock agreed to host the celebrity auction portion of the evening. And as raffle prizes, Madonna's friends volunteered their talents—batting practice with New York Yankees star Alex Rodriguez, an hour of soccer with David Beckham, and aerobics with Gwyneth Paltrow, among others.[5]

Attending the $2,500-a-plate gathering were international entertainment, business, philanthropy, and sports royalty.[6] The event was an opportunity for Madonna to introduce her powerful friends to her powerless friends: one million children in need in Malawi. For her, the evening was as much about education as fundraising.[7] She said,

> The more you know, the more you realize you don't know... the more you cannot turn your back on things... I suppose that's why people generally don't want to know more, because at a soul level they understand that the more they know, the more they have to do.[8]

The event raised more than $5 million and made headlines around the world: in both the entertainment press, because of the attendees, and on news pages, because of the latest Madonna "controversy." She was accused of misusing the UN premises because Gucci had sponsored the event and because part of the funds went to Raising Malawi, which was associated with the Kabbalah Centre. The UN responded that it was sure the money would be spent wisely, and it was not bothered by Gucci.[9]

Madonna and Gucci teamed up again for a less virtuous cause when many of those same people gathered later that month in Los Angeles. A writers' strike in Hollywood forced the cancellation of the annual *Vanity Fair* Oscar after-party. Madonna, Guy Oseary, and Demi Moore stepped into the A-list breach and threw one of their own. Oseary's home was the location for the invitation-only, no-cameras-allowed, anything-goes event. Gucci provided the swag bags. Madonna picked the theme.[10]

It was a protected space. Tom Cruise and Katie Holmes, Ellen DeGeneres and Portia de Rossi, Cameron Diaz, Owen Wilson, Elton John and David Furnish, Leonardo DiCaprio, Jack Nicholson, Sean Penn—in short, celebrities who zealously guarded their personal lives—came to partake of the absinthe that poured from fountain stations. The Madonna-Oseary event became a coveted post-Oscars invitation through the next decade.[11]

It was not Hollywood Madonna who appeared in Berlin that month but Madonna the novice director. Her decision to premiere *Filth and Wisdom* at the Berlin International Film Festival was as audacious as appearing on national television to play guitar a month after she had learned to strum one. On both occasions, the student Madonna was prepared to risk appearing foolish because she so loved the art.

James Christopher, in the London *Times,* said the film showed that "Madonna has real potential as a director."[12] But almost no other critic said anything good about it. The *Guardian* critic wrote,

> Madonna has been a terrible actor in many, many films and now...she has graduated to being a terrible director. She has made a movie so incredibly bad that Berlin festivalgoers were staggering around yesterday in a state of clinical shock.[13]

Without doubt, Madonna was prepared for the bad press. She had even considered releasing the film directly to the internet.[14] She knew that skill arose from practice and dedication, and she was prepared to finally dedicate herself to film the way she had dedicated herself to music.

That year, 2008, Madonna marked the twenty-fifth anniversary of her debut album, which meant she was eligible to be inducted into the Rock & Roll Hall of Fame. It wasn't a given that she would be. In purist rock circles, Madonna was considered a pop star. The hall was also a boys' club. Of the 156 individuals or groups inducted since 1986, only sixteen were women solo performers or all-female groups. Of those, nine were legacy inductions, recognizing women from the '50s and '60s who no longer performed. But Madonna's place in music history was undeniable, and she could not be ignored.[15]

On March 10, in New York, Madonna, Leonard Cohen, John Mellencamp, the Dave Clark Five, and the Ventures were inducted into the Rock & Roll Hall of Fame. Inductees were allowed to select the people who would introduce them at the ceremony and, if they didn't perform themselves, they could choose the artists who would represent their work onstage. Madonna's choices reflected her musical past and her musical present. She picked Iggy Pop to perform "Burning Up" and "Ray of Light." To introduce her, she picked Justin Timberlake.

Timberlake nervously tripped through his introductory remarks, reminding the audience that Madonna was "the biggest name on the planet," a person who had achieved success "the old-fashioned way: she earned it." Along with his praise, he apparently felt it necessary to get dirty and add some innuendo-filled jokes that received almost no response. When Madonna finally appeared onstage, the relief was almost palpable.[16]

Her look that night was subdued. There was nothing in her appearance to suggest a rock star, much less the woman who had, in Timberlake's words, "changed the way our world sounded...the way our world looked." Madonna that night looked like a middle-aged woman dressed up for an evening out. And that meant that fortysomething women could see themselves in her achievements.

Madonna thanked everyone who had helped her, going back to Christopher Flynn and the Gilroys. She thanked the people who criticized her, "ones who said I was talentless, that I was chubby, that I couldn't sing, that I was a one-hit wonder. They helped me, too. They helped me because they made me question myself repeatedly and they pushed me to be better." She thanked the people who were still with her, like Liz Rosenberg, and the people who were no longer in her entourage, like Freddy DeMann. And she thanked Guy Oseary, who had become her sole manager after Angela Becker left that job to have a child with Stuart Price.[17]

Madonna told the hall that her career had been the result of collaboration. "I did not get here on my own," she said, looking very much alone as she did so. Guy Ritchie did not attend the ceremony. In fact, he was scarce during all Madonna's events early that year.[18] She told a German magazine, "We no longer have the idealistic expectation of a relationship. I gave up the dream that he is the perfect husband. He gave up the expectation that I am the ideal wife." She said instead that they had "a deep affection for each other."[19]

Hard Candy was released soon after the Hall of Fame induction, and it confirmed her status in the music world for anyone who still doubted. The first single released from the album, "4 Minutes," climbed its way up the charts. When it breached the top ten, Madonna dethroned Elvis as the rock-era artist with the most top ten hits: she had thirty-seven.[20]

The "4 Minutes" video helped. Shot in January in London, it was created by a French team in their early twenties known as Jonas & François— Jonas Euvremer and François Rousselet.[21] "4 Minutes" would be only their fourth video.[22]

They came up with the concept of a void, or what Madonna called an "amorphous graphic line slowly eating up the world."[23] The video begins with Timbaland performing the song's introduction and Madonna and Timberlake seen separately from behind—she in a flesh-colored corset, he in leather jacket and jeans. That is the end of reality as we know it.

The video switches to Madonna pushing a car, walking briskly across tabletops, making an escape as a black screen, representing the fragile fabric of existence, disappears behind her. Interspersed throughout the action are shots of people who pop up like cartoon speech balloons: eating, bathing, kissing. Some of them, too, melt down to their anatomical parts.

Everything in the video is fleeting, and everyone in the video is unaware of the danger except Madonna and Timberlake.[24]

The set piece of the shoot involves one of the most demanding performances of her career. She and Timberlake navigate an obstacle course of cars—jumping through windows and up onto car roofs, presumably outrunning Armageddon.[25] They did all their own stunt work, and Madonna emerged from the video with bruises and skin burns. It did, however, give her a chance to display her hyperfit body, which became an important part of the *Hard Candy* promotion.[26]

The album arrived in stores featuring a cover photograph taken by Steven Klein showing Madonna as a boxer, wearing a black bodysuit, lace-up boots, a brass-knuckle ring that read M-DOLLA (Williams's nickname for her), and a heavyweight championship belt bearing the initial *M*. "It's quite a sort of tough stance," she said.[27] In the dozens of interviews she gave to promote the album, she seemed anything but.

Normally, when Madonna did an interview alongside a collaborator, she dominated the discussion. Her artistic partners generally stood mute. But while promoting *Hard Candy,* Madonna was the silent partner as Timberlake or Williams pontificated on the project or as Timbaland embarked on his own promotional interviews. The result distanced Madonna even more from the record, and maybe that was intentional. Or maybe she wanted to duck the inevitable questions about her private life.

There was also the matter of age. As her clock ticked toward fifty, the press was obsessed with it. Every article and most TV appearances began with the writer or interviewer commenting on how great she looked, meaning *for her age.* Madonna had never been so condescended to. There were plenty of other people, not sitting across from her, who hinted that she didn't look so good—that she'd had facial work; that her hands showed her years. One even dared to ask if the "urgency" in the song "4 Minutes" had to do with her age. Madonna said, "I think the state of the world has to do with my sense of urgency."[28]

Hard Candy, meanwhile, debuted at number 1 in thirty-seven countries, but that enthusiasm didn't last. Its worldwide sales of four million copies made it the lowest-selling studio album of Madonna's career to that point. That, however, wasn't a problem that overly concerned her. Malawi was. She was rescued from the superficial world of promotions and sales by her film about that country. She was ready to show it to the world.

I Am Because We Are premiered at the Tribeca Festival on April 24. The project and the night were about family. The film's music was composed by Pat Leonard, and Madonna attended the event with its director, Nathan Rissman, and her New York contingent, led by Rosie O'Donnell.

Madonna said the film "is closer to my heart than anything I've ever done...because it's about children in need and because while making this film I met my son."[29]

The following month, on May 21, Madonna took her message and her movie to the Cannes film festival, where it showed out of competition. Not since *Truth or Dare* had she been there to promote her own film.

Guy hadn't attended Madonna's UN event or the *Filth and Wisdom* premiere or her Hall of Fame induction, but he was with her at Cannes, looking pained on the red carpet as she was greeted warmly by festival organizers.[30] Inside the hall, that gathering of the global film industry elite loved her movie, at times gasping at its harrowing images and at others being moved to tears and near cheers by the heroism of some of its characters.[31]

"It's impossible to tear your eyes away from the screen," wrote Rosamund Witcher in London's *Sunday Times.* "If Madonna wants us to see her as more than the gyrating, gym-obsessed Queen of Pop, she has succeeded powerfully."[32] Wrote *The Guardian*'s Mark Brown, "Madonna the documentary-maker came, saw, and conquered the world's biggest film festival yesterday with a powerful polemic on the effects of disease and poverty on Malawi."[33]

The response of the humanitarian and activist community well beyond Cannes was mixed. Some saw it as reinforcing the "rescue" narrative the white world recited about the Global South and perpetuating the idea that Africa was a decaying continent. But others found reason to commend Madonna for her emphasis on local efforts to solve Malawi's problems and her insistence that only the empowerment of the population — from its children to its leaders — would ensure a better future.[34]

Seven days after Cannes, Madonna and Guy learned that the High Court in Malawi had finally approved their adoption of David. Social workers who had monitored the child described him as "lively, happy and thriving" and the family as a "warm and loving" environment.[35] Madonna equated the long, emotional process with childbirth.

> It was painful and a big struggle and I didn't understand it. But in the end I rationalized that when a woman has a child and goes through natural childbirth, she suffers an enormous amount...So I went through my own kind of birthing pains, dealing with the press on my doorstep, accusing me of kidnapping or whatever.[36]

Madonna and Guy's marriage had been difficult for years, but they had remained together in part because of David. During the eighteen-month adoption process, they tried as much as possible to keep the depth of their problems private. And in fact they were working to save their marriage, not as lovers but as friends. Earlier that year, Madonna bought the Mayfair pub that Ritchie frequented, the Punchbowl.[37]

But after David became legally part of their family, the facade could be dropped. "Sources," "insiders," and "friends" began leaking details of their difficulties. If the press reports were to be believed, it came down to a matter of money, career, and respect.[38]

Madonna had ten times Ritchie's wealth but felt that in a marriage of equals they should try to share financial responsibilities. Guy also believed that, stating repeatedly that he did not want her money. But questions arose about his contributions to Rocco's expenses — school fees and his nanny. And then there was the matter of $2 million that Madonna had given him to make a film about Kabbalah. When she learned that Ritchie had suspended the project, she wanted the money back.[39]

In an interview with the *Daily Mirror,* a source defended Ritchie, saying of the missed payments, "Guy was just engrossed in his work and he may have just taken his eye off the ball rather than intentionally not pay." On the subject of the film advance, the source said, "A lot of Guy's money is tied up and because of Madonna's wealth, she could effectively call upon the cash very quickly ... Guy just felt the way Madonna behaved over the loan wasn't like a loving wife should."[40]

Mostly, though, Ritchie was described as tired of Madonna's celebrity, her focus on her career, and the presence of her handlers, who, he said, "worshipped at the altar of Madonna." He had also grown tired of her causes. "I went along with all the 'heal the world' rubbish at first," he was quoted as saying. "Blokes do anything to keep the missus sweet. But when she started getting a bit up herself about it, I would take the piss. There was a time when she used to have a sense of humor about herself. In the last few years, she just got angry."[41]

Some women heard in Ritchie's litany of woes a familiar story. People had recognized the workplace "glass ceiling" that women could not breach. But in the early 2000s, a new impediment was identified: the "maternal wall." The pressure was not only external (companies created "mommy tracks" that excluded women with children from advancement) but also internal, which manifested itself in the form of guilt. Women who had careers and a family were expected to cut back on their professional responsibilities for the sake of the family. It was the "natural" and "normal" thing to do.[42]

Madonna loved her children and wanted her marriage to succeed, but she didn't think she had to sacrifice who she was and what she did to prove it. British journalist Fiona Phillips, attempting to balance the uncritical coverage of Ritchie's marital complaints, wrote, "Madonna is being blamed for the collapse of her marriage because she still loves the buzz her career gives her." Phillips added that if what Ritchie wanted was a " 'regular husband and wife thing'... Madonna isn't likely to be No. 1 on your list, is she?"[43]

The press reported that spring that Madonna had consulted a divorce lawyer, Fiona Shackleton. She had represented Prince Charles in his divorce from Diana and Paul McCartney in his messy split with Heather Mills. And then in June, Madonna told Guy, "I'm sorry, I want a divorce." He agreed. A friend said, "It was all quite painless but very sad."[44]

By 2008, Madonna believed she had done everything possible to save the marriage but concluded that it would not survive: "I didn't want to stay unhappy and miserable."[45] Ritchie had lived with Madonna for more than eight years, but he still didn't understand her, partly because she had tried to be who he wanted her to be.[46] The real Madonna was obscured by the role of wife, which she had tried to master aided by the teachings of Kabbalah. It told her that her ego and personal desires stood in the way of her happiness.

The person Ritchie believed stood in the way of *his* happiness was Madonna the artist, Madonna the provocateur.[47] As much as she wanted to please him, there was simply no possibility that she could become the person he needed, that she would stop working, stop creating. "It's inexplicable; it's like breathing, and I can't imagine not doing it," she said.

> That was one of the arguments I would get into with [Ritchie], who used to say to me, "But why do you have to do this again? Why do you have to make another record? Why do you have to go on tour? Why do you have to make a movie?" And I'm like, "Why do I have to explain myself?"
>
> I feel like that's a very sexist thing to say... Does somebody ask Steven Spielberg why he's still making movies? Hasn't he had enough success? Hasn't he made enough money?... Did somebody go to Pablo Picasso and say, "Okay, you're eighty years old. Haven't you painted enough paintings?" No. I'm so tired of that question. I just don't understand it. I'll stop doing everything that I do when I don't want to do it anymore. I'll stop when I run out of ideas. I'll stop when you fucking kill me. How about that?[48]

Madonna said that at times she "felt incarcerated" in her marriage. "I wasn't really allowed to be myself... It doesn't mean marriage is a bad thing... but if you're an artist, you've got to find someone who accepts who you are and is comfortable with that."[49]

★   ★   ★

In early July, Christopher Ciccone received an email from Madonna that was completely unlike her: the words were misspelled, the sentence structure was incorrect, even the font was different. It ended with an unspecified threat, telling him he'd "be sorry." The fury she directed his way was because of his book. After years of thinking about it, he had finally written the story of his life at Madonna's side, and it was about to be published. He had wanted to call it *The Queen and I,* but Simon and Schuster chose the more modest *Life with My Sister Madonna.*[50]

Reading the bizarre email, Christopher thought,

> You know what? There is so much more happening in her world than just this book. This was scaring the shit out of her, and she went to the worst possible place. It made me frightened for her, so I emailed her a week before the book came out. I said, "I love you. I would never do anything intentionally to hurt you . . . I hope you are safe. If you need me, I will be there in a heartbeat."[51]

Madonna's emails stopped. They were replaced by phone calls from lawyers trying to halt the book's publication. What hurt Christopher most was that he had been at her side for forty-plus years—half of them professionally—yet she still didn't trust him. She thought his intention was malign, that he wanted to spill her deepest secrets. "It is the stuff that makes her human that frightens her the most," he said. "I am not knocking her off her pedestal. I am gently helping her back down to earth. Welcome back to the human race, OK?"[52]

Christopher had considered writing the book for six years, ever since Madonna chose not to include him in the Drowned World tour. "I was really angry, so I was writing the angry version." After finishing one chapter, he realized it wasn't the story he wanted to tell. In 2006, he was ready to try again. By then his relationship with Madonna had deteriorated to the point where, he said, "We weren't really talking at all."[53]

At that time, Ingrid Casares was once again part of Madonna's life. Christopher said she seemed to want to embrace him, perhaps bring him back into the fold. He had a large design job in Miami, and in November of 2006, Ingrid offered to throw him a birthday party.[54]

During Madonna's Miami sojourn in the 1990s, Christopher's birthday parties were major social events. For his forty-sixth, Ingrid put together a small party at a Miami Beach hotel. "I arrived there with some friends," he said, "and she hadn't really done anything. She'd gotten cheap vodka, and I was kind of an asshole. I was totally an asshole. I was like, 'What the fuck is this? I don't drink that shit vodka.' I was just a fucker. I walked out saying, 'Fuck you, we're leaving.'" Then Christopher went home and had what he called an epiphany.[55]

"I'm an angry guy at this point. It's not on the surface; it's sort of bubbling underneath, and it comes out once in a while. I'm doing a lot of drugs, sort of killing the pain." He recognized that night that "something's wrong here that needs to be fixed." In the meantime, Ingrid told Madonna about the episode. Madonna called, gave him the name of a psychiatrist, and told him to get into rehab because he was a drug addict. Christopher wasn't sure about that, but he knew he needed help. He stopped taking drugs and agreed to go into therapy.[56]

Madonna had been part of other such interventions, notably with Ingrid. But more recently, she had helped Donatella Versace. The fashion industry, like the music industry — like all industries — had consolidated, and individual houses like Versace faced nearly insurmountable odds against conglomerates if they did not join one. By 2004, Versace was struggling under a weight of debts. Donatella was struggling, too. Her drug habit had only grown as the company's fortunes diminished, and by that year, she was mixing cocaine with serious prescription sedatives. When people came to her show, they did so partly to see if she would physically survive it.[57]

Through the intervention of her family and Elton John, she entered rehab in the summer of 2004. By the fall, she was clean and strong enough to mount a successful runway show of designs that once again associated the name Versace with elegance. But one show would not restore the company's position. That was where Madonna came in. Donatella asked her to be the face of Versace's critical 2005 collection. Over the Thanksgiving holiday, ten years after their first such shoot, Madonna and Mario Testino were reunited in London to photograph her wearing Versace designs. The photos featured Madonna as a businesswoman, chic and serious, like the new Donatella, who would remain sober for the rest of her life.[58]

Christopher had begun his drug use in the Miami circle around Donatella, and Madonna wanted him clean, too. He had given his doctor permission to discuss his findings with Madonna. But he said that when the psychiatrist and blood tests both concluded that Christopher was not an addict, she refused to believe the psychiatrist. "She accused him of being a fraud and a quack," Christopher said. He began seeing another therapist at her behest. The new therapist agreed with the psychiatrist that Christopher wasn't unstable or addicted to drugs. Madonna "totally disagreed." When she demanded that he see someone else, Christopher hung up on her. "It was at that point I realized that if you don't agree with her...," he said, trailing off.[59]

On his own, Christopher continued therapy, and his anger dissipated. "It was right at that point that I realized that I needed to write something. I needed to tell my story from a good place," he said. "I knew that I had to do something because I just felt like, I'm going to be out in the world and I'm going to be her brother for my entire life. I needed to make a change in my life. The way that I was living was making me a horrible person to myself and to others."[60]

At around that time, Christopher met a British writer named Wendy Leigh, who agreed to help with the book. "I laid down the ground rules. It was not going to be an 'I hate Madonna' book. That's not how I feel." It wasn't even really a "Madonna" book; it was about Christopher. "I knew I could relate our relationship and my position in her world and my position in *the* world in a positive way. I wasn't going to drag her through the mud."[61]

Christopher and Leigh engaged in stealth writing for seven months, fearful that if Madonna learned of the project, she would work to stop it. He would arrive at Leigh's Key Biscayne apartment under an assumed name—Mr. Blake. He managed to keep the book a secret until shortly before its publication, in 2008, when Madonna heard about it.[62]

She would have objected to it in any case. But during a year when she was on an emotional roller coaster over David's adoption, her marriage, and her career, she could not take the added strain.[63] She emailed Christopher with two words: "Call me." He did not and refused to take her phone calls. "Unfortunately, she then chose to drag my father into it and started emailing him" because he had given Christopher photographs to use in his book.[64]

Madonna, however, could not stop its publication. *Life with My Sister Madonna* appeared in bookstores on July 14 and became a bestseller in the United States and England. There was little in it that she wouldn't have revealed herself if someone had asked. The book was new, though, in that it described that previously mysterious figure Christopher Ciccone and Madonna from the perspective of a family member and close associate.

Few of Madonna's inner circle ever spoke to the press at length without her approval. She, like other celebrities, asked her associates to sign confidentiality agreements. Christopher's book was, therefore, the first candid glimpse into her world. It was told with humor and warmth, and the only person who came out lesser in the telling was Ritchie. Christopher didn't spare him.

Prepublication reports hinted that it included salacious details of drug use and wild sex. It did not, but it didn't matter. Based on the advance buzz, Madonna prepared herself for Christopher's "ultimate betrayal."[65] Liz Rosenberg issued a statement saying that Madonna hadn't read the book but found it so "upsetting" that it precluded any future relationship between them.[66] Ritchie dismissed it as an act of desperation and denied the book's insinuations that he was antigay, telling *The Observer,* "You'd be hard pushed to be a homophobe and marry Madonna."[67]

When she finally had Christopher's book in hand, Madonna said, she "hurled it across the room at a wall, that's how enraged I was about it. Then I thought, OK, I'm not really mad about this book, I'm mad about other stuff, and this damn book just happens to be the thing in my hand that I can throw."[68]

Life with My Sister Madonna also happened to appear the week that newspapers trumpeted headlines about Madonna's friendship with one of the most controversial sports stars in the United States, New York Yankees third baseman Alex Rodriguez. His wife had filed for divorce that Monday, citing, among other alleged transgressions, a relationship with Madonna. The rumors had been circulating in the tabloids for weeks but rose to the level of news because of the divorce.[69]

Madonna issued a statement denying an affair (she often said she would never date a married man), and the Rodriguez divorce papers did not claim one, but the Madonna angle was the juiciest morsel from A-Rod's divorce, and so it became the headline.[70]

Madonna escaped the fallout from Christopher's book and the most recent tabloid onslaught by going to Gwyneth Paltrow's place in the Hamptons. Madonna had injured her knee during rehearsals and was diagnosed as anemic. She needed to restore her mind and relax her body.[71] She was going back out on the road, and her tour was scheduled to begin the next month. It would require her to perform eighty-five two-hour shows through the end of the year and into 2009.

The tour, called Sticky & Sweet, was essentially a traveling corporation, with 250 people on staff, and because of Live Nation's involvement, there were a lot more people in decision-making positions, mostly about money. At $375 per ticket for the most expensive seats, Madonna's concert was the highest-priced of any artist's that year. (Elton John's came in second.)[72] And yet the crew felt cheated by poor accommodations and low-cost flights. By the second stop, Nice, some of them threatened to quit.[73]

On August 23, in Cardiff, Wales—opening night—there were grumbles from inside the stadium, too. Audience members had waited ninety minutes for the show to begin, and their jocularity upon arrival had turned into boos. When Madonna finally appeared, though, the sheer scale and intensity of the performance overrode concerns about ticket prices or waiting babysitters or early starts to the next morning's workday. The production was overwhelming.[74]

People looking for familiar faces on the tour's roster would have found few. Jamie King was back as tour director, but Kevin Antunes had replaced Stuart Price as musical director. He was from the Justin Timberlake camp, having worked with him for nine years, including as musical director on Timberlake's successful 2007 FutureSex/LoveShow tour.[75]

The only returning band member was Monte Pittman. Nicki Richards sang backup again, but Donna De Lory was replaced by Kiley Dean, who had toured with Britney Spears and was once signed to Timbaland's record label. Also missing was Gaultier. Arianne Phillips had gathered a group of designers and couture houses to outfit the tour: Givenchy's Riccardo Tisci, Tom Ford, Miu Miu, Stella McCartney, Moschino, Yves Saint Laurent, Roberto Cavalli, and Jeremy Scott.[76]

The dance staff was also largely new. Stefanie Roos returned as lead choreographer, but she had twenty-four other choreographers working with her to develop specialized types of movement. Onstage, five Re-Invention and Confessions tour dancers were back, but twelve other dancers were new to Madonna's show.[77]

Everything about the tour felt bigger, more professional in a corporate way, more complex. The challenge for Madonna was to do a blockbuster show and still connect with members of the audience—to infuse the vast production with the intimacy her fans expected.

Because the concert was a Jamie King production, video was paramount. Sticky & Sweet featured seventeen screens. The three largest, measuring twenty feet by twenty feet, could be moved together to create a continuous sixty-foot image. There were also three massive circular screens that descended from a grid above the stage. Jason Harvey, who with his crew managed the video production, said there were only around five minutes in the show without a video: "Basically, when Madonna is talking to the audience."[78]

In the past, screens had been used in Madonna's concerts as backdrops—to create the illusion of space or to deliver messages. In Sticky & Sweet, they became artist-delivery devices for Madonna collaborators who couldn't make the tour. The screens were also used both behind and in front of the live performers, to engulf them in the visuals.

Sticky & Sweet's first act, called pimp, opened to musical hints of "4 Minutes" and a marvel of lights and images until Madonna rotated into view on a throne (looking very much like Prince), singing "Candy Shop" and giving that song new life.[79] In fact, one of the most exciting aspects of the concert was Madonna's performance of *Hard Candy* songs. Gone was the monotony that characterized the album. New arrangements and her performance finally turned them into "Madonna songs." "Beat Goes On," the second number in the concert, became a loopy call to dance. Pharrell

Williams joined Madonna via video in the performance. It was a little strange seeing him floating over the proceedings like Marley's ghost, but after the audience saw similar apparitions in the form of Kanye West during the same song, it began to seem less paranormal.[80]

After the two offerings from her new album, Madonna picked up a guitar and sang "Human Nature," with images of Britney Spears trapped in an elevator projected on several screens behind her. Madonna's decision to feature her during that famous refusal-to-apologize number was a nod to Spears's troubles. She had had a series of crises, including the loss of her children in a custody battle and booze- and drug-fueled meltdowns. At the time she appeared in Madonna's concert video, she was trying to rehabilitate herself. Disheveled but smiling as the elevator representing her life took her up and down, she was roughed up but would survive.[81]

The next section, old school, began with on-screen images of Keith Haring–like figures and Madonna jumping rope in front of them as she sang "Into the Groove," the song she wrote with Steve Bray so many years before. The scene onstage re-created the Roxy, where the B-boys and B-girls decked out in athletic gear tore up the dance floor.[82] The song "Heartbeat," from *Hard Candy,* came next. It was about feeling alive on the dance floor and recalled the New York clubs where "Madonna" as the world knew her was born.[83]

Remaining in that era, Madonna delivered a rockin' version of "Borderline" that turned the puppy-love song into an angry woman's anthem. "She's Not Me," in which Madonna stayed in sassy mode, denouncing a love rival — or pop-music newcomers vying to replace her — followed. During the song, four dancers posed as iconic Madonna characters from "Material Girl," "Open Your Heart," "Like a Virgin," and "Express Yourself." She revealed them as impostors. Unable to seduce or destroy them, she threw a choreographed tantrum on the stage.[84]

A pair of Japanese dancers Madonna had discovered on YouTube, Riki "Rickiccho" Onodera and Yuki "Da-Yoshi" Yoshida, entertained the audience during an interlude with a fusion of "Rain" and the Eurythmics' "Here Comes the Rain Again." Madonna returned with a ballad, "Devil Wouldn't Recognize You," which she sang atop a piano. Once again, a *Hard Candy* song became musically more complex in concert, and her nuanced performance gave the lyrics, about the end of a relationship, the weight they deserved.[85]

That song introduced the concert's gypsy segment. It might have been called her world segment, because in it, Madonna traversed the globe culturally, beginning with "Spanish Lessons" and continuing into "Miles Away." She was joined onstage by a trio of Romany musicians she had met at her most recent birthday party through her musician-actor friend

Eugene Hütz. Alexander Kolpakov, the most famous Romany guitarist in Russia; his guitarist nephew, Vadim Kolpakov; and violinist Arkady Gips backed her up on "You Must Love Me" and a Romany-esque version of "La Isla Bonita."[86]

Between the gypsy segment and the final portion of the concert, the rave segment, the audience was treated to a taped mash-up of "4 Minutes," "Give It 2 Me," "Voices," and "Beat Goes On" while on-screen, a video shot by Steven Klein for a song called "Get Stupid" played. As it critiqued Western society's addiction to fossil fuels, cheap consumer products, and fast money, Madonna's voice urged political action by repeating "It's time," "Let's go," "Use your mind," "Before it's too late." There was good cause for urgency. In 2008, tremors were emanating from US financial markets, and some economists predicted an earthquake.

The video was the only controversial part of the concert. It created a bad guy–good guy roster, positioning Republican US presidential candidate John McCain within a rogues' gallery that included Adolf Hitler, Zimbabwe's Robert Mugabe, and Iran's Ayatollah Ali Khamenei, whose photos were interspersed with scenes of war, civil strife, and starvation. A subsequent set of images featured the peacemakers: Mother Teresa, Gandhi, Nelson Mandela, and Barack Obama, whose image, repeated across several screens, ended the video.

Hillary Clinton had suspended her presidential campaign that June. Obama was a formidable opponent and a singular figure in US history, but Clinton would have failed to advance even against a lesser opponent. The United States was not ready for a female leader.[87] In her absence, Madonna became a fervid Obama supporter, and while he no doubt appreciated it, he didn't approve of her concert video. His campaign officially criticized the depiction of his political rival McCain.[88]

The "Get Stupid" video served as a segue into "4 Minutes," which featured Timbaland and Timberlake on-screen. Madonna and her dancers, wearing American football–style shoulder pads, performed with them. Then, having traded her shoulder pads for a metallic breastplate, Madonna reappeared as a futuristic Joan of Arc to sing "Like a Prayer" as inspirational messages in several languages flashed behind her. The concert's closing number, "Give It 2 Me," was electrifying. As Madonna danced across the stage, no one doubted when she declared in the song that she could not be stopped.[89]

Madonna was onstage for two hours. There were no aerial hijinks, no overhead walkways, and there was only one catwalk into the audience. Aside from the screens, the show featured old-school song and dance, and it was outstanding. She had chosen music from her latest and arguably weakest album and re-created it. She had performed in massive arenas on stages filled with dozens of people and still made the show intimate. She connected with the crowd in a way she hadn't since the Girlie Show — speaking with them, taking song requests, and singing with them. During that period, she needed their love.

Guy's film *RocknRolla* premiered on September 1 in England, with indications from Warner Bros. that it would not be released widely in the States and that the promotion would be limited.[90] Madonna had two days free between shows and flew back to London from Zurich to be with Ritchie on the red carpet. She arrived an hour late, leaving him waiting outside the Odeon in Leicester Square making jokes about her absence. At the premiere party afterward, Madonna only stayed briefly. She was due in Amsterdam the next day for her tour, but the press reported her early departure as a slight to Ritchie.[91]

Just the month before, he had organized a fiftieth birthday party for her at a central London club called Volstead. Billed as an intimate gathering of ninety, it included Madonna's three children and looked like a possible last attempt at a reconciliation. Guy reportedly spared no expense on the event: £100,000 for the party, £250,000 for a Bulgari necklace and bracelet, £450,000 for a Banksy portrait of Madonna. He even had a garden dug at Ashcombe so she could grow organic vegetables. Toasting Madonna, Guy said, "I'm so proud. I love her so much."[92] The sentiment behind the gestures was a mystery to observers. In truth, the relationship was over. Mrs. Ritchie had left the building.

After seventeen European dates, the Sticky & Sweet tour arrived in the States in October. Not long afterward, while Madonna was performing in Boston, Liz Rosenberg made official what the press in Britain had already reported — that Madonna and Guy Ritchie had agreed to divorce.[93] They had reportedly planned to hold off on the announcement until the end of her tour, but Ritchie's friends told the press that he wanted it over and done with.[94]

Before they were married, when the question of a prenuptial agreement arose, Guy stated, "I do not want a single penny of the money if this marriage dies." He even offered to help support *her* if they split. Those remarks were made during his salad days.[95] Times had changed. A friend of Madonna's said, "Guy feels entitled to get a lot of money from her. He feels like it's a partnership, and when a partnership ends, you divide things up." The issue would come down to English law, which could award Guy half of Madonna's estimated £380 million ($600 million) fortune.[96]

At that point in the negotiations, however, money was less important than the question of the children. Madonna had sole custody of Lourdes, according to her arrangement with Carlos Leon, but she shared custody of

Rocco and David with Guy.[97] Conscious that the news of the divorce was global, a week after the announcement, Madonna sent two representatives to Malawi to speak with Yohane Banda to explain the situation and to reassure him that David's well-being would not be affected.[98]

Guy, meanwhile, had begun filming *Sherlock Holmes* in England, "relieved," a friend said, that "he doesn't have to fake it anymore." The tabs there embraced their wounded lad and painted Madonna as an aging, needy control freak. Ritchie's only crime in that narrative was that he spent too much time at the pub.[99] Happily for Madonna, she was spared the coverage. She was in New York with the children, who helped ground her. Her tour did, too. "She said the other night, 'When I go onstage, I forget all my troubles.' Offstage, it's back to reality," a source told *People* magazine at the time.[100]

Sticky & Sweet took Madonna to San Diego on November 4, the day the United States stood poised on the verge of history: it might elect its first Black president. The hope Obama inspired at a time of social and financial upheaval was palpable. That fall, the catastrophe that some economists feared had transpired: US banking giant Lehman Brothers collapsed, precipitating the worst global financial crisis since the 1930s Great Depression.[101]

By October, in the United States, the financial system seized up, banks failed, companies went bust, ten million people lost their homes, and nine million people lost their jobs. In western Europe, whole countries were affected, causing crises that would last years. The sacrifice and suffering were borne by people who had nothing remotely to do with the cause. The United States and the world desperately needed a healer, and Obama's supporters believed he was that person. When TV networks broadcast the news that he had defeated John McCain, it sparked jubilation from coast to coast and around the world.

Madonna heard about his victory just before going onstage. "I said, 'I feel like I'm living a dream.' I got down and kissed the ground."[102] She bounded out onto the stage, shouting to the crowd, "I'm so fucking happy right now! Woo!" but she didn't say why. Forty-five minutes into the concert, she did, asking the crowd, "Are you as happy as I am? . . . Let's hear it for Obama! It's the best day of my life." In honor of the new president, Madonna added "Express Yourself" to her set list that night. The crowd sang along.[103]

At the end of the concert, three massive images of Obama appeared on screens behind the stage bearing the words WE WON. Madonna closed the show by saying, "Thank you, thank you, thank you for making it possible." In liberal-leaning California, her pronouncements were greeted with roars and ovations. One young mother told a local reporter, "This is a pivotal moment in my life, to have Madonna tell me that Barack is my next president…It doesn't get better than this—my past (Madonna) introducing my future (Obama)."[104]

Madonna's tour continued through the States, infused with fresh energy. The bitter shadow of divorce was lifted and replaced by that much greater victory. Madonna responded to light, and Obama was it. She prepared to return to live in the United States, which was once again a country she could be proud of.

Covering her November 26 show for the *Miami New Times,* Jose Duran wrote,

> I'm half-convinced that the Madonna show was the most astonishing concert I've ever seen. Not in any musical way…but because of the lady herself…Madonna came out dancing tonight, and she didn't stop until long after the ordinary rules of biology would have dropped any sane performer.[105]

After each performance, Madonna sat in an ice bath for ten minutes. "I'm an athlete," she said. "My ankles get taped before the shows, and I have treatments and physical therapists. It's from years and years of abuse, dancing in high heels, which is not great on your knees. All dancers have injuries, but we just deal with them."[106]

The tour left North America for Mexico, then went on to South America, where Madonna performed in Argentina, Chile, and Brazil to crowds so large that extra dates were added to her schedule. She had not been in Argentina in nearly thirteen years, since filming *Evita.* In the interim, the country had elected a woman president, Cristina Fernández de Kirchner. She invited Madonna to the presidential palace to meet her and former Colombian presidential candidate Ingrid Betancourt, who had recently been freed after six years as a hostage of the FARC guerrilla group.[107]

The headlines in the Argentinean press from their meeting read TRES MUJERES—three women. Concerning Madonna, Betancourt said, "Who hasn't danced listening to Madonna?…It was a beautiful moment then, because when I saw her, I thought how curious, I am here in the palace where Evita lived, and it is she who played Evita."[108]

Later, at the River Plate Stadium before nearly seventy thousand people, Madonna recalled in song the months she spent as Eva Perón. When she performed "You Must Love Me," from that film, the response in Buenos Aires was near silence for the first few seconds as the crowd processed what she was singing. When it did, rather than cheer, the audience bellowed, and many wept. The song ended with chants of "We love you, we love you."[109]

For that audience, Madonna performed an additional song—"Don't Cry for Me Argentina." Again silence, followed that time by a roar. It wasn't Eva Perón singing to her people; it was Madonna singing to her fans. William Langley, in the *Daily Telegraph* that August, described Madonna as having "changed the world's social history, done more things as more different people than anyone else is ever likely to."[110]

Chapter 51

London, Lilongwe, Marseille, Bucharest, Rio de Janeiro, 2009

Show me the goddamn wall I have to get through to get to the place I want to be and I'll take the wall down with my teeth and fingernails if necessary.[1]

— *Harry Crews*

IN JANUARY, WITH her divorce finalized, Madonna began picking up the pieces of her life. She kept the apartment in New York that she had bought during her marriage to Sean, the house in Beverly Hills, and the home in London. Guy reportedly kept the Ashcombe house, in Wiltshire; a London town house; and the Punchbowl pub. Liz Rosenberg said that, including those properties, he walked away from the marriage with around £60 million — $92 million. That was the most any man had ever received in a divorce settlement from a woman.[2]

Within days of that figure being released, Ritchie's side protested that the amounts were "wide of the mark." Madonna and Ritchie next issued a joint statement saying that the figures released were "inaccurate" and that the financial details would remain private.[3] For people who followed Madonna, though, the joint statement and protestations rang hollow.

Rosenberg had handled Madonna's press for twenty-five years. She would not have released inaccurate details concerning a story of that magnitude. And she would certainly not have done so without Madonna's permission.[4] A source told *The Guardian* that the figures were released because "it got to the point where everyone in the UK and out there was thinking Guy didn't ask for any money."[5] Joking about the settlement years later, Madonna said, "If I think about it for even five seconds it's more than I can take. Did he deserve a hundred million dollars for putting up with me? Hell, if I thought he was going to get *that* much, I would have been a *much bigger* bitch to him. *Much bigger!*"[6]

One aspect of the divorce settlement that was not disputed initially concerned the children. Madonna and Guy agreed to share custody of Rocco and David, who would split their time between Britain and the United States. Madonna's sole custody of Lourdes was undisputed.[7]

There was no question that the divorce had been agonizing. It represented the death of love between two adults. It meant the death of a family for the children in it. It signified a failure, both personal and spiritual. The split was inevitable, but she and Guy—despite their differences—still felt affection for each other, which made it all even more wrenching.[8]

Near the end of her marriage, Madonna had begun writing a screenplay for a film she hoped to make about an American divorcée who, in 1936, cost a British king his throne. She had been mildly obsessed with the story of Wallis Simpson and King Edward VIII since she arrived in London. "In England, people are still polarized about her," Madonna said of Simpson.[9] When she mentioned the Duke and Duchess of Windsor at dinner parties, it was "like throwing a Molotov cocktail onto the table. Suddenly the table would erupt, and everyone would get into an argument about who they were."[10] "I decided to really take it on and do research and find out about English history and learn about the royal family."[11]

After delving into the subject and reading every book she could find about the Windsors, Madonna concluded that the generally accepted story of Edward's abdication was distorted. Simpson, she believed, had been reduced to a cliché of an evil temptress and Edward to something less than human because, as a royal, he was considered something greater.[12] She was also struck by the romance of their story. "Men want power and they'll kill to have it," Madonna said. "How many wars were waged to win the throne? And here's a man who walked away from that for love. And so, for a romantic like me, I would say, 'Wow, to be loved like that!'"[13]

But mostly Madonna was moved by a strong sympathy for Simpson, who understood that when Edward chose her over his duty to his country she became "the most hated woman in the world."[14] Most depictions of the Wallis–Edward relationship focused on what *he* had sacrificed. Madonna recognized what the free-living Wallis had lost by being linked to the fallen king. She would forever be *that woman*. She would never be herself.[15]

To tell the story, Madonna borrowed a narrative device used by author A. S. Byatt. In her award-winning 1990 book, *Possession,* Byatt tells the story of a love affair between two fictional nineteenth-century poets as seen through the eyes of two modern-day scholars researching them. Over the course of Byatt's book, the lives of the four characters become entangled as the past influences the present. Madonna would do the same in her film. Viewers would discover Wallis and Edward through the eyes of an unhappily married late twentieth-century New Yorker, who (like Madonna) becomes obsessed with Simpson and looks to that other woman's life to find the strength to survive her own.

Madonna didn't set out to make a "woman's film," just as she didn't set out to make feminist statements in her music. But in both cases, that was what happened. "I believe sometimes we aren't always in charge of everything that we do creatively," Madonna said. "We submit to things as we're going on our own journey. Wally [her film's modern character] was learning about herself, and so was I—on my own journey and the journey of all women. I don't work any other way."[16]

After her divorce, Madonna began working on the project in earnest, writing during the day so she could see her children at night.[17]

In March, a New York judge approved the custody agreement Madonna and Guy had reached in Britain. That meant Madonna could focus on bringing home the child she already thought of as her daughter: three-year-old Chifundo (Mercy) James. Mercy's grandmother Lucy Chekechiwa and Mercy's uncle Peter Baneti had finally agreed to allow Madonna to adopt her.[18]

Madonna said she "put my armor on" and prepared to battle the same forces that had tried to prevent her adoption of David.[19] Emailing a friend, the actor Ben Fellows, as she traveled to Malawi to make a formal adoption request, Madonna wrote, "Let the storm commence."[20] And it did.

Charities again denounced her for supposedly bypassing Malawi's legal system.[21] The press in the States and Britain published fresh diatribes against her. Columnist Sue Carroll, writing in London's *Daily Mirror,* was particularly shrill:

> This increasingly desperate woman is unable to do anything—let alone adopt another poor child—with an iota of dignity or decorum...Here [in England] a single mother with three children by different fathers and a gargantuan self-regard would stand about as much chance of adopting as the Yorkshire Ripper—and maybe that's a good thing.[22]

Leaving that chatter behind, Madonna and her children arrived in Lilongwe for a March 30 hearing before High Court judge Esme Chombo. Having stated her case, Madonna was told she would receive the court's ruling later in the week.[23]

The Malawian government backed Madonna's application, saying she supported more than twenty-five thousand orphans through charitable donations and had proved herself to be a good mother to David.[24] But the political climate in Malawi had changed amid corruption scandals and alleged coup plots. The fallout from Madonna's adoption of David also lingered. Malawi's educated urban residents still suspected her motives. And she was now a divorced single mother. In predominantly Christian Malawi, that would complicate the adoption.[25]

Journalist Jacques Peretti traveled to Malawi to make a documentary about Mercy's adoption for Britain's Channel 4. He visited the places and people who had benefited from Madonna's projects. He found that in rural Malawi, people revered her. There she was known as "'Ma Donor,' the Giver," and was "nothing short of a holy figure." Peretti said that many people tracking Mercy's adoption imagined her as the "next Barack Obama."[26]

Madonna didn't think of herself as a savior. She admitted that when she first arrived, in 2006, she had thought, "I have to help, I have to save these people. And then I thought, 'Wait a minute. I think it's the other way around. I think they might be saving me.'" She thought of herself as a supplicant and student wanting to share what she had, not only to fill a need but also to express her gratitude.[27]

Five days after Madonna appeared before Judge Chombo, her lawyers were summoned back to Malawi's High Court while she stayed at the Kumbali Lodge, near the capital, with Mercy, David, Rocco, and Lourdes, preparing for a celebration.[28] Instead, the judge said, "I must decline to grant the application to Madonna."[29] Citing Malawi's requirement that an adoptive parent be a resident in the country for eighteen months, she said that such regulations were necessary to protect children from traffickers and that ignoring the rule in Madonna's case could inadvertently pave the way for "unscrupulous individuals."[30] The judge also noted that Madonna was a single parent.[31]

Chombo acknowledged that Mercy's family and other "well-wishers" were eager for the child to experience the "unlimited opportunities" that would come from being adopted by Madonna. In deciding that Mercy should remain in Malawi, she prayed that the child would be among those benefiting from Madonna's generosity there.[32]

Rights campaigners cheered the ruling, but Malawians gathered outside the court did not. "Madonna was going to give that child the chance of her life," one said. "Now she may turn her back on Malawi."[33] Madonna's lawyer Alan Chinula, meanwhile, rushed to the Kumbali Lodge to tell Madonna. When he did, she howled in grief and disbelief, burying her head in her hands and crying out, "Whaaaat?" "She kept wringing her hands and covering her face in her hands," a source said. "She was really in shock." She also didn't know how to break the news to the children, who were bonding with Mercy as a sister.[34]

It was telling that in Madonna's recollection of the judge's decision, the part she felt was most unjustified was the comment about her marital status, which supposedly prevented her from being a good mother. Several years later, she was still aggrieved. Recalling the moment, she said, "She informed me, as a divorced woman, I was not fit to raise children and that Mercy James was better off growing up in an orphanage."[35]

It took Madonna but a moment to decide to appeal. "If you cannot give me a logical reason for the word 'no,' then I will not accept the word 'no.'" After arranging for Mercy to remain at Kumbali Lodge with a nurse and a nanny and hiring lawyers to argue the case at Malawi's Supreme Court of Appeal, Madonna left the country to mobilize for the fight.[36]

Security forces blocked journalists from the Malawi airport as her convoy passed areas where coffins sat by the side of the road. These held the bodies of dead adults. The country's dead orphans were often buried in pits.[37] Those images haunted Madonna as she flew home without Mercy.

"The last week has been one of the hardest in her life," a friend said of Madonna when she reached London.[38] She was not allowed to publicly discuss her appeal, but she wrote a letter to the Malawi newspaper *The Nation* stating her case anyway.

> I want to provide Mercy with a home, a loving family environment and the best education and healthcare possible...And it's my hope that she, like David, will one day return to Malawi to help the people of their country.[39]

The appeal was to be heard by three supreme court judges in Blantyre on May 4. Madonna argued that Malawi's 1940s adoption laws requiring extended residency were "archaic." On the question of being a single mother, she argued that women through the centuries had raised children alone and she offered herself—a single mother of three—as an example. Her lawyers also argued that Madonna's commitment to Malawi and her support for its children meant that she should be treated as a resident of the country.[40]

Then, two days before the judges were to rule on her appeal, Mercy's father reappeared to claim custody. James Kambewa had disappeared three years earlier, after his girlfriend and fellow student, fourteen-year-old Mwandida Maunde, died days after giving birth to Mercy. The villagers in Zaone had collected money to send Mwandida to school and hoped she would return as a doctor. When she became pregnant and perished instead, they accused eighteen-year-old Kambewa of "bewitching" her. Fearing they would kill him, he fled. He said he did not know Mercy was alive until a British tabloid reporter found him. The judges considering Madonna's appeal delayed the case for an agonizing month to consider his petition. In the end, Kambewa decided not to fight for custody.[41]

Finally, on June 11, Malawi's Supreme Court of Appeal ruled in Madonna's favor. In overturning the lower court decision, Chief Justice Lovemore Munlo said, "Madonna has been judged to be a compassionate, intelligent and articulate person. Her adoption of Mercy James is not a selfish act. No Malawian family has expressed their intention to adopt her." Ultimately, he said, the ruling came down to the question of Mercy's future: "Either to stay at the orphanage without the love of family and live with the possibility of destitution or be with Madonna where she is assured of love. Every child has the right to love."[42]

Madonna heard the news at 3:00 a.m. in New York, when lawyer Alan Chinula called her from Malawi. She whooped with joy. "I fought for Mercy," Madonna said, "and I won."[43] "I still got the shit kicked out of me, but it didn't hurt as much." She added, "I do not regret one moment of the fight."[44] Mercy's uncle Peter Baneti said the family was happy, too, and hoped that "Mercy will be joining Madonna soon."[45]

Madonna and her children flew to Malawi to collect Mercy and throw a "thank you" party for the people who helped make the adoption possible and for her charity, Raising Malawi. On June 20, when she was back in London, a source close to Madonna quoted her as saying, "My family is finally complete, we're all together at last." To give her time with Mercy, Guy took the boys to the countryside for the weekend, leaving the three Ciccone women together in the city.[46]

Madonna described her house as

> like a Benetton ad. I have French nannies, my security guards are Israeli, I have assistants from Argentina and Puerto Rico as well as a Japanese assistant and chef, and another chef from Italy. It's wonderful, I love it. I wouldn't have it any other way. My life is a cacophony of different languages and music.[47]

Those scenes played out at the house in London and, when they were in the States, in a new place Madonna purchased that spring on the Upper East Side of Manhattan. The latter had thirteen bedrooms, a large back garden, and an elevator.[48] "She sees this as a new chapter in her life," a friend said. "She has all her children around her now, and feels she's really moved on from the divorce. The new house means a new beginning for her family... They all feel it's a great place for new memories to be made."[49]

While in London, Madonna began preparing for the second stage of her tour. It was there that she heard the news. Michael Jackson was dead. As a child in Michigan, she had been inspired and challenged by him. As an adult in California, she had befriended him, partly because he was so vulnerable that he risked being crushed by the weight of his talent and lost to the unreality of his fame.

Since 1969, when eleven-year-old Michael and his brothers sang "I Want You Back" on *The Ed Sullivan Show,* he had been a phenomenon. Madonna said, "His music had an extra layer of inexplicable magic that didn't just make you want to dance, it made you believe you could fly, dare to dream, be anything you wanted to be."[50] His voice, his movement, and his spirit exuded joy and optimism after a decade of protests, assassinations, riots, and war. That child pointed a way out. Other children around the world heard him, saw themselves in him, and felt courage, Madonna among them.

Michael Jackson the young man continued to create pop music masterpieces that shaped lives, but by the mid-'90s, it was impossible to separate his art from scandal. It was during that tabloid decade that rumors of child molestation surfaced. In 2003, he was arrested. The *New York Times's* Frank Rich described the press orgy surrounding his arrest as "a base morality tale with no heroes." The press was *outraged* by his alleged depravity and yet couldn't stop talking about it in salacious detail. By the time Jackson was acquitted, in 2005, the charges had become his legacy. Michael Jackson the genius performer was a distant relative of Michael Jackson the alleged pedophile.[51]

By 2009, after years in relative seclusion personally and creatively, Jackson had decided to emerge in a big way with a world tour. The pressure was enormous because the expectations were so high. At fifty, he was exhausted, but he couldn't sleep and had begun taking a cocktail of sedatives along with the powerful anesthetic propofol. On June 25, it killed him. The official cause of death was heart attack, but it was brought on by the drugs. His doctor was convicted of involuntary manslaughter.[52]

Few entertainment friends had been willing to speak up on his behalf during his molestation ordeal. Elizabeth Taylor did. So did Madonna. Hearing of his death, she could not stop crying.[53] "The first thing that comes into my head was the word abandoned," she said. "I feel like we all abandoned him and put him in a box and labelled him a strange person."[54] Madonna's sons were "obsessed with Michael Jackson." Too young to understand the scandal, they discovered the artist. Of that Jackson, Madonna said, "Long live the king."[55]

Madonna's Sticky & Sweet tour resumed in Europe on July 4. Holding her family close, she packed up her children and hit the road.[56] It would be little Mercy's introduction to her mother's world as they traveled through England, Italy, and France, then east to Romania, Hungary, Estonia, and

Serbia, then north to Finland, Sweden, and St. Petersburg, Russia. One million tickets, worth $100 million, had sold in a matter of days.[57]

It was almost inevitable that a show of that size traveling for so many months would encounter problems, and it did. Sometimes it was the video. Sometimes it was the sound. And then in Marseille, on July 16, tragedy struck. While the stage was being constructed at the Velodrome stadium, part of the roof collapsed and a crane toppled, killing fifty-two-year-old Frenchman Charles Criscenzo and twenty-three-year-old Charles Prow of Leeds, England. Eight others were seriously hurt, and more than thirty people suffered less serious injuries.[58]

Madonna was in Udine, Italy, preparing to perform when the news reached her. Once onstage, she stopped the concert, choking back tears and saying, "I just wanted to take a moment to acknowledge and pay tribute to two people who lost their lives today...I feel so devastated to be in any way associated with anyone's suffering. Let's all just take a moment to say a prayer for Charles Criscenzo and Charlie Prow."[59]

The July 19 concert in Marseille was canceled. Instead, Madonna met privately with Criscenzo's family, then visited injured crew members who were being treated in two Marseille hospitals. She slipped in and out of all her stops without making a statement and without an official escort other than a bodyguard.[60] Later, she met with Faith Prow, the mother of Charlie Prow. She had flown to Marseille, and Madonna sent her a note asking to speak with her. "It wasn't a publicity stunt," said Chris Prow, Charlie's father. "The meeting was a quiet affair with just the two of them."[61]

Madonna was shaken to her core. Once upon a time, she controlled her shows. By 2009, her tour was so huge that it was impossible for her to know whom she was responsible for, whom to thank, and sometimes why she went on tour at all. But then the fans reminded her. In Munich, she spotted a father with his daughter on his shoulders. "She was completely enraptured," Madonna said. At another concert, she saw two shirtless men covered in Madonna tattoos.[62]

There was also her larger purpose—the responsibility that came with her fame. In Romania, home to the largest population of Romany people in Europe, she was booed and jeered when she decried discrimination against them.[63] The hostility of the Bucharest crowd's response shocked her Romany musical trio, who stood beside her. "Being on stage and experiencing that," said guitarist Vadim Kolpakov, "we're very thankful to Madonna for bringing it up. She always wants to do the right thing, and I love her for that."[64]

But to end her longest, most difficult tour, during which her emotions ricocheted from despair brought on by divorce and death to elation over Mercy's adoption and Obama's election, she spent two nights onstage in

Tel Aviv without controversy or commentary. She simply sang and danced.[65]

Sticky & Sweet was a commercial success. It grossed $408 million, the largest amount for a tour by any solo artist up to that point and, as of 2022, still the largest ever for a tour by a woman.

That fall, Madonna cemented her artistic place in the world of music by releasing her final album for Warner Bros. Records. The thirty-six-track collection, *Celebration,* featured a range of work from her earliest to her latest. Upon its release, it debuted in the top ten around the world. Praise for the album was nearly universal.

Madonna shared her musical bounty with the constituency that helped put her on top. In October, news came that she had given the rights to her entire musical catalog to the groundbreaking gay-friendly television series *Glee.* The show's producer and cocreator, Ryan Murphy, had asked Madonna if he could feature her work in an upcoming one-hour episode. She agreed and gave him everything.[66]

If Madonna was smiling again, it wasn't merely because of career successes. That spring the world got a look at what her romantic life postmarriage might look like. While she was on tour in Brazil the previous December, Steven Klein joined her for a two-day photo shoot for *W.* The spread, called "Blame It on Rio," featured Madonna looking every bit her sultry, spectacular fifty-year-old self surrounded by gorgeous young men. It was a comical inverse of the usual narrative—a rich middle-aged man in a hotel room surrounded by young women. By the end of the photo essay, and in reality, Madonna had selected a friend for an intimate interlude. He was a twenty-two-year-old Brazilian model named Jesus Luz.[67]

If a doctor could have written a prescription for a drug to boost Madonna's spirits, quicken her metabolism, and revive her sex life after a reported drought with Ritchie, Jesus Luz would have been it. Buff, curly-haired, with piercing blue eyes, he was charming, sweet, fun, easy—as in uncomplicated by burdens—and therefore free, which was a state Madonna had only experienced onstage of late. Also, he had studied Kabbalah for two years prior to their meeting, he was an aspiring DJ, and he was discreet.[68]

The tabs and bloggers were ecstatic to be able to write about Madonna's love life. It had been a while since she had been so *Madonna.* She even had a new battleground: ageism. "Once you reach a certain age you are not allowed to be adventurous, you're not allowed to be sexual. I mean, is there a rule?" she asked. "Are you supposed to just die?"[69]

Madonna had done fashion shoots occasionally through the years, but in 2009 and 2010, after passing fifty, she became the face of four collections created by two of the highest-profile fashion houses in the world. In photos shot by Steven Meisel for Louis Vuitton and by Steven Klein for Dolce & Gabbana, she showed what a fiftysomething woman looks like lounging in a Parisian café, eating pasta with her hands in an Italian kitchen, even doing the dishes.[70]

She embodied beauty, sensuality, and playfulness, but most of all confidence. And she likely scared the pants off all those commentators who tried to dismiss her as "desperate," "over the hill," "pathetic." Madonna, quite convincingly, was not. What made that scary, if history is any guide, was that other women might see those possibilities in themselves, too.

PART SIX

LISBON

2010–2020

Chapter 52

New York, London, Paris, Chinkhota, Venice, 2010–2011

A lot of people have problems with Madonna. In fact, pretty much the entire history of Madonna has been the history of people having various problems with her![1]

—*Jude Ellison S. Doyle*

AN EARLY TWENTIETH-CENTURY British period piece should not have generated controversy. The film that would become *W.E.* did because it was Madonna's, because she was an American who dared to put her spin on a controversial moment in British history, and because the film at its core is about the complexities of women. In *Shot/Countershot,* a study of women and film, author Lucy Fischer remarked that women's art by its very nature is subversive because it represents an alternative to the dominant male worldview and narrative.[2] Madonna's movie constituted just such a revolt. She would present history from a woman's point of view and through the filter of a woman's imagination.[3]

One could argue that women in film were everywhere. Or were they? Madonna's costar in *A League of Their Own,* Geena Davis, had founded the Geena Davis Institute on Gender in Media, which, among other things, sponsors research about popular entertainment. A 2008 study of films released between 1990 and 2006 found that 73 percent of speaking roles featured men and that the women characters fell largely into two groups—traditional (wives, mothers) and "hypersexual." The latter category was the only one in which women outnumbered men on-screen—by 500 percent—even in children's animation.[4]

If women were without a voice in films, another Davis Institute study found the reason: women comprised only 7 percent of feature-film directors, 13 percent of writers, and 20 percent of producers. Men created and paid for what the world saw on-screen.[5] Madonna decided to challenge that status quo by directing a film.

She wasn't alone. Her friend Sofia Coppola was directing her fourth film, two of them highly acclaimed. Jane Campion became the first woman to earn the Palme d'Or at Cannes, for the 1993 film *The Piano*. Kimberly Peirce's heartbreaking 1999 movie, *Boys Don't Cry,* won awards while busting norms. Kathryn Bigelow became the first woman to win Best Director and Best Picture Oscars, for her 2008 film, *The Hurt Locker* (about men). But those women were rare exceptions.[6] Madonna would do what she had done with other underground phenomena. By her entry into that world and the attention she attracted—good, bad, but never indifferent—she helped mainstream the idea of a woman at the helm of a movie.

After working on her script for several years, Madonna realized in 2010 that the story of Wallis Simpson and King Edward VIII was much larger than she imagined.[7] Portraying the couple as human rather than as historical clichés made them infinitely more complex, and the world they inhabited vast—socially, politically, and geographically. To do it justice, she needed to film throughout Europe as well as in New York, where a present-day tandem story was set. It would be through the character there, a fictional woman named Wally Winthrop, that the narrative would unfold and discoveries would be made.

Madonna decided she needed someone to help her write it. She called Alek Keshishian. "Not only is it lonely to do things on your own creatively, it's also kind of arrogant," Madonna said. "I guess some people are brilliant enough to be brilliant on their own and never doubt anything and come up with fabulous things." She believed that for her, it was beneficial during the creative process to be forced to justify and explain decisions, to have "a sounding board." She said that at that point she and Alek had a "brother-sister relationship" that made working together easy and fun.[8] Keshishian said, "It was like getting back into an old jacket that fits you so well."[9]

Sometimes they wrote in the same room, sharing a laptop. Sometimes they worked alone and emailed what they had written to each other or discussed it by phone. If the children were away "and I have a chunk of time when I'm a single woman living in my house for a miraculous week," Madonna said, "I will get to write at different hours. I mean, we've burned the candle. We've stayed up all night. We've done it every which way. But generally, we schedule chunks of time to be together and work on it."[10]

Madonna did not set out to make a documentary or even a "historical" movie. She had done the research and could have taken that path, but she was more interested in telling a story. *W.E.* would therefore be a depiction of what "moved and inspired" her in the life of Wallis Simpson and the larger issues Simpson represents: the distorting nature of fame, the blindness of passion, the frailty of love, the value of freedom. The fact that the film travels along two story lines—a duality—makes it a Madonna movie.[11]

Madonna's twentysomething art expert, Wally Winthrop, lives in a gilded cage in 1998 New York as the wife of a wealthy psychiatrist who does not want her to work because he wants children.[12] After Wally's relationship with her husband comes to blows, she abandons her "perfect" life in search of something better. But first, she must find herself.

Named after Wallis Simpson, Wally has an idealized vision of Wallis's life. At a Sotheby's auction, she sifts through a collection of artifacts that had belonged to the Duke and Duchess of Windsor, looking for a clearer understanding of Wallis's life and her own.

Through Wally's musings, viewers meet the historical Wallis, first in an abusive relationship as a soldier's wife, and then in a second marriage, to the decent but dull businessman Ernest Simpson. He gives Wallis license to socialize, and she is masterful at it.[13] Her parties are updated versions of the legendary nineteenth-century Parisian salons, where men and women of note exchange ideas while amusing themselves with drugs, alcohol, and love affairs.[14]

The man who would be her soulmate, the future King Edward VIII, is the first royal to be recognized as a champion of the people and to express his opinions irrespective of the monarchy's, making him the first modern king.[15] But his family and the British government will not countenance his too-modern desire to marry an American divorcée who is, in fact, still wedded to another man. Telling his kingdom that he cannot live without her, Edward relinquishes his throne to his younger brother.

As Wally roams Sotheby's, she befriends a Ukrainian immigrant pianist named Evgeni, who works as a security guard. Madonna describes Wally and Evgeni as "lost souls."[16] Wallis and Edward become lost souls, too. His abdication defines their story.[17]

After the auction, Wally travels to Paris to meet with Harrods owner Mohamed Al-Fayed so she can gain access to Wallis's letters. (In reality, Al-Fayed did own some of the letters, and he allowed Madonna to read them, which gave her a unique perspective into Simpson's thoughts and life.)[18] Wally discovers in Wallis's letters that the romance of the century was not perfect, that she was tormented by doubt, and that she often felt trapped but ultimately accommodated those feelings.

Wally returns to New York, having divorced her husband, to find that she is pregnant by Evgeni. Is she happy? It would seem so. As happy as Wallis. The women each discover that love is both less than and greater than what they imagined. What Wally achieves that Wallis didn't is freedom.

The character who is not in the film, Madonna, is everywhere. She is Wallis, the American who becomes the most infamous woman in Britain. She is Wally, obsessed with Simpson.[19] She is both women as they face wrenching decisions involving children, divorce, marriage, career, and what society expects versus what a woman needs. That is why the film ultimately rings so true and feels so moving.

Among the first people Madonna contacted about the film was German cinematographer Hagen Bogdanski, whose work she had seen in the Oscar-winning 2006 movie *The Lives of Others* and in 2009's *The Young Victoria*. The former is about voyeurism, the latter about exhibitionism. One is intimate, the other majestic. One is relatively contemporary, the other a period piece. *W.E.* would incorporate all those elements, and Bogdanski had shown he could shoot them brilliantly. In February, he received a call from a person who asked, "Would you have time to meet with a very well-known woman?" He read the script and went the following day to meet Madonna.[20]

They sat for two hours as she described the project and showed him books and objects relating to Wallis and Edward. In the process, she and Bogdanski sized each other up and concluded that there was sufficient chemistry between them to sustain the project. He said their relationship was entirely collaborative. He could give Madonna his ideas with the certainty that she would listen.[21]

To decide on the *look* they wanted for the film, they pored through books, photographs, and art and watched other movies, from French New Wave to the 2007 Edith Piaf biopic, *La Vie en Rose*.[22]

Despite their personal differences, Madonna consulted Guy Ritchie about technical matters related to cameras and film.[23] She said she wanted to use historical footage, 16mm film for intimate shots, and Super 8 to create a feeling of "home movies" for flashback scenes.[24]

Music was as important as the film's visuals. Madonna wanted it to be integrated into the film as part of the atmosphere the characters breathed.[25] She hired Polish composer Abel Korzeniowski, whose work she admired in the 2009 film *A Single Man,* to create a similarly "melancholic, sweeping, emotional" score for her film.[26]

Next came the casting. Madonna said finding the actor to play Simpson was nearly impossible because Simpson's speech and mannerisms were singular and subtle and because the actor had to portray her from age twenty-eight to age seventy. "When Andrea Riseborough walked into the room, I knew she was the one." At twenty-eight, she was young, but her face could evoke many ages and emotions. Like Wallis, she was both fragile *and* fierce.[27]

Riseborough, who had played British prime minister Margaret Thatcher in a 2008 TV series, read Madonna's script and found it "unique and brave."[28] "It's an industry that's very strongly dominated by males," she said, "and so to be part of a creative endeavor with a strong woman at the helm, a film about strong women, was, I thought, important and genuinely humbling."[29]

Actor James D'Arcy wasn't Madonna's first choice to play King Edward VIII, and he knew it. "A lot of my friends were up for it," D'Arcy said. Originally, he wanted to try out for the part simply to meet Madonna, but when he read the script, he became genuinely interested in the role.[30] D'Arcy had been in numerous television series and several big movies, but he had never been the lead. By the time Madonna gave him the part, she envisaged him as a king. She referred to him as "Your Royal Highness" and curtsied when she saw him.[31]

Madonna said she cast Australian actor Abbie Cornish as Wally because so much of what occurs in the film happens inside Wally's head, and Cornish's face was so expressive that she was able to convey a story without words.[32]

Originally Madonna had planned to cast Eugene Hütz as the security guard who would be Wally's love interest, which was why she made the character Ukrainian. But Hütz dropped out to go on tour. For Evgeni, she turned instead to Oscar Isaac, who had just worked with Cornish on a film called *Sucker Punch*.[33]

His background was one Madonna understood well. Born in Guatemala, he was raised in Miami in a strict Christian household. He had played in a punk band, and his early roles onstage and in film had tended toward the edgy and the political.[34] "I was summoned to Madonna's 'lair,' her house up in New York, and met with her for a few hours," Isaac said. "We just had a great conversation and off of that she hired me."[35]

Before filming started, the actors had to go to school. Madonna wanted them to know as much as she did about their characters.[36] "She was more prepared than any director I've ever worked with, except possibly Peter Weir," D'Arcy said.[37] "You'd get emails from her at two in the morning and then another one at six in the morning...I don't know how she's doing it because she's not sleeping."[38]

Isaac, who had never played the piano, spent a month and a half working with piano teachers to learn to play three complex songs. Riseborough concentrated on the French language, dancing, and mastering Simpson's voice. D'Arcy learned to clay shoot, ride horses, dance, and play the bagpipes. He was told by a teacher, "You can't do it in six weeks—it takes at least a year—[so] the only thing I can teach you is how to look like you're playing them." D'Arcy told Madonna, who wrote him a note saying, "Just because somebody says you can't do something doesn't mean you should listen to them."[39]

It fell to Arianne Phillips to dress the characters. In her lifetime, Wallis Simpson was a walking runway show—not unlike Madonna herself. She wore Schiaparelli, Valentino, Dior, Vionnet, and Balenciaga creations. (Edward was just as stylish. Dunhill provided his suits for the film.)[40] Phillips and Madonna visited the archives of the Victoria and Albert Museum, which agreed to re-create four dresses for the production, including a hand-beaded chiffon gown and a silver-and-gold lamé dress for Wallis.[41]

Jewelry was so important that it was almost a character in the film. Simpson was a trendsetter, with a taste for large, colorful, expensive pieces.[42] Some of the jewelry in *W.E.* was re-created by Cartier and Van Cleef & Arpels, but some was original and had belonged to Simpson. When Riseborough wore those, six security guards followed her.[43]

With preproduction scheduled, Madonna took a break to travel to the village of Chinkhota, around ten miles from Malawi's capital, Lilongwe, to lay the first brick for the girls' school she planned to build there. She had been at the site with her children the previous October to plant three Moringa trees. Known as the "miracle tree," the Moringa is prized for its ability to nourish the body. Madonna hoped the Raising Malawi Academy for Girls, which would stand in the trees' shadow, would nourish five hundred young minds beginning in 2011.[44]

Madonna's involvement in Malawi had deepened, even in the few months since her contentious adoption of Mercy. Her Raising Malawi charity funded six orphanages, including providing nearly the entire operating budget at the Home of Hope orphanage where David had lived. With Jeffrey Sachs, she helped develop two Millennium Villages in Malawi, with the goal of making them self-sustainable. And she funded community centers so that orphans who remained with extended families in villages could access food and health-care services. Some aid organizations promoted that alternative to adoption as a way to maintain community cohesion.[45]

Her projects were not without controversy. Her planned school in Chinkhota was criticized for forcing two hundred villagers off the land. They were given $500,000 in compensation by Raising Malawi, and by the spring of 2010, when Madonna arrived, the site was ready for construction to begin.[46]

With Mercy and Lourdes beside her, Madonna laid a brick inscribed with the phrase DARE TO DREAM. She hoped to educate girls to become doctors, lawyers, and leaders. "Having seen the determination in the eyes of these children," she said, "I know they have the strength to save Malawi. They just need to be given the tools."[47] Her goal was to offer students an "internationally competitive education while incorporating local values."[48]

To some, Madonna was known as "Saint Madonna of Malawi."[49] But in May she irritated government officials by publicly criticizing a Malawian court's sentencing of two gay men to fourteen years in prison for violating the country's antigay laws. Madonna called on "progressive men and women of Malawi—and around the world—to challenge this decision in the name of human dignity."[50] Not long afterward, questions were raised about a lack of progress at the site for her school. There were three trees and a brick but no building.[51]

When Madonna returned to London and her film, the word she encountered most often was *no.* "When you make a movie," she said, "it seems like there's nothing but resistance." The film's budget was around $20 million, but the project she envisioned would require double that. She had to be creative to make it work.[52]

For the interior sets in London, Madonna said, "I literally robbed my own house to dress [it]. Half the paintings and drapes came from my home. Every day we would go there and pick up different bits of furniture." She used her relationship with fashion houses to secure haute couture on the cheap, persuading them to make costumes and allow her to borrow others. Stella McCartney also lent a hand. And when additional jewelry was needed, Madonna used some of her own.[53] Eventually, enough people said yes to allow her to begin four months of filming in July.

W.E. was shot in dozens of locations: London, the English countryside, Wales, Manhattan, Brooklyn, Cap d'Antibes, Portofino. Mohamed Al-Fayed allowed Madonna to film on his Bois de Boulogne property in Paris, where Wallis and Edward had lived for decades. She said she had no idea when she wrote the script how difficult shooting at all those locations would be.

> I wrote it from a place of inspiration. "Oh, they were in the south of France, and now they're in Paris, and now they're in the countryside in England." I never once thought that means I'm going to have to go to all these places... to create all these locations...I was naive while I was writing it.[54]

Cinematographer Bogdanski said filming went smoothly in England because most of the shots were interior. When they arrived in France, however, the situation became almost untenable. The streets were clogged with bystanders and paparazzi. "We had to stop shooting twice in Nice. Suddenly there were a thousand people on the set, and we had to flee," Bogdanski said. "She's used to it. She just can't go anywhere without people freaking out."[55] At one point Madonna used the chaos in her film. "When Wallis gets off the boat in France and waves to the people," Bogdanski said, "there were really paparazzi and hundreds of maniacs to the left and right of the picture. That was absurd."[56]

Bogdanski's camerawork reflects the madness. It seems continually in motion, befitting the tumultuous story as well as a crucial part of Madonna's world: dance.[57] There is a lot of dancing in *W.E.* Wallis does a modified Charleston to "Pretty Vacant," by the Sex Pistols. In New York, Wally and Evgeni dance amid Wallis's precious things at Sotheby's. But the last dance of the film is perhaps the most poignant. As Edward lies on his deathbed, he asks Wallis, by then slightly hunched and stiff, to dance for him. It is 1972. She drops the needle on a Chubby Checker record and does the twist.

Madonna wrapped up her filming in Europe in late July, with the shoot scheduled to move to New York in September. In between, in early August, she introduced a line of Material Girl clothing with thirteen-year-old Lourdes at Macy's in Herald Square—the same location where, in 1985, Andy Warhol had presided over a Madonna look-alike contest. Now a new generation of girls lined up to buy clothing designed by Lourdes but inspired by that earlier period: short dresses, short skirts, crop tops, bangles, and torn tights. The look was vintage Madonna, from her *Desperately Seeking Susan* era. Less overtly sexual than sassy and tough, Lourdes's creations reasserted Madonna's original message of empowerment.[58]

Stella McCartney had introduced Lourdes to fashion design when she was around eight.[59] Five years later, Lourdes was working on the Material Girl creations with the design team at the brand management firm Iconix Brand Group and attending meetings with Macy's executives. "I didn't really do anything," Madonna said. "I couldn't even say it was a collaboration. It was 90 percent Lola. I respect her style. It's for a junior line, and that's who she is."[60]

The publicity surrounding Material Girl clothing provided a rare glimpse into Madonna's relationship with her daughter. It included television interviews and even a video promotion that showed the two of them interacting. Madonna came across as a proud but far from lenient mother. Taking a page from her father's book of parenting, she said, she monitored what Lourdes wore to school. "School's not a nightclub; that's what I always say to her," she explained.[61]

Seeming at times wise and poised beyond her years, Lourdes, likewise, had veto power over her mother's clothing. Before an event in New York, she intervened to tell her that the outfit she planned to wear—a corset and fishnet stockings in lieu of pants—was a nonstarter. Madonna acquiesced but told an interviewer, "I'm not going to let [parenthood] completely censor me. I say to my kids all the time, I'm an artist, this is what I do, this is what I've always done. And they need to learn to separate it."[62]

As Madonna the mother taught her children life lessons, she did so through her experience as an artist. To Rocco, she said, "There's a couple of things you've got to remember. One is to have good manners...I don't care if you become a revolutionary: please have manners."[63] She used the same rationale for school.

> I say, "You want to change the world? You want to be somebody?...Being educated is a big part of being a rebel." And also discipline, starting a project and finishing through to the end, is key to making something out of your life.[64]

Madonna believed that the policing of a child's development was a parent's most difficult job. For a single working parent, it was nearly impossible, always exhausting, and often guilt-inducing, especially if the parent *liked* her work. During an appearance on *The Late Show with David Letterman* the previous year, Madonna was asked whether parenting was her most important job. She answered without conviction, "Uh, yes. That's the politically correct answer."[65]

Madonna's candor resonated with women. Feminist author Jude Ellison S. Doyle wrote at the time in *bitchmedia,*

> It's refreshing to hear a female celebrity say this stuff, especially in an environment where getting married, getting impregnated...is de rigueur... where women whose lives don't and may never include a husband and baby are portrayed as pathetic lost souls...[66]
>
> The fact that Madonna evidently believes she would be a success at life whether or not she had children makes me absurdly happy.[67]

Madonna had hoped her school in Malawi would open in 2011, but by the fall of 2010, though nearly $4 million had been spent on fees and staff, ground had still not been broken. She had entrusted the oversight of the school to her Raising Malawi organization, headed by former Kabbalah Centre development director Philippe van den Bossche.[68]

Amid criticism over his handling of the project, van den Bossche left his job without publicly responding because of a confidentiality agreement. Madonna, meanwhile, hired Global Philanthropy Group to evaluate her organization. Its director, Trevor Neilson, who had cornered the market on celebrity charities, concluded, "Madonna was misled by multiple people about what was happening on the ground in Malawi."[69]

Neilson's group gave Madonna a report that alleged a "startling lack of accountability on the part of the management team in Malawi and the management team in the United States." GPG's investigators reportedly found that only around $850,000 of the $3.8 million spent on the academy made it to Malawi and that much of that money had gone to architects, designers, and staff.[70]

In February of 2011, Raising Malawi's board of directors, including the Kabbalah Centre's Michael Berg, was replaced by three people: Madonna, Guy Oseary, and Madonna's accountant, Richard Feldstein. The organization also planned to move out of the Kabbalah Centre, where it had been headquartered. Such was the shake-up that in March, Madonna announced she would not build her Raising Malawi Academy for Girls. Instead, she would use the $18 million she had raised ($11 million of it her own money) to build not one school but many.[71]

"There's a real education crisis in Malawi," she said. "Sixty-seven percent of girls don't go to secondary school, and this is simply unacceptable."[72] "My original vision is now on a much bigger scale...I want to do more and I want to do it better."[73] Partnering with the US charity buildOn, which had already constructed more than fifty schools in Malawi, she hoped to fund ten new schools to educate one thousand boys and girls each year.[74]

The fallout for the Kabbalah Centre in the United States, meanwhile, continued. That spring, the *Los Angeles Times* reported that the Berg family's operation was the subject of a federal criminal tax probe involving both the IRS and the US Attorney's Office for the Southern District of New York. Investigators were looking into whether the Bergs "enriched themselves with members' donations."[75]

Raising Malawi became part of the investigation. Its new board cooperated fully with federal officials.[76] But the story of alleged financial improprieties, coming so soon after Madonna abandoned her girls'-school plans, undermined her previous three years of trust building in Lilongwe. Headlines didn't help. Some erroneously implied that Madonna herself was the target of US investigators: FBI PROBES MADONNA'S MALAWI AID read one.[77]

Against the backdrop of that crisis, Madonna had managed to nearly finish *W.E.,* working with British film editor Danny Tull. By that point, Tull was Madonna's "house" editor. They first collaborated on the DVD of her Confessions tour, in 2006, and in the years since, he had edited all Madonna's major visual work, including her Malawi film, *I Am Because We Are.*

She was also back in the music studio with another trusted associate, William Orbit, working on a song called "Masterpiece." Guy Oseary had persuaded an already overstretched Madonna to write a song for *W.E.,* which she reluctantly did. "Masterpiece" would appear during the closing credits of the film, almost as Madonna's postscript to her movie.[78]

Writing with Orbit for the first time in ten years and working on a record for the first time in four years reminded Madonna how much she had missed what she called her "day job"—making music. "To sit down and play my guitar and sing a song—I almost cried," she said.[79] She decided to team with Orbit again on what would be her twelfth studio album.

After leaving Warner Bros. Records, in 2007, Madonna was without a record label. Her Live Nation deal did not include recording her music. That changed in December of 2010, when Interscope Records offered her a three-album deal worth $40 million. Madonna immediately took to Facebook: "It's official…I need to move. I need to sweat. I need to make new music! Music I can dance to. I'm on the lookout for the maddest, sickest, most bad ass people to collaborate with."[80]

Orbit filled the "maddest" role. His career as a solo artist, composer, and producer had grown enormously after the paradigm-shifting album *Ray of Light.* But his life had spun out of control. "Success tore me up, to be honest," he said.[81] After producing and remixing songs by some of the biggest names in the business and getting caught up in that world, Orbit found his way back to semi-sanity by creating a work of art for himself. He composed a nine-movement seventy-minute-long symphonic piece, *Orchestral Suite,* which was performed by the BBC Philharmonic.[82]

For Madonna's part, *Hard Candy* had been such a disappointment commercially, the sound so un-Madonna, and her collaborators ultimately so ill suited to her work that she needed to be in the studio with someone who understood her. Orbit was that person. He would work on six tracks.[83] Perhaps also in reaction to *Hard Candy,* on which Madonna worked with "known" artists, she returned to her tradition of bringing relative unknowns into her world. In addition to Orbit, three Europeans would be crucial to her new album: Italian DJ Benny Benassi; his producer cousin, Alessandro "Alle" Benassi; and French producer Martin Solveig.

Benny Benassi had won a Grammy for Best Remixed Recording in 2008 for the Public Enemy song "Bring the Noise" and opened for Madonna during her Sticky & Sweet tour in Rome.[84] She called on him the following year to remix her single "Celebration," and then came the call to work with her on three tracks for her next studio album. Benny told the Italian newspaper *La Stampa*:

She explained she wanted us because this record is meant to be a declaration of love to the world of disco, in which she was born. An album that gathers together all the styles and atmospheres that have characterized international night life over the last ten years. And to her, we represent Italian Dance music...the one "made in Reggio Emilia" in which melody is the vital element.[85]

Martin Solveig had been on the French scene since the late '90s making music that tapped several genres: house, pop, R&B. He called himself "100-percent club-friendly...and 100-percent pop-friendly."[86] A song he did called "Boys and Girls" for a Jean Paul Gaultier runway show caught Madonna's attention. They agreed to work on one track, which turned into three. They had so much fun that she invited him to help her produce her album. He dropped what he was doing and joined her, he said, "shaking in my shiny shoes."[87]

Solveig was a little like Stuart Price—self-deprecating yet cocky, so nerdy he was hip—and he shared Madonna's sense of humor. He said,

We worked together for three months between London and New York, and sent texts, ideas back and forth.[88] We did six or seven tracks and, by today's standards, our studio collaboration was old school. Now it's people who have never met emailing...tracks to each other. [This] was organic in comparison.[89]

The Madonna-Solveig song "Give Me All Your Luvin'" would be the album's first single. It was as unstoppable as "Hung Up," but a lot frothier. On the first day they met, Solveig played Madonna a demo. "She told me: 'I like this song but if we're going to do it together we're going to redo it together, too.' We took everything out of the demo she didn't like: the snare drum, the vocal, and from that skeleton track we built a new song."[90] Then, he added, "her manager and I thought about including M.I.A. on the song and Madonna thought about Nicki Minaj, because she loves her."[91] The two women rappers would be the "badass" elements in Madonna's creative equation.

Twenty-eight-year-old Trinidad-born, Queens-raised Onika Maraj, a.k.a. Nicki Minaj, would work on two tracks. By 2011, she was considered the most successful female rapper in the United States and one of the artists whose style and drive best mirrored Madonna's own. Minaj was a take-no-prisoners feminist—sassy, sexy on her own terms and for her own pleasure, and funny. Unlike pop women who resided in a mancentric world, Minaj lived in Nicki's world. She ruled it. "I'm an artist in every mother-fucking sense of the word," she said.[92]

Minaj was about to produce her second album and felt, she said, the way Madonna must have in the early '80s. "She was mentally where I am now, feeling like 'If people would just leave me alone and let me do me, they'll see the great things I have to offer.'" To prepare to work with Madonna, she watched *Truth or Dare* and came away from it feeling connected to her before they even reached the studio.[93]

Also called in to collaborate was the British–Sri Lankan artist Mathangi "Maya" Arulpragasam, who performed as M.I.A.[94]

Nicki Minaj rapped about the street, being a woman on it, and being an artist in a world ruled by men. M.I.A. added radical politics to that mix.[95] By the time she was in the studio with Madonna, she had a global following and had racked up awards and nominations: the BRITs, the Turner Prize, the Grammys, MTV Video Music Awards, even an Oscar nomination for Best Original Song from the 2008 film *Slumdog Millionaire*. But in 2010, she did what Madonna had often done. She risked everything by making a nine-minute video for the song called "Born Free."[96]

Created with the French director Romain Gavras, it was an unflinching depiction of violence suffered by ethnic and racial minorities. In her video, the "other" was, ironically, represented by redheaded people who were rounded up in Los Angeles by paramilitary groups—some wearing US flags on their uniforms—and taken to the desert to be beaten, tortured, and killed. Throughout, there were references to real resistance groups and ongoing conflicts. M.I.A.'s politically poignant film was banned nearly everywhere, including on YouTube. She took the ban in stride. "If I'm honest, I find the new Justin Bieber video...more of an assault to my eyes and senses than what I've made."[97]

Madonna had wanted to call her album *L.U.V.,* but M.I.A. came up with an alternative, *MDNA,* an abbreviation of Madonna's name that was also a playful reference to Ecstasy.[98] On July 4, 2011, Madonna began recording it.[99]

Critics and Madonna fans would see it as the divorce album that *Hard Candy* failed to be. It was about overcoming obstacles, pushing past disappointment, despair, and defeat—quietly at times, angrily at others. When she started *MDNA,* Madonna said, between her divorce, the complications in Malawi, and the demands of her film, "I felt like a caged animal."[100]

"Girl Gone Wild" is about busting free of that cage. Madonna worked on it with Benny and Alle Benassi. The sound is joyous Italian electropop. "Gang Bang," produced by William Orbit, takes a hairpin turn in the opposite direction. It's safe to say no one would dance to that one. It is Madonna's most pointedly rageful song.

Growling like a vengeful Marianne Faithfull, screaming like the banshee Patti Smith, wielding a gun like Cher in her 1966 "Bang Bang (My Baby Shot Me Down)," Madonna in "Gang Bang" uses her weapon on an ex-lover who had taken her "jack"—her money—and tried to entomb her. Distance isn't enough to obliterate his memory. In the song, she puts a bullet in the fellow's head. She doesn't regret it, even if it means going to hell (where she says she happens to have a lot of friends).

Madonna said she improvised the vocals. "I felt like I had to just scream, to let myself become possessed by this kind of Russ Meyer, Quentin Tarantino kind of character. It was all very tongue-in-cheek, but I just went off...obviously, I had to get some things off my chest."[101]

On the first three tracks of Madonna's album, she introduces listeners to Italian sounds and British sounds. On the fourth track, "Turn Up the Radio," they encounter Martin Solveig's French exuberance. The Benassis kept listeners on the dance floor. Solveig puts them in their cars and tells them to drive. The song is a tribute to music as the true opium of the people—the soothing balm, the restorative medicine, the portal through which they flee their woes, if only for three and a half minutes.

"I Don't Give A" is possibly the first pop song to describe the bitter reality of a divorced single mother's life—the custody battles and messy fights over money. Unlike "Gang Bang," "I Don't Give A" isn't angry but mutedly triumphant. That is thanks partly to Solveig's production and partly to Nicki Minaj's defiant rap. Her message: she has Madonna's back.

"Madonna's the only humungous artist I ever worked with who actually sat with me in the studio," Minaj said.

> [She was] 100,000-percent involved. Did not leave the studio until it was done. I mean her children even came by after school. I was just like, that's the epitome of who I want to be. If I can balance a family and career, then I win.[102]

Orbit said that during the writing and recording of *MDNA,* Madonna "was on form and better than ever...We had songs lined up that were breathtaking."[103] Her album and the joy she experienced writing it would be a buffer for the months ahead as she prepared to show her movie to the world.

In June, Madonna arranged a test screening of *W.E.* at the AMC Loews Lincoln Square in New York. The small audience was given no advance material, meaning there was no mention of Madonna. After the screening, the group completed a two-page questionnaire about the film: Did they like it? If it lagged, where? What about the performances? Madonna and Harvey Weinstein, whose company would distribute the film in the

United States, sat at the back of the room and listened as audience members discussed their responses. *W.E.* was compared favorably with popular period pieces such as *The Duchess, The King's Speech,* and *Marie Antoinette* as well as with thought-provoking contemporary films about relationships, like *Babel* and *Revolutionary Road.*[104]

All went well until one audience member said he liked the film because of its director. Others asked who that was. When he said Madonna, the mood in the room turned instantly negative. Madonna left. Weinstein stayed to hear what the now semihostile group had to say. The takeaway from the screening: the film was fine; Madonna would be a problem.[105]

Having missed the deadline for Cannes, the film premiered at the Venice International Film Festival on September 1, 2011. Madonna arrived at the Lido by speedboat, dressed in one of Wallis Simpson's favorite designers, Vionnet. In her gray gown covered in red butterflies, she was mid-twentieth-century elegance personified: flowing blond hair, red sunglasses, red platform heels.[106] Hundreds of photographers descended upon her as she chatted with the film's actors. Hundreds of fans shouted her name.[107] It was her evening, a chance to finally be recognized for her contribution to the world of film that she loved.

Madonna and the audience settled into the Palazzo del Cinema to watch her movie.[108] It was nearly impossible to imagine that the woman who directed *W.E.* was the same person who had directed *Filth and Wisdom* just a few years earlier. The new film was beautifully shot, tightly edited, and brilliantly acted at some points. The music was superb. Madonna had reason to be proud, which was why the response was so shocking. The criticism coming out of Venice was *venomous.* The *Daily Telegraph* said the film was greeted in Venice "as warmly as a six-foot rise in sea levels."[109]

Some of it could be attributed to the inevitable comparison between *W.E.* and the Oscar-winning 2010 film *The King's Speech,* which involves the monarchy in the aftermath of Edward's abdication. *W.E.* was not that film and had no pretensions to be, but it would be judged the lesser for it. Some of the criticism, however, just felt personal.

> The *Los Angeles Times:* "What we have is an overwrought historical drama" with a "too simplistic and borderline offensive" plot.[110]
> The *Guardian:* "What an extraordinarily silly, preening, mishandled film this is…Her direction is so all over the shop it barely qualifies as direction at all."[111]
> The *Daily Telegraph:* "*W.E.* is a…stultifyingly vapid film, festooned with moments of pure aesthetic idiocy."[112]

Instead of being applauded for expanding the Wallis and Edward story beyond the accepted narrative, based on her research and Wallis's letters,

Madonna was mocked and criticized for historical inaccuracy. What mattered, apparently, was not what Wallis said but what history said *about* her.

Anne Sebba, who also read Wallis's letters, for her 2011 book, *That Woman,* agreed with Madonna's take on Simpson. "For a long time Wallis has been mistreated by history," Sebba said. "So it is nice to see this interpretation of her...Madonna has really understood a critical part of Wallis...It is what Wallis called her dual nature; her fearfulness on the one hand and on the other hand her driving ambition."[113]

Feminist author Naomi Wolf also defended Madonna, writing a scathing opinion piece in *The Guardian* about the response to the film. "The reliable media theme of 'Hating Madonna,' whenever she steps out of her pretty-girl-pop-music bandwidth, is so consistent that it deserves scrutiny in its own right," she said.[114] As for the film itself, Wolf wrote:

> *W.E.* does not apologize for female centrality the way most works of art by women still feel they must do: she places Wallis and Wally's journeys right at the center of the narrative. The men are peripheral, sometimes two-dimensional images (The Abuser, The Great Lover) but this works in the story just the way that female Muse figures, or Whores with Hearts of Gold, often work in films about male self-realization.[115]

Diego Semerene, writing in *Slant,* was one of the very few critics who appreciated the film. He said that if critics put aside their "heterosexist anxieties," they would see that *W.E.* "makes a mockery out of 'man's cinema'...

> Madonna handles this film like a masterful aesthetician. The absolutely enthralling soundtrack patches everything together along with the grainy handheld close-ups that tend to follow every establishing shot.[116]

But Wolf and Semerene were voices in the wilderness. The consensus was that the film stank. As always, Madonna persisted. "I'm well aware that everything I say and do is judged with a different measuring stick to most other people," she said. "I'm under the magnifying glass...but I can also use that. I can influence people."[117]

In October, *W.E.* screened in Leicester Square at the British Film Institute's London Film Festival. Madonna was booed by fans who felt snubbed along the red carpet and criticized by filmgoers inside the theater. A *Guardian* writer who saw *W.E.* there called it "inescapably ridiculous" and a "clumsily assembled jigsaw of bad movie cliches...trite, misguided" and yet "not as bad as I expected."[118]

After each screening, Madonna went back into her film—which she called a "work in progress"—and tweaked it.[119] In December, it was finished. It was that version that she brought to New York to screen at the Museum of Modern Art.

The 450 people in the audience at the event, sponsored by the Cinema Society and Piaget, were mostly art, entertainment, and fashion notables. It was Madonna's kind of crowd, but she was nervous. "I think being nervous means you care about something and want the outcome to be good," she said. "I come to the art of filmmaking with great humility. I respect it immensely as an art form and I know I have a lot to learn."[120]

Taking the podium, Harvey Weinstein defended Madonna against bad reviews, saying that if she were "Joe Smith" she would be considered a great filmmaker. "Thanks Harvey," Madonna replied after taking the microphone from him, "but I would never want to be Joe Smith."[121]

Two hours later, when the lights went up, Patti Smith gave *W.E.* a standing ovation. (She had seen it at the Venice film festival and liked it there, too.) At the after-party, other audience members swarmed around Madonna with congratulations.[122] Thomas Wolfe once said you can't go home again. For a New York artist, sometimes that's the only place you *can* go.

Chapter 53

Indianapolis, New York, 2012

> Art opens up alternative realities, and that's extremely helpful
> when we have a crisis and multiple failures of the political
> imagination.[1]
>
> — *Nadya Tolokonnikova*

WHILE MADONNA WAS being booed at the *W.E.* screening in London, Sean
Lennon and Rufus Wainwright were leading protesters in lower Manhattan in a rendition of "Material Girl," which they dedicated to the Federal
Reserve chairman, Ben Bernanke. The Occupy Wall Street protests were
the manifestation of the anger and frustration young people felt in the aftermath of the 2008–2009 financial crisis, when the inequities that governed
the system were laid bare and it became clear that the people who caused so
much hardship would go unpunished. Madonna said she was "excited" by
the protests, and not just because they featured her song.[2]

Revolution was in the air. In fact, Occupy was a belated US response to
anti-austerity protests that had rocked Europe in the aftermath of the US
financial meltdown and, more important, the Arab Spring. That uprising
began in December of 2010, when a twenty-six-year-old Tunisian street
vendor set himself on fire to protest the actions of police who had tried to
prevent him from making a living. His self-immolation went viral and
ignited anger throughout Tunisia over corruption, the cost of living, auto-
cratic rule — basically a future without hope for people who were not born
to privilege. Less than a month after Mohamed Bouazizi's death, the
twenty-three-year reign of Tunisia's president was over. For the first time
in history, an Arab leader was forced from office by a public that said it had
had enough.

Streets throughout the Arab world — in Egypt, Bahrain, Morocco,
Jordan, the Palestinian territories, Libya, Syria, Sudan, and Yemen —
exploded in protests that were spread on social media. In some places,
decades-old dictatorships ended. Democracy and individual freedom —
the ideals that US president Barack Obama had preached in an extraordinary speech to students in Cairo in June of 2009 — suddenly seemed
within reach.

Young people around the world watched as their Arab counterparts risked their lives to create a better world. And though only one of those revolts would ultimately give rise to a functioning, albeit faltering, democracy—in the place where it all started, Tunisia—they all awakened a generation to the reality that change was possible through unity and courage.

By mid-October of 2011, New York's own revolt, the Occupy movement, had spawned demonstrations in eighty other cities and countries and a global Day of Rage during which millions of people took to the streets. Like the Arab Spring protests, the Occupy Movement was unsuccessful in achieving its goals, but the seeds were planted. The dialogue had begun.

Madonna wanted to be part of it. In 2012, using the powerful platform of a world tour, she would travel from city to city, speaking her mind about a range of issues, daring authorities to stop her. She chose to start her tour that spring in the region where the protests were happening, in the Middle East. Before she did, however, she agreed to perform on the high holy day of American culture at its most sacred secular event: the Super Bowl.

Historically, Super Bowl halftime shows featured big names who seemed overwhelmed by the scale of the performance. At first, Madonna was, too. She had just a few weeks to create the ultimate spectacle under the strictest possible conditions. "I have eight minutes to set up my stage, twelve minutes to put on the greatest show on earth, and...seven minutes to take it down...How do you do that?"[3] Madonna did what she always did. She hired the best people to help, and she rehearsed—for 320 hours.[4]

Swedish fashion designer Bea Åkerlund, who was married to Jonas, had the daunting task of outfitting the show's one hundred drum-line performers, 150 gladiators, and two hundred choir members in addition to Madonna's guest artists. They included EDM duo LMFAO (Stefan Kendal Gordy and Skyler Austen Gordy), Nicki Minaj, M.I.A., and Atlanta rapper CeeLo Green.[5]

The last time a woman headlined the Super Bowl halftime show was in 1996, when Diana Ross starred in the event.[6] The last time a halftime show made news was in 2004, when during a joint performance by Janet Jackson and Justin Timberlake a tiny portion of Jackson's breast was exposed for a few seconds. That "controversy" "outraged" America. An appearance by Madonna, the queen of controversy, promised more delicious scandal worthy of more faux outrage. But America would be disappointed. Super Bowl Madonna was as wholesome as apple pie. She told the press that she planned to dedicate her performance to her father, because "I'm sure that of all the things I've ever done in my life, this will be the thing he's most excited about."[7]

The Super Bowl would become part of the highly choreographed rollout of Madonna's new album, *MDNA*. Its first single, "Give Me All Your Luvin'," was released just ahead of the game. The radio behemoth Clear Channel, which normally shunned Madonna songs, partnered with her to debut the "Super Bowl single" on one hundred stations. The song's video, meanwhile, premiered on sixteen hundred digital billboards around the world and on YouTube, where it clocked three million views on the first day and more than twelve million in the first week. Not surprisingly, "Give Me All Your Luvin'" charted in the top ten in twenty-two countries.[8]

The video, which featured Nicki Minaj and M.I.A., blended womanly sass appeal with a football theme and offered a preview of what viewers might expect on February 5 in Indianapolis. That was the day the New York Giants faced the New England Patriots and Madonna led an army onstage.

Her performance consisted of a twelve-minute medley of new and old material. Opening with "Vogue," the song in her repertoire most associated with gay and trans culture, she gave a nod to American football players' historical roots in the gladiators of ancient Rome. "Music" followed as the Roman Empire onstage became a massive LED jukebox.[9]

Joined by Minaj, M.I.A., and a troupe of female dancers dressed as cheerleaders, Madonna sang "Give Me All Your Luvin'." Minaj and M.I.A. stood on either side of her and rapped their own verses of the song. That section ended with another football staple, a marching band, led by CeeLo Green. It arrived to a few lines from "Open Your Heart" and "Express Yourself."[10]

With the next song, Madonna acknowledged the sport's sacred place in US culture. She, Green, and a black-robed choir let loose with "Like a Prayer." The darkened stadium was illuminated by what seemed like thousands of candles and echoed with what sounded like scores of celestial voices. The song and the scene were meant to transport the audience spiritually, and without doubt they did. On the field in gold lights, the words WORLD PEACE appeared.[11]

Super Bowl XLVI was the most-watched game in US television history, but even more people—114 million—tuned in for Madonna's halftime show.[12] She had been so nervous before and during the performance that she collapsed in the bathroom when it was over.[13] "I laid down on the floor and cried...because I got through it and I knew everything went off without a hitch."[14] Not exactly. Madonna didn't know that M.I.A. had let loose a middle finger while singing the lyrics "I don't give a shit."[15]

A few eagle eyes spotted it. Out of the tens of millions of people who saw the show, 222 of them complained about M.I.A.'s finger to the Federal Communications Commission. The NFL responded by suing M.I.A. for nearly $17 million for allegedly violating league "values." Surprisingly,

Madonna didn't defend M.I.A. In a morning-after interview, she called the gesture "punk rock" but said it was "a teenager, irrelevant thing to do...What was the point? It was just out of place."[16]

M.I.A. didn't apologize. Instead, she publicly accused the NFL of hypocrisy. In the twelve months prior to her "offense," twenty NFL players had been accused of, charged with, or convicted of battery, domestic violence, sexual assault, or drug possession. And as the NFL's suit against M.I.A. slowly made its way through the legal system, a quarterback who flipped the bird at a game was fined $12,000.[17] "If you're talking about racism and sexism," M.I.A. said years later, "that moment in my life showed the cracks in everyone I knew."[18]

The controversy dogged M.I.A. for two years until the two sides settled for an undisclosed amount. It did not hurt Madonna. Preorders for *MDNA* were so great that it went to number 1 in more than forty countries. Even her back catalog got a boost from the Super Bowl. *Billboard* reported that some of her digital tracks saw sales increase "over 1,700 percent."[19]

Amid enormous anticipation, her second single, "Girl Gone Wild," appeared on March 2, and three weeks later, its video was released. And that *did* hurt Madonna. Not since "American Life," in 2003, had a Madonna video caused such a stir. Not since "Justify My Love," in 1990, had the controversy been about sex. YouTube, the new home of music videos, only allowed access to over-eighteens, saying it was too "raunchy" to show on open view.[20]

The video was directed by the fashion world's next-generation hot photographers Mert Alas and Marcus Piggott, who had also shot Madonna's *MDNA* album cover.[21] "Girl Gone Wild" mockingly played off the concept of Girls Gone Wild, the humilitainment franchise in which drunken young women are encouraged to expose their breasts and perform "lesbian" sex acts for the benefit of leering men and the cameras. Unlike Madonna's video, the Girls Gone Wild thirty-minute infomercials were not restricted—they aired on E!, BET, Fox Sports Net, and Comedy Central, among other places. Its videos sold in the millions.[22]

Madonna's video features the gender-bending Ukrainian synth-pop boy band and dance group Kazaky. Think Eastern European New York Dolls. Shot in black and white, it references "Justify My Love," "Vogue," and "Express Yourself." It also plays with the kind of religious imagery that had gotten Madonna in hot water before: one of her bare-chested men wears a crown of thorns. But there is no doubt that what disturbed the sleep of YouTube censors is the homoeroticism of the video and Madonna's reveling in it.

Madonna's video controversy was a little like M.I.A.'s finger. In M.I.A.'s case, the target was the hypocrisy of the NFL; in Madonna's, it was the hypocrisy of the entertainment business. It was also a pointed embrace of gay fans who had felt abandoned by British country lady Madonna during her Guy Ritchie period. In an interview with *The Advocate*'s Ari Karpel before the video's release, she said, "I'm back...Never fear."[23]

MDNA was released on March 26. It sold more than 350,000 copies in the first week, Madonna's best performance since *Music* and her eighth number 1 album. But during the second week, sales fell off a cliff. Speculation was that the initial burst came from "bundling": the album was included in the price of a concert ticket. No doubt record-setting preorders were also responsible for the strong start. Whatever the reason, the numbers didn't improve. By the end of the year, *MDNA* had only sold two million copies and ranked even lower than *Hard Candy*.[24]

William Orbit felt that the record hadn't been promoted properly. Madonna was pressed for time with her commitments to her film, the Material Girl fashion line, a perfume line, a shoe line, an international gym franchise, and workout DVDs.[25] Ageism, he believed, also had an extremely negative impact on sales.[26] Writing in the *Village Voice,* Maura Johnston, who didn't like the album, agreed. She noted that *Forbes* called *MDNA* "Madonna's Mighty Menopausal Comeback."[27] But mostly, Orbit blamed the album's poor reception on the way it was created.[28]

Numbers told that story. *Ray of Light* had twenty-six people on the music side of the album. *MDNA* had ninety-two. If, as some critics said, it lacked unity, that was part of the reason. Orbit had wanted to mix the album himself, or only with Madonna. He wanted to drop some of the tracks and add "more depth" to others, he said.[29] He had not been allowed to do any of that. "[I would] lie down in the mud if she didn't want to get her shoes messed up," he said, but "it's hard to be an effective knight when your hands are bound."[30]

Madonna rarely expressed regret over a record's performance, and she almost never gave up on a project if the initial response was criticism. She simply presented it another way. That was what she did with *MDNA*. She took her album on the road. It would be her ninth tour, and it would be unlike any other.

It wasn't that the show was so different, it was that Madonna and the times had changed. She used her tour to draw back the curtain on social and political grievances in many of the countries she visited without regard for the consequences. Some would call it reckless. Madonna considered it necessary. MDNA would be the most political tour of Madonna's career.

She was fully aware of the blowback she would receive and the demands she faced: eight months on the road, eighty-eight shows across the Middle East, Europe, the United States, and South America. Hundreds of people in the cast and crew who relied on her. Millions of dollars invested and hundreds of millions of dollars to be earned, all dependent upon her performance. But more important than all that were her children. Their well-being was paramount. And that weighed on Madonna, too.

That she was able to do her tour at all could be attributed to her drive, commitment, and need to create as well as to a battalion of trusted helpers, among them a new man in her life. Brahim Zaibat was from a banlieue of Lyon, France, and had been part of a group of break-dancers and hip-hop artists who traveled the world performing. He and Madonna met in September of 2010, when he was picked to perform at the launch party for Lourdes's Material Girl clothing line.[31] When Madonna made her relationship with the twenty-four-year-old dancer public, in October, he said, he received "more than a thousand telephone calls" in one day.[32]

The media and the late-night comics relished the chance to make more May–December jokes. But according to Madonna, there was nothing unusual about it. They met. They liked each other. They began dating. As for the desire to have a man in her life, that, too, was simple.

> My children fill me up in many ways and inspire me in many ways, but I need a partner in life. I've never really lived a conventional life, so I think it's quite foolish for me or for anyone else to start thinking that I'm going to start making conventional choices.[33]

Zaibat became a constant presence in Madonna's life. He danced in the Super Bowl show, performed in her videos, and would join her on her tour. He also helped with the children. Madonna wanted the boys, especially, to have a male role model other than just their father. Zaibat, a young Muslim of Algerian descent, was it. Just as Madonna had studied British history when she began her relationship with Guy Ritchie, she introduced herself to Zaibat's world by studying the Qur'an with an Islamic scholar because she believed it was "important to study all the holy books. As my friend Yaman always tells me, a good Muslim is a good Jew, and a good Jew is a good Christian...I couldn't agree more."[34]

The Super Bowl production was such a success that Madonna invited many members of the team that helped her create it to join her on tour. The Moment Factory, which had used LED lighting and animation to turn a football field into a canvas, would be back to do the same to her stage.[35] Michel Laprise, a Cirque du Soleil veteran who helped guide nearly four hundred people onstage for twelve minutes and make it seem effortless, would be the MDNA tour's show director.[36]

Helping those newcomers were Madonna's tour stalwarts. Jamie King would reprise his role as creative director, Kevin Antunes would return as musical director, Monte Pittman would be on guitar, and Jason Young and Alison Faulk, who had both been with her since the Confessions tour, would be the two main choreographers. Arianne Phillips once again oversaw costumes. "We're taking seven hundred shoes on the road," she said. "Madonna changes outfits seven or eight times and the dancers change ten to fifteen times."[37]

Phillips designed some of the pieces herself, including a Joan of Arc outfit for Madonna and a majorette costume, which she based on a 1940s photo she found.[38] But Jean Paul Gaultier was also summoned to help. "I love Madonna. She is the only woman I have asked to marry me. She refused, of course," he said. "But when she asked me to do a costume for her for this tour, I couldn't refuse."[39]

Gaultier's decades of designs for Madonna represented not only a chronology of their careers but also the history of women. While performing "Vogue" during the MDNA tour, she would wear the latest iteration of Gaultier's corset over a white shirt and black tie. It illustrated that though women had made strides in a man's world, they were still constrained by tradition. "We played with the ideas of a suit and a corset," Gaultier said. "But the corset is now like a cage."[40]

For the first time, the tour wardrobe also included Madonna's own designs: her intimate apparel, which was sold under the name Truth or Dare, and shoes from a forthcoming footwear line of that name. Also contributing costuming were Jeremy Scott and Alexander Wang. Dolce & Gabbana created suits for the band. Fausto Puglisi made bandolier vests and ram's-head masks for the dancers, and Prada designed high-heeled boots for the male dancers to wear during "Vogue."[41]

On each tour, the number of dancers increased. For Blond Ambition, there were seven; for Confessions, fourteen; for MDNA, there would be twenty-two dancers and two slackliners, who taught other members of the cast to walk a two-inch-wide length of webbed fiber that was as dangerous as a tightrope but as bouncy as a trampoline. "Tours of this scale, the dancers that are hired are typically the veterans," said choreographer Faulk. "Madonna doesn't like to do that. She likes to take a few veterans, and then she likes to take people that have *never* been in this situation and pluck them out of their world, where they're, like, the best, and then drop them into her world and say, 'Okay, go for it!' "[42]

Rehearsals were held from March to May in New York. "Every single day there's a schedule that's three run-throughs a day," said James "Winky"

Fairorth, CEO of TAIT Towers, which provided all the show's staging elements. "The set list is made...and by the time she gets to the first show she knows where she's going to take every single step for the rest of the ninety-three shows on the tour. I mean, she is locked and loaded."[43]

Even with that schedule and focus, Madonna's work revolved around her children's lives. "The only time she raised her voice during rehearsal," said Michel Laprise, "was when the schedule wasn't allowing her to see her kids."[44] To keep the older ones close, Madonna put Lourdes in the costume department and Rocco onstage with her. David and Mercy, both six years old at the start of the tour, had playrooms set up wherever Madonna worked and nannies to keep an eye on them as they traveled with their mother.[45]

The show, consisting of around twenty songs per concert and four video interludes, was designed around four acts: transgression, prophecy, masculine/feminine, and redemption.[46] Starting in February, the Moment Factory dedicated twenty people to "nonstop" work with Madonna and Laprise on the visuals to help tell that story. The stage design, meanwhile, was underway in New York, Belgium, and China.[47]

For each venue, crews worked in teams, as if on a construction site, building a small city that might only exist for one night before they tore it all down and built it again someplace else. The precision of their work was crucial because, as had been tragically demonstrated in Marseille during Madonna's Sticky & Sweet tour, lives depended on it.[48]

The most challenging aspect of the MDNA stage construction was the task of assembling a matrix of multicolored LED lifts, essentially thirty-six cubes that moved eight feet up or down to create a smooth floor, raised platforms, steps, or escape hatches. If even one of the cubes had a mechanical problem—if it did not lower back into place or did not rise completely—the stage became a flashing-red danger zone.[49]

The area below the stage—the "underworld"—was just as complicated and potentially dangerous. In addition to tech areas, dressing rooms, and hydraulics systems, there were two "coal miners' dollies" that ran on rails in areas where headroom was a problem. Madonna or a dancer would lie on top and be given a push to send the dolly speeding from one end of the underworld to the other. Madonna had tiny Zohars taped to mechanisms throughout the underground. "I'm so superstitious," she said, "and I don't trust stages."[50]

The show began with church bells, hooded monks, a Christian cross, a giant golden censer spewing incense, and three robed men solemnly chanting "Mah-doh-nah." She answered with the beginning of the prayer that Catholics recite during confession. But religion could not contain her.

To the sound of broken glass, Madonna emerged in a bodysuit of black patent leather singing "Girl Gone Wild." The show had begun.[51]

That opening number was Madonna's gayest since the Blond Ambition tour. Her monks, stripped of their robes, shimmied bare-chested in tight trousers and sequined high-heeled ankle boots, reveling in sin along with Madonna. If that song was about the sin of sexuality, the next two numbers were about the sin of violence.[52]

Rather than the dystopian future of Madonna's Drowned World tour, MDNA's violence took place in the real world. It began with "Revolver" and Madonna, armed with a replica assault rifle, surrounded by "badass bitches" also packing heat. The theme continued during "Gang Bang." Madonna described herself in that sequence as a "super vixen bent on revenge." The segment was set in a room at the "Paradise Motel."[53]

Madonna picked off intruders with relish and performed some convincing hand-to-hand combat before finishing one of them off with a bullet to the head. Bang. Bang. "He deserved it!" she shouted amid a wail of police sirens with a car-chase video on the screen behind her.[54] Music journalist Carol Cooper called the segment vintage Madonna.

> Unlike lesser pop stars who also think their song-writing is strong enough to support artistic, "attitudinal" staging, only Madonna sustains the palpable strength of character to pair the blood-splatter visuals of "Dexter" to a homicidal song about her ex-husband and somehow make it a gleeful collective catharsis.[55]

As if anticipating the criticism the segment was sure to provoke, "Papa Don't Preach" followed. Man-beasts appeared onstage to chain her up and toss her around. As they did, she sang a medley: "Hung Up," "Girl Gone Wild," and "Sorry." It was during that part of the show that Madonna walked a slackline. "Every time I do shows, I learn a new skill," she said, adding, "The slackline...was a nightmare."[56] Michel Laprise said that during the first few weeks of rehearsals, Madonna "hurt her ankle and broke her little finger. I asked to slow down [the] pace. She said, 'No Michel. That's the job.'"[57]

Madonna's medley, sung while she was trussed up (a metaphor for marriage), was about a living hell. Her next song was about what came after: divorce. She was joined by a vocal and percussion trio from France's Basque Country who called themselves Kalakan. She had met them the previous summer while visiting friends to celebrate her birthday. As a treat, Kalakan had performed Ravel's *Bolero* for her, and she asked them to join her on tour.[58]

Playing electric guitar with backup from the Basque musicians,

Madonna sang "I Don't Give A." It was a good song on her album, but it was infinitely better live. She didn't sing the verses as much as spit them. She wasn't a survivor of a bad relationship; she was triumphant in having—as the song implies—shed a man who dragged her down. Nicki Minaj appeared by video. Seated on a throne while delivering her own rap, she commiserated with Madonna about writing checks for an unworthy man.[59]

The first section of the show closed with a stunning image of Madonna rising on a platform in front of an illuminated cross. Lying on the floor like a human sacrifice, she raised her fist. She was bruised but still breathing.[60]

While Madonna left the stage for a costume change, dancers performed a new type of dance—bone breaking, or flexing—which involved twisting the body's joints to the point of contortion. Having originated in the reggae scene in Jamaica, it moved to clubs in Brooklyn before making its way to Madonna's stage. It was not yet a craze but soon would be. To the strains of "Heartbeat" and "Best Friend," MDNA dancers formed pretzels of their bodies before merging, bound by twisted limbs, to create a living sculpture. Images from a cemetery appeared on-screen behind them. The marriage that had required Madonna to become a contortionist had ended. That part of the show had, too.[61]

The second section, prophecy, looked to the future. It began with a brief history lesson: Madonna dressed as a 1940s baton-twirling majorette singing "Express Yourself" with a cohort of female dancers similarly attired. Behind them flashed period animation that charted the course of women from 1920s flappers to 1940s Rosie the Riveters (fist now flipping a finger) to 1970s college graduates.[62]

Madonna, meanwhile, offered a mini lesson in pop music by cheekily inserting Lady Gaga's hit song "Born This Way" into "Express Yourself." Gaga's melody was so close to Madonna's classic that it took a few seconds to realize that Madonna had switched songs. Point made, she transitioned to "She's Not Me."[63]

People who had been hankering for a throwdown between Madonna and Lady Gaga saw that medley as the opening salvo. Liz Rosenberg said, "Whether it's an homage or a smack in the face or just being funny, I don't know...People can decide what it means. Madonna isn't one to explain herself." Most likely, she was just playing around. During a tour stop in Atlantic City, she would tell the crowd that she loved Gaga.[64]

Having dispatched with the "competition," Madonna and her cheerleaders sang "Give Me All Your Luvin'." She had earned it. As classic video clips flashed on-screen, the sound of a vintage radio teased listeners by playing a second or two each of some of Madonna's biggest hits:

"Holiday," "Into the Groove," "Like a Virgin," and "Music," among others. Madonna reappeared to sing "Turn Up the Radio."[65]

Joined again by Kalakan, she performed "Open Your Heart" as a French street scene. Eleven-year-old Rocco appeared with her for that number, doing a backflip and some B-boy moves as the cast danced. It is not an overtly rebellious song, but it became one when paired with the Basque song "Sagarra jo!" (smash the apple). Wearing black berets, Madonna and her dancers became outlaws whose crime might only be that they were part of a minority.[66]

At that juncture in the concert, Madonna gave herself time to greet the audience and inject a political or social message, which would change according to the venue. Her point, however, remained the same. It was about the sanctity of the individual and the right to be who you are without censure, to say what you feel without fear. Each person is a masterpiece—and "Masterpiece" was Madonna's next song. It was written for *W.E.* and earned her a Golden Globe but was otherwise lost in the deluge of criticism for her movie. Performed in concert, it created a poignant moment.[67]

The video interlude between that section and the next, masculine/feminine, saw a return of the thugs who plagued her during "Girl Gone Wild." They performed a dance-mime to a video of Madonna (as Lana Turner) singing a William Orbit remix of "Justify My Love." Madonna returned to the stage to sing "Vogue."[68]

Through the years, that song in performance had strayed far from the mood of its glamour-soaked black-and-white video. During MDNA, the original sensibility returned. Madonna and company posed onstage in what could only be described as a Gaultier retrospective.[69] Madonna remained in the land of hot and sexy in the next song.

On her *Hard Candy* album, "Candy Shop" was one of the least memorable songs. In concert, spiced up with a few lines from "Erotica," it was riveting. Madonna performed a sensual pas de deux with her dancer boyfriend, Brahim Zaibat, in what was meant to be a Parisian brothel. Displaying for the world—or at least the audience—the sexual chemistry between an older woman and her much younger man, she answered critics who shuddered at the thought of such a coupling. Madonna showed that it was natural, beautiful, and very real.[70]

It made sense that the next song on her set list was her most famous non-apology, "Human Nature," which she performed as a striptease while on the video screen behind her a man in a suit drilled a peephole into a wall to better see her. Madonna said a man once asked her, " 'Why do you have to show your ass on stage?' And I said to him, 'Why does anyone have to show their ass on stage? So that you pay attention.' " Having gotten the audience's attention by stripping, she at that point revealed political statements written on her back.[71]

That moment was followed by "Like a Virgin," which Madonna sang, partly astride a piano played by Ric'key Pageot, to the tune of Abel Korzeniowski's *W.E.* composition, "Evgeni's Waltz." It became a woman's languid tale of finding love when experience told her that that was no longer possible. The song's transformation was remarkable. It would be one of the highlights of the concert.[72]

"Love Spent," Madonna's song about a lover who valued her for her money, came next during her US tour. As she sang, dancer Marvin Gofin laced her into a corset. Too tired to fight, she stood limp and allowed him to take control. But resistance hadn't been entirely squeezed out of her. She described the final section of her show as "a strange marriage between martial arts and Joan of Arc." She would come back fighting and righteous.[73]

The video interlude between sections prepared the audience. To a remix of "Nobody Knows Me," three slackliners dressed in prison orange performed until five dancer "guards" beat them into submission. Meanwhile, on-screen behind them, a video of faces superimposed over Madonna's appeared: she was the pope, then former North Korean leader Kim Jong-il, then French politician Marine Le Pen, then Democratic Republic of the Congo dictator Mobutu Sese Seko.[74]

On either side of those faces were images of the chaos caused by ill-intentioned leaders along with images of the victims of their misguided rule. Most poignant among them was a reference to Trayvon Martin, an innocent Black youth shot dead in Florida that year, and the faces of seven gay children and teenagers who killed themselves after being bullied. With the permission of their parents, Madonna showed their pictures, gave their names, and listed the dates of their births and tragic deaths. All those children, including Trayvon, died because of who they were, not what they did.[75]

The "Nobody Knows Me" interlude ended with a message of hope. By the end of the song, the imprisoned dancers and their guards made peace. All stood on slacklines in front of an awe-inspiring photo of Earth from space. They were suspended with a choice to make—get back down in the mire or reach for the stars. A magnificent image, it introduced the final segment of the concert: redemption.[76]

Madonna appeared in medieval-style battle dress to sing "I'm Addicted" and "I'm a Sinner." During the latter, she and her dancers stood atop raised cubes in front of a video of a railroad track in India, creating the illusion that they were riding the tops of the trains. The dancers threw themselves and one another between the cubes in a truly death-defying performance. In recognition of Hindu tradition, in front of a video, they then ritually washed themselves in what was presumably the Ganges. They ended the performance as holy men and women.[77]

All Madonna's concerts built to a grand finale. In MDNA, "Celebration" was it. Having retired her medieval gear, she appeared on a raised cube in black pants and sneakers, inviting the audience to "join the party." It was a riotous ending. Rocco formed part of the troupe, dancing directly in front of his mother. "He's disconcertingly comfortable onstage," she said. "I was thrilled to see him every night. He gave me a little boost of energy."[78]

There was almost no respite for Madonna during the show, which clocked in at just under two hours. Her energy and passion were on full display. She *loved* performing. It is nearly impossible to imagine that anything offstage could give her such a rush or as much pleasure.

The MDNA project manager, James Erwin, said that so many people put so much into the show and turned so many impossible ideas into reality that the result was nothing short of a miracle. When it came time for an audience to see it, it wasn't applause that made him realize they had succeeded; it was the rare moment of silence. That meant the audience was in awe of what Madonna and her team had done.[79]

Chapter 54

Tel Aviv, Istanbul, Paris, Moscow, St. Petersburg, Denver, Medellín, 2012

You think we're a civilization that's moving forward...I'm sorry, my friend, we are not.[1]

— *Madonna*

MADONNA'S MDNA TOUR opened on May 31 in Tel Aviv. Before she left the States, her team wondered if she should cancel because there were fears that Israel planned to bomb Iran's nuclear facilities, which could lead to regional war. Madonna refused. "I said we're going, we're going...The threat of war's not keeping me out of a country. Actually, it's an invitation." Madonna had fans and friends in Israel and Iran, and she thought of them all as victims of their governments' disputes.[2]

Upon arriving in Israel, she began with an obligatory peace gesture, meeting with Israeli and Palestinian activists. It made news, but it wasn't considered particularly noteworthy. And when, during her show, she told the crowd that she opened her tour in Israel to promote peace, her words were met with a shrug. "They all give that speech when they come to Israel," said an Israeli blogger.[3]

That might have been the end of the conversation except for the replica assault rifles onstage. Madonna delivered her peace lessons while holding a gun. (A *Jerusalem Post* reporter labeled her "Jihad Madonna.") Her dichotomous message of peace and war, of nonviolence and violence, of the world that might be and the world as it was, got the audience's and the press's attention. Love her or hate her, respect her or dismiss her, Tel Aviv couldn't stop talking about her.[4]

Madonna's first-ever performance in an Islamic country occurred in Abu Dhabi three days later and created more rumbles. She was more than an hour and a half late arriving onstage, which left her forty-five thousand fans baking in nearly one-hundred-degree heat. She felt the heat, too, shouting from the stage at one point, "It's too damn hot but we're going to have fun anyway."[5]

Many people in the crowd were part of Abu Dhabi's large expat community and would not have been shocked by Madonna's language, her dancers' attire, and the sexuality expressed onstage. Others, however, were scandalized by her perceived cultural insensitivity and delighted by her boldness in equal measure.[6] Said one female blogger,

> The Material Girl couldn't care less about the fact that she was performing in the Middle East. Her performance contained sexual gestures, hints at religious aspects, and even a scene that looked somewhat like a striptease! I think she definitely deserved applause for her courage, it is the Middle East after all you know, you're penalized for almost anything![7]

With each tour stop, it seemed that Madonna's provocations became more focused. In Istanbul, she tested the Turkish government's support of women's independence. That May, Turkey became the first signatory of the Istanbul Convention, a treaty aimed at preventing violence against women and prosecuting those who engaged in it. The Turkish prime minister, Recep Tayyip Erdoğan, appeared to be a new kind of modern Muslim leader, devout but perhaps tolerant and prepared to be inclusive. Madonna decided to see for herself.[8]

During all her concerts, while singing "Human Nature," she partially stripped as she strolled down the catwalk into the audience. In Istanbul she went further, casually exposing a breast as if that were the most natural thing in the world for a woman to do. The crowd's astonishment was followed by a roar of approval. Turning away from the audience, she showed a message written on her back: NO FEAR. It was directed at Turkish women, whose clothing and actions had long been dictated by their government.[9]

Madonna's several seconds of nipple exposure made headlines around the world, but not in Turkey, where it would not have been discussed openly. Word spread anyway. Emrah Güler, writing a review of the concert for Turkey's largest-circulation newspaper, *Hürriyet,* called MDNA "the best show anyone could hope to see."[10]

From Turkey, Madonna returned to familiar territory in western Europe. In most of those places, her concerts began with fans furious over the delayed start of her show. With each tour, she took greater liberties with time. She refused to appear onstage until she was ready, because once there, she had to be at her physical and mental best. She wanted the show "to be perfect," she said. "My fans deserve it, and quite frankly I deserve it."[11] The DJs enlisted to pacify the crowds often did so to boos.

Hometown boy Martin Solveig was the opener outside Paris when Madonna appeared on Bastille Day to a sold-out show of sixty-two thousand people at the Stade de France. The French were among Madonna's most enthusiastic fans, so the anticipation for the concert would have been great in any case. But her arrival in France had set up a showdown with Marine Le Pen, the leader of the country's largest and most powerful far-right party. The audience eagerly awaited Madonna's next move.

Le Pen had been trying to mainstream the National Front, founded by her father, by publicly rejecting his extreme anti-Semitic and racist views. Her effort had succeeded. In that year's presidential race, she came in third. Critics accused her of merely softening the party's facade but not changing its fascist core. It was a charge she denied. Madonna was among those who didn't believe her. In her "Nobody Knows Me" concert video, she flashed an image of Le Pen with a swastika on her forehead. In post–World War II France, that was a sign that a woman had collaborated with the Nazis.

Le Pen heard about the image and threatened to sue if Madonna didn't remove it by the time she arrived in France. Taking a dig at Madonna, she said, "We understand how old singers who need to get people talking about them go to such extremes."[12] Madonna didn't flinch. The "Nobody Knows Me" video she showed at the Stade de France included Le Pen and the swastika. The next day, a National Front spokesman said Le Pen planned to sue Madonna for the French equivalent of defamation.[13]

The French antiracism group SOS Racisme supported Madonna's effort to identify politicians who spread hatred, especially in France, where anti-Semitic and anti-immigrant attacks were up significantly that year. During the hard-fought presidential race, even some centrist politicians had felt the need to pander to the xenophobic right.[14]

Madonna left that controversy brewing in France and traveled north to the UK and Ireland. Guy Ritchie was in the audience to see Rocco perform in her London show. The previous September, Ritchie had a son by the new woman in his life, a thirty-year-old model named Jacqui Ainsley, who was described in the British press as "a younger, firmer, sexier, less gobby and way more obedient version of his ex-wife."[15] Madonna sent a "huge bouquet" and congratulations to the new parents.[16]

Madonna had never performed in Scotland, so fans were frenzied ahead of her appearance in Edinburgh. Police had asked her in advance to respect Scotland's firearms laws and not use replica weapons in her show. The UK's tough antigun laws were enacted after a mass shooting at a school in Dunblane, Scotland, in 1996, that killed sixteen five- and six-year-old children and their teacher. With that request still pending, the day before Madonna's concert and half a world away, a gunman opened fire at a movie theater in Aurora, Colorado, killing twelve people and wounding fifty-eight. Scottish police again advised Madonna not to use guns in her show. She refused to change her program.[17]

A member of her team said, "Madonna would rather cancel her show than censor her art. Her entire career, she has fought against people telling her what she can and cannot do. She's not about to start listening to them now." The British antigun lobbying group Mothers Against Guns denounced her. A Scottish member of Parliament called her decision "crass and insensitive." The local *Daily Record* newspaper, reporting on the controversy, neatly summed up Madonna's tour: "Controversial as always. Dull, never."[18]

While Madonna was in London, her tour promoter announced that a special performance would be added to her schedule. She would return to Paris on July 26 for a forty-five-minute show at the Olympia theater, where the likes of Edith Piaf and Billie Holiday had performed.

The Olympia guaranteed a far more intimate show than the other tour stops. Sixty thousand people saw Madonna perform at the Stade de France, for example, while the Olympia seated fewer than two thousand. Madonna used that smaller concert in that historic hall to address the Marine Le Pen controversy.

She talked about freedom of expression and France's history of supporting artists. She pointed out that France had opened its doors to Black artists fleeing racial repression in the States.[19] And then she said,

> We are entering very scary times in the world...People all over the world are suffering and people are afraid. And what happens when people are afraid?...They become intolerant. They start pointing the finger at other people...
>
> I know that I made a certain Marine Le Pen very angry with me. And it's not my intention to make enemies...It's my intention to promote tolerance.[20]

But, she warned, people who speak of making a country great by scapegoating others through repression or exclusion are frightening reminders of a past that shouldn't be repeated. "So the next time you want to point the finger at somebody and blame them for a problem in your life, take that finger and point it back at you. And fix it."[21]

The Olympia concert had been created quickly, which meant that some of its problems hadn't been resolved. Under the intense spotlights, the heat onstage was extreme. Madonna's dancers were coated in sweat. At one point she came back from a costume change, and within a minute, her shirt was soaked through. During "Candy Shop" and "Human Nature," dancers and Madonna alike wiped the sweat off their bodies.[22]

Despite the heat, despite the hall being filled well past its capacity, and despite having waited for as long as two days outside the theater for tickets, the crowd was with her. Arms from the audience were outstretched along the catwalk and waving in the air as she sang "Beautiful Killer," her tribute to French actor Alain Delon.[23] Madonna then surprised the audience by singing Serge Gainsbourg's "Je t'aime...moi non plus," which she performed in a "duet" with Marvin Gofin, who lip-synched Gainsbourg's part.

The song was about a relationship that was over and yet could not end because the attraction remained. In Madonna's reenactment of it, the problem was solved. She bound her lover to a chair and shot him in the mouth. The words JE T'AIME appeared on the screen with a heart. With that confusing climax still being digested by the audience, Madonna dropped her weapon and walked off the stage.[24]

The show had ended, but the audience didn't know it. Cheering, chanting, clapping, the crowd was on its feet waiting for the next set. When it became clear that the forty-nine-minute show was all there was, the mood turned to confusion, disappointment, and anger. Some people said concert organizers had not explained that the "special concert" would be shorter than Madonna's stadium shows. People began to boo. Plastic bottles were tossed at the stage. Chants of "*Rembourser!*" (refund) mingled with shouts of "*Salope!*" (slut).[25]

A core group of agitators made the most noise, and their protest didn't appear to be spontaneous. They came prepared with printed signs, which they held up—along with their middle fingers—as they initiated chants that were then picked up throughout the theater.[26] Madonna later said skinheads "sent there by Marine Le Pen...were 'Heil Hitlering'" at the back of the hall.[27]

The passions aroused in France seemed to inspire more attacks on Madonna as she traveled eastward in Europe, where the political divisions were even deeper. In Kyiv, Madonna learned from fans about Ukraine's effort to break ties with Russia and become integrated into the West. Ukrainian opposition leaders had been poisoned and imprisoned, elections rigged, rights curtailed, and corruption allowed to run rampant to keep the Ukrainian oligarchy in Moscow's pocket. Madonna posted a YouTube video urging Ukrainians to fight despite the consequences. "Are you brave? Do you have courage? Are you willing to fight for what's right?" she asked.[28]

At her next stop, Russia, she put herself to that very test.

The previous February in Moscow, five young women wearing minidresses, brightly colored tights, and perky-colored balaclavas ran onto the sanctuary in the Russian Orthodox Cathedral of Christ the Saviour, jerking their heads, kicking their legs, and playing air guitar while singing "A Punk Prayer," entreating the Virgin Mary to rid Russia of Vladimir Putin.

It lasted forty seconds. Security guards hustled them away as nuns in veils and parishioners, mostly old women with heads covered by babushkas, watched in alarm and confusion.[29]

The five were part of a group of eleven women who played punk music and staged zap actions in defense of women's rights and gay rights—in short, freedom. In a world driven by brands, the name they chose for themselves, Pussy Riot, was a doozy. They were angry third wave feminists with a funny bone. "Smile as an act of resistance," band member Nadya Tolokonnikova wrote. "Smile and say fuck you at the same time."[30]

Band members were charged with "premeditated hooliganism inspired by religious hatred." Three were jailed: Tolokonnikova, twenty-two; Maria "Masha" Alyokhina, twenty-three; and Yekaterina Samutsevich, twenty-nine. If convicted, they faced up to seven years in prison. Samutsevich was ultimately released, but Alyokhina and Tolokonnikova, who both had young children, were remanded to jail until trial. They immediately began a hunger strike, demanding they be freed to be with their children. The state said no.[31]

Trial for the three women began on July 20. Their court appearances provided more occasions for them to show their contempt for Putin's Russia. They laughed during what they implied were kangaroo court proceedings. "Some would say that we should just rearrange our private lives [and be good girls] and it'll be fine," wrote Tolokonnikova. "I say that's like making the bed in your cabin on the *Titanic* when the ship is already underwater."[32]

The world media generally didn't begin to pay attention to their case until August 2, when a group of British musicians led by Pete Townshend of the Who and Neil Tennant of the Pet Shop Boys wrote an open letter about it to the London *Times* while Putin was in the city on an official visit. Other entertainers picked up their cause, including Patti Smith, Yoko Ono, and the Red Hot Chili Peppers.[33]

After her arrival in Moscow, Madonna said, she tried to decide how to respond—whether to go to court to bring attention to the trial.

> These three girls were put in this cage and put on this monkey trial for singing thirty seconds of a song that basically said that Putin was oppressing artists and women and a hypocrite and aligning himself with the church when he wasn't a man of God himself...I was thinking, "How can I be of service, what can I do?"[34]

Though the US embassy warned of threats of violence at her August 7 concert, Madonna decided to use the occasion to make a statement on behalf of Alyokhina, Samutsevich, and Tolokonnikova.[35] Interrupting her show, she said, "So I just want to say a few words about Pussy Riot." The crowd erupted in wild applause and cheers.

> Now, I know there are many sides to every story, and I mean no disrespect to the church or the government, but I think that these three girls—Masha, Katya, Nadya [wild cheers]...have done something courageous. I think that they have paid the price for this act, and I pray for their freedom [cheers, applause]...I know everyone in this auditorium, if you're here as my fan, feels they have the right to be free. [Shouts, cheers][36]

Later, during "Human Nature," Madonna stripped down to show the words PUSSY RIOT written across her back, just as NO FEAR had been in the Middle East. The crowd roared again while she stood still for a full minute so they could take it in and, more important, capture it on their phones to ensure that it would spread throughout social media in Russia and far beyond. Then, putting on a black balaclava in solidarity with the group, PUSSY RIOT still visible, Madonna sang her slow, angst-ridden version of "Like a Virgin."[37]

After her performance, the Western media became obsessed with Pussy Riot. It wasn't that government repression in Russia was news, but now the people protesting it were attractive young women with a naughty name. Commentators could not resist saying it. Their smirks told that story. The Russian government, however, wasn't amused. In a tweet, then deputy prime minister Dmitry Rogozin called Madonna a slut or a whore—depending upon the translation—who was in no position to lecture Russia about morality.[38]

Two nights later, Madonna was due in St. Petersburg, where she planned to make a statement about gay rights. A Russian Orthodox priest urged his followers to call in bomb threats while she was performing. She also received death threats and was told by St. Petersburg police that anyone (presumably including Madonna and her cast members) carrying or wearing Pride flags or colors or displaying gay-rights slogans would be arrested.[39]

The city had passed a law that year that banned the promotion of "non-traditional" sexual relations. The so-called propaganda law was part of broader efforts to crack down on liberal Western ideas, including gay rights, that had gained popularity after the collapse of the Soviet Union. Similar laws had been passed in other Russian cities, and the Duma was considering making the muzzling of gay expression the law of the land.[40]

Like Pussy Riot's free speech, the gay-rights issue was tailor-made for Madonna. She had been fighting for those causes since the start of her career. In the United States, it was still possible in twenty-nine states to fire or refuse to hire people because of their sexual orientation, and eight states banned the "promotion of homosexuality in school," which meant that it couldn't be discussed in sex-education classes. It was no surprise that gay teenagers were the targets of bullying and that 30 percent of all adolescent suicides were committed by LGBTQ children.[41]

With Rocco at her side onstage in St. Petersburg, Madonna and the MDNA cast members raised clenched fists as she defended gay rights and called Russia's antigay legislation absurd. "It's a very strange time in the world," Madonna told the audience.[42]

> I'm traveling around...and I'm feeling in the air, I feel that people are becoming more and more afraid of people who are different. People are becoming more and more intolerant...We can change this. We have the power. And we don't have to do it with violence. We just have to do it with love...If you're with me, I want to see your pink armbands. Raise your arms.[43]

Madonna was the first to raise hers, as did her cast and Rocco, who pointed to his armband for people who didn't understand English well enough to catch her drift.[44] Meanwhile, rainbow posters that had been distributed to audience members in defiance of the law appeared throughout the stadium, waved by concertgoers who were on their feet. On one side of the poster were the words NO FEAR. The audience was ecstatic. Many recorded that rebellious solidarity to spread the message on social media.[45]

Outside the concert, authorities stood ready. Madonna learned that eighty-seven people were arrested.[46] She was not arrested, but three Russian activist groups sued her for more than $10 million for allegedly "damaging morals" in violation of St. Petersburg's antigay law and inflicting "psychological stress and emotional shock" well beyond her concert venue.[47]

Six nights later, Madonna was in liberal Oslo. She should have been able to enjoy the show without fear of violence, but Norway was on high alert, awaiting the verdict in the trial of a right-wing extremist charged in the country's worst massacre since World War II. The previous summer, Anders Behring Breivik systematically murdered seventy-five people, most of them teenagers attending a youth camp for political leadership.[48]

Breivik was a celebrity among the far right. The 1,500-page manifesto he published on the day of his attacks had become another must-read in the literature fueling Western extremists. In it, he had included Madonna on a "hit list" because he said she "propagated and glorified race mixing."[49] Madonna's MDNA concert, which truly did glorify all races, would have horrified him and his followers. During "Like a Virgin," Madonna turned her bare back to the audience. Again, it said, NO FEAR.

Between Oslo and Madonna's next stop, in Zurich, she learned that the three Pussy Riot women were sentenced to two years in a penal colony for their forty-second-long protest. Madonna joined the list of celebrities, rights groups, and Western governments denouncing the sentence, but the effort seemed futile. After hearing the verdict, Nadya Tolokonnikova's husband, Pyotr Verzilov, said, "Whatever Putin wants, Putin gets."[50]

Madonna's final European date brought her back to France, where she was scheduled to perform on August 21 in Nice. The area around that city was a far-right stronghold. Madonna's advisers decided that it wasn't prudent to march into a National Front enclave and brand its leader a Nazi sympathizer. Posters for the concert had been defaced in the run-up to the show. In response, and for the first time since she discarded her Iraq War video, in 2003, Madonna publicly censored herself. She exchanged the image of Le Pen with a swastika on her forehead for a less incendiary one of Le Pen with question marks. Le Pen's supporters claimed victory. The suit against Madonna was not pursued.[51]

Madonna left Europe, shaken.

> I'm going from city to city saying, "Okay, this world is changing very rapidly, and maybe it's always been like this, but it's like time, space, and motion is speeding everything up."
>
> And so I was feeling not only that I was being oppressed or censored as an artist but also as a human being and also the rights of other human beings were very visibly . . . — whether you were gay or you were Muslim or whatever — and I couldn't not just pay attention to it.[52]

Before the tour's first US concert, in Philadelphia, Madonna wrote a statement in verse that the press called a "manifesto." Some of the negative reactions she had encountered on the road occurred because people didn't understand what she was trying to say in her show. She thought that if she could explain, her message might be understood as an effort "to make the world a better place."[53]

It was also, perhaps, a strategic move because the wounds caused by the massacre at the Aurora, Colorado, movie theater were still fresh. In fact, between that July 20 rampage and her August 28 concert in Philadelphia, there had been three more mass shootings in the United States. One of them involved a neo-Nazi who killed six people at a Sikh temple in

Wisconsin. Madonna's use of guns in her show was sure to be criticized in that environment.

In her statement, Madonna described her concert as a journey "from darkness to light / from anger to love / from chaos to order." She said the guns she used were wielded to illustrate that weapons did not bestow true power, that violence did not solve problems but created new ones, and that change could not be imposed on others but had to arise from within. Finally, she said, the point was not to hurt but to heal. And that required love.[54]

She felt a real sense of urgency. But during that first date, in Philadelphia, she came up against a new obstacle: complacency. In three months, the United States would elect a president—either Obama or his Republican challenger, Mitt Romney. Looking at her audience, she did not sense engagement about the vote or a recognition of the responsibility individuals have to exercise their right to it as citizens in a democracy.[55]

"So here was a new fight," she said later. The people she met abroad took their right to vote seriously, because "it is life and death. If you're getting thrown in jail for holding a guy's hand, then you're going to be paying attention to gay rights. If you're not allowed to vote for who you want to vote for, then you're gonna care about democracy."[56] Madonna didn't think Americans did, so she hammered the point home in concert after concert.

As she did so, a violent act in South Asia showed just how precious freedom was. On October 9, 2012, a fifteen-year-old in Pakistan was shot in the head and neck by the Pakistani Taliban because she openly advocated for girls' education. The cowardice of her shooters and the bravery of the teenager who stood up to them crystallized the global struggle for women's rights and the forces arrayed against them.

As Malala Yousafzai clung to life in the hospital, activists, government leaders, and celebrities—Madonna among them—recognized her and her cause.[57] During her Los Angeles concerts, Madonna's body writing read MALALA, and she spoke to the crowd about the attack. "Do you realize how sick this is?...Support education! Support women!"[58] The crowd cheered, but the press, almost without exception, criticized Madonna for being "tone deaf" to religious sensitivities in Pakistan by using a "striptease" to bring attention to Malala's case. In essence, she was accused of offending the Taliban.[59]

Press reports noted that Madonna's performance was used by the group to justify its attack on Malala because it "proved" that the child was a proponent of corrupt Western values. Among the problems with those stories was that attempts to slur Malala by associating her with the West began *before* Madonna's show. The Taliban had also listed Barack Obama, Angelina Jolie, and then Afghan president Hamid Karzai as enemies of Islam, but who would read a story about the Taliban criticizing Obama? And wasn't it delicious to suggest that Madonna's outspokenness had only made things worse? In defense of women's rights, *for God's sake, silence her!*[60] Madonna ignored the criticism and continued to talk about the attack. "The shooting of Malala was a... really, really big thing for me," she said.[61]

On the second night of her sold-out Staples Center show, in LA, Sean Penn was in the front row. As Madonna took incoming attacks for her political statements, Sean was there to commiserate with her. They were still the "Poison Penns," no longer because the press found them bratty but because both used their celebrity to further causes greater than themselves. They were portrayed as naive dilettantes, self-promoters, aid tourists. And yet their commitment was beyond question.

Sean had been to Iraq, Iran, Cuba, and Venezuela as a citizen journalist writing about war, poverty, and the possibility of dialogue across cultures. In 2005, he was in New Orleans after Hurricane Katrina, driving a boat through flooded streets, rescuing people. More recently, after the January 2010 earthquake in Haiti that killed three hundred thousand, he lived in a camp established to house fifty thousand displaced people.[62]

Madonna's fans fantasized about a Penn-Ciccone reunion. One MDNA concertgoer in LA told *Us Weekly,* "Madonna seemed to be performing entirely for Sean. And he was saying things like 'Amazing!' and 'She's so hot!'"[63] His fourteen-year marriage to Robin Wright had ended in 2010, but there was no plan to rekindle the Madonna-Sean relationship. They were close friends who publicly expressed their love for each other and supported and consulted each other in times of need and at life-changing moments.[64]

In Gus Van Sant's 2008 movie *Milk,* about San Francisco's slain gay political leader Harvey Milk, the script called for Penn to kiss actor James Franco. Franco said that immediately afterward, "Sean texted Madonna and said, 'I just popped my cherry kissing a guy. I thought of you. I don't know why.'" She wrote back with one word: "Congratulations." (Penn won his second Best Actor Oscar for the role.)[65] In January of 2010, they met for a three-hour dinner. He was on his way into the unknown in Haiti, and she was about to begin working on *W.E.* "I talked to Sean about making the film," she said. "He's always been supportive of me."[66] It was support she needed during that most controversial tour.

Madonna left LA on October 12 for two nights in Las Vegas, then went on to Phoenix, where after stripping, she revealed the name AMANDA on her back. That was a reference to a fifteen-year-old gay Canadian who had killed herself after being bullied.[67] Madonna's next stop was Denver, where the controversy over her use of fake guns began long before her arrival. Appeals had been made for her to drop them during her Colorado performance, not just because of Aurora but also out of respect for the families and victims of the 1999 massacre at nearby Columbine High School. Again, she refused.[68]

The Denver audience at the sold-out concert knew what was coming, and still many people were stunned by what they saw. "We all just stood there," said one concertgoer. "Everybody who was around me all had shock on their face." A local sports-radio announcer said he saw people gather their things and leave.[69] But others appreciated Madonna for doing what she always did, confronting difficult subjects head-on. "We can't let a psycho's actions determine how entertainers are allowed to perform," one attendee told the *Denver Post*.[70]

The mood lifted in Pittsburgh. It was election night, November 6. When it seemed likely that Obama would win reelection, Madonna giddily told the crowd that she was so happy that she might not remember the rest of her show. By the last number, "Celebration," she knew for sure. Singing "Madonna-Obama," she jumped around the stage.[71]

Madonna's next stop was South America. She opened that leg of her tour in Medellín, Colombia. Prior to her appearance, no major international artist had ever performed there.[72] The city had long been known as the heart of Colombia's drug trade, the front line of a decades-old rebel insurgency, and the murder and kidnapping capital of the world. One journalist called it the "most dangerous city on earth."[73]

In 2012, the FARC rebels were negotiating with the government and had forsworn kidnappings (though not violence), and the major drug traffickers had either been killed or extradited to the United States to stand trial. Medellín was on the mend. Mayor Aníbal Gaviria said that with her show, Madonna and Medellín would make history. Interest was so great that a second performance was added. One hundred and eighty thousand people bought tickets to Madonna's concerts.[74]

The event was a success. Others followed. The next year, Beyoncé performed in Medellín, and it would be named "the most innovative city in the world."[75]

Near the end of Madonna's tour, in December, she had two performances scheduled in Buenos Aires, with a rare day off between concerts. Steven Klein and a camera crew were with her to do an ad campaign for the lingerie and shoe line she had been working on. At the last minute, Madonna said, the ad was canceled because the US company distributing her designs thought they were too "edgy." "I was outraged...I had all this fire inside of me about everything that I had witnessed, so I said, 'We're shooting something anyway.'"[76]

Madonna and Klein decided to make a short film using some of her tour dancers, the lingerie she designed, and a set that she described as a series of interrogation rooms. The film would be about the stifling of artistic expression, whether on religious, political, or commercial grounds.[77]

The project was inspired by one of Madonna's favorite movies: Italian director Liliana Cavani's 1974 classic *The Night Porter.* It is about a former Nazi guard and a concentration camp survivor who meet by chance thirteen years after the war and together reenact that time, from which neither can escape. It was telling that at that moment, Madonna chose to reference a movie by a woman about the ambiguities of love and the clarity of hate.[78]

Madonna's film became *secretprojectrevolution.* It would be more than a statement on artistic freedom. It was an artist's statement on creating in a world spinning out of control.[79]

On the very day Madonna and her team were filming in Buenos Aires, a tragedy was unfolding in the States that would make the turmoil she had seen during her tour seem trivial. A twenty-year-old killed his mother and then drove to the Sandy Hook Elementary School, in Newtown, Connecticut, where he shot and killed six adults and twenty children, ages six and seven, before killing himself. Even gun-rights proponents were stunned, at least temporarily, by the depravity of that killing. The cliché "epidemic of gun violence" had twenty small, innocent faces. Surely something would change.

Madonna's tour had been about a journey from darkness to light, but as it ended—on December 22, in Argentina—that light wasn't simply dim: it was nearly extinguished, especially after Malala and Newtown. Madonna had had intimations of the change along the way. "The dial got turned up everywhere," she said. "The stakes were higher... There were more passes and tags and checkpoints."[80]

> Sometimes I just felt I didn't have the strength to go on and sing and dance and pretend like crazy shit wasn't happening in the world, but I thought, You know what?... The world needs to be inspired, and so when there's shitty things happening in the world, it's my job, it's all of our jobs, to raise people up.[81]

When asked by a fan at a news conference what she planned to do after her tour, Madonna said, "Start a revolution of love, baby!"[82]

Chapter 55

New York, Menton, Los Angeles, 2013–2014

It is the artist's job to not only reflect the world that he or she
lives in, but...to shape the world that he or she lives in.[1]

— *Madonna*

MADONNA'S MDNA TOUR was the highest-grossing tour of the year,
bringing in more than $300 million.[2] In her first two outings for Live
Nation, she proved that the people who questioned the company's ten-year
investment in a fiftysomething woman were wrong. She also muted critics
who suggested that "Grandma" should pack it in because she was no longer relevant. But proving herself, performing at her best over such a long
period, had taken a toll. Madonna said MDNA was the hardest tour she'd
ever undertaken.[3]

When Madonna finally did go home, she collapsed. During two weeks
of recovery, she tried to make sense of the fear she had encountered during
her travels and the joy she had seen on the faces of her fans, despite the
social turmoil around them. Art had been her escape out of a life of pain
and longing when she was a child. She believed art could similarly help
people on a much larger scale. That had been one of its functions historically. Artists existed to help people find their way. Madonna had always
done that, with greater and lesser degrees of intention. In 2013, that mission became the stated purpose of her work.[4]

"I want to give these people a voice. I want to give *all* people who are
being persecuted and oppressed a voice," she explained. "I want to fight
for people's rights." Fully aware that she might sound simultaneously naive
and grandiose, she defended the statement because she meant it. When
asked by VICE's Eddy Moretti how far she was willing to go, she said, "As
far as I have to go. That's how far I'm willing to go." That battle, she said,
"and the education and livelihood of my children," were the most important things in her life.[5]

The first project Madonna embarked on with her new sense of purpose
was the film she shot in Buenos Aires with Steven Klein. In New York, she
and editor Danny Tull created a rough cut so she could see what they had

and put words to the images. She decided that the film wasn't finished. She and Klein went back to work.[6]

While she was creating her film, GLAAD (Gay and Lesbian Alliance Against Defamation) asked Madonna to present CNN journalist Anderson Cooper with its annual Vito Russo Award. Cooper had come out the previous year and was at that point the highest-profile gay journalist on television.[7] He was seen around the world, even in places where being gay amounted to a death sentence. That was why his pride in who he was and his candor in talking about it were paradigm-shifting.

No doubt Madonna would have presented Cooper with the award even if she had not just launched her revolution, but it seemed particularly appropriate to do so at that moment and to do so in memory of Vito Russo.

Twenty-five years earlier, that gay journalist, who had been diagnosed with AIDS, refused to accept the cloak of victimhood. Instead, during a speech in Albany, he made one of the most powerful statements of the early AIDS era.

> I wanted to speak out today as a person with AIDS who is not dying...If I'm dying from anything, I'm dying from homophobia. If I'm dying from anything, I'm dying from racism. If I'm dying from anything, it's from indifference and red tape...If I'm dying from anything, I'm dying from the sensationalism of newspapers and magazines and television shows, which are interested in me as a human-interest story—only as long as I'm willing to be a helpless victim, but not if I'm fighting for my life.[8]

His words shook the community and became a rallying cry for gay-rights activists, Cooper and Madonna among them.

The changed reality for people outside the heterosexual "norm" in the years since Russo had thrown down his gauntlet was breathtaking, especially given the conservative headwinds the community faced during many of them. A whole new language had developed to describe gender and sexual orientation.[9] Some teenagers in the 2010s believed they didn't have to define themselves by gender at all. They could be something truly remarkable: themselves.[10]

But while the vocabulary around being LGBTQ had changed, and some people felt more comfortable using it, acceptance was far from universal.[11] The National Coalition of Anti-Violence Programs, which tracked gender-related hate crimes, found that violent attacks on LGBTQ people were up in both severity and number in 2013 and that people of color and transgender women were the most frequent targets.[12] Those were the adults. As Madonna had discovered, LGBTQ children and teen-agers suffered physical assault and bullying that resulted in a range of con-sequences, from homelessness and exploitation on the street to suicide.

Madonna used her speech introducing Anderson Cooper to address that intolerance. She appeared in a Boy Scout uniform to highlight the fact that the largest boys' organization in the United States—one whose oath stressed kindness, charity, trust, and ethics—banned openly gay youths. The issue was increasingly divisive, and the Scouts planned to use their annual meeting in Texas that May to decide whether to end the prohibition.[13]

Madonna expressed her belief that it was unfamiliarity that bred con-tempt and distrust of "others" and that the internet had made the situation worse. After reciting a litany of abuses, from racism to sexism to homopho-bia, she said, "I don't know about you, but I can't take this shit anymore... It's 2013, people—we live in America. Land of the free, home of the brave? That's a question, not a statement." She also praised Cooper for "giving voice to the LGBTQ community" and called him "a badass mother-fucker...The world needs more people like you."[14]

The Boy Scouts lifted its ban on gay scouts during its meeting that spring. Maybe there was hope.[15]

Madonna often said that if she hadn't been a performer, she would have been a teacher. She saw a lack of education globally as a contributing factor in social and political turmoil. "Until you learn to read and write, you cannot think for yourself," she said.[16] The focus of her philanthropic work was, therefore, education, and it began in Malawi. In April, she traveled there with her children to check on the progress of the schools she had helped refurbish, expand, or build, which provided classrooms for four thousand children.[17]

By 2013, she had donated more money to Malawi than any other single benefactor and had been back to the country many times to oversee her work, meet with officials, and allow her Malawian children to visit their birth country and their biological families. After her adoption sagas, her trips caused little commotion and drew scant press attention. That spring, however, a statement released by the office of Malawi's new president, Joyce Banda, put Madonna once again in the middle of a controversy in which she was cast as a villain.[18]

Banda became president the year before, after the death of her predeces-sor, Bingu wa Mutharika. As a former educator, women's rights activist, and only the second elected female head of state in Africa, Banda should have had a productive relationship with Madonna. But complications arose almost immediately.[19] The president said shortly after taking office, "I have a problem" with Madonna's adoption of David and Mercy, her decision not to build a girls' academy, "and then coming back to build community schools."[20]

After Madonna's April 2013 visit, Banda's office issued an extraordinary statement accusing Madonna of lying about her work in Malawi and of demanding VIP treatment while there. The statement described Madonna as "a musician who desperately thinks she must generate recognition by bullying state officials instead of playing decent music on the stage." In response, Madonna said she was surprised and saddened by the "lies about what we've accomplished, my intentions, how I personally conducted myself while visiting Malawi and other untruths."[21]

In the background of that exchange was the fact that Banda's sister, Anjimile Mtila-Oponyo, had been the director of Madonna's Raising Malawi Academy for Girls but was dismissed during the shake-up over the use of funds. She was not implicated in any wrongdoing, but her name was associated with the controversy, and she reportedly sued Raising Malawi. Oponyo also worked in Malawi's education ministry, overseeing primary-school education. That position theoretically put her in control of, if not in opposition to, Madonna's projects.[22]

The controversy took yet another turn on the day after the damning statement from Banda's office was released. The president was reportedly "incandescent with anger" over the statement because she knew nothing about it and had not approved it. She did not, however, apologize, because she said she still had questions about Madonna's charities.[23] Madonna continued her work in Malawi undeterred. She even expanded it well beyond the country's borders.

Through her private Ray of Light Foundation, under the directorship of her sister Melanie, Madonna had begun funding schools for girls in Pakistan and Afghanistan. To help pay for them, she sold the 1921 painting *Trois femmes à la table rouge,* by French artist Fernand Léger, for more than $7 million. Purchased in 1990, it had been one of the most important pieces in her collection. She said of its sale, "I want to trade something valuable for something invaluable."[24]

Madonna took that message to London in June, appearing at a concert called the Sound of Change Live, to benefit the global charity Chime for Change. Gucci, with Beyoncé and Salma Hayek, had established it that year to improve women's access to education and health care and to lobby for women's rights. The lineup for the concert was unlike that of most charity performance extravaganzas because it featured primarily women, with Beyoncé, Mary J. Blige, Rita Ora, and Jennifer Lopez headlining. Madonna didn't perform. Rather, like Gloria Steinem, who also appeared onstage, she preached the virtues of education.

"What happens when we educate girls?" Madonna asked the crowd of fifty thousand at Twickenham Stadium. "We empower them. They have jobs. They have opportunities. They know their rights. They have the ability to defend themselves, support their families, take care of their health." She said that while those rights were taken for granted in some parts of the world, in others women "get shot for writing blogs. They have acid thrown in their faces for wanting to go to school. They are assassinated for being schoolteachers."[25]

Madonna introduced a young Pakistani woman named Humaira Bachal, who received an education only because of her mother's sacrifices; she was beaten by Humaira's father for allowing the child to go to school. At the age of sixteen, Bachal began teaching in a three-room classroom in a run-down building on the outskirts of Karachi. Within eight years, she had taught two thousand students in those three rooms.[26]

"I think Humaira needs a bigger school, don't you?" Madonna asked the London audience. She challenged them to donate enough to build the first floor, and she would fund the rest of the building. She also said she would double donations to the Afghan Institute of Learning, an eighteen-year-old project run by Afghan women to promote the education and health of Afghan girls. The following year, Bachal's state-of-the-art Dream Model Street School opened.[27] Madonna's foundation would continue to support both organizations.

In 2013, *Forbes* ranked Madonna the highest-paid musician in the world. (Lady Gaga was a distant second.) Madonna also ranked number 5 on *Forbes*'s list of the one hundred most powerful celebrities. (Oprah Winfrey was first.)[28] But there were still some corners of the world where Madonna wasn't known. The Church of St. Patrick in Monkstown, a suburb south of Dublin, was one of them. When Madonna was there for a funeral, a nun asked if she was part of the family. "No," she said. "I'm Madonna." The nun smiled and said, "Grand, Donna, would you like to go and meet David's mam?"[29]

The David in question was David Collins. Madonna learned in July that the friend who had shared her life during some of her highest times in Miami and New York and her lowest moments in London had died three weeks after being diagnosed with skin cancer.[30] Like many of the most important people in Madonna's life, Collins lived within her orbit but somehow managed to escape the scrutiny of even the most persistent journalists. His name rarely appeared in stories about her, yet beginning in the late '90s, he was one of her closest and most trusted friends.

He was like Christopher Flynn—a cultured gay Irishman with a wicked sense of humor. He was like Martin Burgoyne and Herb Ritts in that everyone loved him. He was like her brother Christopher because he had great taste, was utterly loyal, and kept Madonna grounded. And he was like Madonna.

Growing up as a self-described "precocious child," he spent hours poring over photos of Hollywood's golden era and dreaming of a life away from County Dublin where he could truly be someone. He chose London as Madonna chose New York and design as she did performance.[31] And, like Madonna's, Collins's career took off in 1985. As bangers-and-mash Britain evolved into a sophisticated international culinary destination, he designed many of its most famous restaurants. One writer said he was the "set designer for 'Cool Britannia,'" that he "transformed the very 'look'" of London.[32]

Madonna met him in Miami in 1995, but it wasn't until she arrived in London to shoot *Evita* that they became close. And then, after she and Christopher fell out, Collins became her interior designer of choice, and she became his extra-special client. Collins kept a six-foot-by-eight-foot photo of her outside the boardroom of his Mayfair studio.[33]

When he died, a friend described Madonna as "beside herself with grief."[34] She rarely attended the funerals of people she loved. She had missed the services for Martin Burgoyne, Christopher Flynn, and even her beloved grandmother Elsie Fortin. She knew her presence would turn any memorial into a press circus. But she showed up for David Collins, arriving at church in time for the final hymns and following the funeral party to a nearby luncheon, where she spoke about her friend and how much she would miss him. "What am I going to do now?" she asked that gathering of mostly strangers.[35]

Madonna turned fifty-five that year and spent her birthday at a villa in Menton, in the South of France, with her children, Brahim Zaibat, and a garden full of revelers. The party's theme was the French Revolution. Madonna appeared in a Marie Antoinette wig, a black eye patch, a silver grill covering her teeth, and a purple bustier—*sans culottes,* as befitting a political radical. She and Steven Klein had been working on their film *secretprojectrevolution* for months and were ready to show it that night during her party.[36]

The seventeen-minute, black-and-white film incorporates voice-over dialogue, snippets of speeches from Madonna's concerts, and music by *W.E.* composer Abel Korzeniowski. It begins with an image of Madonna behind bars and a voice-over from her concert explaining that fear leads to intolerance, blame, and discrimination. Armed with a gun, she shows the next stage in that progression—violence—as she shoots her dancers one by one.[37]

The second scene shows Madonna in a dark trench coat, being dragged down a hallway by four policemen and left facedown on the floor of a jail cell. In a voice-over, she complains that people don't take her call to revolution seriously because she is a blond woman (a person whom society is conditioned not to fear) and because she is a performer (who should not have political opinions).[38]

She expresses her opinion anyway, describing the ways in which "corporate branding" and "what's trending" destroy beauty, talent, and creativity and her fear that democracy itself was dead. "It's time to wake up, before it's too late," Madonna says. "We live in a very scary time. Or should I say we don't really live at all."[39]

To the sound of "Evgeni's Waltz," Madonna describes her revolution as one of "thinking for yourself, of having your own opinion and not giving a damn what people say." It is a revolution without envy, because people are happy with who they are. As dancer Chaz Buzan describes that idyllic society through balletic movements in space, images of police are superimposed over him. His is still a dream.[40]

In the film's final scene, it becomes evident that the bars of the cell that incarcerated Madonna are in her mind and made from her own prejudices and fears. Freed of those, her cell door opens. The people she killed come back to life. "I want to start a revolution. Are you with me?" she asks. But she is under no illusion that it will be easy. The last scene shows Madonna on the floor of a freight elevator surrounded by police. The doors slam closed. A gunshot is heard. Her fate and the fate of her revolution are uncertain.[41]

Madonna's film is dark. One might have expected her to throw viewers a bone of hope in the last moments, but she doesn't. The goal was to shake people from their lethargy, not placate them. One can imagine the silence that greeted it in the garden in Menton where Madonna's party guests, dressed in eighteenth-century revolutionary costumes, were invited to sample her extreme real-world political statement along with their champagne.

From the garden to the world. Bypassing theaters, museums, and critics, Madonna took her movie directly to the street. Beginning on September 23, in an act of what can only be described as guerrilla cinema, she projected it on walls in thirteen cities: Chicago, Toronto, Paris, New York, Los Angeles, San Francisco, London, Berlin, Rome, Tel Aviv, Jericho, Rio de Janeiro, and Vigo, Spain.

Rental vans loaded with sound and projection equipment showed up in commercial districts, arts districts, poor neighborhoods, rich neighborhoods—any high-traffic area with good clean wall space. As they were for the underground raves and the Arab Spring protests, the times and locations were posted on social media with little advance warning. Some people arrived intentionally, but many others stumbled upon the events and were dumbstruck by the ideas rarely spoken in public and the strange images on the wall.

In Jericho, a Palestinian watching the film said it was the first movie of its kind ever to be shown there. In Rio, it was screened in the heart of the city's feared favelas. In Paris and Rome, people in cars, on motorbikes, and on foot stopped to watch. (Police near the Pompidou Centre and the Vatican shut down the film.) In mercantile Chicago, viewers sat on a curb as Madonna's call to revolution appeared projected on the side of a bank.[42]

Her words echoed through the dark: disturbing, ominous, and strangely beautiful. When Madonna asked, "Are you with me?" the answer on the streets was tears, applause, and sometimes shouts of *amar, amour, amore, Liebe*—love. One man, energized by what he saw in London, said, "I believe everybody has to take action now." Another asked, "What's next, a movement?"[43] Tens of thousands of people saw the film in person. Within three weeks, more than a million people had downloaded it for free on BitTorrent.[44]

As the film was being projected around the world, its official New York premiere occurred at the Gagosian Gallery in Chelsea. It, too, was (relatively) guerrilla. There were no chairs, just the concrete floor for the A-list crowd to sit on. Guests may have been further disconcerted by the presentation. Waiters appeared with drinks, but they were wearing gas masks. Madonna didn't want attendees to feel cozy. She wanted them uncomfortable and wondering why.

In a lengthy introduction before the screening, she announced a new project called Art for Freedom. Established in partnership with VICE Media, it gave a platform to writers, painters, photographers, and filmmakers who did not have representation or recognition. To submit their work, artists needed to write a statement describing their notion of freedom. Those selected would receive a $10,000 donation to the nonprofit organization of their choice.[45]

Madonna's film was *her* definition of freedom, or at least an expression of her concerns about it. She told the Gagosian gathering that in her travels she had discovered that people generally fell into two categories. They were either "not free and fighting for it, or free and taking it for granted, and both of those situations made me extremely agitated, and that's why I made this film." Citing persecuted artists Pussy Riot in Russia and Ai Weiwei in China, Madonna said she considered such repression a crime against God.[46]

She warned the hundred or so people seated before her that she and they were witnessing the start of the "collapse of civilization as we know it. I know that sounds dramatic, but it's happening . . . It's really happening."[47]

When the film ended, Madonna was dragged in shackles onto a portion of the gallery floor that had been designated as a stage. She then sang a cover of the late Elliott Smith's melancholy song "Between the Bars." As she knelt on the floor, a dancer wearing a black balaclava spun behind her. The dancer then knelt down, unlocked her handcuffs, and helped Madonna to her feet. As they stood side by side, he removed his face covering. It was Rocco. Her child had freed her.[48]

For the rest of the evening, Madonna mingled with the crowd. Sean Penn was there, and his presence garnered more media attention than Madonna's film or what she said about it. The paparazzi that plagued them in the '80s were replaced that evening by people with phones who captured Penn's arm around Madonna's shoulder and their warm exchange. That night or soon afterward, Sean asked Madonna if she'd like to visit him in Haiti. She said yes, and in November, she and Rocco flew to Port-au-Prince and traveled by car to Pétion-Ville, a sprawling community where Sean had become the unofficial mayor.[49]

Aside from time he spent in other countries shooting movies and lobbying for more earthquake relief, Sean had been in Haiti since January of 2010. When he arrived, there was less than nothing. Bodies lay where they fell in the street or, mostly, where they were buried under piles of rubble. The stench of death was so strong and the misery and despair so thick that there was no doubt he had arrived in hell. But hell didn't frighten him. Six months later, a UN organization named him camp manager in charge of tens of thousands of people.[50]

By 2013, when Madonna and Rocco arrived, he no longer lived in a tent. He and his J/P Haitian Relief Organization had moved what he estimated to be forty thousand of the original fifty thousand people from the tent city into a new camp. Homes were repaired, new ones were built, and two health clinics, a school, and a police substation were established. Sean's organization also supported a bakery.[51]

Working out of a former school, with a fleet of trucks, heavy equipment, and three hundred staff members, the actor-director turned mayor-marshal had become one of the largest employers in the area.[52] Sean said he hoped Madonna might find a cause in Haiti worth adopting.[53] As expected, she brought attention to the needs of the Haitian people through the press that trailed her and through her Instagram posts. She also pledged Ray of Light Foundation funds to help build a large, bright multistory school at Pétion-Ville.[54]

Madonna had devoted the months after her eye-opening MDNA tour to addressing some of the problems she encountered. But that was only the beginning. The more she looked, the more need she found. In May, she sold the apartment she had bought with Sean on Central Park West, and in October she sold the Beverly Hills house she had bought with Guy Ritchie. Each went for just under $20 million.[55]

Madonna was consolidating. She didn't need so much stuff. One of the biggest misconceptions about her, according to the people who know her best, is the Material Girl image. Possessing things had never been important to her. "I think she understood that there are so many people out there hurting that why would she do that and why would she try to glorify that when you know the disparity is killing us?" said Niki Haris. "She always *liked* the finer things, but I never remember her feeling that she needed to *have* them."[56] In the previous two years, those things had come to mean even less.

Madonna's activism continued in early February 2014, when she appeared onstage at the Barclays Center, in Brooklyn, to join Maria Alyokhina and Nadya Tolokonnikova, the two newly freed members of Pussy Riot, at an Amnesty International–sponsored concert. Tolokonnikova said they were released one month shy of their full two-year sentence because Vladimir Putin wanted high-profile inmates out of prison before the start of his "pet project"—the Winter Olympics in Sochi. Though they were free to walk the street, they were still under strict surveillance. They were also physically harassed and assaulted by police.[57] "It makes you realize that the conditions we endured in prison aren't actually that different from the conditions we're faced with now that we're free," Tolokonnikova told *The Guardian*.[58]

One thing they were able to do was travel, which was what brought them to New York.[59] The Amnesty International event, called Bringing Human Rights Home, was held on the eve of the Sochi Olympics. It was Madonna's job to introduce Alyokhina and Tolokonnikova. Wearing a black stocking cap and walking with a cane because of a dance injury, she mused aloud, "Isn't it strange that we have the phrase 'human rights' in our lexicon? Because it's not something we should have to fight for."[60]

She told the gathering that she had thought of herself as a freedom fighter since the early '80s, when she realized she had a voice people listened to.

> What I realized when I went to Russia...was how lucky I was and am to live in a country where I can speak my mind...I can criticize the government. I can speak out against religious fundamentalists...and I don't have to fear being thrown in jail. Not yet, anyway.[61]

She commended Nadya and Masha for their courage because they did not have those rights in Russia, yet they dared to speak. "It's time for the rest of the world to be as brave as Pussy Riot."[62] Having been introduced, the two young women took turns addressing the audience in Russian, which was then translated into English. Proudly and recklessly they expressed their disdain for a government that silenced and sometimes killed the voices of dissent. They also read ten statements from political prisoners who were about to be sentenced for protesting Putin and Russia's rigged elections. When they had finished, the women led the crowd in an anti-Putin chant: "Russia will be free. Russia will be free. Russia will be free."[63]

For the New York audience, Alyokhina and Tolokonnikova were a sight to behold and a thrill to hear. But some in the Pussy Riot collective in Russia criticized them for appearing at an event with Madonna.[64] Tolokonnikova dismissed the criticism. "I feel very positive about how Madonna helps us." Onstage in Brooklyn Tolokonnikova said that after their arrest, "we were so overjoyed when we heard that she had spoken out in our support." They knew that the key to political change was communication and that Madonna's voice resonated throughout the world.[65]

The young women were feted in the States and could have remained on the lecture circuit as the darlings of the Western left. Instead, they returned to Russia shortly afterward and participated in a Pussy Riot demonstration in Sochi to protest corruption in Olympic funding. The protesters were met with whips and beatings. Alyokhina and Tolokonnikova continued as voices of opposition anyway. "I suppose we have nothing more to lose," Nadya said.[66]

Madonna had a three-album deal with Interscope, but she had only produced one album. After all the turmoil she had seen on tour, and after a year of concentrating on her film, her family, and her activism, she was ready to go back into the studio. All the elements that had consumed her, especially her commitment to human rights and artistic freedom, would form part of the record she would make. "There was a time when art reflected what was happening in society," she said that spring. "Artists like Marvin Gaye, Stevie Wonder, Richard Pryor, or Jean-Luc Godard made political statements through their art."[67]

With her thirteenth studio album, *Rebel Heart,* Madonna would criticize the commodification of art, describe the perilous state of the world, and most of all express the anger she felt rising among women everywhere.

She began the album thinking about old-school songwriting. It was "part of my Armageddon thinking right now," she said. If Madonna found herself alone after the apocalypse, she said, she wanted to be able to play her music, just her voice and a piano or a guitar.[68] But to help her achieve that simplicity, she would employ teams of DJs, producers, writers, and engineers. That's how it was done.

The songwriting method born in Stockholm at Cheiron Studios in the early '90s, which involved pop hitmakers working in music labs to create infectious noise, had relocated to Los Angeles and by 2014 was the music-industry norm. A generation of artists had grown up knowing no other way to create a song except by committee during what were called "writing camps." Those weeklong sessions were organized by record companies just as an advertising agency might gather teams to create a new marketing campaign. One writers' group was pitted against another to see who came up with the best songs in the shortest time. Soulless in, soulless out, and utterly forgettable.[69]

Just as Jamie King and his disciples had come to dominate the music-tour business, the hot DJ-producers of pop, hip-hop, and EDM overwhelmed those genres. The stars' names and faces changed, but the producers listed in the credits didn't.

"Everything has become generic and homogenized," Madonna said. "If the majority of artists follow a formula, who's pushing the envelope?... Who's being revolutionary in their thinking?"[70] And yet, as she had with *Hard Candy* and as she did on her tours with Jamie King, she chose producers from that pool anyway. She believed her vision was strong enough to overpower theirs. In *Rebel Heart,* she succeeded. As Joe Levy wrote in *Billboard,* "*Rebel Heart* has fourteen producers working in seven different teams and still it sounds exactly like a Madonna album."[71]

The first producer in the pack was twenty-four-year-old Tim Bergling, known professionally as Avicii. Guy Oseary suggested that Madonna work with him. Avicii had begun mixing tracks in his Stockholm bedroom when he was a child. By the time he was twenty-two, he had written the chart-topping single "Levels" and had an international reputation as a DJ on the EDM circuit.[72]

Madonna had worked with him that spring in Miami at the Ultra Music Festival, where he remixed "Girl Gone Wild." During her MDNA tour, he was the opening DJ at her Los Angeles shows. Avicii was on the road continually, a manic existence that did not suit his introverted, ethereal temperament. He loved the music, but he thought of himself as more of a songwriter than a DJ. Madonna appealed to that side of him when she asked him to help her create her album.

Avicii would oversee two songwriting groups—one working on upbeat songs and one working on introspective pieces. Madonna traveled between them, adding her words and ideas.[73] Though he was known for EDM,

Avicii's first love was melody. He infused his music with folk, country, soul, and funk.[74] Those sounds were at the forefront in his work with Madonna. "Everything was very simple—vocals and piano, vocals and guitar," she said.[75]

> I wrote a lot of good songs with Avicii's writing team…I ended up writing a lot of personal and very soulful songs with them, [the people] I refer to as my Viking Harem—who are all really wonderful, intelligent, soulful people. And they made me feel really comfortable. I guess I felt like I was safe enough to write these kinds of songs, and that surprised me.[76]

They were well on their way, but as they worked, Avicii's health deteriorated. Madonna wasn't aware of the struggle going on in the mind and body of that sweet young man.

Avicii suffered from acute pancreatitis as a result of heavy drinking, exacerbated by prescription opioids. He successfully kicked the pills for a time in 2014, when he began working with Madonna, but in March he was rushed to the hospital with a burst appendix. Having had it and his gallbladder removed, he was given opioids for the pain, and that started a new downward spiral. He dropped out of that year's Ultra Music Festival and cut back on his workload, Madonna's album included.[77]

"So a lot of the songs that I wrote with him or his song writing team, I ended up having to go out and find other producers to work on them, to finish the songs with me," she said. "And then Diplo came along."[78] Born Thomas Wesley Pentz in Tupelo, Mississippi, thirty-five-year-old Diplo was a prince of the electrodance world. In 2012, *Billboard* called him one of the three "most powerful—and arguably, revolutionary—figures to hit pop culture in years."[79]

Diplo was a DJ, a producer, and a curator who discovered new music and put it on his Mad Decent label, where, he said, "you can find the weirdest things on the outskirts of the Internet." He was also an author, filmmaker, and photographer. He had a weekly Las Vegas residency, was scheduled for hundreds of dates each year at clubs, festivals, and parties, and worked with everyone, the big and the small.[80] But Madonna didn't want *that* Diplo. She wanted a new sound, one that went beyond anything he had done before.[81] "You can't stay relevant unless you're pushing yourself out onto the razor's edge of life on a regular basis," she said.[82]

It was Madonna's openness to traveling in a new direction—in fact her requirement that her collaborators do so—that excited Diplo. He said it usually took him a week to decide if there was enough chemistry between himself and an artist to make it work. With Madonna, he knew instantly.[83]

She's the queen of making music...I've always loved how she's a forward-thinking motherfucking beast. She was the first person to really bring in different sounds and co-opt things for her own sound, and I've always loved her for that.[84]

But more important for the immediate project, he sensed that "she was up for anything...We really pushed the envelope with some of the stuff we were doing."[85]

Unfortunately, Diplo's many commitments meant that he could not sit with Madonna, as William Orbit, Mirwais Ahmadzaï, and Stuart Price had. Madonna had to catch him on the fly and try to create with him in the moment.[86]

As Nicki Minaj once said, Madonna "schooled" her collaborators. What she taught Diplo and his team was focus. "I never leave the room," she said. "Sometimes I think that makes them mad. Like, 'Don't you have to go to the bathroom? Don't you have somewhere to go?'" The answer was always no. It was her name on the record, ultimately her work of art, and she would oversee every aspect of it.[80]

Madonna had written tracks with Avicii and his teams and with Diplo and his crew, but she had other songs that still needed producers. Avicii and Diplo were both EDM-based. She wanted to add some hip-hop to her mix, but she wasn't interested in working with a "conventional hip-hop producer." She discovered DJ Dahi, who had worked on a Kendrick Lamar record she liked. Dahi in turn brought in people he knew from the hip-hop world.[88]

Madonna said that "revolving door of creativity" made it difficult to keep the record on track and unified.[89]

> The whole writing process was like a train that kept running. I kept picking people up. Some people stayed on the train longer than others...We're living in an age when these DJ/producers are working with lots of artists...So I was going crazy thinking, *"Can't I just have you for a whole week? Why do I just get you for two days?"* There was a constant battle...That drove me bonkers.[90]

There was also a battle for the producers' attention when they were finally in the studio. Some brought what seemed like their "entire families or twenty of their closest friends," she said. "They need to be surrounded by a posse, they need to have craziness around them."[91]

One of the people who stayed on the train was Toby Gad. A Munich native, he grew up on US jazz played by his musician parents. After success in Europe writing music, he made the leap to New York in 2000, sending his studio equipment over in a shipping container and landing in the city ready for a challenge. It did not come. For half a year, he said, he lived on instant soup and a bagel a day and was so desperate that he posted signs on traffic lights that read, ARE YOU A SINGER? DO YOU WANT TO WORK WITH ME? His Sony contact in Europe sent him an email saying, "You will never make it in America and you're going to come home crying."[92]

But a music publisher in LA knew of Gad and gave him a break. "He set me up with Fergie, and we wrote 'Big Girls Don't Cry' together in 2001," Gad said. "That was probably the most important introduction of my career." The song wasn't released until 2007, but when it was, it went platinum six times. Doors opened. Beyoncé came in. She recorded his song "If I Were a Boy." In 2008, it went double platinum, and then everybody wanted to work with him.[93] He made the Madonna connection through an Interscope executive.[94]

Gad was someone Madonna felt comfortable with. She said he was "very open-hearted...extremely musical, not inhibited."[95] His work ethic was as all-consuming as hers. Madonna said that of all the artists she had worked with through the years, Gad "pushed" her the most as a songwriter.[96] During five weeks in the studio, they created thirteen songs, seven of which made it onto the album, including "Illuminati," "Joan of Arc," and "Living for Love."[97]

Kanye West was also back, roaming in and out of sessions as a writer, producer, and general "beautiful mess," according to Madonna. "He's a brilliant madman. He can't help himself...I don't always agree with the things he says or does—I don't always like his music, even." But she said she "loved him."[98]

Madonna compared the process of songwriting to "that exercise where you stand with your eyes closed and you let yourself fall back, and you just, like, trust that someone is going to catch you."[99] "It's almost like writing your diary in front of somebody and reading it aloud."[100] "Some people you immediately have a connection with and they get your sense of humor," Madonna said. "You click into their frequency. Other people are strangely uptight and you're thinking, 'OK I can't wait until this is over.'" But of Mozella, who would work with Madonna on eleven *Rebel Heart* tracks, she said, "She's a Michigan girl. I clicked with her immediately."[101]

Thirty-three-year-old Detroit-born Maureen McDonald was a Maverick artist in the early 2000s and had released a couple of soulful, breezy, lyrics-driven albums on the label just as Madonna was parting ways with it. In 2013, she wrote Miley Cyrus's biggest hit, "Wrecking Ball."[102] Its success should have produced a breakthrough for her and for women songwriters generally, but, Mozella said, even two years later, top-of-the-line male songwriter-producers still outnumbered female songwriter-producers ten to one.[103] When she began to work with Madonna, her expected two-day studio stint lasted a month. "I feel like being around a woman that strong made me feel stronger...It kind of changed my life."[104]

In addition to the legions of writers and producers on *Rebel Heart,* Madonna invited guest artists to join the party. Nicki Minaj returned to rap. Veteran rapper Nas (Nasir bin Olu Dara Jones) and rising rap star Chance the Rapper (Chancelor Johnathan Bennett) made contributions, as did Madonna's old friend Mike Tyson.

She had just seen his one-man show, *Undisputed Truth,* in which he talked about his life in a thoughtful, thought-provoking, humble, and genuinely funny way. Madonna said, "I wanted him to be in the song that I wrote, called 'Iconic,' because I do believe that he is iconic...He is one of those people that survived so much...been to hell and back...There's no one like him."[105]

When she called him in Las Vegas and invited him into the studio, he accepted.[106] Tyson said,

> Madonna calls and tells you to come somewhere, you go...I didn't know what the hell I was going there for...I didn't know if she wanted me to talk or rap. I just go in there and start talking. I'm talking about my life and things that I have endured...[107]

Those characters, and dozens more, would help Madonna create *Rebel Heart.* Munich, Stockholm, Chicago, Detroit, New York, Los Angeles, Tupelo, Las Vegas; women and men; Black and white; young and not so young—they all had a part in it. Crazy as the situation was, it worked. When the album finally made it to the critics, it would be heralded as Madonna's best in a decade.

Chapter 56

New York, Los Angeles, London, 2014–2015

She has broken the cardinal rule of female celebrity by refusing to be tragic.[1]

—Ellen Willis

VENTURING UPON A Madonna album, a listener can expect certain themes: love, loss, vulnerability, irony, anger, resilience. That listener can also expect to dance. And, eventually, sing. It's impossible not to. *Rebel Heart* contains all those elements, but its overall theme is survival—from surviving a failed relationship to surviving the apocalypse. In a way, it is an updated version of the music Madonna wrote during the 1980s AIDS crisis, when the present was utterly bleak and the future for many was nonexistent. At that time, Madonna sang to inspire. She is a romantic optimist, that is her appeal, and it comes through again in *Rebel Heart*. The world is a mess, all the more reason to celebrate joy and beauty when and where you find them.

Madonna described her "home base" as "pop music and the Catholic Church." They were her inspirations as a child and remained so. Also sex. But by *Rebel Heart,* her use of it in her work had become a naughty joke.[2] The other aspect of a Madonna album that hadn't changed was her commitment. "There's that level of pride in the music," Diplo said. "It's like, she's already sold billions of records and she's still treating this one as if it's her first."[3]

The album's first track and first single is an example of that. "Living for Love" went through ten iterations, according to Madonna. Twenty, according to Diplo. They agreed that they wanted to make a dance record and that it would be timeless.[4] The lyrics, she said, were about "having your heart broken and instead of being bitter about it, learning about it and rising above it. Recognizing that you deserve better."[5]

The song is worthy of comparison to "Like a Prayer," and not just because it includes a choir. "Living for Love" makes love and loss into a religious experience and expresses it as a hymn. It is more cynical than "Like a Prayer," but it isn't angry. It preaches acceptance of reality. It swells with the sounds of survival. The song is a testimonial to Madonna's ability to persevere. It might also be considered the anthem for her "revolution of love."

On all Madonna's albums, her collaborators' vision helped her find her musical direction. On *Rebel Heart,* it was Diplo's contribution that gave the album its path, Madonna said. Prior to that, she wasn't sure where she was headed. Then "he started adding these monster beats and punch-you-in-the-stomach bass sounds and 808s like you've never heard before, and that pushed me in a certain direction."[6]

The beat in "Unapologetic Bitch" isn't meant to make you move your feet: it is meant to shake your core like the drums of early Jamaican reggae or the original 808 drum machines of early-'80s hip-hop. With the song's lyrics, Madonna lands a sucker punch to the gut. She said it is about a "guy who fucked me over."[7] "You think you're going to ruin my life and you think that it's over for me, but guess what? It's not. Life goes on."[8]

Fans saw Madonna's breakup with Brahim Zaibat as the song's inspiration. The official reason for the split was heavy workloads, which kept them apart, but some accounts described Madonna as feeling "used" by Zaibat to further his career. The split was characterized as acrimonious.[9] She also said the song was inspired partly by the *Playboy-Penthouse* photo crisis, in the mid-1980s.[10] But mostly, she said, it arose out of the song's "crazy-ass bass line."[11] Like "Living for Love," "Unapologetic Bitch" is a survival song, but the woman in it has exchanged the church for a club.

The anger of "Unapologetic Bitch" dissipates in "Hold Tight." Written with Diplo, Mozella, and Toby Gad, among others, but produced by Madonna alone, it is both sweeping and embracing. It rushes past in orchestral grandeur and stops short—or holds tight—in drumbeats that sound like heartbeats. "Hold Tight" is a mother's song of devotion, describing love that is unconditional and protective. It is one of Madonna's most tender and compelling songs.

"Veni Vidi Vici" provides a musical retrospective of her career, the way the videos at her concerts sped through her old photographs. Madonna said it was the "right time" to think about her past in a song—the people she had known, loved, worked with, and lost, people like Basquiat and Michael Jackson and Tupac. "I survived and they didn't and it's bittersweet for me to think about that . . . It's kind of like survivor guilt."[12]

She wanted a guest artist to feature on it, and thought of Nas. In the business, he was considered one of the best rappers of all time.[13] "He just turned up one day all by himself," Madonna said, "no bodyguards, no assistants, nothing—and listened to the track before saying, 'Yes, I'm in. I'll do it.'" After that meeting, they became friends based on their shared musical background. "He also came up at a time when I felt like rap music was peaking," Madonna said, "back when the bulk of rappers were still talking about their real lives and reflecting on what was going on in society."[14]

Of all the songs on Madonna's album, "Veni Vidi Vici" is most often criticized because it is self-referential, tracing her path from the streets of New York to stardom, and because she (like male artists who aren't criticized) name-checks her most popular songs. She was also mocked for rapping, just as she was when she rapped on *American Life*. The commentary was ageist, sexist, and gratuitous, especially considering some of the moronic rap that was heralded by critics. "Veni Vidi Vici" isn't Madonna's best song on the album—as a song. But as a work of art, it is ingenious.

Using a deep rap voice for the street and a light, girlish voice to describe her aspirations, "Veni Vidi Vici" forms a collage of sounds and words. Nas, meanwhile, raps his own difficult life story into the middle of hers. The result is a portrait of two artists and their stories of survival, which are not so different at all.

Diplo and Madonna had written around seven or eight songs, and on their last night in the studio, they were goofing around, drinking a little rosé.[15] Diplo recalled Madonna saying, "'Yo, give me some of the craziest shit you've got right now' and we literally wrote a song that night."[16] It became "Bitch I'm Madonna" and includes a rap from her sister in sedition Nicki Minaj.[17]

If Madonna's album were divided between the "rebel" and the "heart," the songs she wrote with Diplo generally fall into the former category, while those she wrote with Avicii and his mostly European team belong in the latter category. One of them is the album's title track, "Rebel Heart." Should Madonna ever climb onto a roadhouse stage and begin strumming her guitar, "Rebel Heart" would be the song she would sing. It is her most convincingly country-western composition.

"Devil Pray" remains in guitar-music country. Madonna said it's about people trying to achieve a higher state of consciousness and taking a shortcut to do so. "I'm certainly not judging people who take drugs but ultimately, you're going to be lost."[18] Musically, "Devil Pray" is what Madonna had hoped to do with her album. If she wanted to, she could perform the song with only her voice and a guitar.[19]

"HeartBreakCity" switches out the guitar of "Devil Pray" for a piano and slows down the tempo. The song returns to the breakup story covered in "Unapologetic Bitch," but the anger is muted because the wounds are still fresh. The lyrics are sharp, crisp, and direct, as are Madonna's delivery and the musical interludes between the song's soaring choruses. That kind of simplicity isn't easy. The song required ten writers, the primary one being Iranian-Swedish songwriter-producer Ash Pournouri, and six producers.

Rebel Heart's second single, "Ghosttown," was written over three days with three Californians: Evan Bogart, Sean Douglas, and Jason Evigan.

She called the track they produced together a "post-apocalyptic love song."[20] "We all got in a room together. They start playing their chords and then we just start thinking," Madonna said. They were looking for a way to tell the story of Armageddon and the few people who would survive it. "Kind of dramatic," she admitted, "but not entirely impossible at this stage of the game."[21]

Madonna remained in the studio with Bogart, Douglas, and Evigan to write "Inside Out," which she produced with Houston hip-hop songwriter and producer Mike Dean. His roots in the genre were deep, and he worked frequently with Kanye West. After *Rebel Heart,* he would become a trusted member of Madonna's creative family.

Musically, "Inside Out" is one of the most accomplished tracks on the album. Madonna's voice becomes an instrument, traveling a range from pop to jazz to ska. The music stops listeners' breath in one moment and sends their hearts soaring in the next.

It follows two seriously silly songs about seduction. "Holy Water" is Madonna's requisite mixture of religious imagery and sexuality. "Whenever I write about sex, I always do it tongue-in-cheek," she said. "'Holy Water' is obviously meant to be funny."[22] So is "Body Shop." "I liked the idea: a car—the body of a car—it's a kind of sexual metaphor...lots of innuendos, lots of fun."[23]

"S.E.X." is a more serious commentary on what Madonna called the "lack of intimacy" in the hookup scene.[24] Its description of a sexual encounter sounds the way sex scenes in many films look—pretend heat, surface passion. Its literal shopping list of sex toys, from rope to soap to latex thong, describes the commercialized nature of sex in a pornified culture.

Toby Gad said that Madonna sometimes started a writing team's creative juices flowing by encouraging them to throw around controversial ideas, swear, dare to say something stupid. It was part mental calisthenics, part group therapy. That is how they began working on "Living for Love" and again on "Illuminati."[25]

Madonna wrote the song because she was annoyed that people used the word *illuminati* to describe a conspiracy theory involving an imagined group of rich and powerful people bent on cultural domination when in fact it can refer to any enlightened group of scientists, artists, and philosophers, especially those who flourished during the fifteenth and seventeenth centuries in Europe. "They were illuminating people," Madonna said. "It had nothing to do with money and power."[26]

Madonna remained in the fifteenth century with another Gad and Mozella song, "Joan of Arc." She was drawn to the strength of the Maid of Orléans's story. "In the face of death, she did not back down," Madonna explained. In the song, she compares herself to the saint—unfavorably. "I'm not ready to be burned at the stake," she said, only half jokingly.[27]

In May, Madonna took a break from working on her album to travel with her children to Michigan for her father's birthday and to visit the University of Michigan at Ann Arbor. Lourdes planned to study dance and theater there in the fall. (Lourdes paid her own tuition and room and board.)[28] Madonna said she and Lourdes had had many discussions about "being an artist, being creative, where to put energy...she's an incredible singer and dancer." In fact, all her children were musical, Madonna said. Rocco danced and produced music. David played guitar, sang, and danced. Mercy played piano "beautifully...This is a very musical household."[29]

Madonna was proud of the children she loved, educated, nurtured, and advised. "Sometimes I make mistakes," she admitted. "Sometimes things don't go the way I planned, and I ask my sister [Melanie] for her advice because she was raised by my grandmother and she's a good mother."[30]

To be that kind of mother, Madonna said, "I tend to take a lot of breaks and deal with my kids, and then go back to work."[31] As her children grew older, they became part of that work.

Sometimes they inspired her. Madonna told a friend, the illusionist and performance artist David Blaine, that one of her sons came to the studio "and said he didn't want to go home. I said, 'No, you have to go home; it's time for bed.' And he said, 'Mom, I feel like I'm isolated from your heart.' I was like, 'Oh, that's a good line. I have to use that.'"[32]

Sometimes they influenced her by telling her what new music to listen to. And sometimes they critiqued hers. Lourdes's and Rocco's favorite song on her new album was "Bitch I'm Madonna." David's was "Devil Pray."[33] Madonna said David was her biggest fan and Lola her biggest critic.[34] Rocco didn't care about her "accomplishments," she said. "He just wants me to cook for him."[35]

At home, she harassed them about homework. She required them to clean their rooms. And at night, they bonded over TV shows or movies. *Game of Thrones* was a favorite.[36] So was the movie *Whiplash,* about a music academy and the obsessive drive of a young drummer.[37] The movie reiterated Madonna's own message: nothing worth doing comes easily. And in the morning, they prayed together, not addressing the God of any one religion but the spirit of all religions.

Madonna said she tried to instill in them what she called

> my rebel heart...They see a woman who fights for gay rights, for children orphaned by AIDS, for the right of Muslim women to get an education. They see me never backing down an inch from who I am and what I believe

in…Obviously, they're also aware of the criticism. They read insults aimed at me on social media and they get hurt by it, but they also understand how important it is to follow one's path.[38]

She demanded much of them, and they demanded much of her, too. That summer, they got her up on a surfboard, and in the winter, they got her on skis. "And I say, 'Well, why not? I'm going to suck at it, so that's OK.' I'm good with that…Failure is a challenge. Failure is an invitation."[39]

That summer marked a turning point for Madonna as Lourdes prepared to leave home for college. Like the death of her mother, the birth of her daughter had fundamentally changed who Madonna was. She and Lola had been together through adventures and misadventures for nearly eighteen years. Friends and colleagues came and went. Men came and went. Lola stayed.

Before Lourdes left, Madonna marked her fifty-sixth birthday with a blowout 1920s-themed party at a villa near Cannes, then traveled with her children and some of the revelers to Ibiza. She and Lourdes spent an evening dancing at a club in one of their last outings together before Lourdes went off to school.[40]

When she moved out of my house, in the autumn, it was the hardest day of my life…Even when my long-term relationships ended, I didn't feel the pain I felt at that moment. It almost tore the heart out of my chest…I miss my daughter every day.[41]

When Madonna's heartbreak softened from acute pain to a gnawing ache, she was able to call that moment a "lesson in letting go. I can no longer dominate her. She gets to do what she wants to do, and that has helped me become less domineering."[42]

Madonna was back in the studio in New York with Diplo in early November to mix some of their songs, and then she left the States for Malawi.[43] The country had a new president, Peter Mutharika, with whom Madonna had a good relationship. The trip would have been entirely pleasant except that, two days after Thanksgiving, she learned that forty seconds of one or two early *Rebel Heart* demos had leaked.[44]

At first, she wasn't overly concerned. Leaks had occurred with nearly every album of hers since the late '90s. The internet made intellectual-property theft easy. Initially, the *Rebel Heart* leaks seemed minor. Guy Oseary sent out a tweet asking fans to help find the culprit, and that was that.[45] And then on December 16, there was another leak. Thirteen unfinished *Rebel Heart* songs, as well as the album's artwork, began circulating on the internet.

A Madonna album release was plotted with the precision of a military campaign. The songs might be tweaked up to the last minute, but the overall schedule was regimented.[46] A single and video were released, which she promoted during select TV, print, and Web interviews; there was an album release party; another single appeared and usually another video. "Everything [is] set up just so," Madonna said. "That's the kind of person I am."[47] *Rebel Heart*'s first single, "Living for Love," wasn't supposed to be available until Valentine's Day of 2015.[48] The leaked songs exploded Madonna's campaign.

Madonna said she was devastated. To illustrate the point, she posted a photo of a smashed iPod on Instagram and called it "a symbol of my broken heart!…#fuckedupshit."[49] On the internet, people were passing judgment on the songs that were still in the process of being created. Good comments or bad, Madonna didn't want to hear them. She began "second-guessing everything."[50]

Guy Oseary said his team tried to "pull down as many leaks as we could." Soon it was "unstoppable…You could not seal this leak."[51] On the morning of December 17, the vice chairman of Interscope was on a call with Madonna and Oseary. "She was in a very angry, upset, emotional place," said Steve Berman. "She told me, 'Steve, I care about my music. I can't have the songs being heard the wrong way.'"[52] Adding to her anxiety was the question of who did it. "I was worried it was an engineering assistant or somebody that had access to everything," she said.[53]

Oseary contacted a private investigator in Israel named Asher Wizman, whose firm handled international cases. Ironically, an expert Wizman sent to New York to examine Madonna's computers discovered that the hack had originated in Israel.[54] It was believed that the suspect, who was put under surveillance, may have had access to Madonna's computer and phone "for more than a decade." The investigation uncovered evidence that private photos had also been stolen.[55]

Madonna's focus was her album. She wanted as much of the finished work released as soon as possible. "There was a lot of talk about the many reasons why it didn't make sense," Oseary said, "but she was adamant that she didn't want people to think those were the finished tracks."[56] Interscope's Berman thought Apple could be pressed into releasing the material that Madonna felt was ready. But Apple's servers would be shut down from December 19 until January 5. That gave executives from Interscope, Universal Music Group, and Apple two days to agree to the premature release and make it happen. "There was a chance that technically it was not possible because it was so last minute," Oseary said.[57]

While Apple worked on making the songs available, Madonna wasn't sure that the six slated for release—"Living for Love," "Ghosttown," "Devil Pray," "Illuminati," "Unapologetic Bitch," and "Bitch I'm Madonna"—were finished. Her producers, meanwhile, were busy with other projects all over the world and couldn't be summoned back to New York on such short notice to help. Madonna went into the studio alone to master and mix the tracks herself.

She described going into "overdrive," not sleeping or seeing her children. "It was pandemonium, confusion, paranoia, and hysteria."[58] Christmas was approaching, and for the Ciccones, that normally involved elaborate tree trimming, decorating, and gift making. That year would be different. Madonna called the period "living hell."[59]

Meanwhile, a new wrinkle arose. Robert Kondrk, the Apple executive who needed to sign off on the agreement, was already away with his family in Mexico. Kondrk intervened anyway. At eight thirty on the night of December 19, just hours before the scheduled release, Madonna got the call saying, "We are good."[60] That meant that at midnight Eastern time, people who preordered the *Rebel Heart* album on iTunes would be able to download six tracks immediately.[61]

The next day, the album registered at number 1 on the iTunes charts in forty-one countries, and the six songs landed at or near the top of various charts around the world. Madonna called it a "miracle." If she took time to celebrate, it didn't last. Fourteen more demos were leaked beginning on December 24.[62]

Madonna always turned adversity into a lesson. She banned the internet if she and her crew were working on a song on computers. Hard drives were hand-delivered. "It sucks, but," she said, "it's just the age that we're living in."[63]

In late January of 2015, the FBI and Israeli police announced the arrest in Tel Aviv of the suspected hacker. He was a thirty-eight-year-old aspiring singer named Adi Lederman. Reports said that a search of his computers found he had hacked into the cloud accounts of three members of Madonna's staff as well as Guy Oseary's office email and fifteen other email accounts. The probe also revealed that Lederman had hacked an early version of "Give Me All Your Luvin'" in 2012 from Madonna's *MDNA* album and that Madonna may not have been his only target. He allegedly hacked other artists to access their work, and police suspected that he tried to sell the material. Lederman would be indicted in February on four counts and would ultimately confess as part of a plea agreement. He was sentenced to fourteen months in prison.[64]

On the day of his arrest, Madonna said, "Strangely I don't feel thrilled. I'm happy he's caught, but he's been hacking into my server and the servers of people around me for more than a decade. It's a deeply disturbing viola-tion. This is only the beginning."[65]

The arrest ended one impediment to the smooth launch of her album. But there would be others that so detracted from the work that at times the album seemed cursed.

Madonna hadn't promoted *MDNA,* and it didn't sell, which meant that her songs weren't heard. She would not make that same mistake with *Rebel Heart.* She set about promoting the hell out of it, appearing on seemingly any TV show that would have her, performing her songs on stages large and small, enduring days of print media interviews. And she took her campaign to the digital world.

Sometimes it worked, and sometimes it didn't. Social media is an unfor-giving space where decisions made in the second it takes to press Send quickly become a major crisis. That happened with memes based on Madonna's album cover. *Rebel Heart* featured an arresting image of her face bound in black cord. It had both Christian and Jewish antecedents, but she said its message was secular: it represented the constraints placed on artists. The image spread through social media as fans reproduced various faces wrapped in cord. Madonna reposted some, but when she reposted images of Nelson Mandela, Martin Luther King Jr., and Bob Marley with their faces bound, she ignited a firestorm.[66]

Her idea was that they were rebel hearts. But that was too fine a point. Madonna was called disrespectful for misusing the images of revered figures such as King and Mandela in her promotion. She was called arrogant for seemingly comparing herself to them and racist for showing Black men in restraints. The deluge of criticism began on social media and spread through mainstream media, which was hungry for a good old Madonna outrage.[67]

Though Madonna wasn't inclined to defend herself against fabricated controversy, she did so in this case because it threatened to torpedo her album at the start of its promotion, because she would never do anything to disrespect those figures, and because it could affect her children. The previous year, she had had to apologize for a hashtag below an Instagram photo that showed Rocco boxing. In it, she had used the N-word. She wrote it playfully, she said, and as a term of "endearment toward her son who is white," but she understood the consternation it provoked. "I am not a racist," she wrote. "There's no way to defend the use of the word." Now, to head off fresh charges of racism, Madonna quickly posted another apology, saying her intent was to pay tribute to cultural icons.[68]

Some argued that Madonna would do herself a favor by staying away from social media. Instead, she dove in. On February 5, she released the first video from her new album on Snap Channel, a new platform from

Snapchat. "Living for Love" appeared for twenty-four hours, to be shared among fans as well as people who wouldn't otherwise go out of their way to look at a Madonna video. She was the first major artist to use that platform for a video launch.[69]

Madonna had hired the French directors Julien Choquart and Camille Hirigoyen to help create it. Having made a name shooting edgy commercials, in 2014 they created a visually stunning video for the song "Saint Claude," by the French singer-songwriter Christine and the Queens. Against a cadmium-red background, on a red stage, Chris (Héloïse Adélaïde Letissier) danced and sang alone. Little enhanced his performance technically except an occasional camera distortion that elongated his body and the illusion in the finale that he was hanging suspended in an aerial backbend high above the stage.[70]

The video for "Living for Love" re-created that saturated red background and red stage as well as some of Chris's movements as Madonna danced. But the setting was much more elaborate. It depicted a bullfight in which Madonna, as matador, tames into submission a herd of man-bulls. Since 1994's "Take a Bow," she had returned regularly to the bullfight theme. "Living for Love" was the most stylized version, shot and edited to the point of abstraction. And that abstraction was its essence. Madonna saw it as a "painting that came to life."[71]

Just as each of Madonna's best albums reflects its producer's influence, each of her album promotions and tours reflects a particular visual image. The "Living for Love" video's images became the theme of the *Rebel Heart* promotions. Three days after the video's release, they came to life at the Grammy's. Madonna performed "Living for Love" as a matador surrounded by twenty-two male dancers wearing bull's horns and jeweled face masks, with backup from a twenty-eight-member choir.

When she took the stage that night at the Staples Center, she didn't do so as a mere icon. By 2015, she was an archetype. As T. Cole Rachel would write that year in *Pitchfork,*

> She essentially built the house that everyone else—Britney, Beyoncé, Nicki, Gaga, Sky, Rihanna, Katy, Ariana, even Kanye—all now get to call home. She devised the archetype of pop stardom as we know and understand it today. And, with the exception of Michael Jackson...Madonna's enduring impact on popular culture remains pretty much unequaled.[72]

The performance that night would be a reminder why. It culminated in Madonna hanging by a harness in an "extreme backbend," silhouetted against a red backdrop high above the stage.[73] The segment was unforgettable visually. It was a display by a woman who was quite simply without fear.

She hoped that her message about courage and daring resonated with her audience, because that was the difference between commerce and art, and the current environment fostered the former over the latter. "If you're a pop star and want to get your records played and reach the masses, you have to play it very safe," she said. "Keeping your brand going and not rocking the boat—that's what is encouraged."[74]

Some of the major stars in mainstream pop had begun to make statements. In 2014, Beyoncé stood onstage at the MTV Video Music Awards in front of a screen emblazoned with the word FEMINIST. For her part, Lady Gaga had made gay rights central to her work. But generally, until an artist was several years into a career and had a bank balance as big as the bank's own, politics were too risky. Riskier still was anger, especially for women.[75]

The formula for a female pop star's success was, by then, well established. According to Emerson College music-industry expert Kristin Lieb, the star must sing and dance, be likable and attractive, embrace diversity, have experienced conflict, and hint at vulnerability. "If you can't pose near naked on the cover of a magazine and be well received, that's a career roadblock," Lieb said.[76] The goal of the industry was not to support a female pop star as an artist but to grow her "brand" into a conglomerate. In the entertainment business, it was called the "Madonna effect," yet that wholesale packaging was the antithesis of what she represented.[77]

Madonna saw Nile Rodgers at the Grammys that night. "I just gave him the longest, biggest hug," she said. "I feel like I've survived so much, and been through so much. And sometimes I miss the innocence of those times. Life was different. New York was different. The music business was different. I miss the simplicity of it, the naiveté of everyone around me."[78]

Amid all that industry-controlled "individualism," Madonna couldn't resist a bit of mischief. During her arrival on the red carpet, she flipped the skirt on her Givenchy matador costume and treated the media to a look at her nearly bare derriere. The statement was an unsubtle "Kiss my ass" to those who said that her "brand" had expired, that she was too old to perform, to be sexual, to be attractive, to be heard. "This is me. This is who I wanna be," she said. "I can do what I want, OK?"[79]

Germaine Greer wrote in her book *The Change* that Western society has an "irrational fear and hatred" of aging women, who, postmenopause, are supposedly no longer useful. And yet she saw those women as not *less* but *more* powerful, possessing "experience, strength, staying power, character, sexual self-knowledge." Greer challenged women to embark on the "grand spiritual adventure" of middle age.[80]

Madonna had begun hers, and, as it was in her youth, it was about rebellion. "I don't follow the rules. I never did, and I'm not going to start," she said. "This is what a fifty-six-year-old ass looks like, motherfuckers."[81] An interviewer suggested that perhaps her well-toned behind wasn't typical for a woman her age. Madonna snapped back,

> You know what? It *could* be the average one day…So if I have to be the person who opens the door for women to believe and understand and embrace the idea that they can be sexual and look good and be as relevant in their fifties or their sixties as they were in their twenties, then so be it.[82]

Madonna's cheeky display went viral and appeared in the press around the world.[83] Whether outraged or amused, people responded. They looked and listened, but more important, they thought.

With the entertainment world still preoccupied with Madonna's Grammy performance onstage and off, she released three more songs, "Joan of Arc," "Iconic," and "Hold Tight." And she promoted her work in unconventional places, including the gay dating app Grindr, where she launched a contest asking entrants to re-create her album cover — despite the controversy such memes had already caused. The prize for the five winners was a Grindr chat with Madonna. She also took to Instagram to announce that she would appear at that year's BRIT Awards.[84]

Remarkably, despite her attachment to Great Britain, her huge fan base there, and the importance of the UK music market — it was second only to that of the States — Madonna had only performed once before at the British equivalent of the Grammys, and that was twenty years previously, when she sang "Bedtime Story." The 2015 BRITs were to be held in the O2 Arena, which could accommodate twenty thousand people. Five million more were expected to watch on TV.

Rehearsals — one for her vocals and one with the dancers — went late into the night on the eve of the performance.[85] She would again be a matador, but for her entrance, Armani had made a black satin hooded cape. The idea was that she would walk along a catwalk through the audience, a mysterious presence with her face hidden under the hood and two dancers holding the cape's long train. The cloak was held closed by magnets, but it was so heavy that something else was needed to secure it at the neck. Madonna suggested a silk string tied loosely in a bow and began rehearsing the show with that wardrobe change. "We rehearsed it twenty thousand times," Madonna said. It worked every time. The show was ready.[86]

The next day, just hours before the performance was scheduled to begin,

Madonna was told she couldn't approach the stage as planned. The adjustment meant she had to walk farther, which added to the time her heavy cape had to be carried and increased the risk that the bow would come undone. Madonna and her stylist, Bea Åkerlund, tied the bow slightly tighter and gave it a tug to make sure it wouldn't loosen prematurely.[87]

Madonna's performance was the last of the evening. It began as her Grammy act did—with the audience hearing a voice-over describing her revolution of love. She marched in on four-inch heels along the catwalk, with dancers holding her cape from what looked like fifteen feet behind her. She ascended three stairs onto the stage, then another four up to her performance platform.[88]

At the top, on cue, Madonna threw back her hood, and the dancers knelt facedown before her. As she sang, she tugged on her bow to release her cape. It wouldn't give. On the phrase "I let down my guard," the two women carrying her cape responded to the cue, as rehearsed, and yanked her cape with full force to free it from her shoulders. Instead, Madonna tumbled backward down four high stairs.[89] "I had a choice: I could either be strangled or fall with the cape, and I fell."[90] Madonna said she hit her head, "but I had so much adrenaline pumping...that I just was, OK, I have to keep going. So I just got back onstage."[91] Ironically, the line she came back in on was "Love's gonna lift me up."[92]

The audience, which gasped when it saw her tumble, gasped again when only seconds later she was up, singing and dancing as if nothing had happened. She continued to do so for the remainder of her five-minute performance. "That's one thing you learn, and the one thing my dance teacher always told me: that when you make a mistake, you can never telegraph that to the audience...They're gonna believe what you tell them to believe."[93] At the end of her song, the audience was on its feet, clapping.

Social media, meanwhile, was on fire with commentary. There were jokes, and some people who didn't trust the veracity or sincerity of anything Madonna did called the fall a publicity stunt because it was timed so perfectly to the song's lyrics.[94] But mostly there was admiration. One headline read, MADONNA FELL DOWN THE STAIRS BUT KEPT PERFORMING BECAUSE SHE'S A G.D. PRO.[95] Cher tweeted, "This is Something we all dread. Madge, you are a champ for finishing your song."[96] *The Guardian*'s Ben Beaumont-Thomas wrote:

> As befits Madge, who has risen phoenix-like more times than anyone can remember, she's a proper trooper [sic] and completes the song...Many lesser performers would have missed an entire verse at such a nasty fall. Kudos![97]

For friends and colleagues, however, seeing her fall pained them. "If it was us seven dancers, we would have done something—we would have reacted," said Blond Ambition dancer Salim Gauwloos. "I wouldn't have let her lie there on her back."[98]

Because Madonna hit her head, her doctor worried about a concussion. She was monitored for several hours to see if she was okay. "I could have hurt so many things, and I didn't," she said.[99]

The fall dominated the dozens of interviews she had scheduled to promote her album. Again and again, she had to explain what happened. Again and again, she laughed off bad jokes about that night. What was most remarkable about the incident wasn't mentioned. In hundreds of performances requiring treacherous onstage feats over the course of thirty years, an accident like that had never happened before. "I rehearse everything to death, and I never do anything live that I haven't rehearsed," Madonna said. "I broke that rule that one time, and I've learned my lesson. I will never do it again."[100]

After the leaks, after the album-cover meme controversy, after the BRITs, after Madonna was in the news for everything *but* music, *Rebel Heart* was finally released in March. As befitting an album with such an explosive preamble, she didn't release just one album; she released many. There were two standard editions, five deluxe editions (one French and one Japanese), a superdeluxe edition, a special German edition, and a Japanese tour edition. The albums' tracks made listeners dance, think, swoon, laugh, feel sad, feel sexy, and come away defiant. Madonna had learned to harness the producer-heavy music and technology that made anything possible in the studio and marry them to lyrics and a sound that were quintessentially her own.[101]

She had been promoting the album since the first of the year, but as extensive as that campaign was, it didn't help. For the first time in Madonna's career, critics generally loved the album, but her fans didn't—or at least not enough of them did—and nonfans didn't hear it. In Britain, BBC Radio 1, one of the most influential pop stations in the world, wouldn't play "Living for Love." The station's playlist committee didn't think Madonna appealed to its target audience—people between the ages of eighteen and thirty.[102]

Ageism was just one factor in the declining sales of Madonna's music. Globally, the record industry lost $10 billion between 2002 and 2015 because of streaming services. People listened to music more than ever; they just didn't necessarily pay for it.[103] *Rebel Heart* became one of Madonna's lowest-selling albums at its launch: only 250,000 copies were sold in the United States (fewer than *MDNA*), along with sixty-seven thousand in the UK and fifty thousand in France.[104]

Madonna knew the album was good, so she became an evangelist for it. In March, she spent a full week on *The Ellen DeGeneres Show,* made a first-ever stop at Howard Stern's radio show, and appeared on the *Today* show and *The Tonight Show Starring Jimmy Fallon.* Overseas, she appeared on *The Jonathan Ross Show* (UK), *Che tempo che fa* (Italy), *Le Grand Journal* (France), and *Today* (Australia), among others.[105]

She also turned up at events where she joined other artists onstage. On March 29, she was at the Shrine Auditorium, in Los Angeles, for an unannounced performance with Taylor Swift at the iHeartRadio Music Awards. Madonna sang "Ghosttown" with Swift accompanying her on guitar. In April, at Coachella, Madonna made a guest appearance during Drake's set. His album that year included a mixtape cut called "Madonna," during which he promised to make a girl in the song "as big as Madonna." Madonna joked that her unfulfilled "lifelong ambition" was to kiss him.[106] At Coachella, she did.

Wearing a hat that said THREAT and a T-shirt that read BIG AS MADONNA, she sang "Human Nature" and "Hung Up." The sound system was terrible, and the crowd disengaged as Madonna gamely sang and danced alone onstage. When Drake joined her, sitting in a chair in what was obviously a staged move, Madonna leaned over him to collect her kiss. Maybe he had expected a peck. That wasn't what was on offer. After nearly sucking the life out of him, Madonna stopped, turned away, and said, "Bitch, I'm Madonna." Drake was left looking shocked. He leaned forward and wiped his mouth. Later he said it wasn't the kiss but Madonna's lipstick that made him grimace.[107]

That time the social media sphere lit up with indignation over the way Madonna had mistreated the lad and what it meant. Was she really that sexually aggressive? Or was it all choreographed because she was simply tired of talking about her fall? If so, it worked. "The kiss" became a new topic as she made the interview circuit.

Amid all that nonsensical jabber, Madonna and Jonas Åkerlund teamed up on two videos that reflected the rebel and the heart at the center of her work. They hadn't shot anything together since the Confessions tour, in 2006. She called him out of the blue, wondering if he'd be interested in directing a video for her new album. "I was very excited about 'Ghosttown,'" he said. "I connected to it creatively." The song's concept was life after the apocalypse. They worked together on what that would look like. "We've built trust between us through the years," Åkerlund said. "Every time we do videos, we want to change the world. A lot of artists don't do that."[108]

Åkerlund begins the video with images on a vintage TV screen of nuclear detonations and warnings about the end of the world. There are three survivors—Madonna, actor Terrence Howard, and an Asian child—scavenging for life in Edwardian attire amid the urban blight of bombed-out buildings. Their introduction does not involve words but dance. By the end of it, the couple and the child walk off together into the gloom.[109]

Åkerlund said they enjoyed working together again, so Madonna asked him to shoot another video. That time it was for something much lighter—"Bitch I'm Madonna." It would be a cathartic crescendo to *Rebel Heart*'s bumpy rollout. "We thought, 'Let's [gather] some friends and family and go crazy with it!'"[110]

At the Standard, High Line hotel in New York, Åkerlund filmed a party that looked spontaneous but was in fact tightly choreographed. "Everyone had cues, and everyone was ready," Åkerlund said.[111] The camera followed Madonna from floor to floor of the hotel as pop-culture notables—Chris Rock, Katy Perry, Kanye West, Miley Cyrus, Nicki Minaj, Diplo, Rita Ora, Beyoncé, Alexander Wang, and many others—celebrated alongside her. Her sons David, who did a solo dance number, and Rocco were in the crowd, too. "When we left the shoot," Åkerlund said, "we thought, 'If the video feels half as good as we feel, then it's a home run.'"[112] It was a New Year's Eve party in June marking the end of one creative endeavor and heralding the start of the next. Madonna announced her tenth tour.

Chapter 57

Paris, New York, Montreal, Stockholm, London, Melbourne, 2015–2016

Je suis Charlie.[1]

— Madonna

THE THREAT OF violence that Madonna felt boiling just below the surface during her MDNA tour had erupted like a volcano in the three years since. Girls. Political liberty. Free expression. All were under attack. In northern Nigeria, the militant Islamist group Boko Haram kidnapped 275 schoolgirls. Revolution and counterrevolution in Ukraine were followed by Russia's invasion of Crimea and the threat of a greater war in Europe. In Asia, pro-democracy protesters took to the streets of normally peaceful Hong Kong when it became clear that China planned to curtail and then eliminate the city's cherished political freedoms.

In the Middle East, the promise of the Arab Spring had been burned to embers in the civil wars raging in Syria and Libya and beaten into submission elsewhere, especially in Egypt, where a new military strongman ruled. In Iraq, the Islamic State terrorist network that arose out of the chaos and carnage of war inspired followers around the world as it perpetrated medieval-type horrors on its way to establishing an imagined caliphate.

A group of those followers struck the offices of the satirical newspaper *Charlie Hebdo* and a Jewish supermarket in Paris in January of 2015, killing seventeen people. The paper was targeted over a cartoon depicting Prophet Muhammad. Madonna said of those murders, "Artists who foster discussion through provocation are the ones most at risk at the moment."[2]

In the United States during the Obama administration, in response to the election of the nation's first Black president, the population of aggrieved white men that had arisen in the '90s became more militant. The Department of Homeland Security reported a 50 percent increase in hate groups, from neo-Nazis and the KKK to militias and white separatists. Their profiles were consistent: white men mostly in their twenties who saw no future for themselves, which they extrapolated into no future for "their people." The canon of that extreme right was encapsulated in the Fourteen Words: "We must secure the existence of our people and a future for white children." While the news media focused on the threat from Islamist militants, the growing—and truly homegrown—threat was from angry white men.[3]

At the same time, the systematic mistreatment of Blacks by police sparked major protests from coast to coast. Two women started the Black Lives Matter movement in 2013 following the acquittal of the Florida man accused of killing seventeen-year-old Trayvon Martin. The movement grew as extrajudicial killings by police claimed one Black life after another.[4] In 2015 alone, there were more than a dozen known police killings of Black men and women.

Not since the 1960s had racial tensions been expressed so openly on the street and in the media. In 2015, the internet was an accelerant, spreading hate speech and inspiring acts of violence so extreme that they caused a nation jaded by murder to pause in horror. On June 17, 2015, a twenty-one-year-old white supremacist sat amid a Bible study group at the Emanuel African Methodist Episcopal Church in Charleston, South Carolina, casually pulled out a Glock handgun, and killed nine Black worshippers.

Ten days later, a Black woman named Bree Newsome climbed the flagpole at the South Carolina State House, where the flag of the racist Confederacy still flew, and removed it. She was arrested, and the flag was restored to the top of the pole, but not for long. In the wake of the Charleston shooting, Confederate flags across the South disappeared. The Confederate leaders still standing in stone and metal began to tumble, too.[5] And when President Obama visited the site of the June slaughter, singing "Amazing Grace" alone and a cappella from the depths of his grieving heart, it seemed like the country might have reached a turning point. It lasted for only a moment.

The events of that year had a profound effect on Madonna, because so much of the violence was done in the name of religion. By 2015, her immersion in three of the world's main religions—Judaism, Christianity, and Islam—was complete. She did not see herself as a member of any one group but as a person who embraced aspects of them all.[6] The message from all three was love for one's neighbor, yet extremists of all religions perpetrated acts of violence in God's name. Madonna said,

> With all the things that have happened here in America, what happened in Paris, what's happening around the world with Boko Haram...I really can't take it. I feel personally wounded by it, and I feel like it's my job as a human being, as an artist, as a mother, as a woman, to fight for all these people.[7]

While she was in France promoting her album on the TV show *Le Grand Journal,* the host, Antoine de Caunes, challenged her over her willingness to confront social problems. He asked if she was tempted by a career in politics. Madonna replied, "I'm *in* politics. You're watching it."[8]

De Caunes noted that Madonna had been one of the first artists to publicly declare solidarity with the *Charlie Hebdo* staff. At that point on the show, she was introduced to Rénald Luzier, a cartoonist who had survived the attack and who, a week after the carnage, drew another cartoon of Prophet Muhammad for the newspaper's cover. On it, the Prophet declared, "Je suis Charlie," and said, "All is forgiven." That first postattack newspaper—"the survivors' issue"—also featured a column describing the best things that had come out of the assault, Madonna's support among them. By contrast, in the States and the UK, she had been pilloried for an Instagram post declaring, "Je suis Charlie."[9]

Madonna and Luzier embraced tightly, spoke quietly, and then, as they took their places at the table to speak with de Caunes, Madonna wiped tears from her eyes. On behalf of his colleagues, Luzier thanked her for her support. She thanked him for "being a freedom fighter," to which he responded wearily, "Yeah, we try." Madonna said the people who died did not do so in vain. "They walk in the footsteps of giants...So, bravo." And then she said, "Art for freedom."[10] That was the message she would take on her tour.

The Rebel Heart tour would comprise eighty-two shows in North America, Europe, Asia, and Oceania. Madonna would appear in Japan for the first time in almost ten years, Australia for the first time in twenty-three years, and in the Philippines, China, Hong Kong, Macao, Singapore, Taiwan, Thailand, and New Zealand for the first time ever.[11]

Over the course of the previous year, she had been gathering ideas for her tour from "art, fashion, music, all of it," she said. Other sources of inspiration were her own short performances, even her cameos with other artists. But her "Living for Love" video was critical. It "became the catalyst for what I did at the Grammys, becomes the catalyst for what I do at the BRITs. It just starts spinning from there," she said.[12]

The themes of Madonna's show would cover familiar ground: four segments, traveling from introspection to celebration. She described the first as "empowerment." "Medieval warrior bitch goddess, that's what I'm going for," she said.[13] "We're using 'Iconic' as the opening. It talks about being a warrior and fighting for what you believe in." The show also explored "themes of sex and religion, because they are things in our society that are always separated. And, to me, sex is a sacred gift that was given to us." Finally, the show was an expression of love. She said she wanted people to leave her concert inspired, "like they've seen something they've never seen before, felt something they've never felt before."[14]

She would do that musically by presenting a thirty-year career retrospective. She said she preferred her "more abstract, less commercial songs," but she knew her audience wanted to sing along. "So, I have to balance that out and not just do a creative show that's going to please me."[15] The formula she devised to make the greatest number of people happy—including herself—was the simplest. In the past, when she performed her classics, she completely reworked them. During Rebel Heart, the songs—"True Blue," "La Isla Bonita," and "Who's That Girl," among others—sounded like the originals.

Madonna reassembled her tour team to make that happen. There were a few familiar faces among the cast and crew: Jamie King as show director, Kevin Antunes as musical director, Monte Pittman on guitar, Ric'key Pageot on keyboards, and Nicki Richards and Kiley Dean singing backup. The dance staff was thirty-seven strong, with eighteen people designated as "additional choreographer." Some of those, too, were returnees: Jason Young, Valeree Young, Chaz Buzan, Sébastien Ramirez, and Marvin Gofin. But the vast majority of dancers were new to Madonna's world. Five thousand people in Paris, New York, and Los Angeles had auditioned for twenty slots in the show.[16]

Madonna's management team featured her trusted colleagues Guy Oseary and Sara Zambreno. But Liz Rosenberg shared publicity duty with a newcomer, Brian Bumbery. That was because after thirty years, Liz had decided to leave Madonna's employ. "I think two centuries is long enough, don't you?" she joked in making the announcement in late June to the *New York Post*'s Page Six.[17]

Liz was the last of Madonna's original professional family. Aside from a brief period after 9/11 when, in the wake of that terrible day, she felt the need to reevaluate her life, she had been at Madonna's side during every high and every low. During the worst of the lows, it had been Liz's clever maneuvering that saved Madonna from an even worse press shellacking than she received. That was because while the press may have disliked Madonna, it loved Liz. Reporters knew Liz was often fibbing on Madonna's behalf, but she told her tales so convincingly and with such good humor that she would go unchallenged for at least a few news cycles.[18] With Liz's departure, Madonna lost one of the people in her life on whom she had most depended. Rebel Heart would be her first tour without her.

Tour planning had begun the previous November, but rehearsals didn't start until midsummer in New York.[19] "Six days a week, 120 people working with Madonna at the helm," said the Live Nation tour director, Tres

Thomas.[20] Madonna called it a "vicious cycle of working late and then sleeping late." To ensure she stayed healthy, she was followed by a woman Madonna called "the food police. 'Are you eating? Did you drink enough water?' "[21]

Most days, rehearsals began at 9:00 or 10:00 a.m. and might run until two o'clock the following morning. The rigor for the newcomers came as a shock, but so did Madonna's participation in it. She was the boss, but she was also one of the cast, working hour after hour among them, despite being twice the age of most of the dancers. "I mean, you cannot tell. She's so fit," said French hip-hop choreographer Honji Wang. The pay (undisclosed) and the perks made the process less painful. Masseurs, good food. Wang said, "You are in a golden cage."[22]

Meanwhile, the stage design had progressed from the concepts of January and the mock-ups of the first half of the year to a seemingly living, moving, breathing character in the drama. It was based on a sketch Madonna drew that incorporated ideas from the *Rebel Heart* album cover: an arrow, a cross, and a heart.

Extending one hundred feet into the arena, the stage allowed Madonna and her dancers to interact more closely with more of the audience than ever before.[23] Around eighty people, whose numbers were augmented by one hundred local crew members hired in each city along the route, built the stage and installed the 130,000 pounds of equipment that hung from the ceiling.[24] As for the living, breathing part, that was a matter of light and film magic.

Moment Factory again took charge of video production. With each show, that dimension of a Madonna concert became increasingly integrated into the performance. It began with Drowned World's screen behind the stage. By Rebel Heart, the video *became* the stage. The twenty-eight-foot-wide, sixteen-foot-high, twenty-five-ton video deck served as the stage floor, a raised platform, and an angled wall that performers could use during their flips and tumbles.[25]

Only well into the rehearsal process, after the dances had been choreographed, the story lines established, and the stage dimensions understood, did the focus turn to the tour's costumes.[26] Arianne Phillips was once again the master of style, contributing her own creations and adjusting designs by Prada, Gucci, Fausto Puglisi, Moschino, Nicolas Jebran, and Alexander Wang to make them all "show ready." That meant reinforcing the clothing from the inside so it could withstand the rigors of the performance.[27]

The tour required nine hundred costumes. Madonna alone changed hers every ten minutes during the show. Helping her was her longtime

dresser, Tony Villanueva, who also oversaw the tour's wardrobe department, including seamsters who repaired the costumes and the tour's
in-house launderers, who washed them.[28]

By late summer, the Rebel Heart tour was road-ready. It would take
twenty-four semis and three Boeing 747s to move it.[29] The stage itself
filled eight trucks; lighting filled another eight.[30] One full truck and a half
were dedicated to Madonna's "dressing-room compound": furniture,
paintings, photographs, and a gym.[31] The man in charge of setting that
scene from city to city was the ambience director, Jaime Laurita. His job,
he said, was to create a "home away from home for Madonna. There's a
perfect flow of energy that gets her from the car to the room and from the
room to the stage."[32]

Even though tickets were the highest-priced of any tour that year—the
average on many stops was more than $450—fans snapped them up.[33] In
Italy, concerts in Turin sold out in three minutes. In Paris, five minutes. In
Taiwan, fifteen minutes. Hong Kong fans made history, buying up
Madonna tickets in thirty minutes.[34] The show would ultimately sell out
everywhere, which meant that more than one million people would see it
live. It had been scheduled to begin in August in Miami, but the first five
shows were rescheduled, to the consternation of fans. Instead, it opened in
Montreal on September 9.

The first glimpse the audience had of Madonna was on video. She was
in a cage, dressed in the outfit she wore to the Academy Awards so many
years before when she vamped "Sooner or Later" from *Dick Tracy*. It was
Madonna as Jean Harlow, Marilyn Monroe—all the intelligent women
who had graced the silver screen but who were appreciated primarily for
their bodies.[35]

Madonna's video image was replaced with that of Mike Tyson (another
supposedly brainless body), who recited his dialogue from "Iconic" until
Madonna herself appeared onstage, descending from the ceiling in a cage,
not as a Hollywood star but as a samurai warrior. She picked up where
Tyson left off on "Iconic."[36]

Having declared her intention to start a revolution, she introduced herself with "Bitch I'm Madonna." The scene was menacing and saturated in
red, but the tone was playful. Madonna was up to mischief, not martial
arts—despite all the warriors around her. Chance the Rapper had made a
video appearance during "Iconic." Nicki Minaj did the same during
"Bitch I'm Madonna," her pixie face beneath a pink wig looming over the
stage.[37]

Madonna exchanged *Rebel Heart* Samurai Madonna for a 1980s Rocker

Madonna. Striding down the catwalk in thigh-high boots, she picked up her black Gibson Flying V guitar and treated the audience to a faithful rendition of one of her earliest songs, "Burning Up." And then she became Sister Madonna.[38]

Madonna and four female dancers dressed as nuns (if nuns wore frilly white underwear and black leather bras under their miniskirted habits) stepped demurely down the stage, hands held as if in prayer. As Madonna sang "Holy Water," the four nuns pole danced on crosses. When the song switched to "Vogue," it was Madonna's turn to mount the pole. She didn't dance; rather, she "surfed" the horizontal body of the nun stretched out like a board beneath her. "Vogue" then became "Holy Water" again, and the action returned to the main stage for a bacchanalian Last Supper, complete with chalices, halos, crowns of thorns, and a lot of naked flesh. The scene was worthy of Pasolini. At the end of it, Madonna was left alone on the table, on her back, her hands and arms bound in red rope.[39]

Beginning with Blond Ambition, each of Madonna's concerts featured an act of contrition. In Blond Ambition, it came after her infamous "Like a Virgin" masturbation scene. During Rebel Heart, it occurred after she defiled the Last Supper. Madonna sang her ode to higher consciousness, "Devil Pray," as an appeal for mercy made to a dancer dressed as a priest, with three other dancers dressed in religious garb: Jewish, Muslim, Hindu.[40]

The first act of the concert ended with a similarly religious interlude featuring a song Madonna wrote with Avicii, "Messiah." Madonna appeared on video while a twenty-one-year-old Californian named Ahlamalik Williams danced alone onstage with a piece of fabric that blew like a flame as his partner. He was new to Madonna's tour but had worked with Jamie King and Kevin Antunes on the 2013 Cirque du Soleil show *Michael Jackson ONE*. Marvin Gofin, who had been with Madonna since the MDNA tour, took the stage from Williams, and the single flame, which had represented the fire of inspiration, grew to become the flames of hell. Video flames engulfed Gofin until he was consumed by them.[41]

The second act began with a new song that, as performed, was filled with delightful nostalgia. First came a visual reference to the industrial scene in the video for "Express Yourself" and the opening act of Blond Ambition. But in Rebel Heart, the pistons and engines weren't part of a factory but a car mechanic's shop, a "Body Shop."[42]

It made sense that "True Blue" would follow. That was nostalgic, too. Madonna performed it playing a ukulele with Monte Pittman. As a love song, it was her simplest and maybe her purest. Her dancers paired off in couples to dance while she sang. The audiences along her tour route did, too.[43]

Love could be quiet, or it could be raucous. The next song, "Deeper and Deeper," celebrated the latter, as Madonna reassembled her gang for a full-on song-and-dance number. The song's club roots made it irresistible in concert. And then a gunshot sounded as Madonna put a finger to her temple and shot herself. Darkness descended upon the dance floor. The joy of falling in love was shattered. That had been her experience in life. Romance didn't last.[44]

Madonna turned somber for "HeartBreakCity." From atop a spiral staircase, she angrily directed the lyrics at dancer Marvin Gofin, who, playing her foil, climbed the staircase only to have Madonna reject him. At the end of the number, she made it final, pushing him off the stairs and watching him tumble sixteen feet below. Remorse? Not really. Madonna shouted, "Nobody fucks with the queen." That was soon followed by "Like a Virgin."[45]

Madonna performed alone, but she had thousands of voices accompanying her. She sang the song straight, the way she had originally recorded it. As she danced down the catwalk, she looked as joyous as her Virgin tour self. She also became her naughty Blond Ambition self, mock-masturbating for a few beats without the help of eunuchs. She was having a ball as she ripped open her shirt to cool off, stuck her thumb in her mouth, and gyrated to the rhythm that every single person in her audience knew so well.[46]

And then she disappeared. The interlude between acts featured Madonna on-screen as Dita Parlo, whispering portions of "Justify My Love" before her dancers paired off on four beds (not all couples hetero) and engaged in pretend (and slightly robotic) intercourse to her critique of hookup culture, "S.E.X."[47]

The third act began with Madonna tempting fate by re-creating her performance from the BRIT Awards. Having marched down the hundred-foot-long catwalk, her cape carried by two dancers, as it had been in London, she mounted three steps, then four more, took off her hood, and sang a few words that cued her dancers to pull the cape away from her. There was no doubt that the audience watched the scene with trepidation, and when she completed it successfully—as she did at every tour stop—they and she experienced the joy of the song "Living for Love" even more.[48]

Madonna remained in exuberant mode for the next number, "La Isla Bonita." It was the fifth tour in which she performed it. The song had followed her through all her personas and had been sung with her onstage by various traditional artists. During Rebel Heart, there were no vocal guests—the traditional element appeared in the form of dance. Madonna and her troupe performed a flamenco.[49]

In gypsy attire—fringed cape, skirt, black hat with a flower—she launched into a medley of "Dress You Up," "Into the Groove," and "Lucky Star." Psychedelics flashed on the screen behind her and her female dancers, who exuded 1960s flower power. One was even dressed as a flower. The visuals were riotous. Madonna added a drinking game to the party, challenging her dancers to throw back shots of tequila. During the *Rebel Heart* promotion, she had challenged journalists who asked dumb or obvious questions to do the same.[50]

It was at that point in the show, more than three-quarters of the way through, that Madonna spoke to her audience. Sitting on a chair at the end of the long catwalk, she talked about her life and her difficult personal and professional journey. That direct interaction continued with her next song, "Rebel Heart," her tale about tough love, social ostracism, and finding inner strength.[51]

The interlude between the third act and the final segment of the show featured the song "Illuminati" and was the most awe-inspiring of the evening. On-screen, historical footage of laborers and capitalists, war and peace, protests and repression, formed a backdrop for Madonna's dancers, dressed as robber barons in top hats and tuxes. They marched along the catwalk while five dancers on twenty-foot-high flexible poles showed that the solid ground on which those capitalists walked was far from stable.[52]

Their death-defying bends out over the audience were inspired by Cirque du Soleil and elicited gasps, howls, and applause from the crowd. At one point, the rebellious dancers atop the poles reached down and plucked a tuxedoed dancer off the stage, lifting her high above it. In the end, the robber barons won, using their canes to shoot the dancers on the poles, but one had the sense that their victory was only temporary.[53]

Before the crash came the party. Madonna and her dancers reappeared in flapper finery to perform "Music." The setting was European, vaguely Parisian—a café in Josephine Baker's Montmartre, perhaps—or the Berlin of *Cabaret*'s Sally Bowles. But the action was pure Hollywood slapstick, with top-hatted tap dancers, fedora-wearing gangsters, and Madonna as a Louise Brooks burlesque star. "And now, something special," she said. "I'm going to play my favorite instrument." Ric'key Pageot hit individual keys of the piano as Madonna "played" her pelvic region. It was genuinely funny.[54]

Staying in the land of bawdy, she launched into "Candy Shop," with its unsubtle sexual innuendos, and played a gal on the make in "Material Girl." For the first time since her Mary Lambert video of 1985, Madonna performed the song with men in tuxedos, plucking cash from their pockets as she once had. As was the case then, none of the men suited her, and she was left alone in a wedding veil with a bouquet of flowers, wondering aloud about husband number three. She had several criteria: he had to be single, he couldn't be a felon, and he had to have talent.[55]

After throwing her bouquet into the audience, she sang "La Vie en rose" in French, accompanying herself on the ukulele. Madonna called it the greatest love song ever written and the woman who made it famous, Edith Piaf, one of her favorite performers. She ended that tribute to Piaf with a reference to another predecessor. She sang the line "Diamonds are a girl's best friend," but only to make a point.[56] She wasn't Marilyn Monroe. She was an "Unapologetic Bitch." Which was her next song.[57]

Near the end of the concert, Madonna invited a celebrity in the audience to join her onstage to dance, sing, or act the straight man in a comic routine. During her tour, these celebrities included Anderson Cooper, Jean Paul Gaultier, Stella McCartney, Adele, Jessica Chastain, Amy Schumer, Idris Elba, and Ariana Grande. Her ten-year-old children, David and Mercy, who traveled along with her on tour, made occasional appearances onstage, too.[58]

During her most recent tours, Madonna had shunned encores. In Rebel Heart, she came back with "Holiday," wearing the flag of whatever country she was in. Though it occurred nearly two hours into the show, her dancing during that encore was her most vigorous of the night. It was the kind of closer her fans expected, starring the Madonna they all loved.[59] One critic said the concert seemed "crafted to blow [them] away."[60]

The Rebel Heart tour was surprising because it was old-school, and not just in its musical choices. There was a good deal of video, but it didn't overwhelm the show. It was as if Madonna had made a conscious decision to step away from the world she had occupied in her tours since 2001. The secret to Rebel Heart's success was that it felt real. She and her cast expressed themselves without the intervention of too much technology.

The concert also felt retro, like a Broadway revue or a 1980s performance. In fact, not since the Who's That Girl tour had Madonna simply danced and sung. During Rebel Heart, she didn't fly, perform extreme yoga, or undertake complicated or dangerous choreography. And that may have been by necessity. Though Madonna was on her feet through nearly the entire concert, her movement seemed to be restricted. Her dancers, rather than the star of the show, performed feats of derring-do. And yet it was impossible to take your eyes off her.

Each Rebel Heart show was slightly different. In previous tours, every aspect was set in stone as much as humanly possible. But in Rebel Heart, the set list changed, as did the costumes and the people Madonna performed with. To open her show in New York, she deviated from her usual DJs and picked a comedian who was another of her creative off-spring. Amy Schumer had built her career exposing "womanly" qualities such as likability, modesty, and timidity for what they were: restraints that prevent girls and women from being full human beings. Madonna loved her.[61]

Schumer had had an incredible year, writing and starring in her first film, *Trainwreck,* and winning an Emmy Award and a Peabody Award for her TV series *Inside Amy Schumer.* In the spring, it got a lot better. "It was the craziest thing," she recalled. "Chris Rock called me and... was like 'Madonna wants your phone number.' I'm like, I can't believe *you* have my phone number." Then it was Madonna's turn to call. To the question of whether she would like to be Madonna's opening act, Schumer said, "'*Of course.*'...There is no one in the world I'd want to open for more." She hung up and called her high school girlfriends with the news.[62]

The New York audience was full of stars, most of them Madonna's friends. Standing near the stage on the second night of her show was a very special one—Sean Penn, along with his twenty-four-year-old daughter, Dylan. Some of the songs Madonna sang that night were written during her marriage to him and reflected both love and loss. After the performance, he took Dylan backstage to meet the woman he routinely referred to not by name but as his first wife. "Madonna and Sean have stayed close friends over the years," a source said, "so of course she embraced Dylan."[63]

Madonna left New York for sixteen more North American stops. After all those cities, she was only a third of the way into the tour. She said it was like going to war every night. Sometimes the venue was a problem; sometimes she had personal problems; sometimes a dancer was hurt. "When you do live shows, you never know what can happen," she said, "so you have to have that warrior-going-into-battle mentality."[64]

Each night after her show she spent twenty minutes in the hotel coming down. She did vocal "cool-downs," drank tea to soothe her throat, and waited for the ringing in her ears to stop. "Then I come back down to earth." Sometimes she had a massage or acupuncture, sometimes dinner with friends. But her socializing never involved parties or clubs. The demands of the tour were too great. "I watch films—things that get me out of my head and stop worrying...It takes me a couple of hours to unwind."[65]

Among the most difficult issues that Madonna faced was personal and involved fifteen-year-old Rocco. A tour was still a novelty for Mercy and David. For Rocco, not as much.[66] Like any teenager, he seemed most interested in testing the limits of his independence, which with Madonna did not extend very far. From the tour's start, reports described mother and elder son as being at odds.[67]

Rebel Heart reached Europe in early November. Sixteen cities, twenty-five shows, six weeks, beginning with Cologne, Prague, and Berlin. It was on arrival in a fourth city, Stockholm, on November 13 that she heard the news from Paris.

It began at nine twenty that Friday night at the Stade de France, where France was playing Germany in a soccer match. French president François Hollande was in the stands when a man wearing a suicide belt blew himself up at a security gate and killed a bystander. Within minutes, a second man detonated another suicide belt at another security gate. The crowd poured onto the soccer pitch. They feared the stadium was under assault.[68]

Outside, five minutes after the first Stade blast, a series of attacks was unleashed by gunmen in a car who sprayed five bars, restaurants, and cafés with hundreds of bullets. Thirty-nine people were killed and thirty-two gravely wounded. Four minutes after the last of those attacks, three men wearing suicide vests and carrying Kalashnikovs stormed the fifteen-hundred-seat Bataclan theater during a sold-out concert by the American band Eagles of Death Metal.[69]

People inside the theater had no idea that the city was under siege. They heard gunfire, but thought it was firecrackers detonated by rowdy fans. When the screaming began and men with assault rifles moved through the crowd, the reality of the situation became terrifyingly clear.[70] The siege lasted two hours and forty minutes. Eighty-nine dead. Ninety-nine in critical condition.[71]

France declared a state of emergency and reinforced the country's borders. Some of the perpetrators were dead, but not the men in the car. And certainly an operation of that scope had to have been the work of a larger cell. Almost immediately, officials blamed ISIS for the attacks. They were the deadliest in western Europe since the Madrid train bombings in 2004, and the deadliest coordinated terrorist attacks on civilians since the assaults in Mumbai in 2008, when twelve locations were hit by Islamist militants who killed 175 people.[72]

After that night in Paris, events around Europe were canceled because no one was certain whether the cell would strike elsewhere. Madonna took the stage in Stockholm the next night anyway. Her voice quavering, tears streaming down her face, she told the audience,

> I was going to cancel my show tonight, but then I thought, "Why should I give that to them?... Why should I allow them to stop me, to stop us, from enjoying freedom?"[73]

After a moment of silence for the victims and their families, Madonna said, "So here's what I know how to do...I hope that you will all join me, and we will sing this prayer together." With Monte Pittman on guitar, she led the audience in "Like a Prayer." Thousands of arms held lit mobile phones. Thousands of voices joined that song.[74]

Madonna continued the tour, which had become difficult professionally because it was so grueling, difficult emotionally because of the murderous attacks in Paris, and difficult personally because of Rocco. When the tour arrived in London, on December 1, he broke away from it. Madonna had reportedly taken away his phone because he wasn't doing his homework. "I feel the need to protect my kids more, and get them to focus on relationships with humans, not gadgets and technology," she said. She also worried about her sons being exposed to online porn, and she regretted giving her older children phones when they were thirteen. Madonna had since established meals as a "no-phone zone."[75]

Rocco accused her of being too controlling and said he wanted to live with his father. Guy and Jacqui, who by then had three small children, had married that summer. Within that traditional structure, Guy gave Rocco latitude to be his laddish fifteen-year-old self. Ritchie took Rocco's side in the argument. Rocco stayed in London, and Madonna left with her tour. The first stop was Amsterdam; the second was Paris.[76]

The city had been all but shuttered since the November 13 attacks. The only major performers to appear there were U2, and that wasn't until December 7.[77] Rebel Heart was due to open in Paris two nights later. There was no chance that Madonna would cancel. With the Bataclan suspects still at large, her two shows at the AccorHotels Arena had a massive security presence. But after her first performance, on December 9, she left that protective bubble.

Accompanied by Monte Pittman, her son David, and two plainclothes guards, she went to the heart of the city, to the Place de la République, which had become a memorial site for those killed on November 13. Flowers, candles, toys, cards, handmade signs, and the French flag all covered the base of the iconic statue of Marianne, France's revolutionary mother, who held an olive branch in one hand and the Declaration of the Rights of Man in the other. Madonna joined those gathered there in the rain to remember and mourn.

It was a small crowd, maybe twenty people, who heard her perform an impromptu concert. It was less a concert, in fact, than a show of respect. Singing without a microphone, she started with the postapocalyptic "Ghosttown." John Lennon's "Imagine" followed. It had been thirty-five years that week since Lennon was shot dead in New York. She ended her set with "Like a Prayer." By then, the crowd had grown, and so had the number of voices singing.[78]

By late December, Madonna was ready for her scheduled two-week break. Uppermost in her mind were her frayed relationship with Rocco and his welfare. She wanted custody. After reviewing the case, the judge sided with Madonna and ordered Rocco to return to New York, saying, "If he wants to stay with his father, he must return to his mother." But Guy's lawyer intervened.[79] And, most important, Rocco didn't want to rejoin her. He defied the judge's order and remained in London. Madonna spent Christmas without him.[80]

There was a reason Sean had been in the audience at Madonna's New York show. He needed her help. The day before, an article had appeared in the *Hollywood Reporter* that revived the old claims that Sean had physically abused Madonna.[81] The rumors concerning what happened between them in December of 1988 had, through the years, remained rumors. But Sean wanted to clear the record. His friend the historian Douglas Brinkley said that as Sean became more involved in philanthropic and political causes, he had begun to consider his legacy and didn't "want to go down in history as the guy who beat up Madonna."[82]

Sean asked Madonna to help put the story to rest. He planned to file a $10 million defamation suit against director Lee Daniels for claiming in the *Hollywood Reporter* that Sean had a history of domestic violence. Sean needed Madonna to make a statement saying otherwise.[83] She did, declaring, "Sean has never struck me, 'tied me up,' or physically assaulted me, and any report to the contrary is completely outrageous, malicious, reckless and false." Five months later, the case was settled. Daniels apologized and made a donation to Sean's Haiti charity.[84]

Long before that case was resolved, however, Sean found himself in much more serious legal and potentially physical danger. Again, he turned to Madonna when it erupted.

In October of 2015, he was writing an article for *Rolling Stone* about the costly and ineffectual "war on drugs" and had traveled to Mexico to interview a fugitive drug lord who was among the most wanted men in the world. When Joaquín "El Chapo" Guzmán was captured in Mexico three months later, a tale was spun by the Mexican government that Sean's meeting with him had been "essential" to the drug lord's capture. Even though that wasn't true, Sean feared that the Sinaloa cartel would target him as a traitor and perhaps target his family. The Mexican government, meanwhile, considered launching a criminal investigation of Sean's association with the fugitive.[85]

The day after Guzmán's arrest and on the eve of the publication of his

Rolling Stone article, Sean was scheduled to hold a high-profile fundraiser in Beverly Hills for his Help Haiti Home charity. He had asked Madonna to attend and, if she wanted to, perform. She was in Mexico City on tour but had three days before she was due in San Antonio. She said she'd come to Los Angeles and sing.[86] In the wake of the El Chapo events, her role became more important. At the fundraiser, she would deflect attention, something that came easily to her, as well as do something she rarely did: normalize things.

After her fall at the BRITs, she recalled Christopher Flynn's observation that an audience would believe whatever a performer wanted it to believe. That night at the Montage Beverly Hills hotel, Madonna wanted the crowd to think everything was fine. The focus was on Haiti and helping people in need there. Not on Mexico and the arrest of the biggest drug dealer in the Americas and Sean's alleged role in that arrest. And not on Sean's disappointment that the focus of his article, the reason he had taken chances with his life, was being lost in the controversy over his interview. He had wanted to reopen a debate about the war on drugs. No one was interested. He believed he had failed.[87]

Madonna took it upon herself to focus on his accomplishments. During a brief speech, she described the work Sean had done in Haiti and the vast and effective organization he had created. "I'm so proud of you," she said, "so proud to know you...I wanna say Sean, I love you. From the moment that I laid eyes on you, and I still love you just the same. I just wish you'd stop smoking so many cigarettes." She then sang "La Vie en rose," apologizing in advance if she forgot some of the words. "I have a lot on my mind," she explained.[88]

The song was about a lifelong romance, which was how she viewed her relationship with Sean. Both had been and would be involved with other people. But he was family, and that endured. During her performance, Madonna played the ukulele. She offered it up for auction, and it fetched $300,000. Sean, meanwhile, raised $7 million that night.[89] As for the El Chapo case, Sean, to his relief, was not targeted by the cartel, and the Mexican government didn't arrest him.

Between her twelve North American shows in early 2016 and the start of a heavy schedule in Asia and Oceania, Madonna flew to London to talk to Rocco. She could not persuade him to change his mind and live with her in New York. Heartbroken, she left for Taiwan. While she was there, a photo surfaced in the press showing Rocco smoking what was either a hand-rolled cigarette or a joint.[90]

Since living with his father, he had shaved his head and broken his wrist, and Madonna reportedly worried that he wasn't going to school. She feared that Ritchie was too lenient. Press reports described Ritchie as thinking Madonna's parenting methods "old-school" and harmful to Rocco's "self-esteem." A source close to Madonna said, "This is not a custody battle at all. This is about a mother desperately trying to protect her son." But the tour was a major impediment. "Until she is home-based, it's a hard argument for her to say, 'Come back to New York' when there's not a parent there," a friend told *People* magazine.[91]

Judges on both sides of the Atlantic urged Madonna and Guy to settle the "highly unfortunate and deeply regrettable" dispute. Until they did, a New York judge ruled that Rocco should reside with his father.[92] Other than in her songs, Madonna rarely discussed her personal problems onstage. But after that ruling, she broadcast her pain to the world.

During an early March show in New Zealand, she dedicated "La Vie en rose" to Rocco, saying, "There is no love stronger than a mother for her son...I hope he hears this somewhere and knows how much I miss him." Rocco posted on Instagram that he was staying in London and reportedly blocked Madonna from his account.[93]

Five nights later, in Melbourne, she devoted an entire show to her aching heart. Called Tears of a Clown, the special event featured Madonna dressed as a clown, performing without backup singers and with only a few band members.

The show had been scheduled to begin at 10:00 p.m. At eleven she was still rehearsing. It finally began at ten minutes to one. Some fans had left well before that, but those who remained for the two-hour show were treated to an unfiltered, emotional performance by Madonna. "If anyone thinks they came here to see a finished final show, there's the door," she declared. "This is some brand spanking new shit." She added a warning: "I didn't say this was going to be a cheerful show."[94]

The performance was so unlike Madonna that some people thought she was drunk. (A postconcert headline read: MADONNA SAYS PLAYING CHARACTER, NOT DRUNK IN AUSTRALIA SHOW.)[95] She rode a tricycle, started and stopped songs as if she were rehearsing, bantered with the audience, and candidly described the ongoing tribulations involving her teenage son. This time, she dedicated the song "Intervention" to Rocco, saying,

> There's no end to the mistakes I've made. Anyway, everybody knows the saga of me and my son, Rocco. It's not a fun story to tell or think about. I probably could have enjoyed myself a little bit more on this tour if he hadn't disappeared so suddenly, and also if I knew when I would see him again.[96]

As she sang, pictures of Rocco were projected behind her.[97] Fans didn't know what to make of it. Wrote Jon Lisi in *PopMatters,* "Is this show, the most intimate of Madonna's long career, a vulnerable cry for help and understanding, or is Madonna just screwing with us?"[98] Cameron Adams, who covered it for News Corp Australia, said,

> It was the sort of thing you never thought you'd see a superstar do…That's what made it fascinating—and difficult—to watch…she's publicly reflecting what's going on in her…personal life with a show that was out of her comfort zone and uncharacteristically loose…If you weren't a diehard Madonna fan, you were…wasting a ticket someone would have walked over cut glass for.[99]

Madonna had six more performances in Australia before her tour—all seven months, eighty-two shows, and twenty-four countries of it—was over. In Brisbane, on March 15 and 16, fans were furious that the scheduled 9:00 p.m. start was delayed until eleven thirty, just a half hour before public transportation stopped running. Hundreds walked out, demanding a refund. When she finally appeared, some people in the audience were incensed that she joked about their inconvenience. "She's just rude, she's swearing, it's just not the Madonna I know," said one.[100] The *Brisbane Times* critic called her "breathtakingly arrogant."[101]

Madonna was coming undone, but she managed to pull herself together for her last performance in Australia. She had wanted to document her tour and asked her longtime editor Danny Tull and director Nathan Rissman to shoot it. They saved the concert portion of the film for Madonna's final show, in Sydney on March 20.

Madonna started late, but she compensated her audience by performing for two and a half hours. There was no fatigue on display, no references to Rocco, no acrimonious exchanges with the audience. She was in performance mode for posterity, and she was relieved that she could finally see the light at the end of that long Rebel Heart tunnel.

Front-row seats went for just under $2,000. Despite the bad press leading up to the concert, there were no empty chairs among them.[102] What the audience witnessed that night was possibly the last big arena gig of Madonna's career, her last foray onto the megastage that she had helped create, which had become the standard for nearly every pop star after her. But she wasn't abandoning live performance. After Rebel Heart, it would just be different. An artist reflects the times, and the times, as Mr. Dylan said, were changing.

Madonna earned nearly $170 million on the Rebel Heart tour, bringing her tour total since 1990's Blond Ambition to $1.31 billion. That made her the highest-grossing solo recording artist ever and the third-highest-grossing overall, behind the Rolling Stones and U2.[103] Having sold 335 million records, she was also named the bestselling female recording artist of all time by *Guinness World Records*.[104]

Those milestones were for Madonna's music. Her brand, though, stretched across a vast landscape. She had an MDNA skin-care line; fragrances; children's books; a film production company; a clothing line for H&M; an MG Icon clothing line at Macy's; sunglasses with Dolce & Gabbana; a Truth or Dare product line, which encompassed lingerie, shoes, and purses; Hard Candy Fitness gyms and DVDs; and a stake in Jay-Z's music streaming service, TIDAL, and Live Nation's Artist Nation division, among other entities.[105] *Forbes* estimated her net worth at $520 million. She told Howard Stern that she wasn't a billionaire because "I have big overhead and I share my money with people. I take care of countries, come on."[106]

Her work, carried out at manic pace by any standard, allowed her to do good, which was a large part of the reason she did it. But the price was high. Her late compatriots in the music business told that story.

On April 21, Prince died of an accidental fentanyl overdose at his home and creative compound in Minnesota. Nearly forty years of dancing onstage — mostly in heels — had wrecked his naturally frail body. In the years before his death, he had relied on pain medication and eventually developed an addiction to opioids. A European tour had been in the works, but the idea was abandoned after the Bataclan attack.[107]

Instead, he embarked on a pared-down tour called Piano & a Microphone, which would allow him to perform without too much physical stress and in very small venues. Dan Piepenbring, who was helping Prince write an autobiography at the time, described the show as "just him and his pain and intimate settings." But even that was too much. He left the tour with what his handlers called the flu and returned home to Paisley Park, where, not long afterward, he was found dead.[108] Madonna was the last of the class of 1958 still standing.

The music business was brutal, even for someone like Prince, who had built himself a protective cocoon. For every moment of joy in the studio or onstage there existed hours of misery. The work was hard, the attention unremitting, the life dislocating. People lost themselves and the people they loved. If artists have trouble enduring the rigors of that life, the people around them often — it might even be safe to say *most* often — find it intolerable.

Madonna's crisis with Rocco was an example. On one level, he was a typical teenager rebelling against a parent. On another, he was a teenager rebelling against his superstar mother's life. In late March, just after her tour ended, a judge in Britain appealed again to Madonna and Guy to settle their custody battle.[109] It wouldn't be easy. Their relationship was described by a source in the Madonna camp as "toxic."[110]

Carlos Leon was a grounding force for Madonna during the crisis. In 2013, he had married a Danish model and fashion designer named Betina Holte, and in February of 2015 they had a son. Carlos advised Madonna to move on from her anger with Guy, and she did. She called him and said she wanted to work things out.[111]

In late April of 2016, Madonna was at her home in London when paparazzi spotted Guy Ritchie there twice in one week. The visits were brief, but they meant, presumably, that the two were talking. Rocco and Madonna were talking, too. The mother and son visited a photo exhibition at the Barbican Centre with some of Rocco's friends. The ice was thawing, but it would take until September for a final custody arrangement to be agreed upon, and it would be bittersweet. Rocco would live in London with Ritchie but make regular visits to New York to be part of his mother's life, too.[112]

Chapter 58

Washington, Havana, Miami, New York, 2016

There is still no "right" way to be a woman in public power without being considered a you-know-what.[1]

— *Gloria Steinem*

By May of 2016, it wasn't yet official, but it was clear who the candidates to replace Barack Obama as president of the United States would be: Democrat Hillary Clinton and Republican Donald Trump. It was hard to imagine two more polarizing figures. It was hard to imagine two who more clearly embodied the political, social, and gender divides in the United States. It was hard to imagine two who had more divergent visions for the country's future. As an excuse for choosing not to vote, Americans often say that voting doesn't matter because politicians are all the same. In the 2016 election, that was most definitely not the case.

Clinton's politics were born in the radical movements of the '60s, second wave feminism, and social justice campaigns. From the moment she declared — in Beijing in 1995 — that "human rights are women's rights and women's rights are human rights" (a statement remarkable for being considered remarkable), she became a global leader for women. She had done the work and made the sacrifices. Few modern US political figures had ever been so reviled, not because of what she did but because of who she was — a powerful woman who, no matter how many times she had been defeated, even humiliated, did not surrender. Feminist poet Katha Pollitt said the right had a "quasi-pornographic obsession" with her.[2]

After the shame of Bill Clinton's impeachment (which should have been his alone), she won a US Senate seat in New York. After being defeated in the 2008 Democratic primary race by Barack Obama, she accepted his offer to be secretary of state. By the time she entered the presidential campaign, in 2015, not everyone in the party loved her or agreed with her, but few would dispute that she was uniquely qualified for the job.

Trump, by contrast, was a political novice and a social dinosaur, a relic of a patriarchal past in which one's worth was measured by wealth and the ability to dominate. It wasn't public service that motivated him but an egotism that made the notoriously swelled heads in Washington seem modest by comparison. Trump was a property developer who, thanks to a TV reality show, had become a pop culture demigod. As a politician, he was a big daddy–style boss who would turn back the clock to an age when white people needn't apologize for racism, when women knew their place, and when gays and lesbians resided deep inside the closet. Every presidential contest has a crackpot candidate. It seemed at first that Trump was 2016's.[3]

Twenty-two people had put themselves forward as Republican presidential candidates: twenty-one men and one woman. From the start, Trump, the showman, commanded the field. While the traditional candidates talked policy, Trump riffed about himself, about his opponents' appearance, about his apocalyptic vision of the world. His every utterance was outrageous and largely fact-free. Even when he was demonstrably lying, the media let him natter on unchallenged. It was a phenomenon that became known as letting Trump be Trump. TV ratings soared. Trump's spotlight grew brighter, his rally crowds larger. He made politics *fun*. Earnest Hillary Clinton wasn't fun, and when she tried to be, it usually backfired.

Hillary Clinton wasn't allowed to be Hillary Clinton. Few American women who had attained positions of power did so by being themselves. They had to become creatures who were likable, attractive, and did not show anger or annoyance or fatigue or ill health. A powerful woman could be a defender but not an aggressor, and her speeches could be conciliatory and embracing but never expressions of raw strength. In the hot glare of a presidential race, a woman who tried to become that Stepford-wife version of a leader would undoubtedly appear false. Clinton did, and people hated her for it. "I just don't trust her" was a common refrain.

For Madonna, there was no question whom she would support. Since 2005, she had spoken publicly of a President Hillary Clinton. She also knew Donald Trump the way New Yorkers knew him—as a playboy, a club guy, a blowhard, part of the '80s developer crowd who bought Manhattan out from under the people who lived there.[4] Madonna became an early and fervent Clinton advocate.

The US presidential election was all-consuming. Very little news broke through the wall-to-wall coverage, and when it did, it was not good. In June, a lone gunman who claimed to have pledged allegiance to ISIS, burst into Pulse, a gay club in Orlando, Florida, during Gay Pride month and sprayed the dance floor with an assault rifle and a semiautomatic pistol. During the more than three-hour siege, forty-nine people were killed and fifty-three wounded. It was at the time the deadliest mass shooting in modern US history and the deadliest attack ever against the LGBTQ community in the United States.[5]

The response to the shooting was horror, then support for the victims, their families, and the gay community. The year before, on June 26, 2015, the Supreme Court had made marriage equality the law of the land. By then, polls showed that most Americans were ready for gays and lesbians to become part of the broad American family. Public vigils after the Pulse attack were held throughout the United States and indeed the world. In New York, One World Trade Center was illuminated in rainbow colors. So was the Eiffel Tower in Paris.[6]

In the aftermath of the murders, Madonna partnered with the National LGBTQ Task Force by helping fund its violence-prevention program, especially its work on behalf of transgender women of color.[7] Less than a month later, having corralled her four children, she left the States. For the rest of the summer, she did her best to escape the madness.

The first stop was Malawi, in early July. By 2016, she had been working there for a decade, building classrooms and schools that educated thousands of children, funding orphanages and community programs that cared for children in need. And while there was some notable progress, medical care for children was still lacking. For example, few of the doctors in district hospitals were trained to perform surgery, yet they were required to do so anyway.

Madonna met a Malawi-born pediatric surgeon named Dr. Eric Borgstein, based at the Queen Elizabeth Central Hospital, in Blantyre, who was trying to change that by going into rural areas to supplement and organize surgical care there. Madonna described him as "an angel" who dedicated his life to children. After seeing him work without adequate space and equipment, she decided to build a new wing at the Queen Elizabeth hospital and hire surgeons to help him.[8]

She got to work immediately, planning an auction fundraiser for December's Art Basel Miami Beach in the hopes of raising $7.5 million toward the project. Madonna would perform a much less angst-ridden version of her Tears of a Clown show, while friends would contribute auction items: a private poker game with Edward Norton and Jonah Hill, a week at Leonardo DiCaprio's Palm Springs home, a private performance by illusionist David Blaine, and art by Cindy Sherman, Marilyn Minter, and Ai Weiwei, among others.[9] Her son David would put the importance of the event into perspective by telling his own life story, and Sean Penn would join her onstage for pranks to keep the auction lively.[10]

But first, in August, Madonna went to Cuba to celebrate her fifty-eighth birthday. She traveled with all her children and members of the family she had created, people like Debi Mazar, Rosie O'Donnell, Jonas and Bea Åkerlund, Arianne Phillips, and Steven Klein.[11] It was a pleasure trip from start to finish. Madonna drove from the airport in a caravan of vintage convertibles and danced on a table at Havana's La Vitrola restaurant.[12] That holiday was the last calm moment before a tumultuous, even calamitous autumn.

During Madonna's journeys, the presidential race moved into the home stretch. It was a race unlike any in US history, played out across the lawless Wild West of social media. Truth was whatever you wanted it to be. Ugly and sometimes violent political rallies moved online to become hate-filled forums where outlandish conspiracy theories flourished. Meanwhile, allegations of corruption, deceit, sexual assault, financial misdeeds, and potentially illegal foreign influence dogged both campaigns. (In the case of the sex, Bill Clinton's escapades returned to haunt Hillary.)

After the two political-party conventions that summer, Clinton's candidacy survived intact, and she was seen as the front-runner. But in the United States, the metaphorical glass ceiling was made of hardened steel.[13] The sexism embedded in US life became clear during the campaign. In fact, misogyny that election season was so thick that it was choking.

On October 7, the *Washington Post* released a videotape of a conversation that took place in 2005 between Donald Trump and *Access Hollywood* host Billy Bush in which Trump boasted that he could "do anything" to women, even "grab 'em by the pussy."[14] At least twenty-four women had leveled charges against him for behavior of that nature over the course of the previous thirty years. He denied them all.[15]

Then, two nights after the *Access Hollywood* tape release, Clinton and Trump met for a presidential debate. As Hillary spoke, Trump paced behind her in full aggressor mode, hovering, invading her space. Clinton later described her emotions at those moments. Her options, she said, were to "stay calm, keep smiling" or turn around and "say loudly and clearly, 'Back up you creep, get away from me.'" She chose the former. A lifetime of training had taught her, she said, to stay calm, bite her tongue, and smile.[16]

At that moment, Hillary had a chance to show her strength as a woman leader, but she blinked. She couldn't express anger toward Trump, even when he physically menaced her. She had a chance to defend and embolden all women who were subjected to sexual harassment and assault, who out of fear for their jobs or for their lives didn't have the power or courage to say no. She had a chance to convince skeptical younger women that she was the warrior they wanted to lead them. Hillary could have, but she chose the womanly course of politesse instead. It was painful to watch. A simple "Fuck off" might have changed history. It most certainly would have changed the lives of women.

After the final debate, the odds still overwhelmingly favored Clinton. But women had been there before—not as close to the White House as Clinton had come but as close to solidifying political gains only to see them lost. Nothing could be taken for granted.

Madonna went into overdrive to support Hillary.[17] On November 7, she and other performers, from Bruce Springsteen to Lady Gaga, used music to make last-ditch appeals for support on Hillary's behalf. Most of the concerts at venues around the country were scheduled. Madonna's solo performance was a surprise.[18]

The crowd in Washington Square Park in Greenwich Village knew it was a Hillary event. Security seemed to indicate that whoever was coming was notable. At seven thirty that evening, Madonna appeared with an acoustic guitar, her eleven-year-old son, David, and Monte Pittman.[19] A woman in the crowd said, "I feel like my heart's going to explode."[20]

Wearing an American-flag stocking cap and a huge smile, Madonna said the concert was about "*keeping* American great, not *making* America great" by electing a president who did not discriminate against women, the LGBT community, or racial and ethnic minorities.[21]

Madonna acknowledged that there was an "opponent. But you know what? In life, there is always an opponent, and we have to fight against that opponent...Are we going to settle for second best?" That was her introduction to "Express Yourself."[22]

Madonna's set list during her thirty-minute concert comprised old favorites, including "Don't Tell Me" and "Like a Prayer," and that made the event a sing-along as Monte and David played guitar and Madonna sang, played guitar, and danced around the fountain. Few late-fall evenings in New York felt so warm. For those moments it seemed possible. Maybe Hillary would win. Maybe the gay and trans people in the crowd had nothing to fear. Maybe young women could envision a future free of sexual harassment, and maybe people of color could be freed from dread.

Madonna knew the audience's dreams in advance, because they were her own. She worked John Lennon's "Imagine" into her show. She said Americans had a way of killing their sages and angels, Lennon among them. A man in the crowd shouted, "What about us?" Madonna replied, "We're here to keep the fire going, to keep the flame going."[23]

Between songs, Madonna spoke, reminding the crowd that it wasn't just a concert. She had a purpose. She spoke of the chauvinism that still ruled the country, and the racism, and what a Trump victory might mean.[24] She closed her concert with two songs, "If I Had a Hammer" and "Rebel Heart."

The first was a protest song from decades past, the second her own protest story from 2015, but the message was the same: using one's voice to speak for and support one another, following one's heart, and being true to oneself. With tears in her eyes, Madonna ended the concert beseeching the crowd to vote "with your heart, with your mind, vote with your spirit, vote with your soul. Save this country, please. Vote for Hillary Rodham Clinton."[25]

Election night: November 8, 2016. Madonna's agent received updates from someone she knew in the Clinton campaign. "At one point she was like, 'It's not looking good.' It was just like watching a horror show," Madonna said. "We were doing everything: lighting candles, meditating, praying, offering our lives to God forever, if only."[26]

She went to bed not knowing the outcome. Clinton won the popular vote, but Trump prevailed in the electoral college. He would be the next president of the United States.[27] "Since that night, I wake up every morning and it's like when you break up with somebody who has really broken your heart," Madonna said.

> You wake up and for a second you're just you, and then you go, "Oh, the person I love more than anything has just broken my heart, and I'm devastated...I'm lost." That's how I feel every morning. I wake up and I go, "Wait a second. Donald Trump is the president."...It's like being dumped by a lover and also being stuck in a nightmare.[28]

When details about the voting emerged, the news became even more depressing. Women comprised 55 percent of the electorate and could have delivered the election to Clinton. Black and Hispanic women voted in record numbers for her, but a plurality of white women, who represented the vast majority of women voters, cast their ballots for Trump.[29] "It feels like women betrayed us," Madonna said. The low voter turnout—below 55 percent—was also galling. Madonna said of those people who sat out the vote, "They took their hands off the wheel and then the car crashed... We're fucked."[30]

Madonna told an interviewer weeks after the election that she was trying to figure out her response to Trump.[31] "Since Hillary lost the election, it's really important for me to make a stand and speak my mind about the importance of women, and women empowering themselves, and believing in themselves and understanding their worth."[32] She decided to "get way more vocal and become a little bit less mysterious."[33]

On December 9, she began. She used her own life as an allegory to describe a woman's journey in a sexist world made more pernicious because it was supposedly postsexist. In that environment, women were reluctant to call out misogyny where they saw it, even among themselves, for fear of appearing weak or uptight or *troublesome*. Madonna decided to start the conversation women needed to have by describing what she had lived through on her way to the top. It was without doubt the most memorable and affecting speech of her career, delivered at a time when women most needed to hear it.

Madonna had been named Billboard Woman of the Year. Begun in 2007, the award honored women who made significant contributions to the world of music. If the Rock & Roll Hall of Fame skewed toward men, the Billboard Woman of the Year award seemed to favor young artists. Reba McEntire was the award's first recipient, but in the years since, the women recognized for their achievements represented the youth wing of the industry: Beyoncé, Fergie, Taylor Swift (twice), Katy Perry, Pink, and Lady Gaga among them. In 2016, it was finally Madonna's turn.

Introduced by Anderson Cooper, she took the stage in New York and spoke words that no one had ever heard her utter. What had set Madonna apart from past stars was her invulnerability. Sure, she sang about heartbreak and wounds that would not heal, but she did it as a woman so tough that almost nothing—after thirty-four years in an unforgiving spotlight—had derailed her, much less made her crack. And yet she *had* suffered, and she was there to describe it in order to help other women embrace their pain, feel free to talk about it, and confront the forces that inflicted it.

She told her story to that audience of mostly women, some of whom had been among her harshest critics, questioning her motives, her talent, and her intelligence even as she fought bruising battles to expose sexism and discrimination. She spoke to young women in music, whom she had tried to support when she saw them being misused by the industry. She spoke, and no audience had ever listened so closely to what she had to say.

"I stand before you as a doormat. Oh, I mean as a female entertainer," said the most successful female artist of all time. "Thank you for acknowledging my ability to continue my career . . . in the face of blatant misogyny, sexism, constant bullying, and relentless abuse."[34]

Madonna described her early years in New York—being robbed and raped and losing almost every friend she had to AIDS or drugs or violence. At the start of her career, she said, she didn't think of herself as a woman but as an artist, and though she was inspired by other women, like Debbie Harry, Chrissie Hynde, and Aretha Franklin, her real inspiration was David Bowie.[35]

He embodied creative freedom, but Madonna soon realized that that kind of freedom only belonged to men. Women artists had to "play the game." They had to look good, be sexy, act stupid, stay young, and appear nonthreatening to other women when around their men.[36]

She described the period after the release of her *Erotica* album and *Sex* book as devastating. Her eyes filled with tears and her voice quavered as she described feeling paralyzed by the backlash.[37] During those moments of extreme vulnerability, she said, she wished she had a woman she could turn to for support, but she felt abandoned by women. Many of them chastised and ostracized her for supposedly undermining feminism. Madonna recalled thinking, "Fuck it. I'm a different kind of feminist. I'm a *bad* feminist.

> What I would like to say to all the women here today is this: women have been so oppressed for so long they believe what men have to say about them, and they believe they have to back a man to get the job done. And there are some very good men worth backing…not because they're men, but because they're worthy.
>
> As women, we have to start appreciating our own work and each other's work. Seek out strong women to befriend, to align yourself with, to learn from, to be inspired by, to collaborate with, to support, to be enlightened by.[38]

At times unable to speak through her emotion, Madonna tearfully thanked the people who had stood by her through the years but also those who "said I could not, that I would not, that I must not." She said their resistance made her who she was, a formidable woman. "So thank you."[39] Madonna received a standing ovation.

Her speech was reported in newspapers, online, and during television news shows around the world. It was called searing, heartfelt, caustic, funny, blunt, brutally honest, powerful, inspiring, an "emotional manifesto," a major feminist statement. What Madonna offered was what she had always offered—herself. By her example that day, she gave women license to express vulnerability without the fear that this made them "a girl." The *New York Times*'s Patrick Healy called Madonna and Hillary Clinton "sisters in arms…I can imagine Mrs. Clinton listening to that speech and just saying 'Yaaaas' over and over."[40]

The faces in the Billboard audience—some tear-streaked, some smiling—nearly all registered recognition. Madonna spoke to an audience that knew exactly what she was saying. In 1976, only 10 percent of artists with top ten hits were women. Four decades later, that figure was still a mere 27 percent. What those women had had to endure to reach minority status in an industry built around the *ideal* of women was a tale that each person in that audience could tell, ranging from simple sexism to rape. One survey found that 72 percent of female musicians experienced gender discrimination and 67 percent experienced sexual harassment.[41]

"I think women need to embrace one another," Madonna said.

> In our society, we have always wanted to pit women against each other. Strong, powerful women aren't comfortable in a room with other strong, powerful women—or they're two bitches that have to fight each other or be competitive with one another. And I think we need to get rid of those stereotypes...and be more vocally supportive of one another. Be happy for other women's success.[42]

During the '70s, when women escaped the isolation of their homes and began talking to one another about their quiet desperation, they found strength and comfort. In 2016, when Donald Trump's victory, as much as Hillary Clinton's loss, made clear how perilous the state of womanhood still was, it was time to resume that dialogue. It was time to share pain, share joy, share strength, and share knowledge. Women writers, painters, musicians, and songwriters passed that knowledge along in their work. Women on the street, in the home, in the office, in front of a classroom, on the deck of a navy ship, or in the cockpit of a plane needed to be heard, too. There were lessons of strength and survival to be learned from all of them.

Trump bizarrely congratulated himself for shattering the glass ceiling.[43] What he really did was reawaken feminism.

Chapter 59

Washington, New York, Blantyre, Charlottesville, Lisbon, 2017–2018

> To the men scratching their heads in concern and confusion: The rage you see right now, the rage bringing down previously invulnerable men today, barely scratches the surface. You think we might be angry? You have no idea how angry we are.[1]
>
> — *Ijeoma Oluo*

THE DAY BEFORE Trump's inauguration, Madonna appeared on a stage at the Brooklyn Museum with artist Marilyn Minter and poet Elizabeth Alexander. Dressed in heavy black, like a widow, she wore a shirt that read FEMINIST.[2] What feminism looked like on that day and what it might look like six months later was anyone's guess. Who would have predicted the previous six months?

Madonna was grumpy. Second wave pioneer Andrea Dworkin once said of herself, "I'm a radical feminist. Not the fun kind."[3] That was who Madonna was onstage that night. She wasn't laughing. Still smarting from the defection of white women to Trump, she feared for women, saying, "In many respects, we're still in the Dark Ages."[4]

It was in her nature to find light in darkness and a path beyond pain and disappointment. In the weeks since the election, she had found hers, though it didn't make her less angry. She told the gathering in Brooklyn that her way forward was to make a "habit" of revolution. "Start where you are...Just every day [say], 'I'm going to do something...that's going to make a small change or a big change. I'm going to think outside the box. I'm going to act outside the box.'"[5]

She said she believed Donald Trump's election was an opportunity to reject political lethargy and become united. She said there were only two paths to take, "destruction [or] creation...I'm going down the road of creation and you're all welcome to join me."[6]

Donald Trump was inaugurated the forty-fifth president of the United States the next day, January 20, 2017. He delivered a sixteen-minute speech that was as ominous as the rain clouds roiling overhead. Afterward, former president George W. Bush, a Republican, was overheard saying, "That was some weird shit."[7] And that was just the beginning.

The previous November, as the election results sank in, a Hawaiian retiree named Teresa Shook wrote on Facebook that women needed to respond to Trump's victory with a good old-fashioned protest march. Thousands of women soon agreed. As veteran organizers watched those numbers swell, they decided to make it official and give it a date: January 21, the day after Trump's inauguration. The main event would be in Washington, but marches were encouraged throughout the States.[8]

The Women's March embraced the concerns of all people worried that their rights would be curtailed by the new administration. The idea of the march was to build bridges, not walls. But women's rights—the right to one's own body, the right to determine one's future free of harassment, discrimination, and legislative interference—was the central issue.[9]

Meanwhile, a secondary project evolved alongside the march planning. Its organizers wanted to create a "sea of pink" on that day: pink scarves, pink banners and signs, and pink "pussyhats," topped with catlike "ears." The Pussyhat Project, organized by Krista Suh and Jayna Zweiman in LA, married the color associated with femininity to traditional womanly handcrafts and created a radical feminist statement. "It does reference Donald Trump and those comments," said Zweiman of Trump's *Access Hollywood* boast, "but it's so much more. It's reappropriating the word 'pussy' in a positive way."[10]

By late December, march organizers had received sixty thousand hats handmade from a single pattern and donated by women across the country.[11] Organizers had no idea whether there would be enough heads to wear them. But on the morning of the march, it became clear that the response would be massive.

More than four million people participated in 650 marches held across the United States, in big cities and small, even in areas that Trump had won. Some called it the largest single-day protest in US history. Globally, streets swelled, too, as an estimated three hundred thousand people in thirty countries, from Antarctica to Norway, from South Korea to Saudi Arabia, showed solidarity with their US siblings. Even people in Scotland's Isle of Eigg, population eighty-eight, wore pink that day.[12]

The epicenter, though, was Washington. The Women's March on Washington attracted five hundred thousand people who poured onto the Mall, chanting and carrying signs. Many read, NOT MY PRESIDENT. One sign listed the seven stages of grief, with the last stage, acceptance, replaced by the word RESISTANCE. In that city of mostly male-authored legislation, another sign read KEEP YOUR LAWS OUT OF MY DRAWERS. A new century had awakened a new women's movement. Women claimed their political power through the language of their sexual power. They were finally one and the same.

The DC gathering was thick with notable figures. A few of them climbed up onto the dais to speak during the three-hour-plus rally. Some had names synonymous with resistance. Some were politicians; some were celebrities; some, such as the Mothers of the Movement, whose sons had been killed by police, were joined by grief. Madonna wasn't on the roster, but she made a surprise appearance as the event's closer. Wearing a black pussyhat, a shirt that said FEMINISM: THE RADICAL NOTION THAT WOMEN ARE PEOPLE, and Guantánamo-orange cargo pants, she asked the crowd, "Are you ready to shake up the world?"

Speaking slowly and clearly to reach that vast audience, Madonna said that Americans had mistakenly believed that justice and goodness would prevail.

> Well, good did not win this election, but good will win in the end…The revolution starts here…There is power in our unity…no opposing force stands a chance in the face of true solidarity…So my question to you today is, "Are you ready?"[13]

The crowd hollered yes and repeated it again and again. Madonna continued,

> Yes, I'm angry. Yes, I am outraged. Yes, I have thought an awful lot about blowing up the White House, but I know that this won't change anything. We cannot fall into despair.[14]

Backed by the event's band and Monte Pittman, Madonna shouted, "Come on, girls, do you believe in love?" That was the introduction to "Express Yourself." The acoustics were terrible, it was impossible to hear the band, and the sound system was erratic, but the crowd was dancing. Thousands of pink hats moved up and down, and thousands of bodies were swaying. Madonna followed "Express Yourself" with "Human Nature," which she dedicated to Trump. The applause line came when Madonna sang, "I'm not your bitch don't hang your shit on me." She had the audience repeat it over and over. At one point she inserted the phrase "Donald Trump suck a dick." It didn't make a heck of a lot of sense, but apparently she couldn't help herself.[15]

The next morning Kellyanne Conway, the campaign strategist who helped put Trump on the road to victory, referred to Madonna's comments as a way to belittle the entire march. She criticized her "profanity-laced insults" and her joke that she thought of "blowing up the White

House." The media outlets that were uncomfortable with the phenomenon of millions of angry women seized on Conway's cue.

Republican pundit and former House Speaker Newt Gingrich said Madonna should be arrested. The White House floated the idea that the Secret Service might investigate the "threat." Even Trump piped in, employing a word he often used to describe women, *disgusting*. Wrote feminist journalist Rebecca Traister, "It was as if a massive political eruption of women had happened, and the male dominated media *hadn't even seen it*."[16]

Women, however, weren't discouraged. Revolution was in the air. In the next election, women would run for office and win. On the street, women spearheaded more protests, and very shortly the campaign for women's rights became extremely personal.

In 2006, an activist named Tarana Burke realized that women could help one another survive sexual violence simply by sharing their stories of abuse. It didn't seem like a revolutionary step, but it was. Part of the power men had over girls and women was that girls and women remained silent. Burke formed a group on social media to break the silence. She called it Me Too.[17] Ten years later, that phrase, with an added hashtag, became front-page news.

Fissures had begun to appear in the wall of male entitlement as early as 2011, when a thirty-two-year-old West African immigrant named Nafissatou Diallo, who worked as a hotel housekeeper in New York, accused the former chairman of the International Monetary Fund and the front-runner in the French presidential race of sexual assault and attempted rape. The charges were ultimately dismissed (though a civil settlement was reached), but the events brought an end to Dominique Strauss-Kahn's political career.[18]

In 2015, "America's Dad," Bill Cosby, was charged with aggravated indecent assault. In August of 2016, a group of young gymnasts, including members of the US national gymnastics team, exposed team doctor Larry Nassar's decades of sexual abuse.[19] During that same summer, women at Fox News forced the resignation of the company's CEO, Roger Ailes, over several charges of sexual harassment. Six months later, Fox's top-rated host, Bill O'Reilly, was similarly forced out (he denied the allegations). And then, on October 5, 2017, the *New York Times* carried the headline HARVEY WEINSTEIN PAID OFF SEXUAL HARASSMENT ACCUSERS FOR DECADES.[20]

Women came out of the shadows to accuse one of the most powerful men in Hollywood, and as they did so, the details became increasingly lurid and the charges increasingly serious. It wasn't simply harassment: it was rape. The dominoes began to fall. More than two hundred prominent men lost their jobs within the first year after the Weinstein headline appeared. Some of them faced criminal and civil charges. Some, including Weinstein, were convicted.[21]

For the first time in US history, men quaked at the power of women, joking nervously that they didn't know how to behave in order to avoid awakening female wrath. And rightly so. The movement spread nationally and internationally,[22] and a new generation of young women leaders was emerging.

Many came of age after September 11, 2001, during a period defined by calamities: war and terrorism; natural disasters exacerbated by climate change; the rise of populism, nationalism, and autocracy. The young women recognized their power. It resided in their brains, their voices, their hearts and spirits, their physical strength, and their examples.

Malala Yousafzai in Pakistan, Greta Thunberg in Sweden, Rahaf Mohammed in Saudi Arabia, Vanessa Nakate in Uganda, Jamie Margolin in the United States. In New York, a twenty-eight-year-old waitress named Alexandria Ocasio-Cortez decided to take her activism to Washington by running for Congress. In California, thirty-year-old World Cup soccer player Megan Rapinoe fearlessly faced the blowback over her very public stands against homophobia, sex-based discrimination, and racism on the field and off.

Those girls and young women were in the minority, but they made news by speaking eloquently and forcefully, and they allowed other young women to see themselves as leaders, too. Wrote Egyptian feminist Mona Eltahawy, "We must teach [girls] to be as loud, as visible, as troublesome, as unruly, as angry as they want so that the world knows to ignore their voice at their peril."[23] In other words, teach them to be like Madonna.

Madonna's first two decades in the spotlight were spent empowering women with her music. Beginning in 2005, she committed her time and money to helping women in places where the need was much greater than could be addressed in song. There, she focused on health and education, the best areas in which to start helping women understand their value and change their world. By 2017, her work had expanded into Gaza, Kabul, Karachi, Manila, Nairobi, the Democratic Republic of the Congo, Mali, Nigeria, and Haiti.[24]

Her work in Malawi had not abated. She had teamed with the organization buildOn and Malawi's Ministry of Education to build sixteen primary schools and one secondary school that served ten thousand children, half of them girls. And she continued to support the country's orphans.[25]

While the number of orphans had declined since 2006, as treatments for AIDS became more readily available, young women and girls remained at risk. As a matter of financial survival, they often married older men, unaware that the men were infected. Because Malawi was a conservative religious country, they could not access condoms to protect themselves or contraceptives to avoid pregnancy. "It is a vicious cycle," said Dr. Linda A. Nyondo, a health systems specialist in Malawi. "You've got issues to do with education, issues to do with poverty."[26]

It was after a visit to the Home of Hope orphanage in the summer of 2016 that Madonna decided to help two more children escape that cycle. She had met twin girls there in 2014 and reconnected with them two years later during the family's summer visit. When she returned home, she looked around and felt that something was missing. The place was too quiet. David and Mercy still lived at home, but twenty-year-old Lourdes lived on her own in New York and sixteen-year-old Rocco lived with his father in London. She thought, "Why isn't my kitchen filled with dancing children? There's so many children that need a home." Her next thoughts were "Why wait?" and "Just do it."[27]

Madonna described her decision to embark on another adoption as "inexplicable," but she had fallen in love with the girls.[28] Psychoanalysts might see another reason. Madonna's mother had given birth to six children. Now Madonna would have six of her own.

Sisters Stella and Estere Mwale were four. They had been placed in the orphanage as infants by their grandparents following the death of their mother and their father's remarriage. Madonna wanted to give them a permanent home, but she needed the permission of her children, the twins' family, and the court.[29]

She started with her own children, asking them what they thought about expanding their family. "Mercy and David were excited," Madonna said. For the older two, "there might have been, 'Oh, we have to share you with more people'—not jealousy, just an adjustment." But "eventually everyone was supportive. Lola said, 'Mom, if that's what you want and it's going to make you happy, let's go.'"[30]

Madonna arrived in Malawi to plead her case five days after the Women's March on Washington. The twins' father, identified as AM, gave his permission and said he did so without receiving any "incentives." The court's approval was the most difficult to secure. In addition to the past impediments Madonna had faced, the judge noted that at fifty-eight, Madonna was "above the age normally considered within the ranges of parenting." She required Madonna to provide medical proof that she was healthy and to designate a person who would care for the children if anything befell her.[31]

Madonna received a "clean bill of health," and her sister Melanie and her husband, Joe Henry, assured the court that they would become the girls' guardians in case of emergency.[32] After that, the court's decision came quickly. Madonna was in the courtroom with her lawyer and the twins' father when High Court judge Fiona Mwale called her a "good friend of the country" and ruled that she could conditionally adopt the twins. A government-appointed guardian would travel with them to observe the girls in Madonna's home. If all was well, the adoptions would be finalized in a year.[33]

The next day, Madonna made it public. "I am overjoyed they are now part of our family," she wrote in an Instagram post that showed her walking down a dirt road with the two girls.[34] Another post featured Madonna and all four of her adopted children, the two youngest wearing T-shirts bearing the slogan THE FUTURE IS FEMALE.[35]

Madonna returned to Malawi in July. The medical facility that she had long dreamed of building so that Dr. Eric Borgstein and the children he served could have a proper place to work and heal was ready.[36] Her idea was not simply to build a building but also to educate and train Malawians to be doctors and nurses.[37] "There is not enough indigenous staff," said Dr. Nyondo. "Most of the medical doctors that we have, within the public facility, they're either heading the institution or bogged down with administrative work. They rely on physician assistants—that's the backbone of the Malawi health system."[38]

At Madonna's hospital, medical students would receive training in pediatric health so they could bolster the ranks of the country's medical staff. "It's made some tremendous improvement," Dr. Nyondo said three years after the opening. Of the facility itself, she said, "Children come in from around the country."[39]

Madonna named the hospital after one of Malawi's children, her daughter Mercy.[40] The Mercy James Institute for Pediatric Surgery and Intensive Care was located at the Queen Elizabeth Central Hospital, in Blantyre. It was the first of its kind in the country. The sixty-bed, state-of-the-art facility had three operating theaters, which meant that very sick children, many with head injuries, no longer needed to be sent abroad for treatment. By way of thanks, President Peter Mutharika said to Madonna, "You started by adopting four Malawian children, now we are adopting you as the daughter of this nation."[41]

Dr. Nyondo said Madonna had passed "beyond the stage of a celebrity in Malawi...For me, the way I see her is as a mother whose children come from this particular area." She said Madonna's decision to name the facility after Mercy was a

game changer from my [previous] perception of her...She could have chosen to build it and name it Madonna Hospital, something like that. But to

call it Mercy James shows that she still values the links these children have . . .
She has maintained their names and broadened the horizons of these children without transforming them and dividing them off from their roots. I
think, for me, it's quite amazing.[42]

At the opening ceremony, eleven-year-old Mercy took the podium,
poised, confident, beaming. "It is a great honor to know that this hospital
is named after me, but what's more important is that it will heal many kids
and save many lives. I want to thank those who started this amazing journey with us and continue to help Raising Malawi." She thanked Dr. Borgstein, the "hands" that built the building, the artists (Rocco among them)
who painted murals, the doctors and nurses who staffed the hospital, the
president of Malawi, who supported it, and Madonna. "Thank you, Mom;
you're the bomb." Mercy ended her speech with an unexpected flourish —
a hip-hop dab. Mercy's innocence, as much as her words, was greeted with
applause and ululation.[43]

Being one of Madonna's children meant having a life of wealth. In addition, Madonna tried to give each of them what she called "world knowledge" through vast and varied experiences.[44] The downside of being
Madonna's child was that everything he or she did was scrutinized and
compared to their mother's outsize success.

Lourdes, who had left college, found her way from dance into modeling.
She decided she could make a statement about body image and diversity and
help move the profession away from using models as "silent clothing racks" to
seeing them as "personalities and artists."[45] She made her debut in 2016 in a
Stella McCartney print ad and would appear for the first time on the runway
during New York's Fashion Week. "I have a lot of people judging my every
move," she said. "It's important for me not to let it rule my life."[46]

Madonna told her, "'Remember, this shit is not real. It's not about the
money or your face or how hot you look. It's about what you're bringing
into the world and what you're going to leave behind.'" Lourdes said, "That
always shakes me awake when I get too caught up in everything."[47]

Lourdes said she inherited Madonna's "control issues" but not her work
ethic.[48] Of all her children, Madonna saw that latter quality most reflected
in David. "What he has more than anything is focus and determination,"
she said.[49] But David and the three younger children had an added difficulty that Madonna's older children did not experience: racism. Madonna
said,

For instance, if my younger children go to a place to sign up for a dance class
or gymnastics class, and they're with their nanny, who is West African,

they're told, "No, no, classes are full." Then I'll show up and say, "Are you going to tell me you have no room?" And they'll say, "Of course we have some space.". . . If people don't know they are my kids, then they are treated differently.[50]

Madonna was ready for that fight. "My family is everything," she told an interviewer that year. "Whatever I'm fighting for, it's for my daughters and my sons. I want them to have a good future. I've created an unconventional family."[51] But it was starting to look like that family had no place in Donald Trump's America.

In August, white demonstrators aligned with the nihilistic alt-right, the KKK, and neo-Nazis—all emboldened by the Trump White House—descended on Charlottesville, Virginia, spouting anti-Semitism and race hatred.[52] A counterprotester was killed, but Trump refused to blame the white supremacists for the violence.[53]

In September, Madonna packed up her family and moved to Portugal. "This is not America's finest hour," she explained. "I felt like we needed a change, and I wanted to get out of America for a minute."[54]

Chapter 60

Lisbon, London, New York, Las Vegas, 2018–2019

I think we were both just possessed, possessed by the Holy Spirit of creativity.[1]

— *Madonna*

THE DECISION TO move to Portugal was also made because David, who would turn twelve that year, dreamed of being a professional soccer player. Madonna didn't think the level of playing in the United States was as high as it was in Europe, so she scouted around for a city they could all enjoy that also had a soccer academy. She narrowed her choices to Barcelona, Turin, and Lisbon. Lisbon, she decided, offered something for everyone.[2]

The family moved into a four-story eighteenth-century neo-Arabic home in Sintra, near Lisbon, on an estate with its own lake and extensive gardens.[3] The children picked up Portuguese and entered into Lisbon life, and David joined the Benfica soccer team's youth academy.[4] Madonna prepared to explore, too. "I like putting myself in strange places and trying to survive," she once said. "I like knowing that I could figure out a way to live anywhere."[5]

Among her first discoveries were places to ride. Her favorite was the beach, "feeling at one with my horse, feeling the salt of the ocean splashing my face, getting drenched with it," she said. That and "playing with my children and hearing their laughter; the joy that brings me is my happy place."[6]

But engaging with people her own age during those first months was difficult. Hampered by the language, she said, "[I] found myself going to school and football matches. I was Billy-no-mates. I got a little bit depressed."[7] She joked that, sitting on cinder-block risers in a hoodie and sneakers, she had become "an official soccer mom."[8] That wasn't going to work for long. "I started asking around. Where's the music? Eventually I got an invitation to a living-room session" where people gathered, drank wine, and played music.[9] "You walk [in] . . . and there's this rolling, very intimate performance happening where people play, they sing, they recite poetry."[10] Madonna said, "Money had nothing to do with it. Fame had nothing to do with it. Instagram followers had nothing to do with it. It was really about passion and music and art."[11]

Cape Verde–born singer, composer, and Afro-electro pioneer Dino D'Santiago introduced Madonna to everybody, she said. He showed her *his* Lisbon, which happened to be exactly the one she was after. She felt like she was back in New York in the early '80s. "People didn't treat me any differently in Lisbon," she said. "They didn't act like I was a famous pop star or anything...I felt like I was just like everybody else."[12]

Almost immediately, she began thinking about how her own music might reflect her new life and inspirations. She told an interviewer that fall that she wanted to work with new genres and artists from a vast array of musical traditions. "It's time for me to take a different approach and really get back down to the beauty and simplicity of music and lyrics and intimacy."[13]

Madonna kept the home in Sintra, but in early 2018, she moved closer to the action, into Lisbon's Lapa Quarter, where she occupied the storied Ramalhete Palace.[14] The area was weighted with history. Even the aged trees that provided much-needed shade seemed to have stories to tell. There was also a lively café and restaurant scene. Madonna's lonely life in Sintra had ended. She told an interviewer at the time,

> On any given night you'll get a phone call saying these musicians are performing at this house, come by at 11—everything happens late in Lisbon. Sometimes there would be food, other times there would just be port to drink. Usually, all the doors would be open and depending on where you are, you can look across the River Tagus to the Atlantic Ocean. Sometimes there would be gypsies flamenco dancing.[15]

Madonna had long loved the work of the legendary Cape Verdean singer Cesária Évora and the poetic, melodic genre called morna. Through Guinea-Bissau artist Kimi Djabaté, she discovered the rhythm-heavy gumbe music brought to West Africa in the nineteenth century from Jamaica by formerly enslaved people. Through Dino D'Santiago, she heard the funaná music of Cape Verde, which often featured the accordion and lyrics that conveyed personal and political messages in coded language. And in the bars, she heard fado, the Portuguese music that described longing and loss through voice and strings: twelve-string guitars, basses, and violas. "There's something about fado and also morna. There's a kind of melancholy and a kind of sadness that is a perfect palette for me to paint from, so to speak," she said.[16]

The antidote to all that melancholy was kuduro, which she also heard in bars and clubs. That Afro-electronic music, born out of Angola's civil war, was designed to lift people up. As fast, hot, and danceable as the music in the discos and dance clubs of '70s and '80s New York, it is, in the words of musician Coréon Dú, "a celebration of being alive."[17]

For Madonna, all those sounds were fascinating and exhilarating, and then Dino blew her away. He called her and said that he had something special to show her, but he wouldn't say what. Madonna went to the designated bar. It was a rather derelict place that didn't look as though it had been used for a while, but it was full of people.[18]

A DJ played kuduro, a woman sang, people danced, and then the music stopped. The attention shifted to a group of women sitting on chairs in a semicircle. They began to play drums that they held in their laps, and then their rhythm became song as they took turns singing, and their music became dance as—one by one—they let their bodies respond to the sound.[19]

> I marveled at the age range of the women—from teenage girls to women who looked like they could be grandmothers. It was an amazing, immersive, musical, familial, matriarchal experience.[20]

The women were called the Orquestra Batukadeiras. Madonna couldn't get their music out of her head. She saw them a second time and asked Dino to contact them about collaborating with her.[21] In fact, she wanted to collaborate with *everyone* she had met and bring their music to the world.

> It was a little bit like when I saw, you know, voguers or voguing for the first time and I was like, "Whoa, this is insane."[22] I wanted to take the folk music I was listening to but make it more modern sounding, something you could dance to...I was first inspired by it, then I turned it into a challenge.[23]

Madonna went to school. She learned to sing in Creole and Portuguese, play the twelve-string guitar, and sing fado. "I also learned and understood how limited I am," she said, "and how far I have to go as a musician and singer."[24] Next, she summoned the collaborator who could best appreciate how that Lisbon sound could be applied to the troubled times.

Madonna and Mirwais Ahmadzaï hadn't worked together in ten years, but she sent him some recordings of living-room sessions. "Samples of Portuguese music—morna mostly, and some fado. And I said, 'Does this inspire you and can we make something *new* out of it?' And he did—like in a week."[25] She told veteran music writer Danny Eccleston that what Mirwais created excited her all over again.

> He comes from a school of making a whole album with an artist, an album, a body of work—not just a track. And he doesn't have any rules about how music should sound...He's also very philosophical, highly intellectual, very existential, loves to argue and debate about things, which sparks great ideas for songs. Super-political.[26] It just happens that us together is like a combustible, political, musical manifesto. If I dare say so.[27]

As soon as they began working together, Mirwais said, their "musical connection" was restored. "I was astonished, just like we never stopped."[28] Their personal relationship also slid back into familiar territory. "She thinks I'm crazy, so I'm allowed to say that I kind of see her as a slightly nuts sister."[29] "I remember one exchange with her on WhatsApp where I had to invoke Spinoza and Freud to have the last word."[30]

They started with what the music would *sound* like, not necessarily what a song would say. "We agreed on the Portuguese and Latino influences she wanted to explore," Mirwais said. It was also a given that they would break rules.[31]

> We live in a stifling mainstream world where Pop Stars bring out the same sort of song every 3 months...They change a chord, slightly change the text around and then the marketing labels take care of shouting about how great the new song is—so new and revolutionary etc...! Whereas in fact it's...more or less the same harmless banal song...Clearly, Madonna wanted to get away from the traditional "pop" format in both lyrics and in the form.[32]

Musically, her album would be about the new sounds she had been exposed to. Lyrically, it would be less about Madonna than any album she ever made. Her point of view was outward. She sang about what she saw.[33]

The first track she wrote with Mirwais, for what would be her fourteenth studio album, was an example. Madonna said the track, called "Killers Who Are Partying," was about the "unity" of marginalized people whom society tried to separate in order to more easily deprive them of their rights. It was also about her willingness to put herself on the "front line" of the fight.[34] "I felt it was really important to reflect my rage, my sense of betrayal," she told journalist Charlotte Gunn, and to assert in the lyrics that she would "take on the burdens of all marginalized people."[35]

Some critics would question how a "white woman of privilege" could know what it was like to be the Palestinian, African, or Native American in her song. Madonna responded:

> I'm a human being and they're human beings. And I've always fought for the rights of marginalized people so it's not like I woke up one day and decided I was going to be the voice of a certain minority... I am saying "No, we belong together." It's a song about unifying the soul of all humans. And I have the right to say that I want to do that.[36]

The song was inspired by morna and fado—string-heavy, slow, weary, yet hopeful. Madonna sang part of it in Portuguese, but only as much as Dino D'Santiago had taught her. To help communicate with musicians who did not speak English, he acted as studio interpreter. Madonna also sent him copies of some Portuguese- and African-inspired tracks. She wanted his opinion about their authenticity. "His approval was very important to me," she said.[37]

"Come Alive" was one of them. It was based on Gnawa music and used "percussion instruments—the krakebs—that are really distinctive," Madonna said.[38] They were made from the shackles enslaved people wore. "Once they were free, they turned what enslaved them into music... I wanted to bring that instrument back into the story."[39] The lyrics she wrote for "Come Alive" were about rejecting limitations, refusing to stifle oneself in speech or action. The track included the Tiffin Children's Chorus, which made the song a powerful combination of a hymn sung by angelic voices and the looping work song or field call sung by laborers and enslaved people.

"Ciao Bella" featured Guinea-Bissau musician Kimi Djabaté. Madonna said that as a child, he had wanted to play music, but his family and the people in his village discouraged him. He played anyway and eventually moved to Lisbon.[40] Hearing him there, she was so taken with his art that "Ciao Bella" became Djabaté's song. She ceded it to his voice and appeared almost as a guest artist.

As exciting as those collaborations were, Madonna's work with the Orquestra Batukadeiras was unforgettable. She, her son David, and Mirwais wrote what she considered a "feminist manifesto." She said she called it "Batuka" because "that's the style of music that it is... Created by women, played by women." It was an expression of joy, solidarity, and freedom.[41]

The lyrics described fighting for one's rights in the face of what felt like a coming storm. One line, about putting an "old man" in jail, sounded like a reference to Trump. But Madonna said it wasn't limited to him. "Oh gosh, pick a head of state—I think you might have a few."[42]

The Batukadeiras approved of Madonna's song because, historically, the music they played was born of rebellion. She said the batuque tradition arose out of communities of enslaved women who created music while washing their clothes in the river by forming a drum out of a ball of cloth. The "instrument" evolved: the women covered the ball of cloth in leather. And when it was taken away by "authorities and slaveowners," the women beat out rhythms on their legs. "I just love that story," Madonna said. "Their music is proof that the human spirit cannot be kept down."[43]

She described being in the studio with those women as "a religious experience...Even my children were there singing along with them. It was just a total celebration of life...You could feel the matriarchal power of these women; you could feel history."[44]

Madonna's previous three albums had been knee-deep in young producers sharing their talents on the fly with as many artists as would pay them. By contrast, the people she worked with on her new album, from the musicians she met in Lisbon's bars and living rooms to the Cape Verdean women who joined her in the studio, belonged to another world and another time — a precious world and a precious time. But there were artists from outside that world whom she wanted to bring on to the project who could help her marry the traditional sounds she heard in Lisbon to contemporary life.[45]

Madonna had let languish one of the first songs she wrote for the album as she became involved with the artists in Lisbon. When she picked it up again, she knew she needed a male collaborator to help her tell its story of desire. She thought of Swae Lee (Khalif Malik Ibn Shaman Brown), a twenty-four-year-old hip-hop artist from Mississippi. Just three years into his professional career, he had been nominated for a Grammy and had worked with Diplo, Nicki Minaj, and Beyoncé, among others. Madonna "liked the tone of his voice" and considered him a "very good writer [and] a great singer."[46]

"It was dope to hear that she loved MY music," Swae Lee recalled. "I jumped to whatever she wanted me to do."[47] The song she wanted his help with was called "Crave." Its subject was lust and longing. Lyrically, there was nothing terribly sexual about it, but its delivery was intensely erotic because both woman and man sounded like coiled springs. "Crave" managed to combine fado and the Atlanta hip-hop genre called trap convincingly and easily. It became one of the most hypnotic songs on the album.[48]

Rebel Heart alum Mike Dean, who worked on "Crave," was crucial to the new album. He helped write and produce five songs. Diplo was also back to work on a track. It was in part through him that Madonna was introduced to rapper Starrah (Brittany Hazzard), who would help her write five songs. Starrah had only been making a living from music for around three years, but in that short window she went from selling clothes at Urban Outfitters to writing songs with and for some of the biggest names in the business—Diplo, Camila Cabello, Rihanna, Drake, and, in 2018, Madonna.[49]

Many of Madonna's new songs featured a powerful sense of passion restrained, and that sound was distinctive to Starrah's music and her life. In an entertainment world where people clamored to be seen, she did her best to remain in the shadows, obscuring her face in photos, revealing only scant details about her life. Fame did not interest her. When ASCAP named her Pop Music Songwriter of the Year, in 2018—the first woman to be so honored in sixteen years—she wore a mask to accept the award.[50] She told one interviewer that she protected her privacy because "I love my day to day."[51]

Madonna had begun working with Starrah in January of 2018 in London, sorting through bits of songs and singing melodies until the pair selected five that they could develop together.[52] One of them was a prayer called "Looking for Mercy." Both simple and grand, it began as Madonna's nightly prayer and swelled into an orchestral rhapsody that transformed her personal appeal into a plea for humankind. Another was "Crazy," which she and Starrah wrote with Jason Evigan (of "Ghosttown") and Mike Dean. It perfectly blended the accordion-rich funaná musical tradition of Cape Verde, the Lisbon scene Madonna loved, and twenty-first-century America. Anyone could relate to its story about finding self-worth after a bad relationship.

As good as that song was, it felt familiar because it covered ground Madonna had traveled on *Rebel Heart*. But that was a rare moment of nostalgia. The most powerful statements on the new album were fiercely of the moment and created in response to world events.

On Valentine's Day—February 14, 2018—a nineteen-year-old hopped out of an Uber outside the Marjory Stoneman Douglas High School, in Parkland, Florida, wearing a shirt bearing the school's logo and carrying a backpack. In it, he had an AR-15 semiautomatic assault rifle and ammunition. Within six minutes, seventeen people were dead and seventeen others wounded. It was the worst high school shooting in US history.[53]

Since the massacre of mostly young children at Sandy Hook Elementary School, in 2012, there had been hundreds of deaths in mass shootings in the United States. Just five months before the Parkland murders, a gunman in Las Vegas positioned himself at a hotel window and fired one thousand bullets into a crowd of outdoor concertgoers, killing sixty people and wounding more than four hundred. The following month, in Sutherland Springs, Texas, a man with a semiautomatic assault rifle fired seven hundred rounds into a church service, killing twenty-six people and wounding twenty-two.

The response to such violence involved the recitation of a meaningless script and official inaction. Not since 1994's federal ban on assault rifles (which Congress allowed to lapse in 2004) and a relatively toothless 2007 background-check law had a US politician had the courage to do something about gun violence. By the time the Parkland gunman was headed to a fast-food joint to top up after his shooting spree, US politicians had essentially decided that the right to own weapons of war was more sacred than life itself.[54] The teenage survivors of the Marjory Stoneman Douglas massacre thought otherwise.

Their generation had never known a life without fear of violence at school; at churches, synagogues, temples, and mosques; at concerts and movie theaters. And it wasn't just in the States. The previous spring, in Manchester, England, as Ariana Grande finished the closing song of her concert there, a young man detonated a suicide vest, killing twenty-two concertgoers and injuring more than one hundred. The youngest victim was an eight-year-old girl.

The Parkland students cried out in agony for all those victims and in fury demanded action. One hundred students took buses to the Florida state capitol to force lawmakers to look them in the eye and explain their opposition to gun control. High school senior Emma González spoke through tears of rage during that event.

> They say a good guy with a gun stops a bad guy with a gun, we call BS. They say guns are tools just like knives and are as dangerous as cars. We call BS. They say no laws could have been able to prevent the hundreds of senseless tragedies that have occurred. We call BS. That us kids don't know what we're talking about, that we're too young to understand how the government works, we call BS.[55]

In record time, using social media, the Parkland students organized a national anti–gun violence event on March 24. Eight hundred cities around the globe held March for Our Lives rallies. In Washington, DC, hundreds of thousands of people showed up to demand action. And still, the Parkland students did not stop. They organized a fifty-city tour to keep the issue alive. By the end, they had registered an army of ten thousand new voters.[56] The passion of the children shook politicians, however momentarily, the way men were shaken in the wake of #MeToo.

Twenty-five states passed some form of gun-control legislation, including Florida.[57]

Stirred by González's speech, Madonna sampled part of it in a song called "I Rise." "I see Emma as a spokeswoman and pioneer of her generation," she said.[58] She had intended the song as an LGBTQ anthem, but after Parkland, the message became broader. She wanted to give "hope and courage" to hurting people who believed they were voiceless.[59] In another song, Madonna tackled gun control head-on.

Mirwais called "God Control" perhaps the first "Disco Protest Song."[60] It is the album's major political statement and one of its two most experimental tracks. Accompanied by the Tiffin Children's Chorus, Madonna sings through gritted teeth about daily life in a world gone mad. "I wanted to sing as if someone had wired my jaw shut and I wasn't allowed to speak but I *had* to speak and I was coming from a very angry place...Nowhere is safe anymore...No public gathering is safe." Gun-rights advocates argued that guns didn't kill people—people killed people. Madonna said, okay, then, control *them*. "People feel like gods when they have guns in their hands." And control *him*. Madonna's song includes a dig at Trump and his obsession with building a wall to "protect" Americans when murderers were already within the wall and had access to all the guns they wanted.[61]

The song might have become bogged down by proselytizing, but Mirwais and Madonna didn't allow it to. After her bitter spoken-sung reproach, a gunshot is followed by Madonna as a chipper morning newscaster beseeching listeners to "wake up"; Madonna reciting a childish—though crazed—rhyme; and Madonna as a crone whispering, "Everybody knows the damn truth," until finally the music crests and breaks into full-on 1970s disco. "It's a hustle, yeah...It's a con."[62]

The genius of the song is the discordance between the lyrics and the music. The lyrics are dire indeed, but the music is thrillingly kinetic. And that reflected twenty-first-century life, at least in the United States. People heard the warnings, saw the signs, and yet for the most part ignored them in pursuit of escape—in the form of food, stuff, drugs, booze, and, yes, music. Critic Sal Cinquemani called "God Control" "a euphoric, densely layered samba-disco-gospel mash-up...the most exhilaratingly batshit thing she's done in years."[63]

The major *artistic* statement on the album was a song Madonna and Mirwais wrote called "Dark Ballet." "Mirwais played the piano solo and then I started thinking about Joan of Arc burning at the stake," Madonna said. "I don't know why...that's how we inspire each other."[64] The magnificent result was unlike anything she had ever done. Cinquemani wrote, "A multi-part suite that shifts abruptly from electro-pop dirge to classical ballet and back again, 'Dark Ballet' is a Kafkaesque treatise on faith and her lifelong crusade against the patriarchal forces of religion, gender, and celebrity."[65]

Part of what makes "Dark Ballet" so new is that it successfully encapsulates more than a century of music in just over four minutes.[66] Madonna and Mirwais use "Dance of the Reed Flutes" from Tchaikovsky's *The Nutcracker* in the same way that Stanley Kubrick uses classical music in his story of social apocalypse, *A Clockwork Orange* (one of Madonna's favorite films).[67] "And then I become the storyteller who's telling a kind of Grimms' Fairy Tale... It's kind of like the way someone would tell a story on a radio show." Madonna said she wasn't singing so much as acting with her voice.[68]

In May, Madonna debuted part of "Dark Ballet" at the seventieth Met Gala, the annual glamorous fundraiser for the Metropolitan Museum of Art's Costume Institute. That year, the title of the accompanying exhibition was *Heavenly Bodies: Fashion and the Catholic Imagination,* which was also the theme of the gala. The artist who consistently embodied that theme was asked to perform: Madonna. The designer she chose to create her costume was her high priest, Jean Paul Gaultier.

They had not worked together on a performance since the MDNA tour, six years previously. By 2018, the sixty-six-year-old whom the press still referred to as the "bad boy" of fashion was winding down. He hadn't tired of fashion, but he decried the industry that required designers to churn out more products than people could wear. He was ready to look back, to assess his life's work. That year, at the Folies Bergère, in Paris, Gaultier created a cabaret show that told his colorful life story. He called it *Fashion Freak Show.*[69]

For the Met Gala, Gaultier created two costumes for Madonna. The first was a black dowager-queen dress—or what Madonna's stylist, Eyob Yohannes, called "Immaculate Goth Queen"—with a fitted bodice, a cross-shaped cutout traveling vertically from neck to navel and horizontally across her breasts, and a full floor-length skirt. The second was a virginal, diaphanous white dress with a satin cone-bra corset and a sleeve of medieval armor covering her left shoulder and arm—like something Joan of Arc might have worn.

Madonna the performance artist would finally "show" in a museum. Appearing at the top of the Metropolitan Museum's grand staircase in a brown monk's cowl, surrounded by more than two dozen similarly clad figures, she sang one of her most familiar songs, "Like a Prayer." As Joan of Arc, she followed it with a song no one had heard yet, "Dark Ballet," before ending with a cover of the late Leonard Cohen's moving hymn "Hallelujah."[70]

Madonna's mix of old and new influences continued at Donatella Versace's after-party, at the Mark hotel. Madonna was there to relax as well as to listen to the three-member Georgia hip-hop group Migos. Madonna had met Migos' twenty-seven-year-old front man, Quavo, in March at her own annual Oscar after-party, and they agreed to work together.[71] She would appear on his first solo album that fall, and he would appear as a guest artist on her new album.

Madonna said he had a large following of young people who, she believed, might be more willing to receive a lesson about the state of the world from one of their own. Diplo and his associates the Picard Brothers were tapped to produce "Future," the song that Quavo appeared on. That meant it combined southern hip-hop, trap, reggae, and French electropop. Asked if Madonna was cool in the studio, Quavo said, "She fire, actually."[72]

Her *Rebel Heart* song "Ghosttown" was about the people who survived the apocalypse. "Future" warned that, unless individuals change themselves and change the world, many people will *not* survive. That was made painfully clear that spring when Avicii, Madonna's collaborator on *Rebel Heart,* killed himself. The twenty-eight-year-old was found dead in a hotel in Muscat, Oman. His family said simply, "He could not go on any longer. He wanted to find peace. Tim was not made for the business machine he found himself in."[73]

Madonna turned sixty on August 16, 2018. Media outlets finally had legitimate reason to run stories about her age. There were profiles, pieces about her decades of influence, and collections of commentary on every aspect of her life and career. Remarkably, most of the coverage was positive. For a moment, the commentariat that routinely called her desperate (for appearing alongside younger artists she supported) and unseemly (for dating younger men she enjoyed) and who dismissed her need to create as a mere addiction to the spotlight finally cut her some slack.

Her resilience and defiance at sixty were as inspiring as the courage she had shown at twenty-six. British AIDS activist Matthew Hodson said he appreciated that Madonna owned "every element of herself" and made no excuses for any of it.

I'm a gay man living with HIV, and what I've learned is that rather than hide those bits of myself away which may make other people uncomfortable, I empower myself, and I empower other people, by being open, shameless, and perhaps even brazen about it...I'm not saying Madonna gave me that, but I look at what Madonna does, and it's the same thing, particularly now around sexuality and aging.[74]

Madonna celebrated her birthday in Marrakech. Before traveling there, she launched a $60,000 fundraising appeal for Malawi.[75] And then came the party in the desert. The guests — all dressed in traditional Moroccan attire — included her six children, old friends, and her extended professional world. The only thing that was forbidden as the party continued until dawn was Madonna's own music. She wanted a break from that self.[76]

While Madonna was in Morocco — in fact, on her birthday — seventy-six-year-old Aretha Franklin died of pancreatic cancer at her home in Detroit, the city where she famously began her singing career at her father's church. She had slowed down during the previous two years, but not by much. Aretha had released an album in 2017 and performed at an Elton John AIDS event that fall. As tributes came in from around the world, it didn't quite seem real that the woman who had entertained generations and buoyed the civil rights movement at a critical moment was gone, that her incomparable voice would be replaced by silence.

On August 20, just after Madonna's return to the States, the media's birthday moratorium on Madonna bashing ended. She was scheduled to announce the Video of the Year at the MTV Video Music Awards in New York. Organizers asked her at the last minute to mention Franklin in her remarks and describe her effect on Madonna's own career.

She appeared onstage wearing the headdress, jewelry, and caftan of North Africa's Berber, or Imazighen (free), people. The clothing was not merely a reminder of where Madonna had been — Morocco — but also represented who she and Aretha were. "A beautiful Amazigh woman is one that is fierce and strong and powerful and can work hard," said Cynthia Becker, a Boston University expert on North African art. The coin necklaces Imazighen women wore were musical, creating sounds when the wearer moved, allowing her to become her own instrument.[77] The press pulled out the old chestnut of cultural appropriation, then accused Madonna of disrespecting Aretha during her two-minute remarks by talking about Franklin's impact on her own career (as organizers had asked her to do).

Unquestionably, she went on longer than necessary recounting her own creative "birth" narrative, but the uproar certainly did not fit the crime. The same thing happened when Madonna performed a tribute to Prince at the 2016 Billboard Music Awards. Her renditions of his songs (one of which she performed with Stevie Wonder) supposedly stained the memory of the Purple One. Did Madonna ever do *anything* without criticism? Not often. But in a way, it was confirmation of her power that she remained a lightning rod for controversy. Critics said Madonna always made any event about herself. But by making her the headline story, they did, too.[78] "The pressure to be silenced comes and goes," Madonna remarked. "Let's see what happens when my record comes out."[79]

David remained in school in Portugal while Madonna and her three younger daughters lived in London during the week and traveled on the weekends to see him. Madonna had been in the studio toiling twelve to eighteen hours a day and "living in a permanent state of guilt" about the children.[80] "In the back of my mind, I'm always thinking, *OK, what is my son doing right now? What is my daughter doing right now? I haven't spoken to David yet. I've got to be there for them*...My head is in a whirl."[81]

Finally, after eighteen months of work in Lisbon, London, New York, and Los Angeles, she, Mirwais, and Mike Dean were putting together the final mixes. The project was still "shrouded in secrecy." Thanks to leaks, *Rebel Heart* contained almost no surprises on its official release date. On the new album, by contrast, nothing was revealed that Madonna did not want revealed. It wasn't just a matter of business; it was also in keeping with the album's theme.[82]

Lisbon was a city of secrets and spies. During World War II, it was called the Capital of Espionage because all sides of the conflict hid spies among the diplomatic corps and because writers who specialized in spy thrillers took up residence there. Madonna became one of their characters. In April, she announced the title of her album, *Madame X*. That person was many things: a professor, a dancer, an equestrian, a prisoner, a "secret agent traveling around the world changing identities, fighting for freedom." The list was extensive and ended with "a spy in the house of love." Oh, and the lady wore an eye patch.[83]

Around the time that she disclosed the name of her new project, she also announced her collaboration with twenty-five-year-old Colombian superstar Maluma (Juan Luis Londoño Arias). He was a reggaetonero, an artist who combined hip-hop, rap, and EDM with Latin American and Caribbean sounds.[84] They had met at the VMAs, where Madonna was criticized for her Aretha Franklin comments. Maluma may have missed that controversy because he was at the show to make history as the first solo Latino artist to perform entirely in Spanish. Before he took the stage, his manager arranged for him to meet Madonna. They spoke, and Maluma kissed her, took her hand, and thanked her for making "music history." Then he took the stage.[85]

VMAs performances were either so choreographed that they felt like Las Vegas revues or designed to deliver a moment so "shocking" that an artist could be assured of making the next day's headlines. Maluma's act was neither. It was old-school sexy and intimate. When he went into the audience to dance with Camila Cabello and invited her mother to join them, he teleported the crowd out of Radio City Music Hall and into a bar in Medellín. Madonna told him afterward that he was "ready for the next level."[86]

Not long after the VMAs, Madonna and Maluma were both in London, she in the studio, he onstage. "She texted me...and she told me that she wanted to do a song with me that was called 'Medellín'...I almost had a heart attack." That was his hometown.[87] They went into the studio immediately and got to work. Maluma proposed beginning the rap portion of the song in a macho, aggressive style. "But she said, 'No. That's not who you are. You are sensuality. Try to do it as if you had the woman of your dreams in front of you.'"[88]

Maluma and Madonna had several studio sessions, some in Los Angeles, some in London, starting in the evening and lasting until four in the morning. They created two songs, "Medellín" and a playful track called "Bitch I'm Loca." For both songs, with Maluma's help, Madonna learned to sing some of the lyrics in Spanish. She also recorded vocals for Maluma's single "Soltera," which would be on his forthcoming album, *11:11*.[89] "We just had a beautiful connection," Maluma said.[90]

Their partnership was so rich that Madonna asked Maluma to perform with her in a video for "Medellín" and at the Billboard Music Awards that May. He accepted both invitations eagerly. "I think this is something big for our [Latin music] industry," he said. "I want the whole world to feel pride at this step I'm taking—not just as an artist, but culturally."[91]

In March, Madonna moved out of the rented palace in the Lapa Quarter. The promotion of her album meant that, for the next few months, "at home" would mean "on airplanes." The *Madame X* publicity campaign had all the precision that the *Rebel Heart* release lacked. After a drip feed of teasers on Instagram, it officially kicked off on April 14 with a ninety-second video.

Created by Portuguese director Nuno Xico, featuring Steven Klein images, it introduced Madonna's multifaceted character Madame X. Three days later, Madonna released "Medellín" as the album's first single. Mirwais said,

> In Trump's America, where the Latinos are insulted just about every day, and where the minorities are provoked all the time, the fact that one of the principal American superstars, who's white, has chosen a lead single duo in English and Spanish with a Colombian is a very strong political sign.[92]

Written by Madonna, Mirwais, Maluma, and the Mexican songwriter-producer Edge (Edgar Barrera), "Medellín" combines Latin pop and house with a classic Cuban cha-cha-cha beat.

Upon its release, some critics expressed surprise, and some expressed outright delight. Charlotte Gunn, writing in *NME,* said, "Madonna is back, bitches...the track is everything we want from a Madonna come-back: it's fresh (arguably her best work in years), it sets the tone for a brand-new era."[93] Madonna would argue that it wasn't a *new* era—that she had come "full circle." She was the person she had been at the start of her career, creating in an environment of pure inspiration.[94]

"Medellín" charted in the top ten in eleven countries and extended Madonna's dominance of the Billboard Dance Club Songs chart by giving her a forty-seventh number 1 single.[95] The video for "Medellín" helped it reach those peaks. Its directors, Barcelona-based Diana Kunst and Mau Morgó, were new to Madonna's world. She had seen Kunst's work and was impressed by her painterly style, her color palette, and the fact that she was inspired by women surrealist painters. "I wanted this video to look like a painting," Madonna said. "I just vibed with what she was interested in culturally."[96]

Kunst and Morgó shot the video at the Quinta Nova da Assunção palace, near Madonna's home in Sintra. "We worked eighteen hours a day and it was freezing cold," Madonna said, "and I had to ride a horse at six o'clock in the morning with one eye [covered by an eye patch]. I had a ball."[97]

The story line features a woman disappointed in life and love who has been kidnapped, abused, hurt, and humiliated. That information is imparted by Madonna in silhouette, kneeling in prayer, before declaring that she must take charge of her life. "From now on I am Madame X," she announces. "And Madame X loves to dance because you can't hit a mov-ing target." She is, in other words, Madonna. Let the show begin.[98]

Wearing a black bob wig, red leather eye patch, crisp white shirt, black tie, and slim black midcalf skirt, Madonna counts out a cha-cha beat alone in a tiled and mirrored room in an eighteenth-century palace. But not for long. Maluma and his crew of a dozen dancers come in to join her. Madonna and Maluma's dance-floor seduction lands them in bed for champagne and hijinks, which soon lead to a Dionysian wedding banquet peopled with characters wearing jeweled masks, facial markings, and an array of colorful attire representing many cultures.[99] It is an otherworldly scene worthy of Hieronymus Bosch, James Ensor, or Peter Greenaway—if those painters and that director had worked in the saturated colors of the Renaissance.

Meanwhile, clad in a wedding dress, a white cowboy hat, and a silver eye patch, Madonna dances down a long table overflowing with libations. At dawn, bride and groom—she in her wedding dress on a black horse, he in a red velvet jacket on a white horse—ride through the countryside together, presumably en route to a happy ending.[100]

Several memorable moments in the video raised eyebrows, including Madonna's decision to lick Maluma's toe during their bedroom scene. She said it wasn't planned, but she found him "a beautiful man from head to toe."[101] The closing horse segment was Madonna's idea, too. She feared that Maluma had never ridden; when she pointed to an Arabian stallion and told him to hop on, he hesitated. He owned horses, but not stallions. "Fuck it," he said to himself. "Let's go." After a night of magic, what was there to fear? He galloped away.[102]

The chemistry between Madonna and Maluma was so strong that, remarkably, the vast majority of critics reviewing the video did not mention the difference in age between the bride and groom. The video was so good—or at least so visually overwhelming—that they forgot to be ageist.[103]

A week after the video's release, Madonna and Maluma performed together at the Billboard Music Awards. But it wasn't just one Madonna onstage. Four holograms representing various *Madame X* personae danced with them. Artists had played with the hologram concept for years. In 2007, Celine Dion performed a duet with a hologram of Elvis; in 2012, a life-size Tupac Shakur performed with Snoop Dogg and Dr. Dre; and in 2014, the late Michael Jackson moonwalked across the Billboard Music Awards stage. But no one before Madonna had performed with several holograms, and no one had re-created themselves in that form.[104]

The rehearsals for the performance began months earlier in London.[105] The first challenge for the Billboard show was to scan and reproduce Madonna in three dimensions performing as four characters: a bride, a secret agent, a dance instructor, and a funaná musician. The next step was to make the holograms perform alongside Madonna, Maluma, and a dozen dancers.[106] By the time Maluma came into the process, changes were still being made. He said that after most rehearsals, he wouldn't get home until two in the morning. "I was like, 'Oh shit, I've never rehearsed like this in my life.'"[107]

In the days before the show, held at the MGM Grand Garden Arena, in Las Vegas, the buzz raised expectations to nearly unattainable heights. Madonna's five-minute segment, which cost $5 million to create, was billed as "one of the most ambitious performances ever attempted on live TV." Details leaked about behind-the-scenes concerns. "Obviously, a lot could go wrong," one insider offered.[108] In the end, the performance was flawless.

It began with Madonna awakening in a CGI Garden of Eden. As she sang, her first "hologram self" appeared—the secret agent—followed by the musician, the bride, and the dance instructor. Maluma entered from another part of the stage, singing and dancing with Madonna's holograms on a set designed to look like a street in Lisbon. It only became clear that none of the Madonnas onstage were human when she emerged singing from the building behind Maluma.[109]

By that point, Madonna and Maluma were so comfortable together that they performed like the storied dance partners of the 1940s and 1950s. Maluma moved out of the center spotlight for a moment while Madonna danced with her four hologram selves. The scene then shifted downstage to a Lisbon bar interior with a dozen real dancers and Maluma singing his verses alone. When Madonna arrived at the bar, their performances converged.[110]

The couple led the cast, musicians included, into the audience in a conga line, Madonna's arm over Maluma's shoulder as they sang.[111] At the end of the number, Madonna and Maluma were left alone onstage, holding on to each other. "Maluma, baby, thank you," Madonna said. "Madonna, baby," he replied, grinning.[112]

Because of the nature of the technology, TV viewers were treated to the full hologram experience. The people in the arena, however, only saw it if they watched the performance on the screens above the stage. Onstage, there were no holograms, just people doing a song-and-dance routine and sometimes gesturing strangely into the void.[113] That was one area where technology robbed the live performance of its magic. Cell-phone use was another.

People close to the performance were on their feet dancing. Elsewhere in the hall, however, thousands of people stood stock-still recording the event on their phones, trading the intensity of the live performance for the ability to relive it in absurd miniature on another day.

Reviews of the performance, meanwhile, were mixed and appeared largely on social media. Increasingly, that world drove mainstream media coverage. Some entertainment outlets relinquished the critic's chair altogether to a Greek chorus of Twitter and Instagram posts—the more extreme the better. Instead of articles about the artistry of a performance, coverage was reduced to: I love it. I hate it. She's too old.

But *Forbes* magazine recognized in the "Medellín" performance a signpost of two important cultural trends. First, it acknowledged the emerging global music market. Second, it showed that technology could create a "mixed reality" free of cumbersome headsets and goggles. Technology expanded an artist's repertoire, the article said, but the social implications were ominous because it undermined the trustworthiness of reality itself.[114]

★   ★   ★

The Billboard performance ended the first part of Madonna's *Madame X* prerelease campaign. It was time to drop another single. On May 3, she did, with "I Rise."[115] Mirwais had said the decision to release "Medellín" first could be seen as a rebuke to the anti-immigration hysteria gripping the States. Releasing "I Rise" as the second single was a response to the virulent antigay rhetoric abroad in the land.

The debut was also tied to an event that took place the following day. GLAAD selected Madonna to receive its Advocate for Change Award. She was only the second person ever to receive it; the first was former president Bill Clinton, in 2013. In announcing the 2019 award, GLAAD president, Sarah Kate Ellis, said, "Madonna always has and always will be the LGBTQ community's greatest ally."[116]

Each generation has its female "gay icon," from Mae West to Elizabeth Taylor to Judy Garland to Bette Midler. But for many—perhaps most— LGBTQ people born between 1960 and 1980, *the* female icon is Madonna. Said British author Matt Cain,

> A friend of mine and I always joke that if you get more than two gay men of a certain age—over about forty-two, forty-three—in a room, the conversation has turned to Madonna within half an hour, sometimes within ten minutes, every time. What she has meant to us, what she meant to us growing up on a kind of fundamental, primal, existential level, is impossible to exaggerate.[117]

GLAAD's thirtieth-anniversary event was held at the New York Hilton Midtown. Madonna received the award from three people: Anderson Cooper, queer hip-hop star Mykki Blanco, and Rosie O'Donnell. Cooper and Madonna often traded introductions at awards shows. That night, his was personal as he described Madonna's decades of work on behalf of the gay community and her importance in his own life as a gay teenager confused and struggling with his identity. Cooper said, "No single ally has been a better friend or had a bigger impact on acceptance for the LGBTQ community than Madonna, it's that simple." Blanco followed.[118]

Like Madonna, Blanco, who uses the pronouns "they" and "them," lived in Lisbon to escape "Trump's reign of terror."[119] One day, Madonna called to say she wanted to talk to them about her video for "Dark Ballet." She envisioned them playing Joan of Arc *and* Mykki Blanco.[120] Proposing the idea to Blanco, she said, "Think about if you had existed in her time, you would have been burned at the stake as well."[121] In some cultures they would still be killed for being themselves.

Born Michael Quattlebaum Jr., they fled North Carolina at sixteen, bound for New York. Blanco was ready for its streets. "When you've been called a faggot every single day since you were six years old, there comes a point when you stop crying and you become quite hard," they said. Blanco became a most unusual rapper—a six-foot-plus Black man in full drag—and created a genre called queer rap.[122]

For all their brave honesty, Blanco was being eaten alive by a secret. In 2011, just as they made their breakthrough as a rapper, they were diagnosed as HIV-positive. In 2015, they decided they could no longer bear the weight of it. Risking what they expected to be a career-ending move, they announced they were positive. Instead of being shunned, Blanco said, the support they received "surprised the fuck out of me."[123]

And then, a few years later, Madonna came calling, and Blanco agreed to appear in her video. "For her to reach her hand out and lift me up creatively to her level…that does mean something to me. This project has exposed me to an audience that might not have been within my reach."[124]

At the GLAAD awards, Blanco refused to divulge their top-secret project, but they described the thrill of being directed by Madonna. Blanco also described the ways in which Madonna had opened the door for queer artists—with her example and tenaciousness and friendship. After Blanco, it was time for one of Madonna's oldest friends to tell her story.[125]

Rosie O'Donnell and Madonna had remained central to each other's lives since they met, in 1990. Rosie recalled those early days as relatively innocent. It was before social media, when "Trump was just an asshole who lived in a gold apartment." Of Madonna, she said, she had watched her grow from a "motherless daughter" to a mother of six, from pop star to "global philanthropist," all without changing who she was—a person who does what she thinks is right, even if everyone else thinks she's wrong.

> I want to thank you Madonna, the big sister I never had…for helping me live my most authentic and meaningful life…Madonna, MoMo, I love you more than I can say.[126]

Madonna approached the podium as "I Rise" played through the hall. It was her turn to tell her tale, which, it is safe to say, nearly everyone in that audience knew by heart. Detroit. Christopher Flynn. Her first gay club and the joy she felt there. The exhilaration of early New York and the way AIDS had killed it.

> It made me want to shout from the top of the Empire State Building, "What the fuck is going on? Why are we losing all the beautiful people?"…I decided to take up the bullhorn and really fight…I had to get on the frontline no matter the cost.[127]

She linked her work in Malawi directly to her experiences during the early days of the AIDS crisis and described her activism in that country as its natural extension. She also saw the irony of meeting four of her "beautiful children" amid that misery. "Death and loss brought me new life, brought me to life, brought me to love."[128]

When she finished, the crowd was on its feet applauding, faces stained with tears. Madonna's was, too. The GLAAD speech was a companion to her Billboard Woman of the Year speech, given the previous year. In the latter, she spoke of the travails of being a woman. At the GLAAD awards, she expressed her joy at being an artist and being alive.

On the day of her GLAAD award, Madonna announced her plan to take *Madame X* on the road. For years, she had talked about an intimate tour in small venues, where she could interact with the audience in a club setting, mixing music, humor, and dance. She wasn't alone in thinking small. Prince's 2016 tour, Piano & a Microphone, had played at theaters. Bruce Springsteen performed a Tony Award–winning show on Broadway in 2017. But Madonna said that what persuaded her to finally do it was Gaultier's *Fashion Freak Show,* in which he combined all the elements they both loved with a healthy dose of madness.[129]

Chapter 61

Tel Aviv, New York, 2019

It is no longer a question of how many records she sells, but of continuing to do what she has always done better than anyone else: to make us think. To inspire us to take action.[1]

—*Donatella Versace*

THE *MADAME X* rollout had been unusually controversy-free. That ended with Madonna's decision to perform on the closing night of the Eurovision Song Contest. An Israeli won in 2018, which meant that Israel would host the 2019 event in Tel Aviv. Immediately, pro-Palestinian activists called for a boycott. The European Broadcasting Union, which organized the Eurovision event, stood by its decision, saying that Israel had won the right to host the show. Meanwhile, no contestant who was scheduled to compete withdrew.[2] Just as the boycott effort started to fizzle, it revived with the news that Madonna might perform. Pro-Palestinian groups pleaded with her not to.[3]

Madonna's relationship with Israel was long and deep—through Kabbalah, through her many visits to the country, and through her associations with its leaders, from opposition figure Tzipi Livni to Prime Minister Benjamin Netanyahu. What was less recognized was her involvement with Palestinians. Madonna's Ray of Light Foundation supported projects in the West Bank and Gaza and paid teachers' salaries at UN-funded schools in Gaza after the Trump White House cut funding. In fact, as her work on behalf of Palestinians became known, she earned the enmity of some Israelis who joined the chorus of critics telling her to stay home.[4]

She ignored them all, saying, "I'll never stop playing music to suit someone's political agenda, nor will I stop speaking out against violations of human rights wherever in the world they may be."[5] Arriving in Tel Aviv with Quavo, twenty-five dancers, forty backup singers, and thirty tons of props, she then annoyed event organizers because she wouldn't allow them to approve the content of her act.[6] Madame X didn't divulge secrets, and Madame X did as she pleased.

★   ★   ★

The challenge of the Eurovision performance was not unlike that of the Super Bowl. The crew had only a few minutes in the middle of an ongoing production to build and disassemble an elaborate stage set, in this case one that re-created the grand stairway at the Metropolitan Museum of Art through a combination of props, lights, and video. The segment's opening would basically follow the script written for the Met Gala. Brown-clad monks lined the stairs, chanting as a cloaked Madonna appeared at the top, singing "Like a Prayer."[7]

As she descended the stairs to the first landing, five monks broke away from the pack, as they had in New York, to reveal themselves as virgins. In Israel, the young women wore white dresses, crowns of flowers, and gas masks. Madonna, too, had changed since that earlier performance. She had gone full Joan of Arc, and because she was Madame X, she wore an eye patch. Alone with her gas-masked virgins, she spoke the ominous words from "Dark Ballet," using the *Grimms' Fairy Tales* voice of her recording.[8]

Behind her on a screen were projections of men dressed in the ceremonial garments of the world's major religions. As Madonna intoned the word *howl,* a mighty gust knocked over everyone onstage, and the screens behind them showed raging fires. With that, she began "Future," and the screens showed cities destroyed by war. Quavo picked up the song as Madonna danced with her revived virgins and six male dancers (also in gas masks) to the reggae beat that felt, after "Dark Ballet," like a chance at rebirth.[9]

The scenes of devastation on-screen turned into a starry night sky. The dancers removed their gas masks. Peace and reconciliation were in the air. The dancers mounted the stairs in pairs, supporting one another as a picture of the Earth taken from space floated on-screen. Finally, a man and woman climbed the stairs arm in arm, their backs to the audience. One displayed a Palestinian flag, the other an Israeli flag. The silhouettes of a mosque, a synagogue, and a church appeared, followed by the words WAKE UP. Madonna and Quavo disappeared.[10]

Duncan Laurence of the Netherlands won the Eurovision Song Contest that night, but his triumph was drowned out by the global rant over Madonna's performance: what she wore (inappropriate) and how she sang (badly). Most egregious of all, however, was what she said. *She seemed to have an opinion about the state of the world that she wanted to express!* Much of that criticism came from people who hadn't followed her career, who had no idea about her involvement in the region, and who didn't know that Palestinian and Israeli symbols had featured in her shows for at least fifteen years. Her admonition to "wake up" wasn't random: it came from her song "God Control." Under the circumstances, it didn't seem like bad advice.

*   *   *

Madame X would be one of the most visual albums Madonna had created in years. For *Rebel Heart,* she made only three videos. For *Madame X,* she would release six videos based on songs and two promotional films.

Video number two, "Crave," dropped in late May. It was the work of Portuguese director Nuno Xico, who would be responsible for many of the *Madame X* visual materials. An unfinished version of the video had leaked ahead of the Eurovision show, but it barely registered. When it was officially released, the video still caused a stir because it was as daring as the song.

In it, Madonna is back in New York on a rooftop, the scene of her rape as a young woman. Now, so many years later, she puts herself in that place as a grown woman, powerful and whole, one who knows what she wants. That is one part of the song's message, described in notes Madonna sends in the video via carrier pigeons. The first and last messages bear the title of Carson McCullers's 1940 novel, *The Heart Is a Lonely Hunter.* On the receiving end of her notes is Swae Lee. His entry into the video tells the other side of the story and returns the song to its roots: pure lust.

Madonna's romantic contretemps with Maluma in "Medellín" is frisky. She moves into more dangerous territory with Swae Lee and "Crave." It isn't that they interact sexually. In fact, they barely interact at all, only coming together in the last frame of the video to touch forefingers. But the visuals project heat involving a white woman and a man of color less than half her age. That kind of pairing occurs routinely in videos by male musicians. In fact it would be a major statement if those men cavorted with a woman *their own age* on-screen. But for Madonna to reverse that equation in the first two videos from her album was exceptional.

There was one more event on the *Madame X* prerelease calendar, and it remained in groundbreaking territory. The video for "Dark Ballet," which became available on June 6, was a visual reminder of how far from the mainstream the album was. Among other things, Madonna made only a cameo appearance in it. She had relinquished the starring role of Joan of Arc to Mykki Blanco.

The video was directed by a thirty-year-old Ghanaian-Dutch filmmaker named Emmanuel Adjei, with Madonna, according to Mykki, acting as the video's "co-director and chief choreographer."[11] It began with a written quotation attributed to Joan of Arc:

One life is all we have and we live it as we believe in living it. But to sacrifice what you are and to live without belief, that is a fate more terrible than dying.[12]

That was the video's theme. The opening shot shows that living one's beliefs isn't easy, even for a person prepared to accept martyrdom. Mykki—at the stake, about to be burned—stands sobbing. The video flashes back to events that brought them to that point. Wearing a simple tunic, alone in a cell, possessing only a cross and their fear, Mykki must face a religious tribunal consisting of men in elaborate clerical garb.[13]

In a variation of Christ's words on the cross, Mykki calls out, "Help me, God." The video then becomes their wild imaginings, as they dance and plead their case to religious figures who mock and reject them. Mykki/Joan is sentenced to death. A group of silent nuns watches them burn. But Joan of Arc/Mykki Blanco/Madonna—like all artists, spiritual guides, and political figures with the courage of their convictions—does not die, so the video implies, because they live through the people they have inspired. The final quotation is Mykki's:

> I have walked this earth, Black, Queer and HIV positive, but no transgression against me has been as powerful as the hope I hold within.[14]

On June 14, the waiting ended. *Madame X* was released. It would be Madonna's first truly international album, sung in English, Spanish, and Portuguese, with African, Portuguese, Spanish, Colombian, Brazilian, Caribbean, French, and North American influences. Mirwais called it a "global futuristic album"—"global" because it was about sharing cultures and repudiating the cultural nationalism favored by autocrats and populists and futuristic because it foretold where the music industry was headed.[15]

Madame X represented a marker in Madonna's career as important as *Like a Prayer* and *Ray of Light*.[16] Like those previous albums, it took an entirely new direction lyrically and musically. In fact, it showed Madonna speeding down the highway called Artistic Risk. Rob Sheffield, in *Rolling Stone,* wrote, "*Madame X* is so admirably bizarre that all you can do is stand back and watch the girl go."[17]

The album went to number 1 on the Billboard 200 chart in the States, her ninth studio album to do so. It also reached the first or second spot in ten other countries. Erica Russell, at MTV, saw Madonna's continued success as reason for all women artists to celebrate, especially young women. "She remains relevant because, quite frankly, she's still here; still uncompromising and still reinventing; still flipping off a culture that seeks to push her out. And still breaking new ground for the artists who came after her."[18]

Madonna said simply, "I'm going to make it easier for all those girls behind me when they turn sixty. I hope they appreciate it."[19]

★   ★   ★

Five days after the album's release, the video for "I Rise" was released. "Dark Ballet" depicts an ancient battle. "I Rise" features a montage of modern horrors, from the Parkland school shooting to the contaminated-water crisis in Flint, Michigan; from the arrest of Philippine journalist Maria Ressa to the heartbreak of war; from the fires and floods of climate change to the dislocation of millions of migrants.[20]

It also features moments of courage: Emma González at the start of the video, challenging the government with her accusation "We call BS"; the Women's March, Black Lives Matter protests, pro-immigration rallies; gay marriage triumphs, gay rights marches; and Olympic gymnast Aly Raisman's brave testimony against Larry Nassar.[21] Madonna, who does not appear in the video, said she wanted to empower people by showing that honesty with oneself and unity with others open the door to change, if not revolution.

The release of the "Dark Ballet" and "I Rise" videos were gifts to the gay community, which was gearing up that month to celebrate the fiftieth anniversary of the LGBTQ big bang, the Stonewall uprising. That year, the international festival called WorldPride would be held in New York in honor of the 1969 rebellion.

Planning in the States had been underway for ten years. Madonna had been named a Stonewall ambassador and kicked off the 2019 celebration during a surprise performance at the Stonewall Inn on New Year's Eve. By then, the dive bar had become a national monument, designated as such by President Obama. Madonna and her son David sang "Like a Prayer" and covered Elvis's 1961 hit "Can't Help Falling in Love." After that, gay-themed art and historical exhibitions, performances, and readings were held every month. In June, that trickle of events became a great cascade.

Politicians, entertainers, and the media stumbled over themselves in the rush to be part of WorldPride. New York City's police commissioner, James O'Neill, issued a belated apology for the police actions in 1969 that caused the uprising.[22] That peace offering set the tone for the festivities. Crowds throughout Pride month expressed anger at the Trump administration and Republican lawmakers throughout the country for trying to curtail gay and trans rights, but the overall feeling was unfettered joy. By June 28, the uprising's anniversary, five million people had converged on Manhattan to celebrate. It would be the largest LGBTQ event in history.[23]

To mark it, Madonna released one of the most powerful and controversial videos of her career: the one for "God Control." Directed by Jonas Åkerlund, it begins with a warning: the viewer is about to see graphic violence. But, the text says, that violence reflects real life, "and it has to stop."

The sound of police sirens follows. A time stamp says it is 3:00 a.m. That is when the June 2016 attack on the Pulse nightclub in Orlando, Florida, ended, and that is when Madonna and Åkerlund's fictional retelling of that tragedy begins.[24]

The video is split into four parts. The viewer sees the nightclub dance floor and revelers dressed to the nines partying to Madonna's song. She dances in a blond bob wig among them while a gunman with an assault weapon opens fire at close range. Bodies drop where they are, one on top of another. The second narrative begins six hours earlier, as Madonna prepares to go out for a night of fun. That is not possible in a world awash in weapons. She is mugged at gunpoint on the way to the club.[25]

The third and fourth parts of the video take place outside that club narrative. One shows Madonna sitting in a room at a typewriter, surrounded by photos of Frida Kahlo, Simone de Beauvoir, Angela Davis, and Martha Graham, holding her head in despair, typing out the words to "God Control." The other features footage of protests after the Parkland shooting and antigun rallies after *all* the mass shootings. Signs read, WE ARE NOT TARGET PRACTICE; BAN ASSAULT RIFLES; AM I NEXT?[26]

Toward the end of the video, Madonna, at the typewriter, looks straight into the camera as tears spill down her cheek. The screen goes dark. Two words appear: WAKE UP. The video ends with two sets of text. One is a quotation by Angela Davis:

> I am no longer accepting the things I cannot change. I am changing the things I cannot accept.

It is followed by statistics: thirty-six thousand people are killed by guns in the United States each year, and approximately one hundred thousand more are wounded. Words appear on the screen: "No one is safe. Gun control. Now."[27]

The video was released on Wednesday, June 26. By the following morning, one million people had watched it.[28] Madonna was immediately condemned for apparent insensitivity to the forty-nine Pulse victims' families and the many people wounded in the attack.[29] Parkland survivor and gun-control activist Emma González criticized her, calling the video "fucked up" and "horrible." "This is not the way to talk about gun violence," she said. "If you want to support the gun violence prevention movement, donate to the places who need it."[30]

In fact, upon releasing the video, Madonna had posted lists of gun-control and anti–gun violence organizations that she supported and encouraged others to as well. But that was lost in the social media furor.

Some of that criticism was knee-jerk Madonna hate, but much of it was heartfelt. No matter.

In her battle against sexual violence, Andrea Dworkin once said that in order to get and hold the attention of a public inured to the misogyny of modern life, she would "have to write a prose more terrifying than rape, more abject than torture, more insistent and destabilizing than battery, more desolate than prostitution, more invasive than incest, more filled with threat and aggression than pornography." She said she had to be "smarter, deeper, colder."[31] That was what Madonna did with her "God Control" video.

Like Dworkin, Madonna was not afraid to shock, even offend, in service of a greater good, and she was not prone to understatement. If she had something to say, she said it as boldly and loudly as she could. And she had something to say about gun violence, which she called "the biggest problem in America right now." Pleas for sensible laws hadn't worked. Protests hadn't worked. Madonna wagered that showing the horror, instead of merely talking about it, might. "I cannot take it anymore," she said of the violence.

> I send my children to school with the same fear that every mother in this era has... It's really scary to me that the once-safe spaces where we gather, worship, and learn are targets. Nobody's safe. So, of course, as a mother I acutely feel the worry.[32]

Madonna was the closing act of New York's Pride month celebrations. The location was Pier 97, a once notorious gay cruising spot in Hell's Kitchen. The crowd was ecstatic, but Madonna struck a cautious note. Her role at WorldPride was not unlike Larry Kramer's in 1983, at the start of the AIDS crisis, when he wrote, "If this article doesn't scare the shit out of you, we're in real trouble." Then as now, people had to awaken to a reality they would rather ignore. Death by AIDS. Death by guns. Death if trans. The American Medical Association that year called violence against transgender women an "epidemic."[33]

"Even though we have a lot to celebrate," Madonna told the gathering, "we have a lot of work to do."[34] The community had struggled to win the right of full citizenship. That did not mean that right was etched in stone.

She opened her nearly half-hour performance with a backstory video that was part of a twenty-two-minute documentary shot by Nuno Xico in Portugal called *World of Madame X*. Through the years, she had commissioned behind-the-scenes shorts about the creation of certain videos and certain albums, in addition to her tour documentaries. But *World of Madame X* was the first to describe an album's inspiration. The musical cultures represented in it were so new that she wanted to provide listeners with an introduction to them while describing the excitement she felt when *she* discovered them.

Education, however, was only part of the reason Madonna was in New York. She was there for a party. Her film tribute to Lisbon's music scene ended with a voice-over that cheekily asked, "What are you looking at?" and the opening strains of "Vogue."[35] A figure in a blond wig, dark glasses, and trench coat appeared onstage and sat down at a typewriter. More "Madonnas" turned up, similarly dressed. They were her ten dancers (mostly men) in heels and trench coats. Finally, Madonna appeared, singing and dancing to "Vogue."[36]

After much Rockettes-style leg action, the next number was an odd choice: "American Life." She rarely performed that song, which had been so heavily criticized upon its release. Times, however, had changed.[37] Relieved of her trench coat, Madonna appeared in a modified military uniform. Instead of a bandolier, her body was crisscrossed in the rainbow colors of Queer Nation. Her dancers, meanwhile, formed a fearsome army in black leather uniforms and provided the song's percussion by stomping their boots. Behind them, Madonna's controversial "American Life" video appeared, ending with the image of a white-gloved hand, middle finger raised, as she repeated the words "Fuck it."[38] With that, she paused to talk to the audience, *her* audience.

> Fifty years, people...Fifty years of revolution. Fifty years of freedom-fighting. Fifty years of putting up with discrimination, hatred, and indifference. Fifty years of blood, sweat, and tears. Fifty years of not bowing down to fear...Fifty fucking years. It's insane...Are you happy? Are you proud?[39]

After each question, the audience shouted, "Yeah!" "So am I," Madonna said. "It's as if I've been waiting my whole life for this moment."[40]

The next part of the show being more physically demanding, Madonna changed out of her heels and into combat boots made for the occasion by Donatella Versace. Madonna laughed it off, but it was one of the first indications that she was having trouble with her legs. More than two decades of stress from dancing in heels had taken a toll.[41] Beseeching her audience to join her, she cried out, "Disco god, help us." That was the cue for "God Control."[42]

Madonna did not show the full video for "God Control" as she and her dancers, dressed as soldiers and riot police, performed. Instead, she flashed bits of it on the screen—religious imagery, protests, coffins, the Tiffin Children's Chorus—interspersed with dance-club scenes. There was little carnage, but everyone knew what she wasn't showing.[43] Madonna and her dancers left the stage. When they returned, a portion of Emma González's "We call BS" speech blasted from the sound system. That was the signal for "I Rise."[44]

Madonna wrote that song with the LGBTQ community in mind. Now she was singing it to them. The number ended with her and her cast standing in a row, fists raised, the word RESIST on the screen behind them. As they danced offstage to "I Don't Search I Find," a Pride flag fluttered on-screen and fireworks exploded overhead.[45]

The audience at the concert, which had been sold out since March, was filled with diehard Madonna fans. One observer said that the crowd of around seven thousand seemed to be made up mostly of shirtless, well-heeled gay men of a certain age. But there were young folks there, too, some of whom had never seen Madonna perform live. Writer Rose Dommu was one, and she was not disappointed. In *Out* magazine, she said, "I was struck more than ever by the surety that Madonna isn't an ally. She's one of us...To quote a friend, 'Madame X is a faggot.'" [46]

It had been seven long months since Madonna left the comfort of the studio and the musicians from Lisbon whom she had assembled there. On July 19, the release of the video for her song "Batuka" brought it all wonderfully back to life. Madonna said her aim was to re-create her first meeting with the women of the Orquestra Batukadeiras and the journey they had taken together.[47]

Madonna and Emmanuel Adjei, who had also directed the video for "Dark Ballet," chose to shoot in an abandoned whitewashed house on a windswept beach near Sintra to replicate the Cape Verde shore from which slave ships once sailed.[48] The video introduces that painful history in text and black-and-white historical footage before bursting into color with the modern Batukadeiras and Madonna's song.[49]

The scene, like the song, begins with expressions of defiance and ends with the pin-drop silence of prayer. In the video, as the women stand hand in hand looking out to sea toward ghost ships destined for an uncertain future, the music and their faces become mournful. A hawk flies from a pole. They only experience such liberty in their music.[50]

Madonna wasn't ready to give that up. She invited the Orquestra women to join the Madame X tour. She wanted the audience to see them and be inspired the way she was. Many of the Batukadeiras weren't able to travel because of family or work. Fourteen could, and they agreed to become part of her show.[51]

★　　★　　★

Rehearsals began in earnest in July at a studio in Brooklyn's Greenpoint neighborhood. Madonna kept her fans apprised of the progress via Instagram. Her excitement was palpable. For the first time since Blond Ambition, she was her tour's creator and director. Jamie King was back as creative producer and Kevin Antunes as musical director, but the show represented the breadth of Madonna's artistic vision in a way no tour had for three decades.

The performance would be equal parts music, dance, painting, video, film, and the written word. The venues would be small. "Intimacy...the thing we've become allergic to thanks to social media" was what she was after, she said.[52] On that stage, Madonna would, as usual, celebrate human diversity, but for the first time, she would also celebrate age. Joining her onstage were people whose lives spanned six decades. Finally, she wanted to make serious political and artistic statements while indulging her love of ribald humor.

Normally, by the end of tour rehearsals, the people involved felt like family. In the case of Madame X, the cast and crew were that close from the start. Madonna and company had been collaborating all year on special performances and videos that would become the tour's foundation. Now they needed to stitch those pieces together, add extraordinary visuals and cutting-edge choreography, and they would have their show.

The result wouldn't be a concert: it would be something new, which was what Madonna, left to her own devices, always did. *Rolling Stone* called the Madame X show "a testament to the genius in her madness... Madonna will never be the kind of superstar who repeats her successes, sticks to her strengths, or plays it safe. Instead, she's getting weirder with age. Thank all the angels and saints for that."[53]

Madonna asked two old friends—Monte Pittman and Ric'key Pageot—to join her on tour, but most of the musicians she invited were people she had met in Portugal. In addition to the Batukadeiras, those who agreed to help her re-create the Lisbon music scene onstage included her cultural guide, Dino D'Santiago, trumpet player Jéssica Pina, and fifteen-year-old guitarist Gaspar Varela.[54]

The dancers were all Madonna alumni who had either worked with her on previous tours and performances or on films and videos. The newest arrival among them was a twenty-six-year-old Neapolitan named Daniele Sibilli, whom Madonna first met when he performed at her fifty-ninth birthday party, in Puglia. When she turned sixty, she called him to Marrakech, and again he danced for her. Her next call was to invite him on tour.[55]

One of the show's choreographers was also a newcomer. Madonna asked the extraordinary Belgian-French artist Damien Jalet to create four of the

show's dance segments. Like hers, his work incorporated film, video, theater, music, and fashion, and his inspirations were multicultural and spiritual. As for sexuality, gender, to him, was "a state of mind," he said. "The
traditional pas de deux between men and women doesn't interest me at
all."[56] Jalet's contributions would help raise the show to the level of true
performance art.[57]

Jalet said he discovered Madonna when he was thirteen. "She's someone
who has had enormous influence on the person I've become."[58] Thirty
years later, he was surprised when he received a call asking if he'd like to
collaborate with her. His mark on the show was evident from its very first
moments. It would be Jalet who choreographed Madame X's dramatic and
stark opening.[59]

The show began with the sound of typing and the images of a woman in
silhouette bent over a desk and a young Black man dressed in black suit,
black tie, white shirt, and spectacles. The words being typed were written
by James Baldwin—"Art is here to prove that all safety is an illusion"—
and appeared in white on a black screen. The sound of keystrokes was met
with the sound of bullets fired. A shot hit its target; the dancer fell dead.
But Baldwin's words live. Art, unlike bodies, is impervious to bullets.
That was the theme of Madonna's show: art cannot be silenced.

The opening segment finished, Madonna appeared onstage in a tricorne
and a Revolutionary War naval uniform in front of a tattered US flag singing
her anti-gun anthem "God Control." She was greeted by riot police. The
"God Control" video covered the stage set behind her, and when the song
cut to the bloodied club section, Madonna's dancers joined her onstage for
the first time. That was also the moment when the audience got a first look at
the set, created by the British production specialists Stufish.

The inspiration was Dutch artist M. C. Escher's Impossible Construc-
tions, in which descent and ascent are indistinguishable, background is
foreground, and what one thinks one sees becomes, on close inspection,
something else entirely. The set was as simple and stark as an off-off-
Broadway play's: a set of staircases. But those staircases could be moved and
reconfigured to create a wall, a multilevel structure, a fado club with bal-
conies, or a labyrinth.[60]

They also became a screen on which words and images—videos, photographs, tile patterns, paintings—were projected. At the end of "God
Control," Madonna stood at the top of the staircase, enveloped in videos,
seemingly lost among filmed protesters. The effect was stunning,
tumultuous—a collage of video images and real people as the Batukadeiras stood on the stairs singing on either side of her. That scene ended
abruptly with the words WAKE UP. The set went dark.

After a reworking of her "Dark Ballet" performance from the Eurovision contest, Madonna was seized by two men in gas masks and dragged away, shouting, "Traitor...I fought for you...Death to the patriarchy!" That was the introduction to "Human Nature."

The scene referenced Jean-Baptiste Mondino's video for that song, but instead of being confined inside a box, she was inside a blue-lit circle surrounded by the giant silhouettes of hands pointing fingers of accusation and disapprobation. Meanwhile, high above, the silhouettes of women danced, defying the judgment of the fingers. The hands were replaced by the graffiti message FUCK OFF, written small and large dozens of times across the stage.

As the song neared its end, Madonna summoned all the women in her cast to join her onstage, including her daughters Estere, Stella, and Mercy.[61] As the group danced to "Human Nature," their shadows did, too, courtesy of a yellow spotlight that created a full moon and made their gathering seem pagan. They were dangerous because they were free. "Have we made ourselves clear?" Madonna asked. "Nobody is anybody's bitch. I can't spell it out any clearer than that."[62] She ended the segment with an a cappella version of "Express Yourself."

Madonna followed that with "Vogue." It was the performance from her WorldPride set, in which she and the dancers wore blond wigs and trench coats as images of Hollywood stars flashed on the screen. Her next song, "I Don't Search I Find," described how she went from being a child dreaming about those stars' lives to living her own.

The image projected onto the stage was that of the skyline of New York City, Madonna's creative birthplace. Two men in trench coats and fedoras appeared, representing the forces that would try to impede her career. They were figures of authority who handcuffed and interrogated her after finding a sheet of forbidden words in her pocket—her words. It was their mission to silence her, but they could not.

Madonna continued that theme of patriarchal authority with "Papa Don't Preach," and it served as an example of the layers of meaning she built into her work. In the Madame X concert, she performed the song against a backdrop of paintings by the brilliant but neglected seventeenth-century Italian artist Artemisia Gentileschi.

Gentileschi's *Susanna and the Elders,* one of the works Madonna used, was the first known portrayal of rape by a female painter. Unlike the ravishment scenes traditionally painted by men, the image is not about lust and power but about coercion and fear. Gentileschi was seventeen when she created it. The next year, the artist was raped by a friend of her father. A public trial; an unsuccessful forced marriage to the rapist; marriage to another man, which meant more submission—none of that destroyed

Gentileschi. She once said, "You will find the spirit of Caesar in the soul of a woman."[63]

The teenager of Madonna's song was also determined to make her own decisions. In the Madame X version of "Papa Don't Preach," though, she decided *not* to keep her baby. During the tour, Madonna would use the song to introduce a discussion of abortion rights, which were under threat as the Trump administration named conservative judges to the Supreme Court. "That's right, I made up my mind! You don't mind if I choose what I do with my body, do you?" she asked the audience.[64]

"American Life" followed and, in a sense, concluded Madonna's American creative journey. Against an image of the US flag and with her "American Life" video playing behind her, she sang and played guitar with Monte Pittman as dancers leaped around them in camouflage uniforms. To their right, uniforms dropped one by one from the rafters into a heap, a symbol of people who had died in war. Fresh recruits wearing T-shirts picked up the uniforms and put them on. One by one, they died, too. A flag-draped coffin was carried across the stage.

With that, Madonna disappeared, and the Lisbon portion of her show began with the image of a sixteenth-century slave-trading map. The video for Madonna's song "Batuka" replaced the map, and as its images filled the stage, fourteen women of the Orquestra Batukadeiras walked through the audience and took their places onstage in a semicircle to perform. Madonna said being with them every night "was like an ecstatic experience...I felt like they were there to share their message of love and unity and female empowerment."[65]

As they sang, the stage behind the curtain was transformed into a tiled Lisbon bar, complete with a grand piano and café tables. Musicians sat in the chairs, ready for a session. Madonna, playing guitar and seated on top of the piano, joined Dino D'Santiago to sing the morna song "Sodade" (Longing), which was made famous by Cesária Évora. Everyone in the band joined in. It was Madonna's tribute to Lisbon and to the wanderers from all parts—herself included—who had found their way there. The song's ending was ecstatic. All those cultures, all those sounds and voices, came together, and it worked. "Sodade" would be one of the highlights of the show.

Madonna asked, "Where should we go next?" Dino D'Santiago's answer was "Colombia." It was time for "Medellín." Madonna sat down at a typewriter and tapped out the beat. Maluma would not join Madonna on tour, but his video image loomed above the stage as Madonna and the cast da͏   ͏ow.

three extraordinary numbers could be called the Damien Jalet as unique, both within the concert and within the history of k. Taken as a set, they described her life up to 1996 and the hter Lourdes.

The first, "Extreme Occident," about Madonna's journey from Michigan to fame, had her lost in a labyrinth. Jalet made the set's staircase come to life by having dancers move its pieces, as if they were giant building blocks, to form new angles and avenues as Madonna sang about her quest to find herself. Finally, she found an opening and fled through the narrowest of passages toward her future.

Her flight was the start of Jalet's next segment. Called "Rescue Me/ Breathwork," it began with dancer Daniele Sibilli alone onstage in front of a black screen in an open white shirt and dark pants, inhaling and exhaling. His breath dictated his movement and represented his most important percussive instrument, his heart. He was soon joined by eight other dancers similarly attired, standing in a line, taking deliberate breaths.

Their bodies responded in jerks and jolts as they were thrown to the floor one minute and twisted upright the next. The only music was the occasional drumbeat. The only other sound was Madonna's voice-over as she recited the lyrics of "Rescue Me," which as recorded began with a heartbeat and a breath. That song celebrated the saving power of love. The love that had rescued her from a decade of confusion was the birth of her eldest daughter, in 1996.

Just as "Rescue Me" ended, the first strains of "Frozen" were heard. That was also the beginning of Jalet's final segment, and it was perhaps the most poignant, beautiful, and memorable in the show.

With the "Rescue Me/Breathwork" dancers still in place, a black-and-white image that covered the entire height and width of the stage loomed over them. It was a barefoot woman, dressed in a black tank top and leggings, seated with her legs apart, her head bowed, and her face obscured by her hair. The reflection of her arms on the floor created the letter *m*. She moved her legs to create the letter *x*. Across the fingers of one hand was tattooed the word MOM, and on the fingers of the other hand was tattooed the word DAD. Those hands separated to reveal a tiny figure: Madonna. The dancer parted her hair to reveal who she was: twenty-three-year-old Lourdes.

The dance was a duet between a massive Lourdes on-screen and Madonna onstage alone. And yet mother and daughter were completely intertwined. Standing under a scrim, Madonna seemed to be enveloped by Lourdes. That aspect of the performance was mesmerizing. On its own merits, Lourdes's dance was, too. It was a dance of arms, legs, and hair; shadows, light, and reflection. When Lourdes rolled onto her back and looked at the camera faceup, her reflection on the floor created a second face—a Janus face—that was disconcertingly more real than the one attached to her body. Extending her arms upward into an X shape, she became a totem. The video then split into two Lourdeses dancing.

The next shot was iconic. With Lourdes's cheek on the floor, her bare shoulder and hand visible from out of the darkness, Madonna sang beneath the image of Lourdes's upraised hand as Lourdes watched and listened. Then, newly awakened, one Lourdes, two Lourdeses, three Lourdeses spun and danced above and around Madonna as she sang. Lourdes became a kaleidoscope of shifting forms, as Madonna had been in her video for "Frozen." Gradually, Lourdes's figure, now wet—or thawed—became still. The song ended.

It was a breathtaking piece of art and a window into Madonna's family. She had worked with Lourdes on fashion projects, philanthropic events, and even tours, but the "Frozen" performance was the first time Lourdes collaborated with her mother as an equal.

Lourdes told Debi Mazar a few years later,

> My experience with my mom's music has changed so much as I've gotten older, because I'm increasingly able to recognize how influential and amazing this woman is, and how empowering to other women and ahead of her time she has always been. I didn't fully comprehend that until I realized the importance of empowerment and what it means to be a woman.[66]

The trip through Madonna's world via Damien Jalet's choreography having ended, the next segment evoked North Africa. The stage filled with people dressed in colorful caftans, while the screen behind them displayed constantly shifting images of equally colorful tiles. Madonna appeared in a headscarf and crystal-encrusted robe to sing "Come Alive." The instruments onstage were traditional, as was the dancing. The overall feeling was tribal and spiritual, and when the Orquestra Batukadeiras and Madonna's musicians joined her at the front of the stage to repeat the phrase "Come alive, come alive" for a full minute, the performance became a revival meeting.

The tone shifted dramatically for the next song, "Future." For the first time ever in concert, Madonna played the piano. The already ominous song sounded even darker as she quietly sang the words "Oh no, oh no" with storm clouds and flames on the screen behind her. Dancers in black gas masks with red eye holes menaced her. Hope was enough to repel them temporarily.

Against a backdrop of bombed-out buildings, the masked figures returned, climbing onto the piano, leaning over Madonna from behind as she played. She continued undaunted. They could not shake her. The destroyed buildings on-screen were replaced with the image of an intact New York housing project that fans would recognize from her video for "Crave." That was the next song. The version performed in concert was a remix created by Madonna's friend the Miami DJ Tracy Young, and it was a reason to dance.

The stage became pure late-'70s disco. A golden disco ball sent out hundreds of points of light, and the floor was moving. Black feather boas and superfly coats; shirtless gay boys in tight shorts, or pocketless pants and skintight polyester shirts; women covered in silk and sequins. Madonna was still wearing her robe from "Come Alive," but she had added a leather hat. Greeting two dancers, she said, "Hey, ladies, how we doin'?" Her daughters Stella and Estere joined her at the front of the pack for a line dance.

While the disco crowd milled about onstage after that song, a choir began singing "Like a Prayer." In the old days in New York, the Saturday night discos closed as the Sunday morning churches opened. Clubbers stumbling home crossed paths with the righteous. The same happened on Madonna's stage. As the dancers made for the wings, the Batukadeiras took up position on the staircases, which were arranged in the shape of an X at the back of the stage.

During that transition, Madonna changed into a monk's cloak covered in jeweled crosses. The images on the screen behind her were from her original "Like a Prayer" video, featuring her thirty-year-old self. She joined the Batukadeiras on the X, climbing the steps to take the central position on a landing. When she reached it, the X turned red. That might have been a fitting concert ending. But Madonna had one more song that was just as moving and better suited to the times.

A portion of the James Baldwin quotation that opened the show appeared once again on a blackened screen, introducing the ending. The next sounds were a heartbeat, a piano, and a fragment of Emma González's "We call BS" speech. Madonna appeared in a military-style Versace jacket bearing a soldier's name tag: MADAME X. The song was "I Rise."

Behind her and her dancers, who wore white shirts, black ties, and black pants, the video for "I Rise" played. Gradually, it was replaced by the rainbow flag of Gay Pride. That was why Madonna wrote the song. She and her dancers stood with fists raised in front of it. "I will rise."

Madonna's tour was scheduled to open at the Brooklyn Academy of Music's Howard Gilman Opera House and remain there for seventeen performances. The tour would then move from city to city and take up residence in each for between three and eleven days.[67] But by late August, it became clear that the show would not be ready for the scheduled September 12 premiere, in Brooklyn. Madonna canceled three performances and added two at the end of her New York residency by way of compensation.[68]

That rescheduling was the first indication that something was wrong. Madonna — the showgirl who never disappointed, the workhorse who never tired — was struggling physically. She began her eleven-city, six-month tour praying that she would be able to finish it.

Chapter 62

New York, Las Vegas, Los Angeles, Lisbon, London, 2019–2020

No one set of circumstances completes you. Maybe nothing ever
does. So you work on your life, and you work on your work, and
you try to live every single day like it's your last.[1]

— *Madonna*

ON SEPTEMBER 17, Madonna's Madame X tour opened in Brooklyn. At
the door, people were given a "radical" choice: surrender their phones and
smartwatches to sealed Yondr pouches or be denied entry. For many, it
represented a moment of extreme crisis, tantamount to asking them to sacrifice an arm—or part of their brains.[2] Madonna had her reasons. She
wanted audiences to be there with her, experiencing the show, not busily
recording it for posterity. As the tour progressed, the grumbles would be
replaced by praise from concertgoers who enjoyed the experience of a hall
free of phone lights and an audience engaged in a communal experience.
Said *Rolling Stone*'s Rob Sheffield, "Honestly, all shows should be this
way."[3]

In New York, the opera house's two thousand seats were filled with
friends—Rosie O'Donnell, Debi Mazar, Anderson Cooper, and Spike
Lee among them—and diehard fans.[4] Madonna could pretty much say and
do what she wanted in Brooklyn.[5] The crowd loved her. Generally, critics
loved Madame X, too. Rhian Daly, in *NME,* called the show "a mind-
blowing riot of theatrics and powerful political messaging."[6]

The tour was off to a spectacular start. And then life intervened. Opening her September 19 show two and a half hours late, Madonna made a
joke of her tardiness, saying, "I don't like to keep you waiting. But I have
an injury. I have six kids. I have a LOT of wigs."[7] On October 7, she postponed a show because of a knee injury.[8]

The concert did not require her to do an extraordinary amount of tricky
dancing, aside from a handstand, but Madonna had to climb and descend
ladders and steep steps. In fact, the set seemed designed to aggravate whatever physical problems she had.

Having concluded her long New York run on October 12, Madonna would have only two days off before beginning a six-night residency in Chicago. She needed more time. Whether the reason was the officially stated "highly specialized production elements" or Madonna's health, the start date was pushed back a night, with an extra date added. That, in turn, affected the scheduled start of the concert at her next stop, San Francisco.[9]

Once there, Madonna told the audience that she had a cold, a torn ligament, and a bad knee. It was clear that she was stiff. When she pulled herself up from a kneeling position, she did so slowly. When she did a "butterfly" dance atop the piano, her legs made only a reference to a flutter. Not without cause, Madonna was cranky.[10]

She expressed annoyance at a fan's illuminated crown in the otherwise darkened theater, the opening and closing of a door used to access the restrooms, and audience chatter. "Don't talk while I'm talking," she snapped before adding, "Don't talk while I'm not talking." According to Aidin Vaziri, who covered the show for the *San Francisco Chronicle,* she also accused the crowd of being lazy. She could do that in San Francisco. It was, like New York, Madonna territory. She would be forgiven. Vaziri called the show "spectacular."[11]

Las Vegas, her show's next stop, was not Madonna territory. On her opening night, at the Colosseum at Caesars Palace, she finally took the stage at 12:30 a.m. The audience was raging, and the angriest of them were escorted out by security. Among those who stayed, many complained about the heat because Madonna had ordered the air-conditioning turned off. Soon, nearly half the audience was heckling her. They didn't want to hear her talk—certainly not about social and political issues. It was *Vegas*. They wanted a *show*.[12]

Josh Bell, who reviewed the performance for the *Las Vegas Weekly,* said Madonna "did not seem to care [that the] crowd of rowdy drunks who just want to hear 'Material Girl'" interrupted her repeatedly. She persevered, at one point telling the audience, "I still love you, in spite of your hostility." She wore them down. By the end of the concert, in the wee hours of November 8, many pricey seats in the front were empty. Fans from the ramparts wandered down to fill them. It was then that the show became truly intimate. Bell called it "cathartic." The social media war waged by the disgruntled multitude, however, continued: "Complete waste of money." "Worse [sic] concert ever." "Shame on Madonna."[13]

Madonna struggled through two more nights in Las Vegas. She was due in Los Angeles for eleven shows beginning on November 12, but Live Nation issued a statement saying that the first concert would be canceled. When her sojourn at the Wiltern theater finally began, she could count on the industry people, entertainers, fashionistas, and young artists who wanted to be her—as well as her vast gay fan base—to support her, even if her body did not.

In 1976, the Band's lead guitarist, Robbie Robertson, looked into the camera during the filming of Martin Scorsese's documentary *The Last Waltz* and said, "The road will kill you." He was thirty-three. For artists double that age, the rigors of touring were literally fatal. In 2017, sixty-six-year-old Tom Petty overdosed on fentanyl after suffering through an agonizing fifty-three-date tour with a hip injury. It was the same drug that killed Prince, who also took it for pain.[14]

And yet artists did it anyway. Despite injuries, they hit the road. For some, it was a matter of money. For most, the expression of their art and the interaction with an audience were what they lived for. In those cases, physical pain became mental anguish when they could not perform at their best. That was Madonna's problem. She was a perfectionist, but her body was in rebellion against her will. She soldiered on. Ice baths at 3:00 a.m. had become part of her routine. Her costumes featured knee supports.[15]

On the final night of her LA residency, Swae Lee joined Madonna onstage for "Crave." Smiling broadly and embracing him, she said, "The bird has returned." Draped in black boas, they danced to the disco version of the song. Madonna seemed genuinely happy. Joy had momentarily eased the pain. But it was only temporary. Two days later, she canceled her entire three-show Boston run. Releasing a statement, she said, "Please forgive this unexpected turn of events. Doing my show every night brings me so much joy and to cancel is a kind of punishment for me. But the pain I'm in right now is overwhelming." She said she needed to rest to survive the remainder of her tour.[16] She was only halfway through it.

Madonna performed four nights in Philadelphia before reaching the last city on the US leg of her tour, Miami. She was booked to play at the Fillmore in South Beach for seven nights. Before she arrived, a Miami man filed suit against Live Nation, claiming that even though the concert's start time had changed, the tour organizer would not refund the price of his tickets.

The case received widespread publicity and soured the mood of some concertgoers who showed up grumpy on December 14. They became grumpier still when Madonna started her first show three hours late. Others were angry over Madonna's no-air-conditioning policy.[17] The heat in the Fillmore was unbearable. To the crowd's shouts of "A/C! A/C! A/C!" Madonna responded, "Fuck you, I'm cold. Take your fucking clothes off." But unlike the Las Vegas banter, the Miami banter was mostly familial. The crowed loved Madonna, and she loved them—until December 22.[18]

Fans had arrived by plane, by car, and on foot to see Madonna's final Fillmore show on that night only to discover that, with less than two hours' notice, it had been canceled. They were furious. With no explanation given, rumors circulated on social media.[19] The fury was compounded by published photos of Madonna and her new paramour canoodling on a balcony during her Miami residency and her social media posts showing their private playtime. The man in question was twenty-five-year-old dancer Ahlamalik Williams.

Their romance was headline news: he was Madonna's new "boy toy." The relationship, however, was not a casual fling. Williams had worked with Madonna on the Rebel Heart tour and on nearly every performance since then. Over that period, their relationship evolved. But that was not the story that made the news. The story became their thirty-six-year age difference and, after the Miami cancellation, the betrayal felt by fans who saw Madonna having fun while supposedly abandoning them.[20]

Madonna let crucial days pass before explaining herself. Finally, in an Instagram post, she detailed her "indescribable" pain. The night before her canceled performance, as she climbed the ladder to sing "Batuka," she said, it was so bad that she was in tears. Each night, she prayed she could make it through the show. Madonna spent two days with doctors: "Scans, ultrasounds, X-rays. Poking and probing and more tears." Their immediate prescription was rest. Madonna agreed. She thanked her fans for their patience, but some had already reached their limit. More lawsuits were filed.[21]

Madonna had a three-week break before the start of the European portion of her tour. Over New Year's she took her family, Williams, and her entourage to the Maldives for some "water therapy." What she was after was rest, warmth, and fun. If a series of her Instagram posts is any indication, she found all three.[22] She was so revived that on January 12, she was ready to get back onstage in Lisbon for eight shows at the Coliseu dos Recreios theater. She appeared to be a new, improved version of herself. Though Lisbon was one city where a 12:30 a.m. start time wouldn't raise eyebrows, her show opened just before ten.[23]

Her banter with the crowd in what she called her "second home" was easy and seemed to be helped by the port she drank during the concert. She joked about her "twenty-five injuries" and advised the audience not to "pay attention to what goes on from the waist down." Limping, she moved more cautiously than she had during previous shows.[24]

There was a warmth about the concert that had been missing from some of her US outings. Fans were happy that she had made it at all, because the possibility that she would cancel the rest of her tour was very real. On the third night, she assured the crowd that she was still game, declaring, "I won't stop 'til I drop."[25]

The first indication that her crippling pain had returned occurred

during the fourth Lisbon show. The start time slipped back without explanation. And then, the next day, just forty-five minutes before the performance, ticket holders received an email telling them that the concert was
canceled. Unlike the Miami fans, who raged over a last-minute cancellation, the Portuguese audience outside the historic theater was sympathetic
and concerned. A star of Madonna's caliber did not cancel eight shows
over the course of her tour unless she was seriously injured.[26] Before she
left Lisbon, she would be forced to cancel a ninth.[27]

Half a world away in Los Angeles, the Grammy Awards were held in the
gap between Madonna's Lisbon shows and her next commitments, in London. There was a time when she would have flown in for the ceremony.
But the male club that bestowed the golden gramophones only nominated
Madame X, which many critics called her best album in two decades, in
one category: Best Remixed Recording. It was for DJ and producer Tracy
Young's remix of "I Rise." As much as Madonna admired and supported
Young, and had for decades, she skipped the show. It was a good year to
miss it.

Ten days before the awards ceremony, Deborah Dugan, the newly hired
CEO of the Recording Academy, which oversees the Grammys, was fired.
Dugan, a longtime Bono philanthropic associate, then filed a complaint
with the federal government against the academy, alleging corruption,
malpractice, and systemic sexism and racism.[28]

At the time, Grammy nominees were selected by a thirteen-thousand-
member voting body that was "overwhelmingly" white and male. A
report released in 2018 found that between 2013 and 2018, just over 9 percent of nominees for the most prestigious categories were women. In the
wake of that damning report, the 2018 Grammys were heralded as usher-
ing in the "year of the woman." Most of the major awards found their way
into the hands of female artists, as if to prove the report wrong. But Dugan
said the culture had not changed. The academy defended itself against
Dugan's charges by calling her "problematic" and "bullying."[29]

Madonna often said she didn't care about awards. She thought they were
arbitrary. How could a work of art be the "best"? Who painted better
skies—van Gogh or the English Romantic J. M. W. Turner? That had
been Madonna's attitude from the start of her career, and it was lucky for
her that it was. Her acting-award snubs were well documented. Less well
known was how few Grammys she had received. During her nearly four-
decade career, she had won just seven, and only three of them were for her
music.

She was ignored despite being the bestselling female recording artist of
all time and the highest-grossing solo musical artist of all time.[30] Even

more important than her ability to sell her music, however, was her role in the history of music. She was ignored by the academy despite having fundamentally changed pop music and culture *globally*. Or maybe that was precisely why she was ignored. She was too powerful for the boys.

All the women who took the stage at the Grammys that year—and many of the men—were indebted to her for influencing the way they had built their careers, the way they created their art, the way they chose to present themselves, and the issues that they dared to champion. "She was writing the playbook for them," said Emerson College's Kristin Lieb. "One of the things that can be frustrating when you look at popular music today is you get the sense that those who are ripping pages from that playbook don't even know that they are doing it. She doesn't get the credit she deserves, and some are quite dismissive of her."[31]

Tracy Young's "I Rise" remix win was sweet because it was historic. Young was the first woman to ever be nominated in that production category, much less win it. As a lesbian, she thanked the LGBTQ community for its support. And she thanked Madonna. In interviews over the years, Young said she wouldn't be where she was if not for her. "She really handed me a career."[32]

While the Grammys ignored her, Madonna racked up another first. A remix of her song "I Don't Search I Find" earned her a fiftieth number 1 single on the Billboard Dance Club Songs chart. No other artist even came close (Rihanna was number 2, with thirty-three). Madonna also became the only artist—solo or as a member of a group—to have fifty number 1 singles in any category. Her closest rival was George Strait, who topped the country chart forty-four times.[33] Madonna's position in music was undeniable, yet there were people who tried to deny it.

The mood as Madonna headed to London, where she had fifteen shows scheduled, was apprehensive. Fans poured into England from around the world, knowing at that point that possessing a ticket did not mean they would see her. Two days before the January 27 opening, she canceled the show.[34] She would open her London residency on January 29.

The theater she chose to perform in, the London Palladium, in Soho, was known as one of the best variety stages in London. It wasn't a natural home for a show as avant-garde as Madonna's. Just before her arrival, Andrew Lloyd Webber and Tim Rice's *Joseph and the Amazing Technicolor Dreamcoat* had a fiftieth-anniversary run there. But what the Palladium had was history, more than one hundred years of it. Legends had performed there: Houdini, Louis Armstrong, Frank Sinatra, Diana Ross, the Beatles.[35]

It was at the Palladium in 1951 that Judy Garland won over her audience and revived her career with an onstage tumble that became a metaphor for the vicissitudes of her life. Madonna needed that same understanding from her audience. It was in no way assured. As she took the stage on opening night, she knew that if her performance was less than perfect, the British press would gleefully try to destroy her with ageist headlines.

That did not happen. The reviews of her show ranged from good to great. Only the *Financial Times* found reason to grumble, and that was over the show's content, not the lady responsible for it.

Madonna's opening in London wasn't perfect, but like Judy Garland's fall, that imperfection made it more intimate and "live." The lights didn't quite work. Madonna needed a hand on the stairs and on and off a piano top. Sometimes her exchanges with the audience fell flat, often because the people she spoke to were so tongue-tied that they couldn't respond.[36]

BBC arts correspondent Will Gompertz, who was there for her opening night, said the show's flaws made it art. "It was perfectly imperfect, like one of those sketchy landscapes by Cézanne where you can see his under-drawings and misplaced lines, making it so much more beautiful and real... Truth is the point of art, not perfection." Gompertz concluded that the Madame X show was great. "Five-star great... an adventurous piece of contemporary theatre and a match for any of the Tony and Olivier-winning shows currently playing the West End and Broadway."[37]

The *Daily Telegraph*'s Neil McCormick seconded Gompertz on most points. "The show's slightly anarchic nature only added to the fun. It was like a cross between experimental theater and showbiz extravaganza." But what sold McCormick on the show and earned it a five-star rating was Madonna's pure pleasure in doing it. "I've been watching her live for four decades and this may not have been her slickest or most spectacular—but her wacky joy in performance made it the most entertaining Madonna show ever."[38]

Alexis Petridis, in *The Guardian,* though more measured in his enthusiasm (four stars), wrote, "It's hard to imagine another star of her stature even thinking about trying anything as clearly experimental as this."[39] But it was El Hunt, in *NME,* who got to the heart of the show's power.

> Tonight is largely about Madonna herself. By the end, it feels like we know her a lot better... As disorienting as it feels, the tension of seeing an untouchable legend letting her guard down makes this show incredibly special. It also feels like a brave move from an artist who could do just about anything. Then again, risk-taking and reinvention is what makes Madonna an icon.[40]

That Madonna was able to perform at all was attributable to six hours of physical therapy a day—three before the show and three after it. But doctors were concerned about the possibility of permanent injury and advised her against working on two consecutive nights. That would mean canceling half her London shows. She said no, so they struck a compromise. She would perform two nights and take the third off. Announcing the schedule change, Madonna told her fans, "It's a miracle I have gotten this far. I'm determined that I will make it to the end if I pace myself. God willing."[41]

In London, Madonna's shows started almost on time, not by choice but because of the city's strict 11:00 p.m. curfew. If a performance continued past that time, the curtain fell, and the show was preemptively declared over. On February 5, Madonna learned just how closely city officials watched the clock. At eleven, while she was performing, the houselights came on and the curtain closed. But she hadn't sung her final number.

The crowd began chanting her name. She and her cast appeared, bouncing out from behind the curtain, singing and dancing to "I Rise." The dance was freestyle, rebellious, wild. A city ordinance had serendipitously created an unforgettable guerrilla-theater performance. One fan called it a "glorious moment. She finished the show a cappella in front of the curtain like a champ!"[42]

The curfew controversy, which Madonna equated with censorship, enlivened her. When she took the stage the next night, she did so fueled by indignation, and she ignited her fans.

The average age of the people in the audience was forty. They had been the children who discovered Madonna in their early teens and had grown up with her, shocked and elated by her fearlessness, using her words, work, and life as their guides. They were the adults who had turned up in Brixton twenty years previously to watch her puncture the myth that a woman could not be at once a mother and an artist, a fully functioning member of society, and gloriously sexual. Now approaching what society called old age, they were back to watch Madonna rip to shreds a new set of prejudices, and they cheered her on again.

The once taut bodies of her gay male audience had softened and expanded around the middle. Baldness was a fact of life rather than a fashion statement. Some of the women in the audience nostalgically wore *Desperately Seeking Susan*–era rags in their graying hair. There were men dressed as monks and people of all genders dressed as nuns. There were feathers, fishnets, ill-fitting corsets, and a preponderance of Madame X–style X's on jackets, shirts, and even handmade ponchos. One man, dressed as a character from *The Night Porter,* roamed the hall in a Nazi hat and powdered face.

Without phones to distract them, the fans mingled and chatted. The moments before the show felt like a homecoming, but for most people the only thing that connected them was their admiration for the woman they awaited. There was a sense that they might not see her again onstage.

Three fado musicians warmed up the crowd, leading them through "Like a Virgin" as if it were a pregame school fight song. And then Madonna appeared, and the audience jumped out of its seats and stood for the duration of the concert, waiting to be transported, waiting to dance, even though it wasn't that kind of concert and even though she admonished the crowd to be seated. It didn't matter. With Madonna, you had to be ready, because you never knew what was in store.

When, near the end of her show, she sang "Like a Prayer," the crowd joined her in celebration of their shared past and the improbable, extraordinary journey they had all taken and would continue to take—as Madonna said, God willing. And when she sang "I Rise," the crowd joined her, too, in celebration as well as in defiance. Celebration because they had all risen. Defiance because the Gay Pride flag projected behind Madonna and her troupe still needed protecting. Racked with pain, as she pushed her way through the crowd, fist-bumping fans, her determination was as clear as her message. Fight on.

Epilogue

MADONNA SURVIVED HER London shows and had one more city on her tour — Paris, where she was scheduled to give fourteen performances. Almost immediately she canceled the opening date. And without the threat of the London curfew, when her shows did start, they began late. On the second night, the performance began three hours late. "I was in more pain than I've ever been in in my life," Madonna explained.[1]

She had begun using a black cane with a silver skull handle. She said it hid a sword — maybe to ward off whiners. There were many people, mostly on social media, who complained about the cancellations, her tardiness. Paris, though, was Madonna country, home to some of her most ardent followers and her beloved French collaborators: Jean-Baptiste Mondino, Mirwais Ahmadzaï, and Jean Paul Gaultier.

Gaultier saw the second night of Madonna's Paris show. "What are you doing here?" she asked as she sat next to him during one of her excursions into the audience.

"I came to see you," he said shyly, sweetly.

"Do you like the show?"

"I *love* it," he replied. Madonna confessed that he was partly the inspiration for it, as he had been for shows throughout her career.[2] That was a high point for her in Paris, though.

Madonna canceled her next Paris concert, but the patchwork of rest she tried to build into her schedule was never enough. And then, on February 27, injury was added to injury. Each night, near the end of "Vogue," a dancer pulled out a chair so Madonna could sit at her famous typewriter. On that night, the chair was mistakenly pulled out too far. Madonna missed it and landed on her tailbone.

Pain was written on her face. She could not get up without assistance. A fan said at one point, Madonna burst into tears and could not stop crying. Remarkably, she continued that show and even performed the next night before she hit a wall. In a post, she said, "Here I Am — Flesh and Blood. If only knees didn't twist and cartilage didn't tear and nothing hurt and tears never fell out of our eyes." She described herself as a "broken doll held together with tape and glue."[3]

She performed two more shows before abruptly canceling another on March 7. And then, just as abruptly, the agony of Madame X was over.

A new virus first identified in China was spreading rapidly around the world. Health authorities weren't sure how it was transmitted. The only thing they knew was that it was highly contagious and potentially deadly. Governments began quarantining whole regions where COVID-19 cases were detected. France announced a ban on all gatherings of more than one thousand people. After her March 8 performance, Live Nation announced the cancellation of the last two dates of Madonna's tour.[4]

As Madonna left Paris, she realized that she and many members of her tour had the virus. "We all thought we had a very bad flu," she said.[5] It would have been almost impossible not to be exposed to it. While she was at the Palladium, apparently unbeknownst to British health experts, the disease was already rampant in London. That closed, small concert space became an incubator for the virus. The same was true in Paris.

For people like Madonna, who had lived through the early days of AIDS, there was a déjà vu aspect to the new crisis. Intimacy, which had killed so effectively in the '80s, was taking its toll again, but this time it didn't require risky behavior. Even the response to the crisis was eerily familiar: some of the same faces at the same government agencies expressed impotent bewilderment while people died. Madonna was back where she started, donating money to help stop a plague. That spring, she sent $1 million to the Bill & Melinda Gates Foundation to help fund research into a COVID vaccine.

Meanwhile, she packed up and went home to restore her body with regenerative knee treatments and hip replacement surgery and to think about where she had been, what she had done, and the state of the world.[6]

With much of the planet in a COVID lockdown, and the death toll from the virus mounting, the United States was in the midst of another presidential campaign that could see Donald Trump win reelection. Political tensions between pro-Trump and anti-Trump forces threatened to tear the country apart. Social tensions over COVID restrictions only exacerbated them. The stakes felt terrifyingly high and the future at best uncertain.

Madonna was once asked what she would tell her six-year-old self. She answered: "Shit's going to get better...Everything's going to be all right...don't despair."[7] That optimism was a large part of her appeal. Her fans, like her six-year-old self, wanted to hear her say, "Shit's going to get better." Especially in 2020, when that was very hard to imagine.

What they needed was a bedtime story, a "once upon a time" tale that carried them back to the place where she and they began. Madonna would do that.

In September, she announced her next project. She decided to climb back into the director's chair and make a movie. Her subject would be inspirational, because that's what the world needed. The movie would be about herself. And then in 2023 she made another announcement. Madonna was headed back out on tour. It, too, would be a look into the rearview mirror of her life. She called it simply Celebration.

Copyright and Permissions Acknowledgments

WastedTalent: Excerpts from Jeffrey Ferry's "Madonna: The Glamourous Life," *The Face* (February 1985); Sheryl Garratt's "Je ne regrette rien…," *The Face* (October 1994); Miranda Sawyer's "The Future Sound of London," *The Face* (August 2000); and Gavin Herlihy's "Driving Miss Ravey," *MixMag* (December. 2005).

The Wylie Agency: Excerpts from Ingrid Sischy's "Madonna and Child," *Vanity Fair* (March 1998). Copyright © Ingrid Sischy 1998, used by permission of The Wylie Agency (UK) Limited; excerpts from unpublished drafts of Norman Mailer's article "Like A Lady." Norman Mailer Papers, University of Texas. Copyright © Norman Mailer, used by permission of The Wylie Agency LLC.

Estates

Permission Granted by Copyright Holders

Estate of Jean-Michel Basquiat through ADAGP Paris/IVARO Dublin: Reproduction of the painting *A Panel of Experts,* 1982. The Montreal Museum of Fine Arts.

Estate of John Gruen represented by Julia Gruen: Excerpts from *Keith Haring: The Authorized Biography* by John Gruen. New York: Prentice Hall Press, 1991. John Gruen, "Madonna Interview," *The John Gruen Papers,* Tape 26. Keith Haring Foundation, New York, New York.

Estate of Edwin Miller represented by Eric Edwin Miller: Excerpts from Edwin Miller's "Interview with Madonna," October. 10, 1984. Edwin Miller Papers, Interviews for *Seventeen* magazine, MSSCol 22968, Box 24, F 10, New York Public Library Archives and Manuscripts.

Estate of Tseng Kwong Chi represented by Muna Tseng: Photographs by Tseng Kwong Chi of Madonna performing at the Paradise Garage, 1984, and Keith Haring drawing in the NYC Subway, 1983. Copyright © Muna Tseng Dance Projects, Inc.

Film / Media / Web Sites

Permission Granted by Copyright Holders

ABCNEWS VideoSource: Madonna on ABC's *Nightline,* interviewed by Forrest Sawyer (recorded December 3, 1990).

BackPages Limited: Quotes from Steven Daly's audio interview "Madonna," *Rock's Backpages* (2002).

Luis Camacho: For his quotes in Ester Gould and Reijer Zwann's film *Strike a Pose,* 2016; and "Let Your Body Go with the Flow," MadonnaTribe Meets Luis Camacho.

CBS News Archives: Excerpts from "Madonna at 40," Madonna interviewed by Charlie Rose for *60 Minutes II* (aired March 17, 1999).

Copyright Agency Rights Portal: Excerpts from Cameron Adams's "Review: Madonna Is Late, Loose, and Ultra Personal at Her Fans Only Tears of a Clown Show in Melbourne," news.com.au (May 11, 2016).

Oliver Crumes: For his quotes in Ester Gould and Reijer Zwann's film *Strike a Pose,* 2016.

CTM Docs and The Other Room in co-production with Serendipity Films and SWR: Quotes from Ester Gould and Reijer Zwann's film *Strike a Pose,* 2016.

Guy Guido: Quotes from his film *Madonna and the Breakfast Club.* The Orchard (2019).

Nine Entertainment: Quotes from "Unlike a Virgin," Madonna interviewed by Richard Carleton for *60 Minutes Australia,* 1992.

Paolo Olivi and Mario John: Excerpts from MadonnaTribe interviews, "MadonnaTribe Meets Stephen Bray and the Breakfast Club" (April 23, 2016); "'Starlight, Star Bright,' MadonnaTribe meets Nicki Richards" (2006); and "Let Your Body Go with the Flow, MadonnaTribe meets Luis Camacho" (2005–2008).

Kimberly van Pinxteren: Excerpts from interview with Donna De Lory. Madonnaunderground, 2017.

Helen Terry: Quotes from documentary *Madonna: Naked Ambition*. Directed by Angus Cameron, produced by Helen Terry. Diverse Productions, 2000.

Sue Trupin: For her quotes in Ester Gould and Reijer Zwann's film *Strike a Pose,* 2016.

Foundations

Andy Warhol Foundation: For use of Andy Warhol acetate of Sean Penn and Madonna at the Live Aid concert, Philadelphia, 1985; Andy Warhol and Keith Haring, *Untitled,* 1985; and photograph of Madonna and Jellybean Benitez, 1984. Copyright © The Andy Warhol Foundation for the Visual Arts, Inc. / Licensed by Artists Rights Society (ARS), New York.

Keith Haring Foundation: Haring, Keith, Journal entry July 7, 1986. Copyright © Keith Haring Foundation. Photograph of Sean Penn and Madonna at the Live Aid concert, Philadelphia, 1985. Photograph copyright © Keith Haring Foundation. Andy Warhol and Keith Haring, Untitled, 1985. Art copyright © Keith Haring Foundation. Artwork represented in the 1983 photo of Keith Haring painting in the New York subway by Tseng Kwong Chi, copyright © Keith Haring Foundation.

Acknowledgments

Every book involves a cast of characters the reader will not meet directly in its pages but who were essential to its creation. These are the generous, brilliant people who sit for interviews, patiently field written questions, offer advice and direction, and help ensure that the book looks great and reads well. I often feel that an author's name on a book should be followed by a link directing readers to a list of collaborators without whom it would not exist. Here are a few of the people who, in a more perfect world, would appear on the list following my name on *Madonna: A Rebel Life*.

During multiple interview sessions, Christopher Ciccone shared his own story and his unique perspective on Madonna's, and in the process helped me better understand the first four decades of her life. Through words and pictures, Whit Hill, Linda Alaniz, Peter Sparling, and Peter Kentes offered insights into Madonna's college years. Whit and Linda also provided details about Madonna's early life in New York, as did Whit's delightful father, Ed Setrakian. Catherine Underhill, Lawrence Monoson, and the late Marcus Leatherdale filled in another side of that early New York picture, describing the joy and tragedy of that period when AIDS changed all their lives. Among the people I spoke with who worked and toured with Madonna were Donna De Lory, Niki Haris, Kevin Stea, and Carlton Wilborn. All had incredible personal and professional stories to tell. Sue Trupin did not work with Madonna, but she shared her memories of her son, Gabriel, who did.

Some people outside Madonna's circle helped me understand her broader life. Mike McGuinness gave me a crash course on the social history of southern Michigan and patiently answered questions as they arose throughout this project. Jeffrey Deitch painted an unforgettable portrait of the cultural happenings arising out of lower Manhattan in the late '70s and early '80s. Brian Antoni, Tom Austin, and Louis Canales helped me re-create the scene that inspired Madonna in Miami Beach in the 1990s. Dr. Linda A. Nyondo helped me understand the complexities of life in Malawi. Through their own stories, Matt Cain and Matthew Hodson explained the impact Madonna had on the LGBTQ community. Kristin Lieb provided insight into the backstage workings of the entertainment industry and the precarious life of women in music. And Marilyn Minter and Betty Tompkins described the joys and travails of being a woman artist who dared to express herself.

The list of people who generously shared their *work* with me is too long for this section and can be found on the copyright acknowledgments page and in the bibliography, but I want to mention a few of them because their books, articles, and films were invaluable in recounting Madonna's story and because of their kindness to me. Among them are Vince Aletti, Danny Eccleston, Ester Gould, Julia Gruen, Guy Guido, Charlotte Gunn, Eric Edwin Miller, Lucy O'Brien, Matthew Rettenmund, Don Shewey, Helen Terry, Kimberly van Pinxteren, and Jonathan Van Meter. A few people at organizations and foundations were likewise extremely generous with their time and guidance. They include Barney Hoskyns and Mark Pringle at Rock's Backpages, Emily King and Annelise Ream at the Keith Haring Foundation, and Matt Gray and Patrick Seymour at the Andy Warhol Museum. I would also like to thank Cari Taplin for spending days in the University of Texas archives mining for gold in Norman Mailer's and Liz Smith's papers.

I have had the privilege, once again, of having my book published by Hachette Book Group and Little, Brown. With each of my last three books, I fear I have tested the limits of the editorial staff's endurance and the publisher's willingness to give me the time and space I need to tell the story I want to tell. Each time, I have received nothing but support.

As the primary editor on this project, Asya Muchnick accompanied me on every step along the six-decade-plus journey through the cultural and social history that is Madonna's life. As always, Asya's suggestions were unfailingly apt. As always, I felt fortunate to work with someone I trust so completely. Liese Mayer, as an editor several steps removed, was called in to help shape the book, and it was left to Betsy Uhrig and her team to copyedit and fact-check it. I cannot thank Betsy, Ben Allen, Alison Kerr Miller, Jeffrey Gantz, and Barbara Clark enough for their careful attention—especially Barbara, who shouldered the burden of much of the job and did so with wisdom and patience. I would also like to thank Hachette Book Group creative director Mario Pulice. He not only made the book beautiful, he helped make the process fun. And finally, Lena Little, Bryan Christian, Mariah Dwyer, and Maya Guthrie. They have the gargantuan task of taking this book when all that early work is finished and presenting it to the world. Somehow, despite that heavy responsibility, they manage to make it seem easy.

There would not be a book without the support and encouragement of

Brettne Bloom at The Book Group. I also thank TBG's DJ Kim, who seemingly hasn't met a problem too large to be solved.

I thank Nick Keane for his help keeping the computers running and Vincent Knight for years of patiently piling books and journals at my gate.

Finally, I would like to thank my family. To write a book of this scope requires a yearslong, seven-days-a-week, six-to-nine-hours-per-day commitment. I have been blessed with a family that understands that kind of work. To John, who has created beautiful paintings and written remarkable books while I sat hunched over a computer, I say thank you for your support, your understanding, and your love. To my mother, Rosemary, I say forgive me for being an absentee daughter and thank you for having the grace to never make me feel guilty about it. To her husband, Ken, I say thank you for your patience when I descend upon your household and take over the kitchen table, the phones, and the internet. To Gemma, Russ, Kai, Zoe, Teagan, and Quinn I say let's start creating our own stories together again.

Bibliography

The bibliography for this book can be found at https://www.hachette bookgroup.com/titles/mary-gabriel/madonna/9780316456470/.

Notes

The endnotes for this book can be found at https://www.hachettebook
group.com/titles/mary-gabriel/madonna/9780316456470/.

Index

Note: The abbreviation M in subheadings refers to Madonna.

About the Author

Mary Gabriel is the author of *Ninth Street Women—Lee Krasner, Elaine de Kooning, Grace Hartigan, Joan Mitchell, and Helen Frankenthaler: Five Painters and the Movement That Changed Modern Art,* which won the 2022 NYU/Axinn Foundation Prize for narrative nonfiction and the 2019 Library of Virginia and Virginia Museum of Fine Arts's Mary Lynn Kotz Award. Gabriel's book *Love and Capital: Karl and Jenny Marx and the Birth of a Revolution* was a finalist for the Pulitzer Prize, the National Book Award, and the National Book Critics Circle Award. She is also the author of *Notorious Victoria: The Life of Victoria Woodhull, Uncensored* and *The Art of Acquiring: A Portrait of Etta and Claribel Cone.* She worked in Washington and London as a Reuters editor for nearly two decades and lives in Ireland.